The New York State Directory

2015–2016

The New York State Directory

Grey House
Publishing

AMENIA, NY 12501

PUBLISHER: Leslie Mackenzie
EDITOR: Richard Gottlieb
EDITORIAL DIRECTOR: Laura Mars
EDITORIAL RESEARCH: Jael Bridgemahon

PRODUCTION MANAGER: Kristen Thatcher
PRODUCTION ASSISTANTS: Jael Bridgemahon; Brittany O'Brien
COMPOSITION: David Garoogian
MARKETING DIRECTOR: Jessica Moody

Grey House Publishing, Inc.
4919 Route 22
Amenia, NY 12501
518.789.8700
FAX 518.789.0545
www.greyhouse.com
e-mail: books @greyhouse.com

The New York State directory. — [1st ed.] (1983)-

Annual
ISSN: 0737-1314

1. New York (State)—Officials and employees—Directories. 2. Government executives—New York (State)—Directories. 3. Legislators—New York (State)—Directories.

JK3430 .N52
353.9747002

New York State Directory
2 Volume Set (*New York State Directory* and *Profiles of New York State*)

ISBN: 978-1-61925-563-0
ISBN: 978-1-61925-564-7

TABLE OF CONTENTS

TABLE OF CONTENTS

INTRODUCTION

This 2015/2016 edition of *The New York State Directory* is a comprehensive guide to public officials and private sector organizations and individuals who influence public policy in the state of New York. Fully updated with current addresses and office holders, this edition includes dozens of four-color maps—Demographic and Congressional Maps that show population, race, employment, home value, education, income, voter distribution, and break outs of New York's congressional districts.

Arrangement

The New York State Directory includes 45 chapters, arranged in eight sections, plus Appendices. A list of detailed sources appears in the Organization of Data that follows this introduction.

Section One includes three chapters: Executive Branch, Legislative Branch, and the Judicial Branch of New York State government. This section profiles the public officials in the state's executive departments, administrative agencies, and court system. Detailed listings of departments and agencies appear in Section Two.

Section Two includes 25 chapters covering the most significant public policy issue areas from Agriculture to Veterans & Military. Arranged in alphabetical order, each Policy Area chapter identifies the state, local, and federal agencies and officials that formulate or implement policy. Each chapter ends with a list of Private Sector experts and advocates who influence the policy process.

Section Three is comprised of four chapters with state and local government information: Public Information Offices; U.S. Congress Membership & Committees; County Government; and Municipal Government.

Section Four includes three chapters—Political Parties, Lobbyists, and Political Action Committees—all with comprehensive contact information.

Section Five has two Business chapters—Chambers of Commerce and Economic & Industrial Development Organizations. All listings have valuable contact information and key executives.

Section Six is News Media—detailed listings for Newspapers, News Services, News Magazines, News Radio and News Television stations that serve New York State. Listings include current contact information, plus valuable key executives.

Section Seven covers Education in two chapters—New York State Colleges & Universities, and Public School Districts in the state.

Section Eight includes 245 current, comprehensive Biographies of all New York state lawmakers: Executive; New York Senate; New York Assembly; U.S. Senate; and U.S. House of Representatives. All profiles include office addresses with phone numbers, fax numbers and email addresses, making it easy to contact these influential individuals.

Appendices

- **Financial Plan Overview:** Cash Disbursements by Department, projected to FY 2019.

- **Three Indexes:** Name Index; Organization Index; and Geographic Index.

- **Demographic & Reference Maps:** four-color maps that show political districts, physical features, racial breakdown, age, income, education, congressional districts, and more.

Every reasonable effort has been made to ensure that information in *The New York State Directory* is as accessible and accurate as possible. Organizational, agency, and key official updates and verification were made as late as June 2015. Continuing assistance and cooperation from state, regional, county, municipal, and federal officials and staff have helped make *The New York State Directory* a unique and valuable resource. We are grateful to these individuals and the private sector sources listed for their generous contributions of time and insight.

In addition to this latest edition of the *Directory,* Grey House offers a companion volume, *Profiles of New York State.* This comprehensive volume provides demographic, economic, religious, geographic, and historical details on the more than 2,500 places that make up New York state—counties, cities, towns, and villages. In addition, *Profiles of New York State* includes chapters on Education, Ancestry, Hispanic & Asian Populations, Climate, plus four-color maps, comparative statistics and rankings.

ORGANIZATION OF DATA

Section 1: New York State Branches of Government

Executive Branch. Outlines key staff in the Governor's and Lieutenant Governor's offices and senior officials in New York state executive departments and agencies. Biographies for the senior executive branch officials appear in the Biographies section at the back of the book.

Legislative Branch. Covers the state Senate and Assembly leadership, membership, administrative staff, and standing committees and subcommittees. Committee listings include the Chairperson, Ranking Minority Member, Majority and Minority committee members, committee staff, and key Senate or Assembly Majority and Minority staff assignments. Biographies with district office information for Senators and Assembly members appear in the Biographies section at the back of the book.

Judicial Branch. Identifies the state courts, judges who currently sit on these courts, and the clerk of each court. Includes the Court of Appeals, Appellate Division courts, Supreme Court, Court of Claims, New York City courts, county courts, district courts and city courts outside New York City. The county judge section identifies the specific court with which the judge is associated.

Section 2: Policy Areas

This section classifies New York state government activity into 25 major policy areas. Each policy area lists key individuals in the New York state government, federal government, and the private sector who have expertise in the area of government activity. All entries show organization name, individual name, title, address, telephone number, and fax number. Internet and e-mail addresses are included where available.

Each policy area includes the following information:

New York State
Governor's Office. Identifies the Governor's legal and program staff assigned to the policy area.

Executive Department & Related Agencies. Provides a complete organizational description of the primary state departments and agencies responsible for the policy area. Also includes those state departments and agencies whose activities relate to the policy area.

Corporations, Authorities & Commissions. Covers independent public and quasi-private sector agencies in the state, as well as intrastate bodies to which New York sends a representative.

Legislative Standing Committees. Lists committees and subcommittees which oversee governmental activities in that policy area, their respective chairpersons, and ranking minority members.

U.S. Government
Executive Departments & Related Agencies. Identifies federal departments and agencies located in or assigned to the New York region.

U.S. Congress. Lists congressional committees which oversee federal activities in that policy area, their respective chairpersons, ranking minority members, and NY delegation members.

Private Sector Sources
Includes an alphabetized list of public interest groups, trade and professional associations, corporations, and academia, with the associated individuals who have expertise in the policy area.

Section 3: State & Local Government Public Information

Public Information Offices. Lists key contacts in state government public information offices and libraries.

U.S. Congress. Lists all New York State delegates to the Senate and the House of Representatives with their Washington, DC office, phone and fax numbers, and e-mail addresses. Biographies with district office information for each New York Senator and Representative appear in the *Biographies* section at the back of the book. Provides a comprehensive list of all Senate and House standing, select, and special committees and subcommittees. Each committee and subcommittee entry includes the chairperson, ranking minority member, and assigned members from the New York delegation.

County Government. Identifies senior government officials in all New York counties.

Municipal Government. Identifies senior public officials for cities, towns, and villages in New York with populations greater than 20,000. All New York City departments are included in the city listing.

Section 4: Political Parties & Related Organizations

Political Parties. Lists statewide party officials and county chairpersons for the Conservative, Democratic, Independence and Republican parties.

Lobbyists. Identifies registered lobbyists and clients.

Political Action Committees. Lists registered political action committees and their treasurers.

Section 5: Business

Chambers of Commerce. Lists contact information for chambers of commerce, and economic and industrial development organizations and their primary officials.

Section 6: News Media

Identifies daily and weekly newspapers in New York, major news services with reporters assigned to cover state government, radio stations with a news format, and television stations with independent news staff. Newspapers are categorized by the primary city they serve. Staff listings include managing, news, and editorial page editors, and political reporters. News service entries include bureau chiefs and reporters. Radio and television entries include the news director.

Section 7: Education

SUNY and Other Universities and Colleges. Includes the board of trustees, system administration, the four University Centers, and all colleges and community colleges in the SUNY system; the central administration and all colleges in the CUNY system; and independent colleges and universities. Each college includes the name of its top official, usually the president or dean, as well as address, telephone number and Internet address.

Public School Administrators. Lists school district administrators by county and school district. The New York City School's subsection includes officials in the Chancellor's office. Following are BOCES District Superintendents by supervisory district and the education administrators of schools operated by the state or other public agencies.

Section 8: Biographies

Includes political biographies of all individuals representing New York state's Executive Branch, New York state Assembly members, New York state Senate members, US Senators from New York, and US Representatives from New York

Appendices

Financial Plan Overview
Cash Disbursements By Function—All Government Funds. Provides information excerpted from the New York State FY 2016 Executive Budget Financial Plan.

Indexes

Name Index. Includes every official and executive name listed in The New York State Directory.

Organizations Index. Includes the names of the top three organization levels in all New York state executive departments and agencies, as well as public corporations, authorities, and commissions. In addition, this index includes all organizations listed in the Private Sector section of each policy chapter, as well as lobbyist organizations and political action committees, chambers of commerce, newspapers, news services, radio and television stations, SUNY and CUNY locations, and private colleges.

Geographic Index. Includes the organizations listed in the *Government and Private Sector Organizations Index* (see above) arranged by the city location.

Demographic & Reference Maps
Populated Places, Transportation & Physical Features
Congressional Districts
Federal Lands & Indian Reservations
Core Based Statistical Areas, Counties, and Independent Cities
Economic Losses from Hazard Events
Population
Percent White
Percent Black
Percent Asian
Percent Hispanic
Median Age
Median Household Income
Median Home Value
Percent High School Graduates
Percent College Graduates
Percent of Population who Voted for Barack Obama in 2008

ACRONYMS

AAA	Automobile Association of America
AAAA	Army Aviation Association of America
AARP	American Association of Retired Persons
AFA	Air Force Association
AFL-CIO	American Federation of Labor/Congress of Industrial Organizations
AFSA	Air Force Sergeants Association
AFSCME	American Federation of State, County & Municipal Employees
AFWOA	Air Force Women Officers Association
AHRC	Association for the Help of Retarded Children
AIA	American Institute of Architects
AIVF	Association of Independent Video & Filmmakers
AMAC	Association for Metroarea Autistic Children
AMSUS	Association of Military Surgeons of the US
ASPCA	American Society for the Prevention of Cruelty to Animals
AUSA	Association of the US Army
BAC	Bricklayers & Allied Craftsmen
BIANYS	Brain Injury Association of NYS
BLS	Bureau of Labor Statistics
BOCES	Board of Cooperative Educational Services
CASES	Center for Alternative Sentencing & Employment Services
CBVH	Commission for the Blind & Visually Handicapped
CGR	Center for Governmental Research
CHIP	Community Housing Improvement Program
CIO	Chief Information Office
COA	Commissioned Officers Association
COMPA	Committee of Methadone Program Administrators
COPE	Committee on Political Education
CPB	Customs & Border Protection
CPR	Institute for Conflict Prevention and Resolution
CSD	Central School District
CUNY	City University of New York
DHS	Department of Homeland Security
FEGS	Federation Employment & Guidance Service
FEMA	Federal Emergency Management Agency
FRA	Fleet Reserve Association
FRIA	Friends & Relatives of Institutionalized Aged
HANNYS	Hunger Action Network of New York State
HFA	Housing Finance Agency
IBPAT	International Brotherhood of Painters & Allied Trades
IBT	International Brotherhood of Teamsters
ILGWU	International Ladies' Garment Workers' Union
IOLA	Interest on Lawyers Account
IUE	International Union of Electrical, Radio & Machine Workers
IUOE	International Union of Operating Engineers
MADD	Mothers Against Drunk Driving
MBBA	Municipal Bond Bank Agency
MCA	Military Chaplains Association
MCL	Marine Corps League
MOAA	Military Officers Association of America
MOPH	Military Order of the Purple Heart
MTA	Metropolitan Transportation Authority

NAIFA	North American Insurance & Finance Association
NERA	National Enlisted Reserve Association
NGAUS	National Guard Association of the US
NLN	National League for Nursing
NLUS	Navy League of the US
NMFA	National Military Family Association
NOFA	Northeast Organization Farming Association
NOW	National Organization for Women
NRA	National Reserve Association
NYC	New York City
NYANA	New York Association for New Americans
NYAPRS	New York Association of Psychiatric Rehabilitation Services
NYATEP	New York Association of Training & Employment Professionals
NYCCT	New York Community College Trustees
NYS	New York State
NYSARC	New York State Association for Retarded Citizens
NYSANA	New York State Association of Nurse Anesthetists
NYSHESC	New York State Higher Education Services Corp
NYSIR	New York State Insurance Reciprocal
NYSID	New York State Industries for the Disabled
NYSSMA	New York State School Music Association
NYSEG	New York State Electric & Gas Corporation
NYSTEC	New York State Technology Enterprise Corporation
NYSTEA	New York State Transportation Engineering Alliance
NYU	New York University
OOA	Office of Administration
PAC	Political Action Committee
PACE	Political Action for Candidates' Election
PAF	Political Action Fund
PAT	Political Action Team
PBA	Patrolmen's Benevolent Association
PCNY	Police Conference of New York
PEF	Political Education Fund - and - Public Employees Federation
PRLDEF	Puerto Rican Legal Defense and Education Fund
PSRC	Professional Standards Review Council
RCIL	Resource Center for Independent Living
RID	Rid Intoxicated Drivers
RIOC	Roosevelt Island Operating Corporation
ROA	Reserve Officers Association
SCAA	Schuyler Center for Analysis & Advocacy
SEMO	State Emergency Management Office
SENSES	Statewide Emergency Network for Social & Economic Security
SIFMA	Securities Industry and Financial Markets Association
SONYMA	State of New York Mortgage Agency
SUNY	State University of New York
UNYAN	United New York Ambulance Network
USWA	United Steel Workers of America
VESID	Vocational & Educational Services for Individuals with Disabilities Office
VFW	Veterans of Foreign Wars
VISN	Veterans Integrated Service Network
VWIN	Veterans Widows International Network
WHEDCO	Women's Housing & Economic Development Corporation

Section 1:
BRANCHES OF GOVERNMENT

EXECUTIVE BRANCH

This chapter provides a summary of officials in the Executive Branch. For a more detailed listing of specific executive and administrative departments and agencies, refer to the appropriate policy area in Section 2 or to the Organizations Index. Biographies for the senior Executive Branch officials appear in a separate section in the back of the book.

NEW YORK STATE

Governor (also see Governor's Office):
    Andrew M Cuomo 518-474-8390
Lieutenant Governor:
    Kathleen C Hochul 518-402-2292
Chief Information Officer & Director, Office of Information Technology Services (also see CIO Office & Office of Information Technology Services):
    Maggie Miller 518-408-2140
Comptroller (also see State Comptroller, Office of the):
    Thomas P DiNapoli . . . . 518-474-4044 or 212-681-4491
Attorney General (also see Law Department):
    Eric T Schneiderman . . . . 518-474-7330 or 212-416-8000
Secretary of State (also see State Department):
    Cesar A Perales 518-474-0050

Governor's Office
Executive Chamber
State Capitol
Albany, NY 12224
518-474-8390 Fax: 518-474-1513
Web site: www.governor.ny.gov; www.ny.gov

Governor:
    Andrew M Cuomo 518-474-8390
Secretary to the Governor:
    William Mulrow 518-474-4246
Counsel to the Governor:
    Alphonso David 518-474-8343
Director, Communications:
    Melissa DeRosa . . . . 518-474-8418 or 212-681-4640

Office of the Secretary
Secretary to the Governor:
    William Mulrow 518-474-4246
Director, State Operations:
    James Malatras 518-486-9871
Executive Deputy Secretary to the Governor:
    Joseph Percoco 518-486-3940
Counselor to the Governor:
    Linda Lacewell 518-474-4623
Special Counsel to the Governor:
    Rick Cotton 518-474-8434
Special Advisor to the Governor:
    Rodney Capel 212-681-4580
Special Advisor to the Governor:
    Christine Quinn 212-681-4580
Deputy Director of State Operations:
    Joseph Rabito 518-408-2051
Deputy Director of State Operations:
    Andrew Kennedy 518-474-3478
Deputy Director of State Operations:
    Matthew Millea 518-474-9883
Deputy Secretary for Labor:
    Elizabeth de Leon Bhargava 212-681-4584
Deputy Secretary, Health:
    Courtney Burke 518-408-2500

Deputy Secretary for Civil Rights:
    Patricia Gatling 212-681-4584
Deputy Secretary, Food & Agriculture:
    Patrick Hooker 518-486-3960
Deputy Secretary, Transportation:
    Ron Thaniel 518-408-2555
Chairman of Energy & Finance for New York:
    Richard Kauffman 518-681-4580
Deputy Secretary, Environment:
    Basil Seggos 518-408-2552
Deputy Secretary, Public Safety:
    Terrence O'Leary 518-474-3522
Deputy Secretary, Education:
    Elana Sigall 518-474-9883
Deputy Secretary, Technology:
    Rachel Haot 212-681-4573
Director of Policy:
    John Maggiore 518-408-2576
Deputy Secretary for Financial Services:
    George Haggerty 518-474-5442

Communications
Director, Communications:
    Melissa DeRosa 518-474-8418

Counsel
Counsel to the Governor:
    Alphonso David 518-474-8343
First Assistant Counsel:
    Sandi Toll 518-474-8434

New York City Office
633 Third Ave, 38th Fl, New York, NY 10017
212-681-4580
Governor:
    Andrew M Cuomo 212-681-4580

Washington Office of the Governor
444 N Capitol St NW, Washington, DC 20001
202-434-7100
Director:
    Alexander Cochran 202-434-7100

Lieutenant Governor's Office
Executive Chamber
State Capitol
Albany, NY 12224
518-402-2292 Fax: 518-474-1513

633 Third Ave
New York, NY 10017
212-681-4575

Lieutenant Governor:
    Kathleen C Hochul . . . . 518-402-2292 or 212-681-4575
Chief of Staff:
    Jeffrey Pearlman 518-402-2292
Deputy Chief of Staff:
    Melissa Bochenski 518-402-2292
Press Secretary:
    Jason Elan 518-402-2292
Director, Policy:
    Brian Quiara 518-402-2292
Director, Constituent Services:
    Jeffrey Lewis 212-681-4571

Offices and agencies generally appear in alphabetical order, except when specific order is requested by listee.

EXECUTIVE DEPARTMENTS AND RELATED AGENCIES

Aging, Office for the
2 Empire State Plaza
Albany, NY 12223
518-474-4425 or 800-342-9871 Fax: 518-474-0608
e-mail: nysofa@aging.ny.gov
Web site: www.aging.ny.gov

Director:
  Corinda Crossdale 518-474-4425
Executive Deputy Director:
  Greg Olsen 518-474-7012
Counsel:
  Jennifer Seehase 518-474-0388
Deputy Director, Agency Operations:
  John Cochran 518-486-3661
Deputy Director, Division of Aging Network Operations:
  John J Lynch 518-473-4808
Deputy Director, Division of Policy, Planning, Program & Outcomes:
  Laurie Pferr 518-474-7012
Public Information Officer:
  Reza Mizbani 518-474-7181
  e-mail: reza.mizbani@aging.ny.gov
Director of Aging Projects:
  Kelly Mateja 518-473-7424
Federal Relations/FOIL Officer, Staff Liaison:
  Stephen Syzdek 518-474-5041

Agriculture & Markets Department
10B Airline Dr
Albany, NY 12235
518-457-3880 or 800-554-4501 Fax: 518-457-3087
e-mail: info@agriculture.ny.gov
Web site: www.agriculture.ny.gov

Commissioner:
  Richard Ball 518-457-8876
First Deputy Commissioner:
  Jen McCormick 518-457-2771
  e-mail: jen.mccormick@agriculture.ny.gov
Deputy Commissioner:
  Ron Rausch 518-485-7728
  e-mail: ron.rausch@agriculture.ny.gov
Deputy Commissioner:
  Jackie Moody-Czub 518-485-7728
  e-mail: jackie.moody-czub@agriculture.ny.gov
Counsel:
  Susan Rosenthal 518-457-1059
  e-mail: susan.rosenthal@agriculture.ny.gov
Public Information Officer:
  Jola Szubielski 518-485-7728/fax: 518-457-3087
  e-mail: jola.szubielski@agriculture.ny.gov

New York State Liquor Authority (Division of Alcoholic Beverage Control)
317 Lenox Ave
New York, NY 10027
212-961-8300 Fax: 212-961-8299
Web site: www.sla.ny.gov

80 S Swan St
Ste 900
Albany, NY 12210-8002
518-474-3114
Fax: 518-402-4015

Chair:
  Vincent Bradley .212-961-8300 or 518-473-6559
Commissioner:
  Jeanique Greene . . . . .518-474-3114 or 212-961-8300
Commissioner:
  Kevin Kim . . . . .518-474-3114 or 212-961-8300
Director, Information Technology:
  Michael Drake .518-474-3114/fax: 518-402-4015
CEO:
  Kerri O'Brien 518-474-3114
Director, Enforcement:
  Noel Colon 518-474-3114
Counsel:
  Jacqueline Flug .518-474-3114/fax: 518-402-2304
  e-mail: legal@sla.ny.gov
Director, Public Affairs:
  William Crowley . . . . .518-474-3114 or 518-474-4875
  fax: 518-473-9565
  e-mail: press.office@sla.ny.gov

Alcoholism & Substance Abuse Services, Office of
1450 Western Ave
Albany, NY 12203
518-473-3460 Fax: 518-457-5474
e-mail: communications@oasas.ny.gov
Web site: www.oasas.ny.gov

501 7th Ave
8th Fl
New York, NY 10018
646-728-4533

Commissioner:
  Arlene Gonzalez-Sanchez 518-457-2061
Executive Deputy Commissioner:
  Sean M. Byrne 518-457-1758
Office of the Medical Director (Acting):
  Charles W Morgan MD 845-359-8500
Chief Counsel, Office of Counsel & Internal Controls:
  Robert Kent 518-485-2312
Acting Assoc Cmsr, Division of Prevention, Housing & Management
  Service:
  Mary Ann DiChristopher 518-485-6022
Associate Commissioner, Fiscal Administration Division:
  P David Sawicki 518-457-5312
Associate Commissioner, Treatment & Practice Innovation Division:
  Steve Hanson . . . . .518-457-7077 or 585-461-0410
Associate Commissioner, Quality Assurance & Performance Improvement
  Division:
  Charles W Monson 518-485-2257
Director, Governmental Affairs, Grants Management:
  Patricia Zuber-Wilson 518-485-2317
Associate Commissioner, Outcome Management & System Information
  Division:
  William F. Hogan 518-485-2322
Director, Public Information & Communications:
  Susan A Craig, MPH 518-457-8299/fax: 518-485-6014

Financial Services Department
One State Street
New York, NY 10004-1511
212-709-3500 or 877-226-5697
e-mail: public-affairs@dfs.ny.gov
Web site: www.dfs.ny.gov

Superintendent:
  Benjamin M. Lawsky . . . . .212-709-3501 or 518-474-4567
  fax: 212-709-3520

Offices and agencies generally appear in alphabetical order, except when specific order is requested by listee.

Deputy Superintendent & General Counsel:
   Marjorie Gross....................212-709-1640/fax: 212-480-5256
Deputy Superintendent, Community Regional Banks:
   Martin Cofsky....................................212-709-1610
Deputy Superintendent, Property/Casual Markets:
   Michael Moriarty 212-480-5127
Director, Criminal Investigations Bureau:
   Ricardo Velez....................................212-709-3554
Chief Information Officer:
   William Rachmiel................................212-709-5420
Director, Frauds:
   Frank Orlando....................................212-480-5770
Acting Director, Capital Markets Division:
   Matti Peltonen 212-480-5071/fax: 212-480-6085
Director, Public Affairs:
   Andrew Mais..................212-480-5257/fax: 212-480-6077

Budget, Division of the
State Capitol
Albany, NY 12224
518-473-3885 Fax: 518-474-9041
Web site: www.budget.ny.gov

Director:
   Mary Beth Labate 518-474-2300
First Deputy Director:
   Dominic Colafati................................518-474-8282
Deputy Director:
   David Lara 518-402-4246
Budget Services Head:
   Bob Brondi 518-473-0580
Public Protection Head:
   Anne Bink......................................518-474-4313
Press Officer:
   Morris Peters 518-473-3885/fax: 518-474-9041
   e-mail: dob.sm.press@budget.ny.gov

CIO & Office of Information Technology Services (ITS)
State Capitol
Empire State Plaza
PO Box 2062
Albany, NY 12220-0062
518-402-2537 or 866-789-4638 Fax: 518-474-1196
e-mail: customer.relations@its.ny.gov
Web site: www.its.ny.gov

Chief Information Officer/Director of ITS:
   Maggie Miller 518-408-2140
Executive Deputy Chief Information Officer:
   Mahesh Nattanmai 518-408-2140
Chief Technology Officer:
   Kishor Bagul....................................518-486-9200
Counsel & Legal Services:
   Karen Geduldig..................................518-408-2484
Director, Administration:
   Terri Papa 518-408-2484
Chief Data Officer:
   Barbara Cohn 518-474-3019
Director, Enterprise Information Security Office:
   Thomas D Smith..................................518-242-5200
   e-mail: eiso@its.ny.gov
Director, Public Information:
   Michelle McDonald 518-408-3899

Children & Family Services, Office of
52 Washington St
Rensselaer, NY 12144
518-473-7793 Fax: 518-486-7550
Web site: www.ocfs.ny.gov

Acting Commissioner:
   Sheila Poole....................................518-402-3108
Executive Deputy Commissioner:
   Sheila Poole....................................518-402-3108
Assisant Commissioner, Communications:
   Jennifer Givner...............518-402-3130 or 518-473-7793
   fax: 518-486-7550
   e-mail: info@ocfs.state.ny.us
Acting Deputy Commissioner, Legal Affairs & General Counsel:
   Lee Prochera 518-473-8418
Associate Commissioner, Administration/Human Resources:
   James Barron....................................518-486-6942
Deputy Commissioner, Child Welfare & Community Service:
   Laura Velez.....................................518-474-3377
Deputy Commissioner, Juvenile Justice & Opportunity for Youth:
   Ines Neives 518-473-1786
CIO:
   Rick Ryan 518-402-3194
Associate Commissioner, Blind & Visually Handicapped Commission:
   Brian S Daniels.................................518-474-7812

Council on Children & Families .... fax: 518-473-2570
52 Washington Street, West Bldg, Ste 99, Rensselaer, NY 12144
518-473-3652 Fax: 518-473-2570
e-mail: council@ccf.ny.gov
Web site: www.ccf.ny.gov
Executive Director:
   Deborah Benson 518-473-3652/fax: 518-473-2570
   e-mail: debbie.benson@ccf.ny.gov
Deputy Director & Counsel:
   Elana Marton....................................518-473-3652
   e-mail: elena.marton@ccf.ny.gov
Project Director, Head Start Collaboration:
   Patricia Persell.................................518-474-9352
   e-mail: patricia.persell@ccf.ny.gov
Project Director, Kids Count:
   Mary DeMasi 518-473-3652
   e-mail: mary.demasi@ccf.ny.gov

Civil Service Department
Alfred E Smith State Ofc Bldg
Albany, NY 12239
518-457-2487 or 877-697-5627
Web site: www.cs.ny.gov

Commissioner:
   Jerry Boone.....................................518-457-3701
Executive Deputy Commissioner:
   Vacant..518-473-5698
Deputy Commissioner, Operations:
   Vacant..518-473-5711
Deputy Commissioner, Administration:
   Deirdre Taylor..................................518-473-5694
Deputy Commissioner/General Counsel:
   Ilene Lees 518-473-2624
Director, Workforce & Occupational Planning:
   Vacant..518-473-6411
Director, Financial Administration:
   Vacant..518-473-2269
Director, Employee Benefits:
   Robert Dubois 518-473-1977/fax: 518-473-3292
Human Resources & Administrative Planning:
   Valerie Morrison................................518-473-4306
Public Information Officer:
   Ed Walsh 518-457-9375/fax: 518-473-2372
   e-mail: pio@cs.state.ny.us

Civil Service Commission
President:
   Jerry Boone.....................................518-457-3701

Offices and agencies generally appear in alphabetical order, except when specific order is requested by listee.

Commissioner:
   Caroline Ahl 518-473-6326
Commissioner:
   Dennis Hanrahan. 518-473-6326

Consumer Protection, Division of
One Commerce Plaza
99 Washington Ave
Albany, NY 12231
518-474-8583 or 800-697-1220 Fax: 518-473-9055
Web site: www.dos.ny.gov/consumerprotection/

Executive Deputy Director, Consumer Protection:
   Aiesha Battle. 518-474-2363

Corrections & Community Supervision Department
1220 Washington Ave
Bldg 2 State Campus
Albany, NY 12226-2050
518-457-8126 Fax: 518-457-7252
Web site: www.doccs.ny.gov

Acting Commissioner:
   Anthony Annucci 518-457-8134
Assistant Commissioner & Executive Assistant:
   Diane L Van Buren. 518-457-1281
Special Assistant to Commissioner:
   Terri Pratt 518-457-8134
Executive Deputy Commissioner:
   Anthony Annucci . . . . .518-457-1748 or 518-485-9613
Deputy Commissioner & Counsel:
   Maureen Boll 518-485-9613
Deputy Commissioner, Administrative Services:
   Daniel F. Martuscello III 518-457-8188
Deputy Commissioner, Correctional Facility Operations:
   Joseph Bellnier 518-457-8138
Deputy Commissioner, Health Services Division/Chief Medical Officer:
   Carl Koenigsmann 518-457-7073
Assistant Commissioner, Program Services:
   Vacant. 518-408-5825
Director, Public Information:
   Thomas Mailey 518-457-8182/fax: 518-457-7070

Council on the Arts
300 Park Avenue South
10th Floor
New York, NY 10010
212-459-8800 or 800-510-0021
Web site: www.nysca.org

Chair:
   Aby Rosen. 212-459-8800
Vice Chair:
   Dr Barbaralee Diamonstein-Spielvogel 212-459-8800
Executive Director:
   Lisa Robb 212-459-8808
   e-mail: executive.director@arts.ny.gov
Deputy Executive Director, Programs:
   Megan White. 212-459-8806
   e-mail: megan.white@arts.ny.gov
Director, Agency Operations:
   Brenda Brown. 212-459-8827
   e-mail: brenda.brown@arts.ny.gov
Manager, Information Technology:
   Lenn Ditman 212-459-8810
   e-mail: lenn.ditman@arts.ny.gov
Director, Administrative Services:
   Tracy Hamilton-Thompson. 212-459-8822
   e-mail: tracy.hamilton@arts.ny.gov

Victim Services, Office of
55 Hanson Place
10th Fl
Brooklyn, NY 11217-1523
718-923-4325 or 800-247-8035 Fax: 718-923-4347
Web site: www.ovs.ny.gov

805 Swan Street
2nd Floor
Albany, NY 12210
518-457-8727
Fax: 518-457-8658

65 Court Street
Buffalo, NY 14202
716-847-7992
Fax: 716-847-7995

Director:
   Elizabeth Cronin Esq 518-485-5719
General Counsel/Legal Unit:
   John Watson 518-457-8066/fax: 518-457-8658
Deputy Director for Administration:
   Danny Morgan 518-457-8050
Director, MIS:
   Susan Nardolillo 518-485-9299
Crime Victim Compensation Investigations (Brooklyn):
   Claudette Christian Bullock 718-923-4348
Crime Victim Compensation Investigations (Albany & Buffalo):
   Noreen Yvie 518-457-8176

Criminal Justice Services, Division of
80 South Swan Street
Albany, NY 12210
518-457-5837 or 800-262-3257 Fax: 518-457-3089
e-mail: info@dcjs.ny.gov
Web site: www.criminaljustice.ny.gov

Executive Deputy Commissioner:
   Michael C Green. 518-457-1260
Deputy Commissioner, Program Development & Funding:
   Anne Marie Strano 518-457-8462
Deputy Commissioner, Administration:
   Vacant 518-457-6105
Deputy Commissioner & Counsel:
   Gina Bianchi. 518-457-4181
Deputy Commissioner, Public Safety:
   Melvin Perez 518-485-7620
Deputy Commissioner, Justice Information Systems:
   Anne Roest 518-485-7176
Director, Human Resources Management:
   Karen Davis 518-485-1704
Director, Finance:
   Kimberly J Szady 518-457-6105
Deputy Commissioner, Bureau of Justice Stats & Performance:
   Terry Salo 518-457-7301
Deputy Director, Public Information:
   Janine Kava 518-457-8828/fax: 518-485-7715
   e-mail: janine.kava@dcjs.ny.gov

Developmental Disabilities Planning Council
99 Washington Ave
12th Fl, Ste 1230
Albany, NY 12210
518-486-7505 or 800-395-3372 Fax: 518-402-3505
e-mail: ddpc@ddpc.ny.gov
Web site: www.ddpc.ny.gov

Offices and agencies generally appear in alphabetical order, except when specific order is requested by listee.

Chairperson:
Rose Marie Toscano 518-486-7505
Vice Chairperson:
Ansley Bacon, PhD..............................518-486-7505
Executive Director:
Sheila M Carey 518-486-7505
e-mail: sheila.carey@ddpc.ny.gov
Deputy Director-Program Development Specialist:
Anna Lobosco....................................518-486-7505
e-mail: anna.lobosco@ddpc.ny.gov
Public Information Officer:
Thomas F Lee 518-486-7505/fax: 518-486-3505
e-mail: thomas.lee@ddpc.ny.gov

Education Department
State Education Bldg
89 Washington Ave
Albany, NY 12234
518-474-3852 Fax: 518-486-5631
Web site: www.nysed.gov

Commissioner & University President:
MaryEllen Elia 518-474-5844
Executive Deputy Commissioner:
Elizabeth Berlin 518-473-8381
General Counsel & Deputy Commissioner:
Richard Trautwein 518-474-6400
e-mail: legal@mail.nysed.gov
Deputy Commissioner, Higher Education:
John D'Agati....................................518-486-3633
Deputy Commissioner, Cultural Education Office:
Jeffrey Cannell.........518-474-5976/fax: 518-486-4850
e-mail: jcannell@mail.nysed.gov
Deputy Commissioner, Office of the Professions:
Douglas Lentivech 518-486-1765
Deputy Commissioner, Office of P-12 Education:
Ken Slentz......................................518-474-3862
Deputy Commissioner, Adult Career & Continuing Ed Svcs (ACCES):
Kevin Smith 518-474-2714
Deputy Commissioner, Performance Improvement & Mgmnt Svcs:
Sharon Cates-Williams..........................518-473-4706
Chief, External Affairs (Communications):
Dennis Tompkins.............518-474-1201/fax: 518-473-2977

Elections, State Board of
40 N Pearl Street
Suite 5
Albany, NY 12207
518-474-6220 or TTY: 800-367-8683 Fax: 518-486-4068
e-mail: info@elections.ny.gov
Web site: www.elections.ny.gov

Co-Chair:
James A Walsh 518-474-8100
Co-Chair:
Douglas A Kellner 518-474-8100
Commissioner:
Andrew J Spano 518-474-8100
Commissioner:
Gregory P Peterson..............................518-474-8100
Co-Executive Director:
Todd Valentine 518-474-6336/fax: 518-474-1008
Co-Executive Director:
Robert A Brehm 518-474-6336/fax: 518-474-1008
Special Counsel:
Kimberly Galvin................................518-474-6367
Election Law Enforcement Counsel:
Elizabeth C Hogan 518-474-2063
Director, Election Operations:
Anne E Svizzero 518-473-5086/fax: 518-486-4546

Director, Public Information:
John W Conklin...........518-474-1953/fax: 518-473-8315
Coordinator, NVRA:
Gregory Fiozzo 518-474-1953

Homeland Security & Emergency Services, Division of
1220 Washington Ave
Bldg. 7A
Suite 710
Albany, NY 12242
518-242-5000 Fax: 518-322-4978
Web site: www.dhses.ny.gov

633 Third Ave
32nd Fl
New York, NY 10017
212-867-7060

Commissioner & Director, Office of Counterterrorism:
Jerome M Hauer 518-292-2301
Assistant Director, Office of Counterterrorism:
David Sheppard.................................518-242-5121
Director, Fire Prevention Bureau & State Fire Administrator:
Bryant Stevens 518-474-6746
e-mail: fire@dhses.ny.gov
Director, State Office of Emergency Management:
Steven Kuhr 518-292-2301
First Deputy Director, Emergency Management:
Greg Brunelle 518-242-5000
Assistant Director, OEM Training:
Richard French 518-292-2357
Executive Assistant to the Director:
Angela Groelz...................................518-292-2301
Director, Office of Interoperable & Emergency Communications:
Robert Barbato 518-292-4913
e-mail: dhsesoiec@dhses.ny.gov
Public Information Officer:
Rachel McEneny 518-242-5133/fax: 518-322-4978

Empire State Development Corporation
633 Third Ave
New York, NY 10017
212-803-3100 Fax: 212-803-3131
e-mail: esd@esd.ny.gov
Web site: www.esd.ny.gov

625 Broadway
Albany, NY 12207
518-292-5200

95 Perry Street
Ste 500
Buffalo, NY 14203
716-846-8200
Fax: 716-846-8260

President & CEO:
Howard Zemsky ....212-803-3700 or 518-292-5100
Public Affairs:
Kay Sarlin Wright..............................800-260-7313
e-mail: esdpressoffice@esd.ny.gov
Chief of Staff & COO:
Mehul Patel....................212-803-3700 or 518-292-5100
Business Attraction & Expansion:
John Gilstrap...................................212-803-3700
General Counsel:
Liz Fine..212-803-3100

Offices and agencies generally appear in alphabetical order, except when specific order is requested by listee.

Employee Relations, Governor's Office of
Two Empire State Plz
Ste 1201
Albany, NY 12223
518-473-8766 Fax: 518-473-6795
e-mail: info@goer.ny.gov
Web site: www.goer.ny.gov

Director:
  Gary Johnson 518-474-6988/fax: 518-486-7304
Deputy Director, Contract Negotiations & Administration:
  Vacant 518-473-3130/fax: 518-486-7304
Acting General Counsel:
  Michael N Volforte 518-474-4090/fax: 518-486-7304
Director, Administration:
  Mary Hines 518-473-3467/fax: 518-473-6725
CIO/Information Technology Division:
  Moses M Kamya PhD 518-486-1305/fax: 518-473-6294

Environmental Conservation Department
625 Broadway
Albany, NY 12233-0001
518-402-8545 Fax: 518-402-9016
Web site: www.dec.ny.gov

Commissioner:
  Joseph J Martens 518-402-8545/fax: 518-402-8541
Executive Deputy Commissioner:
  Marc Gerstman 518-402-9401
General Counsel:
  Ed McTiernan 518-402-9185/fax: 518-402-9018
Assistant Commissioner, Hearings & Mediation:
  Louis Alexander 518-402-8537
Assistant Commissioner, Natural Resources:
  Kathy Moser 518-402-2797
Deputy Commissioner, Administration:
  Anne Reynolds 518-402-9401
Assistant Commissioner, Public Protection & Regional Affairs:
  Chris Walsh .518-402-8549/fax: 518-402-9016
Deputy Commissioner, Remediation & Materials Management:
  Gene Leff 518-402-2794
Assistant Commissioner, Air Resources, Climate Change & Energy:
  Jared Snyder 518-402-8537
Assistant Commissioner, Water & Watershed:
  James Tierney 518-402-8545
Director, Public Affairs:
  Michael Bopp 518-402-8000

General Services, Office of
Corning Tower, 41st Fl
Empire State Plaza
Albany, NY 12242
518-474-3899 Fax: 518-474-1546
Web site: www.ogs.ny.gov

Commissioner:
  RoAnn Destito 518-474-5991/fax: 518-486-9179
Executive Deputy Commissioner:
  Joseph J Rabito 518-473-6953
Deputy Commissioner, Administration:
  Gail Hammond 518-474-3199
Deputy Commissioner, Design & Construction:
  Vacant 518-474-0337/fax: 518-486-9135
Deputy Commissioner, Information Technology & Procurement Services:
  Vacant 518-473-3933/fax: 518-486-9166
Deputy Commissioner, Legal Services & Counsel:
  Howard Zwickel 518-474-5988/fax: 518-473-4973
Director, Real Estate Planning & Development Group:
  James Sproat 518-474-4944

Director, Public Affairs:
  Heather Groll 518-474-5987/fax: 518-402-5146
  e-mail: heather.groll@ogs.ny.gov

Health Department
Corning Tower
Empire State Plaza
Albany, NY 12237
518-474-2011
Web site: www.health.ny.gov

Commissioner:
  Howard Zucker, MD, JD 518-474-2011
Executive Deputy Commissioner:
  Sally Dreslin, MS, RN 518-474-2011
Assistant Commissioner, Governmental & External Affairs:
  Amy Nickson 518-473-1124/fax: 518-473-9674
Acting Health Cluster CIO:
  Robert Pennacchia 518-474-8373/fax: 518-474-2288
Deputy Commissioner & State Medicaid Director:
  Jason A Helgerson 518-474-3018/fax: 518-486-1346
General Counsel:
  James E Dering 518-474-7553/fax: 518-473-2802
Deputy Commissioner, Public Health:
  Guthrie S Birkhead MD MPH .518-402-5382
Director, Health Emergency Preparedness:
  Michael J Primeau. 518-474-2893
Director, AIDS Institute:
  Dan O'Connell 518-474-6399
Director, Center for Community Health:
  Bradley J Hutton 518-473-4371/fax: 518-473-8389
Director, Family Health:
  Rachel de Long 518-474-6968/fax: 518-474-7054
Deputy Commissioner, Primary Care & Health Systems Management:
  Daniel B Sheppard 518-474-1686
Director, The Wadsworth Center:
  Jill Taylor, PhD 518-474-3157/fax: 518-474-3439
Director, Public Affairs:
  Vacant 518-474-7354 x1
Deputy Director, Public Affairs:
  Marci Natale. 518-474-7354 x1

Housing & Community Renewal
Hampton Plaza
38-40 State St
Albany, NY 12207
866-275-3427 or 518-473-2526
Web site: www.nyshcr.org

25 Beaver St
New York, NY 10004
866-275-3427

Commissioner/CEO:
  Darryl C Towns. 518-486-3370
President, Office of Community Renewal:
  Matthew Nelson 212-480-6707
President, Office of Finance & Development:
  Marian Zucker . . . . .518-486-3370 or 212-480-6772
  fax: 518-473-9462
Director, Fair Housing & Equal Opportunity:
  Wanda Graham 518-474-2057/fax: 518-474-5247
Chief Public Information Officer:
  Charni Sochet 212-872-0681

Hudson River Valley Greenway
625 Broadway, 4th Fl
Albany, NY 12207

Offices and agencies generally appear in alphabetical order, except when specific order is requested by listee.

518-473-3835 Fax: 518-473-4518
e-mail: hrvg@hudsongreenway.ny.gov
Web site: www.hudsongreenway.ny.gov

Greenway Conservancy for the Hudson River Valley
Acting Chair:
  Sara Griffen. 518-473-3835
Executive Director (Acting):
  Mark Castiglione. 518-473-3835

Hudson River Valley Greenway Communities Council
Board Chair:
  Barnabas McHenry Esq. 518-473-3835/fax: 212-681-4552
Executive Director (Acting):
  Mark Castiglione. 518-473-3835

Human Rights, State Division of
1 Fordham Plaza, 4th Fl
Bronx, NY 10458
718-741-8400 or 888-392-3644 Fax: 718-741-8279
e-mail: infobronx@dhr.ny.gov
Web site: www.dhr.ny.gov

Commissioner:
  Helen Diane Foster. 718-741-8326
First Deputy Commissioner:
  Valerie P. Dent 718-741-8330
PR & Communications:
  Leticia Theodore-Greene .718-741-3223
  e-mail: lgreene@dhr.ny.gov
Deputy Commissioner, Federal Programs:
  Edward A Watkins 718-741-8440
Deputy Commissioner, Enforcement:
  Melissa Franco 718-741-8400
Director, Housing Investigations Unit:
  William Lamot 718-741-8435
General Counsel:
  Caroline Downey 718-741-8398
Director, Equal Opportunity & Diversity:
  Rockwell Chin 718-741-8309

Inspector General (NYS), Office of the
Empire State Plaza
Bldg 2, 16th Fl
Albany, NY 12223
518-474-1010 or 800-367-4448 Fax: 518-486-3745
e-mail: igpress@ig.ny.gov
Web site: www.ig.ny.gov

61 Broadway
12th Floor
New York, NY 10006
212-635-3150
Fax: 212-809-6287

State Inspector General:
  Catherine Leahy Scott . . . . .212-635-3150 or 518-474-1010
  e-mail: inspector.general@ig.ny.gov
Executive Inspector General:
  Spencer Freeman. 212-635-3150
Deputy Inspector General - Investigations:
  Bernard Cosenza. 212-635-3150
Director, Communications:
  William P. Reynolds. 518-474-1010

Insurance Fund (NYS)
15 Computer Drive West
Albany, NY 12205

518-437-5220
Web site: www.nysif.com

199 Church St
New York, NY 10007
212-587-9000

Executive Director:
  Eric Madoff. . . . . .212-312-7004 or 518-437-5220
Deputy Executive Director:
  Dorothy Carey. 212-312-9933
Deputy Executive Director:
  Colleen Gardner 212-587-9000
Deputy Executive Director:
  Shirley Stark 212-312-9917
Chief Fiscal Officer:
  Susan D Sharp. 518-437-6168
Public Information Officer:
  Robert Lawson. 518-437-3504/fax: 518-437-1849
General Attorney:
  Gregory Allen 518-437-5220
Director, Administration:
  Joseph Mullen 518-437-5220

Insurance Fund Board of Commissioners
Acting Chair:
  Vacant. 518-437-5220
Vice Chair:
  Vacant. 518-437-5220
Secretary to the Board:
  Michael Miliano 212-312-7408

Labor Department
Building 12, Room 500
Harriman State Office Campus
Albany, NY 12240
518-457-9000 Fax: 518-457-6908
e-mail: nysdol@labor.ny.gov
Web site: www.labor.ny.gov

Commissioner:
  Peter M. Rivera. 518-457-9000
Executive Deputy Commissioner:
  Mario Musolino 518-457-4318
Acting Counsel:
  Pico Ben-Amotz 518-457-3665
Director, Special Investigations:
  John Dormin 518-457-7012
Acting Deputy Commissioner, Employment Security:
  Mary Batch 518-457-5124
Acting Deputy Commissioner, Workforce Development:
  Karen Coleman 518-457-4317
Deputy Commissioner, Worker Protection:
  Pico Ben-Amotz 518-457-4317
Director, Communications:
  Leo Rosales 518-457-5519/fax: 518-485-1126
  e-mail: leo.rosales@labor.ny.gov
Director, Personnel:
  Carol Owsiany 518-457-1020

Law Department
120 Broadway
New York, NY 10271-0332
212-416-8000 or 800-771-7755
Web site: www.ag.ny.gov

State Capitol
Albany, NY 12224-0341

Offices and agencies generally appear in alphabetical order, except when specific order is requested by listee.

518-474-7330
Fax: 518-473-9909

Attorney General:
Eric T Schneiderman . . . . .212-416-8050 or 518-776-2000
Chief Deputy Attorney General & Counsel:
Harlan Levy 212-416-8525
Solicitor General:
Barbara D Underwood . . . . .212-416-8016 or 518-776-2002
Executive Deputy Attorney General, Criminal Justice:
Kelly Donovan 212-416-8050
Executive Deputy Attorney General, Economic Justice:
Karla Sanchez. 212-416-8050
Executive Deputy Attorney General, Social Justice:
Alvin L Braggs, Jr. 212-416-8450/fax: 212-416-8942
Executive Deputy Attorney General, Regional Affairs:
Martin J Mack. 716-852-6274
Press Secretary:
Fernando Aquino. 212-416-8060/fax: 212-416-6005

New York State Gaming Commission
One Broadway Center
PO Box 7500
Schenectady, NY 12301-7500
518-388-3300 Fax: 518-388-3423
Web site: www.nylottery.ny.gov

Executive Director:
Robert Williams 518-388-3400
General Counsel:
Edmund Burns 518-388-3408
Deputy Director/COO:
Gardner Gurney 518-388-3406
Director, Communications & Public Information Officer:
Christy Calicchia. 518-388-3415/fax: 518-388-3423
Manager, Lottery Games Operations:
Jim Nielsen. 518-388-1266
Executive Director:
Robert Williams 518-395-5400
Public Information Officer:
Lee Park. .518-395-5400/fax: 518-453-8867
e-mail: lee.park@racing.ny.gov

Mental Health, Office of
44 Holland Ave
Albany, NY 12229
518-474-4403 or 800-597-8481 Fax: 518-474-2149
Web site: www.omh.ny.gov

Acting Commissioner:
Ann Marie T Sullivan MD 518-474-4403
Executive Deputy Commissioner:
Martha Schaefer Hayes 518-474-7056/fax: 518-473-4690
Deputy Commissioner & Counsel:
Joshua Pepper 518-474-1331/fax: 518-473-7863
Medical Director:
Lloyd I Sederer, MD .212-330-1650 x. 360
Chief Financial Officer:
Emil Slane. 518-474-3631
Director, Center for Human Resource Management:
J. Lynn Heath 518-474-0171
Director, Public Affairs:
Benjamin Rosen. 518-474-6540/fax: 518-473-3456

NYS Office for People with Developmental Disabilities
44 Holland Avenue
Albany, NY 12229
866-946-9733 or TTY: 866-933-4889 Fax: 518-474-1335
Web site: www.opwdd.ny.gov

Acting Commissioner:
Kerry Delaney. 518-473-1997
Executive Deputy Commissioner:
Kerry Delaney. 518-473-1997
General Counsel:
Roger Bearden 518-473-1873
Director of Internal Audit:
James Nellegar 518-474-4376
Director, Advocacy Services:
Deborah Franchini 518-473-1997
Director, Communications & Public Affairs:
Jennifer Givner 518-474-6601
e-mail: communications.office@opwdd.ny.gov

Military & Naval Affairs, Division of
330 Old Niskayuna Rd
Latham, NY 12110
518-786-4786 or 518-489-6188 Fax: 518-786-4649
Web site: www.dmna.ny.gov

Adjutant General:
Major Gen Patrick Murphy. .518-786-4502
e-mail: pat.murphy@us.army.mil
Assistant Adjutant General - Air:
Anthony P. German 518-786-4317
Executive Officer:
Donald McKnight 518-786-4388
e-mail: bob.epp@us.army.mil
Legal Counsel:
Robert G Conway, Jr 518-786-4541
Joint Chief of Staff:
Col. Raymond L. Shields 518-786-4417
e-mail: renwick.payne@us.army.mil
Director, Governmental Community Affairs:
James M Huelle. 518-786-4580
Director, Public Affairs:
Eric Durr 518-786-4581/fax: 518-786-4649
e-mail: eric.d.durr@nfg@mail-mil
Director, Budget & Finance:
Robert A Martin 518-786-4514

Motor Vehicles Department
6 Empire State Plaza
Albany, NY 12228
Web site: www.dmv.ny.gov

Commissioner:
Barbara J Fiala. 518-486-9786/fax: 518-474-9578
Executive Deputy Commissioner:
J David Sampson. 518-474-0846/fax: 518-474-0712
Deputy Commissioner, Administration:
Gregory J Kline 518-474-6876/fax: 518-474-0712
Deputy Commissioner, Legal Affairs:
Neal Schoen. 518-473-1965/fax: 518-474-0712
Deputy Commissioner, Operations & Customer Service:
Yomika Bennett 518-474-0846
Deputy Commissioner, Safety, Consumer Protection & Clean Air:
Terri Egan 518-402-4860/fax: 518-474-0712
Director, Information Technology:
Adam Gigandet. 518-474-0605
Director, Driver Safety Programs:
Kathy McHale. 518-474-0855
Associate Commissioner, Communications:
Jackie McGinnis 518-473-7000/fax: 518-473-1930

NYSTAR - Division of Science, Technology & Innovation
30 South Pearl St
11th Fl
Albany, NY 12207

Offices and agencies generally appear in alphabetical order, except when specific order is requested by listee.

518-292-5700 Fax: 518-292-5798
e-mail: nystarsupport@esd.ny.gov
Web site: www.csd.ny.gov/nystar

Director:
Edward Reinfurt 518-292-5700
Deputy Director:
Edward J Hamilton 518-292-5700
Director, Communications/Government Affairs:
Jannette Rondo 518-292-5700/fax: 518-292-5798
Director, Regional Technology Development:
Matthew Watson 518-292-5700
Counsel:
Paul Jesep 518-292-5700

Parks, Recreation & Historic Preservation, NYS Office of
Empire State Plaza, Bldg 1
625 Broadway, 12207
Albany, NY 12238
518-486-0456 Fax: 518-486-2924
Web site: www.nysparks.com

Commissioner:
Rose Harvey 518-474-0443
Executive Deputy Commissioner:
Andrew Beers 518-474-0020/fax: 518-474-4492
Deputy Commissioner, Finance & Administration:
Melinda Scott 518-474-0414
Director, Operations & Programs:
Marc Talluto 518-474-0440
Deputy Commissioner, Historic Preservation:
Ruth Pierpont 518-237-8643 x3269
Secretary:
Virginia Davis 518-474-0443
General Counsel:
Patrick Bradford 518-474-0414
Park Police/Director, Law Enforcement:
Chief Richard O'Donnell 518-474-4029/fax: 518-408-1032
Deputy Public Information Officer:
Dan Keefe 518-486-1868

Parole Board, The
Corrections & Community Supervision
97 Central Ave
Albany, NY 12206
518-473-9548 Fax: 518-473-6037
Web site: www.parole.ny.gov; doccs.ny.gov

Acting Commissioner:
Anthony J Annucci 518-473-9548
Chief Counsel:
Terrence X Tracy 518-473-5671/fax: 518-473-9760
Public Information Offficer:
Vacant .518-486-4631/fax: 518-473-6037
Director, Administrative Services:
Jeffrey Nesich 518-473-3901/fax: 518-486-5858
Deputy Commissioner, Community Supervision:
Angela Jiminez . . . . .518-473-9672 or 212-239-5730
Director, Internal Operations:
Timothy O'Brien 518-408-3473

Prevention of Domestic Violence, Office for the
80 South Swan Street
11th Fl Rm 1157
Albany, NY 12210
518-457-5800 Fax: 518-457-5810
e-mail: opdvpublicinfo@opdv.ny.gov
Web site: www.opdv.ny.gov

90 Church St, 13th Fl
New York, NY 10007
212-417-4477
Fax: 212-417-4972

Executive Director:
Gwen Wright 518-457-5800
Director, NYC Program:
Sujata Warrier 212-417-4477
Counsel:
Johanna Sullivan 518-457-5800
Director, Prevention & Human Services:
Gwen Wright 518-457-5916
Fiscal Officer:
Linda Cassidy 518-457-7995
Public Information Officer:
Suzanne Cecala 518-457-5744
e-mail: suzanne.cecala@opdv.ny.gov

Public Employment Relations Board
80 Wolf Rd
Albany, NY 12205
518-457-2578 Fax: 518-457-2664
e-mail: perbinfo@perb.ny.gov
Web site: www.perb.ny.gov

Chair:
Jerome Lefkowitz 518-457-2578
Member:
Sheila S Cole 518-457-2578
Executive Director:
Anthony Zumbolo 518-457-2676
Deputy Chair & Counsel:
William A Herbert 518-457-2614
Secretary to the Board:
Sheila Talavera 518-457-2578
Director, Conciliation Office:
Kevin B. Flanigan 518-457-6014
Director, Employment Practices & Representation:
Monte Klein 518-457-5973

Public Service Commission
NYS Dept of Public Service
3 Empire State Plaza
Albany, NY 12223-1350
518-474-7080 Fax: 518-474-0421
Web site: www.dps.ny.gov

90 Church St
New York, NY 10007-2919
212-417-2378

Ellicott Sq Bldg
295 Main St
Room 1050
Buffalo, NY 14203
716-847-3941

Chairman:
Garry A Brown 518-474-2523/fax: 518-473-2838
Commissioner:
Maureen F Harris . . . . .518-474-2503 or 212-417-3168
fax: 518-473-2838
Commissioner:
Gregg C. Sayre . . . . .518-474-2503 or 212-417-3168
fax: 518-473-2838

Offices and agencies generally appear in alphabetical order, except when specific order is requested by listee.

Commissioner:
  Patricia L Acampora................518-474-2503 or 212-417-3168
  fax: 518-473-2838
Commissioner:
  James L Larocca...................518-474-2503 or 212-417-3168
  fax: 518-473-2838
Secretary to the Commission:
  Kathleen H Burgess.................518-474-6530/fax: 518-486-6081
  e-mail: secretary@dps.ny.gov
Executive Deputy:
  Judith Lee 518-408-1978/fax: 518-473-2838
General Counsel:
  Peter McGowan....................518-474-2510/fax: 518-486-5710
Director, Consumer Services Office:
  Sandra Sloane 518-474-3280
  e-mail: csd@dps.ny.gov
Acting Director, Energy Efficiency & the Environment:
  Colleen Gerwitz 518-474-2350
Director, Electric, Gas & Water:
  Thomas Dvorsky 518-473-6080/fax: 518-473-4992
Director, Office of Administration:
  Sorelle Brauth 518-474-2508/fax: 518-474-0413
Director, Telecommunications:
  Chad Hume 518-474-1668/fax: 518-474-5616
Director, Accounting & Finance:
  Doris Stout ....518-474-4508 or 212-417-2136
Director, Public Affairs:
  James Denn 518-474-7080/fax: 518-474-0421
  e-mail: james.denn@dps.ny.gov

Real Property Tax Services, Office of
NYS Dept of Tax & Finance
WA Harriman State Campus
Bldg 8A
Albany, NY 12227
518-474-3793 Fax: 518-474-4242

Acting Secretary of Board & Assistant Deputy Commissioner:
  Susan Savage 518-474-3793
State Board Member:
  John M Bacheller 518-474-3793
State Board Member (Chair):
  Matthew Rand...............................518-474-3793
State Board Member:
  Edgar A King 518-474-3793
Assistant to the Board:
  Darlene Maloney
  e-mail: darlene.maloney@tax.ny.gov

State Comptroller, Office of the
110 State St, 15th Fl
Albany, NY 12236-0001
518-474-4044 Fax: 518-473-3004
e-mail: contactus@osc.state.ny.us
Web site: www.osc.state.ny.us

633 Third Ave, 31st Fl
New York, NY 10017-6754
212-681-4491
Fax: 212-681-4468

State Comptroller:
  Thomas P DiNapoli ....518-474-4040 or 212-681-4491
First Deputy Comptroller:
  Pete Grannis....................518-474-2909 or 212-681-4469
Chief of Staff:
  Shawn Thompson 518-474-4044
Deputy Comptroller & Chief Information Officer:
  Kevin Belden 518-486-4349

Information Enterprise Applications & IT Business Management:
  Mary Anne Barry 518-474-8089
Director, Communications:
  Jennifer Freeman ....518-474-4015 or 212-681-4840
Assistant Comptroller, Business Communications:
  Ellen Evans....................518-474-4040 or 212-681-4489
Deputy Comptroller, Human Resources & Administration:
  Angela Dixon 518-474-5512
Inspector General - Internal Audit:
  Stephen Hillerman 518-549-2393
General Counsel:
  Nancy Groenwegen...........................518-474-3444
Executive Deputy Comptroller, Operations:
  Joan Sullivan..............................518-402-4103
Deputy Comptroller, City of New York:
  Ken Bleiwas 212-383-3905
  e-mail: osdc@osc.state.ny.us
Deputy Comptroller, Budget & Policy Analysis:
  Robert Ward...............................518-473-4333
Deputy Comptroller, Intergovernmental Relations:
  Cathy Calhoun 518-402-3234

State Department
One Commerce Plaza
99 Washington Avenue
Albany, NY 12231-0001
518-474-4750 Fax: 518-474-4597
e-mail: info@dos.ny.gov
Web site: www.dos.ny.gov

123 William Street
New York, NY 10038-3804
212-417-5800
Fax: 212-417-2383

Secretary of State:
  Cesar A Perales...............................518-474-0050
First Deputy Secretary of State:
  Daniel Shapiro 518-474-4750
General Counsel:
  Susan Watson 518-474-6740/fax: 518-473-9211
Deputy Secretary, Licensing:
  Marcos Vigil................................518-4743-2728
Deputy Secretary of State, Local Government Services:
  Dierdre Scozzafava 518-473-3355/fax: 518-474-6572
Deputy Secretary, Communications & Community Affairs:
  Vacant 518-486-9846/fax: 518-474-4765
  e-mail: info@dos.state.ny.us

State Police, Division of
Bldg 22, State Campus
1220 Washington Ave
Albany, NY 12226-2252
518-457-2180
e-mail: nyspmail@troopers.ny.gov
Web site: www.troopers.ny.gov

Superintendent:
  Joseph A D'Amico 518-457-6721
First Deputy Superintendent:
  Kevin T Gagan 518-457-6711/fax: 518-485-7505
Counsel:
  Vacant 518-457-6137/fax: 518-485-1164
Assistant Deputy Superintendent, Administration:
  Terence P O'Mara..............518-457-6622/fax: 518-485-5051
Deputy Superintendent, Employee Relations:
  Francis P Christensen 518-457-3572/fax: 518-485-7505
Deputy Superintendent, Field Command:
  John P Melville 518-457-6554/fax: 518-457-4779

Offices and agencies generally appear in alphabetical order, except when specific order is requested by listee.

Deputy Superintendent, Technology & Communications:
  Steven F Cumoletti 518-457-6621
Deputy Superintendent, Internal Affairs:
  Anthony G Ellis 518-485-6018
Director, Public Information:
  Darcy Wells 518-457-2180/fax: 518-485-7818
  e-mail: pio@troopers.ny.gov

Tax Appeals, Division of
Agency Building 1
Empire State Plaza
Albany, NY 12223
518-266-3000 Fax: 518-271-0886
e-mail: nysdota@nysdta.org
Web site: www.nysdta.org

Tax Appeals Tribunal
President & Commissioner:
  James H Tully Jr (2016) 518-266-3050
Commissioner:
  Charles H Nesbitt (2013) 518-266-3050
Counsel:
  Nicholas A Behuniak 518-266-3052
Secretary to the Tribunal:
  Jean A McDonnell 518-266-3036

Administrative Law Judges & Officers
Supervising Administrative Law Judge:
  Daniel J Ranalli 518-266-3000
Presiding Officer:
  Barbara J Russo 518-266-3000

Taxation & Finance Department
State Campus
Bldg 9, Rm 227
Albany, NY 12227
518-457-4242 Fax: 518-457-2486
Web site: www.tax.ny.gov

Commissioner:
  Thomas H Mattox 518-457-2244
Executive Deputy Commissioner:
  Nonie Manion 518-457-7358
Deputy Commissioner & Counsel:
  Amanda Hiller 518-457-3746/fax: 518-457-8247
Deputy Commissioner & Treasurer:
  Aida M Brewer 518-474-4250/fax: 518-402-4118
Deputy Commissioner, Criminal Enforcement:
  Risa Sugarman . . . . 518-457-9692 or 800-225-5829
Deputy Commissioner, Tax Policy Analysis:
  Robert D Plattner 518-457-4357
Deputy Commissioner, Processing & Taxpayer Svcs:
  Edward Chaszczewski 518-457-1000
Chief Financial Officer & Budget/Management Analysis:
  Eric Mostert 518-485-5080
Director, Public Information:
  Geoffrey Gloak 518-457-7377

Temporary & Disability Assistance, Office of
40 N Pearl St
Albany, NY 12243
518-473-1090 or 518-474-9516 Fax: 518-486-6255
e-mail: nyspio@otda.ny.gov
Web site: www.otda.ny.gov

Commissioner:
  Kristin M. Proud 518-474-4152/fax: 518-486-6255
Deputy Commissioner, Center for Child Well-Being:
  Eileen Stack 518-474-1078

Deputy Commissioner, Center for Specialized Services:
  Linda L Glassman 518-486-4151
Director, Budget, Finance & Data Management:
  Nancy Maney 518-474-0183
Deputy Commissioner, Operations & Program Support:
  Wilma Brown Phillips 518-473-3912
CIO, Information Technology:
  Rick Ryan 518-486-1012
Deputy Commissioner, Center for Employment & Economic Supports:
  Phyllis Morris 518-474-9222/fax: 518-474-5281
General Counsel:
  Krista Rock 518-474-9502
Acting Director, Intergovernmental Affairs Office:
  Ryan Richard 518-486-1012
Director, Public Information:
  Kristi L. Berner 518-474-9516/fax: 518-486-6935
  e-mail: nyspio@otda.ny.gov

Transportation Department
50 Wolf Road
Albany, NY 12232
518-457-5100 or 518-457-6195 Fax: 518-457-5583
Web site: www.dot.ny.gov

Commissioner:
  Joan McDonald 518-457-4422
Executive Deputy Commissioner:
  Stanley Gee 518-457-4422
CIO/Information Technology Division:
  Nancy Mulholland 518-485-8853
Operations & Asset Management Division:
  Roderic Sechrist 518-485-0887
Director, Legal Affairs Division:
  Janice A McLachlan 518-457-2411
CFO/Finance Office:
  Ron Epstein 518-457-2320
Director, Administrative Services Division:
  Pete Snyder 518-457-6300
Acting Director, Policy & Planning Division:
  Ron Epstein 518-457-2320
Director, Audit & Civil Rights Division:
  John Samaniuk 518-457-1590
Chief Engineer/Engineering Division:
  Phillip Eng 518-457-4430
Director, Communications Office:
  Beau Duffy 518-457-6400/fax: 518-457-6506
  e-mail: beau.duffy@dot.ny.gov

Veterans' Affairs, Division of
2 Empire State Plaza
17th Fl
Albany, NY 12223-1551
518-474-6114 or 888-838-7697 Fax: 518-473-0379
e-mail: dvainfo@veterans.ny.gov
Web site: www.veterans.ny.gov

Director:
  Eric J. Hesse 518-474-6114
  e-mail: ehesse@veterans.ny.gov
Executive Deputy Director:
  Vacant 518-474-6114
Secretary to the Director:
  Mary Quay 518-474-6114
  e-mail: m.quay@veterans.ny.gov
Deputy Director, Administration & Budget:
  Michelle LaRock 518-474-6114
  e-mail: mlarock@veterans.state.ny.us
Deputy Director, Programs, Operations & Training:
  Christine Tarnowski 518-474-6784
  e-mail: ctarnowski@veterans.state.ny.us

Offices and agencies generally appear in alphabetical order, except when specific order is requested by listee.

Counsel:
  Samuel Spitzberg 518-474-6114
  e-mail: sspitzberg@veterans.ny.gov
Assistant Director, Communications:
  Casey Lumbra 518-486-5251
  e-mail: clumbra@veterans.state.ny.us
Deputy Director, Eastern Region:
  Andrew Roberts 718-722-2584
Deputy Director, Western Region:
  Vacant 716-847-3414/fax: 716-847-3410

Welfare Inspector General, Office of NYS

Shirley Chisholm State Offc Bldg
55 Hanson Place
Room 650
Brooklyn, NY 11217
718-923-4290 or 800-682-4530 Fax: 718-923-4310
e-mail: owig@dfa.state.ny.us
Web site: www.owig.ny.gov

Acting Welfare Inspector General:
  Catherine Leahy Scott...............718-923-4290/fax: 718-923-4310
Chief Investigator:
  Joseph Bucci 718-923-4290
Confidential Assistant/Office Manager:
  Joy Quiles 718-923-4290/fax: 718-923-4310
  e-mail: joy.quiles@owig.ny.gov

Workers' Compensation Board

328 State Street
Schenectady, NY 12305
518-462-8880 or 877-632-4996 Fax: 518-473-1415
e-mail: publicinfo@wcb.ny.gov
Web site: www.wcb.ny.gov

Executive Director:
  Mark Wade 518-408-0469
Chair, Board of Commissioners:
  Robert E Beloten 518-408-0469/fax: 518-473-1415
Vice Chair:
  Fran Libous 518-408-0469/fax: 518-473-1415
Secretary to the Board:
  Sandra M Olson 518-402-6070
Director, Security:
  John Dale 518-402-0172/fax: 518-402-6100
Director, Information Management Systems:
  Matthew Ancin 518-474-6557/fax: 518-474-9367
General Counsel:
  Vacant 518-486-9564/fax: 518-402-0113
Director, Public Information:
  Rachel McEneny 518-408-5592/fax: 518-473-1415
  e-mail: publicinfo@wcb.ny.gov
Advocate for Injured Workers:
  Edwin Ruff ....800-580-6665 or 518-474-8182
  fax: 518-486-7510

Offices and agencies generally appear in alphabetical order, except when specific order is requested by listee.

LEGISLATIVE BRANCH SENATE

Members of the Senate welcome e-mail correspondence from the public. They may reply by e-mail, or by mail when more extensive follow-up is necessary. Please include both an e-mail and mailing address in all correspondence. Biographies of Senate Members appear in a separate section in the back of the book.

STATE SENATE LEADERSHIP

State Capitol
Albany, NY 12247
Web site: www.nysenate.gov

ADMINISTRATION

Francis W Patience 518-455-2051/fax: 518-455-3332
Title: Secretary of the Senate

Kathy Pendergast 518-455-2201/fax: 518-455-6742
Title: Director, Appointments Office

General Information 800-342-9860
Title: Bill Status Hotline

Christopher J Cook 518-455-2246/fax: 518-426-6842
Title: Director, Chamber Operations

Mary Carey 518-455-2245/fax: 518-426-6842
Title: Journal Clerk

Douglas J Breakell 518-455-2521/fax: 518-426-6743
Title: Director, Legislative Services

James Giliberto 518-455-2468/fax: 518-426-6901
Title: Legislative Librarian, Legislative Library

George Federoff 518-455-2338/fax: 518-455-3332
Title: Sergeant-at-Arms

Nicholas Parrella 518-455-7150/fax: 518-426-6827
Title: Director, Student Programs Office

Tracy Starr 518-455-3145/fax: 518-426-6831
Title: District Office Coordinator

Dawn Harrington 518-455-3376/fax: 518-426-6927
Title: Personnel Officer

James Bell 518-455-2313/fax: 518-455-7339
Title: Director, Technology Services

REPUBLICAN CONFERENCE LEADERSHIP

John J Flanagan (R) 518-455-2071
e-mail: flanagan@nysenate.gov
Title: Temporary President of the Senate

John A DeFrancisco (R) 518-455-3511
e-mail: jdefranc@nysenate.gov
Title: Chair of Senate Finance Committee

Thomas W Libous (R) 518-455-2677
e-mail: senator@senatorlibous.com
Title: Deputy Majority Leader; Legislative Operations

Catharine M Young (R) 518-455-3563
e-mail: cyoung@nysenate.gov
Title: Assistant Senate Majority Whip

James L Seward (R) 518-455-3131
e-mail: seward@nysenate.gov
Title: Chairman, Majority Program Development Committee

Kemp Hannon (R) 518-455-2200
e-mail: hannon@nysenate.gov
Title: Assistant Majority Leader, Operations

Kenneth P LaValle (R) 518-455-3121
e-mail: lavalle@nysenate.gov
Title: Chair, Senate Majority Conference

Hugh T Farley (R) 518-455-2181
e-mail: farley@nysenate.gov
Title: Vice President Pro Tempore

William J Larkin Jr (R) 518-455-2770
e-mail: larkin@nysenate.gov
Title: Assistant Majority Leader for House Operations

Andrew Lanza (R) 518-455-3215
e-mail: lanza@nysenate.gov
Title: Deputy Majority Leader for Government Oversight & Accountability

Michael F Nozzolio (R) 518-455-2366
e-mail: nozzolio@nysenate.gov
Title: Majority Whip of the Senate

Carl L Marcellino (R) 518-455-2390
e-mail: marcelli@nysenate.gov
Title: Vice Chair, Senate Majority Conference

Michael Ranzenhofer (R) 518-455-3161
e-mail: ranz@nysenate.gov
Title: Deputy Majority Leader for Economic Development

Patrick M Gallivan (R) 518-455-3471
e-mail: gallivan@nysenate.gov
Title: Liaison to the Executive Branch

Martin J Golden (R) 518-455-2730
e-mail: golden@nysenate.gov
Title: Secretary of the Senate Majority Conference

Joseph A. Griffo (R) 518-455-2015
e-mail: griffo@nysenate.gov
Title: Deputy Majority Leader for Policy

Elizabeth O'C Little (R) 518-455-2811
e-mail: little@nysenate.gov
Title: Deputy Majority Whip for the Senate

Joseph Robach (R) 518-455-2909
e-mail: robach@nysenate.gov
Title: Chairman, Majority Steering Committee

Patricia Ritchie (R) 518-455-3438
e-mail: ritchie@nysenate.gov
Title: Deputy Majority Leader for Senate/Assembly Relations

John J Bonancic (R) 518-455-3181
e-mail: bonacic@nysenate.gov
Title: Deputy Majority Leader, State/Federal Relations

REPUBLICAN CONFERENCE STAFF

Diane Burman 518-455-2675/fax: 518-426-6830
Title: Counsel to the Republican Conference

Irene Villacci 518-455-2533/fax: 518-426-6974
Title: Counsel to the Majority Leader

Thomas Dunham 518-455-2381/fax: 518-426-6818
Title: Director of Majority Operations

Offices and agencies generally appear in alphabetical order, except when specific order is requested by listee.

Joseph Sorbero 518-455-3171/fax: 518-426-6950
Title: Special Advisor to Republican Conference Leader

Janet L Reilly 518-455-2589/fax: 518-426-6965
Title: Majority Calendar Clerk

Robert Mujica......................518-455-2675/fax: 518-426-6830
Title: Secretary to the Finance Committee & Senior Advisor for Policy

Kelly Cummings...................518-455-2264/fax: 518-455-2260
Title: Director, Republican Conference

Eileen Miller 518-455-3545/fax: 518-426-6917
Title: Director, Media Services

Douglas Breakell 518-455-2550/fax: 518-426-6743
Title: Director, Legislative Services

INDEPENDENT DEMOCRATIC CONFERENCE LEADERSHIP

Jeffrey D. Klein (D-R-W-I) 518-455-3595
e-mail: jdklein@nysenate.gov
Title: Independent Democratic Conference Leader

David J. Valesky (D-W-I) 518-455-2838
e-mail: valesky@nysenate.gov
Title: Independent Democratic Conference Leader for Legislative Operations

David Carlucci (D-W-I) 518-455-2991
e-mail: carlucci@nysenate.gov
Title: Independent Democratic Conference Whip

Diane J. Savino (D-W-I)......................518-455-2437
e-mail: savino@nysenate.gov
Title: Independent Democratic Conference Liason to the Executive Branch

Tony Avella (D-W-I)...........................518-455-2210
e-mail: savino@nysenate.gov
Title: Assistant Conference Leader, Policy & Administration of Independent Democratic Conference

DEMOCRATIC CONFERENCE LEADERSHIP

Andrea Stewart-Cousins (D).........................518-455-2585
e-mail: scousins@nysenate.gov
Title: Democratic Leader

Michael Gianaris (D) 518-455-3486
e-mail: gianaris@nysenate.gov
Title: Deputy Democratic Leader

Toby Ann Stavisky (D)...........................518-455-3461
e-mail: stavisky@nysenate.gov
Title: Assistant Democratic Leader for Conference Operations

Martin M Dilan (D)...............................518-455-2177
e-mail: dilan@nysenate.gov
Title: Assistant Democratic Leader for Policy & Administration

Jose M. Serrano (D) 518-455-2795
e-mail: serrano@nysenate.gov
Title: Chair of Democratic Conference

Ruth Hassell-Thompson (D) 518-455-2061
e-mail: hassellt@nysenate.gov
Title: Vice Chair of Democratic Conference

Kevin S. Parker (D)..............................518-455-2580
e-mail: parker@nysenate.gov
Title: Assistant Democratic Leader, Intergovernmental Affairs

Jose Peralta (D) 518-455-2529
e-mail: jperalta@nysenate.gov
Title: Democratic Conference Whip

Timothy Kennedy (D)...............................518-455-2426
e-mail: kennedy@nysenate.gov
Title: Assistant Democratic Conference Whip

Bill Perkins (D)..................................518-455-2441
e-mail: perkins@nysenate.gov
Title: Deputy Democratic Conference Whip

Velmanette Montgomery (D) 518-455-3451
e-mail: montgome@nysenate.gov
Title: Secretary of the Senate Democratic Conference

Neil D. Breslin (D)..............................518-455-2225
e-mail: breslin@nysenate.gov
Title: Assistant Democratic Leader, Floor Operations

Daniel Squadron (D)..............................518-455-2625
e-mail: squadron@nysenate.gov
Title: Deputy Democratic Conference Floor Leader

Gustavo Rivera (D) 518-455-3395
e-mail: grivera@nysenate.gov
Title: Chair, Democratic Program Development

DEMOCRATIC CONFERENCE STAFF

John Tomlin 518-455-2800
Title: Chief of Staff to the Democratic Leader

Celeste Knight....................518-455-3401/fax: 518-455-2816
Title: Special Assistant

Keith St John 518-455-2711/fax: 518-426-6955
Title: Deputy Counsel

Mary K Berger 518-455-2636/fax: 518-455-2816
Title: Director, Minority Operations

Joseph Pennisi....................518-455-2217/fax: 518-426-6839
Title: Comptroller, Senate Minority

Tracey Pierce-Smith 518-455-2501/fax: 518-426-6930
Title: Director, Minority Conference Services

Vacant..........................518-455-2415/fax: 518-426-6933
Title: Press Secretary to the Minority Leader

STATE SENATE ROSTER

Multiple party abbreviations following the names of legislators indicate that those legislators ran as the Senate candidate for each identified party.
Source: NYS Board of Elections. Party abbreviations: Conservative (C), Democrat (D), Green (G), Independent (I), Liberal (L), Republican (R), Working Families (WF)

Joseph P Addabbo Jr (D) 518-455-2322/fax: 518-426-6875
District: 15 *Room:* 613 LOB *e-mail:* addabbo@nysenate.gov
Committees: Aging; Civil Service & Pensions; Education; Labor; Racing, Gaming & Wagering (Ranking Member); Veterans, Homeland Security & Military Affairs (Ranking Member)
Senior Staff: Patricia McCabe

George Amedore, Jr (R) 518-455-2350/fax: 518-426-6751
District: 46 *Room:* 802 LOB *e-mail:* amedore@nysenate.gov
Committees: Alcoholism & Drug Abuse (Chair); banks; Consumer Protection; Elections; Judiciary; Social Services; Veterans' Affairs
Senior Staff: Douglas Breakell

Tony Avella (D-WF) 518-455-2210/fax: 518-426-6736
District: 11 *Room:* 902 LOB *e-mail:* avella@nysenate.gov
Committees: Banks; Cultural Affairs, Tourism, Parks & Recreation;, Education; Elections; Environmental Conservation; Ethics (Chair); Housing,

---

Offices and agencies generally appear in alphabetical order, except when specific order is requested by listee.

Construction & Community Development; Insurance; Judiciary; Transportation
Senior Staff: Seth Urbinder

John J Bonacic (R) 518-455-3181/fax: 518-426-6948
District: 42 *Room:* 509 LOB *e-mail:* bonacic@nysenate.gov
Title: Republican Leader, State/Federal Relations
Committees: Alcoholism & Drug Abuse; Banks; Children & Families; Finance; Housing, Construction & Community Dvlpmnt; Judiciary (Chair); Racing, Gaming & Wagering (Chair); Rules; Cultural Affrs Tourism, Parks & Recreation
Senior Staff: Andrew Winchell

Philip M. Boyle (R) 518-455-3411/fax: 518-426-6973
District: 4 *Room:* 814 LOB *e-mail:* pboyle@nysenate.gov
Committees: Codes; Consumer Protection; Commerce, Economic Development & Small Business (Chair); Housing, Construction & Community Development; Local Government; Racing, Gaming & Wagering
Senior Staff: Tom Connolly

Neil D Breslin (D) 518-455-2225/fax: 518-426-6807
District: 44 *Room:* 414 CAP *e-mail:* breslin@nysenate.gov
Title: Assistant Democratic Leader, Floor Operations
Committees: Banks; Education; Finance; Higher Education; Insurance (Ranking Member); Judiciary; Rules
Senior Staff: Maureen Cetrino

David Carlucci (D-W-I) 518-455-2991/fax: 518-426-6737
District: 38 *Room:* 815 LOB *e-mail:* carlucci@nysenate.gov
Title: Independent Democratic Conference Whip
Committees: Alchlsm & Drg Abuse; Enrgy & Telecomm.; Infrstrctre & Cptl Invstmnt; Insrnce; Invstgtns & Gov't Ops., Mntl Hlth & Dvlpmntl Dsblts; Social Services (Chair); Racing, Gaming & Wgring; Rules; Vtrn's Affrs; Hmlnd Scrty & Mltry Affrs
Senior Staff: Jay Martin

Leroy Comrie (D) 518-455-2701
District: 14 *Room:* 617 LOB *e-mail:* comrie@nysenate.gov
Committees: Agriculture; Civil Service & Pensions; Consumer Protection; Elections; Infrastructure & Capital Investments; Judiciary; Racing & Wagering; Veterans, Homeland Security & Military Affrs
Senior Staff: Derrick Davis

Thomas D Croci (R) 518-455-2215/fax: 518-426-6745
District: 55 *Room:* 905 LOB *e-mail:* croci@nysenate.gov
Committees: Alcoholism & Drug Abuse; Civil Service & Pensions; Energy & Telecommunications; Higher Education; Infrastructure & Capital Investments; Veterans, Homeland Security & Military Affairs (Chair)
Senior Staff: Christopher Molluso

John A DeFrancisco (R) 518-455-3511/fax: 518-426-6952
District: 50 *Room:* 416 CAP *e-mail:* jdefranc@nysenate.gov
Title: Chair, Finance Committee
Committees: Banks; Cities; Codes; Crime Victims, Crime & Correction; Finance (Chair); Judiciary; Labor
Senior Staff: Dorothy Pohlid

Ruben Diaz Sr (D) 518-455-2511/fax: 518-426-6945
District: 32 *Room:* 606 LOB *e-mail:* diaz@nysenate.gov
Committees: Aging (Ranking Member); Banks; Finance; Investigations & Government Operations; Judiciary; Transportation
Senior Staff: Helen Jacome

Martin M Dilan (D) 518-455-2177/fax: 518-426-6947
District: 18 *Room:* 711B LOB *e-mail:* dilan@nysenate.gov
Title: Asst Democratic Leader, Policy & Administration
Committees: Civil Service & Pensions; Elections; Energy & Telecommunications; Finance; Infrastructure & Capital Investments; Judiciary; Labor; Rules; Transportation (Ranking Member)
Senior Staff: Heath Heimroth

Adriano Espaillat (D) 518-455-2041/fax: 518-426-6847
District: 31 *Room:* 513 LOB *e-mail:* espailla@nysenate.gov
Committees: Codes; Finance; Higher Education; Housing, Construction & Community Development (Ranking Member); Insurance; Judiciary; Rules
Senior Staff: Aneiry Batista

Hugh T Farley (R-C-I) 518-455-2181/fax: 518-455-2271
District: 49 *Room:* 711 LOB *e-mail:* farley@nysenate.gov
Title: Chair, Republican Conference Program Development Committee
Committees: Banks (Vice Chair); Education; Ethics; Finance; Health; Rules; Social Services
Senior Staff: Patricia Pietrusza

Simcha Felder (D) 518-455-2754/fax: 518-426-6931
District: 17 *Room:* 944 LOB *e-mail:* felder@nysenate.gov
Committees: Aging; Children & Families (Chair); Commerce, Economic Development & Small Business; Health; Infrastructure & Capital Investments; Mental Health & Developmental Disabilities
Senior Staff: Cirel Neumann

John J Flanagan (R-I-C) 518-455-2071/fax: 518-426-6904
District: 2 *Room:* 330 CAP *e-mail:* flanagan@nysenate.gov
Title: Deputy Republican Conference Leader, Policy
Committees: Rules (Chair)
Senior Staff: Raymond Bennardo

Rich Funke (R-C-I) 518-455-2215/fax: 518-426-6745
District: 55 *Room:* 905 LOB *e-mail:* funke@nysenate.gov
Committees: Aging; Agriculture; Cities; Commerce, Economic Development & Small Business; Consumer Protection; Elections (Chair); Environmental Conservation; Higher Education
Senior Staff: Matt Nelligan

Patrick M. Gallivan (R) 518-455-3471/fax: 518-426-6949
District: 59 *Room:* 947 LOB *e-mail:* gallivan@nysenate.gov
Title: Deputy Republican Conference Leader, Senate Assembly Relations
Committees: Agriculture; Codes; Commerce, Econ Development & Small Business; Crime Victims, Crime & Correction (Chair); Elections; Finance; Higher Education; Housing Construction & Community Development; Infrastructure & Capital Investment; Labor; Transportation
Senior Staff: A.J. Baynes

Michael N Gianaris (D) 518-455-3486/fax: 518-426-6929
District: 12 *Room:* 413 CAP *e-mail:* gianaris@nysenate.gov
Title: Deputy Democratic Leader
Committees: Ethics; Finance
Senior Staff: Michael Sais

Martin J. Golden (R-C) 518-455-2730/fax: 518-426-6910
District: 22 *Room:* 409 LOB *e-mail:* golden@nysenate.gov
Title: Chairman, Republican Conference Steering Committee
Committees: Aging; Civil Service & Pensions (Chair); Banks; Codes; Finance; Health; Insurance; Investigations & Government Operations; Veterans, Homeland Security & Military Affairs
Senior Staff: Gerard Kassar

Joseph A Griffo (R-C) 518-455-3334/fax: 518-426-6921
District: 47 *Room:* 612 LOB *e-mail:* griffo@nysenate.gov
Title: Liaison to the Executive Branch
Committees: Codes; Cmmrce, Ecnmc Dvlpmnt & Smll Bsness; Crime Vctms,Crime& Crrctn; Cltrl Affrs, Tourism, Prks & Rec.; Enrgy & Telecomm (Chair); Finance; Hgher Ed; Rcing, Gming & Wgrnig; Vtrns', Hmlnd Scrty & Mltry Affrs
Senior Staff: Dwight Evans

Jesse Hamilton (D) 518-455-2431/fax: 518-426-6856
District: 20 *Room:* 608 LOB *e-mail:* hamilton@nysenate.gov
Committees: Agriculture; Banks; Codes; Commerce, Economic Development & Small Business; Education; Energy & Telecommunications; Mental Health & Developmental Disabilities
Senior Staff: Jarvis Houston

Offices and agencies generally appear in alphabetical order, except when specific order is requested by listee.

Kemp Hannon (R-I-C) 518-455-2200/fax: 518-426-6954
District: 6 *Room:* 420 CAP *e-mail:* hannon@nysenate.gov
Title: Assistant Republican Conference Leader, Conference Operations
Committees: Finance; Health (Chair); Judiciary; Labor; Mental Health &
Developmental Disabilities; Rules
Senior Staff: Phil Hecken

Ruth Hassell-Thompson (D-WF) 518-455-2061/fax: 518-426-6998
District: 36 *Room:* 707 LOB *e-mail:* hassellt@nysenate.gov
Title: Vice Chair, Democratic Conference
Committees: Alcoholism & Drug Abuse; Commerce, Economic Development
& Small Business; Crime Victims, Crime & Correction (Ranking Member);
Finance; Health; Rules
Senior Staff: Gerard Savage

Brad Hoylman (D) 518-455-2451/fax: 518-426-6846
District: 27 *Room:* 413 LOB *e-mail:* hoylman@nysenate.gov
Committees: Aging; Crime Victim, Crime & Correction; Environmental
Conservation (Ranking Member); Health; Investigations & Government
Operations (Ranking Member); Judiciary; Local Governments; Cultural
Affairs; Tourism, Parks & Recreation
Senior Staff: Peter Ajemian

Timothy Kennedy (D) 518-455-2426/fax: 518-426-6851
District: 63 *Room:* 506 LOB *e-mail:* kennedy@nysenate.gov
Committees: Banks; Commerce, Economic Development & Small Business
(Ranking Member); Cultural Affairs, Tourism, Parks & Recreation; Energy &
Telecommunications; Finance; Insurance; Infrastructure & Capital
Investment; Transportation
Senior Staff: Lauren Rivett

Jeffrey D Klein (D) 518-455-3595/fax: 518-426-6887
District: 34 *Room:* 913 LOB *e-mail:* jdklein@nysenate.gov
Title: Independent Democratic Conference Leader
Committees:
Senior Staff: John Emrick

Liz Krueger (D-WF) 518-455-2297/fax: 518-426-6874
District: 28 *Room:* 808 LOB *e-mail:* lkrueger@nysenate.gov
Committees: Codes; Elections; Finance (Ranking Member); Higher
Education; Housing, Construction & Community Development; Mental
Health & Developmental Disabilities; Rules
Senior Staff: Brad Usher

Kenneth P LaValle (R-I-C) 518-455-3121/fax: 518-426-6826
District: 1 *Room:* 806 LOB *e-mail:* lavalle@nysenate.gov
Title: Chair, Senate Republican Conference
Committees: Aging; Education; Environmental Conservation; Finance;
Higher Education (Chair); Insurance; Judiciary; Rules; Social Services
Senior Staff: Joann Scalia

Andrew J Lanza (R-I) 518-455-3215/fax: 518-426-6852
District: 24 *Room:* 708 LOB *e-mail:* lanza@nysenate.gov
Title: Deputy Republican Conference Leader, Policy
Committees: Cities (Chair); Civil Service & Pensions; Codes; Education;
Ethics; Finance; Insurance; Judiciary
Senior Staff: John Turoski

William J Larkin Jr (R-C) 518-455-2770/fax: 518-426-6923
District: 39 *Room:* 502 CAP *e-mail:* larkin@nysenate.gov
Title: Republican Conference Whip
Committees: Corporations, Authorities & Commissions; Finance; Health;
Insurance; Rules; Transportation; Veterans, Homeland Security & Military
Affairs
Senior Staff: Jennifer Downs

George S. Latimer (D) 518-455-2031/fax: 518-455-6860
District: 37 *Room:* 615 LOB *e-mail:* latimer@nysenate.gov
Committees: Banks; Consumer Protection; Education (Ranking Member);
Environmental Conservation; Insurance; Local Government; Racing, Gaming
& Wagering
Senior Staff: Victor Mallison

Thomas W Libous (R-I-C) 518-455-2677/fax: 518-455-2065
District: 52 *Room:* 429 CAP *e-mail:* senator@senatorlibous.com
Title: Deputy Republican Conference Leader, Legislative Operations
Committees: Rules (Vice Chair)
Senior Staff: James Thomas

Elizabeth O'C Little (R-I-C) 518-455-2811/fax: 518-426-6873
District: 45 *Room:* 310 LOB *e-mail:* little@nysenate.gov
Title: Assistant Senate Republican Conference Whip
Committees: Energy & Telecommunications; Consumer Protection; Crime
Victims, Crime & Correction; Cultural Affairs, Tourism, Parks & Recreation
(Chair); Education; Environmental Conservation; Health; Finance; Rules
Senior Staff: Daniel MacEntee

Carl L Marcellino (R) 518-455-2390/fax: 518-426-6975
District: 5 *Room:* 811 LOB *e-mail:* marcelli@nysenate.gov
Title: Secretary, Senate Republican Conference
Committees: Investigations & Government Operations (Chair); Banks;
Cultural Affairs, Tourism, Parks & Recreation; Education; Environmental
Conservation; Finance; Labor; Rules; Infrastructure & Capital Investment
(Chair); Transportation (Vice Chair)
Senior Staff: Kirk Ives

Kathleen A. Marchione (R-C) 518-455-2381/fax: 518-426-6985
District: 43 *Room:* 918 LOB *e-mail:* marchione@nysenate.gov
Committees: Consumer Protection; Cultural Affairs; Tourism, Parks &
Recreation; Elections; Labor; Local Government (Chair); Racing, Gaming &
Wagering; Aging; Banks
Senior Staff: Joshua Fitzpatrick

Jack Martins (R) 518-455-3265/fax: 518-426-6739
District: 7 *Room:* 915 LOB *e-mail:* martins@nysenate.gov
Committees: Banks; Civil Service & Pensions; Corporations, Authorities &
Commissions; Finance; Health; Insurance; Labor (Chair); Social Services
Senior Staff: Paul Ehrlich

Velmanette Montgomery (D) 518-455-3451/fax: 518-426-6854
District: 25 *Room:* 903 LOB *e-mail:* montgome@nysenate.gov
Title: Secretary of the Senate Democratic Conference
Committees: Agriculture; Children & Families (Ranking Member); Crime
Victims, Crime & Correction; Education; Finance; Health; Rules
Senior Staff: Susan Leung

Terrence Murphy (R) 518-455-3111/fax: 518-426-6977
District: 40 *Room:* 817 LOB *e-mail:* murphy@nysenate.gov
Committees: Banks; Ethics; Health; Investigations & Government
Operations; Labor; Local Governments; Mental Health & Developmental
Disabilities
Senior Staff: Matthew Slater

Michael F Nozzolio (R-C) 518-455-2366/fax: 518-426-6953
District: 54 *Room:* 503 CAP *e-mail:* nozzolio@nysenate.gov
Title: Vice Chairman, Senate Republican Conference
Committees: Codes (Chair); Elections; Crime Victims, Crime & Correction;
Finance; Housing, Construction & Community Development; Investigations
& Government Operations; Judiciary; Racing, Gaming & Wagering; Rules;
Transportation
Senior Staff: Joan Grela

Thomas F O'Mara (R) 518-455-2091/fax: 518-426-6976
District: 58 *Room:* 848 LOB *e-mail:* omara@nysenate.gov
Committees: Agriculture; Banks; Codes; Energy & Telecommunications;
Environmental Conservation (Chair); Finance; Insurance; Investigations &
Government Operations; Judiciary; Transportation
Senior Staff: Pierson Ellis

Robert G Ortt (R) 518-455-2024/fax: 518-426-6987
District: 62 *Room:* 815 LOB *e-mail:* ortt@nysenate.gov
Committees: Cities; Civil Service & Pensions; Corporations, Authorities &
Commissions; Environmental Conservation; Local Government; Mental
Health & Developmental Disabilities (Chair); Veterans, Homeland Security
& Military Affairs
Senior Staff: Scott Kiedrowski

Offices and agencies generally appear in alphabetical order, except when specific order is requested by listee.

Marc Panepinto (D)................518-455-2760/fax: 518-426-6760
District: 60 *Room:* 302 LOB *e-mail:* panepinto@nysenate.gov
Committees: Agriculture (Ranking Member); Codes; Health; Housing, Construction & Community Development; Insurance; Local Government (Ranking Member); Transportation; Veterans, Homeland Security & Military Affairs
Senior Staff: Danny Corum

Kevin S Parker (D-WF)...........518-455-2580/fax: 518-426-6843
District: 21 *Room:* 604 LOB *e-mail:* parker@nysenate.gov
Title: Assistant Democratic Leader, Intergovernmental Affairs
Committees: Alcoholism & Drug Abuse (Ranking Member); Banks; Cultural Affairs, Tourism, Parks & Recreation; Energy & Telecommunications (Ranking Member); Finance; Higher Education; Insurance; Rules
Senior Staff: Vaughn Mayers

Jose Peralta (D)...................518-455-2529/fax: 518-455-6909
District: 13 *Room:* 415 LOB *e-mail:* jperalta@nysenate.gov
Title: Democratic Conference Whip
Committees: Cities; Consumer Protection; Crime Victims, Crime & Correction; Education; Finance; Higher Education; Labor (Ranking Member)
Senior Staff: Nancy Conde

Bill Perkins (D-WF)...............518-455-2441/fax: 518-426-6809
District: 30 *Room:* 517 LOB *e-mail:* perkins@nysenate.gov
Title: Deputy Democratic Conference Whip
Committees: Crime Victims, Crime & Correction; Codes; Corporations, Authorities & Commissions (Ranking Member); Finance; Judiciary; Labor; Rules; Transportation
Senior Staff: Cordell Cleare

Michael H Ranzenhofer (R-I-C)......518-455-3161/fax: 518-426-6963
District: 61 *Room:* 609 LOB *e-mail:* ranz@nysenate.gov
Title: Deputy Republican Conference Leader, Economic Development
Committees: Agriculture; Corporations, Authorities & Commissions (Chair); Education; Finance; Judiciary; Racing, Gaming & Wagering; Transportation
Senior Staff: Kathy Donner

Patricia Ritchie (R)................518-455-3438/fax: 518-426-6740
District: 48 *Room:* 412 LOB *e-mail:* ritchie@nysenate.gov
Committees: Agriculture (Chair); Alcoholism & Drug Abuse; Civil Service & Pensions; Crime Victims, Crime & Corrections; Cultural Affairs, Tourism, Parks & Recreation; Energy & Telecommunications; Finance; Higher Education; Local Government; Transportation
Senior Staff: Sarah Compo

J Gustavo Rivera (D)...............518-455-3395/fax: 518-426-6858
District: 33 *Room:* 408 LOB *e-mail:* grivera@nysenate.gov
Title: Chair of Democratic Conference Program Development
Committees: Crime Victims, Crime & Corrections; Ethics; Finance; Health (Ranking Member); Higher Education; Labor; Mental Health & Developmental Disabilities
Senior Staff: Katrina Asante

Joseph E Robach (R-I-C)...........518-455-2909/fax: 518-426-6938
District: 56 *Room:* 803 LOB *e-mail:* robach@nysenate.gov
Title: Deputy Republican Conference Whip of the Senate
Committees: Commerce, Economic Development & Small Business; Consumer Protection; Education; Finance; Higher Education; Infrastructure & Capital Investment; Labor; Transportation (Chair)
Senior Staff: Kate Munzinger

John L Sampson (D)...............518-455-2788/fax: 518-426-6806
District: 19 *Room:* 808 LOB *e-mail:* sampson@nysenate.gov
Committees:
Senior Staff: Michelle Trotman

James Sanders (D)................518-455-3531/fax: 518-426-6859
District: 10 *Room:* 508 LOB *e-mail:* sanders@nysenate.gov
Committees: Banks; Civil Service & Pensions (RM); Commerce, Economic Development & Small Business; Cultural Affairs, Tourism, Parks &

Recreation; Insurance; Labor; Racing, Gaming & Wagering; Veterans, Homeland Security & Military Affairs
Senior Staff: Clyde Vaneo

Diane J Savino (D).................518-455-2437/fax: 518-426-6943
District: 23 *Room:* 315 LOB *e-mail:* savino@nysenate.gov
Title: Independent Democratic Conference Liaison to the Executive Branch
Committees: Banks (Chair); Children & Families; Cities; Codes; Civil Service & Pensions; Consumer Protection; Crime Victims, Crime & Correction; Finance; Judiciary; Labor
Senior Staff: Robert Cataldo

Sue Serino (R).....................518-455-2945/fax: 518-426-6770
District: 41 *Room:* 812 LOB *e-mail:* serino@nysenate.gov
Committees: Aging (Chair; Children & Families; Cultural Affairs, Tourism, Parks & Recreation; Education; Higher Education; Judiciary; Mental Health & Developmental Disabilities
Senior Staff: Caroline Chauvin

Jose M Serrano (D)................518-455-2795/fax: 518-426-6886
District: 29 *Room:* 406 LOB *e-mail:* serrano@nysenate.gov
Title: Chair of Democratic Conference
Committees: Aging; Agriculture; Children & Families; Consumer Protection; Cultural Affairs, Tourism, Parks & Recreation (Ranking Member); Environmental Conservation; Mental Health & Developmental Disabilities; Veterans, Homeland Security & Military Affairs
Senior Staff: Gregory Meyer, Esq.

James L Seward (R-I-C)...........518-455-3131/fax: 518-455-3123
District: 51 *Room:* 430 CAP *e-mail:* seward@nysenate.gov
Title: Assistant Republican Conference Leader, Operations
Committees: Agriculture; Education; Finance; Health; Higher Education; Insurance (Chair); Mental Health & Developmental Disabilities; Rules
Senior Staff: Duncan S Davie

Dean G Skelos (R-IP-C)...........518-455-3171/fax: 518-426-6950
District: 9 *Room:* 909 LOB *e-mail:* skelos@nysenate.gov
Title: Republican Conference Leader
Committees:
Senior Staff: Thomas K Dunham

Daniel Squadron (D-WF)...........518-455-2625/fax: 518-426-6956
District: 26 *Room:* 515 LOB *e-mail:* squadron@nysenate.gov
Title: Deputy Democratic Floor Leader
Committees: Cities; Codes (Ranking Member); Corporations, Authorities & Commissions; Finance; Investigations & Government Operations; Social Services; Transportation
Senior Staff: Adrian Gonzalez

Toby Ann Stavisky (D-WF).........518-455-3461/fax: 518-426-6857
District: 16 *Room:* 706 LOB *e-mail:* stavisky@nysenate.gov
Title: Assistant Democratic Leader for Conference Operations
Committees: Education; Finance; Health; Higher Education (Ranking Member); Judiciary; Transportation
Senior Staff: Michael Favilla

Andrea Stewart-Cousins (D).........518-455-2585/fax: 518-426-6811
District: 35 *Room:* 907 LOB *e-mail:* scousins@nysenate.gov
Title: Democratic Leader
Committees: Rules (Ranking Member)
Senior Staff: Jeffery Pearlman

David J Valesky (D)................518-455-2838/fax: 518-426-6885
District: 53 *Room:* 512 LOB *e-mail:* valesky@nysenate.gov
Title: Independent Democratic Conference Leader, Legislative Operations
Committees: Aging; Agriculture; Commerce, Economic Development & Small Business; Education; Health; Higher Education; Finance; Local Government; Rules; Transportation
Senior Staff: Jessica DeCerce

Offices and agencies generally appear in alphabetical order, except when specific order is requested by listee.

Michael Venditto (R)................518-455-3341/fax: 518-426-6823
District: 8   *Room:* 946 LOB   *e-mail:* venditto@nysenate.gov
Committees: Consumer Protection (Chair); Crime Victims, Crime &
Correction; Insurance; Judiciary; Labor;
Senior Staff: John Banville

Catharine M Young (R-C-I)........518-455-3563/fax: 518-426-6905
District: 57   *Room:* 307 LOB   *e-mail:* cyoung@nysenate.gov
Committees: Agriculture; Children & Families; Environmental Conservation;
Finance; Health; Housing, Construction & Community Development (Chair);
Insurance; Rules; Transportation
Senior Staff: Jessica Jeune

STATE SENATE STANDING COMMITTEES

Aging
Chair:
  Sue Serino (R).................................518-455-2945
Ranking Minority Member:
  Ruben Diaz Sr (D).............................518-455-2511

Committee Staff
Committee Director:
  Caroline Chauvin..............................518-455-2945
Republican Assistant Counsel:
  Barbara McRedmond.............................518-455-2484

Membership

Majority
Kathleen A. Marchione	Martin J Golden
Kenneth P LaValle	Rich Funke

Minority
Simcha Felder	Brad Hoylman
Joseph P Addabbo Jr	Jose Serrano
David Valesky	

Agriculture
Chair:
  Patricia Ritchie (R)..........................518-455-3438
Ranking Minority Member:
  Marc Panepinto (D)............................518-455-2760

Committee Staff
Committee Director:
  Todd Kusnierz.................................518-455-3438

Key Senate Staff Assignments
Republican Assistant Counsel:
  Paul Midey....................................518-455-2599

Membership

Majority
Patrick Gallivan	Thomas O'Mara
Michael Ranzenhofer	Rich Funke
James L Seward	Catharine Young

Minority
Jose Serrano	David Valesky
Jesse Hamilton	Leroy Comrie
Valmanette Montgomery	

Alcoholism & Drug Abuse
Chair:
  George Amedore Jr (R).........................518-455-2350
Ranking Minority Member:
  Kevin Parker (D)..............................518-455-2580

Membership

Majority
Thomas Croci	Patricia Ritchie
John J Bonacic	

Minority
David Carlucci	Ruth Hassell-Thompson

Banks
Chair:
  Diane J Savino (D)............................518-455-2437
Ranking Minority Member:
  Jesse Hamilton (D)............................518-455-2431

Committee Staff

Key Senate Staff Assignments
Republican Senior Counsel:
  Robert Farley.................................518-455-3127
Democratic Associate Counsel:
  Richard Jacobson

Membership

Majority
Kathleen Marchione	Hugh T Farley
Jack Martins	John J Bonacic
John A DeFrancisco	Martin Golden
Carl L Marcellino	Thomas O'Mara
Terrence Murphy	

Minority
George Latimer	Kevin S. Parker
James Sanders, Jr.	Tony Avella
Neil D Breslin	Ruben Diaz Sr
Timothy M Kennedy	

Children & Families
Chair:
  Simcha Felder (D).............................518-455-2754
Ranking Minority Member:
  Velmanette Montgomery (D).....................518-455-3451

Membership

Majority
John J. Bonacic	Catharine M Young
Sue Serino	

Minority
Diane Savino	Jose Serrano

Cities
Chair:
  Andrew Lanza (R)..............................518-455-3215
Ranking Minority Member:
  Daniel Squadron (D)...........................518-455-2625

Committee Staff
Clerk:
  Nancy Probst..................................518-455-3215

Key Senate Staff Assignments
Republican Assistant Counsel:
  Skip Piscitelli...............................518-455-2595

Membership

Majority
John A DeFrancisco	Rich Funke
Robert G Ortt	

Minority
Jose Peralta	Diane J Savino

Offices and agencies generally appear in alphabetical order, except when specific order is requested by listee.

Civil Service & Pensions
Chair:
Martin J Golden (R) 518-455-2730
Ranking Minority Member:
James Sanders, Jr. (D) 518-455-3531

Committee Staff
Clerk:
Meg Brown 518-455-2730

Key Senate Staff Assignments
Republican Senior Counsel:
Lisa Harris 518-455-2751

Membership

Majority
Patricia Ritchie   Robert G Ortt
Andrew Lanza   Jack Martins
Thomas Croci

Minority
Joseph Addabbo Jr.   Martin Malave Dilan
Leroy Comrie   Diane J Savino
James Sanders, Jr.

Codes
Chair:
Michael F. Nozzolio (R) 518-455-2366
Ranking Minority Member:
Daniel L. Squadron (D) 518-455-2625

Committee Staff
Clerk:
Meg Fitzgerald 518-455-2366

Key Senate Staff Assignments
Republican Senior Counsel:
NancyLynn Thiel 518-455-2576
Democratic Associate Counsel:
Alejandra Paulino 518-455-2628

Membership

Majority
Philip Boyle   John A DeFrancisco
Patrick Gallivan   Martin Golden
Joseph A Griffo   Thomas O'Mara

Minority
Diane J Savino   Jesse Hamilton
Liz Krueger   Adriano Espaillat
Bill Perkins   Marc Panepinto

Commerce, Economic Development & Small Business
Chair:
Philip Boyle (R) 518-455-3411
Ranking Minority Member:
Timothy Kennedy (D) 518-455-2426

Committee Staff
Clerk:
Deanna Schneider 518-455-3411

Key Senate Staff Assignments
Republican Senior Counsel:
Ryan McAllister 518-455-2483
Democratic Budget Analyst:
Paul Alexander 518-455-2695

Membership

Majority
Patrick M. Gallivan   Joseph A Griffo

Rich Funke   Joseph E Robach
Minority
Jesse Hamilton   Simcha Felder
David J Valesky   Ruth Hassell-Thompson
James Sanders, Jr.

Consumer Protection
Chair:
Michael Venditto (R) 518-455-3341
Ranking Minority Member:
Leroy Comrie (D) 518-455-2701

Committee Staff

Key Senate Staff Assignments
Republican Senior Counsel:
Lisa Harris 518-455-2751
Democratic Associate Counsel:
Richard Jacobson 518-455-2711

Membership

Majority
Kathleen Marchione   Philip Boyle
Rich Funke   Joseph E Robach
George Amedore Jr

Minority
Diane Savino   George Latimer
Jose Peralta   Jose M. Serrano

Corporations, Authorities & Commissions
Chair:
Michael Ranzenhofer (R) 518-455-3161
Ranking Minority Member:
Bill Perkins (D) 518-455-2441

Committee Staff
Committee Director:
Jessica Pollack 518-455-3161

Key Senate Staff Assignments
Repulican Assistant Counsel:
James Curran 518-455-2486
Democratic Associate Counsel:
Dan Ranellone 518-455-2852

Membership

Majority
Robert G Ortt   Jack Martins
William L. Larkin, Jr.

Minority
Daniel L. Squadron

Crime Victims, Crime & Correction
Chair:
Patrick M. Gallivan (R) 518-455-3471
Ranking Minority Member:
Ruth Hassell-Thompson (D) 518-455-2061

Committee Staff
Clerk:
Zach Primeau 518-455-3471

Key Senate Staff Assignments
Republican Assistant Counsel:
Kenneth Connolly 518-455-2342

Membership

Majority
Elizabeth O'C. Little   Patricia Ritchie

Offices and agencies generally appear in alphabetical order, except when specific order is requested by listee.

John A. DeFrancisco   Michael Venditto
Joseph Griffo   Michael Nozzolio

Minority
Velmanette Montgomery   Bill Perkins
Jose Peralta   Diane J Savino
J Gustavo Rivera

Cultural Affairs, Tourism, Parks & Recreation
Chair:
  Elizabeth O'C Little (R) 518-455-2811
Ranking Minority Member:
  Jose Serrano (D) 518-455-2795

Committee Staff
Clerk:
  Mary Pat McDonald 518-455-2811

Key Senate Staff Assignments
Republican Assistant Counsel:
  Skip Piscitelli 518-455-2595
Policy Analyst:
  Andrew Postiglione 518-455-2977

Membership

Majority
Kathleen Marchione   John J. Bonacic
Carl L. Marcellino   Sue Serino
Patricia Ritchie   Joseph A. Griffo

Minority
Tony Avella   James Sanders Jr
Brad Hoylman   Kevin Parker
Timothy Kennedy

Education
Chair:
  Carl L Marcellino (R) 518-455-2390
Ranking Minority Member:
  George Latimer (D) 518-455-2031

Committee Staff
Committee Clerk:
  Robin Mueller 518-455-2631

Key Senate Staff Assignments
Republican Assistant Counsel:
  James Curran 518-455-2486
Director, Budget Studies:
  Felix Muniz 518-455-2641

Membership

Majority
Elizabeth O'C. Little   James L Seward
Kenneth P. LaValle   Hugh T Farley
Andrew Lanza   Sue Serino
Michael H Ranzenhofer   Joseph E Robach

Minority
Tony Avella   Joseph P Addabbo Jr
Velmanette Montgomery   Neil D Breslin
Jose Peralta   Jesse Hamilton
Toby Ann Stavisky   David Valesky

Elections
Chair:
  Rich Funke (R) 518-455-2215
Ranking Minority Member:
  Leroy Comrie (D) 518-455-2701

Committee Staff
Clerk:
  Lisa Sams 518-455-2215

Key Senate Staff Assignments
Republican Senior Counsel:
  John Ciampoli 518-455-2565
Democratic Senior Counsel:
  Christopher Higgins 518-455-3447

Membership

Majority
George Amedore Jr   Kathleen Marchione
Patrick Gallivan   Michael Nozzolio

Minority
Tony Avella   Martin Malave Dilan
Liz Krueger

Energy & Telecommunications
Chair:
  Joseph A Griffo (R) 518-455-3334
Ranking Minority Member:
  Kevin Parker (D) 518-455-2580

Committee Staff
Clerk:
  Regina Boyd 518-455-2024
Chief of Staff:
  Dwight Evans 518-455-3334

Key Senate Staff Assignments
Replican Senior Counsel:
  Emma Maceko 518-455-2908
Democratic Budget Analyst:
  Paul Alexander

Membership

Majority
Thomas Croci   Patricia Ritchie
Elizabeth O'C Little   Thomas O'Mara

Minority
David Carlucci   Timothy Kennedy
Jesse Hamilton   Martin Malave Dilan

Environmental Conservation
Chair:
  Thomas O'Mara (R) 518-455-2091
Ranking Minority Member:
  Brad Hoylman (D) 518-455-2451

Committee Staff
Chief of Staff:
  Pierson Ellis 518-455-2091

Key Senate Staff Assignments
Republican Assistant Counsel:
  Paul Midey 518-455-2599

Membership

Majority
Elizabeth O'C Little   Catharine M Young
Kenneth P LaValle   Robert G Ortt
Rich Funke

Minority
Joseph Adabbo   Carl Marcellino
Jose M Serrano   George Latimer

Offices and agencies generally appear in alphabetical order, except when specific order is requested by listee.

Ethics
Chair:
Tony Avella (D) 518-455-2210
Ranking Minority Member:
Michael Gianaris (D) 518-455-3486

Key Senate Staff Assignments
Democratic Deputy Counsel:
Keith St John...................................518-455-2711
Republican Assistant Counsel:
Adam Richardson 518-455-2506

Membership

Majority

Andrew Lanza	Terrence Murphy
Hugh T Farley	

Minority

Gustavo Rivera

Finance
Chair:
John A DeFrancisco (R) 518-455-3511
Ranking Minority Member:
Liz Krueger (D)................................518-455-2297

Committee Staff
Secretary to the Committee & Chief of Staff:
Robert Mujica..................................518-455-2880

Key Senate Staff Assignments
Director of Budget Studies:
Felix Muniz 518-455-2642
Democratic Secretary to Finance:
Louie Tobias...................................518-455-2641

Membership

Majority

Hugh T Farley	Kenneth P LaValle
Carl L Marcellino	Michael F Nozzolio
Joseph E Robach	Joseph A Griffo
Thomas O'Mara	James L Seward
Kemp Hannon	William J Larkin Jr
Michael N. Ranzenhofer	Patricia Ritchie
Patrick Gallivan	Jack Martins
John J Bonacic	Martin J Golden
Andrew J Lanza	Elizabeth O'C Little
Catharine M Young	

Minority

Neil D Breslin	Martin Malave Dilan
Velmanette Montgomery	Kevin S Parker
Jose Peralta	Adriano Espaillat
Ruben Diaz Sr	David Valesky
Diane Savino	Bill Perkins
Ruth Hassell-Thompson	Toby Ann Stavisky
Timothy Kennedy	Daniel L Squadron
J Gustavo Rivera	

Health
Chair:
Kemp Hannon (R)................................518-455-2200
Ranking Minority Member:
J. Gustavo Rivera (D) 518-455-3395

Committee Staff
Committee Director:
Kristin Sinclair 518-455-2200

Key Senate Staff Assignments
Republican Program Director:
J Thomas Wickham Jr 518-455-2675
Republican Assistant Counsel:
David Previte 518-455-2604

Membership

Majority

Terrence Murphy	Martin J Golden
James L Seward	Hugh T Farley
William J Larkin Jr	Catharine M Young
Elizabeth O'C Little	Jack Martins

Minority

Brad Hoylman	Velmanette Montgomery
Ruth Hassell-Thompson	Marc Panepinto
Toby Ann Stavisky	Simcha Felder

Higher Education
Chair:
Kenneth P LaValle (R)...........................518-455-3121
Ranking Minority Member:
Toby Ann Stavisky (D)...........................518-455-3461

Committee Staff
Committee Director:
Kristin Sinclair 518-455-2200

Key Senate Staff Assignments
Republican Program Director:
Tom Wickham 518-455-2068
Democratic Associate Counsel:
Dan Leinung...................................518-455-2821

Membership

Majority

Patrick Gallivan	Joseph A Griffo
Rich Funke	James L Seward
Robert G Ortt	Joseph E Robach
Sue Serino	Thomas Croci
Patricia Ritchie	

Minority

Adriano Espaillat	David Valesky
J Gustavo Rivera	Kevin S Parker
Jose Peralta	Liz Krueger
Neil D Breslin	

Housing, Construction & Community Development
Chair:
Catharine M Young (R) 518-455-3563
Ranking Minority Member:
Adriano Espaillat (D) 518-455-2041

Committee Staff
Clerk:
Chelsey Watroba................................518-455-3563

Key Senate Staff Assignments
Republican Senior Counsel:
Robert Gibbon 518-455-2876
Democratic Special Counsel:
John Allen.....................................518-455-5545

Membership

Majority

Philip Boyle	John J. Bonacic
Patrick Gallivan	Michael Nozzolio

Minority

Liz Krueger	Tony Avella

Offices and agencies generally appear in alphabetical order, except when specific order is requested by listee.

Marc Panepinto

Infrastructure & Capital Investment
Chair:
   Carl L Marcellino (R) 518-455-2390
Ranking Member:
   Timothy Kennedy (D) 518-455-2426

Committee Staff
Committee Director:
   Deborah Peck Kelleher 518-455-2390
Republican Senior Counsel:
   Adam Richardson 518-455-2406

Membership

Majority
   Patrick Gallivan   Thomas Croci
   Joseph Robach

Minority
   David Carlucci   Simcha Felder
   Martin Malave Dilan   Leroy Comrie

Insurance
Chair:
   James L Seward (R) 518-455-3131
Ranking Minority Member:
   Neil D Breslin (D) 518-455-2225

Committee Staff
Committee Director:
   Natalie Bernardi 518-455-3131

Key Senate Staff Assignments
Republican Senior Counsel:
   Robert Farley 518-455-3127
Republican Assistant Counsel:
   Frank Alleva 518-455-2488
Democratic Associate Counsel:
   Richard Jacobson

Membership

Majority
   William J Larkin Jr   Catharine M Young
   Martin J Golden   Kenneth P LaValle
   Michael Venditto   Jack Martins
   Andrew J Lanza   Thomas O'Mara

Minority
   Timothy Kennedy   Marc Panepinto
   Adriano Espaillat   David Carlucci
   James Sanders Jr   George Latimer
   Kevin S Parker   Tony Avella

Investigations & Government Operations
Chair:
   Carl L Marcellino (R) 518-455-2390
Ranking Minority Member:
   Brad Hoylman (D) 518-455-2451

Committee Staff
-lerk:
   Deborah Peck Kelleher

Key Senate Staff Assignments
Republican Senior Counsel:
   Ryan McAllister 518-455-2914
Democratic Senior Counsel:
   Christopher Higgins

Membership

Majority
   Martin J Golden   Michael F Nozzolio
   Terrence Murphy   Thomas O'Mara

Minority
   David Carlucci   Daniel Squadron
   Ruben Diaz Sr

Judiciary
Chair:
   John J Bonancic (R) 518-455-3181
Ranking Minority Member:
   Ruth Hassell-Thompson (D) 518-455-2061

Committee Staff
Legislative Assistant:
   Conor Gillis......................................518-455-3181

Membership

Majority
   Michael Venditto   Andrew J Lanza
   Michael H Ranzenhofer   John A DeFrancisco
   Kenneth P LaValle   Michael F Nozzolio
   Kemp Hannon   George Amedore Jr
   Thomas O'Mara   Sue Serino

Minority
   Tony Avella   Bill Perkins
   Neil D Breslin   Martin Malave Dilan
   Diane Savino   Adriano Espaillat
   Toby Ann Stavisky   Ruben Diaz Sr
   Leroy Comrie   Brad Hoylman

Labor
Chair:
   Jack Martins (R) 518-455-3265
Ranking Minority Member:
   Jose R Peralta (D) 518-455-2529

Committee Staff
Legislative Director:
   Peter Faherty.....................................518-455-3265

Key Senate Staff Assignments

Membership

Majority
   Terrence Murphy   Kemp Hannon
   Kathleen Marchione   Carl L Marcellino
   Michael Venditto   John A DeFrancisco
   Patrick Gallivan   Joseph Robach

Minority
   Joseph P Addabbo Jr   Martin Malave Dilan
   Bill Perkins   Diane J Savino
   James Sanders, Jr.   J Gustavo Rivera

Local Government
Chair:
   Kathleen Marchione (R) 518-455-2381
Ranking Minority Member:
   Marc Panepinto (D) 518-455-2760

Committee Staff
Legislative Director:
   Daphne Jordan 518-455-2381

Key Senate Staff Assignments
Republican Assistant Counsel:
   Robert Gibbon 518-455-2876

Offices and agencies generally appear in alphabetical order, except when specific order is requested by listee.

Democratic Budget Analyst:
Teria Cooper....................................518-455-2793

Membership

Majority

Terrence Murphy	Philip Boyle
Patricia Ritchie	Robert G Ortt

Minority

Brad Hoylman	George Latimer
David Valesky	

Mental Health & Developmental Disabilities

Chair:
Robert G Ortt (R) 518-455-2024
Ranking Minority Member:
Jesse Hamilton (D) 518-455-2431

Committee Staff

Legislative Director:
Joe Erdman 518-455-2024

Key Senate Staff Assignments
Republican Assistant Counsel:
Carmen Barber 518-455-2480

Membership

Majority

Terrence Murphy	Sue Serino
Kemp Hannon	James Seward

Minority

J Gustavo Rivera	Liz Krueger
Jose Serrano	David Carlucci
Simcha Felder	

Racing, Gaming & Wagering

Chair:
John J Bonacic (R) 518-455-3181
Ranking Minority Member:
Joseph Addabbo Jr. (D) 518-455-2322

Committee Staff

Legislative Assistant:
Conor Gillis.....................................518-455-3181

Membership

Majority

Kathleen Marchione	Michael Ranzenhofer
Joseph Griffo	Philip Boyle
Michael F Nozzolio	

Minority

David Carlucci	George Latimer
Leroy Comrie	James Sanders, Jr.

Rules

Chair:
John J Flanagan (R) 518-455-2071
Ranking Minority Member:
Andrea Stewart-Cousins (D)..................518-455-2585

Membership

Majority

Hugh T Farley	William J Larkin Jr
Catharine Young	Kenneth P LaValle
James L Seward	Carl L Marcellino
Michael F Nozzolio	John Bonacic
Kemp Hannon	Elizabeth O'C. Little

Minority

Neil D Breslin	Bill Perkins
David Carlucci	Martin Malave Dilan
Velmanette Montgomery	Kevin S Parker
Liz Krueger	Ruth Hassell-Thompson
Adriano Espaillat	Michael Gianaris
David Valesky	

Social Services

Chair:
David Carlucci (D) 518-455-2991

Committee Staff

Committee Director:
Evan Sullivan 518-455-2991

Key Senate Staff Assignments
Republican Program Associate:
Niko Ladopoulos 518-455-2482
Democratic Budget Analyst:
Cheryl Halter

Membership

Majority

George Amedore Jr	Jack Martins
Kenneth P LaValle	Hugh T Farley

Minority

Daniel L Squadron	Velmanette Montgomery

Transportation

Chair:
Joseph E Robach (R) 518-455-2909
Ranking Minority Member:
Martin Malave Dilan (D) 518-455-2177

Committee Staff

Committee Clerk:
Michelle Cameron

Key Senate Staff Assignments
Republican Senior Counsel:
Lisa Harris 518-455-2751
Democratic Associate Counsel:
Dan Ranellone 518-455-2852

Membership

Majority

Patrick Gallivan	William J Larkin Jr
Michael F Nozzolio	Catharine M Young
Patricia Ritchie	Jack Martins
Thomas O'Mara	Michael H Ranzenhofer

Minority

Marc Panepinto	Bill Perkins
Timothy Kennedy	David J Valesky
Ruben Diaz Sr	Daniel L Squadron
Tony Avella	Toby Ann Stavisky

Veterans, Homeland Security & Military Affairs

Chair:
Thomas Croci (R) 518-455-3570
Ranking Minority Member:
Joseph P Addabbo Jr (D) 518-455-2322

Committee Staff

Legislative Director:
Jennifer Slagen 518-455-4265

Key Senate Staff Assignments
Democratic Associate Counsel:
Nic Rangel 518-455-7925

Offices and agencies generally appear in alphabetical order, except when specific order is requested by listee.

Republican Senior Counsel:
  Bob Farley 518-455-3111

Membership

Majority

Martin J Golden	William J Larkin Jr
Joseph A Griffo	Robert G Ortt
George Amedore Jr	

Minority

Marc Panepinto	Jose Serrano
David Carlucci	Leroy Comrie
James Sanders, Jr.	

SENATE SELECT & SPECIAL COMMITTEES & SPECIAL TASK FORCES

Libraries, Select Committee on

Chair:
  Hugh T Farley (R) 518-455-2181/fax: 518-455-2271

Science, Technology, Incubation & Entrepreneurship, Select Committee on

Chair:
  Martin J Golden (R) 518-455-2730

JOINT LEGISLATIVE COMMISSIONS

Administrative Regulations Review, Legislative Commission on

Senate Co-Chair:
  Terrence Murphy (R) 518-455-3111
Assembly Co-Chair:
  Kenneth Zebrowski (D) 518-455-5735
Assembly Program Manager:
  Rich Murphy .518-455-5091/fax: 518-455-4175

Demographic Research & Reapportionment, Legislative Task Force on

Senate Co-Chair:
  Michael F Nozzolio (R) 518-455-2366
Assembly Co-Chair:
  Phil Ramos (D) 518-455-5185
Co-Executive Director:
  Debra Levine 212-618-1100/fax: 212-618-1135
Co-Executive Director:
  Karen Blatt. 212-618-1100/fax: 212-618-1135

Ethics Committee, Legislative

Senate Co-Chair:
  Andrew Lanza (R) 518-455-3215
Assembly Co-Chair:
  Charles D Lavine (D) 518-455-4546
Executive Director/Counsel:
  Lisa P Reid 518-432-7837
  e-mail: lreid@nysenate.gov

Government Administration, Legislative Commission on

Senate Vice-Chair:
  Vacant 518-455-0000
Assembly Chair:
  Brian Kavanagh (D) 518-455-5506

Rural Resources, Legislative Commission on

Senate Chair:
  Catharine Young (D) 518-455-3563
  e-mail: ruralres@nysenate.gov
Assembly Chair:
  Frank Skartados (D) 518-455-5762
Republican Counsel:
  Barbara McRedmond. 518-455-2069/fax: 518-486-6919

Offices and agencies generally appear in alphabetical order, except when specific order is requested by listee.

LEGISLATIVE BRANCH ASSEMBLY

STATE ASSEMBLY LEADERSHIP

Members of the Assembly welcome e-mail correspondence from the public. They may reply by e-mail, or by mail when more extensive follow-up is necessary. Please include both an e-mail and mailing address in all correspondence. Biographies of Assembly Members appears in a separate section in the back of the book.

State Capitol
Albany, NY 12248
Web site: www.assembly.ny.gov

ADMINISTRATION

Laurene R Kretzler 518-455-4242/fax: 518-455-4935
Title: Clerk of the Assembly

Wayne P Jackson 518-455-3797/fax: 518-455-4445
Title: Sergeant-at-Arms, Chamber

Michael Kane 518-455-5767/fax: 518-455-4963
Title: Director, Communication Information Services (CIS)

Vicki Chase 518-455-5767/fax: 518-455-4963
Title: Director, Information Services

John P Wellspeak 518-455-4411/fax: 518-455-4298
Title: Director, Administration

Kathleen McCarty 518-455-4704/fax: 518-455-4705
Title: Director, Internship Program

Mike Gaffney 518-455-5165/fax: 518-455-4741
Title: Director, Document Room

Robin Marilla 518-455-4218/fax: 518-455-5175
Title: Public Information Officer

Vacant 518-455-2468/fax: 518-426-6901
Title: Reference Librarian, Legislative Library

Jim Devine 518-455-5190/fax: 518-455-4517
Title: Director, Operations

MAJORITY LEADERSHIP

Carl E Heastie (D) 518-455-3791
e-mail: speaker@assembly.state.ny.us
Title: Speaker

Joseph Morelle 518-455-5373
e-mail: morellej@assembly.state.ny.us
Title: Majority Leader

Herman D Farrell, Jr (D) 518-455-5491
e-mail: farrelh@assembly.state.ny.us
Title: Chair, Ways & Means Committee

Earlene Hooper (D) 518-455-5861
e-mail: hoopere@assembly.state.ny.us
Title: Deputy Speaker

Jeffrion L. Aubrey (D) 518-455-4561
e-mail: aubryj@assembly.state.ny.us
Title: Speaker Pro Tempore

N Nick Perry (D) 518-455-4166
e-mail: perryn@assembly.state.ny.us
Title: Assistant Speaker Pro Tempore

Felix Ortiz (D) 518-455-3821
e-mail: ortizf@assembly.state.ny.us
Title: Assistant Speaker

Vivian E Cook (D) 518-455-4203
e-mail: cookv@assembly.state.ny.us
Title: Chair, Committee on Standing Committees

Phil Ramos (D) 518-455-5185
e-mail: ramosp@assembly.state.ny.us
Title: Deputy Majority Leader

Dov Hikind (D) 518-455-5721
e-mail: hikindd@assembly.state.ny.us
Title: Assistant Majority Leader

William Colton (D) 518-455-5828
e-mail: coltonw@assembly.state.ny.us
Title: Majority Whip

Barbara Clark (D) 518-455-4711
e-mail: clarkb@assembly.state.ny.us
Title: Deputy Majority Whip

Jose Rivera (D) 518-455-5414
e-mail: RiveraJ@assembly.state.ny.us
Title: Assistant Majority Whip

Michelle Schimel (D) 518-455-5192
e-mail: schimelm@assembly.state.ny.us
Title: Chair, Majority Conference

Aravella Simotas (D) 518-455-5014
e-mail: simotasa@assembly.state.ny.us
Title: Vice Chair, Majority Conference

David I Weprin (D) 518-455-5806
e-mail: weprind@assembly.state.ny.us
Title: Secretary, Majority Conference

Barbara Lifton (D) 518-455-5444
e-mail: liftonb@assembly.state.ny.us
Title: Chair, Majority Steering

Alec Brook-Krasny (D) 518-455-4811
e-mail: brookkrasnya@assembly.state.ny.us
Title: Vice Chair, Majority Steering

Carmen Arroyo (D) 518-455-5402
e-mail: arroyoc@assembly.state.ny.us
Title: Chair, Majority Program

Michael Miller (D) 518-455-4621
e-mail: millermg@ssembly.state.ny.us
Title: Chair, Majority House Operations

MAJORITY STAFF

Judy R Rapfogel 212-312-1400/fax: 212-312-1418
Title: Chief of Staff to the Speaker

Michael Whyland 518-455-3888/fax: 518-455-3858
Title: Press Secretary to the Speaker

Neil Fisher 518-455-4736/fax: 518-455-5428
Title: Director, Index Services

John Hudder 518-455-4386/fax: 518-455-5573
Title: Executive Director, Program Development

Bill Collins 518-455-4191/fax: 518-455-4103
Title: Counsel to the Majority

Matthew Howard 518-455-3786/fax: 518-455-4445
Title: Secretary to the Committee on Ways & Means

Offices and agencies generally appear in alphabetical order, except when specific order is requested by listee.

MINORITY LEADERSHIP

Brian M Kolb (R) 518-455-3751
e-mail: kolbb@assembly.state.ny.us
Title: Minority Leader

Jane Corwin (R) 518-455-4601
e-mail: corwinj@assembly.state.ny.us
Title: Minority Leader Pro Tempore

Tom McKevitt (R) 518-455-5341
e-mail: mckevit@assembly.state.ny.us
Title: Assistant Minority Leader Pro Tempore

Marc Butler (R) 518-455-5393
e-mail: butlerm@assembly.state.ny.us
Title: Ranking Minority Member, Committee on Standing Committees

William Barclay (R) 518-455-5841
e-mail: barclaW@assembly.state.ny.us
Title: Deputy Minority Leader

Gary Finch (R) 518-455-5878
e-mail: finchG@assembly.state.ny.us
Title: Assistant Minority Leader

Stephen Hawley (R) 518-455-5811
e-mail: hawleys@assembly.state.ny.us
Title: Assistant Minority Leader

James Tedisco (R) 518-455-5772
e-mail: tediscj@assembly.state.ny.us
Title: Minority Whip

Andrew Raia (R) 518-455-5952
e-mail: raiaA@assembly.state.ny.us
Title: Deputy Minority Whip

Michael Montesano (R) 518-455-4684
e-mail: montesanom@assembly.state.ny.us
Title: Assistant Minority Whip

Clifford W Crouch (R) 518-455-5741
e-mail: crouchc@assembly.state.ny.us
Title: Chair, Minority Conference

Peter Lopez (R) 518-455-5363
e-mail: lopezp@assembly.state.ny.us
Title: Vice Chair, Minority Conference

Philip Palmesano (R 518-455-5791
e-mail: palmesanop@assembly.state.ny.us
Title: Secretary, Minority Conference

Michael Fitzpatrick (R) 518-455-5021
e-mail: fitzpatrickm@assembly.state.ny.us
Title: Chair, Minority Joint Conference Committee

David McDonough (R) 518-455-4633
e-mail: mcdonod@assembly.state.ny.us
Title: Vice Chair, Minority Joint Conference Committee

Joseph Giglio (R) 518-455-5241
e-mail: giglioj@assembly.state.ny.us
Title: Chair, Minority Steering Committee

Edward Ra (R) 518-455-4627
e-mail: rae@assembly.state.ny.us
Title: Vice Chair, Minority Steering Committee

Joseph Saladino (R) 518-455-5305
e-mail: saladij@assembly.state.ny.us
Title: Chair, Minority Program Committee

Janet Duprey (R) 518-455-5943
e-mail: palmesanop@assembly.state.ny.us
Title: Vice Chair, Program Committee

Vacant (R) 518-455-0000
e-mail: reilicw@assembly.state.ny.us
Title: Chair, Minority House Operations

Robert Oaks (R) 518-455-5655
e-mail: oaksR@assembly.state.ny.us
Title: Ranking Minority Member, Ways & Means

MINORITY STAFF

Doug Finch 518-455-3751/fax: 518-455-3750
e-mail: finchd@assembly.state.ny.us
Title: Chief of Staff

Judy Skype 518-455-4211/fax: 518-455-3758
Title: Deputy Chief of Staff

Michael Fraser 518-455-3751/fax: 518-455-3750
e-mail: fraserm@assembly.state.ny.us
Title: Director, Minority Communications

Harry MacAvoy 518-455-5002/fax: 518-455-5829
Title: Director, Minority Research & Program Development

Rebecca D'Agati 518-455-5161/fax: 518-455-4550
Title: Director, Minority Ways & Means Staff

STATE ASSEMBLY ROSTER

Multiple party abbreviations following the names of legislators indicate that those legislators ran as the Assembly candidate for each identified party. Source: NYS Board of Elections. Party abbreviations: Conservative (C), Democrat (D), Green (G), Independent (I), Liberal (L), Republican (R), Right to Life (RL), Veterans (VE), Working Families (WF)

Peter J Abbate, Jr (D) 518-455-3053/fax: 518-455-5524
District: 49   *Room:* 839 LOB   *e-mail:* abbatep@assembly.state.ny.us
Committees: Aging; Banks; Consumer Affairs & Protection; Governmental Employees (Chair); Labor

Thomas Abinanti (D) 518-455-5753/fax: 518-455-5920
District: 92   *Room:* 744 LOB   *e-mail:* abinantit@assembly.state.ny.us
Committees: Codes; Corporations, Authorities & Commissions; Election Law; Environmental Conservation; Health; Libraries & Education Technology (Chair)
Senior Staff: Joanne Sold

Carmen E Arroyo (D) 518-455-5402/fax: 518-455-4681
District: 84   *Room:* 734 LOB   *e-mail:* arroyoc@assembly.state.ny.us
Title: Chair, Majority Program
Committees: Aging; Alcoholism & Drug Abuse; Children & Families; Education
Senior Staff: Isamar Rodriguez

Jeffrion L Aubry (D) 518-455-4561/fax: 518-455-4565
District: 35   *Room:* 646 LOB   *e-mail:* aubryj@assembly.state.ny.us
Title: Speaker Pro Tempore
Committees: Governmental Employees; Rules; Social Services; Ways & Means
Senior Staff: Mary C Nicholson

William A Barclay (R-I-C) 518-455-5841/fax: 518-455-5362
District: 120   *Room:* 521 LOB   *e-mail:* barclaw@assembly.state.ny.us
Title: Deputy Minority Leader
Committees: Energy; Insurance (Ranking Minority Member); Judiciary; Rules; Ways & Means
Senior Staff: Jennifer Cook

Offices and agencies generally appear in alphabetical order, except when specific order is requested by listee.

Didi Barrett (D) .518-455-5177/fax: 518-455-5418
District: 106 *Room:* 553 LOB *e-mail:* barrettd@assembly.state.ny.us
Committees: Aging; Agriculture; Economic Development, Job Creation;
Commerce & Industry; Mental Health; Tourism, Parks, Arts & Sports
Development; Veterans' Affairs
Senior Staff: Nick Melson

Charles Barron (D) 518-455-5912
District: 60 *Room:* 532 LOB *e-mail:* barronc@assembly.state.ny.us
Committees: Aging; Alcoholism & Drug Abuse; Economic Development, Job
Creation, Commerce & Industry; Energy; Small Business; Social Services
Senior Staff: Viola Plummer

Michael R Benedetto (D) 518-455-5296/fax: 518-455-4641
District: 82 *Room:* 842 LOB *e-mail:* benedettom@assembly.state.ny.us
Committees: Agriculture; Cities (Chair); Education; Governmental
Operations; Labor; Ways & Means
Senior Staff: Ben Randazzo

Rodneyse Bichotte (D) 518-455-5385
District: 42 *Room:* 833 LOB *e-mail:* bichotter@assembly.state.ny.us
Committees: Banks; Economic Development, Job Creation, Commerce &
Industry; Governmental Ops; Housing; Small Business; Social Services
Senior Staff: Rona Taylor

Michael Blake (D) 518-455-5272
District: 79 *Room:* 919 LOB *e-mail:* blakem@assembly.state.ny.us
Committees: Banks; Correction; Election Law; Governmental Ops; Housing;
Veterans' Affairs
Senior Staff: Aaron Carr

Kenneth Blankenbush (R) 518-455-5797/fax: 518-455-5289
District: 117 *Room:* 322 LOB *e-mail:* blankenbushk@assembly.state.ny.us
Committees: Agriculture (Ranking Member); Corporations, Authorities &
Commissions; Insurance; Tourism, Parks, Arts & Sports Development
Senior Staff: Brian Peck

Joseph Borelli (R) 518-455-4495/fax: 518-455-4501
District: 62 *Room:* 428 LOB *e-mail:* borellij@assembly.state.ny.us
Committees: Cities (Ranking Member); Energy; Health; Housing
Senior Staff: Frank Mascia

Karl Brabenec (R) 518-455-5991/fax: 518-455-5929
District: 98 *Room:* 523 LOB *e-mail:* brabeneck@assembly.state.ny.us
Committees: Aging; Cities; Election Law; Labor; Local Governments
Senior Staff: Joseph Coleman

Edward C. Braunstein (D) 518-455-5425/fax: 518-455-4648
District: 26 *Room:* 557 LOB *e-mail:* braunsteine@assembly.state.ny.us
Committees: Aging; Cities; Health; Insurance; Judiciary; Small Business
Senior Staff: David Fischer

James F Brennan (D) 518-455-5377/fax: 518-455-5592
District: 44 *Room:* 422 LOB *e-mail:* brennanj@assembly.state.ny.us
Committees: Codes; Corporations, Authorities & Commissions (Chair);
Education; Real Property Taxation
Senior Staff: Melanie Hirsch Riback

Anthony J Brindisi (D) 518-455-5454/fax: 518-455-5928
District: 119 *Room:* 538 LOB *e-mail:* brindisia@assembly.state.ny.us
Committees: Aging; Economic Development, Job Creation, Commerce &
Industry; Energy; Higher Education; Transporation; Veterans' Affairs
Senior Staff: Caitlin Calogero

Harry Bronson (D) 518-455-4527/fax: 518-455-5342
District: 138 *Room:* 502 LOB *e-mail:* bronsonh@assembly.state.ny.us
Committees: Agriculture; Economic Development, Job Creation, Commerce
& Industry; Labor; Local Governments; Transportation
Senior Staff: Jen Skoog-Harvey

Alec Brook-Krasny (D) 518-455-4811/fax: 518-455-5654
District: 46 *Room:* 639 LOB *e-mail:* brookkrasnya@assembly.state.ny.us
Title: Vice Chair, Majority Steering
Committees: Aging; Cities; Election Law; Governmental Employees;
Housing; Social Services
Senior Staff: Kate Cucco

David Buchwald (D) 518-455-5397/fax: 518-455-5041
District: 93 *Room:* 331 LOB *e-mail:* buchwaldd@assembly.state.ny.us
Committees: Consumer Affairs & Protection; Corporations, Authorities &
Commissions; Election Law; Governmental Operations; Judiciary; Local
Governments
Senior Staff: Daniel Weisfield

Marc W Butler (R-I-C) 518-455-5393/fax: 518-455-5889
District: 118 *Room:* 525 LOB *e-mail:* butlerm@assembly.state.ny.us
Title: Ranking Minority Member, Committee on Standing Committees
Committees: Agriculture; Economic Development, Job Creation, Commerce
& Industry; Environmental Conservation; Higher Education; Insurance;
Rules
Senior Staff: Deborah Dempsey Scialdo

Kevin A Cahill (D) 518-455-4436/fax: 518-455-5576
District: 103 *Room:* 716 LOB *e-mail:* cahillk@assembly.state.ny.us
Committees: Ethics & Guidance; Economic Development, Job Creation,
Commerce & Industry; Health; Higher Education; Insurance (Chair); Ways &
Means
Senior Staff: Evan Gallo

John D Ceretto (R) 518-455-5284/fax: 518-455-5694
District: 145 *Room:* 320 LOB *e-mail:* cerettoj@assembly.state.ny.us
Committees: Cities; Education; Energy; Labor; Tourism, Parks, Arts & Sports
(Ranking Member)
Senior Staff: William Angus

Barbara M Clark (D) 518-455-4711/fax: 518-455-3740
District: 33 *Room:* 547 LOB *e-mail:* clarkb@assembly.state.ny.us
Title: Deputy Majority Whip
Committees: Children & Families; Education; Health; Labor; Libraries &
Education Technology; Rules
Senior Staff: Tyrone Benton

William Colton (D-WF) 518-455-5828/fax: 518-455-5706
District: 47 *Room:* 733 LOB *e-mail:* coltonw@assembly.state.ny.us
Title: Majority Whip
Committees: Correction; Environmental Conservation; Governmental
Employees; Labor; Rules; Ways & Means
Senior Staff: Susan Zhuang

Vivian E Cook (D) 518-455-4203/fax: 518-455-3606
District: 32 *Room:* 939 LOB *e-mail:* cookv@assembly.state.ny.us
Title: Chair, Committee on Standing Committees
Committees: Codes; Corporations, Authorities & Commissions; Housing;
Insurance; Rules; Ways & Means
Senior Staff: Joyce Corker

Jane L Corwin (R) 518-455-4601/fax: 518-455-5257
District: 144 *Room:* 446 LOB *e-mail:* corwinj@assembly.state.ny.us
Title: Minority Leader Pro Tempore
Committees: Corporations, Authorities & Commissions (Ranking Member);
Education; Environmental Conservation; Mental Health; Ways & Means
Senior Staff: Kim Laurie

Marcos Crespo (D) 518-455-5514/fax: 518-455-5827
District: 85 *Room:* 454 LOB *e-mail:* crespoM@assembly.state.ny.us
Committees: Alcoholism & Drug Abuse; Cities; Energy; Environmental
Conservation; Insurance; Transportation
Senior Staff: Matthew Shuffler

Offices and agencies generally appear in alphabetical order, except when specific order is requested by listee.

Clifford W Crouch (R) 518-455-5741/fax: 518-455-5864
District: 122 *Room:* 450 LOB *e-mail:* crouchc@assembly.state.ny.us
Title: Chair, Minority Conference
Committees: Agriculture; Economic Development, Job Creation, Commerce
& Industry; Labor; Rules; Ways & Means
Senior Staff: Kathleen Mami-Moore

Brian Curran (R) 518-455-4656/fax: 518-455-4643
District: 21 *Room:* 318 LOB *e-mail:* curranb@assembly.state.ny.us
Committees: Banks; Ethics & Guidance (Ranking Member); Insurance;
Labor; Veterans Affairs
Senior Staff: Leslie Rothschild

Michael J Cusick (D) 518-455-5526/fax: 518-455-4760
District: 63 *Room:* 724 LOB *e-mail:* cusickm@assembly.state.ny.us
Committees: Election Law (Chair); Governmental Employees; Higher
Education; Mental Health; Transportation; Veterans' Affairs; Ways & Means
Senior Staff: Sharon L Grobe

Steven H Cymbrowitz (D) 518-455-5214/fax: (518) 455-5738
District: 45 *Room:* 824 LOB *e-mail:* cymbros@assembly.state.ny.us
Committees: Aging; Codes; Environmental Conservation; Health; Insurance
Senior Staff: Adrienne Knoll

Maritza Davila (D) 518-455-5537/fax: 518-455-5789
District: 53 *Room:* 631 LOB *e-mail:* davilaM@assembly.state.ny.us
Committees: Alcoholism & Drug Abuse; Children & Families; Correction;
Economic Development, Job Creation, Commerce & Industry; Housing;
Social Services
Senior Staff: Rachel Fuentes

Michael G DenDekker (D) 518-455-4545/fax: 518-455-4547
District: 34 *Room:* 841 LOB *e-mail:* dendekkerm@assembly.state.ny.us
Committees: Aging; Alcoholism & Drug Abuse; Governmental Employees;
Labor; Transportation; Veterans' Affairs (Chair)
Senior Staff: Maureen Allen

Erik M Dilan (D) 518-455-5821
District: 54 *Room:* 921 LOB *e-mail:* dilane@assembly.state.ny.us
Committees: Cities; Consumer Affairs & Protection; Corporations,
Authorities & Commissions; Governmental Operations; Housing; Insurance
Senior Staff: Videsh Persaud

Jeffrey Dinowitz (D-WF) 518-455-5965/fax: 518-455-4437
District: 81 *Room:* 941 LOB *e-mail:* dinowij@assembly.state.ny.us
Committees: Consumer Affairs & Protection (Chair); Election Law; Health;
Judiciary; Rules
Senior Staff: Randi Martos

David DiPietro (R-C) 518-455-5314/fax: 518-455-5761
District: 147 *Room:* 543 LOB *e-mail:* dipietrod@assembly.state.ny.us
Committees: Alcoholism & Drug Abuse; Economic Development, Job
Creation, Commerce & Industry; Labor; Small Business (Ranking Member);
Transportation
Senior Staff: Loren Gierlinger

Janet L Duprey (R) 518-455-5943/fax: 518-455-5761
District: 115 *Room:* 635 LOB *e-mail:* dupreyj@assembly.state.ny.us
Title: Vice Chair, Program Committee
Committees: Correction; Governmental Operations (Ranking Minority
Member); Higher Education; Rules; Ways & Means
Senior Staff: Jill Abdallah

Steven C Englebright (D) 518-455-4804/fax: 518-455-5795
District: 4 *Room:* 621 LOB *e-mail:* engles@assembly.state.ny.us
Committees: Environmental Conservation (Chair); Education; Energy;
Higher Education; Rules
Senior Staff: Maria Hoffman

Patricia Fahy (D) 518-455-4178
District: 109 *Room:* 452 LOB *e-mail:* fahyp@assembly.state.ny.us
Committees: Banks; Children and Families; Environmental Conservation;
Higher Education; Tourism, Parks, Arts & Sports Development
Senior Staff: Catherine Fahey

Herman D Farrell, Jr (D) 518-455-5491/fax: 518-455-5776
District: 71 *Room:* 923 LOB *e-mail:* farrelh@assembly.state.ny.us
Title: Chair, Ways & Means Committee
Committees: Rules; Ways & Means (Chair)
Senior Staff: Marcia Coleman

Gary D Finch (R-C) 518-455-5878/fax: 518-455-3895
District: 126 *Room:* 448 LOB *e-mail:* finchg@assembly.state.ny.us
Title: Assistant Minority Leader
Committees: Agriculture; Banks; Correction; Insurance; Rules
Senior Staff: Suzanne Redmond

Michael J Fitzpatrick (R-C) 518-455-5021/fax: 518-455-4394
District: 8 *Room:* 458 LOB *e-mail:* fitzpatrickm@assembly.state.ny.us
Title: Chair, Minority Joint Conference Committee
Committees: Higher Education; Housing (Ranking Minority Member); Labor;
Ways & Means
Senior Staff: Kathy Albrecht

Christopher Friend (R) 518-455-4538/fax: 518-455-5922
District: 124 *Room:* 938 LOB *e-mail:* friendc@assembly.state.ny.us
Committees: Aging; Children & Families (Ranking Member); Corporations
Authorities & Commissions; Housing; Local Governments (Ranking
Member)
Senior Staff: Scott Esty

Sandra R Galef (D-I) 518-455-5348/fax: 518-455-5728
District: 95 *Room:* 641 LOB *e-mail:* galefs@assembly.state.ny.us
Committees: Corporations Authorities & Commissions; Election Law;
Governmental Operations; Health; Real Property Taxation (Chair)
Senior Staff: Dana Levenberg

David F Gantt (D) 518-455-5606/fax: 518-455-5419
District: 137 *Room:* 830 LOB *e-mail:* ganttd@assembly.state.ny.us
Committees: Economic Development, Job Creation, Commerce & Industry;
Local Governments; Rules; Transportation (Chair); Ways & Means
Senior Staff: Nick Thony

Andrew R Garbarino (R-I-C) 518-455-4611
District: 7 *Room:* 529 LOB *e-mail:* garbarinoa@assembly.state.ny.us
Committees: Banks; Health; Environmental Conservation; Higher Education;
Racing & Wagering
Senior Staff: Josh Ringel

Joe Giglio (R-I-C) 518-455-5241/fax: 518-455-5869
District: 148 *Room:* 439 LOB *e-mail:* giglioj@assembly.state.ny.us
Title: Chair, Minority Steering Committee
Committees: Aging; Children & Families; Codes; Correction (Ranking
Minority Member); Ethics & Guidance
Senior Staff: Michael Brisky

Mark Gjonaj (D) 518-455-8444/fax: 518-455-4649
District: 80 *Room:* 633 LOB *e-mail:* gjonajm@assembly.state.ny.us
Committees: Banks; Local Government; Real Property Taxation; Small
Business; Tourism, Parks, Arts & Sports Development
Senior Staff: Renee Montminy

Deborah J Glick (D) 518-455-4841/fax: 518-455-4649
District: 66 *Room:* 717 LOB *e-mail:* glickd@assembly.state.ny.us
Committees: Environmental Conservation; Governmental Operations; Higher
Education (Chair); Rules; Ways & Means
Senior Staff: Sarah Sanchala

Phillip Goldfeder (D) 518-455-4292/fax: 518-455-4723
District: 23 *Room:* 542 LOB *e-mail:* goldfederp@ assembly.state.ny.us
Committees: Aging; Corporations, Authorities & Commissions;
Governmental Employees; Insurance; Mental Health; Racing & Wagering
Senior Staff: Angela Katz

Andrew Goodell (R) 518-455-4511/fax: 518-455-4328
District: 150 *Room:* 545 LOB *e-mail:* goodella@assembly.state.ny.us
Committees: Governmental Operations; Health; Judiciary; Social Services
Senior Staff: Michele Krege

Offices and agencies generally appear in alphabetical order, except when specific order is requested by listee.

Richard N Gottfried (D-WF)........ 518-455-4941/fax: 518-455-5939
District: 75 *Room:* 822 LOB *e-mail:* gottfriedr@assembly.state.ny.us
Committees: Health (Chair); Higher Education; Rules
Senior Staff: Richard Conti

Alfred C Graf (R).................. 518-455-5937/fax: 518-455-4784
District: 5 *Room:* 433 LOB *e-mail:* grafa@assembly.state.ny.us
Committees: Codes; Housing (Ranking Member); Education; Judiciary
Senior Staff: Angela Ventrice

Aileen M Gunther (D-C)............ 518-455-5355/fax: 518-455-5239
District: 100 *Room:* 826 LOB *e-mail:* gunthea@assemby.state.ny.us
Committees: Agriculture; Environmental Conservation; Health; Mental
Health (Chair); Racing & Wagering; Real Property Taxation
Senior Staff: Allison Horan

Stephen Hawley (R)................ 518-455-5811/fax: 518-455-5558
District: 139 *Room:* 329 LOB *e-mail:* hawleys@assembly.state.ny.us
Title: Assistant Minority Leader
Committees: Agriculture; Insurance; Veterans' Affairs; Ways & Means
Senior Staff: Eileen Banker

Carl E Heastie (D) 518-455-3791/fax: 518-455-4812
District: 83 *Room:* 932 LOB *e-mail:* speaker@assembly.state.ny.us
Title: Speaker
Committees: Rules
Senior Staff: Jevonni Brooks

Andrew Hevesi (D).................. 518-455-4926/fax: 518-455-5173
District: 28 *Room:* 844 LOB *e-mail:* hevesia@assembly.state.ny.us
Committees: Energy; Health; Insurance; Labor; Social Services (Chair)
Senior Staff: Christopher Kaznowski

Dov Hikind (D) 518-455-5721/fax: 518-455-5948
District: 48 *Room:* 551 LOB *e-mail:* hikindd@assembly.state.ny.us
Title: Assistant Majority Leader
Committees:
Senior Staff: Marc B Kronenberg

Earlene Hooper (D-I) 518-455-5861/fax: 518-455-4329
District: 18 *Room:* 739 LOB *e-mail:* hoopere@assembly.state.ny.us
Title: Deputy Speaker
Committees: Education; Rules; Ways & Means
Senior Staff: Arndreia M Goodbee

Ellen Jaffee (D).................... 518-455-5118/fax: 518-455-5119
District: 97 *Room:* 650 LOB *e-mail:* jaffeee@assembly.state.ny.us
Committees: Children & Families; Economic Development, Job Creation,
Commerce & Industry; Environmental Conservation; Health; Higher
Education; Mental Health; Oversight, Analysis & Investigation (Chair)
Senior Staff: Tiffany Card

Kimberly Jean-Pierre (D)........... 518-455-5787/fax: 518-455-3976
District: 11 *Room:* 530 LOB *e-mail:* jeanpierrek@assembly.state.ny.us
Committees: Banks; Economic Development, Job Creation, Commerce &
Industry; Mental Health; Transportation
Senior Staff: Bilal Malik

Mark Johns (R) 518-455-5784/fax: 518-455-4639
District: 135 *Room:* 549 LOB *e-mail:* johnsm@assembly.state.ny.us
Committees: Aging; Alcoholism & Drug Abuse; Governmental Employees;
Governmental Operations; Housing
Senior Staff: Sean Delehanty

Latoya Joyner (D) 518-455-5671/fax: 518-455-5461
District: 77 *Room:* 427 LOB *e-mail:* joynerl@assembly.state.ny.us
Committees: Aging; Consumer Affairs; Housing; Insurance; Judiciary; Social
Services
Senior Staff: Jamie Gilkey

Todd Kaminsky (D) 518-455-3028
District: 20 *Room:* 827 LOB *e-mail:* kaminskyt@assembly.state.ny.us
Committees: Consumer Affairs & Protection; Environmental Conservation;
Judiciary; Transportation; Veterans' Affairs
Senior Staff: Halie Meyers

Steve Katz (R)......................518-455-5783/fax: 518-455-5543
District: 94 *Room:* 718 LOB *e-mail:* katzs@assembly.state.ny.us
Committees: Aging; Alcoholism & Drug Abuse; Economic Development, Job
Creation, Commerce & Industry; Housing; Mental Health
Senior Staff: Tara Keegan

Brian P Kavanagh (D)............... 518-455-5506/fax: 518-455-4801
District: 74 *Room:* 419 LOB *e-mail:* kavanaghb@assembly.state.ny.us
Committees: Cities; Corporations, Authorities & Commissions; Election
Law; Environmental Conservation; Housing; Labor
Senior Staff: Anna Pycior

Michael P Kearns (D)................................518-455-4691
District: 142 *Room:* 431 LOB *e-mail:* kearnsm@assembly.state.ny.us
Committees: Banks; Cities; Housing; Oversight, Analysis & Investigation
Senior Staff: Kelly Krug

Ron Kim (D) 518-455-5411/fax: 518-455-4650
District: 40 *Room:* 429 LOB *e-mail:* kimr@assembly.state.ny.us
Committees: Children & Families; Corporations, Authorities & Commissions;
Education; Governmental Operations; Housing; Social Services
Senior Staff: Yuh-Line Niou

Brian M Kolb (R-I-C)............... 518-455-3751/fax: 518-455-4650
District: 131 *Room:* 933 LOB *e-mail:* kolbb@assembly.state.ny.us
Title: Minority Leader
Committees: Rules (Ranking Member)
Senior Staff: Judy Skype

Kieran Michael Lalor (R-I-C)........ 518-455-5725/fax: 518-455-5729
District: 105 *Room:* 531 LOB *e-mail:* lalork@assembly.state.ny.us
Committees: Banks; Governmental Operations; Real Property Taxation
(Ranking Member); Small Business; Veterans' Affairs
Senior Staff: Chris Covucci

Charles D Lavine (D) 518-455-5456/fax: 518-455-5467
District: 13 *Room:* 441 LOB *e-mail:* lavinec@assembly.state.ny.us
Committees: Codes; Ethics & Guidance (Chair); Health; Higher Education;
Insurance; Judiciary
Senior Staff: Tara Butler-Sahai

Peter Lawrence (R) 518-455-4664/fax: 518-455-3093
District: 134 *Room:* 722 LOB *e-mail:* lawrencep@assembly.state.ny.us
Committees: Ethics & Guidance; Higher Education; Oversight, Analysis &
Investigation; Racing & Wagering; Small Business
Senior Staff: Aaron Baker

Joseph R Lentol (D)................ 518-455-4477/fax: 518-455-4599
District: 50 *Room:* 632 LOB *e-mail:* lentolj@assembly.state.ny.us
Committees: Codes (Chair); Election Law; Rules; Ways & Means
Senior Staff: Catherine E Peake

Barbara S Lifton (D)............... 518-455-5444/fax: 518-455-4640
District: 125 *Room:* 555 LOB *e-mail:* liftonb@assembly.state.ny.us
Title: Chair, Majority Steering
Committees: Agriculture; Education; Election Law; Environmental
Conservation; Higher Education; Rural Resources
Senior Staff: Linda Smith

Guillermo Linares (D) 518-455-5807
District: 72 *Room:* 534 LOB *e-mail:* linaresg@assembly.state.ny.us
Committees: Aging; Banks; Cities; Housing; Mental Health
Senior Staff: Herminio Martinez

Legislative
Branch

Peter D Lopez (R) 518-455-5363/fax: 518-455-5856
District: 102 *Room:* 402 LOB *e-mail:* lopezp@assembly.state.ny.us
Title: Vice Chair Minority Conference
Committees: Agriculture; Alcoholism & Drug Abuse; Corporations,
Authorities & Commissions; Education; Environmental Conservation
Senior Staff: Hannah Roberti

Donna A Lupardo (D).................518-455-5431/fax: 518-455-5693
District: 123 *Room:* 626 LOB *e-mail:* lupardod@assembly.state.ny.us
Committees: Children & Families (Chair); Economic Development, Job
Creation, Commerce & Industry; Environmental Conservation; Higher
Education; Transportation
Senior Staff: Joan Marcy

Chad A Lupinacci (R-C-I-WF) 518-455-5732/fax: 518-455-5553
District: 10 *Room:* 937 LOB *e-mail:* lupinaccic@assembly.state.ny.us
Committees: Election Law; Higher Education; Judiciary; Tourism, Parks,
Arts & Sports Development; Transportation
Senior Staff: Frances Spatafora

William Magee (D-I) 518-455-4807/fax: 518-455-5237
District: 121 *Room:* 828 LOB *e-mail:* mageew@assembly.state.ny.us
Committees: Aging; Agriculture (Chair); Banks; Higher Education; Local
Governments
Senior Staff: Laura Martino

William B Magnarelli (D-WF-VE) 518-455-4826/fax: 518-455-5498
District: 129 *Room:* 837 LOB *e-mail:* magnarw@assembly.state.ny.us
Committees: Economic Development, Job Creation, Commerce & Industry;
Education; Oversight, Analysis & Investigation; Local Governments (Chair);
Rules
Senior Staff: Christine H Slocum

Nicole Malliotakis (R-C)............518-455-5716/fax: 518-455-5970
District: 64 *Room:* 725 LOB *e-mail:* malliotakisn@assembly.state.ny.us
Committees: Banks; Corporations, Authorities & Commissions; Government
Employees (Ranking Member); Transportation; Ways & Means
Senior Staff: Paul Marrone

Margaret M Markey (D) 518-455-4755/fax: 518-455-5032
District: 30 *Room:* 712 LOB *e-mail:* markeym@assembly.state.ny.us
Committees: Labor; Racing & Wagering; Tourism, Parks, Arts & Sports
Development (Chair); Rules; Ways & Means
Senior Staff: Eileen Boland

Shelly Mayer (D) 518-455-3662/fax: 518-455-5499
District: 90 *Room:* 327 LOB *e-mail:* mayers@assembly.state.ny.us
Committees: Children & Families; Cities; Health; Education; Labor; Social
Services
Senior Staff: Rachel A. Estroff

John T McDonald III (D) 518-455-4474/fax: 518-455-4727
District: 108 *Room:* 417 LOB *e-mail:* mcdonaldj@assembly.state.ny.us
Committees: Aging; Alcoholism & Drug Abuse; Cities; Mental Health; Real
Property Taxation; Insurance
Senior Staff: Emily Shover

David G McDonough (R-C-I) 518-455-4633/fax: 518-455-5559
District: 14 *Room:* 443 LOB *e-mail:* mcdonod@assembly.state.ny.us
Title: Vice Chair, Minority Joint Conference Committee
Committees: Consumer Affairs & Protection; Education; Health;
Transportation (Ranking Minority Member); Veterans' Affairs
Senior Staff: Lynette Liverani

Tom McKevitt (R) 518-455-5341/fax: 518-455-4346
District: 17 *Room:* 546 LOB *e-mail:* mckevit@assembly.state.ny.us
Title: Assistant Minority Leader Pro Tempore
Committees: Codes; Consumer Affairs & Protection; Election Law; Local
Governments
Senior Staff: Lynn Schaefering

Steve McLaughlin (R)...............518-455-5777/fax: 518-455-5923
District: 107 *Room:* 533 LOB *e-mail:* mclaughlins@assembly.state.ny.us
Committees: Children & Families; Economic Development, Job Creation,
Commerce and Industry (RM); Education; Social Services
Senior Staff: Jennifer Polaro

Michael Miller (D) 518-455-4621/fax: 518-455-5361
District: 38 *Room:* 542 LOB *e-mail:* millermg@assembly.state.ny.us
Title: Chair, House Operations
Committees: Aging; Banks; Education; House Operations (Chair); Labor;
Racing & Wagering; Veterans' Affairs
Senior Staff: Angel Vazquez

Michael Montesano (R-I-C).........518-455-4684/fax: 518-455-5477
District: 15 *Room:* 437 LOB *e-mail:* montesanom@assembly.state.ny.us
Title: Assistant Minority Whip
Committees: Codes; Corporations, Authorities & Commissions; Ethics &
Guidance; Judiciary (Ranking Member); Oversight, Analysis & Investigation
(Ranking Member)
Senior Staff: Ida McQuair

Joseph D Morelle (D)...............518-455-5373/fax: 518-455-5647
District: 136 *Room:* 926 LOB *e-mail:* morellej@assembly.state.ny.us
Title: Majority Leader
Committees:
Senior Staff: Kristin Anderson

Walter T Mosley (D) 518-455-5325/fax: 518-455-3684
District: 57 *Room:* 528 LOB *e-mail:* mosleyw@assembly.state.ny.us
Committees: Banks; Codes; Correction; Education; Housing
Senior Staff: Gigi Elliott-Davis

Francisco Moya (D) 518-455-4567/fax: 518-455-5375
District: 39 *Room:* 727 LOB *e-mail:* moyaf@assembly.state.ny.us
Committees: Corporations, Authorities & Commissions; Energy; Housing;
Insurance; Labor; Ways & Means
Senior Staff: Meghan Tadio

Dean Murray (R) 518-455-4901/fax: 518-455-5908
District: 3 *Room:* 430 LOB *e-mail:* murrayd@assembly.state.ny.us
Committees: Aging; Education; Small Business; Tourism, Parks, Arts &
Sports Development; Transportation
Senior Staff: Ed Flood

Bill Nojay (R-I) 518-455-5662/fax: 518-455-5918
District: 133 *Room:* 527 LOB *e-mail:* nojayw@assembly.state.ny.us
Committees: Consumer Affairs & Proteection; Election Law (Ranking
Member); Mental Health; Transportation
Senior Staff: Barbara Collins

Catherine T Nolan (D) 518-455-4851/fax: 518-455-3847
District: 37 *Room:* 836 LOB *e-mail:* nolanc@assembly.state.ny.us
Committees: Corporations, Authorities & Commissions; Education (Chair);
Rules; Veterans' Affairs; Ways & Means
Senior Staff: Kathleen Whynot

Daniel J O'Donnell (D) 518-455-5603/fax: 518-455-3812
District: 69 *Room:* 526 LOB *e-mail:* odonnelld@assembly.state.ny.us
Committees: Codes; Correction (Chair); Education; Environmental
Conservation; Judiciary; Tourism, Parks, Arts & Sports
Senior Staff: Nicholas O'Neill

Robert C Oaks (R-C)...............518-455-5655/fax: 518-455-5407
District: 130 *Room:* 444 CAP *e-mail:* oaksr@assembly.state.ny.us
Title: Ranking Minority Member, Ways & Means
Committees: Rules; Ways & Means (Ranking Member)
Senior Staff: Myra Brown

Felix W Ortiz (D) 518-455-3821/fax: 518-455-3828
District: 51 *Room:* 731 LOB *e-mail:* ortizf@assembly.state.ny.us
Title: Assistant Speaker
Committees: Correction; Labor; Rules; Ways & Means
Senior Staff: Jeffrey Wice

Offices and agencies generally appear in alphabetical order, except when specific order is requested by listee.

Steven Otis (D) 518-455-4897/fax: 518-455-4861
District: 91 *Room:* 325 LOB *e-mail:* otiss@assembly.state.ny.us
Committees: Agriculture; Corporations Authorities & Commissions;
Environmental Conservation; Libraries & Education Technology; Local
Governments; Tourism, Parks, Arts & Sports Development
Senior Staff: Debra Lagapa

Philip Palmesano (R) 518-455-5791/fax: 518-455-4644
District: 132 *Room:* 723 LOB *e-mail:* palmesanop@assembly.state.ny.us
Title: Secretary, Minority Conference
Committees: Corporations, Authorities & Commissions; Energy (Ranking
Member); Libraries & Education Technology; Real Property Taxation;
Tourism, Parks, Art & Sports Development
Senior Staff: Sperry Navone

Anthony H Palumbo (R) 518-455-5294/fax: 518-455-4740
District: 2 *Room:* 719 LOB *e-mail:* palumba@assembly.state.ny.us
Committees: Consumer Affairs & Protection (Ranking Member);
Environmental Conservation; Governmental Employees; Judiciary; Social
Services
Senior Staff: Jennine Kubik

Amy R Paulin (D) 518-455-5585/fax: 518-455-5409
District: 88 *Room:* 713 LOB *e-mail:* paulina@assembly.state.ny.us
Committees: Energy (Chair); Education; Health; Higher Education
Senior Staff: Nancy Fisher

Crystal D Peoples-Stokes (D) 518-455-5005/fax: 518-455-5471
District: 141 *Room:* 625 LOB *e-mail:* peoplec@assembly.state.ny.us
Committees: Alcoholism & Drug Abuse; Environmental Conservation;
Governmental Operations (Chair); Health; Higher Education; Insurance
Senior Staff: Mark Boyd

N Nick Perry (D) 518-455-4166/fax: 518-455-5478
District: 58 *Room:* 736 LOB *e-mail:* perryn@assembly.state.ny.us
Title: Assistant Speaker Pro Tempore
Committees: Banks; Codes; Labor; Rules; Transportation; Ways & Means
Senior Staff: Joyce Elie

Roxanne Persaud (D) 518-455-5211
District: 59 *Room:* 324 LOB *e-mail:* persaudr@assembly.state.ny.us
Committees: Children & Families; Higher Education; Libraries & Education
Technology; Real Property Taxation; Social Services
Senior Staff: Jaime Rivas-Williams

Victor Pichardo (D) 518-455-5511/fax: 518-455-5449
District: 86 *Room:* 920 LOB *e-mail:* pichardov@assembly.state.ny.us
Committees: Cities; Higher Education; Housing; Real Property Taxation;
Small Business; Social Services
Senior Staff: Nicole Lauterbach

James Gary Pretlow (D) 518-455-5291/fax: 518-455-5447
District: 89 *Room:* 845 LOB *e-mail:* pretloj@assembly.state.ny.us
Committees: Codes; Insurance; Racing & Wagering (Chair); Rules; Ways &
Means
Senior Staff: Janet E Edwards

Dan Quart (D) 518-455-4794/fax: 518-455-4629
District: 73 *Room:* 741 LOB *e-mail:* quartd@assembly.state.ny.us
Committees: Alcoholism & Drug Abuse; Consumer Affairs & Protection;
Corporations, Authorities & Commissions; Insurance; Judiciary; Tourism,
Parks, Arts & Sports Development
Senior Staff: Amanda Wallwin

Edward Ra (R) 518-455-4627/fax: 518-455-4643
District: 19 *Room:* 544 LOB *e-mail:* rae@assembly.state.ny.us
Title: Vice Chair, Minority Steering Committee
Committees: Codes; Education (Ranking Member); Health; Higher
Education; Transportation
Senior Staff: Vacant

Andrew P Raia (R-C-I) 518-455-5952/fax: 518-455-5804
District: 12 *Room:* 629 LOB *e-mail:* raiaa@assembly.state.ny.us
Title: Deputy Minority Whip
Committees: Banks; Environmental Conservation; Health; Housing; Rules
Senior Staff: Judy VanAmburgh

Philip R Ramos (D-I-WF) 518-455-5185/fax: 518-455-5236
District: 6 *Room:* 648 LOB *e-mail:* ramosp@assembly.state.ny.us
Title: Deputy Majority Leader
Committees: Aging; Education; Local Governments; Ways & Means
Senior Staff: Erik Vasquez

Diane C Richardson (WF) 518-455-5262
District: 43 *Room:* 834 LOB *e-mail:* richardsond@assembly.state.ny.us
Committees: Banks; Corporations, Authorities & Commissions; Economic
Development, Job Creation, Commerce & Industry; Mental Health; Small
Business
Senior Staff: Vacant

Jose Rivera (D) 518-455-5414/fax: 518-455-5322
District: 78 *Room:* 536 LOB *e-mail:* riveraj@assembly.state.ny.us
Title: Assistant Majority Whip
Committees: Aging; Agriculture; Insurance; Small Business
Senior Staff: Jasmin Clavasquin

Samuel D Roberts (D) 518-455-5383/fax: 518-455-5417
District: 128 *Room:* 510 CAP *e-mail:* robertss@assembly.state.ny.us
Committees: Aging; Labor; Libraries & Education Technology; Small
Business; Tourism, Arts & Sports Development; Transportation
Senior Staff: Lanessa Owens

Annette Robinson (D) 518-455-5474/fax: 518-455-5857
District: 56 *Room:* 424 LOB *e-mail:* robinsona@assembly.state.ny.us
Committees: Aging; Banks (Chair); Children & Families; Housing;
Oversight, Analysis & Investigation; Real Property Taxation; Small Business
Senior Staff: Adrienne Johnson

Robert J Rodriguez (D) 518-455-4781/fax: 518-455-3893
District: 68 *Room:* 729 LOB *e-mail:* rodriguezrj@assembly.state.ny.us
Committees: Banks; Corporations, Authorities & Commissions; Housing;
Labor; Mental Health; Ways & Means
Senior Staff: Maggie McDermott

Linda B Rosenthal (D-WF) 518-455-5802/fax: 518-455-5015
District: 67 *Room:* 627 LOB *e-mail:* rosentl@assembly.state.ny.us
Committees: Agriculture; Alcoholism & Drug Abuse (Chair); Education;
Energy; Health; Housing; Tourism, Parks, Arts & Sports Development
Senior Staff: Lauren Schuster

Nily Rozic (D-WF) 518-455-5172/fax: 518-455-5479
District: 25 *Room:* 820 LOB *e-mail:* rozicn@assembly.state.ny.us
Committees: Children & Families; Corporations, Authorities & Commissions;
Correction; Environmental Conservation; Labor
Senior Staff: Erin Rogers

Addie J Russell (D-WF) 518-455-5545/fax: 518-455-5751
District: 116 *Room:* 456 LOB *e-mail:* russella@assembly.state.ny.us
Committees: Agriculture; Corporations, Authorities & Commissions;
Economic Development, Job Creation, Commerce & Industry; Energy; Local
Governments; Veterans' Affairs
Senior Staff: Mark Pacilio

Sean Ryan (D) 518-455-4886/fax: 518-455-4890
District: 149 *Room:* 540 LOB *e-mail:* ryans@assembly.state.ny.us
Committees: Banks; Education; Energy; Environmental Conservation; Local
Governments; Veterans' Affairs
Senior Staff: Joshua Pennel

Joseph S Saladino (R) 518-455-5305/fax: 518-455-5024
District: 9 *Room:* 720 LOB *e-mail:* saladij@assembly.state.ny.us
Title: Chair, Minority Program Committee
Committees: Environmental Conservation; Governmental Employees; Labor;
Libraries & Education Technology (Ranking Member); Ways & Means
Senior Staff: Victoria Ventura

Offices and agencies generally appear in alphabetical order, except when specific order is requested by listee.

Angelo Santabarbara (D)............518-455-5197/fax: 518-455-5024
District: 111 *Room:* 654 LOB *e-mail:* santabarbaraa@assembly.state.ny.us
Committees: Agriculture; Energy; Governmental Employees; Racing &
Wagering; Small Business; Veterans' Affairs
Senior Staff: Gerard Parisi

Michelle Schimel (D)...............518-455-5192/fax: 518-455-4921
District: 16 *Room:* 702 LOB *e-mail:* schimelm@assembly.state.ny.us
Title: Chair, Majority Conference
Committees: Environmental Conservation; Governmental Operations; Local
Governments; Transportation; Veterans' Affairs
Senior Staff: Nicole Duckham

Robin L Schimminger (D-I-C).......518-455-4767/fax: 518-455-4724
District: 140 *Room:* 847 LOB *e-mail:* schimmr@assembly.state.ny.us
Committees: Codes; Economic Development, Job Creation, Commerce &
Industry (Chair); Health; Ways & Means
Senior Staff: Kenneth L Berlinski

Rebecca Seawright (D)....................518-455-5676
District: 76 *Room:* 818 LOB *e-mail:* seawrightr@assembly.state.ny.us
Committees: Banks; Consumer Affairs & Protection; Corporations,
Authorities & Commissions; Judiciary; Tourism, Parks, Arts & Sports
Development
Senior Staff: Cali Madia

Luis R Sepulveda (D)...............518-455-5102/fax: 518-455-5459
District: 87 *Room:* 432 LOB *e-mail:* sepulvedal@assembly.state.ny.us
Committees: Aging; Agriculture; Banks; Correction; Housing
Senior Staff: Thomas Musich

Sheldon Silver (D-WF).............518-455-3640/fax: 518-455-7092
District: 65 *Room:* 704 LOB *e-mail:* silvers@assembly.state.ny.us
Committees:
Senior Staff: Judy R Rapfogel

Michael Simanowitz (D)....................518-455-4404
District: 27 *Room:* 742 LOB *e-mail:* simanowitzm@assembly.state.ny.us
Committees: Aging; Agriculture; Consumer Affairs & Protection; Economic
Development, Job Creation, Commerce & Industry; Higher Education; Small
Business
Senior Staff: Scott Wolff

Jo Anne Simon (D)....................518-455-5426
District: 52 *Room:* 326 LOB *e-mail:* simonj@assembly.state.ny.us
Committees: Consumer Affairs & Protection; Higher Education; Judiciary;
Labor; Transportation
Senior Staff: Ptahra Jeppe

Aravella Simotas (D)...............518-455-5014/fax: 518-455-4044
District: 36 *Room:* 652 LOB *e-mail:* simotasa@assembly.state.ny.us
Title: Vice Chair, Majority Conference
Committees: Banks; Consumer Affairs & Protection; Corporations,
Authorities & Commissions; Energy
Senior Staff: Samantha Darche

Frank Skartados (D)...............518-455-5762/fax: 518-455-5593
District: 104 *Room:* 435 LOB *e-mail:* skartadosf@assembly.state.ny.us
Committees: Agriculture; Economic Development; Local Governments;
Small Business; Tourism, Parks, Arts & Sports Development; Transportation
Senior Staff: Steve Gold

James Skoufis (D)...............518-455-5441/fax: 518-455-5884
District: 99 *Room:* 821 LOB *e-mail:* skoufisj@assembly.state.ny.us
Committees: Agriculture; Local Governments; Insurance; Labor;
Transportation; Veterans' Affairs
Senior Staff: Laurie Tautel

Michaelle C Solages (D)...........518-455-4465/fax: 518-455-5560
District: 22 *Room:* 619 LOB *e-mail:* solagesm@assembly.state.ny.us
Committees: Consumer Affairs & Protection; Governmental Employees;
Libraries & Education Technology; Racing & Wagering; Social Services
Senior Staff: Marthe Desdunes

Dan Stec (R-I-C)....................518-455-5565/fax: 518-455-7710
District: 114 *Room:* 940 LOB *e-mail:* stecd@assembly.state.ny.us
Committees: Banks, Environmental Conservation (Ranking Member); Local
Governments; Social Services; Tourism, Parks, Arts & Sports Development
Senior Staff: Debbie Capezzuti

Phil Steck (D)....................518-455-5931/fax: 518-455-5840
District: 110 *Room:* 819 LOB *e-mail:* steckp@assembly.state.ny.us
Committees: Children & Families; Health; Insurance; Judiciary;
Transportation
Senior Staff: Thad Rutherford

Al Stirpe (D)....................518-455-4505/fax: 518-455-5593
District: 127 *Room:* 656 LOB *e-mail:* stirpea@assembly.state.ny.us
Committees: Agriculture; Alcoholism & Drug Abuse; Economic
Development, Job Creation, Commerce & Industry; Higher Education;
Tourism, Parks, Arts & Sports Development
Senior Staff: Dorothy Money

James N Tedisco (R-I-C)...........518-455-5772/fax: 518-455-3750
District: 112 *Room:* 404 LOB *e-mail:* tediscj@assembly.state.ny.us
Title: Minority Whip
Committees: Banks; Economic Development, Job Creation, Commerce &
Industry; Racing & Wagering; Rules
Senior Staff: Adam Kramer

Claudia Tenney (R)...............518-455-5334/fax: 518-455-5391
District: 101 *Room:* 426 LOB *e-mail:* tenneyc@assembly.state.ny.us
Committees: Banks (Ranking Member); Codes; Education; Social Services;
Veterans' Affairs
Senior Staff: Karen Newton

Fred W Thiele, Jr (D)...............518-455-5997/fax: 518-455-5963
District: 1 *Room:* 746 LOB *e-mail:* thielef@assembly.state.ny.us
Committees: Education; Environmental Conservation; Small Business
(Chair); Oversight, Analysis & Investigation; Transportation; Ways & Means
Senior Staff: Lisa Lombardo

Matthew Titone (D-WF).............518-455-4677/fax: 518-455-5946
District: 61 *Room:* 643 LOB *e-mail:* titonem@assembly.state.ny.us
Committees: Education; Environmental Conservation; Health; Judiciary;
Social Services; Tourism, Parks, Arts & Sports Development
Senior Staff: Chris Bauer

Michele R Titus (D)...............518-455-5668/fax: 518-455-3892
District: 31 *Room:* 522 LOB *e-mail:* titusm@assembly.state.ny.us
Committees: Children & Families; Codes; Education; Ethics & Guidance;
Labor (Chair); Judiciary
Senior Staff: A Richard McKoy

Latrice Walker (D)....................518-455-4466
District: 55 *Room:* 628 LOB *e-mail:* walkerl@assembly.state.ny.us
Committees: Correction; Economic Development, Job Creation, Commerce &
Industry; Election Law; Energy; Housing
Senior Staff: Alicha Ampry-Samuel

Raymond Walter (R)...............518-455-4618/fax: 518-455-5023
District: 146 *Room:* 550 LOB *e-mail:* walterr@assembly.state.ny.us
Committees: Economic Development, Job Creation, Commerce & Industry;
Health; Housing; Insurance; Ways & Means
Senior Staff: Erin Baker

Helene E Weinstein (D)...........518-455-5462/fax: 518-455-5752
District: 41 *Room:* 831 LOB *e-mail:* weinsth@assembly.state.ny.us
Committees: Aging; Codes; Judiciary (Chair); Rules; Ways & Means
Senior Staff: Yehuda Schupper

David I Weprin (D)...............518-455-5806/fax: 518-455-5977
District: 24 *Room:* 602 LOB *e-mail:* weprind@assembly.state.ny.us
Title: Secretary, Majority Conference
Committees: Banks; Cities; Codes; Election Law; Judiciary; Ways & Means
Senior Staff: Janna Davis

Offices and agencies generally appear in alphabetical order, except when specific order is requested by listee.

Carrie Woerner (D).............518-455-5404/fax: 518-455-3727
District: 113   *Room:* 323 LOB   *e-mail:* woernerc@assembly.state.ny.us
Committees: Agriculture; Local Governments; Racing & Wagering; Small
Business; Tourism, Parks, Arts & Sports Development
Senior Staff: Mark Luciano

Angela M Wozniak (C)..........518-455-5921/fax: 518-455-3962
District: 143   *Room:* 721 LOB   *e-mail:* wozniaka@assembly.state.ny.us
Committees: Aging; Children & Families; Cities; Labor; Local Governments
Senior Staff: Beth Bochiechio

Keith L T Wright (D) 518-455-4793/fax: 518-455-3890
District: 70   *Room:* 943 LOB   *e-mail:* wrightk@assembly.state.ny.us
Committees: Codes; Correction; Housing (Chair); Rules; Ways & Means
Senior Staff: Jeanine Johnson

Kenneth Zebrowski (D-I-C-WF) 518-455-5735/fax: 518-455-5561
District: 96   *Room:* 637 LOB   *e-mail:* zebrowskik@assembly.state.ny.us
Committees: Codes; Environmental Conservation; Ethics & Guidance;
Government Employees; Judiciary; Labor
Senior Staff: Chris Bresnan

STATE ASSEMBLY STANDING COMMITTEES

Aging
Chair:
  Steven Cymbrowiz (D)............................518-455-5214
Ranking Minority Member:
  Angela M Wozniak (C)...........................518-455-5921

Committee Staff
Clerk:
  Lena DeThomasis................................518-455-5965

Key Assembly Staff Assignments
Majority Program Analyst:
  Erin Cunningham................................518-455-4355

Membership
Majority
Peter Abbate, Jr.	Carmen Arroyo
Edward Braunstein	Anthony Brindisi
John McDonald III	Helene Weinstein
Michael DenDekker	Phillip Goldfeder
Didi Barrett	Alec Brook-Krasny
William Magee	Michael Miller
Annette Robinson	Jose Rivera
Phil Ramos	Samuel Roberts
Charles Barron	Latoya Joyner
Guillermo Linares	Luis Sepulveda
Michael Simanowitz	

Minority
Christopher Friend	Joseph Giglio
Dean Murray	Mark Johns
Steve Katz	Karl Brabenec

Agriculture
Chair:
  William Magee (D)..............................518-455-4807
Ranking Minority Member:
  Kenneth Blankenbush (R) 518-455-5797

Committee Staff
Clerk:
  Connie Groves 518-455-4807

Key Assembly Staff Assignments
Majority Program & Legislative Analyst:
  Robert Stern 518-455-4928

Minority Analyst/Counsel:
  Nicholas Forst.................................518-455-4515
Majority Associate Counsel:
  Felicia Reid...................................518-455-4285

Membership
Majority
Didi Barrett	Harry Bronson
Michael Benedetto	Aileen Gunther
Barbara Lifton	Steven Otis
Linda Rosenthal	Jose Rivera
Addie Russell	Angelo Santabarbara
Luis Sepulveda	Michael Simanowitz
Frank Skartados	James Skoufis
Carrie Woerner	Al Stirpe

Minority
Marc Butler	Clifford Crouch
Gary Finch	Stephen Hawley
Peter Lopez	

Alcoholism & Drug Abuse
Chair:
  Linda Rosenthal (D) 518-455-5802
Ranking Minority Member:
  Mark Johns (R) 518-455-5784

Committee Staff
Clerk:
  Holly Francisco................................518-455-5802

Key Assembly Staff Assignments
Majority Program Analyst:
  Alexis Conti...................................518-455-4371
Majority Associate Counsel:
  Jennifer Sacco
Minority Analyst/Counsel:
  Sarah Shearer 518-455-4285

Membership
Majority
Carmen Arroyo	Maritza Davila
Marcos Crespo	Michael G DenDekker
Charles Barron	John McDonald III
Crystal D Peoples-Stokes	Dan Quart
Al Stirpe	

Minority
David DiPietro	Steven Katz
Peter Lopez	

Banks
Chair:
  Annette Robinson (D)...........................518-455-5474
Ranking Minority Member:
  Claudia Tenney (R).............................518-455-5334

Committee Staff
Clerk:
  Virginia Rawlins...............................518-455-5474

Key Assembly Staff Assignments
Majority Principal Analyst:
  Peter Hoffman..................................518-455-4928
Majority Associate Counsel:
  Teri Kleinmann.................................518-455-4928
Minority Analyst/Counsel:
  Michelle Pellegri-Buono 518-455-5230

Offices and agencies generally appear in alphabetical order, except when specific order is requested by listee.

Membership

Majority

Peter J Abbate, Jr	Rodneyse Bichotte
Patricia Fahy	Mark Gjonaj
Michael Kearns	Michael Blake
William Magee	Michael Miller
Walter Mosley	N. Nick Perry
Robert Rodriguez	Kimberly Jean-Pierre
Sean Ryan	Rebecca Seawright
Luis Sepulveda	Aravella Simotas
Guillermo Linares	David Weprin

Minority

Gary Finch	Brian Curran
Andrew Garbarino	Nicole Malliotakis
Dan Stec	Diana Richardson (WF)
James Tedisco	Andrew Raia
Keiran Michael Lalor	

Children & Families
Chair:
> Donna Lupardo (D) 518-455-5431

Ranking Minority Member:
> Steven McLaughlin (R) 518-455-5777

Committee Staff
Clerk:
> Jeff Quain 518-455-4451

Majority Assistant Secretary:
> Rebecca Mudie 518-455-4881

Key Assembly Staff Assignments
Majority Program & Counsel Legislative Analyst:
> Naomi Schultz 518-455-4371

Membership

Majority

Carmen Arroyo	Barbara M. Clark
Patricia Fahy	Maritza Davila
Ellen Jaffee	Ron Kim
Shelley Mayer	Roxanne Persaud
Annette M. Robinson	Nily Rozic
Phil Steck	Michele R Titus

Minority

Joe Giglio	Angela M Wozniak
Christopher Friend	

Cities
Chair:
> Michael Benedetto (D) 518-455-5296

Ranking Minority Member:
> Joseph Borelli (R) 518-455-4495

Committee Staff
Clerk:
> Judith Talar 518-455-5296

Key Assembly Staff Assignments
Majority Assistant Secretary:
> Julia Mallalieu

Minority Analyst/Counsel:
> Edmund V Wick 518-455-4262

Membership

Majority

Alec Brook-Krasny	Edward Braunstein
Marcos Crespo	Victor Pichardo
Brian P. Kavanagh	Michael Kearns
Erik Dilan	Shelley Mayer
John McDonald III	Guillermo Linares

David Weprin

Minority

John Ceretto	Karl Brabenec
Angela M Wozniak	

Codes
Chair:
> Joseph R Lentol (D) 518-455-4477

Ranking Minority Member:
> Al Graf (R) 518-455-5937

Committee Staff
Clerk:
> Wilda Lang 518-455-4477

Key Assembly Staff Assignments
Senior Team Counsel:
> Marty Rosenbaum 518-455-4313

Counsel:
> Jonathan Bailey 518-455-4313

Majority Program Analyst:
> Nathaniel Jenkins

Minority Analyst/Counsel:
> Lori Smith

Membership

Majority

Thomas Abinanti	James F. Brennan
Vivian E Cook	Steven Cymbrowitz
Charles D Lavine	Walter Mosley
Daniel J. O'Donnell	N Nick Perry
James Gary Pretlow	Robin L. Schimminger
Michele R. Titus	Helene Weinstein
David Weprin	Keith L. Wright
Kenneth Zebrowski	

Minority

Joseph Giglio	Claudia Tenney
Tom McKevitt	Michael Montesano
Edward Ra	

Consumer Affairs & Protection
Chair:
> Jeffrey Dinowitz (D) 518-455-5965

Ranking Minority Member:
> Anthony Palumbo (R) 518-455-5294

Committee Staff
Clerk:
> William Schwartz 518-455-5965

Key Assembly Staff Assignments
Majority Legislative Analyst:
> Michael Szydlo 518-455-4355

Minority Analyst/Counsel:
> Edmund V Wick 518-455-4262

Membership

Majority

Peter J Abbate, Jr	David Buchwald
Erik Dilan	Todd Kaminsky
Latoya Joyner	Dan Quart
Michael Simanowitz	Jo Anne Simon
Aravella Simotas	Rebecca Seawright
Michaelle Solages	

Minority

Tom McKevitt	Bill Nojay
David McDonough	

Offices and agencies generally appear in alphabetical order, except when specific order is requested by listee.

Legislative Branch

Corporations, Authorities & Commissions
Chair:
James F Brennan (D) 518-455-5377
Ranking Minority Member:
Jane Corwin (R) 518-455-4601

Committee Staff
Clerk:
Lisa Forkas 518-455-5753

Key Assembly Staff Assignments
Majority Assistant Secretary:
Christian Malagna 518-455-4881
Majority Associate Counsel:
Gregory Berck 518-455-4881

Membership

Majority
Thomas Abinanti	Vivian E Cook
Sandra R Galef	David Buchwald
Philip Goldfeder	Erik Dilan
Brian P. Kavanagh	Ron Kim
Francisco Moya	Catherine T. Nolan
Steven Otis	Dan Quart
Robert Rodriguez	Aravella Simotas
Nily Rozic	Addie J. Russell

Minority
Ken Blankenbush	Christopher Friend
Nicole Malliotakis	Michael Montesano
Philip Palmesano	Diana Richardson (WF)
Peter Lopez	

Correction
Chair:
Daniel O'Donnell (D)............................518-455-5603
Ranking Minority Member:
Joseph Giglio (R) 518-455-5241

Committee Staff
Clerk:
Cheryl Myers 518-455-4548

Key Assembly Staff Assignments
Majority Counsel:
Dianna Goodwin..................................518-455-4313
Minority Analsyt/Counsel:
Lori Smith.......................................518-455-5002

Membership

Majority
William Colton	Maritza Davila
Felix W Ortiz	Michael Blake
Nily Rozic	Luis Sepulveda
Walter Mosley	Latrice Walker
Keith L. T. Wright	

Minority
Janet L Duprey	Gary Finch

Economic Development, Job Creation, Commerce & Industry
Chair:
Robin L Schimminger (D) 518-455-4767
Ranking Minority Member:
Raymond Walter (R)..............................518-455-4618

Committee Staff
Clerk:
Patrice Mago....................................518-455-4767

Key Assembly Staff Assignments
Majority Program Analyst:
Lekeya Martin....................................518-455-4928
Minority Analyst/Counsel:
Michelle Pellegri-Buono

Membership

Majority
Didi Barrett	Maritza Davila
Anthony Brindisi	Harry Bronson
Kevin A Cahill	David F Gantt
Frank Skartados	William B Magnarelli
Al Stirpe	Charles Barron
Donna Lupardo	Rodneyse Bichotte
Michael Simanowitz	Latrice Walker
Kimberly Jean-Pierre	Addie J Russell
Ellen Jaffee	

Minority
Marc Butler	Clifford W Crouch
Diana Richardson (WF)	David DiPietro
Steven McLaughlin	Steve Katz
James Tedisco	

Education
Chair:
Catherine Nolan (D) 518-455-4851
Ranking Minority Member:
Edward Ra (R) 518-455-4627

Committee Staff
Committee Clerk:
Kimberly Shannon

Key Assembly Staff Assignments
Majority Program Analyst:
Diane Girourard
Minority Analyst/Counsel:
Kristin Frank....................................518-455-4258

Membership

Majority
Carmen E Arroyo	Michael Benedetto
James F Brennan	Walter Mosley
Barbara M Clark	Steven C Englebright
Linda Rosenthal	Earlene Hooper
Barbara Lifton	William B Magnarelli
Ron Kim	Shelley Mayer
Michael Miller	Sean Ryan
Daniel J O'Donnell	Amy R Paulin
Philip R Ramos	Fred W Thiele, Jr
Matthew Titone	Michele Titus

Minority
Jane L Corwin	Al Graf
John Ceretto	Peter Lopez
David McDonough	Steven McLaughlin
Dean Murray	Claudia Tenney

Election Law
Chair:
Michael Cusick (D).............................518-455-5526
Ranking Minority Member:
Bill Nojay (R) 518-455-5662

Committee Staff
Legislative Director:
Sharon Grobe 518-455-4313

Offices and agencies generally appear in alphabetical order, except when specific order is requested by listee.

Key Assembly Staff Assignments

Majority Program Analyst:
  Matthew Aumand 518-455-4313

Majority Assistant Secretary:
  Daniel Salvin

Majority Counsel:
  Jessica Norgrove

Minority Analyst/Counsel:
  James Walsh

Membership

Majority

Thomas Abinanti	Alec Brook-Krasny
David Buchwald	Michael Blake
Jeffrey Dinowitz	Sandra R. Galef
Brian P. Kavanagh	Joseph R Lentol
Barbara Lifton	Latrice Walker
David Weprin	

Minority

Karl Brabenec	Chad Lupinacci
Tom McKevitt	

Energy

Chair:
  Amy Paulin (D) 518-455-5585
Ranking Minority Member:
  Philip Palmesano (R) 518-455-5791

Committee Staff

Clerk:
  Andrew Buder 518-455-3786

Key Assembly Staff Assignments

Majority Associate Consel:
  Nairobi Vives

Minority Analyst/Counsel:
  Jennifer Grasso

Membership

Majority

Anthony Brindisi	Marcos Crespo
Steven C. Englebright	Charles Barron
Andrew Hevesi	Francisco Moya
Linda Rosenthal	Addie Russell
Sean Ryan	Aravella Simotas
Angelo Santabarbara	Latrice Walker

Minority

William Barclay	John Ceretto
Joseph Borelli	

Environmental Conservation

Chair:
  Steven Englebright (D) 518-455-4804
Ranking Minority Member:
  Dan Stec (R) 518-455-5565

Committee Staff

Clerk:
  Ryan Vineyard 518-455-2091

Key Assembly Staff Assignments

Majority Program Analyst:
  Michelle Milot

Minority Analyst/Counsel:
  Nicholas Forst 518-455-4515

Membership

Majority

William Colton	Steven Cymbrowitz

Majority (second column)

Deborah J Glick	Aileen M Gunther
Ellen Jaffee	Brian P Kavanagh
Thomas Abinanti	Marcos Crespo
Sean Ryan	Patricia Fahy
Barbara S Lifton	Donna Lupardo
Nily Rozic	Steven Otis
Daniel J O'Donnell	Fred W Thiele, Jr
Crystal D Peoples-Stokes	Michelle Schimel
Matthew Titone	Todd Kaminsky
Kenneth Zebrowski	

Minority

Marc Butler	Jane Corwin
Andrew Raia	Andrew Garbarino
Peter D. Lopez	Joseph S. Saladino
Anthony Palumbo	

Ethics & Guidance

Chair:
  Charles Lavine (D) 518-455-5456
Ranking Minority Member:
  Brian Curran (R) 518-455-4656

Membership

Majority

Kevin A Cahill	Michele R. Titus
Kenneth Zebrowski	

Minority

Peter Lawrence	Jospeh Giglio
Michael Montesano	

Governmental Employees

Chair:
  Peter J Abbate, Jr (D) 518-455-3053
Ranking Minority Member:
  Nicole Malliotakis (R) 518-455-5716

Committee Staff

Clerk:
  Christine Eppelmann 518-455-3053

Key Assembly Staff Assignments

Majority Assistant Secretary:
  Jennifer Best 518-455-4311

Minority Analyst/Counsel:
  Douglas Goldman 518-455-4637

Membership

Majority

Jeffrion L Aubry	Alec Brook-Krasny
William Colton	Michael J Cusick
Michael G DenDekker	Philip Goldfeder
Michaelle Solages	Angelo Santabarbara
Kenneth Zebrowski	

Minority

Anthony Palumbo	Mark Johns
Joseph Saladino	

Governmental Operations

Chair:
  Crystal Peoples-Stokes (D) 518-455-5005
Ranking Minority Member:
  Janet L Duprey (R) 518-455-5943

Committee Staff

Clerk:
  Leah Halton-Pope 518-455-5436

Offices and agencies generally appear in alphabetical order, except when specific order is requested by listee.

Key Assembly Staff Assignments
Majority Assistant Secretary:
　Aaron Suggs
Majority Associate Counsel:
　Kerryanne Burke 518-455-4355
Minority Analyst/Counsel:
　Logan Smith 518-455-4626

Membership

　Majority
　　Michael Benedetto　　　　Michael Blake
　　Sandra R Galef　　　　　　Deborah Glick
　　Michelle Schimel　　　　　Ron Kim
　　ErikM Dilan　　　　　　　Rodneyse Bichotte
　　David Buchwald

　Minority
　　Kieran Michael Lalor　　　Andrew Goodell
　　Mark Johns

Health
Chair:
　Richard N Gottfried (D) 518-455-4941
Ranking Minority Member:
　Andrew Raia (R) 518-455-4495

Committee Staff
Clerk:
　Helen Dong 518-455-4941

　Key Assembly Staff Assignments
　Majority Assistant Secretary:
　　Rebecca Mudie 518-455-4311
　Majority Program Analyst:
　　Michelle Newman
　Minority Analyst/Counsel:
　　Sarah Shearer

Membership

　Majority
　　Ellen Jaffee　　　　　　　Kevin A Cahill
　　Steven Cymbrowitz　　　　Jeffrey Dinowitz
　　Sandra R Galef　　　　　　Aileen M Gunther
　　Andrew Hevesi　　　　　　Thomas Abinanti
　　Charles D Lavine　　　　　Matthew Titone
　　Shelley Mayer　　　　　　Barbara Clark
　　Amy R Paulin　　　　　　　Crystal D Peoples-Stokes
　　Edward Braunstein　　　　Linda B Rosenthal
　　Robin L Schimminger　　　Phil Steck

　Minority
　　Joseph Borelli　　　　　　Andrew Goodell
　　Edward Ra　　　　　　　　David G McDonough
　　Raymond Walter　　　　　Andrew Garbarino

Higher Education
Chair:
　Deborah J Glick (D) 518-455-4841
Ranking Minority Member:
　Chad Lupinacci (R) 518-455-5732

Committee Staff
Clerk:
　Charles LuDuc 518-455-4841
Legislative Director:
　Teresa Swidorski 518-455-4841

　Key Assembly Staff Assignments
　Majority Associate Counsel:
　　Gregory Berck

Minority Analyst/Counsel:
　Kristin Frank 518-455-4258

Membership

　Majority
　　Roxanne Persaud　　　　　Kevin A Cahill
　　Patricia Fahy　　　　　　　Michael J Cusick
　　Steven C Englebright　　　Richard N Gottfried
　　Ellen Jaffee　　　　　　　Charles D Lavine
　　Barbara S Lifton　　　　　Donna Lupardo
　　William Magee　　　　　　Jo Anne Simon
　　Al Stirpe　　　　　　　　Michael Simanowitz
　　Victor Pichardo　　　　　Amy R Paulin
　　Crystal D Peoples-Stokes　Anthony Brindisi

　Minority
　　Marc W Butler　　　　　　Andrew Garbarino
　　Peter Lawrence　　　　　　Edward Ra
　　Michael J Fitzpatrick　　　Janet Duprey

Housing
Chair:
　Keith L.T. Wright (D) 518-455-4793
Ranking Minority Member:
　Michael J Fitzpatrick (R) 518-455-5021

Committee Staff
Clerk:
　Francisco Polanco 518-455-5537

　Key Assembly Staff Assignments
　Majority Program Analyst:
　　Anthony Kergaravat 518-455-4355
　Majority Associate Counsel:
　　Felicia Reid 518-455-4355
　Minority Analyst/Counsel:
　　Edmund V Wick 518-455-4262

Membership

　Majority
　　Rodneyse Bichotte　　　　Victor Pichardo
　　Michael Blake　　　　　　Alec Brook-Krasny
　　Joseph Borelli　　　　　　Vivian E Cook
　　Erik Dilan　　　　　　　Michael Kearns
　　Latoya Joyner　　　　　　Ron Kim
　　Francisco Moya　　　　　Brian P Kavanagh
　　Robert Rodriguez　　　　Linda B Rosenthal
　　Walter Mosley　　　　　Maritza Davila
　　Guillermo Linares　　　　Latrice Walker
　　Annette M Robinson　　　Luis Sepulveda

　Minority
　　Al Graf　　　　　　　　Andrew P Raia
　　Mark Johns　　　　　　Steve Katz
　　Raymond Walter　　　　Christopher Friend

Insurance
Chair:
　Kevin Cahill (D) 518-455-4436
Ranking Minority Member:
　William A Barclay (R) 518-455-5841

Committee Staff
Clerk:
　Vincent Rossetti 518-455-4436

　Key Assembly Staff Assignments
　Majority Assistant Secretary:
　　Jennifer Best 518-455-4311
　Majority Program Analyst:
　　Dallas Trombley

Offices and agencies generally appear in alphabetical order, except when specific order is requested by listee.

Minority Analyst/Counsel:
Douglas Goldman............................518-455-4637

Membership

Majority

Erik Dilan	Vivian E Cook
Steven H Cymbrowitz	Philip Goldfeder
Marcos Crespo	Charles D Lavine
Crystal D Peoples-Stokes	Latoya Joyner
James Gary Pretlow	Edward Braunstein
James Skoufis	Francisco Moya
Dan Quart	Jose Rivera
John McDonald III	Phil Steck
Andrew Hevesi	

Minority

Marc W Butler	Brian Curran
Stephen Hawley	Gary Finch
Raymond Walter	Ken Blankenbush

Judiciary

Chair:
Helene E. Weinstein (D)...........................518-455-5462
Ranking Minority Member:
Michael Montesano (R)...........................518-455-4684

Committee Staff

Clerk:
Sarah Beaver................................518-455-5462

Key Assembly Staff Assignments
Counsel:
Richard Ancowitz..............................518-455-4313
Team Counsel:
Clayton Rivet................................518-455-4313
Associate Counsel:
Amy Naggs..................................518-455-4313
Minority Analyst:
Nicholas Forst...............................518-455-4515

Membership

Majority

Edward Braunstein	Jeffrey Dinowitz
David Buchwald	Latoya Joyner
Charles D Lavine	Todd Kaminsky
Phil Steck	Matthew Titone
Dan Quart	Rebecca Seawright
Jo Anne Simon	David Weprin
Michele R Titus	Kenneth Zebrowski

Minority

William A Barclay	Al Graf
Chad Lupinacci	Andrew Goodell
Anthony Palumbo	

Labor

Chair:
Michele Titus (D)..............................518-455-5668
Ranking Minority Member:
Karl Brabenec (R)..............................518-455-5991

Committee Staff

Clerk:
Claude Nelson................................518-455-5668

Key Assembly Staff Assignments
Majority Assistant Secretary:
Jennifer Best................................518-455-4311
Minority Analyst/Counsel:
Douglas Goldman..............................518-455-4637

Membership

Majority

Peter J Abbate, Jr	Michael Benedetto
Barbara M Clark	William Colton
Michael DenDekker	Andrew Hevesi
Brian P Kavanagh	Shelley Mayer
Francisco Moya	Margaret M Markey
Nily Rozic	James Skoufis
Jo Anne Simon	Felix W Ortiz
Harry Bronson	Michael Miller
Samuel Roberts	Robert Rodriguez
N Nick Perry	Kenneth Zebrowski

Minority

John Ceretto	David DiPietro
Brian Curran	Michael Fitzpatrick
Angela M Wozniak	Joseph Saladino
Clifford W Crouch	

Libraries & Education Technology

Chair:
Thomas Abinanti (D)............................518-455-5753
Ranking Minority Member:
Joseph Saladino (R)............................518-455-5305

Committee Staff

Clerk:
Doug Rosenthal...............................518-455-5585

Key Assembly Staff Assignments
Majority Program Analyst:
Steve McCutcheon.............................518-455-3786
Minority Analyst/Counsel:
Kristin Frank................................518-455-4258

Membership

Majority

Barbara M Clark	Michaelle Solages
Steven Otis	Roxanne Persaud
Samuel Roberts	

Minority

Philip Palmesano

Local Governments

Chair:
William B Magnarelli (D).......................518-455-4826
Ranking Minority Member:
Christopher Friend (R).........................518-455-4583

Committee Staff

Committee Director:
Craig Swiecki................................518-455-4826

Key Assembly Staff Assignments
Majority Assistant Secretary:
Julia Mallalieu..............................518-455-4363
Majority Program Analyst:
Alice Baumgartner
Minority Analyst/Counsel:
Logan Smith.................................518-455-4626

Membership

Majority

Harry Bronson	Kimberly Jean-Pierre
David F Gantt	Steven Otis
Mark Gjonaj	David Buchwald
William Magee	James Skoufis
Carrie Woerner	Philip R Ramos
Addie J Russell	Michelle Schimel
Sean Ryan	Frank Skartados

Offices and agencies generally appear in alphabetical order, except when specific order is requested by listee.

Minority
Karl Brabenec	Tom McKevitt
Dan Stec	Angela M Wozniak

Mental Health
Chair:
Aileen Gunther (D) 518-455-5355
Ranking Minority Member:
Steve Katz (R) 518-455-5783

Committee Staff
Clerk:
Tom Gatto 518-455-5102

Key Assembly Staff Assignments
Majority Program Analyst:
Willie Sanchez 518-455-3786
Minority Analyst/Counsel:
Sarah Shearer 518-455-4285

Membership
Majority
Guillermo Linares	Michael J Cusick
Kimberly Jean-Pierre	Didi Barrett
John McDonald III	Philip Goldfeder
Ellen Jaffee	Robert Rodriguez

Minority
Jane L Corwin	Diana Richardson (WF)
Bill Nojay	

Oversight, Analysis & Investigation
Chair:
Ellen Jaffee (D) 518-455-5118
Ranking Minority Member:
Peter Lawrence (R) 518-455-4664

Membership
Majority
William B Magnarelli	Michael Kearns
Annette Robinson	Fred W. Thiele, Jr.

Minority
Michael Montesano

Racing & Wagering
Chair:
James Gary Pretlow (D) 518-455-5291
Ranking Minority Member:
Andrew Garbarino (R) 518-455-4611

Committee Staff
Clerk:
Kaitesi Munroe

Key Assembly Staff Assignments
Majority Assistant Secretary:
Jennifer Best 518-455-4311
Minority Analyst/Counsel:
Edmund V Wick 518-455-4262

Membership
Majority
Aileen Gunther	Margaret M Markey
Michaelle Solages	Philip Goldfeder
Angelo Santabarbara	Carrie Woerner
Michael Miller	

Minority
James Tedisco	Peter Lawrence

Real Property Taxation
Chair:
Sandra R Galef (D) 518-455-5348
Ranking Minority Member:
Kieran Michael Lalor (R) 518-455-5725

Committee Staff
Clerk:
Rebecca Southard-Kreiger 518-455-5348

Key Assembly Staff Assignments
Majority Program Analyst:
Lauren Denison .518-455-4363
Minority Analyst/Counsel:
Logan Smith 518-455-4265

Membership
Majority
James F Brennan	John McDonald III
Aileen M Gunther	Victor Pichardo
Mark Gjonaj	Roxanne Persaud
Annette M Robinson	

Minority
Philip Palmesano

Rules
Chair:
Carl Heastie (D) 518-455-3791
Ranking Minority Member:
Brian M Kolb (R) 518-455-3751

Membership
Majority
Jeffrion L Aubry	Vivian E Cook
Herman D Farrell, Jr	David F Gantt
Deborah J Glick	Richard N Gottfried
Earlene Hooper	Margaret Markey
Joseph R Lentol	William Colton
Joseph D Morelle	Catherine T Nolan
William Magnarelli	Jeffrey Dinowitz
Keith L T Wright	Felix W Ortiz
James Gary Pretlow	Barbara Clark
N Nick Perry	Steve Englebright
Helene E Weinstein	

Minority
Clifford W Crouch	William Barclay
Marc Butler	Janet Duprey
Gary Finch	Andrew Raia
James Tedisco	Robert C Oaks

Small Business
Chair:
Fred Thiele, Jr (D) 518-455-5997
Ranking Minority Member:
David DiPietro (R) 518-455-5314

Committee Staff
Clerk:
Lisa Lombardo 518-455-5997

Key Assembly Staff Assignments
Majority Associate Counsel:
Victoria Choi 518-455-4928

Membership
Majority
Charles Barron	Rodneyse Bichotte
Jose Rivera	Annette M Robinson
Victor Pichardo	Mark Gjonaj

Offices and agencies generally appear in alphabetical order, except when specific order is requested by listee.

Samuel Roberts
Michael Simanowitz
Angelo Santabarbara

Frank Skartados
Carrie Woerner

Minority

Peter Lawrence
Dean Murray

Diane Richardson (WF)
Kieran Michael Lalor

Social Services

Chair:
    Andrew Hevesi (D)..518-455-4926
Ranking Minority Member:
    Andrew Goodell (R)..518-455-4511

Committee Staff

Clerk:
    Rebecca Rasmussen...518-455-4926

Key Assembly Staff Assignments

Majority Assistant Secretary:
    Rebecca Mudie...518-455-4371
Majority Associate Counsel:
    Jennifer Sacco
Minority Analyst/Counsel:
    Lori Smith..518-455-4265

Membership

Majority

Maritza Davila
Jeffrion Aubry
Ron Kim
Victor Pichardo
Roxanne Persaud
Michaelle Solages

Shelley Mayer
Alec Brook-Krasny
Charles Barron
Rodneyse Bichotte
Latoya Joyner
Matthew Titone

Minority

Steven McLaughlin
Claudia Tenney

Anthony Palumbo
Dan Stec

Tourism, Parks, Arts & Sports Development

Chair:
    Margaret Markey (D).......................................518-455-4755
Ranking Minority Member:
    John Ceretto (R)..518-455-5284

Committee Staff

Clerk:
    Alyssa McCoy..518-455-5373

Key Assembly Staff Assignments

Majority Assistant Secretary:
    Aaron Suggs...518-455-4355
Majority Program Analyst:
    Yolanda Bostic..518-455-4928

Membership

Majority

Al Stirpe
Rebecca Seawright
Dan Quart
Frank Skartados
Daniel J O'Donnell
Carrie Woerner
Linda Rosenthal

Didi Barrett
Mark Gjonaj
Samuel Roberts
Patricia Fahy
Steven Otis
Matthew Titone

Minority

Ken Blankenbush
Dean Murray
Dan Stec

Chad Lupinacci
Philip Palmesano

Transportation

Chair:
    David F Gantt (D)...518-455-5606
Ranking Minority Member:
    David G McDonough (R).....................................518-455-4633

Committee Staff

Clerk:
    Kathryn F Curren..518-455-5606

Key Assembly Staff Assignments

Majority Principal Analyst:
    Julie Barney..518-455-4881
Majority Associate Counsel:
    Michael Hernandez...518-455-4881
Minority Analyst/Counsel:
    Jennifer Grasso...518-455-4264

Membership

Majority

Kimberly Jean-Pierre
Michael Cusick
Jo Anne Simon
Todd Kaminsky
Michelle Schimel
Marcos Crespo
Samuel Roberts
James Skoufis

Michael G DenDekker
Anthony Brindisi
Donna Lupardo
N Nick Perry
Harry Bronson
Frank Skartados
Fred W Thiele, Jr.
Phil Steck

Minority

Chad Lupinacci
Nicole Malliotakis
David DiPietro

Bill Nojay
Edward Ra
Dean Murray

Veterans' Affairs

Chair:
    Michael DenDekker (D).....................................518-455-4545
Ranking Minority Member:
    Stephen Hawley (R)..518-455-5811

Committee Staff

Clerk:
    Kenny Mendoza...518-455-4545

Key Assembly Staff Assignments

Majority Program Analyst:
    Joanne Martin...518-455-4355
Minority Analyst/Counsel:
    Logan Smith...518-455-4626

Membership

Majority

Michael J Cusick
Todd Kaminsky
Catherine T Nolan
Addie J Russell
Sean Ryan
Michelle Schimel

Michael Blake
Angelo Santabarbara
Didi Barrett
Michael Miller
Anthony Brindisi
James Skoufis

Minority

Brian Curran
David McDonough

Kieran Michael Lalor
Claudia Tenney

Ways & Means

Chair:
    Herman D Farrell, Jr (D)..................................518-455-5491
Ranking Minority Member:
    Bob Oaks (R)..518-455-5655

Offices and agencies generally appear in alphabetical order, except when specific order is requested by listee.

Committee Staff
Clerk:
   Debra Devine 518-455-3786

Key Assembly Staff Assignments
Director of Economic Studies:
   Audra Nowosielski 518-455-4006
Secretary:
   Blake G Washington 518-455-4054

Membership

Majority

Jeffrion L Aubry	Kevin A Cahill
William Colton	Vivian E Cook
Michael Benedetto	David F Gantt
Deborah J Glick	Earlene Hooper
Michael Cusick	Edward Braunstein
Felix Ortiz	Keith L T Wright
Phil Ramos	Joseph R Lentol
Robert Rodriguez	Francisco Moya
Catherine T Nolan	N Nick Perry
James Gary Pretlow	David Weprin
Robin L Schimminger	Margaret Markey
Fred W Thiele, Jr.	Helene E Weinstein

Minority

William A Barclay	Janet Duprey
Nicole Malliotakis	Clifford W Crouch
Raymond Walter	Jane Corwin
Michael Fitzpatrick	Stephen Hawley
Joseph Saladino	

ASSEMBLY TASK FORCES & CAUCUS

Food, Farm & Nutrition, Task Force on
Chair:
   Addie Russell (D) 518-455-5545
Program Manager:
   Robert Stern 518-455-5203

People with Disabilities Task Force
Chair:
   David Weprin (D) 518-455-5806

Puerto Rican/Hispanic Task Force
Chair:
   Marcos Crespo (D) 518-455-5514
Legislative Director:
   Guillermo Martinez 518-455-3608

Skills Development & Career Education, Legislative Commission on
Assembly Chair:
   Vacant 518-455-0000
Program Manager:
   Brenda Carter 518-455-4865/fax: 518-455-4175

State-Federal Relations, Legislative Task Force on
Assembly Chair:
   Matthew Titone (D) 518-455-4677
Program Manager:
   Robert Stern 518-455-3632

University-Industry Cooperation, Task Force on
Chair:
   Samuel Roberts (D) 518-455-5383
Coordinator:
   Maureen Schoolman 518-455-3632/fax: 518-455-4175

Women's Issues, Task Force on
Chair:
   Aravella Simotas (D) 518-455-5014
Coordinator:
   Christina Williams 518-455-3632/fax: 518-455-4574

JOINT LEGISLATIVE COMMISSIONS

Administrative Regulations Review, Legislative Commission on
Assembly Co-Chair:
   Kenneth Zebrowski (D) 518-455-5735
Senate Co-Chair:
   Terrence Murphy (R) 518-455-3111
Assembly Program Manager:
   Rich Murphy .518-455-5091/fax: 518-455-4175

Demographic Research & Reapportionment, Legislative Task Force on
Assembly Co-Chair:
   Philip Ramos (D) 518-455-5185
Senate Co-Chair:
   Michael F Nozzolio (D) 518-455-2366
Co-Executive Director:
   Karen Blatt 212-618-1100/fax: 212-618-1135
Co-Executive Director:
   Debra Levine 212-618-1100/fax: 212-618-1135

Ethics Committee, Legislative
Assembly Co-Chair:
   Charles D. Lavine (D) 518-455-4546
Senate Co-Chair:
   Andrew Lanza (R) 518-455-3215
Director/Counsel:
   Lisa P Reid 518-432-7837
   e-mail: lreid@nysenate.gov

Government Administration, Legislative Commission on
Assembly Chair:
   Brian Kavanagh (D) 518-455-5506
Senior Program Manager:
   Philip Johnson 518-455-3632/fax: 518-455-4574

Rural Resources, Legislative Commission on
Assembly Chair:
   Frank Skartados (D) 518-455-5762
Senate Chair:
   Catharine Young (R) 518-455-3563
Republican Counsel:
   Barbara McRedmond 518-455-2069

Science & Technology, Legislative Commission on
Assembly Chair:
   Francisco Moya (D) 518-455-4567
Senior Program Manager:
   Philip Johnson 518-455-5081/fax: 518-455-4859

Offices and agencies generally appear in alphabetical order, except when specific order is requested by listee.

JUDICIAL BRANCH

COURT OF APPEALS

The Court of Appeals is the highest court in New York State, hearing both civil and criminal appeals. This court consists of the Chief Judge and six Associate Judges. Judges are appointed by the Governor for fourteen-year terms or until age seventy, whichever comes first. The Court of Appeals receives direct appeal on matters where the only question relates to the constitutionality of a State or Federal statute. The Court also establishes policy for administration of the New York State Unified Court System.

Court of Appeals

20 Eagle Street
Albany, NY 12207-1095
518-455-7700
Web site: www.nycourts.gov/ctapps/

Clerk of the Court/Legal Counsel:
Andrew W Klein.....................................518-455-7700
e-mail: coa@courts.state.ny.us
Deputy:
John P Asiello.......................................518-455-7700
Public Information Officer:
Gary Spencer.......................................518-455-7711
e-mail: gspencer@courts.state.ny.us
Chief Judge:
Jonathan Lippman

Associate Judges

Jenny Rivera
Sheila Abdus-Salaam
Susan Phillips Read

Leslie E Stein
Eugene F Pigott
Eugene M Fahey

APPELLATE DIVISIONS

The Appellate Divisions of the Supreme Court exist for each of New York State's four Judicial Departments. Each Judicial Department is comprised of one or more of the State's twelve judicial districts and has Governor appointed Presiding and Associate Justices. The Presiding Justice serves the duration of his/her term as a Supreme Court Justice. Associate Justices serve for the shorter of a five-year term or the balance of their term. Supreme Court Justices are required to retire at age seventy, unless they become "Certificated" by the Administrative Board of the Courts. Justices may serve after age seventy under Certification for two-year terms, until age seventy-six. The Appellate Divisions review appeals from the Superior Court decisions in civil and criminal cases, and from Appellate Terms and County Courts in civil cases.

1st Department
Judicial Districts 1, 12
Courthouse
27 Madison Ave
New York, NY 10010
212-340-0400 Fax: 212-889-4412

Clerk of the Court:
Suzanna Molina Rojas 212-340-0422
Presiding Justice:
Luis A Gonzalez

Associate Justices
Rolando T Acosta
Barbara R Kapnick
Helen E Freedman
Angela M Mazzarelli
Dianne T Renwick

Richard T Andrias
Leland G DeGrasse
David Friedman
Karla Moskowitz
Rosalyn H Richter

David B Saxe
Peter Tom
Paul G. Feinman
Darcel D. Clark

John W Sweeny Jr
Sallie Manzanet-Daniels
Judith J. Gische

2nd Department
Judicial Districts 2, 9, 10, 11, 13
45 Monroe Pl
Brooklyn, NY 11201
718-875-1300

Deputy Clerk:
Aprilanne Agostino ....718-722-6324 or 718-722-6307
fax: 212-419-8457
e-mail: ad2clerk@courts.state.ny.us
Justice:
Randall T. Eng

Associate Justices
Colleen Duffy
Hector D LaSalle
Cheryl E Chambers
Mark C Dillon
John M Leventhal
Sheri S Roman
L. Priscilla Hall
Leonard B. Austin
Plummer E. Lott
William F. Mastro

Ruth C Balkin
Joseph J Maltese
Thomas A Dickerson
Robert J Miller
Reinaldo E Rivera
Peter B Skelos
Sylvia C. Hinds-Radix
Jeffrey A. Cohen
Sandra L. Sgroi

3rd Department
Judicial Districts 3, 4, 6
Capitol Station
PO Box 7288
Albany, NY 12224-0288
518-471-4777

Clerk of the Court:
Robert D Mayberger 518-471-4777/fax: 518-471-4750
e-mail: ad3clerksoffice@nycourts.gov
Presiding Justice:
Karen K Peters

Associate Justices
John A Lahtinen
Robert S Rose
John C Egan Jr.

William E McCarthy
Leslie E Stein
Elizabeth A. Garry

4th Department
Judicial Districts 5, 7, 8
50 East Ave
Rochester, NY 14604-2214
585-530-3100 Fax: 585-530-3247

Clerk of the Court:
Frances E Cafarell................................585-530-3100
Presiding Justice:
Henry J Scudder

Associate Justices
Edward D. Carni
Salvatore R Martoche
John V Centra
Stephen K. Lindley
Rose H. Sconiers

Eugene M Fahey
Nancy E Smith
Erin M Peradotto
Gerald J Whalen
Joseph D. Valentino

Offices and agencies generally appear in alphabetical order, except when specific order is requested by listee.

SUPREME COURT

The Supreme Court consists of twelve Judicial Districts, which are comprised of County Courts within NYS (See County Court information in related section). Justices are elected by their Judicial Districts for fourteen-year terms, unless they reach age seventy before term expiration. Justices may serve beyond age seventy if Certificated (see Apellate Divisions for definition). The Supreme Court generally hears cases outside the jurisdiction of other courts, such as: civil matters with monetary limits exceeding that of the lower courts; divorce, separation and annulment proceedings; equity suits; and criminal prosecutions of felonies.

1st Judicial District
New York County
Administrative Judge, Civil:
    Sherry Klein Heitler
Administrative Judge, Criminal:
    Michael Obus
Chief Clerk, Civil Branch:
    Norman Goodman...............................646-386-5955
Chief Clerk, Criminal Branch:
    Barry Clarke, Esquire 646-386-3900/fax: 212-374-3177
    e-mail: amurphy@courts.state.ny.us

Judges
Kathryn E. Freed	Margaret Chan
Ellen M. Coin	Carol R Edmead
Nancy M. Bannon	Lucy Billings
Arlene Bluth	Sherry Klein Heitler
Eileen Bransten	Richard Brown
Matthew Cooper	Tandra Dawson
Laura E. Drager	Arthur F. Engoron
Fern Fisher	Marcy S. Friedman
Ira Gammerman	Phyllis Gangel-Jacob
Ellen Gesmer	Shlomo S. Hagler
Douglas E. Hoffman	Carol E. Huff
Alexander Hunter	Barbara Jaffe
Deborah Kaplan	Debra A. James
Barbara R. Kapnick	Tanya Kennedy
Cynthia Kern	Shirley Kornreich
Jeffrey K. Oing	Martin Shulman
Raymond Guzman (Cert)	Joan Kenny
Kelly O'Neill Levy	Doris Ling-Cohan
Joan B. Lobis	Joan A. Madden
Lawrence Marks	Milton A. Tingling
Michael Stallman	George Silver
Peter Moulton	Manuel Mendez
Paul Wooten	Geoffrey D.S. Wright
Rena Uviller (Cert)	Ronald A. Zweibel (Cert)
Lois B. York	

2nd Judicial District
Kings County
Administrative Judge, Criminal:
    Barry Kamin
Administrative Judge, Civil:
    Lawrence Knipel
Chief Clerk, Criminal Division:
    Daniel M. Alessandrino
Chief Clerk, Civil Division:
    Charles A. Small, Esq.

Judges
Rachel A. Adams	Sylvia Ash
Jack Battaglia	Gloria Dabiri
Noach Dear	Carolyn DeMarest
Laura Lee Jacobson	Joseph J. Maltese
Larry Martin	Ann Pfau
Karen B. Rosenberg	Karen Rothenberg
David Schmidt	Kenneth Sherman

Debra Silber	Ellen Spodek
Jeffrey Sunshine	Peter Sweeney
Delores Thomas	Carl J. Landicino
Mark I Partnow	Michelle Weston
Michael L Pesce	Eric I Prus
Francois A Rivera	Leon Ruchelsman
Wayne P Saitta	Arthur M Schack
Martin M Solomon	James P Sullivan
David B Vaughan	

3rd Judicial District
Albany, Columbia, Greene, Rensselaer, Schoharie, Sullivan & Ulster Counties
Administrative Judge:
    Thomas A. Breslin
District Executive:
    Carol Schongar 518-285-8300/fax: 518-285-6169
    e-mail: 3rdjdadministration@nycourts.gov

Judges
Christopher E Cahill	George B Ceresia Jr
Eugene Devine	Raymond Elliott
Michael C Lynch	Richard J McNally Jr
Patrick J McGrath	Stephan G. Schick
Joseph C Teresi	James Gilpatric
Richard Mott	

4th Judicial District
Counties: Clint, Essex, Frankln, Fultn, Hamiltn, Montg, St Lawr, Saratga, Schenectady, Warren & Wash
Administrative Judge:
    Vito C Caruso
District Executive:
    Joanne B. Haelen, Esq. 518-285-5099/fax: 518-587-3179

Judges
Richard T Aulisi	Stan Pritzker
David R Demarest	John Ellis
Stephen A Ferradino	Joseph Sise
Robert J Muller	Thomas D Nolan, Jr.
Vincent J Reilly, Jr.	Robert J. Chauvin
Ann C. Crowell	Christine M. Clark
Thomas Buchanan	Barry D. Kramer
David B. Krogmann	

5th Judicial District
Herkimer, Jefferson, Lewis, Oneida, Onondaga & Oswego Counties
Administrative Judge:
    James C Tormey III
District Executive:
    Michael A Klein 315-671-2111/fax: 315-671-1175
    e-mail: 5thjdadministration@nycourts.gov

Judges
Bernadette T. Clark	Brian F DeJoseph
Hugh A Gilbert	Donald A Greenwood
Deborah H Karalunas	Samuel D Hester
Patrick F MacRae	Kevin G Young
James P Murphy	David A. Murad
Anthony J Paris	Norman W Seiter Jr
James McCarthy	James P. McClusky
Charles C. Merrell	Norman I. Siegel
Erin P. Gall	

6th Judicial District
Broome, Chemung, Chenango, Cortland, Delaware, Madison, Otsego, Schuyler, Tioga & Tompkins Counties
Administrative Judge:
    Robert C. Mulvey

Offices and agencies generally appear in alphabetical order, except when specific order is requested by listee.

District Executive:
 Karen A Ambrozik 607-240-5350/fax: 212-295-4927

Judges

Kevin M Dowd	Ferris D Lebous
Donald F. Cerio, Jr.	Eugene D. Faughnan
Judith F O'Shea	Phillip R Rumsey
Jeffrey A Tait	Molly Fitzgerald
Michael V. Coccoma	

7th Judicial District
Cayuga, Livingston, Monroe, Ontario, Seneca, Steuben, Wayne & Yates Counties

Administrative Judge:
 Craig J. Doran
District Executive:
 Ronald Pawelczak. 585-371-3266

Judges

Francis A Affronti	John J. Ark
Kenneth R Fisher	Evelyn Frazee
John Owens	William P Polito
Matthew A Rosenbaum	Thomas A Stander
Ann Marie Taddeo	Elma A. Bellini
Daniel Doyle	Thomas Moran
J. Scott Odorisi	Alex R. Renzi
Richard Dollinger	Joanne Winslow

8th Judicial District
Allegany, Cattaraugus, Chautauqua, Erie, Genesee, Niagara, Orleans & Wyoming Counties

Administrative Judge:
 Paula L. Feroleto
District Executive:
 Andrew B Isenberg 716-845-2505/fax: 716-845-7500

Judges

Tracey A Bannister	M William Boller
Ralph A Boniello, III	Christopher J Burns
Russell Buscaglia	Frank Caruso
John M Curran	Diane Y Devlin
James Dillon	Kevin M Dillon
Timothy Drury	Jeremy J. Moriarty, III
Joseph R Glownia	Deborah A Haendiges
Richard C Kloch Sr	Frederick J Marshall
John A Michalek	Patrick H NeMoyer
John F O'Donnell	Deborah A. Chimes
Sharon S. Townsend	Mark A. Montour
John L. Michalski	Donna M Siwek
Timothy Walker	Henry Nowak
Penny Wolfgang	Catherine Nugent-Panepinto
Shirley Troutman	

9th Judicial District
Dutchess, Orange, Putnam, Rockland & Westchester Counties

Administrative Judge:
 Alan B Sheinkman
District Executive:
 Nancy M. Mangold 914-824-5100/fax: 914-995-4946
 e-mail: 9thjdadministration@nycourts.gov
Chief Clerk:
 Michael Thompson 845-431-1710/fax: 845-431-1743

Judges

Lester B Adler	Catherine M. Bartlett
Victor J. Alfieri	Orazio Bellantoni
James V Brands	Linda Christopher
Robert H Freehill	Margaret Garvey
William J Giacomo	Linda S Jamieson
William A Kelly	Robert M. Berliner

John Colangelo	Robert M. Dibella
Victor Grossman	Joan B Lefkowitz
Lewis Lubell	Francesca Connolly
Lawrence H. Ecker	Gerald Loehr
Paul I. Marx	J Emmett Murphy
James D. Pagones	Francis A. Nicolai
Robert A. Onofry	Maria G. Rosa
Sandra Sciortino	Elaine Slobod
Mary H Smith	Christine A Sproat
Bruce E Tolbert	Maria S. Vazquez-Doles
Sam Walker	Charles D. Wood

10th Judicial District
Nassau & Suffolk Counties

Administrative Judge, Nassau:
 Thomas A. Adams
Administrative Judge, Suffolk:
 C. Randall Hinrichs
Chief Clerk, Nassau:
 Kathryn Driscoll Hopkins, Esq. 516-493-3400
Chief Clerk, Suffolk:
 Michael Scardino 631-852-2334

Judges

W. Gerard Asher	Richard Ambro
Paul J Baisley, Jr	Stacy D. Bennett
Jeffrey S. Brown	John C Bivona
Robert A. Bruno	Stephen A Bucaria
John B. Collins	William J. Condon
Andrew A. Crecca	Robert B Cozzens, Jr.
Vito M. DeStefano	Timothy S. Driscoll
Arthur M Diamond	Antonio Brandveen
Martin I. Efman	Elizabeth H Emerson
Jerry Garguilo	Thomas Feinman
John Michael Galasso	Angela G Iannacci
Jeffrey A. Goodstein	Randy S. Marber
Steven M. Jaeger	William J Kent
Norman Janowitz	Gary F. Knobel
H. Patrick Leis III	Roy S Mahon
Anthony Marano	Hector D. LaSalle
John J. Leo	Edward A. Maron
Carol MacKenzie	Karen Murphy
Peter H. Mayer	James McCormack
Anthony L Parga	Thomas P Phelan
Emily Pines	Arthur G Pitts
William B Rebolini	Jerome Murphy
Daniel Palmieri	Sondra K. Pardes
Sandra L Sgroi	Joseph C. Pastoressa
David Reilly	Margaret C. Reilly
A. Gail Prudenti	Denise Sher
Joseph A. Santorelli	Leonard Steinman
Thomas F Whelan	Hope Zimmerman
F Dana Winslow	Michele M Woodard

11th Judicial District
Queens County

Administrative Judge, Civil:
 Jeremy S. Weinstein
Administrative Judge, Criminal:
 Joseph Zayas
Chief Clerk, Civil:
 Tracy Catapano-Fox 718-298-1000
Chief Clerk, Criminal:
 Maureen D'Aquila 718-298-1408

Judges

Augustus C Agate	Michael B Aloise
Pam Jackman Brown	Valerie Brathwaite Nelson
Denis J. Butler	Richard Lance Buchter
Arthur J Cooperman (Cert)	Anna Culley
Timothy Duffiey	Darrell L. Gavin

Offices and agencies generally appear in alphabetical order, except when specific order is requested by listee.

David Elliot
William M Erlbaum
Phyllis Orlikoff Flug
Stephen Knopf
Howard G Lane
Ronald D Hollie
Lee A. Mayersohn
Robert C Kohm
Robert Nahman
Daniel Lewis
Leslie J. Purificacion
Steven W. Paynter
Jaime Antonio Rios
Martin E Ritholtz
Frederick D R Sampson
Sidney F Strauss
Jeremy S Weinstein

Rudolph Greco
Kevin Kerrigan
James J Golia
Marguerite A Grays
Duane A Hart
Jeffrey D. Lebowitz
Orin R Kitzes
Gregory L Lasak
Diccia Pineda-Kirwan
Robert J McDonald
Peter O'Donoghue
Thomas Raffaele
Bernice D. Siegal
Roger N Rosengarten
Martin J Schulman
Janice A Taylor
Allan B Weiss

12th Judicial District
Bronx County
Chief Administrative Judge, Civil:
  Douglas E. McKeon
Administrative Judge, Criminal:
  Douglas McKeon
Chief Clerk, Criminal Division:
  Steven B Clark...................718-618-3000/fax: 718-618-3585
Chief Clerk, Civil Division:
  Tracy Pardo.....................................718-618-1400

Judges
John A Barone
Wilma Guzman
Dominic R. Massaro (Cert)
Larry Schachner
Yvonne Gonzalez
Howard H. Sherman
La Tia W Martin
Richard L Price (Cert)
Robert A Sackett (Cert)
Kenneth Thompson, Jr
Alison Y Tuitt

Sharon Aarons
Mary Briganti-Hughes
Laura G Douglas
Mark Friedlander
Alexander W Hunter
George Villegas
Douglas E McKeon
Norma Ruiz
Barry Salman
Robert E Torres

13th Judicial District
Richmond County
Administrative Judge:
  Judith N. McMahon
Chief Clerk:
  Joseph Como......................................718-675-8700

Judges
Thomas P. Aliotta
Catherine M. DiDomenico
Joseph J. Maltese
Barbara I. Panepinto
Stephen J. Rooney

Robert J. Collini
John A. Fusco
Philip G. Minardo
Leonard P. Rienzi
Charles Troia

COURT OF CLAIMS

The Court of Claims is a special trial court that hears and determines only claims against the State of New York. Court of Claims judges are appointed by the Governor for nine-year terms. Certain judges of this court, as designated herein by an *, also serve as acting Supreme Court Justices for the assigned judicial district.

Court of Claims
Robert Abrams Justice Bldg
Capitol Station
PO Box 7344
Albany, NY 12224

518-432-3441 Fax: 518-432-3483
Clerk of the Court:
  Robert T DeCataldo.................518-432-3411/fax: 518-432-3483
  e-mail: rdecatal@nycourts.gov
Presiding Judge:
  Richard E Sise.....................518-432-3435/fax: 518-432-3428

Judges
W. Brooks De Bow
John J Brunetti*
Russell P Buscaglia
Thomas J Carroll
Robert J Collini*
James H. Ferreira
Vincent M Del Guidice*
Stephen J. Lynch
Judith A Hard
Michael E Hudson
Richard C Kloch
Christopher McCarthy
Martin Marcus*
Daniel Martin*
Thomas J McNamara*
Stephen J Mignano
Richard Molea*
Michael F Mullen*
Richard Platkin
Stephen J Rooney*
Terry J Ruderman
Thomas H Scuccimarra
Richard E Sise
Gina Lopez-Summa
David A. Weinstein

Antonio I Brandveen*
Glen T. Bruening
Gregory Carro*
Margaret L Clancy*
Francis T Collins
Matthew J D'Emic*
Diane L Fitzpatrick
Philip M Grella*
Alan L Honorof*
John G Ingram*
Albert Lorenzo*
Guy J Mangano, Jr*
Alan C Marin
Frank P. Milano
Nicholas V Midey Jr
Renee Forgensi Minarik
Jeremiah J Moriarity III
Juanita B Newton
Philip J Patti
Catherine C. Schaewe
Melvin Schweitzer
Norman I Siegel*
Faviola Soto
O. Peter Sherwood
Maxwell T Wiley*

NEW YORK CITY COURTS

New York City has its own Civil, Criminal and Family courts, separate from the County Court system. The NYC Civil Court hears civil cases involving amounts up to $25,000, and its judges are elected for ten-year terms. The NYC Criminal Court conducts trials of misdemeanors and violations. Criminal Court judges act as magistrates for all criminal offenses and are appointed by the City's Mayor for ten-year terms. The NYC Family Court hears matters involving children and families, such as: child protection, delinquency, domestic violence, guardianship, parental rights and spousal and child support. Family Court judges are appointed by the City's Mayor for ten-year terms. Certain judges of the Civil Court, as designated herein by an *, are also assigned to serve in other courts.

Civil Court, NYC
Deputy Chief Administrative Judge:
  Fern A Fisher
Chief Clerk:
  Carol Alt.................646-386-5409/fax: 212-374-5709

Bronx County
851 Grand Concourse, Bronx, NY 10451
Clerk of the County:
  Eddy Valdez.....................................718-618-2500

Kings County
141 Livingston St, Brooklyn, NY 11201
Clerk of the County:
  Lydia Grima....................................347-404-9133

New York County
111 Centre St, New York, NY 10013
Clerk of the County:
  Serena Spingle.................................646-386-5730

Offices and agencies generally appear in alphabetical order, except when specific order is requested by listee.

Queens County
89-17 Sutphin Blvd, Jamaica, NY 11435
Clerk of the County:
Maurien Giddens

Richmond County
927 Castleton Ave, Staten Island, NY 10310
Clerk of the County:
Deborah Torforice 718-675-8458

Judges

Rachel Amy Adams*
Frederick Arriaga*
Ben R. Barbato
Loren Baily-Schiffman*
Arthur Birnbaum
Reginald A. Boddie
Joseph Capella*
Joseph Capella
David P. Cohen
Noach Dear
Mary K. Dollard
Raymond L. Bruce*
Raul Cruz
Dena E. Douglas*
Timothy J. Dufficy
Genine D. Edwards
Saralee Evans*
Paul G. Feinman*
Fern A. Fisher
Marcy S. Friedman*
Michael Gerstein*
Doris Gonzalez*
Stephen S. Gottlieb
Rudolph E. Greco
Stanley Green*
Maureen Healy
Dawn M. Jimenez-Salta
Barbara Jaffe*
Ingrid Joseph*
Deborah A. Kaplan*
Robert Kalish*
Kathy J. King*
Sarah L. Krauss*
Richard Latin
Katherine A. Levine
Diana A. Lebedeff*
Andrea Masley
Ira H. Margulis*
Orlando Marrazzo, Jr.
Donald A. Miles
Peter K. Moulton
Kelly O'Neill*
Lisa S. Ottley
Jodi Orlow
Barbara I. Panepinto*
Mary O'Donoghue*
Linda Poust-Lopez*
Robert R. Reed
Julia I. Rodriguez*
Laura Safer-Espinoza*
Saliann Scarpulla*
Barry Schwartz
Jennifer Schecter*
Debra Silber*
Shawndaya L. Simpson*
Karen Smith*
Michael D. Stallman*
Peter Paul Sweeney*
Elizabeth Taylor
Analisa Torres*

Harold Adler*
Francis M Alessandro
Nancy Bannon
Johnny Lee Baynes
Arlene P Bluth
Cheree A. Buggs
Margaret A. Chan
Devin P. Cohen
Mitchell Danziger
Laura G. Douglas*
Dorothy K. Chin Brandt*
Matthew F. Cooper*
Marilyn G. Diamond*
James E. D'Auguste*
Arthur F. Engoron
Joseph J. Esposito*
Carol Feinman*
Pamela Fisher
Kathryn E. Freed
Robin S. Garson
Ellen Frances Gesmer*
Lizbeth Gonzalez
Bernard J. Graham*
Desmond A. Green*
Liana Gruebel*
Shlomo S. Haggler*
Pam Jackman-Brown*
Debra A. James*
Tanya Kennedy
Joan M. Kenney*
Michael Katz*
Lynn R. Kotier*
Dennis Lebwhol*
Evelyn J. LaPorte*
Gerald Lebovitz*
Charles Lopresto
Nelinda Malave-Gonzalez
Shari Michels*
Rita Mella*
Manuel J. Mendez*
Frank Nervo*
Ann E. O'Shea*
Terrence O'Connor
Jose A. Padilla
Kibbie F. Payne*
Geraldine Pickett*
Leslie J. Purificacion
Eileen A. Rakower*
Leticia Ramirez*
Debrarose Samuels
Larry S. Schachner*
Robin K. Sheares
Kenneth Sherman
George J. Silver*
Anil C. Singh*
Charles Solomon*
Philip S. Straniere
Fernando Tapiat*
Harriet Thompson
Wavny Toussaint*

Carmen R. Velasquez
William A. Viscovich
Jacqueline Williams
John H. Wilson*

Carolyn E. Wade
Edgar G. Walker
Betty J. Williams*

Housing Court Judges

Paul L. Alpert
Gilbert Badillo
Hannah Cohen
Timmie E. Elsner
Marc Finkelstein
Cheryl Gonzalez
Sheldon J. Halprin
David J. Kaplan
Jerald R. Kline
Joel Kullas
John S. Lansden
Andrew Lehrer
Jaya Madhavan
Rubin Martino
Kevin McClanahan
Kimberly Moser
Eleanora Ofshtein
Eardell J. Rashford
Jose Rogriguez
Phyllis Saxe
Jean T. Schneider
Marcia Sikowitz
John Stanley
Louis J. Villella
Steven A. Weissman
Elizabeth J. Yalin Tao

Susan Avery
Ronni D Birnbaum
Marian C. Doherty
Anthony J. Fiorella
Thomas M. Fitzpatrick
Arlene H. Hahn
Inez Hoyos
Anne Katz
Sabrina B. Kraus
Lydia C. Lai
Laurie L. Lau
Ulysses B. Leveret
Laurie Marin
Gary Marton
Maria Milin
Marina Mundy
Michael J. Pinckney
Maria Ressos
Verna Saunders
Bruce E. Scheckowitz
Michelle D. Schreiber
Brenda S. Spears
Jack Stoller
Deighton S. Waithe
Peter Wendt

Criminal Court, NYC
Administrative Judge:
Barry Kamins
Chief Clerk:
Justin Barry 646-386-4600/fax: 212-374-4835

Bronx County
215 E 161st St., Bronx, NY 10451
Chief Clerk:
William Kalish 718-618-2460/fax: 718-537-5164

Kings County
120 Schermerhorn St, Brooklyn, NY 11201
Borough Chief Clerk:
Antonio Diaz 347-404-9400/fax: 718-643-5234

New York County
100 Centre St, New York, NY 10013
Borough Chief Clerk:
Donald Vasti 646-386-4511/fax: 212-374-5293

Queens County
125-01 Queens Blvd, Kew Gardens, NY 11415
Borough Chief Clerk:
Carey Wone 718-298-0792/fax: 718-520-4712

Richmond County
67 Targee St, Staten Island, NY 10304
Borough Chief Clerk:
Ada Molina 718-675-8558/fax: 718-390-8405

Judges

Bruce Allen
A. Kirke Bartley
Peter J. Benitez
Joel L. Blumenfeld
James M. Burke
Gregory Carro
John Cataldo

Efrain L. Alvarado
Lewis Bartstone
Miriam Best
Denis J. Boylet
Alexander Calabrese
Richard D. Carruthers
Danny K. Chun

Offices and agencies generally appear in alphabetical order, except when specific order is requested by listee.

Judicial Branch

Ellen M. Coin
Daniel Conviser
Joseph J. Dawson
Laura E. Drager
Thomas A. Farber
Anthony J. Ferrara
Daniel P. Fitzgerald
Lenora Gerald
Joel M. Goldberg
James P. Griffin
Josephe Gubbay
Roger S. Hayes
Douglas E. Hoffman
Melissa C. Jackson
Diane R. Kiesel
Barry Kron
Judith S. Lieb
Juan Marchan
Alan D. Marrus
Daniel McCullough
Edward McLaughlin
Suzanne J. Melendez
Salvatore J. Modica
Suzanne M. Mondo
Cassandra Mullen
Barbara F. Newman
Mary O'Donoghue
Eugene Oliver
Ann Pfau
Leonard P. Rienzi
Jennifer Schecter
Charles H. Solomon
Larry R. Stephen
Megan Tallmer
Renak Uviller
Richard M. Weinberg
Maxwell Wiley
Bonnie G. Wittner
Alvin M. Yearwood
Ronald Zweibel

John P. Collins
Myriam Cyrulnik
Tandra Dawson
Ralph A. Fabrizio
Joann Ferdinand
Neil Jon Firetog
William E. Garnett
Arlene D. Goldberg
Ethan Greenberg
Michael A. Gross
William S. Harrington
Patricia E. Henry
Nicholas Iacovetta
Marcy L. Kahn
Jill Konviser
John B. Latella
Gene R. Lopez
Lawrence Marks
Seth L. Marvin
William L. McGuire, Jr.
Alan J. Meyer
William Miller
William I. Mogulescu
John S. Moore
Pauline Mullings
Patricia M. Nunez
Michael J. Obus
Eduardo Padro
Ruth Pickholz
Neil E. Ross
Matthew Sciarrino, Jr.
Michael R. Sonberg
Robert M. Stolz
Analisa Torres
Laura A. Ward
Renee A. White
Patricia Anne Williams
Douglas S. Wong
Joseph A. Zayas

Family Court, NYC

Administrative Judge:
    Edwina G. Richardson-Mendelson
Chief Clerk:
    George Cafasso . . . . 646-386-5170 or 212-374-3700
    fax: 212-374-3257

Bronx County
900 Sheridan Ave, Bronx, NY 10451
e-mail: bronxfamilycourt@nycourts.gov
Clerk of Court:
    Michael J. Williams 718-618-2098/fax: 718-590-7875

Kings County
330 Jay St, Brooklyn, NY 11201
e-mail: kingsfamilycourt@nycourts.gov
Clerk of Court:
    Robert Ratanski 347-401-9600/fax: 347-401-9609

New York County
60 Lafayette St, New York, NY 10013
e-mail: manhattanfamilycourt@nycourts.gov
Clerk of Court:
    Evelyn Hasanoeddin 646-386-5200/fax: 212-748-5272

Queens County
151-20 Jamaica Ave, Jamaica, NY 11432
e-mail: queensfamilycourt@nycourts.gov
Clerk of Court:
    Vaunda L. Harris-Shrachan 718-298-0197/fax: 718-297-2826

Richmond County
100 Richmond Terrace, Staten Island, NY 10301
e-mail: richmondfamilycourt@nycourts.gov
Clerk of Court:
    William J Quirk 718-675-8800/fax: 718-390-5247

Judges
Michael A Ambrosio
Stephen J Bogacz
Guy P. DePhillips
Sidney Gribetz
John M. Hunt
Arnold Lim
Ruben A. Martino
Emily M. Olshansky
Jeanette Reitz
Edwina G. Richardson-Mendelson
Gayle P. Roberts
Barbara Salinitro
Carol Ann Stokinger
Stewart H. Weinstein

Mary E Bednar
Tandra L. Dawson
Monica Drinane (Supervising)
Douglas Hoffman
Susan R. Larabee
Fran L. Lubow
Martin P. Murphy
Jane Pearl
Clark V. Richardson
Marybeth S. Richroath
Helene Sacco
Gloria Sosa-Lintner
Daniel Turbow

COUNTY COURTS

NYS has three types of courts designated at a county level: County Court, Family Court and Surrogate's Court. The County Court is authorized to handle criminal prosecutions of offenses committed within the county and hears civil cases involving amounts up to $25,000. County Court judges are elected for ten-year terms. The Family Court hears matters involving children and families (for types of court matters see NYC Courts). Family Court judges are elected for ten-year terms. The Surrogate's Court hears cases involving the affairs of decedents, including the probate of wills, and administration of estates and adoptions. Surrogates are elected for ten-year terms. This section also includes Supreme Court clerks and their addresses. Additional information and a list of judges for the NYS Supreme Court is provided in the related Section.

Albany County

Judges
County:
    Peter Lynch
Surrogate:
    Stacy Pettit
Family:
    Susan Kushner
County:
    Stephen W Herrick
Family:
    Richard Rivera
Family:
    Gerard E Maney
Family:
    Margaret T Walsh

County Court
Albany County Judicial Center, 6 Lodge Street, Albany, NY 12207
Chief Clerk:
    Charles E Diamond 518-285-8777/fax: 518-436-3986

Family
30 Clinton Ave, Albany, NY 12207
Chief Clerk:
    Cynthia Robinson 518-285-8600/fax: 518-462-4248
Deputy Chief Clerk-Surrogate:
    Deborah Kearns 518-285-8585/fax: 518-462-0194

Supreme Court & Surrogate
Courthouse, Room 102, 16 Eagle St, Albany, NY 12207

Offices and agencies generally appear in alphabetical order, except when specific order is requested by listee.

Chief Clerk-Supreme/County:
Charles E Diamond 518-285-8989/fax: 518-487-5020

Allegany County

Judges
Multi-Bench:
Thomas Paul Brown
Multi-Bench:
Terrence M. Parker

Supreme, County, Family & Surrogate's Courts
7 Court St, Belmont, NY 14813-1084
Chief Clerk-County/Supreme:
Laura Gabler 585-268-5941
e-mail: lgabler@nycourts.gov
Chief Clerk-Family:
April Din 585-268-5859
e-mail: adin@nycourts.gov
Chief Clerk-Surrogate's:
Dorine Jacobs 585-268-5815
e-mail: dgjacobs@nycourts.gov

Bronx County

Judges
Surrogate:
Nelinda Malave-Gonzalez

COUNTY & FAMILY COURTS: See New York City Courts

Supreme & Surrogate's Courts
851 Grand Concourse, Bronx, NY 10451
Clerk-Civil Division:
Eddy Valdez 718-618-2500
Chief Clerk-Surrogate:
Michael P. Hausler 718-618-2300

Broome County

Judges
Family:
Richard H Miller II
Family (Supervising):
Rita Connerton
County:
Joseph Cawley
Surrogate:
David H. Guy
Family:
Spero Pines
County:
Martin E Smith

County, Family
65 Hawley St, Binghamton, NY 13902
Chief Clerk-Family:
Debbi D Singer 607-240-5799/fax: 607-240-5904
Chief Clerk-County/Supreme:
Karen K. Stephens 607-240-5800/fax: 607-240-5940

Surrogate & Supreme Court
92 Court St, Binghamton, NY 13901
607-840-5789
Chief Clerk-Surrogate:
Rebecca A Malmquist 607-778-2111/fax: 607-778-2308

Cattaraugus County

Judges
Multi-Bench:
Ronald D Plaetz

Multi-Bench:
Michael L Nenno

Supreme & Family Court
One Leo Moss Dr, Olean, NY 14760
Chief Clerk-Family:
Denise Filjones 716-373-8035/fax: 716-373-0449
e-mail: dfiljone@nycourts.gov

Supreme, County & Surrogate's Courts
Courthouse, 303 Court St, Little Valley, NY 14755
Chief Clerk-Surrogate:
Christine Wrona 716-938-2327
e-mail: cwrona@nycourts.gov
Chief Clerk-Supreme:
Verna Dry 716-938-2388/fax: 716-938-6413
e-mail: vdry@nycourts.gov

Cayuga County

Judges
Multi-Bench (Acting):
Mark H Fandrich
County/Family:
Thomas G Leone

Family Court
152 Genesee St, Auburn, NY 13021
e-mail: cayugafamilycourt@courts.state.ny.us
Chief Clerk:
L.D. Serafino . . . . 315-237-6450 or 315-237-6400
fax: 315-237-6451

Chautauqua County

Judges
Surrogate:
Stephen W Cass
Family:
Jeffrey Piazza
Family:
Judith S Claire
County:
John T Ward

Family Court
2 Academy Street, Ste 5, Mayville, NY 14757
Chief Clerk-Family:
Frank Baggiano 716-753-4351/fax: 716-753-4350
e-mail: fbaggian@nycourts.gov

Supreme & County Courts
County Courthouse, 3 North Erie Street, PO Box 292, Mayville, NY
14757-0292
Chief Clerk:
Kathleen Krauza 716-753-4266/fax: 716-753-4993
e-mail: kkrauza@nycourts.gov

Surrogate Court
Gerace Bldg, Courthouse, PO Box C, Mayville, NY 14757
Chief Clerk:
Curt N Meeder 716-753-4339/fax: 716-753-4600

Chemung County

Judges
Family:
Mary M Tarantelli
County:
Richard W Rich
County/Surrogate:
James T Hayden

Offices and agencies generally appear in alphabetical order, except when specific order is requested by listee.

Family Court
203-209 William St, PO Box 588, Elmira, NY 14902-0558
Chief Clerk:
Rebecca Walp 607-873-9500/fax: 212-884-8950

Supreme & County Courts
Courthouse, 224 Lake St, PO Box 588, Elmira, NY 14902-0588
Chief Clerk-County/Supreme:
Nancy Kreisler 607-737-2084/fax: 646-963-6605

Surrogate Court
224 Lake St, PO Box 588, Elmira, NY 14902-0588
e-mail: 6jdchmsurr@courts.state.ny.us
Chief Clerk-Surrogate:
Laurie Hubbard 607-837-9440/fax: 646-963-6606

Chenango County

Judges
Multi-Bench:
Frank B. Revoir

Supreme, County, Family & Surrogate's Courts
5 Court St, Norwich, NY 13815
Chief Clerk-Surrogate:
Linda Wiley 607-337-1827/fax: 607-337-1834
Chief Clerk-Family:
Carole S Dunham 607-337-1824/fax: 607-337-1835
Chief Clerk-County/Supreme:
Catherine A Schell . . . . 607-337-1457 or 607-337-1825
fax: 917-522-3447
e-mail: cschell@courts.state.ny.us

Clinton County

Judges
Family:
Timothy J Lawliss
County:
Patrick R McGill
Surrogate:
Kevin K. Ryan

Supreme, County, Family & Surrogate's Courts
137 Margaret St, Plattsburgh, NY 12901
Chief Clerk-Family:
Cathy Williams 518-565-4658/fax: 518-285-4545
Chief Clerk-County/Supreme:
Jan M Lavigne 518-565-4715/fax: 518-285-8504
Chief Clerk-Surrogate:
Debra Babbie 518-565-4630

Columbia County

Judges
Multi-Bench:
Richard Koweek
Multi-Bench:
Jonathan D Nichols

Supreme, County, Family & Surrogate's Courts. fax: 518-851-7615
621 State Road, 32B, Claverack, NY 12513
518-267-3150 Fax: 518-851-7615
Chief Clerk-Multi:
Diana Morelock 518-267-3150
Chief Clerk-Surrogate:
Teresa Slemp 518-267-3150

Cortland County

Judges
Multi-Bench:
William F Ames
Multi-Bench:
Julie A Campbell

Supreme, County, Family & Surrogate's Courts
Courthouse, 46 Greenbush St, Ste 301, Cortland, NY 13045-2725
Chief Clerk-Family:
Laurie L Case 607-753-5353/fax: 646-963-6452
e-mail: lcase@courts.state.ny.us
Chief Clerk-County/Supreme:
Karen Jordan 607-753-5013/fax: 646-963-6452
e-mail: kjordan@nycourts.gov
Chief Clerk-Surrogate:
Lynne Day 607-753-5355/fax: 212-457-2661
e-mail: lday@courts.state.ny.us

Delaware County

Judges
Multi-Bench:
Carl F Becker

Supreme, County, Family & Surrogate's Courts
Courthouse, 3 Court St, Delhi, NY 13753
Chief Clerk-County/Supreme:
Kelly Sanfilippo 607-746-2131/fax: 646-963-6402
Chief Clerk-Surrogate:
Lisa Hulse 607-746-2126/fax: 646-963-6403
Chief Clerk-Family:
Lori Metzko 607-746-2298/fax: 646-963-6400

Dutchess County

Judges
County:
Peter M. Forman
Family:
Denise M. Watson
County:
Stephen Greller
Surrogate:
James D Pagones
Family:
Joan Posner
Family:
Joseph Egitto

Family Court
50 Market St, Poughkeepsie, NY 12601
Chief Clerk-Family:
Peter A Palladino 845-431-1850/fax: 845-486-2510

Supreme, County & Surrogate's Courts
Courthouse, 10 Market St, Poughkeepsie, NY 12601
Chief Clerk-Surrogate:
Erica DeTraglia, Esq. 845-431-1770/fax: 845-476-3659
Chief Clerk-County/Supreme:
Michael Thompson 845-431-1710/fax: 845-431-1743

Erie County

Judges
Family:
Robert Merino
Family:
Mary Carney
Family:
Kevin M Carter

Offices and agencies generally appear in alphabetical order, except when specific order is requested by listee.

County:
    Michael L D'Amico
Family:
    Sharon LoVallo
County:
    Sheila DiTullio
Family:
    Lisa Bloch Rodwin
Family:
    Deanne Tripi
Surrogate:
    Barbara Howe
County:
    Thomas P Franczyk
County:
    Michael F Pietruszka
Family:
    Margaret O Szczur
County:
    Kenneth Case

Family Court
One Niagara Plz, Buffalo, NY 14202
Chief Clerk:
    Frank J Boccio 716-845-7444/fax: 716-845-7546
    e-mail: fboccio@nycourts.gov

Surrogate's Court . . . . fax: 716-845-7566
Erie County Hall, 92 Franklin St, Buffalo, NY 14202
716-845-2560 Fax: 716-845-7566
Chief Clerk-Surrogate (Temporary):
    Joseph Shifflett 716-845-9454/fax: 716-845-7565
    e-mail: jshiffle@courts.state.ny.us

Supreme & County Court
25 Delaware Ave, Buffalo, NY 14202
Chief Clerk-County/Supreme:
    Ellis W. Bozzolo 716-845-9301/fax: 716-851-3293
    e-mail: ebozzolo@courts.state.ny.us

Essex County

Judges
Multi-Bench:
    Richard D Meyer

Supreme, County, Family & Surrogate's Courts
Courthouse, 7559 Court St, PO Box 217, Elizabethtown, NY 12932
Chief Clerk-Surrogate:
    Mary Ann Badger 518-873-3384/fax: 518-451-8740
Chief Clerk-Family (Acting):
    Mary Ann Badger 518-873-3320/fax: 518-451-8739
Chief Clerk-Supreme/County:
    Terry A Stoddard. 518-873-3370/fax: 518-451-8738

Franklin County

Judges
Multi-Bench:
    Robert G Main, Jr

Supreme, County, Family & Surrogate's Courts
Courthouse, 355 W Main St, Malone, NY 12953
Chief Clerk-Surrogate:
    Martha A LaBarge. 518-481-1736/fax: 518-481-1443
Chief Clerk-Family:
    Janice F Mock 518-481-1742/fax: 518-481-5453
Chief Clerk-Supreme/County:
    Jodi L. Wood 518-481-1748/fax: 518-481-5456

Fulton County

Judges
County/Surrogate:
    Richard C Giardino
County/Surrogate:
    Polly A Hoye
Family:
    Edward F. Skoda

Supreme, County, Family & Surrogate's Courts
223 W Main St, Johnstown, NY 12095
Chief Clerk-County/Supreme (Acting):
    Lisa Tricozzi 518-736-5662/fax: 518-762-5078
Chief Clerk-Surrogate:
    Barbara Shattuck 518-736-5685/fax: 518-451-8746
Chief Clerk-Family:
    Lisa Tricozzi 518-762-3840/fax: 518-451-8745

Genesee County

Judges
Family:
    Eric R Adams
Multi-Bench:
    Robert C Noonan

Supreme, County, Family & Surrogate's Courts
County Courts Facility, 1 W Main St, Batavia, NY 14020
Chief Clerk-Family:
    Laurie Johnston 585-344-2230/fax: 585-344-8520
    e-mail: ljohnsto@nycourts.gov
Chief Clerk-County/Supreme:
    Mary Lou Strathearn 585-344-2550 x2239/fax: 585-344-8517
    e-mail: mstrathe@nycourts.gov
Chief Clerk-Surrogate:
    Michele Westfall-Owens 585-344-2550 x2240/fax: 585-344-8517
    e-mail: mawestfa@nycourts.gov

Greene County

Judges
Multi-Bench:
    Charles M. Tailleur
Multi-Bench:
    Terry J. Wilhelm

Supreme, County, Family & Surrogate's Courts
Courthouse, 320 Main St, Catskill, NY 12414
Chief Clerk-County/Supreme:
    Michelle Carroll 518-625-3160
Chief Clerk-Surrogate:
    Eric Maurer. 518-625-3150
Chief Clerk-Family:
    Brenda VanDermark. 518-625-3180

Hamilton County

Judges
Multi-Bench:
    S Peter Feldstein

County, Family & Surrogate's Courts
139 White Birch Lane, PO Box 780, Indian Lake, NY 12842
Chief Clerk:
    Araina Eldridge 518-648-5411/fax: 518-453-8687

Herkimer County

Judges
County/Surrogate:
    John H. Crandall

Offices and agencies generally appear in alphabetical order, except when specific order is requested by listee.

Family:
John J. Brennan

Family Court
County Office & Court Facility, 301 N Washington St, Suite 2501,
Herkimer, NY 13350
Chief Clerk:
Lynn M Kohl...................315-867-1139/fax: 315-867-1369

Supreme, County & Surrogate's Courts
County Office & Court Facility, 301 N Washington St, Herkimer, NY 13350
Chief Clerk - Supreme:
Paul B. Heintz................315-867-1346/fax: 315-866-1802
Chief Clerk:
Mary T. Grogan.................315-867-1367/fax: 315-866-1722

Jefferson County

Judges
Family:
Richard V Hunt
County:
Kim H Martusewicz
Surrogate:
Peter A Schwerzmann

County, Family & Surrogate's Courts
163 Arsenal St, Watertown, NY 13601
Chief Clerk-Family:
Valerie Boyle 315-785-3001/fax: 315-266-4776
Chief Clerk-Surrogate:
Benjamin Cobb 315-785-3019/fax: 315-785-5194

Supreme Court
State Office Bldg, 317 Washington St, Watertown, NY 13601
Chief Clerk-County/Supreme:
Deanna L. Morse................315-785-7906/fax: 315-266-4779

Kings County

Judges
Surrogate:
Margarita Lopez Torres
Surrogate:
Diana A. Johnson

COUNTY & FAMILY COURTS: See New York City Courts

Supreme Court
Civil: 360 Adams St, Criminal: 320 Jay St, Brooklyn, NY 11201
Chief Clerk-Criminal:
Daniel M. Allessandrino..........................347-396-1100
Chief Clerk-Civil:
Charles A. Small, Esq..........................718-675-7699

Surrogate's Court
2 Johnson St, Brooklyn, NY 11201
Chief Clerk-Surrogate:
Doreen Quinn....................718-643-7098 or 347-404-9700

Lewis County

Judges
Multi-Bench:
Daniel R. King

Supreme, County, Family & Surrogate's Courts
Courthouse, 7660 N State St, Lowville, NY 13367
Chief Clerk-Family:
Lori Pfendler...................315-376-5345/fax: 315-376-5189
Chief Clerk-Surrogate:
Lori Pfendler...................315-376-5344/fax: 315-376-1647

Chief Clerk-County/Supreme:
Bart R Pleskach ....315-376-5366 or 315-376-5347
fax: 315-376-4198

Livingston County

Judges
County:
Dennis S Cohen
County:
Robert B Wiggins

Supreme, County, Family & Surrogate's Courts
Courthouse, 2 Court St, Geneseo, NY 14454-1030
e-mail: livingstonfamilycourt@courts.state.ny.us
Chief Clerk - Family:
Robert M. Lewis 585-371-3919/fax: 585-371-3933

Madison County

Judges
Multi-Bench:
Biagio J DiStefano
Multi-Bench:
Dennis K McDermott

Supreme, County, Family & Surrogate's Courts
Courthouse, N Court St, Wampsville, NY 13163-0545
Chief Clerk-Family:
Cheryl Collins.................315-366-2291/fax: 315-366-2828
e-mail: madisonfamilycourt@courts.state.ny.us
Chief Clerk-County/Supreme:
Marianne Kincaid 315-366-2267/fax: 646-963-6588
Chief Clerk-Surrogate:
Deborah Samoyedny..............315-366-2392/fax: 646-963-6594
e-mail: dsamoyed@courts.state.ny.us

Monroe County

Judges
Multi-Bench:
Patricia Gallaher
Multi-Bench:
Joan S. Kohout
Multi-Bench:
Gail A. Donofrio
Multi-Bench:
Joseph G. Nesser
Multi-Bench:
John Gallagher
Multi-Bench:
Dandrea L. Ruhlmann
Surrogate:
Edmund A. Calvaruso

Supreme, County, Family & Surrogate's Courts. fax: 585-371-3780
Hall of Justice, 99 Exchange Blvd, Rochester, NY 14614
585-371-3758 Fax: 585-371-3780
Chief Clerk-Surrogate:
Mark L. Annunziata............................585-371-3289
e-mail: mannunzi@courts.state.ny.us
Chief Clerk-County:
Lisa Preston ....585-428-2020 or 585-428-2331
fax: 585-428-2190
e-mail: monroe_superior@courts.state.ny.us
Chief Clerk-Family:
Loreen Nash 585-371-3544/fax: 585-371-3585
e-mail: monroefamilycourt@courts.state.ny.us

Offices and agencies generally appear in alphabetical order, except when specific order is requested by listee.

Montgomery County

Judges
County:
  Felix J Catena
Family:
  Philip V Cortese
Surrogate:
  Guy P Tomlinson

Supreme, County, Family & Surrogate's Courts
Courthouse, 58 Broadway, PO Box 1500, Fonda, NY 12068-1500
Chief Clerk-Surrogate:
  Ella Bowerman 518-853-8108/fax: 518-853-8230
Chief Clerk-Family:
  Laurie Furnare 518-853-8133/fax: 518-238-4370
Chief Clerk-County/Supreme:
  Timothy J Riley 518-853-4516/fax: 518-853-3596

Nassau County

Judges
County:
  David J Ayres
County:
  Meryl J Berkowitz
County:
  Angelo A. Delligatti
County:
  Joseph Calabrese
County:
  Jerald S Carter
Family:
  Julianne S Eisman
Family:
  Teresa K. Corrigan
County:
  Robert H. Spergel
County:
  Steven M Jaeger
County:
  John M. Galasso
Family:
  Edmund M. Dane
Family:
  Ellen R. Greenberg
Family:
  Robin M. Kent
County:
  James P McCormack
Family:
  Merik A. Aaron
County:
  George R Peck
Surrogate:
  Edward W. McCarthy, III
County:
  Tammy S Robbins
County:
  David P Sullivan
Family:
  Conrad D. Singer

County & Surrogate's Courts
262 Old Country Rd, Mineola, NY 11501
516-493-3800 or 516-493-3710
Chief Clerk-County:
  Donald F. Vetter 516-493-3710
Chief Clerk-Surrogate:
  Michael Murphy 516-493-3805

Family Court
1200 Old Country Rd, Westbury, NY 11590
516-493-4000
Chief Clerk:
  Rosalie Fitzgerald 516-493-4000

Supreme Court
Supreme Court Bldg, 100 Supreme Court Dr, Mineola, NY 11501
Chief Clerk:
  Kathryn D Hopkins 516-493-3400

New York County

Judges
Surrogate:
  Nora S. Anderson

COUNTY & FAMILY COURTS: See New York City Courts

SUPREME COURT, Civil Term
60 Centre St, New York, NY 10007
Clerk:
  Norman Goodman 646-386-5955

SUPREME COURT, Criminal Term
100 Centre St, New York, NY 10013
Clerk:
  Barry Clarke 646-386-3900/fax: 212-748-5129

Surrogate's Court
31 Chambers St, New York, NY 10007
Chief Clerk:
  Diana Sanabria 646-386-5000

Niagara County

Judges
Family:
  Kathleen Wojtaszek-Gariano
County/Surrogate:
  Matthew J Murphy
Family:
  John F. Batt
County/Surrogate:
  Sara Sheldon Farkas

County, Family & Surrogate's Courts
Courthouse, 175 Hawley St, Lockport, NY 14094
Chief Clerk-Family:
  William F McCarthy 716-278-1880/fax: 716-278-1877
  e-mail: wmccarth@nycourts.gov
Chief Clerk-County/Supreme:
  Michael C. Veruto, Esq. 716-278-1800/fax: 716-278-1809
  e-mail: mveruto@nycourts.gov
Chief Clerk-Surrogate:
  Angela Stamm-Philipps, Esq. 716-439-7130/fax: 716-439-7157

County, Supreme & Family Courts
Delsignore Civic Bldg, 775 Third St, Niagara Falls, NY 14301

Oneida County

Judges
Family:
  Randall B Caldwell
County (Supervising):
  Barry M Donalty
County:
  Michael L Dwyer
Surrogate:
  Louis P. Gigliotti

Family:
 James R Griffith
Family (Rome):
 Joan E. Shkane

Supreme, County & Family Courts
Courthouse, 200 Elizabeth St, Utica, NY 13501
Chief Clerk-Supreme/County:
 Kathleen Aiello 315-266-4200/fax: 315-798-6047
Chief Clerk-Family:
 Barbara A Porta 315-266-4444/fax: 315-798-6404

Surrogate's Court
County Office Bldg, 800 Park Ave, 8th Fl, Utica, NY 13501
Chief Clerk:
 Kristine K Pecheone 315-266-4550/fax: 315-797-9237

Onondaga County

Judges
County:
 Anthony F Aloi
County:
 Joseph E Fahey
Family:
 Michael Hanuszczak
Family:
 Julie A. Cecile
Family:
 Michele Pirro Bailey
Family:
 Martha E Mulroy
Surrogate:
 Ava S Raphael
County:
 Thomas J. Miller
Family (Supervisory):
 Martha Walsh Hood

Supreme, County, Family & Surrogate's Courts
Courthouse, 401 Montgomery St, Syracuse, NY 13202
Chief Clerk-Family:
 David Primo, Esq. 315-671-2000/fax: 315-671-1163
Chief Clerk-Supreme/County:
 Patricia J Noll . . . . .315-671-1030 or 315-671-1020
 fax: 315-671-1176
Chief Clerk-Surrogate:
 Ellen S Weinstein Esq 315-671-2100/fax: 315-671-1162

Ontario County

Judges
Multi-Bench:
 Craig Doran
Multi-Bench:
 Williamk F Kocher
Multi-Bench:
 Frederick G Reed
Family (Acting):
 Stephen D. Aronson

Supreme, County, Family & Surrogate's Courts
Courthouse, 27 N Main St, Canandaigua, NY 14424-1459
Chief Clerk-County:
 Nicole Botti .585-396-4239/fax: 585-396-4576
Chief Clerk - Family:
 Lynda Wood 585-412-5299/fax: 585-412-5327
 e-mail: ontariofamilycourt@courts.state.ny.us

Orange County

Judges
County:
 Jeffrey G Berry
Family:
 Andrew P Bivona
County:
 Nicholas DeRosa
Family:
 Debra Kiedaisch
Family:
 Carol S Klein
County:
 Robert H. Freehill
Surrogate:
 Robert A Onofry
Family:
 Lori Currier Woods

Supreme, County & Family Courts
285 Main St, Goshen, NY 10924
Chief Clerk-County/Supreme:
 Lynn McKelvey 845-476-3500
Chief Clerk-Family:
 Elizabeth Holbrook 845-476-3520

Surrogate's Court
Courthouse, 30 Park Pl, Goshen, NY 10924
Chief Clerk:
 Jeanne Smith 845-476-3655/fax: 845-291-2196

Orleans County

Judges
Multi-Bench:
 James P Punch

Supreme, County, Family & Surrogate's Courts
Courthouse Square, 1 S. Main Street, Suite 3, Albion, NY 14411-1497
Chief Clerk-Surrogate:
 Deborah Berry 585-589-4457/fax: 585-589-0632
 e-mail: dberry@nycourts.gov
Chief Clerk-Family:
 Laurie A Bower 585-589-4457/fax: 585-589-0632
 e-mail: lbower@nycourts.gov
Chief Clerk-County/Supreme:
 Kristin Nicholson 585-589-5458/fax: 585-589-0632
 e-mail: knichols@nycourts.gov

Oswego County

Judges
Surrogate:
 Spencer Ludington
County:
 Walter W Hafner, Jr
County:
 Donald E. Todd
Family:
 Kimberly M. Seager

Family Court
Public Safety Ctr, 39 Churchill Rd, Oswego, NY 13126
Chief Clerk-Family:
 Kathleen L. Halstead 315-349-3350/fax: 315-349-3457

Supreme, County & Surrogate's Courts
Courthouse, 25 E Oneida St, Oswego, NY 13126
Chief Clerk-Surrogate:
 Cheryl Blake 315-349-3295/fax: 315-349-8514

Offices and agencies generally appear in alphabetical order, except when specific order is requested by listee.

Chief Clerk-County/Supreme:
Sonya Malone 315-349-3277/fax: 315-266-4519

Otsego County

Judges
Multi-Bench:
Brian D Burns
Multi-Bench:
John F Lambert

Supreme, County, & Surrogate's Courts
197 Main St, Cooperstown, NY 13326
Chief Clerk-County/Supreme:
Christy Bass 607-547-4364/fax: 646-963-6663
e-mail: cbass@courts.state.ny.us
Chief Clerk-Family:
Karen A Nichols 607-547-4264/fax: 212-457-2956
e-mail: otsegofamilycourt@courts.state.ny.us
Chief Clerk-Surrogate:
Lisa Weite 607-547-4213/fax: 607-547-7566

Family Court
County Annex Building, 32 Chestnut Street, Cooperstown, NY 13326

Putnam County

Judges
Multi-Bench:
James F Reitz
Multi-Bench:
James T Rooney

Supreme, County & Family Courts
20 County Center, Carmel, NY 10512

Surrogate's Court
44 Gleneida Ave, Carmel, NY 10512
Chief Clerk-Family:
Karen O'Connor 845-208-7805/fax: 845-228-9614
Chief Clerk-County/Supreme:
Karen O'Connor 845-208-7830/fax: 845-208-7869
Chief Clerk-Surrogate:
Linda M Schwark 845-208-7860/fax: 845-228-5761

Queens County

Judges
Surrogate:
Peter Kelly

COUNTY & FAMILY COURTS: See New York City Courts

Supreme & Surrogate's Courts
88-11 Sutphin Blvd, Jamaica, NY 11435
Chief Clerk:
Margaret Gribbon. . . . . .718-298-0400 or 718-298-0500

Rensselaer County

Judges
Family:
Catherine Cholakis
Family:
Elizabeth Marie Walsh
County - Part Time:
Henry F. Zwack
Surrogate:
Paul V. Morgan Jr.
County:
Debra J Young

County:
Andrew G. Ceresia
County - Part Time:
Michael Melkonian

Family Court
1504 Fifth Ave, Troy, NY 12180
Deputy Chief Clerk:
Lee Bridenbeck 518-435-5515/fax: 518-272-6573

Supreme, County & Surrogate's Courts
Courthouse, 80 Second Street, Troy, NY 12180
Chief Clerk-Surrogate:
Vacant 518-285-6100/fax: 518-272-5452
Chief Clerk-County/Supreme:
Richard F Reilly, Jr. 518-285-5025/fax: 518-270-3714

Richmond County

Judges
Surrogate:
Robert J. Gigante

COUNTY & FAMILY COURTS: See New York City Courts

Supreme & Surrogate's Courts
County Courthouse, 18 Richmond Terrace, Staten Island, NY 10301
Chief Clerk-Surrogate:
Ronald M Cerrachio. 718-675-8500
Chief Clerk-Supreme:
Joseph Como 718-675-8700

Rockland County

Judges
County:
Charles A Apotheker
Family:
Sherri L. Eisenpress
County:
William K Nelson
Surrogate:
Thomas E Walsh, II
Family:
William P Warren

Supreme, County, Family & Surrogate's Courts
Courthouse, 1 S Main St, New City, NY 10956
Chief Clerk-Family:
Anna Kosovych. 845-483-8210/fax: 845-638-5319
Chief Clerk-County/Supreme:
John F Hussey 845-483-8310/fax: 845-638-5312
Chief Clerk-Surrogate:
Virginia Athens 845-483-8260/fax: 845-638-5632

Saratoga County

Judges
Family:
Courtenay W Hall
Family:
Jennifer Jensen Bergan
County:
Jerry J Scarano
Surrogate:
Richard Kupferman

Family Court
35 W High St, Ballston Spa, NY 12020
Chief Clerk:
Susan Samascott 518-451-8888/fax: 518-453-5942

Offices and agencies generally appear in alphabetical order, except when specific order is requested by listee.

Supreme, County & Surrogate's Courts
30 McMaster St, Bldg 3, Ballston Spa, NY 12020
Chief Clerk-Surrogate:
    Catharine Ruggles..............518-451-8830/fax: 518-453-8693
Chief Clerk-County/Supreme:
    Carianne Brimhall..............518-451-8840/fax: 518-453-5937

Schenectady County

Judges
County:
    Karen A Drago
Surrogate:
    Vincent W. Versaci
Family:
    Mark L Powers
Family:
    Kevin A. Burke

Family Court
County Office Bldg, 620 State St, Schenectady, NY 12305
Chief Clerk:
    Melissa Mills...................518-285-8435/fax: 518-393-1565

Supreme, County & Surrogate's Courts
Courthouse, 612 State St, Schenectady, NY 12305
Chief Clerk-Surrogate:
    Paula Miller....................518-285-8455/fax: 518-451-8732
Chief Clerk-County/Supreme:
    Mary Adams 518-285-8401/fax: 518-451-8731

Schoharie County

Judges
Multi-Bench:
    George R Bartlett, III

Supreme, County, Family & Surrogate's Courts
Courthouse, 290 Main St, PO Box 669, Schoharie, NY 12157-0669
Chief Clerk-Surrogate/Family/County/Supreme:
    F Christian Spies................518-453-6998/fax: 518-453-6982

Schuyler County

Judges
Multi-Bench:
    Dennis J. Morris

Supreme, County, Family & Surrogate's Courts
Courthouse, 105 9th St, Unit 35, Watkins Glen, NY 14891
Chief Clerk-Family:
    Amanda Riley 607-535-7143/fax: 646-963-6590
    e-mail: alriley@courts.state.ny.us
Chief Clerk-County/Supreme:
    Rita S Decker 607-535-7760/fax: 646-963-6590
    e-mail: rdecker@nycourts.gov
Chief Clerk-Surrogate:
    Michele Ormsbee 607-535-7144/fax: 646-963-6590

Seneca County

Judges
Multi-Bench:
    Dennis F Bender

Supreme, County, Family & Surrogate's Courts
Courthouse, 48 W Williams St, Waterloo, NY 13165
Chief Clerk:
    Conchetta M Brown 315-539-7021/fax: 315-539-3267
    e-mail: senecafamilycourt@courts.state.ny.us

St Lawrence County

Judges
Family:
    Cecily L. Morris
County:
    Jerome J Richards
Surrogate:
    Kathleen Martin Rogers

Supreme, County, Family & Surrogate's Courts
Courthouse, 48 Court St, Canton, NY 13617-1194
Chief Clerk-County/Supreme:
    Mary B Curran 315-379-2219/fax: 315-379-2423
    e-mail: mcurran@courts.state.ny.us
Chief Clerk-Family:
    Rhonda Poupore 315-379-2410/fax: 315-386-3197
Chief Clerk-Surrogate:
    Debra Dow 315-379-2217/fax: 315-379-2372

Steuben County

Judges
Multi-Bench:
    Peter C Bradstreet
Multi-Bench:
    Marianne Furfure
Multi-Bench:
    Joseph W Latham

Supreme, County, Family & Surrogate's Courts
Courthouse, 3 E Pulteney Sq, Bath, NY 14810
Chief Clerk - Family:
    Pamela Gardner..................607-622-8218/fax: 607-622-8239
    e-mail: steubenfamilycourt@courts.state.ny.us

Suffolk County

Judges
County/Acting Surrogate Judge:
    Stephen L Braslow
Family:
    Marlene Budd
County:
    Stephen M. Behar
Surrogate:
    John M Czygier, Jr
County:
    Joseph Farnetti
Family:
    David Freundlich
County:
    Ralph T Gazzillo
Family:
    Denise F. Molia
Family:
    Richard Hoffman
County:
    James C Hudson
County:
    Barbara Kahn
Family:
    John Kelly
Family:
    Martha L Luft
Family:
    Caren Loguercio
County:
    Jeffrey Arlen Spinner
Family:
    Bernard Cheng

Offices and agencies generally appear in alphabetical order, except when specific order is requested by listee.

Family:
  Andrew G Tarantino Jr
County:
  John Iliou
Family:
  Theresa Whelan
County:
  James F. Quinn

County Court
210 Center Dr, Riverhead, NY 11901
Chief Clerk:
  Frank L. Tropea 631-852-2120/fax: 631-852-2568

Family Court
Courthouse, 400 Carleton Ave, Central Islip, NY 11722
Chief Clerk:
  Terry Matyszczyk 631-853-4289

Supreme Court
235 Griffing Ave, Riverhead, NY 11901
Chief Clerk:
  Michael Scardino 631-852-2334

Surrogate's Court
320 Center Dr, Riverhead, NY 11901
Chief Clerk:
  Michael Cipollino 631-852-1746

Sullivan County

Judges
County:
  Frank J LaBuda
Surrogate:
  Michael McGuire
Family:
  Mark M Meddaugh

Surrogate's & Family Courts
Government Ctr, 100 North St, Monticello, NY 12701
Chief Clerk-Surrogate:
  Rita Guarnaccia 845-807-0690/fax: 845-794-0310
Chief Clerk-Family:
  Christina Benson 845-807-0650/fax: 845-794-0199

Supreme & County Court
Courthouse, 414 Broadway, Monticello, NY 12701
Chief Clerk-Supreme/County:
  Sarah Katzman 845-794-4066/fax: 845-791-6170

Tioga County

Judges
Multi-Bench:
  Gerald Keene

Supreme County, Family & Surrogate's Courts
Court Annex, 20 Court St, PO Box 10, Owego, NY 13827
Chief Clerk-Family:
  Denise Marsili 607-689-6077/fax: 646-963-6399
Chief Clerk-Surrogate:
  Deborah Stone 607-689-6099/fax: 646-963-6398
Chief Clerk-Supreme/County:
  Janean Cook 607-689-6102/fax: 212-401-5970

Tompkins County

Judges
Multi-Bench:
  John C Rowley
Multi-Bench:
  Joseph R. Cassidy

Supreme, County, Family & Surrogate's Courts
Courthouse, 320 N Tioga St, Ithaca, NY 14850
Chief Clerk-Surrogate:
  Lori S Decker 607-216-6655/fax: 212-457-2952
Deputy Chief Clerk-County/Supreme:
  Mary C Hodges 607-272-0466/fax: 212-401-9071
Chief Clerk-Family:
  Cheryl Lidell Obenauer 607-216-6640/fax: 212-457-2951
  e-mail: clidell@courts.state.ny.us

Ulster County

Judges
County:
  Donald Williams
Family:
  Marianne O Mizel
Surrogate:
  Mary MacMaster Work
Family:
  Anthony McGinty

Family Court
16 Lucas Ave, Kingston, NY 12401
Chief Clerk:
  Kathy Lasko 845-340-3600/fax: 845-340-3626
  e-mail: ulsterfamilycourt@nycourts.gov

Supreme & County Courts
Courthouse, 285 Wall St, Kingston, NY 12401
Chief Clerk:
  Claudia Jones 845-340-3377/fax: 845-340-3387

Surrogate's Court
240 Fair St, Kingston, NY 12401
Chief Clerk:
  Mary Ellen Sullivan 845-340-3348/fax: 845-340-3352
  e-mail: ulstersurrogatecourt@nycourts.gov

Warren County

Judges
Family:
  J Timothy Breen
County/Surrogate:
  John S Hall Jr

Supreme, County, Family & Surrogate's Courts
Municipal Ctr, 1340 State Rte 9, Lake George, NY 12845
Chief Clerk-Family:
  Sally Boivin 518-761-6500/fax: 518-761-6230
Chief Clerk-Surrogate:
  Deborah Ricci 518-761-6514/fax: 518-761-6511
Chief Clerk-County/Supreme:
  Joanne Mann 518-761-6431/fax: 518-761-6253

Washington County

Judges
Multi-Bench:
  Kelly S McKeighan

Supreme, County, Family & Surrogate's Courts
Courthouse, 383 Broadway, Fort Edward, NY 12828-1015
Chief Clerk-County/Supreme:
  Tricia Robarge 518-746-2521/fax: 518-746-2519
Chief Clerk-Family:
  Josephine Doll 518-746-2501/fax: 518-746-2503
Chief Clerk-Surrogate:
  Barbara Smith 518-746-2545/fax: 518-746-2547

Offices and agencies generally appear in alphabetical order, except when specific order is requested by listee.

Wayne County

Judges
Multi-Bench:
Dennis M Kehoe
Multi-Bench:
John B Nesbitt
Multi-Bench:
Daniel G. Barrett

Supreme, County, Family & Surrogate's Courts
Hall of Justice, 54 Broad St, Rm 106, Lyons, NY 14489-1199
Chief Clerk:
Lorraine T. Fodera 315-946-5459/fax: 315-946-5456
e-mail: waynefamilycourt@courts.state.ny.us

Westchester County

Judges
County:
Susan M Capeci
County:
David F. Everett
County:
Susan Cacace
County:
Barry Warhit
County:
David S. Zuckerman
Surrogate:
Anthony A Scarpino Jr
County:
James W Hubert
County:
Barbara G Zambelli

Supreme, County & Family Courts
111 Dr Martin Luther King Jr Blvd, White Plains, NY 10601
Chief Clerk-Family:
James McAllister.................914-824-5500/fax: 914-995-8650
Chief Clerk-County/Supreme:
Nancy J. Barry, Esq................914-824-5300 or 914-824-5400
fax: 914-995-3427

Surrogate's Court
111 Dr Martin Luther King Jr Blvd, 19th Fl, White Plains, NY 10601
Chief Clerk:
Joseph Accetta..................914-824-5656/fax: 914-995-3728

Wyoming County

Judges
Multi-Bench:
Michael Mohun
Multi-Bench:
Michael F Griffith

Supreme, County, Family & Surrogate's Courts
Courthouse, 147 N Main St, Warsaw, NY 14569
Chief Clerk-Surrogate:
William D Beyer................585-786-3148/fax: 585-786-3800
e-mail: wbeyer@nycourts.gov
Chief Clerk-Family:
Jacqueline DiAngelo.............585-786-3148/fax: 585-786-3800
e-mail: jdiangel@nycourts.gov
Chief Clerk-County/Supreme:
Rebecca Miller...................585-786-3148 or 585-786-2253
fax: 585-786-2818
e-mail: rmmiller@nycourts.gov

Yates County

Judges
Multi-Bench:
W Patrick Falvey

Supreme, County, Family & Surrogate's Courts
Courthouse, 415 Liberty St, Penn Yan, NY 14527-1191
Chief Clerk:
Robert Peelle...................315-536-5126/fax: 315-536-5190
e-mail: yatesfamilycourt@courts.state.ny.us

DISTRICT COURTS

District Courts exist in Nassau County and in five western towns of Suffolk County. District Courts have civil jurisdiction up to $15,000, and criminal jurisdiction for misdemeanors, violations and lesser offenses. Judges are elected for six-year terms by their judicial districts.

Nassau County
Chief Clerk:
Eileen Bianchi...................................516-493-4162

1st, 2nd & 4th District Courts
99 Main St, Hempstead, NY 11550
516-493-4200
Deputy Chief Clerk, 4th:
Michael Beganskas............................516-572-2355
Deputy Chief Clerk, 1st & 2nd:
Kenneth Roll....................................516-572-2355

3rd District Court
435 Middle Neck Rd, Great Neck, NY 11023
District Executive:
Paul Lamanna, Esq..............516-493-3000/fax: 516-493-3390

Judges

Valerie Alexander	Anna Anzalone
Michael A. Ciaffa	Eric Bjorneby
Andrew M. Engel	Tricia M. Ferrell
Rhonda E. Fischer	Scott Fairgrieve
David Goodsell	Sharon MJ Gianelli
Fred J. Hirsch	Susan T. Kluewer
Gary F Knobel	Douglas J. Lerose
David W. McAndrews	Martin J Massell
Terence P. Murphy	William J O'Brien
Anthony W Paradiso	Colin F. O'Donnell
Erica L Prager	Anthony W. Paradiso
Andrea Phoenix	Francis Ricigliano
David P. Sullivan	Helen Voutsinas
(Supervising):	
Norman St George	
Joy M. Watson	

Suffolk County
Chief Clerk:
Michael Paparatto.................................631-853-4530

1ST DISTRICT COURT, Civil Term ....fax: 631-854-9681
3105 Veterans Memorial Hwy, Ronkonkoma, NY 11779
631-854-9676 Fax: 631-854-9681

1ST DISTRICT COURT, Criminal Term ....fax: 631-853-4505
Courthouse, 400 Carleton Ave, Central Islip, NY 11722
631-853-7500 Fax: 631-853-4505

2nd District Court ....fax: 631-854-1127
30 East Hoffman Avenue, Lindenhurst, NY 11757
631-854-1121 Fax: 631-854-1127

Offices and agencies generally appear in alphabetical order, except when specific order is requested by listee.

3rd District Court . . . . .fax: 631-854-4549
   1850 New York Ave, Huntington Station, NY 11746
   631-854-4545 Fax: 631-854-4549

4th District Court . . . . .fax: 631-853-5951
   Veterans' Memorial Highway, North County Cplx Bldg C158, Hauppauge,
   NY 11787
   631-853-5400 Fax: 631-853-5951

5th District Court . . . . .fax: 631-854-9681
   3105 Veterans Memorial Hwy, Ronkonkoma, NY 11779
   631-854-9676 Fax: 631-854-9681

6th District Court . . . . .fax: 631-854-1444
   150 W Main St, Patchogue, NY 11772
   631-854-1440 Fax: 631-854-1444

Judges

Richard I. Horowitz	John Andrew Kay
Janine A. Barbera-Dalli	Toni A Bean
Chris Ann Kelley	Karen Kerr
James McDonough	Richard T. Dunne
William G. Ford	Patricia M Filiberto
Philip Goglas	James P Flanagan
C Stephen Hackeling	Paul M Hensley
Jennifer A. Henry	Steven A Lotto
Gaetan B Lozito	Glenn A Murphy
Vincent J. Martorana	G Ann Spelman
David A. Morris	Stephen L. Ukeiley

CITY COURTS OUTSIDE NEW YORK CITY

City Courts outside New York City have civil jurisdiction up to $15,000 and criminal jurisdiction over misdemeanors or lesser offenses. City Court judges are either elected or appointed for terms of ten years for full-time judges and six years for part-time judges.

Albany

Judges
   Criminal:
     William A Carter
   Traffic/Civil:
     Helena Heath
   Criminal:
     Thomas K Keefe
   Criminal:
     Rachel L Kretser
   Traffic/Civil:
     Gary F Stiglmeier

Civil Court
   Albany City Hall, Room 209, 24 Eagle Street, Albany, NY 12207
   Chief Clerk:
     Anthony Mancino 518-453-4640/fax: 518-453-8679
     e-mail: albanycivilcourt@nycourts.gov

Criminal Court
   Public Safety Bldg, 1 Morton Ave, Albany, NY 12202
   Chief Clerk:
     Anthony Mancino 518-453-5520/fax: 518-453-8989
     e-mail: albanycriminalcourt@nycourts.gov

Traffic Court
   Albany City Hall Basement, 24 Eagle St, Albany, NY 12207
   Chief Clerk:
     Anthony Mancino 518-453-4630/fax: 518-453-8699
     e-mail: albanytrafficcourt@nycourts.gov

Amsterdam

Judges
Howard M Aison	Lisa W Lorman

Civil & Criminal Courts
   Public Safety Bldg, Rm 208, 1 Guy Park Ave Ext, Amsterdam, NY 12010
   Chief Clerk:
     Melanie Hartman. 518-842-9510/fax: 518-453-8646

Auburn

Judges
Michael F McKeon	Thomas J Shamon

Civil & Criminal Courts
   157 Genesee St, Auburn, NY 13021
   315-237-6420
   Chief Clerk:
     Deborah L Robillard 315-253-1570/fax: 315-253-1085

Batavia

Judges
Robert J Balbick	Durin B Rogers

Civil & Criminal Courts . . . . .fax: 585-344-8556
   Facility Bldg, 1 W Main St, Batavia, NY 14020
   585-344-2550 x2417 Fax: 585-344-8556
   Chief Clerk:
     Paula DaBella 585-344-2550 x2426
     e-mail: pdabella@nycourts.gov

Beacon

Judges
Rebecca S Mensch	Timothy G Pagones

Civil & Criminal Courts
   1 Municipal Plz, Ste 2, Beacon, NY 12508
   Chief Clerk:
     Debra Antonelli. 845-431-1900/fax: 845-838-5041

Binghamton

Judges
Carol A Cocchiola	William C Pelella
Daniel L Seiden	

Civil & Criminal Courts
   City Hall, Governmental Plz, 38 Hawley St, 5th Fl, Binghamton, NY
   13901
   Chief Clerk:
     Sherry L Baker 607-772-7006/fax: 607-772-7041
     e-mail: sbaker@nycourts.gov

Buffalo

Judges
   (Chief):
     Thomas P Amodeo

Patrick M Carney	Joseph A Fiorella
Betty Calvo-Torres	Debra L Givens
Craig D Hannah	Kevin J Keane
Susan Eagan	James A McLeod
JaHarr Pridgen	Diane Wray
Barbara Johnson-Lee	Robert T Russell Jr
Amy C. Martoche	

Civil & Criminal Courts . . . . .fax: 716-847-8257
   50 Delaware Ave, Buffalo, NY 14202
   716-845-2600 Fax: 716-847-8257

Offices and agencies generally appear in alphabetical order, except when specific order is requested by listee.

Judicial Branch

Chief Clerk:
> Sharon A Thomas.............................716-845-2689
> e-mail: sthomas@nycourts.gov

Canandaigua

Judges

Stephen D Aronson (Acting)   John A Schuppenhauer (Acting)

Civil & Criminal Courts

City Hall, 2 N Main St, Canandaigua, NY 14424
585-412-5170
Chief Clerk:
> Lisa Schutz 585-412-5170/fax: 585-412-5172

Cohoes

Judges

Richard R Maguire   Stephen J Van Ullen

Civil, Criminal & Traffic Courts

City Hall, 97 Mohawk St, PO Box 678, Cohoes, NY 12047
Chief Clerk:
> Vacant.......................518-453-5501/fax: 518-233-8202
> e-mail: cohoescitycourt@nycourts.gov

Corning

Judges

Robert H Cole, Jr (Acting)   David B Kahl

Civil & Criminal Courts

500 Nasser Civic Ctr Plaza, Ste 101, Corning, NY 14830
Chief Clerk:
> Julie L Machuga 607-654-6033/fax: 607-654-6030

Cortland

Judges

Lawrence J Knickerbocker   Elizabeth A Burns

Civil & Criminal Courts

City Hall, 25 Court St, Cortland, NY 13045
Chief Clerk:
> Diana L Davis 607-428-5420/fax: 607-428-5435

Dunkirk

Judges

Walter F Drag   John M Kuzdale (Acting)

Civil & Criminal Courts

City Hall, 342 Central Ave, Dunkirk, NY 14048-2122
Chief Clerk:
> Jean Dill 716-366-2055/fax: 716-366-3622
> e-mail: jdill@nycourts.gov

Elmira

Judges

Steven W Forrest   Ottavio Campanella

Civil & Criminal Courts

317 E Church St, Elmira, NY 14901
e-mail: elmiracitycourt@courts.state.ny.us
Deputy Chief Clerk:
> Casey Johnson..................607-837-9520/fax: 212-401-9240

Fulton

Judges

David H. Hawthorne   Jerome A Mirabito

Civil & Criminal Courts

Municipal Bldg, 141 S First St, Fulton, NY 13069
e-mail: fulton_city@courts.state.ny.us
Chief Clerk:
> Maureen Ball...................315-593-8400/fax: 315-266-4753
> e-mail: mball@courts.state.ny.us

Geneva

Judges

Timothy J Buckley   Elisabeth A Toole
Bram S. Lehman

Civil & Criminal Courts

255 Exchange St, Geneva, NY 14456
315-237-6575
Chief Clerk:
> Josephine Guard 315-789-6575/fax: 315-781-2802

Glen Cove

Judges

Joseph D McCann   Richard J McCord

Civil & Criminal Courts

13 Glen St, Glen Cove, NY 11542
Chief Clerk:
> Stacey Gallo 516-403-2441/fax: 516-676-1570

Glens Falls

Judges

Gary C Hobbs   Nikki J Moreschi

Civil & Criminal Courts

City Hall, 42 Ridge St, 3rd Fl, Glens Falls, NY 12801
Chief Clerk:
> Lisa Ghenoiu....................518-798-4714/fax: 518-453-8623

Gloversville

Judges

Traci Di Mezza   Cory Dalmata

Civil & Criminal Courts

City Hall, 3 Frontage Rd, Gloversville, NY 12078
Chief Clerk:
> Jodi L Ferguson.................518-773-4527/fax: 518-773-4599

Hornell

Judges

Joseph E Damrath   David A Shults

Civil & Criminal Courts

PO Box 627, 82 Main St, Hornell, NY 14843
Chief Clerk:
> Love Griffin 607-324-7531/fax: 607-324-6325

Hudson

Judges

John Connor, Jr.   Mark Portin

City Court

429 Warren St, Hudson, NY 12534
Chief Clerk:
> Rosemary Zukowski 518-828-3100/fax: 518-828-3628
> e-mail: hudsoncitycourt@nycourts.gov

Offices and agencies generally appear in alphabetical order, except when specific order is requested by listee.

Ithaca

Judges

Scott A. Miller   Richard M Wallace

Civil & Criminal Courts

118 E Clinton St, Ithaca, NY 14850
607-216-6660
e-mail: ithacacitycourt@nycourts.gov
Chief Clerk:
Ronna J Collins 607-216-6660/fax: 607-277-3702

Jamestown

Judges

John J LaMancuso   Frederick A Larson

Civil & Criminal Courts

Municipal Bldg, 200 E 3rd St, Jamestown, NY 14701
Chief Clerk:
Lisa Meacham 716-483-7561/fax: 716-483-7519
e-mail: lmeacham@nycourts.gov

Johnstown

Judges

Frederick R Stortecky   Thomas C Walsh

Civil & Criminal Courts

City Hall, 33-41 E Main St, Johnstown, NY 12095
Chief Clerk:
Stephen Russo 518-762-0007/fax: 578-453-8651

Kingston

Judges

Lawrence E Ball   Philip W. Kirschner

City Court

Kingston City Court, 1 Garraghan Dr, Kingston, NY 12401
Chief Clerk:
Nicole Murphy 845-481-9350/fax: 845-483-8113
e-mail: kingstoncitycourt@nycourts.gov

Lackawanna

Judges

(Chief):
Frederic J Marrano
Norman LeBlanc Jr (Associate)

Civil & Criminal Courts . . . . fax: 716-845-7599

City Hall, 714 Ridge Rd, Lackawanna, NY 14218
716-845-7220 Fax: 716-845-7599
Chief Clerk:
Vacant 716-845-7216

Little Falls

Judges

Joy Malone   Mark Rose

Civil & Criminal Courts

City Hall, 659 E Main St, Little Falls, NY 13365
Chief Clerk:
Patrice M Gleim 315-823-1690/fax: 315-266-4711

Lockport

Judges

William J Watson   Thomas M DiMillo

Civil & Criminal Courts

1 Locks Plz, Lockport, NY 14094
Chief Clerk:
Colleen Wagner 716-280-6207/fax: 716-439-6684
e-mail: cjwagner@nycourts.gov

Long Beach

Judges

Frank Dikranis   Roy Tepper

Civil & Criminal Courts

1 W Chester St, Long Beach, NY 11561
516-442-8544
Chief Clerk:
Robert Davis 516-442-8555/fax: 516-889-3511

Mechanicville

Judges

John H Ciulla Jr   Joseph W Sheehan

Civil & Criminal Courts

City Hall, 36 N Main St, Mechanicville, NY 12118
Chief Clerk:
Francine Baker 518-453-5959/fax: 518-453-8678

Middletown

Judges

Steven Brockett   Robert Moson

Civil & Criminal Courts

2 James St, Middletown, NY 10940
Chief Clerk:
Linda Padden 845-476-3630/fax: 845-343-5737

Mount Vernon

Judges

William Edwards   Helen M Blackwood
Adam Seiden

Civil & Criminal Courts

2 Roosevelt Square N, 2nd Floor, Mount Vernon, NY 10550
Chief Clerk:
Lawrence Darden 914-831-6440/fax: 914-824-5511

New Rochelle

Judges

Susan I. Kettner   Anthony A. Carbone

Civil & Criminal Courts

475 North Ave, New Rochelle, NY 10801
Chief Clerk:
James Generoso 914-358-8000/fax: 914-654-0344

Newburgh

Judges

Peter M Kulkin   Paul D Trachte
E. Loren Williams

Civil & Criminal Courts

300 Broadway, Newburgh, NY 12550
Chief Clerk:
Jasmin Reyes-Finch 845-483-8100/fax: 845-565-0230

Niagara Falls

Judges

Angelo J Morinello   Robert Merino

Offices and agencies generally appear in alphabetical order, except when specific order is requested by listee.

Mark A Violante (Chief)   Diane Vitello

Civil & Criminal Courts ....fax: 716-278-9809
1925 Main Street, Niagara Falls, NY 14305
716-278-9800 Fax: 716-278-9809
Chief Clerk:
     Maureen Hourihan 716-278-9810/fax: 716-278-9869
     e-mail: mhourina@nycourts.gov

North Tonawanda

Judges
Jeffrey N Mis   William R Lewis

Civil & Criminal Courts
City Hall, 216 Payne Ave, North Tonawanda, NY 14120
Chief Clerk:
     Jennifer Steele...................716-845-7240/fax: 716-743-1754
     e-mail: jasteele@nycourts.gov

Norwich

Judges
James G. Cushman   James Downey

Civil & Criminal Courts
1 Court Plz, Norwich, NY 13815
Chief Clerk:
     Irene Williams...................607-334-1224/fax: 607-334-8494

Ogdensburg

Judges
Gary R. Alford   William Small

Civil & Criminal Courts
330 Ford St, Ogdensburg, NY 13669
Chief Clerk:
     Lisa Marie Meyer 315-393-3941/fax: 315-393-6839

Olean

Judges
William H Mountain III   Daniel R Palumbo (Acting)

Civil & Criminal Courts
101 E State St, PO Box 631, Olean, NY 14760
Acting Chief Clerk:
     Rhonda Eaton 716-376-5620/fax: 716-376-5623
     e-mail: reaton@nycourts.gov

Oneida

Judges
Anthony P Eppolito   Michael J Misiaszek

Civil & Criminal Courts
Municipal Bldg, 108 N Main St, Oneida, NY 13421
e-mail: oneidacitycourt@courts.state.ny.us
Chief Clerk:
     Lynne Mondrick 315-266-4740/fax: 646-963-6435

Oneonta

Judges
Lucy P Bernier   Richard W. McVinney

Civil & Criminal Courts
Public Safety Bldg, 81 Main St, Oneonta, NY 13820
Chief Clerk:
     Catherine J Tisenchek............607-432-4480/fax: 646-963-6433

Oswego

Judges
James M Metcalf   David J Roman

Civil & Criminal Courts
Conway Municipal Ctr, 20 W Oneida St, Oswego, NY 13126
e-mail: osw_city_ct@courts.state.ny.us
Chief Clerk:
     Cassie Kinney 315-343-0415/fax: 315-266-4752

Peekskill

Judges
Thomas R Langan   Reginald Johnson

Civil & Criminal Courts
2 Nelson Ave, Peekskill, NY 10566
Chief Clerk:
     Concetta (Tina) Cardinale.........914-831-6480/fax: 914-736-1889

Plattsburgh

Judges
John F. Niles   Mark J Rogers

Civil & Criminal Courts
24 US Oval, Plattsburgh, NY 12903
Chief Clerk:
     Kimberly Crow 518-563-7870/fax: 518-453-8624

Port Jervis

Judges
James M Hendry III   Matthew D. Witherow

Civil & Criminal Courts
20 Hammond St, Port Jervis, NY 12771
Chief Clerk:
     Catherine Quinn 845-476-3700/fax: 845-476-3691

Poughkeepsie

Judges
Frank M. Mora   Katherine A. Moloney

Civil & Criminal Courts
62 Civic Ctr Plaza, Poughkeepsie, NY 12601
Chief Clerk:
     Jean Jicha 845-483-8200/fax: 845-451-4094

Rensselaer

Judges
Kathleen L Robichaud   Carmelo Laquidara

Civil & Criminal Courts
City Hall, 62 Washington Street, Rensselaer, NY 12144
e-mail: rensselaercitycourt@nycourts.gov
Chief Clerk:
     Barbara Agans..................518-453-4680/fax: 518-453-8996

Rochester

Judges
Melchor E Castro (Acting)   Charles F Crimi
Mija Dixon   Teresa D Johnson
Stephen T Miller   Thomas R Morse
John R Schwartz   Ellen Yacknin

Civil Court ....fax: 585-428-2588
99 Exchange Boulevard, 6 Hall of Justice, Rochester, NY 14614
585-371-3412 Fax: 585-428-2588

Offices and agencies generally appear in alphabetical order, except when specific order is requested by listee.

Chief Clerk:
Sandra Petrella 585-428-3527

Criminal Court . . . . .fax: 585-371-3430
123 Public Safety Bldg, Rochester, NY 14614
585-371-3413 Fax: 585-371-3430
Chief Clerk:
Sandra Petrella 585-428-3527

Rome

Judges
John C Gannon   Gregory J. Amoroso

Civil & Criminal Courts
100 W Court St, Rome, NY 13440
Chief Clerk:
James Jecen .315-337-6440/fax: 315-338-0343

Rye

Judges
Joseph L. Latwin   Robert S. Cypher

Civil & Criminal Courts
21 McCullough Pl, Rye, NY 10580
Chief Clerk:
Antoinette Cipriano 914-831-6400/fax: 914-831-6546

Salamanca

Judges
William J Gabler   Alan L Spears

Civil & Criminal Courts
225 Wildwood Ave, Salamanca, NY 14779
Chief Clerk:
Stella Johnston 716-945-4153/fax: 716-945-2362
e-mail: ssjohnst@courts.state.ny.us

Saratoga Springs

Judges
James E Doern   Jeffrey D. Wait

Civil & Criminal Courts
City Hall, 474 Broadway, Ste 3, Saratoga Springs, NY 12866
Chief Clerk:
Susan Lewis 518-451-8780/fax: 518-453-8686

Schenectady

Judges
Mark W. Blanchfield   Guido A Loyola
Mark J Caruso   Robert W Hoffman

Civil Court
City Hall, 105 Jay St, Schenectady, NY 12305
Chief Clerk:
Robin Farmer 518-453-6989/fax: 518-285-8983

Criminal Court
531 Liberty St, Schenectady, NY 12305
Chief Clerk:
Robin Farmer 518-382-5077/fax: 518-453-8984

Sherrill

Judges
James W Betro

Civil & Criminal Courts
373 Sherrill Rd, Sherrill, NY 13461

Chief Clerk:
Carol A Shea 315-363-0996/fax: 315-363-1176

Syracuse

Judges
Vanessa E Bogan   James H Cecile
Stephen J Dougherty   Rory A. McMahon
Theodore H. Limpert   Mary Anne Doherty
Kate Rosenthal   Ross P Andrews
Karen M Uplinger

Civil & Criminal Courts
505 S State St, Syracuse, NY 13202
Chief Clerk:
Lucia Sander 315-671-2700/fax: 315-671-2741

Tonawanda

Judges
Joseph J Cassata   Dean Lilac

Civil & Criminal Courts . . . . .fax: 716-845-7590
200 Niagara St, Tonawanda, NY 14150
716-845-2160 Fax: 716-845-7590
Chief Clerk:
Mary Strobel 716-845-2164
e-mail: mstrobel@nycourts.gov

Troy

Judges
Christopher T Maier   Jill Kehn
Matthew J Turner

Civil & Criminal Court
51 State St, 2nd & 3rd Floors, Troy, NY 12180
Chief Clerk:
Karen DeBenedetto 518-453-5900/fax: 518-274-2816
e-mail: troycitycourt@nycourts.gov

Utica

Judges
John S Balzano   Ralph J Eannace
Gerald J Popeo

Civil & Criminal Courts
411 Oriskany St W, Utica, NY 13502
315-266-4600
Chief Clerk:
Steven V Pecheone 315-266-4606/fax: 315-792-8038

Watertown

Judges
Catherine J. Palermo   Eugene R Renzi

Civil & Criminal Courts
Municipal Bldg, 245 Washington St, Watertown, NY 13601
Chief Clerk:
Benjamin Cobb 315-785-7785/fax: 315-785-7856

Watervliet

Judges
Thomas Lamb   Susan B Reinfurt

Civil & Criminal Courts
2 - 15th St, Watervliet, NY 12189
Chief Clerk:
Robin Robillard 518-453-5550/fax: 518-453-8995
e-mail: watervlietcitycourt@nycourts.gov

Offices and agencies generally appear in alphabetical order, except when specific order is requested by listee.

White Plains

Judges

JoAnn Friia

Barbara A Leak

Brian Hansbury

Eric P Press

Civil & Criminal Courts

77 S Lexington Ave, White Plains, NY 10601

Chief Clerk:

Eileen Byrne .914-824-5675/fax: 914-824-5858

Yonkers

Judges

Robert C Cerrato

Arthur J Doran, III

Edward J. Gaffney

Michael A Martinelli

Thomas R Daly

MaryAnne Scattaretico-Naber

Evan Inlaw

Civil & Criminal Courts

100 S Broadway, Yonkers, NY 10701

Chief Clerk:

Marisa Garcia 914-831-6450/fax: 914-377-6395

Offices and agencies generally appear in alphabetical order, except when specific order is requested by listee.

Section 2:
POLICY AREAS

AGRICULTURE

NEW YORK STATE

GOVERNOR'S OFFICE

Governor's Office
Executive Chamber
State Capitol
Albany, NY 12224
518-474-8390 Fax: 518-474-1513
Web site: www.ny.gov

Governor:
Andrew M Cuomo 518-474-8390
Secretary to the Governor:
William Mulrow 518-474-4246
Counsel to the Governor:
Alphonso David 518-474-8343
Director, Communications:
Melissa DeRosa . . . . .518-474-8418 or 212-681-4640
Deputy Secretary, Food & Agriculture:
Patrick Hooker 518-486-3960
Chairman of Energy & Finance for New York:
Richard Kauffman. 518-681-4580

EXECUTIVE DEPARTMENTS AND RELATED AGENCIES

Agriculture & Markets Department
10B Airline Dr
Albany, NY 12235
518-457-3880 Fax: 518-457-3087
e-mail: info@agriculture.ny.gov
Web site: www.agriculture.ny.gov

Commissioner:
Richard Ball 518-457-8876
First Deputy Commissioner:
Jen McCormick. 518-457-2771
e-mail: jen.mccormick@agriculture.ny.gov
Deputy Commissioner, Administration:
Phil Giltner 518-457-2771
e-mail: phil.giltner@agriculture.ny.gov
Deputy Commissioner:
Ron Rausch. 518-485-7728
e-mail: ron.rausch@agriculture.ny.gov
Deputy Commissioner:
Jackie Moody-Czub .518-485-7728
e-mail: jackie.moody-czub@agriculture.ny.gov
Director, Internal Audit:
Joe Morrissey 518-485-2771
e-mail: j.morrissey@agriculture.ny.gov
Agency Emergency Management Coordinator:
Kelly Nilsson 518-457-2771
e-mail: kelly.nilsson@agriculture.ny.gov
Special Assistant:
Geoff Palmer. 518-457-2771
e-mail: geoff.palmer@agriculture.ny.gov
Special Assistant:
Sue Gold 518-457-2771
e-mail: sue.gold@agriculture.ny.gov
Special Assistant:
Frank Rooney 518-485-7728
e-mail: frank.rooney@agriculture.ny.gov
Public Information Officer:
Jola Szubielski. 518-485-7728/fax: 518-457-3087
e-mail: jola.szubielski@agriculture.ny.gov

Agricultural Development Division
Director, Agricultural Development:
Kevin King 518-457-7076/fax: 518-457-2716
e-mail: kevin.king@agriculture.ny.gov

Agricultural Districts
Manager:
Bob Somers. 518-457-2713
e-mail: bob.somers@agriculture.ny.gov

Animal Industry . . . . .fax: 518-485-7773
Director:
Dr. David Smith 518-457-3502
e-mail: david.smith@agriculture.ny.gov
Companion Animal & Dog Licensing:
Peter Leal 518-485-7965
Milk Ring Tests:
Erin Bond 518-457-7757
DAHP & Pullorum:
Mary Beth Fitzgerald 518-457-5558
NYSCHAP, Tuberculosis & Brucellosis:
Vacant. 518-457-5365
Animal Exports & Imports:
Sharon Blanch 518-457-3971
Veterinarian Accreditation:
Pam Hull 518-485-9964

Counsel's Office . . . . .fax: 518-457-8842
Counsel:
Susan Rosenthal .518-457-1059
e-mail: susan.rosenthal@agriculture.ny.gov
Supervising Attorney:
Michael McCormick. 518-457-2449
Penalty Litigation Unit:
Nancy Bogaard 518-485-8741

Fiscal Management . . . . .fax: 518-485-7750
Director:
Lucy Roberson 518-457-2080
e-mail: lucy.roberson@agriculture.ny.gov

Food Laboratory . . . . .fax: 518-485-8097
Director:
Daniel Rice 518-457-4477
e-mail: daniel.rice@agriculture.ny.gov
Assistant Director:
Debra Oglesby 518-485-5012
Associate Food Chemist:
Robert Sheridan .518-457-8885
Associate Food Chemist:
Virginia Greene. .518-485-8098

Food Safety & Inspection . . . . .fax: 518-485-8986
Director:
Stephen Stich 518-457-4492
e-mail: stephen.stich@agriculture.ny.gov
Assistant Director:
John Luker 518-457-5382
Director, Field Operations:
Erin Sawyer. 518-457-5380
Food Products Quality Manager:
William Lyons 518-457-2090
Supervisor, Compliance:
Vacant. 518-457-2840
Poultry, Fruit & Vegetable Inspector:
Michael Jones 518-457-2090

Field Operations
Brooklyn . . . . .fax: 718-722-2510
55 Hanson Place, Rm 378, Brooklyn, NY 11217-1583
Chief Inspector:
Richard Olson 718-722-2876

Offices and agencies generally appear in alphabetical order, except when specific order is requested by listee.

Buffalo ....fax: 716-847-3155
535 Washington Ave, Ste 203, Buffalo, NY 14203
Supervising Inspector:
Dan Gump 716-847-3185
Albany
10B Airline Drive, Albany, NY 12235
Vacant
Rochester ....fax: 716-424-1248
900 Jefferson Rd, Rochester, NY 14623
Supervising Food Inspector:
Evelyn Miles 585-427-0200
Syracuse ....fax: 315-487-1064
Art & Home Center, New York State Fairgrounds, Syracuse, NY 13209
Supervising Food Regional Supervisor:
Vacant 315-487-0852

Human Resources ....fax: 518-457-8852
Director:
Mark Vanderpoel 518-457-3216
e-mail: mark.vanderpoel@agriculture.ny.gov

Information Systems ....fax: 518-457-7815
Director:
Wendy Scheening 518-457-7368
e-mail: wendy.scheening@agriculture.ny.gov

Kosher Law Enforcement
Rabbi/Director:
Rabbi Aaron Metzger 718-722-2852
e-mail: aaron.metzger@agriculture.ny.gov

Milk Control & Dairy Services ....fax: 518-485-8730
Director, Milk Control:
Casey McCue 518-457-1772
e-mail: casey.mccue@agriculture.ny.gov
Director, Dairy Services:
Charles Huff 518-457-1772
e-mail: charlie.huff@agriculture.ny.gov
Market Research Information & Reporting:
David Del Cogliano 518-457-1772
e-mail: david.delcogliano@agriculture.ny.gov

New York City Office ....fax: 718-722-2510
55 Hanson Place, Brooklyn, NY 11217-1583
Chief, Food Safety & Inspection:
Rich Olson 718-722-2876

Plant Industry ....fax: 518-457-1204
Director:
Christopher Logue 518-457-2087
e-mail: christopher.logue@agriculture.ny.gov

Soil & Water Conservation Committee ....fax: 518-457-3412
10B Airline Dr, Albany, NY 12235
518-457-3738 Fax: 518-457-3412
Web site: www.nys-soilandwater.org
Chair:
George Proios 518-457-3738
Executive Director:
Michael Latham 518-457-3738
e-mail: michael.latham@agriculture.ny.gov
Coordinator, Agricultural Environmental Management Program:
Greg Albrecht 607-330-1242
e-mail: greg.albrecht@agriculture.ny.gov

State Fair ....fax: 315-487-9260
581 State Fair Blvd, Syracuse, NY 13209
315-487-7711 Fax: 315-487-9260
Web site: www.nysfair.org
Acting Director:
Troy Waffner 315-487-7711 x1200

Statistics ....fax: 518-453-6564
Fax: 518-453-6564
e-mail: naas-ny@nass.usda.gov
Web site: www.nass.usda.gov/ny
Director:
Blair Smith 518-487-5570
e-mail: blair.smith@nass.usda.gov

Weights & Measures ....fax: 518-457-5693
Director:
Mike Sikula...............................518-457-3146
e-mail: mike.sikula@agriculture.ny.gov
Metrologist:
Edward Szesnat............................518-457-4781

NEW YORK STATE LEGISLATURE

See Legislative Branch in Section 1 for additional Standing Committee and Subcommittee information.

Assembly Standing Committees

Agriculture
Chair:
William Magee (D)........................518-455-4807
Ranking Minority Member:
Kenneth Blankenbush (R) 518-455-5797

Assembly Task Force

Food, Farm & Nutrition, Task Force on
Chair:
Addie Russell (D)........................518-455-5545
Program Manager:
Robert Stern 518-455-5203

Senate Standing Committees

Agriculture
Chair:
Patricia Ritchie (R).....................518-455-3438
Ranking Minority Member:
Marc Panepinto (D) 518-455-2350

Senate/Assembly Legislative Commissions

Rural Resources, Legislative Commission on
Senate Chair:
Catharine Young (R)......................518-455-3563
Assembly Chair:
Frank Skartados (D) 518-455-5762
Republican Counsel:
Barbara McRedmond..............518-455-2069/fax: 518-426-6919

U.S. GOVERNMENT

EXECUTIVE DEPARTMENTS AND RELATED AGENCIES

Commodity Futures Trading Commission
Three Lafayette Centre
1155 21st Street, NW
Washington, DC 20581
202-418-5000 Fax: 202-418-5521
e-mail: questions@cftc.gov
Web site: www.cftc.gov

Offices and agencies generally appear in alphabetical order, except when specific order is requested by listee.

Eastern Region
One World Trade Center, Suite 3747, New York, NY 10048
212-466-2071
Deputy Regional Counsel:
Terry S. Arbit

US Commerce Department
1401 Constitution Avenue, NW
Washington, DC 20230
202-482-2000
Web site: www.commerce.gov

National Oceanic & Atmospheric Administration
1401 Constitution Avenue, NW, Room 5128, Washington, DC 20230

National Weather Service, Eastern Region
630 Johnson Ave, Bohemia, NY 11716
e-mail: erhwebmaster@noaa.gov
Web site: www.nws.noaa.gov
Deputy Chief ERH:
Jason Tuell, P.H.D. 631-244-0101
e-mail: jason.tuell@noaa.gov
Regional Program Manager:
John Koch. 631-244-0104
e-mail: john.koch@noaa.gov
Meteorologist:
Jeff Waldstreicher. 631-244-0131
e-mail: jeff.waldstreicher@noaa.gov
Chief, Meteorological Services Division:
John Guiney 631-244-0121
e-mail: john.guiney@noaa.gov
Chief, Regional Hydrology Division:
Reggina Cabrera
e-mail: reggina.cabrera@noaa.gov
Chief, Scientific Services Division:
Kenneth Johnson 631-244-0136
e-mail: kenneth.johnson@noaa.gov

US Department of Agriculture
1400 Independence Avenue SW
Washington, DC 20250
Web site: www.usda.gov

Agricultural Marketing Service
1445 Federal Drive, Montgomery, AL 36107
334-223-7488
e-mail: amsadministratoroffice@ams.usda.gov

Dairy Programs
Web site: www.ams.usda.gov/AMSv1.0/dairy
Northeast Marketing Area
302A Washington Avenue Extension, Albany, NY 12203-7303
e-mail: MAAlbany@fedmilk1.com
Web site: www.fmmone.com
Market Administrator:
Erik F Rasmussen 518-452-4410

Fruit & Vegetable Division
e-mail: http://www.ams.usda.gov/AMSv1.0/fv
Fresh Products Branch—Bronx Field Office . . . . . fax: 718-589-5108
465B New York City Terminal Market, Bronx, NY 10474-7351
718-991-7665 or 888-213-5151 Fax: 718-589-5108
Officer-in-Charge:
Geno DeSanto 718-991-7665
Fresh Products Branch—Albany Office . . . . fax: 518-485-8986
10B Airline Drive, Albany, NY 12235
518-485-8764 Fax: 518-485-8986
Director, Food Product Quality:
William Lyons 518-485-8764

USDA-AMS Poultry Grading Branch
Gastonia Region—New York Office . . . . .fax: 518-459-5163
21 Aviation Rd, Albany, NY 12205
Federal-State Supervisor:
Dennis McAuliffe. 518-459-5487/fax: 518-459-5163
e-mail: dennis.mcauliffe@ams.usda.gov

Agricultural Research Service

North Atlantic Area
Ithaca NY Research Units
Robert W Holley Center for Agriculture & Health . fax: 607-225-2459
Tower Road, Cornell University, Ithaca, NY 14853
607-255-4549 Fax: 607-225-2459
Center Director & Research Leader:
Leon V. Kochian 607-255-2454
e-mail: Leon.Kochian@ars.usda.gov
Geneva NY Research Units
Plant Genetic Resources & Grape Genetic Research Units . . . . fax:
315-787-2483
Grape Genetics Research Unit, USDA, ARS, 630 West North Street,
Geneva, NY 14456
315-787-2442 Fax: 315-787-2483
Research Leader (BIPMR):
Donna Gibson 607-255-2359/fax: 607-255-1132

Animal & Plant Health Inspection Service
Web site: www.aphis.usda.gov

Plant Protection Quarantine (PPQ) Programs-Eastern Region . . . . fax:
919-855-7295
920 Main Campus Dr, Ste 200, Raleigh, NC 27606
919-855-7250 Fax: 919-855-7295
Regional Domestic Program Manager:
Ronald D. Weeks Jr., Ph.D.
Avoca Work Unit . . . . .fax: 607-566-2081
8237 Kanona Rd, Avoca, NY 14809-9729
Director:
Daniel J Kepich 607-566-2212
e-mail: daniel.j.kepich@aphis.usda.gov
Batavia Work Station . . . . .fax: 585-343-5538
29 Liberty St, Ste 1, Batavia, NY 14020
PPQ Officer:
Lewis Tandy 585-343-9167 x1033
e-mail: lewis.tandy@aphis.usda.gov
Big Flats Work Station . . . . .fax: 607-562-3470
USDA Plant Material Ctr, 3266-B State Rte 352, Corning, NY 14830
PPQ Officer:
Lawrence R Kershaw. 607-562-3459
Canandaigua Work Station .fax: 585-394-8367
3037 County Rd 10, Canandaigua, NY 14424
Senior PPQ Officer:
Cynthia A Estey 585-394-0525 x5
e-mail: cynthia.a.estey@aphis.usda.gov
JFK International Airport Inspection Station
230-59 Intl Airport Ctr Blvd, Jamaica, NY 11430
Supervisory VMO:
Dr. Lori Harms 718-553-3570/fax: 718-553-3572
New York State Office . . . . .fax: 518-218-7545
500 New Karner Rd, 2nd Floor, Albany, NY 12205-3857
State Plant Health Director:
Diana Hoffman 518-218-7510
e-mail: Diana.L.Hoffman@aphis.usda.gov
Oneida Work Station
248 Main St, 1st Fl, Oneida, NY 13421
Senior PPQ Officer:
Paul F Wrege 315-361-4281/fax: 315-363-3657
e-mail: paul.f.wrege@usda.gov
Westhampton Beach Work Station . . . . .fax: 631-288-6021
4 Stewart Ave, Westhampton Beach, NY 11978-1103
PPQ Officer:
Willy Hsiang 631-288-4191

Offices and agencies generally appear in alphabetical order, except when specific order is requested by listee.

Veterinary Services
NY Animal Import Center . . . . fax: 845-564-1075
474 International Blvd, Rock Tavern, NY 12575
845-564-2950 Fax: 845-564-1075
e-mail: http://www.aphis.usda.gov/animal health/
Supervisory VMO:
Dr. Kenneth Davis 845-838-5500/fax: 845-838-5516
New York Area Office
500 New Karner Rd, 2nd Fl, Albany, NY 12205
Veterinarian-in-Charge, New York Area:
Dr Roxanne C Mullaney 518-218-7540/fax: 518-218-7545

Cornell Cooperative Extension Service
Cornell University, Roberts Hall, Room 365, Ithaca, NY 14853

Farm Service Agency, New York State Office . . . fax: 315-477-6323
441 S Salina St, Suite 536, Syracuse, NY 13202
State Executive Director:
James Barber. 315-477-6301
e-mail: james.barber@ny.usda.gov

Food & Nutrition Service

Albany Field Office . . . . fax: 518-431-4271
O'Brien Federal Bldg, Rm 752, Clinton Ave & N Pearl St, Albany, NY
12207
518-431-4274 Fax: 518-431-4271
Regional Administrator:
James Arena-DeRosa 617-565-6370

New York City Field Office . . . . fax: 212-620-6948
201 Varick St, Rm 609, New York, NY 10014
212-620-7360 Fax: 212-620-6948
Assistant Director:
Denise Thomas 212-620-7360

Food Safety & Inspection Service
Web site: www.fsis.usda.gov

National Agricultural Statistics Service-NY Field Office . . . . . fax:
518-485-8719
10B Airline Dr, Albany, NY 12235
800-821-1276 or 518-457-5570 Fax: 518-485-8719
e-mail: nass-ny@nass.usda.gov
Director:
King J. Whetstone 518-457-5570

Office of the Inspector General, Northeast Region . . . . fax:
301-504-2437
26 Federal Plaza, Room 1409, New York, NY 10278-0004
Special Agent-in-Charge:
William Squires 212-264-8400
Assistant Special Agent-in-Charge:
Beth Dinkins

Rural Development
Web site: www.rurdev.usda.gov/ny

New York State Regional Offices . . . . fax: 315-477-6438
441 South Salina Street, Suite 357, Syracuse, NY 13202
315-477-6400 or TTY:315-477-6447 Fax: 315-477-6438
State Director:
Stanley Telega 315-477-6437
Eastern Region Area Director:
Ronda Falkena . . . . 845-343-1872 ext. 4
Northern Region Area Director:
Brian Murray . . . . 315-386-2401 ext. 4
Western Region Area Director:
Jim Walfrand 585-343-9167 x.2200
Regional Director:
Elkin Parker 404-562-5840
e-mail: elkin.w.parker@usda.gov

US Department of Homeland Security (DHS)
Web site: www.dhs.gov

Customs & Border Protection (CBP)
877-272-5511
Web site: www.cbp.gov

Agricultural Inspections (AI)
Albany, Port of . . . . fax: 518-431-0203
445 Broadway, Room 216, Albany, NY 12207
518-431-0200 Fax: 518-431-0203
Port Director:
Andrew Westcott 518-431-0200/fax: 518-431-0203
Alexandria Bay . . . . fax: 315-482-5304
46735 Interstate Route 81, Alexandria Bay, NY 13607
315-482-2065 Fax: 315-482-5304
Supervisory CBPO:
Darren Erwin . . . . 315-482-5004 x. 2390
Binghamton Airport . . . . fax: 607-763-4292
2534 Airport Road, Box 4, Johnson City, NY 13790
607-763-4294 Fax: 607-763-4292
Port Director:
Vacant
Buffalo, Port of
726 Exchange Street, Suite 400, Buffalo, NY 14210
Supervisory CBP Officer:
Gary Friedman
Champlain, Port of . . . . fax: 518-298-8395
237 West Service Road, Champlain, NY 12919
518-298-8311 Fax: 518-298-8395
Public Affairs Liaison:
Richard Misztal. . . . . 716-626-0400 x. 204
JFK International Airport Area Office . . . . fax: 718-487-5191
John F. Kennedy International Airport, Building #77, Jamaica, NY
11430
718-487-5164 Fax: 718-487-5191
OFO Public Affairs Liasion:
John Saleh 646-733-3215
Customs Supervisor:
James Armstrong
Massena, Port of
30M Seaway International Bridge, Rooseveltown, NY 13683
315-769-3091
SCBPO:
Tracey S. Casey 315-769-3091 x.7041
Ogdensburg, Port of
Ogdensburg Bridge Plaza, 104 Bridge Approach, Ogdensburg, NY
13669
315-393-1390
Public Affairs Liaison:
Richard Misztal 716-626-0400 x.204/fax: 716-626-1164
Rochester, Port of . . . . fax: 585-263-5828
1200 Brooks Avenue, Rochester, NY 14624
585-263-6293 Fax: 585-263-5828
Port Director:
Charles Junta 585-263-6293
Syracuse, Port of
152 Air Cargo Road, Suite 201, North Syracuse, NY 13212
315-455-8446
Port Director:
Patrick Cohan. 315-455-8446
Trout River, Port of . . . . fax: 518-483-3717
17013 State Route 30, Constable, NY 12926
518-483-0821 x.229 Fax: 518-483-3717
Port Director:
Marry Ellen O'Shea 518-483-0821 x.229/fax: 518-483-3717

Offices and agencies generally appear in alphabetical order, except when specific order is requested by listee.

U.S. CONGRESS

See U.S. Congress Chapter for additional Standing Committee and Subcommittee information.

House of Representatives Standing Committees

Agriculture
Committee Chair:
Frank D. Lucas (R-OK-3)
Ranking Member:
Collin C. Peterson

Appropriations
Chair:
Hal Rogers (R-KY)
Ranking Minority Member:
Nita Lowey (D-NY)
New York Delegate:
Bill Owens (D)
New York Delegate:
Jose E Serrano (D)

Subcommittee
Agriculture, Rural Development, FDA & Related Agencies
Chair:
Robert Aderholt (R-AL) 202-225-2638
Ranking Member:
Sam Farr (D-CA)

Senate Standing Committees

Agriculture, Nutrition & Forestry
Chair:
Debbie Stabenow (D-MI)
Ranking Member:
Thad Cochran (R-MI)

Appropriations
Chair:
Barbara Mikulski (D-MD) 202-224-7363
Vice Chair:
Richard Shelby (R-AL)

Subcommittee
Agriculture, Rural Development, FDA & Related Agencies
Chair:
Mark Pryor (D-AR) 202-224-7363
Ranking Member:
Roy Blount (R-MO)

PRIVATE SECTOR

Agricultural Affiliates
638 Lake St, PO Box 10, Wilson, NY 14172-0010
716-751-9331 Fax: 716-751-6141
e-mail: agaffiliat@aol.com
Advise & inform agriculture industry on labor issues & related public policy
Peter Russell, President

American Farmland Trust, New York Office
112 Spring Street, Suite 207, Saratoga Springs, NY 12866
518-581-0078 Fax: 518-581-0079
e-mail: newyork@farmland.org
Web site: www.farmland.org/newyork
Advocacy & education to protect farmland & promote environmentally sound farming practices
David Haight, New York State Director
Tammy Holtby, Operations Coordinator

American Society for the Prevention of Cruelty to Animals (ASPCA)
424 E 92nd St, New York, NY 10128-6804
212-876-7700 x4552 Fax: 212-360-6875
e-mail: government@aspca.org
Web site: www.aspca.org
Promoting humane treatment of animals, education & advocacy programs & conducting statewide anti-cruelty investigation & enforcement
Lisa Weisberg, Senior Vice President, Government Affairs & Public Policy, Senior Policy Advisor

Associated New York State State Food Processors Inc
16 Loretta Dr, Ste 100, Spencerport, NY 14559
585-352-7766 Fax: 585-349-2334
e-mail: jackie@nyfoodprocessors.org
Web site: www.nyfoodprocessors.org
Jacqueline J Arnold, Executive Secretary

Birds Eye Foods Inc
90 Linden Oaks, PO Box 20670, Rochester, NY 14602-0670
585-383-1850
e-mail: media@birdseyefoods.com
Web site: www.birdseyefoods.com
Produces & markets processed food products
Bea Slizewski, Vice President, Corporate Communications

Christmas Tree Farmers Association of New York Inc
646 Finches Corners Rd, Red Creek, NY 13143
315-754-8132 Fax: 315-754-8499
Web site: www.christmastreesny.org
Fresh Christmas trees & evergreen wreaths
Robert D Norris, Executive Director

Consumers Union
101 Truman Ave, Yonkers, NY 10703-1057
914-378-2000 Fax: 914-378-2900
Web site: www.consumerreports.org; www.consumersunion.org
Food safety issues including genetically engineered food, microbial safety of food, toxic chemical issues, pesticides, integrated pest management, sustainable agriculture
Jean Halloran, Director, Consumer Policy Institute

Community & Regional Development Institute (CaRDI)
Cornell Cooperative Extension
365 Roberts Hall, Cornell University, Ithaca, NY 14853-5905
607-255-2170 Fax: 607-255-0788
e-mail: rlh13@cornell.edu
Web site: www.cce.cornell.edu
Extension educational system & outreach
Rod Howe,

Community & Regional Development Institute
43 Warren Hall, Cornell University, Ithaca, NY 14853
607-255-9510 Fax: 607-255-2231
e-mail: cardi@cornell.edu
Web site: www.cardi.cornell.edu
Provides research, education & policy analysis on critical community & regional development issues
Rod Howe, Executive Director

Cornell Cooperative Extension, Pesticide Management Education Program
5142 Comstock Hall, Cornell University, Ithaca, NY 14853-0901
607-255-1866 Fax: 607-255-3075
e-mail: rdg5@cornell.edu
Web site: pmep.cce.cornell.edu
Ronald D Gardner, Senior Extension Associate

Offices and agencies generally appear in alphabetical order, except when specific order is requested by listee.

Cornell Cooperative Extension, Urban Agriculture & Markets Program
Cornell University, 16 East 34th St, New York, NY 10016
212-340-2946 Fax: 212-340-2908
e-mail: jma20@cornell.edu
Web site: www.cce.cornell.edu
Farmer recruitment & training for urban farmers' markets; community gardens advisory; food access/food security policy
John Ameroso, Extension Educator

Cornell Farmedic Training Program
Cornell University, 777 Warren Rd, Ithaca, NY 14850
800-437-6010 Fax: 607-253-3907
e-mail: farmedic@cornell.edu
Web site: www.farmedic.com
Training programs for emergency providers & agricultural workers to reduce mortality, injury & property loss from agricultural emergencies
Eric Hallman, Director Ag. Health & Safety Program

Cornell University, Department of Applied Economics & Management
357 Warren Hall, Ithaca, NY 14853-7801
607-255-4534 Fax: 607-255-1589
e-mail: ell4@cornell.edu
Web site: www.aem.cornell.edu/profiles/ladue.htm
Agricultural finance
Eddy L LaDue, W I Myers Professor of Agricultural Finance
Duncan Hilchey, Agricultural Development Specialist

Cornell University, FarmNet Program
Dept of Applied Economics & Management, 415 Warren Hall, Ithaca, NY 14853-7801
607-255-4121 or 800-547-3276 Fax: 607-254-7435
e-mail: nyfarmnet@cornell.edu
Web site: www.nyfarmnet.org
Farm family resource library; financial & family consultations; workshops for agricultural services professionals & farmers
Ed Staehr, Program Director

Cornell University, Program on Dairy Markets & Policy
Agriculture & Life Sciences, 316 Warren Hall, Ithaca, NY 14853-7801
607-255-7602 Fax: 607-255-9984
e-mail: amn3@cornell.edu
Web site: www.cpdmp.cornell.edu
Applied research and extension education program
Andrew Novakovic, Director

Dairylea Cooperative Inc
PO Box 4844, Syracuse, NY 13221-4844
315-433-0100 or 800-654-8838 Fax: 315-433-2345
e-mail: clyde.rutherford@dairylea.com
Web site: www.dairylea.com
Maximizes net returns at the farm by preserving and enhancing milk markets and milk-marketing relationships, and by providing services and programs that create real economic value.
Clyde Rutherford, President

Empire State Honey Producers Association
273 Randall Rd, Lisbon, NY 13658
315-322-4208
e-mail: harmonydeb@starband.net
Web site: www.eshpa.org
Promote & protect the interests of beekeepers in NYS
Deborah Kalicin, Secretary/Treasurer

Empire State Potato Growers Inc
PO Box 566, Stanley, NY 14561-0566
585-526-5356 Fax: 585-526-6576
e-mail: mwickham@hypotatoes.org
Web site: www.hypotatoes.org
To foster the potato industry in NYS
Melanie Wickham, Executive Secretary

Farm Sanctuary
PO Box 150, Watkins Glen, NY 14891
607-583-2225 Fax: 607-583-2041
e-mail: info@farmsancturary.org
Web site: www.farmsanctuary.org
Farm animal rescue; public information programs & advocacy for the humane treatment of animals
Gene Baur, President

Farmers' Market Federation of NY
2100 Park St, Syracuse, NY 13208
315-475-1101 Fax: 315-362-5012
e-mail: diane.eggert@verizon.net
Web site: www.nyfarmersmarket.com
Education & services to NY's farmers markets.
Diane Eggert, Director

Food Industry Alliance of New York State Inc
130 Washington Ave, Albany, NY 12210
518-434-1900 Fax: 518-434-9962
e-mail: michael@fiany.com
Web site: www.fiany.com
Assn of retail grocery, wholesale & supplier/manufacturer food companies
Michael Rosen, Vice President for Government Relations & General Counsel

Fund for Animals (The)
200 W 57th St, New York, NY 10019
212-757-3425 or 212-246-2096 Fax: 212-246-2633
Web site: www.fund.org
Working to protect all animals through education, legislation, litigation & hands-on care
Marian Probst, Chair

New York State Flower Industries Inc
Garden Gate Greenhouse
11649 W Perrysburg Rd, Perrysburg, NY 14129
716-532-6282
Greenhouse plant production
Gary Patterson, President

Global Gardens Program, New York Botanical Garden (The)
200th St & Kazimiroff Blvd, Bronx, NY 10458-5126
718-817-8700 Fax: 718-817-8178
e-mail: emccarthy@nybg.org
Web site: www.nybg.org
Promoting understanding of ethnic diversity & the interconnectedness of cultures through gardening
Toby Adams, Family Garden Manager

GreenThumb
49 Chambers Street, Room 1020, New York, NY 10007
212-788-8070 Fax: 212-788-8052
e-mail: edie@greenthumbnyc.org
Web site: www.greenthumbnyc.org
Development & preservation of community gardens; reclamation of urban land for green space
Edie Stone, Director

Greenmarket/Council on the Environment of NYC
51 Chambers Street, Room 228, New York, NY 10007
212-788-7900 Fax: 212-788-7913
e-mail: info@grownyc.org
Web site: www.grownyc.org
Direct to consumer farmers' markets, sustainable agriculture
Marcel Van Doyen, Executive Director

Hill & Gosdeck
99 Washington Ave, Ste 400, Albany, NY 12210-2823
518-463-5449 x3102 Fax: 518-463-0947
e-mail: tomgosdeck@hillandgoosdeck.com
Workers compensation, group self insurance and food industry regulation
Thomas J Gosdeck, Partner

Offices and agencies generally appear in alphabetical order, except when specific order is requested by listee.

Humane Society of the United States, Mid Atlantic Regional Office
270 US Hwy 206, Flanders, NJ 07836
973-927-5611 Fax: 973-927-5617
e-mail: maro@hsus.org
Web site: www.hsus.org
Nina Austenberg, Regional Director

Long Island Farm Bureau
104 Edwards Ave, Suite 3, Calverton, NY 11923
631-727-3777 Fax: 631-727-3721
e-mail: askus@lifb.com
Web site: www.lifb.com
Provides strong, networked and allied Farm Bureau organizations at the local, state and national organization levels. Goal is to protect and strengthen the nation's agricultural industry.
Joseph M Gergela, III, Executive Director

Long Island Nursery & Landscape Association Inc
PO Box 1165, Farmingdale, NY 11735
516-249-0545 Fax: 516-249-0740
e-mail: linla@nysnla.com
A professional association serving retail garden center, nursery and landscape businesses on Long Island. Fosters professionalism in the green industry while cultivating a high standard of business ethics.
Kim Psinakis, Executive Secretary

National Potato Board
McCormick Farms Inc
4189 Route 78, Bliss, NY 14024
585-322-7274 Fax: 585-322-7495
James P McCormick, NYS Delegate

My-T Acres Inc
8127 Lewiston Rd, Batavia, NY 14020
585-343-1026 Fax: 585-343-2051
Vegetable crops & grain
Peter Call, Co-Owner

NOFA-NY Certified Organic LLC
840 Upper Front St, Binghamton, NY 13905-1542
607-724-9851 Fax: 607-724-9853
e-mail: certifiedorganic@nofany.org
Web site: www.nofany.org
Organic farming certification
Carol King, Certification Director

NY Farms!
125 Williams Rd, Candor, NY 13743
607-659-3710 or 888-NYFARMS Fax: 607-659-3710
e-mail: nyfarms@nyfarms.info
Web site: www.nyfarms.info
Campaign to promote farming & protect farmland in NYS
Gene Pierce, President

NYS Agricultural Society
493 Charlton Rd, Ballston Spa, NY 12020
518-384-1715
e-mail: penny@nysagsociety.org
Web site: www.nysagsociety.org
To improve the condition of agriculture through education, leadership development & recognition programs
Penny Heritage, Executive Secretary

NYS Arborists
PO Box 306, Pawling, NY 12564-0306
845-855-0225 Fax: 845-855-0387
e-mail: execsec@newyorkstatearborists.com
Web site: www.newyorkstatearborists.com
Professional arborists & educators; promote public interest, foster research & education in the care & benefits of trees, shrubs & their environment
David Hayner, Executive Secretary

NYS Association for Food Protection
Cornell University, Dept of Food Science, 116 Stocking Hall, Ithaca, NY 14853
607-255-2892 Fax: 607-255-7619
e-mail: jgg3@cornell.edu
Web site: www.foodscience.cornell.edu/nysfsanit/index.html
Janene Lucia, Executive Secretary

NYS Association of Veterinary Technicians Inc
119 Washington Ave, 2nd Floor, Albany, NY 12210
518-426-7920 Fax: 518-432-5902
e-mail: nysavt@aol.com
Web site: www.nysavt.org
Jan Dorman, Executive Director

NYS Berry Growers Association
14 State Street, Bloomfield, NY 14469
585-657-5328 Fax: 585-657-4642
e-mail: goodberries@frontiernet.net
Web site: www.nysbga.org
Jim Altemus, Executive Secretary

NYS Cheese Manufacturers Association, Department of Food Science
Cornell University, 116 Stocking Hall, Ithaca, NY 14853
607-255-2892 Fax: 607-255-7619
e-mail: jgg3@cornell.edu
Web site: www.newyorkcheese.org
Cheese manufacturing education & product promotion
Janene Lucia, Secretary

NYS Grange
100 Grange Place, Cortland, NY 13045
607-756-7553 Fax: 607-756-7757
e-mail: nysgrange@nysgrange.org
Web site: www.nysgrange.org
Advocacy, education & services for farm, rural & suburban families
Oliver J Orton, President

NYS Horticultural Society
630 W. North Street, Geneva, NY 14456
315-787-2404 Fax: 315-787-2216
e-mail: wilsonk36@hotmail.com
Web site: www.nyshs.org
Advocacy, education & member services for the fruit industry
Paul Baker, Executive Director

NYS Nursery/Landscape Association
24 Martin Road, Voorheesville, NY 12186
518-320-8760 or 877-210-4518 Fax: 518-694-4431
e-mail: nysnla@aol.com; suzannemm@nycap.rr.com
Web site: www.nylandscaper.com
Trade Association
Kimberly Tiberia, Executive Director

NYS Turfgrass Association
PO Box 612, Latham, NY 12110
518-783-1229 Fax: 518-783-1258
e-mail: nysta@nysta.org
Web site: www.nysta.org
Grow & manage turf for golf courses, ball fields & landscape
Beth Same, Executive Director

NYS Vegetable Growers Association Inc
PO Box 70, Kirkville, NY 13082-0070
315-687-5734 Fax: 315-687-5734
e-mail: nysvga@twcny.rr.com
Jeff & Lindy Kubecka, Co-Contacts

Offices and agencies generally appear in alphabetical order, except when specific order is requested by listee.

Policy Areas

NYS Weights & Measures Association
8292 State Rt 3, Harrisville, NY 13648
315-543-2820 Fax: 315-376-5874
e-mail: bcooper@lewiscountyny.org
Web site: lewiscountyny.net/wt-measures
Promote uniformity in measure accuracy, enforcement standards & legal requirements
Barbara J Cooper, Director

National Coffee Association
15 Maiden Ln, Ste 1405, New York, NY 10038
212-766-4007 Fax: 212-766-5815
e-mail: info@ncausa.org
Web site: www.ncausa.org
Robert F Nelson, President & Chief Executive Officer

National Grape Cooperative-Welch Foods Inc
575 Virginia Rd, 3 Concord Farms, Concord, MA 01742-9101
978-371-1000 Fax: 978-371-3707
Web site: www.welchs.com
Manufacturers of juices, jams and jellies.
Dave Lukiewski, President & Chief Executive Officer

New York Agriculture in the Classroom
Cornell University, Dept of Horticulture, 106 Kennedy Hall, Ithaca, NY 14853
607-255-9253 Fax: 607-255-7905
e-mail: nyaitc@cornell.edu
Web site: www.nyaged.org/aitc
An agricultural literacy program providing resources and professional development opportunities for teachers to facilitate the integration of food and fiber systems education into the curriculum

New York Apple Association Inc
7645 Main St, PO Box 350, Fishers, NY 14453-0350
585-924-2171 Fax: 585-924-1629
e-mail: jimallen@nyapplecountry.com
Web site: www.nyapplecountry.com
Promote NYS apples & apple products
James Allen, President

New York Beef Industry Council Inc
PO Box 250, Westmoreland, NY 13490
315-339-6922 Fax: 315-339-6931
e-mail: cgillis@nybeef.org
Web site: www.nybeef.org
Producer-directed & funded organization conducting beef promotion & information programs
Carol Gillis, Executive Director

New York Center for Agricultural Medicine & Health, Bassett Healthcare
1 Atwell Rd, Cooperstown, NY 13326
800-343-7527 or 607-547-6023 Fax: 607-547-6087
e-mail: info@nycamh.com
Web site: www.nycamh.com
Occupational health & medicine in agriculture
John May, MD, Director

New York Farm Bureau
159 Wolf Road, PO Box 5330, Albany, NY 12205-0330
518-436-8495 Fax: 800-342-4143
Web site: www.nyfb.org
Resources, education, advocacy, services & programs for the farming industry & community
Julie Suarez, Contact

New York Field Corn Growers Association
2269 DeWindt Rd, Newark, NY 14513
315-331-7791 Fax: 315-331-1294
e-mail: svanvoo338@aol.com
Web site: www.nycorn.org
Steven VanVoorhis, President

New York Holstein Association
957 Mitchell St, Ithaca, NY 14850
607-273-7591 or 800-834-4644 Fax: 607-273-7612
e-mail: pgifford@nyholsteins.com
Web site: www.nyholsteins.com
Promoting the Holstein breed for the economic & social benefit of junior & senior members
Patricia G Gifford, Executive Manager

New York Pork Producers Coop
4124 MacDougall Road, Waterloo, NY 13165
315-585-6276 Fax: 315-585-6278
e-mail: amsinc@wildblue.net
Web site: www.newyorkpork.org
Education & promotion of pork industry in NY
Jamie Mesmer, Executive Secretary/State Contact

New York Seed Improvement Project, Cornell University, Plant Breeding Department
103C Leland Lab, Cornell University, Ithaca, NY 14853
607-255-9869 Fax: 607-255-9048
e-mail: aaw4@cornell.edu
Web site: SeedPotato.NewYork.cornell.edu
Official seed certifying agency for the state of NY & foundation seedstocks agency
Alan Westra, Manager

New York State Association of Agricultural Fairs Inc
67 Verbeck Ave, Schaghticoke, NY 12154
518-753-4956 Fax: 518-753-0208
e-mail: carousels4@aol.com
Web site: www.nyfairs.org
Norma W Hamilton, Executive Secretary

New York State Dairy Foods Inc
201 S Main St, Suite 302, North Syracuse, NY 13212
315-452-6455 Fax: 315-452-1643
Web site: www.nysdfi.org
Full service trade association representing dairy processing/distribution industry
Bruce W Krupke, Executive Vice President

New York State Maple Producers Association Inc
PO Box 210, Watkins Glens, NY 14891
607-535-9790 Fax: 607-535-9794
Web site: www.nysmaple.com
Promoting quality maple products through education & research
Mary Jeanne Packer, Secretary

New York State Veterinary Medical Society
9 Highland Ave, Albany, NY 12205-5417
518-437-0787 or 800-876-9867 Fax: 518-437-0957
e-mail: info@nysvms.org
Web site: www.nysvms.org
Julie Lawton, Executive Director

New York Thoroughbred Breeders Inc
Saratoga Spa State Park, 19 Roosevelt Drive, Saratoga Springs, NY 12866
518-580-0100 Fax: 518-580-0500
e-mail: nybreds@nybreds.com
Web site: www.nybreds.com
Martin G Kinsella, Executive Director

Offices and agencies generally appear in alphabetical order, except when specific order is requested by listee.

New York Wine & Grape Foundation
800 South Main Street, Suite 200, Canadaigua, NY 14424
585-394-3620 Fax: 585-394-3649
e-mail: info@newyorkwines.org
Web site: www.newyorkwines.org
Promotion of winery products & tours; research for wine & grape related products
James Trezise, President

Northeast Organic Farming Association of New York
PO Box 880, Cobleskill, NY 12043
607-652-6632
e-mail: office@nofany.org
Web site: www.nofany.org
Education for farmers, gardeners & consumers; organic certification program
Greg Swartz, Executive Director

Community & Economic Development
PathStone Corporation
400 East Ave, Bronx, NY 14607-1910
585-340-3366 Fax: 585-340-3309
e-mail: lbeaulac@pathstone.org
Web site: www.pathstone.org
Lee Beaulac, Senior VP, CED

Public Markets Partners / Baum Forum
5454 Palisade Ave, Bronx, NY 10471
718-884-5716
e-mail: hilarybaum@aol.com
Web site: www.baumforum.org
Partnerships with communities to develop & manage public markets to revitalize urban areas & promote regional agriculture; educational programs
Hilary Baum, President

Regional Farm & Food Project
PO Box 8628, Albany, NY 12208
518-271-0744
e-mail: cheryl@farmandfood.org
Web site: www.farmandfood.org
Building supply and demand for farm fresh local foods in the Hudson-Mohawk Valley foodshed.
Cheryl Nechoma, Chair

Rural Opportunities, Inc
400 East Ave, Rochester, NY 14607-1910
585-340-3366 Fax: 585-340-3309
e-mail: lbeaulac@ruralinc.org
Web site: www.ruralinc.org
Housing & related assistance for farmworkers, seniors & the rural poor

Lee Beaulac, Senior Vice President

Seneca Foods Corporation
3736 South Main St, Marion, NY 14505
315-926-8100 Fax: 315-926-8300
e-mail: webmaster@senecafoods.com
Web site: www.senecafoods.com
Vegetable food products
Kraig H Kayser, President & CEO

NYS Bar Association
Special Committee on Animals & the Law
1 Elk Street, Albany, NY 12207
518-463-3200 Fax: 518-463-4276
e-mail: hkpassantino@aol.com
Web site: www.nysba.org
Holly Kennedy Passantino, Chair

Tea Association of the USA Inc
420 Lexington Ave, Suite 825, New York, NY 10170
212-986-9415 Fax: 212-697-8658
e-mail: info@teausa.com
Web site: www.teausa.com
Trade association for the tea industry
Joe Simrany, President

United Dairy Cooperative Services Inc
12 North Park St, Seneca Falls, NY 13148
315-568-2750 Fax: 315-568-2752
e-mail: unitedag@flare.net
Management, accounting & payroll services to agriculture industry
James G Patsos, Chief Executive Officer

Upstate Niagara Cooperative Inc
25 Anderson Rd, Buffalo, NY 14225
716-892-3156 Fax: 716-892-3157
Web site: www.upstateniagara.com
Bob Hall, General Manager & Chief Executive Officer

Venture Vineyards Inc
PO Box 185, Lodi, NY 14860
607-582-6774 Fax: 607-582-6342
e-mail: venturev@capital.net
Produce wholesaler of grapes/juices
Melvin P Nass, President

Offices and agencies generally appear in alphabetical order, except when specific order is requested by listee.

BANKING AND FINANCE

NEW YORK STATE

GOVERNOR'S OFFICE

Governor's Office
Executive Chamber
State Capitol
Albany, NY 12224
518-474-8390 Fax: 518-474-1513
Web site: www.ny.gov

Governor:
Andrew M Cuomo 518-474-8390
Secretary to the Governor:
William Mulrow. 518-474-4246
Counsel to the Governor:
Alphonso David 518-474-8343
Deputy Secretary, Technology:
Rachel Haot. 212-681-4573
Deputy Secretary for Financial Services:
George Haggerty. 518-474-5442
Director, Communications:
Melissa DeRosa . . . . .518-474-8418 or 212-681-4640

EXECUTIVE DEPARTMENTS AND RELATED AGENCIES

Financial Services Department
One State St
New York, NY 10004-1511
212-480-6400 or 518-474-6600
e-mail: public-affairs@dfs.ny.gov
Web site: www.dfs.ny.gov

Superintendent:
Benjamin M. Lawsky 212-709-3501/fax: 212-709-3520
Chief Administrative Officer:
Cheryl Aini 518-473-6160
Assistant Director, Administration & Operations:
Lori Fraser. 518-486-4737
Deputy Superintendent & General Counsel:
Marjorie Gross 212-709-1640
Deputy Superintendent, Community Regional Banks:
Martin Cofsky 212-709-1610
Director, Criminal Investigations Bureau:
Ricardo Velez 212-709-3554
Chief Information Officer:
William Rachmiel. 212-709-5420
Director, Public Affairs:
Andrew Mais. 212-480-5257/fax: 212-480-6077
e-mail: public-affairs@dfs.ny.gov
Senior Public Information Specialist:
Ronald Klug 212-480-2285
Consumer Representative, State Charter Advisory Board:
Vacant 212-709-3500

Banking Division
Deputy Superintendent:
Vacant 212-709-1690

Insurance Division
Deputy Superintendent, Property & Casual Markets:
Michael Moriarty. 212-480-5127/fax: 212-480-2310
Chief, Life Insurance Bureau:
Gail Keren 212-480-5030/fax: 212-480-5329

Chief, Health Insurance Bureau:
Vacant 518-486-2970
Chief Insurance Examiner 3:
Michael Maffei 212-480-5023

Financial Frauds & Consumer Protection Division
Director, Frauds:
Frank Orlando 212-480-5770/fax: 212-480-6066
Assistant Director, Frauds:
Angelo Carbone 212-480-5688

Capital Markets Division
Acting Director, Capital Markets:
Matti Peltonen 212-480-5071/fax: 212-480-6085

Real Estate Finance Division
Deputy Superintendent, Mortgage Banking:
Rhonda Ricketts 212-709-5540

Law Department
120 Broadway
New York, NY 10271-0332
212-416-8000 or 800-771-7755
Web site: www.ag.ny.gov

State Capitol
Albany, NY 12224-0341
518-474-5481
Fax: 518-473-9909

Attorney General:
Eric T Schneiderman . . . . .212-416-8050 or 518-474-7330
Director, Public Information:
Shawn Morris 518-776-2357/fax: 518-650-9401
Press Secretary:
Fernando Aquino . . . . .518-473-5525 or 212-416-8060
fax: 518-402-2271

Economic Justice
Executive Deputy Attorney General:
Karla Sanchez. 212-416-8050

Antitrust Bureau
Bureau Chief:
Eric J Stock .212-416-8262/fax: 212-416-6015
e-mail: eric.stock@ag.ny.gov

Consumer Frauds & Protection Bureau
Bureau Chief:
Jane Azia. 212-416-8300/fax: 212-416-8003

Internet Bureau
Bureau Chief:
Kathleen McGee 212-416-8433/fax: 212-416-8369
e-mail: ifraud@ag.ny.gov

Investor Protection Bureau
Bureau Chief:
Chad Johnson 212-416-8225/fax: 212-416-8816

Real Estate Finance Bureau
Bureau Chief:
Marissa Piesman 212-416-8102/fax: 212-416-8136

CORPORATIONS, AUTHORITIES AND COMMISSIONS

New York State Homes & Community Renewal
25 Beaver Street
New York, NY 10004

Offices and agencies generally appear in alphabetical order, except when specific order is requested by listee.

212-480-6700
e-mail: hcrinfo@nyshcr.org
Web site: www.nyshcr.org

Hampton Plaza
38-40 State Street
Albany, NY 12207
518-473-2526

Commissioner & CEO:
  Darryl C Towns.....................................212-480-6705
President, Office of Finance & Development:
  Marian Zucker......................................212-480-6700
President, Office of Community Renewal:
  Matthew Nelson...................................212-480-6700
President, Office of Professional Services:
  Sharon Devine.....................................212-480-6700
COO:
  Kevin Kelly..212-480-6700
Director, Fair Housing & Equal Opportunity:
  Wanda Graham....................................212-480-6700

NEW YORK STATE LEGISLATURE

See Legislative Branch in Section 1 for additional Standing Committee and Subcommittee information.

Assembly Standing Committees

Banks
Chair:
  Annette Robinson (D)..............................518-455-5474
Ranking Minority Member:
  Claudia Tenney (R)................................518-455-5334

Senate Standing Committees

Banks
Chair:
  Diane J Savino (D).................................518-455-2437
Ranking Minority Member:
  Jesse Hamilton (D)................................518-455-2431

U.S. GOVERNMENT

EXECUTIVE DEPARTMENTS AND RELATED AGENCIES

Export Import Bank of the United States
Web site: www.exim.gov

Northeast Regional Office......................fax: 212-809-2687
  Ted Weiss Federal Building, 290 Broadway, 13th Floor, New York, NY 10004
  212-809-2650 Fax: 212-809-2687
Regional Director:
  Thomas Cummings................................212-809-2652
  e-mail: thomas.cummings@exim.gov

Federal Deposit Insurance Corporation
877-275-3342
Web site: www.fdic.gov

Division of Depositor and Consumer Protection
  350 Fifth Avenue, Suite 1200, New York, NY 10118-0110
  800-334-9593 or 917-320-2500
Regional Director:
  John Vogel

Deputy Regional Director:
  Scott Strockoz

Federal Reserve System

Federal Reserve Bank of New York
  33 Liberty St, New York, NY 10045
  212-720-6130
  e-mail: general.info@ny.frb.org
  Web site: www.newyorkfed.org
President:
  William C Dudley
First Vice President:
  Christine M Cumming
  e-mail: peter.bakstansky@ny.frb.org
Chair:
  Emily K Rafferty

National Credit Union Administration
Web site: www.ncua.gov

Albany Region
  9 Washington Square, Suite 6, Albany, NY 12205
  518-862-7400
  e-mail: region1@ncua.gov
Regional Director:
  L J Blankenberger..................518-862-7400/fax: 518-862-7420

US Treasury Department
Web site: www.treasury.gov

Comptroller of the Currency
  Web site: www.occ.treas.gov

  Northeastern District Office.....................fax: 212-790-4058
  340 Madison Avenue, 5th Floor, New York, NY 10173-0002
  212-790-4000 Fax: 212-790-4058
  Deputy Comptroller:
    Toney Bland 212-790-4001/fax: 212-790-4058
  Assistant Deputy Comptroller, Specialties/Operations:
    Maureen Whalen 212-790-4003
  District Counsel:
    Jonathan Rushdoony 212-790-4010

US Mint
  Web site: www.usmint.gov
Plant Manager:
  Ellen McCullom 845-446-6201

U.S. CONGRESS

See U.S. Congress Chapter for additional Standing Committee and Subcommittee information.

House of Representatives Standing Committees

Financial Services
Chair:
  Jeb Hensarling (R-TX)
Ranking Member:
  Maxine Waters (D-CA)
New York Delegate:
  Peter T. King (R)
New York Delegate:
  Michael G. Grimm (R)
New York Delegate:
  Carolyn B. Maloney (D)
New York Delegate:
  Nydia M. Velazquez (D)

Offices and agencies generally appear in alphabetical order, except when specific order is requested by listee.

New York Delegate:
  Gregory W. Meeks (D)
New York Delegate:
  Carolyn McCarthy (D) 202-225-5516

Senate Standing Committees

Banking, Housing & Urban Affairs
Chair:
  Tim Johnson (D-SD) 202-224-7391/fax: 202-224-5137
Ranking Member:
  Mike Crapo (R-ID)
New York Delegate:
  Charles E Schumer (D) 202-224-6542

PRIVATE SECTOR

Alliance Bank
Tower II, 120 Madison St 18th Floor, Syracuse, NY 13202
315-475-2100 or 800-310-6275 Fax: 315-475-4421
e-mail: abnaweb@alliancebankna.com
Web site: www.alliancebankna.com
Jack H Webb, President & Chief Executive Officer

American Express Company
200 Vesey St, 48th Fl, New York, NY 10285-4811
212-640-5028 Fax: 212-640-9602
Web site: www.americanexpress.com
*Consumer lending, travel services, proprietary database marketing,
insurance underwriting & investment services*
Stephen Lemson, Vice President, State & Government Affairs

American International Group Inc
70 Pine St, 36th Fl, New York, NY 10270
212-770-6114 Fax: 212-785-4214
e-mail: ned.cloonan@aig.com
Web site: www.aig.com
International business, government & financial services
Edward T Cloonan, Vice President International & Corporate Affairs

Antalek & Moore Insurance Agency
340 Main St, Beacon, NY 12508
845-831-4300 or 866-894-1026 Fax: 845-831-5631
e-mail: fantalek@antalek-moore.com
Web site: www.antalek-moore.com
NYS Banking Board member
Frederick N Antalek, Sr, President

Apple Banking for Savings
122 East 42nd St, 9th Fl, New York, NY 10168
212-224-6410 Fax: 212-224-6580
Web site: www.applebank.com
NYS Banking Board member
Alan Shamoon, President & Chief Executive Officer

**Community Bankers Assn of NY State, Banking Law &
Regulations Cmte**
Astoria Federal Savings & Loan
1 Astoria Federal Plaza, Lake Success, NY 11042-1085
516-327-3000 Fax: 516-327-7860
e-mail: banking@astoriafederal.com
Web site: www.astoriafederal.com
Alan P Eggleston, Member

Bank of Akron
46 Main St, Akron, NY 14001
716-542-5401 Fax: 716-542-5510
Web site: www.bankofakron.com
*NYS Banking Board member/ Director - Independent Bankers Association of
New York State (IBANYS)*
E Peter Forrestel, II, President & Chief Executive Officer

Bear Stearns & Co Inc
383 Madison Ave, 11th Fl, New York, NY 10179
212-272-2000 Fax: 212-272-5188
e-mail: bforan@bear.com
Web site: www.bearstearns.com
Public finance
James E Cayne, Chairman & Chief Executive Officer

SIFMA
Bond Market Association (The)
360 Madison Ave, Ste 18, New York, NY 10017-7111
646-637-9200 or 212-808-1000 Fax: 646-637-9126
e-mail: namiel@bondmarkets.com
Web site: www.bondmarkets.com
*Represent securities firms & banks that underwrite, trade & sell debt
securities*
Jon Teall, Vice President, Media Relations

**Brown Brothers Harriman & Co, Bank Asset Management
Group**
140 Broadway, New York, NY 10005-1101
212-483-7907 Fax: 212-493-7657
e-mail: andrew.hofer@bbh.com
Web site: www.bbh.com
Andrew P Hofer, Managing Director/Head of Insurance Asset Management

Canandaigua National Bank & Trust Co
72 S Main St, Canandaigua, NY 14424
585-394-4260 or 800-724-2621 Fax: 585-396-1355
e-mail: ghamlin@cnbank.com
Web site: www.cnbank.com
Full service banking
George W Hamlin, Chairman/CEO
Frank H Hamlin, President

Citigroup
399 Park Avenue, New York, NY 10043
212-559-5248 or 800-285-3000 Fax: 212-793-8011
e-mail: thomsonte@citi.com
Web site: www.citigroup.com

Citigroup Inc
399 Park Ave, 2nd Fl, New York, NY 10043
212-793-0141 Fax: 212-793-2008
e-mail: schleinm@citigroup.com
Web site: www.citigroup.com
Commercial & retail banking
Michael Schlein, Senior Vice President, Global Corporate Affairs, Human
    Resources & Business Practices

The Clearing House Association, LLC
100 Broad St, New York, NY 10004
212-612-9205 Fax: 212-612-9253
e-mail: norm.nelson@theclearinghouse.org
Web site: www.theclearinghouse.org
Electronic funds transfer
Norman R Nelson, General Counsel

Cornell University, Economics Department
450 Uris Hall, Ithaca, NY 14853-7601
607-255-6283 Fax: 607-255-2818
e-mail: dae3@cornell.edu
Web site: www.arts.cornell.edu/econ
Microeconomic theory, financial economics
David Easley, Professor

Offices and agencies generally appear in alphabetical order, except when specific order is requested by listee.

Credit Advocate Counseling Corporation
237 First Ave, Ste 305, New York, NY 10003
212-260-2776 or 866-MYBILLS Fax: 646-218-4599
e-mail: info@creditadvocates.com
Web site: www.creditadvocates.com
*Advice & assistance in eliminating credit card debt by consolidating &
handling bill payments while reducing interest rates*
Steve Burman, President

Credit Union Association of New York (CUANY)
1021 Watervliet-Shaker Road, P.O. Box 15118, Albany, NY 12212-5118
518-437-8122 or 800-342-9835 Fax: 518-782-4212
e-mail: amy.kramer@cuany.org
Web site: www.cuany.org
Serving & support credit unions
Amy Kramer, Vice President/Governmental Affairs

Deutsche Bank
60 Wall Street, New York, NY 10005
212-250-2500
e-mail: thomas.curtis@db.com
Web site: www.db.com
Thomas Curtis, Global Head of Business Development & Strategic Planning
    & Communications

Federal Home Loan Bank of New York
101 Park Ave, New York, NY 10178-0599
212-681-6000 Fax: 212-441-6890
Web site: www.fhlbny.com
Alfred A DelliBovi, President

Financial Services Forum
601 Thirteenth Street NW, Suite 750 South, Washington, DC 20005
202-457-8765 Fax: 202-457-8769
Web site: www.financialservicesforum.org
*NYS Banking Board member; organization of CEOs of twenty one of the
largest & most diversified financial institutions*
Rob Nichols, President/COO

Goldman Sachs & Co
101 Constitution Avenue NW, Suite 1000 East, Washington, DC 20001
202-637-3700 Fax: 202-637-3773
Web site: www.gs.com
Ann S Costello, Managing Director & Head of Global Government Affairs

HSBC USA Inc
452 Fifth Ave, New York, NY 10018
212-525-3800 Fax: 212-525-0109
e-mail: linda.s.recupero@us.hsbc.com
Web site: www.us.hsbc.com
Bank holding company
Linda Recupero, Executive Vice President, Public Affairs-North America

IRX Therapeutics Inc
140 West 57th, Ste 9-C, New York, NY 10019
212-582-1199 Fax: 212-582-3659
e-mail: jhwang@irxtherapeutics.com
Web site: www.irxtherapeutics.com
Jeffrey Hwang, Chief Financial Officer

Independent Bankers Association of NYS
125 State St, Albany, NY 12207
518-436-4646 Fax: 518-436-4648
e-mail: info@ibanys.net
Web site: ibanys.net
Representing New York's community banks
William Y Crowell, III, Executive Director

Kudlow & Company LLC
301 Tahmore Drive, Fairfield, CT 06825
203-228-5050 Fax: 203-228-5040
e-mail: svarga@kudlow.com
Web site: www.kudlow.com
NYS Banking Board member

Lake Shore Savings
128 East Fourth St, Dunkirk, NY 14048
716-366-4070 Fax: 716-366-2965
e-mail: dave.mancuso@lakeshoresavings.com
Web site: www.lakeshoresavings.com
David C Mancuso, President & Chief Executive Officer

M&T Bank Corporation
One M&T Plaza, Buffalo, NY 14203-2399
716-842-5425 Fax: 716-842-5220
e-mail: rwilmers@MTB.com
Web site: www.MTB.com
Commercial, savings & mortgage banking services
Robert G Wilmers, Chairman/CEO

MBIA Insurance Corporation
113 King St, Armonk, NY 10504
914-273-4545 Fax: 914-765-3555
e-mail: ethel.geisinger@mbia.com
Web site: www.mbia.com
Insure municipal bonds & structured transactions
Ethel Z Geisinger, Vice President, Government Relations

Mallory Factor Inc
555 Madison Ave, New York, NY 10022
212-350-0000 Fax: 212-350-0001
NYS Banking Board member
Mallory Factor, President

Merrill Lynch & Co Inc
222 Broadway, 16th Fl, New York, NY 10038-2510
212-670-0302 Fax: 212-670-4501
e-mail: andrew_kandel@ml.com
Web site: www.ml.com
Securities, capital markets & financial services
Andrew Kandel, First Vice President & Assistant General Counsel, State
    Regulation, Legislation & Government Relations

Morgan Stanley
1585 Broadway, New York, NY 10036
212-761-4000 Fax: 212-762-7994
Web site: www.morganstanley.com
Investment banking
John Mack, Chairman & Chief Executive Officer

Municipal Credit Union
22 Cortlandt St, New York, NY 10007-3107
212-238-3361 Fax: 212-416-7050
Web site: www.nymcu.org
NYS Banking Board member
Thomas G Siciliano, General Counsel

NBT Bancorp Inc.
PO Box 351, Norwich, NY 13815
607-337-2265 Fax: 607-336-6545
e-mail: customerservice@nbtbank.com
Web site: www.nbtbank.com
Commercial banking
Martin A Dietrich, President & Chief Executive Officer

National Federation of Community Development Credit Unions
116 John St, 33rd Fl, New York, NY 10038
212-809-1850 Fax: 212-809-3274
e-mail: rmorales@cdcu.coup
Web site: www.cdcu.coop
Cliff Rosenthal, Executive Director

New York Bankers Association
99 Park Ave, 4th Fl, New York, NY 10016-1502
212-297-1664 Fax: 212-297-1622
e-mail: bbosies@nyba.com
Web site: www.nyba.com
Advocacy for commercial banking industry
William J Bosies, Senior Vice President, Legislation & Regulation

Community Bankers Assn of NY State, Mortgages & Real Estate Cmte
New York Community Bank
615 Merrick Ave, Westbury, NY 11590
516-683-4100 Fax: 516-683-8344
Web site: www.mynycb.com
Joseph R Ficalora, Chairman/President/Chief Executive Officer

New York State Credit Union League Inc
19 British American Blvd, Latham, NY 12110
800-342-9835 Fax: 518-782-8284
e-mail: mlanotte@nyscul.org
Web site: www.nyscul.org
Trade association for over 600 not-for-profit, member owned credit unions in New York
Michael A Lanotte, Senior Vice President, Governmental & Regulatory
    Affairs

New York Stock Exchange
Government Relations, 11 Wall St, 6th Fl, New York, NY 10005
212-656-3000 Fax: 212-656-5605
e-mail: pagurto@nyse.com
Web site: www.nyse.com
Richard G Ketchum, Chief Regulatory Officer

Norddeutsche Landesbank Girozentrale
1114 Ave of the Americas, 37th Fl, New York, NY 10036
212-398-7300 Fax: 212-812-6860
e-mail: thomas.buerkle@nordlb.com
Web site: www.nordlbnewyork.com
Thomas S Buerkle, Executive Vice President & General Manager

Community Bankers Assn of NY State, Bank Operations & Admin Cmte
North Country Savings Bank
127 Main St, Canton, NY 13617
315-386-4533 Fax: 315-386-3739
e-mail: bgraham@northcountrysavings.com
Web site: www.northcountrysavings.com
Brandi Graham, Deposit Operations Manager

Community Bankers Assn of NY State, Accounting & Taxation Cmte
North Fork Bank
275 Broadhollow Road, Melville, NY 11747
631-844-1004 Fax: 631-531-2759
Web site: www.northforkbank.com
Carolyn Dresel, Co-Chair

Community Bankers Assn of NY State, Government Relations Cmte
Pioneer Savings Bank
21 Second St, Troy, NY 12180
518-274-4800 Fax: 518-274-1060
e-mail: troybranch@pioneersb.com
Web site: www.pioneersb.com
Dawn Gendron, Sales Development Officer/Senior Branch Manager

Securities Industry Association (SIA)
120 Broadway, 35th Fl, New York, NY 10271-0800
212-608-1500 Fax: 212-968-0703
e-mail: info@sia.com
Web site: www.sia.com
Mark Lackritz, President

Sullivan & Cromwell
125 Broad St, New York, NY 10004
212-558-3534 Fax: 212-558-4000
Web site: www.sullcrom.com
Bank regulation & acquisition law
H Rodgin Cohen, Partner & Senior Chairman
Joseph Shenker, Partner & Chairman

TD Banknorth
One Old Loudon Road, Latham, NY 12110
518-786-2522 Fax: 518-786-2528
e-mail: jeffrey.rivenburgh@TDBanknorth.com
Web site: www.TDBank.com
Commercial, retail & investment banking
Jeffrey Rivenburg, President/Senior Loan Officer

Todtman, Nachamie, Spizz, & Johns, P.C.
425 Park Avenue, 5th Floor, New York, NY 10022
212-754-9400 or 212-751-7100 Fax: 212-754-6262
e-mail: wchenlaw@tnsj-law.com
Web site: www.tnsj-law.com
NYS Banking Board member
Wesley Chen, Special Counsel

Tompkins Financial Corporation
110 N Tioga St, PO Box 460, Ithaca, NY 14851
607-273-3210 Fax: 607-273-0063
e-mail: sromaine@tompkinstrust.com
Web site: www.tompkinsfinancial.com
$3.4 Billion financial services holding company headquartered in Ithaca, NY. Parent company to three community banks, Tompkins Trust Company, The Bank of Castile and Mahopac National Bank, as well as Tompkins Insurance Agencies & Tompkins Financial.
Stephen S Romaine, President & CEO

Ulster Savings Bank
180 Schwank Dr, Kingston, NY 12401
845-338-6322 or 800-762-0449 Fax: 845-339-9008
Web site: www.ulstersavings.com
NYS Banking Board member
Clifford Miller, President & Chief Executive Officer

Union State Bank
100 Dutch Hill Rd, Orangeburg, NY 10962
845-365-4605 or 800-616-3491 Fax: 845-365-2130
e-mail: customerservices@unionstate.com
Web site: www.unionstate.com
NYS Banking Board member
Thomas E Hales, Pres & Chief Executive Officer

Valley National Bank
1460 Valley Road, Wayne, NJ 07470
973-686-5034 Fax: 973-694-2261
e-mail: rfraser@valleynationalbank.com
Web site: www.valleynationalbank.com
Full-service banking, cash management, municipal leasing & public finance

---

Offices and agencies generally appear in alphabetical order, except when specific order is requested by listee.

Ronald Fraser, FVP Corporate & Government

Washington Mutual
589 5th Avenue, New York, NY 10117-1923
212-353-6230 Fax: 212-673-5118
Web site: www.wamu.com
National financial services company that provides a diversified line of products to consumers & small to mid-sized businesses
Donna Wilson, Senior Vice President, Regional President

White & Case LLP
1155 Ave of the Americas, New York, NY 10036-2787
212-819-8200 Fax: 212-354-8113
e-mail: dwall@whitecase.com
Web site: www.whitecase.com
Advises domestic & foreign banks on the nature & structure of their operations & activities in the US & abroad

Duane D Wall, Partner

Wilber National Bank
245 Main St, PO Box 430, Oneonta, NY 13820
607-432-1700 Fax: 607-433-4161
e-mail: dgulotty@wilberbank.com
Web site: www.wilberbank.com
Commercial & retail banking
Douglas C Gulotty, President & Chief Executive Officer

COMMERCE, INDUSTRY & ECONOMIC DEVELOPMENT

NEW YORK STATE

GOVERNOR'S OFFICE

Governor's Office
Executive Chamber
State Capitol
Albany, NY 12224
518-474-8390 Fax: 518-474-1513
Web site: www.ny.gov

Governor:
   Andrew M Cuomo 518-474-8390
Secretary to the Governor:
   William Mulrow 518-474-4246
Counsel to the Governor:
   Alphonso David 518-474-8343
Deputy Secretary for Financial Services:
   George Haggerty................................518-474-5442
First Assistant Counsel:
   Sandi Toll 518-474-8434
Director, Communications:
   Melissa DeRosa ....518-474-8418 or 212-681-4640

EXECUTIVE DEPARTMENTS AND RELATED AGENCIES

New York State Liquor Authority (Division of Alcoholic Beverage Control)
80 S Swan St
Ste 900
Albany, NY 12210-8002
518-474-3114 Fax: 518-402-4015
Web site: www.sla.ny.gov

317 Lenox Ave
New York, NY 10027
212-961-8300
Fax: 212-961-8299

Chair:
   Vincent Bradley ....212-961-8300 or 518-473-6559
Commissioner:
   Jeanique Greene ....212-961-8300 or 518-474-3114
Commissioner:
   Kevin Kim ....212-961-8300 or 518-474-3114
Director, Enforcement:
   Noel Colon 518-474-3114
Counsel:
   Jacqueline Flug 518-474-3114/fax: 518-402-2304

Administration
Secretary to the Authority:
   Jacqueline Held................................518-473-6559
Deputy Commissioner, Administration:
   Chad Loshbaugh................................518-473-0365
Director, Public Affairs:
   William Crowley ....518-474-3114 or 518-474-4875
   fax: 518-473-9565
   e-mail: press.office@sla.ny.gov

Licensing & Enforcement

Albany (Zone II)
80 S Swan St, Ste 900, Albany, NY 12210-8002
CEO:
   Kerri O'Brien 518-474-3114/fax: 518-402-2304
Deputy Counsel:
   Lisa Bonacci................................518-474-3114
Director, Information Technology:
   Michael Drake 518-474-3114

Buffalo (Zone III)
Iskalo Electric Tower, 535 Washington St, Ste 303, Buffalo, NY 14203
Deputy Commissioner, Licensing:
   David L Edmunds Jr................................716-847-3001
Supervising Beverage Control Investigator:
   Gary Bartikofsky 716-847-3035

New York City (Zone I)
317 Lenox Avenue, New York, NY 10027
Deputy Chief Executive Officer:
   Michael Jones................................212-961-8300
Supervising Beverage Control Investigator:
   Franklin Englander................................212-961-8376

Budget, Division of the
State Capitol
Albany, NY 12224
518-473-0580 or 518-473-3885 Fax: 518-474-9041
Web site: www.budget.ny.gov

Director:
   Mary Beth Labate................................518-474-2300
First Deputy Director:
   Dominic Colafati................................518-474-8282
Deputy Director:
   David Lara 518-402-4246
Budget Services Head:
   Bob Brondi 518-473-0580
Public Protection Head:
   Anne Bink................................518-474-4313
Press Officer:
   Morris Peters 518-473-3885/fax: 518-474-9041
   e-mail: dob.sm.press@budget.ny.gov

Consumer Protection, Division of
One Commerce Plaza
99 Washington Ave
Albany, NY 12231
518-474-8583 or 800-697-1220 Fax: 518-473-9055
Web site: www.dos.ny.gov/consumerprotection/

Executive Deputy Director, Consumer Protection:
   Aiesha Battle................................518-474-2363

Empire State Development Corporation
633 Third Ave
New York, NY 10017
212-803-3100 Fax: 212-803-3131
e-mail: esd@esd.ny.gov
Web site: www.esd.ny.gov

625 Broadway
Albany, NY 12207
518-292-5100

95 Perry Street
Ste 500
Buffalo, NY 14203

Offices and agencies generally appear in alphabetical order, except when specific order is requested by listee.

716-846-8200
Fax: 716-846-8260

President & CEO:
  Howard Zemsky 212-803-3700
  e-mail: president@esd.ny.gov
Business Expansion:
  John Gilstrap . . . . .212-803-3700 or 518-292-5100
Chief of Staff & COO:
  Mehul J. Patel 212-803-3700
Public Affairs:
  Kay Sarlin Wright 800-260-7313
  e-mail: esdpressoffice@esd.ny.gov

Law Department
120 Broadway
New York, NY 10271-0332
212-416-8000 or 800-771-7755
Web site: www.ag.ny.gov

State Capitol
Albany, NY 12224-0341
518-474-7330
Fax: 518-473-9909

Attorney General:
  Eric T Schneiderman . . . . .212-416-8050 or 518-474-7330
Chief of Staff:
  Micah Lasher 212-416-8050
COO:
  Jeanette Moy .518-776-2500/fax: 518-915-7753
Press Secretary:
  Fernando Aquino 212-416-8060/fax: 212-416-6005
Solicitor General:
  Barbara D Underwood . . . . .212-416-8016 or 518-402-2074

Economic Justice
Executive Deputy Attorney General:
  Karla Sanchez 212-416-8050

Antitrust Bureau
Bureau Chief:
  Eric J Stock 212-416-8282/fax: 212-416-6015
  e-mail: eric.stock@ag.ny.gov

Consumer Frauds Bureau
Bureau Chief:
  Jane Azia . . . . .212-416-8300 or 518-776-2307
  fax: 212-416-6003

Internet Bureau
Bureau Chief:
  Kathleen McGee 212-416-8433/fax: 212-416-8369

Investor Protection Bureau
Bureau Chief:
  Chad Johnson 212-416-8225/fax: 212-416-8816

State Counsel
Chief Deputy Attorney General:
  Harlan Levy 212-416-8525

Claims Bureau
Bureau Chief:
  Katharine Brooks . . . . .518-776-2300 or 212-416-8913

NYSTAR - Division of Science, Technology & Innovation
30 South Pearl St
11th Fl
Albany, NY 12207

518-292-5700 Fax: 518-292-5798
Web site: www.esd.ny.gov/nystar

Director:
  Edward Reinfurt 518-292-5700
Deputy Director:
  Edward J Hamilton 518-292-5700
Director, Communications/Government Affairs:
  Jannette Rondo 518-292-5700/fax: 518-292-5798
Regional Technology Development:
  Matthew Watson 518-292-5700
Counsel:
  Paul Jesep 518-292-5700

Centers for Advanced Technology

Center for Advanced Ceramic Technology at Alfred University
2 Pine Street, Alfred, NY 14802-1296
e-mail: cactinfo@alfred.edu
Web site: cact.alfred.edu
Director:
  Dr Matthew M Hall 607-871-2486/fax: 607-871-3469
  e-mail: hallmm@alfred.edu

Center for Advanced Materials Processing at Clarkson Univ
CAMP, Box 5665, Potsdam, NY 13699-5665
Web site: www.clarkson.edu/camp
Director:
  S V Babu .315-268-2336/fax: 315-268-7615
  e-mail: babu@clarkson.edu

Center for Advanced Tech in Biomedical & Bioengineering
University at Buffalo, 701 Ellicott St, Buffalo, NY 14203
Web site: www.bioinformatics.buffalo.edu/cat
Co-Director:
  Alexander N. Cartwright PhD 716-645-0312
Co-Director:
  Marnie LaVigne PhD 716-645-0312
  e-mail: lavigne2@buffalo.edu

Sensor CAT-Diagnostic Tools & Sensor Systems
SUNY Stony Brook, Suffolk Hall, Room 115B, Stony Brook, NY
  11794-3717
e-mail: sensor@ece.sunysb.edu
Web site: sensorcat.sunysb.edu
Director:
  Serge Luryi . . . . .631-632-1368 or 631-632-8420
  fax: 631-632-8529

Center for Emerging & Innovative Sciences
Univ of Rochester, Taylor Hall, 260 Hutchinson Rd, Rochester, NY
  14627-0194
Web site: www.ceis.rochester.edu
Director:
  Mark Bocko 585-275-0547
  e-mail: mark.bocko@seas.rochester.edu

Center for Advanced Information Management
Columbia University, 630 W 168th St, Bldg 130, New York, NY 10032
Web site: www.cat.columbia.edu
Director:
  George Hripcsak 212-305-2944/fax: 212-305-0196

Center for Advanced Technology in Life Science Enterprise
Cornell University, 130 Biotechnology Bldg, Ithaca, NY 14853-2703
Web site: www.biotech.cornell.edu/cat
Director:
  George Grills 607-255-9693
  e-mail: biotech@cornell.edu

Center for Advanced Technology in Photonics Applications
CUNY, Steinman Hall T606, 160 Convent Avenue, New York, NY 10031
Web site: www.cunycat.org

Offices and agencies generally appear in alphabetical order, except when specific order is requested by listee.

Director:
>   David T. Crouse, PhD 212-650-5330/fax: 212-650-7760
>   e-mail: crouse@cunycat.org

Ctr for Advanced Tech in Telecommunications at Polytech Univ
5 MetroTech Center, 9th Floor, Brooklyn, NY 11201
Web site: catt.poly.edu
Director:
>   Shivendra S Panwar . . . . .718-260-3050 or 718-260-3740
>   fax: 718-260-8687
>   e-mail: panwar@catt.poly.edu

Center for Automation Technologies & Systems at Rensselaer
CII 8011, 110 8th Street, Troy, NY 12180
e-mail: cats-info@rpi.edu
Web site: www.cats.rpi.edu
Director:
>   John Wen 518-276-8744/fax: 518-276-4897

Center for Advanced Medical Biotechnology
Biotechnology Building, 2nd Floor, Stony Brook, NY 11790
Web site: www.biotech.sunysb.edu
Director:
>   Clinton T Rubin PhD 631-632-8521/fax: 631-632-8577

Center for Computer Applications & Software Engineering
Syracuse University, 2-212 Ctr for Science & Tech, Syracuse, NY 13244
Web site: www.case.syr.edu
Director:
>   Pramod Varshney 315-443-1060/fax: 315-443-4745
>   e-mail: varshney@syr.edu

Center in Nanomaterials and Nanoelectronics
251 Fuller Road, Albany, NY 12203
Director:
>   Michael Fancher 518-437-8686/fax: 518-437-8687

Future Energy Systems CAT at Rensselaer Polytechnic Inst
110 8th Street, Troy, NY 12180
e-mail: cfes@rpi.edu
Web site: www.rpi.edu/cfes
Director:
>   Dr. Jian Sun 518-276-8297/fax: 518-276-6844
>   e-mail: jsun@ecse.rpi.edu

Integrated Electronics Engineering Center at Binghamton
IEEC, Vestal Pkwy East, PO Box 6000, Binghamton, NY 13902-6000
e-mail: ieec@binghamton.edu
Web site: www.binghamton.edu/ieec/
Director:
>   Daryl Santos 607-777-4769/fax: 607-777-4683

Regional Technology Development Centers

Alliance for Manufacturing & Technology
59 Court St, 6th Fl, State St Entrance, Binghamton, NY 13901
e-mail: info@amt-mep.org
Web site: www.amt-mep.org
Executive Director:
>   Edward Gaetano 607-774-0022 x304/fax: 607-774-0026

Center for Economic Growth
30 Pearl Street, Ste 100, Albany, NY 12207
e-mail: ceg@ceg.org
Web site: www.ceg.org
President/CEO:
>   F Michael Tucker 518-465-8975/fax: 518-465-6681
>   e-mail: miket@ceg.org

Central New York Technology Development Organization
445 Electronics Pkwy, Ste 206, Liverpool, NY 13088
Web site: www.tdo.org

President/CEO:
>   Robert I Trachtenberg 315-425-5144/fax: 315-233-1259
>   e-mail: rtrachtenberg@tdo.org

Council for Interntl Trade, Tech, Education & Communication
Peyton Hall, Box 8561, Main St, Clarkson University, Potsdam, NY 13669
Web site: www.citec.org
Executive Director:
>   William P. Murray 315-268-3778 x29/fax: 315-268-4432
>   e-mail: murray@citec.org

High Technology of Rochester
150 Lucius Gordon Drive, Suite 100, West Henrietta, NY 14586
Web site: www.htr.org
President:
>   Jim Sendall 585-214-2400
>   e-mail: info@htr.org

Hudson Valley Technology Development Center
1450 Route 300, Building 1, Newburgh, NY 12550
Web site: www.hvtdc.org
Executive Director:
>   Thomas G Phillips, Sr 845-391-8214 x3006/fax: 845-845-8218
>   e-mail: tom.phillips@hvtdc.org

Industrial & Technology Assistance Corp
39 Broadway, Suite 100, New York, NY 10006
Web site: www.itac.org
President:
>   Sara Garretson 212-809-3900/fax: 646-588-5156
>   e-mail: sgarretson@itac.org

Long Island Forum for Technology
510 Grumman Road West, Bay Shore, NY 11706
e-mail: info@lift.org
Web site: www.lift.org
Executive Director:
>   William Wahlig 631-969-3700/fax: 631-846-2789
>   e-mail: bwahlig@lift.org

Mohawk Valley Applied Technology Corp
207 Genesee St, Ste 405, Utica, NY 13501
Web site: www.mvatc.com
President:
>   Paul MacEnroe 315-793-8050/fax: 315-793-8057
>   e-mail: paulm@mvatc.com

INSYTE Consulting (Western NY Technology Development Ctr)
726 Exchange St, Ste 812, Buffalo, NY 14210
Web site: www.insyte-consulting.com
President:
>   Benjamin Rand 716-636-3626/fax: 716-845-6418
>   e-mail: brand@insyte-consulting.com

State Department

One Commerce Plaza
99 Washington Avenue
Albany, NY 12231
518-474-4750 Fax: 518-474-4765
Web site: www.dos.ny.gov

123 William St
New York, NY 10038
212-417-5801
Fax: 212-417-5805

Secretary of State:
>   Cesar A Perales 518-474-0050
First Deputy Secretary of State:
>   Daniel Shapiro 518-474-4750
Deputy Secretary of State, Public Affairs:
>   Vacant 212-417-5800

Offices and agencies generally appear in alphabetical order, except when specific order is requested by listee.

Assistant Secretary of State, Communications:
Vacant 518-474-4752/fax: 518-474-4597
e-mail: info@dos.state.ny.us
Counsel:
Samuel L. Watson 518-474-6740/fax: 518-473-9211
Deputy Secretary of State, Local Government & Community Services:
Robert Elliott .518-486-9888/fax: 518-474-6572

Licensing Services Division
Deputy Secretary of State:
Marcos Vigil .518-473-2728/fax: 518-473-2730
e-mail: licensing@dos.state.ny.us

Administrative Rules Division
Manger, Publications:
Maribeth St. Germain 518-474-6957/fax: 518-473-9055
e-mail: adminrules@dos.state.ny.us

Cemeteries Division
Director:
Richard D Fishman . . . . .518-474-6226 or 212-417-5713
fax: 518-473-0876
e-mail: cemeteries@dos.state.ny.us

Corporations, State Records & UCC Division
Director:
Sandra J. Tallman 518-473-2492/fax: 518-474-1418
e-mail: corporations@dos.ny.gov

Taxation & Finance Department
State Campus
Bldg 9, Rm 227
Albany, NY 12227
518-457-4242 Fax: 518-457-2486
Web site: www.tax.ny.gov

Commissioner:
Thomas H Mattox 518-457-2244
Executive Deputy Commissioner:
Nonie Manion 518-457-7358
Deputy Commissioner & Counsel:
Amanda Hiller .518-457-3746/fax: 518-457-8247
Director, Conciliation & Mediation Services:
Kevin Law. 518-485-8063
Director, Executive Correspondence & Legislative Affairs:
Maryann Tucker 518-457-2398
Director, Public Information:
Geoffrey Gloak 518-457-7377

Office of Processing & Taxpayer Services (OPTS)
Deputy Commissioner:
Edward Chaszczewski 518-457-1000

Human Resources Management
Director:
Gina Lysyczyn 518-457-2786

Operations Support Bureau
Director:
Lisa Negus 518-457-4250

Office of Budget & Management Analysis
Chief Financial Officer:
Eric Mostert 518-485-5080

Planning & Management Analysis Bureau
Director:
Mary Ellen Nagengast 518-457-8660

Office of Information Technology Services
Chief Information Officer:
Daniel Chan 518-292-7808

Office of Processing & Taxpayer Services
Director:
Helen Pelersi 518-591-1944

Office of State Treasury
Deputy Commissioner & Treasurer:
Aida Brewer. .518-474-4250/fax: 518-402-4118

Office of Criminal Enforcement
Deputy Commissioner:
Risa Sugarman 518-457-9692

Audit Division
Director, Tax Audits:
Joe Carzo 518-451-8910

Collections & Civil Enforcement
Director:
Patricia Coneys. 518-457-1138

Office of Tax Policy Analysis
Deputy Commissioner:
Robert D Plattner 518-457-4357

CORPORATIONS, AUTHORITIES AND COMMISSIONS

Central New York Regional Market Authority
2100 Park St
Syracuse, NY 13208
315-422-8647 Fax: 315-422-6897
Web site: cnyrma.com

Acting Commissioner of Agricultural Markets:
Richard A Ball 315-422-8647
Commissioner's Representative:
Troy Waffner 315-422-8647
e-mail: genedemos@gmail.com

Development Authority of the North Country
317 Washington Street
Watertown, NY 13601
315-661-3200
e-mail: info@danc.org
Web site: www.danc.org

Chair:
Gary Turck 315-661-3200
Executive Director:
James Wright 315-661-3200
Deputy Executive Director:
Thomas R Sauter. 315-661-3200
e-mail: tsauter@danc.org
Director, Engineering:
Carrie Tuttle. 315-661-3210/fax: 315-786-2971
Telecom Division Manager:
David Wolf 315-661-3200
e-mail: oatn@danc.org
Landfill Superintendent:
Steve McElwain 315-661-3230
Director, Regional Development:
Michelle Capone 315-661-3200

Great Lakes Commission
2805 S Industrial Hwy
Ste 100
Ann Arbor, MI 48104-6791
734-971-9135 Fax: 734-971-9150
e-mail: teder@glc.org
Web site: www.glc.org

Offices and agencies generally appear in alphabetical order, except when specific order is requested by listee.

Chairman:
  Kelvin Burch.....................................814-332-6816
  e-mail: keburch@state.pa.us
Vice Chair:
  Jon W Allan 517-284-5035
  e-mail: allanj@michigan.gov
New York State Commissioner:
  Joseph Martens 518-402-8540
  e-mail: joseph.martens@dec.ny.gov
Executive Director:
  Tim A Eder 734-971-9135
  e-mail: teder@glc.org
Deputy Director:
  Thomas R Crane 734-971-9135
  e-mail: tcrane@glc.org
CIO:
  Stephen J Cole 734-971-9135
  e-mail: scole@glc.org
Program Director:
  Victoria Pebbles 734-971-9135
  e-mail: vpebbles@glc.org
Communications Director:
  Christine Manninen 734-971-9135
  e-mail: manninen@glc.org
Policy Director:
  Matthew Doss.....................................734-971-9135
  e-mail: mdoss@glc.org

United Nations Development Corporation

Two United Nations Plaza, 27th Fl
New York, NY 10017
212-888-1618 Fax: 212-588-0758
e-mail: info@undc.org
Web site: www.undc.org

Chair, Board of Directors:
  George Klein.....................................212-888-1618
Sr VP & General Counsel/Secretary:
  Robert Cole......................................212-888-1618
Controller/Treasurer:
  Jorge Ortiz......................................212-888-1618
Vice President:
  Kenneth Coopersmith..............................212-888-1618

NEW YORK STATE LEGISLATURE

See Legislative Branch in Section 1 for additional Standing Committee and Subcommitee information.

Assembly Standing Committees

Cities
Chair:
  Michael Benedetto (D)............................518-455-5296
Ranking Minority Member:
  Joseph Borelli (R)...............................518-455-4495

Consumer Affairs & Protection
Chair:
  Jeffrey Dinowitz (D).............................518-455-5965
Ranking Minority Member:
  Anthony Palumbo (R)..............................518-455-5294

Corporations, Authorities & Commissions
Chair:
  James F Brennan (D) 518-455-5377
Ranking Minority Member:
  Jane Corwin (R) 518-455-4601

Economic Development, Job Creation, Commerce & Industry
Chair:
  Robin L Schimminger (D) 518-455-4767
Ranking Minority Member:
  Raymond Walter (R)...............................518-455-4618

Small Business
Chair:
  Fred Thiele, Jr (D)..............................518-455-5997
Ranking Minority Member:
  David DiPietro (R) 518-455-5314

Assembly Task Forces

University-Industry Cooperation, Task Force on
Chair:
  Samuel Roberts (D)...............................518-455-5383
Coordinator:
  Maureen Schoolman 518-455-3632/fax: 518-455-4175

Senate Standing Committees

Cities
Chair:
  Andrew Lanza (R) 518-455-3215
Ranking Minority Member:
  Daniel Squadron (D)..............................518-455-2625

Commerce, Economic Development & Small Business
Chair:
  Philip Boyle (R) 518-455-3411
Ranking Minority Member:
  Timothy Kennedy (D)..............................518-455-2426

Consumer Protection
Chair:
  Michael Venditto (R) 518-455-3341
Ranking Minority Member:
  Leroy Comrie (D) 518-455-2701

Corporations, Authorities & Commissions
Chair:
  Michael Ranzenhofer (R) 518-455-3161
Ranking Minority Member:
  Bill Perkins (D).................................518-455-2441

Senate/Assembly Legislative Commissions

Rural Resources, Legislative Commission on
Senate Chair:
  Catharine Young (R)..............................518-455-3563
Assembly Vice Chair:
  Frank Skartados (D) 518-455-5762
Counsel:
  Barbara McRedmond 518-455-2069

U.S. GOVERNMENT

EXECUTIVE DEPARTMENTS AND RELATED AGENCIES

Commodity Futures Trading Commission
Web site: www.cftc.gov

Eastern Region
One World Trade Center, Suite 3747, New York, NY 10048
212-466-2071
Deputy Regional Counsel:
  Lenel Hickson 646-746-9700/fax: 646-746-9938

Offices and agencies generally appear in alphabetical order, except when specific order is requested by listee.

Consumer Product Safety Commission
609-927-1840 Fax: 609-927-4013
Web site: www.cpsc.gov

Eastern Regional Center
201 Varick St, Rm 903, New York, NY 10014
212-620-4120
Acting Director:
Vacant

Export Import Bank of the United States
Web site: www.exim.gov

Northeast Regional Office . . . . fax: 212-809-2687
Ted Weiss Federal Building, 290 Broadway, 13th Floor, New York, NY 10007
212-809-2650 Fax: 212-809-2687
Regional Director:
Thomas Cummings 212-809-2652/fax: 212-809-2687
e-mail: thomas.cummings@exim.gov

Federal Trade Commission
212-607-2828 Fax: 212-607-2822
Web site: www.ftc.gov

Northeast Regional Office . . . . fax: 212-607-2822
1 Bowling Green, New York, NY 10004
877-382-4357 Fax: 212-607-2822
Regional Director:
William H. Efron 212-607-2829

Small Business Administration
Web site: www.sba.gov

Region II New York . . . . fax: 212-264-4963
26 Federal Plaza, Ste 3108, New York, NY 10278
212-264-1450 Fax: 212-264-4963
Regional Administrator:
Jorge Silva-Puras
Regional Communications Director:
Justine Cabulong

District Offices
Buffalo . . . . fax: 716-551-4418
Niagara Center, 130 S Elmwood Avenue, Suite 540, Buffalo, NY 14202
716-551-4301 Fax: 716-551-4418
District Director:
Franklin J Sciortino 716-551-4301 x.313/fax: 716-551-4418
e-mail: franklin.sciortino.sba.gov
New Jersey . . . . fax: 973-645-6265
2 Gateway Center, Suite 1501, Newark, NJ 07102
973-645-2434 Fax: 973-645-6265
District Director:
Alfred Titone
New York City . . . . fax: 212-264-4963
26 Federal Plaza, Ste 3100, New York, NY 10278
212-264-4354 Fax: 212-264-4963
Acting District Director:
Vacant
Syracuse . . . . fax: 315-471-9288
224 Harrison Street, 5th Floor, Syracuse, NY 13202
315-471-9393 Fax: 315-471-9288
District Director:
Bernard J Paprocki

New York Business Information Center
1 Computer Dr South, Albany, NY 12205
Director:
Daniel O'Connell 518-446-1118 x231/fax: 518-446-1228
e-mail: daniel.oconnel@sba.gov

Small Business Development Center . . . . fax: 518-485-8223
State University Plaza, Corporate Woods Building, 3rd Floor, Albany, NY 12246
800-732-SBDC (7232) or 518-443-5398 Fax: 518-485-8223
Director:
William Brigham

US Commerce Department
Web site: www.doc.gov

Census Bureau
Web site: www.census.gov

New York Region
395 Hudson St, Ste 800, New York, NY 10014
212-584-3400 or 800-991-2520
e-mail: new.york.regional.office@census.gov
Regional Director:
Jeff T. Behler 212-584-3400/fax: 212-478-4800

Economic Development Administration
Web site: www.eda.gov

Philadelphia Region (includes New York)
The Curtis Center, Suite 140 South, 601 Walnut Street, Philadelphia, PA 19106
267-687-4313
Regional Director:
Willie C Taylor 215-597-4603/fax: 215-597-1063
e-mail: willie.c.taylor@eda.gov

Minority Business Development Agency
e-mail: nyro-info@mbda.gov
Web site: www.mbda.gov

New York Region
26 Federal Plaza, Room 3720, New York, NY 10278
212-264-3262
Regional Director:
Heyward B Davenport 212-264-3262/fax: 212-264-0725

National Oceanic & Atmospheric Administration

National Weather Service, Eastern Region
630 Johnson Ave, Bohemia, NY 11716
Web site: www.nws.noaa.gov
Director:
Dean Gulezian 631-244-0100/fax: 631-244-0109
e-mail: dean.gulezian@noaa.gov
Deputy Director:
Mickey J Brown 631-244-0100
Public Affairs Officer:
Marcie Katcher 631-244-0149/fax: 631-244-0167
Chief, Meteorological Services Division:
John Guiney 631-244-0121
e-mail: john.guiney@noaa.gov
Chief, Regional Hydrology Division:
Reggina Cabrera
e-mail: reggina.cabrera@noaa.gov
Chief, Scientific Services Division:
Kenneth Johnson 631-244-0136
e-mail: kenneth.johnson@noaa.gov

National Weather Service
Center for Environmental Science & Tech, 251 Fuller Rd, Ste B300, Albany, Ny 12203-3640
Science Operations Officer:
Warren Snyder 518-435-9568

US Commercial Service - International Trade Administration
Web site: www.export.gov

Buffalo US Export Assistance Center
130 South Elmwood Ave, Suite 530, Buffalo, NY 14202

Offices and agencies generally appear in alphabetical order, except when specific order is requested by listee.

e-mail: office.buffalo@trade.gov
Web site: http://www.export.gov/newyork/bflorochsyr
Director:
Rosanna Masucci 716-551-4191/fax: 716-551-5290
e-mail: rosanna.masucci@trade.gov

Harlem US Export Assistance Center . . . . fax: 212-860-6203
163 West 125th St, Ste 901, New York, NY 10027
212-860-6200 Fax: 212-860-6203
e-mail: office.harlem@mail.trade.gov
Web site: http://www.export.gov/newyork/harlem/
USEAC Director:
K L Fredericks. 212-860-6200/fax: 212-860-6203
e-mail: kl.fredericks@trade.gov

Long Island US Export Assistance Center
c/o College at Old Westbury, POB 210, Academic Village Marshall
Hallam Building 10, 233 Store Hill Road, Old Westbury, NY
1568-0210
Web site: http://www.export.gov/newyork/longisland
Director:
Shakir Farsakh . . . . .646-722-0182 or 516-876-3418
fax: 516-876-7563
e-mail: shakir.farsakh@trade.gov

New York US Export Assistance Center
Ted Weiss Federal Building, 290 Broadway, Suite 1312, New York, NY
10007
USEAC Director:
Carmela Mammas 212-809-2676/fax: 212-809-2687
e-mail: carmela.mammas@trade.gov

US Department of Agriculture

Rural Development
Web site: www.rurdev.usda.gov

New York State Office. . . . . .fax: 315-477-6438
441 S Salina St, Ste 357, Syracuse, NY 13202
315-477-6400 Fax: 315-477-6438
New York State Director:
Stanley Telega 315-477-6437
Assistant to the New York State Director:
Scott Collins
Special Projects Coordinator:
Chris Stewart

US Justice Department
Web site: www.usdoj.gov

Antitrust Division-New York Field Office . . . . fax: 212-335-8021
26 Federal Plaza, Rm 3630, New York, NY 10278-0004
212-335-8000 Fax: 212-335-8021
e-mail: newyork.atr@usdoj.gov
Chief:
Dierdre A. McEvoy
Assistant Chief:
Elizabeth B. Prewitt

Civil Division-Commercial Litigation Branch
950 Pennsylvania Avenue, NW, Washington, DC 20530-0001
202-514-2000
e-mail: civil.feedback@usdoj.gov
Deputy Assistant Attorney General:
Joyce Branda

Community Relations Service
600 E St NW, Ste 600, Washington, DC 20004
202-305-2935
Director of Community Relations Services:
Grande H. Lum

Community Relations Service-Northeast & Carribean Region
26 Federal Plaza, Ste 36-118, New York, NY 10278
CRS Conciliator:
Linda Ortiz

US Securities & Exchange Commission
Web site: www.sec.gov

New York Regional Office
233 Broadway, New York, NY 10279
646-428-1500
e-mail: newyork@sec.gov
Regional Director:
Mark Schoenfeld. 646-428-1500

Enforcement Division
Acting Director:
George Canellos 202-551-4500

Investment Management
Director:
Norm Champ 202-551-6720

U.S. CONGRESS

See U.S. Congress Chapter for additional Standing Committee and Subcommittee information.

House of Representatives Standing Committees

Energy & Commerce
Chair:
Fred Upton (R-MI)
Ranking Member:
Henry Waxman (D-CA)
New York Delegate:
Eliot L Engel (D) 202-225-2464
New York Delegate:
Paul Tonko (D)

Foreign Affairs
Chair:
Ed Royce (R-CA)
Ranking Member:
Eliot L. Engel (D-NY)
New York Delegate:
Gregory W. Meeks (D)
New York Delegate:
Brian Higgins (D)
New York Delegate:
Grace Meng (D)

Small Business
Chair:
Sam Graves (R-MO)
Ranking Member:
Nydia Velazquez (D-NY)
New York Delegate:
Chris Collins (R)

Joint Senate & House Standing Committees

Economic Committee, Joint
Chair:
Kevin Brady (R-TX)
Vice Chair:
Sen. Amy Klobuchar (D-MN)
Ranking Member:
Sam Brownback (R-KS) 202-224-6521

Offices and agencies generally appear in alphabetical order, except when specific order is requested by listee.

Senate Standing Committees

Commerce, Science & Transportation
Chair:
John D Rockefeller IV (D-WV) 202-224-6472
Ranking Member:
Sen. John Thune (R-SD)

Finance
Chair:
Max Baucus (D-MT) 202-224-2651
Ranking Member:
Orrin G. Hatch (R-UT)

Foreign Relations
Chair:
Sen. Robert Mendez (D-NJ)
Ranking Member:
Sen. Bob Corker (R-TN)

Small Business & Entrepreneurship
Chair:
Mary L Landrieu (D-LA) 202-224-5824
Ranking Minority Member:
James E. Risch (R-ID)

PRIVATE SECTOR

AeA New York Council
255 Fuller Rd, Albany Nanotechnology Complex, Albany, NY 12203
518-437-8820 Fax: 518-437-8821
e-mail: justin-wright@aeanet.org
Web site: www.aeanet.org
Electronics, software & information technology industries; support of high tech industry goals
Justin Wright, Executive Director

Altria Corporate Services
120 Park Ave, 16th Fl, New York, NY 10017
917-663-4000
Web site: www.altria.com
Manufacturing & marketing of foods, tobacco, alcoholic beverages
Louis C Camilleri, Chairman & Chief Executive Officer

American Chemistry/American Plastics Council
One Commerce Plaza, 99 Washington Ave, Ste 701, Albany, NY 12210
518-432-7835 Fax: 518-426-2276
e-mail: steve_rosario@americanchemistry.com
Web site: www.americanchemistry.com
Stephen Rosario, Director

American Council of Engineering Companies of NY (ACEC New York)
6 Airline Drive, Albany, NY 12205
518-452-8611 Fax: 518-452-1710
e-mail: jay@acecny.org
Web site: www.acecny.org
Business association for consulting engineering
Jay J Simson, Executive Director

American Institute of Architects (AIA) New York State Inc
52 S Pearl St, 3rd Fl, Albany, NY 12207
518-449-3334 Fax: 518-426-8176
e-mail: aianys@aianys.org
Web site: www.aianys.org
Architectural regulations, state policy, smart growth & affordable housing
Edward C Farrell, Executive Director

American Management Association International
1601 Broadway, New York, NY 10019
212-586-8100 or 800-262-9699 Fax: 212-903-8168
Web site: www.amanet.org
Business education & management development programs for individuals & organizations
Edward T Reilly, President & Chief Executive Officer

Associated Builders & Contractors, Empire State Chapter
6369 Collamer Dr, East Syracuse, NY 13057-1115
315-463-7539 or 800-477-7743 Fax: 315-463-7621
e-mail: empire@abcnys.org
Web site: www.abcnys.org
Merit shop construction trade association
Stephen Lefebvre, President

Associated General Contractors of America, NYS Chapter
10 Airline Dr, Ste 203, Albany, NY 12205-1025
518-456-1134 Fax: 518-456-1198
e-mail: agcadmin@agcnys.org
Web site: www.agcnys.org
Michael J Elmendorf II, President/CEO

Association Development Group Inc
119 Washington Ave, Ste 300, Albany, NY 12210
518-465-7085 Fax: 518-427-9495
e-mail: info@adgcommunications.com
Web site: www.adgcommunications.com
Association management, communications, education & training, strategic planning, graphic design, web design, database design
Kathleen A Van De Loo, President

Association for a Better New York
355 Lexington Ave, 8th Fl, New York, NY 10017
212-370-5800 Fax: 212-661-5877
e-mail: info@abny.org
Web site: www.abny.org
NYC public policy issues forums & committees
Michelle Adams, Executive Director

Association of Graphic Communications
330 Seventh Ave, 9th Fl, New York, NY 10001
212-279-2100 x108 Fax: 212-279-5381
e-mail: spindrvrk@agcomm.org
Web site: www.agcomm.org
Promote the economic well-being & public perception of printing & graphic communications within the NY/NJ/CT metro area
Vicki R Keenan, VP, Public Affairs

Better Business Bureau of Metropolitan New York
257 Park Ave South, 4th Fl, New York, NY 10010-7384
212-533-6200 Fax: 212-477-4912
e-mail: inquiry@newyork.bbb.org
Web site: www.newyork.bbb.org
Membership organization promoting ethical business practices
Susan D McMillan, President

NYS Bar Assn, Public Relations Cmte
Brown & Kelly, LLP
424 Main St, 1500 Liberty Bldg, Buffalo, NY 14202-3615
716-854-2620 Fax: 716-854-0082
e-mail: phassett@brownkelly.com
Paul Michael Hassett, Chair

Building Contractors Association
451 Park Ave South, 4th Fl, New York, NY 10016
212-683-8080 Fax: 212-683-0404
e-mail: pobrien@ny-bca.com
Web site: www.ny-bca.com
Commercial contractors
Paul J O'Brien, Managing Director

Offices and agencies generally appear in alphabetical order, except when specific order is requested by listee.

Policy Areas

Building Industry Association of NYC Inc
3130 Amboy Road, Staten Island, NY 10306
718-720-3070 Fax: 718-720-3088
e-mail: nshea@webuildnyc.com
Web site: www.webuildnyc.com
Nina Shea, Office Manager

Business Council for International Understanding
1212 Ave of the Americas, 10th Fl, New York, NY 10036
212-490-0460 Fax: 212-697-8526
Web site: www.bciu.org
Promoting dialogue & action between the business & government communities to expand international commerce
Peter J Tichansky, President & Chief Executive Officer

Business Council of New York State Inc
152 Washington Ave, Albany, NY 12210
518-465-7511 or 800-358-1202 Fax: 518-465-4389
e-mail: kenneth.adams@bcnys.org
Web site: www.bcnys.org
Kenneth Adams, President/CEO

Center for Economic Growth Inc
63 State Street, Albany, NY 12207
518-465-8975 Fax: 518-465-6681
e-mail: ceg@ceg.org
Web site: www.ceg.org
Business membership nonprofit promoting economic & business development in the Capital Region and Tech Valley
F Michael Tucker, President/Chief Executive Officer

Columbia University, Science & Technology Ventures
80 Claremont Avenue, 4th Fl, New York, NY 10027
212-854-6777 Fax: 212-854-8463
e-mail: mc1378@columbia.edu
Web site: www.stv.columbia.edu
Identify & patent new inventions & copyright materials; interact with industry to setup collaborative research agreements
Michael Cleare, Executive Director

Conference Board (The)
845 Third Ave, New York, NY 10022
212-339-0300 Fax: 212-836-3805
e-mail: gail.fosler@conference-board.org
Web site: www.conference-board.org
Research for business
Gail Fosler, Executive Vice President & Chief Economist

Construction Contractors Association of the Hudson Valley Inc
330 Meadow Ave, Newburgh, NY 12550
845-562-4280 Fax: 845-562-1448
e-mail: jjb@ccahv.com
Web site: www.ccahv.com
Association of building commercial and industrial contractors.
James Jay Bodrato, Executive Director

Consumers Union
101 Truman Ave, Yonkers, NY 10703-1057
914-378-2000 Fax: 914-378-2905
Web site: www.consumerreports.org; www.consumersunion.org
Publisher of Consumer Reports magazine; independent, nonprofit testing & information organization serving only consumers
Jean Halloran, Director, Consumer Policy Institute

Cornell University, Economics Department
450 Uris Hall, Ithaca, NY 14853-7601
607-255-6283 Fax: 607-255-2818
e-mail: dae3@cornell.edu
Web site: www.arts.cornell.edu/econ
Microeconomic theory, financial economics
David Easley, Professor

Dale Carnegie & Associates Inc
290 Motor Parkway, Hauppauge, NY 11788-5102
631-415-9300 or 800-231-5800 Fax: 631-415-9358
e-mail: peter_handal@dale-carnegie.com
Web site: www.dale-carnegie.com
Executive leadership training
Peter Handal, President & Chief Executive Officer

Davis Polk & Wardwell
450 Lexington Ave, New York, NY 10017
212-450-4284 Fax: 212-450-5545
e-mail: henry.king@davispolk.com
Web site: www.dpw.com
Securities litigation & antitrust law
Henry L King, Senior Counsel

Decision Strategies Group
111 Washington Ave, Ste 409, Albany, NY 12210
518-436-0607 Fax: 518-432-4359
e-mail: lynnmueller@dsgny.com
Web site: www.decisionstrategiesgroup.com
Strategic planning & communications consulting
I Lynn Mueller, President

Development Counsellors International
215 Park Ave S, 10th Floor, New York, NY 10003
212-725-0707 Fax: 212-725-2254
e-mail: andy.levine@dc-intl.com
Web site: www.aboutdci.com
Marketing services for economic development & tourism
Andrew T Levine, President

EVCI Career Colleges Holding Corp
1 Van Der Donck St, Yonkers, NY 10701-7049
914-623-0700 Fax: 914-964-8222
e-mail: info@evcinc.com
Web site: www.evcinc.com
Own & operate accredited career & college centers in NY & PA emphasizing business, technology & allied health programs
Dr John J McGrath, President/Chief Executive Officer

Eastern Contractors Association Inc
6 Airline Dr, Albany, NY 12205-1095
518-869-0961 Fax: 518-869-2378
e-mail: info@ecainc.org
Web site: www.ecainc.org
Commercial development & construction
Todd G Helfrich, Managing Director

Eastman Kodak Company
1250 H Street, Ste 800, Washington, DC 20005
202-857-3474 Fax: 202-857-3401
e-mail: stephen.ciccone@kodak.com
Web site: www.kodak.com
Manufactures & markets imaging systems & related services
Stephen J Ciccone, Director & Vice President of Public Affairs

Empire Center for New York State Policy
PO Box 7113, Albany, NY 12224
518-434-3100 Fax: 518-434-3130
e-mail: info@empirecenter.org
Web site: www.empirecenter.org
An independent nonpartisan research organization dedicated to fostering greater economic growth, opportunity, and individual responsibility in the Empire State. The Empire Center is a project of the Manhattan Inst for Policy Research.
Edmund J McMahon, Director

Empire State Restaurant & Tavern Association Inc
12 Sheridan Ave, Albany, NY 12207
518-436-8121 Fax: 518-436-7287
e-mail: esrta@verizon.net
Web site: www.esrta.org
Scott Wexler, Executive Director

Empire State Society of Association Executives Inc
991 Broadway, Suite 208, Albany, NY 12204
518-463-1755 Fax: 518-463-5257
e-mail: penny@essae.org
Web site: www.essae.org
Education, information, research & networking for professional staff of not-for-profit trade business & professional associations
Penny Murphy, President & Chief Executive Officer

Eric Mower & Associates
500 Plum St, Syracuse, NY 13204
315-466-1000 Fax: 315-466-2000
e-mail: csteenstra@mower.com
Web site: www.mower.com
Marketing communications & issues management
Chris Steenstra, Senior Partner

NYS Bar Assn, Antitrust Law Section
Federal Trade Commission
One Bowling Green, Ste 318, New York, NY 10004
212-607-2828
e-mail: banthony@ftc.gov
Barbara Anthony, Chair

Food Industry Alliance of New York State Inc
130 Washington Ave, Albany, NY 12210
518-434-8144 Fax: 518-434-9962
e-mail: michael@fiany.com
Web site: www.fiany.com
Assn of retail grocery, wholesale & supplier/manufacturer food companies
Michael Rosen, Vice President for Government Relations & General Counsel

General Contractors Association of NY
60 East 42nd St, Rm 3510, New York, NY 10165
212-687-3131 Fax: 212-808-5267
e-mail: ffarber@gcany.net
Heavy construction, transportation
Felice Farber, Director, External Affairs

Gilbert Tweed Associates Inc
415 Madison Ave, 20th Fl, New York, NY 10017
212-758-3000 Fax: 212-832-1040
e-mail: spinson@gilberttweed.com
Web site: www.gilberttweed.com
Executive searches & recruitment in public transit, transportation, energy, utilities, communication & insurance
Stephanie L Pinson, President

NYS Bar Assn, Intellectual Property Law Section
Hartman & Winnicki, PC
115 W Century Rd, Paramus, NJ 7654
201-967-8040 Fax: 201-967-0590
e-mail: rick@ravin.com
Richard L Ravin, Chair

IBM Corporation
80 State St, Albany, NY 12207
518-487-6733 Fax: 518-487-6679
Web site: www.ibm.com
Steve LaFleche, Managing Director, NYS Government

Intermagnetics General Corporation
450 Old Niskyuna Rd, PO Box 461, Latham, NY 12110-0461
518-782-1122 Fax: 518-786-8216
e-mail: corporate@igc.com
Web site: www.igc.com
Kathy Sheehan, Vice President & General Counsel

International Flavors & Fragrances Inc
521 West 57th Street, New York, NY 10019-2960
212-765-5500 Fax: 212-708-7132
Web site: www.iff.com
Create & manufacture flavors & fragrances for consumer products
Dennis M Meany, Senior Vice President, General Counsel & Secretary

Macy's East Inc
151 W 34th St, 18th Fl, New York, NY 10001
212-494-5568 Fax: 212-494-1857
e-mail: ed.goldberg@macys.com
Retail department/specialty stores
Edward Jay Goldberg, Senior Vice President Government & Consumer Affairs

Manhattan Institute for Policy Research
52 Vanderbilt Avenue, 2nd Floor, New York, NY 10017
212-599-7000 x315 Fax: 212-599-3494
e-mail: communications@manhattan-institute.org
Web site: www.manhattan-institute.org
Think-tank promoting the development & dissemination of new ideas that foster greater economic choice & individual responsibility
Lindsay Y Craig, Executive Director, Communications

Manufacturers Association of Central New York
One Webster's Landing, 5th Fl, Syracuse, NY 13202-1044
315-474-4201 Fax: 315-474-0524
e-mail: kburns@macny.org
Web site: www.macny.org
Training, education, compensation data & government relations services, HR services, consulting, purchasing consortiums
Karyn E Burns, Director, Communications & Government Relations

NYS Bar Assn, Business Law Section
Menaker & Herrmann LLP
10 East 40th Street, New York, NY 10016
212-545-1900 Fax: 212-545-1656
e-mail: sfa@mhjur.com
Web site: www.mhjur.com
Advice and counsel in Commercial Litigation, Corporate Securities & Finance and Commodities and Derivitives
Samuel F Abernethy, Partner

Mid-Hudson Pattern for Progress
6 Albany Post Rd, Newburgh, NY 12550-1439
914-565-4900 Fax: 914-565-4918
e-mail: mditullo@pfprogress.org
Web site: www.pattern-for-progress.org
Regional planning, research & policy development
Jonathan Drapkin, President

NYS Bar Assn, Commercial & Federal Litigation Section
Montclare & Wachtler
67 Wall St, 22nd Fl, New York, NY 10005
212-509-3900 Fax: 212-509-7239
e-mail: ljwachtler@montclarewachtler.com
Web site: www.montclarewachtler.com
Lauren J Wachtler, Chair

NY Society of Association Executives Inc (NYSAE)
322 Eighth Avenue, Suite 501, New York, NY 10001-8001
212-206-8230 Fax: 212-645-1147
e-mail: jdolci@nysaenet.org
Web site: www.nysaenet.org
Joel A Dolci, President & Chief Executive Officer

Offices and agencies generally appear in alphabetical order, except when specific order is requested by listee.

NYS Association of Electrical Contractors
16 Wade Rd, Latham, NY 12110
518-785-3676 or 800-724-1904 Fax: 518-785-0912
Web site: www.nysaec.org
Jay Mangione, Managing Director

NYS Builders Association Inc
One Commerce Plaza, Ste 704, Albany, NY 12210
518-465-2492 Fax: 518-465-0635
e-mail: phill@nysba.com
Web site: www.nysba.com
Advocate for building and housing industry on all legislative & regulatory issues impacting builders and housing
Philip A LaRocque, Executive Vice President

NYS Building & Construction Trades Council
71 West 23 St, New York, NY 10010
212-647-0700 Fax: 212-647-0705
Edward J Malloy, President

NYS Clinical Laboratory Association Inc
62 William St, 2nd Fl, New York, NY 10005
212-664-7999 Fax: 212-248-3008
e-mail: info@nyscla.com
Web site: www.nyscla.com
Promote the common business and regultaory interests of clinical laboratories located or operated within the state
Tom Rafalsky, President

NYS Economic Development Council
111 Washington Avenue, 6th Floor, Albany, NY 12210
518-426-4058 Fax: 518-426-4059
e-mail: mcmahon@nysedc.org
Web site: www.nysedc.org
Economic development professionals membership organization
Brian McMahon, Executive Director

NYS Society of Certified Public Accountants
3 Park Ave, 18th Fl, New York, NY 10016-5991
212-719-8300 or 800-633-6320 Fax: 212-719-3364
e-mail: lgrumet@nysscpa.org
Web site: www.nysscpa.org
Louis Grumet, Executive Director

NYS Trade Adjustment Assistance Center
81-85 State Street, 4th Floor, Binghamton, NY 13901
607-771-0875 Fax: 607-724-2404
e-mail: information@nystaac.org
Web site: www.nystaac.org
Advises US manufacturers on competing with foreign imports
Louis G McKeage, Director

National Association of Black Accountants, NY Chapter
PO Box 2791, Grand Central Station, New York, NY 10163
212-969-0560 Fax: 646-349-9620
e-mail: info@nabany.org
Web site: www.nabany.org
Represents the interest of African Americans & other minorities in accounting, auditing, business, consulting, finance & information technology
L Matthew Perry, President

National Federation of Independent Business
1 Commerce Plaza, Suite 803, Albany, NY 12260-1000
518-434-1262 or 877-434-1262 Fax: 518-426-8799
e-mail: mike.elmendorf@NFIB.org
Web site: www.nfib.org
Small business advocacy; supporting pro-small business candidates at the state & federal levels
Michael Elmendorf, State Director

New York Association of Convenience Stores
130 Washington Ave, Suite 300, Albany, NY 12210-2219
518-432-1400 Fax: 518-432-7400
e-mail: info@nyacs.org
Web site: www.nyacs.org
Retail & small business issues
Jim Calvin, President

New York Biotechnology Association (The)
25 Health Sciences Drive, Ste 202, Stony Brook, NY 11790
631-444-8895 Fax: 631-444-8896
e-mail: info@nyba.org
Web site: www.nyba.org
Development & growth of NYS-based biotechnology-related industries & institutions; strengthen competitiveness of the state as a location for biotech/biomed research, education & industry
Nathan P Tinker PhD, Executive Director

New York Building Congress
44 W 28th St, 12th Fl, New York, NY 10001-4212
212-481-9230 Fax: 212-447-6037
e-mail: rtanders55@aol.com
Web site: www.buildingcongress.com
Coalition of design, construction & real estate organizations
Richard T Anderson, President

New York Business Development Corporation
50 Beaver St, 6th Fl, Albany, NY 12207
518-463-2268 Fax: 518-463-0494
e-mail: mackrell@nybdc.com
Web site: www.nybdc.com
Small business lending
Patrick Mackrell, President & Chief Executive Officer

New York Mercantile Exchange Inc
1 North End Ave, New York, NY 10282-1101
212-299-2000 Fax: 212-301-4568
Web site: www.nymex.com
Commodity trading
Mitchell Steinhause, Chair

New York State Auto Dealers Association
37 Elk St, Albany, NY 12207
518-463-1148 x204 Fax: 518-432-1309
e-mail: bob@nysada.com
Web site: www.nysada.com
Robert Vancavage, President

New York State Restaurant Association
409 New Karner Rd, Albany, NY 12205
518-452-4222 Fax: 518-452-4497
e-mail: ricks@nysra.org
Web site: www.nysra.org
Rick J Sampson, President & Chief Executive Officer

Berkley Center for Entrepreneurial Studies NYU, Stern School of Business
44 West Fourth Street, Suite 7-91, New York, NY 10012-1126
212-998-8943 Fax: 212-995-4211
e-mail: william.baumol@nyu.edu
Web site: http://pages.stern.nyu.edu/~wbaumol
Productivity growth, downsizing, scale economies; trade, anti-trust; economics of industry, the environment, the arts & entrpreneurship
William J Baumol, Professor of Economics & Academic Director of B.C.E.S.

Northeast Equipment Dealers Association Inc
128 Metropolitan Park Dr, Liverpool, NY 13088
315-457-0314 or 800-932-0607 Fax: 315-451-3548
e-mail: rgaiss@ne-equip.com
Web site: www.ne-equip.com
Agricultural, industrial & outdoor power equipment
Ralph F Gaiss, CEO

Offices and agencies generally appear in alphabetical order, except when specific order is requested by listee.

Partnership for New York City
One Battery Park Plaza, 5th Fl, New York, NY 10004-1479
212-493-7403 or 212-493-7564 Fax: 212-493-7778
Web site: www.partnershipfornyc.org
Government Affairs; Business organization working in partnership with government, labor & the nonprofit sector to enhance the NYC economy
MarySol Rodriguez, Vice President, Government Affairs

Pepsi Co
700 Anderson Hill Rd, MD 3/1-311, Purchase, NY 10577
914-253-2609 Fax: 914-249-8203
e-mail: pwilcox@pepsi.com
Web site: www.pepsi.com
Manufacture, sell & distribute soft drinks, concentrates, syrups, snack foods & beverages
Peter G Wilcox, Director, Government Affairs

Perry Davis Associates
25 W 45th St, Suite 1405, New York, NY 10036
212-840-1166 Fax: 212-840-1514
e-mail: perry@perrydavis.com
Web site: www.perrydavis.com
Economic development & fundraising & management consulting for nonprofit organizations
Perry Davis, President

NYS Bar Assn, Multi-jurisdictional Practice Cmte
Proskauer Rose LLP
1585 Broadway, New York, NY 10036-8299
212-969-2900 Fax: 212-969-2900
e-mail: keppler@proskauer.com
Web site: www.proskauer.com
Klaus Eppler, Chair

Public Policy Institute of NYS Inc
152 Washington Ave, Albany, NY 12210
518-465-7511 Fax: 518-432-4537
e-mail: david.shaffer@bcnys.org
Web site: www.ppinys.org
Conduct & publish research on NYS economic development issues
David Shaffer, President

Regional Plan Association
4 Irving Place, 7th Fl, New York, NY 10003
212-253-2727 Fax: 212-253-5666
e-mail: yaro@rpa.org
Web site: www.rpa.org
Develops & implements land-use, community design, transportation, open-space preservation, economic development & social equity proposals
Robert D Yaro, President

Retail Council of New York State
258 State St, PO Box 1992, Albany, NY 12201
518-465-3586 or 800-442-3589 Fax: 518-465-7960
e-mail: info@retailcouncilnys.com
Web site: www.retailcouncilnys.com
James R Sherin, President & Chief Executive Officer

Sawchuk Brown Associates
41 State St, Ste 500, Albany, NY 12207
518-462-0318 Fax: 518-462-0688
e-mail: caseys@sawchukbrown.com
Web site: www.sawchukbrown.com
Public affairs, public relations, marketing, association communication
Sean Casey, Senior Vice President, Public Affairs

Society of Professional Engineers Inc (NYS)
6 Airline Drive, Albany, NY 12205
518-283-7490 Fax: 518-283-7495
e-mail: kknorris@nysspe.org
Web site: www.nysspe.org
Promotes and defends the lawful and ethical practice of engineering
Kelly K Norris, Executive Director

Software & Information Industry Association
1090 Vermont Ave, NW, 6th Fl, Washington, DC 20005-4095
202-289-7442 Fax: 202-289-7097
Web site: www.siia.net
Issues affecting the software & information industry, in particular electronic commerce & the digital marketplace
Ken Wasch, President

Support Services Alliance Inc
107 Prospect St, PO Box 130, Schoharie, NY 12157
800-322-3920 or 518-295-7966 Fax: 518-295-8556
e-mail: info@ssamembers.com
Web site: www.smallbizgrowth.com
Provides representation & group purchasing for small businesses
Steven Cole, President

UHY Advisors
66 State St, Albany, NY 12207
518-449-3166 Fax: 518-449-5832
e-mail: rkotlow@uhy-us.com
Web site: www.uhyadvisors-us.com
Professional financial, tax, business & tax advisory services for mid-sized to larger companies
Richard Kotlow, Chief Executive Officer

Wegmans Food Markets Inc
1500 Brooks Ave, PO Box 30844, Rochester, NY 14603-0844
585-464-4760 Fax: 585-464-4669
e-mail: comments@wegmans.com
Web site: www.wegmans.com
Mary Ellen Burris, Senior Vice President, Consumer Affairs

Women's Business Training Center of New York State
200 Genesee St, Utica, NY 13502
315-733-9848 or 877-844-9848 Fax: 315-733-0247
e-mail: nywbc@aol.com
Web site: www.nywbc.org
Dedicated to helping women reach their entrepreneurial goals & aspirations through assistance and training
Donna L Rebisz, Project Director

Women's Venture Fund Inc
545 5th Ave, 17th Fl, New York, NY 10018
212-563-0499 Fax: 212-868-9116
e-mail: info@wvf-ny.org
Web site: www.womensventurefund.org
Multi-service micro-lender that targets women entrepreneurs in under-served urban communities
Maria Otero, President & Founder

Zogby International
901 Broad St, Utica, NY 13501
315-624-0200 or 877-462-7655 Fax: 315-624-0210
e-mail: marketing@zogby.com
Web site: www.zogby.com
Political polling & analysis; social science research; business & consumer public opinion surveys & market research
John Zogby, President/CEO

Offices and agencies generally appear in alphabetical order, except when specific order is requested by listee.

CORPORATIONS, AUTHORITIES & COMMISSIONS

NEW YORK STATE

Adirondack Park Agency
1133 NYS Route 86
PO Box 99
Ray Brook, NY 12977
518-891-4050 Fax: 518-891-3938
Web site: www.apa.ny.gov

Chair:
Leilani Ulrich 518-891-4050
Executive Director:
Terry Martino 518-891-4050
Counsel:
James Townsend 518-891-4050
Public Relations:
Keith McKeever 518-891-4050
e-mail: keith.mckeever@apa.y.gov

Agriculture & NYS Horse Breeding Development Fund
1 Broadway Center
Suite 602
Schenectady, NY 12305
518-395-5484 Fax: 518-347-1483
e-mail: info@nysirestakes.com
Web site: www.nysirestakes.com

Executive Director:
Mike Mullaney 518-395-5484
e-mail: mike.mullaney@nysirestakes.com
Counsel:
Mark Stuart 518-395-5484

Albany County Airport Authority
Albany International Airport
Administration Building
2nd Floor
Albany, NY 12211
518-242-2222 x1 Fax: 518-242-2641
e-mail: info@albanyairport.com
Web site: www.albanyairport.com/airport_authority.php

Chief Executive Officer:
John A O'Donnell PE 518-242-2222 x1
Chief Financial Officer:
William O'Reilly 518-242-2222 x1
Director, Public Affairs:
Douglas I. Myers 518-242-2222 x1
Counsel:
Peter F Stuto 518-242-2222 x1
Airport Planner:
Stephen A Iachetta 518-242-2222 x1
Administrative Services:
Liz Charland 518-242-2222 x1

Albany Port District Commission
106 Smith Blvd, Admin Bldg
Port of Albany
Albany, NY 12202
518-463-8763 Fax: 518-463-8767
e-mail: portofalbany@portofalbany.us
Web site: www.portofalbany.us

Chair:
Georgette Steffens. 518-463-8763
General Manager:
Richard Hendrick 518-463-8763
e-mail: rhendrick@portofalbany.us
Counsel:
Thomas Owens 518-694-0910

Atlantic States Marine Fisheries Commission
1050 N. Highland Street
Ste 200 A-N
Arlington, VA 22201
703-842-0740 Fax: 703-842-0741
e-mail: info@asmfc.org
Web site: www.asmfc.org

Chair, NC:
Dr. Louis Daniel III
Administrative Commissioner, New York:
James Gilmore. 631-444-0433
Governor's Appointee, New York:
Emerson C Hasbrouck, Jr 631-928-1524
Executive Director:
Robert E Beal 703-842-0740
e-mail: rbeal@asmfc.org
Director Communications:
Tina Berger 703-842-0740
e-mail: tberger@asmfc.org

Battery Park City Authority (Hugh L Carey)
One World Financial Center, 24th Fl
200 Liberty Street
New York, NY 10281
212-417-2000 Fax: 212-417-2001
e-mail: info@bpca.ny.gov
Web site: www.bpca.ny.gov

Chairman & CEO:
Dennis Mehiel. 212-417-2000
President & Chief Operating Officer:
Shari Hyman 212-417-4205/fax: 212-417-4153
Vice Chair:
Donald Cappocia. 212-417-2000
Member/Vice Chair:
Frank J Branchini 212-417-2000
Member:
Lester Petracca 212-417-2000
Member:
Martha J Gallo. 212-417-2000
VP External Relations:
Robin Forst 212-417-2276/fax: 212-417-2279
e-mail: robin.forst@bpca.ny.gov

Brooklyn Navy Yard Development Corporation
63 Flushing Ave, Unit #300
Bldg 292, 3rd Fl
Brooklyn, NY 11205
718-907-5900 Fax: 718-643-9296
e-mail: info@brooklynnavyyard.org
Web site: www.brooklynnavyyard.org

Chair:
Henry Gutman. 718-907-5900
President & Chief Executive Officer:
David Ehrenberg 718-907-5900
Executive Vice President/Chief Operating Officer:
Elliot S. Matz 718-907-5900
Vice President/Deputy General Counsel:
Martin H. Baker 718-907-5900

Offices and agencies generally appear in alphabetical order, except when specific order is requested by listee.

Chief of Staff:
  Clare Newman 718-907-5900
Senior Vice President, External Affairs:
  Richard Drucker 718-907-5900

Buffalo & Fort Erie Public Bridge Authority (Peace Bridge Authority)
One Peace Bridge Plaza
Buffalo, NY 14213-2494
716-884-6744 Fax: 716-884-2089
Web site: www.peacebridge.com

Chair (US):
  William Hoyt....................716-884-6744/fax: 716-883-7246
Vice Chair (Canada):
  Anthony M Annunziata..............716-884-6744/fax: 716-883-7246
General Manager:
  Ron Rienas 716-884-6744

Capital District Regional Off-Track Betting Corporation
510 Smith St
Schenectady, NY 12305
518-344-5266 or 800-292-2387 Fax: 518-370-5460
e-mail: customerservice@capitalotb.com
Web site: www.capitalotb.com

Chair:
  Marcel Webb..518-344-5225
Board Secretary & Director:
  F James Mumpton....................................518-344-5225
President & Chief Executive Officer:
  John F Signor 518-344-5225
VP, Corporate Operations:
  Tod Grenci 518-344-5408
VP, Legal Affairs/General Counsel:
  Robert Hemsworth 518-344-5298
VP, Finance/Comptroller:
  Nancy Priputen-Madrian 518-344-5233
VP, Human Resources:
  Robert Dantz.......................................518-344-5301

Capital District Regional Planning Commission
One Park Place
Suite 102
Albany, NY 12205
518-453-0850 Fax: 518-453-0856
e-mail: cdrpc@cdrpc.org
Web site: www.cdrpc.org

Executive Director:
  Rocco A Ferraro 518-453-0850
  e-mail: rocky@cdrpc.org
Information Services:
  Tim Canty 518-453-0850
  e-mail: d1wardle@cdrpc.org

Capital District Transportation Authority
110 Watervliet Ave
Albany, NY 12206
518-437-8300 or 518-482-8822 Fax: 518-437-8318
Web site: www.cdta.org

Chair:
  David M Stackrow 518-437-8311
Vice Chair:
  Georgeanna Nugent Lussier 518-437-8311
CEO:
  Carm Basile......................518-437-6840/fax: 518-437-8349
  e-mail: carmb@cdta.org

General Counsel:
  Amanda A Avery...................518-437-8315/fax: 518-437-8318
  e-mail: amandaa@cdta.org
VP, Finance & Administration:
  Michael P Collins 518-437-8380/fax: 518-437-8347
  e-mail: mikec@cdta.org
Director of Transportation:
  Gary Cook.......................518-437-8372/fax: 518-437-8328
  e-mail: garyc@cdta.org
VP, Planning & Infrastructure:
  Christopher G Desany 518-437-8320/fax: 518-437-8328
  e-mail: chrisd@cdta.org

Catskill Off-Track Betting Corporation
Park Place
Box 3000
Pomona, NY 10970
845-362-0407 Fax: 845-362-0419
e-mail: otb@interbets.com; customerservice@interbets.com
Web site: www.interbets.com

President:
  Donald J Groth 845-362-0400

Central New York Regional Market Authority
2100 Park St
Syracuse, NY 13208
315-422-8647 Fax: 315-422-6897
Web site: cnyrma.com

Acting Commissioner of Agricultural Markets:
  Richard A Ball 315-422-8647
Commissioner's Representative:
  Troy Waffner 315-422-8647
  e-mail: genedemos@gmail.com

Central New York Regional Transportation Authority
200 Cortland Ave
PO Box 820
Syracuse, NY 13205-0820
315-442-3400 Fax: 315-442-3337
Web site: www.centro.org

Chair, Board of Directors:
  Brian M Schultz 315-442-3300
Executive Director:
  Frank Kobliski 315-442-3360
  e-mail: fkobliski@centro.org
VP, Finance:
  Christine LoCurto..................................315-442-3355
Manager, Procurement & Grants Administration:
  EJ Moses...315-442-3368

Central Pine Barrens Joint Planning & Policy Commission
624 Old Riverhead Road
Westhampton Beach, NY 11978
631-288-1079 Fax: 631-288-1367
e-mail: info@pb.state.ny.us
Web site: www.pb.state.ny.us

Chair & Governor's Appointee & Region 1 Director DEC:
  Peter A Scully.....................................631-288-1079
Member & Suffolk County Executive:
  Steve Bellone 631-288-1079
Member & Brookhaven Town Supervisor:
  Edward P. Romaine 631-288-1079

Offices and agencies generally appear in alphabetical order, except when specific order is requested by listee.

Policy Areas

Member & Riverhead Town Supervisor:
Sean M Walter 631-288-1079
Member & Southampton Town Supervisor:
Anna E Throne-Holst 631-288-1079

City University Construction Fund
555 W 57th St, 10th Fl
New York, NY 10019
212-541-0171 Fax: 212-541-0175

Interim Executive Director:
Judith Bergtraum..............................646-664-2605
e-mail: iris.weinshall@mail.cuny.edu
Counsel:
Frederick Schaffer...............................646-664-9210
e-mail: frederick.schaffer@mail-cuny.edu

Delaware River Basin Commission
25 State Police Drive
PO Box 7360
West Trenton, NJ 08628-0360
609-883-9500 Fax: 609-883-9522
Web site: www.state.nj.us/drbc

New York Member/Chair:
Andrew M Cuomo 518-474-8390
Executive Director:
Steve Tambini 609-883-9500 x200
e-mail: steve.tambini@drbc.state.nj.us
Deputy Executive Director:
Vacant 609-883-9500 x208
Commission Secretary & Assistant General Counsel:
Pamela Bush 609-883-9500 x203
e-mail: pamela.bush@drbc.state.nj.us
General Counsel:
Kenneth J Warren 484-383-4834
e-mail: kwarren@warrenenvcounsel.com
Communications Manager:
Clarke Rupert..............................609-883-9500 x260
e-mail: clarke.rupert@drbc.state.nj.us

Development Authority of the North Country
317 Washington Street
Watertown, NY 13601
315-661-3200
e-mail: info@danc.org
Web site: www.danc.org

Chair:
Gary Turck 315-661-3200
Executive Director:
James Wright 315-661-3200
Deputy Executive Director:
Thomas R Sauter................................315-661-3200
e-mail: tsauter@danc.org
Director, Engineering:
Carrie Tuttle 315-661-3210
Telecom Division Manager:
David Wolf 315-661-3200
e-mail: oatn@danc.org
Landfill Superintendent:
Steve McElwain 315-661-3230
Director, Regional Development:
Michelle Capone................................315-661-3200

Empire State Development Corporation
633 Third Avenue
New York, NY 10017

518-270-1130 Fax: 518-270-1141
e-mail: capitaldist@esd.ny.gov
Web site: www.esd.ny.gov

625 Broadway
Albany, NY 12207
518-292-5200

95 Perry Street
Ste 500
Buffalo, NY 14203
716-846-8200
Fax: 716-846-8260

President & CEO:
Howard Zemsky 212-803-3700
e-mail: president@esd.ny.gov
Business Expansion:
John Gilstrap.................................212-803-3700
Public Affairs:
Kay Sarlin Wright.............................800-260-7313
e-mail: esdpressoffice@esd.ny.gov
Chief of Staff & COO:
Mehul J. Patel 212-803-3700

Great Lakes Commission
2805 S Industrial Hwy
Ste 100
Ann Arbor, MI 48104-6791
734-971-9135 Fax: 734-971-9150
e-mail: teder@glc.org
Web site: www.glc.org

Chairman:
Kelvin Burch.................................814-332-6816
e-mail: keburch@state.pa.us
Vice Chair:
Jon W Allan 517-284-5035
e-mail: allanj@michigan.gov
New York State Commissioner:
Joseph Martens 518-402-8540/fax: 518-402-8541
e-mail: joseph.martens@dec.ny.gov
Executive Director:
Tim A Eder....................................734-971-9135
e-mail: teder@glc.org
Deputy Director:
Thomas R Crane 734-971-9135
e-mail: tcrane@glc.org
CIO:
Stephen J Cole 734-971-9135
e-mail: scole@glc.org
Program Director:
Victoria Pebbles 734-971-9135
e-mail: vpebbles@glc.org
Communications Director:
Christine Manninen 734-971-9135
e-mail: manninen@glc.org
Policy Director:
Matthew Doss 734-971-9135
e-mail: mdoss@glc.org

Hudson River-Black River Regulating District
Hudson River Area Office
350 Northern Blvd, Ste 304
Albany, NY 12204
518-465-3491 Fax: 518-432-2485
e-mail: hrao@hrbrrd.com
Web site: www.hrbrrd.com

Offices and agencies generally appear in alphabetical order, except when specific order is requested by listee.

Chair:
  Mark M Finkle 518-465-3491
Executive Director:
  Michael A Clark 518-465-3491
Chief Engineer:
  Robert S Foltan 518-465-3491
Chief Fiscal Officer:
  Richard J Ferrara 518-465-3491
General Counsel:
  Robert P Leslie 518-465-3491

Interest on Lawyer Account (IOLA) Fund of the State of NY
11 East 44th St
Ste 1406
New York, NY 10017
646-865-1541 or 800-222-4652 Fax: 646-865-1545
e-mail: iolaf@iola.org
Web site: www.iola.org

Chair:
  Benito Romano 646-865-1541
Executive Director:
  Christopher O'Malley 646-865-1541
General Counsel:
  Christine M Fecko 646-865-1541
Director of Administration:
  Michele D Agard 646-865-1541

Interstate Environmental Commission
247 West 30th St
Ste 6B
New York, NY 10001
212-967-1414 Fax: 212-967-1430
e-mail: iecmail@iec-nynjct.org
Web site: www.iec-nynjct.org

Chair (CT):
  Patricia Sesto 212-967-1414
Vice Chair (NY):
  Judith L Baron 212-967-1414
Vice Chair (NJ):
  John M Scagnelli 212-967-1414
Associate Director:
  Bill Shadel 212-967-1414

Interstate Oil & Gas Compact Commission
PO Box 53127
900 NE 23rd St
Oklahoma City, OK 73152-3127
405-525-3556 Fax: 405-525-3592
e-mail: iogcc@iogcc.state.ok.us
Web site: www.iogcc.ok.gov

Chair:
  Governor Gary R Herbert (UT) .405-525-3556
Vice Chair:
  Hal Fitch 405-525-3556
Executive Director:
  Mike Smith 405-525-3556
New York State Official Representative:
  Bradley J Field 518-402-8076
Communications Manager:
  Carol Booth 405-525-3556

Lake George Park Commission
75 Fort George Rd
PO Box 749
Lake George, NY 12845
518-668-9347 Fax: 518-668-5001
e-mail: info@lgpc.state.ny.us
Web site: www.lgpc.state.ny.us

Chair:
  Bruce E Young 518-668-9347
Executive Director:
  David Wick 518-668-9347
  e-mail: dave@lgpc.state.ny.us
Counsel:
  Eileen Haynes 518-668-9347
Director of Law Enforcement:
  Lt William Bramlage 518-668-9347
  e-mail: ben@lgpc.state.ny.us
Director, Operations:
  Keith Fish 518-668-9347
  e-mail: opdir@lgpc.state.ny.us

Lawyers' Fund for Client Protection
119 Washington Ave
Albany, NY 12210
518-434-1935 or 800-442-FUND Fax: 518-434-5641
e-mail: info@nylawfund.org
Web site: www.nylawfund.org

Chair:
  Eric A Seiff 518-434-1935
Vice Chair:
  Nancy Burner 518-434-1935
Executive Director & Counsel:
  Timothy O'Sullivan 518-434-1935

Legislative Bill Drafting Commission
Capitol, Rm 308
Albany, NY 12224
518-455-7500 Fax: 518-455-7598

Commissioner:
  Randall G Bluth 518-455-7506
  e-mail: bluth@lbdc.state.ny.us

Legislative Retrieval System .fax: 518-455-7679
  1450 Western Ave, Albany, NY 12203
  800-356-6566 Fax: 518-455-7679
Director:
  Burleigh McCutcheon 518-455-7672
  e-mail: mccutcheon@lbdc.state.ny.us

MTA (Metropolitan Transportation Authority)
347 Madison Ave
New York, NY 10017
212-878-7000 Fax: 212-878-7264
Web site: www.mta.info

Chairman/CEO:
  Thomas F. Prendergast 212-878-7200
Chief Operating Officer:
  Nuria I. Fernandez 212-878-7274
Director of Security:
  Raymond Diaz 212-878-7155
Director, Government & Community Affairs:
  Robert Brennan 212-878-7160
Senior Director, Human Resources:
  Margaret M. Connor

Offices and agencies generally appear in alphabetical order, except when specific order is requested by listee.

Policy Areas

Director, Labor Relations:
  Anita Miller. 212-878-7438
Auditor General:
  Michael J Fucilli. .212-878-7000
Director, Special Project Development & Planning:
  William Wheeler. .212-878-7278
Chief Financial Officer:
  Robert E. Foran
General Counsel:
  Jerome F Page 212-878-7313/fax: 212-878-7050
Chief of Staff:
  Catherine A. Rinaldi 212-878-7206
Director, External Communications:
  Adam Lisberg 212-878-7440

MTA Bridges & Tunnels
2 Broadway
22nd Floor
New York, NY 10004-2801
646-252-7000 Fax: 646-252-7408
Web site: www.mta.info/bandt

Chairman/CEO:
  Thomas F. Prendergast. 212-878-7200
COO:
  Nuria I. Fernandez 212-878-7200
President:
  James Ferrara 212-360-3100
Chief Engineer:
  Joseph Keane 212-878-7200
Vice President, Labor Relations:
  Sharon Gallo-Kotcher. 212-360-3015
Vice President, Operations:
  James Fortunato 212-878-7200
Chief Procurement Officer:
  Anthony Koestler .646-252-7084
Vice President, Staff Services & Chief of Staff:
  Catherine T Sweeney 646-252-7421
Executive Vice President:
  David T Moretti 646-252-7100
Chief Financial Officer:
  Don Spero 646-252-7132
Chief Technology Officer:
  Tariq Habib. 646-252-7230
General Counsel:
  M. Margaret Jerry. 212-878-7200
Manager, Public Affairs:
  Judith Glave 646-252-7276

MTA Bus Company
2 Broadway
New York, NY 10004
212-878-7174 Fax: 212-878-0205
Web site: www.mta.info/busco

Chairman/CEO:
  Thomas F. Prendergast. 212-878-7200
President:
  Darryl Irick. 212-878-7174

MTA Capital Construction Program
2 Broadway
8th Floor
New York, NY 10002
646-252-4575
Web site: www.mta.info/capital

Chairman/CEO:
  Thomas F. Prendergast 212-878-7200

President:
  Dr Michael Horodniceanu 646-252-4277
Chief of Staff:
  Ayala Malinovitz .646-252-4011
Senior Director, Government & Community Affairs:
  Richard Mulieri 646-252-4197
Executive Vice President:
  William Goldstein. 646-252-4277
Senior Vice President & General Counsel:
  Evan Eisland 646-252-4274
Senior Director/Chief Procurement Officer:
  David Cannon 646-252-2321
Vice President/Chief Engineer:
  Mike Kyriacou 646-252-4500
Senior Vice President & Program Executive, East Side Access:
  Alan Paskoff. 212-967-0118
Senior Vice President & Program Executive, 2nd Ave Subway:
  William Goodrich. 212-510-2661
VP & Program Executive, #7 Subway Line Extension:
  Mark Schiffman 646-252-3723
Director, System Safety & Security:
  Eric Osnes. 646-252-4556
Vice President, Program Controls & Quality Safety:
  Raymond Schaeffer. 646-252-5393
Vice President, Planning, Development & External Relations:
  Joseph Petrocelli .646-252-3813

MTA Long Island Rail Road
Jamaica Station
Jamaica, NY 11435
718-558-7400 Fax: 718-558-8212
Web site: www.mta.info/lirr

Chairman/CEO:
  Thomas F. Prendergast. 212-878-7200
President:
  Helena E Williams 718-558-8252
Executive Vice President:
  Albert Cosenza 718-558-7993
  e-mail: accosen@lirr.org
Chief Information Officer:
  Scott Dieterich 718-588-8166
Vice President, General Counsel & Secretary:
  Richard Gans. 718-558-8264
Vice President, Labor Relations:
  Michael Chirillo 718-558-7405
Vice President, Market Development & Public Affairs:
  Joseph Calderone .718-558-7301
Vice President, ESA/Special Projects:
  John Coulter 718-558-7363
  e-mail: jwcoult@lirr.org
Director, System Safety:
  Frank Lo Presti 718-558-7711
General Manager, Public Affairs:
  Susan McGowan 718-558-7400

MTA Metro-North Railroad
347 Madison Ave
New York, NY 10017
212-340-2677 Fax: 212-340-4995
Web site: www.mta.info/mnr

Chairman/CEO:
  Thomas F. Prendergast 212-878-7200
President:
  Joseph Giulietti 212-340-2677
General Counsel:
  Seth Cummins. 212-340-4933
VP, Finance & Informational Systems:
  D. Kim Porcelain .212-340-2636

Offices and agencies generally appear in alphabetical order, except when specific order is requested by listee.

Senior VP, Operations:
Robert Lieblong 212-499-4300
Senior Director, Capital Planning & Program:
John Kennard 212-340-2500
Chief of Staff & Operations:
David Treasure 212-340-2677
Chief Safety & Security Officer:
Anne Kirsch 212-340-4913
Senior Director, Capital Programs:
Timothy McCartney 212-340-4913
Vice President, Business Operations:
Thomas Tendy 212-672-1251
Senior Director, Corporate & Public Affairs:
Mark Mannix 212-340-2142

MTA New York City Transit
2 Broadway
New York, NY 10004
718-330-3000 Fax: 718-596-2146
Web site: www.mta.info/nyct

Chairman/CEO:
Thomas F. Prendergast 212-878-7200
Acting President:
Carmen Bianco 646-252-5800
Chief Transportation Officer:
Herbert Lambert 718-330-3000
Vice President, Labor Relations:
Christopher Johnson 718-330-3000
Vice President, Corporate Communications:
Paul Fleuranges 646-252-5873
Vice President, Technology & Information Services:
Signey Gellineau 718-330-3000
Vice President & General Counsel:
Martin Schnabel 718-694-3900
Director, Labor Relations:
Andrew Paul 646-252-5880

MTA Office of the Inspector General
2 Penn Paza, 5th Fl
New York, NY 10121
212-878-0000 or 800-682-4448 Fax: 212-878-0003
e-mail: complaints@mtaig.org
Web site: www.mtaig.state.ny.us

Inspector General:
Barry L Kluger 212-878-0000

Nassau Regional Off-Track Betting Corporation
139 Liberty Ave
Mineola, NY 11501
516-572-2800 Fax: 516-572-2840
e-mail: webmaster@nassauotb.com
Web site: www.nassauotb.com

President:
Joseph G. Cairo, Jr. 516-572-2800
Director, Facilities Development:
John J Sparacio 516-572-2800

New England Interstate Water Pollution Control Commission
Wannalancit Mills
650 Suffolk Street
Suite 410
Lowell, MA 01854

978-323-7929 Fax: 978-323-7919
e-mail: mail@neiwpcc.org
Web site: www.neiwpcc.org

Chair:
Yvonne Bolton 978-323-7929
Vice Chair (MA):
Bethany Card 978-323-7929
Commissioner, New York State:
Joseph J Martens 518-485-8940
Executive Director:
Ronald F Poltak 978-323-7929
e-mail: rpoltak@neiwpcc.org
Deputy Director:
Susan Sullivan 978-323-7929
e-mail: ssullivan@neiwpcc.org

New York City Housing Development Corporation
110 William St
10th Fl
New York, NY 10038
212-227-5500 Fax: 212-227-6865
e-mail: info@nychdc.com
Web site: www.nychdc.com

Chairperson:
Vicki Been 212-863-6100
President:
Gary D Rodney 212-227-3600
Executive VP/COO & General Counsel:
Richard Froehlich 212-227-7435
Executive VP, Real Estate & Chief of Staff:
Joan Tally 212-227-6846
Senior Vice President, Portfolio Management:
Teresa Gigliello 212-227-9133
Senior Vice President, Loan Servicing:
Eileen O'Reilly 212-227-7494
Chief Credit Officer:
Urmas Naeris 212-227-9724
Communications/Press Office:
Christina Sanchez 212-227-2644
e-mail: csanchez@nychdc.com

New York City Residential Mortgage Insurance Corporation
Chair:
Vicki Been 212-863-6100
President:
Gary D Rodney 212-227-3600

New York City School Construction Authority
30-30 Thomson Ave
Long Island City, NY 11101-3045
718-472-8000 Fax: 718-472-8840
Web site: www.nycsca.org

Chair/Chancellor:
Carmen Farina 718-472-8000
President & Chief Executive Officer:
Lorraine Grillo 718-472-8001
Executive Vice President & General Counsel:
Ross J Holden 718-472-8220
VP, Finance:
Marianne Egri 718-472-8012
VP, Construction Management:
George Toma 718-472-8359
VP, Architecture & Engineering:
E Bruce Barrett, RA 718-472-8710
VP, Administration:
Craig Collins 718-472-8149

Offices and agencies generally appear in alphabetical order, except when specific order is requested by listee.

New York Convention Center Operating Corporation
655 W 34th St
New York, NY 10001-1188
212-216-2000 Fax: 212-216-2588
e-mail: moreinfo@javitscenter.com
Web site: www.javitscenter.com

Chair:
Henry Silverman...................................212-216-2130
President/CEO:
Alan Steel..212-216-2000
SVP/Chief Financial Officer:
Edward B MacDonald Jr...........................212-216-2369
SVP/General Counsel:
Elizabeth Bradford................................212-216-2125
SVP, Sales & Marketing:
Doreen Guerin.....................................212-216-2335

New York Metropolitan Transportation Council
199 Water St, 22nd Fl
New York, NY 10038
212-383-7200 Fax: 212-383-2418
e-mail: nymtc-web@dot.ny.gov
Web site: www.nymtc.org

Executive Director:
Joel Ettinger.....................................212-383-7236
Acting Director, Administration:
Anthony Gawrych..................................212-383-2412
e-mail: anthony.gawrych@dot.ny.gov
Director, Planning:
Gerard J Bogacz..................................212-383-7260
e-mail: gerry.bogacz@dot.ny.gov
PIO:
Lisa Daglian......................................212-383-7241
e-mail: lisa.daglian@dot.ny.gov

New York Power Authority
123 Main Street
Mailstop 10-H
White Plains, NY 10601-3170
914-681-6200 Fax: 914-390-8190
e-mail: info@nypa.gov
Web site: www.nypa.gov

Chairman:
John R. Koelmel...................................914-287-3636
President & Chief Executive Officer:
Gil C Quiniones...................................914-287-3501
Vice President, Public & Regulatory Affairs:
Jill Anderson.....................................518-433-6700
Chief Operating Officer:
Edward A Welz.....................................518-433-6700
Acting General Counsel:
Arthur Cambouris..................................914-681-6200

New York State Assn of Fire Districts
PO Box 1419
Massapequa, NY 11758
631-947-2079 or 800-520-9594 Fax: 631-207-1655
Web site: www.firedistnys.com

President:
Thomas E Herlihy Jr...............................315-683-5309
e-mail: teherlih@yahoo.com
First Vice President:
Anthony Gallino...................................631-831-6875
e-mail: digndad@aol.com

Second Vice President:
Thomas J Rinaldi.................................518-664-6538
e-mail: tom@rinaldi1.com
Secretary & Treasurer:
Joseph P DeStefano...............................631-947-2079
e-mail: dacomish@aol.com
Counsel:
William N Young.................800-349-2904 or 518-456-6767
fax: 518-456-4644
e-mail: byoung@yfkblaw.com

New York State Athletic Commission
123 William St
2nd Floor
New York, NY 10038
212-417-5700 Fax: 212-417-4987
e-mail: info@dos.ny.gov
Web site: www.dos.ny.gov/athletic

Chair:
Melvina Lathan...................................212-417-5700

New York State Board of Law Examiners
Corporate Plaza Bldg 3
254 Washington Ave Ext
Albany, NY 12203-5195
518-453-5990 Fax: 518-452-5729
Web site: www.nybarexam.org

Chair:
Diane F Bosse.....................................518-453-5990
Executive Director:
John J McAlary....................................518-453-5990
Deputy Director/Counsel:
Cara J. Brousseau

New York State Bridge Authority
Mid-Hudson Bridge Plaza
PO Box 1010
Highland, NY 12528
845-691-7245 Fax: 845-691-3560
e-mail: info@nysba.ny.gov
Web site: www.nysba.ny.gov

Chair:
Richard A. Gerentine.............................845-691-7245
Vice Chair:
Joseph Ramaglia..................................845-691-7245
Executive Director:
Joseph Ruggiero..................................845-691-7245
Director, IT:
Gregory J Herd...................................518-828-4107
Director, Toll Collections & Operations:
Wayne V Ferguson.................................845-691-7245

New York State Commission of Correction
80 South Swan St
12th Fl
Albany, NY 12210
518-485-2346 Fax: 518-485-2467
e-mail: infoscoc@scoc.ny.gov
Web site: www.scoc.ny.gov

Chairman:
Thomas A Beilein.................................518-485-2330
Commissioner:
Phyllis Harrison-Ross M.D.

Offices and agencies generally appear in alphabetical order, except when specific order is requested by listee.

Commissioner:
  Thomas Loughren
Assistant to Chair:
  Patricia Amati 518-485-2330
Counsel:
  Brian Callahan 518-485-2346
Chair, Citizens' Policy & Complaint Review Council:
  Thomas Loughren. 518-485-2346
Chair, Medical Review Board:
  Phyllis Harrison-Ross. 518-485-2346
Director, Operations:
  James Lawrence 518-485-2346
Deputy Director, Operations:
  Richard Kinney. 518-457-6110
Deputy Director, Public Information:
  Walter McClure 518-485-2346

New York State Commission on Judicial Nomination

c/o Greenberg Traurig LLP
54 State Street
Albany, NY 12207
518-689-1400 Fax: 518-689-1499
Web site: www.nysegov.com/cjn/

Chair:
  Vacant. 212-735-3680
Counsel:
  Henry Greenberg. 518-689-1400
  e-mail: greenbergh@gtlaw.com

New York State Commission on the Restoration of the Capitol

Corning Tower, 31st Fl
Empire State Plaza
Albany, NY 12242
518-473-0341 Fax: 518-486-5720

Executive Director:
  Andrea J Lazarski 518-473-0341
  e-mail: andrea.lazarski@ogs.ny.gov

New York State Disaster Preparedness Commission

Building 22, Suite 101
1220 Washington Ave
Albany, NY 12226-2251
518-292-2301 or 518-292-2200 Fax: 518-322-4978
Web site: www.dhses.ny.gov/oem/disaster-prep/

Chairman/Director:
  Jerome M Hauer 518-292-2301

New York State Dormitory Authority

515 Broadway
Albany, NY 12207-2964
518-257-3000 Fax: 518-257-3100
e-mail: dabonds@dasny.org
Web site: www.dasny.org

One Penn Plaza
52nd Fl
New York, NY 10119-0098
212-273-5000
Fax: 212-273-5121

539 Franklin St
Buffalo, NY 14202-1109

716-884-9780
Fax: 716-884-9787

Chair:
  Alfonso L Carney Jr 518-257-3000/fax: 518-257-3100
President/CEO:
  Paul T Williams Jr. 518-257-3180/fax: 518-257-3183
Vice President:
  Michael T Corrigan 518-257-3192/fax: 518-257-3183
Acting Chief Financial Officer:
  Linda H Button .518-257-3562/fax: 518-257-3100
General Counsel:
  Michael Cusack. 518-257-3120/fax: 518-257-3101
Managing Director, Construction:
  Stephen D Curro, PE 518-257-3271/fax: 518-257-3100
  e-mail: scurro@dasny.org
Managing Director, Public Finance & Portfolio Monitoring:
  Portia Lee. 518-257-3362/fax: 518-257-3100
  e-mail: plee@dasny.org
Public Information Officer:
  John Chirlin. 518-257-3380
  e-mail: jchirlin@dasny.org

New York State Energy Research & Development Authority

17 Columbia Circle
Albany, NY 12203-6399
518-862-1090 Fax: 518-862-1091
Web site: www.nyserda.ny.gov

Chairman:
  Richard L Kauffman. 518-862-1090
President & CEO:
  John B Rhodes. 518-862-1090 x3278
General Counsel & Secretary:
  Hal Brodie 518-862-1090 x3280
  e-mail: hb1@nyserda.ny.gov
Program Manager, Economic Development & Community Outreach:
  Kelly Tyler . . . . .716-842-1522 x 3005
  e-mail: kat@nyserda.ny.gov
Director, Communications:
  Kate Muller. 518-862-1090 x3582/fax: 518-862-1091
  e-mail: ktm@nyserda.ny.gov

New York State Environmental Facilities Corp

625 Broadway
Albany, NY 12207-2997
518-402-6924 or 800-882-9721 Fax: 518-486-9323
e-mail: press@efc.ny.gov
Web site: www.nysefc.org

President/CEO:
  Matthew J Driscoll 518-402-6951
Legal Division/General Counsel:
  James R Levine. 518-402-6969
Director, Engineering & Program Management:
  Timothy P Burns. 518-402-7396
Director, Technical Advisory Services:
  Vacant 518-402-7461
Director, PIO:
  Jon Sorensen 518-402-6924
  e-mail: press@efc.ny.gov; jon.sorensen@efc.ny.gov
Controller & Director, Corporate Operations:
  Michael Malinoski 518-486-9267

New York State Gaming Commission

PO Box 7500
Schenectady, NY 12301-7500

Policy Areas

Offices and agencies generally appear in alphabetical order, except when specific order is requested by listee.

518-395-5400 or 518-388-3415 Fax: 518-347-1250
e-mail: info@gaming.ny.gov
Web site: www.gaming.ny.gov

Chair:
  Mark Gearan 518-395-5400
    e-mail: info@gaming.ny.gov
Member:
  John A Crotty 518-395-5400
    e-mail: info@gaming.ny.gov
Member:
  John J Poklemba 518-395-5400
    e-mail: info@gaming.ny.gov
Executive Director:
  Robert Williams 518-395-5400
    e-mail: info@gaming.ny.gov
Public Information Officer:
  Lee Park 518-395-5400
    e-mail: lee.park@gaming.ny.gov

Joint Commission on Public Ethics (JCOPE)
540 Broadway
Albany, NY 12207
518-408-3976 Fax: 518-408-3975
e-mail: jcope@jcope.ny.gov
Web site: www.jcope.ny.gov

Executive Director:
  Letizia Tagliafierro .518-408-3976
Chair:
  Daniel J Horwitz 518-408-3976
Training & Education Services:
  Shari Calnero 518-408-3976
Chief of Staff/Deputy Counsel:
  Monica Stamm 518-408-3976/fax: 518-408-3975

New York State Financial Control Board
123 William St
23rd Fl
New York, NY 10038-3804
212-417-5046 Fax: 212-417-5055
e-mail: nysfcb@fcb.state.ny.us
Web site: www.fcb.state.ny.us

Acting Executive Director:
  Jeffrey Sommer 212-417-5066
Deputy Director, Expenditure & Covered Organization Analysis:
  Dennis DeLisle 212-417-5069
Deputy Director, Finance & Capital Analysis:
  Jewel A Douglas 212-417-5067
Acting Deputy Director, Economic & Revenue Analysis:
  Martin Fischman 212-417-5068
Associate Director, Administration:
  Mattie W Taylor 212-417-5053

New York State Higher Education Services Corp (NYSHESC)
99 Washington Ave
Albany, NY 12255
888-697-4372
Web site: www.hesc.ny.gov

Executive Vice President & Acting President:
  Elsa Magee .518-474-5592/fax: 518-474-5593
    e-mail: elsa.magee@hesc.ny.gov
Senior Vice President, Customer Relations:
  John Austin .518-473-0810/fax: 518-474-2839
    e-mail: john.austin@hesc.ny.gov

Director, Federal Relations:
  Frank Ballmann 202-721-1186
    e-mail: frank.ballmann@hesc.ny.gov
Director, Audit:
  Matt Downey 518-473-2287/fax: 518-486-6515
    e-mail: matt.downey@hesc.ny.gov
General Counsel:
  Thomas Brennan 518-473-1585/fax: 518-486-6515
    e-mail: thomas.brennan@hesc.ny.gov
Senior Vice President, Communications:
  Kathy Crowder 518-402-1448/fax: 518-474-5593
    e-mail: kathy.crowder@hesc.ny.gov
Director, Federal Options:
  Victor Stucchi 518-486-5885/fax: 518-402-3276
    e-mail: victor.stucchi@hesc.ny.gov
Administrative Officer & CFO:
  Warren Wallin 518-474-7505/fax: 518-474-4301
    e-mail: warren.wall@hesc.ny.gov

New York State Homes & Community Renewal
25 Beaver Street
New York, NY 10004
212-480-6700
e-mail: hcrinfo@nyshcr.org
Web site: www.nyshcr.org

Hampton Plaza
38-40 State Street
Albany, NY 12207
518-473-2526

Commissioner & CEO:
  Darryl C Towns 212-480-6705
President, Office of Finance & Development:
  Marian Zucker 212-480-6700
President, Office of Community Renewal:
  Matthew Nelson 212-480-6700
COO:
  Kevin Kelly 212-480-6700
President, Office of Professional Services:
  Sharon Devine 212-480-6700
Director, Fair Housing & Equal Opportunity:
  Wanda Graham 212-480-6700
Public Information:
 212-872-0338

New York State Judicial Conduct Commission
61 Broadway
12th Floor
New York, NY 10006
646-386-4800 Fax: 646-458-0037
e-mail: cjc@cjc.ny.gov
Web site: www.cjc.ny.gov

Corning Tower
Suite 2301
Empire State Plaza
Albany, NY 12223
518-453-4600
Fax: 518-486-1850

Chair:
  Thomas Klonick, Esq 646-386-4800
Vice Chair:
  Terry Jane Ruderman 646-386-4800
Administrator & Counsel:
  Robert H Tembeckjian 646-386-4800

Offices and agencies generally appear in alphabetical order, except when specific order is requested by listee.

Deputy Administrator in Charge, Albany Office:
    Cathleen Cenci 518-453-4600
Deputy Administrator in Charge, Rochester Office:
    John J Postel 585-232-5756
Deputy Administrator in Charge, New York City Office:
    Mark Levine 646-386-4800
Deputy Administrator, Litigation:
    Edward Lindner 518-474-5617
Clerk:
    Jean M Savanyu, Esq 646-386-4800

New York State Law Reporting Bureau
17 Lodge Street
Albany, NY 12207
518-453-6900 Fax: 518-426-1640
Web site: www.courts.state.ny.us/reporter

State Reporter:
    William J Hooks 518-453-6900
Deputy State Reporter:
    Michael S Moran 518-453-6900
    e-mail: Reporter@courts.state.ny.us
Assistant State Reporter:
    Katherine D. LaBoda 518-453-6900
    e-mail: Reporter@courts.state.ny.us

New York State Law Revision Commission
80 New Scotland Ave
Albany, NY 12208
518-472-5858 Fax: 518-445-2303
e-mail: nylrc@albanylaw.edu
Web site: www.lawrevision.state.ny.us

Chairman:
    Peter J Kiernan 518-472-5858
Executive Director:
    Rose Mary Bailly 518-472-5858

New York State Liquor Authority
80 S Swan St, Ste 900
9th Floor
Albany, NY 12210
518-474-3114
Web site: www.sla.ny.gov

Chairman:
    Vincent Bradley . . . . .518-473-6559 or 212-961-8300
Commissioner:
    Jeanique Greene . . . . .518-474-3114 or 212-961-8300
Commissioner:
    Kevin Kim . . . . .518-474-3114 or 212-961-8300
Counsel:
    Jacqueline Flug 518-474-3114/fax: 518-402-2304
    e-mail: legal@sla.ny.gov
CEO:
    Kerri O'Brien 518-474-3114
    e-mail: licensing.information@sla.ny.gov
Director, Public Affairs:
    William Crowley . . . . .518-474-3114 or 518-474-4875
    fax: 518-473-9565
    e-mail: press.office@sla.ny.gov

New York State Olympic Regional Development Authority
Olympic Center
2634 Main Street
Lake Placid, NY 12946

518-523-1655 Fax: 518-523-9275
e-mail: info@orda.org
Web site: www.orda.org/corporate

President & CEO:
    Ted Blazer 518-523-1655 x201
    e-mail: blazer@orda.org
Vice President:
    Jeffrey Byrne 518-523-1655 x203
    e-mail: byrne@orda.org
Olympic Center Manager:
    Dennis Allen 518-523-1655 x222
    e-mail: allen@orda.org
Director, Corporate Development:
    Jeff Potter 518-523-1655
    e-mail: jpotter@orda.org
Director, Events:
    Katie Million 518-523-1655 x212
    e-mail: kmillion@orda.org
Director, Finance:
    Padraig Power 518-523-1655 x217
    e-mail: ppower@orda.org
Communications Manager:
    Jon Lundin 518-523-1655
    e-mail: jlundin@orda.org

New York State Teachers' Retirement System
10 Corporate Woods Dr
Albany, NY 12211-2395
518-447-2900 or 800-348-7298 Fax: 518-447-2695
e-mail: media@nystrs.org
Web site: www.nystrs.org

Executive Director:
    Thomas K Lee 518-447-2726
General Counsel:
    Joseph J. Indelicato, Jr. 518-447-2722
Actuary:
    Richard Young 518-447-2692
Managing Director Operations:
    Kevin Schaefer 518-447-2730
Director, Member Relations:
    Sheila Gardella 518-447-2684
Manager, Public Information:
    John Cardillo 518-447-4743/fax: 518-447-2875
    e-mail: john.cardillo@nystrs.org
Managing Director, Real Estate:
    David C. Gillian 518-447-2751

New York State Thoroughbred Breeding & Development Fund Corporation
One Broadway Center
Suite 601
Schenectady, NY 12305
518-388-0174 Fax: 518-395-5499
e-mail: nybreds@nybreds.com
Web site: www.nybreds.com

Executive Director:
    Tracy Egan 518-388-0174

New York State Thruway Authority
200 Southern Blvd
PO Box 189
Albany, NY 12201
518-436-2700 Fax: 518-436-2899
Web site: www.thruway.ny.gov

Policy Areas

Offices and agencies generally appear in alphabetical order, except when specific order is requested by listee.

Chair:
    Joanne M Mahoney................................518-436-3000
Acting Executive Director:
    Robert Megna 518-436-2900
General Counsel:
    Gordon Cuffy 518-436-2840
Interim Director, Maintenance & Operations:
    Maria Lehman.....................................518-436-2840
Director, Media Relations & Communications:
    Dan Weiller.......................................518-471-5300

New York State Canal Corporation
    Web site: www.canals.ny.gov
Acting Executive Director:
    Robert Megna 518-436-3055/fax: 518-471-5023
Director of Canals:
    Brian U. Stratton..................................518-436-3055

New York State Tug Hill Commission
Dulles State Office Bldg
317 Washington St
Watertown, NY 13601
315-785-2380 Fax: 315-785-2574
e-mail: tughill@tughill.org
Web site: www.tughill.org

Chair:
    Jan Bogdanowicz 315-785-2380
Executive Director:
    John K Bartow, Jr.................................315-785-2570
    e-mail: john@tughill.org

Niagara Falls Bridge Commission
5365 Military Rd
Lewiston, NY 14092
716-285-6322 Fax: 716-282-3292
e-mail: general_inquiries@niagarafallsbridges.com
Web site: www.niagarafallsbridges.com

Chair:
    Kathleen L Neville 716-285-6322
Vice Chair:
    Kenneth E Loucks................................716-285-6322
Treasurer:
    Linda L McAusland 716-285-6322
Secretary:
    Russell G Quarantello............................716-285-6322

Niagara Frontier Transportation Authority
181 Ellicott St
Buffalo, NY 14203
716-855-7300 or 800-622-1220 Fax: 716-855-6655
e-mail: info@nfta.com
Web site: www.nfta.com

Chair:
    Howard Zemsky 716-855-7232
Executive Director:
    Kimberley A Minkel..............................716-855-7470
Chief Financial Officer:
    John Cox...716-855-7300
General Counsel:
    David J State.....................................716-855-7686
Director, Aviation:
    William Vanecek 716-630-6030
Director, Human Resources:
    Karen Novo.......................................716-855-7343
Director, Public Transit:
    Thomas George...................................716-855-7390

Director, Engineering:
    Michael Bykowski 716-855-7389
Director, Public Affairs:
    C Douglas Hartmayer 716-855-7420
Chief, NFTA Police:
    George W. Gast...................................716-855-7666

Northeastern Forest Fire Protection Commission
21 Parmenter Terrace
PO Box 6192
China Village, ME 04926
207-968-3782 Fax: 207-968-3782
e-mail: info@nffpc.org
Web site: www.nffpc.org

Chair of Commissioners:
    Sen. Elizabeth O. Little...........................518-455-2811
    e-mail: little@senate.state.ny.us
Executive Director/Center Manager:
    Thomas G Parent.................................207-968-3782
    e-mail: necompact@fairpoint.net
Operations Committee, Chair:
    Luc Dugas..418-871-3341
    e-mail: ldugas@sopfeu.qc.ca
New York Fire Prevention:
    David Russell 518-483-2836
    e-mail: dgrussel@gw.dec.state.ny.us

Ogdensburg Bridge & Port Authority
One Bridge Plaza
Ogdensburg, NY 13669
315-393-4080 Fax: 315-393-7068
e-mail: obpa@ogdensport.com
Web site: www.ogdensport.com

Chair:
    Samuel J LaMacchia.............................315-393-4080
Executive Director:
    Wade A Davis....................................315-393-4080
    e-mail: wadavis@ogdensport.com

Ohio River Valley Water Sanitation Commission
5735 Kellogg Ave
Cincinnati, OH 45230
513-231-7719 Fax: 513-231-7761
e-mail: info@orsanco.org
Web site: www.orsanco.org

New York State Commissioner:
    Douglas E Conroe................................513-231-7719
New York State Commissioner:
    Michael P Wilson 513-231-7719
New York State Commissioner:
    Joseph J Martens.................................513-231-7719
Executive Director:
    Richard Harrison ....513-231-7719 ext 105
    e-mail: rharrison@orsanco.org
Source Water Protection/Emergency Response:
    Jerry Schulte.............................513-231-7719 ext 104
    e-mail: jschulte@orsanco.org
Communications Coordinator:
    Lisa Cochran ....513-231-7719 ext 102
    e-mail: lcochran@orsanco.org

Port Authority of New York & New Jersey
225 Park Ave South
18th Fl
New York, NY 10003

Offices and agencies generally appear in alphabetical order, except when specific order is requested by listee.

212-435-7000 Fax: 212-435-4032
Web site: www.panynj.gov

Chair, New Jersey:
    John J Degnan....................................212-435-7000
Vice Chair, New York:
    Scott H Rechler..................................212-435-7000
Executive Director:
    Patrick Foye 212-435-7271
Acting COO:
    Stephanie E Dawson.............................212-435-7887
Director, Government & Community Affairs - NJ:
    Tina Lado 212-435-6903
General Counsel:
    Darrell Buchbinder 212-435-3515
Chief Financial Officer:
    Elizabeth McCarthy 212-435-7738
Acting Public Information Officer/Media Relations:
    Steve Coleman...............212-435-7777/fax: 212-435-4032
Director, Public Safety/Superintendent of Police:
    Michael A Fedorko 212-435-7000
Chief Engineer:
    Peter J Zipf 212-435-7449
Office of Secretary:
    Karen E Eastman................................212-435-6528

Port of Oswego Authority
1 East Second St
Oswego, NY 13126
315-343-4503 Fax: 315-343-5498
e-mail: shipping@portoswego.com
Web site: www.portoswego.com

Chairman:
    Terrence Hammill.................................315-343-4503
    e-mail: chairman@portoswego.com
Executive Director & CEO:
    Zelko N. Kirincich........................315-343-4503 x111
    e-mail: zkirincich@portoswego.com
Manager, Administrative Services/Facility Security Officer:
    William Scriber 315-343-4503 x108
    e-mail: wscriber@portoswego.com
Supervisor of Marina Operations:
    Bernie Bacon.....................................315-343-4503
    e-mail: oswegomarina@yahoo.com

Rochester-Genesee Regional Transportation Authority-RTS
1372 E Main St
PO Box 90629
Rochester, NY 14609
585-654-0200 or 585-288-1700 Fax: 585-654-0224
Web site: www.myrts.com

Chief Executive Officer:
    Bill Carpenter 585-654-0200
Chief Operating Officer:
    Miguel A Velazquez.............................585-654-0200
Chief Financial Officer:
    Scott Adair 585-654-0200
General Counsel/CAO:
    Daniel DeLaus 585-654-0200
Media Contact:
    Carole Downing 585-654-0730
    e-mail: cdowling@myrts.com

Roosevelt Island Operating Corporation (RIOC)
591 Main St
Roosevelt Island, NY 10044

212-832-4540 Fax: 212-832-4582
e-mail: information@rioc.ny.gov
Web site: www.rioc.ny.gov

President/CEO:
    Charlene M Indelicato 212-832-4540 x319
Director Island Operations:
    Cyril Opperman 212-832-4583
    e-mail: cyril.opperman@rioc.ny.gov
VP/General Counsel:
    Donald D. Lewis 212-832-4540 x311
    e-mail: donald.lewis@rioc.ny.gov
VP/Chief Financial Officer:
    Frances Walton 212-832-4540 x350
Director Public Safety:
    Captain Estrella Suarez.......................212-832-4545
    e-mail: keith.guerra@rioc.ny.gov

State University Construction Fund
353 Broadway
Albany, NY 12246
518-320-3200 Fax: 518-443-1008
Web site: www.sucf.suny.edu

General Manager:
    Robert M Haelen.................................518-320-1502
General Counsel/Director Legal Svcs:
    William K Barczak 518-320-1746

Suffolk Regional Off-Track Betting Corporation
5 Davids Dr
Hauppauge, NY 11788-2004
631-853-1000 Fax: 631-853-1086
e-mail: customerservice@suffolkotb.com
Web site: www.suffolkotb.com

President/CEO:
    Philip C. Nolan 631-853-1000
Vice President:
    Anthony Pancella 631-853-1000
General Counsel:
    James McManmon 631-853-1000
Director Governmental & Public Affairs:
    Debbie Pfeifer...................................631-853-1000

Thousand Islands Bridge Authority
PO Box 428, Collins Landing
43530 Interstate 81
Alexandria Bay, NY 13607
315-482-2501 or 315-658-2281 Fax: 315-482-5925
e-mail: info@tibridge.com
Web site: www.tibridge.com

Chair:
    Robert Barnard 315-482-2501
Executive Director:
    Robert G Horr, III...............................315-482-2501
    e-mail: roberthorr@tibridge.com
Legal Counsel:
    Dennis Whelpley.................................315-482-2501

Uniform State Laws Commission
c/o Coughlin & Gerhart LLP
99 Corporate Drive
PO Box 2059
Binghamton, NY 13902-2039
607-723-9511 Fax: 607-723-1530

Offices and agencies generally appear in alphabetical order, except when specific order is requested by listee.

Policy Areas

Chair:
Richard B Long 607-821-2202
e-mail: rlong@cglawoffices.com
Member:
Sandra Stern 212-207-8150
Member:
Norman L. Greene 212-661-5030
Member:
Justin L. Vigdor . . . . 585-232-5300 ext 228
Member:
Mark F Glaser 518-689-1413

United Nations Development Corporation

Two United Nations Plaza, 27th Fl
New York, NY 10017
212-888-1618 Fax: 212-588-0758
e-mail: info@undc.org
Web site: www.undc.org

Chair, Board of Directors:
George Klein 212-888-1618
Sr VP & General Counsel/Secretary:
Robert Cole 212-888-1618
Controller/Treasurer:
Jorge Ortiz 212-888-1618
Vice President:
Kenneth Coopersmith 212-888-1618

Waterfront Commission of New York Harbor

39 Broadway, 4th Fl
New York, NY 10006
212-742-9280 Fax: 212-480-0587
Web site: www.wcnyh.org

Commissioner, New York:
Ronald Goldstock 212-742-9280
Commissioner, New Jersey:
Michael Murphy 212-742-9280
Executive Director:
Walter M Arsenault 212-905-9201
General Counsel:
Phoebe S Sorial 212-742-8965

Western Regional Off-Track Betting Corp

8315 Park Road
Batavia, NY 14020
585-343-3750 Fax: 585-343-6873
e-mail: info@westernotb.com
Web site: www.westernotb.com

Chair:
Richard D Bianchi 585-343-3750
President & Chief Executive Officer:
Michael D Kane 585-343-3750
VP-Administration:
William R White 585-343-3750
General Counsel/Secretary:
Henry Wojtaszek 585-343-3750
Director, Video Gaming:
Mark Wolf 585-343-3750
Director, Marketing:
Ryan Hasenauer 585-343-3750
Manager, Branch Operations:
Edward Merriman 585-343-3750

CRIME & CORRECTIONS

NEW YORK STATE

GOVERNOR'S OFFICE

Governor's Office
Executive Chamber
State Capitol
Albany, NY 12224
518-474-8390 Fax: 518-474-1513
Web site: www.ny.gov

Governor:
Andrew M Cuomo 518-474-8390
Secretary to the Governor:
William Mulrow 518-474-4246
Counsel to the Governor:
Alphonso David 518-474-8343
First Assistant Counsel:
Sandi Toll 518-474-8434
Director, Communications:
Melissa DeRosa . . . . 518-474-8418 or 212-681-4640

EXECUTIVE DEPARTMENTS AND RELATED AGENCIES

Corrections & Community Supervision Department
1220 Washington Ave
Bldg 2 State Campus
Albany, NY 12226-2050
518-457-8126 Fax: 518-457-7252
Web site: www.doccs.ny.gov

Acting Commissioner:
Anthony Annucci 518-457-8134
Executive Deputy Commissioner:
Anthony Annucci . . . . 518-457-1748 or 518-485-9613
Deputy Commissioner & Counsel:
Maureen Boll 518-485-9613
Assistant Commissioner & Executive Assistant:
Diane L Van Buren 518-457-1281
Special Assistant to Commissioner:
Terri Pratt 518-457-8134
Health Services Deputy Commissioner/Chief Medical Officer:
Carl Koenigsmann MD 518-457-7073
Deputy Commissioner, Program Services:
Jeffrey McKoy 518-457-5555
Asst Commissioner, Program Services:
Vacant 518-408-5825
Director, Public Information:
Thomas Mailey 518-457-8182/fax: 518-457-7070

Administrative Services
Deputy Commissioner:
Daniel F. Martuscello III 518-457-8188
Assistant Commissioner:
Thomas Corcoran 518-457-7135

Budget & Finance Division
Director:
Sandy Downey 518-457-5562

Diversity Management
Director:
Deborah E. Nazon 518-485-5806

Human Resources Management Division
Director, Personnel:
Darren Ayotte 518-457-9887
Support Operations
550 Broadway, Menands, NY 12204
Director:
Nannette Ferri 518-436-7886

Inmate Grievance
Director:
Karen Bellamy 518-457-1885
Deputy Commissioner, Correctional Industries & Accreditation:
Osbourne A McKay 518-485-2858

Internal Controls
Director:
Peter Berezny 518-485-1394
Special Assistant for Labor Relations:
Gary Simpson 518-457-7291

Training Academy
1134 New Scotland Rd, Albany, NY 12208
Director:
Joseph Tewksbury 518-489-9072

Correctional Facility Operations
Deputy Commissioner:
Joseph Bellnier 518-457-8138
Assistant Commissioner:
Patricia Le Coney 518-457-5902
Assistant Commissioner:
Vacant 518-457-5902
Assistant Commissioner:
Vacant 518-457-4118
Chief of Investigations & Inspector General:
Vernon Fonda 518-457-2653
Associate Commissioner, Population Management:
Ann Marie McGrath 518-457-7261

Correctional Industries Division . . . . fax: 518-436-6007
Corcraft Products, 550 Broadway, Albany, NY 12204
Fax: 518-436-6007
Web site: www.corcraft.org
Director:
Michael Hurt 518-436-6321 x2305

Facilities
Adirondack Correctional Facility
196 Ray Brook Rd, Box 110, Route 86, Ray Brook, NY 12977-0110
Superintendent:
Jeffrey Tedford 518-891-1343
Albion Correctional Facility
3595 State School Rd, Albion, NY 14411
Superintendent:
William Powers 585-589-5511
Altona Correctional Facility
555 Devils Den Rd, Altona, NY 12910
Superintendent:
John Demars 518-236-7841
Attica Correctional Facility
639 Exchange Street, Attica, NY 14011-0149
Superintendent:
Mark Bradt 585-591-2000
Auburn Correctional Facility
135 State St, Auburn, NY 13024
Superintendent:
Harold Graham 315-253-8401
Bare Hill Correctional Facility
Caller Box #20 181 Brand Rd, Malone, NY 12953
Superintendent:
Bruce Yelich 518-483-8411
Bayview Correctional Facility
550 West 20th St, New York, NY 10011

Policy Areas

Offices and agencies generally appear in alphabetical order, except when specific order is requested by listee.

Superintendent:
Vacant 212-255-7590

Beacon Correctional Facility
50 Camp Beacon Rd, PO Box 780, Beacon, NY 12508-0780
Superintendent:
Gail Thomas. 845-831-4200

Bedford Hills Correctional Facility
247 Harris Rd, Bedford Hills, NY 10507
Superintendent:
Sabina Kaplan 914-241-3100

Butler Correctional Facility
PO Box 388, 14001 Westbury Cutoff Rd, Red Creek, NY 13143
Superintendent:
Sheryl Zenzen 315-754-8001

Cape Vincent Correctional Facility
36560 Route 12E, Box 599, Cape Vincent, NY 13618
Superintendent:
Patricia LeConey 315-654-4100

Cayuga Correctional Facility
PO Box 1150, 2202 Route 38A, Moravia, NY 13119-1150
Superintendent:
David Stallone 315-497-1110

Chateaugay Correctional Facility
PO Box 320, 7874 Route 11, Chateaugay, NY 12920
Superintendent:
Michael Lira. 518-497-3300

Clinton Correctional Facility
PO Box 2000, 1156 Route 374, Cook St, Dannemora, NY 12929
Superintendent:
Thomas LaValley 518-492-2511 x2099

Collins Correctional Facility
PO Box 490, Middle Rd, Collins, NY 14034-0490
Superintendent:
Michael Graziano. 716-532-4588

Coxsackie Correctional Facility
11260 Route 9W, Box 200, West Coxsackie, NY 12051-0200
Superintendent:
Daniel Martuscello. 518-731-2781

Downstate Correctional Facility
121 Red Schoolhouse Rd, PO Box 445, Fishkill, NY 12524-0445
Superintendent:
Ada Perez. 845-831-6600

Eastern NY Correctional Facility
30 Institution Rd, Box 338, Napanoch, NY 12458-0338
Superintendent:
Thomas Griffin 845-647-7400

Edgecombe Correctional Facility
611 Edgecombe Ave, New York, NY 10032-4398
Superintendent:
Shelda Washington 212-923-2575

Elmira Correctional Facility
1879 Davis St, PO Box 500, Elmira, NY 14902-0500
Superintendent:
Paul Chappius 607-734-3901

Fishkill Correctional Facility
18 Strack Dr, PO Box 307, Prospect Street, Beacon, NY 12508
Superintendent:
William Connolly 845-831-0400

Five Points Correctional Facility
Caller Box 400, 6000 State Rte 96, Romulus, NY 14541
Superintendent:
Michael Sheahan 607-869-5111

Franklin Correctional Facility
62 Bare Hill Rd, PO Box 10, Malone, NY 12953
Superintendent:
Darwin LaClair 518-483-6040

Gouverneur Correctional Facility
112 Scotch Settlement Rd, PO Box 370, Gouverneur, NY 13642-0370
Superintendent:
Elizabeth O'Meara. 315-287-7351

Gowanda Correctional Facility
PO Box 350, South Rd, Gowanda, NY 14070-0350
Superintendent:
John Lempke 716-532-0177

Great Meadow Correctional Facility
11739 State Rte 22, Box 51, Comstock, NY 12821
Superintendent:
Steve Racette 518-639-5516

Green Haven Correctional Facility
594 Rte 216, Stormville, NY 12582
Superintendent:
William Lee 845-221-2711

Greene Correctional Facility
PO Box 8, 165 Plank Rd, Coxsackie, NY 12051-0008
Superintendent:
Brandon Smith. 518-731-2741

Groveland Correctional Facility
7000 Sonyea Rd, PO Box 50, Sonyea, NY 14556
Superintendent:
Sandra Amoia-Kowalczyk. 585-658-2871

Hale Creek ASACTC
279 Maloney Rd, Johnstown, NY 12095
Superintendent:
David Hallenbeck 518-736-2094

Hudson Correctional Facility
Box 576, 56 East Court St, Hudson, NY 12534-0576
Superintendent:
Donna Lewin 518-828-4311

Lakeview Shock Incarceration Correctional Facility
9300 Lake Ave, PO Box T, Brocton, NY 14716
Superintendent:
Malcolm Cully. 716-792-7100

Lincoln Correctional Facility
31-33 West 110th St, New York, NY 10026-4398
Superintendent:
Wendy Featherstone .212-860-9400

Livingston Correctional Facility
7005 Sonyea Rd, PO Box 49, Sonyea, NY 14556-0049
Superintendent:
Michelle Artus 585-658-3710

Marcy Correctional Facility
PO Box 5000, 9000 Old River Rd, Marcy, NY 13403
Superintendent:
Charles Kelly. 315-768-1400

Mid-State Correctional Facility
PO Box 216, 9005 Old River Rd, Marcy, NY 13403-0216
Superintendent:
John Colvin 315-768-8581

Mohawk Correctional Facility
6100 School Road, PO Box 8451, Rome, NY 13440
Superintendent:
Paul Gonyea. 315-339-5232

Monterey Shock Incarceration Correctional Facility
2150 Evergreen Hill Rd, RD #1, Beaver Dams, NY 14812-9718
Superintendent:
Leroy Fields. 607-962-3184

Moriah Shock Incarceration Correctional Facility
PO Box 999, Mineville, NY 12956-0999
Superintendent:
Bruce McCormick 518-942-7561

Mt McGregor Correctional Facility
1000 Mt McGregor Rd, Box 2071, Wilton, NY 12831-5071
Superintendent:
William Haggett. 518-587-3960

Ogdensburg Correctional Facility
One Correction Way, Ogdensburg, NY 13669-2288
Superintendent:
Larry Frank 315-393-0281

Orleans Correctional Facility
3595 Gaines Basin Rd, Albion, NY 14411

Offices and agencies generally appear in alphabetical order, except when specific order is requested by listee.

Superintendent:
Sandra Dolce 585-589-6820
Otisville Correctional Facility
57 Sanitorium Rd, Box 8, Otisville, NY 10963-0008
Superintendent:
Kathleen Gerbing 845-386-1490
Queensboro Correctional Facility
47-04 Van Dam St, Long Island City, NY 11101-3081
Superintendent:
Dennis Breslin 718-361-8920
Riverview Correctional Facility
PO Box 158, 1110 Tibbits Dr, Ogdensburg, NY 13669
Superintendent:
Calvin Rabsatt 315-393-8400
Rochester Correctional Facility
470 Ford St, Rochester, NY 14608-2499
Superintendent:
Sheryl Zenzen 585-454-2280
Shawangunk Correctional Facility
200 Quick Rd, PO Box 750, Wallkill, NY 12589-0750
Superintendent:
Joseph Smith 845-895-2081
Sing Sing Correctional Facility
354 Hunter St, Ossining, NY 10562
Superintendent:
Michael Capra 914-941-0108
Southport Correctional Facility
236 Bob Masia Dr, PO Box 2000, Pine City, NY 14871
Superintendent:
Stephen Wenderlich 607-737-0850
Sullivan Correctional Facility
Box 116, 325 Riverside Dr, Fallsburg, NY 12733-0116
Superintendent:
Patrick Griffin 845-434-2080
Taconic Correctional Facility
250 Harris Rd, Bedford Hills, NY 10507-2498
Superintendent:
Patty Nelson 914-241-3010
Ulster Correctional Facility
750 Berme Rd, PO Box 800, Napanoch, NY 12458
Superintendent:
Jerome Nicolato 845-647-1670
Upstate Correctional Facility
PO Box 2000, 309 Bare Hill Rd, Malone, NY 12953
Superintendent:
David Rock 518-483-6997
Wallkill Correctional Facility
50 McKenderick Rd, PO Box G, Wallkill, NY 12589-0286
Superintendent:
Timothy Laffin Sr 845-895-2021
Washington Correctional Facility
72 Lock 11 Lane, Box 180, Comstock, NY 12821-0180
Superintendent:
Tim Sheehan 518-639-4486
Watertown Correctional Facility
23147 Swan Rd, Watertown, NY 13601-9340
Superintendent:
Barry McArdle 315-782-7490
Wende Correctional Facility
3040 Wende Rd, PO Box 1187, Alden, NY 14004-1187
Superintendent:
Dale Artus 716-937-4000
Willard Drug Treatment Center
7116 County Route 132, PO Box 303, Willard, NY 14588
Superintendent:
Ricky Bartlett 607-869-5500
Woodbourne Correctional Facility
99 Prison Rd, PO Box 1000, Woodbourne, NY 12788
Superintendent:
Robert Cunningham 845-434-7730

Wyoming Correctional Facility
3203 Dunbar Rd, PO Box 501, Attica, NY 14011
Superintendent:
David Unger 585-591-1010

Security Staffing Unit
Director:
Philip Battiste 518-485-5407

Special Operations
Director, Corrections Emergency Response Team (Cert):
Col. Michael Kirkpatrick 518-457-2006
Director, CIU:
James O'Gorman 518-457-2006
Director, Special Housing/Inmate Disciplinary Program:
Albert Prack 518-457-2337

Health Services Division
Deputy Commissioner/Chief Medical Officer:
Carl Koenigsmann MD 518-457-7072
Assistant Commissioner, Health Services:
Elizabeth Ritter 518-457-7072

Correctional Health Services
Director:
Nancy Lyng 518-457-7072

Dental Services
Director:
Mary D'Silva DDS 518-457-7072

Mental Health
Director:
Doris Ramirez-Romero 518-408-0281

Population Management
Chief of Investigations:
Vernon Fonda .518-457-2653 or 518-457-2653

Management Information Services
Director/CIO:
Thomas Herzog 518-457-2540

Program Planning, Research & Evaluation
Director:
Paul Korotkin 518-408-0424

Program Services
Deputy Commissioner:
Jeffrey McKoy 518-457-5555
Assistant Commissioner:
Cathy Jacobson 518-457-8134

Education
Director:
Linda Hollmen 518-402-0092

Guidance & Counseling
Director:
Joanne Nigro 518-402-1813

Library Services
Supervising Librarian:
Vacant 518-402-1739

Ministerial, Family & Volunteer Services
Director:
Cheryl V Morris 518-402-1700

Substance Abuse Treatment Services
Director:
Rachael Young 518-402-1744

Offices and agencies generally appear in alphabetical order, except when specific order is requested by listee.

Victim Services, Office of

1 Columbia Circle, Ste 200
Albany, NY 12203-6383
518-457-8727 or 800-247-8035 Fax: 518-457-8658
Web site: www.ovs.ny.gov

55 Hanson Place
10th Fl
Brooklyn, NY 11217-1523
718-923-4325
Fax: 718-923-4347

65 Court St
Rm 308
Buffalo, NY 14202
716-847-7992
Fax: 716-847-7995

Director:
  Elizabeth Cronin Esq 518-485-5719
Deputy Director for Administration/Advocacy/Grants:
  Virginia A Miller 518-485-5719
Crime Victim Compensation Investigations:
  Claudette Christian Bullock 718-923-4348
General Counsel/Legal Unit:
  John Watson 518-457-8066/fax: 518-457-8658
Director, MIS:
  David Loomis 518-485-5719

Criminal Justice Services, Division of

80 S. Swan St
Albany, NY 12210
518-457-5837 or 800-262-3257 Fax: 518-457-3089
e-mail: info@dcjs.ny.gov
Web site: www.criminaljustice.ny.gov

Acting Commissioner:
  Sean M Byrne 518-457-1260
Executive Deputy Commissioner:
  Michael C Green 518-457-6091
Affirmative Action Officer:
  Wanda Trouche 518-485-7962
Director, Public Information:
  John Caher 518-457-8828/fax: 518-485-7715
  e-mail: john.caher@dcjs.ny.gov

Administration Office

Deputy Commissioner, Administration:
  Vacant 518-457-6105

Administrative Services
Director:
  Vacant 518-457-4168

Human Resources Management
Director:
  Dennis Langley 518-485-7964

State Finance & Budget
Director, Finance:
  Kimberly J Szady 518-457-6105
Director, Internal Audit & Compliance:
  Bob Wright 518-485-5823

Advisory Groups

Juvenile Justice Advisory Group
Chair:
  Vacant 518-457-3670

NYS Motor Vehicle & Insurance Fraud Prevention Board
Chair:
  Vacant 518-485-8462

Legal Services
Deputy Commissioner & Counsel:
  Gina Bianchi 518-457-4181

Missing & Exploited Children Clearinghouse
Director:
  Kenneth R Buniak 518-485-7641

Commission on Forensic Science

Office of Forensic Services
Director:
  Vacant 518-457-4181

Office of Criminal Justice Operations
Director, Human Resources Management:
  Dennis Langley 518-485-1704

Office of Operations
Assistant Director:
  Vacant 518-457-6050
Chief, Operations:
  Dona Call 518-485-7688
Manager, State Identification:
  Ann Sammons 518-457-3700

Office of Justice Information Services
Deputy Commissioner:
  Anne Roest 518-485-7176

Information Technology Development Group
Director:
  Connie Snyder 518-485-7154

Information Technology Services Group
Assistant Director:
  Alex Roberts 518-457-3743

Office of Sex Offender Management
Director:
  Risa Sugarman 518-457-6985

Office of Justice Statistics & Performance
Director:
  Terry Salo 518-457-7301
Chief, Crimestat Unit:
  Paula K Lockhart 518-485-7122
Chief, Crime Reporting & Statistical Services Unit:
  Adam Dean 518-457-8381

Office of Public Safety

Law Enforcement Accreditation Council

Municipal Police Training Council

State Committee for Coordination of Police Services for Elderly (TRIAD)

Statewide Law Enforcement Telecommunications Committee
Deputy Commissioner:
  Tony Perez 518-485-7620
Supervisor, Program Services:
  John R Digman 518-485-1411
Supervisor, Administrative Services & Security Guard Advisory Council:
  Debra Bourque 518-485-1416

Office of Strategic Planning

Justice Systems Analysis Unit
Chief:
  David vanAlstyne 518-457-7301

Offices and agencies generally appear in alphabetical order, except when specific order is requested by listee.

Funding & Program Assistance Office
Director:
 AnneMarie Strano 518-457-8462
Assistant Director:
 Ron Dickens..................................518-457-8406

Operation IMPACT Coordinator
Director:
 Julie Pasquini 518-485-7923

Inspector General (NYS), Office of the
Empire State Plaza
Bldg 2, 16th Fl
Albany, NY 12223
518-474-1010 or 800-367-4448 Fax: 518-486-3745
Web site: www.ig.ny.gov

61 Broadway
12th Fl
New York, NY 10006
212-635-3150
Fax: 212-809-6287

State Inspector General:
 Catherine Leahy Scott ....212-635-3150 or 518-474-1010
 e-mail: inspector.general@ig.ny.gov
First Deputy Inspector General:
 Michael C Clarke 212-635-3150
Chief Investigator:
 William Hebert 212-635-3150
Director, Public Information:
 Kate Gurnett 518-474-1010

Law Department
120 Broadway
New York, NY 10271-0332
212-416-8000 or 800-771-7755
Web site: www.ag.ny.gov

State Capitol
Albany, NY 12224-0341
518-474-5481
Fax: 518-473-9909

Attorney General:
 Eric T Schneiderman ....212-416-8050 or 518-474-7330
COO:
 Jeanette Moy......................212-416-8050 or 518-473-7900
Press Secretary:
 Fernando Aquino..................212-416-8060/fax: 212-416-6005

Appeals & Opinions
Solicitor General:
 Barbara D Underwood ....212-416-8016 or 518-402-2074
Deputy Solicitor General, Criminal Appeals:
 Nikki Kowalski..................................212-416-8370
Deputy Solicitor General:
 Anisha Dasgupta................................212-416-8921
Deputy Solicitor General:
 Steven Wu.......................212-416-6312/fax: 212-416-8962

Law Library
Chief, Library Services:
 Patricia Partello.................518-776-2566/fax: 518-915-7737
Legal Support Analyst:
 Vacant 212-416-8012/fax: 212-416-6130

Criminal Justice
Executive Deputy Attorney General:
 Kelly Donovan 212-416-8050

Criminal Enforcement & Financial Crimes Bureau
Bureau Chief:
 Gary Fishman...................212-416-8750 or 518-776-2370

Medicaid Fraud Control Unit
120 Broadway, 13th Fl, New York, NY 10271-0007
Deputy Attorney General:
 Vacant.......................518-474-3032/fax: 518-474-4519

Organized Crime Task Force
Bureau Chief:
 Vacant.......................518-474-1620/fax: 518-474-7258

Guns, Gangs & Drugs Initiative
Special Deputy Attorney General:
 Carl J Boykin 315-793-2502

Economic Justice
Executive Deputy Attorney General:
 Karla Sanchez..................................212-416-8050
Deputy Attorney General:
 Virginia Chavez Romano 212-416-8389

Antitrust Bureau
Bureau Chief:
 Eric J Stock 212-416-8282/fax: 212-416-6015
 e-mail: eric.stock@ag.ny.gov

Consumer Frauds Bureau
Bureau Chief:
 Jane Azia......................212-416-6067/fax: 212-416-6003

Social Justice
Executive Deputy Attorney General:
 Alvin L Braggs, Jr 212-416-8075/fax: 212-416-8942

Civil Rights Bureau
Bureau Chief:
 Kristen Clarke...................212-416-8250/fax: 212-416-8074

Investigations
Chief, Investigations:
 Dominick Zarrella...............212-416-6328 or 518-486-4540
 fax: 212-416-8773

State Counsel
First Deputy Attorney General:
 Harlan Levy 212-416-8525

Civil Recoveries Bureau
Bureau Chief:
 John Cremo 518-776-2173/fax: 518-915-7731

Claims Bureau
Bureau Chief:
 Katharine Brooks ....518-776-2300 or 212-416-8913

Litigation Bureau
Bureau Chief:
 Lisa Dell......................518-776-2300 or 212-416-8610

Real Property Bureau
Bureau Chief:
 Alison Crocker 518-776-2700

Parole Board, The
Corrections & Community Supervision
97 Central Ave
Albany, NY 12206

Offices and agencies generally appear in alphabetical order, except when specific order is requested by listee.

518-473-9400 Fax: 518-473-6037
Web site: www.parole.ny.gov; doccs.ny.gov

Executive Office
Acting Commissioner:
  Anthony J Annucci 518-473-9548
Secretary to the Chair:
  Rachael Seguin 518-473-9548
Public Information Officer:
  Vacant 518-486-4631/fax: 518-473-6037
Administrative Assistant:
  Lorraine Morse 518-473-5424/fax: 518-473-6037

Administrative Services
Director:
  Jeffrey Nesich 518-473-3901/fax: 518-486-5858
Director, Human Resource Management:
  Barbara Farley 518-473-3901
Labor Relations Representative:
  Vacant 518-474-5612

Clemency Unit
97 Central Ave, Albany, NY 12206
Director:
  Frank Herman 518-485-8953

Information Services
Director:
  John Armitage 518-445-7558/fax: 518-445-7553

Office of Counsel
Chief Counsel:
  Terrence X Tracy 518-473-5671/fax: 518-473-9760

Parole Operations Unit
Deputy Commissioner, Community Supervision:
  Angela Jiminez 212-239-5730
Director, Internal Operations:
  Timothy O'Brien 518-408-3473
Deputy Director, Sex Offenders Mgmt Unit:
  Mary Osborne 518-473-5572
Regional Dir-Region I:
  Michael Falk 212-736-9880
Regional Dir-Region II:
  Milton Brown 718-558-5227
Regional Dir-Region III:
  Steven Claudio 914-654-8690
Regional Dir-Region IV:
  Michael Burdi 518-459-7469
Regional Dir-Region V:
  Eugenio Russi 585-232-6927

Policy Analysis
Director:
  Michael R Buckman 518-445-6071

Victim Impact Unit . . . . .fax: 518-493-9659
Parole Officer:
  Barbara Tobin 518-486-4400
Parole Officer:
  Christine Robinson 518-486-4400

Prevention of Domestic Violence, Office for the
80 South Swan Street
11th Fl Rm 1157
Albany, NY 12210
518-457-5800 Fax: 518-457-5810
e-mail: opdvpublicinfo@opdv.ny.gov
Web site: www.opdv.ny.gov

90 Church St, 13th Fl
New York, NY 10007
212-417-4477
Fax: 212-417-4972

Executive Director:
  Gwen Wright 518-457-5800
Fiscal Officer:
  Linda Cassidy 518-457-7995
Public Information Officer:
  Suzanne Cecala 518-457-5744
  e-mail: suzanne.cecala@opdv.ny.gov

State Police, Division of
Building 22, State Campus
1220 Washington Ave
Albany, NY 12226-2252
518-457-2180
e-mail: nyspmail@troopers.ny.gov
Web site: www.troopers.ny.gov

Superintendent:
  Joseph A D'Amico 518-457-6721
First Deputy Superintendent:
  Kevin T Gagan 518-457-6711/fax: 518-485-7505
Counsel:
  Glenn Valle 518-457-6137/fax: 518-485-1164

Administration
Director:
  Terence P O'Mara 518-457-6622/fax: 518-485-5051

  Forensic Investigation Center
  Director, Staff Inspector:
    Gerald M Zeosky 518-457-2466/fax: 518-457-2477

  Public Information
  Director, Technical Lieutenant:
    Glenn R Miner 518-457-2180/fax: 518-485-7818
    e-mail: nyspmail@troopers.ny.gov

Employee Relations
Deputy Superintendent:
  Francis P Christensen 518-457-3572/fax: 518-485-7505

  Human Resources
  Deputy Superintendent:
    Bryon Christman 518-485-5044/fax: 518-485-2293

  State Police Academy
  Director:
    Major Ellwood A Sloat, Jr 518-457-7254/fax: 518-485-1454

Field Command
Deputy Superintendent:
  John P Melville 518-457-6554/fax: 518-457-4779

Internal Affairs
Deputy Superintendent:
  Anthony G Ellis 518-485-6018

CORPORATIONS, AUTHORITIES AND COMMISSIONS

New York State Commission of Correction
80 South Swan St
12th Fl
Albany, NY 12210
518-485-2346 Fax: 518-485-2467
e-mail: infoscoc@scoc.ny.gov
Web site: www.scoc.ny.gov

Offices and agencies generally appear in alphabetical order, except when specific order is requested by listee.

Chairman:
   Thomas A Beilein 518-485-2330
Assistant to Chair:
   Patricia Amati 518-485-2330
Counsel:
   Brian Callahan 518-485-2346
Chair, Citizens' Policy & Complaint Review Council:
   Thomas Loughren 518-485-2346
Chair, Medical Review Board:
   Phyllis Harrison-Ross .518-485-2346
Deputy Director, Operations:
   Richard Kinney 518-457-6110
Director, Operations:
   James Lawrence 518-485-2346
Deputy Director Public Information:
   Walter McClure 518-485-2346

NEW YORK STATE LEGISLATURE

See Legislative Branch in Section 1 for additional Standing Committee and Subcommittee information.

Assembly Standing Committees

Alcoholism & Drug Abuse
Chair:
   Linda Rosenthal (D) 518-455-5802
Ranking Minority Member:
   Mark Johns (R) 518-455-5784

Codes
Chair:
   Joseph R Lentol (D) 518-455-4477
Ranking Minority Member:
   Al Graf (R) 518-455-5937

Correction
Chair:
   Daniel O'Donnell (D) .518-455-5603
Ranking Minority Member:
   Joe Giglio (R) 518-455-5241

Senate Standing Committees

Codes
Chair:
   Michael F Nozzolio (R) 518-455-2366
Ranking Minority Member:
   Daniel Squadron (D) 518-455-2625

Crime Victims, Crime & Correction
Chair:
   Patrick M Gallivan (R) 518-455-3471
Ranking Minority Member:
   Ruth Hassell-Thompson (D) 518-455-2061

U.S. GOVERNMENT

EXECUTIVE DEPARTMENTS AND RELATED AGENCIES

US Justice Department
Web site: www.usdoj.gov

Bureau of Alcohol, Tobacco, Firearms & Explosives
Web site: www.atf.gov

New York Field Division . . . . .fax: 646-335-9001
Financial Square, 32 Old Slip, Suite 3500, New York, NY 10005

646-335-9000 Fax: 646-335-9001
e-mail: nydiv@atf.gov
Special Agent-in-Charge:
   Joseph Anarumo
Public Information Officer:
   Charles Mulham

Drug Enforcement Administration - New York Task Force
99 Tenth Ave, New York, NY 10011
212-337-3900
Web site: www.dea.gov
Associate Special Agent-in-Charge:
   James J. Hunt
Associate Special Agent-in-Charge:
   Wilbert L Plummer 212-337-2901
Associate Special Agent-in-Charge:
   Jimmy S Fox 212-620-4910
Associate Special Agent-in-Charge:
   Daniel S Anderson 212-337-2903

Federal Bureau of Investigation - New York Field Offices
Web site: www.fbi.gov

Albany . . . . .fax: 518-431-7463
200 McCarty Ave, Albany, NY 12209
518-465-7551 Fax: 518-431-7463
Web site: www.albany.fbi.gov
Special Agent-in-Charge:
   Andrew Vale 518-465-7551

Buffalo . . . . .fax: 716-843-5288
One FBI Plaza, Buffalo, NY 14202-2698
716-856-7800 Fax: 716-843-5288
Web site: www.buffalo.fbi.gov
Special Agent-in-Charge:
   Richard M. Frankel 716-856-7800

New York City . . . . .fax: 212-384-2745
26 Federal Plaza, 23rd Fl, New York, NY 10278-0004
212-384-1000 Fax: 212-384-2745
Assistant Director-in-Charge:
   George Venizelos 212-384-1000

Federal Bureau of Prisons
Web site: www.bop.gov

Brooklyn Metropolitan Detention Center . . . . .fax: 718-840-5005
80 29th St, Brooklyn, NY 11232
718-840-4200 Fax: 718-840-5005
Warden:
   Frank Strada 718-840-4200/fax: 718-840-5005

CCM New York . . . . .fax: 718-840-4207
100 29th St, Brooklyn, NY 11232
718-840-4219 Fax: 718-840-4207

Federal Correctional Institution at Otisville
Two Mile Drive, PO Box 600, Otisville, NY 10963
Warden:
   Howard L. Hufford

Metropolitan Correctional Center . . . . .fax: 646-836-7751
150 Park Row, New York, NY 10007
646-836-6300 Fax: 646-836-7751
Warden:
   Catherine Stareck Linaweaver

Ray Brook Federal Correctional Institution
PO Box 300, Ray Brook, NY 12977
Warden:
   Russell Perdue 518-897-4000/fax: 518-897-4216

Offices and agencies generally appear in alphabetical order, except when specific order is requested by listee.

Secret Service - New York Field Offices

Albany
39 N Pearl St, Ste 2, Albany, NY 12207-2785
Resident Agent-in-Charge:
William Leege....................518-436-9600/fax: 518-436-9635

Buffalo
610 Main St, Ste 300, Buffalo, NY 14202
Special Agent-in-Charge:
Michael Bryant..................716-551-4401/fax: 716-551-5075

JFK/LGA.......................................fax: 718-553-7626
230-59 Rockaway Blvd, Bldg 59, Suite 265, Springfield Gardens, NY 11413
718-553-0911 Fax: 718-553-7626
Resident Agent-in-Charge:
Kenneth J Cronin 718-553-0911

Melville.......................................fax: 631-293-4389
145 Pinelawn Rd, Ste 200N, Melville, NY 11747
631-293-4028 Fax: 631-293-4389
Resident Agent-in-Charge:
Kenneth Pleasant 631-293-4028

New York City.................................fax: 718-840-1001
335 Adams St, Brooklyn, NY 11201
718-840-1000 Fax: 718-840-1001
Special Agent-in-Charge:
A T Smith....................................718-840-1000

Rochester
1820 HSBC Plaza, 100 Chestnut St, Rochester, NY 14604
585-232-4160
Resident Agent:
Michael de Stefano 585-232-4160/fax: 585-232-4662

Syracuse.......................................fax: 315-448-0302
100 S Clinton St, PO Box 7006, Syracuse, NY 13261
315-448-0304 Fax: 315-448-0302
Resident Agent-in-Charge:
Timothy Kirk 315-448-0304

White Plains
140 Grand St, White Plains, NY 10601
914-682-6300
Resident Agent-in-Chg:
Milton D Johnson 914-682-6300/fax: 914-682-6182

US Attorney's Office - New York

Eastern District ....fax: 718-254-6479
271 Cadman Plaza East, Brooklyn, NY 11201
718-254-7000 Fax: 718-254-6479
US Attorney:
Loretta E. Lynch 718-254-7000/fax: 718-254-6479
Chief Assistant United States Attorney:
Eric Covngold....................718-254-7000/fax: 718-254-6300
Executive Assistant United States Attorney:
William J Muller..................718-254-7000/fax: 718-254-6329
Administrative Assistant United States Attorney:
John Lenior.....................................718-254-6255
Chief Assistantt United States Attorney, Criminal Division:
Bridget Rohde 718-254-6238/fax: 718-254-6150
Chief Assistant United States Attorney, Civil Division:
Susan Riley 718-254-6037/fax: 718-254-7483
Chief Assistant United States Attorney, Appeals Division:
Peter Norling 718-254-6280
Administrative Officer:
Charles Dunne

Northern District ....fax: 518-431-0249
518-431-0247 Fax: 518-431-0249

Albany
445 Broadway, Room 218, Albany, NY 12207
Assistant United States Attorney:
Tom Spina
Binghamton ....fax: 607-773-2901
319 Federal Building, Binghamton, NY 13901
607-773-2887 Fax: 607-773-2901
Assistant United States Attorney:
Miro Lovric
Syracuse ....fax: 315-448-0689
100 S Clinton St, PO Box 7198, Syracuse, NY 13261-7198
315-448-0672 Fax: 315-448-0689
United States Attorney:
Glenn Suddaby.............................315-448-0672
Assistant United States Attorney:
Charles E Roberts 315-448-0672
Assistant United States Attorney, Chief Civil Division:
William H Pease 315-448-0672
Administrative Officer:
Martha Stratton.............315-448-0672/fax: 315-448-0689

Southern District ....fax: 212-637-2685
1 Saint Andrews Plaza, New York, NY 10007
212-637-2200 Fax: 212-637-2685
New York City
United States Attorney:
Preet Bahara
Associate United States Attorney:
John M McEnany........................212-637-2571
Chief United States Appellate Attorney:
Celeste Koeleveld 212-637-1044
Chief, Civil Division:
James Cott.................................212-637-2695
Chief, Criminal Division:
Lev Dassin.................................212-637-2508
Administrative Officer:
Edward Tyrrell 212-637-2269/fax: 212-637-0084
White Plains ....fax: 914-993-1980
300 Quarropas St, White Plains, NY 10601
914-993-1000 Fax: 914-993-1980
Chief Assistant United States Attorney:
Margery Feinzig..........................914-993-1909

Western District
Buffalo ....fax: 716-551-3052
138 Delaware Ave, Buffalo, NY 14202
716-843-5700 Fax: 716-551-3052
United States Attorney:
William J. Hochul, Jr.
First Assistant United States Attorney:
Kathleen M Mehltretter 716-843-5817
Assistant United States Attorney, Civil Division Chief:
Mary Pat Fleming 716-843-5867
Assistant United States Attorney, Narcotics & Violent Crime Division Chief:
Joseph M Guerra, III 716-843-5824
Assistant United States Attorney, Strike Force Division Chief:
Anthony M Bruce 716-843-5886
Assistant United States Attorney, White Collar & General Crimes Division Chief:
Paul J Campana 716-843-5819
Administrative Officer:
Barbara A Sweitzer 716-843-5826/fax: 716-551-3170
Rochester ....fax: 585-263-6226
620 Federal Bldg, 100 State St, Rochester, NY 14614
585-263-6760 Fax: 585-263-6226
Assistant United States Attorney-in-Charge:
Bradley E Tyler 585-263-5717

Offices and agencies generally appear in alphabetical order, except when specific order is requested by listee.

US Marshals' Service - New York

Eastern District

Brooklyn

US Courthouse, 225 Cadman Plaza, Brooklyn, NY 11201
718-260-0440
United States Marshal:
   Charles Dunne

Central Islip

100 Federal Plaza, Central Islip, NY 11722
631-712-6000
United States Marshal:
   Charles Dunne

Northern District

Albany

James T. Foley Courthouse, 445 Broadway, Albany, NY 12207
518-472-5401
United States Marshal:
   David McNulty

Syracuse

100 S Clinton St, Syracuse, NY 13261
Unitede States Marshal:
   David McNulty 315-473-7601

Southern District

500 Pearl St, Ste 400, New York, NY 10007
United States Marshal:
   Joseph R Guccione 212-331-7200/fax: 212-637-6130

Western District

Buffalo

2 Niagara Street, Buffalo, NY 14202

Rochester

US Courthouse, Rm 284, 100 State St, Rochester, NY 14614
United States Marshal:
   Charles Salina

US Parole Commission

90 K Street, NE, 3rd Floor, Washington, DC 20530
Chairman:
   Isaac Fulwood, Jr. 202-346-7000

U.S. CONGRESS

See U.S. Congress Chapter for additional Standing Committee and Subcommittee information.

House of Representatives Standing Committees

Judiciary

Chair:
   Bob Goodlatte (R-VA)
Ranking Member:
   John Conyers, Jr. (D-MI)
New York Delegate:
   Hakeem Jeffries (D)
New York Delegate:
   Jerrold Nadler (D). 202-225-5635

Subcommittee

Crime, Terrorism & Homeland Security

Chair:
   Jim Sensebrenner (D-WI)
Ranking Member:
   Louie Gohmert (R-TX) 202-225-3035

Senate Standing Committees

Judiciary

Chair:
   Patrick J. Leahy (D-VT) 202-224-4242
Ranking Member:
   Charles Grassley (R-IA)
New York Delegate:
   Charles E Schumer (D) 202-224-6542

PRIVATE SECTOR

American Society for the Prevention of Cruelty to Animals (ASPCA)

424 E 92nd St, New York, NY 10128-6804
212-876-7700 x4552 Fax: 212-360-6875
e-mail: government@aspca.org
Web site: www.aspca.org
Promoting humane treatment of animals, education & advocacy programs & conducting statewide anti-cruelty investigation & enforcement
Lisa Weisberg, Sr VP, Government Affairs & Public Policy, Sr Policy Advisor

Associated Licensed Detectives of New York State

575 Madison Avenue, Suite 1006, New York, NY 10022
646-320-0143 Fax: 212-605-0222
e-mail: info@aldonys.org
Web site: www.aldonys.org
Licensed NYS private investigators & watch, guard & patrol license holders
William C Vassell, President

Berkshire Farm Center & Services for Youth

13640 Route 22, Canaan, NY 12029
518-781-4567 Fax: 518-781-4577
e-mail: dharrington@berkshirefarm.org
Web site: www.berkshirefarm.org
Multi-function agency for troubled youth & families
Timothy Giacchetta, Chief Executive Officer

CUNY John Jay College of Criminal Justice

899 10th Ave, Room 625, New York, NY 10019
212-237-8600 or 212-237-8606 Fax: 212-237-8607
e-mail: jtravis@jjay.cuny.edu
Web site: www.jjay.cuny.edu
Criminal justice, police & fire science, forensic science & psychology, international criminal justice, public administration
Jeremy Travis, President

Center for Alternative Sentencing & Employment Services (CASES)

346 Broadway, 3rd Fl, New York, NY 10013
212-732-0076 Fax: 212-571-0292
e-mail: jcopperman@cases.org
Web site: www.cases.org
Advocacy for the use of community sanctions that are fair, affordable & consistent with public safety
Joel Copperman, President/Chief Executive Officer

Center for Law & Justice

Pine West Plaza, Bldg 2, Washington Ave Ext, Albany, NY 12205
518-427-8361 Fax: 518-427-8362
e-mail: cflj@verizon.net
Web site: www.timesunion.com/communities/cflj
Advocacy for fair treatment of poor people & communities of color by the legal & criminal justice systems; referral, workshops, community lawyering & education
Alice P Green, Executive Director

Policy Areas

Coalition Against Domestic Violence, NYS
350 New Scotland Ave, Albany, NY 12208
518-482-5465 Fax: 518-482-3807
e-mail: vasquez@nyscadv.org
Web site: www.nyscadv.org
Jessica Vasquez, CEO

Coalition Against Sexual Assault (NYS)
28 Essex Street, Albany, NY 12206
518-482-4222 Fax: 518-482-4248
e-mail: lafo@nyscasa.org
Web site: www.nyscasa.org
Advocacy, public education, technical assistance & training
Anne Liske, Executive Director

Correctional Association of New York
2090 Adam Clayton Powell Jr Blvd, Suite 200, New York, NY 10027
212-254-5700 Fax: 212-473-2807
e-mail: rgangi@correctionalassociation.org
Web site: www.correctionalassociation.org
Drug law reform/improved prison conditions
Soffiyah Elijah, Executive Director

NYS Bar Assn, Public Trust & Confidence in the Legal System
Debevoise & Plimpton LLP
919 Third Ave, New York, NY 10022
212-909-6096 Fax: 212-909-6836
e-mail: elieberman@debevoise.com
Web site: www.debevoise.com
Ellen Lieberman,

Education & Assistance Corporation Inc
50 Clinton St, Ste 107, Hempstead, NY 11550
516-539-0150 Fax: 516-539-0160
e-mail: lelder@eacinc.org
Web site: www.eacinc.org
Rehabilitation for nonviolent offenders; advocacy, education & counseling programs for youth, elderly & families
Lance W Elder, President & CEO

Fortune Society (The)
53 W 23rd St, 8th Fl, New York, NY 10010
212-691-7554 x501 Fax: 212-255-4948
e-mail: jpfortune@aol.com
Web site: www.fortunesociety.org
Education & vocational training for ex-offenders, alternatives to incarceration, counseling, drug treatment & HIV/AIDS services & referrals & transitional housing facility
JoAnne Page, Executive Director

Hofstra University, School of Law
121 Hofstra University, Hempstead, NY 11549-1210
212-864-6092
e-mail: lawdny@hofstra.edu
Web site: www.hofstra.edu/law
Antitrust, criminal law, evidence
David N Yellen, Emeritus Professor of Law

Law Offices of Stanley N Lupkin
98 Cutter Mill Road, Suite 52N, Great Neck, NY 11021
516-482-1223 Fax: 516-466-2799
e-mail: slupkin@gnlaw.com
Corporate, criminal & financial investigations, integrity monitorships
Stanley N Lupkin, White Collar Criminal Defense

Legal Action Center
225 Varick Street, 4th Floor, New York, NY 10014
212-243-1313 Fax: 212-675-0286
e-mail: lacinfo@lac.org
Web site: www.lac.org
Legal & policy issues, alcohol/drug abuse, AIDS & criminal justice
Paul N Samuels, President & Director

Legal Aid Society
199 Water Street, New York, NY 10013
212-557-3300 Fax: 212-509-8761
e-mail: jpreble@legal-aid.org
Web site: www.legal-aid.org
Criminal defense & appeals
Judith Preble, Supervising Attorney, Criminal Defense Practice

NYS Bar Assn, Criminal Justice Section
Michael T Kelly, Esq
1217 Delaware Ave, Apt 1003, Buffalo, NY 14209
716-886-1922 Fax: 716-886-1922
e-mail: mkelly1005@aol.com
Michael T Kelly, Chair

Mothers Against Drunk Driving (MADD) of NYS
790 Watervliet-Shaker Road, Suite #6, Latham, NY 12110
518-785-6233 or 800-245-6233 Fax: 518-782-1806
e-mail: ny.state@madd.org
Web site: www.madd.org
Advocacy, public education & victim support
Donna Kopec, Executive Director

NYS Association of Chiefs of Police Inc
2697 Hamburg Street, Schenectady, NY 12303
518-355-3371 Fax: 518-356-5767
e-mail: nysacop@nycap.rr.com
Web site: www.nychiefs.org
John Grebert, Executive Director

NYS Correctional Officers & Police Benevolent Association Inc
102 Hackett Blvd, Albany, NY 12209
518-427-1551 or 888-484-7279 Fax: 518-426-1635
e-mail: nyscopba@nyscopba.org
Web site: www.nyscopba.org
Mary Gulino,

NYS Council of Probation Administrators
c/o Council of Community Svcs of NYS, Box 2, 272 Broadway, Albany, NY 12204-2941
518-434-9194 Fax: 518-434-0392
e-mail: president@nyscopa.org
Web site: www.nyscopa.org
Provide supervision & investigation services to courts
Patricia Aikens, President

NYS Defenders Association
194 Washington Ave, Ste 500, Albany, NY 12210-2314
518-465-3524 Fax: 518-465-3249
e-mail: info@nysda.org
Web site: www.nysda.org
Criminal defense
Jonathan E Gradess, Executive Director

NYS Deputies Association Inc
61 Laredo Dr, Rochester, NY 14624
585-247-9322 Fax: 585-247-6661
e-mail: tross1@rochester.rr.com
Web site: www.nysdeputy.org
Thomas H Ross, Executive Director

NYS Law Enforcement Officers Union, Council 82, AFSCME, AFL-CIO
Hollis V Chase Bldg, 63 Colvin Ave, Albany, NY 12206
518-489-8424 or 800-724-0482 Fax: 518-435-1523
e-mail: c82@council82.org
Web site: www.council82.org
Provides the professional working men and women that protect the citizens of New York State with the best possible working conditions.
James Lyman, President

Offices and agencies generally appear in alphabetical order, except when specific order is requested by listee.

NYS Sheriffs' Association
27 Elk St, Albany, NY 12207
518-434-9091 Fax: 518-434-9093
e-mail: pkehoe@nysheriffs.org
Web site: www.nysheriffs.org
Peter R Kehoe, Executive Director

New York State Law Enforcement Council
One Hogan Place, New York, NY 10013
212-335-8927 Fax: 212-335-3808
Web site: www.nyslec.org
Founded in 1982 as a legislative advocate for NY's law enforcement community. The members represent leading law enforcement professionals throughout the state. An active voice and participant in improving the quality of justice and a safer NY.
Leroy Frazer, Jr, Coordinator

Osborne Association
809 Westchester Avenue, Bronx, NY 10455
718-707-2600 or 718-842-0500 Fax: 718-707-3102
e-mail: info@osborneny.org
Web site: www.osborneny.org
Career/educational counseling, job referrals & training for recently released prisoners, substance abuse treatment, case management, HIV/AIDS counseling & prevention, family services, parenting education, re-entry services, housing placement assistan
Elizabeth A Gaynes, Executive Director

Pace University, School of Law, John Jay Legal Services Inc
80 N Broadway, White Plains, NY 10603-3711
914-422-4333 Fax: 914-422-4391
e-mail: jjls@law.pace.edu
Web site: www.law.pace.edu
Law school clinical program with programs in the areas of health law, poverty law, domestic violence, immigration, criminal justice, and investor rights.
Margaret M Flint, Executive Director

Palladia Inc
2006 Madison Avenue, New York, NY 10035
212-979-8800 Fax: 212-979-0100
e-mail: info@palladiainc.org
Web site: www.palladiainc.org
Outpatient treatment, substance abuse treatment & counseling, alternatives to incarceration & parole transitional services
Susan Ohanesian, Vice President, Residential Services

Patrolmen's Benevolent Association
40 Fulton St, 17th Fl, New York, NY 10038
212-233-5531 Fax: 212-233-3952
e-mail: union@nycpba.org
Web site: www.nycpba.org
NYC patrolmen's union
Patrick Lynch, President

Police Conference of NY Inc (PCNY)
112 State St, Ste 1120, Albany, NY 12207
518-463-3283 Fax: 518-463-2488
e-mail: pcnyinfo@pcny.org
Web site: www.pcny.org
Advocacy for law enforcement officers
Richard Wells, President

Prisoners' Legal Services of New York
114 Prospect St, Ithaca, NY 14850-5616
607-273-2283 Fax: 607-272-9122
e-mail: kmmonks@plsny.org
Karen L Murtagh, Executive Director

Remove Intoxicated Drivers (RID-USA Inc)
1013 Nott St, PO Box 520, Schenectady, NY 12301
518-372-0034 or 518-393-4357 Fax: 518-370-4917
e-mail: daiken2@nycap.rr.com
Web site: www.rid-usa.org
Victims' rights, alcohol policy & public awareness
Doris Aiken, President

Pearls' Prison Families of NY
Rochester Interfaith Jail Ministry Inc
130 Plymouth Avenue South, Rochester, NY 14614
585-428-3802
e-mail: rochesterjail/ministry@yahoo.com
Support services for ex-offenders, the incarcerated & their families
Harry Bronson, Executive Director

SUNY at Stony Brook, NY State Drinking Driver Program
Social & Behavioral Sciences, Rm North 231, Stony Brook, NY 11794-4326
631-632-7060 Fax: 631-632-4224
e-mail: spd.ddp@notes.cc.sunysb.edu
Drinking & driving education & prevention
Judith Forde, Director

Stillman, Friedman & Shechtman PC
425 Park Ave, New York, NY 10022
212-223-0200 Fax: 212-223-1942
e-mail: cstillman@stillmanfriedman.com
Web site: www.stillmanfriedman.com
White collar criminal law
Charles A Stillman, Partner

Trooper Foundation-State of New York Inc
3 Airport Park Blvd, Latham, NY 12110-1441
518-785-1002 Fax: 518-785-1003
e-mail: rmincher@nystf.org
Web site: www.nystrooperfoundation.org
Supports programs & services of the NYS Police
Rachel L Mincher, Foundation Administrator

Vera Institute of Justice
233 Broadway, 12th Fl, New York, NY 10279-1299
212-334-1300 Fax: 212-941-9407
e-mail: mgolden@vera.org
Web site: www.vera.org
Research, design & implementation of demonstration projects in criminal justice & social equity in partnership with governmental community organizations
Michael Jacobson, Director

Women's Prison Association & Home Inc
110 Second Ave, New York, NY 10003
646-336-6100 Fax: 212-677-1981
Web site: www.wpaonline.org
Community corrections & family preservation programs
Ann Jacobs, Executive Director

Offices and agencies generally appear in alphabetical order, except when specific order is requested by listee.

EDUCATION

NEW YORK STATE

GOVERNOR'S OFFICE

Governor's Office
Executive Chamber
State Capitol
Albany, NY 12224
518-474-8390 Fax: 518-474-1513
Web site: www.ny.gov

Governor:
Andrew M Cuomo 518-474-8390
Secretary to the Governor:
William Mulrow 518-474-4246
Counsel to the Governor:
Alphonso David 518-474-8343
Director of Policy:
John Maggiore 518-408-2576
Deputy Secretary, Education:
Elana Sigall 518-474-9883
Director, Communications:
Melissa DeRosa . . . . .518-474-8418 or 212-681-4640

EXECUTIVE DEPARTMENTS AND RELATED AGENCIES

Board of Regents
89 Washington Ave
EB, Rm 110
Albany, NY 12234
518-474-5889 Fax: 518-486-2405
e-mail: regentsoffice@mail.nysed.gov
Web site: www.regents.nysed.gov

Chancellor:
Merryl H Tisch (2016) 518-474-5889
e-mail: regent.Tisch@nysed.gov
Vice Chancellor:
Anthony S. Bottar (2016) 315-422-3466
e-mail: regent.Bottar@nysed.gov
Education Commissioner, USNY President:
MaryEllen Elia 518-474-5844
Secretary to the Board:
Anthony Lofrumento 518-474-5889
Member:
James E Cottrell (2019) 718-270-2331
e-mail: regent.cottrell@nysed.gov
Member:
Charles R Bendit (2017). 212-220-9945
e-mail: regent.bendit@nysed.gov
Member:
Josephine Finn (2019). 518-474-5889
e-mail: regentFinn@mail.nysed.gov
Member:
Kathleen M Cashin (2020) .518-474-5889
e-mail: regent.cashin@nysed.gov
Member:
Andrew T Brown (2017) 585-454-3667
e-mail: regent.brown@nysed.gov
Member:
Judith Johnson (2020). 518-474-5889
e-mail: regentchapey@mail.nysed.gov
Member:
Wade S Norwood (2019) 585-436-2944
e-mail: regent.norwood@nysed.gov

Member:
Catherine Collins (2020). 518-474-5889
e-mail: regent.collins@nysed.gov
Member:
Judith Chin (2018) 518-474-5889
e-mail: regent.chin@nysed.gov
Member:
Christine D Cea (2019). 718-494-5306
e-mail: regent.Cea@nysed.gov
Member:
Betty A Rosa (2018). 718-664-8052
e-mail: regent.rosa@nysed.gov
Member:
Beverly Ourderkirk (2020) .315-375-8596
e-mail: regent.ouderkirk@nysed.gov
Member:
James R Tallon, Jr (2017). .212-494-0777
e-mail: regent.tallon@nysed.gov
Member:
Roger B Tilles (2020) 516-364-2533
e-mail: regent.tilles@nysed.gov
Member:
Lester W Young, Jr (2020) .718-722-2796
e-mail: regent.young@nysed.gov

Children & Family Services, Office of
52 Washington St
Rensselaer, NY 12144
518-473-7793 Fax: 518-486-7550
Web site: www.ocfs.state.ny.us

Acting Commissioner:
Sheila Poole 518-402-3108
Executive Secretary:
Nancy Degree 518-402-3108
Executive Deputy Commissioner:
Sheila Poole 518-402-3108
Assistant Commissioner, Communications:
Jennifer Givner 518-402-3130
e-mail: cfspio@dfa.state.ny.us
Bureau of Policy Analysis:
Rayana Gonzales. 518-473-1776
Deputy Commissioner, Juvenile Justice & Opportunity for Youth:
Ines Neives 518-473-1786
Deputy Commissioner, Child Welfare & Community Service:
Laura Velez 518-474-3377
Director of Regional Operations:
Jim Hart. 518-473-1790

Regional Operations
Deputy Commissioner, Childcare Services:
Janice Molnar 518-486-6247
Acting Associate Commissioner, Youth Programs & Services:
Joseph Tomassone 518-486-6766

Education Department
State Education Bldg
89 Washington Ave
Albany, NY 12234
518-474-3852 Fax: 518-486-5631
Web site: www.nysed.gov

Commissioner & University President:
MaryEllen Elia 518-474-5844
Chief, External Affairs (Communications):
Dennis Tompkins 518-474-1201
Executive Deputy Commissioner:
Valerie Grey 518-473-8381

Offices and agencies generally appear in alphabetical order, except when specific order is requested by listee.

General Counsel:
Robert Trautwein 518-474-6400
 e-mail: legal@mail.nysed.gov
Chief of Staff:
James N Baldwin 518-474-5844
Associate Commissioner, Special Education:
Rebecca Cort. 518-473-4818

Cultural Education Office
10A 33 Cultural Education Center, Madison Avenue, Albany, NY 12230
Web site: www.oce.nysed.gov
Deputy Commissioner:
Jeffrey Cannell 518-474-5976
 e-mail: jcannell@mail.nysed.gov

Educational Television & Public Broadcasting
Director:
Elizabeth Hood. 518-474-5862

State Archives
e-mail: archinfo@mail.nysed.gov
Assistant Commissioner & State Archivist:
Christine Ward 518-474-6926
 e-mail: cward@mail.nysed.gov
Coordinator, Training & Publications:
Mary Beth Sullivan. 518-474-6926
 e-mail: archtrain@mail.nysed.gov
Archival Services:
Maria Holden 518-474-6276
Reference & Research Services:
James Folts 518-474-8955
 e-mail: archref@mail.nysed.gov
State Records Center Services:
Maggi Gonsalves 518-457-3171
 e-mail: records@mail.nysed.gov
Government Records Services:
Geof Huth 518-474-6926
Administrative & Technical Services:
Michelle Arpey. 518-474-6926
Public Programs & Outreach:
Julie Daniels 518-473-8037
 e-mail: archedu@mail.nysed.gov

State Library
222 Madison Ave, Cultural Education Center, Albany, NY 12230
Web site: www.nysl.nysed.gov
Assistant Commissioner & State Librarian:
Bernard Margolis 518-474-5930
 e-mail: bmargolis@mail.nysed.gov
Director, Research Library:
Loretta Ebert 518-473-1189
 e-mail: lebert@mail.nysed.gov
Technical Services & Systems:
Liza Duncan 518-474-5946
 e-mail: lduncan@mail.nysed.gov
Coordinator Statewide Library Services:
Carol Ann Desch 518-474-7196
 e-mail: cdesch@mail.nysed.gov
Talking Book & Braille Library:
Sharon Phillips 518-474-5935
 e-mail: sphillip@mail.nysed.gov

State Museum Office
www.nysm.nysed.gov,
Director:
Mark A Schaming. 518-474-5812
 e-mail: mschamin@mail.nysed.gov
Coordinator, Public Programs:
Nicole LaFountain 518-474-0575
 e-mail: nlafount@mail.nysed.gov

State Historian:
Robert Weible. 518-473-1299
 e-mail: rweible@mail.nysed.gov

Research and Collections
Director:
Dr. John P. Hart 518-474-5816
 e-mail: jhart@mail.nysed.gov
Assistant Director:
Robert Daniels 518-473-8121
 e-mail: rdaniels@mail.nysed.gov
Collections Database Manager:
Ellen Stevens 518-474-5816
 e-mail: estevens@mail.nysed.gov
State Archaeologist:
Christina B Reith 518-402-5975
 e-mail: creith@mail.nysed.gov
Deputy Commissioner:
Sharon Cates-Williams. 518-473-4706
Chief Financial Officer:
Donald Juron. 518-474-7751
Diversity, Ethics & Access:
Steven Earle 518-474-1265
Facilities & Business Services:
Tom Casey 518-474-7770
Human Resources Management:
Annette Franchini. 518-474-5883
Grant Finance:
Margaret Zollo 518-474-4875
Audit Services:
James Conway 518-473-4516
Budget Coordination & Financial Administration:
Andrew Klippel 518-486-1708
Education Finance Director:
Joseph Conroy 518-486-2422
State Review:
Justyn Bates 518-485-9373
Rate Setting Unit:
Ann Marsh 518-474-3227
STAC (Systems to Track & Account for Children):
Harold Matott 518-474-7116

Information Technology Services
Chief Information Officer:
Benny Thottam. 518-474-4660
Information Technology Services (ITS) Director:
Benny Thottam. 518-474-4640

Office of P-12 Education
89 Washington Ave, EB West 2nd Fl Mezzanine, Albany, NY 12234
Web site: www.p12.nysed.gov
Deputy Commissioner:
Ken Slentz. 518-474-3862/fax: 518-473-2056
Basic Educational Data System (BEDS):
Ken Wagner 518-474-7965
Striving Readers:
Meg McNiff 518-474-5807
Title 1 School & Community Service:
Roberto Reyes. 518-473-0295
School Innovation:
Sally Bachofer. 518-474-4817
Native American Education & Services:
Adrian Cooke 518-474-0537

School Operations & Management Services
Assistant Commissioner:
Charles Szuberla 518-474-2238
Child Nutrition Program Administration
 Lead Contact:
 Frances O'Donnell. 518-473-8781

Offices and agencies generally appear in alphabetical order, except when specific order is requested by listee.

Educational Management Services
Lead Contact:
 Charles Szuberla 518-474-6541
Facilities & Planning
Lead Contact:
 Carl Thurnau 518-474-3906
Grants Management
Lead Contact:
 Maureen Lavare.........................518-474-3936

Office of Higher Education
89 Washington Ave, Room 977 EB Annex, Albany, NY 12234
e-mail: oheweb@mail.nysed.gov
Web site: www.highered.nysed.gov
Deputy Commissioner:
 John D'Agati.............................518-486-3633

Office of K-16 Initiatives & Access Programs
Executive Director:
 Stanley S Hansen, Jr 518-474-3719/fax: 518-474-7468
e-mail: kiap@mail.nysed.gov
College & University Evaluation
Coordinator:
 Vacant..................518-474-2593/fax: 518-486-2779
e-mail: ocueinfo@nysed.gov
Research & Information Systems
Coordinator:
 Glenwood Rowse.........................518-474-5091
e-mail: growse@mail.nysed.gov

Office of Teaching Initiatives
Teacher Certification, Teacher Policy & School Personnel Review
Assistant Commissioner:
 Deborah Marriott.........................518-473-2998

Office of the Professions....................fax: 518-474-1449
89 Washington Ave, EB, 2nd Fl, West Mezz, Albany, NY 12234
Fax: 518-474-1449
Web site: www.op.nysed.gov
Deputy Commissioner:
 Douglas Lentivech 518-486-1765

Office of Professional Responsibility
Professional Examinations
475 Park Ave South, New York, NY 10016
Director:
 Harrison Fisher 518-474-3817
Director, Investigations:
 Donald Dawson 212-951-6444
Director, Legal Services:
 Andrew Tolkoff.........................212-951-6550
Director, Prosecutions:
 George Ding.........................212-951-6401

Professional Education Program Review
Director:
 William Murphy 518-474-3817 x300
e-mail: opprogs@mail.nysed.gov

Professional Licensing Services
Acting Director:
 Susan Naccarato 518-474-3817 x340
e-mail: opdpls@mail.nysed.gov

Office of Adult Career & Continuing Education Services
(ACCES)....................................fax: 518-474-8802
One Commerce Plaza, Rm 1606, Albany, NY 12234
Fax: 518-474-8802
Web site: www.acces.nysed.gov
Deputy Commissioner:
 Kevin Smith 518-474-2714
Assistant Commissioner:
 Debora Brown-Jackson.........................518-402-3955

Director, Proprietary School Supervision:
 Carole Yates 518-474-3969/fax: 518-473-3644
e-mail: cyates@mail.nysed.gov
Director, Adult Education Program & Policy:
 Mark Leinung.........................518-474-8892
e-mail: adulted@mail.nysed.gov

Fiscal & Administrative Services
Coordinator:
 Rosemary Johnson 518-486-4038

Vocational Rehabilitation Operations
Assistant Commissioner:
 Debora Brown-Johnson.........................518-402-3955
e-mail: dbrowngr@mail.nysed.gov
Manager, Independent Living Centers:
 Robert Gumson.........................518-474-2925
e-mail: rgumson@mail.nysed.gov
Albany District Office
80 Wolf Road, Ste 200, Albany, NY 12205
District Office Manager:
 Barbara Arisohn.........................518-485-8558
e-mail: barisonn@mail.nysed.gov
Bronx District Office
1215 Zerega Ave, Bronx, NY 10462
District Office Manager:
 Judith Pina 718-931-3500
e-mail: jpina@mail.nysed.gov
Brooklyn District Office
55 Hanson Pl, Brooklyn, NY 11217-1578
District Office Manager:
 Mark Weinstein 718-722-6700
e-mail: mweinste@mail.nysed.gov
Buffalo District Office
508 Main St, Buffalo, NY 14202
Director of Counseling:
 Noreen Murphy 716-848-3013
e-mail: nmurphy@mail.nysed.gov
Hauppauge District Office
State Office Bldg, 250 Veterans Memorial Hwy, Room 3A-12,
 Hauppauge, NY 11788
District Office Manager:
 Sandy Silver.........................631-952-6357
e-mail: ssilver@mail.nysed.gov
Garden City District Office
711 Stewart Ave, Ste 4, Garden City, NY 11530
Regional Coordinator:
 Aurora Farrington 516-227-6801
e-mail: afarring@mail.nysed.gov
Malone District Office
209 W Main St, Malone, NY 12953
Regional Coordinator:
 Michelle Snell 518-483-3530
e-mail: msnell@mail.nysed.gov
Manhattan District Office
116 West 32nd St, 6th Fl, New York, NY 10001
Assistant District Manager:
 JoAnne Schwartz.........................212-630-2300
e-mail: jschwar2@mail.nysed.gov
Mid-Hudson District Office
Manchester Mill Ctr, 301 Manchester Rd, Ste 200, Poughkeepsie,
 NY 12603
District Office Manager:
 Daniel O'Shea 845-452-4935
e-mail: doshea@mail.nysed.gov
Queens District Office
One LeFrak City Plaza, 20th Fl, 59-17 Junction Blvd, Corona, NY
 11368
District Office Manager:
 John Nardozzi 347-510-3101
e-mail: jnardozz@mail.nysed.gov

Offices and agencies generally appear in alphabetical order, except when specific order is requested by listee.

Rochester District Office
109 S Union St, 2nd Fl, Rochester, NY 14607
Regional Coordinator:
Nicolette Leathersich 585-238-2900
e-mail: nleather@mail.nysed.gov

Southern Tier District Office
44 Hawley St, Binghamton, NY 13901
District Office Manager:
Richard Bohman 607-721-8400
e-mail: rbohman@mail.nysed.gov

Syracuse District Office
333 E Washington St, 2nd Fl, Rm 230, Syracuse, NY 13202-1428
District Office Manager:
Duane Watson 315-428-4179
e-mail: dwatson2@mail.nysed.gov

Utica District Office
207 Genesee St, Rm 801, Utica, NY 13501-2812
Business Manager:
Edward Vincent 315-793-2536
e-mail: evincent@mail.nysed.gov

White Plains District Office
75 South Broadway, Ste 200, White Plains, NY 10601
District Office Manager:
Mark Ridgeway 914-946-1313
e-mail: mridgewa@mail.nysed.gov
Director:
Edward Reinfurt 518-292-5700
Deputy Director:
Edward J Hamilton 518-292-5700
Director, Communications/Government Affairs:
Jannette Rondo 518-292-5700/fax: 518-292-5798
Regional Technology Development:
Matthew Watson 518-292-5700
Counsel:
Paul Jesep 518-292-5700

Centers for Advanced Technology

Center for Advanced Ceramic Technology at Alfred University
2 Pine Street, Alfred, NY 14802-1296
e-mail: cactinfo@alfred.edu
Web site: cact.alfred.edu
Director:
Dr Matthew M Hall. 607-871-2486/fax: 607-871-3469

Center for Advanced Materials Processing at Clarkson Univ
CAMP, Box 5665, Potsdam, NY 13699-5665
Web site: www.clarkson.edu/camp
Director:
S V Babu 315-268-2336/fax: 315-268-7615
e-mail: babu@clarkson.edu

Center for Advanced Tech in Biomedical & Bioengineering
Univeristy at Buffalo, 701 Ellicott Street, Buffalo, NY 14203
Web site: www.bioinformatics.buffalo.edu/
Co-Director:
Alexander N. Cartwright PhD .716-645-0312
Co-Director:
Marnie LaVigne PhD 716-645-0312
e-mail: lavigne2@buffalo.edu

Sensor CAT-Diagnostic Tools & Sensor Systems
SUNY at Stony Brook, Suffolk Hall, Room 115B, Stony Brook, NY 11794-3717
e-mail: sensor@ece.sunysb.edu
Web site: sensorcat.sunysb.edu
Director:
Serge Luryi. . . . . .631-632-1368 or 631-632-8420
fax: 631-632-8529

Center for Emerging & Innovative Sciences
Univ of Rochester, 2 Taylor Hall, 260 Hutchison Rd, Rochester, NY 14627

Web site: www.ceis.rochester.edu
Director:
Mark Bocko 585-275-0547
e-mail: mark.bocko@seas.rochester.edu

Center for Advanced Information Management
Columbia University, 630 W 168th St, Bldg 30, New York, NY 10032
Web site: www.cat.columbia.edu
Director:
George Hripcsak 212-305-2944/fax: 212-305-0196

Center for Advanced Technology in Life Science Enterprise
Cornell University, 130 Biotechnology Bldg, Ithaca, NY 14853-2703
Web site: www.biotech.cornell.edu/cat
Director:
George Grills 607-255-9693
e-mail: biotech@cornell.edu

Center for Advanced Technology in Photonics Applications
CUNY, Steinman Hall T606, 16D Convent Avenue, New York, NY 10031
Web site: www.cunycat.org
Director:
David T. Crouse, PhD 212-650-5330
e-mail: crouse@cunycat.org

Center for Automation Technologies & Systems at Rensselaer
CII 8011, 110 8th Street, Troy, NY 12180
e-mail: cats-info@rpi.edu
Web site: www.cats.rpi.edu
Director:
John Wen. .518-276-8744/fax: 518-276-4897

Center for Advanced Medical Biotechnology
Biotechnology Building, 2nd Floor, Stony Brook, NY 11790
Web site: www.biotech.sunysb.edu
Director:
Clinton T Rubin PhD 631-632-8521/fax: 631-632-8577

Center for Computer Applications & Software Engineering
Syracuse University, 2-212 Ctr for Science & Tech, Syracuse, NY 13244
Web site: www.case.syr.edu
Director:
Pramod Varshney 315-443-1060/fax: 315-443-4745
e-mail: varshney@syr.edu

Center in Nanomaterials and Nanoelectronics
251 Fuller Road, Albany, NY 12203
Web site: csne.albany.edu
Director:
Michael Fancher 518-437-8686/fax: 518-437-8687

Ctr for Advanced Tech in Telecommunications at Polytech Univ
5 MetroTech Center, 9th Floor, Brooklyn, NY 11201
Web site: catt.poly.edu
Director:
Shivendra S Panwar . . . . .718-260-3050 or 718-260-3740
fax: 718-260-3074
e-mail: panwar@catt.poly.edu

Future Energy Systems CAT at Rensselaer Polytechnic Inst
110 8th Street, Troy, NY 12180
e-mail: cfes@rpi.edu
Web site: www.rpi.edu/cfes
Director:
Dr. Jian Sun. 518-276-8294/fax: 518-276-6844
e-mail: jsun@ecse.rpi.edu

Integrated Electronics Engineering Center at Binghamton
IEEC, Vestal Pkwy East, PO Box 6000, Binghamton, NY 13902-6000
e-mail: ieec@binghamton.edu
Web site: www.binghamton.edu/ieec/
Director:
Daryl Santos 607-777-4769/fax: 607-777-4683

Offices and agencies generally appear in alphabetical order, except when specific order is requested by listee.

Policy Areas

Regional Technology Development Centers

Alliance for Manufacturing & Technology
69 Court St, 6th Fl, State St Entrance, Binghamton, NY 13901
e-mail: info@amt-mep.org
Web site: www.amt-mep.org
Executive Director:
  Edward Gaetano 607-774-0022 x304/fax: 607-774-0026

Center for Economic Growth
30 Pearl St, Ste 100, Albany, NY 12207
e-mail: ceg@ceg.org
Web site: www.ceg.org
President/CEO:
  F Michael Tucker 518-465-8975/fax: 518-465-6681
  e-mail: miket@ceg.org

Central New York Technology Development Organization
445 Electronics Pkwy, Ste 206, Liverpool, NY 13088
e-mail: mail@tdo.org
Web site: www.tdo.org
President/CEO:
  Robert I Trachtenberg 315-425-5144/fax: 315-233-1259
  e-mail: rtrachtenberg@tdo.org

Council for Interntl Trade, Tech, Education & Communication
Peyton Hall, Box 8561, Main St, Clarkson University, Potsdam, NY 13669
Web site: www.citec.org
Executive Director:
  William P. Murray 315-268-3778 x29/fax: 315-268-4432
  e-mail: murray@citec.org

High Technology of Rochester
150 Lucius Gordon Dr, Suite 100, West Henrietta, NY 14586
Web site: www.htr.org
President:
  Jim Sendall 585-214-2400
  e-mail: info@htr.org

Hudson Valley Technology Development Center
1450 Route 300, Building 1, Newburgh, NY 12550
e-mail: info@hvtdc.org
Web site: www.hvtdc.org
Executive Director:
  Thomas G Phillips, Sr 845-391-8214 x3006/fax: 845-845-8218
  e-mail: tom.phillips@hvtdc.org

Industrial & Technology Assistance Corp
39 Broadway, Suite 1110, New York, NY 10006
Web site: www.itac.org
President:
  Sara Garretson 212-809-3900/fax: 646-588-5156
  e-mail: sgarretson@itac.org

Long Island Forum for Technology
510 Grumman Road West, Bethpage, NY 11714
e-mail: info@lift.org
Web site: www.lift.org
Executive Director:
  William Wahlig 631-969-3700/fax: 631-846-2789
  e-mail: bwahlig@lift.org

Mohawk Valley Applied Technology Corp
207 Genesee St, Ste 405, Utica, NY 13501
Web site: www.mvatc.com
President:
  Paul MacEnroe 315-793-8050/fax: 315-793-8057
  e-mail: paulm@mvatc.com

INSYTE Consulting (Western NY Technology Development Ctr)
726 Exchange St, Ste 812, Buffalo, NY 14210
Web site: www.insyte-consulting.com

President:
  Benjamin Rand 716-636-3626/fax: 716-845-6418
  e-mail: brand@insyte.org

CORPORATIONS, AUTHORITIES AND COMMISSIONS

City University Construction Fund
555 W 57th St
11th Fl
New York, NY 10019
212-541-0171 Fax: 212-541-1014

Interim Executive Director:
  Judith Bergtraum. 646-664-2605
  e-mail: iris.weinshall@mail.cuny.edu
Counsel:
  Frederick Schaffer. 646-664-9210
  e-mail: frederick.schaffer@mail.cuny.edy

New York City School Construction Authority
30-30 Thomson Ave
Long Island City, NY 11101-3045
718-472-8000 Fax: 718-472-8840
Web site: www.nycsca.org

Chair/Chancellor:
  Carmen Farina. 718-472-8000
President & Chief Executive Officer:
  Lorraine Grillo 718-472-8001
Executive Vice President & General Counsel:
  Ross J Holden 718-472-8220
VP, Finance:
  Marianne Egri 718-472-8012
VP, Construction Management:
  George Toma 718-472-8359
VP, Architecture & Engineering:
  E Bruce Barrett, RA 718-472-8710
VP, Administration:
  Craig Collins 718-472-8149

New York State Dormitory Authority
515 Broadway
Albany, NY 12207-2964
518-257-3000 Fax: 518-257-3100
e-mail: dabonds@dasny.org
Web site: www.dasny.org

One Penn Plaza
52nd Fl
New York, NY 10119-0098
212-273-5000
Fax: 212-273-5121

539 Franklin St
Buffalo, NY 14202-1109
716-884-9780
Fax: 716-884-9787

Chair:
  Alfonso L Carney Jr 518-257-3000/fax: 518-257-3100
President/CEO:
  Paul T Williams Jr. 518-257-3180/fax: 518-257-3183
Vice President:
  Michael T Corrigan 518-257-3192/fax: 518-257-3183
Acting Chief Financial Officer:
  Linda H Button 518-257-3562/fax: 518-257-3100
General Counsel:
  Michael Cusack 518-257-3120/fax: 518-257-3101

Offices and agencies generally appear in alphabetical order, except when specific order is requested by listee.

Managing Director, Construction:
    Stephen D Curro, PE 518-257-3271/fax: 518-257-3100
    e-mail: scurro@dasny.org
Managing Director, Public Finance & Portfolio Monitoring:
    Portia Lee. 518-257-3362/fax: 518-257-3100
    e-mail: plee@dasny.org
Public Information Officer:
    John Chirlin. 518-257-3380
    e-mail: jchirlin@dasny.org

New York State Higher Education Services Corp (NYSHESC)
99 Washington Ave
Albany, NY 12255
888-697-4372
Web site: www.hesc.ny.gov

Executive Vice President & Acting President:
    Elsa Magee 518-474-5592/fax: 518-474-5593
    e-mail: elsa.magee@hesc.ny.gov
Director, Federal Relations:
    Frank Ballmann. 202-721-1186
    e-mail: frank.ballmann@hesc.ny.gov
Director, Audit:
    Matt Downey. 518-473-2287/fax: 518-486-6515
    e-mail: matt.downey@hesc.ny.gov
General Counsel:
    Thomas Brennan 518-473-1585/fax: 518-486-6515
    e-mail: thomas.brennan@hesc.ny.gov
Senior Vice President, Communications:
    Kathy Crowder 518-402-1448/fax: 518-474-5593
    e-mail: kathy.crowder@hesc.ny.gov
Director, Federal Options:
    Victor Stucchi 518-486-5885/fax: 518-402-3276
    e-mail: victor.stucchi@hesc.ny.gov
Administrative Officer & CFO:
    Warren Wallin 518-474-7505/fax: 518-474-4301
    e-mail: victor.stucchi@hesc.ny.gov
Senior Vice President, Customer Relations:
    John Austin 518-473-0810/fax: 518-474-2839
    e-mail: john.austin@hesc.ny.gov

New York State Teachers' Retirement System
10 Corporate Woods Dr
Albany, NY 12211-2395
518-447-2900 or 800-348-7298 Fax: 518-447-2695
e-mail: media@nystrs.org
Web site: www.nystrs.org

Executive Director:
    Thomas K Lee. 518-447-2726
General Counsel:
    Joseph J. Indelicato, Jr. 518-447-2722
Actuary:
    Richard Young 518-447-2692
Managing Director Operations:
    Kevin Schaefer 518-447-2730
Director, Member Relations:
    Sheila Gardella 518-447-2684
Manager, Public Information:
    John Cardillo 518-447-4743/fax: 518-447-2875
    e-mail: john.caradillo@nystrs.org
Managing Director, Real Estate:
    David C. Gillian 518-447-2751
Managing Director, Private Equity:
    John W. Virtanen 518-447-2751

State University Construction Fund
353 Broadway
Albany, NY 12246
518-320-3200 Fax: 518-443-1008
Web site: www.sucf.suny.edu

General Manager:
    Robert M Haelen. 518-320-1502
General Counsel/Director Legal Svcs:
    William K Barczak 518-320-1746

NEW YORK STATE LEGISLATURE

See Legislative Branch in Section 1 for additional Standing Committee and Subcommittee information.

Assembly Standing Committees

Education
Chair:
    Catherine T Nolan (D) 518-455-4851
Ranking Minority Member:
    Edward Ra (R) 518-455-4627

Higher Education
Chair:
    Deborah J Glick (D) 518-455-4841
Ranking Minority Member:
    Chad Lupinacci (R). 518-455-5732

Libraries & Education Technology
Chair:
    Thomas Abinanti (D) 518-455-5753
Ranking Minority Member:
    Joseph Saladino. 518-455-5305

Assembly Task Forces

Skills Development & Career Education, Legislative Commission on
Assembly Chair:
    Vacant. 518-455-0000
Program Manager:
    Brenda Carter. 518-455-4865/fax: 518-455-4175

University-Industry Cooperation, Legislative Task Force on
Chair:
    Samuel Roberts (D). 518-455-5383
Coordinator:
    Maureen Schoolman 518-455-3632/fax: 518-455-4175

Senate Standing Committees

Education
Chair:
    Carl L Marcellino (R). 518-455-2390
Ranking Minority Member:
    George Latimer (D). 518-455-2031

Higher Education
Chair:
    Kenneth P LaValle (R). 518-455-3121
Ranking Minority Member:
    Toby Ann Stavisky (D). 518-455-3461

Offices and agencies generally appear in alphabetical order, except when specific order is requested by listee.

U.S. GOVERNMENT

EXECUTIVE DEPARTMENTS AND RELATED AGENCIES

National Archives & Records Administration

Franklin D Roosevelt Presidential Library & Museum
4079 Albany Post Rd, Hyde Park, NY 12538
846-486-7770
Web site: www.fdrlibrary.marist.edu
Director:
Lynn Bassanese.....................................845-486-7770
e-mail: roosevelt.library@nara.gov

US Defense Department
e-mail: www.defenselink.mil

US Military Academy
Building 600, West Point, NY 10996
845-938-3507
Web site: www.usma.edu
Superintendent:
David H. Huntoon
Director, Public Affairs:
Sherri Reed

US Education Department
Web site: www.ed.gov

Region 2 - NY, NJ, PR, Vi.....................fax: 646-428-3904
32 Old Slip, 25th Floor, New York, NY 10005
646-428-3906 Fax: 646-428-3904
e-mail: OCR.NewYork@ed.gov
Communications Director:
Jacquelyn Pitta 646-428-3907
Deputy Secretary's Regional Representative:
Orysia Dmytrenko....................................646-428-3906

Civil Rights
Regional Director:
Linda Colon 800-368-1019
e-mail: randolph.wills@ed.gov
Chief Civil Rights Attorney:
Rachel Pomerantz................................646-428-3835

Federal Student Aid
NY Team Area Case Director:
William Swift.....................................646-428-3755
e-mail: william.swift@ed.gov
Director, Loan Client Account Management Group Team Leader:
David A Sola..................617-565-5810/fax: 617-565-8636
e-mail: david.sola@ed.gov

Financial Partner Services
Director, Eastern Regions:
Robin Shinn 646-428-3770

Office of Inspector General
Regional Inspector General, Audit:
Daniel Schultz 646-428-3888
e-mail: daniel.schultz@ed.gov
Special Agent-in-Charge:
Brian Hickey....................................646-428-3874

Regional Grants Representative
Regional Grants Representative:
Earl Williams 646-428-3935
e-mail: earl.williams@ed.gov

US Transportation Department

US Merchant Marine Academy.................fax: 516-773-5774
300 Steamboat Road, Kings Point, NY 11024
516-773-5800 Fax: 516-773-5774
Web site: www.usmma.edu
Superintendent:
Real Admiral James A. Helis

U.S. CONGRESS

See U.S. Congress Chapter for additional Standing Committee and Subcommittee information.

House of Representatives Standing Committees

Education & Labor
Chair:
John Klein (R-MN)................................202-225-2271
Ranking Member:
George Miller (D-CA) 202-225-2095
New York Delegate:
Timothy H Bishop (D) 202-225-3826
New York Delegate:
Carolyn McCarthy (D) 202-225-5516

Senate Standing Committees

Health, Education, Labor & Pensions
Chair:
Tom Harkin (D-IA)...............................202-224-9369
Ranking Member:
Lamar Alexander (R-TN).........................202-224-4944

PRIVATE SECTOR

ASPIRA of New York Inc
520 Eighth Ave, 22nd Fl, New York, NY 10018
212-564-6880 Fax: 212-564-7152
e-mail: hgesualdo@ny.aspira.org
Web site: www.nyaspira.org
Foster the social advancement of the PuertoRican/Latino community by supportig its youth through community & leadership development
Hector Gesualdo, Executive Director

Advocates for Children of New York Inc
151 West 30th St, 5th Fl, New York, NY 10001
212-947-9779 Fax: 212-947-9790
e-mail: info@advocatesforchildren.org
Web site: www.advocatesforchildren.org; www.insideschools.org
Advocacy for public school students
Kim Sweet, Executive Director

Africa-America Institute (The)
420 Lexington Ave, Suite 1706, New York, NY 10170-0002
212-949-5666 Fax: 212-682-6174
e-mail: aainy@aaionline.org
Web site: www.aaionline.org
Promoting enlightened engagement between Africa & America through education, training & dialogue
Mora McLean, President & Chief Executive Officer

After-School Corporation (The)
925 Ninth Ave, New York, NY 10019
212-547-6950 Fax: 212-548-6983
e-mail: info@tascorp.org
Web site: www.tascorp.org
Non-profit organization dedicated to enhancing the quality, availability & sustainability of in-school, after-school programs in NYS

Offices and agencies generally appear in alphabetical order, except when specific order is requested by listee.

John P Albert, Vice President, External Relations

Agudath Israel of America
42 Broadway, 14th Fl, New York, NY 10004
212-797-7385 Fax: 646-254-1650
e-mail: dzwiebel@agudathisrael.org
Religious school education; Orthodox Judaism
David Zwiebel, Executive Vice President, Government & Public Affairs

American Higher Education Development Corporation
Two Penn Plaza, Suite 1500, New York, NY 10121
212-292-5658 Fax: 212-292-4957
e-mail: jdevaney@ahed.com
Web site: www.ahed.com
Acquisition of & investment in post-secondary education institutions
James M Devaney, Chief Executive Officer

New York Community Colleges Association of Presidents
c/o Onondaga Community College, 4585 W Seneca Tpk, Syracuse, NY 13215-4585
315-498-2214 Fax: 315-469-4475
Debbie L Sydow PhD, President

Associated Medical Schools of New York
10 Rockefeller Plaza, Suite 1120, New York, NY 10020
212-218-4610 Fax: 212-218-5644
Web site: www.amsny.org
AMS NY is a consortium of the fifteen public and private medical schools in New York State. Our mission is to support quality health care, education and research in New York State.
Jo Wiederhorn, Executive Director

Association of Proprietary Colleges
121 State Street, Albany, NY 12207
518-437-1867 Fax: 518-436-4751
e-mail: apc@apc-colleges.org
Web site: www.apc-colleges.org
Karen K Dyer, Administrator

Board of Jewish Education of Greater New York
520 - 8th Ave, New York, NY 10018
646-472-5300 Fax: 646-472-5421
e-mail: judyopp@bjeny.org
Web site: www.bjeny.org
Chaim Lauer, Executive Vice President

Campaign for Fiscal Equity, Inc
110 William St, Ste 2602, New York, NY 10038
212-867-8455 Fax: 212-867-8460
e-mail: cfeinfo@cfequity.org
Web site: www.cfequity.org
Geri Palart, Executive Director

Catholic School Administrators Association of NYS
406 Fulton St, Ste 512, Troy, NY 12180
518-273-1205 Fax: 518-273-1206
e-mail: nysadm@csdsl.net
Web site: www.csaanys.org
Carol Geddis, Executive Director

Center for Educational Innovation - Public Education Association
28 W 44th St, Ste 300, New York, NY 10036-6600
212-302-8800 Fax: 212-302-0088
e-mail: info@pea-online.org
Web site: www.cei-pea.org
Advocacy & public information for NYC public education
Judy Roth Berkowitz, Chairman

Cerebral Palsy Associations of New York State
330 W 34th St, New York, NY 10001
212-947-5770 x201 Fax: 212-356-0746
e-mail: sconstantino@cpofnys.org
Web site: www.cpofnys.org
Advocate & provide direct services with & for individuals with cerebral palsy & other significant disabilities, & their families through a Statewide Affiliate network
Susan Constantino, President & CEO

Coalition of New York State Career Schools (The)
437 Old Albany Post Rd, Garrison, NY 10524
845-788-5070 Fax: 845-788-5071
e-mail: tzaleski@sprynet.com
Web site: www.coalitionofnewyorkstatecareerschools.com
Licensed post-secondary career schools
Terence M Zaleski, Special Counsel

Commission on Independent Colleges & Universities
17 Elk St, PO Box 7289, Albany, NY 12224
518-436-4781 Fax: 518-436-0417
e-mail: abe@cicu.org
Web site: www.cicu.org
Represent public policy interests of member colleges & universities
Abraham M Lackman, President

Conference of Big 5 School Districts
74 Chapel Street, Albany, NY 12207
518-465-4274 Fax: 518-465-0638
e-mail: big5@big5schools.org
Georgia Asciutto, Executive Director

Cornell University
314 Day Hall, Ithaca, NY 14853
607-255-9029 Fax: 607-255-5572
e-mail: spj2@cornell.edu
Web site: www.govrelations.cornell.edu
Stephen Philip Johnson, Vice President for Government & Community Relations

Cornell University, Rural Schools Association of NYS
111 Kennedy Hall, Cornell University, Ithaca, NY 14853
607-255-8709 or 607-255-8056 Fax: 607-255-7905
e-mail: lak35@cornell.edu
Web site: rsa.cornell.edu
Advocacy for small & rural schools throughout New York
Lawrence Kiley, Executive Director

Cornell University, School of Industrial & Labor Relations
368 Ives Hall, Ithaca, NY 14853-3901
607-255-2742 or 607-257-1402 Fax: 607-255-1836
e-mail: jhb5@cornell.edu
Web site: www.ilr.cornell.edu
Education, workforce preparedness; student peer culture, employee training, recruitment & selection practices
John Bishop, Professor

Council of School Supervisors & Administrators
16 Court St, 4th Fl, Brooklyn, NY 11241
718-852-3000 Fax: 718-403-0278
e-mail: ernest@csa-nyc.org
Web site: www.csa-nyc.org
Ernest Logan, President

Council on the Environment of NYC, Environmental Education
51 Chambers St, Rm 228, New York, NY 10007
212-788-7900 or 212-788-7932 Fax: 212-788-7913
e-mail: info@grownyc.org
Web site: www.grownyc.org
Environmental education & action training programs for students
Marcel Van Doyen, Executive Director

Policy Areas

Office of Government Relations and Urban Affairs
Fordham University
Admin Bldg, 441 E Fordham Rd, Rm 220, Bronx, NY 10458
718-817-3023 or 718-817-0180 Fax: 718-817-0698
e-mail: massiah@fordham.edu
Web site: www.fordham.edu
Lesley A Massiah-Arthur, Associate Vice President, Government Relations
and Urban Affairs

Learning Leaders
80 Maiden Lane, 11th Fl, New York, NY 10038
212-213-3370 Fax: 212-213-0787
e-mail: mduitz@learningleaders.org
Web site: www.learningleaders.org
*Helps NYC public school students (K-12) succeed in school by training
volunteers who provide tutoring and other school-based support, and by
equipping parents to foster their own children's educational development*
Mindy Duitz, President

MDRC
16 East 34th St, 19th Floor, New York, NY 10016-4326
212-532-3200 Fax: 212-684-0832
e-mail: information@mdrc.org
Web site: www.mdrc.org
*Nonprofit research & field testing of education & employment programs for
disadvantaged adults & youth*
Gordon Berlin, President

Museum Association of New York
265 River St, Troy, NY 12180
518-273-3400 Fax: 518-273-3416
e-mail: info@manyonline.org
Web site: www.manyonline.org
An information and advocacy resource for the state's museum community.
Anne Ackerson, Director

**NYC Board of Education Employees, Local 372/AFSCME,
AFL-CIO**
125 Barclay Street, 6th Fl, New York, NY 10007
212-815-1372 Fax: 212-815-1347
Web site: www.local372.com
Veronica Montgomery-Costa, President, District Council 37/372

NYS Alliance for Arts Education
PO Box 2217, Albany, NY 12220-0217
800-ARTS-N-ED or 518-473-0823 Fax: 518-486-7329
e-mail: info@nysaae.org
Web site: www.nysaae.org
*State & local advocacy, professional development, technical assistance &
information for educators, organizations, artists, parents & policymakers*
Jeremy Johannesen, Executive Director

**NYS Association for Health, Physical Education, Recreation &
Dance**
77 North Ann St, Little Falls, NY 13365
315-823-1015 Fax: 315-823-1012
e-mail: ccorsi@nysahperd.org
Web site: www.nysahperd.org
*Promoting, educating & creating opportunites for physical education, health,
recreation & dance professionals*
Colleen Corsi, Executive Director

NYS Association for the Education of Young Children
230 Washington Ave Ext, Albany, NY 12203-5390
518-867-3517 Fax: 518-867-3520
e-mail: nysaeyc@capital.net
Web site: www.nysaeyc.org
*Supporting the development of professionals to promote quality care &
education for the well-being of all young children & their families*
Patricia A Myers, Executive Director

NYS Association of Library Boards
PO Box 11048, Albany, NY 12211
518-445-9505 Fax: 518-426-8240
Web site: www.nysalb.org
Margaret Malicki, Association Manager

NYS Association of School Business Officials
7 Elk St, #1, Albany, NY 12207-1002
518-434-2281 Fax: 518-434-1303
e-mail: steve@nysasbo.org
Web site: www.nysasbo.org
Leadership in the practice of school business management
Steve Van Hoesen, Director of Governement Relations

NYS Association of Small City School Districts
c/o Biggerstaff Law Firm, Main Sq, 318 Delaware Ave, Delmar, NY 12054
518-475-9500
e-mail: reb@biggerstaff-form.com
Web site: scsd.neric.org
Advocacy for small city school districts
Robert Biggerstaff, Executive Director

NYS Head Start Association
230 Washington Ave Ext, Albany, NY 12203
518-452-0897 Fax: 518-452-0898
e-mail: nyshsa@capital.net
Web site: www.nysheadstart.org
*Educational program designed to meet the needs of low-income children &
their families*
Steven Moskowitz, Executive Director

NYS Public High School Athletic Association
8 Airport Park Blvd, Latham, NY 12110
518-690-0771 Fax: 518-690-0775
e-mail: nvanerk@nysphsaa.org
Web site: www.nysphsaa.org
*Provide equitable & safe competition through interschool athletic activities
at secondary schools*
Nina Van Erk, Executive Director

NYS Reading Association
PO Box 874, Albany, NY 12201-0874
518-434-4748 Fax: 518-434-4748
e-mail: information@capital.net
Web site: www.nysreading.org
*Literacy education advocacy & professional development programs for
educators*
Dolores Watford, President

NYS Theatre Institute
37 First Street, 1218 O, Troy, NY 12180
518-274-3200 Fax: 518-274-3815
e-mail: nysti@capital.net
Web site: www.nysti.org
*Professional theater productions for family and school audiences; training &
education, internships, community/school outreach & cultural exchange
programs*
Patricia Di Benedetto Snyder, Producing Artistic Director

Nelson A Rockefeller Inst of Govt, Higher Education Program
411 State St, Albany, NY 12203
518-443-5835 or 518-443-5843 Fax: 518-443-5788
e-mail: burkejo@rockinst.org
Web site: www.rockinst.org
*Accountability & autonomy in public higher education; system governance;
performance funding, budgeting, reporting & assessment*
Joseph C Burke, Director

Offices and agencies generally appear in alphabetical order, except when specific order is requested by listee.

New York Community College Trustees (NYCCT)
State University Plaza, Room N110, Albany, NY 12246-0001
518-320-1175 or 518-443-5133 Fax: 518-443-5100
e-mail: cynthia.demarest@suny.edu
Web site: www.nycctrustees.org
Trustee education, legislative advocacy & communication
Anton Kasanof, President

New York Library Association (The)
252 Hudson Ave, Albany, NY 12210-1802
518-432-6952 Fax: 518-427-1697
e-mail: director@nyla.org
Web site: www.nyla.org
Advocacy on behalf of public, college and school libraries on funding and legislation.
Michael J Borges, Executive Director

New York State Association of Independent Schools
12 Jay St, Schenectady, NY 12305-1913
518-346-5662 Fax: 518-346-7390
e-mail: annie@nysais.org
Web site: www.nysais.org
Accreditation and professional development.
Elizabeth P Riegelman, Executive Director

New York State Catholic Conference
465 State St, Albany, NY 12203-1004
518-434-6195 Fax: 518-434-9796
e-mail: info@nyscatholic.org
Web site: www.nyscatholic.org
Identify, formulate & implement public policy objectives of the NYS Bishops in health, education, welfare, human & civil rights
Richard E Barnes, Executive Director

New York State Congress of Parents & Teachers Inc
One Wembley Court, Albany, NY 12205-3830
518-452-8808 Fax: 518-452-8105
e-mail: office@nyspta.org
Web site: www.nyspta.org
Advocating education, health, welfare of children & parent involvement
Maria L DeWald, President

New York State Council of School Superintendents
7 Elk St, 3rd Floor, Albany, NY 12207-1002
518-449-1063 Fax: 518-426-2229
Web site: www.nyscoss.org
Thomas L Rogers, Executive Director

New York State School Boards Association
24 Century Hill Drive, Ste 200, Latham, NY 12110-2125
518-783-0200 Fax: 518-783-0211
e-mail: info@nyssba.org
Web site: www.nyssba.org
Public school leadership advocates
Timothy G Kremer, Executive Director

New York State School Music Association (NYSSMA)
718 The Plain Rd, Westbury, NY 11590-5931
516-997-7200 Fax: 516-997-1700
e-mail: executive@nyssma.org
Web site: www.nyssma.org
Advocacy for a quality school music education for every student
Steven Schopp, Executive Director

New York State United Teachers/AFT, NEA, AFL-CIO
800 Troy-Schenectady Road, Latham, NY 12110-2455
518-213-6000 or 800-342-9810 Fax: 518-213-6428
Web site: www.nysut.org
Representing employees & retirees of NY's public schools, colleges & healthcare facilities
Richard Iannuzzi, President

New York University
25 West 4th St, 5th Fl - Rm 503, New York, NY 10012
212-998-6840 Fax: 212-995-4021
e-mail: john.beckman@nyu.edu
Web site: www.nyu.edu
Office of Public Affairs
John Beckman, Vice President

Niagara University
Alumni Hall, Niagara University, NY 14109-2014
716-286-8360 Fax: 716-286-8349
e-mail: mpf@niagara.edu
Web site: www.niagara.edu
Dr Marilynn P Fleckenstein, Associate Vice President for Academic Affairs

ProLiteracy Worldwide
1320 Jamesville Ave, Syracuse, NY 13210-4224
315-422-9121 Fax: 315-422-6369
e-mail: info@proliteracy.org
Web site: www.proliteracy.org
Sponsors educational programs & services to empower adults & families through the acquisition of literacy skills & practices
Rochelle A Cassella, Director, Corporate Communications

Rensselaer Polytechnic Institute
110 8th St, Troy, NY 12180-3590
518-276-2840 Fax: 518-276-6091
e-mail: bourgt@rpi.edu
Web site: www.rpi.edu
Assistant to the President for Media & Public Relations
Theresa Bourgeois, Director, Media Relations

Research Foundation of SUNY
State University Plz, Albany, NY 12246
518-434-7066 Fax: 518-434-9108
e-mail: cathy.kaszluga@rfsuny.org
Web site: www.rfsuny.org
Facilitate research, education & public service at SUNY campuses
Cathy Kaszluga, Vice President, Corporate Communications

Rochester School for the Deaf
1545 St Paul St, Rochester, NY 14621
585-544-1240 Fax: 585-544-0383
e-mail: hmowl@rsdeaf.org
Web site: www.rsdeaf.org
Complete educational program for deaf children to age 21
Dr. Harold Mowl, Jr, Superintendent

Schuyler Center for Analysis & Advocacy (SCAA)
150 State St, 4th Fl, Albany, NY 12207
518-463-1896 x25 Fax: 518-463-3364
e-mail: joconnor@scaany.org
Web site: www.scaany.org
Advocacy, analysis & forums on education, child welfare, health, economic security, mental health, revenue & taxation issues.
Karen Schimke, President/CEO

School Administrators Association of NYS
8 Airport Park Blvd, Latham, NY 12110
518-782-0600 Fax: 518-782-9552
e-mail: kcasey@saanys.org
Web site: www.saanys.org
Kevin S Casey, Executive Director

Sports & Arts in Schools Foundation
58-12 Queens Blvd, Suite 1 - 59th Entrance, Woodside, NY 11377
718-786-7110 Fax: 718-786-7635
e-mail: info@sasfny.org
Web site: www.sasfny.org
After-school, summer camps & clinics, winter-break festival
James R O'Neill, Executive Director

Policy Areas

Offices and agencies generally appear in alphabetical order, except when specific order is requested by listee.

Syracuse University, Maxwell School of Citizenship & Public Affairs
426 Eggers Hall, Syracuse, NY 13244-1020
315-443-3114 Fax: 315-443-1081
e-mail: ctrpol@syr.edu
Web site: www.maxwell.syr.edu/opr.aspx
Education, healthcare, entrepreneurship policies, social welfare, income distribution & comparative social policies
Christine L Himes, Professor/Director

Syracuse University, Office of Government & Community Relations
Room 2-212, Center for Science & Technology, Syracuse, NY 13244-4100
315-443-3919 Fax: 315-443-3676
e-mail: edperson@syr.edu
Web site: gcr.syr.edu
Eric Persons, Associate VP, Government & Community Relations

Teachers College, Columbia University
525 W 120th St, Box 7, New York, NY 10027
212-678-3000 Fax: 212-678-3682
e-mail: ts171@columbia.edu
Web site: www.tc.columbia.edu
Education policy
Thomas Sobol, Professor

Teaching Matters Inc
475 Riverside Dr, Ste 1270, New York, NY 10115-0122
212-870-3505 Fax: 212-870-3516
e-mail: lguastaferro@teachingmaters.org
Web site: www.teachingmatters.org
Technology planning & professional development for NYC public schools
Lynette Guastaferro, Executive Director

United Federation of Teachers
52 Broadway, New York, NY 10004
212-777-7500 Fax: 212-260-6393
e-mail: rweigarte@aol.com
Web site: www.uft.org
Randi Weingarten, President

United University Professions
PO Box 15143, Albany, NY 12212-5143
518-640-6600 or 800-342-4206 Fax: 518-640-6698
e-mail: contact@uupmail.org
Web site: www.uupinfo.org
SUNY labor union of academic & other professional faculty
William E Scheuerman, President

Western New York Library Resources Council
4455 Genesee St, PO Box 400, Buffalo, NY 14225-0400
716-633-0705 Fax: 716-633-1736
e-mail: sknab@wnylrc.org; www.wnyinfo.org
Web site: www.wnylrc.org; www.wnylibraries.org;www.askus247.org
Dedicated to enhancing access to information, encouraging resource sharing & promoting library interests
Sheryl Knab, Executive Director

Offices and agencies generally appear in alphabetical order, except when specific order is requested by listee.

ELECTIONS

NEW YORK STATE

GOVERNOR'S OFFICE

Governor's Office
Executive Chamber
State Capitol
Albany, NY 12224
518-474-8390 Fax: 518-474-1513
Web site: www.ny.gov

Governor:
Andrew M Cuomo 518-474-8390
Secretary to the Governor:
William Mulrow 518-474-4246
Counsel to the Governor:
Alphonso David 518-474-8343
Director, Communications:
Melissa DeRosa . . . . .518-474-8418 or 212-681-4640
Deputy Secretary for Civil Rights:
Patricia Gatling 212-681-4584
First Assistant Counsel:
Sandi Toll 518-474-8434

EXECUTIVE DEPARTMENTS AND RELATED AGENCIES

Elections, State Board of
40 N Pearl Street
Suite 5
Albany, NY 12207-2729
518-474-6220 Fax: 518-486-4068
e-mail: info@elections.ny.gov
Web site: www.elections.ny.gov

Co-Chair:
Peter S Kosinski 518-474-8100
Co-Chair:
Douglas A Kellner 518-474-8100
Commissioner:
Andrew J Spano 518-474-8100
Commissioner:
Gregory P Peterson 518-474-8100
Co-Executive Director:
Todd Valentine 518-474-6336/fax: 518-474-1008
Co-Executive Director:
Robert A Brehm 518-474-6336/fax: 518-474-1008
Director, Public Information:
John W Conklin 518-474-1953/fax: 518-473-8315

Administrative Services
Administrative Officer:
Thomas A Jarose 518-474-6336/fax: 518-474-1008
Special Counsel:
Kimberly Galvin 518-474-6367/fax: 518-486-4068
Deputy Counsel:
Brian M Quail 518-474-6367

Campaign Finance
Campaign Finance:
Vacant 518-474-8200/fax: 518-486-6627
e-mail: cfinfo@elections.ny.gov

Counsel/Enforcement
Counsel:
Risa Sugarman 518-486-7858
e-mail: enforcement@elections.ny.gov

Deputy Enforcement Counsel:
William McCann 518-474-2063

County Boards of Elections

Albany . . . . .fax: 518-487-5077
32 N Russell Rd, Albany, NY 12206
Fax: 518-487-5077
e-mail: boardofelections@albanycounty.com
Web site: www.albanycounty.com
Commissioner:
Matthew Clyne (D) 518-487-5060
Commissioner:
Rachel L Bledi (R) 518-487-5060
Deputy Commissioner:
Kathleen A Donovan (D) 518-487-5060
Deputy Commissioner:
Ellen Graziano (R) 518-487-5060

Allegany . . . . .fax: 585-268-9406
6 Schuyler Street, Belmont, NY 14813
Fax: 585-268-9406
e-mail: acboe@alleganyco.com
Web site: www.alleganyco.com
Commissioner:
Michael J McCormick (D) 585-268-9295
e-mail: mccormm@alleganyco.com
Commissioner:
Richard Hollis (R) 585-268-9294
e-mail: hollisrg@alleganyco.com
Deputy Commissioner:
Barbara Broughton (D) 585-268-9295
e-mail: broughB@alleganyco.com
Deputy Commissioner:
Marcy Crawford (R) 585-268-9294
e-mail: crawfoMJ@alleganyco.com

Broome . . . . .fax: 607-778-2174
Gov't Plaza, 60 Hawley St, PO Box 1766, Binghamton, NY 13902
Fax: 607-778-2174
e-mail: bcboe@co.broome.ny.us
Commissioner:
John Perticone (D) 607-778-2172
Commissioner:
Robert N Nielsen, Jr (R) 607-778-2172
Deputy Commissioner:
Mary E Pines (D) 607-778-2172
Deputy Commissioner:
Karen A Davis (R) 607-778-2172

Cattaraugus . . . . .fax: 716-938-2775
207 Rock City St, Ste 100, Little Valley, NY 14755
Fax: 716-938-2775
e-mail: boe-support@cattco.org
Web site: www.cattco.org
Commissioner:
Kevin Burleson (D) 716-938-2404
e-mail: KCBurleson@cattco.org
Commissioner:
Sue A Fries (R) 716-938-2405
e-mail: SAFries@cattco.org
Deputy Commissioner:
Karen L Byrne (D) 716-938-2403
e-mail: klbyrne@cattco.org
Deputy Commissioner:
Gina L Shields (R) 716-938-2401
e-mail: glshields@cattco.org

Cayuga . . . . .fax: 315-253-1289
157 Genesee Street (Basement), Auburn, NY 13021
Fax: 315-253-1289
e-mail: election@cayugacounty.us
Web site: www.co.cayuga.ny.us/election

Offices and agencies generally appear in alphabetical order, except when specific order is requested by listee.

Commissioner:
  Katie Lacey (D) 315-253-1285
  e-mail: klacey@cayugacounty.us
Commissioner:
  Cherl Heary (R) 315-253-1285
  e-mail: cheary@cayugacounty.us
Deputy Commissioner:
  Deborah Calarco (D) 315-253-1285
  e-mail: dcalarco@cayugacounty.us
Deputy Commissioner:
  Roberta Massarini (R) 315-253-1285

Chautauqua ....fax: 716-753-4111
7 North Erie St, Mayville, NY 14757
716-753-4580 Fax: 716-753-4111
e-mail: vote@co.chautauqua.ny.us
Web site: www.co.chautauqua.ny.us
Commissioner:
  Norman P Green (D).........................716-753-4580
  e-mail: GreenN@co.chautauqua.ny.us
Commissioner:
  Brian C Abram (R)..........................716-753-4580
  e-mail: AbramB@co.chautauqua.ny.us
Commissioner:
  Doris Parment (D) 716-753-4580
Commissioner:
  Nacole Ellis (R) 716-753-4580

Chemung................................fax: 607-737-5499
378 S Main Street, PO Box 588, Elmira, NY 14902-0588
607-737-5475 Fax: 607-737-5499
e-mail: votechemung@co.chemung.ny.us
Web site: www.chemungcounty.com
Commissioner:
  Cindy Emmer (D)............................607-737-5475
Commissioner:
  Robert D Siglin (R) 607-737-5475
  e-mail: rsiglin@co.chemung.ny.us
Deputy Commissioner:
  Mary Collins (D) 607-737-5475
  e-mail: marycollins@co.chemung.ny.us
Deputy Commissioner:
  Linda A Forrest (R) 607-737-5475
  e-mail: lforrest@co.chemung.ny.us

Chenango ....fax: 607-337-1766
5 Court Street, Norwich, NY 13815
607-337-1760 Fax: 607-337-1766
Web site: www.co.chenango.ny.us
Commissioner:
  Carol A Franklin (D) 607-337-1765
  e-mail: carolf@co.chenango.ny.us
Commissioner:
  Mary Lou A Monahan (R) 607-337-1764
Deputy Commissioner:
  Carly J Hendricks (D).......................607-337-1764
Deputy Commissioner:
  Laura C Chapin (R) 607-337-1764

Clinton ....fax: 518-565-4508
County Gov't Center, 137 Margaret St, Ste 104, Plattsburgh, NY 12901
Fax: 518-565-4508
e-mail: boe@co.clinton.ny.us
Web site: www.clintoncountygov.com
Commissioner:
  Susan R Castine (D)........................518-565-4740
Commissioner:
  Gregory Campbell (R) 518-565-4740
Deputy Commissioner:
  Mary R. Dyer (D) 518-565-4740
Deputy Commissioner:
  Kara McBrayer (R)..........................518-565-4740

Columbia ....fax: 518-828-2624
401 State St, Hudson, NY 12534
Fax: 518-828-2624
e-mail: elections@columbiacountyny.com
Web site: www.columbiacountyny.com
Commissioner:
  Virginia Martin (D) 518-828-3115
Commissioner:
  Jason Nastke (R)...........................518-828-3115
Deputy Commissioner:
  Hilary Hillman (D).........................518-828-3115
  e-mail: hilary.hillman@columbiacountyny.com
Deputy Commissioner:
  Kathy L Harter (R).........................518-828-3115
  e-mail: kathy.harter@columbiacountyny.com

Cortland ....fax: 607-758-5513
112 River Street, Ste 1, Cortland, NY 13045
607-758-5032 Fax: 607-758-5513
e-mail: elections@cortland-co.org
Web site: www.cortland-co.org
Commissioner:
  Thomas Henry Brown (D) 607-753-5033
  e-mail: tbrown@cortland-co.org
Commissioner:
  Robert C Howe (R)..........................607-753-5031
  e-mail: rhowe@cortland-co.org

Delaware...............................fax: 607-746-6516
3 Gallant Ave, Delhi, NY 13753
Fax: 607-746-6516
e-mail: boe.move@co.delaware.ny.us
Web site: www.co.delaware.ny.us
Commissioner:
  Judith Garrison (D)........................607-746-2315
Commissioner:
  William J Campbell (R) 607-746-2315
Deputy Commissioner:
  Paula Schermerhorn (D).....................607-746-2315
Deputy Commissioner:
  Robin L Alger (R) 607-746-2315

Dutchess ....fax: 845-486-2483
47 Cannon St, Poughkeepsie, NY 12601
Fax: 845-486-2483
e-mail: dutchesselections@dutchessny.gov
Web site: www.dutchesselections.com
Commissioner:
  Marco Caviglia (D).........................845-486-2473
Commissioner:
  Erik Haight (R)............................845-486-2473
  e-mail: ehaight@dutchessny.gov
Deputy Commissioner:
  Daniel Miller (D) 845-486-2389
Deputy Commissioner:
  Christopher Baiano (R) 845-486-2471
  e-mail: cbaiano@dutchessny.gov

Erie ....fax: 716-858-8282
134 West Eagle St, Buffalo, NY 14202
Fax: 716-858-8282
Web site: elections.erie.gov
Commissioner:
  Leonard Lenihan (D) 716-858-7787
Commissioner:
  Ralph M Mohr (R) 716-858-7786
Deputy Commissioner:
  Arthur O Eve Jr (D) 716-858-8891
Deputy Commissioner:
  Robin Sion (R) 716-858-8891

Offices and agencies generally appear in alphabetical order, except when specific order is requested by listee.

Essex . . . . .fax: 518-873-3479
7551 Court Street, PO Box 217, Elizabethtown, NY 12932
518-873-3474 Fax: 518-873-3479
e-mail: essexelections@co.essex.ny.us
Web site: www.co.essex.ny.us/elect.asp
Commissioner:
    Mark C. Whitney (D) 518-873-3475
    e-mail: mwhitney@co.essex.ny.us
Commissioner:
    Allison McGahay (R) 518-873-3478
    e-mail: amcgahay@co.essex.ny.us
Deputy Commissioner:
    Holly Rollins (D) 518-873-3477
    e-mail: hrollins@co.essex.ny.us
Deputy Commissioner:
    Shona Doyle (R) 518-873-3476
    e-mail: sdoyle@co.essex.ny.us

Franklin . . . . .fax: 518-481-6018
335 West Main St, Ste 161, Malone, NY 12953-1823
518-481-1663 Fax: 518-481-6018
e-mail: boe@co.franklin.ny.us
Web site: franklincony.org
Commissioner:
    Kelly Cox (D) 518-481-1662
    e-mail: kcox@co.franklin.ny.us
Commissioner:
    Veronica King (R) 518-481-1661
    e-mail: vking@co.franklin.ny.us
Deputy Commissioner:
    Linda S. Maneely (D) 518-481-1663
Deputy Commissioner:
    Ruth Besio (R) 518-481-1663

Fulton . . . . .fax: 518-736-1612
2714 State Highway 29, Ste 1, Johnstown, NY 12095-9946
Fax: 518-736-1612
e-mail: boe@co.fulton.ny.us
Web site: www.fultoncountyny.org
Commissioner:
    Lynne Rubscha (D) 518-736-5526
Commissioner:
    Lee A Hollenbeck (R) .518-736-5526
Deputy Commissioner:
    Michele Miller (D) 518-736-5526
Deputy Commissioner:
    Linda M Madison (R) .518-736-5526

Genesee . . . . .fax: 585-344-8562
County Bldg One, 15 Main St, PO Box 284, Batavia, NY 14021
Fax: 585-344-8562
e-mail: election@co.genesee.ny.us
Web site: www.co.genesee.ny.us
Commissioner:
    Lorie J Longhany (D) 585-344-2550
Commissioner:
    Richard Siebert (R) 585-344-2550
Deputy Commissioner:
    Karen S Gannon (D) 585-344-2250
Deputy Commissioner:
    Melissa L Gaebler (R) .585-344-2250

Greene . . . . .fax: 518-719-3784
411 Main Street, Ste 437, Catskill, NY 12414
Fax: 518-719-3784
e-mail: elections@discovergreene.com
Web site: greenegovernment.com
Commissioner:
    Thomas J Burke (D) 518-719-3550
    e-mail: tburke@discovergreene.com

Commissioner:
    Brent Bogardus (R) 518-719-3550
    e-mail: bbogardus@discovergreene.com
Deputy Commissioner:
    Marie Metzler (D) 518-719-3550
Deputy Commissioner (Acting):
    Carol Engelmann (R) 518-719-3550

Hamilton . . . . .fax: 518-548-6345
Route 8, PO Box 175, Lake Pleasant, NY 12108
Fax: 518-548-6345
e-mail: elections@hamiltoncountyny.gov
Web site: www.hamiltoncounty.com
Commissioner:
    Cathleen E Rogers (D) .518-548-4684
Commissioner:
    Marie Buanno (R) 518-548-4684
Deputy Commissioner:
    William Parslow (D) 518-548-4684
Deputy Commissioner:
    Virginia E Morris (R) .518-548-4684

Herkimer . . . . .fax: 315-867-1106
109 Mary Street, Suite 1306, Herkimer, NY 13350
315-867-1102 Fax: 315-867-1106
e-mail: boeinfo@herkimercounty.org
Web site: herkimercounty.org
Commissioner:
    Connie L Shepherd (D) 315-867-1103
Commissioner:
    Louis Patrick Christie (R) 315-867-1104
Deputy Commissioner:
    Robert Drumm (D) 315-867-1102
Deputy Commissioner:
    Jennifer Williams (R) .315-867-1102

Jefferson . . . . .fax: 315-785-5197
175 Arsenal St, 4th Floor, Watertown, NY 13601
Fax: 315-785-5197
Web site: www.co.jefferson.ny.us
Commissioner:
    Babette M. Hall (D) 315-785-3027
    e-mail: babetteh@co.jefferson.ny.us
Commissioner:
    Jude Seymour (R) 315-785-3027
Deputy Commissioner:
    Michelle LaFave (D) 315-785-3027
Deputy Commissioner:
    Trina L Kampnich (R) .315-785-3027

Lewis . . . . .fax: 315-376-2860
7660 N. State St, Lowville, NY 13367
Fax: 315-376-2860
e-mail: elections@lewiscountyny.org
Web site: www.lewiscountyny.org
Commissioner:
    Lindsay Burris (D) 315-376-5329
    e-mail: lburris@lewsicountyny.org
Commissioner:
    Ann M Nortz (R) 315-376-5329
    e-mail: anortz@lewiscountyny.org

Livingston . . . . .fax: 585-243-7015
County Government Ctr, 6 Court St, Rm 104, Geneseo, NY 14454-1043
Fax: 585-243-7015
e-mail: elections@co.livingston.ny.us
Commissioner:
    David DiPasquale (D) .585-243-7090
Commissioner:
    Nancy L Leven (R) 585-243-7090
    e-mail: nleven@co.livingston.ny.us

Policy Areas

Offices and agencies generally appear in alphabetical order, except when specific order is requested by listee.

Deputy Commissioner:
Laura Schoonover (D) 585-243-7090
e-mail: lschoonover@co.livingston.ny.us
Deputy Commissioner:
Diana Farrell (R)..............................585-243-7090

Madison ....fax: 315-366-2532
North Court St, County Office Bldg, PO Box 666, Wampsville, NY 13163
Fax: 315-366-2532
e-mail: boecommissioner@madisoncounty.ny.gov
Web site: www.madisoncounty.org
Commissioner:
Laura P Costello (D)............................315-366-2231
Commissioner:
Kelley S Hood (R) 315-366-2231
Deputy Commissioner:
Ann L Jones (D) 315-366-2231
Deputy Commissioner:
Mary Egger (R).................................315-366-2231

Monroe ....fax: 585-324-1612
39 Main St West, Rochester, NY 14614
585-753-1550 Fax: 585-324-1612
Web site: www.monroecounty.gov
Commissioner:
Thomas F Ferrarese (D) 585-753-1550/fax: 585-753-1531
e-mail: tFerrarese@monroecounty.gov
Commissioner:
David Van Varick (R)............585-753-1550/fax: 585-753-1521
Deputy Commissioner:
Colleen Anderson (D)............585-753-1550/fax: 585-753-1531
Deputy Commissioner:
Douglas E French (R) 585-753-1550/fax: 585-753-1521

Montgomery.....................................fax: 518-853-8392
Old Court House, 9 Park St, PO Box 1500, Fonda, NY 12068-1500
518-853-8180 Fax: 518-853-8392
e-mail: boe@co.montgomery.ny.us
Commissioner:
Jamie M Duchessi (D) 518-853-8181
Commissioner:
Terrance J Smith (R)............................518-853-8182
Deputy Commissioner:
Caroline Swartz (D) 518-853-8183
Deputy Commissioner:
Wendy D. Shaver (R).............................518-853-8183

Nassau ....fax: 516-571-2058
240 Old Country Rd, 5th Fl, Mineola, NY 11501
Fax: 516-571-2058
e-mail: fedmil@nassaucountyny.gov
Web site: www.nassaucountyny.gov
Commissioner:
David J Gugerty (D)............................516-571-2411
Commissioner:
Louis G Savinetti (R)...........................516-571-2411
Deputy Commissioner:
Michael Santeramo (D) 516-571-2411
Deputy Commissioner:
Carol Demauro Busketta (R) 516-571-2411

New York City ....fax: 212-487-5349
32 Broadway, 7th Fl, New York, NY 10004
Fax: 212-487-5349
Web site: www.vote.nyc.ny.us
Executive Director:
Michael J Ryan (D) 212-487-5300
Deputy Executive Director:
Dawn Sandow (R) 212-487-5300
Administrative Manager:
Pamela Green Perkins (D) 212-487-5300

Bronx ....fax: 718-299-2140
1780 Grand Concourse, 5th Fl, Bronx, NY 10457
Commissioner:
Bianca Perez (D) 718-299-9017
Commissioner:
Michael A Rendino (R) 718-299-9017
Deputy Chief Clerk:
Marricka Scott-McFadden (D) 718-299-9017
Deputy Chief Clerk:
Anthony J Ribustello (R).......................718-299-9017

Kings ....fax: 718-246-5958
345 Adams St, 4th Fl, Brooklyn, NY 11201
Commissioner:
John Flateau (D)..............................718-797-8800
Commissioner:
Simon Shamoun (R).............................718-797-8800
Deputy Chief Clerk:
BettyAnn Canizio (D) 718-797-8800
Chief Clerk:
Diane Haslett Rudiano (R) 718-797-8800

New York
200 Varick St, 10th Fl, New York, NY 10014
Commissioner:
Alan Schulkin (D) 212-886-2100
Commissioner:
Frederic M Umane (R).........................212-886-2100
e-mail: fumane@boe.nyc.ny.us
Chief Clerk:
Greg Lehman (R) 212-886-2100
Deputy Chief Clerk (Acting):
Alvin Samuels (D)............................212-886-2100

Queens ....fax: 718-459-3384
126-06 Queens Blvd, Kew Gardens, NY 11415
Commissioner:
Jose M Araujo (D) 718-730-6730
Commissioner:
Michael Michel (R)...........................718-730-6730
Chief Clerk:
Barbara Conacchio (D) 718-730-6730
Deputy Chief Clerk:
Bart Haggerty (R) 718-730-6730

Richmond ....fax: 718-876-0912
1 Edgewater Plaza, Staten Island, NY 10305
Commissioner:
Maria R Guastella (D) 718-876-0079
Commissioner:
Ronald Castorina, Jr (R) 718-876-0079
Chief Clerk:
Sheila Del Giorno (D) 718-876-0079
Deputy Chief Clerk:
Anthony Andruili (R) 718-876-0079

Niagara ....fax: 716-438-4054
111 Main Street, Ste 100, Lockport, NY 14094
716-438-4040 Fax: 716-438-4054
e-mail: ncboe@niagaracounty.com
Web site: www.elections.niagara.ny.us
Commissioner:
Lora A. Allen (D)............................716-438-4041
e-mail: lora.allen@niagaracounty.com
Commissioner:
Jennifer Fronczak (R).........................716-438-4040
e-mail: jennifer.fronczak@niagaracounty.org
Deputy Commissioner:
Darryl DiNoto (D) 716-438-4041
Deputy Commissioner:
Michael Carney (R) 716-438-4040

Oneida ....fax: 315-798-6412
Union Station, 321 Main St, 3rd Fl, Utica, NY 13501

Offices and agencies generally appear in alphabetical order, except when specific order is requested by listee.

Fax: 315-798-6412
e-mail: boardofelections@ocgov.net
Web site: www.ocgov.net
Commissioner:
  Jordan S Karp (D).................................315-798-5761
Commissioner:
  Rose Grimaldi (R) 315-798-5763
    e-mail: rgrimaldi@ocgov.net
Deputy Commissioner:
  Carolann N. Cardone (D)..........................315-798-5765
Deputy Commissioner:
  Catherine A Dumka (R)...........................315-798-5765

Onondaga...fax: 315-435-8451
1000 Erie Boulevard West, Syracuse, NY 13204
Fax: 315-435-8451
e-mail: elections@ongov.net
Web site: www.ongov.net
Commissioner:
  Dustin M. Czarny (D).............................315-435-3312
Commissioner:
  Helen M Kiggins-Walsh (R) 315-435-3312

Ontario...fax: 585-393-2941
74 Ontario St, Canandaigua, NY 14424
Fax: 585-393-2941
e-mail: boe@co.ontario.ny.us
Web site: www.co.ontario.ny.us/elections
Commissioner:
  Mary Q Salotti (D)...............................585-396-4005
    e-mail: mary.salotti@co.ontario.ny.us
Commissioner:
  Michael J Northrup (R) 585-396-4005
    e-mail: michael.northrup@co.ontario.ny.us
Clerk to Commissioner:
  Karen Reed (D)...................................585-396-4005
Clerk to Commissioner:
  Karen Bodine (R).................................585-396-4005

Orange ....fax: 845-291-2437
25 Court Lane, PO Box 30, Goshen, NY 10924
Fax: 845-291-2437
e-mail: elections@orangecountygov.com
Web site: www.orangecountygov.com
Commissioner:
  Susan Bahren (D)................................845-291-2444
Commissioner:
  David C Green (R) 845-291-2444
Deputy Commissioner:
  Louise Vandemark (D)............................845-291-2444
Deputy Commissioner:
  Courtney Canfield Greene (R) 845-291-2444

Orleans ....fax: 585-589-2771
14012 State Rte 31, Albion, NY 14411
Fax: 585-589-2771
Web site: www.orleansny.com
Commissioner:
  Janice E Grabowski (D)...........................585-589-3274
    e-mail: janice.grabowski@orleansny.com
Commissioner:
  Dennis J Piedimonte (R)..........................585-589-3274
    e-mail: dennis.piedimonte@orleansny.com
Deputy Commissioner:
  Eileen Aina (D).................................585-589-3274
Deputy Commissioner:
  Clara L Martin (R)..............................585-589-3274

Oswego ....fax: 315-349-8357
185 E Seneca St, Box 9, Oswego, NY 13126
Fax: 315-349-8357
Web site: www.co.oswego.ny.us/boe/index.html

Commissioner:
  Richard Atkins (D)...............................315-349-8350
Commissioner:
  Peggy Bickford (R) 315-349-8350
Deputy Commissioner:
  Teresa Munger (D)...............................315-349-8350
Deputy Commissioner:
  Marianne B. Ingerson (R).........................315-349-8350

Otsego ....fax: 607-547-4248
140 County Hwy 33W, Ste 2, Cooperstown, NY 13326
Fax: 607-547-4248
e-mail: boe_move@otsegocounty.com
Web site: www.otsegocounty.com/depts/boe
Commissioner:
  Richard D Abbate (D) 607-547-4247
Commissioner:
  Sheila M Ross (R) 607-547-4247
Deputy Commissioner:
  Michael Henrici (D).............................607-547-4247
    e-mail: henricim@otsegocounty.com
Deputy Commissioner:
  Lori L Lehenbauer (R) 607-547-4247
    e-mail: lehenbauerl@otsegocounty.com

Putnam ....fax: 845-808-1920
25 Old Rte 6, Carmel, NY 10512
Fax: 845-808-1920
e-mail: putnamcountyelections@putnamcountyny.gov
Web site: www.putnamcountyny.com/boe/index.htm
Commissioner:
  Catherine Croft (D).............................845-808-1300
Commissioner:
  Anthony G Scannapieco, Jr (R) 845-808-1300
Deputy Commissioner:
  Andrea Basli (D)................................845-808-1300
Deputy Commissioner:
  Nancy M Quis (R) 845-808-1300

Rensselaer..fax: 518-270-2909
Ned Pattison Govt Ctr, 1600 Seventh Ave, Troy, NY 12180
Fax: 518-270-2909
e-mail: renscoboe@rensco.com
Commissioner:
  Edward G McDonough (D) 518-270-2990
Commissioner:
  Larry A Bugbee (R) 518-270-2990

Rockland..fax: 845-638-5196
11 New Hempstead Rd, New City, NY 10956
Commissioner:
  Kristen Zebrowski (D) 845-638-5172
Commissioner:
  Louis C Babcock (R) 845-638-5172
Deputy Commissioner:
  Kathleen Pietanza (D)...........................845-638-5172
Deputy Commissioner:
  Gerard Rogers (R) 845-638-5172

Saint Lawrence ....fax: 315-386-2737
48 Court St, Canton, NY 13617
Fax: 315-386-2737
Web site: www.co.st-lawrence.ny.us
Commissioner:
  Jennie H Bacon (D).............................315-379-2202
    e-mail: jbacon@stlawco.org
Commissioner:
  Thomas A Nichols (R) 315-379-2202
    e-mail: tnichols@stlawco.org
Deputy Commissioner:
  Seth Belt (D)..................................315-379-2202
    e-mail: sbelt@stlawco.org

Policy Areas

Offices and agencies generally appear in alphabetical order, except when specific order is requested by listee.

Deputy Commissioner:
    Nicole R Maxner (R) 315-379-2202
    e-mail: nmaxner@stlawco.org

Saratoga . . . . .fax: 518-884-4751
50 W High St, Ballston Spa, NY 12020
Fax: 518-884-4751
e-mail: saratogacounty.ny.gov/departments
Web site: www.co.saratoga.ny.us
Commissioner:
    William Fruci (D) 518-885-2249
Commissioner:
    Roger J Schiera (R) 518-885-2249
Deputy Commissioner:
    Carol Turney (D) 518-885-2249
Deputy Commissioner:
    John Marcellus (R) 518-885-2249

Schenectady . . . . .fax: 518-377-2716
388 Broadway, Ste E, Schenectady, NY 12305-2520
Fax: 518-377-2716
e-mail: boe@schenectadycounty.com
Web site: www.schenectadycounty.com
Commissioner:
    Amy M Hild (D) 518-377-2469
Commissioner:
    Art Brassard (R) 518-377-2469
Deputy Commissioner:
    Laura Fronk (D) 518-377-2469
Deputy Commissioner:
    Darlene D Harris (R) 518-377-2469

Schoharie . . . . .fax: 518-295-8419
County Office Bldg, 284 Main St, PO Box 99, Schoharie, NY 12157
Fax: 518-295-8419
e-mail: boe@co.schoharie.ny.us
Commissioner:
    Clifford C Hay (D) 518-295-8388
Commissioner:
    Lewis L Wilson (R) 518-295-8388
Deputy Commissioner:
    Richard Shultes (D) 518-295-8388
    e-mail: rich.shultes@co.schoharie.ny.us
Deputy Commissioner:
    Sara Davies-Griffin (R) 518-295-8388
    e-mail: griffins@co.schoharie.ny.us

Schuyler . . . . .fax: 607-535-8364
County Ofc Bldg, 105 Ninth St, Unit 13, Watkins Glen, NY 14891-9972
Fax: 607-535-8364
e-mail: elections@co.schuyler.ny.us
Commissioner:
    John L Vona (D) 607-535-8195
Commissioner:
    Joseph Fazzary (R) 607-535-8195
Deputy Commissioner:
    Carolyn Elkins (D) 607-535-8195
Deputy Commissioner:
    Cindy L Cady (R) 607-535-8195

Seneca . . . . .fax: 315-539-3710
1 DiPronio Dr, Waterloo, NY 13165
Fax: 315-539-3710
e-mail: boe@co.seneca.ny.us
Web site: www.co.seneca.ny.us/boe
Commissioner:
    Ruth V Same (D) 315-539-1760
    e-mail: rsame@co.seneca.ny.us
Commissioner:
    Tiffany Folk (R) 315-539-1760

Deputy Commissioner:
    Carl J Same (D) 315-539-1760
    e-mail: csame@co.seneca.ny.us
Deputy Commissioner:
    Sherrill A O'Brien (R) 315-539-1760

Steuben . . . . .fax: 607-664-2376
3 E Pulteney Square, Bath, NY 14810
607-664-2260 Fax: 607-664-2376
e-mail: elections@co.steuben.ny.us
Web site: www.steubencony.org
Commissioner:
    Kelly J Penziul (D) 607-664-2260
Commissioner:
    Veronica Olin (R) 607-664-2260
    e-mail: veronica@co.steuben.ny.us
Deputy Commissioner:
    Colleen A Hauryski (D) 607-664-2260
Deputy Commissioner:
    Angelia M Cornish (R) 607-664-2260

Suffolk . . . . .fax: 631-852-4590
Yaphank Ave, PO Box 700, Yaphank, NY 11980
Commissioner:
    Anita S Katz (D) 631-852-4500
Commissioner:
    Nick LaLota (R) 631-852-4500
Deputy Commissioner:
    Jeanne O'Rourke (D) 631-852-4500
Deputy Commissioner:
    William J Ellis (R) 631-852-4500

Sullivan . . . . .fax: 845-807-0410
Government Ctr, 100 North St, PO Box 5012, Monticello, NY 12701-5192
Commissioner:
    Ann Prusinski (D) 845-807-0400
Commissioner:
    Rodney Gaebel (R) 845-807-0400
Deputy Commissioner:
    Honora Wohl (D) 845-807-0400
Deputy Commissioner:
    Pam Murran (R) 845-807-0400

Tioga . . . . .fax: 607-687-6348
1062 State Rte 38, PO Box 306, Owego, NY 13827
607-687-8261 Fax: 607-687-6348
e-mail: votetioga@co.tioga.ny.us
Web site: www.tiogacountyny.com
Commissioner:
    John J Langan (D) 607-687-8261
    e-mail: langanj@co.tioga.ny.us
Commissioner:
    Bernadette M Toombs (R) 607-687-8261
    e-mail: toombsb@co.tioga.ny.us
Deputy Commissioner:
    Sandra Saddlemire (D) 607-687-8261
    e-mail: saddlemires@co.tioga.ny.us
Deputy Commissioner:
    Lin Layman (R) 607-687-8261
    e-mail: laymanl@co.tioga.ny.us

Tompkins . . . . .fax: 607-274-5533
Court House Annex, 128 E Buffalo St, Ithaca, NY 14850
Fax: 607-274-5533
e-mail: movehelp@tompskins-co.org
Web site: www.tompkins-co.org/boe
Commissioner:
    Stephen M DeWitt (D) 607-274-5522
    e-mail: sdewitt@tompkins-co.org
Commissioner:
    Elizabeth W Cree (R) 607-274-5522
    e-mail: ecree@tompkins-co.org

Offices and agencies generally appear in alphabetical order, except when specific order is requested by listee.

Deputy Commissioner:
  Laura Norman (D) 607-274-5522
Deputy Commissioner:
  Kari L Stamm (R)..............................607-274-5522

Ulster.................................fax: 845-334-5434
284 Wall Street, Kingston, NY 12401
Fax: 845-334-5434
e-mail: elections@co.ulster.ny.us
Web site: www.co.ulster.ny.us/elections/
Commissioner:
  C Victor Work (D) 845-334-5470
Commissioner:
  Thomas F Turco (R)............................845-334-5470
Deputy Commissioner:
  Timothy Gay (D) 845-334-5470
Deputy Commissioner:
  Patty Jacobsen (R) 845-334-5470

Warren ....fax: 518-761-6480
County Municipal Center, 1340 State Rte 9, 3rd Fl, Lake George, NY
  12845
518-761-6456 Fax: 518-761-6480
e-mail: boe@warrencountyny.gov
Web site: www.warrencountyny.gov/boe
Commissioner:
  Elizabeth J McLaughlin (D)....................518-761-6459
Commissioner:
  Mary Beth Casey (R) 518-761-6458
Deputy Commissioner:
  Kimberly Ross (D) 518-761-6456
Deputy Commissioner:
  Emily Kladis (R)..............................518-761-6457

Washington............................fax: 518-746-2179
383 Broadway, Fort Edward, NY 12828
518-746-2180 Fax: 518-746-2179
e-mail: boardofelections@co.washington.ny.us
Commissioner:
  Jeffrey J Curtis (D)..........................518-746-2180
Commissioner:
  Leslie Allen (R) 518-746-2180
Deputy Commissioner:
  Melinda Suprenant (D).........................518-746-2180
Deputy Commissioner:
  Thomas Rogers (R).............................518-746-2180

Wayne.................................fax: 315-946-7409
7376 State Route 31, PO Box 636, Lyons, NY 14489
Fax: 315-946-7409
e-mail: elections@co.wayne.ny.us
Web site: www.co.wayne.ny.us
Commissioner:
  Mark H Alquist (D) 315-946-7400
Commissioner:
  Marjorie M Bridson (R) 315-946-7400
Deputy Commissioner:
  Joyce A Krebbeks (D) 315-946-7400
  e-mail: jkrebbeks@co.wayne.ny.us
Deputy Commissioner:
  Kelley M Borrelli (R).........................315-946-7400

Westchester ....fax: 914-995-3190
25 Quarropas Street, White Plains, NY 10601
Fax: 914-995-3190
e-mail: boe-west@westchestergov.com
Commissioner:
  Reginald A LaFayette (D).........914-995-5700/fax: 914-995-7753
Commissioner:
  Douglas A Colety (R)..........................914-995-5700
Deputy Commissioner:
  Jeannie L Palazola (D) 914-995-5700

Deputy Commissioner:
  Nancy Meehan (R) 914-995-5700

Wyoming................................fax: 585-786-8843
4 Perry Avenue, Warsaw, NY 14569-1329
Fax: 585-786-8843
e-mail: boewyoming@wyomingco.net
Web site: www.wyomingco.net
Commissioner:
  Anna Mae Balmas (D) 585-786-8931
Commissioner:
  James E Schlick (R) 585-786-8931
Deputy Commissioner:
  Jeanne M Williams (D) 585-786-8931
  e-mail: jewilliams@frontiernet.net
Deputy Commissioner:
  Wendy Simpson (R) 585-786-8931
  e-mail: wlsimpson@frontiernet.net

Yates ....fax: 315-536-5523
417 Liberty St, Ste 1124, Penn Yan, NY 14527
Fax: 315-536-5523
e-mail: boardofelections@yatescounty.org
Commissioner:
  Robert Brechko (D) 315-536-5135
Commissioner:
  Amy J Daines (R)..............................315-536-5135
Deputy Commissioner:
  Sandra P McKay (D) 315-536-5135
Deputy Commissioner:
  Helen J Scarpechi (R).........................315-536-5135

Election Operations
Director:
  Anna E Svizzero 518-473-5086/fax: 518-486-4546

General Information
Coordinator, NVRA:
  Gregory Fiozzo 518-474-1953

Information Technology Unit
Manager, Data Processing/CTO:
  Vacant..518-473-4803

CORPORATIONS, AUTHORITIES AND COMMISSIONS

Joint Commission on Public Ethics (JCOPE)
540 Broadway
Albany, NY 12207
518-408-3976 Fax: 518-408-3975
e-mail: jcope@jcope.ny.gov
Web site: www.jcope.ny.gov

Executive Director:
  Letizia Tagliafierro..........................518-408-3976
Chair:
  Daniel J Horwitz..............................518-408-3976
Training & Education Services:
  Shari Calnero 518-408-3976
Chief of Staff/Deputy Counsel:
  Monica Stamm......................518-408-3976/fax: 518-408-3975

NEW YORK STATE LEGISLATURE

See Legislative Branch in Section 1 for additional Standing Committee and Subcommittee information.

Offices and agencies generally appear in alphabetical order, except when specific order is requested by listee.

Assembly Standing Committees

Election Law
Chair:
  Michael Cusick (D).................................518-455-5526
Ranking Minority Member:
  Bill Nojay (R) 518-455-5662

Senate Standing Committees

Elections
Chair:
  Rich Funke (R) 518-455-2215
Ranking Minority Member:
  Leroy Comrie (D) 518-455-2701

Senate/Assembly Legislative Commissions

Demographic Research & Reapportionment, Legislative Task Force on
Senate Co-Chair:
  Michael F Nozzolio (R) 518-455-2366
Assembly Co-Chair:
  Phil Ramos (D)...................................518-455-5185
Assembly Program Manager:
  Karen Blatt....................212-618-1100/fax: 212-618-1135
Executive Director:
  Debra Levine..................212-618-1110/fax: 212-618-1135

U.S. GOVERNMENT

EXECUTIVE DEPARTMENTS AND RELATED AGENCIES

Federal Election Commission
999 E St NW
Washington, DC 20463
202-694-1000 or 800-424-9530
Web site: www.fec.gov

Chair:
  Ellen W. Weintraub
  e-mail: commissionerweintraub@fec.gov
Vice Chair:
  Donald F. McGahan II
  e-mail: commissionermcgahn@fec.gov
Commissioner:
  Caroline C. Hunter
  e-mail: commissionerhunter@fec.gov
Commissioner:
  Matthew S. Petersen
  e-mail: commissionerpetersen@fec.gov
Commissioner:
  Steven T. Walther
  e-mail: commissionerwalther@fec.gov

US Commission on Civil Rights
Web site: www.usccr.gov

EASTERN REGION (includes New York State)
624 9th St NW, Ste 500, Washington, DC 20425
Regional Director:
  Ivy L. Davis ....202-376-7533 or TTY: 202-376-8116

U.S. CONGRESS

See U.S. Congress Chapter for additional Standing Committee and Subcommittee information.

House of Representatives Standing Committees

Oversight & Government Reform
Chair:
  Darrell E Issa (R-CA)..............................202-225-3906
Ranking Member:
  Elijah Cummings (D-MD) 202-225-4741
New York Delegate:
  Carolyn B Maloney (D) 202-225-7944

Subcommittee
Federal Workforce, Postal Service and the District of Columbia
    Chair:
      Elijah Cummings (D-MD)..................202-225-4741
    Ranking Member:
      Stephen F. Lynch (D-MA)..................202-225-8273

Ethics
Chair:
  K. Michael Conway (R-TX)..........................202-225-3605
Ranking Member:
  Linda T. Sanchez (D-CA)...........................202-225-6676

Senate Standing Committees

Ethics, Select Committee on
Chair:
  Barbara Boxer (D-CA) 202-224-3553
Ranking Member:
  Johnny Isakson (R-GA) 202-224-3643

Homeland Security & Governmental Affairs
Chair:
  Tom Carper (D-DE) 202-224-2441
Ranking Member:
  Tom A. Coburn, M.D. (R-OK).......................202-224-5754

PRIVATE SECTOR

Arthur J Finkelstein & Associates Inc
16 N Astor, Irvington, NY 10533
914-591-8142 Fax: 914-591-4013
Election polling & consulting
Arthur J Finkelstein, President

Branford Communications
611 Broadway, New York, NY 10012
212-260-9905 Fax: 212-260-9908
Media consulting; print production & advertising
Ernest Lendler, Principal

Bynum, Thompson, Ryer
44 Travis Corners, Garrison, NY 10524
845-424-4300 Fax: 845-424-3850
e-mail: bynum@btrsc.com
Web site: www.btrsc.com
Campaign communication, strategy & media production
Peter Bynum, President

CUNY Graduate School, Center for Urban Research
365 5th Ave, New York, NY 10016-4309
212-817-2046 Fax: 212-817-1575
e-mail: jmollenkopf@gc.cuny.edu
Web site: www.gc.cuny.edu
Political participation, voting behavior, NYC politics & urban economic & demographic change
John Hull Mollenkopf, Director

Offices and agencies generally appear in alphabetical order, except when specific order is requested by listee.

Century Foundation (The)
41 East 70th St, New York, NY 10021
212-535-4441 Fax: 212-879-9197
e-mail: info@tcf.org
Web site: www.tcf.org
Sponsor the Federal Election Reform Network; co-organizer of the National Commission on Federal Election Reform; provide policymakers with new ideas to address challenges facing the nation
Christy Hicks, Vice President, Public Affairs

Citizen Action of New York
94 Central Ave, Albany, NY 12206
518-465-4600 x113 Fax: 518-465-2890
e-mail: rkirsch@citizenactionny.org
Web site: www.citizenactionny.org
Campaign finance reform; health care advocacy & consumer protection; education
Richard Kirsch, Executive Director

Columbia Law School, Legislative Drafting Research Fund
435 W 116th St, New York, NY 10027-7297
212-854-2640 or 212-854-2638 Fax: 212-854-7946
e-mail: rb34@columbia.edu
Web site: www.law.columbia.edu
State & local government law, property law & election law
Richard Briffault, Professor of Legislation

Common Cause/NY
155 Ave of the Americas, 4th Fl, New York, NY 10013
212-691-6506 Fax: 212-807-1809
e-mail: cocauseny@aol.com
Web site: www.commoncause.org/ny
Campaign finance reform, ballot access, political gift disclosure & public interest lobbying
Rachel Leon, Executive Director

Conservative Party of NYS
325 Parkview Dr, Schenectady, NY 12303
518-356-7882 Fax: 518-356-3773
e-mail: cpnys@nycap.rr.com
Web site: www.cpnys.org
Campaign consulting services & funding for Conservative Party political candidates
Shaun Marie Levine, Executive Director

Cookfair Media Inc
536 Buckingham Ave, Syracuse, NY 13210
315-478-3359 Fax: 315-478-5236
e-mail: cookfair@aol.com
Campaign media production, print production & advertising
John R Cookfair, III, President

Democratic Congressional Campaign Committee
430 South Capitol St, SE, Washington, DC 20003
202-863-1500 Fax: 202-485-3436
Web site: www.dccc.org
Funding for Democratic congressional candidates; campaign strategy
Rahm Emanuel, Chair

Election Computer Services Inc
197 County Route 7, Pine Plains, NY 12567-9664
518-398-8844 or 212-750-8844 Fax: 518-398-9370
e-mail: ecs@taconic.net
Computer services, voter lists & direct mail
Margo Marabon, President

EMILY's List
1120 Connecticut Ave NW, Ste 1100, Washington, DC 20036-3949
202-326-1400 Fax: 202-326-1415
Web site: www.emilyslist.org
Political network for pro-choice Democratic women political candidates
Johnathan Parker, Political Director

Garth Group Inc (The)
1 W 67th St, #206, New York, NY 10023-6200
212-838-8800 Fax: 212-873-5252
e-mail: garthgroup@aol.com
Political & media consulting
David Garth, Chairman

Harris Interactive Inc
60 Corporate Woods, Rochester, NY 14623-1457
585-272-8400 or 800-866-7655 Fax: 585-272-8763
e-mail: info@harrisinteractive.com
Web site: www.harrisinteractive.com
Market research
Greg Novak, President & Chief Executive Officer

League of Women Voters of New York State
62 Grand Street, Albany, NY 12207-2712
518-465-4162 Fax: 518-465-0812
e-mail: rob@lwvny.org
Web site: www.lwvny.org
Public policy issues forum; good government advocacy
Kristen Hansen, Executive Director

Marist Institute for Public Opinion
Marist College, 3399 North Road, Poughkeepsie, NY 12601
845-575-5050 Fax: 845-575-5111
e-mail: lee.miringoff@marist.edu
Web site: www.maristpoll.marist.edu
Develops & conducts nonpartisan public opinion polls on elections & issues
Lee M Miringoff, Director

NY League of Conservation Voters/NY Conservation Education Fund
30 Broad Street, 30th Floor, New York, NY 10004
212-361-6350 x208 Fax: 212-361-6363
e-mail: mbystryn@nylcv.org
Web site: www.nylcv.org
Endorsement of pro-environmental candidates; environmental advocacy & education statewide
Marcia Bystryn, President

NYC Campaign Finance Board
40 Rector St, 7th Fl, New York, NY 10006-1705
212-306-7100 Fax: 212-306-7143
e-mail: info@nyccfb.info
Web site: www.nyccfb.info
Public funding of candidates for NYC elective offices
Amy M Loprest, Executive Director

NYS Right to Life Committee
41 State St, Ste 100, Albany, NY 12207
518-434-1293 Fax: 518-426-1200
e-mail: admin@nysrighttolife.com
Web site: www.nysrighttolife.org
Lori Kehoe, Executive Director

National Organization for Women, NYS
1500 Central Avenue, Albany, NY 12205
518-452-3944 Fax: 518-452-3861
e-mail: newyorkstatenow@aol.com
Web site: www.nownys.com
Campaign assistance & funding for political candidates who support feminist agenda; legislative lobbying on women's issues
Marcia Pappas, President

New School University, Department of Political Science
65 5th Ave, New York, NY 10011
212-229-5784 Fax: 212-807-1669
e-mail: hattamv@newschool.edu
Web site: www.newschool.edu
Business unionism in the US; political parties & elections
Victoria Hattam, Associate Professor of Political Science

Offices and agencies generally appear in alphabetical order, except when specific order is requested by listee.

New York Republican State Committee
315 State St, Albany, NY 12210
518-462-2601 Fax: 518-449-7443
Web site: www.nygop.org
Joseph N Mondello, Chairman

New York State Democratic Committee
60 Madison Ave, Ste 1201, New York, NY 10010
212-725-8825 Fax: 212-725-8867
e-mail: rodneyc@nysdems.org
Web site: www.nydems.org
Edna Ishayik, Executive Director

New York University, Departmentt of Politics
19 West 4th Street, New York, NY 10012-9580
212-998-8500 or 646-284-7161 Fax: 212-995-4184
e-mail: russell.hardin@nyu.edu
Web site: www.nyu.edu/gsas/dept/politics
Collective action & social movements; nationalism & ethnic conflict; constitutionalism
Russell Hardin, Professor of Politics

New York University, Graduate School of Journalism
20 Cooper Square, 6th Floor, New York, NY 10003
212-998-7980 Fax: 212-995-4148
e-mail: jr3@nyu.edu
Web site: www.journalism.nyu.edu
Political role of the press
Jay Rosen, Chair, Journalism Department

New York Wired
One Commerce Plz, Ste 301, PO Box 3945, Albany, NY 12203
518-462-1780 x211
Web site: www.newyorkwired.com
Tom Owens, Consulting & Legal

Nostradamus Advertising
884 West End Ave, Ste 2, New York, NY 10025
212-581-1362
e-mail: nos@nostradamus.net
Web site: www.nostradamus.net
Print production, media consulting, direct mail development
Barry N Sher, President

Public Agenda
6 East 39th St, 9th Fl, New York, NY 10016
212-686-6610 Fax: 212-889-3461
e-mail: info@publicagenda.org
Web site: www.publicagenda.org
Nonpartisan, nonprofit organization dedicated to conducting unbiased public opinion research & producing fair-minded citizen education materials
Alex Trilling, VP/General Manager

SUNY at Albany, Nelson A Rockefeller College
135 Western Ave, Albany, NY 12222
518-442-5378 or 518-439-9440 Fax: 518-442-5298
e-mail: zimmer@albany.edu
Web site: www.albany.edu/rockefeller
Intergovernmental relations; NY state & local government; ethics in government; election systems & voting

Joseph F Zimmerman, Professor

SUNY at New Paltz, College of Liberal Arts & Sciences
1 Hawk Drive, New Paltz, NY 12561-2499
845-257-3520 Fax: 845-257-3520
e-mail: benjamig@newpaltz.edu
Web site: www.newpaltz.edu
Local & state government process & structure; regionalism; politics & election law
Gerald Benjamin, Director CRREO/Distinguished Professor of Political Science

Sheinkopf Communications
152 Madison Avenue, Suite 1603, New York, NY 10016
212-725-2378 Fax: 212-725-6896
e-mail: info@scheinkopf.com
Web site: www.sheikopf.com
Strategic message counseling for corporate & political clients
Henry A Sheinkopf, President

US Term Limits Foundation
240 Waukegan Road, Suite 200, Glenview, IL 60025
847-657-7429 or 800-733-6440 Fax: 847-657-7502
e-mail: howrch@cs.com
Web site: www.ustermlimits.org
Publishers of
Howard Rich, President

Women's Campaign Fund
734 15th St NW, Ste 500, Washington, DC 20005
202-393-8164 or 800-446-8170 Fax: 202-393-0649
e-mail: susanmedalie@wcfonline.org
Web site: www.wcfonline.org
Training, education & funding for pro-choice women political candidates
Ilana Goldman, Executive Director

Women's City Club of New York
307 Seventh Ave, Ste 1403, New York, NY 10001
212-353-8070 Fax: 212-228-4665
e-mail: info@wccny.org
Web site: www.wccny.org
Nonpartisan, nonprofit civic organization whose mission is to shape public policy through education, advocacy and citizen participation
Ruth Acker, President

Working Families Party
2-4 Nevins Street, 3rd Flr, Brooklyn, NY 11217
718-222-3796 Fax: 718-246-3718
e-mail: wfp@workingfamiliesparty.org
Web site: www.workingfamiliesparty.org
Dan Cantor, Executive Director

Zogby International
901 Broad St, Utica, NY 13501
315-624-0200 Fax: 315-624-0210
e-mail: mail@zogby.com
Web site: www.zogby.com
Political polling & analysis; social science research; business & consumer public opinion surveys & market research
John Zogby, President

Offices and agencies generally appear in alphabetical order, except when specific order is requested by listee.

ENERGY, UTILITY & COMMUNICATION SERVICES

NEW YORK STATE

GOVERNOR'S OFFICE

Governor's Office
Executive Chamber
State Capitol
Albany, NY 12224
518-474-8390 Fax: 518-474-1513
Web site: www.ny.gov

Governor:
　Andrew M Cuomo 518-474-8390
Secretary to the Governor:
　William Mulrow 518-474-4246
Counsel to the Governor:
　Alphonso David 518-474-8343
Chairman of Energy & Finance for New York:
　Richard Kauffman. 518-408-2552
Deputy Secretary, Technology:
　Rachel Haot. 212-681-4573
Director, Communications:
　Melissa DeRosa .518-474-8418 or 212-681-4640

EXECUTIVE DEPARTMENTS AND RELATED AGENCIES

CIO & Office of Information Technology Services (ITS)
State Capitol, ESP
PO Box 2062
Albany, NY 12220-0062
518-402-2537 or 866-789-4638 Fax: 518-474-1196
e-mail: customer.relations@its.ny.gov
Web site: www.its.ny.gov

Chief Information Officer & Director:
　Maggie Miller. 518-408-2140
Executive Deputy CIO:
　Mahesh Nattanmai 518-408-2140
Counsel & Legal Services:
　Karen Geduldig. 518-408-2484
Director, Public Information:
　Michelle McDonald 518-408-3899

Administration
Chief Operating Officer:
　Pat Bennison. 518-402-7000
Director, Administration:
　Terri Papa 518-408-2484
Chief Technology Officer:
　Kishor Bagul. 518-408-2484
Chief Data Officer:
　Barbara Cohn. 518-474-3019/fax: 518-486-7923
Director, Enterprise Information Security Office:
　Thomas D Smith. 518-242-5200
　e-mail: eiso@its.ny.gov
Chief Portfolio Officer:
　Nancy Mulholland 518-473-9450

Consumer Protection, Division of
One Commerce Plaza
99 Washington Avenue
Albany, NY 12231

518-474-8583 or 800-697-1220 Fax: 518-473-9055
Web site: www.dos.ny.gov/consumerprotection/

Executive Deputy Director:
　Aiesha Battle. 518-474-2363

Law Department
120 Broadway
New York, NY 10271-0332
212-416-8000 or 800-771-7755
Web site: www.ag.ny.gov

State Capitol
Albany, NY 12224-0341
518-474-7330
Fax: 518-473-9909

Attorney General:
　Eric T Schneiderman . . . . .212-416-8050 or 518-474-7330
Chief of Staff:
　Micah Lasher 212-416-8050
Director, Public Information:
　Shawn Morris 518-776-2357/fax: 518-650-9401
Press Secretary:
　Fernando Aquino. 212-416-8060/fax: 212-416-6005

Economic Justice
Executive Deputy Attorney General:
　Karla Sanchez. 212-416-8050

Internet Bureau
Bureau Chief:
　Kathleen McGee 212-416-8433/fax: 212-416-8369

Public Service Commission
NYS Dept of Public Service
3 Empire State Plaza
Albany, NY 12223-1350
518-474-7080 Fax: 518-474-0421
Web site: www.dps.ny.gov

90 Church St
New York, NY 10007-2919
212-417-2378

Ellicott Sq Bldg
295 Main St
Room 1050
Buffalo, NY 14203
716-847-3941

Chairman:
　Garry A Brown .518-474-2523/fax: 518-473-2838
Executive Deputy:
　Judith Lee 518-408-1978/fax: 518-473-2838
Policy & Legal Affairs:
　Jeff Cohen 518-408-1978/fax: 518-473-2838
Manager of Utility Rates & Services:
　William Bouteiller. 518-402-5674/fax: 518-473-2838
General Counsel:
　Peter McGowan 518-474-2510
Secretary to the Commission:
　Kathleen H Burgess. 518-474-6530/fax: 518-486-6081
　e-mail: secretary@dps.ny.gov
Director, Public Affairs:
　James Denn 518-474-7080/fax: 518-473-2838
　e-mail: james.denn@dps.ny.gov

Offices and agencies generally appear in alphabetical order, except when specific order is requested by listee.

Accounting & Finance Office
Director:
Doris Stout . . . . .518-474-4508 or 212-417-2136

Consumer Policy Office
Director:
Douglas Elfner .518-402-5786/fax: 518-473-5685

Consumer Services Office
Director:
Sandra Sloane 518-474-3280
e-mail: csd@dps.ny.gov

Consumer Complaints 1-800-342-3377
e-mail: csd@dps.ny.gov

Energy Efficiency & the Environment
Acting Director:
Colleen Gerwitz 518-474-2350
Deputy Director:
James Austin 518-473-4635/fax: 518-473-5026
Chief, Renewable Energy:
Christina Palmero 518-474-1612/fax: 518-474-5026
Chief, Analysis & Modeling:
Steven Keller 518-486-2430/fax: 518-473-1498

Electric, Gas & Water Office
Director:
Thomas Dvorsky 518-473-6080/fax: 518-473-4992
Deputy Director, Electric:
Raj Addepalli 518-473-8986/fax: 518-473-2420
Deputy Director, Gas, Water & Steam:
Michael Scott 518-474-1372/fax: 518-473-4992
Chief, Electric Rates & Tariffs:
Bruce Alch 518-486-2400/fax: 518-473-5204
Chief, Distribution Systems:
Michael Worden 518-486-2498/fax: 518-473-2420
Chief, Bulk Electric Systems:
Tammy Mitchell 518-486-2462/fax: 518-473-2420
Chief, Policy Coordination:
William Heinrich 518-473-3402/fax: 518-473-2420
Chief, Gas Rates & Tariffs:
Thomas Coonan 518-473-6694/fax: 518-473-4992
Chief, Gas Policy & Supply:
Cynthia McCarran 518-474-1396/fax: 518-473-4992
Chief, Water:
James Evensen 212-417-2321/fax: 212-417-2324
Chief, Safety, Electric, Gas & Steam:
Gavin S Nicoletta 518-486-2496/fax: 518-473-1498
Chief, Utility Security:
John Sennett .518-402-5445/fax: 518-473-5685

Hearings & Alternative Dispute Resolution Office
Chief Administrative Law Judge:
Elizabeth Liebschutz 518-474-4520/fax: 518-473-3263

Industry & Governmental Relations Office
Managing Director:
Michael Corso 518-474-4686

Office of Administration
Director:
Sorelle Brauth 518-474-2508/fax: 518-474-0413
Adminstrative Management:
Judy Regan .518-474-1990/fax: 518-474-0413
Finance & Budget:
Carole Gnacik 518-474-2516/fax: 518-473-9990
Human Resources:
Janice Nissen 518-486-2626/fax: 518-473-9990
Information Services Director:
Carmela Turpin 518-486-4960/fax: 518-473-7815

Internal Audit:
Theresa Schillaci 518-473-2079/fax: 518-486-6081

Regulatory Economics Office
Director:
Mark Reeder 518-474-1721

Office of Telecommunications
Director:
Chad Hume .518-474-1668/fax: 518-474-5616

CORPORATIONS, AUTHORITIES AND COMMISSIONS

Interstate Oil & Gas Compact Commission
PO Box 53127
900 NE 23rd St
Oklahoma City, OK 73152-3127
405-525-3556 Fax: 405-525-3592
e-mail: iogcc@iogcc.state.ok.us
Web site: www.iogcc.ok.gov

Chair:
Governor Gary R Herbert (UT) 405-525-3556
Vice Chair:
Hal Fitch 405-525-3556
Executive Director:
Mike Smith 405-525-3556
New York State Official Representative:
Bradley J Field 518-402-8076
Communications Manager:
Carol Booth 405-525-3556

New York Power Authority
123 Main Street
Mailstop 10-H
White Plains, NY 10601-3170
914-681-6200 Fax: 914-390-8190
e-mail: info@nypa.gov
Web site: www.nypa.gov

Chairman:
John R. Koelmel 914-287-3636
President & Chief Executive Officer:
Gil C Quiniones 914-287-3501
Vice President, Public & Regulatory Affairs:
Jill Anderson 518-433-6700
Chief Operating Officer:
Edward A Welz 518-433-6700
Acting General Counsel:
Arthur Cambouris 914-681-6200

New York State Energy Research & Development Authority
17 Columbia Circle
Albany, NY 12203-6399
518-862-1090 Fax: 518-862-1091
Web site: www.nyserda.ny.gov

Chairman:
Richard L Kauffman 518-862-1090
President & CEO:
John B Rhodes 518-862-1090 x3278
General Counsel & Secretary:
Hal Brodie 518-862-1090 x3280
e-mail: hb1@nyserda.ny.gov
Program Manager, Economic Development & Community Outreach:
Kelly Tyler . . . . .716-842-1522 x. 3005
e-mail: kat@nyserda.ny.gov

Offices and agencies generally appear in alphabetical order, except when specific order is requested by listee.

Director, Communications:
Kate Muller. 518-862-1090 x3582/fax: 518-862-1091
e-mail: ktm@nyserda.ny.gov

NEW YORK STATE LEGISLATURE

See Legislative Branch in Section 1 for additional Standing Committee and Subcommittee information.

Assembly Standing Committees

Energy
Chair:
Amy Paulin (D). 518-455-5585
Ranking Minority Member:
Philip Palmesano (R) 518-455-5791

Senate Standing Committees

Energy & Telecommunications
Chair:
Joseph A Griffo (R) 518-455-3334
Ranking Minority Member:
Kevin Parker (D). 518-455-2580

U.S. GOVERNMENT

EXECUTIVE DEPARTMENTS AND RELATED AGENCIES

Federal Communications Commission
e-mail: fccinfo@fcc.gov
Web site: www.fcc.gov

Office of Media Relations . . . . .fax: 866-418-0232
445 12th St SW, Washington, DC 20554
888-225-5322 Fax: 866-418-0232
Director:
Tammy Sun

Nuclear Regulatory Commission
Web site: www.nrc.gov

REGION I (includes New York State)
475 Allendale Rd, King of Prussia, PA 19406-2713
Regional Administrator:
William Dean
Deputy Regional Administrator:
David Lew
Senior Public Affairs Officer:
Diane Serenci

US Department of Agriculture
Web site: www.usda.gov

Rural Development
Web site: www.rurdev.usda.gov/ny

New York State Office. . . . . .fax: 315-477-6438
The Galleries of Syracuse, 441 S Salina St, Ste 357, 5th Fl, Syracuse, NY 13202-2425
TTY: 315-477-6447 or 315-477-6400 Fax: 315-477-6438
State Director:
Stanley Telega 315-477-6437
Program Director, Rural Utilities Service:
David Miller 315-477-6427
e-mail: david.miller@ny.usda.gov

Eastern New York Office . . . . .fax: 845-987-8111
26 Jessup Road, Warwick, NY 10090-2540
845-987-8111 Fax: 845-987-8111
Director:
Ronda Falkena. . . . . .845-343-1872 x. 4

Western New York Office. .fax: 315-677-0072
2571 US Rte 11, Ste 4, Lafayette, NY 13084
315-677-3552 Ext.4 Fax: 315-677-0072
Director:
Jim Walfrand . . . . .585-343-9167 Ext. 4

US Department of Energy
Web site: www.doe.gov

Federal Energy Regulatory Commission

New York Regional Office
19 W 34th St, Ste 400, New York, NY 10001-3006
Acting Regional Engineer:
Gerald L. Cross

Office of External Affairs
888 First St NE, Washington, DC 20426
202-502-8200
Director:
Leonard Tao 202-502-8004/fax: 202-208-2106

Laboratories

Brookhaven National Laboratory
Community Involvement/Public Affairs
Building 400 C, Upton, NY 11973-5000
Community Relations Manager:
Nora Detweiler
Office of the Director
2 Center Street, Upton, NY 11973
Director:
Doon Gibbs

Knolls Atomic Power Laboratory- KAPL Inc
2401 River Road, Schenectady, NY 12309

U.S. CONGRESS

See U.S. Congress Chapter for additional Standing Committee and Subcommittee information.

House of Representatives Standing Committees

Appropriations
Chair:
Harold Rogers (R-KY) 202-225-4601
Ranking Member:
Nita M. Lowey (D-NY) 202-225-6506
New York Delegate:
Bill Owens (D) 202-225-4611
New York Delegate:
Jose E Serrano (D) 202-225-4361

Subcommittee
Energy & Water Development
Chair:
Rodney Frelinghuysen (R-NJ). 202-225-5034
Ranking Member:
Marcy Kaptur (D-OH). 202-225-4146

Energy & Commerce
Chair:
Fred Upton (R-MI) 202-225-3761
Ranking Member:
Henry Waxman (D-CA) 202-225-3976

Offices and agencies generally appear in alphabetical order, except when specific order is requested by listee.

New York Delegate:
   Eliot L Engel (D) 202-225-2464
New York Delegate:
   Paul Tonko (D) 202-225-5076

   Subcommittee
    Energy & Power
     Chair:
      Ed Whitfield (R-KY)........................202-225-3115
     Ranking Member:
      Bobby L. Rush (D-IL) 202-225-4372
     New York Delegate:
      Eliot L Engel (D) 202-225-2464
     New York Delegate:
      Paul Tonko (D) 202-225-5076

Natural Resources
Chair:
   Doc Hastings (R-WA) 202-225-5816
Ranking Member:
   Edward J. Markey (D-MA)........................202-225-2836

   Subcommittees
    Energy & Mineral Resources
     Chair:
      Doug Lamborn (R-CO) 202-225-4422
     Ranking Member:
      Rush Holt (D-NJ)...........................202-225-5801
    Water & Power
     Chair:
      Tom McClintock (R-LA)....................202-225-2511
     Ranking Member:
      Grace F. Napolitano (D-CA) 202-225-8331

Science & Technology
Chair:
   Lamar Smith (R-TX)...............................202-225-4326
Ranking Member:
   Eddie Bernice Johnson 202-225-8885

   Subcommittee
    Energy
     Chair:
      Cynthia Lummis (R-TX) 202-225-2311
     Ranking Member:
      Eric Swalwell (D-CA) 202-225-5065

Senate Standing Committees

Appropriations
Chair:
   Barbara A. Mikulski (D-MD).....................202-224-4654
Vice Chair:
   Richard C. Shelby (R-AL) 202-224-5065

   Subcommittee
    Energy & Water Development
     Chair:
      Dianne Feinstein (D_CA) 202-224-3841
     Ranking Member:
      Lamar Alexander (R-TN) 202-224-4944

Commerce, Science & Transportation
Chair:
   John D Rockefeller IV (D-WV) 202-224-6472
Ranking Member:
   John Thune (R-SD)...............................202-224-2321

   Subcommittee
    Aviation Operations, Safety & Security
     Chair:
      Maria Cantwell (D-WA) 202-224-3441

Ranking Member:
   Kelly Ayotte (R-NH).......................202-224-3324
Science & Space
   Chair:
    Bill Nelson (D-FL)..........................202-224-5724
   Ranking Member:
    Ted Cruz (R-TX) 202-224-5922

Energy & Natural Resources
Chair:
   Ron Wyden (D-OR) 202-224-5244
Ranking Member:
   Lisa Murkowski (R-AK)..........................202-224-6665

PRIVATE SECTOR

AT&T Corporation
One AT&T Way, Bedminster, NJ 7921
908-532-1835 Fax: 908-532-1702
e-mail: morrisse@lga.att.com
Web site: www.att.com
Telecommunications services & systems
Michael Morrissey, Vice President, Law & Government Affairs

AeA New York Council
255 Fuller Rd, Albany Nanotechnology Complex, Albany, NY 12203
518-437-1530 Fax: 732-340-1533
e-mail: justin-wright@aeanet.org
Web site: www.aeanet.org
Electronics, software & information technology industries; support of high tech industry goals
Justin Wright, Executive Director

Amerada Hess Corporation
1185 Ave of the Americas, New York, NY 10036
212-997-8500 Fax: 212-536-8390
Web site: www.hess.com
Manufacture & market petroleum products; operate gasoline outlets
John B Hess, Chief Executive Officer

Association of Public Broadcasting Stations of NY Inc
33 Elk St, Ste 200, Albany, NY 12207
518-462-1590 Fax: 518-462-1390
e-mail: apbs@wxxi.org
Public television
Peter Repas, Executive Director

CBS Corporation
51 W 52nd St, New York, NY 10019
212-975-4321 Fax: 212-975-6035
Web site: www.cbs.com
TV & radio broadcasting, news, entertainment
Martin Franks, Executive Vice President, CBS Television & Senior Vice President, Viacom

Cable Telecommunications Association of New York, Inc
54 State St, Suite 800, Albany, NY 12207
518-463-6676 Fax: 518-463-0574
e-mail: allison_lee@dkcnews.com
Web site: www.cabletvny.com
Advocate & represent the interests of the cable television industry
Allison Lee, President

Cablevision Systems Corporation
1111 Stewart Ave, Bethpage, NY 11714-3581
516-803-2580 Fax: 516-803-2585
e-mail: lrosenbl@cablevision.com
Web site: www.cablevision.com
Own & operate cable television systems & programming networks, telecommunications, Madison Square Garden, Radio City Music Hall, pro sports teams

Offices and agencies generally appear in alphabetical order, except when specific order is requested by listee.

Lisa Rosenblum, Senior Vice President, Government Relations

Central Hudson Gas & Electric Corporation
284 South Ave, Poughkeepsie, NY 12601
845-486-5218 Fax: 845-486-5544
e-mail: jglusko@cenhud.com
Web site: www.cenhud.com
Governmental relations, corporate relocations & economic development
John P Glusko, Director, Governmental Affairs & Economic Development

Consolidated Edison Energy
4 Irving Pl, Rm 1650S, New York, NY 10276-0138
212-460-2706 or 800-752-6633 Fax: 212-614-1821
e-mail: banksjo@coned.com
Web site: www.coned.com
John H Banks, Vice President, Government Relations

Constellation NewEnergy Inc
Metro-North Region, 810 7th Avenue, Suite 400, New York, NY 10019
212-885-6400 Fax: 212-883-5888
e-mail: cnesalesny@constellation.com
Web site: www.newenergy.com
Retail energy supply & energy services
Charles C Sutton, Vice President

Crane, Parente & Cherubin
90 State Street, Ste 1515A, Albany, NY 12207
518-432-8000 Fax: 518-432-0086
e-mail: jcrane@cpclaw.net
*Governmental relations, banking & financial services, corporate law,
construction law, energy, utilities, communications, land use, environmental
& wireless telecommunications law*
James B Crane, II, Managing Partner

Educational Broadcasting Corporation
450 West 33rd St, New York, NY 10001
212-560-1313 Fax: 212-560-1314
e-mail: rae@thirteen.org
Web site: www.thirteen.org
Kathleen Rae, Director Governmental Affairs

Empire State Petroleum Association Inc
80 Wolf Rd, St 308, Albany, NY 12205
518-449-0702 Fax: 518-449-0779
e-mail: tpeters@espa.net
Web site: www.espa.net
Petroleum industry lobby & trade association
Thomas J Peters, CEO

Energy Association of New York State
111 Washington Ave, Suite 601, Albany, NY 12210
518-449-3440 Fax: 518-449-3446
Electric & gas utility companies
Patrick J Curran, Executive Director

Entek Power Services
11 Satterly Rd, East Setauket, NY 11733
631-751-9800 Fax: 631-980-3759
e-mail: info@entekpower.com
Web site: www.entekpower.com
Energy consulting
Harry Davitian, President

Entergy Nuclear Northeast
440 Hamilton Ave, White Plains, NY 10601
914-272-3200 Fax: 914-272-3205
Web site: www.entergy.com
Second largest operator of nuclear power plants in the US
Michael R Kansler, President

Exxon Mobil Corporation
1400 Old Country Rd, Ste 203, Westbury, NY 11590
516-333-3177 Fax: 516-333-3428
e-mail: donald.l.clarke@exxonmobil.com
Web site: www.exxonmobil.com
Donald L Clarke, Manager, Public Affairs Northeast

Frontier, A Citizens Communications Co
19 John St, Middletown, NY 10940
845-344-9801 Fax: 845-343-3768
e-mail: claudia.maroney@frontiercorp.com
Web site: www.frontieronline.com
Full service telecommunications provider
Claudia Maroney, Operations Director

Fund for the City of New York, Center for Internet Innovation
121 Ave of the Americas, 6th Fl, New York, NY 10013
212-925-6675 Fax: 212-925-5675
e-mail: mmccormick@fcny.org
Web site: www.fcny.org
*Developing technology systems & applications that help nonprofits &
government streamline operations, expand services, improve performance*
Mary McCormick, President

Getty Petroleum Marketing Inc
1500 Hempstead Turnpike, East Meadow, NY 11554
516-542-5055 Fax: 516-832-8443
e-mail: mlewis@getty.com
Web site: www.getty.com
Petroleum products sales & distribution
Michael G Lewis, Vice President & General Counsel

NYS Bar Assn, Electronic Communications Task Force
Heslin Rothenberg Farley & Mesiti PC
5 Columbia Cir, Albany, NY 12203
518-452-5600 Fax: 518-452-5579
e-mail: dpm@hrfmlaw.com
Web site: www.hrfmlaw.com
David P Miranda, Chair

NYS Bar Assn, Media Law Committee
Hogan & Hartson LLP
875 3rd Ave, 25th Fl, New York, NY 10022
212-918-3637 Fax: 212-918-3100
e-mail: srmetcalf@hhlaw.com
Slade R Metcalf,

Independent Oil & Gas Association of New York
5743 Walden Drive, Lake View, NY 14085
716-627-4250 Fax: 716-627-4375
e-mail: brgill@iogany.org
Web site: www.iogany.org
*Trade association representing oil & natural gas producers, drillers &
affiliated service companies*
Bradley Gill, Executive Director

Independent Power Producers of NY Inc
19 Dove Street, Ste 302, Albany, NY 12210
518-436-3749 Fax: 518-436-0369
e-mail: gavin@ippny.org
Web site: www.ippny.org
*Companies developing alternative, environmentally friendly electric
generating facilities*
Gavin J Donohue, President & Chief Executive Officer

KeySpan Corporation
1377 Motor Parkway, Hauppauge, NY 11749
631-300-3700 Fax: 631-300-3702
e-mail: tdejesu@keyspanenergy.com
Electric generation & gas utility
Thomas DeJesu, Director, Government Relations

Offices and agencies generally appear in alphabetical order, except when specific order is requested by listee.

Komanoff Energy Associates
636 Broadway, Rm 602, New York, NY 10012-2623
212-260-5237
e-mail: kea@igc.org
Web site: www.carbontax.org
Energy, utilities & transportation consulting
Charles Komanoff, Director

Mechanical Technology Incorporated
431 New Karner Road, Albany, NY 12205
518-533-2200 Fax: 518-533-2201
Web site: www.mechtech.com
New energy technologies, precision measurement & testing instruments
Cynthia A Scheuer, Chairman & Chief Executive Officer

Municipal Electric Utilities Association
6652 Hammersmith Drive, East Syracuse, NY 13057
315-453-7851 Fax: 315-453-7849
e-mail: info@meua.org
Web site: www.meua.org
Tony Modafferi, Executive Director

NY Oil Heating Association
183 Madison Avenue, Ste 1403, New York, NY 10122
212-695-1380 Fax: 212-594-6583
e-mail: nyoilheating@nyoha.org
Web site: www.nyoha.org
Fuel dealers & auxiliary industries
John Maniscalco, CEO

NY Press Association
1681 Western Ave, Albany, NY 12203
518-464-6483 Fax: 518-464-6489
e-mail: mkrea@nynewspapers.com
Web site: www.nynewspapers.com
Weekly community & ethnic newspaper publishers
Michelle Rea, Executive Director

NY Propane Gas Association
PO Box 760, Clifton Park, NY 12065
518-383-3823 Fax: 518-383-3824
e-mail: nypga1@aol.com
Web site: www.nypropane.com
Provides services that communicate, promote and educate the propane industry in New York.
John Hamilton, President; Roland Penta, State/National Director

NYS Broadcasters Association
1805 Western Ave, Albany, NY 12203
518-456-8888 Fax: 518-456-8943
Web site: www.nysbroadcasters.org
Trade association for NYS Broadcasters
Joseph Reilly, President

NYS Technology Enterprise Corporation (NYSTEC)
540 Broadway, 3rd Floor, Albany, NY 12207
518-431-7028 Fax: 518-431-7037
e-mail: nystec@nystec.com
Web site: www.nystec.com
Technology acquisition, technology management & engineering services to government clients
Mike Donovan, President/CEO

National Economic Research Associates
308 N Cayuga St, Ithaca, NY 14850
607-277-3007 Fax: 607-277-1581
e-mail: alfred.kahn@nera.com
Web site: www.nera.com
Utility & transportation regulation, deregulation & antitrust
Alfred E Kahn, Professor Emeritus & Special Consultant

National Fuel Gas
800 North 3rd Street, Ste 410, Box 1145, Harrisburg, PA 17108
717-232-7236 Fax: 717-232-8238
e-mail: morrisong@nat.fuel.com
Web site: www.nationalfuel.com
Gary L Morrison, General Manager, Government Affairs

NYS Bar Assn, Public Utility Law Committee
National Fuel Gas Distribution
Legal Department, 6363 Main Street, Buffalo, NY 14221
716-857-7313
Michael W Reville, Chair

National Grid
300 Erie Blvd West, Syracuse, NY 13202
315-428-5430 Fax: 315-428-3406
e-mail: susan.crossett@us.ngrid.com
Susan Crossett, Vice President Energy Solutions Services

Nelson A Rockefeller Inst of Government, NY Forum for Info
411 State St, Albany, NY 12203-1003
518-443-5001 Fax: 518-443-5006
e-mail: gbenson@nysfirm.org
Web site: www.nysfirm.org
Information management; public access to government information; privacy & confidentiality; intellectual property; public/private partnerships
Gregory M Benson Jr, Executive Director

New York Independent System Operator - Not For Profit
10 Krey Blvd, Rensselaer, NY 12144
518-356-8728 Fax: 518-356-7524
e-mail: trumsey@nyiso.com
Web site: www.nyiso.com
Grid operator
Tom Rumsey, Vice President, External Affairs

New York News Publishers Association
50 Colvin Avenue, Suite 102, Albany, NY 12206
518-449-1667 Fax: 518-449-5053
e-mail: diane@nynpa.com
Web site: www.nynpa.com
Diane Kennedy, President

New York Press Photographers Association
225 E 36th St, Ste 1-P, New York, NY 10016
212-889-6633 Fax: 212-889-6634
e-mail: nyppa@aol.com
Web site: www.nyppa.org
Bernie Nunez, President

Rochester Gas and Electric Corporation
New York State Electric & Gas Corporation (NYSEG)
18 Link Drive, Box 5224, Binghamton, NY 13902-5224
607-762-7310 Fax: 585-340-1659
e-mail: ctchadwick@nyseg.com
Web site: www.nyseg.com
Cindy T Chadwick, Manager, Public Affairs

New York State Petroleum Council
150 State St, Albany, NY 12207
518-465-3563 Fax: 518-465-4022
e-mail: nyspc@nycap.rr.com
Web site: www.api.org
Petroleum industry lobby
Michael R Doyle, Executive Director

New York State Telecommunications Association Inc
100 State St, Ste 650, Albany, NY 12207
518-443-2700 Fax: 518-443-2810
e-mail: rpuckett@nysta.com
Web site: www.nysta.com
Robert R Puckett, President

Offices and agencies generally appear in alphabetical order, except when specific order is requested by listee.

Northeast Gas Association
75 Second Ave, Ste 510, Needham, MA 02494-2824
781-455-6800 Fax: 781-455-6828
e-mail: tkiley@northeastgas.org
Web site: www.northeastgas.org
Gas Industry Trade Association
Thomas M Kiley, President & CEO

Oil Heat Institute of Long Island
200 Parkway Drive S, Ste 202, Hauppauge, NY 11788
631-360-0200 Fax: 631-360-0781
e-mail: info@ohili.org
Web site: www.ohili.org
Heating oil industry association
Kevin M Rooney, Chief Executive Officer

Orange & Rockland Utilities Inc
One Blue Hill Plz, Pearl River, NY 10965
845-352-6000 Fax: 845-577-6914
e-mail: struckr@oru.com
Web site: www.oru.com
New business development
John D McMahon, President & Chief Executive Officer

Plug Power Inc
968 Albany-Shaker Rd, Latham, NY 12110
518-782-7700 x1970 Fax: 518-782-9060
Web site: www.plugpower.com
Fuel cell research & development for small stationary applications
Gerard L Conway, Jr, General Counsel

Public Utility Law Project of New York Inc
194 Washington Ave, Ste 420, Albany, NY 12210-2314
518-449-3375 Fax: 518-449-1769
e-mail: info@pulp.tc
Web site: www.pulp.tc
Advocacy of universal service, affordability & customer protection for residential utility consumers
Gerald A Norlander, Executive Director

Rochester Gas & Electric Corporation
89 East Ave, Rochester, NY 14649
585-771-2230 Fax: 585-724-8799
e-mail: marion@rge.com
Web site: www.rge.com
Dick Marion, Manager, Corporate Communications

Sithe Energies Inc
335 Madison Ave, New York, NY 10017
212-351-0266 Fax: 212-351-0800
Web site: www.sithe.com
Independent electric power producer & generator
Frank Gomez, Office Manager

Spanish Broadcasting System Network Inc
26 W 56th St, New York, NY 10019
646-710-2629 Fax: 212-541-9295
Web site: www.lamusica.com
Spanish language FM radio stations
Luis A Miranda, Jr, Director, Public Affairs

Sunwize Technologies Inc
1155 Flatbush Rd, Kingston, NY 12401
845-336-0146 x124 Fax: 845-336-0457
e-mail: sunwize@sunwize.com
Web site: www.sunwize.com
Solar electric energy development & product distribution
Bruce Gould, Vice President, Sales

Verizon Communications
140 West Street, New York, NY 10007
518-396-1086 Fax: 518-436-0141
Web site: www.verizon.com
Telecommunications services for northeastern US
David Lamendola, Director, Government Affairs-State of NY

Viacom Inc
1515 Broadway, New York, NY 10036
212-258-6000
Web site: www.viacom.com
International media, entertainment
Sumner M Redstone, Chairman & Chief Executive Officer

Wall Street Journal (The)
200 Liberty St, New York, NY 10281
212-416-2000 Fax: 212-416-2720
e-mail: paul.steiger@dowjones.com
Web site: www.wsj.com
Paul E Steiger, Managing Editor

Policy Areas

Offices and agencies generally appear in alphabetical order, except when specific order is requested by listee.

ENVIRONMENT & NATURAL RESOURCES

NEW YORK STATE

GOVERNOR'S OFFICE

Governor's Office
Executive Chamber
State Capitol
Albany, NY 12224
518-474-8390 Fax: 518-474-1513
Web site: www.ny.gov

Governor:
    Andrew M Cuomo 518-474-8390
Secretary to the Governor:
    William Mulrow. 518-474-4246
Counsel to the Governor:
    Alphonso David 518-474-8343
Chairman of Energy & Finance for New York:
    Richard Kauffman. 518-408-2552
Deputy Secretary, Environment:
    Basil Seggos. 518-408-2552
Director, Communications:
    Melissa DeRosa . . . . .518-474-8418 or 212-681-4640

EXECUTIVE DEPARTMENTS AND RELATED AGENCIES

Empire State Development Corporation
633 Third Ave
New York, NY 10017
212-803-3100 Fax: 212-803-3131
Web site: www.esd.ny.gov

625 Broadway
Albany, NY 12207
518-292-5200

95 Perry Street
Ste 500
Buffalo, NY 14203
716-846-8200
Fax: 716-846-8260

President & CEO:
    Howard Zemsky 212-803-3700
Public Affairs:
    Kay Sarlin Wright. 800-260-7313
    e-mail: esdpressoffice@esd.ny.gov

Environmental Conservation Department
625 Broadway
Albany, NY 12233
518-402-8545 Fax: 518-402-9016
Web site: www.dec.ny.gov

Commissioner:
    Joseph J Martens 518-402-8545/fax: 518-402-8541
Executive Deputy Commissioner:
    Marc Gerstman 518-402-9401
Public Affairs:
    Michael Bopp 518-402-8000
Deputy Commissioner, Administration:
    Anne Reynolds 518-402-9401
Director, Internal Audit & Investigation:
    Anne Lapinski. 518-402-9147

Secretary to the Commissioner:
    Dawn Sherwin. 518-402-8545

Air Resources, Climate Change & Energy Office
Assistant Commissioner:
    Jared Snyder 518-402-8552

Air Resources Division
Director:
    David Shaw .518-402-8452/fax: 518-402-9035

Climate Change Office
Acting Director:
    Lois New. 518-402-8448

Office of Remediation & Materials Management
Deputy Commissioner:
    Gene Leff. 518-402-2794/fax: 518-402-9016

Environmental Remediation Division
Director:
    Robert Schick 518-402-9706/fax: 518-402-9020

Mineral Resources Division
Director:
    Bradley J Field 518-402-8076/fax: 518-402-8060

Materials Management Division
Director:
    Sal Ervolina. .518-402-8651/fax: 518-402-9024

General Counsel's Office
General Counsel:
    Ed McTiernan 518-402-9185/fax: 518-402-9018

Hearings & Mediation Services Office
Asst Commissioner:
    Louis Alexander 518-402-8537

Natural Resources Office
Assistant Commissioner:
    Kathy Moser .518-402-2797/fax: 518-402-9016

Fish, Wildlife & Marine Resources Division
Director:
    Patricia Riexinger 518-402-8924/fax: 518-402-9027

Lands & Forests Division
Director:
    Robert Davies 518-402-9405/fax: 518-402-9028

Water Resources Office
Assistant Commissioner:
    James Tierney. 518-402-8545

Water Division
Director:
    Mark Klotz 518-402-8233/fax: 518-402-9029

Information Services Division
Director:
    Leslie Brennan 518-402-9860/fax: 518-402-9031

Management & Budget Division
Director:
    Nancy Lussier 518-402-9228/fax: 518-402-9023

Operations Division
Director:
    Mark Malinoski. 518-402-9055/fax: 518-402-9053

Public Affairs & Education Division
Director:
    Laurel Remus 518-402-8049/fax: 518-402-9036
    e-mail: dpaweb@gw.dec.state.ny.us

Offices and agencies generally appear in alphabetical order, except when specific order is requested by listee.

Office of Employee Relations
Director:
　Mark Cadrette 518-402-9388/fax: 518-486-9957

Public Information
Press Operations:
　Emily DeSantis 518-402-8000/fax: 518-402-9016

Public Protection Office
Assistant Commissioner:
　Chris Walsh .518-402-8549/fax: 518-402-9016

Forest Protection & Fire Management Division
Director:
　Joe Zeglan 518-402-8839/fax: 518-402-8840

Law Enforcement Division
Director:
　Peter Fanelli 518-402-8829/fax: 518-402-8830

Regional Offices

Region 1
SUNY - 50 Circle Rd, Stony Brook, NY 11790
Director:
　Peter A Scully 631-444-0345/fax: 631-444-0349

Region 2
One Hunters Pt Plaza, 47-40 21st St, Long Island City, NY 11101-5407
Director:
　Venetia Lannon 718-482-4949/fax: 718-482-4026

Region 3
21 S Putt Corners Rd, New Paltz, NY 12561-1696
Acting Director:
　Thomas Rudolph 845-256-3000/fax: 845-255-3042

Region 4
1130 N Westcott Rd, Schenectady, NY 12306-2014
Director:
　Gene Kelly 518-357-2068/fax: 518-357-2398

Region 5
1115 Rte 86, PO Box 296, Ray Brook, NY 12977
e-mail: r5info@gw.dec.state.ny.us
Director:
　Robert Stegemann 518-897-1211/fax: 518-897-1394

Region 6
317 Washington St, Watertown, NY 13601-3787
Director:
　Judy Drabicki 315-785-2239/fax: 315-785-2242

Region 7
615 Erie Blvd West, Syracuse, NY 13204-2400
Director:
　Kenneth Lynch 315-426-7403/fax: 315-426-7408

Region 8
6274 E Avon-Lima Rd, Avon, NY 14414-9519
Director:
　Paul D'Amato 585-226-5366/fax: 585-226-9485

Region 9
270 Michigan Ave, Buffalo, NY 14203
Director:
　Abby Snyder 716-851-7000/fax: 716-851-7211

Special Programs

Great Lakes Program
Region 9 NYS DEC, 270 Michigan Ave, Buffalo, NY 14203
Coordinator:
　Donald Zelazny 716-851-7220/fax: 716-851-7226

Hudson River Estuary Program
Region 3 NYS DEC, 21 S Putt Corners Rd, New Paltz, NY 12561
Special Asst:
　Frances Dunwell 845-256-3016/fax: 845-255-3649
　e-mail: hrep@gw.dec.state.ny.us

Health Department
Corning Tower
Empire State Plaza
Albany, NY 12237
518-474-2011
Web site: www.health.ny.gov

Commissioner:
　Howard Zucker, MD, JD 518-474-2011
Executive Deputy Commissioner:
　Sally Dreslin, MS, RN 518-474-2011
Deputy Commissioner, Administration:
　Michael J. Nazarko 518-474-8565

Public Affairs
Director:
　Vacant 518-474-7354 x1
Deputy Director:
　Marci Natale. .518-474-7354 x1

Center for Environmental Health
547 River St, Troy, NY 12180
Director:
　Dr. Nathan Garber. 518-402-7500

Division of Environmental Health Assessment
Director:
　Kevin Gleason 518-402-7511

Division of Environmental Health Investigation
Director:
　Vacant. 518-402-7510

Division of Environmental Health Protection
Director:
　Michael Cambridge 518-402-7500

Wadsworth Center
Director:
　Jill Taylor, PhD 518-474-3157/fax: 518-474-3439
Deputy Director:
　Victoria Derbyshire. 518-474-7592
Associate Director, Administration:
　Carlene Van Patten 518-474-7592
Associate Director, Research & Technology:
　Erasmus Schneider 518-473-4856
Associate Director, Medical Affairs:
　Elizabeth Mahoney 518-474-7592

Environmental Health Sciences
Director:
　Ken Aldous 518-474-7161/fax: 518-473-2895
Deputy Director:
　Patrick Parsons 518-474-7161

Hudson River Valley Greenway
625 Broadway
4th Floor
Albany, NY 12207
518-473-3835 Fax: 518-473-4518
e-mail: hrvg@hudsongreenway.ny.gov
Web site: www.hudsongreenway.ny.gov

Offices and agencies generally appear in alphabetical order, except when specific order is requested by listee.

Greenway Conservancy for the Hudson River Valley
Acting Chair:
Sara Griffen...................................518-473-3835
Executive Director (Acting):
Mark Castiglione...............................518-473-3835

Hudson River Valley Greenway Communities Council
Board Chair:
Barnabas McHenry...............................518-473-3835
Executive Director (Acting):
Mark Castiglione...............................518-473-3835

Law Department
120 Broadway
New York, NY 10271-0332
212-416-8000 or 800-771-7755
Web site: www.ag.ny.gov

State Capitol
Albany, NY 12224-0341
518-474-7330
Fax: 518-473-9909

Attorney General:
Eric T Schneiderman ....212-416-8050 or 518-474-7330
Chief of Staff:
Micah Lasher 212-416-8050
Press Secretary:
Fernando Aquino...................212-416-8060/fax: 212-416-6005
Bureau Chief, Litigation Bureau:
Lisa Dell ....518-776-2300 or 212-416-8610

Social Justice
Executive Deputy Attorney General:
Alvin L Braggs, Jr.................212-416-8450/fax: 212-416-8942

Environmental Protection Bureau
Bureau Chief:
Lisa Burianek....................518-776-2400 or 212-416-8446
fax: 518-416-6007

Parks, Recreation & Historic Preservation, NYS Office of
Empire State Plaza, Bldg 1
625 Broadway, 12207
Albany, NY 12238
518-486-0456 Fax: 518-486-2924
Web site: www.nysparks.com

Commissioner:
Rose Harvey 518-474-0443
Executive Deputy Commissioner:
Andrew Beers 518-474-0020
Deputy Commissioner, Finance & Administration:
Melinda Scott 518-474-0414
Deputy Commissioner, Natural Resources:
Tom Alworth....................................518-474-0414
Counsel:
Patrick Bradford 518-474-0414
Public Information Officer:
Randy Simmons 518-486-1868
Chief Park Police/Director, Law Enforcement:
Richard O'Donnell 518-474-4029/fax: 518-408-1032

Field Services
Peebles Island, PO Box 189, Waterford, NY 12118
Deputy Commissioner:
Ruth Pierpont 518-237-8643

Historic Sites Bureau
Peebles Island, Waterford, NY 12188

Acting Director:
Mark Peckham 518-237-8643

Marine & Recreational Vehicles
Director:
Brian Kempf 518-474-0445/fax: 518-408-1030

Environmental Management
Director:
Pamela Otis 518-474-0409/fax: 518-474-7013

State Comptroller, Office of the
110 State St, 15th Fl
Albany, NY 12236-0001
518-474-4044 Fax: 518-473-3004
Web site: www.osc.state.ny.us

633 Third Ave, 31st Fl
New York, NY 10017-6754
212-681-4491
Fax: 212-681-4468

State Comptroller:
Thomas DiNapoli...................518-474-4040 or 212-681-4469

Executive Office
First Deputy Comptroller:
Pete Grannis ....518-474-2909 or 212-681-4469
Chief of Staff:
Shawn Thompson 518-474-4044
General Counsel:
Luke Bierman 518-474-3444

Oil Spill Fund Office
Executive Director:
David J Hasso 518-474-6657/fax: 518-474-9979

State Department
123 William St
New York, NY 10038
212-417-5801 Fax: 212-417-5805
Web site: www.dos.ny.gov

One Commerce Plaza
99 Washington Avenue
Albany, NY 12231
518-474-0050
Fax: 518-474-4765

Secretary of State:
Cesar A Perales..................................518-474-0050
First Deputy Secretary of State:
Daniel Shapiro 518-474-4750
Assistant Secretary of State, Communications:
Vacant 518-474-4752/fax: 518-474-4597
e-mail: info@dos.state.ny.us
Deputy Secretary of State, Public Affairs:
Vacant 212-417-5800
Counsel:
Ruth Colon........................518-474-6740/fax: 518-473-9211

Local Government & Community Services
Deputy Secretary of State:
Dierdre Scozzafava...............................518-473-3355

Coastal Resources & Waterfront Revitalization Division
Director:
George Stafford..................518-474-6000/fax: 518-473-2464
e-mail: coastal@dos.state.ny.us

Offices and agencies generally appear in alphabetical order, except when specific order is requested by listee.

Community Services Division
Director:
  Veronica Cruz 518-474-5741/fax: 518-486-4663
  e-mail: commserv@dos.state.ny.us

CORPORATIONS, AUTHORITIES AND COMMISSIONS

Adirondack Park Agency
1133 NYS Route 86
PO Box 99
Ray Brook, NY 12977
518-891-4050 Fax: 518-891-3938
Web site: www.apa.ny.gov

Chair:
  Leilani Ulrich 518-891-4050
Executive Director:
  Terry Martino 518-891-4050
Counsel:
  James Townsend 518-891-4050
Public Relations:
  Keith McKeever 518-891-4050
  e-mail: keith.mckeever@apa.ny.gov

Atlantic States Marine Fisheries Commission
1050 N Highland Street
Ste 200 A-N
Arlington, VA 22201
703-842-0740 Fax: 703-842-0741
e-mail: info@asmfc.org
Web site: www.asmfc.org

Chair, NC:
  Dr. Louis Daniel III
Administrative Commissioner, New York:
  James Gilmore 516-444-0433
Governor's Appointee, New York:
  Emerson C Hasbrouck, Jr 631-928-1524
Executive Director:
  Robert E. Beal 703-842-0740
  e-mail: rbeal@asmfc.org
Director Communications:
  Tina Berger 703-842-0740
  e-mail: tberger@asmfc.org

Central Pine Barrens Joint Planning & Policy Commission
624 Old Riverhead Road
Westhampton Beach, NY 11978
631-288-1079 Fax: 631-228-1367
e-mail: info@pb.state.ny.us
Web site: www.pb.state.ny.us

Chair & Governor's Appointee & Region 1 Director DEC:
  Peter A Scully 631-288-1079
Member & Suffolk County Executive:
  Steve Bellone 631-288-1079
Member & Brookhaven Town Supervisor:
  Edward P. Romaine 631-288-1079
Member & Riverhead Town Supervisor:
  Sean M Walter 631-288-1079
Member & Southampton Town Supervisor:
  Anna E Throne-Holst 631-288-1079

Delaware River Basin Commission
25 State Police Dr
PO Box 7360
West Trenton, NJ 08628-0360

609-883-9500 Fax: 609-883-9522
Web site: www.state.nj.us/drbc

New York Member/Chair:
  Andrew M Cuomo 518-474-8390
Executive Director:
  Steve Tambini 609-883-9500 x200
  e-mail: steve.tambini@drbc.state.nj.us
Deputy Executive Director:
  Vacant 609-883-9500 x208
Commission Secretary & Assistant General Counsel:
  Pamela Bush 609-883-9500 x203
  e-mail: pamela.bush@drbc.state.nj.us
General Counsel:
  Kenneth J Warren 484-383-4834
  e-mail: kwarren@warrenenvcounsel.com
Communications Manager:
  Clarke Rupert 609-883-9500 x260
  e-mail: clarke.rupert@drbc.state.nj.us

Great Lakes Commission
2805 S Industrial Hwy
Ste 100
Ann Arbor, MI 48104-6791
734-971-9135 Fax: 734-971-9150
e-mail: teder@glc.org
Web site: www.glc.org

Chairman:
  Kelvin Burch 814-332-6816
  e-mail: keburch@state.pa.us
Vice Chair:
  Jon W Allan 517-284-5035
  e-mail: allanj@michigan.gov
New York State Commissioner:
  Joseph Martens 518-402-8540
  e-mail: joseph.martens@dec.ny.gov
Executive Director:
  Tim A Eder 734-971-9135
  e-mail: teder@glc.org
Deputy Director:
  Thomas R Crane 734-971-9135
  e-mail: tcrane@glc.org
CIO:
  Stephen J Cole 734-971-9135
  e-mail: scole@glc.org
Program Director:
  Victoria Pebbles 734-971-9135
  e-mail: vpebbles@glc.org
Communications Director:
  Christine Manninen 734-971-9135
  e-mail: manninen@glc.org
Policy Director:
  Matthew Doss 734-971-9135
  e-mail: mdoss@glc.org

Hudson River-Black River Regulating District
Hudson River Area Office
350 Northern Blvd, Ste 304
Albany, NY 12204
518-465-3491 Fax: 518-432-2485
e-mail: hrao@hrbrrd.com
Web site: www.hrbrrd.com

Chair:
  Mark M Finkle 518-465-3491
Executive Director:
  Michael A Clark 518-465-3491

Offices and agencies generally appear in alphabetical order, except when specific order is requested by listee.

Policy Areas

Chief Engineer:
  Robert S Foltan 518-465-3491
Chief Fiscal Officer:
  Robert J Ferrara. 518-465-3491
General Counsel:
  Robert P Leslie 518-465-3491

Interstate Environmental Commission

247 West 30th Street
Ste 6B
New York, NY 10001
212-967-1414 Fax: 212-967-1430
e-mail: iecmail@iec-nynjct.org
Web site: www.iec-nynjct.org

Chair (CT):
  Patricia Sesto. 212-967-1414
Vice Chair (NY):
  Judith L Baron 212-967-1414
Vice Chair (NJ):
  John M Scagnelli 212-967-1414
Associate Director:
  Bill Shadel. 212-967-1414

Interstate Oil & Gas Compact Commission

PO Box 53127
900 NE 23rd St
Oklahoma City, OK 73152-3127
405-525-3556 Fax: 405-525-3592
e-mail: iogcc@iogcc.state.ok.us
Web site: www.iogcc.ok.gov

Chair:
  Governor Gary R Herbert (UT) 405-525-3556
Vice Chair:
  Hal Fitch 405-525-3556
Executive Director:
  Mike Smith 405-525-3556
New York State Official Representative:
  Bradley J Field 518-402-8076
Communications Manager:
  Carol Booth. 405-525-3556

Lake George Park Commission

75 Fort George Rd
PO Box 749
Lake George, NY 12845
518-668-9347 Fax: 518-668-5001
e-mail: info@lgpc.state.ny.us
Web site: www.lgpc.state.ny.us

Chair:
  Bruce E Young 518-668-9347
Executive Director:
  David Wick. 518-668-9347
  e-mail: dave@lgpc.state.ny.us
Counsel:
  Eileen Haynes 518-668-9347
Director of Law Enforcement:
  Lt William Bramlage 518-668-9347
  e-mail: ben@lgps.state.ny.us
Director, Operations:
  Keith Fish 518-668-9347
  e-mail: opdir@lgpc.state.ny.us

New England Interstate Water Pollution Control Commission

Wannalacit Mills
650 Suffolk Street
Suite 410
Lowell, MA 01854
978-323-7929 Fax: 978-323-7919
e-mail: mail@neiwpcc.org
Web site: www.neiwpcc.org

Chair:
  Yvonne Bolton 978-323-7929
Vice Chair (MA):
  Bethany Card 978-323-7929
Commissioner, New York State:
  Joseph J Martens. 518-485-8940
Executive Director:
  Ronald F Poltak 978-323-7929
  e-mail: rpoltak@neiwpcc.org
Deputy Director:
  Susan Sullivan. 978-323-7929
  e-mail: ssullivan@neiwpcc.org

New York State Energy Research & Development Authority

17 Columbia Circle
Albany, NY 12203-6399
518-862-1090 Fax: 518-862-1091
Web site: www.nyserda.ny.gov

Chairman:
  Richard L Kauffman 518-862-1090
President & CEO:
  John B Rhodes. 518-862-1090 x3278
General Counsel:
  Hal Brodie 518-862-1090 x3280
  e-mail: hb1@nyserda.ny.gov
Program Manager, Economic Development & Community Outreach:
  Kelly Tyler. . . . . .716-842-1522 x. 3005
  e-mail: kat@nyserda.ny.gov
Director, Communications:
  Kate Muller. 518-862-1090 x3582/fax: 518-862-1091
  e-mail: ktm@nyserda.ny.gov

New York State Environmental Facilities Corp

625 Broadway
Albany, NY 12207-2997
518-402-6924 or 800-882-9721 Fax: 518-486-9323
e-mail: press@efc.ny.gov
Web site: www.nysefc.org

President/CEO:
  Matthew J Driscoll 518-402-6951
Legal Division/General Counsel:
  James R Levine. 518-402-6969
Director, Engineering & Program Management:
  Timothy P Burns. 518-402-7396
Director, Technical Advisory Services:
  Vacant 518-402-7461
Director, PIO:
  Jon Sorensen 518-402-6924
  e-mail: press@efc.ny.gov; jon.sorensen@efc.ny.gov
Controller & Director, Corporate Operations:
  Michael Malinoski 518-486-9267

Offices and agencies generally appear in alphabetical order, except when specific order is requested by listee.

New York State Tug Hill Commission

Dulles State Office Bldg
317 Washington St
Watertown, NY 13601
315-785-2380 Fax: 315-785-2574
e-mail: tughill@tughill.org
Web site: www.tughill.org

Chair:
    Jan Bogdanowicz 315-785-2380
Executive Director:
    John K Bartow, Jr...............................315-785-2570
    e-mail: john@tughill.org

Northeastern Forest Fire Protection Commission

21 Parmenter Terrace
PO Box 6192
China Village, ME 04926
207-968-3782 Fax: 207-968-3782
e-mail: info@nffpc.org
Web site: www.nffpc.org

Chair of Commissioners:
    Se. Elizabeth O. Little..........................518-455-2811
    e-mail: little@senate.state.ny.us
Executive Director/Center Manager:
    Thomas G Parent...............................207-968-3782
    e-mail: necompact@fairpoint.net
Operations Committee, Chair:
    Luc Dugas.....................................418-871-3341
    e-mail: ldugas@sopfeu.qc.ca
New York State Fire Prevention:
    David Russell 518-483-2836
    e-mail: dgrussel@gw.dec.state.ny.us

Ohio River Valley Water Sanitation Commission

5735 Kellogg Ave
Cincinnati, OH 45230
513-231-7719 Fax: 513-231-7761
e-mail: info@orsanco.org
Web site: www.orsanco.org

New York State Commissioner:
    Douglas E Conroe................................513-231-7719
New York State Commissioner:
    Michael P Wilson 513-231-7719
New York State Commissioner:
    Joseph J Martens...............................518-457-3446
Executive Director:
    Richard Harrison ....513-231-7719 ext 105
    e-mail: rharrison@orsanco.org
Source Water Protection/Emergency Response:
    Jerry Schulte..............................513-231-7719 ext 104
    e-mail: jschulte@orsanco.org
Communications Coordinator:
    Lisa Cochran..............................513-231-7719 ext 102
    e-mail: lcochran@orsanco.org

NEW YORK STATE LEGISLATURE

*See Legislative Branch in Section 1 for additional Standing Commit-
tee and Subcommittee information.*

Assembly Standing Committees

Environmental Conservation

Chair:
    Steven Englebright (D).............................518-455-4804
Ranking Minority Member:
    Dan Stec (R) 518-455-5565

Senate Standing Committees

Environmental Conservation

Chair:
    Thomas O'Mara (R)...............................518-455-2091
Ranking Minority Member:
    Brad Hoylman (D) 518-455-2451

Senate/Assembly Legislative Commissions

Rural Resources, Legislative Commission on

Senate Chair:
    Catharine Young (R)..............................518-455-3563
Assembly Vice Chair:
    Frank Skartados (D) 518-455-5762
Counsel:
    Barbara McRedmond 518-455-2069

U.S. GOVERNMENT

EXECUTIVE DEPARTMENTS AND RELATED AGENCIES

US Commerce Department

Web site: www.doc.gov

National Oceanic & Atmospheric Administration

National Marine Fisheries Svc, Northeast Region Headquarters
55 Great Republic Drive, Gloucester, MA 01930
978-281-9300
Web site: www.nero.noaa.gov/nero/
John K. Bullard

National Weather Service, Eastern Region
630 Johnson Ave, Ste 202, Bohemia, NY 11716
Web site: www.nws.noaa.gov
Director:
    Dean Gulezian...................631-244-0100/fax: 631-244-0109
    e-mail: dean.gulezian@noaa.gov
Deputy Director:
    Mickey J Brown 631-244-0102
Public Affairs Specialist:
    Marcie Katcher 631-244-0149/fax: 631-244-0167
Chief, Meteorological Services Division:
    John Guiney 631-244-1021
    e-mail: john.guiney@noaa.gov

US Defense Department

e-mail: www.defenselink.mil

Army Corps of Engineers

Web site: www.usace.army.mil

Great Lakes & Ohio River Division (Western NYS)
550 Main St, PO Box 10524, Cincinnati, OH 45202-3222
Commander:
    BG Margaret W. Burcham........................513-684-3010
    Buffalo District Office ....fax: 716-879-4195
      1776 Niagara St, Buffalo, NY 14207
      716-879-4200 or 800-833-6390 ext. 3 Fax: 716-879-4195
      Deputy Commander:
      Michael A. Busby

Policy Areas

Offices and agencies generally appear in alphabetical order, except when specific order is requested by listee.

District Commander:
  LTC Owen J. Beaudoin

North Atlantic Division
302 General Lee Ave, Brooklyn, NY 11252
Commanding General:
  BG Kent D. Saure
Colonel:
  Christopher J. Larsen 718-765-7001
Senior Civilian:
  David I. Leach
Acting Director of Business:
  Vacant
Public Affairs Officer:
  David J Lipsky 718-765-7018/fax: 718-765-7173
Program Directorate
  Director of Programs:
    Lloyd Caldwell 718-765-7129
  Supervisory Civil Engineer, Civil Works Integration Div:
    Larry Petrosino 718-765-7060
  Supervisory Civil Engineer, Military Integration Div:
    Bob Mawhinney 718-765-7120
  Supervisory Civil Engineer, Program Support Div:
    Joseph Vietri 718-765-7080
Regional Business Directorate
  Regional Business Director:
    Robert J. Bauer
  Director/Financial Manager:
    Irma Nanez 718-765-7033
  Supervisory Program Manager, Business Mgmt Div:
    Larry Mazzola 718-765-7127
  Supervisory Civil Engineer, Business Technical Div:
    John Bianco 718-765-7086

US Department of Agriculture

Forest Service-Northeastern Area State & Private Forestry
11 Campus Blvd, Newtown Square, PA 19073
Area Director:
  Tony L. Ferguson 610-557-4103
Deputy Director:
  James S. Barresi 610-557-4103
Asst Director, Forest Health & Economics:
  Mark Buccowich 610-557-4029
Asst Director, Fire Management:
  Dan Zimmerman 610-557-4145
Asst Director, WERC:
  Steve Milouskas
Deputy Director, WERC:
  Edward T. Cesa 304-487-1510 x.233

Forest Service-Northern Research Station
11 Campus Blvd, Ste 200, Newton Square, PA 19073
Director:
  Michael T Rains 610-557-4017
Deputy Director:
  Robin Morgan 610-557-4118

Forest Service-Region 9
Web site: www.fs.fed.us

Green Mountain & Finger Lakes . . . . fax: 802-747-6766
231 N Main St, Rutland, VT 05701
802-747-6700 Fax: 802-747-6766
  Finger Lakes National Forest . . . . fax: 607-546-4474
    5218 State Route 414, Hector, NY 14841
    District Ranger:
      Jodie Vanselow

Natural Resources Conservation Service . . . . fax: 315-477-6550
441 S Salina St, Suite 354, Syracuse, NY 13202-2450

Fax: 315-477-6550
Web site: www.ny.nrcs.usda.gov
State Conservationist:
  Donald Pettit

US Department of Homeland Security (DHS)

National Urban Security Technology Laboratory
201 Varick St, 5th Fl, New York, NY 10014-7447
Director:
  Dr. Adam Hutter
  e-mail: mitchell.erickson@dhs.gov

Administration
Director:
  Richard Larsen 212-620-3524/fax: 212-620-3600
  e-mail: richard.larsen@dhs.gov

Systems Division
Director:
  Lawrence Ruth 212-620-3609/fax: 212-620-3600
  e-mail: lawrence.ruth@dhs.gov

Testbeds Division
Director:
  Adam Hutter 212-620-3619/fax: 212-620-3651
  e-mail: adam.hutter@dhs.gov

US Department of the Interior
e-mail: webteam@ios.doi.gov
Web site: www.doi.gov

Bureau of Land Management
  e-mail: woinfo@blm.gov
  Web site: www.blm.gov

Eastern States Office (includes New York State) . . . . fax: 703-440-1701
7450 Boston Blvd, Springfield, VA 22153
703-440-1600 Fax: 703-440-1701
State Director:
  Dr. John Lyon

Fish & Wildlife Service . . . . .fax: 413-253-8303
413-253-8200 Fax: 413-253-8303
e-mail: northeast@fws.gov
Web site: www.fws.gov

Northeast Region (includes New York State) . . . . . . .fax: 413-253-8308
300 Westgate Center Dr, Hadley, MA 01035-9589
Regional Director:
  Wendi Weber

Geological Survey
  Web site: ny.usgs.gov

Water Resources Division - New York State District Office
425 Jordan Rd, Troy, NY 12180-8349
District Chief:
  David Russ 703-648-6660
  Coram Sub-District Office .fax: 631-736-4283
    2045 Rte 112, Bldg 4, Coram, NY 11727
    Sub-District Chief:
      Steve Terracciano 631-736-0783
  Ithaca Sub-District Office .fax: 607-266-0521
    30 Brown Rd, Ithaca, NY 14850-1573
    Sub-District Chief:
      Edward Bugliosi 607-266-0217 x3005

National Park Service-Northeast Region
200 Chestnut St, US Custom House, Philadelphia, PA 19106
  Web site: www.nps.gov
Northeast Regional Director:
  Dennis R. Reidenbach 215-597-7013/fax: 215-597-0815

Offices and agencies generally appear in alphabetical order, except when specific order is requested by listee.

Fire Island National Seashore . . . . fax: 631-289-4898
120 Laurel St, Patchogue, NY 11772-3596
631-687-4750 Fax: 631-289-4898
Superintendent:
  Chris Soller

Office of the Secretary, Environmental Policy & Compliance

Northeast Region (includes New York State)
408 Atlantic Ave, Rm 142, Boston, MA 02210-3334
Regional Environmental Officer:
  Andrew L Raddant 617-223-8565/fax: 617-223-8569

Office of the Solicitor

Northeast Region (includes New York State) . . . . fax: 617-527-6848
One Gateway Center, Ste 612, Newton, MA 02458-2881
Regional Solicitor:
  Anthony R Conte 617-527-3400
Deputy Regional Solicitor:
  James E Epstein 617-527-3400
Attorney Advisor:
  Martha F Ansty 802-872-0629 x17
Attorney Advisor:
  Mark D Barash 617-527-3400
Attorney Advisor:
  Marcia F Gittes 617-527-3400
Attorney Advisor:
  J Robin Lepore 617-527-3400
Attorney Advisor:
  Katherine Buttolph 617-527-3400
Attorney Advisor:
  David Rothstein 617-527-3400
Attorney Advisor:
  Katharine M Costenbader 617-527-3400
Attorney Advisor:
  Andrew Tittler 617-527-3400

US Environmental Protection Agency
Web site: www.epa.gov

Region 2 - New York . . . . fax: 212-637-3526
290 Broadway, New York, NY 10007-1866
212-637-3660 Fax: 212-637-3526
Regional Administrator:
  Judith A. Enck. 212-637-5000
Acting Deputy Regional Administrator:
  George Pavlov

Caribbean Environmental Protection Division (CEPD)
Director:
  Jose Font

Division of Enforcement & Compliance Assistance (DECA)
Director:
  Dore LaPosta 212-637-4031

Division of Environmental Planning & Protection (DEPP)
Director:
  Patricia Pechko. 212-637-3796

Division of Environmental Science & Assessment (DESA)
2890 Woodbridge Ave, Edison, NJ 08837-3679
Contact:
  Corrine Spinks 732-632-4764
  e-mail: spinks@corrine@epa.gov

Emergency & Remedial Response Division (ERRD)
Director:
  Walter Mugdan

Inspector General, Office of (OIG)
Divisional Inspector General, Investigation:
  Paul Zammit 212-637-3042/fax: 212-637-3071
  e-mail: zammit.paul@epa.gov

OCEFT/Criminal Investigations Division
Special-Agent-In-Charge:
  William V Lometti 212-637-3610
  e-mail: lometti.william@epa.gov

Policy & Management, Office of
Asst Regional Administrator for Policy & Management:
  Donna Vizian 212-637-3581

Public Affairs Division (PAD)
Director:
  Bonnie Bellow. 212-637-3660/fax: 212-637-5046
  e-mail: bellow.bonnie@epa.gov

Regional Counsel, Office of (ORC)
Deputy Regional Counsel:
  Eric Schaaf 212-637-3107
  e-mail: schaaf.eric@epa.gov

U.S. CONGRESS

See U.S. Congress Chapter for additional Standing Committee and Subcommittee information.

House of Representatives Standing Committees

Agriculture
Chair:
  Frank D. Lucas (R-OK) 202-225-5565
Ranking Member:
  Collin C. Peterson (D-MN). 202-225-2165

Subcommittees
Department Operations, Oversight, Nutrition & Forestry
  Chair:
    Steve King (R-IA) 202-225-4426
  Ranking Member:
    Marcia L. Fudge (D-OH). 202-225-7032
General Farm Commodities & Risk Management
  Chair:
    K. Michael Conway (R-TX) 202-225-3605
  Ranking Member:
    David Scott (D-GA). 202-225-2939
Horticulture and Organic Agriculture
  Chair:
    Austin Scott (R-GA) 202-225-6531
  Ranking Member:
    Kurt Schrader (D-OR) 202-225-5711
Livestock, Rural Development & Credit
  Chair:
    Eric A. Crawford (R-AZ) 202-225-4076
  Ranking Member:
    Jim Costa (D-CA) 202-225-3341

Energy & Commerce
Chair:
  Fred Upton (R-MI) 202-225-3761
Vice Chair:
  Marsha Blackburn (D-TN) 202-225-2811
New York Delegate:
  Eliot L Engel (D) 202-225-2464
New York Delegate:
  Paul Tonko (D) 202-225-5076

Offices and agencies generally appear in alphabetical order, except when specific order is requested by listee.

Subcommittees
Environment & the Economy
  Chair:
    John Shimkus (R-IL) 202-225-5271
  Ranking Member:
    Paul Tonko (D-NY) 202-225-5076

Natural Resources
Chair:
  Doc Hastings (R-WA) 202-225-5816
Ranking Member:
  Edward J. Markey (D-MA) 202-225-2836

Science & Technology
Chair:
  Lamar Smith (R-TX) 202-225-4236
Ranking Member:
  Eddie Bernice Johnson (D-TX) 202-225-8885
New York Delegate:
  Dan Maffei 202-225-3701

Subcommittee
Environment
  Chair:
    Chris Stewart (R-UT) 202-225-9730
  Ranking Member:
    Suzanne Bonamici (D-OR) 202-225-0855

Transportation & Infrastructure
Chair:
  Bill Shuster (R-PA) 202-225-2431
Ranking Member:
  Nick J. Rahall II (D-WV) 202-225-3452
New York Delegate:
  Timothy Bishop (D) 202-225-3826
New York Delegate:
  Richard L. Hanna (R) 202-225-3665
New York Delegate:
  Sean Patrick Maloney (D) 202-225-5441
New York Delegate:
  Jerrold Nadler (D) 202-225-5635

Subcommittee
Water Resources & Environment
  Chair:
    Bob Gibbs (R-OH) 202-225-6265
  Ranking Member:
    Timothy H. Bishop (D-NY) 202-225-3826
  New York Delegate:
    Sean Patrick Maloney (D) 202-225-5441
  New York Delegate:
    Richard L. Hannon (R) 202-225-3665

Senate Standing Committees

Agriculture, Nutrition & Forestry
Chair:
  Debbie Stabenow (D-MI) 202-224-4822
Ranking Member:
  Thad Cochran (R-MI) 202-224-5054

Subcommittee
Conservation, Forestry & Natural Resources
  Chair:
    Heidi Heitkamp (D-ND) 202-224-2043
  Ranking Minority Member:
    Mike Johanns (R-NE) 202-224-4224

Commerce, Science & Transportation
Chair:
  Jay Rockefeller (D-WV) 202-224-6472
Vice Chair:
  John Thune (R-SD) 202-224-2321

Subcommittee
Oceans, Atmosphere, Fisheries and Coast Guard
  Chair:
    Mark Begich (D-AK) 202-224-3004
  Ranking Minority Member:
    Marco Rubio (R-FL) 202-224-3041

Energy & Natural Resources
Chair:
  Ron Wyden (R-OR) 202-224-5244
Ranking Member:
  Lisa Murkowski (R-AK) 202-224-6665

Environment & Public Works
Chair:
  Barbara Boxer (D-CA) 202-224-8832
Ranking Member:
  David Vitter (R-LA) 202-224-4623
New York Delegate:
  Kirsten Gillibrand (D) 202-224-4451

PRIVATE SECTOR

Adirondack Council Inc (The)
103 Hand Ave, Ste 3, Box D-2, Elizabethtown, NY 12932
518-873-2240 Fax: 518-873-6675
e-mail: info@adirondackcouncil.org
Web site: www.adirondackcouncil.org
The Council's mission is to ensure the ecological integrity and wild character of the Adirondack Park.
Brian L Houseal, Executive Director

American Farmland Trust, New York Office
112 Spring Street, Suite 207, Saratoga Springs, NY 12866
518-581-0078 Fax: 518-581-0079
e-mail: newyork@farmland.org
Web site: www.farmland.org/newyork
Advocacy & education to protect farmland & promote environmentally sound farming practices
Tammey Holtby, Operations Coordinator

American Museum of Natural History
Central Park West at 79th St, New York, NY 10024-5192
212-769-5100 Fax: 212-769-5018
e-mail: info@amnh.org
Web site: www.amnh.org
Education, exhibition & scientific research
Ellen V Futter, President

Audubon New York
200 Trillium Lane, Albany, NY 12203
518-869-9731 Fax: 518-869-0737
e-mail: nasny@audubon.org
Web site: ny.audubon.org
Protecting birds, other wildlife & their habitats
Albert E Caccese, Executive Director

Audubon Society of NYS Inc (The) / Audubon International
Hollyhock Hollow Sanctuary, 46 Rarick Rd, Selkirk, NY 12158
518-767-9051 x20 Fax: 518-767-0069
e-mail: hjack@auduboninternational.org
Web site: www.auduboninternational.org
Wildlife & water conservation; environmental education; sustainable land management
Howard A Jack, Vice President & Chief Operating Officer

Offices and agencies generally appear in alphabetical order, except when specific order is requested by listee.

Brooklyn Botanic Garden
1000 Washington Ave, Brooklyn, NY 11225-1099
718-623-7200 Fax: 718-857-2430
Web site: www.bbg.org
Comprehensive study of plant biodiversity in metropolitan New York; home gardener's resource center
Scot Medbury, President & CEO

Business Council of New York State Inc
152 Washington Ave, Albany, NY 12210
518-465-7511 x205 Fax: 518-465-4389
e-mail: ken.pokalsky@bcnys.org
Web site: www.bcnys.org
Taxation, economic development, workers' compensation
Kenneth J Pokalsky, Senior Director, Government Affairs

CWM Chemical Services LLC
1550 Balmer Rd, PO Box 200, Model City, NY 14107
716-754-8231 Fax: 716-754-0211
e-mail: cwmmdc@wm.com
Web site: www.cwmlandfill.com
Hazardous waste treatment, storage & disposal
Michael Mahar, District Manager

Catskill Center for Conservation & Development, The
PO Box 504, Route 28, Arkville, NY 12406-0504
845-586-2611 Fax: 845-586-3044
e-mail: cccd@catskillcenter.org
Web site: www.catskillcenter.org
Advocacy for environmental & economic health of the Catskill Mountain region
Alan White, Executive Director

Center for Environmental Information Inc
55 St Paul St, Rochester, NY 14604-1314
585-262-2870 Fax: 585-262-4156
e-mail: cei@ceinfo.org
Web site: www.ceinfo.org
Public information & education on environmental topics

Citizens' Environmental Coalition
33 Central Avenue, 3rd Floor, Albany, NY 12210
518-462-5527 Fax: 518-465-8349
e-mail: cectoxic@igc.org
Web site: www.cectoxic.org
Organizing & assistance for communities concerned about toxic waste, air & water contamination & pollution prevention
Barbara Warren, Executive Director

Colgate University, Department of Geology
13 Oak Dr, Hamilton, NY 13346
315-228-7201 Fax: 315-228-7187
e-mail: aleventer@colgate.edu
Web site: departments.colgate.edu/geology
Metamorphic and igneous petrology, Isotope geochemistry
William Peck, Chair, Department of Geology

Columbia University, MPA in Environmental Science & Policy
420 W 118th St, Rm 1314, New York, NY 10027
212-854-4445 or 212-854-3142 Fax: 212-864-4847
e-mail: sc32@columbia.edu
Web site: www.columbia.edu/~sc32
Urban & environmental policy; public management
Steven Cohen, Director

Commodore Applied Technologies Inc
150 East 58th St, Ste 3238, New York, NY 10155-0001
212-308-5800 Fax: 212-753-0731
e-mail: jdeangelis@commodore.com
Web site: www.commodore.com
Develops technologies for destroying hazardous waste, PCBs, dioxins, mixed waste & chemical weapons

James DeAngelis, Senior Vice President/Chief Financial & Administration Officer

Cornell Cooperative Extension, Environment & Natural Resources Initiative
108 Fernow Hall, Cornell University, Ithaca, NY 14853
607-255-2115 Fax: 607-255-2815
e-mail: cce-nat-res@cornell.edu
Web site: www.dnr.cornell.edu/extension
Working to improve the quality & sustainability of human environments & natural resources
Diana Bryant, Department Extension Assistant

Cornell Cooperative Extension, NY Sea Grant
Cornell University, 112 Rice Hall, Ithaca, NY 14853-5601
607-255-2832 Fax: 607-255-2812
e-mail: drb17@cornell.edu
Web site: www.nyseagrant.org
Research, education & training related to ocean, coastal & Great Lakes resources
Dale Baker, Program Leader

Cornell University Center for the Environment
200 Rice Hall, Ithaca, NY 14853-5601
607-255-7535 Fax: 215-701-1844
Web site: environment.cornell.edu
Environmental research
Mark B Bain, Director

Council on the Environment of NYC (The)
51 Chambers St, Rm 228, New York, NY 10007
212-788-7900 Fax: 212-788-7913
e-mail: info@grownyc.org
Web site: www.grownyc.org
Promotes environmental awareness & develops solutions to environmental problems
Marcel Van Doyen, Executive Director

Dakota Software Corporation
95 Allens Creek Rd, #2-302, Rochester, NY 14618
585-244-3300 Fax: 585-244-3301
e-mail: info@dakotasoft.com
Web site: www.dakotasoft.com
Environmental health & safety regulatory software systems design
Arlene Davidson, Marketing Director

Dionondehowa Wildlife Sanctuary & School - Not For Profit
148 Stanton Rd, Shushan, NY 12873
518-854-7764 Fax: 518-854-3648
e-mail: dionondehowa@yahoo.com
Web site: www.dionondehowa.org
Conservation & land use issues, conscious living, nature studies & healing & expressive arts
Bonnie Hoag, Co-Founder & Director

ENSR
3495 Winton Place, Suite E295, Rochester, NY 14623
585-381-2210 Fax: 585-381-5392
e-mail: pnielsen@ensr.aecom.com; askensr@ensr.aecom.com
Web site: www.ensr.aecom.com
Environmental consulting, engineering, remediation & related services
Peter Nielsen, Senior Program Manager

Ecology & Environment Inc
368 Pleasant View Dr, Lancaster, NY 14086-1397
716-684-8060 Fax: 716-684-0844
e-mail: dcastle@ene.com
Web site: www.ene.com
Environmental scientific & engineering consulting
Gerhard J Neumaier, President

Offices and agencies generally appear in alphabetical order, except when specific order is requested by listee.

Empire State Forest Products Association
47 Van Alstyne Drive, Rensselaer, NY 12144
518-463-1297 x2 Fax: 518-426-9502
e-mail: mburns@esfpa.org
Web site: www.esfpa.org
Michael J. Burns, Deputy Director

Environmental Advocates of New York
353 Hamilton St, Albany, NY 12210
518-462-5526 x238 Fax: 518-427-0381
e-mail: info@eany.org
Web site: www.eany.org
New York's government watchdog, in the state capital holding lawmakers and agencies' accountable for enacting and enforcing laws that protect natural resources and safeguard public health.
Erica Ringewald, Communications Director

Environmental Business Association of NYS Inc
991 Broadway, Suite 207, Albany, NY 12204
518-432-6400 x227 Fax: 518-432-1383
e-mail: suzanne@eba-nys.org
Web site: www.eba-nys.org
Supports businesses that provide products & services to prevent, monitor, control or remediate pollution or generate, conserve and/or recycle energy & resources
Suzanne Maloney, Executive Director

Environmental Defense
257 Park Ave South, 17th Fl, New York, NY 10010
212-505-2100 Fax: 212-505-2375
e-mail: adarrell@environmentaldefense.org
Web site: www.environmentaldefense.org
Andrew Darrell, NY Regional Director

Ethan C Eldon Associates Inc
1350 Broadway, New York, NY 10018
212-967-5400 Fax: 212-967-2747
e-mail: info@ethanceldon.com
Web site: www.ethanceldon.com
Environmental, EIS, traffic, hazardous & solid waste consulting
Ethan C Eldon, President

Great Lakes United
Buffalo State College, Cassety Hall, 1300 Elmwood Ave, Buffalo, NY 14222
716-886-0142 Fax: 716-204-9521
e-mail: glu@glu.org
Web site: www.glu.org
Great Lakes & St Lawrence River issues
Derrick Stack, Executive Director

GreenThumb
49 Chambers Street, Room 1020, New York, NY 10007
212-788-8070 Fax: 212-788-8052
e-mail: edie@greenthumbnyc.org
Web site: www.greenthumbnyc.org
Development & preservation of community gardens; reclamation of urban land for green space
Edie Stone, Director

Greene County Soil & Water Conservation District
907 County Office Building, Cairo, NY 12413
518-622-3620 Fax: 518-622-0344
e-mail: jeff@gcswcd.com
Web site: www.gcswcd.com
Natural resource conservation & water quality programs & public access to Hudson River, stormwater management, wetland mitigation
Jeff Flack, Executive Director

Greenmarket/Council on the Environment of NYC
51 Chambers Street, Room 228, New York, NY 10007
212-788-7900 Fax: 212-788-7913
e-mail: info@grownyc.org
Web site: www.grownyc.org
Direct to consumer farmers' markets, sustainable agriculture, recycling; environmental education; open space greening, community gardens
Marcel Van Doyen, Executive Director

Hawk Creek Wildlife Center Inc
PO Box 662, East Aurora, NY 14052
716-652-8646 Fax: 716-652-8646
e-mail: info@hawkcreek.org
Web site: www.hawkcreek.org
Hawk Creek's mission is to create understanding & knowledge of the natural world & its relationship to humankind through conservation, environmental education & research
Loretta C Jones, President

Hofstra University, School of Law
121 Hofstra University, Hempstead, NY 11549
212-864-6092
Web site: www.hofstra.edu
Land use & environmental law
William R Ginsberg, Emeritus Professor of Law

Hudson River Environmental Society, Inc
PO Box 279, Marlboro, NY 12542
e-mail: hudsonriverenvironmental@gmail.com
Web site: www.hres.org
Facilitates & coordinates research in the physical & biological sciences, environmental engineering & resource management in the Hudson River region
Dr Robert Daniels, Vice President

Hudson River Sloop Clearwater Inc
112 Little Market St, Poughkeepsie, NY 12601
845-454-7673 Fax: 845-454-7953
e-mail: office@clearwater.org
Web site: www.clearwater.org
Hudson River water quality, environmental education & advocacy
Gregg Swanzey, Executive Director

Hudson Valley Grass Roots Energy & Environmental Network
PO Box 208, Red Hook, NY 12571
845-486-7070
e-mail: hvgreentimes@hotmail.com
Web site: www.hvgreentimes.org
Public environmental education & journalism
Brian Reid, Board Member

INFORM Inc
5 Hanover Square, New York, NY 10004
212-361-2400 Fax: 212-361-2412
e-mail: inform@informinc.org
Web site: www.informinc.org
Advocacy, research & education on practical methods to protect natural resources & public health
Katherine O'Dea, Interim Executive Director

Institute of Ecosystem Studies
PO Box A B, Millbrook, NY 12545
845-677-5359 Fax: 845-677-6455
e-mail: quillenl@ecostudies.org
Web site: www.ecostudies.org
Ecosystem research; curriculum development & on-site ecology education
Lori Quillen, Director & President

Offices and agencies generally appear in alphabetical order, except when specific order is requested by listee.

Land Trust Alliance Northeast Program
112 Spring St, Suite 205, PO Box 792, Saratoga Springs, NY 12866
518-587-0774 Fax: 518-587-9586
e-mail: newyork@lta.org
Web site: www.lta.org
Promotes voluntary land conservation; provides leadership, information, skills & resources needed by land trusts
Kevin Case, Northeast Director

Messinger Woods Wildlife Care & Education Center Inc
PO Box 508, Orchard Park, NY 14127
716-648-8091
e-mail: mike@messingerwoods.org
Web site: www.messingerwoods.org
Promoting community awareness, education, instruction, involvement, understanding, appreciation & acceptance of our wildlife in order to conserve it
Michael Olek, President

Modutank Inc
41-04 35th Ave, Long Island City, NY 11101
718-392-1112 Fax: 718-786-1008
e-mail: info@modutank.com
Web site: www.modutank.com
Rent & sell modular storage tanks for potable water, wastewater & liquid chemicals
Reed Margulis, President

NY League of Conservation Voters/NY Conservation Education Fund
30 Broad Street, 30th Floor, New York, NY 10006-3201
212-361-6350 x208 Fax: 212-361-6363
e-mail: info@nylcv.org
Web site: www.nylcv.org
Endorsement of pro-environmental candidates; environmental advocacy & education statewide
Marcia Bystryn, President

NYC Neighborhood Open Space Coalition
232 E 11th St, New York, NY 10003
212-228-3126 Fax: 212-471-9987
e-mail: nosc@treebranch.com
Web site: www.treebranch.com; www.walkny.org
Works to preserve/expand NYC's parks, waterfront, community gardens & other public open space
David Lutz, Executive Director

NYS Association of Solid Waste Management
PO Box 13461, Albany, NY 12212
518-783-2827 Fax: 518-786-7331
e-mail: info@newyorkwaste.org
Web site: www.newyorkwaste.org
Waste management & recycling professionals providing advocacy & education for responsible integrated solid waste management
Michael Wolak, President

NYS Water Resources Institute of Cornell University
Cornell University, 207 Rice Hall, Ithaca, NY 14853-5601
607-255-5941
e-mail: nyswri@cornell.edu
Web site: wri.eas.cornell.edu
Education, research, investigation & technical assistance to agencies & communities concerned with water resources
Keith S Porter, Director

National Wildlife Federation
1400 16th Street NW, Suite 501, Washington, DC 20036
202-797-6800 Fax: 202-797-6646
e-mail: spencer@nwf.org
Web site: www.nwf.org
Conservation education, litigation & advocacy for policies to restore habitat & return wildlife to natural environs

Rick Spencer, Regional Representative

Natural Resources Defense Council
40 W 20th St, 11th Fl, New York, NY 10011
212-727-2700 Fax: 212-727-1773
e-mail: nrdcinfo@nrdc.org
Web site: www.nrdc.org
Litigation, legislation advocacy & public education to preserve & protect the environment & public health
Frances Beinecke, President

Nature Conservancy (The)
195 New Karner Rd, Ste 200, Albany, NY 12205
518-690-7850 Fax: 518-869-2332
e-mail: kmoser@tnc.org
Web site: www.nature.org
Preserve plants, animals & natural communities by protecting the land & water which they need to survive
Kathy Moser, New York State Director (Acting)

New York Forest Owners Association Inc
PO Box 541, Lima, NY 14485
800-836-3566
e-mail: info@nyfoa.org
Web site: www.nyfoa.org
Promote & nurture private woodland owners stewardship
Mary Jeanne Packer, Executive Director

New York Public Interest Research Group
9 Murray St, 3rd Fl, New York, NY 10007
212-349-6460 Fax: 212-349-1366
e-mail: nypirg@nypirg.org
Web site: www.nypirg.org
Environmental preservation, public health, consumer protection & government reform
Christopher Meyer, Executive Director

New York State Conservation Council
8 E Main St, Ilion, NY 13357-1899
315-894-3302 Fax: 315-894-2893
e-mail: nyscc@nyscc.com
Web site: www.nyscc.com
Promotes conservation & wise use & management of natural resources
Harold l Palmer, President

New York State Woodsmen's Field Days Inc
PO Box 123, 118-120 Main St, Boonville, NY 13309
315-942-4593 Fax: 315-942-4452
e-mail: fielddays@aol.com
Web site: www.starinfo.com/woodsmen/
Promoting the forest products industry
Phyllis W White, Executive Coordinator

New York Water Environment Association Inc (NYWEA)
525 Plum Street, Suite 102, Syracuse, NY 13204
315-422-7811 Fax: 315-422-3851
e-mail: pcr@nywea.org
Web site: www.nywea.org
Promoting sustainable clean water quality management through science, education and training.
Patricia Cerro-Reehil, Executive Director

Northeastern Loggers' Association
PO Box 69, Old Forge, NY 13420
315-369-3078 Fax: 315-369-3736
e-mail: nela@northernlogger.com
Web site: www.northernlogger.com
Joseph E Phaneuf, Executive Director & Treasurer

Offices and agencies generally appear in alphabetical order, except when specific order is requested by listee.

Open Space Institute
1350 Broadway, Ste 201, New York, NY 10018-7799
212-290-8200 Fax: 212-244-3441
Web site: www.osiny.org
*Protects scenic, natural and historic landscapes to ensure public enjoyment,
conserve habitats and sustain community character. OSI achieves its goal
through land acquisition, conservation, easements, special loan programs,
fiscal sponsorships.*
Christopher J Elliman, President/Chief Executive Officer

**Pace University, School of Law Center for Environmental Legal
Studies**
78 N Broadway, White Plains, NY 10603
914-422-4244 Fax: 914-422-4261
e-mail: nrobinson@law.pace.edu
Web site: www.law.pace.edu
US & international environmental law
Nicholas Robinson, Co-Director

Proskauer Rose LLP
Eleven Times Square, New York, NY 10036-8299
212-969-3000 Fax: 212-969-2900
e-mail: info@proskauer.com
Web site: www.proskauer.com
Joseph M Leccese, Chairman

Radiac Environmental Services
261 Kent Ave, Brooklyn, NY 11211
718-963-2233 Fax: 718-388-5107
e-mail: jtekin@radiacenv.com
Radioactive & chemical waste disposal, decontamination & remediation
John V Tekin, Jr, Operations Manager

Radon Testing Corp of America Inc
2 Hayes St, Elmsford, NY 10523
914-345-3380 or 800-457-2366 Fax: 914-345-8546
e-mail: rtca97@att.net
Web site: www.rtca.com
*Radon detection services for health departments, municipalities,
homeowners; manufacture canister detectors*
Nancy Bredhoff, President

**Rensselaer Polytechnic Inst, Ecological Economics, Values &
Policy Program**
Dept of Science & Tech Studies, 110 Eighth St, Troy, NY 12180
518-276-8509 Fax: 518-276-2659
e-mail: hessd@rpi.edu
Web site: www.rpi.edu/dept/sts/eevp
Educating leaders for a sustainable future

**Riverhead Foundation for Marine Research & Preservation
(The)**
467 E Main St, Riverhead, NY 11901
631-369-9840 Fax: 631-369-9826
Web site: www.riverheadfoundation.org
*Preservation & protection of the marine environment through education,
rehabilitation & research*
Robert DiGiovanni Jr, Foundation Director/Senior Biologist

Riverkeeper Inc
828 South Broadway, Suite 101, Tarrytown, NY 10591
914-478-4501 Fax: 914-478-4527
e-mail: info@riverkeeper.org
Web site: www.riverkeeper.org
*Nonprofit member supported environmental organization protecting the
ecological integrity of the Hudson and its tributaries, also safeguards NYC
drinking water supply watershed.*
Alex Matthiessen, Hudson Riverkeeper & President

Rural Water Association
PO Box 487, Claverack, NY 12513-0487
518-828-3155 Fax: 518-828-0582
Patricia C Scalera, Executive Director

SCS Engineers PC
140 Rte 303, Valley Cottage, NY 10989-1923
845-353-5727 Fax: 845-353-5731
e-mail: pkuniholm@scsengineers.com
Web site: www.scsengineers.com
Environmental consulting
Peter Kuniholm, Vice President

**SUNY at Cortland, Center for Environmental & Outdoor
Education**
PO Box 2000, Cortland, NY 13045
607-753-5488 Fax: 607-753-5985
e-mail: robert.rubendall@cortland.edu
Web site: www.cortland.edu
Robert Rubendall, Director

**NYS Bar Assn, Environmental Law Section
Sahn Ward & Baker, PLLC**
333 Earle Ovington Blvd, Suite 601, Uniondale, NY 11553
516-228-1300 Fax: 516-228-0038
e-mail: mvillani@sahnwardbaker.com
Web site: www.sahnwardbaker.com
Miriam Villani, Partner

Scenic Hudson
1 Civic Center Plaza, #200, Poughkeepsie, NY 12601
845-473-4440 Fax: 845-473-2648
e-mail: info@scenichudson.org
Web site: www.scenichudson.org
*Environmental advocacy, air & water quality, riverfront protection,
land/historic preservation, smart growth planning*
Ned Sullivan, President

Sierra Club, Atlantic Chapter
353 Hamilton St, Albany, NY 12210-1709
518-426-9144
e-mail: john.stouffer@sierraclub.org
Web site: www.sierraclub.org/chapters/ny/
Environmental protection advocacy & education; outdoor recreation
John Stouffer, Legislative Director

Spectra Environmental Group Inc
19 British American Blvd, Latham, NY 12110
518-782-0882 Fax: 518-782-0973
e-mail: rclafleur@spectraenv.com
Web site: www.spectraenv.com
*Environmental & infrastructure engineering, architecture, surveying, air
quality, ground penetrating radar & power generation consulting & services*
Robert C Lafleur, President

St John's University, School of Law
8000 Utopia Pkwy, Jamaica, NY 11439
718-990-6628 Fax: 718-990-6649
e-mail: weinberp@stjohns.edu
Environmental law
Philip Weinberg, Professor

Syracuse University Press
621 Skytop Rd, Syracuse, NY 13244-5290
315-443-5541 Fax: 315-443-5545
e-mail: supress@syr.edu
Web site: www.syracuseuniversitypress.syr.edu
Adirondack & regional NYS studies series
Alice R Pfeiffer, Director

Offices and agencies generally appear in alphabetical order, except when specific order is requested by listee.

Syracuse University, Maxwell School of Citizenship & Public Affairs
200 Eggers Hall, Syracuse, NY 13244-1020
315-443-2252 Fax: 315-443-1075
e-mail: whlambri@maxwell.syr.edu
Web site: www.maxwell.syr.edu
Environmental policy; science, technology & public policy
W Henry Lambright, Director & Professor

Trees New York
51 Chambers St, Ste 1412A, New York, NY 10007
212-227-1887 Fax: 212-732-5325
e-mail: info@treesny.com
Web site: www.treesny.com
Planting, preserving & protecting street trees; urban forestry resources & reference materials & programs in NYC
Susan Gooberman, Executive Director

University of Rochester School of Medicine
Box EHSC, Rochester, NY 14642
585-275-3911 Fax: 585-256-2591
e-mail: tom_clarkson@urmc.rochester.edu
Web site: www2.envmed.rochester.edu
Mercury poisoning
Thomas Clarkson, Professor, Department of Environmental Medicine

Upstate Freshwater Institute
PO Box 506, Syracuse, NY 13214
315-431-4962 Fax: 315-431-4969
e-mail: sweffler@upstatefreshwater.org
Web site: www.upstatefreshwater.org
Freshwater water quality research
Steven Effler, Executive Director

Waterkeeper Alliance
50 South Buckhout Street, Suite 302, Irvington, NY 10533
914-674-0622 Fax: 914-674-4560
e-mail: info@waterkeeper.org
Web site: www.waterkeeper.org
Protect & restore the quality of the world's waterways
Steve Fleischli, Executive Director

Whiteman Osterman & Hanna LLP
One Commerce Plaza, Albany, NY 12260
518-487-7619 Fax: 518-487-7777
e-mail: druzow@woh.com
Web site: www.woh.com
Environmental & zoning law
Daniel A Ruzow, Senior Partner

Wildlife Conservation Society
2300 Southern Blvd, Bronx, NY 10460
718-220-5100 Fax: 718-220-6890
e-mail: jcalvelli@wcs.org
Web site: www.wcs.org
John Calvelli, Senior Vice President, Public Affairs

Policy Areas

Offices and agencies generally appear in alphabetical order, except when specific order is requested by listee.

GOVERNMENT OPERATIONS

NEW YORK STATE

GOVERNOR'S OFFICE

Governor's Office
Executive Chamber
State Capitol
Albany, NY 12224
518-474-8390 Fax: 518-474-1513
Web site: www.ny.gov

Governor:
  Andrew M Cuomo 518-474-8390
Secretary to the Governor:
  William Mulrow 518-474-4246
Counsel to the Governor:
  Alphonso David 518-474-8343
Deputy Director of State Operations:
  Joseph Rabito 518-408-2051
Director of Policy:
  John Maggiore 518-408-2576
Deputy Secretary, Public Safety:
  Terrence O'Leary 518-474-3522
Director, Communications:
  Melissa DeRosa . . . . 518-474-8418 or 212-681-4640

New York City Office
  633 Third Ave, 38th Fl, New York, NY 10017

Washington Office of the Governor
  444 N Capitol St NW, Washington, DC 20001
Director:
  Alexander Cochran 202-434-7100

Lieutenant Governor's Office
Executive Chamber
State Capitol
Albany, NY 12224
518-402-2292 Fax: 518-474-1513

633 Third Ave
New York, NY 10017
212-681-4575

Lieutenant Governor:
  Kathleen C Hochul . . . . 518-402-2292 or 212-681-4575

EXECUTIVE DEPARTMENTS AND RELATED AGENCIES

Budget, Division of the
State Capitol
Albany, NY 12224
518-473-0580 Fax: 518-474-9041
Web site: www.budget.ny.gov

Director:
  Mary Beth Labate 518-474-2300
First Deputy Director:
  Dominic Colafati. 518-474-8282
Deputy Director:
  David Lara 518-402-4246
Budget Services Head:
  Bob Brondi 518-473-0580
Public Protection Head:
  Anne Bink 518-474-4313

Press Officer:
  Morris Peters 518-473-3885
  e-mail: dob.sm.press@nysemail.state.ny.us

CIO & Office of Information Technology Services (ITS)
State Capitol, ESP
PO Box 2062
Albany, NY 12220-0062
518-402-2537 or 866-789-4638 Fax: 518-474-1196
Web site: www.its.ny.gov

Chief Information Officer & Director:
  Maggie Miller 518-408-2140
Executive Deputy CIO:
  Mahesh Nattanmai 518-408-2140
Counsel & Legal Services:
  Karen Geduldig 518-408-2484
Director, Public Information:
  Michelle McDonald 518-408-3899
Chief Portfolio Officer:
  Nancy Mulholland 518-473-9450
COO:
  Pat Bennison 518-402-7000
Director, Administration:
  Terri Papa 518-408-2484
Chief Technology Officer:
  Kishor Bagul 518-408-2484
Chief Data Officer:
  Barbara Cohn 518-474-3019

Homeland Security & Emergency Services, Division of
1220 Washington Ave
Bldg. 7A
Suite 710
Albany, NY 12242
518-242-5000 Fax: 518-322-4978
Web site: www.dhses.ny.gov

633 Third Ave
32nd Fl
New York, NY 10017
212-867-7060

Commissioner & Director, Office of Counterterrorism:
  Jerome M Hauer 518-292-2301
Assistant Director, Office of Counterterrorism:
  David Sheppard. 518-242-5121
Director, State Office of Emergency Management:
  Steven Kuhr 518-292-2301
First Deputy Director, Emergency Management:
  Greg Brunelle 518-242-5000
State Fire Administrator & Director, Fire Prevention:
  Bryant Stevens. 518-474-6746/fax: 518-474-3240
  e-mail: fire@dhses.ny.gov
Director, Office of Interoperable & Emergency Communications:
  Robert Barbato 518-292-4913
  e-mail: dhsesoiec@dhses.ny.gov
Public Information Officer:
  Rachel McEneny. 518-242-5133

General Services, Office of
Corning Tower, 41st Fl
Empire State Plaza
Albany, NY 12242
518-474-3899 Fax: 518-474-1546
Web site: www.ogs.ny.gov

Offices and agencies generally appear in alphabetical order, except when specific order is requested by listee.

Commissioner:
RoAnn Destito 518-474-5991
Ex. Deputy Commissioner:
Joseph J Rabito 518-473-6953
Deputy Commissioner, Counsel:
Howard Zwickel 518-474-5988/fax: 518-473-4973
Director, Public Affairs:
Heather Groll 518-474-5987/fax: 518-402-5146
e-mail: heather.groll@ogs.ny.gov

Administration
Deputy Commissioner:
Gail Hammond 518-474-3199
CFO, Administration:
Franklin A Hecht 518-474-4546/fax: 518-486-3651
Assistant Director, Financial Administration:
Vacant 518-473-4522
Director, Human Resources Management:
Dan Cunningham 518-474-5995/fax: 518-473-8610
Director, Personnel:
Christina Gavin 518-474-5995
Director, Bureau of Risk, Insurance & Fleet Management:
Tomlynn Yacono 518-474-4725

Support Services
Director, Support Services Operations:
Thomas Osterhout 518-402-5557
Printing & Mailing Services:
Annemarie Pingelski 518-457-6593
Assistant Director, State & Federal Surplus Property:
Terrance Flynn 518-457-6335
Director, Food Distribution & Warehousing:
Annemarie Garceau 518-474-5122
Project Manager, Alternative-Fueled Vehicles:
Tom Osterhout 518-453-6594
e-mail: nys.alt.fuel@cgs.ny.gov
Director, Mail & Freight Security Services:
Arthur Hasson 518-474-6707

Design & Construction
Deputy Commissioner:
Vacant 518-474-0337
e-mail: design.construction@cgs.ny.gov
Director, Construction:
Robert Palmer 518-474-0331/fax: 518-474-8201
Director, Contract Administration:
John D Lewyckyj 518-474-0201/fax: 518-473-5221
Director, Design:
James Dirolf 518-474-0222

Information Technology & Procurement Services
Deputy Commissioner:
Vacant 518-473-3933/fax: 518-486-9166

Information Resource Management
Director:
Kevin Baxter 518-473-4788
Asst Director, Technical Services:
Eliel Mamousette 518-473-4788

Procurement Services Group
Director:
Vacant 518-474-3695/fax: 518-486-6099
Assistant Director:
Bruce Hallenbeck 518-408-1705
Acting Assistant Director:
Kathleen McAuley 518-474-1994
Assistant Director:
Anne Samson 518-474-3855

Real Estate Planning & Development Group
Director, Real Estate Planning & Development:
James Sproat 518-474-4944

Asst Director, Real Estate Planning & Development:
Robert W Lazarou 518-474-4944
Bureau Chief, Land Management:
Charles Scheifer 518-474-2195
Bureau Chief, Real Estate Planning - Upstate:
Leah Nicholson 518-486-1484

Real Property Management Group
Executive Director:
Eric S. McShane 518-474-6057/fax: 518-474-1523
Director, Empire State Plaza & Downtown Buildings:
Kevin O'Connor 518-474-6148
Director, Downstate Regional Buildings:
Kevin Cahill 718-923-4448/fax: 718-923-4451
Assistant Director, Empire State Plaza & Downtown Buildings:
Roger Fortune 518-474-8860/fax: 518-474-4182
Director, Upstate Harriman State Office Campus:
Louis Salerno 518-457-2290/fax: 518-457-8297
Director, Utilities Management:
Paul Cleveland 518-474-5585/fax: 518-485-1678

Empire State's Convention & Cultural Events Office
Director:
Heather Flynn 518-474-0549
Manager, Convention Center:
Vacant 518-474-0558/fax: 518-473-2190
Director, Curatorial & Tour Services:
Dennis Anderson 518-473-7521/fax: 518-474-0984
NYS Vietnam Memorial:
Information 518-474-2418

Inspector General (NYS), Office of the
Empire State Plaza
Bldg 2, 16th Fl
Albany, NY 12223
518-474-1010 or 800-367-4448 Fax: 518-486-3745
Web site: www.ig.ny.gov

State Inspector General:
Catharine Leahy Scott . . . . 212-635-3150 or 518-474-1010
e-mail: inspector.general@ig.ny.gov
Executive Deputy Inspector General:
Spencer Freedman 212-635-3150
Deputy Inspector General, Investigations:
Bernard Cosenza 212-635-3150
Director, Communications:
William P. Reynolds 518-474-1010

Law Department
120 Broadway
New York, NY 10271-0332
212-416-8000 or 800-771-7755
Web site: www.ag.ny.gov

State Capitol
Albany, NY 12224-0341
518-474-7330
Fax: 518-473-9909

Attorney General:
Eric T Schneiderman . . . . 212-416-8050 or 518-474-7330
Chief Deputy Attorney General & Counsel:
Harlan Levy 212-416-8525
COO:
Jeanette Moy . . . . 212-416-8050 or 518-473-7900
fax: 518-474-0680
Executive Deputy Attorney General for Criminal Justice:
Kelly Donovan 212-416-8050

Offices and agencies generally appear in alphabetical order, except when specific order is requested by listee.

Policy Areas

State Comptroller, Office of the
110 State St, 15th Fl
Albany, NY 12236-0001
518-474-4044 Fax: 518-473-3004
e-mail: contactus@osc.state.ny.us
Web site: www.osc.state.ny.us

633 Third Ave, 31st Fl
New York, NY 10017-6754
212-681-4491
Fax: 212-681-4468

State Comptroller:
  Thomas P DiNapoli . . . . .518-474-4040 or 212-681-4469
Deputy Comptroller, Budget & Policy Analysis:
  Robert Ward 518-473-4333
Assistant Comptroller, Labor Affairs:
  Kathy McCormack 518-473-8409

Executive Office
First Deputy Comptroller:
  Pete Grannis .518-474-2909 or 212-681-4469
Chief of Staff:
  Shawn Thompson 518-474-4044
Deputy Comptroller & Chief Information Officer:
  Kevin Belden 518-486-4349
Enterprise Applications & IT Business Management:
  Mary Anne Barry 518-474-8089
Director, Communications:
  Jennifer Freeman . . . . .518-474-4015 or 212-681-4840
Assistant Comptroller, Business Communications:
  Ellen Evans .518-474-4040 or 212-681-4489
Deputy Comptroller, Office of the State Deputy Comptroller for the City of
  New York:
  Ken Bliewas 212-383-3905

Human Resources & Administration
Deputy Comptroller, Human Resources & Administration:
  Angela Dixon 518-474-5512
Assistant Comptroller, Administration:
  Larry Appel. 518-402-3043
Director, Financial Administration:
  Brian Matthews 518-474-2709
Assistant Director, Management Services:
  Beth Bristol 518-486-7433

Inspector General
Inspector General - Internal Audit:
  Stephen Hillerman 518-549-2393

Intergovernmental Affairs
Deputy Comptroller:
  Cathy Calhoun 518-402-3234

Legal Services
General Counsel:
  Nancy Groenwegen. 518-474-3444
Special Counsel for Ethics:
  Barbara Smith 518-408-3855

Operations
Executive Deputy Comptroller:
  Joan Sullivan. 518-402-4103
Deputy Comptroller, Contracts & Expenditures:
  Margaret N. Becker. 518-486-9544
Deputy Comptroller, Payroll, Accounting & Revenue Services (PARS):
  Chris Gorka. 518-408-4149

Pension Investment & Cash Management
Assistant Comptroller, Real Estate Investments:
  Marjorie Tsang 212-681-2589

Retirement
Deputy Comptroller:
  Kevin Murray 518-474-2600

Local Government & School Accountability
Deputy Comptroller:
  Steve Hancox 518-474-4037

State Government Accountability
Executive Deputy Comptroller:
  Andrew San Filippo 518-474-4593
Deputy Comptroller:
  Elliot Pagliaccio 518-473-3596
Assistant Comptroller:
  Jerry Barber. 518-473-0334

State Department
One Commerce Plaza
99 Washington Ave
Albany, NY 12231
518-474-4750 Fax: 518-474-4765
Web site: www.dos.ny.gov

123 William St
New York, NY 10038
212-417-5801
Fax: 212-417-5805

Secretary of State:
  Cesar A Perales. 518-474-0050
First Deputy Secretary of State:
  Daniel Shapiro 518-474-4750
Deputy Secretary of State, Public Affairs:
  Vacant. 212-417-5800
Counsel:
  Susan L. Watson 518-474-6740/fax: 518-473-9211
Assistant Secretary of State, Communications:
  Vacant 518-474-4752/fax: 518-474-4597
  e-mail: info@dos.state.ny.us

Licensing Services Division
Deputy Secretary of State:
  Marcos Vigil 518-473-2728/fax: 518-473-2730
  e-mail: licensing @dos.state.ny.us

Administrative Rules Division
Manager, Publications:
  Maribeth St. Germain 518-474-6957/fax: 518-473-9055
  e-mail: adminrules@dos.state.ny.us

Cemeteries Division
Director:
  Richard D Fishman . . . . .518-474-6226 or 212-417-5713
  fax: 518-473-0876
  e-mail: cemeteries@dos.state.ny.us

Corporations, State Records & UCC Division
Director:
  Sandra J. Tallman 518-473-2492/fax: 518-474-1418
  e-mail: corporations@dos.ny.gov

Local Government & Community Services
Deputy Secretary of State:
  Dierdre Scozzafava. 518-473-3355

Coastal Resources & Waterfront Revitalization Division
Director:
  George Stafford 518-474-6000
  e-mail: coastal@dos.state.ny.us

Offices and agencies generally appear in alphabetical order, except when specific order is requested by listee.

Code Enforcement & Administration Division
Director:
Ronald E Piester 518-474-4073/fax: 518-486-4487
e-mail: codes@dos.state.ny.us

Community Services Division
Director:
Veronica Cruz 518-474-5741/fax: 518-486-4663
e-mail: commserv@dos.state.ny.us

Local Government Services Division
Deputy Secretary of State:
Dierdre Scozzafava 518-473-3355/fax: 518-474-6572
e-mail: localgov@dos.ny.gov

Open Government Committee
Executive Director:
Robert J Freeman. 518-474-2518/fax: 518-474-1927
e-mail: opengov@dos.state.ny.us

Operations
Director, Administration & Management:
Judith E Kenny 518-474-4751/fax: 518-474-4765

Administrative Support Services
Director:
Rebecca Sebesta 518-473-8221/fax: 518-473-7182

Affirmative Action . . . . .fax: 518-473-3294
Affirmative Action Officer:
Teneka Frost-Amusa 518-474-6740

Fiscal Management
Director:
George Lupe .518-474-2754/fax: 518-474-4777

Human Resources Management
Director:
Philip Kelly 518-474-2752/fax: 518-473-3294

Internal Audit
Acting Director:
Louis Canter 518-474-1859

Information Technology Management
Director:
Steven S Lovelett 518-474-8512/fax: 518-474-6239

Regional Services
Assistant Director:
Brian S. Tollisen 518-474-4073/fax: 518-474-5788

Regional Offices
Region 9 - Capital District Office . . . . .fax: 518-477-2369
One Commerce Plaza, 99 Washington Avenue, Albany, NY 12231
518-474-7497 Fax: 518-477-2369
Regional Representative:
Joseph McGrath. 518-477-7497
Region 4 - Kingston Office . . . . .fax: 845-334-9373
One Albany Avenue, Suite G-%, Kingston, NY 12401
845-334-9768 Fax: 845-334-9373
Regional Representative:
Dan Nichols 845-334-9768/fax: 845-334-9373
Region 1 - Buffalo Office. . . . . .fax: 716-847-7941
65 Court St, Room 208, Buffalo, NY 14202
716-847-7611 or 716-847-7612 Fax: 716-847-7941
Regional Representative:
Kumar Vijaykumar 716-847-7611
Regional Representative:
Andrew Hvisdak 716-847-7612
Region 12/13 - Long Island Office . . . . .fax: 631-952-4911
Suffolk State Office Bldg., 250 Veterans Memorial Highway,
Hauppauge, NY 11788
631-952-4915 Fax: 631-952-4911

Regional Representative:
Courtney Nation 631-952-4915/fax: 631-952-4911
Regional Representative:
Richard Smith 631-952-4912
Region 10 - Northern New York Office
PO Box 341, Lake George, NY 12845
Regional Representative:
Whitney Russell 518-441-1895/fax: 518-668-5369
Region 2 - Peekskill Office
2 John Walsh Blvd., Suite 206, Peekskill, NY 10566
Regional Representative:
Erika Krieger 914-734-1347/fax: 914-734-1763
Region 5 - Syracuse Office
St Ofc Bldg, 333 E Washington St, Rm 514, Syracuse, NY 13202
Regional Representative:
James King 315-428-4434/fax: 578-428-4655
Region 6 - Utica Office
State Office Bldg, 207 Genesee St, Utica, NY 13501
Regional Representative:
Thomas Romanowski. 315-793-2526/fax: 315-793-2569
Region 7/8 - Western New York Office
PO Box 141, Conesus, NY 14435
585-402-3017
Regional Representative:
Deborah Babbitt. 585-402-3017

State Athletic Commission
123 William St, 2nd Fl, New York, NY 10038
Chair:
Melvina Lathan 212-417-5700/fax: 212-417-4987
e-mail: athletic@dos.ny.gov

Welfare Inspector General, Office of NYS
Chisholm State Office Bldg.
55 Hanson Place
Room 650
Brooklyn, NY 11217
718-923-4290 or 800-682-4530 Fax: 718-923-4310
e-mail: owig@dfa.state.ny.us
Web site: www.owig.state.ny.us

Acting Welfare Inspector General:
Catherine Leahy Scott. 718-923-4290
Chief Investigator:
Joseph Bucci 718-923-4290
Confidential Assistant:
Joy Quiles 718-923-4290
e-mail: joy.quiles@owig.ny.gov

CORPORATIONS, AUTHORITIES AND COMMISSIONS

Legislative Bill Drafting Commission
Capitol, Rm 308
Albany, NY 12224
518-455-7500 Fax: 518-455-7598

Commissioner:
Randall G Bluth 518-455-7506
e-mail: bluth@lbdc.state.ny.us

Legislative Retrieval System .fax: 518-455-7679
1450 Western Ave, Albany, NY 12203
800-356-6566 Fax: 518-455-7679
Director:
Burleigh McCutcheon. 518-455-7672
e-mail: mccutcheon@lbdc.state.ny.us

Offices and agencies generally appear in alphabetical order, except when specific order is requested by listee.

New York State Athletic Commission
123 William St
2nd Fl
New York, NY 10038
212-417-5700 Fax: 212-417-4987
e-mail: info@dos.ny.gov
Web site: www.dos.ny.gov/athletic

Chair:
   Melvina Lathan...................................212-417-5700

New York State Commission on the Restoration of the Capitol
Corning Tower, 31st Fl
Empire State Plaza
Albany, NY 12242
518-473-0341 Fax: 518-486-5720

Executive Director:
   Andrea J Lazarski............................518-473-0341
   e-mail: andrea.lazarski@ogs.ny.gov

New York State Disaster Preparedness Commission
Building 22, Suite 101
1220 Washington Ave
Albany, NY 12226-2251
518-292-2301 or 518-292-2200 Fax: 518-322-4978
Web site: www.dhses.ny.gov/oem/disaster-prep/

Chairman/Director:
   Jerome M Hauer...............................518-292-2301

New York State Dormitory Authority
515 Broadway
Albany, NY 12207-2964
518-257-3000 Fax: 518-257-3100
e-mail: dabonds@dasny.org
Web site: www.dasny.org

One Penn Plaza
52nd Fl
New York, NY 10119-0098
212-273-5000
Fax: 212-273-5121

539 Franklin St
Buffalo, NY 14202-1109
716-884-9780
Fax: 716-884-9787

Chair:
   Alfonso L Carney Jr 518-257-3000/fax: 518-257-3100
President/CEO:
   Paul T Williams Jr..................518-257-3180/fax: 518-257-3183
Vice President:
   Michael T Corrigan 518-257-3192/fax: 518-257-3183
Chief Financial Officer:
   Linda H Button 518-257-3562/fax: 518-257-3100
General Counsel:
   Michael Cusack...................518-257-3120/fax: 518-257-3101
Managing Director, Construction:
   Stephen D Curro, PE...............518-257-3271/fax: 518-257-3100
   e-mail: scurro@dasny.org
Managing Director, Public Finance & Portfolio Monitoring:
   Portia Lee........................518-257-3362/fax: 518-257-3100
   e-mail: plee@dasny.org

Public Information Officer:
   John Chirlin....................................518-257-3380
   e-mail: jchirlin@dasny.org

Joint Commission on Public Ethics (JCOPE)
540 Broadway
Albany, NY 12207
518-408-3976 Fax: 518-408-3975
e-mail: jcope@jcope.ny.gov
Web site: www.jcope.ny.gov

Executive Director:
   Letizia Tagliafierro............................518-408-3976
Chair:
   Daniel J Horwitz...............................518-408-3976
Training & Education Services:
   Shari Calnero.................................518-408-3976
Chief of Staff/Deputy Counsel:
   Monica Stamm.................................518-408-3976

New York State Financial Control Board
123 William St
23rd Fl
New York, NY 10038-3804
212-417-5046 Fax: 212-417-5055
e-mail: nysfcb@fcb.state.ny.us
Web site: www.fcb.state.ny.us

Acting Executive Director:
   Jeffrey Sommer................................212-417-5066
Deputy Director, Expenditure & Covered Organization Analysis:
   Dennis DeLisle 212-417-5069
Acting Deputy Director, Economic & Revenue Analysis:
   Martin Fischman...............................212-417-5068
Associate Director, Administration:
   Mattie W Taylor 212-417-5053

New York State Law Reporting Bureau
17 Lodge Street
Albany, NY 12207
518-453-6900 Fax: 518-426-1640
Web site: www.courts.state.ny.us/reporter

State Reporter:
   William J Hooks...............................518-453-6900
Deputy State Reporter:
   Michael S Moran..............................518-453-6900
   e-mail: Reporter@courts.state.ny.us
Assistant State Reporter:
   Katherine D. LaBoda...........................518-453-6900
   e-mail: Reporter@courts.state.ny.us

Uniform State Laws Commission
c/o Coughlin & Gerhart LLP,
99 Corporate Drive
PO Box 2089
Binghamton, NY 13902-2039
607-723-9511 Fax: 607-723-1530

Chair:
   Richard B Long................................607-821-2202
   e-mail: rlong@cglawoffices.com
Member:
   Sandra Stern 212-207-8150
Member:
   Norman L. Greene 212-661-5030
Member:
   Justin L. Vigdor..............................585-232-5300 ext 228

Offices and agencies generally appear in alphabetical order, except when specific order is requested by listee.

Member:
Mark F Glaser 518-689-1413

United Nations Development Corporation
Two United Nations Plaza
27th Fl
New York, NY 10017
212-888-1618 Fax: 212-588-0758
e-mail: info@undc.org
Web site: www.undc.org

Chair, Board of Directors:
George Klein 212-888-1618
Sr VP & General Counsel/Secretary:
Robert Cole 212-888-1618
Vice President:
Kenneth Coopersmith 212-888-1618
Controller/Treasurer:
Jorge Ortiz 212-888-1618

NEW YORK STATE LEGISLATURE

See Legislative Branch in Section 1 for additional Standing Committee and Subcommittee information.

Assembly Standing Committees

Consumer Affairs & Protection
Chair:
Jeffrey Dinowitz (D) 518-455-5965
Ranking Minority Member:
Anthony Palumbo (R) 518-455-5294

Corporations, Authorities & Commissions
Chair:
James F Brennan (D) 518-455-5377
Ranking Minority Member:
Jane Corwin (R) 518-455-4601

Ethics & Guidance
Chair:
Charles Lavine (D) 518-455-5456
Ranking Minority Member:
Brian Curran (R) 518-455-4656

Governmental Operations
Chair:
Crystal Peoples-Stokes (D) 518-455-5005
Ranking Minority Member:
Janet Duprey (R) 518-455-5943

Oversight, Analysis & Investigation
Chair:
Ellen Jaffee (D) 518-455-5118
Ranking Minority Member:
Peter Lawrence (R) 518-455-4664

Rules
Chair:
Carl Heastie (D) 518-455-3791
Ranking Minority Member:
Brian M Kolb (R) 518-455-3751

Ways & Means
Chair:
Herman D Farrell, Jr (D) 518-455-5491
Ranking Minority Member:
Bob Oaks (R) 518-455-5655

Assembly Task Forces & Caucus

State-Federal Relations Task Force
Assembly Chair:
Matthew Titone (D) 518-455-4677
Program Manager:
Robert Stern 518-455-3632

Senate Select Committees

Senate Standing Committees

Civil Service & Pensions
Chair:
Martin J Golden (R) 518-455-2730
Ranking Minority Member:
James Sanders, Jr. (D) 518-455-3531

Consumer Protection
Chair:
Michael Venditto (R) 518-455-3341
Ranking Minority Member:
Leroy Comrie (D) 518-455-2701

Corporations, Authorities & Commissions
Chair:
Michael Ranzenhofer (R) 518-455-3161
Ranking Minority Member:
Bill Perkins (D) 518-455-2441

Ethics
Chair:
Tony Avella (D) 518-455-2210
Ranking Minority Member:
Michael Gianaris (D) 518-455-3486

Finance
Chair:
John A DeFrancisco (R) 518-455-3511
Ranking Minority Member:
Liz Krueger (D) 518-455-2297

Investigations & Government Operations
Chair:
Carl L Marcellino (R) 518-455-2390
Ranking Minority Member:
Brad Hoylman (D) 518-455-2451

Rules
Chair:
John J Flanagan (R) 518-455-2071
Ranking Minority Member:
Andrea Stewart-Cousins (D) 518-455-2585

Senate/Assembly Legislative Commissions

Ethics Committee, Legislative
Senate Co-Chair:
Andrew J Lanza (R) 518-455-3215
Assembly Co-Chair:
Charles Lavine (D) 518-455-4546
Director/Counsel:
Lisa P. Reid
e-mail: lreid@nysenate.gov

Government Administration, Legislative Commission on
Assembly Chair:
Brian Kavanaugh (D) 518-455-5506
Senate Vice Chair:
Vacant 518-455-0000

Offices and agencies generally appear in alphabetical order, except when specific order is requested by listee.

Policy Areas

AMERICAN INDIAN TRIBES

Cayuga Nation of New York
2540 SR-89
PO Box 803
Seneca Falls, NY 13148
315-568-0750 Fax: 315-568-0752
Web site: www.cayuganation-nsn.gov

Federal Representative:
   Clint Halftown

Oneida Indian Nation
2037 Dream Catcher Plaza
Oneida, NY 13421
315-829-8900 or 800-685-6115 Fax: 315-829-8958
e-mail: info@oneida-nation.org
Web site: www.oneidaindiannation.com

Nation Repesentative:
   Ray Halbritter

Onondaga Nation
3951 Route 11
Nedrow, NY 13120
315-492-1922 Fax: 315-469-4717
e-mail: admin@onondaganation.org
Web site: www.onondaganation.org

Chief:
   Irving Powless, Jr

Seneca Nation of Indians
William Seneca Building
12837 Route 438
Irving, NY 14081
716-532-4900
e-mail: sni@sni.org
Web site: www.sni.org

President:
   Maurice A John, Sr

Shinnecock Indian Nation
PO Box 5006
Southampton, NY 11969-5006
631-283-6143 or 631-287-3752 Fax: 631-283-0751
e-mail: sination@optonline.net
Web site: www.shinnecocknation.com

Chairperson:
   Daniel Collins, Sr.
Director of Communications:
   Beverly Jensen
   e-mail: nationsvoice@shinnecock.org

St Regis Mohawk Tribe
412 State Route 37
Akwesasne, NY 13655
518-358-2272 Fax: 518-358-3203
e-mail: communications@srmt-nsn.gov
Web site: www.srmt-nsn.gov

Tribal Clerk:
   Corleen Jacco 518-358-2272

Unkechaug Nation
Poospatuck Reservation
PO Box 86
Mastic, NY 11950
631-281-6464 or 631-281-4143 Fax: 631-281-2125
e-mail: hwal1@aol.com
Web site: http://unkechaug.wordpress.com/

Chief:
   Harry Wallace

U.S. GOVERNMENT

EXECUTIVE DEPARTMENTS AND RELATED AGENCIES

New York Regional Office. . . . . .fax: 212-352-54401
   201 Varick St, Ste 1025, New York, NY 10014
   855-855-1961 or 212-352-5440 Fax: 212-352-54401
   e-mail: nyinfo@peacecorps.gov
Regional Manager:
   Vincent Wickes. 212-352-5440
   e-mail: nyinfo@peacecorps.gov
Public Affairs Specialist:
   Elizabeth Chamberlain 774-330-9200
   e-mail: chamberlain@peacecorps.gov

US Department of Homeland Security (DHS)
Web site: www.dhs.gov

Bureau of Immigration & Customs Enforcement (ICE)
   Web site: www.ice.gov

   New York District Office . . . . .fax: 646-230-3255
   601 W 26th St, 7th Floor, New York, NY 10001
   646-230-3200 Fax: 646-230-3255
   Special Agent-in-Charge:
      James T. Hayes, Jr.
      Albany Sub Office
         1086 Troy-Schenectady Rd, Latham, NY 12110-1010
         Group Supervisor:
            Dean Del Negro
         Resident Agent-in-Charge:
            Matthew Scarpino

Customs & Border Protection (CBP)
202-354-1000
Web site: www.cbp.gov

Agriculture Inspections (AI)
   Brooklyn, Port of
      6405 7th Ave, 3rd Fl, Brooklyn, NY 11220
      Supervising Ag Specialist:
         Willie J Martin. 718-340-5225
   Buffalo, Port of
      1 Peace Bridge Plaza, Room 316, Buffalo, NY 14213
      Supervisor:
         Brent Speicher 716-884-5701/fax: 716-884-5679
   Champlain, Port of. . . . . .fax: 518-298-8395
      237 West Service Rd, Suite 2, Champlain, NY 12919
      518-298-8327 Fax: 518-298-8395
      Ag Specialist:
         Vacant. 518-298-4332/fax: 518-298-4486
   JFK International Airport Area Office . . . . .fax: 718-487-5191
      JFK Int'l Airport, Bldg #77, 2nd Fl, Jamaica, NY 11430
      718-487-5164 Fax: 718-487-5191
      Port Director:
         Camille Polimeni 718-487-5164/fax: 718-487-5191

Buffalo Field Office
300 Airborne Parkway, Suite 300, Buffalo, NY 14225

Offices and agencies generally appear in alphabetical order, except when specific order is requested by listee.

716-626-0400
Director:
    James Engleman............716-626-0400 x201/fax: 716-626-9281
    Albany, Port of
        106 Smith Boulevard, Albany, NY 12202
        518-463-8763
        Port General Manager:
            Rich Hendrick
    Buffalo, Port of
        Larkin at Exchange, 726 Exchange, Suite 400, Buffalo, NY 14210
        716-843-8300
        Port Director:
            Jim Pfohl...............................716-826-7310
    Champlain, Port of...........................fax: 518-298-8395
        237 W Service Rd, Champlain, NY 12919
        518-298-8311 Fax: 518-298-8395
        Area Port Director:
            Christopher Perry...........518-298-8347/fax: 518-298-8314
    Ogdensburg, Port of
        1 Bridge Plaza, Ogdensburg, NY 13669
        Port Director:
            Wade A. Davis............................313-393-1390

New York Field Office.......................fax: 646-733-3245
1 Penn Plaza, 11th Fl, New York, NY 10119
646-733-3100 Fax: 646-733-3245
Director, Field Operations:
    Robert E. Perez
Press Officer:
    Anthony Bucci...............................646-733-3275
    Field Counsel - New York
        Deputy Associate Chief Counsel:
            Colleen Piccone
    Laboratory Division
        Director:
            Laura W. Goldstein.......................973-368-1901

National Urban Security Technology Laboratory
201 Varick St, 5th Fl, New York, NY 10014-7447
Director:
    Adam Hutter

Administration
Director:
    Richard Larsen.................212-620-3524/fax: 212-620-3600
    e-mail: richard.larsen@dhs.gov

Systems Division
Director:
    Dr. Lawrence Ruth.............212-620-3609/fax: 212-620-3600
    e-mail: lawrence.roth@dhs.gov

Testbeds Division
Director:
    Adam Hutter.................212-620-3619/fax: 212-620-3651
    e-mail: adam.hutter@dhs.gov

Federal Emergency Management Agency (FEMA)
TTY: 800-462-7585 or 800-621-3362
Web site: www.fema.gov

National Disaster Medical System................fax: 212-680-3608
26 Federal Plz, Rm 3835, New York, NY 10278
Coordinator:
    Captain Bonita Pyler, USPHS.................212-680-8542
    e-mail: pyler@dhs.gov

New York Regional Office.....................fax: 212-680-3600
26 Federal Plz, New York, NY 10278-0002
Regional Director:
    Lynn Gilmore Canten

Federal Protective Service (The)
26 Federal Plaza, Rm 17-130, New York, NY 10278
Director:
    L. Eric Patterson

Plum Island Animal Disease Center
PO Box 848, Greenport, NY 11944
Director:
    Larry Barrett

Transportation Security Administration (TSA)
201 Varick St, Rm 603, New York, NY 10014
Regional Spokesperson:
    Lisa Farbstein

US Citizenship & Immigration Services (USCIS)
TTY: 800-767-1833 or 800-375-5283
Web site: www.uscis.gov

Buffalo District Office.....................fax: 716-551-3131
Federal Center, 130 Delaware Ave, Buffalo, NY 14202
District Director:
    M Frances Holmes.......................716-551-4741 x6000
    Albany Sub Office
        1086 Troy-Schenectady Rd, Latham, NY 12110
        Field Office Director:
            Kevin Gallagher

CIS Asylum Offices
    New York Asylum Office....................fax: 718-723-1121
        One Cross Island Plaza, 3rd Fl, (133-33 Brookville Boulevard),
            Rosedale, NY 11422
        Director:
            Patricia A Jackson.......................718-723-5954
        Deputy Director:
            Vacant
    Newark Asylum Offc-Including NYS not served by New York City fax:
    201-531-1877
        1200 Wall St, West 4th Fl, Lyndhurst, NJ 07071
        Director:
            Susan Raufer............................201-531-0555
        Deputy Director:
            Aster Zeleke............................201-531-0555

New York City District Office
Jacob J. Javits Federal Building, 26 Federal Plaza, Room 3-120, New
    York, NY 10278
District Director:
    Andrea Quarantillo
    Garden City Satellite Office
        711 Stewart Ave, Garden City, NY 11530
        Acting Field Office Director:
            Sham Chin-Gee..........................516-228-9250

US General Services Administration
Web site: www.gsa.gov

Region 2—New York
26 Federal Plaza, New York, NY 10278
212-264-9290
Regional Administrator:
    Denise L. Pease...............................212-264-2600
    e-mail: denise.pease@gsa.gov
Special Assistant to the Regional Administrator:
    Gita J. Stulberg...............................212-264-2014
    e-mail: gita.stulberg@gsa.gov
Human Resources Officer:
    Mark A. Fuhring...............................212-264-0780
    e-mail: mark.fuhring@gsa.gov
Regional Counsel:
    Carol Latterman..................212-264-8308/fax: 212-264-1987
    e-mail: carol.latterman@gsa.gov

Offices and agencies generally appear in alphabetical order, except when specific order is requested by listee.

Administration
Director, Program Support & Human Resources:
    Joseph J Giorgianni 212-264-0780/fax: 212-264-6798
    e-mail: joseph.giorgianni@gsa.gov

Federal Supply Service
Asst Regional Administrator:
    Charles B Weill 212-264-3590/fax: 212-264-9759

Federal Technology Service
Asst Regional Administrator (Acting):
    Steve Ruggiero 212-264-3590
    e-mail: steve.ruggiero@gsa.gov

Inspector General's Office
Asst Regional Inspector, Investigations:
    Daniel Walsh 212-264-7300/fax: 212-264-7154
Regional Director, Audit:
    Joseph Mastropietro 212-264-8620

Public Buildings Service
PBS Regional Commissioner:
    Joanna Rosato 212-264-4039
    e-mail: joanna.rosato@gsa.gov
Deputy Asst Regional Administrator:
    Vacant 212-264-4285
Director, Property Management:
    David Segermeister 212-264-4273/fax: 212-264-2746
Director, Realty Services:
    Donald W Eigendorff 212-264-4210/fax: 212-264-9400

US Government Printing Office
e-mail: infonewyork@gpo.gov
Web site: www.gpo.gov

Region 2-I (New York)

Printing Procurement Office . . . . fax: 212-264-2413
26 Federal Plaza, Room 2930, New York, NY 10278
212-264-2252 Fax: 212-264-2413
Assistant Manager:
    Debra Rozdzielski

US Postal Service
Web site: www.usps.gov

NORTHEAST AREA (Includes part of New York State) . . . . fax:
860-285-1284
6 Griffin Rd North, Windsor, CT 06006-7010
860-285-7125 Fax: 860-285-1284
Vice President, Area Operations:
    Richard P. Uluski

US State Department
Web site: www.state.gov

Bureau of Educational & Cultural Affairs-NY Pgm Branch . . fax:
212-399-5783
666 Fifth Ave, Ste 603, New York, NY 10103
212-399-5750 Fax: 212-399-5783
Web site: exchanges.state.gov
Director:
    Donna Shirreffs 212-399-5750

US Mission to the United Nations
799 UN Plaza, New York, NY 10017
US Permanent Representative to the United Nations:
    Susan E. Rice
Deputy Permanent Representative to the United Nations:
    Rosemary A. DiCarlo

Alternative Representative of the US for Special Politial Affairs in the United Nations:
    Jeffrey DeLaurenitis
US Representative to ECOSOC:
    Elizabeth M. Cousens
US Representative for UN Management & Reform:
    Joseph M. Torsells

U.S. CONGRESS

See U.S. Congress Chapter for additional Standing Committee and Subcommittee information.

House of Representatives Standing Committees

Oversight & Government Reform
Chair:
    Darrell E. Issa (R-CA) 202-225-3906
Ranking Member:
    Elijah Cummings (D-MD) 202-225-4741
New York Delegate:
    Carolyn B Maloney (D) 202-225-7944

Homeland Security
Chair:
    Michael McCaul (R-TX) 202-225-2401
Ranking Member:
    Bennie G. Thompson (D-MI) 202-225-5876
New York Delegate:
    Yvette D Clarke (D) 202-225-6231
New York Delegate:
    Brian Higgins(D) 202-225-3306
New York Delegate:
    Peter T. King (R). 202-225-7896

Subcommittees
Emergency Communications, Preparedness and Response
    Chair:
        Susan W. Brooks (R-IN) 202-225-2276
    Ranking Member:
        Donald M. Payne (NJ-D). 202-225-3436
Cyber Security, Infrastructure Protection, and Security Technologies
    Chair:
        Patrick Meehan (R-PA) 202-225-2011
    Ranking Member:
        Yvette D. Clarke (D-NY) 202-225-6231
Counterterrorism & Intelligence
    Chair:
        Peter T. King (R-NY) 202-225-7896
    Ranking Member:
        Brian Higgins (D-NY). 202-225-3306
Oversight & Management Efficiency
    Chair:
        Jeff Duncan (R-SC). 202-225-2542
    Ranking Member:
        Ron Barber (D-AZ) 202-225-2542
Transportation Security
    Chair:
        Richard Hudson (R-NC) 202-225-1612
    Ranking Member:
        Cedric L. Richmond (D-LA) 202-225-6636

Intelligence, Permanent Select Committee on
Chair:
    Mike Rogers (R-MI). 202-225-4872
Ruppersberger (D-MD):
    C.A. Dutch"" . . . . Ranking Member or 202-225-3061

Offices and agencies generally appear in alphabetical order, except when specific order is requested by listee.

Subcommittee
Technical & Tactical Intelligence
Chair:
Joe Heck (R-NV)............................202-225-3252
Ranking Member:
Adam Schiff (D-CA)........................202-225-4176

Ethics
Chair:
K. Michael Conway (R-TX)...................202-225-3605
Ranking Member:
Linda T. Sanchez (D-CA)....................202-225-5050

Senate Standing Committees

Ethics, Select Committee on
Chair:
Barbara Boxer (D-CA).......................202-224-3553
Vice Chair:
Johnny Isakson (R-GA)......................202-224-3643

Homeland Security & Governmental Affairs
Chair:
Thomas R. Carper (D-DE)....................202-224-2441
Ranking Member:
Tom Coburn (R-OK)..........................202-224-5754

Indian Affairs, Committee on
Chair:
Maria Cantwell (D-WA)......................202-224-3441
Vice Chair:
John Barrasso (R-WY).......................202-224-6441

Intelligence, Select Committee on
Chair:
Dianne Feinstein (D-CA)....................202-224-3841
Vice Chair:
Saxby Chambliss (R-GA).....................202-224-3521

Judiciary
Chair:
Patrick J Leahy (D-VT).....................202-224-4242
Ranking Member:
Charles Grassley (R-IA)....................202-227-3744
New York Delegate:
Charles E Schumer (D)......................202-227-6542

Subcommittees
Immigration, Refugees and Border Security
Chair:
Patrick J. Leahy (D-VT)....................202-224-3744
Ranking Member:
Chuck Grassley (R-IA)......................202-224-3744
Terrorism & Homeland Security
Chair:
Benjamin L Cardin (D-MD)...................202-224-4524
Ranking Member:
Jon Kyl (R-AZ).............................202-224-4521

PRIVATE SECTOR

Academy of Political Science
475 Riverside Drive, Ste 1274, New York, NY 10115-1274
212-870-2500 Fax: 212-870-2202
e-mail: aps@psqonline.org
Web site: www.psqonline.org
Analysis of government, economic & social issues
Demetrios James Caraley, President

Albany Law School, Government Law Center
80 New Scotland Ave, Albany, NY 12208
518-445-2329 Fax: 518-445-2303
e-mail: psalk@albanylaw.edu
Web site: www.albanylaw.edu
Legal aspects of public policy reform
Patricia Salkin, Associate Dean & Director, Government Law Center

Association of Government Accountants, NY Capital Chapter
PO Box 1923, Albany, NY 12201
518-427-4765 or 212-872-5733
e-mail: lvacarro@kpmg.com
Web site: www.aganycap.org
Education for the government financial management community
Lori Vaccaro, Chapter President

Center for Governmental Research Inc (CGR)
1 South Washington St, Ste 400, Rochester, NY 14614-1135
585-325-6360 Fax: 585-325-2612
e-mail: kgardner@cgr.org
Web site: www.cgr.org
Nonprofit, nonpartisan institution devoted to analyzing public policies to ensure that they benefit the community at large
Kent Gardner, President

Center for Technology in Government, University at Albany, SUNY
187 Wolf Rd, Ste 301, Albany, NY 12205-1138
518-442-3892 Fax: 518-442-3886
e-mail: info@ctg.albany.edu
Web site: www.ctg.albany.edu
Works with government to develop well-informed information strategies that foster innovation and enhance the quality and coordination of public services through applied research and partnership projects
Anthony Cresswell, Director (Acting)

Citizens Union of the City of New York
299 Broadway, Rm 700, New York, NY 10007-1978
212-227-0342 Fax: 212-227-0345
e-mail: citizens@citizensunion.org
Web site: www.citizensunion.org
Government watchdog organization; city and state public policy issues; political and goverment reform.
Dick Dadey, Executive Director

Coalition of Fathers & Families NY, PAC
PO Box 782, Clifton Park, NY 12065
518-383-8202
e-mail: fafny@fafny.org
Web site: www.fafny.org/fafnypac.htm
Political Action for fathers and families in New York
James Hays, Treasurer

Columbia University, Exec Graduate Pgm in Public Policy & Administration
420 W 118th St, Rm 1314, New York, NY 10027
212-854-4445 Fax: 212-854-5765
e-mail: sc32@columbia.edu
Web site: www.columbia.edu/~sc32
Urban & environmental policy; public management
Steven Cohen, Director

Common Cause/NY
155 Ave of the Americas, 4th Fl, New York, NY 10013
212-691-6421 Fax: 212-807-1809
e-mail: cocauseny@aol.com
Web site: www.commoncause.org/ny
Campaign finance reform, ballot access, political gift disclosure & public interest lobbying
Rachel Leon, Executive Director

Offices and agencies generally appear in alphabetical order, except when specific order is requested by listee.

NYS Bar Assn, Task Force to Review Terrorism Legislation Cmte
Connors & Vilardo
1000 Liberty Bldg, 424 Main St, Buffalo, NY 14202-3510
716-852-5533 Fax: 716-852-5649
e-mail: ved@connors-vilardo.com
Web site: www.connors-vilardo.com
Vincent E Doyle, III, Chair

Council of State Governments, Eastern Conference
100 Wall Street, 20th Floor, New York, NY 10005
212-482-2320 Fax: 212-482-2344
e-mail: kimas@csg.org
Web site: www.csgeast.org
Training, research & information sharing for state government officials
Alan V Sokolow, Regional Director

Crane, Parente & Cherubin
90 State Street, Ste 1515A, Albany, NY 12207
518-432-8000 Fax: 518-432-0086
e-mail: jcrane@cpclaw.net
*Governmental relations, banking & financial services, corporate law,
construction law, energy, utilities, communications, land use, environmental
& wireless telecommunications law*
James B Crane, II, Managing Partner

DeGraff, Foy, Kunz & Devine, LLP
90 State St, Albany, NY 12207
518-462-5300 Fax: 518-436-0210
e-mail: firm@degraff-foy.com
Web site: www.degraff-foy.com
*Government relations, administrative law & tax exempt/municipal financing,
education, energy, transportation, public authorities & the environment*
David Kunz, Managing Partner

Fiscal Policy Institute
1 Lear Jet Lane, Latham, NY 12110
518-786-3156
e-mail: mauro@fiscalpolicy.org
Web site: www.fiscalpolicy.org
*Nonpartisan research & education; tax, budget, economic & related public
policy issues that affect quality of life & economic well-being*
Frank Mauro, Executive Director

Fordham University, Department of Political Science
113 W 60th Street, New York, NY 10023
212-636-6334 Fax: 212-636-7153
e-mail: sbeck@fordham.edu
Web site: www.fordham.edu
*Women in public office; importance of gender in understanding modes of
governance*
Susan Beck, Associate Professor of Political Science

Geto & deMilly Inc
276 Fifth Avenue, Suite 806, New York, NY 10001
212-686-4551 Fax: 212-213-6850
e-mail: pr@getodmilly.com
Public & government relations
Ethan Geto, President

NYS Bar Assn, Legislative Policy Cmte
Greenberg Traurig, LLP
MetLife Building, 200 Park Avenue, New York, NY 10166
212-801-9200 Fax: 212-801-6400
e-mail: greenbergh@gtlaw.com
Web site: www.gtlaw.com
Henry M Greenberg, Chair

Institute of Public Administration/NYU Wagner
295 Lafayette St, 2nd Floor, New York, NY 10012-9604
212-998-7400
e-mail: wagner@nyu.edu
Web site: www.wagner.nyu.edu
Non-profit research, consulting & educational institute
David Mammen, President

KPMG LLP
515 Broadway, Albany, NY 12207-2974
518-427-4600 Fax: 518-689-4717
e-mail: rhannmann@kpmg.com
Web site: www.kpmg.com
State & local government audit & advisory service
Ken Dean, Partner

League of Women Voters of New York State
62 Grand Street, Albany, NY 12207-2712
518-465-4162 Fax: 518-465-0812
e-mail: rob@lwvny.org
Web site: www.lwvny.org
Public policy issues forum; good government advocacy
Rob Marchiony, Executive Director

Manhattan Institute for Policy Research
52 Vanderbilt Avenue, 2nd Floor, New York, NY 10017
212-599-7000 x315 Fax: 212-599-3494
e-mail: communications@manhattan-institute.org
Web site: www.manhattan-institute.org
*Think tank promoting the development & dissemination of new ideas that
foster greater economic choice & individual responsibility*
Lindsay M Young, Executive Director, Communications

NYS Bar Assn, Court Structure & Judicial Selection Cmte
McMahon & Grow
301 N Washington St, PO Box 4350, Rome, NY 13442-4350
315-336-4700 Fax: 315-336-5851
e-mail: mgglaw@dreamscape.com
Retired Judge-NYS Court of Appeals
Hon Richard D Simons, Chair

NYS Bar Assn, Federal Constitution & Legislation Cmte
Mulholland & Knapp, LLP
641 Lexington Avenue, New York, NY 10022-4503
212-702-9027 Fax: 212-702-9092
e-mail: robknapp@mklex.com
Web site: www.mklex.com
Robert Knapp, Chair

NY Coalition of 100 Black Women - Not For Profit
PO Box 2555, Grand Central Station, New York, NY 10163
212-517-5700 Fax: 212-772-8771
e-mail: vmontague@cobwfounders.org
*Leadership by example; advocates & agents for changes-improving the
quality of life by focusing resources in education, health & community
services*
Virginia M Montague, President

NY StateWatch Inc
100 State St, Ste 440, Albany, NY 12207
518-449-7425 Fax: 518-449-7431
Web site: www.statewatch.com
Legislative information service/bill tracking
Mike Poulopoulos, Director

NYS Association of Counties
540 Broadway, 5th Floor, Albany, NY 12207
518-465-1473 Fax: 518-465-0506
e-mail: sacquario@nysac.org
Web site: www.nysac.org
Lobbying, research & training services
Stephen J Acquario, Executive Director

Offices and agencies generally appear in alphabetical order, except when specific order is requested by listee.

NYS Bar Assn, Mass Disaster Response Committee
NYS Grievance Committee
Renaissance Plz, 335 Adams St, Ste 2400, Brooklyn, NY 11201
718-923-6300 Fax: 718-624-2978
e-mail: rsaltzma@courts.state.ny.us

NYS Bar Assn, Law Youth & Citizenship Committee
NYS Supreme Court
92 Franklin Street, 2nd Floor, Buffalo, NY 14202
716-845-9327 Fax: 716-851-3229
e-mail: oyoung@courts.state.ny.us
Oliver C Young, Chair

Nelson A Rockefeller Institute of Government
411 State St, Albany, NY 12203-1003
518-443-5522 Fax: 518-443-5788
e-mail: nathanr@rockinst.org
Web site: www.rockinst.org
Management & finance of welfare, health & employment of state & local governments nationally & especially in NY
Richard P Nathan, Co-Director

New York Public Interest Research Group
9 Murray St, 3rd Fl, New York, NY 10007
212-349-6460 Fax: 212-349-1366
e-mail: nypirg@nypirg.org
Web site: www.nypirg.org
Environmental preservation, public health, consumer protection & government reform
Christopher Meyer, Executive Director

New York State Directory
4919 Route 22, PO Box 56, Amenia, NY 12501
518-789-8700 or 800-562-2139 Fax: 518-789-0556
e-mail: books@greyhouse.com
Web site: www.greyhouse.com
State government public policy directory
Leslie Mackenzie, Publisher

Community Bankers Assn of NY State, Government Relations Cmte
Pioneer Savings Bank
21 Second St, Troy, NY 12180
518-274-4800 Fax: 518-274-3560
Web site: www.pioneersb.com
John M Scarchilli, President & CEO

PricewaterhouseCoopers LLP
State St Ctr, 80 State St, Albany, NY 12207
518-462-2030 Fax: 518-427-4499
Web site: www.pwc.com
Rich Grant, Managing Partner

Spec Cmte on Collateral Consequence of Criminal Proceedings
Proskauer Rose LLP
1585 Broadway, New York, NY 10036-8299
212-969-3261 Fax: 212-969-2900
e-mail: psherwin@proskauer.com
Web site: www.proskauer.com
Peter J W Sherwin, Chair

Public Agenda
6 East 39th St, 9th Fl, New York, NY 10016
212-686-6610 Fax: 212-889-3461
e-mail: info@publicagenda.org
Web site: www.publicagenda.org
Nonpartisan, nonprofit organization dedicated to conducting unbiased public opinion research & producing fair-minded citizen education materials
Claudia Feurey, Vice President, Communications & External Relations

SUNY at Albany, Center for Women in Government & Civil Society
135 Western Ave, Draper Hall, Rm 302, Albany, NY 12222
518-442-3900 Fax: 518-442-3877
e-mail: cwig@albany.edu
Web site: www.cwig.albany.edu
Through research, teaching, leadership development, networking & public education, the center works to strengthen women's public policy leadership, broaden access to policy knowledge, skills & influence; advance equity, enhance nonprofit mgmnt
Judith R Saidel, Executive Director

SUNY at Albany, Rockefeller College
135 Western Ave, Albany, NY 12222
518-442-5378 Fax: 518-442-5298
Intergovernmental relations; NY state & local government; ethics in government; election systems & voting
Joseph F Zimmerman, Professor

SUNY at New Paltz, College of Liberal Arts & Sciences
614 Faculty Tower, New Paltz, NY 12561-2499
845-257-3520
e-mail: benjamig@newpaltz.edu
Web site: www.newpaltz.edu
Local & state government process & structure; regionalism; politics & election law
Gerald Benjamin, Dean & Professor of Political Science

SUNY at New Paltz, Department of History
75 South Manheim Blvd, New Paltz, NY 12561
845-257-3523 Fax: 845-257-2735
American Indian policies
Laurence Hauptman, SUNY Distinguished Professor of History

Syracuse University, Maxwell School of Citizenship & Public Affairs
400 Eggers Hall, Syracuse, NY 13244-1020
315-443-2252 Fax: 315-443-1081
e-mail: ctrpol@syr.edu
Web site: www.maxwell.syr.edu
Education, healthcare, entrpreneurship policies, social welfare, income distribution & comparative social policies
Timothy Smeeding, Professor of Public Policy; Director

Offices and agencies generally appear in alphabetical order, except when specific order is requested by listee.

HEALTH

NEW YORK STATE

GOVERNOR'S OFFICE

Governor's Office
Executive Chamber
State Capitol
Albany, NY 12224
518-474-8390 Fax: 518-474-1513
Web site: www.ny.gov

Governor:
   Andrew M Cuomo 518-474-8390
Secretary to the Governor:
   William Mulrow 518-474-4246
Counsel to the Governor:
   Alphonso David 518-474-8343
Deputy Secretary, Health:
   Courtney Burke..................................518-408-2500
Director, Communications:
   Melissa DeRosa ....518-474-8418 or 212-681-4640

EXECUTIVE DEPARTMENTS AND RELATED AGENCIES

Alcoholism & Substance Abuse Services, Office of
1450 Western Ave
Albany, NY 12203
518-473-3460 Fax: 518-457-5474
e-mail: communications@oasas.ny.gov
Web site: www.oasas.ny.gov

501 7th Ave
8th Fl
New York, NY 10018
646-728-4533

Commissioner:
   Arlene Gonzalez-Sanchez.........................518-457-2061
Executive Deputy Commissioner:
   Sean M. Byrne 518-457-1758

Bureau of Public Information & Communications
Director, Public Information & Communications:
   Susan A Craig, MPH 518-457-8299

Office of Counsel & Internal Controls
Director:
   Robert Kent......................................518-485-2312
Office of Audit Services:
   Steven Shrager 518-485-2053
Internal Control Unit:
   Sandra Scleicher 518-485-1109

Office of Governmental Affairs & Grants Mgmt
Director:
   Patricia Zuber-Wilson...........................518-485-2317

Office of NYC Operations, Affirmative Action & Bureau of Recovery
COO:
   Ramon Rodriguez.................................646-728-4720
Affirmative Action Unit Officer:
   Loretta Poole....................................646-728-4530
Recovery Initiatives:
   Lureen McNeil 518-457-6750

Office of Medical Director
Medical Director:
   Charles W Morgan, MD...........................845-359-8500
Director, Health Initiatives:
   Peggy Bonneau...................................518-457-5989

Fiscal Administration Division
Associate Commissioner:
   P David Sawicki 518-457-5312

Bureau of Budget Management
Director:
   Tara Gabriel 518-485-2193

Bureau of Capital Management
Director:
   Jeff Emad 518-457-2545

Bureau of Financial Management
Director:
   Kevin Doherty 518-457-3562

Bureau of Health Care Financing & 3rd Party Reimbursement
Director:
   Laurie Felter....................................518-457-5312

Outcome Management & System Information Division
Associate Commissioner:
   William F. Hogan 518-485-2322

Bureau of State/Local Planning
Director:
   Vacant...518-485-2322

Bureau of Data Analysis, Data Quality & Evaluation
Director:
   Vacant...518-485-7189

Bureau of Research, Epidemiology & Practice Improvement
Director:
   Vacant...518-485-5989

Office of Statewide Field Operations
Director:
   Sean Byrne 518-485-2337

Prevention, Housing & Management Services Division
Acting Associate Commissioner:
   Mary Ann DiChristopher 518-485-6022

Bureau of Housing
Director:
   Henri Williams..................................518-485-0496

Bureau of Prevention Services
Director:
   Scott Brady......................................518-457-4384

Bureau of Management Services
Director:
   Vacant...518-485-6689

Information Technology Services
Director:
   Laura Frost 518-485-2351

Quality Assurance & Performance Improvement Division
Associate Commissioner:
   Charles W Monson................................518-485-2257

Bureau of Certification & Systems Management
Director:
   Janet Paloski 518-485-2250

Offices and agencies generally appear in alphabetical order, except when specific order is requested by listee.

Bureau of Standards Compliance
Director:
    Vacant 518-485-2255

Bureau of Talent Management & Credentializing
Director:
    Julia Fesko 518-485-2033

Treatment & Practice Innovation Division
Associate Commissioner:
    Steve Hanson 518-457-7077

Bureau of Addiction Treatment Centers
Assistant Director:
    Paula Bradwell . . . . .518-457-7077 or 585-461-0410

Education Department
State Education Bldg
89 Washington Ave
Albany, NY 12234
518-474-3852 Fax: 518-486-5631
Web site: www.nysed.gov

Commissioner, University President:
    MaryEllen Elia 518-474-5844
Assistant to the Commissioner:
    Christopher J Halpin .518-474-5845
Acting Counsel & Deputy Commissioner, Legal Affairs:
    Erin O'Grady 518-474-6400
Chief of Staff & Deputy Commissioner, Innovation:
    Allison Armour-Garb .518-486-1713

Office of the Professions . . . . .fax: 518-474-1449
89 Washington Ave, EB, 2nd Fl, West Mezz, Albany, NY 12234
Fax: 518-474-1449
Web site: www.op.nysed.gov
Associate Commissioner:
    Deborah Marriott 518-473-2998

Office of Professional Responsibility
Director:
    Harrison Fisher 518-474-3817

Professional Education Program Review
Supervisor:
    William Murphy .518-474-3817 x300
    e-mail: opprogs@mail.nysed.gov

Professional Licensing Services
Acting Director:
    Susan Naccarato 518-474-3817 x340

Health Department
Corning Tower
Empire State Plaza
Albany, NY 12237
518-474-2011
Web site: wwww.health.ny.gov

Office of the Commissioner
Commissioner:
    Howard Zucker, MD, JD .518-474-2011
Executive Deputy Commissioner:
    Sally Dreslin, MS, RN .518-474-2011

Division of Administration
Deputy Commissioner, Administration:
    Michael J. Nazarko 518-474-8565

AIDS Institute
Director:
    Dan O'Connell . . . . .518-474-6399 or 518-473-6399

Deputy Director, HIV Health Care, Surveillance & Data Systems:
    Mona Scully 518-474-1383
Deputy Director, Office Medicaid Policy & Programs:
    Ira Feldman 518-486-1383
Deputy Director, HIV/STD/Hepatitis C Prevention & Administration:
    Valerie White 518-474-5577
Deputy Director, HIV/STD/Hepatitis C Prevention Services:
    James Tesoriero 518-473-2300
Assistant Director, NYC Office:
    Joan Edwards 212-417-4508
Medical Director, Office of the Medical Director:
    Bruce D Agins 212-417-4536
Deputy Director, Office of the Medical Director:
    Lyn Stevens. 518-473-8815

Center for Community Health
Director:
    Bradley Hutton 518-473-4371
Associate Director:
    Adrienne Mazeau. 518-473-4371/fax: 518-473-8389

Chronic Disease Prevention & Adult Health Division
Director:
    Barbara Wallace 518-474-0512/fax: 518-474-5396
Associate Director:
    Rachel Iverson. 518-474-0512/fax: 518-474-5396

Epidemiology Division
Director:
    Debra Blog, M.D. 518-473-4464/fax: 518-473-2301
Associate Director:
    Stephanie Ostrowski 518-473-4465/fax: 518-473-2301

Family Health Division
Director:
    Rachel de Long 518-474-6968/fax: 518-474-7054
Associate Director:
    Wendy Shaw. 518-474-6968
Medical Director:
    Marilyn Kacica 518-473-9883
Associate Medical Director:
    Christopher A Kus 518-473-9883

Information Technology & Project Management
Director:
    Linh Le 518-473-1809/fax: 518-473-0476
Assistant Director:
    Audra McDonald 518-408-1121

Minority Health
Director:
    Yvonne Graham 518-474-2180/fax: 518-474-4695

Nutrition Division
Director:
    Loretta Santilli. 518-402-7090/fax: 518-402-1149
Associate Director:
    Patricia Race 518-402-7090/fax: 518-402-1149
Associate Director:
    Jill Dunkel 518-402-7090/fax: 518-402-1149

Center for Environmental Health
Director:
    Dr. Nathan Graber. 518-402-7500

Division of Environmental Health Assessment
Director:
    Kevin Gleason 518-402-7511

Division of Environmental Health Investigation
Director:
    Vacant. 518-402-7510

Offices and agencies generally appear in alphabetical order, except when specific order is requested by listee.

Policy Areas

Division of Environmental Health Protection
Director:
  Michael Cambridge 518-402-7500

Executive Offices

Office of Governmental & External Affairs
Assistant Commissioner:
  Amy Nickson 518-473-1124/fax: 518-473-9674
  Division of Council Operations
  Deputy Director:
    Kelly Seebald...............................518-474-8009
  Division of External Affairs
  Deputy Director:
    Angie Corsi 518-473-8007
  Division of Governmental Affairs
  Deputy Director:
    Amy Nickson...............................518-473-1124

Office of Health Insurance Programs
Deputy Commissioner & State Medicaid Director:
  Jason A. Helgerson 518-474-3018/fax: 518-486-1346
Deputy Director:
  Elizabeth Misa...................518-474-8646/fax: 518-486-1346
Medical Director:
  Alda Osinaga, MD 518-486-1042
Medical Director:
  Douglas Fish, MD 518-473-0919
Director, Division of Eligibility & Marketplace Integration:
  Judith Arnold 518-474-0180
Director, Division of OHIP Systems:
  Jonathan Halvorson 518-649-4402
Director, Division of OHIP Operations:
  Jonathan Bick 518-474-8161
Director, Division of Health Plan Contracting & Oversight:
  Vallencia Lloyd 518-474-5737
Director, Division of Program Development & Mngmnt:
  Gregory Allen..............................518-473-0919
Director & CFO, Division of Finance & Rate Setting:
  John Ulberg 518-474-6350
Director, Division of Long Term Care:
  Mark Kissinger............................518-402-5673
Director, Division of Employee & Program Support:
  Ralph Bielefeldt 518-486-5386

Office of Quality & Patient Safety
Director:
  Patrick Roohan 518-473-2941
Deputy Director:
  Joseph Anarella 518-486-9012
Medical Director:
  Foster Gesten, MD, FACP 518-486-6865

Office of Public Health
Deputy Commissioner:
  Guthrie S Birkhead MD MPH 518-402-5382
Deputy Director:
  Ellen Anderson 518-473-0771
Director, Office of Public Health Practice:
  Sylvia Pirani..............................518-473-4223
Director, Health Emergency Preparedness:
  Michael Primeau...........................518-474-2893

School of Public Health, SUNY at Albany ....fax: 518-402-0329
One University Place, Rensselaer, NY 12144
518-402-0283 Fax: 518-402-0329
Dean:
  Philip C Nasca PhD.............518-402-0281/fax: 518-402-0329
Assistant Dean, Administration:
  Larry D Preston 518-402-0281

Health Facilities Management
Director:
  David J Hernandez 518-474-2772/fax: 518-474-0611

Helen Hayes Hospital
Rte 9W, West Haverstraw, NY 10993-1195
845-786-4000
e-mail: info@helenhayeshospital.org
Web site: www.helenhayeshospital.org
CEO:
  Edmund Coletti..................845-786-4202/fax: 845-947-0036
COO:
  Kathleen Martucci 845-786-4201

New York State Veterans' Home at Batavia
220 Richmond Ave, Batavia, NY 14020
585-345-2000
Web site: www.nysvets.org
Administrator:
  Joanne I Hernick 585-345-2076/fax: 585-345-9030
Medical Director:
  Mary Obear MD..............................585-345-2042
Director, Nursing:
  Stephanie Sulyma 585-345-2000 x2041

New York State Veterans' Home at Montrose......fax: 914-788-6100
2090 Albany Post Rd, Montrose, NY 10548
Fax: 914-788-6100
Web site: www.nysvets.org
Administrator:
  Nancy Baa-Danso...........................914-788-6003
Acting Medical Director:
  Ron Ammon, MD............................914-788-6025
Director, Nursing:
  Christene St Paul Joseph 914-788-6021

New York State Veterans' Home at Oxford
4211 State Highway 220, Oxford, NY 13830
607-843-3100
Web site: www.nysvets.org
Administrator:
  James Wyzykowski..............607-843-3129/fax: 607-843-3199
Medical Director:
  Philip Dzwonczyk MD........................607-843-3140

New York State Veterans' Home at St Albans
178-50 Linden Blvd, Jamaica, NY 11434-1467
718-990-0300
Administrator:
  Neville Goldson 718-990-0329
Medical Director:
  Thomas Bizarro MD.........................718-990-0328
Director, Nursing:
  Elaine Boyd-Brown 718-990-0316

Health Research Inc
Riverview Center, 150 Broadway, Ste 560, Menands, NY 12204-2719
Web site: www.healthresearch.org
Executive Director:
  Barbara Ryan 518-431-1204

Office of Primary Care & Health Systems Management
Deputy Commissioner:
  Daniel B Sheppard 518-474-1686
Deputy Director & Director, Office of Professional Medical Conduct:
  Keith W Servis 518-408-1828
Director, Planning & Performance Group (PPG):
  Paul Ambrose 518-486-9177
Director, Administrative Mgmnt Services Group (AMS):
  Karyn Andrade 518-486-9177
Director, Data Management, Analysis & Research Group (DAR):
  Laura Dellahunt 518-473-7019

Offices and agencies generally appear in alphabetical order, except when specific order is requested by listee.

Assistant Director, Center for Health Care Provider Services & Oversight (PSO):
    Jennifer Treacy 518-408-1245
Director, Division of Adult Care Facilities & Assisted Living Surveillance:
    Valerie Deetz 518-408-1133
Deputy Director, Division of Adult Care Facilities & Assisted Living Surveillance:
    Timothy Perry-Coon 518-408-1133
Director, Bureau of Emergency Medical Services:
    Lee Burns 518-402-0997
Deputy Director, Office of Professional Medical Conduct (OPMC):
    Paula M Breen. 518-402-0855
Acting Director, Division of Nursing Homes & Intermediate Care Facilities:
    Shelly Glock 518-408-1267

Human Resources Management Group
Director:
    Joyce M Neznek 518-473-3394/fax: 518-486-7374

Operations Management Group
Director:
    John Reith 518-474-6936/fax: 518-474-8163

Office of Information Technology Services (ITS) Health Cluster
Acting Health Cluster CIO:
    Robert Pennacchia. 518-474-8373/fax: 518-474-2288
Acting Deputy CIO, Health Cluster:
    Linh Le 518-474-8373/fax: 518-474-2288

Legal Affairs
General Counsel:
    James E. Dering. 518-474-7553/fax: 518-473-2802
Director, Bureau of Adjudication:
    James Horan .518-402-0748/fax: 518-402-0751
Director, Bureau of Administrative Hearings:
    Mark Fleischer. 518-473-1707/fax: 518-486-1858
Acting Director, Bureau of House Counsel:
    Sandra Jensen 518-473-3233/fax: 518-473-2019
Director, Bureau of Litigation:
    Richard Zahnleuter 518-473-4631/fax: 518-473-2802
Director, Bureau of Health Insurance Programs:
    Daniel Tarantino 518-408-1495/fax: 518-486-4834
Chief Counsel, Professional Medical Conduct Unit:
    Henry Weintraub. 518-474-8266/fax: 518-473-2430
Acting Records Access Officer:
    Danielle Levine. 518-474-8734

Task Force On Life & The Law
90 Church St, New York, NY 10007
Executive Director:
    Stuart C Sherman 212-417-5444

Public Affairs
Director:
    Vacant 518-474-7354 x1
Deputy Director:
    Marci Natale. 518-474-7354 x1

Regional Offices

Central New York Regional Office
217 S Salina St, Syracuse, NY 13202-1380
315-477-8100
Director:
    David C. Brittain, MD 315-477-8522
Deputy Director:
    Christine Challipnicki. 315-477-8142

Metropolitan Area/Regional Office
90 Church St, New York, NY 10007
212-417-4100
Regional Director:
    Celeste M Johnson 212-417-5550

Deputy Regional Director:
    Ellen Poliski 212-417-5550

Western Regional Office
584 Delaware Ave, Buffalo, NY 14202-1295
716-847-4500
Acting Associate Commissioner:
    Gregory Young. 716-847-4505

Roswell Park Cancer Institute Corporation
Elm & Carlton Streets, Buffalo, NY 14263-0999
716-845-2300
Web site: www.roswellpark.org
President/CEO:
    Candace S Johnson, PhD 716-845-5772/fax: 716-845-8261
Executive Director:
    Vacant 716-845-3385
Chief Medical Officer:
    Boris Kuvshinoff, MD 716-845-7724
Legal Counsel:
    Michael Sexton 716-845-8717
VP, Government Affairs:
    Lisa Damiani. 716-845-3079
    e-mail: lisa.damiani@roswellpark.org

Wadsworth Center
Director:
    Jill Taylor. 518-474-3157/fax: 518-474-3439
Deputy Director:
    Vicky Derbyshire 518-474-7592
Associate Director, Administration:
    Carlene Van Patten 518-474-7592
Associate Director, Research & Technology:
    Erasmus Schneider 518-473-4856
Associate Director, Laboratory Operations:
    Elizabeth Mahoney. 518-474-1002
Associate Director, Medical Affairs:
    Anne Walsh. 518-474-7592

Environmental Health Sciences
Director:
    Ken Aldous .518-474-7161/fax: 518-473-2895
Deputy Director:
    Patrick Parsons 518-474-7161

Genetics
Director:
    Keith Derbyshire 518-473-6079
Deputy Director:
    Michele Caggana 518-473-3854

Herbert W Dickerman Library . . . . .fax: 518-474-3933
518-474-6172 Fax: 518-474-3933

Infectious Disease
Director:
    Ron Limberger 518-474-8660
Deputy Director:
    Kathleen McDonough 518-486-4253

Laboratory Quality Certification
Director:
    Michael Ryan 518-473-3424

Translational Medicine
Director:
    Michael Koonce 518-486-1490
Deputy Director:
    Rajendra Agrawal. 518-486-5797

Financial Services Department
One State Street
New York, NY 10001

Offices and agencies generally appear in alphabetical order, except when specific order is requested by listee.

Policy Areas

212-480-6500 or 518-474-6600
e-mail: public-affairs@dfs.ny.gov
Web site: www.dfs.ny.gov

Superintendent:
  Benjamin M. Lawsky 212-709-3501
Deputy Superintendent & General Counsel:
  Marjorie Gross 212-709-1640
Chief Administrative Officer:
  Cheryl Aini 518-473-6160
Director, Communications:
  David Neustadt 212-480-5265/fax: 212-480-6077
Assistant Director, Administration & Operations:
  Lori Fraser. 518-486-4737

Health Bureau
Chief:
  Vacant 518-486-2970/fax: 518-474-3397

Life Bureau
Chief Examiner:
  Gail Keren .212-480-5030/fax: 212-480-5329

Labor Department
Building 12, Room 500
Harriman State Office Campus
Albany, NY 12240
518-457-9000 Fax: 518-457-6908
e-mail: nysdol@labor.ny.gov
Web site: www.labor.ny.gov

Commissioner:
  Colleen Gardner 518-457-9000
Director, Communications:
  Leo Rosales 518-457-5519/fax: 518-485-1126
  e-mail: leo.rosales@labor.ny.gov

Worker Protection
Deputy Commissioner, Workforce Protection, Standards & Licensing:
  Pico Ben-Amotz 518-457-4317

Safety & Health Division
Director:
  Maureen Cox. 518-457-3518/fax: 518-457-1519
  Asbestos Control Bureau
  Program Manager:
    Robert Perez 518-457-1255/fax: 518-485-8054
  Industry Inspection Unit
  Program Manager, License & Certification:
    Martha Waldman 518-457-2375
  On-Site Consultation Unit
  Program Manager:
    James Rush 518-457-2238/fax: 518-457-3454
  Public Employees Safety & Health (PESH) Unit
  Program Manager:
    Normand Labbe 518-457-1263/fax: 518-457-5545

Law Department
120 Broadway
New York, NY 10271-0332
212-416-8000 or 800-771-7755
Web site: www.ag.ny.gov

State Capitol
Albany, NY 12224-0341
518-474-7330
Fax: 518-473-9909

Attorney General:
  Eric T Schneiderman . . . . .212-416-8050 or 518-474-7330

Chief of Staff:
  Micah Lasher 212-416-8050
Director, Public Information:
  Shawn Morris 518-776-2357/fax: 518-650-9401
Press Secretary:
  Fernando Aquino. 212-416-8060/fax: 212-416-6005

Criminal Justice
Executive Deputy Attorney General:
  Kelly Donovan 212-416-8050

Medicaid Fraud Control Unit
Deputy Attorney General in Charge & Director:
  Vacant 212-417-5250/fax: 212-417-4284
First Asst Attorney General, Legal Affrs:
  Monica Hickey-Martin 212-417-5339/fax: 212-417-4284
First Asst Attorney General, Operations:
  Florence L Finkle 212-417-5850
Regional Director, NYC:
  Richard Harrow. 212-417-5390/fax: 212-417-4725
Deputy Regional Director, Buffalo:
  Gary A Baldauf 716-853-8507/fax: 716-852-8525
Regional Director, Long Island:
  Jane Turkin 631-952-6400/fax: 631-952-6382
Regional Director, Rochester:
  Catherine Wagner 716-262-2860/fax: 716-262-2866
Regional Director, Syracuse:
  Ralph Tortora, III 315-423-1104/fax: 315-423-1120
Deputy Regional Director, Pearl River:
  Anne S Jardine 845-732-7525/fax: 845-732-7555

Social Justice
Executive Deputy Attorney General:
  Alvin L Braggs, Jr 212-416-8450/fax: 212-416-8942

Healthcare Bureau
Bureau Chief:
  Lisa Landau . . . . .518-776-2477 or 212-416-6305
  fax: 518-650-9365

State Counsel
Chief Deputy Attorney General:
  Harlan Levy 212-416-8525

Claims Bureau
Bureau Chief:
  Katharine Brooks . . . . .518-776-2300 or 212-416-8913

Litigation Bureau
Bureau Chief:
  Lisa Dell . . . . .518-776-2300 or 212-416-8610

CORPORATIONS, AUTHORITIES AND COMMISSIONS

New York State Dormitory Authority
515 Broadway
Albany, NY 12207-2964
518-257-3000 Fax: 518-257-3100
e-mail: dabonds@dasny.org
Web site: www.dasny.org

One Penn Plaza
52nd Fl
New York, NY 10119-0098
212-273-5000
Fax: 212-273-5121

539 Franklin St
Buffalo, NY 14202-1109

Offices and agencies generally appear in alphabetical order, except when specific order is requested by listee.

716-884-9780
Fax: 716-884-9787

Chair:
 Alfonso L Carney Jr 518-257-3000/fax: 518-257-3100
President/CEO:
 Paul T Williams Jr 518-257-3180/fax: 518-257-3183
Vice President:
 Michael T Corrigan 518-257-3192/fax: 518-257-3183
Chief Financial Officer:
 Linda H Button 518-257-3562/fax: 518-257-3100
General Counsel:
 Michael Cusack 518-257-3120/fax: 518-257-3101
Managing Director, Construction:
 Stephen D Curro, PE 518-257-3271/fax: 518-257-3100
 e-mail: scurro@dasny.org
Managing Director, Public Finance & Portfolio Monitoring:
 Portia Lee. 518-257-3362/fax: 518-257-3100
 e-mail: plee@dasny.org
Public Information Officer:
 John Chirlin. 518-257-3380
 e-mail: jchirlin@dasny.org

NEW YORK STATE LEGISLATURE

See Legislative Branch in Section 1 for additional Standing Committee and Subcommittee information.

Assembly Standing Committees

Aging
Chair:
 Steven Cymbrowitz (D) 518-455-5214
Ranking Minority Member:
 Angela M Wozniak (C). 518-455-5921

Alcoholism & Drug Abuse
Chair:
 Linda Rosenthal (D) 518-455-5802
Ranking Minority Member:
 Mark Johns (R) 518-455-5784

Children & Families
Chair:
 Donna Lupardo (D). 518-455-5431
Ranking Minority Member:
 Stevenr McLaughlin (R). 518-455-5777

Consumer Affairs & Protection
Chair:
 Jeffrey Dinowitz (D). 518-455-5965
Ranking Minority Member:
 Anthony Palumbo (R). 518-455-5294

Health
Chair:
 Richard N Gottfried (D) 518-455-4941
Ranking Minority Member:
 Andrew Raia (R). 518-455-5952

Senate Standing Committees

Aging
Chair:
 Sue Serino (R). 518-455-2945
Ranking Minority Member:
 Ruben Diaz Sr (D) 518-455-2511

Children & Families
Chair:
 Simcha Felder (D). 518-455-2754
Ranking Minority Member:
 Velmanette Montgomery (D) .518-455-3451

Consumer Protection
Chair:
 Michael Venditto (R) 518-455-3341
Ranking Minority Member:
 Leroy Comrie (D) 518-455-2701

Health
Chair:
 Kemp Hannon (R). 518-455-2200
Ranking Minority Member:
 J. Gustavo Rivera (D) 518-455-3395

Social Services
Chair:
 David Carlucci (D) 518-455-2991

U.S. GOVERNMENT

EXECUTIVE DEPARTMENTS AND RELATED AGENCIES

US Department of Agriculture
Web site: www.usda.gov

Food & Nutrition Service

Albany Field Office
O'Brien Federal Bldg, Rm 752, 1 Clinton Ave & N Pearl St, Albany, NY 12207
Branch Manager:
 Diane Adams

New York City Field Office
201 Varick St, Rm 609, New York, NY 10014
212-620-7360
Branch Manager:
 Denise Thomas 212-620-7360

Rochester Field Office. . . . . fax: 585-263-3146
Federal Bldg, 100 State St, Rm 3180, Rochester, NY 14614-1360
585-263-6744 Fax: 585-263-3146
General Manager:
 Claudia Ortiz 585-263-6748/fax: 585-263-5807
 e-mail: claudia.ortiz@FNS.usda.gov

Food Safety & Inspection Service
Web site: www.fsis.usda.gov

Field Operations-Albany District Office . . . . fax: 518-452-3118
230 Washington Avenue, Albany, NY 12203-6870
District Manager:
 Haroon Mian. 518-452-6870

US Department of Health & Human Services
Web site: www.os.dhhs.gov; www.hhs.gov/region2/

Administration for Children & Families . . . . fax: 212-264-4881
 26 Federal Plaza, Rm 4114, New York, NY 10278
 212-264-2890 Fax: 212-264-4881
 Web site: www.acf.hhs.gov
Regional Administrator:
 Joyce A. Thomas

Administration on Aging . . . . fax: 212-264-0114
 26 Federal Plaza, Rm 38-102, New York, NY 10278

Offices and agencies generally appear in alphabetical order, except when specific order is requested by listee.

212-264-2976 Fax: 212-264-0114
Web site: www.aoa.gov
Regional Administrator:
Kathleen Otte
e-mail: kathleen.otte@aoa.hhs.gov

Centers for Disease Control & Prevention
Web site: www.cdc.gov

Agency for Toxic Substances & Disease Registry-EPA Region 2
290 Broadway North, 20th Floor, New York, NY 10007
Web site: www.atsdr.cdc.gov
Regional Director:
Leah Graziano, RS 212-637-4306
e-mail: escobar.leah@epa.gov

New York Quarantine Station ....fax: 718-553-1524
Terminal 4E, Rm 219 016, JFK Airport, Jamaica, NY 11430-1081
718-553-1685 Fax: 718-553-1524
Officer-in-Charge:
Donald Spatz

Centers for Medicare & Medicaid Services
26 Federal Plaza, Rm 3811, New York, NY 10278-0063
Web site: www.cms.hhs.gov
Regional Administrator:
Raymond Hurd 617-565-1188
e-mail: robosora@cms.hhs.gov
Deputy Regional Administrator:
Dr. Gilbert Kunken 212-616-2205/fax: 212-264-6189
e-mail: gilbert.kunken@cms.hhs.gov

Medicaid and Children's Health (DMCH)
Associate Regional Administrator:
Michael Melendez 212-616-2400
e-mail: ronydmch@cms.hhs.gov

Medicare Financial Management (DMFM)
Associate Regional Administrator:
Vacant

Medicare Survey & Certification Operations Division (CQISCO)
Associate Regional Administrator:
William Robertson 215-861-4287
e-mail: rophidsc@cms.hhs.gov

Food & Drug Administration
888-463-6332
Web site: www.fda.gov

Northeast Region
158-15 Liberty Ave, Jamaica, NY 11433
Deputy Regional Director:
W. Charles Becoat
New York District Office
District Director:
Ronald Pace
Northeast Regional Laboratory
158-15 Liberty Ave, Jamaica, NY 11433
Director:
Michael J Palmieri 718-662-5450/fax: 718-662-5439

Health Resources & Svcs Admin Office of Performance
Review ....fax: 212-264-2673
26 Federal Bldg, Rm 3337, New York, NY 10278
Regional Division Director:
Ron Moss 212-264-2664
e-mail: robert.moss@hrsa.hhs.gov
Operations Director:
Margaret Lee....................................212-264-2571
e-mail: margaret.lee@hrsa.hhs.gov

Director, Office of Engineering Services:
Emilio Pucillo...............................212-264-3600
e-mail: emilio.pucillo@hrsa.hhs.gov

Indian Health Services-Area Office ....fax: 615-467-1501
The Reyes Building, 801 Thompson Avenue, Suite 400, Rockville, MD 20852
Director:
Dr. Yvette Roubideaux.....................301-443-3593

Office of Secretary's Regional Representative-Region 2-NY .. fax: 646-428-3904
32 Old Slip, 25th Floor, New York, NY 10278
646-428-3905 Fax: 646-428-3904
Regional Director:
Jamie R. Torres
Primary Accounting Specialist:
Meredith Bajgier
Communications Director:
Jacquelyn Pitta

Office for Civil Rights.........................fax: 212-264-3039
26 Federal Plaza, Rm 3312, New York, NY 10278
Fax: 212-264-3039
Web site: www.hhs.gov/ocr
Regional Manager:
Linda Colon 212-264-3313

Office of General Counsel
26 Federal Plaza, Rm 3908, New York, NY 10278
Chief Counsel:
Joel Lerner 212-264-6373

Office of Inspector General
Regional Inspector General, Audit:
James P Edert....................................212-264-4620
Regional Inspector General & Regional Coordinator, Investigations:
Thomas O'Donnell...............................212-264-9497
Regional Inspector General, Evaluations & Inspections:
Jodi Nudelman 212-264-1998

Office of Public Health & Science
26 Federal Plaza, Rm 3835, New York, NY 10278
Regional Health Administrator:
Michelle S. Davis...............................212-264-2560
Deputy Regional Health Administrator:
Robert L Davidson...............................212-264-2560
Regional Family Planning Consultant:
Robin Lane......................................212-264-3935
e-mail: rlane@osophs.hhs.gov
Regional Minority Health Consultant:
Claude Colimon 212-264-2560
Regional Women's Health Coordinator:
Sandra Estepa...................................212-264-2560

US Department of Homeland Security (DHS)
Web site: www.dhs.gov

Federal Emergency Management Agency (FEMA)
TTY: 800-462-7585 or 800-621-3362

National Disaster Medical System ....fax: 212-680-3608
26 Federal Plz, Rm 3835, New York, NY 10278
Coordinator:
Captain Bonita Pyler, USPHS 212-680-8542
e-mail: pyler@dhs.gov

New York Regional Office ....fax: 212-680-3681
26 Federal Plz, Ste 1311, New York, NY 10278
Regional Director:
Stephen Kempf, Jr 212-680-3612

Offices and agencies generally appear in alphabetical order, except when specific order is requested by listee.

US Labor Department

Web site: www.dol.gov

Occupational Safety & Health Adminstration (OSHA).......fax: 212-337-2371

201 Varick St, Rm 670, New York, NY 10014
212-337-2378 Fax: 212-337-2371
Web site: www.osha.gov
Regional Administrator:
Robert D. Kulick

Albany Area Office
401 New Karner Rd, Ste 300, Albany, NY 12205-3809
Area Director:
Kim Castillion

Buffalo Area Office
130 South Elmwood Avenue, Suite 500, Browmansville, NY 14026
716-551-3126
Area Director:
Arthur Dube 716-551-3053/fax: 716-551-3126

Long Island Area Office ....fax: 516-334-3326
1400 Old Country Road, Suite 208, Westbury, NY 11590
516-334-3344 Fax: 516-334-3326
Area Director:
Anthony Ciuffo.................516-334-3344/fax: 516-334-3326

Manhattan Area Office
201 Varick St, Rm 908, New York, NY 10014
Area Director:
Kay Gee......................212-620-3200/fax: 212-620-4121

Syracuse Area Office
3300 Vickery Rd, North Syracuse, NY 13212
Area Director:
Christopher Adams 315-451-0808/fax: 315-451-1351

Tarrytown Area Office
660 White Plains Rd, 4th Floor, Tarrytown, NY 10591
Area Director:
Diana Cortez 914-524-7510/fax: 914-524-7515

U.S. CONGRESS

See U.S. Congress Chapter for additional Standing Committee and Subcommittee information.

House of Representatives Standing Committees

Agriculture
Chair:
Frank D. Lucas (R-OK) 202-225-5565
Ranking Member:
Collin C. Peterson (D-MN).........................202-225-2165

Subcommittee
Department Operations, Oversight, Nutrition & Forestry
Chair:
Steve King (R-IA) 202-225-4226
Ranking Member:
Marcia L. Fudge (D-OH) 202-225-7032

Energy & Commerce
Chair:
Fred Upton (R-MI) 202-225-3761
Vice Chair:
Marsha Blackburn (D-TN) 202-225-2811
New York Delegate:
Eliot L Engel (D) 202-225-2464
New York Delegate:
Paul Tonko (D)...................................202-225-5076

Subcommittee
Health
Chair:
Joe Pitts (R-PA) 202-225-2411
Ranking Member:
Frank Pallone, Jr. (D-NJ).....................202-225-8892
New York Delegate:
Eliot L Engel (D) 202-225-2464

Ways & Means
Chair:
Dave Kamp (R-MI)................................202-225-3561
Ranking Member:
Sander Levin (D-MI) 202-225-3880
New York Delegate:
Charles B. Rangel (D).............................202-225-4365
New York Delegate:
Joseph Crowley (D) 202-225-3965
New York Delegate:
Tom Reed (R) 202-225-3161

Subcommittee
Health
Chair:
Kevin Brady (R-TX) 202-225-4901
Ranking Member:
Jim McDermott (D-WA).....................202-225-3106

Senate Standing Committees

Aging, Special Committee on
Chair:
Bill Nelson (D-FL)...............................202-224-5274
Ranking Member:
Susan Collins (R-ME).............................202-224-2523

Agriculture, Nutrition & Forestry
Chair:
Debbie Stabenow (D-MI)..........................202-224-4822
Ranking Minority Member:
Thad Cochran (R-MI)..............................202-224-2402

Health, Education, Labor & Pensions
Chair:
Tom Harkin (D-IA)...............................202-224-3254
Ranking Member:
Lamar Alexander (R-TN).........................202-224-4944

Subcommittees
Primary Health & Aging
Chair:
Bernie Sanders (D-VT) 202-224-5141
Ranking Member:
Richard Burr (R-NC)......................202-224-3154

PRIVATE SECTOR

AIDS Council of Northeastern New York
927 Broadway, Albany, NY 12207-1306
518-434-4686 or 800-201-AIDS Fax: 518-427-8184
e-mail: info@aidscouncil.org
Web site: www.aidscouncil.org
Provide HIV/AIDS education & testing to at-risk individuals; offer direct assistance & service coordination to persons living with HIV; serve as public advocates
Michele McClave, Executive Director

Offices and agencies generally appear in alphabetical order, except when specific order is requested by listee.

Adelphi NY Statewide Breast Cancer Hotline & Support Program
Adelphi University, School of Social Work, 1 South Ave, PO Box 701, Garden City, NY 11530
800-877-8077 or 516-877-4320 Fax: 516-877-4336
e-mail: breastcancerhotline@adelphi.edu
Web site: www.adelphi.edu/nysbreastcancer
Breast cancer support, information & referral hotline for all of New York State; community education, support groups, counseling & advocacy
Hillary Rutter, Director

Alzheimer's Association, Northeastern NY
85 Watervliet Ave, Albany, NY 12206
518-438-2217 Fax: 518-438-2219
e-mail: marvin.leroy@alz.org
Web site: www.alzneny.org
Monika Boekmann, President & Chief Executive Officer

American Cancer Society-Eastern Division
19 Dove St, Ste 103, Albany, NY 12210
518-449-5438 ext13 or 518-454-4023 Fax: 518-449-7283
e-mail: peter.slocum@cancer.org
Web site: www.cancer.org
Peter Slocum, Vice President for Advocacy for NY State

American College of Nurse-Midwives, NYC Chapter
450 Clarkson Ave, Box 1227, Brooklyn, NY 11203-2098
718-270-7759 Fax: 718-270-7634
e-mail: gholmes@downstate.edu
Web site: www.nysmidwives.org; www.nyc.org
Midwifery/women's health
Grace Holmes, Chair

American College of Physicians, New York Chapter
100 State St, Ste 700, Albany, NY 12207
518-427-0366 Fax: 518-427-1991
Web site: www.nyacp.org
Develops & advocates policies on health issues
Linda Lambert, Executive Director

American Congress of Obstetricians & Gynecologists/NYS
152 Washington Ave, Suite 300, Albany, NY 12210
518-436-3461 Fax: 518-426-4728
e-mail: info@ny.acog.org
Web site: www.acogny.org
Women's health care & physician education
Donna Montalto, Executive Director

American Fertility Association
305 Madison Ave, Ste 449, New York, NY 10165
888-917-3777
e-mail: info@americaninfertility.org
Web site: www.theafa.org
Infertility, reproductive disorders, adoption; education, research, advocacy, support & referral
Ken Mosesian, Executive Director (Acting)

American Heart Association Founders Affiliate
17 Technology Place, East Syracuse, NY 13057
315-234-4700 Fax: 315-234-4701
e-mail: fdainquiries@heart.org
Web site: www.heart.org
Research, education & community service to reduce disability & death from heart disease & stroke
Michael Weamer, Executive Vice President

American Liver Foundation, Western NY Chapter
25 Canterbury Rd, Ste 316, Rochester, NY 14607
585-271-2859 Fax: 585-271-8642
e-mail: nkoris@liverfoundation.org
Web site: www.liverfoundation.org
Disease research, public education & patient support

Nancy Koris, Executive Director

American Lung Association of NYS Inc
155 Washington Ave, Ste 210, Albany, NY 12210
518-465-2013 Fax: 518-465-2926
e-mail: mseilback@alanys.org
Web site: www.alanys.org
To prevent lung disease & promote lung health
Michael Seilback, Senior Director of Public Policy/Advocacy

Associated Medical Schools of New York
10 Rockefeller Plaza, Suite 1120, New York, NY 10020
212-218-4610 Fax: 212-218-5644
e-mail: jo.wiederhorn@amsny.org
Web site: www.amsny.org
AMS is a consortium of the fifteen public and private medical schools in New York state. Our mission is to support quality health care in New York State.
Jo Wiederhorn, Executive Director

Association of Military Surgeons of the US (AMSUS), NY Chapter
105 Franklin Ave, Malverne, NY 11565-1926
516-542-0025 Fax: 516-593-3114
e-mail: amsusny@aol.com
Improve federal healthcare service; support & represent military & other health care professionals
Col John J Hassett, USAR, President NY Chapter

Bausch & Lomb Inc
One Bausch & Lomb Place, Rochester, NY 14604-2701
585-338-6000 Fax: 585-338-6007
Web site: www.bausch.com
Development, manufacture & marketing of contact lenses & lens care products, opthalmic surgical & pharmaceutical products
Adam Grossberg, VP, Corporate Communications & Investor Relations

New York University School of Medicine Bellevue Hospital Center, Department of Emergency Medicine
462 First Avenue, Rm A-345, New York, NY 10016
212-562-3346 Fax: 212-562-3001
e-mail: goldfl03@popmail.med.nyu.edu
Emergency medicine; medical toxicology
Lewis Goldfrank, Professor/Chairman Emergency Medicine

Brain Injury Association of NYS (BIANYS)
10 Colvin Ave, Albany, NY 12206
518-459-7911 or 800-228-8201 Fax: 518-482-5285
e-mail: info@bianys.org
Web site: www.bianys.org
Public education & advocacy for brain injury persons & their families
Judith I Avner, Executive Director

Bristol-Myers Squibb Co
PO Box 4755, Syracuse, NY 13221-4755
315-432-2709 Fax: 315-432-2619
Web site: www.bms.com
Develops & markets pharmaceuticals
Pamela M Brunet, Manager of Community Affairs

Bronx-Lebanon Hospital Center
1276 Fulton Ave, Bronx, NY 10456
718-901-8595 Fax: 718-299-5447
Web site: www.bronxcare.org
Errol Schneer, Vice President-Planning, Marketing & Public Relations

Center for Hearing and Communication
50 Broadway, Fl 6, New York, NY 10004-1607
917-305-7700 or TTY: 917-305-7999 Fax: 917-305-7888
e-mail: postmaster@chchearing.org
Web site: www.chchearing.org
Rehabilitation & other services for the deaf & hard of hearing
Laurie Hanin, Executive Director

Offices and agencies generally appear in alphabetical order, except when specific order is requested by listee.

Cerebral Palsy Associations of New York State
90 State St, Albany, NY 12207-1709
518-436-0178 Fax: 518-436-8619
e-mail: malvaro@cpofnys.org
Web site: www.cpofnys.org
Advocate & provide direct services with & for individuals with cerebral palsy & other significant disabilities, & their families through a Statewide Affiliate network.
Michael Alvaro, Executive Vice President

Coalition of Fathers & Families NY
PO Box 782, Clifton Park, NY 12065
518-383-8202
e-mail: fafny@fafny.org
Web site: www.fafny.org/fafnypac.htm
Working to keep fathers and families together
James Hays, President

Columbia University, Mailman School of Public Health
Heilbrunn Dept of Population & Family He, 60 Haven Ave, B-2, New York, NY 10032
212-304-5281 Fax: 212-305-7024
e-mail: lpf1@columbia.edu
Web site: cpmcnet.columbia.edu/dept/sph/popfam
Theory, analysis & development of policy & programs supporting public health & human rights
Lynn P Freedman, Associate Professor & Director

Commissioned Officers Assn of the US Public Health Svc Inc (COA)
8201 Corporate Dr, Ste 200, Landover, MD 20785
301-731-9080 Fax: 301-731-9084
e-mail: gfarrell@coausphs.org
Web site: www.coausphs.org
Committed to improving the public health of the US; supports corps officers & advocates for their interests through leadership, education & communication
Jerry Farrell, Executive Director

Committee of Methadone Program Administrators Inc of NYS (COMPA)
1 Columbia Place, 4th Fl, Albany, NY 12207
518-689-0457 Fax: 518-426-1046
e-mail: compahb@hotmail.com
Web site: www.compa-ny.org
Methadone treatment & substance abuse coalition building; advocacy, community education, standards & regulatory review & policy development
Henry Bartlett, Executive Director

Commonwealth Fund
One E 75th St, New York, NY 10021-2692
212-606-3800 Fax: 212-606-3876
e-mail: cmwf@cmwf.org
Web site: www.commonwealthfund.org
Supports independent research on health access, coverage & quality issues affecting minorities, women, elderly & low income
Karen Davis, President

Community Health Care Association of NYS
254 West 31st Street, 9th Fl, New York, NY 10001
212-279-9686 Fax: 212-279-3851
e-mail: eswain@chcanys.org
Web site: www.chcanys.org
Advocacy, education & services for the medically underserved throughout NYS
Elizabeth Swain, Chief Executive Officer

Community Healthcare Network
79 Madison Avenue, Fl 6, New York, NY 10016-7802
212-366-4500 Fax: 212-463-8411
e-mail: cabate@chnnyc.org
Web site: www.chnnyc.org
Health & social services for low-income, ethnically diverse, medically underserved neighborhoods of NYC
Catherine Abate, President & Chief Executive Officer

Continuum Health Partners Inc
555 West 57th, 18th Fl, New York, NY 10019
212-523-7772 Fax: 212-523-7885
e-mail: jmandler@chpnet.org
Web site: wehealnewyork.org
Hospital system in NYC.
Jim Mandler, Assistant Vice President, Public Affairs

Outreach & Extension
Cornell Cooperative Extension, College of Human Ecology, Nutrition, Health
142 MVR Hall, Cornell University, Ithaca, NY 14853-4401
607-255-2247 Fax: 607-255-3794
e-mail: kapb@cornell.edu
Web site: www.cce.cornell.edu
Promoting nutritional well-being; safe preparation & storage of food; reducing food insecurity; improving access to health services
Karl Pillemer, Associate Dean

County Nursing Facilities of New York Inc
c/o NYSAC, 111 Pine Street, Albany, NY 12207
518-465-1473 Fax: 518-465-0506
e-mail: rmaloney@nysac.org
Web site: www.nysac.org
Richard J Maloney, Executive Director

Dental Hygienists' Association of the State of New York Inc
23 Burton Lane, Massapequa, NY 11758
516-541-4540
e-mail: dhasny@aol.com
Web site: www.dhasny.org
Professional association representing registered dental hygienists; working to improve the oral health of New Yorkers
Jean Hall, Administrative Manager

Doctors Without Borders USA
333 7th Ave, Fl 2, New York, NY 10001-5004
212-679-6800 Fax: 212-679-7016
Web site: www.doctorswithoutborders.org
International medical assistance for victims of natural or man-made disasters & armed conflict
Sophie Delaunay, Executive Director

Empire Blue Cross & Blue Shield
11 West 42nd St, 18th Fl, New York, NY 10036
212-476-1000 Fax: 212-476-1281
e-mail: deborah.bohren@empireblue.com
Web site: www.empireblue.com
Health insurance
Deborah Bohren, Senior Vice President, Communications

Empire State Association of Assisted Living
646 Plank Rd, Ste 207, Clifton Park, NY 12065
518-371-2573 Fax: 518-371-3774
e-mail: lnewcomb1@aol.com
Web site: www.esaal.org
Trade association representing NYS assisted living providers
Lisa Newcomb, Executive Director

Offices and agencies generally appear in alphabetical order, except when specific order is requested by listee.

Policy Areas

Epilepsy Coalition of New York State Inc
111 Washington Ave, Albany, NY 12210
518-434-4360 Fax: 518-434-4542
e-mail: ccnys@epilepsyny.org
Web site: www.epilepsyny.org
Promotes awareness of epilepsy & its consequences
Janice W Gay, President

Excellus Health Plan Inc
165 Court Street, Rochester, NY 14647
585-327-7581 Fax: 585-327-7585
e-mail: stephen.sloan@excellus.com
Web site: www.excellus.com
Health insurance
Stephen R Sloan, Senior Vice President & General Counsel

Eye-Bank for Sight Restoration Inc (The)
120 Wall St, New York, NY 10005-3902
212-742-9000 Fax: 212-269-3139
e-mail: info@ebsr.org
Web site: www.eyedonation.org
Cornea & scleral transplants
Patricia Dahl, Executive Director/Chief Executive Officer

Family Planning Advocates of New York State
17 Elk St, Albany, NY 12207-1002
518-436-8408 Fax: 518-436-0004
e-mail: smitj@fpaofnys.org
Web site: www.fpaofnys.org
Reproductive rights
JoAnn M Smith, President/Chief Executive Officer

Friends & Relatives of Institutionalized Aged Inc (FRIA)
18 John St, Suite 905, New York, NY 10038
212-732-5667 or 212-732-4455 Fax: 212-732-6945
e-mail: fria@fria.org
Web site: www.fria.org
Free telephone helpline for information, assistance and complaints related to nursing homes, assisted living and other long term care issues.
Betti Weimersheimer, Executive Director

Generic Pharmaceutical Association
2300 Clarendon Blvd, Suite 400, Arlington, VA 22201-3367
703-647-2480 Fax: 703-647-2481
e-mail: info@gphaonline.org
Web site: www.gphaonline.org
GPhA's core purpose is to improve the lives of consumers by providing timely access to affordable pharmaceuticals. Toward this end, GPhA advances the interests of our members through initiatives in the scientific, regulatory, fed. & state forums.
Kathleen Jaeger, President & Chief Executive Officer

Gertrude H Sergievsky Center (The)
630 West 168th St, New York, NY 10032
212-305-2391 Fax: 212-305-2518
e-mail: rpm2@columbia.edu
Neurological disease research correlating epidemiological techniques with genetic analysis & clinical investigation
Richard Mayeux, Director

Greater New York Hospital Association
555 W 57th St, New York, NY 10019
212-246-7100 Fax: 212-262-6350
e-mail: raske@gnyha.org
Web site: www.gnyha.org
Trade association representing more than 250 not-for-profit hospitals
Kenneth E Raske, President

Group Health Inc
441 9th Ave, New York, NY 10001
212-615-0891 Fax: 212-563-8561
e-mail: jgoodwin@ghi.com
Affordable, quality health insurance for working individuals & families

Healthcare Association of New York State
1 Empire Dr, Rensselaer, NY 12144
518-431-7600 Fax: 518-431-7915
e-mail: skroll@hanys.org
Web site: www.hanys.org
Representing New York's not-for-profit hospitals, health systems & continuing care providers
Steven Kroll, Vice President, Governmental Affairs & External Relations

Home Care Association of New York State Inc
194 Washington Ave, Suite 400, Albany, NY 12210-2314
518-426-8764 x214 Fax: 518-426-8788
e-mail: mkissinger@hcanys.org
Web site: www.hcanys.org
Advocacy for home health care & related health services
Mark L Kissinger, President

Hospice & Palliative Care Association of NYS Inc
2 Computer Drive West, Suite 105, Albany, NY 12205
518-446-1483 Fax: 518-446-1484
e-mail: info@hpcanys.org
Web site: www.hpcanys.org
Hospice & palliative care information & referral service; educational programs; clinical, psychosocial & bereavement issues
Kathy A McMahon, President & Chief Executive Officer

INFORM Inc
5 Hanover Square, New York, NY 10004
212-361-2400 Fax: 212-361-2412
e-mail: inform@informinc.org
Web site: www.informinc.org
Advocacy, research & education on practical methods to protect natural resources & public health
Katherin O'Dea, Interim Executive Director

Institute for Family Health (The)
16 East 16th St, New York, NY 10003
212-633-0800 ext1255 Fax: 212-691-4610
e-mail: ncalman@institute2000.org
Web site: www.institute2000.org
Family practice healthcare for NYC's underserved; health professions training; research & advocacy
Neil S Calman, President/Chief Executive Officer

Iroquois Healthcare Alliance
17 Executive Park Dr, Clifton Park, NY 12065
518-383-5060 Fax: 518-383-2616
e-mail: gfitzgerald@iroquois.org
Web site: www.iroquois.org
Represents healthcare providers in upstate New York
Gary Fitzgerald, President

Jewish Home & Hospital (The)
120 West 106 St, New York, NY 10025
212-870-4600 Fax: 212-870-4895
e-mail: aweiner@jhha.org
Web site: www.jewishhome.org
Long term care & rehabilitation
Audrey Weiner, President & Chief Executive Officer

Lighthouse International
111 East 59th St, New York, NY 10022
212-821-9484 Fax: 212-821-9712
e-mail: cstuen@lighthouse.org
Web site: www.lighthouse.org
Vision rehabilitation, research, education & awareness

Offices and agencies generally appear in alphabetical order, except when specific order is requested by listee.

Cynthia Stuen, Senior Vice President, Policy & Professional Affairs

Marion S Whelan School of Practical Nursing
Geneva General Hospital, 196 North St, Geneva, NY 14456
315-787-4005 Fax: 315-787-4770
e-mail: VictoriaRecord@flhealth.org
Web site: www.flhealth.org - Services & Programs
Health education/diabetes education
Victoria Record MS, RN, Director

Medical Society of the State of NY, Governmental Affairs Division
One Commerce Plaza, Ste 408, Albany, NY 12210
518-465-8085 Fax: 518-465-0976
e-mail: gconway@mssny.org
Web site: www.mssny.org
Healthcare legislation & advocacy
Gerard L Conway, Senior VP/Chief Legislative Counsel

Memorial Sloan-Kettering Cancer Center
1275 York Ave, New York, NY 10065
212-639-3573 Fax: 212-639-3576
Web site: www.mskcc.org
Nat'l Cancer Institute designated comprehensive cancer center
Christine Hickey, Director, Communications

Mount Sinai Medical Center
One Gustave L Levy Plaza, New York, NY 10029-6514
212-241-6500 Fax: 212-410-6111
e-mail: brad.beckstrom@mssm.edu
Web site: www.mountsinaihospital.org
Brad Beckstrom, Director, Government Affairs

NY Health Information Management Association Inc
19 Aviation Rd, Albany, NY 12205
518-435-0422 Fax: 518-435-0457
e-mail: charrington@nyhima.org
Web site: www.nyhima.org
Christine Harrington, Executive Director

NY Physical Therapy Association
5 Palisades Dr, Ste 330, Albany, NY 12205-1443
518-459-4499 Fax: 518-459-8953
e-mail: lesliew@nypta.org
Web site: www.nypta.org
Leslie Wood, Executive Director

NY State Society of Physician Assistants
251 New Karner Rd, Ste 10A, Albany, NY 12205
877-769-7722 Fax: 856-423-3420
e-mail: info@nysspa.org
Web site: www.nysspa.org
Kenneth Cleveland, Executive Director

NYS Academy of Family Physicians
260 Osborne Rd, Loudonville, NY 12211-1822
518-489-8945 or 800-822-0700 Fax: 518-489-8961
e-mail: fp@nysafp.org
Web site: www.nysafp.org
Vito Grasso, CAE, Executive Vice President

NYS Association of County Health Officials
One United Way, Pine West Plaza, Albany, NY 12205
518-456-7905 Fax: 518-452-5435
e-mail: linda@nysacho.org
Web site: www.nysacho.org
Linda Wagner, Executive Director

NYS Association of Health Care Providers
99 Troy Road, Ste 200, East Greenbush, NY 12061
518-463-1118 Fax: 518-463-1606
e-mail: johnston@nyshcp.org
Web site: www.nyshcp.org
Home health care; health care services for the aging
Christy Johnston, President

NYS Association of Nurse Anesthetists (NYSANA)
PO Box 8867, Albany, NY 12208-0867
518-861-8876 Fax: 518-861-8876
e-mail: webmaster@nysana.com
Web site: www.nysana.com
Kathleen O'Donnell, Executive Secretary

NYS Dental Association
20 Corporate Woods Blvd., Albany, NY 12211
518-465-0044 Fax: 518-465-3219
e-mail: info@nysdental.org
Web site: www.nysdental.org
Mark J Feldman, D.M.D., Executive Director

NYS Federation of Physicians & Dentists
521 5th Ave, Ste 1700, New York, NY 10175-0003
212-986-3859
Larry Nathan, Executive Director

NYS Optometric Association Inc
119 Washington Avenue, Albany, NY 12210
518-449-7300 or 800-342-9836 Fax: 518-432-5902
e-mail: nysoa2020@aol.com
Web site: www.nysoa.org
Jan Dorman, Executive Director

NYS Public Health Association
PO Box 38127, Albany, NY 12203
518-427-5835 Fax: 518-427-5835
e-mail: info@nyspha.org
Web site: www.nyspha.org
Reviewing & advocating for stronger legislation/regulation to protect public health in NYS
Erin Sinisgalli, President

National Amputation Foundation Inc
40 Church St, Malverne, NY 11565
516-887-3600 Fax: 516-887-3667
e-mail: amps76@aol.com
Web site: www.nationalamputation.org
Programs & services geared to help the amputee; donated medical equipment give-away program. Items must be picked up at the office-for anyone in need. Scholarship program for students with major limb amputation attending college full-time.
Paul Bernacchio, President

National League for Nursing (NLN)
61 Broadway, New York, NY 10006
212-363-5555 Fax: 212-812-0392
e-mail: oceo@nln.org
Web site: www.nln.org
Dedicated to excellence in nursing education, the National League for Nursing is the preferred membership organization for nurse faculty and leaders in nursing education.
Dr Beverly Malone, Chief Executive Officer

National Marfan Foundation
22 Manhasset Ave, Port Washington, NY 11050
516-883-8712 Fax: 516-883-8040
e-mail: staff@marfan.org
Web site: www.marfan.org
Marfan syndrome research, education & support
Carolyn Levering, President & Chief Executive Officer

Offices and agencies generally appear in alphabetical order, except when specific order is requested by listee.

New School University, Milano Graduate School of Mgmt & Urban Policy
72 Fifth Ave, 6th Fl, New York, NY 10011
212-229-5311 x1516 Fax: 212-229-5335
Web site: www.newschool.edu
Peter Issinger, Director, Health Policy Research Center

New York AIDS Coalition
231 W 29th St, New York, NY 10001
212-629-3075 Fax: 212-629-8409
e-mail: jdarden@nyaidsc.org
Web site: www.nyaidscoalition.org
HIV/AIDS-related public policy & education
James Darden, Office Manager

New York Association of Homes & Services for the Aging
150 State St, Ste 301, Albany, NY 12207-1698
518-449-2707 Fax: 518-455-8908
e-mail: cyoung@nyahsa.org
Web site: www.nyahsa.org
Long-term care
Carl Young, President

New York Business Group on Health Inc
61 Broadway, Suite 2705, New York, NY 10006
212-252-7440 x223 Fax: 212-252-7448
e-mail: laurel@nybgh.org
Web site: www.nybgh.org
Business employers addressing healthcare cost & quality; Non-profit coalition of 150 businesses devoted to health benefits issues.
Laurel Pickering, Executive Director

New York Counties Registered Nurses Association
120 Wall Street, 23rd Floor, New York, NY 10005
212-673-7110 Fax: 212-673-7762
e-mail: nycrna@aol.com
Web site: www.nysna.org/districts/13.htm
Marlene S Gerber, Executive Director

New York Health Care Alliance
39 Broadway, Ste 1710, New York, NY 10006
212-425-5050 or 877-HI-NYHCA Fax: 212-968-7710
e-mail: njheyman@nyhca.com
Web site: www.nyhca.com
An affiliation of 48 skilled nursing facilities that provide sub-acute, rehabilitation and long term care services in the NY Metropolitan Area. A managed care contracting entity responsible for group contracts with all major health plans in NY Area.
Neil Heyman, CEO

New York Health Plan Association
90 State St, Ste 825, Albany, NY 12207-1717
518-462-2293 Fax: 518-462-2150
e-mail: afogarty@nyhpa.org
Web site: www.nyhpa.org
Promotes the development of managed healthcare plans
Andrew Fogarty, Director, Government Affairs

New York Medical College
Basic Science Bldg, Valhalla, NY 10595
914-594-4110 Fax: 914-594-4944
e-mail: francis_belloni@nymc.edu
Web site: www.nymc.edu
Cardiovascular physiology, graduate education
Francis L Belloni, Dean, Graduate School of Basic Medical Sciences

New York Medical College, Department of Medicine
Munger Pavilion, New York Medical College, Valhalla, NY 10595
914-594-4440 or 914-594-4979 Fax: 914-594-4396
e-mail: lerner@nymc.edu
Web site: www.nymc.edu
Hematology, oncology, research of coagulation & clotting

Robert G Lerner, Professor, Vice Chair-Department of Medicine

New York Medical College, School of Public Health
School of Public Health Building, Valhalla, NY 10595
914-594-4510 or 914-594-4759 Fax: 914-594-4292
e-mail: SHSP_admissions@nymc.edu
Web site: www.nymc.edu/SHSP
Graduate education for public health & the health sciences
Pamela Suett, Director of Recruitment

New York Presbyterian Hospital
Public Affairs Ofc, 525 East 68th St, Box 144, New York, NY 10021
212-821-0560 Fax: 212-821-0576
e-mail: krobinso@med.cornell.edu
Web site: www.med.cornell.edu; www.nyp.org
Kathleen Robinson, Director, Media Relations

New York State Association of Ambulatory Surgery Centers
c/o Harrison Center Outpatient Surgery I, 550 Harrison St, Suite 230, Syracuse, NY 13202
315-472-7315 Fax: 315-475-8056
e-mail: palteri@harrisonsurgery.com
Web site: nysaasc.org
Ambulatory surgery
Margaret M. Alteri, President & Executive Director

New York State Health Facilities Association Inc
33 Elk St, Ste 300, Albany, NY 12207-1010
518-462-4800 x10 Fax: 518-426-4051
e-mail: rherrick@nyshfa.org
Web site: www.nyshfa.org
Nursing homes & adult care services
Richard J Herrick, President & Chief Executive Officer

New York State Nurses Association
11 Cornell Rd, Latham, NY 12110
518-782-9400 x279 Fax: 518-782-1706
e-mail: executive@nysna.org
Web site: www.nysna.org
Labor union & professional association for registered nurses

New York State Ophthalmological Society
10 Colvin Ave, Albany, NY 12206
518-438-2020 Fax: 518-438-3008
e-mail: nysos2020@aol.com
Web site: www.nysos.com
Robin M Pellegrino, Executive Director

New York State Osteopathic Medical Society
1855 Broadway, New York, NY 10023
212-261-1784 Fax: 212-261-1786
e-mail: info@nysoms.org
Web site: www.nysoms.org
Advance the art & science of the osteopathic medical philosophy & practice through continuing medical education programs
Barbara Greenwald, Executive Director

New York State Podiatric Medical Association
1255 Fifth Ave, New York, NY 10029
212-996-4400 Fax: 646-672-9344
e-mail: nyspma@nyspma.org
Web site: www.nyspma.org
To promote and pursue manifest excellence in all aspects of the art and science and podiatric medicine; to promote appreciation for that excellence on the past of patients, policy makers,other health care professionals, and the public.
Leonard Thaler, Executive Director

New York State Radiological Society Inc
9 E 40th St, New York, NY 10016
212-448-1866 Fax: 212-448-1863
e-mail: nysrad@aol.com
Richard Schiffer, Executive Director

Offices and agencies generally appear in alphabetical order, except when specific order is requested by listee.

New York University, Graduate School of Public Service
295 Lafayette St, 2nd Fl, New York, NY 10012
212-998-7455 or 212-998-7440 Fax: 212-995-4166
e-mail: john.billings@nyu.edu
Web site: www.nyu.edu/wagner
Health care reform
John Billings, Director, Center for Health & Public Service Research

New York University, Robert F Wagner Graduate School of Public Service
295 Lafayette, 2nd Floor, New York, NY 10012
212-998-7410 Fax: 212-995-4162
e-mail: jo.boufford@nyu.edu
Web site: www.nyu.edu/wagner
Health policy & management
Jo Ivey Boufford, Professor of Public Administration

Next Wave Inc
24 Madison Ave Ext, Albany, NY 12203
518-452-3351 Fax: 518-452-3358
e-mail: contact@nextwave.info
Web site: www.nextwave.info
Health services research, management consulting & evaluation
John Shaw, President

Nurse Practitioners Assn NYS (The)
12 Corporate Dr, Clifton Park, NY 12065
518-348-0719 Fax: 518-348-0720
e-mail: info@thenpa.org
Web site: www.thenpa.org
Representation, communication & advocacy
Seth Gordon, President/Chief Executive Officer

Pharmacists Society of the State of New York
210 Washington Ave Extenstion, Albany, NY 12203
518-869-6595 Fax: 518-464-0618
e-mail: craigb@pssny.org
Web site: www.pssny.org
Continuing education, public information, health advocacy
Craig Burridge, Executive Director

Professional Standards Review Council of America Inc (PSRC)
200 Madison Ave, Suite 2108, New York, NY 10016
646-419-4020 Fax: 212-779-9307
e-mail: info@psrc-of-america.org
Web site: www.psrc-of-america.org
Health care QA/UR management; credentialing
Carol A Wielk, Executive Director

Radon Testing Corp of America Inc
2 Hayes St, Elmsford, NY 10523
914-345-3380 or 800-457-2366 Fax: 914-345-8546
e-mail: rtca97@att.net
Web site: www.rtca.com
Radon detection services for health departments, municipalities, homeowners; manufacture canister detectors
Nancy Bredhoff, President

Regeneron Pharmaceuticals Inc
777 Old Saw Mill River Rd, Tarrytown, NY 10591-6707
914-345-7400 Fax: 914-345-7688
e-mail: info@regeneron.com
Web site: www.regeneron.com
Discovers, develops & intends to commercialize therapeutic drugs for serious medical conditions, including rheumatoid arthritis, cancer, asthma & obesity
Stephen L Holst, Vice President, Quality Assurance & Regulatory Affairs

Robert P Borsody, PC
666 Fifth, 29th Fl, New York, NY 10103
212-841-0566 Fax: 212-262-5152
e-mail: rborsody@phillipsnizer.com
Web site: www.borsodyhealthlaw.com
Health care law
Robert P Borsody, Attorney

SUNY at Albany, School of Public Health, Center for Public Health Preparedness
One University Pl, Rensselaer, NY 12144-3456
518-486-7921 Fax: 518-402-4656
e-mail: mwatson@albany.edu
Web site: www.ualbanycphp.org
Margaret R Watson, Project Coordinator

The Bachmann-Strauss Dystonia & Parkinson Foundation
551 Fifth Avenue, Suite 520, New York, NY 10176
212-682-9900 Fax: 212-682-6156
e-mail: bachmann.strauss@mssm.edu
Web site: www.dystonia-parkinson.org
Funds research & creates public awareness of dystonia, Parkinson's disease
Sandra F Cahn, Executive Director

True & Walsh, LLP
950 Danby Road, Suite 310, Ithaca, NY 14850
607-273-2301 Fax: 607-272-1901
e-mail: stt@truewalshlaw.com
Web site: www.truewalshlaw.com
Health care, corporate law & estate planning/administration
Sally T True, Partner

United Hospital Fund of New York
1411 Broadway, 12th Floor, New York, NY 10018
212-494-0777 Fax: 212-494-0830
e-mail: jtallon@uhfnyc.org
Web site: www.uhfnyc.org
Health services research & philanthropic organization
James R Tallon, Jr, President

United New York Ambulance Network (UNYAN)
119 Washington Ave, Ste 300, Albany, NY 12210
518-694-4420 Fax: 518-427-9495
e-mail: info@unyan.net
Web site: unyan.net
Ambulance trade association
Kathleen Van De Loo, President

We Move
204 W 84th St, New York, NY 10024
800-437-6682 Fax: 212-875-8389
e-mail: wemove@wemove.org
Web site: www.wemove.org
Education & information about movement disorders for both healthcare providers & patients
Susan B Bressman, President

NYS Bar Assn, Health Law Section
Wilson Elser Moskowitz Edelman & Dicker
677 Broadway, Albany, NY 12207
518-449-8893 Fax: 518-449-4292
e-mail: philip.rosenberg@wilsonelser.com
Philip Rosenberg,

Winthrop University Hospital
286 Old Country Road, Mineola, NY 11501
516-663-2706 Fax: 516-663-2713
e-mail: jbroder@winthrop.org
Web site: www.winthrop.org
John P Broder, Vice President, External Affairs & Development

Policy Areas

Offices and agencies generally appear in alphabetical order, except when specific order is requested by listee.

Yeshiva University, A Einstein Clg of Med, OB/GYN & Wmn's Health
1300 Morris Park Ave, Ste B-502, Bronx, NY 10461
718-430-4192 Fax: 718-430-8813
e-mail: chairobgyn@aol.com
Web site: www.yu.edu
Irwin R Merkatz, The Chella & Maise Safra Professor University Chair

HOUSING & COMMUNITY DEVELOPMENT

NEW YORK STATE

GOVERNOR'S OFFICE

Governor's Office
Executive Chamber
State Capitol
Albany, NY 12224
518-474-8390 Fax: 518-474-1513
Web site: www.ny.gov

Governor:
Andrew M Cuomo 518-474-8390
Secretary to the Governor:
William Mulrow 518-474-4246
Counsel to the Governor:
Alphonso David 518-474-8343
Director, Communications:
Melissa DeRosa . . . . .518-474-8418 or 212-681-4640
Deputy Secretary for Civil Rights:
Patricia Gatling. 212-681-4584

EXECUTIVE DEPARTMENTS AND RELATED AGENCIES

Housing & Community Renewal, Division of
Hampton Plaza
38-40 State St
Albany, NY 12207
866-275-3427 or 518-473-2526
Web site: www.nyshcr.org

25 Beaver St
New York, NY 10004-2319
866-275-3427

Commissioner:
Darryl C. Towns 518-486-3370
Executive Assistant:
Denise Flowers 518-473-0632
Public Information Officer:
Charni Sochet 212-872-0681

Administration
Deputy Commissioner:
Sharon Devine. 518-473-0632

Housing Information Systems
Director:
David Dietrich. 518-473-5681/fax: 518-486-5056

Office of Training & Professional Development
Director:
Katherine Champagne 518-473-6128

Support Services/Processing Services Unit
Director:
Theodore T Minissale 518-486-6166/fax: 518-486-3366

Community Development
Assistant Commissioner, Capital Finance:
Sean Fitzgerald 518-473-8732
Asst Commissioner, Underwriting & Design Services:
Ellen M Coyle 518-473-3890/fax: 518-473-7357
Community Development/Downstate:
Earnest Langhorne 212-480-7473

Community Service Bureau/Technical Assistance Unit
Director:
Pat Doyle. 518-473-3247/fax: 518-486-5186

Energy Rehabilitation Services
Director:
Thom Carey. 518-474-5700/fax: 518-474-9907

Environmental Analysis Unit
Director:
Barbara Wigzell 518-473-0457

Housing Trust Fund Program
Program Manager:
Thomas Koenig. 518-486-7682/fax: 518-486-3410

Regional Offices
Finger Lakes, Western NY, Southern Tier
535 Washington St, Buffalo, NY 14203
Regional Director:
Leonard Skrill 716-847-7955
New York City, Long Island, Hudson Valley
641 Lexington Ave, New York, NY 10022
Regional Director:
Greg Watson 212-688-4000

Fair Housing & Equal Opportunity
Director:
Wanda Graham 518-474-6157/fax: 518-473-3173

Housing Operations
Deputy Commissioner:
Vacant 212-480-6440/fax: 212-480-7169
Asst Commissioner, Section 8:
Alan Smith 518-480-7764
Asst Commissioner, Housing Operations:
Richmond McCurnin. 212-480-6444/fax: 212-480-7169

Manufactured Homes
Director:
Maralyne P Fleischman 518-474-9586

Housing Management Bureau
Director:
Robert D'Amico. 212-480-6266
Mobile Home Unit
Director:
Dominic Cardillo. . . . . .800-432-4210 or 518-486-6267
fax: 518-486-3366
Subsidy Services
Director:
Blanca Cardona 212-480-6674

Legal Affairs
General Counsel:
Gary R Connor 212-480-6707
Deputy General Counsel:
Mark Colon. 212-480-6727

General Law
Managing Attorney:
Sheldon Melnitsky 212-480-6789/fax: 212-480-7416
Supervising Attorney:
Brian P McCartney. 518-486-6337

Policy & Intergovernmental Relations
Deputy Commissioner:
Lorrie Pizzola 518-474-9553/fax: 518-473-9462
Legislative Liaison:
Vacant 518-473-2519/fax: 518-474-5752

Rent Administration
Deputy Commissioner:
Woody Pascal 718-262-4822/fax: 718-262-4008

Offices and agencies generally appear in alphabetical order, except when specific order is requested by listee.

189

Luxury Decontrol/Overcharge
Acting Bureau Chief:
John Lance 718-262-4081

Property Management
Bureau Chief:
Paul Fuller. 718-262-4768/fax: 718-262-7938

Rent Control/ETPA
Bureau Chief/Deputy Counsel:
Michael Rosenblatt 718-262-4713/fax: 718-262-4008

Rent Information Services
Bureau Chief:
Bruce Falbo 718-262-4914/fax: 718-262-4008

Law Department
120 Broadway
New York, NY 10271-0332
212-416-8000 or 800-771-7755
Web site: www.ag.ny.gov

State Capitol
Albany, NY 12224-0341
518-474-5481
Fax: 518-473-9909

Attorney General:
Eric T Schneiderman . . . . .212-416-8050 or 518-474-7330
Chief of Staff:
Micah Lasher 212-416-8050
Press Secretary:
Fernando Aquino212-416-8060/fax: 212-416-6005

Social Justice
Executive Deputy Attorney General:
Alvin L Braggs, Jr 212-416-8075/fax: 212-416-8942

Civil Rights Bureau
Bureau Chief:
Kristen Clarke 212-416-8250/fax: 212-416-8074

Economic Justice
Executive Deputy Attorney General:
Karla Sanchez 212-416-8050

Consumer Frauds & Protection Bureau
Bureau Chief:
Jane Azia 212-416-8300/fax: 212-416-6003

State Counsel
Chief Deputy Attorney General & Counsel:
Harlan Levy 212-416-8525
Executive Deputy Attorney General, State Counsel:
Kent T. Stauffer. 212-416-8252/fax: 212-416-6001

Litigation Bureau
Bureau Chief:
Lisa Dell . . . . .518-776-2300 or 212-416-8610

Real Property Bureau
Bureau Chief:
Alison Crocker 518-776-2700/fax: 518-474-0862

CORPORATIONS, AUTHORITIES AND COMMISSIONS

Capital District Regional Planning Commission
One Park Place
Suite 102
Albany, NY 12205

518-453-0850 Fax: 518-453-0856
e-mail: cdrpc@cdrpc.org
Web site: www.cdrpc.org

Executive Director:
Rocco A Ferraro 518-453-0850
e-mail: rocky@cdrpc.org
Information Services:
Tim Canty 518-453-0850
e-mail: dlwardle@cdrpc.org

Development Authority of the North Country
317 Washington Street
Watertown, NY 13601
315-661-3200
e-mail: info@danc.org
Web site: www.danc.org

Chair:
Gary Turck 315-661-3200
Executive Director:
James Wright 315-661-3200
Deputy Executive Director:
Thomas R Sauter 315-661-3200
e-mail: tsauter@danc.org
Director, Engineering:
Carrie Tuttle 315-661-3210
Telecom Division Manager:
David Wolf 315-661-3200
e-mail: oatn@danc.org
Landfill Superintendent:
Steve McElwain 315-661-3230
Director, Regional Development:
Michelle Capone 315-661-3200

Empire State Development Corporation
633 Third Ave
New York, NY 10017
212-803-3100 Fax: 212-803-3131
Web site: www.esd.ny.gov

625 Broadway
Albany, NY 12207
518-292-5100

95 Perry Street
Ste 500
Buffalo, NY 14203
716-846-8200
Fax: 716-846-8260

President & CEO:
Howard Zemsky 212-803-3700
e-mail: president@esd.ny.gov
Business Expansion:
John Gilstrap 212-803-3700
Public Affairs:
Kay Sarlin Wright 800-260-7313
e-mail: esdpressoffice@esd.ny,gov
Chief of Staff & COO:
Mehul J. Patel . . . . .212-803-3700 or 518-292-5100

New York City Housing Development Corporation
110 William St
10th Fl
New York, NY 10038

Offices and agencies generally appear in alphabetical order, except when specific order is requested by listee.

212-227-5500 Fax: 212-227-6865
e-mail: info@nychdc.com
Web site: www.nychdc.com

Chairman:
  Vicki Been 212-863-6100
President:
  Gary D Rodney. 212-227-3600
Executive VP/COO & General Counsel:
  Richard Froehlich 212-227-7435
Executive VP, Real Estate & Chief of Staff:
  Joan Tally 212-227-6846
Senior Vice President, Portfolio Management:
  Teresa Gigliello. 212-227-9133
Senior Vice President, Loan Servicing:
  Eileen O'Reilly 212-227-7494
Chief Credit Officer:
  Urmas Naeris. 212-227-9724
Communications/Press Office:
  Christina Sanchez 212-227-2644
  e-mail: csanchez@nychdc.com

New York City Residential Mortgage Insurance Corporation
Chair:
  Vicki Been 212-863-6100
President:
  Gary D Rodney. 212-227-3600

Roosevelt Island Operating Corporation (RIOC)
591 Main St
Roosevelt Island, NY 10044
212-832-4540 Fax: 212-832-4582
e-mail: information@rioc.ny.gov
Web site: www.rioc.ny.gov

President/CEO:
  Charlene M Indelicato 212-832-4540 x319
Director Island Operations:
  Cyril Opperman 212-832-4583
  e-mail: cyril.opperman@rioc.ny.gov
VP/General Counsel:
  Donald D. Lewis 212-832-4540 x319
  e-mail: donald.lewis@rioc.ny.gov
VP/Chief Financial Officer:
  Frances Walton 212-832-4540 x350
Director Public Safety:
  Captain Estrella Suarez. 212-832-4545
  e-mail: keith.guerra@rioc.ny.gov

State of New York Mortgage Agency (SONYMA)
641 Lexington Ave
4th Floor
New York, NY 10022
212-688-4000 Fax: 212-872-0789
Web site: www.nyshcr.org

Commissioner & CEO:
  Darryl C. Towns 212-688-4000
President, Finance & Development:
  Marian Zucker. 212-688-4000
Director, Fair Housing & Equal Opportunity:
  Wanda Graham 212-688-4000
Director, Public Information:
  Charni Sochet 212-872-0338

NEW YORK STATE LEGISLATURE

See Legislative Branch in Section 1 for additional Standing Committee and Subcommittee information.

Assembly Standing Committees
Housing
Chair:
  Keith L.T. Wright (D). 518-455-4793
Ranking Minority Member:
  Michael J Fitzpatrick (R) 518-455-5021

Local Government
Chair:
  William B Magnarelli (D). 518-455-4826
Ranking Minority Member:
  Christopher Friend (R) 518-455-4538

Senate Standing Committees

Housing, Construction & Community Development
Chair:
  Catharine M Young (R) 518-455-3563
Ranking Minority Member:
  Adriano Espaillat (D) 518-455-2041

Local Government
Chair:
  Kathleen Marchione (R) 518-455-2381
Ranking Minority Member:
  Marc Panepinto (D) 518-455-2760

U.S. GOVERNMENT

EXECUTIVE DEPARTMENTS AND RELATED AGENCIES

US Department of Agriculture

Rural Development
  Web site: www.rurdev.usda.gov/ny

  New York State Office. . . . . .fax: 315-477-6438
  The Galleries of Syracuse, 441 S Salina St, Suite 357, Syracuse, NY 13202
  TTY: 315-477-6447 or 315-477-6400 Fax: 315-477-6438
State Director:
  Stanley Telega 315-477-6437
Special Projects Representative:
  Christopher Stewart
Program Director, Rural Business-Cooperative Service:
  Walter D Schermerhorn 315-477-6425
  e-mail: walter.schermerhorn@ny.usda.gov
Program Director, Rural Utilities Service:
  David Miller 315-477-6427
  e-mail: david.miller@ny.usda.gov
Administrator:
  Tammye Trevino
  e-mail: george.vonpless@ny.usda.gov

US Housing & Urban Development Department
Web site: www.hud.gov

New York State Office . . . . .fax: 212-264-0246
  26 Federal Plaza, Room 3541, New York, NY 10278-0068
  212-264-8000 Fax: 212-264-0246
Regional Director:
  Vacant. 212-542-7109
Deputy Regional Director:
  Mirza Orriols 212-542-7717
  e-mail: mirza.orriols@hud.gov
Public Affairs Officer:
  Adam Glantz 212-264-8000 x3158
  e-mail: adam.glantz@hud.gov

Policy Areas

Offices and agencies generally appear in alphabetical order, except when specific order is requested by listee.

Administration (Admin Service Center 1)
Deputy Director:
Kathy Brantley 312-353-5944

Community Planning & Development
Director:
Vincent Hom. 212-542-7401
e-mail: vicenthom@hud.gov

Fair Housing & Equal Opportunity Office
Equal Opportunities Specialist:
Amy Apple

Field Offices
Albany Area Office & Financial Operations Center fax: 518-464-4300
52 Corporate Circle, Albany, NY 12203-5121
518-464-4200 Fax: 518-464-4300
Field Office Director:
Jaime Forero
Buffalo Area Office . . . . fax: 716-551-5752
465 Main Street, Lafayette Court, 2nd Floor, Buffalo, NY
14203-1780
Field Office Director:
Joan Spillman. 716-551-5755
Syracuse Area Office . . . . fax: 315-477-0196
100 South Clinton Street, PO Box 7025, Syracuse, NY 13261-7025
315-477-0616 Fax: 315-477-0196
Field Office Director:
Joan Spillman 315-477-0616/fax: 315-477-0196

General Counsel
Regional Counsel:
John Cahill 212-542-7200

Housing
Director:
Brian E Lawlor 212-264-0777 x3701

Inspector General
Special Agent-in-Charge, Investigation:
Ruth A Ritzema 212-264-8062
District Inspector General, Audit:
Alexander C Malloy 212-264-8000 x3976

Public Housing
Director:
Luigi D'Ancona 212-542-7649

U.S. CONGRESS

See U.S. Congress Chapter for additional Standing Committee and Subcommittee information.

House of Representatives Standing Committees

Financial Services
Chair:
Jeb Hensarling (R-TX) 202-225-3484
Ranking Member:
Maxine Waters (D-CA) 202-225-2201
Vice Chairman:
Gary G. Miller. 202-225-3201
New York Delegate:
Peter T King (R) 202-225-7896
New York Delegate:
Michael G. Grimm (R) 202-225-3371
New York Delegate:
Carolyn B Maloney (D) 202-225-7944
New York Delegate:
Carolyn McCarthy (D) 202-225-5516
New York Delegate:
Gregory W Meeks (D) 202-225-3461

New York Delegate:
Nydia M Velazquez (D) 202-225-2361
Subcommittee
Housing & Insurance
Chair:
Randy Neugebauer (R-TX) 202-225-4005
Ranking Member:
Michael E. Capuano (D-MA) 202-225-5111
New York Delegate:
Carolyn McCarthy (D). 202-225-5516
New York Delegate:
Nydia M Velazquez (D). 202-225-2361

Transportation & Infrastructure
Chair:
Bill Shuster (R-PA). 202-225-2431
Ranking Member:
Nick J. Rahall II (D-WV) 202-225-3452
New York Delegate:
Sean Patrick Maloney (D). 202-225-5441
New York Delegate:
Timothy H Bishop (D) 202-225-3826
New York Delegate:
Richard L. Hanna (R) 202-225-3665
New York Delegate:
Jerrold Nadler (D). 202-225-5635
Subcommittee
Economic Development, Public Buildings & Emergency Management
Chair:
Lou Barletta (R-PA). 202-225-6511
Ranking Member:
Eleanor Holmes Norton (D-DC) 202-225-9961

Senate Standing Committees

Banking, Housing & Urban Affairs
Chair:
Tim Johnson (D-SD). 202-224-5842
Ranking Member:
Mike Crapo (R-ID) 202-224-6142
New York Delegate:
Charles E Schumer (D). 202-224-6542

PRIVATE SECTOR

Albany County Rural Housing Alliance Inc
PO Box 407, 24 Martin Road, Voorheesville, NY 12186
518-765-2425 Fax: 518-765-9014
Web site: www.acrha.org
Development & management of low income housing; home repair programs; housing counseling & education
Judith A Eisgruber, Executive Director

American Institute of Architects (AIA) New York State Inc
52 S Pearl St, 3rd Fl, Albany, NY 12207
518-449-3334 Fax: 518-426-8176
e-mail: aianys@aianys.org
Web site: www.aianys.org
Architectural regulations, state policy, smart growth & affordable housing
Edward C Farrell, Executive Director

Association for Community Living
632 Plank Road, Suite 110, Clifton Park, NY 12065
518-688-1682 Fax: 518-688-1686
e-mail: info@aclnys.org
Web site: www.aclnys.org
Membership organization for agencies that provide housing & rehab services to individuals diagnosed with serious mental illness
Antonia Lasicki, Executive Director

Offices and agencies generally appear in alphabetical order, except when specific order is requested by listee.

Association for Neighborhood & Housing Development
50 Broad St, Suite 1125, New York, NY 10004-2376
212-747-1117 Fax: 212-747-1114
e-mail: irene.b@anhd.org
Web site: www.anhd.org
Umbrella organization providing assistance to NYC nonprofits advocating for affordable housing & neighborhood preservation
Irene Baldwin, Executive Director

Association for a Better New York
355 Lexington Ave, 8th Fl, New York, NY 10017
212-370-5800 Fax: 212-661-5877
e-mail: info@abny.org
Web site: www.abny.org
NYC public policy issues forums & committees
Michelle Adams, Executive Director

Brooklyn Housing & Family Services Inc
415 Albemarle Rd, Brooklyn, NY 11218
718-435-7585 Fax: 718-435-7605
e-mail: ljayson@brooklynhousing.org; carol@brooklynhousing.org
Web site: www.brooklynhousing.org
Homelessness prevention, landlord/tenant dispute resolution & advocacy, immigration services, and mortgage foreclosure prevention.
Larry Jayson, Executive Director

CUNY Hunter College, Urban Affairs & Planning Department
695 Park Ave, New York, NY 10021
212-772-5515 Fax: 212-772-5593
e-mail: smoses@hunter.cuny.edu
Web site: www.hunter.cuny.edu
History of planning, employment & education
Stanley Moses, Chair

Center for an Urban Future
120 Wall St, 20th Fl, New York, NY 10005
212-479-3319 Fax: 212-479-3338
e-mail: cuf@nycfuture.org
Web site: www.nycfuture.org
Policy institute dedicated to aggressively pursuing solutions to critical problems facing cities
Johnathan Bowle, Director

Citizens Housing & Planning Council of New York
42 Broadway, Suite 2010, New York, NY 10004
212-286-9211 Fax: 212-286-9214
e-mail: info@chpcny.org
Web site: www.chpcny.org
Jerilyn Perine, Executive Director

Community Housing Improvement Program (CHIP)
377 Broadway, 3rd Floor, New York, NY 10013
212-838-7442 Fax: 212-838-7456
e-mail: info@chipnyc.org
Web site: www.chipnyc.org
Representing NYC apartment building owners
Patrick J Siconolfi, Executive Director

Community Preservation Corporation (The)
28 East 28th Street, 9th Floor, New York, NY 10016-7943
212-869-5300 x511 Fax: 212-683-0694
e-mail: mlappin@communityp.com
Web site: www.communityp.com
Multifamily housing rehabilitation financing for NYC & NJ neighborhoods
Michael D Lappin, President & Chief Executive Officer

Community Service Society of New York
105 E 22nd St, New York, NY 10010
212-614-5492 Fax: 212-614-9441
e-mail: vbach@cssny.org
Web site: www.cssny.org
Research & advocacy for public policies & programs that improve housing conditions & opportunities for low-income NYC residents & communities
Victor Bach, Senior Housing Policy Analyst

Cornell Cooperative Extension, Community & Economic Vitality Program
43 Warren Hall, Cornell University, Ithaca, NY 14853
607-255-2170 Fax: 607-255-2231
e-mail: rlh13@cornell.edu
Web site: www.cce.cornell.edu
Work with community leaders, extension educators & elected officials to strengthen the vitality of New York's communities
Rod Howe, Assistant Director

Council on the Environment of NYC, Open Space Greening Program
51 Chambers St, Rm 228, New York, NY 10007
212-788-7900 or 212-788-7928 Fax: 212-788-7913
e-mail: info@grownyc.org
Web site: www.grownyc.org
Material & technical assistance for housing groups to create & maintain open community gardens & other public open spaces in NYC
Marcel Van Doyen, Executive Director

Federal Home Loan Bank of New York
101 Park Ave, New York, NY 10178-0599
212-681-6000 Fax: 212-441-6890
e-mail: info@fhlbny.com
Web site: www.fhlbny.com
Joseph Gallo, Vice President & Director, Community Investment

Hofstra University, School of Law
121 Hofstra University, Hempstead, NY 11549
212-864-6092
Web site: www.hofstra.edu
Land use & environmental law
William R Ginsberg, Emeritus Professor of Law

Housing Action Council Inc - Not For Profit
55 S Broadway, Tarrytown, NY 10591
914-332-4144 Fax: 914-332-4147
e-mail: rnoonan@affordablehomes.org
Financial feasibility, land use & zoning & affordable housing
Rosemarie Noonan, Executive Director

Housing Works Inc
57 Willoughby Street, Brooklyn, NY 11201
347-473-7400 (x7418) Fax: 347-473-7464
e-mail: smith-caronia@housingworks.org
Web site: www.housingworks.org
Housing, health care, advocacy, job training & support services for homeless NY residents with HIV or AIDS
Terri Smith-Caronia, VP of NYC Policy & Advocacy

Local Initiative Support Corporation
501 7th Ave, Fl 7, New York, NY 10018
212-455-9800 Fax: 212-682-5929
Web site: www.liscnet.org
Support the development of local leadership & the creation of affordable housing, commercial, industrial & community facilities, businesses & jobs
Norman R Bobins, President & Chief Executive Officer

Policy Areas

Offices and agencies generally appear in alphabetical order, except when specific order is requested by listee.

Mid-Hudson Pattern for Progress
6 Albany Post Rd, Newburgh, NY 12550-1439
845-565-4900 Fax: 845-565-4918
e-mail: jdrapkin@pfprogress.org
Web site: www.pattern-for-progress.org
Regional planning, research & policy development
Jonathan Drapkin, President & Chief Executive Officer

NY Housing Association Inc
35 Commerce Ave, Albany, NY 12206
518-435-9858 Fax: 518-435-9839
e-mail: info@nyhousing.org
Web site: www.nyhousing.org
Manufactured, factory built, modular & mobile housing
Nancy Geer, Executive Director

Tenants & Neighbors
236 West 27th St, 4th Fl, New York, NY 10001
212-608-4320 Fax: 212-619-7476
e-mail: info@tandn.org
Web site: www.tandn.org
Organizing support, training, technical assistance, and advocacy around tenants' rights and the preservation of affordable housing.
Maggie Russell-Ciardi, Executive Director

National Trust for Historic Preservation
1785 Massachusetts Avenue NW, Washington, DC 20036-2117
202-588-6000 or 800-944-6847 Fax: 202-588-6038
e-mail: preservation@nthp.org
Web site: www.preservationnation.org
Provides leadership, education, advocacy, and resources to save America's diverse historic places and revitalize our communities.
Richard Moe, President

Neighborhood Preservation Coalition of NYS Inc
40 Colvin Ave, Ste 102, Albany, NY 12206-1104
518-432-6757 Fax: 518-432-6758
e-mail: agostine@npcnys.org
Web site: www.npcnys.org
Community organizations united to preserve & revitalize neighborhoods
Joseph A Agostine, Jr, Executive Director

Nelson A Rockefeller Inst of Govt, Urban & Metro Studies
411 State St, Albany, NY 12203-1003
518-443-5522 Fax: 518-443-5788
e-mail: wrightd@rockinst.org
Web site: www.rockinst.org
Research on community capacity building, impacts of welfare reform on community development corporations, empowerment zone/enterprise communities & neighborhood preservation
David J Wright, Director

New School University, Milano Graduate School of Mgmt & Urban Policy
72 Fifth Ave, New York, NY 10011
212-229-5400
Web site: www.newschool.edu
Research, policy analysis & evaluation on community development & urban poverty
Edwin Melendez, Professor

New York Building Congress
44 W 28th St, 12th Fl, New York, NY 10001-4212
212-481-9230 Fax: 212-447-6037
e-mail: rtanders55@aol.com
Web site: www.buildingcongress.com
Coalition of design, construction & real estate organizations
Richard T Anderson, President

New York Community Bank
One Jericho Plz, PO Box 9005, Jericho, NY 11753
516-942-6994 Fax: 516-942-6995
e-mail: d.coniglio@mynycb.com
Web site: www.mynycb.com
Donna Coniglio, Chair

New York Landmarks Conservancy
1 Whitehall St, 21 Fl, New York, NY 10004
212-995-5260 Fax: 212-995-5268
e-mail: nylandmarks@nylandmarks.org
Web site: www.nylandmarks.org
Technical & financial assistance for preservation & reuse of landmark buildings
Peg Breen, President

New York Lawyers for the Public Interest
151 W 30th Street, 11th Floor, New York, NY 10001
212-244-4664 Fax: 212-244-4570
e-mail: mar@nylpi.org
Web site: www.nylpi.org
Disability rights law; access to health care; pro bono clearingouse; environmental justice and community development
Michael Rothenberg, Executive Director

New York State Community Action Association
2 Charles Blvd, Guilderland, NY 12084
518-690-0491 Fax: 518-690-0498
e-mail: dan@nyscaaonline.org
Web site: www.nyscaaonline.org
Dedicated to the growth & education of community action agencies in NYS to sustain their efforts in advocating & improving the lives of low-income New Yorkers
Daniel Maskin, Chief Executive Officer

New York State Rural Advocates
PO Box 104, Blue Mountain Lake, NY 12812
518-352-7787
Advocacy & education for affordable housing for rural New Yorkers
Nancy Berkowitz, Coordinator

New York State Rural Housing Coalition Inc
79 Pearl Street, 3rd Fl, Albany, NY 12207
518-458-8696 Fax: 518-458-8896
e-mail: rhc@ruralhousing.org
Web site: www.ruralhousing.org
Rural & small city housing; community & economic development
Blair W Sebastian, Executive Director

New York University, Wagner Graduate School
295 Lafayette Street, 2nd Floor, New York, NY 10012
212-998-7400 Fax: 212-995-4162
e-mail: mitchell.moss@nyu.edu
Web site: www.nyu.edu/wagner
Research on urban planning & development, with special emphasis on technology & the future of cities
Mitchell Moss, Professor of Urban Policy & Planning

Park Resident Homeowners' Association Inc
PO Box 68, Ontario, NY 14519
315-524-6703 Fax: 315-524-6703
e-mail: info@prho.com
Web site: www.prho.com
Protecting the rights of homeowners living in mobile/manufactured park communities in NYS
George R Miles, President

Parodneck Foundation (The)
121 6th Ave, Suite 501, New York, NY 10013
212-431-9700 Fax: 212-431-9783
e-mail: info@parodneckfoundation.org
Resident-controlled housing; community development

Offices and agencies generally appear in alphabetical order, except when specific order is requested by listee.

Carlton Collier, Executive Director

Pratt Center for Community Development
200 Willoughby Avenue, 3rd Floor East, Brooklyn, NY 11205
718-636-3486 Fax: 718-636-3709
e-mail: afriedman@pratt.edu
Web site: www.prattcenter.net
Training & technical assistance and advocacy in community economic development & sustainability.
Adam Friedman, Director

Public/Private Ventures
The Chanin Building, 122 East 42nd St, 42nd Fl, New York, NY 10168
212-822-2400 Fax: 212-949-0439
e-mail: kfaulhaber@ppv.org
Web site: www.ppv.org
A national nonprofit, nonpartisan organization that tackles critical challenges facing low-income communities by seeking out and designing innovative programs, rigorously testing them, and promoting the solutions proven to work.
Sheila Maguire, VP, Labor Market Initiatives

Project for Public Spaces
700 Broadway, 4th Fl, New York, NY 10003
212-620-5660 Fax: 212-620-3821
e-mail: pps@pps.org
Web site: www.pps.org
Nonprofit organization providing community planning, design & development services
Fred I Kent, President

Regional Plan Association
4 Irving Place, 7th Fl, New York, NY 10003
212-253-2727 Fax: 212-253-5666
e-mail: yaro@rpa.org
Web site: www.rpa.org
Develops & implements land-use, transportation, open space preservation, economic development & social equity proposals
Robert D Yaro, President

Rent Stabilization Assn of NYC Inc
123 William St, New York, NY 10038
212-214-9200 x222 Fax: 212-732-0618
Web site: www.rsanyc.org
NYC landlord organization
Joseph Strasburg, President

Rural Housing Action Corporation
400 East Ave, Rochester, NY 14607-1910
585-340-3366 Fax: 585-340-3309
e-mail: lbeaulac@ruralinc.org
Web site: www.ruralinc.org
Rental, first-time homebuyer, property management & home improvement programs for farmworkers, seniors & the rural poor
Lee Beaulac, President

Settlement Housing Fund Inc
247 West 37th Street, 4th Fl, New York, NY 10018
212-265-6530 Fax: 212-757-0571
Web site: www.settlementhousingfund.org
Low & moderate income housing development, leasing, community development
Carol Lamberg, Executive Director

Urban Homesteading Assistance Board
120 Wall St, 20th Fl, New York, NY 10005
212-479-3300 Fax: 212-344-6457
e-mail: info@uhab.org
Web site: www.uhab.org
Training, technical assistance & services for development & preservation of low income cooperative housing
Andrew Reicher, Executive Director

Women's Housing & Economic Development Corporation (WHEDCO)
50 E 168th St, Bronx, NY 10452
718-839-1103 Fax: 718-839-1170
e-mail: nbiberman@whedco.org
Web site: www.whedco.org
Non-profit organization dedicated to the economic advancement of low-income women & their families
Nancy Biberman, President

Offices and agencies generally appear in alphabetical order, except when specific order is requested by listee.

HUMAN RIGHTS

NEW YORK STATE

GOVERNOR'S OFFICE

Governor's Office
Executive Chamber
State Capitol
Albany, NY 12224
518-474-8390 Fax: 518-474-1513
Web site: www.ny.gov

Governor:
  Andrew M Cuomo 518-474-8390
Secretary to the Governor:
  William Mulrow 518-474-4246
Counsel to the Governor:
  Alphonso David 518-474-8343
Deputy Secretary for Civil Rights:
  Patricia Gatling 212-681-4584
Director, Communications:
  Melissa DeRosa . . . . .518-474-8418 or 212-681-4640

EXECUTIVE DEPARTMENTS AND RELATED AGENCIES

Civil Service Department
Alfred E Smith State Ofc Bldg
Albany, NY 12239
518-457-2487 or 877-697-5627
Web site: www.cs.ny.gov

Commissioner:
  Jerry Boone 518-457-3701
Executive Deputy Commissioner:
  Vacant 518-473-5698
Deputy Commissioner, Operations:
  Vacant 518-473-5711
Deputy Commissioner, Administration:
  Deirdre Taylor 518-473-5694
Public Information Officer:
  Ed Walsh .518-457-9375/fax: 518-473-2372
  e-mail: pio@cs.state.ny.us

Classification & Compensation Division
Director:
  Patricia A. Itite 518-474-1011/fax: 518-474-0787

Developmental Disabilities Planning Council
99 Washington Ave
12th Fl, Ste 1230
Albany, NY 12210
518-486-7505 or 800-395-3372 Fax: 518-402-3505
e-mail: ddpc@ddpc.ny.gov
Web site: www.ddpc.ny.gov

Chairperson:
  Rose Marie Toscano 518-486-7505
Vice Chairperson:
  Ansley Bacon, PhD 518-486-7505
Executive Director:
  Sheila M Carey 518-486-7505
  e-mail: sheila.carey@ddpc.ny.gov
Deputy Director-Program Development Specialist:
  Anna Lobosco 518-486-7505
  e-mail: anna.lobosco@ddpc.ny.gov

Public Information Officer:
  Thomas F Lee 518-486-7505/fax: 518-486-3505
  e-mail: thomas.lee@ddpc.ny.gov

Human Rights, State Division of
1 Fordham Plaza, 4th Fl
Bronx, NY 10458
718-741-8400 or 888-392-3644 Fax: 718-741-8279
e-mail: infobronx@dhr.ny.gov
Web site: www.dhr.ny.gov

Commissioner:
  Helen Diane Foster 718-741-8326
First Deputy Commissioner:
  Valerie P. Dent 718-741-8330
Deputy Commissioner, Regional Affairs:
  Abena Darkeh 718-741-8324
Deputy Commissioner, Federal Programs:
  Edward Watkins 718-741-8440
Deputy Commissioner, Enforcement:
  Melissa Franco 718-741-8400
General Counsel:
  Caroline Downey 718-741-8402
Equal Opportunity Officer:
  Rockwell J Chin 718-741-8309
Director, Disability Rights:
  John Herrion 718-741-8332
RIO:
  Leticia Theodore-Greene .718-741-3223
  e-mail: lgreene@dhr.ny.gov

Regional Offices

Albany
Empire State Plaza, Agency Bldg., 2nd Floor, Albany, NY 12220
Regional Director:
  Victor DeAmelia 518-474-2705/fax: 518-473-3422
  e-mail: infoalbany@dhr.ny.gov

Binghamton
44 Hawley St, Rm 603, Binghamton, NY 13901
Regional Director:
  Victor DeAmelia 607-721-8467/fax: 607-721-8470
  e-mail: infobinghamton@dhr.ny.gov

Brooklyn
55 Hanson Place, Rm 1084, Brooklyn, NY 11217
Regional Director:
  William Lamot 718-722-2385/fax: 718-722-2869
  e-mail: infobrooklyn@dhr.ny.gov

Buffalo
W J Mahoney State Ofc Bldg, 65 Court St, Ste 506, Buffalo, NY 14202
e-mail: infobuffalo@dhr.ny.gov
Regional Director:
  Tasha Moore 716-847-7632/fax: 716-847-7625

Housing Investigations Unit
1 Fordham Plaza, 4th Fl, Bronx, NY 10458
Regional Director:
  William Lamot . . . . .718-741-8435/fax: 718-741—8103

Manhattan (Upper)
State Ofc Bldg, 163 W 125th St, 4th Fl, New York, NY 10027
Regional Director:
  David Powell 212-961-8650/fax: 212-961-4425

Nassau County
175 Fulton Ave, Ste 404, Hempstead, NY 11550
e-mail: infolongisland@dhr.ny.gov
Regional Director:
  Ronald Brinn 516-538-1360/fax: 516-483-6589

Offices and agencies generally appear in alphabetical order, except when specific order is requested by listee.

Peekskill
8 John Walsh Blvd, Ste 204, Peekskill, NY 10566
Regional Director:
    Roberto Chavez.................914-788-8050/fax: 914-788-8059
    e-mail: infopeekskill@dhr.ny.gov

Rochester
One Monroe Sq, 259 Monroe Ave, Ste 308, Rochester, NY 14607
Regional Director:
    Julia Day.....................585-238-8250/fax: 585-238-8259
    e-mail: inforochester@dhr.ny.gov

Suffolk County
State Office Bldg., 250 Veterans Memorial Highway, Suite 2B-49,
    Hauppauge, NY 11788
Regional Director:
    Ronald Brinn...................631-952-6434/fax: 631-952-6436
    e-mail: infolongisland@dhr.ny.gov

Syracuse
333 E Washington St, Rm 543, Syracuse, NY 13202
e-mail: infosyracuse@dhr.ny.gov
Regional Director:
    Julia Day 315-428-4633/fax: 315-428-4638

Law Department
120 Broadway
New York, NY 10271-0332
212-416-8000 or 800-771-7755
Web site: www.ag.ny.gov

State Capitol
Albany, NY 12224-0341
518-474-5481
Fax: 518-473-9909

Attorney General:
    Eric T Schneiderman ....212-416-8050 or 518-474-7330
Chief of Staff:
    Micah Lasher 212-416-8050
Press Secretary:
    Fernando Aquino212-416-8060/fax: 212-416-6005

Social Justice
Executive Deputy Attorney General:
    Alvin L Braggs, Jr.................212-416-8450/fax: 212-416-8942

Civil Rights Bureau
Bureau Chief:
    Kristen Clarke 212-416-8250/fax: 212-416-8074

Temporary & Disability Assistance, Office of
40 N Pearl St
Albany, NY 12243
518-473-1090
e-mail: nyspio@otda.ny.gov
Web site: www.otda.ny.gov

Commissioner:
    Kristin M. Proud...................................518-474-4152
State Legislative Coordinator:
    Judi West...518-474-7420
Director, Public Information:
    Kristi L. Berner 518-474-9516/fax: 518-486-6935
    e-mail: nyspio@otda.ny.gov

Center for Employment & Economic Supports
Deputy Commissioner:
    Phyllis Morris 518-474-9222/fax: 518-474-5281

Operations & Program Support
Deputy Commissioner:
    Wilma Brown Phillips 518-473-3912

NEW YORK STATE LEGISLATURE

See Legislative Branch in Section 1 for additional Standing Committee and Subcommittee information.

Assembly Standing Committees

Aging
Chair:
    Steven Cymbrowitz (D) 518-455-5214
Ranking Minority Member:
    Angela M Wozniak (C)..............................518-455-5921

Correction
Chair:
    Daniel O'Donnell (D)...............................518-455-5603
Ranking Minority Member:
    Joe Giglio (R) 518-455-5241

Labor
Chair:
    Michele Titus (D) 518-455-5668
Ranking Minority Member:
    Karl Brabenec (R)..................................518-455-5991

Mental Health
Chair:
    Aileen Gunther (D) 518-455-5355
Ranking Minority Member:
    Steven Katz (R) 518-455-5783

Assembly Task Forces

Puerto Rican/Hispanic Task Force
Chair:
    Marcos Crespo (D) 518-455-5514
Executive Director:
    Guillermo Martinez................................518-455-3608

Women's Issues, Task Force on
Chair:
    Aravella Simotas (D) 518-455-5014
Coordinator:
    Christina Williams (R) 518-455-3632/fax: 518-455-4574

Senate Standing Committees

Aging
Chair:
    Sue Serino (R)......................................518-455-2945
Ranking Minority Member:
    Ruben Diaz Sr (D) 518-455-2511

Crime Victims, Crime & Correction
Chair:
    Patrick Gallivan (R) 518-455-3471
Ranking Minority Member:
    Ruth Hassell-Thompson...............................518-455-2061

Labor
Chair:
    Jack Martins (R) 518-455-3265
Ranking Minority Member:
    Jose R Peralta (D) 518-455-2529

Policy Areas

Offices and agencies generally appear in alphabetical order, except when specific order is requested by listee.

Mental Health & Developmental Disabilities
Chair:
Robert G Ortt (R) 518-455-2024
Ranking Minority Member:
Jesse Hamilton (D) 518-455-2431

U.S. GOVERNMENT

EXECUTIVE DEPARTMENTS AND RELATED AGENCIES

Equal Employment Opportunity Commission
Web site: www.eeoc.gov

New York District . . . . fax: 212-336-3790
33 Whitehall St, 5th Fl, New York, NY 10004
800-669-4000 or TTY: 800-669-6820 Fax: 212-336-3790
Director:
Kevin J. Berry . . . . 800-669-4000 or 800-669-6820 TTY
fax: 212-336-3790

Buffalo Local . . . . fax: 716-551-4387
6 Fountain Plaza, Ste 350, Buffalo, NY 14202
800-669-4000 or TTY: 800-669-6820 Fax: 716-551-4387
Director:
John E Thompson Jr 800-669-4000/fax: 716-551-4387

US Commerce Department
Web site: www.doc.gov

Minority Business Development Agency
Web site: www.mbda.gov

New York Region
26 Federal Plaza, New York, NY 10278
212-264-3262
Regional Director:
Suzette C. Bather 212-264-3262

US Commission on Civil Rights
Web site: www.usccr.gov

EASTERN REGION (includes New York State)
624 9th St NW, Ste 500, Washington, DC 20425
Regional Director:
Ivy Davis 202-376-7533/fax: 202-376-7548

US Department of Health & Human Services
Web site: www.os.dhhs.gov; www.hhs.gov/region2/

Office of Secretary's Regional Representative-Region 2-NY . . fax:
212-264-3620
26 Federal Plaza, Rm 3835, New York, NY 10278
Regional Director:
Jaime R. Torres 212-264-4600
e-mail: deborah.konopko@hhs.gov

Office for Civil Rights . . . . fax: 212-264-3039
26 Federal Plaza, Rm 3312, New York, NY 10278
Fax: 212-264-3039
Web site: www.hhs.gov/ocr
Regional Manager:
Linda Colon. 212-264-3313/fax: 212-264-3039

US Department of Homeland Security (DHS)
Web site: www.dhs.gov

US Citizenship & Immigration Services (USCIS)
TTY: 800-767-1833 or 800-375-5283
Web site: www.uscis.gov

Buffalo District Office . . . . fax: 716-551-3131
Federal Center, 130 Delaware Ave, 1st Floor, Buffalo, NY 14202
District Director:
M Frances Holmes. .716-551-4741 x6000
Albany Sub Office
1086 Troy-Schenectady Rd, Latham, NY 12110
Director:
Kevin Gallagher. 518-220-2125

CIS Asylum Offices
New York Asylum Office . . . . fax: 718-723-1121
One Cross Island Plaza, 3rd Fl, Rosedale, NY 11422
Director:
Patricia A Jackson 718-723-5954
Deputy Director:
Mick Dedvukaj 718-723-5954
Newark Asylum Offc-Including NYS not served by New York City fax:
201-531-1877
1200 Wall St, West 4th Fl, Lyndhurst, NJ 07071
Director:
Susan Raufer 201-531-0555
Deputy Director:
Aster Zeleke. 201-531-0555

New York City District Office
26 Federal Plaza, 3rd Floor, Room 3-120, New York, NY 10278
District Director:
Mary Ann Gantner 212-264-3972
Garden City Satellite Office . . . . fax: 914-234-4480
711 Stewart Ave, Garden City, NY 11530
Officer-in-Charge:
Linda Pritchett . . . . .516-228-9242 or 516-288-9243

U.S. CONGRESS

See U.S. Congress Chapter for additional Standing Committee and Subcommittee information.

House of Representatives Standing Committees

Education & the Workforce
Chair:
John Kline (R-MN). 202-225-2271
Ranking Member:
George Miller (D-CA) 202-225-2095
New York Delegate:
Timothy H Bishop (D) 202-225-3826
New York Delegate:
Carolyn McCarthy (D) 202-225-5516

Foreign Affairs
Chair:
Edward R. Royce (R-CA). 202-225-4111
Ranking Member:
Eliot L. Engel (D-NY) 202-225-2464
New York Delegate:
Brian Higgins (D) 202-225-3306
New York Delegate:
Grace Meng (D) 202-225-2601
New York Delegate:
Eliot L Engel (D) 202-225-2464
New York Delegate:
Gregory W Meeks (D) 202-225-3461

Subcommittee
Terrorism, Nonproliferation and Trade
Chair:
Ted Pope (R-TX). 202-225-3121
Ranking Member:
Brad Sherman (D-CA) 202-225-5911

Offices and agencies generally appear in alphabetical order, except when specific order is requested by listee.

Senate Standing Committees

Indian Affairs, Committee on
Chair:
 Maria Cantwell (D-WA)............................202-224-3441
Vice Chair:
 John Barrasso (R-WY)............................202-224-6441

PRIVATE SECTOR

American Jewish Committee
165 E 56th St, New York, NY 10022-2709
212-751-4000 Fax: 212-891-1450
e-mail: pr@ajc.org
Web site: www.ajc.org
*Promoting tolerance, mutual respect & understanding among diverse ethnic,
racial & religious groups*
David Harris, Executive Director

Amnesty International USA
5 Penn Plaza, 16th Floor, New York, NY 10001
212-807-8400 Fax: 212-627-1451
e-mail: aimember@aiusa.org
Web site: www.amnestyusa.org
*Worldwide campaigning movement working to promote internationally
recognized human rights*
Suzanne Nossel, Executive Director

Anti-Defamation League
605 Third Ave, New York, NY 10158
212-885-7707 Fax: 212-697-0109
e-mail: afoxman@adl.org
Web site: www.adl.org
Fighting anti-Semitism worldwide
Abraham H Foxman, National Director

Asian American Legal Defense and Education Fund
99 Hudson St, 12th Fl, New York, NY 10013-2815
212-966-5932 or 800-966-5946 Fax: 212-966-4303
e-mail: info@aaldef.org
Web site: www.aaldef.org
*Defend civil rights of Asian Americans through litigation, legal advocacy &
community education*
Margaret Fung, Executive Director

NYS Bar Assn, Gender Equity Task Force Cmte
Bond Schoeneck & King PLLC
One Lincoln Ctr, Syracuse, NY 13202-1355
315-218-8000 Fax: 315-218-8100
e-mail: crichardson@bsk.com
M Catherine Richardson, Co-Chair

CIDNY - Queens
137-02A Northern Blvd, Flushing, NY 11354
646-442-1520 or TTY 718-886-0427 Fax: 718-886-0428
Web site: www.cidny.org
Rights & advocacy for the disabled
Susan Dooha, Executive Director
Donald Holford, Director of Administration

Cardozo School of Law
55 Fifth Ave, New York, NY 10003
212-790-0200 Fax: 212-790-0205
e-mail: mrosnfld@ymail.yu.edu
Web site: www.cardozo.yu.edu
Law & theory of human rights
Michel Rosenfeld, Justice Sidney L Robins Professor of Human Rights

Center for Constitutional Rights
666 Broadway, 7th Fl, New York, NY 10012
212-614-6464 Fax: 212-614-6499
e-mail: info@ccrjustice.org
Web site: www.ccrjustice.org
*Dedicated to advancing & protecting rights guaranteed by the US
Constitution & the Universal Declaration of Human Rights*
Vincent Warren, Executive Director

Center for Independence of the Disabled in NY (CIDNY)
841 Broadway, Ste 301, New York, NY 10003
212-674-2300 or TTY: 212-674-5619 Fax: 212-254-5953
Web site: www.cidny.org
Rights & advocacy for the disabled
Susan Dooha, Executive Director

Center for Migration Studies of New York Inc
27 Carmine Street, New York, NY 10014
718-351-8800 or 718-255-1111 Fax: 718-667-4598
e-mail: cms@cmsny.org
Web site: www.cmsny.org
*Facilitate the study of sociodemographic, historical, economic, political,
legislative & pastoral aspects of human migration & refugee movements*
Rev Joseph Fugolo, Executive Director

Children's Rights Inc
330 Seventh Avenue, 4th Floor, New York, NY 10001
212-683-2210 Fax: 212-683-4015
e-mail: info@childrensrights.org
Web site: www.childrensrights.org
Advocacy & litigation on behalf of abused & neglected children
Marcia Robinson Lowry, Executive Director

Citizens' Committee for Children of New York Inc
105 E 22nd St, 7th Fl, New York, NY 10010
212-673-1800 Fax: 212-979-5063
e-mail: info@cccnewyork.org
Web site: www.cccnewyork.org
Public policy advocacy for children's rights & services
Jennifer March-Joly, Executive Director

Columbia University, Mailman School of Public Health
Heilbrunn Dept of Population & Family He, 60 Haven Ave, B-2, New York,
NY 10032
212-304-5281 Fax: 212-305-7024
e-mail: lpf1@columbia.edu
Web site: cpmcnet.columbia.edu/dept/sph/popfam
*Theory, analysis & development of policy & programs supporting public
health & human rights*
Lynn P Freedman, Associate Professor & Director

Cornell University, School of Industrial & Labor Relations
Ives Hall, Ithaca, NY 14853-3901
607-255-4381 Fax: 607-255-4496
e-mail: fdb4@cornell.edu
Web site: www.ilr.cornell.edu
Inequality, discrimination & sexual harassment; occupational segregation
Francine Blau, Professor

Drum Major Institute for Public Policy - Not For Profit
40 Exchange Place, Suite 2001, New York, NY 10005
212-909-9663 Fax: 212-909-9493
e-mail: dmi@drummajorinstitute.org
Web site: www.drummajorinstitute.org
*Progressive think tank sponsoring frank dialogue on social problems &
developing public policy to promote social & economic justice & equity*
Andrea Batista Schlesinger, Executive Director

Offices and agencies generally appear in alphabetical order, except when specific order is requested by listee.

Family Planning Advocates of New York State
17 Elk St, Albany, NY 12207-1002
518-436-8408 Fax: 518-436-0004
e-mail: smitj@fpaofnys.org
Web site: www.fpaofnys.org
Reproductive rights
JoAnn M Smith, President/Chief Executive Officer

Filipino American Human Services Inc (FAHSI)
185-14 Hillside Ave, Jamaica, NY 11432
718-883-1295 Fax: 718-523-9606
e-mail: admin@fahsi.org
Web site: www.fahsi.org
FAHSI is a community-based, non-profit organization dedicated to serving the Filipino and Filipino American community of New York City, particularly, marginalized sections such as youth, women, recent immigrants, and the elderly.
Johanna Martinez LMSW, Executive Director

Hispanic Outreach Services
40 North Main Ave, 5th Floor, Albany, NY 12010
518-453-6655 Fax: 518-641-6830
e-mail: elaine.escobales@rcda.org
Web site: www.hispanicoutreachservices.org
Social service, youth guidance, language translation & immigration assistance programs
Elaine Escobales, Executive Director

Human Rights First
333 Seventh Ave, 13th Fl, New York, NY 10001
212-845-5200 Fax: 212-845-5299
e-mail: nyc@humanrightsfirst.org
Web site: www.humanrightsfirst.org
Advocacy for the promotion & protection of fundamental human rights worldwide
Michael Posner, President

Human Rights Watch
350 Fifth Ave, 34th Fl, New York, NY 10118-3299
212-290-4700 Fax: 212-736-1300
e-mail: hrwnyc@hrw.org
Web site: www.hrw.org
Working with victims & activists to prevent discrimination, uphold political freedom, protect people from inhumane conduct in wartime & to bring offenders to justice
Kenneth Roth, Executive Director

International Institute of Buffalo, NY, Inc
864 Delaware Ave, Buffalo, NY 14209
716-883-1900 Fax: 716-883-9529
e-mail: pkefi@iibuff.org
Web site: www.iibuff.org
Assist newly arrived refugees & immigrants to find work, learn English; legal immigration service, translations & interpreting school advocacy
Pamela Kefi, Executive Director

Jewish Community Relations Council of NY Inc
70 W 36th Street, Ste 700, New York, NY 10018
212-983-4800 Fax: 212-983-4084
e-mail: millerm@jcrcny.org
Web site: www.jcrcny.org
JCRC is an umbrella organization for more than 60 Jewish organizations ranging from community based councils to local chapters of national educational, cvic and religious agencies.
Michael Miller, Executive Vice President

Lambda Legal
120 Wall St, Ste 1500, New York, NY 10005-3904
212-809-8585 Fax: 212-809-0055
e-mail: lambda@lambdalegal.org
Web site: www.lambdalegal.org
Gay rights & HIV issues

Frances J. Goldstein, Deputy Director

LatinoJustice PRLDEF
99 Hudson St, 14th Fl, New York, NY 10013-2815
212-219-3360 or 800-328-2322 Fax: 212-431-4276
e-mail: info@latinojustice.org
Web site: www.latinojustice.org
Secure, promote & protect the civil & human rights of the Puerto Rican & wider Latino community through litigation, policy analysis & education
Juan Cartagena, President & General Counsel

Lesbian, Gay, Bisexual & Transgender Community Ctr - Not For Profit
208 West 13th Street, New York, NY 10011-7702
212-620-7310 Fax: 212-924-2657
e-mail: info@gaycenter.org
Web site: www.gaycenter.org
Mental health counseling, out-patient chemical dependency treatment center, after-school youth services, HIV/AIDS services, advocacy, cultural programs, affordable meeting and conference services, and community-building.
Miriam Yeung, Director, Public Policy

NYS Bar Assn, Issues Affecting People with Disabilities Cmte NYS Education Department
Education Bldg, Rm 148, 89 Washington Ave, Albany, NY 12234
518-473-4921 Fax: 518-473-2925
e-mail: ksurgall@mail.nysed.gov
Melinda Saran, Chair

National Council of Jewish Women
53 W 23rd St, 6th Fl, New York, NY 10010
212-645-4048 Fax: 212-645-7466
e-mail: action@ncjw.org
Web site: www.ncjw.org
Human rights & social service advocacy & education
Phyllis Snyder, President

National Organization for Women, NYS
1500 Central Avenue, Albany, NY 12205
518-452-3944 Fax: 518-452-3861
e-mail: newyorkstatenow@aol.com
Web site: www.nownys.com
Legislative lobbying on issues affecting women
Marcia Pappas, President

New School University, Department of Political Science
65 Fifth Ave, New York, NY 10003
212-228-5747 X3088 Fax: 212-807-1669
e-mail: pollis@newschool.edu
Comparative politics, human rights, nationalism & ethnicity
Adamantia Pollis, Professor Emeritus, Political Science

New School University, Intl Center for Migration, Ethnicity & Citizenship
65 Fifth Ave, Room 227, New York, NY 10003
212-229-5399 Fax: 212-989-0504
e-mail: icmec@newschool.edu
Web site: www.newschool.edu/icmec
International migrations, refugees
Aristide R Zolberg, Director

New York Civil Liberties Union
125 Broad Street, 19th Floor, New York, NY 10004
212-607-3300 Fax: 212-607-3318
Web site: www.nyclu.org
Civil rights & civil liberties
Donna Lieberman, Executive Director

Offices and agencies generally appear in alphabetical order, except when specific order is requested by listee.

New York Civil Rights Coalition
3 W 35th Street, Penthouse, New York, NY 10001-2204
212-563-5636 Fax: 212-563-9757
e-mail: nycrc@aol.com
Web site: www.nycivilrights.org
Advocacy of racial equality & multiracial cooperation in advancing social progress through the protection & enforcement of civil rights & the unlearning of stereotypes
Michael Meyers, Executive Director

New York Immigration Coalition (The)
137 W 25th Street, 12th Floor, New York, NY 10001
212-627-2227 x221 Fax: 212-627-9314
e-mail: jwong@thenyic.org
Web site: www.thenyic.org
Nonprofit umbrella advocacy organization for groups assisting immigrants
Chung-Wha Hong, Executive Director

New York Lawyers for the Public Interest
151 W 30th Street, 11th Floor, New York, NY 10001
212-244-4664 Fax: 212-244-4570
e-mail: mmassie@nylpi.org
Web site: www.nylpi.org
Disability justice; health justice; environmental justice, pro bono clearing house
Miranda Massie, Interim Executive Director

New York State Council of Churches
1580 Central Avenue, Albany, NY 12205
518-436-9319 Fax: 518-427-6705
e-mail: nyscoc@aol.com
Web site: www.nyscoc.org
A council; a collaboration, a conscience shared by Christian denominations of many types. Our mission goals focus on social justice, institutional patroal carem and ecumenical cooperation in education, worship, and action.
Rev. Dr. Robert A White, Interim Executive Director

NYS Bar Assn, Minorities in the Profession Cmte
Office of the Attorney General
120 Broadway, New York, NY 10271
212-416-6303 Fax: 212-416-8539
e-mail: lila.kirton@oag.state.ny.us
Lila E Kirton, Chair

Open Society Institute
400 West 59th St, New York, NY 10019
212-548-0600 Fax: 212-548-4600
Web site: www.soros.org
Promotes open societies by shaping government policy & supporting education, media, public health, human & women's rights, as well as social, legal & economic reform
Stewart Paperin, Executive Vice President

Resource Center for Independent Living (RCIL)
401-409 Columbia St, PO Box 210, Utica, NY 13503-0210
315-797-4642 or TTY 315-797-5837 Fax: 315-797-4747
e-mail: rcil@rcil.com
Web site: www.rcil.com
Services & advocacy for the disabled; public information & community education & awareness
Burt Danovitz, Executive Director

SUNY Buffalo Human Rights Center
SUNY Buffalo, School of Law, 523 O'Brian Hall, Buffalo, NY 14260-1100
716-645-6184 Fax: 716-645-2064
e-mail: bhrc@buffalo.edu
Web site: wings.buffalo.edu/law/bhrlc
Fostering scholarship, coursework, research & internships in international & human rights law
Makau Mutua, Professor & Director

Schuyler Center for Analysis & Advocacy (SCAA)
150 State St, 4th Fl, Albany, NY 12207
518-463-1896 x29 Fax: 518-463-3364
e-mail: joconnor@scaany.org
Web site: www.scaany.org
Advocacy, analysis & forums on mental health issues.
Jenn O'Connor, Senior Policy Associate

Self Advocacy Association of NYS
Capital District DSO, 500 Balltown Road, Schenectady, NY 12304
518-382-1454 Fax: 518-382-1594
e-mail: sholmes@earthlink.net
Web site: www.sanys.org
Advocacy for & by persons with developmental disabilities to ensure civil rights & opportunities
Steve Holmes, Administrative Director

Simon Wiesenthal Center, NY Tolerance Center
50 E 42nd St, Ste 1600, New York, NY 10017-5405
212-370-0320 Fax: 212-883-0895
e-mail: swcny@swcny.org
Web site: www.wiesenthal.com
Preserve the memory of the Holocaust by fostering tolerance & understanding through community involvement, educational outreach & social action
Rhonda Barad, Eastern Director

Tanenbaum Center for Interreligious Understanding
254 West 31st Street, New York, NY 10001
212-967-7707 Fax: 212-967-9001
e-mail: info@tanenbaum.org
Web site: www.tanenbaum.org
Puts interreligious understanding into practice; reduces and prevents violence done in the name of religion
Joyce S Dubensky, Executive Vice President

NYS Bar Assn, Gender Equity Task Force Cmte
The Legal Aid Society
One West Main Street, Suite 800, Rochester, NY 14614
585-232-4090 Fax: 585-232-2352
e-mail: cpalumbo@lasroc.org
Carla M Palumbo, Division Director

NYS Bar Assn, Issues Affecting Same Sex Couples
Whiteman Osterman & Hanna LLP
One Commerce Plaza, Albany, NY 12260
518-487-7600 Fax: 518-487-7777
e-mail: lptharp@woh.com
Web site: www.woh.com
Lorraine Power Tharp, Partner

Women's Commission for Refugee Women & Children
122 East 42nd St, New York, NY 10168-1289
212-551-3000 Fax: 212-551-3180
e-mail: wcrwc@womenscommission.org
Web site: www.womenscommission.org
Advocacy on behalf of refugee women & children world-wide
Carolyn Makinson, Executive Director

Offices and agencies generally appear in alphabetical order, except when specific order is requested by listee.

INSURANCE

NEW YORK STATE

GOVERNOR'S OFFICE

Governor's Office
Executive Chamber
State Capitol
Albany, NY 12224
518-474-8390 Fax: 518-474-1513
Web site: www.ny.gov

Governor:
  Andrew M Cuomo 518-474-8390
Secretary to the Governor:
  William Mulrow 518-474-4246
Counsel to the Governor:
  Alphonso David 518-474-8343
Director, Communications:
  Melissa DeRosa ....518-474-8418 or 212-681-4640

EXECUTIVE DEPARTMENTS AND RELATED AGENCIES

Financial Services Department
One State Street
New York, NY 10001
212-480-6400 or 518-474-6600
e-mail: public-affairs@dfs.ny.gov
Web site: www.dfs.ny.gov

Superintendent:
  Benjamin M. Lawsky 212-709-3501
Assistant Director, Administration & Operations:
  Lori Fraser...................................518-486-4737
Deputy Superintendent & General Counsel:
  Marjorie Gross 212-709-1640
Deputy Superintendent, Community Regional Banks:
  Martin Cofsky.................................212-709-1610
Director, Criminal Investigations Bureau:
  Ricardo Velez 212-709-3554
Chief Information Officer:
  William Rachmiel..............................212-709-5420
Senior Public Information Specialist:
  Ronald Klug.................212-480-2285/fax: 212-480-6077
Consumer Representative, State Charter Advisory Board:
  Vacant..212-709-3500

Banking Division
Deputy Superintendent:
  Vacant..212-709-1690

Insurance Division
Deputy Superintendent, Property & Casualty Markets:
  Michael Moriarty.................212-480-5127/fax: 212-480-2310
Chief, Life Insurance Bureau:
  Gail Keren....................................212-480-5030
Chief, Health Insurance Bureau:
  Vacant.....................518-486-2970/fax: 518-474-3397
Insurance Examiner 3:
  Michael Maffei 212-480-5023

Financial Frauds & Consumer Protection Division
Director, Frauds:
  Frank Orlando.................212-480-5770/fax: 212-480-6066
Assistant Director, Frauds:
  Angelo Carbone 212-480-5688

Capital Markets Division
Acting Director, Capital Markets:
  Matti Peltonen...............212-480-5071/fax: 212-480-6085
Deputy Superintendent, Mortgage Banking:
  Rhonda Ricketts 212-480-5540

Insurance Fund (NYS)
15 Computer Drive West
Albany, NY 12205
518-437-5220
Web site: www.nysif.com

199 Church St
New York, NY 10007
212-587-9000

Executive Director:
  Eric Madoff...............212-312-7004 or 518-437-5220
Deputy Executive Director:
  Dorothy Carey.................................212-312-9933
Deputy Executive Director:
  Shirley Stark 212-312-9917
Deputy Executive Director:
  Colleen Gardner 212-587-9000
Chief Fiscal Officer:
  Susan D Sharp.................................518-437-6168
General Attorney:
  Gregory Allen 518-437-5220
Public Information Officer:
  Robert Lawson.................518-437-3504/fax: 518-437-1849

Administration
Director:
  Joseph Mullen.................................518-437-5220

Claims & Medical Operations
Director:
  Edward Hiller 212-312-7880

Confidential Investigations
Director:
  George T Tidona...............................631-756-4007

Field Services
Director:
  Armin Holdorf 212-587-5225

Information Technology Service
Chief Information Officer:
  Sean O'Brien..................................518-437-4361
Director, ITS:
  Laurie Endries................................518-437-3130

Insurance Fund Board of Commissioners
Chair:
  Kenneth R Theobalds 518-437-5220
Vice Chair:
  Barry Swidler 518-437-5220
Secretary to the Board:
  Francine James 212-312-7408
Member (ex-officio)/Commissioner, NYS Dept of Labor:
  Peter M. Rivera...............................518-437-5220
Member:
  Eileen A Frank 518-437-5220
Member:
  Joseph Canovas................................518-437-5220
Member:
  David E Ourlicht..............................518-437-5220

Offices and agencies generally appear in alphabetical order, except when specific order is requested by listee.

Investments
Director:
Miriam Martinez 212-587-6550

NYSIF District Offices

Albany
1 Watervliet Ave Ext, Albany, NY 12206
Business Manager:
Augusto Bortoloni. 518-437-6401/fax: 518-437-8021

Buffalo
225 Oak St, Buffalo, NY 14203
Business Manager:
Ronald Reed 716-851-2004/fax: 716-851-2131

Binghamton
Glendale Technology Park, 2001 E Perimeter Rd, Endicott, NY 13760
Business Manager:
Thomas Racko. 607-741-6023/fax: 607-741-5029

Nassau County, Long Island
8 Corporate Center Dr, 2nd Fl, Melville, NY 11747
Business Manager:
Cliff Meister 631-756-4003/fax: 631-756-4030

Rochester
100 Chestnut St, Ste 1000, Rochester, NY 14604
Business Manager:
Lisa Ellsworth 585-258-2100/fax: 585-258-2065

Suffolk County, Long Island
8 Corporate Center Dr, 3rd Fl, Melville, NY 11747
Business Manager:
Catherine Carillo. 631-756-4330/fax: 631-756-4260

Syracuse
1045 Seventh North St, Liverpool, NY 13088
Business Manager:
Patricia Albert 315-453-8300/fax: 315-453-8313

White Plains
105 Corporate Park Dr, Ste 200, White Plains, NY 10604
Business Manager:
Carl Heitner. 914-701-6292/fax: 914-701-2181

Premium Audit
Director:
Glenn Cunningham. 212-587-7470

Underwriting
Director:
John Massetti 212-312-7012

Labor Department
Building 12, Room 500
Harriman State Office Campus
Albany, NY 12240
518-457-9000 Fax: 518-457-6908
e-mail: nysdol@labor.ny.gov
Web site: www.labor.ny.gov

Commissioner:
Peter M. Rivera 518-457-9000
Executive Deputy Commissioner:
Mario Musolino 518-457-4318
Director, Communications:
Leo Rosales 518-457-5519/fax: 518-485-1126
e-mail: leo.rosales@labor.ny.gov

Hazard Abatement Board
Chair:
Katherine D. Schrier 518-457-7629

Employment Relations Board
Chair:
Jerome Lefkowitz 518-457-2664
e-mail: perbinfo@perb.ny.gov

Industrial Board of Appeals
Chair:
Anne P Stevason 518-474-4785

Unemployment Insurance Appeal Board
Chair:
Leonard Polletta 518-402-0205
Executive Director:
Susan Borenstein. 518-402-0205

State Workforce Investment Board
Chair:
Vacant 518-457-8312/fax: 518-485-8604

Law Department
120 Broadway
New York, NY 10271-0332
212-416-8000
Web site: www.ag.ny.gov

State Capitol
Albany, NY 12224-0341
518-474-7330
Fax: 518-473-9909

Attorney General:
Eric T Schneiderman . . . . .212-416-8050 or 518-474-7330
Chief of Staff:
Micah Lasher 212-416-8050
Press Secretary:
Fernando Aquino212-416-8060/fax: 212-416-6005

State Counsel
Chief Deputy Attorney General & Counsel:
Harlan Levy 212-416-8525
Executive Deputy Attorney General, State Counsel:
Kent T. Stauffer. 212-416-8252/fax: 212-416-6001

Civil Recoveries Bureau
Bureau Chief:
John Cremo 518-776-2173/fax: 518-915-7731

Claims Bureau
Bureau Chief:
Katharine Brooks . . . . .518-776-2300 or 212-416-8913

Litigation Bureau
Bureau Chief:
Lisa Del .518-776-2300 or 212-416-8610
fax: 518-473-1572

Real Property Bureau
Bureau Chief:
Alison Crocker 518-776-2700

Workers' Compensation Board
328 State Street
Schenectady, NY 12305
518-462-8880 or 877-632-4996 Fax: 518-473-1415
e-mail: publicinfo@wcb.ny.gov
Web site: www.wcb.ny.gov

Executive Director:
Mark Wade 518-408-0469
Chair, Board of Commissioners:
Robert E Beloten 518-408-0469/fax: 518-473-1415

Offices and agencies generally appear in alphabetical order, except when specific order is requested by listee.

203

Vice Chair:
Fran Libous 518-408-0469/fax: 518-473-1415
General Counsel:
Vacant 518-486-9564/fax: 518-402-0113
Director, Public Information:
Rachel McEneny 518-408-5592/fax: 518-473-1415
e-mail: publicinfo@wcb.ny.gov
Fraud Inspector General:
Vacant .888-363-6001 or 518-473-4839
fax: 518-402-1059
Advocate for Business:
Neil Gilberg 518-486-3331
Advocate for Injured Workers:
Edwin Ruff .800-580-6665 or 518-471-8182
fax: 518-486-7510

Administration

Facilities Management:
Michael DeBarr. 518-486-9597
Director, Security:
John Dale .518-402-0172/fax: 518-402-6100
Director, Human Resources:
Gilda Hernandez 518-408-0865/fax: 518-486-6364
Affirmative Action Officer:
Jaime Benitez. 518-474-2685/fax: 518-486-6364

Information Management Systems

Director:
Matthew Ancin 518-474-6557/fax: 518-474-9367
Director, Continuous Improvement/MIS:
Thomas Wegener 518-486-5143

Operations

Director, Bureau of Compliance:
K. Brian Collins. 518-474-9598/fax: 518-402-6201

District Offices
Albany
100 Broadway-Menands, Albany, NY 12241
District Manager:
Laurie Hart 866-750-5157/fax: 518-473-9166
Binghamton
State Office Bldg, 44 Hawley St, Binghamton, NY 13901
District Manager:
David Gardiner. 866-802-3604/fax: 607-721-8464
Brooklyn
111 Livingston St, 22nd Fl, Brooklyn, NY 11201
District Manager:
Tom Agostino. 800-877-1373/fax: 718-802-6642
Buffalo
Ellicott Sq Building, 295 Main Street Ste 400, Buffalo, NY 14203
District Manager:
Michelle Hirsch 866-211-0645/fax: 716-842-2171
Long Island
220 Rabro Drive, Ste 100, Hauppauge, NY 11788-4230
District Manager:
Steve Carbone. 866-681-5354/fax: 631-952-7966
Manhattan
215 W 125th St, New York, NY 10027
District Manager:
Sherri Cunningham. 800-877-1373/fax: 212-864-7204
Peekskill
41 N Division St, Peekskill, NY 10566
District Manager:
Luis A Torres 866-746-0552/fax: 914-788-5809
Queens
168-46 91st Ave, 3rd Fl, Jamaica, NY 11432
District Manager:
Bryan Pile. 800-877-1373
Rochester
130 Main St West, Rochester, NY 14614

District Manager:
Joseph Dailor 866-211-0644/fax: 585-238-8351
Syracuse
935 James Street, Syracuse, NY 13203
District Manager:
Marc Johnson 866-802-3730/fax: 315-423-2938

Workers' Compensation Board of Commissioners

Commissioner & Vice Chair:
Fran Libous. 518-408-0469
Commissioner:
Kenneth Munnelly 518-408-0469
Commissioner:
Mark D Higgins 518-408-0469
Commissioner:
Linda Hull. 518-408-0469
Commissioner:
Candace K Finnegan. 914-788-5890
Commissioner:
David Dudley 518-408-0469
Commissioner:
Samuel G Williams. 518-408-0469
Commissioner:
Freida Foster 518-408-0469
Commissioner:
Ellen O Paprocki. 315-423-1276
Commissioner:
Conrad W Lower 518-408-0469
Commissioner:
Richard Bell 315-423-1276
Commissioner:
Loren Lobban 518-408-0469
Secretary to the Board:
Sandra M Olson 518-402-6070

NEW YORK STATE LEGISLATURE

See Legislative Branch in Section 1 for additional Standing Committee and Subcommittee information.

Assembly Standing Committees

Insurance
Chair:
Kevin Cahill (D) 518-455-4436
Ranking Minority Member:
William Barclay (R) 518-455-5841

Labor
Chair:
Michele Titus (D) 518-455-5668
Ranking Minority Member:
Karl Brabenec (R). 518-455-5991

Senate Standing Committees

Insurance
Chair:
James L Seward (R) 518-455-3131
Ranking Minority Member:
Neil D Breslin (D). 518-455-2225

Labor
Chair:
Jack Martins (R) 518-455-3265
Ranking Minority Member:
Jose R Peralta (D) 518-455-2529

Offices and agencies generally appear in alphabetical order, except when specific order is requested by listee.

U.S. GOVERNMENT

U.S. CONGRESS

See U.S. Congress Chapter for additional Standing Committee and Subcommittee information.

House of Representatives Standing Committees

Financial Services
Chair:
  Jeb Hensarling (R-TX) 202-225-3484
Ranking Member:
  Maxine Waters (D-CA) 202-225-2201
Vice Chairman:
  Gary Miller (R-CA) 202-225-3201
New York Delegate:
  Peter T King (R).....................................202-225-7896
New York Delegate:
  Carolyn B Maloney (D) 202-225-7944
New York Delegate:
  Carolyn McCarthy (D) 202-225-5516
New York Delegate:
  Michael G. Grimm (R) 202-225-3371
New York Delegate:
  Gregory W Meeks (D) 202-225-3461
New York Delegate:
  Nydia M Velazquez (D) 202-225-2361

Subcommittee
Capital Markets & Government Sponsored Enterprises
  Chair:
    Scott Garrett (R-NJ).........................202-225-4465
  Ranking Member:
    Carolyn B. Malony (D-NY)...................202-225-7944
  New York Delegate:
    Michael G. Grimm (R).......................202-225-3371
  New York Delegate:
    Peter T King (R) 202-225-7896
  New York Delegate:
    Caroyln B Malony (D)........................202-225-7944

Senate Standing Committees

Finance
Chair:
  Max Baucus (D-MT) 202-224-2651
Ranking Member:
  Orrin G. Hatch (R-UT)............................202-224-5251

Subcommittees
Health Care
  Chair:
    John D Rockefeller, IV (D-WV) 202-224-6472
  Ranking Member:
    Pat Roberts (R-KS) 202-224-4744
Social Security, Pensions and Family Policy
  Chair:
    Michael F. Bennet (D-CO) 202-224-5852
  Ranking Member:
    Michael B. Enzi (R-WY).......................202-224-0359

PRIVATE SECTOR

American International Group Inc
70 Pine St, 36th Fl, New York, NY 10270
212-770-6114 Fax: 212-785-4214
e-mail: ned.cloonan@aig.com
Web site: www.aig.com
International business, government & financial services
Edward T Cloonan, Vice President International & Corporate Affairs

Aon Service Corporation
199 Water St, 35th Fl, New York, NY 10038
212-441-1150 Fax: 212-441-1929
e-mail: ellen_perle@aon.com
Web site: www.aon.com
Regulatory Law Licensing
Ellen Perle, Chief General Counsel/Regulatory Law Licensing

Associated Risk Managers of New York Inc
4 Airline Drive, Suite 205, Albany, NY 12205
518-690-2072 or 800-735-5441 Fax: 518-690-2074
e-mail: arm@armnortheast.com
Web site: www.armnortheast.com
John McLaughlin, Executive Director

Connors & Corcoran PLLC
Times Square Bldg, 45 Exchange St, Ste 250, Rochester, NY 14614
585-232-5885 Fax: 585-546-3631
e-mail: ebuholtz@connorscorcoran.com
Web site: www.connorscorcoran.com
Eileen E Buholtz, Member

DeGraff, Foy, & Kunz, LLP
90 State Street, Albany, NY 12207
518-462-5300 Fax: 518-436-0210
e-mail: firm@degraff-foy.com
Web site: www.degraff-foy.com
Tax law & procedure, administrative law
David Kunz, Managing Partner

Dupee & Monroe, PC
211 Main Street, Box 470, Goshen, NY 10924
845-294-8900 Fax: 845-294-3619
e-mail: law@dupeelaw.com
Web site: www.dupeelaw.com
Litigation, personal injury law, medical malpractice, product liability, civil rights, discrimination, sexual harassment
James E Monroe, Managing Partner

Empire Blue Cross & Blue Shield
11 West 42nd St, 18th Fl, New York, NY 10036
212-476-1000 Fax: 212-476-1281
e-mail: deborah.bohren@empireblue.com
Web site: www.empireblue.com
Health insurance
Deborah Bohren, Senior Vice President, Communications

Equitable Life Assurance Society of the US
1290 Ave of the Americas, New York, NY 10104
212-314-3828 Fax: 212-707-1890
e-mail: wendy.cooper@axa.financial.com
Web site: www.axa-financial.com
Life insurance regulation
Wendy E Cooper, Senior Vice President & Associate General Counsel,
  Government Relations

Excellus Health Plan Inc
165 Court Street, Rochester, NY 14647
585-327-7581 Fax: 585-327-7585
e-mail: stephen.sloan@excellus.com
Web site: www.excellus.com
Health insurance

Offices and agencies generally appear in alphabetical order, except when specific order is requested by listee.

Stephen R Sloan, Senior Vice President & Chief Administrative Officer, General Counsel

Excess Line Association of New York
One Exchange Plz, 55 Broadway, 29th Fl, New York, NY 10006
646-292-5555 Fax: 626-292-5505
e-mail: dmaher@elany.org
Web site: www.elany.org
Industry advisory association; facilitate & encourage compliance with the excess line law
Daniel F Maher, Executive Director

Group Health Inc
441 9th Ave, 8th Fl, New York, NY 10001
212-615-0891 Fax: 212-563-8561
e-mail: jgoodwin@ghi.com
Web site: www.ghi.com
Affordable, quality health insurance for working individuals & families
Jeffrey Goodwin, Director, Governmental Relations

Insurance Brokers' Association of the State of New York
119 Washington Avenue, Suite 300, Albany, NY 12210
518-694-5504
e-mail: info@ibany.org
Web site: www.ibany.org
Dianne Patterson, Executive Director

Life Insurance Council of New York, Inc
551 Fifth Ave, 29th Floor, New York, NY 10176
212-986-6181 Fax: 212-986-6549
e-mail: tworkman@licony.org
Web site: www.licony.org
Promote a legislative, regulatory & judicial environment that encourages members to conduct & grow their business
Thomas E Workman, President & Chief Executive Officer

Marsh & McLennan Companies
1166 6th Ave, New York, NY 10036-2774
212-345-5000
e-mail: barbara.perlmutter@mmc.com
Web site: www.mmc.com
Risk & insurance services; investment management; consulting
Barbara S Perlmutter, Senior Vice President, Public Affairs

Medical Society of the State of New York, Div of Socio-Medical Economics
420 Lakeville Rd, PO Box 5404, Lake Success, NY 11042
516-488-6100 x332 Fax: 516-488-6136
e-mail: rmcnally@mssny.org
Web site: www.mssny.org
Workers compensations; health insurance programs
William Abrams, Executive Vice President

MetLife
27-01 Queens Plaza North, Long Island City, NY 11101
212-578-3968 Fax: 212-578-8869
e-mail: jfdonnellan@metlife.com
Web site: www.metlife.com
MetLife, Inc is a leading provider of insurance and financial services.
James F Donnellan, Vice President Government & Industry Relations

NY Life Insurance Co
51 Madison Ave, Suite 1111, New York, NY 10010
212-576-7000 Fax: 212-576-4473
e-mail: gayle_yeomans@newyorklife.com
Web site: www.newyorklife.com
Insurance products & financial services
Gayle A Yeomans, Vice President Government Affairs

NY Property Insurance Underwriting Association
100 William St, New York, NY 10038
212-208-9700 Fax: 212-344-9676
Web site: www.nypiua.com
Joseph Calvo, President

NYMAGIC Inc
919 3rd Ave, 10th Fl, New York, NY 10022-3919
212-551-0600 Fax: 212-551-0724
e-mail: info@mmo.com
Web site: www.nymagic.com
Marine insurance & excess & surplus lines
A George Kallop, President & CEO

New York Insurance Association Inc
130 Washington Ave, Albany, NY 12210
518-432-4227 Fax: 518-432-4220
Web site: www.nyia.org
Property & casualty insurance
Ellen Melchionni, President

New York Long-Term Care Brokers Ltd
11 Halfmoon Executive Park, Clifton Park, NY 12065
518-371-5522 x116 Fax: 518-371-6131
e-mail: kjohnson@nyltcb.com
Web site: www.nyltcb.com
Long-term care, life & disability insurance; consulting & sales to individual consumers & financial service industry professionals
Kevin Johnson, President & CEO

New York Municipal Insurance Reciprocal (NYMIR)
150 State Street, Albany, NY 12207
518-465-7552 Fax: 518-465-0724
e-mail: jcrawford@kcnymir.org
Web site: www.nymir.org
Property and casualty insurance services for municipalities
Kevin Crawford, Executive Director

New York Schools Insurance Reciprocal (NYSIR)
333 Earle Ovington Blvd, Suite 1030, Uniondale, NY 11553
516-393-2329 or 800-476-9747 Fax: 516-227-2352
e-mail: jgoncalves@wrightrisk.com
Web site: www.nysir.org
Insurance & risk management services for public school districts
Joseph Goncalves, Executive Director

NAIFA - New York State
38 Sheridan Ave, Albany, NY 12210
518-462-5567 Fax: 518-462-5569
e-mail: naifanewyork@aol.com
Web site: www.naifanys.org
Association of individuals engaged in the sale of life, health & property/casualty insurance & related financial services
Mark L Yavornitzki, Executive Vice President & Chief Administrative Officer

Professional Insurance Agents of New York State
25 Chamberlain St, PO Box 997, Glenmont, NY 12077-0997
800-424-4244 Fax: 888-225-6935
e-mail: kenb@piaonline.org
Web site: www.piany.org
Ken Bessette, President/Chief Executive Officer

SBLI USA Mutual Life Insurance Company Inc
460 W 34th St, Suite 800, New York, NY 10001-2320
212-356-0327 Fax: 212-624-0700
e-mail: dklugman@sbliusa.com
Web site: www.sbliusa.com
Corporate insurance regulatory law & government affairs
Vikki Pryor, President & Chief Executive Officer

Offices and agencies generally appear in alphabetical order, except when specific order is requested by listee.

St John's University-Peter J Tobin College of Business, School of Risk Mgmt
101 Murray St, New York, NY 10007
212-962-4111
Web site: www.stjohns.edu
Ellen Thrower, Executive Director

Stroock & Stroock & Lavan LLP
180 Maiden Lane, New York, NY 10038-4982
212-806-5541 Fax: 212-806-2541
e-mail: dgabay@stroock.com
Insurance, reinsurance, corporate & regulatory law
Donald D Gabay, Attorney

Support Services Alliance Inc
107 Prospect St, PO Box 130, Schoharie, NY 12157
800-322-3920 or 518-295-7966 Fax: 518-295-8556
e-mail: info@ssamembers.com
Web site: www.smallbizgrowth.com
Small business support services & insurance

Steven Cole, President

Unity Mutual Life Insurance Co
507 Plum St, PO Box 5000, Syracuse, NY 13250-5000
315-448-7000 Fax: 315-448-7100
e-mail: jwason@unity-life.com
Web site: www.unity-life.com
Jay Wason, Jr, General Counsel

Utica Mutual Insurance Co
PO Box 530, Utica, NY 13503-0530
1-800-274-1914 Fax: 315-734-2662
Web site: www.uticanational.com
Property, casualty insurance
Richard Creedon, Executive Vice President, Claims & General Counsel

Offices and agencies generally appear in alphabetical order, except when specific order is requested by listee.

JUDICIAL & LEGAL SYSTEMS

NEW YORK STATE

GOVERNOR'S OFFICE

Governor's Office
Executive Chamber
State Capitol
Albany, NY 12224
518-474-8390 Fax: 518-474-1513
Web site: www.ny.gov

Governor:
 Andrew M Cuomo 518-474-8390
Secretary to the Governor:
 William Mulrow 518-474-4246
Counsel to the Governor:
 Alphonso David 518-474-8343
Director, Communications:
 Melissa DeRosa . . . . .518-474-8418 or 212-681-4640
Director, State Operations:
 James Malatras 518-486-9871
Deputy Director for State Operations:
 Joseph Rabito 518-408-2051
First Assistant Counsel:
 Sandi Toll 518-474-8434

EXECUTIVE DEPARTMENTS AND RELATED AGENCIES

Criminal Justice Services, Division of
Alfred E. Smith Building
80 South Swan Street
Albany, NY 12210
518-457-5837 or 800-262-3252 Fax: 518-457-3089
e-mail: infodcjsc@dcjs.ny.gov
Web site: www.criminaljustice.ny.gov

Executive Deputy Commissioner:
 Michael C Green 518-457-1260
Affirmative Action Officer:
 Wanda Trouche 518-485-7962
Deputy Director, Public Information:
 Janine Kava 518-457-8906/fax: 518-485-7715
 e-mail: janine.kava@dcjs.ny.gov
Deputy Director, Public Information:
 Walt McClure 518-457-8828
 e-mail: walter.mcclure@dcjs.ny.gov

Human Resources Management
Director:
 Karen Davis 518-485-1704

State Finance & Budget
Director, Finance:
 Kimberly J Szady 518-457-6105

Legal Services
Deputy Commissioner & Counsel:
 Gina Bianchi 518-457-4181

Commission on Forensic Science

Office of Forensic Services
Director:
 Vacant 518-457-4181

Office of Criminal Justice Operations
Director, Criminal Justice Operations:
 Joe Morrissey 518-485-2995

Highway Safety & Technology Unit
518-485-7620

Office of Justice Information Systems
Deputy Commissioner:
 Anne Roest 518-485-7176

Information Technology Development Group

Information Technology Services Group
Director:
 Alex Roberts 518-457-3743

Office of Sex Offender Registry
Director:
 Michelle Mulligan 518-457-3121

Office of Justice Research & Performance
Deputy Commissioner:
 Terry Salo 518-457-3724
Chief, Crimestat Unit:
 Paula K Lockhart 518-485-7122
Chief, Crime Reporting & Statistical Services Unit:
 Adam Dean 518-457-8381

Office of Public Safety

Law Enforcement Accreditation Program

Police & Peace Officer Registry & Training

Missing Persons Clearinghouse

Security Guard Program
Deputy Commissioner:
 Melvin Perez 518-485-7620
Director:
 Julie Pasquini 518-457-2666
 e-mail: julie.pasquini@dcjs.ny.gov

Funding & Program Development Office
Deputy Commissioner:
 AnneMarie Strano 518-457-8462

Operation IMPACT Coordinator
Director:
 Julie Pasquini 518-485-7923

Law Department
120 Broadway
New York, NY 10271-0332
212-416-8000 or 800-771-7755
Web site: www.ag.ny.gov

State Capitol
Albany, NY 12224-0341
518-474-7330
Fax: 518-473-9909

Attorney General:
 Eric T Schneiderman . . . . .212-416-8050 or 518-474-7330

Administration
 Agency Bldg 4, Empire State Plaza, Albany, NY 12224-0341
COO:
 Jeanette Moy 518-776-2500/fax: 518-915-7753
Deputy COO:
 Michael Lefebvre 518-776-2110

Offices and agencies generally appear in alphabetical order, except when specific order is requested by listee.

Budget & Fiscal Management
Director:
Michael Lefebvre 518-776-2110/fax: 518-915-7751

Human Resources Management
Director:
Robert Pablo 518-776-2500

Legal Recruitment
Asst Attorney General in Charge:
Sandra J Grannum 212-416-8080/fax: 212-416-8264

Appeals & Opinions Division
Solicitor General:
Barbara D Underwood . . . . 212-416-8016 or 518-776-2002
Deputy Counsel:
John Amodeo 518-776-2000

Law Library
Chief, Library Services:
Patricia Partello 518-776-2566/fax: 518-915-7737
Legal Support Analyst:
Vacant 212-416-8012/fax: 212-416-6130

Criminal Justice
Executive Deputy Attorney General, Criminal Justice:
Kelly Donovan 212-416-8050

Criminal Enforcement & Financial Crimes Bureau
Bureau Chief:
Gary Fishman . . . . 518-776-2370 or 212-416-8750

Medicaid Fraud Control Unit
120 Broadway, 13th Fl, New York, NY 10271-0007
Deputy Attorney General in Charge & Director:
Vacant 212-417-5250/fax: 212-417-4284
Asst Deputy Attorney General:
Paul J Mahoney 212-417-5254
Deputy Regional Director, Buffalo:
Gary A Baldauf 716-853-8507/fax: 716-852-8525
Regional Director, Long Island:
Jane Turkin 631-952-6400/fax: 631-952-6382
Regional Director, Albany:
Kathleen Boland 518-533-6011/fax: 518-474-4519
Regional Director, Rochester:
Catherine Wagner 585-262-2860/fax: 585-262-2866
Regional Director, Syracuse:
Ralph Tortora, III 315-423-1104/fax: 315-423-1120
Deputy Regional Director, Pearl River:
Anne S Jardine 845-732-7525/fax: 845-732-7555

Economic Justice
Executive Deputy Attorney General, Economic Justice:
Karla Sanchez 212-416-8050

Antitrust Bureau
Bureau Chief:
Eric J Stock 212-416-8282/fax: 212-416-6015
e-mail: eric.stock@ag.ny.gov

Consumer Frauds & Protection Bureau
Bureau Chief:
Jane Azia 212-416-8300/fax: 212-416-6003

Internet Bureau
Bureau Chief:
Kathleen McGee 212-416-8433/fax: 212-416-8369

Investor Protection Bureau
Bureau Chief:
Chad Johnson 212-416-8225/fax: 212-416-8816

Intergovernmental Relations
Deputy Director, Intergovernmental Affairs:
Lilliam Perez 212-416-6044

Director, Intergovernmental Affairs:
Michael Meade 212-416-8985

Office of the Attorney General
Chief of Staff:
Micah Lasher 212-416-8050
Senior Advisor/Director, Operations:
Christina Harvey 212-416-8095
Deputy Counsel:
John Amodeo 518-776-2000
Legislative Policy Advisor:
Kate M Powers 518-776-2444/fax: 518-650-9401
Press Secretary:
Fernando Aquino 212-416-8060/fax: 212-416-6005
Director, Correspondence:
Jennifer Ticknor 518-776-2356
Director, Public Information:
Shawn Morris 518-776-2357/fax: 518-650-9401

Investigations
Chief, Investigations:
Dominick Zarrella 212-416-6328/fax: 212-416-8773
Assistant Chief Investigator - Downstate:
John McManus 212-416-8786
First deputy Chief Investigator:
John Reidy 212-416-6394

Social Justice
Executive Deputy Attorney General, Social Justice:
Alvin L Braggs, Jr 212-416-8450/fax: 212-416-8942

Charities Bureau
Bureau Chief:
James G Sheehan. 212-416-8410/fax: 212-416-8393

Civil Rights Bureau
Bureau Chief:
Kristen Clarke 212-416-8250/fax: 212-416-8074

Environmental Protection Bureau
Bureau Chief:
Lisa Burianek . . . . 518-776-2400 or 212-416-8446

Healthcare Bureau
Bureau Chief:
Lisa Landau . . . . 518-776-2477 or 212-416-6305
fax: 518-650-9365

Regional Offices Division
Executive Deputy Attorney General, Regional Offices:
Martin J Mack. 716-852-6274

Binghamton
State Office Bldg, 44 Hawley St, 17th Fl, Binghamton, NY 13901-4433
Asst Attorney General in Charge:
James E. Shoemaker 607-251-2770/fax: 607-338-1021

Brooklyn
55 Hanson Place, Ste 1080, Brooklyn, NY 11217
Asst Attorney General in Charge:
Lois Booker Williams 718-560-2040/fax: 718-687-1430

Buffalo
Main Place Tower, Ste 300A, 350 Main St, Buffalo, NY 14202
Asst Attorney General in Charge:
Michael J Russo 716-853-8400/fax: 716-853-8571

Harlem
163 West 125th St, Ste 1324, New York, NY 10027
Asst Attorney General in Charge:
Robert G Lebron 212-364-6010/fax: 646-356-3000

Nassau
200 Old Country Rd, Ste 460, Mineola, NY 11501-4241

Offices and agencies generally appear in alphabetical order, except when specific order is requested by listee.

Policy Areas

Asst Attorney General in Charge:
Valerie Singleton.................516-248-3302/fax: 516-747-6432

Plattsburgh
43 Durkee St, Ste 700, Plattsburgh, NY 12901
Asst Attorney General in Charge:
Glen Michaels..................518-562-3288/fax: 518-562-3294

Poughkeepsie
One Civic Ctr Plaza, Suite 401, Poughkeepsie, NY 12601
Asst Attorney General in Charge:
Vincent Bradley 845-485-3900/fax: 845-452-3303

Rochester
144 Exchange Blvd, 2nd Fl, Rochester, NY 14614-2176
Asst Attorney General in Charge:
Debra A Martin.................585-546-7430/fax: 585-546-7514

Suffolk
300 Motor Pkwy, Ste 230, Hauppauge, NY 11788
Asst Attorney General in Charge:
Kimberly Kinirons 631-231-2424/fax: 631-435-4757

Syracuse
615 Erie Blvd West, Suite 102, Syracuse, NY 13204
Asst Attorney General in Charge:
Ed Thompson 315-448-4800/fax: 315-448-4853

Utica
207 Genesee St, Room 508, Utica, NY 13501
Asst Attorney General in Charge:
J Williams 315-864-2000/fax: 315-292-6060

Watertown
Dulles St Ofc Bldg, 317 Washington St, Watertown, NY 13601
Asst Attorney General in Charge:
Deanna Nelson 315-523-6080/fax: 315-955-6311

Westchester
44 S Broadway, White Plains, NY 10601
Asst Attorney General in Charge:
Gary S Brown 914-422-8755/fax: 914-422-8706

State Counsel
Chief Deputy Attorney General & Counsel:
Harlan Levy 212-416-8525
Executive Deputy Attorney General, State Counsel:
Kent T. Stauffer................212-416-8252/fax: 212-416-6001

Civil Recoveries Bureau
Bureau Chief:
John Cremo....................518-776-2173/fax: 518-915-7731

Claims Bureau
Bureau Chief:
Katharine Brooks.................518-776-2300 or 212-416-8913

Litigation Bureau
Bureau Chief:
Lisa Dell.......................518-776-2300 or 212-416-8610

Real Property Bureau
Bureau Chief:
Alison Crocker 518-776-2700

JUDICIAL SYSTEM AND RELATED AGENCIES

Attorney Grievance Committee

1st Judicial Dept, Judicial Dist 1, 12
61 Broadway, 2nd Fl, New York, NY 10006
Chief Counsel:
Jorge Dopico 212-401-0800/fax: 212-287-1045

2nd Judicial Dept, Judicial Dist 2, 9, 10, 11, 13

Judicial Dist 2, 11, 13
Renaissance Plz, 335 Adams St, Ste 2400, Brooklyn, NY 11201-3745
Chief Counsel:
Diana M Kearse..................718-923-6300/fax: 718-624-2978

Judicial Dist 9
399 Knollwood Rd, Ste 200, White Plains, NY 10603
Chief Counsel:
Gary L Casella...................914-824-5070/fax: 914-949-0997

Judicial Dist 10
150 Motor Pkwy, Ste 102, Hauppauge, NY 11788
Chief Counsel:
Robert A. Green 631-231-3775/fax: 516-364-7355

3rd Judicial Dept, Judicial Dist 3, 4, 6
Committee on Professional Standards, 286 Washington Ave Ext, Ste 200, Albany, NY 12203
518-285-8350
Web site: www.nycourts.gov/ad3/cops/index.html
Chief Counsel:
Monica A. Duffy..................518-285-8350/fax: 518-453-4643
e-mail: AD3COPS@nycourts.gov
Deputy Chief Counsel:
Michael G Gaynor...............518-285-8350/fax: 518-453-4643
e-mail: AD3COPS@nycourts.gov

4th Judicial Dept, Dist 5, 7, 8
Web site: www.nycourts.gov/courts/ad4/AG

Judicial Dist 5..............................fax: 315-401-3339
224 Harrison St, Ste 408, Syracuse, NY 13202-3066
Chief Counsel:
Gregory J Huether 315-401-3344
Principal Counsel:
Anthony J Gigliotti............................315-401-3344

Judicial Dist 7..............................fax: 585-530-3191
50 East Ave, Ste 404, Rochester, NY 14604-2206
Chief Counsel:
Gregory J Huether 585-530-3180
Principal Counsel:
Daniel A Drake................................585-530-3180

Judicial Dist 8..............................fax: 716-856-2701
438 Main St, Ste 800, Buffalo, NY 14202
Chief Counsel:
Gregory J Huether 716-845-3630
Principal Counsel:
Roderick Quebral 716-845-3630

Law Guardian Program

3rd Judicial Dept ....fax: 518-471-4757
PO Box 7288, Capital Station, Albany, NY 12224-0288
Fax: 518-471-4757
Web site: www.nycourts.gov/ad3/OAC/index.html
Director:
Betsy R Ruslander 518-471-4825
e-mail: ad3oac@nycourts.gov

4th Judicial Dept ....fax: 585-530-3175
50 East Ave, Ste 304, Rochester, NY 14604
Fax: 585-530-3175
Web site: www.nycourts.gov/courts/ad4/AFC
Director:
Tracy M Hamilton ....585-530-3170 or 585-530-3176
e-mail: thamilto@nycourts.gov
Assistant Program Director:
Christine Constantine 585-530-3178
e-mail: cconstan@nycourts.gov

Offices and agencies generally appear in alphabetical order, except when specific order is requested by listee.

Mental Hygiene Legal Service

1st Judicial Dept
41 Madison Ave, 26th Fl, New York, NY 10010
Director:
Marvin Bernstein 646-386-5891/fax: 212-779-7899
Deputy Director:
Stephen Harkavy 646-386-5891

2nd Judicial Dept
170 Old Country Rd, Rm 500, Mineola, NY 11501
Director:
Michael D Neville 516-493-3976/fax: 646-963-6640
e-mail: mneville@nycourts.gov
Deputy Director:
Dennis Feld 516-493-3975
e-mail: mneville@nycourts.gov

3rd Judicial Dept
40 Steuben St, Ste 501, Albany, NY 12207
Web site: www.nycourts.gov/ad3/mhls/index.html
Director:
Sheila E Shea 518-451-8710/fax: 518-453-6915
Deputy Director:
Shannon Stockwell 518-451-8710

4th Judicial Dept
50 East Ave, Ste 402, Rochester, NY 14604
Web site: www.nycourts.gov/ad4
Director:
Emmett J Creahan 585-530-3050
Deputy Director:
Kevin Wilson 585-530-3050/fax: 585-530-3079

Unified Court System
25 Beaver St
Room 852
New York, NY 10004
212-428-2700 Fax: 212-428-2508
e-mail: questions@nycourts.gov
Web site: www.nycourts.gov

Agency Bldg 4, 20th Fl
Empire State Plaza
Albany, NY 12223
518-474-3828
Fax: 518-473-5514

Administrative Board of the Courts

Appellate Division
1st Judicial Department
Courthouse, 27 Madison Ave, New York, NY 10010
Presiding Justice:
Luis A. Gonzalez 212-340-0400
2nd Judicial Department
45 Monroe Place, Brooklyn, NY 11201
Presiding Justice:
Randall T. Eng 718-875-1300
3rd Judicial Department
Capitol Station, ESP, PO Box 7288, Albany, NY 12224
Presiding Justice:
Karen K. Peters 518-471-4777
4th Judicial Department
50 East Ave, Rochester, NY 14604
Presiding Justice:
Henry Scudder 585-530-3100

Court of Appeals
230 Park Ave, Suite 826, New York, NY 10169

Chief Judge:
Jonathan Lippman 212-661-6787/fax: 212-682-2778

Court Administration
Chief Administrative Judge:
A. Gail Prudenti 212-428-2120
Administrative Director, Office of Court Admin:
Lawrence K Marks 212-428-2884
Deputy Chief Administrative Judge, Courts in NYC:
Fern A. Fisher 646-386-4200
Deputy Chief Administrative Judge, Courts outside NYC:
Michael V. Coccoma 518-474-3828
Chief, Policy & Planning:
Judy Harris Kluger 212-428-2130
Executive Assistant to Deputy Chief Admin Judge, Courts in NYC:
Maria Logus 646-386-4201
Executive Assistant to Deputy Chief Admin Judge, Courts outside NYC:
Peter J. Ryan 518-474-3828
Chief of Staff:
Paul Lewis 212-428-2120
Executive Director:
Ron Younkins 212-428-2126

Administrative Judge to the Court of Claims (NYS). fax: 866-413-1069
Justice Bldg, Capitol Station, PO Box 7344, Albany, NY 12224
Presiding Judge:
Richard E Sise 518-432-3435

Administrative Judges to the Courts in New York City
1st Judicial District (Judicial Department 1)
Administrative Judge, Civil Term:
Sherry Klein-Heitler 646-386-3211
Administrative Judge, Criminal Term:
Michael Obus 646-386-4051
2nd Judicial District (Judicial Department 2)
320 Jay St, Brooklyn, NY 11201
Administrative Judge:
Barry Kamins 347-296-1200
Civil Court
111 Centre St, New York, NY 10013
Administrative Judge:
Lawrence Knipel 646-386-5400/fax: 212-374-5709
Criminal Court
100 Centre St, Rm 549A, New York, NY 10013
Administrative Judge:
Barry Kamins . . . . 646-386-4700 or 347-296-1000
fax: 212-374-3004
Family Court
60 Lafayette St, 11th Floor, New York, NY 10013
Administrative Judge:
Edwina Richardson-Mendelson . 646-386-5190/fax: 212-374-2127

Administrative Judges to the Courts outside New York City
3rd Judicial District (Judicial Department 3)
Courthouse, 80 Second St, Troy, NY 12180
Acting Administrative Judge:
Thomas Mercure 518-285-6152/fax: 518-270-3788
4th Judicial District (Judicial Department 3)
612 State St, Schenectady, NY 12305
Administrative Judge:
Vito Caruso 518-285-8415/fax: 518-347-1972
5th Judicial District (Judicial Department 4)
Onondaga County Court House, 401 Montgomery St, Syracuse, NY 13202
Administrative Judge:
James C Tormey 315-671-2111/fax: 315-671-1183
6th Judicial District (Judicial Department 3)
320 North Tioga Street, Ithaca, NY 14850
Administrative Judge:
Robert Mulvey 607-272-0466

Offices and agencies generally appear in alphabetical order, except when specific order is requested by listee.

7th Judicial District (Judicial Department 4)
Hall of Justice, Civic Center Plz, 99 Exchange Blvd, Rochester, NY 14614
Administrative Judge:
Craig J. Doran 585-396-4239
8th Judicial District (Judicial Department 4)
Erie County Hall, 92 Franklin St, Buffalo, NY 14202
Administrative Judge:
Paula L. Feroleto 716-845-9438/fax: 716-855-1611
9th Judicial District (Judicial Department 2)
County Court House, 111 Dr Martin Luther King Blvd, White Plains, NY 10601
Administrative Judge:
Alan Scheinkman 914-824-5100/fax: 914-995-4111
10th Judicial District (Judicial Department 2)
Administrative Judge, Nassau County:
Thomas Adams..............516-571-2684/fax: 516-571-3713
Administrative Judge, Suffolk County:
C.ÆRandall Hinrichs 631-853-5368/fax: 631-853-7741
11th Judicial District (Judicial Department 2)
88-11 Sutphin Blvd, Jamaica, NY 11435
Administrative Judge, Civil:
Jeremy Weinstein 718-298-1100/fax: 718-520-2499
Administrative Judge, Criminal:
Joseph Zayas
12th Judicial District (Judicial Department 1)
851 Grand Concourse, Bronx, NY 10451
Administrative Judge (Civil & Criminal):
Douglas E. McKeon........................718-618-1441
Deputy Administrative Judge (Criminal):
Robert Torres.............................718-618-3700
13th Judicial District Administrative Judge:
Judith N. McMahon.........................718-618-3700

Counsel's Office
Counsel:
Vacant.....................212-428-2160/fax: 212-428-2155

Management Support
Administrative Services Office
Director:
Laura Weigley Ross 212-428-2860/fax: 212-428-2819
Deputy Director:
Vacant...................212-428-2812/fax: 212-428-2819
Court Operations
Director:
Nancy M Mangold 212-428-2761/fax: 518-428-2768
Coordinator, Alternative Dispute Resolution Program:
Daniel M Weitz 212-428-2892/fax: 212-428-2696
e-mail: dweitz@nycourts.gov
Director, Court Research & Technology:
Chester Mount 212-428-2990/fax: 212-428-2987
Chief of Court Security Services:
Howard Metzdorff 212-428-2766/fax: 212-428-2768
e-mail: ops1@nycourts.gov
Director, Internal Controls Office:
Dennis Donnelly............518-238-4303/fax: 518-238-2086
Inspector General:
Sherrill Spatz...............646-386-3500 or 212-514-7158
e-mail: sspatz@courts.state.ny.us
Deputy Inspector General:
Carol Hamm
e-mail: chamm@courts.state.ny.us
Chief Law Librarian, Legal Info & Records Mgmt:
Ellen Robinson...........518-238-4373/fax: 518-238-2894
Managing Inspector General, Bias Matters:
Kay-Ann Porter Campbell 877-263-2427
e-mail: ieporter@courts.state.ny.us
Managing Inspector General, Fiduciary Appointments:
Elizabeth Candreva 646-386-3514
e-mail: ecandreva@courts.state.ny.us

Financial Management & Audit Services
Empire State Plaza, Bldg 4, Ste 2001, Albany, NY 12223-1450
Director:
Charles Hughes 518-473-5511
Workforce Diversity
Director:
S. Anthony Walters 212-428-2540/fax: 212-428-2545
e-mail: twalters@nycourts.gov
Management Analyst:
Michael J. Moore 212-428-2683/fax: 212-428-2545
e-mail: mmoore@nycourts.gov
Court Analyst:
Doretha L. Jackson 212-428-2540
e-mail: dljackson@nycourts.gov
Deputy Director, Staffing & Security Services:
Gregory J. Salerno 646-386-3400/fax: 212-295-4876
e-mail: gsalerno@courts.stae.ny.us
Chief of Training/Commanding Officer - NYS Court Officers Academy:
Chief Joseph Bacceilieri.......646-386-5660/fax: 212-406-4533
Public Affairs Office
Director:
Gregory Murray 212-428-2116/fax: 212-428-2117
e-mail: opaoutreach@courts.state.ny.us
Director, Communications:
David Bookstaver............212-428-2500/fax: 212-428-2507
e-mail: dbooksta@courts.state.ny.us
Assistant Director, Communications Specialist:
Arlene Hackel...............................212-428-2116
e-mail: ahackel@courts.state.ny.us
Officer:
Gary Spencer 518-455-7711
e-mail: gspencer@courts.state.ny.us

CORPORATIONS, AUTHORITIES AND COMMISSIONS

Interest on Lawyer Account (IOLA) Fund of the State of NY

11 East 44th St
Ste 1406
New York, NY 10017
646-865-1541 or 800-222-4652 Fax: 646-865-1545
e-mail: iolaf@iola.org
Web site: www.iola.org

Chair:
Benito Romano....................................646-865-1541
Executive Director:
Christopher O'Malley..............................646-865-1541
General Counsel:
Christine M Fecko 646-865-1541
Director of Administration:
Michele D Agard 646-865-1541

Lawyers' Fund for Client Protection

119 Washington Ave
Albany, NY 12210
518-434-1935 or 800-442-FUND Fax: 518-434-5641
e-mail: info@nylawfund.org
Web site: www.nylawfund.org

Chair:
Eric A Seiff......................................518-434-1935
Vice Chair:
Nancy Burner 518-434-1935
Executive Director & Counsel:
Timothy O'Sullivan 518-434-1935

Offices and agencies generally appear in alphabetical order, except when specific order is requested by listee.

New York State Board of Law Examiners
Corporate Plaza Bldg 3
254 Washington Ave Ext
Albany, NY 12203-5195
518-453-5990 Fax: 518-452-5729
Web site: www.nybarexam.org

Chair:
    Diane F Bosse 518-453-5990
Executive Director:
    John J McAlary 518-453-5990
Deputy Directory & Counsel:
    Cara J. Brousseau

New York State Commission on Judicial Nomination
c/o Greenberg Traurig LLP
54 State Street
Albany, NY 12207
518-689-1400 Fax: 518-689-1499
Web site: www.nysegov.com/cjn/

Chair:
    Vacant
Counsel:
    Henry Greenberg. 518-689-1400
    e-mail: greenbergh@gtlaw.com

New York State Judicial Conduct Commission
61 Broadway
12th Fl
New York, NY 10006
646-386-4800 Fax: 646-458-0037
e-mail: cjc@cjc.ny.gov
Web site: www.cjc.ny.gov

Corning Tower
Suite 2301
Empire State Plaza
Albany, NY 12223
518-453-4600
Fax: 518-486-1850

Chair:
    Thomas Klonick, Esq 646-386-4800
Vice Chair:
    Terry Jane Ruderman 646-386-4800
Administrator & Counsel:
    Robert H Tembeckjian 646-386-4800
Deputy Administrator in Charge, Albany Office:
    Cathleen Cenci 518-453-4600
Deputy Administrator in Charge, Rochester Office:
    John J Postel 585-232-5756
Deputy Administrator in Charge, New York City Office:
    Mark Levine 646-386-4800
Deputy Administrator, Litigation:
    Edward Lindner 518-474-5617
Clerk:
    Jean M Savanyu, Esq 646-386-4800

New York State Law Reporting Bureau
17 Lodge Street
Albany, NY 12207
518-453-6900 Fax: 518-426-1640
Web site: www.courts.state.ny.us/reporter

State Reporter:
    William J Hooks 518-453-6900

Deputy State Reporter:
    Michael S Moran 518-453-6900
    e-mail: Reporter@courts.state.ny.us
Assistant State Reporter:
    Katherine LaBoda 518-453-6900
    e-mail: Reporter@courts.state.ny.us

New York State Law Revision Commission
80 New Scotland Ave
Albany, NY 12208
518-472-5858 Fax: 518-445-2303
e-mail: nylrc@albanylaw.edu
Web site: www.lawrevision.state.ny.us

Chairman:
    Peter J Kiernan 518-472-5858
Executive Director:
    Rose Mary Bailly 518-472-5858

Uniform State Laws Commission
c/o Coughlin & Gerhart LLP
99 Corporate Drive
PO Box 2039
Binghamton, NY 13902-2039
607-723-9511 Fax: 607-723-1530

Chair:
    Richard B Long. 607-821-2202
    e-mail: rlong@cglawoffices.com
Member:
    Sandra Stern 212-207-8150
Member:
    Norman L. Greene 212-661-5030
Member:
    Justin L. Vigdor . . . . .585-232-5300 ext 228
Member:
    Mark F Glaser 518-689-1413

NEW YORK STATE LEGISLATURE

See Legislative Branch in Section 1 for additional Standing Committee and Subcommittee information.

Assembly Standing Committees

Codes
Chair:
    Joseph R Lentol (D) 518-455-4477
Ranking Minority Member:
    Al Graf (R) 518-455-5937

Judiciary
Chair:
    Helene E Weinstein (D) 518-455-5462
Ranking Minority Member:
    Michael Montesano (R) 518-455-4684

Senate Standing Committees

Codes
Chair:
    Michael F. Nozzolio (R). 518-455-2366
Ranking Minority Member:
    Daniel L. Squadron (D) 518-455-2625

Judiciary
Chair:
    John J Bonacic (R) 518-455-3181

Offices and agencies generally appear in alphabetical order, except when specific order is requested by listee.

Ranking Minority Member:
Ruth Hassell-Thompson (D) 518-455-2061

U.S. GOVERNMENT

EXECUTIVE DEPARTMENTS AND FEDERAL COURTS

US Federal Courts

US Bankruptcy Court - New York

Eastern District
271-C Cadman Plaza East, Suite 1595, Brooklyn, NY 11201-1800
347-394-1700
Web site: www.nyeb.uscourts.gov
Chief Judge:
Carla E. Craig 347-394-1700
Clerk of the Court:
Robert A Gavin Jr 347-394-1700

Northern District
Foley Courthouse, 445 Broadway Ste 330, Albany, NY 12207
518-257-1661
Web site: www.nynb.uscourts.gov
Chief Bankruptcy Judge:
Robert E Littlefield Jr 315-266-1122
Clerk of the Court:
Kim F. LeFebvre 518-257-1661

Southern District
Alexander Hamilton Custom House, 1 Bowling Green, #625, New York,
NY 10004
212-668-2870
Web site: www.nysb.uscourts.gov
Chief Judge:
Cecelia G. Morris 212-668-2870
Clerk of the Court:
Vito Genna 212-668-2870

Western District
300 Pearl St, Ste 250, Buffalo, NY 14202
Web site: www.nywb.uscourts.gov
Chief Bankruptcy Judge:
Carl L Bucki 716-362-3200
Clerk of the Court:
Lisa Bertino Beaser 716-362-3281
e-mail: pwarren@nywb.uscourts.gov

US Court of Appeals for the Second Circuit
Thurgood Marshall U.S. Courthouse, 40 Foley Square, New York, NY
10007
212-857-8500
Web site: www.ca2.uscourts.gov
Circuit Executive:
Karen Greve Milton 212-857-8700/fax: 212-857-8680
Clerk of the Court:
Catherine O'Hagan Wolfe 212-857-8500

US Court of International Trade . . . . .fax: 212-264-1085
One Federal Plaza, New York, NY 10278
212-264-2800 Fax: 212-264-1085
Web site: www.cit.uscourts.gov
Chief Judge:
Donald C. Pogue 212-264-1628
Clerk of the Court:
Tina Potuto Kimble 212-264-2814
e-mail: tina_kimble@cit.uscourts.gov

US DISTRICT COURT - NEW YORK (part of the Second Circuit)
225 Cadman Plaza E, Brooklyn, NY 11201

Eastern District
718-613-2600
Chief District Judge:
Carol Bagley Amon
Clerk of the Court:
Douglas C. Palmer
Chief Magistrate Judge:
Steven M. Gold
District Executive:
Eugene C. Corcoran
Chief Probation Officer:
Edward Kanaley

Northern District
100 S Clinton St, PO Box 7367, Syracuse, NY 13261-7367
315-234-8500
Web site: www.nynd.uscourts.gov
Chief District Judge:
Gary L. Sharpe
Chief Magistrate Judge:
Larry A. Kudrle
Clerk of the Court:
Lawrence K Baerman 315-234-8500
Chief Probation Officer:
Matt Brown

Southern District
300 Quarropas Street, White Plains, NY 10601
914-390-4100
Web site: www.nysd.uscourts.gov
Chief District Judge:
Loretta A. Preska 212-805-0240
Chief Magistrate Judge:
Kevin N. Fox 212-805-6705
District Executive:
Edward Friedland
Clerk of the Court:
Robert J. Krajick
Public Information Officer:
Stephanie Cirkovich

Western District
2 Niagara Street, Buffalo, NY 14202-3350
716-551-1900
Web site: www.nywd.uscourts.gov
Chief District Judge:
William M. Skretny
Clerk of the Court:
Michael J. Roemer
Chief Magistrate Judge:
Hugh B. Scott

US Tax Court
Web site: www.ustaxcourt.gov
Chief Judge:
Michael B Thornton 202-521-0777
Clerk of the Court:
Peter J. Panuthos 202-521-4707

US Justice Department
Web site: www.usdoj.gov

Antitrust Division—New York Field Office
26 Federal Plaza, Rm 3630, New York, NY 10278-0004
Chief:
Deidre A. McEvoy 212-335-8000/fax: 212-335-8021
Assistant Chief:
Elizabeth B. Prewitt 212-335-8000

Offices and agencies generally appear in alphabetical order, except when specific order is requested by listee.

Civil Division - Commercial Litigation Branch
26 Federal Plz, Rm 346, New York, NY 10278
Attorney-in-Charge:
Barbara S Williams 212-264-9240/fax: 212-264-1916

Community Relations Service - Northeast & Caribbean Region
26 Federal Plaza, Suite 36-118, New York, NY 10278
Regional Director:
Reinaldo Rivera, Jr 212-264-0700/fax: 212-264-2143

OFFICE OF INSPECTOR GENERAL (including New York State)

Audit Division
701 Market St, Ste 201, Philadelphia, PA 19106
Audit Director:
Michael T. Hill 215-580-2111/fax: 215-597-1348

Investigations Division
1 Battery Park Plaza, 29th Floor, Jamaica, NY 10004
Spl-Agent-in-Chg:
Vacant

US Attorney's Office - New York

Eastern District . . . . .fax: 718-254-6479
147 Pierrepont St, Brooklyn, NY 11201
718-254-7000 Fax: 718-254-6479
US Attorney:
Roslynn R Mauskopf 718-254-7000/fax: 718-254-6319
Chief Asst US Atty:
Eric Covngold 718-254-7000/fax: 718-254-6300
Executive Asst US Attorney:
William J Muller 718-254-7000/fax: 718-254-6329
Administrative Asst US Attorney:
John Lenior 718-254-6255
Chief Asst US Attorney, Criminal Division:
Bridget Rohde 718-254-6238/fax: 718-254-6150
Chief Asst US Attorney, Civil Division:
Susan Riley 718-254-6037/fax: 718-254-7483
Chief Asst US Attorney, Appeals Division:
Peter Norling 718-254-6280
Administrative Officer:
Peter Kurtin 718-254-6587/fax: 718-254-6550

Northern District
Albany . . . . .fax: 518-431-0249
James T Foley US Courthouse, #218, 445 Broadway, Albany, NY 12207
518-431-0247 Fax: 518-431-0249
Supervising Asst US Attorney:
Grant C Jaquith 518-431-0247/fax: 518-431-0249
Binghamton . . . . .fax: 607-773-2901
US Courthouse, 304 Federal Bldg, 15 Henry St, Binghamton, NY 13901
607-773-2887 Fax: 607-773-2901
Assistant United States Attorney, Chief Criminal Justice:
Thomas P Walsh 607-773-2887/fax: 607-773-2901
Syracuse . . . . .fax: 315-448-0689
J F Hanley Fed Bldg, 100 S Clinton St, Rm 900, Syracuse, NY 13261-7198
315-448-0672 Fax: 315-448-0689
United States Attorney:
Richard S. Hartunian 315-448-0672
First Assistant United States Attorney:
Andrew T Baxter 315-448-0672
Asst US Attorney, Chief Civil Division:
William H Pease 315-448-0672
Administrative Officer:
Martha Stratton 315-448-0672/fax: 315-448-0689

Southern District . . . . .fax: 212-637-2611
212-637-2200 Fax: 212-637-2611

New York City
1 Saint Andrews Plaza, New York, NY 10007
212-637-2200
US Attorney:
Preet Bharara
Deputy US Attorney:
Richard B. Zabel
Chief, Civil Division:
Lorin L. Reisner
Chief, Civil Division:
Sandra L. Shudofsky
White Plains . . . . .fax: 914-682-3392
300 Quarropas St, White Plains, NY 10601-4150
914-993-1900 Fax: 914-682-3392
Chief Asst US Attorney:
Margery B Feinzig 914-993-1909

Western District
Buffalo
138 Delaware Ave, Buffalo, NY 14202
716-843-5700
US Attorney:
William J. Hochul, Jr.
Chief of Appellate Division:
Joseph J. Karaszewski
Asst US Attorney, Civil Division Chief:
Mary Pat Fleming 716-843-5867
Chief, Criminal Division:
Joseph M Guerra, III 716-843-5824
Assistant US Attorney, Narcotics & Violent Crime Division Chief:
Timothy C. Lynch
Chief, General Crimes Division:
Michael DiGiacomo 716-843-5819
Administrative Officer:
Amy L. Smith
Rochester . . . . .fax: 585-263-6226
620 Federal Bldg, 100 State St, Rochester, NY 14614
585-263-6760 Fax: 585-263-6226
Asst US Attorney-in-Charge:
Bradley E Tyler 585-263-5717

US Marshals' Service - New York

Eastern District
Brooklyn
225 Cadman Plaza, Brooklyn, NY 11201
718-260-0440
US Marshal:
Charles Dunne 718-260-0400
Central Islip
100 Federal Plaza, Central Islip, NY 11722
631-712-6000
US Marshal:
Charles Dunne 631-712-6000

Northern District
Albany
James T. Foley Courthouse, 445 Broadway, Albany, NY 12207
US Marshal:
David McNulty 518-472-5401
Syracuse
US District Courthouse, 100 S Clinton St, PO Box 7260, Syracuse, NY 13261
US Marshal:
David McNulty 315-473-7601

Southern District
500 Pearl St, Ste 400, New York, NY 10007
US Marshal:
Joseph R Guccione 212-331-7200/fax: 212-637-6130

Offices and agencies generally appear in alphabetical order, except when specific order is requested by listee.

Western District
Buffalo
Courthouse Bldg, Rm 129, 68 Court St, Buffalo, NY 14202
US Marshal:
Charles Salina 716-551-4851
Rochester
US Courthouse, Rm 2240, 100 State St, Rochester, NY 14614
US Marshal:
Charles Salina 585-263-5787

US Trustee - Bankruptcy, Region 2
33 Whitehall St, 21st Fl, New York, NY 10004-2112
US Trustee:
Tracy Hope Davis 212-510-0500/fax: 212-668-2256

U.S. CONGRESS

See U.S. Congress Chapter for additional Standing Committee and Subcommittee information.

House of Representatives Standing Committees

Judiciary
Chair:
Bob Goodlatte (R-VA) 202-225-5431
Ranking Member:
John Conyers, Jr. (D-MI) 202-225-5126
Ranking Member:
Hakeem Jeffries (D) 202-225-5936
New York Delegate:
Jerrold Nadler (D) 202-225-5635

Senate Standing Committees

Judiciary
Chair:
Patrick J Leahy (D-VT) 202-224-4242
Ranking Member:
Charles Grassley (R-IA) 202-224-3744
New York Delegate:
Charles E Schumer (D) 202-224-6542

PRIVATE SECTOR

Maxwell S Pfeifer, Chair

NYS Bar Assn, International Law & Practice Section
Alston & Bird LLP
90 Park Ave, 15th Fl, New York, NY 10016-1387
212-210-9540 Fax: 212-210-9444
e-mail: pmfrank@alston.com
Jamie Hutchinson, Chair

NYS Bar Assn, Lawyer Referral Service Cmte
Amdursky Pelky Fennell & Wallen
26 E Oneida St, Oswego, NY 13126-2695
315-343-6363 Fax: 315-343-0134
e-mail: apfwlaw@twcny.rr.com
Web site: www.apfwlaw.com
Timothy J Fennell, Chair

Asian American Legal Defense and Education Fund
99 Hudson St, 12th Fl, New York, NY 10013-2815
212-966-5932 or 800-966-5946 Fax: 212-966-4303
e-mail: info@aaldef.org
Web site: www.aaldef.org
Defend civil rights of Asian Americans through litigation, legal advocacy & community education
Margaret Fung, Executive Director

Association of the Bar of the City of New York
42 W 44th St, New York, NY 10036-6689
212-382-6655 Fax: 212-768-8630
e-mail: jbigelsen@nycbar.org
Web site: www.nycbar.org
Jayne Bigelsen, Director, Communications/Legislative Affrs

NYS Bar Assn, Review the Code of Judicial Conduct Cmte
Securities Industry & Financial Markets Association (SIFMA)
360 Madison Ave, 18th Fl, New York, NY 10017-7111
646-637-9200 Fax: 646-637-9126
e-mail: mgross@bondmarkets.com
Web site: www.sifma.org
Herbert H McDade III, Chair

NYS Bar Assn, President's Cmte on Access to Justice
Boylan Brown
2400 Chase Sq, Rochester, NY 14604
585-232-5300 x256 Fax: 585-232-3528
e-mail: info@boylanbrown.com
Web site: www.boylanbrown.com
C Bruce Lawrence, Secretary New York State Bar Association

NYS Bar Assn, Tort System Cmte
Bracken Margolin Besunder LLP
1050 Old Nichols Road, Suite 200, Islandia, NY 11749
631-234-8585 Fax: 631-234-8702
e-mail: jbracken@bmlawllp.com
Web site: www.bmblawllp.com
John P Bracken, Judicial Screening

Brooklyn Law School
250 Joralemon St, Brooklyn, NY 11201
718-780-7900 Fax: 718-780-0393
e-mail: joan.wexler@brooklaw.edu
Web site: www.brooklaw.edu
18 legal clincs include immigration, new media, the arts, criminal defense and prosecution, bankruptcy, real estate, health, and securities arbitration.
Joan G Wexler, Dean

NYS Bar Assn, Cyberspace Law Cmte
Thelen Reid Brown Raysman & Steiner
875 Third Ave, New York, NY 10022
212-603-2196 Fax: 212-603-2001
e-mail: jneuburger@thelen.com
Web site: www.thelen.com
Jeffrey D Neuburger, Chair

CASA - Advocates for Children of NYS
32 Essex St, Albany, NY 12206
518-426-5354 Fax: 518-426-5348
e-mail: mail@casanys.org
Web site: www.casanys.org
Volunteer advocates appointed by family court judges to represent abused & neglected children in court
Penny Page, Executive Director

CPR, The International Institute for Conflict Prevention & Resolution
575 Lexington Ave, 21st Fl, New York, NY 10022
212-949-6490 Fax: 212-949-8859
e-mail: info@cpradr.org
Web site: www.cpradr.org
Alternative dispute resolution
Kathleen A Bryan, President & Chief Executive Officer

Offices and agencies generally appear in alphabetical order, except when specific order is requested by listee.

Center for Court Innovation

520 8th Ave, New York, NY 10018
212-397-3050 Fax: 212-397-0985
e-mail: info@courtinnovation.org
Web site: www.courtinnovation.org
Foster innovation within NYS courts addressing quality-of-life crime,
substance abuse, child neglect, domestic violence & landlord-tenant disputes
Greg Berman, Director

Center for Judicial Accountability Inc (CJA)

283 Soundview Avenue, White Plains, NY 10606-3821
914-421-1200 Fax: 914-684-6554
e-mail: mail@judgewatch.org
Web site: www.judgewatch.org
National, nonpartisan, non-profit citizens' organization documentingthe
politicization & corruption of the judicial selection & discipline processes
Doris L Sassower, President

Center for Law & Justice

Pine West Plaza, Bldg 2, Washington Ave Ext, Albany, NY 12205
518-427-8361 Fax: 518-427-8362
e-mail: cflj@verizon.net
Web site: www.timesunion.com/communities/cflj
Advocacy for fair treatment of poor people & communities of color by the
justice system; referral, workshops, community lawyering & education
Alice P Green, Executive Director

Coalition of Fathers & Families NY, PAC

PO Box 782, Clifton Park, NY 12065
518-383-8202
e-mail: pac@fafny.org
Web site: www.fafny.org/fafnypac.htm
Political Action for fathers and families in New York
James Hays, Treasurer

NYS Bar Assn, Trial Lawyers Section
Connors & Connors, PC

766 Castleton Ave, Staten Island, NY 10310
718-442-1700 Fax: 718-442-1717
e-mail: jpc@connorslaw.com
Web site: www.connorslaw.com
John P Connors, Jr, Chair

NYS Bar Assn, Torts, Insurance & Compensation Law Section
Connors & Corcoran LLP

Times Square Bldg, 45 Exchange St, Ste 250, Rochester, NY 14614
585-232-5885 Fax: 585-546-3631
e-mail: law@connorscorcoran.com
Web site: www.connorscorcoran.com
Eileen E Buholtz, Partner

Cornell Law School, Legal Information Institute

Myron Taylor Hall, Ithaca, NY 14853
607-255-1221 Fax: 607-255-7193
e-mail: lii@lii.law.cornell.edu
Web site: www.law.cornell.edu
Distributes legal documents via the web & electronic mail
Thomas R Bruce, Director

NYS Bar Assn, Judicial Section
Court of Claims

140 Grand St, Ste 507, White Plains, NY 10601
914-289-2310 Fax: 914-289-2313
e-mail: truderma@courts.state.ny.us
Hon Terry Jane Ruderman, Judge

NYS Bar Assn, Federal Constitution & Legislation Cmte
Day Pitney LLP

7 Times Square, New York, NY 10036-7311
973-966-8180 Fax: 973-966-1015
e-mail: jmaloney@daypitney.com
Web site: www.daypitney.com
One Jefferson Road, Parsippany, New Jersey 07054
John C Maloney Jr, Partner

NYS Bar Assn, Trusts & Estates Law Section
Day Pitney LLP

7 Times Square, 41st & 42nd St, New York, NY 10036
212-297-5800 or 212-297-2468 Fax: 212-916-2940
e-mail: gwwhitaker@daypitney.com
Web site: www.daypitney.com
Domestic and international trusts and estates.
G Warren Whitaker,

NYS Bar Assn, Public Trust & Confidence in the Legal System
Debevoise & Plimpton LLP

919 Third Ave, New York, NY 10022
212-909-6000 Fax: 212-909-6836
e-mail: azgorgun@debevoise.com
Web site: www.debevoise.com
Ellen Lieberman,

NYS Bar Assn, Alternative Dispute Resolution Cmte
Elayne E Greenberg, MS, Esq

25 Potters Lane, Great Neck, NY 11024
516-829-5521 Fax: 516-466-8130
e-mail: elayneegreenberg@juno.com
Elayne E Greenberg, Chair

Empire Justice Center

119 Washington Ave, Albany, NY 12210
518-462-6831 Fax: 518-462-6687
e-mail: aerickson@empirejustice.org
Web site: www.empirejustice.org
Policy analysis and research in issues impacting civil legal matters for
low-income residents
Anne Erickson, President & CEO

NYS Bar Assn, Review Judicial Nominations Cmte
Englert, Coffey, McHugh & Fantauzzi LLP

224 State St, PO Box 1092, Schenectady, NY 12305
518-370-4645 Fax: 518-374-5422
e-mail: pcoffey@ecmlaw.com
Web site: www.englertcoffeymchugh.com
Peter V Coffey, Chair

NYS Bar Assn, Cmte on the Jury System
FitzGerald Morris et al

One Broad St Plz, PO Box 2017, Glens Falls, NY 12801-4360
518-745-1400 Fax: 518-745-1576
e-mail: pdf@fmbf-law.com
Peter D FitzGerald, Chair

Fund for Modern Courts (The)

351 W 54th St, New York, NY 10019
212-541-6741 Fax: 212-541-7301
e-mail: justice@moderncourts.org
Web site: www.moderncourts.org
Improve the administration & quality of justice in NYS courts
Dennis R Hawkins, Executive Director

NYS Bar Assn, Court Operations Cmte
Getnick, Livingston, Atkinson, Gigliotti & Priore LLP

258 Genesee St, Ste 401, Utica, NY 13502-4642
315-797-9261 Fax: 315-732-0755
e-mail: mgetnick@glagplawfirm.com
Linda A Juteau, Office Manager

Offices and agencies generally appear in alphabetical order, except when specific order is requested by listee.

Policy Areas

NYS Bar Assn, Labor & Employment Law Section
Goodman & Zuchlewski LLP
500 5th Ave, Ste 5100, New York, NY 10110-5197
212-869-4646 Fax: 212-869-4648
e-mail: pz@kzlaw.net
Pearl Zuchlewski, Chair

Harris Beach LLP
99 Garnsey Rd, Pittsford, NY 14534
585-419-8800 Fax: 585-419-8801
e-mail: vbuzard@harrisbeach.com

NYS Bar Assn, Intellectual Property Law Section
Hartman & Winnicki, PC
115 W Century Rd, Paramus, NJ 7654
201-967-8040 Fax: 201-967-0590
e-mail: rick@ravin.com
Web site: www.hartmanwinnicki.com
Internet and Computer Law, Intellectual Property Law, and Debtors & Creditors Rights.
Richard L Ravin, Chair

NYS Bar Assn, Fiduciary Appointments Cmte
Harvey B Besunder PC
One Suffolk Sq, Ste 315, Islandia, NY 11749
631-234-9240 Fax: 631-234-9278
e-mail: hbb@besunderlaw.com
Harvey Besunder, Owner

NYS Bar Assn, Procedures for Judicial Discipline Cmte
Hollyer Brady et al
380 Madison Avenue, 22nd Fl, New York, NY 10017
212-818-1110 Fax: 212-818-0494
e-mail: hollyer@butzel.com
A Rene Hollyer, Chair

JAMS
620 Eighth Ave, 34th Floor, New York, NY 10018
212-607-2763 Fax: 212-751-4099
e-mail: mshaw@jamsadr.com
Web site: www.jamsadr.com
Mediation of civil, commercial & employment disputes; training & systems design
Margaret L Shaw, Mediator & Arburator

NYS Bar Assn, Real Property Section
Law Office of Anne Reynolds Copps
126 State St, 6th Fl, Albany, NY 12207
518-436-4170 Fax: 518-436-1456
e-mail: arcopps@nycap.rr.com
Web site: arcopps.net
Anne Reynolds Copps, Partner/Owner

NYS Bar Assn, General Practice Section
Law Offices of Frank G. D'Angelo & Associates
901 Stewart Avenue, Suite 230, Garden City, NY 11530
516-742-7601 or 516-222-1122 Fax: 516-742-6070
e-mail: fgdangeloesq@aol.com
Queens Village Office- 224-44 Braddock Ave, Queens Village, NY 11428
Phone; 718-776-7475
Frank G D'Angelo, Elder Law Attorney

Legal Action Center
225 Varick Street, 4th Floor, New York, NY 10014
212-243-1313 Fax: 212-675-0286
e-mail: lacinfo@lac.org
Web site: www.lac.org
Legal & policy issues, alcohol/drug abuse, AIDS & criminal justice
Paul N Samuels, President & Director

Legal Aid Society
199 Water Street, New York, NY 10038
212-577-3277 Fax: 212-809-1574
Web site: www.legal-aid.org
Civil & criminal defense, appeals, juvenile rights, civil legal services
Steven Banks, Attorney-In-Chief

NYS Bar Assn, Legal Aid Cmte/Funding for Civil Legal Svcs Cmte
Legal Services of the Hudson Valley
90 Maple Avenue, White Plains, NY 10601
914-949-1305 x136 Fax: 914-949-6213
e-mail: bfinkelstein@lshv.org
Web site: www.lshv.org
Established to provide free legal representation in civil matters to low-income people. Legal assistance is provided in the following areas; Westchester, Putnam, Dutchess, Orange, Sullivan and Ulster Counties.
Barbara D Finkelstein, Executive Director

Levene, Gouldin & Thompson LLP
PO Box F-1706, 450 Plaza Drive, Binghamton, NY 13902
607-584-5706 Fax: 607-763-9212
e-mail: jpollock@binghamtonlaw.com
Web site: www.binghamtonlaw.com
Commercial and personal injury litigation
John J. Pollock, Managing Partner

NYS Bar Assn, Elder Law Section
Littman Krooks LLP
399 Knollwood Rd, White Plains, NY 10603
914-684-2100 Fax: 914-684-9865
e-mail: hkrooks@lkllp.com
Web site: www.lkrlaw.com
Harold S Krooks, Chair

NYS Bar Assn, Unlawful Practice of Law Cmte
Schlather, Geldenhuys, Stumbar & Salk
200 E Buffalo St, PO Box 353, Ithaca, NY 14851
607-273-2202 Fax: 607-273-4436
e-mail: mjs@lsss-law.com
Web site: www.ithacalaw.com
Mark J Solomon, Chair

NYS Bar Assn, Court Structure & Judicial Selection Cmte
McMahon & Grow
301 N Washington St, PO Box 4350, Rome, NY 13442-4350
315-336-4700 Fax: 315-336-5851
e-mail: mgglaw@dreamscape.com
Web site: www.mgglaw.com
Hon Richard D Simons,

NYS Bar Assn, Resolutions Committee
Meyer Suozzi English & Klein, PC
990Stewart Ave, Garden City, NY 11530-9194
516-592-5704 Fax: 516-741-6706
e-mail: atlevin@nysbar.com
A Thomas Levin, Chair

NYS Bar Assn, Commercial & Federal Litigation Section
Montclare & Wachtler
67 Wall St, 22nd Fl, New York, NY 10005
212-509-3900 Fax: 212-509-7239
e-mail: ljwachtler@montclarewachtler.com
Lauren J Wachtler, Chair

NY County Lawyers' Association
14 Vessey St, New York, NY 10007
212-267-6646 Fax: 212-406-9252
e-mail: mflood@nycla.org
Web site: www.nycla.org
Stewart D Aaron, President

Offices and agencies generally appear in alphabetical order, except when specific order is requested by listee.

NYS Association of Criminal Defense Lawyers
245 Fifth Ave, 19th Fl, New York, NY 10016
212-532-4434 Fax: 212-532-4668
e-mail: nysacdl@aol.com
Web site: www.nysacdl.org
Criminal law
Patricia Marcus, Executive Director

NYS Bar Assn, Cmte on Diversity & Leadership Development
1 Elk St, Albany, NY 12207
518-487-5555 or 212-351-4670 Fax: 212-878-8641
e-mail: kstandard@ebglaw.com
Kenneth G Standard, Co-Chair

NYS Council of Probation Administrators
Box 2 272 Broadway, Albany, NY 12204
518-434-9194 Fax: 518-434-0392
e-mail: president@nyscopa.org
Web site: www.nyscopa.org
Provide supervision & investigation services to courts
Patricia Aikens, President

NYS Court Clerks Association
170 Duane St, New York, NY 10013
212-941-5700 Fax: 212-941-5705
Kevin E Scanlon, Sr, President

NYS Defenders Association
194 Washington Ave, Ste 500, Albany, NY 12210-2314
518-465-3524 Fax: 518-465-3249
e-mail: info@nysda.org
Web site: www.nysda.org
Criminal defense
Jonathan E Gradess, Executive Director

NYS Dispute Resolution Association
255 River St, #4, Troy, NY 12180
518-687-2240 Fax: 518-687-2245
e-mail: nysdra@nysdra.org
Web site: www.nysdra.org
Dispute resolution-mediation, arbitration, facilitation
Lisa U Hicks, Executive Director

NYS Magistrates Association
750 Delaware Ave, Delmar, NY 12054-1124
518-439-1087 Fax: 518-439-1204
e-mail: nysma@juno.com
Web site: www.mysma.net
Association of town & village justices
Tanja Sirago, Executive Director

NYS Bar Assn, Civil Practice Law & Rules Committee
NYS Supreme Court
50 Delaware Ave, Buffalo, NY 14202
716-845-9478 Fax: 716-851-3265
e-mail: sgerstma@courts.state.ny.us
Sharon Stern Gerstman, Chair

National Academy of Forensic Engineers
174 Brady Ave, Hawthorne, NY 10532
914-741-0633 Fax: 914-747-2988
e-mail: nafe@nafe.org
Web site: www.nafe.org
Engineering consultants to legal professionals & expert witnesses in court, arbitration & administrative adjudication proceedings
Marvin M Specter, P.E., L.S, Executive Director

NYS Bar Assn, Public Utility Law Committee
National Fuel Gas Distribution
455 Main St, Buffalo, NY 14203
716-686-6123
Web site: www.natfuel.com
Michael W Reville, Chair

NYS Bar Assn, Municipal Law Section
New York State Court of Claims
500 Court Exchange Bldg, 144 Exchange Blvd, Rochester, NY 14614
585-987-4212 Fax: 585-262-3019
e-mail: rminarik@courts.state.ny.us
Web site: www.nyscourtofclaims.courts.state.ny.us/
Hon Renee Forgensi Minarik,

New York State Law Enforcement Council
One Hogan Place, New York, NY 10013
212-335-8927 Fax: 212-335-3808
Web site: www.nyslec.org
Founded in 1982 as a legislative advocate for NY's law enforcement community. The members represent leading law enforcement professionals throughout the state. An active voice and participant in improving the quality of justice and a safer NY.
Leroy Frazer, Jr, Coordinator

New York State Supreme Court Officers Association
299 Broadway, Suite 1100, New York, NY 10007-1921
212-406-4292 or 212-406-4276 Fax: 212-791-8420
e-mail: lbroderick@nysscoa.org
Web site: www.nysscoa.org
Supreme Court Officers Union
John P McKillop, President

New York State Trial Lawyers
132 Nassau St, 2nd Fl, New York, NY 10038-2486
212-349-5890 Fax: 212-608-2310
e-mail: info@nystla.org
Web site: www.nystla.org
Lawrence Park, Executive Director

New York University School of Law
40 Washington Square South, Rm 413, New York, NY 10012-1099
212-998-6217 Fax: 212-995-4881
e-mail: chase@juris.law.nyu.edu
Web site: www.law.nyu.edu/institutes/judicial
Judicial education & research
Alison Kinney, Program Coordinator-Inst of Judicial Administration

NYS Bar Assn, Media Law Committee
New Yorker
4 Times Square, 20th Fl, New York, NY 10036
212-286-5857 Fax: 212-286-5025
e-mail: lynn_oberlander@newyorker.com
Web site: www.newyorker.com
Lynn Oberlander, Chair

NYS Bar Assn, Courts of Appellate Jurisdiction Cmte
Norman A Olch, Esq
233 Broadway, Suite 705, New York, NY 10279
212-964-6171 Fax: 212-964-7634
e-mail: norman@nolch.com
Norman A Olch, Chair

NYS Bar Assn, Judicial Campaign Monitoring Cmte
Ostertag O'Leary & Barrett
17 Collegeview Ave, Poughkeepsie, NY 12603
845-486-4300 Fax: 845-486-4080
e-mail: r.ostertag@verizon.net
Robert L Ostertag, Chair

Offices and agencies generally appear in alphabetical order, except when specific order is requested by listee.

Pace University, School of Law, John Jay Legal Services Inc
80 N Broadway, White Plains, NY 10603-3711
914-422-4333 Fax: 914-422-4391
e-mail: jjls@law.pace.edu
Web site: www.law.pace.edu
Law school clinical program with programs in the areas of health law, poverty law, domestic violence, immigration, criminal justice, and investor rights.
Margaret M Flint, Executive Director

Prisoners' Legal Services of New York
114 Prospect St, Ithaca, NY 14850-5616
607-273-2283 Fax: 607-272-9122
e-mail: kmmonks@plsny.org
Susan Johnson, Executive Director

Pro Bono Net
151 West 30th St, 10th Fl, New York, NY 10001
212-760-2554 Fax: 212-760-2557
e-mail: info@probono.net
Web site: www.probono.net; www.lawhelp.org
Connects & organizes the public interest legal community in an online environment; a lawyer-to-lawyer network
Mark O'Brien, Executive Director

NYS Bar Assn, Multi-jurisdictional Practice Cmte
Proskauer Rose LLP
1585 Broadway, New York, NY 10036-8299
212-969-3000 Fax: 212-969-2900
e-mail: keppler@proskauer.com
Web site: www.proskauer.com
Business Law, Securities
Klaus Eppler, Partner

Puerto Rican Legal Defense & Education Fund Inc (PRLDEF)
99 Hudson St, 14th Fl, New York, NY 10013-2815
212-219-3360 or 800-328-2322 Fax: 212-431-4276
e-mail: info@prldef.org
Web site: www.prldef.org
Secure, promote & protect the civil & human rights of the Puerto Rican & wider Latino community through litigation, policy analysis & education
Cesar A Perales, President & General Counsel

NYS Bar Assn, Judicial Campaign Conduct Cmte
Supreme Court
401 Montgomery St, Rm 401, Syracuse, NY 13202-2127
315-671-1100 Fax: 315-671-1183
e-mail: maklein@courts.state.ny.us
Michael A Klein, Chair

Vera Institute of Justice
233 Broadway, 12th Fl, New York, NY 10279-1299
212-334-1300 Fax: 212-941-9407
e-mail: contactvera@vera.org
Web site: www.vera.org
Research, design & implementation of demonstration projects in criminal justice & social equity in partnership with government & nonprofit organizations. Involved in child-welfare, cost-benefit analysis, substance abuse and mental health.
Michael Jacobson, Director

NYS Bar Assn, Family Law Section
Vincent F Stempel, Jr Esq
1205 Franklin Ave, Ste 280, Garden City, NY 11530
516-742-8620 Fax: 516-742-6859
e-mail: vstempel@yahoo.com
Vincent F Stempel, Jr, Chair

Volunteers of Legal Service, Inc
281 Park Avenue South, New York, NY 10010
212-966-4400 Fax: 212-219-8943
e-mail: blienhard@volsprobono.org
Providing pro bono civil legal services to poor people in New York City.
Bill Lienhard, Executive Director

NYS Bar Assn, Diversity & Leadership Development Cmte
Whiteman Osterman & Hanna LLP
One Commerce Plaza, Albany, NY 12260
518-487-7600 Fax: 518-487-7777
e-mail: lptharp@woh.com
Web site: www.woh.com
Lorraine Power Tharp, Partner

NYS Bar Assn, Health Law Section
Wilson Elser Moskowitz Edelman & Dicker
677 Broadway, Albany, NY 12207
518-449-8893 Fax: 518-449-4292
e-mail: philip.rosenberg@wilsonelser.com
Philip Rosenberg,

Women's Bar Association of the State of New York
PO Box 936, Planetarium Station, New York, NY 10024-0546
212-362-4445 Fax: 212-721-1620
e-mail: info@wbasny.org
Web site: www.wbasny.org
Linda A Chiaverini, Executive Director

Offices and agencies generally appear in alphabetical order, except when specific order is requested by listee.

LABOR & EMPLOYMENT PRACTICES

NEW YORK STATE

GOVERNOR'S OFFICE

Governor's Office
Executive Chamber
State Capitol
Albany, NY 12224
518-474-8390 Fax: 518-474-1513
Web site: www.ny.gov

Governor:
Andrew M Cuomo 518-474-8390
Secretary to the Governor:
William Mulrow 518-474-4246
Counsel to the Governor:
Alphonso David 518-474-8343
Deputy Secrtary, Labor:
Elizabeth de Leon Bhargava
Director, Communications:
Melissa DeRosa . . . . 518-474-8418 or 212-681-4640

EXECUTIVE DEPARTMENTS AND RELATED AGENCIES

Insurance Fund (NYS)
15 Computer Drive West
Albany, NY 12205
518-437-5220
Web site: www.nysif.com

199 Church St
New York, NY 10007
212-587-9000

Executive Director:
Eric Madoff. . . . . .212-312-7004 or 518-437-5220
Deputy Executive Director:
Dorothy Carey. 212-312-9933
Deputy Executive Director:
Shirley Stark 212-312-9917
Chief Fiscal Officer:
Susan D Sharp. 518-437-6168
General Attorney:
Gregory Allen 518-437-5220
Public Information Officer:
Robert Lawson. 518-437-3504/fax: 518-437-1849
Deputy Executive Director:
Colleen Gardner. 518-437-3504/fax: 518-437-1849

Administration
Director:
Joseph Mullen. 518-437-5220

Claims & Medical Operations
Director:
Edward Hiller 212-312-7880

Confidential Investigations
Director:
George Tidona 631-756-4007

Field Services
Director:
Armin Holdorf 212-587-5225

Information Technology Service
Chief Information Officer:
Sean O'Brien. 518-437-4361
Director, ITS:
Laurie Endries. 518-437-3130

Insurance Fund Board of Commissioners
Chair:
Kenneth R Theobalds .518-437-5220
Vice Chair:
Barry Swidler 518-437-5220
Secretary to the Board:
Francine James 212-312-7408
Member(ex-offico)/Commissioner, NYS Dept of Labor:
Peter M. Rivera. 518-437-5220
Member:
Eileen A Frank 518-437-5220
Member:
Joseph Canovas. 518-437-5220
Member:
David E Ourlicht. 518-437-5220

Investments
Director:
Miriam Martinez. 212-587-6550

NYSIF District Offices

Albany
1 Watervliet Ave Ext, Albany, NY 12206
Business Manager:
Augusto Bortoloni. 518-437-6401/fax: 518-437-8021

Buffalo
225 Oak St, Buffalo, NY 14203
Business Manager:
Ronald Reed .716-851-2004/fax: 716-851-2131

Binghamton
Glendale Technology Park, 2001 E Perimeter Rd, Endicott, NY 13760
Business Manager:
Thomas Racko. 607-741-6023/fax: 607-741-5029

Nassau County, Long Island
8 Corporate Center Dr, 2nd Fl, Melville, NY 11747
Business Manager:
Cliff Meister 631-756-4003/fax: 631-756-4030

Rochester
100 Chestnut St, Ste 1000, Rochester, NY 14604
Business Manager:
Lisa Ellsworth 585-258-2100/fax: 585-258-2065

Suffolk County, Long Island
8 Corporate Center Dr, 3rd Fl, Melville, NY 11747
Business Manager:
Catherine Carillo. 631-756-4330/fax: 631-756-4260

Syracuse
1045 Seventh North St, Liverpool, NY 13088
Business Manager:
Patricia Albert. 315-453-8300/fax: 315-453-8313

White Plains
105 Corporate Park Dr, Ste 200, White Plains, NY 10604
Business Manager:
Carl Heitner. 914-701-6292/fax: 914-701-2181

Premium Audit
Director:
Glenn Cunningham. 212-587-7470

Offices and agencies generally appear in alphabetical order, except when specific order is requested by listee.

Underwriting
Director:
John Massetti 212-312-7012

Labor Department
Building 12, Room 500
Harriman State Office Campus
Albany, NY 12240
518-457-9000 Fax: 518-457-6908
e-mail: nysdol@labor.ny.gov
Web site: www.labor.ny.gov

Commissioner:
Peter M. Rivera 518-457-9000
Executive Deputy Commissioner:
Mario Musolino 518-457-4318

Hazard Abatement Board
Chair:
Katherine D. Schrier 518-457-7629

Employment Relations Board
Chair:
Jerome Lefkowitz 518-457-2664
e-mail: perbinfo@perb.ny.gov

Industrial Board of Appeals
Chair:
Anne P Stevason 518-474-4785

Unemployment Insurance Appeal Board
Chair:
Leonard Polletta 518-402-0205
Executive Director:
Susan Borenstein 518-402-0205

Administration & Public Affairs
Director:
Roger Bailie 518-457-2647
Director, Communications:
Leo Rosales 518-457-5519/fax: 518-485-1126
e-mail: leo.rosales@labor.ny.gov
Director, Personnel:
Carol Owsiany 518-457-1020
Acting Director, Staff & Organization Development:
Sherry Edwards 518-457-7442
Director, Equal Opportunity Development:
Omoye Cooper 518-457-1984

Counsel's Office
Acting Counsel:
Pico Ben-Amotz 518-457-3665

Federal Programs
Deputy Commissioner, Federal Programs:
Bruce Herman 518-485-6410

Employment Services Division
Director:
Vacant 518-457-3584
Assistant Director:
Russell Oliver 518-457-3584

Unemployment Insurance Division
Director:
Richard Marino 518-457-2878/fax: 518-485-8604

Workforce Development & Training Division
Director:
Karen Coleman 518-457-0380/fax: 518-457-9526
Employability Development/Apprentice Training
Acting Director:
Yue Yee 518-457-6820

Labor Planning & Technology
Director, Enterprise Architecture:
David A. Palmisano 518-485-7395

Research & Statistics Division
Chief:
Bohdan Wynnyk 518-485-7990
Chief of Labor Market Information:
Norman Steele 518-457-6638
Statewide Labor Market Analyst:
Kevin Jack 518-457-2919
e-mail: kevin.jack@labor.ny.gov

Special Investigations
Director:
John Dormin 518-457-7012
Director, Internal Audit:
Timothy Burleski 518-457-7012

Veterans Services
Program Coordinator:
Vacant 518-457-1343

Employer Services
Director:
Vacant 518-457-6821
Rural Labor Services:
Valerie Sewell 518-485-8539

Regional Offices
Central/Mohawk Valley . . . . .fax: 315-793-2342
207 Genesee St, Ste 712, Utica, NY 13501
Finger Lakes Region . . . . .fax: 585-258-8859
276 Waring Road, Rochester, NY 14607
Greater Capital District . . . . .fax: 518-462-2777
175 Central Ave, Albany, NY 12206-2902
Hudson Valley . . . . .fax: 914-287-2058
120 Bloomingdale Rd, White Plains, NY 10605
Long Island Region . . . . .fax: 516-934-8553
303 W Old County Rd, Hicksville, NY 11801
New York City . . . . .fax: 212-621-0730
247 West 54th St, New York, NY 10019
Southern Tier . . . . .fax: 607-741-4516
2001 Perimeter Rd East, Ste 3, Endicott, NY 13760
Western Region . . . . .fax: 716-851-2792
284 Main St, Buffalo, NY 14202

Worker Protection
Deputy Commissioner, Workforce Development:
Karen A. Coleman 518-457-4317

Labor Standards Division
Director:
Carmine Ruberto 518-457-4256

Public Work Bureau
Director:
Chris Alund 518-485-5696

Safety & Health Division
Director:
Eileen Franko 518-457-3518/fax: 518-457-1519
Asbestos Control Bureau
Program Manager:
Robert Perez 518-457-1255/fax: 518-485-8054
Industry Inspection Unit
Program Manage, License & Certification:
Martha Waldman 518-457-2735
On-site Consultation Unit
Program Manager:
James Rush 518-457-2238/fax: 518-457-3454

Offices and agencies generally appear in alphabetical order, except when specific order is requested by listee.

Public Employees Safety & Health (PESH) Unit
Program Manager:
Normand Labbe 518-457-1263/fax: 518-457-5545

Law Department
120 Broadway
New York, NY 10271-0332
212-416-8000 or 800-771-7755
Web site: www.ag.ny.gov

State Capitol
Albany, NY 12224-0341
518-474-5481
Fax: 518-473-9909

Attorney General:
Eric T Schneiderman . . . . .212-416-8050 or 518-474-7330
Chief of Staff:
Micah Lasher 212-416-8050
Press Secretary:
Fernando Aquino212-416-8060/fax: 212-416-6005

Social Justice
Executive Deputy Attorney General:
Alvin L Braggs, Jr. 212-416-8450

Civil Rights Bureau
Bureau Chief:
Kristen Clarke 212-416-8250/fax: 212-416-8074

State Counsel
Chief Deputy Attorney General & Counsel:
Harlan Levy 212-416-8525
Executive Deputy Attorney General, State Counsel:
Kent T Stauffer . . . . .212-416-8252 or 518-473-8946
fax: 212-416-6001

Civil Recoveries Bureau
Bureau Chief:
John Cremo .518-776-2173/fax: 518-915-7731

Workers' Compensation Board
328 State Street
Schenectady, NY 12305
518-462-8880 or 877-632-4996 Fax: 518-473-1415
e-mail: publicinfo@wcb.ny.gov
Web site: www.wcb.ny.gov

Executive Director:
Mark Wade 518-408-0469
Chair, Board of Commissioners:
Robert E Beloten 518-408-0469/fax: 518-473-1415
Vice Chair:
Fran Libous 518-408-0469/fax: 518-473-1415
General Counsel:
Vacant 518-486-9564/fax: 518-402-0113
Director, Public Information:
Rachel McEneny 518-408-5592/fax: 518-473-1415
e-mail: publicinfo@wcb.ny.gov
Fraud Inspector General:
Vacant 888-363-6001/fax: 518-402-1059
Advocate for Business:
Neil Gilberg 518-486-3331
Advocate for Injured Workers:
Edwin Ruff . . . . .800-580-6665 or 518-471-8182
fax: 518-486-7510

Administration
Director, Facilities Management:
Michael DeBarr 518-486-9597

Director, Security:
John Dale .518-402-0172/fax: 518-402-6100
Director, Human Resources:
Gilda Hernandez 518-408-0865/fax: 518-486-6364
Affirmative Action Officer:
Jaime Benitez. .518-474-2685/fax: 518-486-6364

Information Management Systems
Director:
Matthew Ancin 518-474-6557/fax: 518-474-9367
Director, Continuous Improvement/MIS:
Thomas Wegener 518-486-5143

Operations
Director, Bureau of Compliance:
K. Brian Collins. 518-474-9598/fax: 518-402-6201

District Offices
Albany
100 Broadway-Menands, Albany, NY 12241
District Manager:
Laurie Hart 866-750-5157/fax: 518-473-9166
Binghamton
State Office Bldg, 44 Hawley St, Binghamton, NY 13901
District Manager:
David Gardiner 866-802-3604/fax: 607-721-8464
Brooklyn
111 Livingston St, 22nd Fl, Brooklyn, NY 11201
District Manager:
Tom Agostino 800-877-1373/fax: 718-802-6642
Buffalo
Ellicott Sq Building, 295 Main Street Ste 400, Buffalo, NY 14203
District Manager:
Michelle Hirsch 866-211-0645/fax: 716-842-2171
Long Island
220 Rabro Drive, Ste 100, Hauppauge, NY 11788-4230
District Manager:
Steve Carbone. 866-681-5354/fax: 631-952-7966
Manhattan
215 W 125th St, New York, NY 10027
District Manager:
Sherri Cunningham. 800-877-1373/fax: 212-864-7204
Peekskill
41 N Division St, Peekskill, NY 10566
District Manager:
Luis A Torres 866-746-0552/fax: 914-788-5809
Queens
168-46 91st Ave, 3rd Fl, Jamaica, NY 11432
District Administrator:
Bryan Pile 800-877-1373/fax: 718-291-7248
Rochester
130 Main St West, Rochester, NY 14614
District Manager:
Joseph Dailor 866-211-0644/fax: 585-238-8351
Syracuse
935 James Street, Syracuse, NY 13203
District Manager:
Marc Johnson 866-802-3730/fax: 315-423-2938

Workers' Compensation Board of Commissioners
Commissioner & Vice Chair:
Fran Libous. 518-408-0469
Commissioner:
Kenneth Munnelly 518-408-0469
Commissioner:
Mark D Higgins 518-408-0469
Commissioner:
Conrad W Lower 518-408-0469
Commissioner:
Loren Lobban 518-408-0469
Commissioner:
Linda Hull. 518-408-0469

Offices and agencies generally appear in alphabetical order, except when specific order is requested by listee.

Commissioner:
 Candace K Finnegan 914-788-5890
Commissioner:
 Freida Foster 518-408-0469
Commissioner:
 David Dudley 518-408-0469
Commissioner:
 Samuel G Williams 518-408-0469
Commissioner:
 Ellen O Paprocki 315-423-1276
Commissioner:
 Richard Bell 315-423-1276
Secretary to the Board:
 Sandra M Olson 518-402-6070

CORPORATIONS, AUTHORITIES AND COMMISSIONS

Waterfront Commission of New York Harbor
39 Broadway
4th Fl
New York, NY 10006
212-742-9280 Fax: 212-480-0587
Web site: www.wcnyh.org

Commissioner, New York:
 Ronald Goldstock 212-742-9280
Commissioner, New Jersey:
 Michael Murphy 212-742-9280
Executive Director:
 Walter M Arsenault 212-905-9201

NEW YORK STATE LEGISLATURE

See Legislative Branch in Section 1 for additional Standing Committee and Subcommittee information.

Assembly Standing Committees

Labor
Chair:
 Michele Titus (D) 518-455-5668
Ranking Minority Member:
 Karl Brabenec (R) 518-455-5991

Assembly Task Forces

Puerto Rican/Hispanic Task Force
Chair:
 Marcos Crespo (D) 518-455-5514
Executive Director:
 Guillermo Martinez 518-455-3608

Skills Development & Career Education, Legislative Commission on
Assembly Chair:
 Vacant 518-455-0000
Program Manager:
 Brenda Carter 518-455-4865

Women's Issues, Task Force on
Chair:
 Aravella Simotas (D) 518-455-5014
Coordinator:
 Christina Williams 518-455-3632/fax: 518-455-4574

Senate Standing Committees

Labor
Chair:
 Jack Martins (R) 518-455-3265
Ranking Minority Member:
 Jose R Peralta (D) 518-455-2529

U.S. GOVERNMENT

EXECUTIVE DEPARTMENTS AND RELATED AGENCIES

Equal Employment Opportunity Commission
Web site: www.eeoc.gov

New York District
33 Whitehall St, 5th Fl, New York, NY 10004
District Director:
 Kevin J. Berry . . . . .800-669-4000 or 800-669-6820 tty
 fax: 212-336-3790

 Buffalo Local
 6 Fountain Plaza, Ste 350, Buffalo, NY 14202
 Director:
  John E Thompson Jr . . . . .800-669-4000 or 800-669-3820 tty
  fax: 716-551-4387

Federal Labor Relations Authority
Web site: www.flra.gov

Boston Regional Office . . . . .fax: 617-565-6262
 O'Neill Federal Bldg, 10 Causeway St, Ste 472, Boston, MA 02222
 617-565-5100 Fax: 617-565-6262
 Regional Director:
  Phillip T. Roberts 617-424-5730/fax: 312-886-5997

Federal Mediation & Conciliation Service
Web site: www.fmcs.gov

Northeastern Region . . . . .fax: 973-297-4860
 1 Newark Center, 16th Floor, Newark, NJ 07102
 732-726-3120 Fax: 973-297-4860
 Regional Director:
  Ken Kowalski 973-645-2000
 Director, Mediation Services:
  Jack Sweeny 973-645-2200
  e-mail: jsweeny@fmcs.gov

National Labor Relations Board
Web site: www.nlrb.gov

Region 2 - New York City Metro Area . . . . .fax: 212-264-2450
 26 Federal Plaza, Rm 3614, New York, NY 10278-0104
 212-264-0300 Fax: 212-264-2450
 Regional Director:
  Karen P. Fernbach 212-264-0300/fax: 212-264-2450

Region 29 - Brooklyn Area .fax: 718-330-7579
 Two MetroTech Center, 100 Myrtle Ave, 5th Fl, Brooklyn, NY 11201-4201
 718-330-7713 Fax: 718-330-7579
 Regional Director:
  James G. Paulsen 718-330-7713/fax: 718-330-7579

Region 3 - Buffalo Area . . . . .fax: 716-551-4972
 Niagara Center Building, 130 South Elmowood Ave, Ste 630, Buffalo, NY 14202-2387
 716-551-4931 Fax: 716-551-4972
 Regional Director:
  Rhonda P. Ley .716-551-4931/fax: 716-551-4972

Offices and agencies generally appear in alphabetical order, except when specific order is requested by listee.

Albany Resident Office . . . . fax: 518-431-4157
Leo W O'Brien Fed Bldg, Rm 342, Clinton Ave and N Pearl St, Albany, NY 12207-2350
518-431-4155 Fax: 518-431-4157
Resident Officer:
    Jon Mackle 518-431-4155/fax: 518-431-4157

US Labor Department
Web site: www.dol.gov

Bureau of Labor Statistics (BLS)
201 Varick St, Rm 808, New York, NY 10014
Web site: www.bls.gov
Regional Commissioner (NY & Boston):
    Deborah A. Brown 617-565-2331
Reg Comm (NY):
    Vacant

Employee Benefits Security Administration (EBSA)
33 Whitehall St, Ste 1200, New York, NY 10004
Regional Director:
    Jonathan Kay 212-607-8600/fax: 212-607-8681

Employment & Training Administration (ETA)
JFK Federal Bldg, Rm E/350, 25 New Sudbury Street, Boston, MA 02203
Regional Administrator:
    Holly O'Brien 617-788-0170/fax: 617-788-0101

Employment Standards Administration

Federal Contract Compliance Programs Office (OFCCP)
26 Federal Plaza, Rm. 36-116, New York, NY 10278
Regional Director:
    Eduardo Fountaine 646-264-3170/fax: 646-264-3009

Labor-Management Standards Office (OLMS)
Web site: www.olms.dol.gov
Buffalo District Office
    130 South Elmwood Street, Suite 510, Buffalo, NY 14202
    District Director:
        Joseph Wasik 716-842-2900/fax: 716-842-2901
New York District Office
    201 Varick St, Rm 878, New York, NY 10014
    District Director:
        Adrianna Vamuateas 646-264-3190/fax: 646-264-3191

Wage-Hour Division (WHD)-Northeast Regional Office
170 So Independence Mall, Ste 850 West, Philadelphia, PA 19106
Regional Admin:
    Corlis L Sellers 215-861-5800/fax: 215-861-5840
Albany District Office
    Leo W O'Brien Fed Bldg, Rm 822, Albany, NY 12207
    District Director:
        Jay Rosenblum 518-431-6460
Long Island District Office
    1400 Old Country Rd, Ste 410, Westbury, NY 11590
    District Director:
        Irv Miljoner 516-338-1890/fax: 516-338-8901
New York City District Office
    26 Federal Plz, Rm 3700, New York, NY 10278
    District Director:
        Maria Rosado 212-264-8185/fax: 212-264-9548

Workers' Compensation Programs (OWCP)
201 Varick St, Rm 740, New York, NY 10014
Regional Director:
    Zev Sapir. 212-868-0844

Inspector General

Inspector General's Office for Audit (OIG-A)
201 Varick St, Rm 871, New York, NY 10014

Audit Director:
    Mark Schwartz 646-264-3511

Occupational Safety & Health Administration (OSHA)
201 Varick St, Rm 670, New York, NY 10014
212-337-2378
Web site: www.osha.gov
Regional Administrator:
    Robert Kulick 212-337-2378

Albany Area Office
401 New Karner Rd, Ste 300, Albany, NY 12205-3809
Area Director:
    Kimberly Castillion. 518-464-4338/fax: 518-464-4337

Buffalo Area Office
130 Elmwood Avenue, Suite 500, Buffalo, NY 14026
Area Director:
    Arthur Dube 716-551-3053/fax: 716-551-3126

Manhattan Area Office
201 Varick St, Rm 908, New York, NY 10014
Area Director:
    Richard Mendelson 212-620-3200/fax: 212-620-4121

Queens Area Office
45-17 Marathon Parkway, Little Neck, NY 11362
Assistant Area Director:
    Kay Gee. 718-279-9060/fax: 718-279-9057

Syracuse Area Office
3300 Vickery Rd, North Syracuse, NY 13212
Area Director:
    Christopher Adams 315-451-0808/fax: 315-451-1351

Tarrytown Area Office
660 White Plains Rd, 4th Floor, Tarrytown, NY 10591-5107
Area Director:
    Diana Cortez 914-524-7510/fax: 914-524-7515

Office of Asst Secretary for Administration & Mgmt (OASAM)
201 Varick St, Rm 815, New York, NY 10014
Regional Administrator (NY & Boston):
    Mark D. Falk. 646-264-5018

Office of the Solicitor . . . . fax: 646-246-3660
201 Varick St, Rm 983, New York, NY 10014
646-264-3650 Fax: 646-246-3660
Reg Solicitor:
    Patricia M Rodenhausen 212-337-2078/fax: 212-337-2112

Region 2 - New York Office of Secretary's Representative
201 Varick St, Rm 605-B, New York, NY 10014
Secretary's Regional Representative (SRR):
    Angelica O Tang 212-337-2317/fax: 212-337-2586

Jobs Corps (JC)
JFK Fed Bldg, Room E350, Boston, NY 02203
Regional Director:
    Joseph A Semansky 617-788-0197/fax: 617-788-0184

Office of Public Affairs (OPA) (serving New York State)
JFK Federal Bldg, Rm E120, Boston, MA 2203
Regional Director, Public Affairs:
    John Chavez 617-565-2072/fax: 617-565-2076

Region 2 New York - Women's Bureau (WB) . . . fax: 646-264-3794
201 Varick St, Rm 602, New York, NY 10014-4811
646-264-3789 Fax: 646-264-3794
Regional Administrator:
    Grace Protos 646-264-3789
    e-mail: protos.grace@dol.gov

Offices and agencies generally appear in alphabetical order, except when specific order is requested by listee.

US Merit Systems Protection Board
Web site: www.mspb.gov

New York Field Office
26 Federal Plaza, Room 3137A, New York, NY 10278
Chief Administrative Judge:
Arthur S. Joseph 212-264-9372/fax: 212-264-1417

US Office of Personnel Management
Web site: www.usajobs.opm.gov

PHILADELPHIA SERVICE CENTER (serving New York)
William J Green Fed Bldg, Rm 3256, 600 Arch St, Philadelphia, PA 19106
Director:
Joseph D Stix.......................215-861-3031/fax: 215-861-3030
e-mail: philadelphia@opm.gov

US Railroad Retirement Board
Web site: www.rrb.gov

New York District Offices

Albany..fax: 518-431-4000
11A Clinton Avenue, Suite 264, Albany, NY 12207-2399
877-772-5772 Fax: 518-431-4000
District Manager:
Daniel M Layton, Jr 877-772-5772/fax: 518-431-4000
e-mail: albany@rrb.gov

Buffalo...fax: 716-551-3802
186 Exchange Streeet, Suite 110, Buffalo, NY 14204-2085
877-772-5772 Fax: 716-551-3802
District Manager:
Philip C Dissek 877-772-5772/fax: 716-551-3802
e-mail: buffalo@rrb.gov

New York ....fax: 212-264-1687
26 Federal Plaza, Rm 3404, New York, NY 10278
877-772-5772 Fax: 212-264-1687
District Manager:
Rose I Jonas....................877-772-5772/fax: 212-264-1687
e-mail: newyork@rrb.gov

Westbury ....fax: 516-334-4763
1400 Old Country Rd, Ste 202, Westbury, NY 11590
877-772-5772 or 716-835-7808 Fax: 516-334-4763
District Manager:
Marie Baran.....................877-772-5772/fax: 516-334-4763

U.S. CONGRESS

See U.S. Congress Chapter for additional Standing Committee and Subcommittee information.

House of Representatives Standing Committees

Education & Labor
Chair:
John Kline (R-MN)..............................202-225-2271
Ranking Member:
George Miller (D-CA) 202-225-2095
New York Delegate:
Timothy H Bishop (D) 202-225-3826
New York Delegate:
Carolyn McCarthy (D) 202-225-5516
New York Delegate: -
Paul Tonko (D).................................202-225-5076

Small Business
Chair:
Sam Graves (R-MO)..............................202-225-7041

Ranking Member:
Nydia Velazquez (D-NY)..........................202-225-2361
New York Delegate:
Grace Meng (D) 202-225-2601

Subcommittees
Contracting and Workforce
Chair:
Richard L. Hanna (R-NY).....................202-225-3665
Ranking Member:
Grace Meng (D-NY) 202-225-2601
Chair:
David Schweikert (R-AZ)....................202-225-2190
Ranking Member:
Yvette Clarke (D-NY) 202-225-6231

Senate Standing Committees

Health, Education, Labor & Pensions
Chair:
Tom Harkin (D-IA)...............................202-224-3254
Ranking Member:
Lamar Alexander (R-TN) 202-224-4944

Small Business & Entrepreneurship
Chair:
Mary L. Landrieu (D-LA).........................202-224-5824
Ranking Member:
James E. Risch (R-ID) 202-224-2752

PRIVATE SECTOR

1199 SEIU United Healthcare Workers East
310 W 43rd St, New York, NY 10036
212-261-2222 Fax: 212-956-5140
Web site: www.1199seiuonline.org
Representing New York State healthcare workers
George Gresham, President

Abilities Inc, Abilities!
201 IU Willets Rd, Albertson, NY 11507-1599
516-465-1400 or 516-747-5355 (TTY) Fax: 516-465-3757
e-mail: jswiesky@abilitiesinc.org
Web site: www.abilitiesinc.org
Provides comprehensive services to help individuals with disabilities reach their employment goals; provides support services & technical assistance to employers who hire persons with disabilities
Alice Muterspaw, Consumer Services/Provider Relations Director

American Federation of Teachers
555 New Jersey Ave NW, Washington, DC 20001
800-238-1133 Fax: 202-393-7479
e-mail: emcelroy@aft.org
Web site: www.aft.org
Edward J McElroy, President

Associated Builders & Contractors, Construction Training Center of NYS
6369 Collamer Drive, East Syracuse, NY 13057-1115
315-463-7539 or 800-477-7743 Fax: 315-463-7621
e-mail: info@abc.org
Web site: www.abc.org/newyork
Merit shop construction trades apprenticeship program
Thomas Schlueter, Vice President of Education Programs

Blitman & King LLP
443 N Franklin St, Ste 300, Syracuse, NY 13204
315-422-7111 Fax: 315-471-2623
e-mail: btking@bklawyers.com
Web site: www.bklawyers.com
Labor & employee benefits

Offices and agencies generally appear in alphabetical order, except when specific order is requested by listee.

Bernard T King, Attorney/Senior Partner

Center for an Urban Future
120 Wall St, 20th Fl, New York, NY 10005
212-479-3319 Fax: 212-479-3338
e-mail: cuf@nycfuture.org
Web site: www.nycfuture.org
A New York City-based think tank that publishes studies about economic development, workforce development and other critical issues facing New York.
Jonathan Bowles, Director

Civil Service Employees Union (CSEA), Local 1000, AFSCME, AFL-CIO
143 Washington Ave, Capitol Station Box 7125, Albany, NY 12210-0125
518-257-1000 or 800-342-4146 Fax: 518-462-3639
Web site: www.csealocal1000.org
Public/private employees union
Danny Donohue, President

Communications Workers of America, District 1
80 Pine St, 37th Floor, New York, NY 10005
212-344-2515 Fax: 212-425-2947
Web site: www.cwa-union.org
Christopher Shelton, Vice President

Cornell University, Institute on Conflict Resolution
412 Dolgen Hall, Ithaca, NY 14853-3901
607-255-5378 Fax: 607-255-6974
e-mail: dbl4@cornell.edu
Web site: www.ilr.cornell.edu
Collective bargaining; dispute resolution, negotiation
David Lipsky, Director

Cornell University, Sch of Industr & Labor Relations Institute for Workplace Studies
16 E 34th Street, 4th Fl, New York, NY 10016
212-340-2850 Fax: 212-340-2893
e-mail: sb22@cornell.edu
Web site: www.ilr.cornell.edu/iws
Substance abuse in the workplace; power & bargaining in organizations
Samuel B Bacharach, McKelvey-Grant Professor & Director

Cornell University, School of Industrial & Labor Relations
Ives Hall, Ithaca, NY 14853-3901
607-255-4375 or 607-255-2223 Fax: 607-255-1836
e-mail: vmb2@cornell.edu
Web site: www.ilr.cornell.edu
Immigration policy; labor market trends & analysis
Vernon Briggs, Professor

Cullen & Dykman LLP
100 Quentin Roosevelt Blvd, Garden City Ctr, Garden City, NY 11530-4850
516-357-3703 Fax: 516-296-9155
e-mail: gfishberg@cullenanddykman.com
Web site: www.cullenanddykman.com
Municipal & labor law
Gerard Fishberg, Partner

Empire State Regional Council of Carpenters
1284 Central Avenue, Ste 1, Albany, NY 12205
518-459-7182 Fax: 518-459-7798
e-mail: jminer@empirestatecarpenters.org
Michael Conroy, Political Director

JAMS
620 Eighth Avenue, 34th Floor, New York, NY 10018
212-751-2700 Fax: 212-751-4099
Web site: www.jamsadr.com
Mediation of civil, commercial & employment disputes: training & systems design
Carol Wittenberg, Arbitrator/Mediator

Kaye Scholer LLP
425 Park Ave, 8th Fl, New York, NY 10022
212-836-8558 Fax: 212-836-6458
e-mail: jwaks@kayescholer.com
Web site: www.kayescholer.com
Chair, Labor & Employment Law Group (representing employers)
Jay W Waks, Partner

NYS Bar Assn, Labor & Employment Law Section
Kraus & Zuchlewski LLP
500 Fifth Ave, Ste 5100, New York, NY 10110
212-869-4646 Fax: 212-869-4648
e-mail: pz@kzlaw.net
Pearl Zuchlewski, Chair

Lancer Insurance Co/Lancer Compliance Services
370 West Park Ave, Long Beach, NY 11561-3245
516-432-5000 Fax: 516-431-0926
e-mail: bcrescenzo@lancer-ins.com
Substance abuse management & testing services for the transportation industry
Bob Crescenzo, Vice President

MDRC
16 East 34th St, 19th Floor, New York, NY 10016-5936
212-532-3200 Fax: 212-684-0832
e-mail: information@mdrc.org
Web site: www.mdrc.org
Nonprofit research & field testing of education & employment programs for disadvantaged adults & youth
Gordon Berlin, President

Manhattan-Bronx Minority Business Enterprise Center
225 W 34th St, Ste 2007, New York, NY 10122
212-947-5351 or 212-947-4900 Fax: 212-947-1506
e-mail: mbmbdc@manhattanmbec.com
Web site: www.manhattanmbec.com
Information & advocacy for local employment & business & contract opportunities
Lorraine Kelsey, Executive Director

NY Association of Training & Employment Professionals (NYATEP)
540 Broadway, 5th Floor, Albany, NY 12207
518-433-1200 Fax: 518-433-7424
e-mail: jtwomey@nyatep.org
Web site: www.nyatep.org
Represent local workforce development partnerships
John Twomey, Executive Director

NYS Building & Construction Trades Council
71 West 23 St, New York, NY 10010
212-647-0700 Fax: 212-647-0705
Edward J Malloy, President

NYS Industries for the Disabled (NYSID) Inc
11 Columbia Circle Dr., Albany, NY 12203
518-463-9706 or 800-221-5994 Fax: 518-463-9708
e-mail: administrator@nysid.org
Web site: www.nysid.org
Business development through 'preferred source' purchasing to increase employment opportunities for people with disabilities
Lawrence L Barker, Jr, President & Chief Executive Officer

National Federation of Independent Business
1 Commerce Plaza, Ste 1119, Albany, NY 12260-1000
518-434-1262 Fax: 518-426-8799
e-mail: mike.elmendorf@nfib.org
Web site: www.nfib.org
Small business advocacy; supporting pro-small business candidates at the state & federal levels
Michael Elmendorf, State Director

Offices and agencies generally appear in alphabetical order, except when specific order is requested by listee.

Policy Areas

National Writers Union
113 University Pl, 6th Fl, New York, NY 10003
212-254-0279 Fax: 212-254-0673
e-mail: nwu@nwu.org
Web site: www.nwu.org
Gerard Colby, President

New York Committee for Occupational Safety & Health
61 Broadway, Suite 1710, New York, NY 10006
212-227-6440 Fax: 212-227-9854
e-mail: nycosh@nycosh.org
Web site: www.nycosh.org
Provide occupational safety & health training & technical assistance
Joel Shufro, Executive Director

New York State Nurses Association
11 Cornell Rd, Latham, NY 12110
518-782-9400 x279 Fax: 518-783-5207
e-mail: executive@nysna.org
Web site: www.nysna.org
Labor union & professional association for registered nurses

New York University, Graduate School of Journalism
20 Cooper Square, 6th Floor, New York, NY 10003
212-998-7980 Fax: 212-995-4148
Web site: www.nyu.edu/gsas/dept/journal
Labor issues & reporting
Bill Serrin, Director, Graduate Studies

Osborne Association
809 Westchester Avenue, Bronx, NY 10455
718-707-2600 Fax: 718-707-3102
e-mail: info@osborneny.org
Web site: www.osborneny.org
Career/educational counseling, job referrals & training for recently released prisoners, substance abuse treatment, case management, HIV/AIDS counseling & prevention, family services, parenting education, re-entry services, housing placement assistan
Tanya L Phillips, Director of Employment & Training

Public/Private Ventures
The Chanin Building, 122 East 42nd St, 42nd Fl, New York, NY 10168
212-822-2400 Fax: 212-949-0439
e-mail: kfaulhaber@ppv.org
Web site: www.ppv.org
A national nonprofit, nonpartisan organization that tackles critical challenges facing low-income communities by seeking out and designing innovative programs, rigorously testing them, and promoting the solutions proven to work.
Sheila Maguire, VP, Labor Market Initiatives

Realty Advisory Board on Labor Relations
292 Madison Ave, New York, NY 10017
212-889-4100 Fax: 212-889-4105
e-mail: jberg@rabolr.com
Web site: www.rabolr.com
Labor negotiations for realtors & realty firms
James Berg, President

Transport Workers Union of America, AFL-CIO
1700 Broadway, 2nd Fl, New York, NY 10019
212-259-4900 Fax: 212-265-5704
Web site: www.twu.com
Bus, train, railroad & airline workers' union
James C Little, International President

UNITE HERE
275 7th Ave, Fl 11, New York, NY 10001-6708
212-265-7000 Fax: 212-765-7751
e-mail: brayor@unitehere.org
Web site: www.uniteunion.org
Bruce Raynor, General President

United Food & Commercial Workers Local 1
5911 Airport Road, Oriskany, NY 13424
315-797-9600 or 800-697-8329 Fax: 315-793-1182
e-mail: organize@ufcwone.org
Web site: www.ufcwone.org
Frank C DeRiso, President

Vedder Price PC
1633 Broadway, New York, NY 10019
212-407-7750 or 917-214-6441 Fax: 212-407-7799
e-mail: akoral@vedderprice.com
Web site: www.vedderprice.com
Representing Management
Alan M Koral, Shareholder

Vladeck, Waldman, Elias & Engelhard PC
1501 Broadway, Suite 800, New York, NY 10036
212-403-7300 Fax: 212-221-3172
e-mail: jvladeck@vladeck.com
Employment law, including discrimination cases
Judith Vladeck, Senior Law Partner

Offices and agencies generally appear in alphabetical order, except when specific order is requested by listee.

MENTAL HYGIENE

NEW YORK STATE

GOVERNOR'S OFFICE

Governor's Office
Executive Chamber
State Capitol
Albany, NY 12224
518-474-8390 Fax: 518-474-1513
Web site: www.ny.gov

Governor:
    Andrew M Cuomo 518-474-8390
Secretary to the Governor:
    William Mulrow.................................518-474-4246
Counsel to the Governor:
    Alphonso David 518-474-8343
Deputy Secretary, Health:
    Courtney Burke.................................518-408-2500
Director, Communications:
    Melissa DeRosa ....518-474-8418 or 212-681-4640

EXECUTIVE DEPARTMENTS AND RELATED AGENCIES

Alcoholism & Substance Abuse Services, Office of
1450 Western Ave
Albany, NY 12203
518-473-3460 Fax: 518-457-5474
e-mail: communications@oasas.ny.gov
Web site: www.oasas.ny.gov

501 7th Ave
8th Fl
New York, NY 10018
646-728-4533

Commissioner:
    Arlene Gonzalez-Sanchez..........................518-457-2061
Executive Deputy Commissioner:
    Sean M. Byrne 518-457-1758
Director, Public Information & Communications:
    Susan A Craig, MPH...............518-457-8299/fax: 518-485-6014
Office & Wellness & Medical Direction (Acting):
    Charles W Morgan, MD...........................845-359-8500
Director, Internal Audit:
    Steven Shrager 518-485-2255
Affirmative Action Officer:
    Loretta Poole..................................646-728-4530
Director, Office of Statewide Field Operations:
    Kathleen Caggiano-Siino 518-457-1758

Fiscal Administration Division
Associate Commissioner:
    P David Sawicki 518-457-5312
Director, Facility Evaluation & Inspection Unit:
    John Van Horn 518-485-2246
Director, Bureau of Capital Management:
    Jeff Emad 518-457-2545
Director, Budget Management:
    Tara Gabriel 518-485-2193
Director, Bureau of Health Care Financing & 3rd Party Reimbursement:
    Laurie Felter 518-457-2545

Quality Assurance & Performance Improvement Division
Associate Commissioner:
    Charles W Monson...............................518-485-2257
Director, Bureau of Standards Compliance:
    William Lachanski 518-485-2255

Prevention, Housing, Technology & Management Services Division
Acting Associate Commissioner:
    Mary Ann DiChristopher 518-485-6022
Director, Management Services:
    Vacant..518-485-6689

Outcome Management & System Information Division
Associate Commissioner:
    William F. Hogan 518-485-2322
Director, Bureau of State/Local Planning & Outcome Mgmt:
    Vacant..518-485-2322
Director, Bureau of Research, Epidemiology & Practice Improvement:
    Vacant..518-485-5989

Developmental Disabilities Planning Council
99 Washington Ave
12th Fl, Ste 1230
Albany, NY 12210
518-486-7505 or 800-395-3372 Fax: 518-402-3505
e-mail: ddpc@ddpc.ny.gov
Web site: www.ddpc.ny.gov

Chairperson:
    Rose Marie Toscano 518-486-7505
Vice Chairperson:
    Ansley Bacon, PhD..............................518-486-7505
Executive Director:
    Sheila M Carey 518-486-7505
    e-mail: sheila.carey@ddpc.ny.gov
Deputy Director-Program Development Specialist:
    Anna Lobosco 518-486-7505
    e-mail: anna.lobosco@ddpc.ny.gov
Public Information Officer:
    Thomas F Lee 518-486-7505/fax: 518-486-3505
    e-mail: thomas.lee@ddpc.ny.gov

Education Department
State Education Bldg
89 Washington Ave
Albany, NY 12234
518-474-3852 Fax: 518-486-5631
Web site: www.nysed.gov

Commissioner, University President:
    MaryEllen Elia 518-474-5844
Assistant to the Commissioner:
    Christopher J Halpin............................518-474-5845
Acting Counsel & Deputy Commissioner, Legal Affairs:
    Erin O'Grady 518-474-6400
Chief of Staff & Deputy Commissioner, Innovation:
    Allison Armour-Garb 518-486-1713

Office of the Professions......................fax: 518-474-1449
    89 Washington Ave, EB, 2nd Fl, West Mezz, Albany, NY 12234
    Fax: 518-474-1449
    Web site: www.op.nysed.gov
Deputy Commissioner:
    Douglas Lentivech 518-486-1765
    e-mail: opopr@mail.nysed.gov

Offices and agencies generally appear in alphabetical order, except when specific order is requested by listee.

Office of Professional Responsibility
Director:
Harrison Fisher 518-474-3817 x440
e-mail: opexdir@mail.nysed.gov

Professional Education Program Review
Director:
William Murphy 518-474-3817 x300
e-mail: opprogs@mail.nysed.gov

Professional Licensing Services
Acting Director:
Susan Naccarato 518-474-3817 x340
e-mail: opdpls@mail.nysed.gov

Office of Adult Career & Continuing Education Services
(ACCES) . . . . .fax: 518-474-8802
One Commerce Plz, Rm 1606, Albany, NY 12234
Fax: 518-474-8802
Web site: www.vesid.nysed.gov
Deputy Commissioner:
Kevin Smith 518-474-2714
Assistant Commissioner:
Deborah Brown-Jackson. 518-473-4818

Fiscal & Administrative Services
Coordinator:
Rosemary Johnson 518-486-4038

Program Development & Special Ed Policy
Coordinator:
Pat Geary 518-486-3220

Quality Assurance - Statewide Special Education
Statewide Coordinator:
James DeLorenzo 518-402-3353

State School for the Blind at Batavia
2A Richmond Ave, Batavia, NY 14020
Superintendent:
Erin Fairben 585-343-5384

Vocational Rehabilitation Operations
Assistant Commsioner:
Debora Brown-Jackson 518-402-3955
e-mail: dbrowngr@mail.nysed.gov

Mental Health, Office of
44 Holland Ave
Albany, NY 12229
518-474-4403 Fax: 518-474-2149
Web site: www.omh.ny.gov

Acting Commissioner:
Ann Marie T Sullivan MD 518-474-4403
Executive Deputy Commissioner:
Martha Schaefer Hayes 518-474-7056/fax: 518-473-4690
Medical Director:
Lloyd I Sederer, MD. . . . . .212-330-1650 x 360
Deputy Commissioner & Counsel:
Joshua Pepper 518-474-1331/fax: 518-473-7863

Division of Adult Services
Senior Deputy Commissioner & Division Director:
Robert Myers, PhD 518-486-4327/fax: 518-473-4690
State Operated Children's & Adult Svcs: Senior Associate
Commissioner/Deputy Director:
Jayne Van Bramer 518-474-4447/fax: 518-473-7926

Division of Integrated Community Services for Children &
Families
Associate Commissioner:
Donna Bradbury 518-473-6328/fax: 518-473-4690

Center for Human Resource Management
Director:
J. Lynn Heath. 518-474-0171/fax: 518-474-7536

Center for Information Technology
Deputy Commissioner & CIO:
John Norton 518-474-7359/fax: 518-473-2778

Division of Forensic Services
Associate Commissioner:
Donna Hall, PhD 518-549-5000/fax: 518-549-5090

Facilities

NYC Children's Center-Bronx Campus
1000 Waters Place, Bronx, NY 10461-2799
Acting Executive Director:
Anita Daniels. 718-239-3600/fax: 718-862-3669

Bronx Psychiatric Center
1500 Waters Place, Bronx, NY 10461-2796
Executive Director:
Pamela Turner 718-862-3300/fax: 718-826-4858

Brooklyn Children's Center
1819 Bergen St, Brooklyn, NY 11233
Acting Executive Director:
Anita Daniels. 718-613-3100/fax: 718-221-4500

Buffalo Psychiatric Center
400 Forest Ave, Buffalo, NY 14213-1298
Acting Executive Director:
Celia Spacone, PhD. 716-816-2001/fax: 716-885-0710

Capital District Psychiatric Center
75 New Scotland Ave, Albany, NY 12208-3474
Executive Director:
William Dickson 518-549-6000/fax: 518-549-6804

Central New York Psychiatric Center
PO Box 300, Marcy, NY 13404-0300
Acting Director:
Peter Russell 315-765-3620/fax: 315-765-3629

Creedmoor Psychiatric Center
79-25 Winchester Blvd, Queens Village, NY 11427-2199
Executive Director:
Ann Marie Barbarotta 718-264-3600/fax: 718-264-3635

Elmira Psychiatric Center
100 Washington St, Elmira, NY 14902-1527
Executive Director:
Mark Stephany 607-737-4738/fax: 607-737-9080

Greater Binghamton Health Center
425 Robinson St, Binghamton, NY 13904-1775
Acting Executive Director:
Mark Stephany 607-773-4082/fax: 607-773-4387

Hutchings Psychiatric Center
620 Madison St, Syracuse, NY 13210-2319
Executive Director:
Mark Cattalani. 315-426-3632/fax: 315-426-3603

Kingsboro Psychiatric Center
681 Clarkson Ave, Brooklyn, NY 11203-2199
Executive Director:
Deborah Parchment. 718-221-7395/fax: 718-221-7206

Kirby Forensic Psychiatric Center
600 East 125th St, Wards Island, NY 10035
Executive Director:
Vinny Miccoli 646-672-5858/fax: 646-672-6446

Manhattan Psychiatric Center
600 East 125th St, Wards Island, NY 10035-6098

Offices and agencies generally appear in alphabetical order, except when specific order is requested by listee.

Executive Director:
   Vinny Miccoli 646-672-5858/fax: 646-672-6446

Mid-Hudson Forensic Psychiatric Center
2834 Route 17-M, New Hampton, NY 10958
Executive Director:
   Joseph Freebern 845-374-8700/fax: 845-374-8861

Mohawk Valley Psychiatric Center
1400 Noyes St, Utica, NY 13502-3082
Acting Executive Director:
   Mark Cattalani 315-738-4404/fax: 315-738-4414

Nathan S Kline Institute for Psychiatric Research
140 Old Orangeburg Rd, Orangeburg, NY 10952-1197
Director:
   Donald C. Goff, MD 845-398-5500/fax: 845-398-5510

New York Psychiatric Institute
1051 Riverside Dr, New York, NY 10032-2695
Director:
   Jeffrey A Lieberman, MD 212-543-5000/fax: 212-543-5200

Pilgrim Psychiatric Center
998 Crooked Hill Rd, West Brentwood, NY 11717-1087
Executive Director:
   Kathy O'Keefe 631-761-2616/fax: 631-761-2194

Queens Children's Psychiatric Center
74-03 Commonwealth Blvd, Bellerose, NY 11426-1890
Acting Executive Director:
   Anita Daniels 718-264-4500/fax: 718-740-0968

Rochester Psychiatric Center
1111 Elmwood Ave, Rochester, NY 14620-3972
Executive Director:
   Elizabeth Suhre 585-241-1594/fax: 585-241-1424

Rockland Children's Psychiatric Center
2 First Avenue, Orangeburg, NY 10962-1199
Acting Executive Director:
   Christopher Tavella PhD 845-359-7400/fax: 845-680-8900

Rockland Psychiatric Center
140 Old Orangeburg Rd, Orangeburg, NY 10962-1196
Executive Director:
   Christopher Tavella, PhD 845-359-1000/fax: 845-680-5580

Sagamore Children's Psychiatric Center
197 Half Hollow Rd, Dix Hills, NY 11746
Acting Executive Director:
   Kathy O'Keefe 631-370-1700/fax: 631-370-1714

South Beach Psychiatric Center
777 Seaview Ave, Staten Island, NY 10305-3499
Executive Director:
   Roseanne Gaylor 718-667-2709/fax: 718-667-2344

St Lawrence Psychiatric Center
1 Chimney Point Dr, Ogdensburg, NY 13669-2291
Executive Director:
   Tim Farrell 315-541-2112/fax: 315-541-2041

Western New York Children's Psychiatric Center
1010 East & West Rd, West Seneca, NY 14224-3699
Acting Executive Director:
   David Privett, LCSW 716-677-7000/fax: 716-675-6455

Office of Consumer Affairs
Director:
   John Allen 518-473-6579/fax: 518-474-8998

Office of Financial Management
Deputy Commissioner & Chief Financial Officer:
   Emil Slane 518-474-3631/fax: 518-473-4690

Office of Public Affairs
Director:
   Benjamin Rosen 518-474-6540/fax: 518-473-3456

Office of Quality Management
Deputy Commissioner:
   Marcia Fazio 518-474-6587

NYS Office for People with Developmental Disabilities
44 Holland Ave
Albany, NY 12229
866-946-9733 or TTY: 866-933-4889 Fax: 518-474-1335
Web site: www.opwdd.ny.gov

Acting Commissioner:
   Kerry Delaney 518-473-1997
Director, Advocacy Services:
   Deborah Franchini 518-473-1997
General Counsel:
   Roger Bearden 518-473-1873
Deputy Commissioner, Enterprise Solutions:
   Kevin Valenchis 518-473-9697
Director, Legislative & Intergovernmental Affairs:
   Greg Roberts 518-473-8084
Affirmative Action/Equal Opportunity:
   Keith Gilmore 518-473-8084
Director, Internal Audit:
   James Nellegar 518-474-4376

New York City Regional Office
75 Morton St, New York, NY 10014
Director:
   Donna Limiti 212-229-3231/fax: 212-229-3234

Information Support Services
Balltown & Consaul Roads, Schenectady, NY 12304
Director:
   Dianne Henk 518-473-1997

Developmental Disabilities Services Offices - State Operations

Bernard Fineson Developmental Disabilities Services Office

Hillside Complex Bldg 12, 80-45 Winchester Blvd, Queens Vlg, NY 11427
Director:
   Jan Williamson 718-217-5890

Brooklyn Developmental Disabilities Services Office
888 Fountain Ave, Brooklyn, NY 11208
Director:
   Sheryl Minter-Brooks 718-642-6000/fax: 718-642-6282

Broome Developmental Disabilities Services Office
249 Glenwood Rd, Binghamton, NY 13905
Director:
   Mark Lankes 607-770-0211/fax: 607-770-8037

Capital District Developmental Disabilities Services Office

Balltown & Consaul Rds, Schenectady, NY 12304
Acting Director:
   Stephanie Dunham 518-370-7331/fax: 518-370-7401

Policy Areas

Offices and agencies generally appear in alphabetical order, except when specific order is requested by listee.

Central New York Developmental Disabilities Services Office

101 W Liberty St, Box 550, Rome, NY 13442
Deputy Director:
Lynette O'Brien . . . . 315-336-2300 or 315-473-2949
fax: 315-339-5456

Finger Lakes Developmental Disabilities Services Office

620 Westfall Rd, Rochester, NY 14620
Director:
Michael Feeney 585-461-8500/fax: 585-461-8764

Hudson Valley Developmental Disabilities Services Office

Admin Bldg, 2 Ridge Rd, PO Box 470, Thiells, NY 10984
Director:
Catherine Varano 845-947-6000/fax: 845-947-6004

Long Island Developmental Disabilities Services Officezz

45 Mall Dr, Ste 1, Commack, NY 11725
Deputy Director:
Barry Ockner 631-493-1701/fax: 631-493-1803

Metro New York Developmental Disabilities Services Office

75 Morton St, New York, NY 10014
Deputy Director:
Joyce White 646-766-3471

Staten Island Developmental Disabilities Services Office

1150 Forest Hill Rd, Staten Island, NY 10314
Director:
Sheryl Minter-Brooks 718-983-5321/fax: 718-983-9768

Sunmount Developmental Disabilities Services Office
2445 State Rte 30, Tupper Lake, NY 12986-2502
Acting Director:
Stephanie Dunham 518-359-3311/fax: 518-359-2276

Taconic Developmental Disabilities Services Office
26 Center Circle, Wassaic, NY 12592
Deputy Director:
Jackie DeVille 845-877-6821/fax: 845-877-9177

Western New York Developmental Disabilities Services Office

1200 East & West Rd, West Seneca, NY 14224

Director:
Kirk Maurer 716-674-6310/fax: 716-674-7488

Institute for Basic Research in Developmental Disabilities
1050 Forest Hill Rd, Staten Island, NY 10314
Director:
Donna Limiti 718-983-5233

JUDICIAL SYSTEM AND RELATED AGENCIES

Mental Hygiene Legal Service

1st Judicial Dept
41 Madison Ave, 26th Fl, New York, NY 10010
Director:
Marvin Bernstein 212-779-1734/fax: 212-779-7899

2nd Judicial Dept
170 Old Country Rd, Rm 500, Mineola, NY 11501
Director:
Michael D Neville 516-493-3976/fax: 646-963-6640

3rd Judicial Dept
40 Steuben St, Ste 501, Albany, NY 12207-2109
Web site: www.nycourts.gov/ad3/mhls/index.html
Director:
Sheila E Shea 518-451-8710/fax: 518-453-6915

4th Judicial Dept
50 East Ave, Ste 402, Rochester, NY 14604
Web site: www.courts.state.ny.us/ad4/mhls/
Director:
Emmett J Creahan 585-530-3050
Deputy Director:
Kevin Wilson 585-530-3050/fax: 585-530-3079

NEW YORK STATE LEGISLATURE

See Legislative Branch in Section 1 for additional Standing Committee and Subcommittee information.

Assembly Standing Committees

Alcoholism & Drug Abuse
Chair:
Linda Rosenthal (D) 518-455-5802
Ranking Minority Member:
Mark Johns (R) 518-455-5784

Mental Health
Chair:
Aileen Gunther (D) 518-455-5355
Ranking Minority Member:
Steven Katz (R) 518-455-5783

Senate Standing Committees

Mental Health & Developmental Disabilities
Chair:
Robert G Ortt (R) 518-455-2024
Ranking Minority Member:
Jesse Hamilton (D) 518-455-2431

Offices and agencies generally appear in alphabetical order, except when specific order is requested by listee.

PRIVATE SECTOR

AIM Services Inc
4227 Route 9, Saratoga Springs, NY 12866
518-587-3208 Fax: 518-587-7236
e-mail: aimservices@aimservicesinc.org
Web site: www.aimservicesinc.org
Residential & home-based services for individuals with developmental disabilities & traumatic brain injuries
June MacClelland, Executive Director

Albert Einstein College of Medicine - Division of Substance Abuse
260 E 161 Street, Track Level, Bronx, NY 10451
718-993-3397 Fax: 718-993-2460
e-mail: schurch@dosa.aecom.yu.edu
Web site: www.einsteinrecovery.org
Sarah Church, PhD, Director

AMAC, Association for Metroarea Autistic Children
25 W 17th St, New York, NY 10011
212-645-5005 Fax: 212-645-0170
e-mail: rica@amac.org
Web site: www.amac.org
Providing lifelong services to austistic & special needs children & adults; specializing in applied behavior analysis (ABA) methodology; serving ages 2 years to adults, schools, camps, group homes
Frederica Blausten, Executive Director

Association for Addiction Professionals of New York
PO Box 4053, Albany, NY 12204
877-862-2769 Fax: 585-394-1111
e-mail: info@appnycounselor.com
Web site: www.aapnycounselor.com
Alcohol & chemical dependency counselor organization; addiction treatment & prevention
Ferd Haverly, President

Association for Community Living
632 Plank Road, Suite 110, Clifton Park, NY 12065
518-688-1682 Fax: 518-688-1686
e-mail: info@aclnys.org
Web site: www.aclnys.org
Membership organization for agencies that provide housing & rehab services to individuals diagnosed with serious mental illness
Antonia Lasicki, Director

Association for Eating Disorders - Capital Region
PO Box 3123, Saratoga Springs, NY 12866
518-464-9043
e-mail: CRAEDOffice@GMail.com
Web site: www.craed.org
Support & referral services, wellness programs & education for recovering individuals, parents & health professionals
William Friske, Treasurer

AHRC New York City
83 Maiden Lane, New York, NY 10038
212-780-2500 or 212-780-2692 Fax: 212-780-2353
e-mail: webmaster@ahrcnyc.org
Web site: www.ahrcnyc.org
Also known as the NYS Chapter of NYSARC, Inc. Social services, education, medical services, advocacy & public information on developmental disabilities
Michael Goldfarb, Executive Director

Brain Injury Association of NYS (BIANYS)
10 Colvin Ave, Albany, NY 12206
518-459-7911 or 800-444-6443 Fax: 518-482-5285
e-mail: info@bianys.org
Web site: www.bianys.org
Public education & advocacy for persons with brain injury & their families

Judith I Avner, Executive Director

Cerebral Palsy Associations of New York State
330 W 34th Street, 15th Floor, New York, NY 10001
212-947-5770 x201 Fax: 212-356-0746
e-mail: sconstantino@cpofnys.org
Web site: www.cpofnys.org
Advocate and provide direct services with and for individuals with cerebral palsy and other significant disabilities and their families through a Statewide Affiliate network.
Susan Constantino, President & CEO

Children's Village (The)
Echo Hills, Dobbs Ferry, NY 10522
914-693-0600 x1201 Fax: 914-674-9208
e-mail: jkohomban@childrensvillage.org
Web site: www.childrensvillage.org
Residential school, located 20 minutes outside of NYC. Treatment & prevention of behavioral problems for youth; residential & community-based services; mental health, education, employment & runaway shelter services
Jeremy Kohomban, PhD, President & Chief Executive Officer

Coalition of Behavioral Health Agencies, Inc (The)
90 Broad St, New York, NY 10004-2205
212-742-1600 x115 Fax: 212-742-2080
e-mail: mailbox@coalitionny.org
Web site: www.coalitionny.org
Advocacy organization representing over 100 nonprofit, community-based mental health and addictions services agencies in NYC.
Phillip A Saperia, Executive Director

Committee of Methadone Program Administrators Inc of NYS (COMPA)
1 Columbus Place, 4th Fl, Albany, NY 12207
518-689-0457 Fax: 518-426-1046
e-mail: compahb@hotmail.com
Web site: www.compa-ny.org
Methadone treatment & substance abuse coalition building; advocacy, community education, standards & regulatory review & policy development
Henry Bartlett, Executive Director

Families Together in NYS Inc
737 Madison Avenue, Albany, NY 12208
518-432-0333 x20 or 888-326-8644 (referr Fax: 518-434-6478
e-mail: info@ftnys.org
Web site: www.ftnys.org
Advocacy for families with children having special social, emotional & behavioral needs; working to improve services & support for children & families
Paige Pierce, Executive Director

Federation Employment & Guidance Service (FEGS) Inc
315 Hudson St, 9th Fl, New York, NY 10013
212-366-8400 Fax: 212-366-8441
e-mail: info@fegs.org
Web site: www.fegs.org
Diversified health & human services system to help individuals achieve their potential at work, at home, at school and in the community
Jonas Waizer, PhD, Chief Operating Officer

Federation of Organizations Inc
One Farmingdale Road, Route 109, West Babylon, NY 11704-6207
631-669-5355 Fax: 631-669-1114
e-mail: bfaron@fedoforg.org
Web site: www.fedoforg.org
Social welfare agency with programs in mental health & aging
Barbara Faron, CEO

Offices and agencies generally appear in alphabetical order, except when specific order is requested by listee.

InterAgency Council of Mental Retardatn & Developmental Disabilities

150 W 30th Street, 15th Floor, New York, NY 10001
212-645-6360 or 917-750-1497 Fax: 212-627-8847
e-mail: mames@iacny.org
Web site: www.iacny.org
A membership association representing non-profit providers of services to individuals with developmental disabilities in the metropolitan NYC area.
Margery E Ames, Executive Director

Jewish Board of Family & Children's Services

120 W 57th St, New York, NY 10019
212-582-9100 or 888-523-2769 Fax: 212-956-5676
e-mail: asiskind@jbfcs.org
Web site: www.jbfcs.org
Mental health services/human services
Alan B Siskind, PhD, Executive Vice President & Chief Executive Officer

Lesbian, Gay, Bisexual & Transgender Community Ctr - Not For Profit

208 W 13th St, New York, NY 10011-7702
212-620-7310 Fax: 212-924-2657
e-mail: enealy@gaycenter.org
Web site: www.gaycenter.org
Mental health counseling, out-patient chemical dependency treatment center, after-school youth services, HIV/AIDS services, advocacy, culutral programs, affordable meeting and conference services, and community-building.
Miriam Yeung, Director, Public Policy

Lifespire

350 5th Ave, Ste 301, New York, NY 10118-0301
212-741-0100 Fax: 212-242-0696
e-mail: info@lifespire.org
Web site: www.lifespire.org
Services for adults with developmental disabilites throughout the five boroughs of New York City
Mark Vanvoorst, Executive Director

Mental Health Association of NYC Inc

666 Broadway, Ste 200, New York, NY 10012
212-254-0333 x307 Fax: 212-529-1959
e-mail: helpdesk@mhaofnyc.org
Web site: www.mhaofnyc.org
Advocacy, public education, community-based services
Giselle Stolper, Executive Director

Mental Health Association of NYS Inc

194 Washington Ave, Ste 415, Albany, NY 12210
518-434-0439 Fax: 518-427-8676
e-mail: info@mhanys.org
Web site: www.mhanys.org
Technical assistance, advocacy, training & resource clearinghouse
Glen Liebman, Chief Executive Officer

NAMI-NYS

260 Washington Ave, Albany, NY 12210
518-462-2000 Fax: 518-462-3811
e-mail: info@naminys.org
Web site: www.naminys.org
Family and consumer advocates for those with mental illness.
Donald P Capone, Executive Director

NY Council on Problem Gambling

100 Great Oaks Boulevard, Suite 126, Albany, NY 12203
518-867-4084 Fax: 518-867-4087
e-mail: jmaney@nyproblemgambling.org
Web site: www.nyproblemgambling.org
Statewide helpline, public information, referral svcs, advocacy for treatment & support svcs, in-service training & workshops
James Maney, Executive Director

NY Counseling Association Inc

PO Box 12636, Albany, NY 12212-2636
518-235-2026 Fax: 518-235-0910
e-mail: nycaoffice@nycounseling.org
Web site: www.nycounseling.org
Counseling professionals in education, mental health, career, employment, rehabilitation & adult development
Donald Newell, Executive Manager

NYS Association of Community & Residential Agencies

99 Pine St, Ste C-110, Albany, NY 12207
518-449-7551 Fax: 518-449-1509
e-mail: nysacra@nysacra.org
Web site: www.nysacra.org
Advocating for agencies that serve individuals with developmental disabilities
Ann M Hardiman, Executive Director

NYS Conference of Local Mental Hygiene Directors

99 Pine Street, Ste C100, Albany, NY 12207
518-462-9422 Fax: 518-465-2695
e-mail: ds@clmhd.org
Web site: www.clmhd.org
Duane Spilde, LCSWR, ACSW, Executive Director

NYS Council for Community Behavioral Healthcare

155 Washington Ave, 2nd Flr, Albany, NY 12210-2329
518-445-2642 Fax: 518-463-2543
e-mail: nyscouncil@nycap.rr.com
Web site: www.nccbh.org
Statewide membertship organization representing community mental health centers
Laurie Cole, Executive Director

NYS Psychological Association

6 Automation Lane, Albany, NY 12205
800-732-3933 Fax: 518-437-0177
e-mail: nyspa@nyspa.org
Web site: www.nyspa.org
Promote & advance profession of psychology; referral service
Tracy Russell, Executive Director

NYSARC Inc

393 Delaware Ave, Delmar, NY 12054
518-439-8311 Fax: 518-439-1893
e-mail: info@nysarc.org
Web site: www.nysarc.org
Developmental disabilities programs, services & advocacy
Marc N Brandt, Executive Director

New York Association of Psychiatric Rehabilitation Services (NYAPRS)

1 Columbia Place, 2nd Floor, Albany, NY 12207
518-436-0008 Fax: 518-436-0044
e-mail: HarveyR@nyaprs.org
Web site: www.nyaprs.org
Promoting the recovery, rehabilitation & rights of New Yorkers with psychiatric disabilities
Harvey Rosenthal, Executive Director

New York Presbyterian Hospital, Department of Psychiatry

180 Fort Washington Ave, Room 270, New York, NY 10032
212-305-9249 Fax: 212-305-4724
e-mail: hjs1@columbia.edu
Psychotherapy & public policy
Herbert J Schlesinger, PhD, Director, Clinical Psychology

Offices and agencies generally appear in alphabetical order, except when specific order is requested by listee.

New York State Rehabilitation Association
155 Washington Ave, Suite 410, Albany, NY 12210
518-449-2976 Fax: 518-426-4329
e-mail: nysra@nyrehab.org
Web site: www.nyrehab.org
Political advocacy, education, communications, networking & referral
services for people with disabilities
Jeff Wise, JD, Vice President

Postgrad Center for Mental Health, Child, Adolescent &
Family-Couples
138 E 26th St, Fl 4, New York, NY 10010-1843
212-576-4190 Fax: 212-576-4129
Psychotherapy & assessment services for children, adolescents & families
Diana Daimwood, Director

Postgraduate Center for Mental Health
344 W 36th St, New York, NY 10018
212-560-6757 Fax: 212-244-2034
e-mail: mholman@pgcmh.org
Web site: www.pgcmh.org
Community-based rehabilitation & employment services for adults with
mental illness
Marcia Holman, CSW/Vice President, Clinical Services

Research Foundation for Mental Hygiene Inc
Riverview Center, 150 Broadway, Suite 301, Menands, NY 12204
518-474-5661 Fax: 518-474-6995
Not-for-profit responsible for administering grants & sponsored research
contracts for the NYS Department of Mental Health & its agencies
Robert E Burke, Managing Director

SUNY at Albany, Professional Development Program, NE States
Addiction
Rockefeller College, 1400 Washington Ave, Room 412A, Albany, NY 12222
518-956-7800 Fax: 518-956-7865
e-mail: lparsons@pdp.albany.edu
Web site: www.pdp.albany.edu
Dissemination of current research & best clinical practice information;
coursework & programs for professionals in the field of addictions
Eugene J Monaco, Director

Samaritan Village Inc
138-02 Queens Blvd, Briarwood, NY 11435
718-206-2000 Fax: 718-657-6982
Web site: www.samaritanvillage.org
Substance abuse treatment; residential & outpatient therapeutic community
Ron Solarz, Executive Director

Schuyler Center for Analysis & Advocacy (SCAA)
150 State St, 4th Fl, Albany, NY 12207
518-463-1896 x29 Fax: 518-463-3364
e-mail: joconnor@scaany.org
Web site: www.scaany.org
Advocacy, analysis & forums on mental health issues.
Jenn O'Connor, Senior Policy Associate

Self Advocacy Association of NYS
Capital District DSO, 500 Balltown Rd, Schenectady, NY 12304
518-382-1454 Fax: 518-382-1594
e-mail: sholmes@earthlink.net
Web site: www.sanys.org
Advocacy for & by persons with developmental disabilities to ensure civil
rights & opportunities
Steve Holmes, Adminstrative Director

Springbrook
2705 State Hwy 28, Oneonta, NY 13820
607-286-7171 Fax: 607-286-7166
e-mail: kennedyp@springbrookny.org
Web site: www.springbrookny.org
Education/mental hygiene
Patricia E Kennedy, Executive Director

St Joseph's Rehabilitation Center Inc
PO Box 470, Saranac Lake, NY 12983
518-891-3950 or 518-891-3801 Fax: 518-891-3986
e-mail: stjoes@sjrcrehab.org
Web site: www.sjrcrehab.org
Inpatient & outpatient alcohol & substance abuse treatment
Robert A Ross, CEO

Statewide Black & Puerto Rican/Latino Substance Abuse Task
Force
2730 Atlantic Ave, Brooklyn, NY 11207-2820
718-647-8275 Fax: 718-647-7889
e-mail: info@nytaskforce.org; nystaskforce@ad.com
Web site: www.nytaskforce.org
Substance abuse, HIV/AIDS & HepC prevention & treatment
Ralph Gonzalez, Executive Director

University at Buffalo, Research Institute on Addictions
1021 Main St, Buffalo, NY 14203-1016
716-887-2566 Fax: 716-887-2252
e-mail: connors@ria.buffalo.edu
Web site: www.ria.buffalo.edu
Alcohol & substance abuse prevention, treatment & policy research
Gerard Connors, Director

YAI/National Institute for People with Disabilities
460 W 34th St, New York, NY 10001-2382
212-273-6110 or 866-2-YAI-LINK Fax: 212-947-7524
e-mail: jmlcares@yai.org
Web site: www.yai.org
Programs, services & advocacy for people with autism, mental retardation &
other developmental disabilities as well as learning disabilities of all ages &
their families; special education & early learning programs
Joel M Levy, Chief Executive Officer

Yeshiva University, A Einstein Clg of Med, Div of Subs Abuse
1510 Waters Place, Bronx, NY 10461
718-409-9450 x312 Fax: 718-892-7115
e-mail: schurch@dosa.aecom.yu.edu
Web site: www.einsteinrecovery.org
Screening, assessment, diagnosis, treatment, support services, research &
teaching & training related to chemical dependency & substance abuse
Sarah Church, PhD, Executive Director

Policy Areas

Offices and agencies generally appear in alphabetical order, except when specific order is requested by listee.

MUNICIPAL & LOCAL GOVERNMENTS

NEW YORK STATE

GOVERNOR'S OFFICE

Governor's Office
Executive Chamber
State Capitol
Albany, NY 12224
518-474-8390 Fax: 518-474-1513
Web site: www.ny.gov

Governor:
  Andrew M Cuomo 518-474-8390
Secretary to the Governor:
  William Mulrow 518-474-4246
Counsel to the Governor:
  Alphonso David 518-474-8343
Director, Communications:
  Melissa DeRosa . . . . .518-474-8418 or 212-681-4640
Director, State Operations:
  James Malatras 518-486-9871

New York City Office
633 Third Ave, New York, NY 10017

EXECUTIVE DEPARTMENTS AND RELATED AGENCIES

Budget, Division of the
State Capitol
Albany, NY 12224
518-473-3885 Fax: 518-474-9041
Web site: www.budget.ny.gov

Director:
  Mary Beth Labate 518-474-2300
First Deputy Director:
  Dominic Colafati. 518-474-8282
Deputy Director:
  David Lara 518-402-4246
Budget Services Head:
  Bob Brondi 518-473-0580
Public Protection Head:
  Ausan Knapp. 518-474-4313
Press Officer:
  Morris Peters. 518-473-3885
  e-mail: dob.sm.press@budget.ny.gov

Civil Service Department
Alfred E Smith State Ofc Bldg
Albany, NY 12239
518-457-2487
Web site: www.cs.ny.gov

Commissioner:
  Jerry Boone. 518-457-3701
Executive Deputy Commissioner:
  Vacant 518-473-5698
Deputy Commissioner, Operations:
  Vacant 518-473-5711
Deputy Commissioner, Administration:
  Deirdre Taylor. 518-473-5694
Deputy Commissioner/General Counsel:
  Ilene Lees 518-473-2624
Director, Workforce & Occupational Planning:
  Vacant 518-473-6411

Director, Financial Administration:
  Vacant 518-473-2269
Director, Human Resources & Administrative Planning:
  Valerie Morrisson 518-473-4306
Public Information Officer:
  Ed Walsh 518-457-9375/fax: 518-473-2372
  e-mail: pio@cs.state.ny.us

Divisions

Classification & Compensation Division
Director:
  Patricia A. Itite 518-474-1011/fax: 518-474-0787

Employee Benefits Division
Director:
  Robert DuBois. 518-473-1977/fax: 518-473-3292
Director, Employee Insurance Programs:
  Mary B Frye 518-457-1771/fax: 518-473-3292
Asst Director, Financial Management & Accounting:
  David Boland 518-402-4264

Employee Health Services Division
Administrator, EHS:
  Maria C Steinbach 518-233-3112/fax: 518-233-3133
Director, Health Services Nursing:
  Mary M McSweeney 518-233-3112

Information Resource Management
Director:
  Frank Slade. 518-473-7516
  e-mail: frank.slade@cs.state.ny.us

Commission Operations & Municipal Assistance Division
Director:
  Nancy B. Kiyonaga 518-473-5022
Local Examinations:
  Will Martin. 518-473-5055

Staffing Services Division
Director:
  Blaine Ryan-Lynch. 518-473-6437
Asst Director:
  Richard Papa. 518-473-6436

Testing Services Division
Director:
  Marcia Dudden. 518-474-2105
Assistant Director:
  Debbi Parrington 518-486-4590

Civil Service Commission
President:
  Jerry Boone. 518-457-3701
Commissioner:
  Caroline Ahl 518-473-6598
Commissioner:
  Dennis Hanrahan. 518-473-6598

Criminal Justice Services, Division of
80 South Swan Street
Albany, NY 12210
518-457-5837 or 800-262-3252 Fax: 518-457-3089
e-mail: infobcjc@dcjs.ny.gov
Web site: www.criminaljustice.ny.gov

Acting Commissioner:
  Sean M Byrne 518-457-1260
Executive Deputy Commissioner:
  Michael C Green. 518-457-1260
Affirmative Action Officer:
  Wanda Trouche. 518-485-7962

Offices and agencies generally appear in alphabetical order, except when specific order is requested by listee.

Deputy Director, Public Information:
Janine Kava.......................518-457-8828/fax: 518-485-7715
e-mail: janine.kava@dcjs.ny.gov

Human Resources Management
Director:
Karen Davis.....................................518-485-1704

State Finance & Budget
Director, Finance:
Kimberly J Szady............................518-457-6105

Legal Services
Deputy Commissioner & Counsel:
Gina Bianchi......................................518-457-4181

Office of Forensic Services
Director:
Vacant...518-457-4181

Office of Criminal Justice Operations
Director, Human Resources Management:
Joe Morrissey...................................518-485-2995

Office of Justice Information Systems
Deputy Commissioner:
Anne Roest......................................518-485-7176

Office of Public Safety

Law Enforcement Accreditation Program
Deputy Commissioner:
Melvin Perez.....................................518-485-7620
Director:
Debra Bourque...................................518-485-1416

Funding & Program Development Office
Deputy Commissioner:
AnneMarie Strano.............................518-457-8462

Homeland Security & Emergency Services, Division of
1220 Washington Ave
Bldg. 7A
Suite 710
Albany, NY 12242
518-242-5000
Web site: www.dhses.ny.gov

633 Third Ave
32nd Fl
New York, NY 10017
212-867-7060

Commissioner & Director, Office of Counterterrorism:
Jerome M Hauer...............................518-292-2301
Assisant Director, Office of Counterterrorism:
David Sheppard................................518-242-5121
Director, State Office of Emergency Management:
Steven Kuhr....................................518-292-2301
First Deputy Director, Emergency Management:
Greg Brunelle..................................518-242-5200
State Fire Administrator & Director, Fire Prevention:
Bryant Stevens...............518-474-6746/fax: 518-474-3240
e-mail: fire@dhses.ny.gov
Director, Office of Interoperable & Emergency Communications:
Robert Barbato................................518-292-4913
e-mail: dhsesoiec@dhses.ny.gov
Public Information Officer:
Rachel McEneny.............518-242-5133/fax: 518-322-4978

Real Property Tax Services, Office of
WA Harriman State Campus
Bldg. 8A
Albany, NY 12227
518-474-2982 Fax: 518-474-9276
e-mail: nysorps@orps.state.ny.us
Web site: www.tax.ny.gov/about/orpts

Acting Secretary of the Board & Assistant Deputy Commissioner:
Susan Savage...................................518-474-6742
State Board Member (Chair):
Matthew Rand..................................518-474-3793
State Board Member:
John M. Bacheller.............................518-474-3793
State Board Member:
Edgar A King...................................518-474-3793
Assistant to the Board:
Darlene Maloney...............................518-474-3793
e-mail: darlene.maloney@tax.ny.gov

Albany (Northern Region)
WA Harriman State Campus, Bldg. 8A, Albany, NY 12227
Regional Director:
Robert Aiken...................518-486-4403/fax: 518-435-8593
e-mail: orpts.northern@tax.ny.gov

Batavia (Western Region)
Genesee County Bldg 2, 3837 W Main Rd, Batavia, NY 14020
Regional Director:
Christine Bannister.............585-343-4363/fax: 585-435-8598
e-mail: orpts.western@tax.ny.gov

Long Island Satellite Office
250 Veterans Memorial Hgwy, Rm 4A-6, Hauppauge, NY 11788
Manager:
Steve Hartnett..................631-595-4071/fax: 518-435-8572
e-mail: orpts.southern@tax.ny.gov

South
44 S. Broadway, 6th Floor, White Plains, NY 10601
Regional Director:
John Wolham...................914-215-6300/fax: 518-435-8498
e-mail: orpts.southern@tax.ny.gov

Ray Brook Satellite Office
884 NYS Rte 86, PO Box 309, Ray Brook, NY 12977
Regional Director:
Robert Aiken...................518-891-1780/fax: 518-435-8593
e-mail: orpts.raybrook@tax.ny.gov

Syracuse (Central Region)
333 E. Washington St, Syracuse, NY 13202
Regional Director:
Teresa Frank...................315-471-2347/fax: 315-435-8583
e-mail: orpts.central@tax.ny.gov

State Comptroller, Office of the
633 Third Ave
31st Fl
New York, NY 10017-6754
212-681-4491 Fax: 212-681-4468

110 State St
15th Fl
Albany, NY 12236-0001
518-474-4044
Fax: 518-473-3004

State Comptroller:
Thomas P DiNapoli.................518-474-4040 or 212-681-4469

Offices and agencies generally appear in alphabetical order, except when specific order is requested by listee.

Deputy Comptroller, Budget & Policy Analysis:
Robert Ward 518-473-4333
Assistant Comptroller, Labor Affairs:
Kathy McCormack 518-473-8409

Executive Office
First Deputy Comptroller:
Pete Grannis .518-474-2909 or 212-681-4469
Chief of Staff:
Shawn Thompson 518-474-4044
Deputy Comptroller & Chief Information Officer:
Kevin Belden 518-486-4349
Director, Enterprise Applications & IT Business Management:
Mary Anne Barry . . . . .518-474-8089 or 212-681-4840
Director, Communications:
Jennifer Freeman . . . . .518-474-4015 or 518-473-8940
Assistant Comptroller, Business Communications:
Ellen Evans . . . . .518-474-4040 or 212-681-4489
Deputy Comptroller, Office of the State Deputy Comptroller for the City of New York:
Ken Bleiwas 212-383-3905

Human Resources & Administration
Deputy Comptroller, Human Resources & Administration:
Angela Dixon 518-474-5512
Assistant Comptroller, Administration:
Larry Appel 518-402-3043
Director, Financial Administration:
Brian Matthews 518-474-2709
Director, Management Services:
Beth Bristol 518-486-7433

Inspector General
Inspector General, Internal Audit:
Stephen Hillerman 518-549-2393

Intergovernmental Affairs
Deputy Comptroller:
Cathy Calhoun 212-402-3234

Legal Services
General Counsel:
Nancy Groenwegen 518-474-3444
Special Counsel for Ethics:
Barbara Smith 518-408-3855

Operations
Executive Deputy Comptroller:
Joan Sullivan 518-408-4103
Deputy Director, Payroll, Accounting and Revenue Services (PARS):
Chris Gorka 518-408-4149

Retirement
Deputy Comptroller:
Kevin Murray 518-474-2600

State Government Accountability
Executive Deputy Comptroller:
Andrew SanFilippo 518-474-4593
Deputy Comptroller:
Elliot Pagliaccio 518-473-3596
Assistant Comptroller:
Jerry Barber 518-473-0334

Local Government and School Accountability
Deputy Comptroller:
Steve Hancox 518-474-4037
Assistant Comptroller:
John Traylor 518-474-4037

State Department
One Commerce Plaza
99 Washington Avenue
Albany, NY 12231
518-474-4750 Fax: 518-474-4765
Web site: www.dos.ny.gov

123 William St
New York, NY 10038
212-417-5801
Fax: 212-417-5805

Secretary of State:
Cesar A Perales 518-474-0050
First Deputy Secretary of State:
Daniel Shapiro 518-474-4750
Deputy Secretary of State, Public Affairs:
Vacant 212-417-5800
Counsel:
Susan L. Watson 518-474-6740/fax: 518-473-9211
Assistant Secretary of State, Communications:
Vacant 518-474-4752/fax: 518-474-4597
e-mail: info@dos.state.ny.us

Local Government & Community Services
Deputy Secretary of State:
Dierdre Scozzafava 518-473-3355

Coastal Resources & Waterfront Revitalization Division
Director:
George Stafford 518-474-6000
e-mail: coastal@dos.state.ny.us

Code Enforcement & Administration Division
Director:
Ronald E Piester 518-474-4073/fax: 518-486-4487
e-mail: codes@dos.state.ny.us

Community Services Division
Director:
Veronica Cruz 518-474-5741/fax: 518-486-4663
e-mail: commserv@dos.state.ny.us

Local Government Services Division
Deputy Secretary of State:
Dierdre Scozzafava 518-473-3355/fax: 518-474-6572
e-mail: localgov@dos.ny.gov

Open Government Committee
Executive Director:
Robert J Freeman 518-474-2518/fax: 518-474-1927
e-mail: opengov@dos.state.ny.us

CORPORATIONS, AUTHORITIES AND COMMISSIONS

New York State Assn of Fire Districts
PO Box 1419
Massapequa, NY 11758
631-947-2079 or 800-520-9594 Fax: 631-207-1655
Web site: www.firedistnys.com

President:
Thomas E Herlihy Jr 315-683-5309
e-mail: teherlih@yahoo.com
First Vice President:
Anthony Gallino 631-831-6875
e-mail: digndad@aol.com
Second Vice President:
Thomas J Rinaldi 518-664-6538
e-mail: tom@rinaldi1.com

Offices and agencies generally appear in alphabetical order, except when specific order is requested by listee.

Secretary & Treasurer:
Joseph P DeStefano . . . . 631-947-2079 or 800-520-9594
fax: 516-799-2516
e-mail: dacomish@aol.com
Counsel:
William N Young . . . . 800-349-2904 or 518-456-6767
fax: 518-456-4644
e-mail: byoung@yfkblaw.com

New York State Disaster Preparedness Commission
Building 22, Suite 101
1220 Washington Ave
Albany, NY 12226-2251
518-292-2301 or 518-292-2200 Fax: 518-322-4978
Web site: www.dhses.ny.gov/oem/disaster-prep/

Chairman/Director:
Jerome M Hauer 518-292-2301

NEW YORK STATE LEGISLATURE

See Legislative Branch in Section 1 for additional Standing Committee and Subcommittee information.

Assembly Legislative Commissions

State Federal Relations, Task Force on
Assembly Chair:
Matthew Titone (D) 518-455-4677
Program Manager:
Robert Stern 518-455-3632

Assembly Standing Committees

Cities
Chair:
Michael Benedetto (D) 518-455-5296
Ranking Minority Member:
Joseph Borelli (R) 518-455-4495

Economic Development, Job Creation, Commerce & Industry
Chair:
Robin L Schimminger (D) 518-455-4767
Ranking Minority Member:
Raymond Walter (D) 518-455-4618

Housing
Chair:
Keith L.T. Wright (D) 518-455-4793
Ranking Minority Member:
Michael J Fitzpatrick (R) 518-455-5021

Local Government
Chair:
William B Magnarelli (D) 518-455-4826
Ranking Minority Member:
Christopher Friend (R) 518-455-4538

Transportation
Chair:
David F Gantt (D) 518-455-5606
Ranking Minority Member:
David G McDonough (R) 518-455-4633

Ways & Means
Chair:
Herman D Farrell, Jr (D) 518-455-5491
Ranking Minority Member:
Bob Oaks (R) 518-455-5655

Senate Standing Committees

Cities
Chair:
Andrew Lanza (R) 518-455-3215
Ranking Minority Member:
Daniel Squadron (D) 518-455-2625

Commerce, Economic Development & Small Business
Chair:
Philip Boyle (R) 518-455-3411
Ranking Minority Member:
Timothy Kennedy (D) 518-455-2426

Finance
Chair:
John A DeFrancisco (R) 518-455-3511
Ranking Minority Member:
Liz Krueger (D) 518-455-2297

Housing, Construction & Community Development
Chair:
Catharine M Young (R) 518-455-3563
Ranking Minority Member:
Adriano Espaillat (D) 518-455-2041

Local Government
Chair:
Kathleen Marchione (R) 518-455-2381
Ranking Minority Member:
Marc Panepinto (D) 518-455-2760

Transportation
Chair:
Joseph E Robach (R) 518-455-2909
Ranking Minority Member:
Martin Malave Dilan (D) 518-455-2177

PRIVATE SECTOR

Association of Fire Districts of the State of NY Inc
948 North Bay Avenue, North Massapequa, NY 11758-2581
516-799-8575 or 800-520-9594 Fax: 516-799-2516
e-mail: FNOC@aol.com
Web site: www.firedistnys.com
Obtain greater economy in the administration of fire district affairs
Frank A Nocerino, Secretary-Treasurer

Association of Towns of the State of New York
150 State St, Albany, NY 12207
518-465-7933 Fax: 518-465-0724
e-mail: jhaber@nytowns.org
Web site: www.nytowns.org
Advocacy, education for local government
G Jeffrey Haber, Executive Director

Citizens Budget Commission
One Penn Plaza, Ste 640, New York, NY 10119
212-279-2605 Fax: 212-868-4745
e-mail: cmb2@ls2.nyu.edu
Web site: www.cbcny.org
Nonpartisan, nonprofit civic organization devoted to influencing constructive change in the finances and services of New York City and New York State government
Charles Brecher, Executive VP & Director, Research

Offices and agencies generally appear in alphabetical order, except when specific order is requested by listee.

Citizens Union of the City of New York
299 Broadway, Rm 700, New York, NY 10007-1978
212-227-0342 Fax: 212-227-0345
e-mail: citizens@citizensunion.org
Web site: www.citizensunion.org
Government watchdog organization; city & state public policy issues;
political and government reform
Dick Dadey, Executive Director

Columbia Law School, Legislative Drafting Research Fund
435 W 116th St, New York, NY 10027-7297
212-854-2640 or 212-854-2638 Fax: 212-854-7946
e-mail: rb34@columbia.edu
Web site: www.law.columbia.edu
State & local government law, property law & election law
Richard Briffault, Vice Dean & Executive Director

Council of State Governments, Eastern Conference
100 Wall St, 20th Fl, New York, NY 10005
212-482-2320 Fax: 212-482-2344
e-mail: alan@csgeast.org
Web site: www.csgeast.org
Training, research & information sharing for state government officials
Alan V Sokolow, Regional Director

Cullen & Dykman LLP
100 Quentin Roosevelt Blvd, Garden City Ctr, Garden City, NY 11530-4850
516-357-3703 Fax: 516-396-9155
e-mail: gfishberg@cullenanddykman.com
Web site: www.cullenanddykman.com
Municipal & labor law
Gerard Fishberg, Partner

Fordham University, Department of Political Science
441 E Fordham Road, Bronx, NY 10458
718-817-3960 Fax: 718-817-3972
e-mail: kantor@fordham.edu
Urban politics, urban economic development and the social condition of
American cities.
Paul Kantor, Professor of Political Science

Fund for the City of New York
121 Ave of the Americas, 6th Fl, New York, NY 10013
212-925-6675 Fax: 212-925-5675
e-mail: mmccormick@fcny.org
Web site: www.fcny.org
Innovations in policy, programs, practice & technology to advance the
functioning of government & nonprofit organizations in NYC & beyond
Mary McCormick, President

Genesee Transportation Council
50 West Main Street, Suite 8112, Rochester, NY 14614-1227
585-232-6240 Fax: 585-262-3106
e-mail: rperrin@gtcmpo.org
Web site: www.gtcmpo.org
Nine-county metropolitan planning organization
Richard Perrin, Executive Director

Hawkins Delafield & Wood LLP
One Chase Manhattan Plaza, 42nd Fl, New York, NY 10005
212-820-9300 Fax: 212-820-9391
e-mail: hzucker@hawkins.com
Web site: www.hawkins.com
Transportation, municipal & local government law
Howard Zucker, Partner

Housing Action Council Inc - Not For Profit
55 S Broadway, Tarrytown, NY 10591
914-332-4144 Fax: 914-332-4147
e-mail: rnoonan@affordablehomes.org
Financial feasibility, land use & zoning & affordable housing
Rosemarie Noonan, Executive Director

Institute of Public Administration/NYU Wagner
295 Lafayette St, 2nd Floor, New York, NY 10012-9604
212-998-7400
e-mail: wagner@nyu.edu
Web site: www.wagner.nyu.edu
Non-profit research, consulting & educational institute
David Mammen, President

KPMG LLP
345 Park Ave, Rm 4095, New York, NY 10154
212-758-9700 Fax: 212-409-8340
e-mail: jrmiller@kpmg.com
Web site: www.kpmg.com
Accounting
Michael D V Rake, Chairman, International & Senior Partner

League of Women Voters of New York State
62 Grand St, Albany, NY 12207-2712
518-465-4162 Fax: 518-465-0812
e-mail: lwvny@lwvny.org
Web site: www.lwvny.org
Public policy issues forum; good government advocacy
Kristen Hansen, Executive Director

MBIA Insurance Corporation
113 King St, Armonk, NY 10504
914-273-4545 Fax: 914-765-3555
e-mail: ethel.geisinger@mbia.com
Web site: www.mbia.com
Insure municipal bonds & structured transactions
Ethel Z Geisinger, Vice President, Government Relations

Manhattan Institute, Center for Civic Innovation
52 Vanderbilt Ave, 2nd Fl, New York, NY 10017
212-599-7000 Fax: 212-599-3494
Web site: www.manhattan-institute.org
Urban policy, reinventing government, civil society
Lindsay Young, Executive Director, Communications

Moody's Investors Service, Public Finance Group
99 Church St, New York, NY 10007
212-553-7780 Fax: 212-298-7113
e-mail: dennis.farrell@moodys.com
Web site: www.moodys.com
Municipal debt ratings & analysis
Dennis M Farrell, Group Managing Director

NY State Association of Town Superintendents of Highways Inc
119 Washington Avenue, Suite 300, Albany, NY 12210
518-694-9313 Fax: 518-694-9314
e-mail: info@nystownhwys.org
Web site: www.nystownhwys.org
Michael K Thompson, Communications Director

NYS Association of Counties
540 Broadway, 5th Floor, Albany, NY 12207
518-465-1473 Fax: 518-465-0506
e-mail: info@NYSAC.org
Web site: www.nysac.org
Lobbying, research & training services
Stephen J Acquario, Executive Director

NYS Conference of Mayors & Municipal Officials
119 Washington Ave, Albany, NY 12210
518-463-1185 Fax: 518-463-1190
e-mail: info@nycom.org
Web site: www.nycom.org
Legislative advocacy for NYS cities & villages
Peter A Baynes, Executive Director

Offices and agencies generally appear in alphabetical order, except when specific order is requested by listee.

NYS Magistrates Association
750 Delaware Ave, Delmar, NY 12054-1124
518-439-1087 Fax: 518-439-1204
e-mail: nysma@juno.com
Web site: www.nysma.net
Association of town & village justices
Tanja Sirago, Executive Director

New York Municipal Insurance Reciprocal (NYMIR)
150 State Street, Albany, NY 12207
518-465-7552 Fax: 518-465-0724
e-mail: kcrawford@kcnymir.org
Web site: www.nymir.org
Property and casualty insurance services for municipalities
Kevin Crawford, Executive Director

New York State Government Finance Officers Association Inc
126 State St, 5th Fl, Albany, NY 12207
518-465-1512 Fax: 518-434-4640
e-mail: info@nysgfoa.org
Web site: www.nysgfoa.org
Membership organization dedicated to the professional management of governmental resources
Maura K Ryan, Executive Director

New York University, Wagner Graduate School
295 Lafayette Street, 2nd Floor, New York, NY 10012
212-998-7400 Fax: 212-995-4162
e-mail: mitchell.moss@nyu.edu
Web site: www.nyu.edu/wagner
Research on urban planning & development, with special emphasis on technology & the future of cities

Mitchell Moss, Professor of Urban Policy & Planning

Syracuse University, Maxwell School of Citizenship & Public Affairs
215 Eggers Hall, Syracuse, NY 13244-1090
315-443-4000 Fax: 315-443-9721
e-mail: sibretsc@maxwell.syr.edu
Capital financing & debt management; public employee pensions; financial management
Stuart Bretschneider, Associate Dean & Chair, Professor of Public
    Administration

Urbanomics
115 Fifth Ave, 3rd Fl, New York, NY 10003
212-353-7464 Fax: 212-353-7494
e-mail: r.armstrong@urbanomics.org
Web site: www.urbanomics.org
Economic development planning studies, market studies, tax policy analyses, program evaluations, economic & demographic forecasts
Regina B Armstrong, Principal

Whiteman Osterman & Hanna LLP
One Commerce Plaza, Albany, NY 12260
518-487-7600 Fax: 518-487-7777
e-mail: lptharp@woh.com
Web site: www.woh.com
Lorraine Power Tharp, Partner

Policy Areas

Offices and agencies generally appear in alphabetical order, except when specific order is requested by listee.

PUBLIC EMPLOYEES

NEW YORK STATE

GOVERNOR'S OFFICE

Governor's Office
Executive Chamber
State Capitol
Albany, NY 12224
518-474-8390 Fax: 518-474-1513
Web site: www.ny.gov

Governor:
　Andrew M Cuomo 518-474-8390
Secretary to the Governor:
　William Mulrow 518-474-4246
Counsel to the Governor:
　Alphonso David 518-474-8343
Deputy Secretary, Public Safety:
　Terrence O'Leary 518-474-3522
Director, Communications:
　Melissa DeRosa . . . . .518-474-8418 or 212-681-4640
First Assistant Counsel:
　Sandi Toll 518-474-8434

EXECUTIVE DEPARTMENTS AND RELATED AGENCIES

Civil Service Department
Alfred E Smith State Ofc Bldg
Albany, NY 12239
518-457-2487 or 877-697-5627
Web site: www.cs.state.ny.us

Commissioner:
　Jerry Boone 518-457-3701
Executive Deputy Commissioner:
　Vacant 518-473-5698
Deputy Commissioner, Operations:
　Vacant 518-473-5711
Deputy Commissioner, Administration:
　Deirdre Taylor 518-473-5694
Deputy Commissioner/General Counsel:
　Ilene Lees 518-473-2624
Director, Workforce & Occupational Planning:
　Vacant 518-473-6411
Director, Financial Administration:
　Vacant 518-473-2269
Director, Human Resources Administrative Planning:
　Valerie Morrison 518-473-4306
Public Information Officer:
　Ed Walsh 518-457-9375/fax: 518-473-2372

Divisions

Classification & Compensation Division
Director:
　Patricia A. Itite 518-474-1011/fax: 518-474-0787

Employee Benefits Division
Director:
　Robert DuBois 518-473-1977/fax: 518-473-3292
Director, Employee Insurance Programs:
　Mary B Frye 518-457-1771/fax: 518-473-3292
Asst Director, Financial Management & Accounting:
　David Boland 518-402-4264

Employee Health Services Division
Administrator, EHS:
　Maria C Steinbach 518-233-3112/fax: 518-233-3133
Director, Health Services Nursing:
　Mary M McSweeney 518-233-3112

Information Resource Management
Director:
　Frank Slade 518-473-7516
　e-mail: frank.slade@cs.state.ny.us

Commission Operations & Municipal Assistance Division
Director:
　Nancy B. Kiyonaya 518-473-5022
Local Examinations:
　Will Martin 518-473-5055

Staffing Services Division
Director:
　Blaine Ryan-Lynch 518-473-6437
Asst Director:
　Richard Papa 518-473-6436

Testing Services Division
Director:
　Marcia Dudden 518-474-2105
Director:
　Debbi Parrington 518-486-4590

Civil Service Commission
President:
　Jerry Boone 518-457-3701
Commissioner:
　Caroline Ahl 518-473-6598
Commissioner:
　Caroline Ahl 518-473-6326
Commissioner:
　Dennis Hanrahan 518-473-6598

Employee Relations, Governor's Office of
Two Empire State Plz
Ste 1201
Albany, NY 12223-1250
518-473-8766 Fax: 518-486-7304
e-mail: info@goer.ny.gov
Web site: www.goer.ny.gov

Director:
　Gary Johnson 518-474-6988/fax: 518-486-7304
Deputy Director, Contract Negotiations & Administration:
　Vacant 518-473-3130/fax: 518-486-7304
Acting General Counsel:
　Michael N Volforte 518-474-4090/fax: 518-486-7304
Director, Administration:
　Mary Hines 518-473-3467/fax: 518-473-6294
Acting Director, Employee Benefits Unit:
　Darryl Decker 518-473-6211/fax: 518-473-6294
Information Security Officer:
　Jeff Reilly 518-486-1305/fax: 518-473-6294
Payroll Benefits Administrator:
　Kelly J. Catman 518-473-3466/fax: 518-486-5602
Director, Workforce & Organizational Development Unit:
　Lori Zwicker 518-474-6772/fax: 518-474-8587
Management/Confidential Affairs:
　Lynda Scalzo 518-473-8317

Labor/Management Committees

Family Benefits Committee
55 Elk St, Rm 301C, Albany, NY 12210-2331
Staff Director:
　Deborah Long Miller 518-473-8091/fax: 518-473-3581

Offices and agencies generally appear in alphabetical order, except when specific order is requested by listee.

NYS/CSEA Discipline Unit.................fax: 518-486-9737
55 Elk St, Rm 301D, Albany, NY 12210-2333
Arbitration Panel Coordinator:
 Linda Ronda...................................518-473-6070

NYS/CSEA Partnership for Education & Training . fax: 518-473-9457
240 Washington Ave Extension, Ste 502, Albany, NY 12203
800-253-4332 or 518-486-7814 Fax: 518-473-9457
Co-Director:
 Jeannine Morell 518-486-7814
Co-Director:
 Peter Trolio...................................518-486-7814

NYS/SSU Joint Labor-Management Committee .... fax: 518-457-9445
55 Elk St, Rm 301-B, Albany, NY 12210
Employee Program Assistant:
 Vacant.......................................518-457-9420

NYS/UUP Labor-Management Committee .... fax: 518-457-9445
55 Elk St, Rm 301-C, Albany, NY 12210
Executive Director:
 Phillip H. Smith..............518-486-4666/fax: 518-486-4667
 e-mail: nysuuplmc@goer.state.ny.us

Statewide Employee Assistance Programs .... fax: 518-486-9796
55 Elk St, Rm 301A, Albany, NY 12210-2316
800-822-0244 Fax: 518-486-9796
Asst Director:
 Karen Dunn 518-486-9769

Public Employment Relations Board
80 Wolf Rd
Albany, NY 12205
518-457-2578 Fax: 518-457-2664
e-mail: perbinfo@perb.ny.gov
Web site: www.perb.ny.gov

Chair:
 Jerome Lefkowitz..............................518-457-2578
Member:
 Sheila S Cole.................................518-457-2578
Executive Director:
 Anthony Zumbolo...............................518-457-2676
Deputy Chair & Counsel:
 William A Herbert 518-457-2614
Secretary to the Board:
 Sheila Talavera...............................518-457-2578

Administration Section
Administrative Officer:
 Mary Beth Purcell.............................518-457-2922

Conciliation Office
Director:
 Kevin B. Flanigan.............................518-457-6014

District Offices

Buffalo
Electric Tower, 535 Washington St, Ste 302, Buffalo, NY 14203
Regional Director:
 Gregory Poland.............716-847-3449/fax: 716-847-3690

New York City
55 Hanson Pl, Ste 700, Brooklyn, NY 11217
Mediator:
 Karen R. Kenney..............718-722-4545/fax: 718-722-4550

Employment Practices & Representation Section
Director:
 Monte Klein 518-457-5973
Asst Director:
 Susan Comenzo.................................518-457-5973

Legal Section
Associate Counsel & Director, Litigation:
 David P Quinn.................................518-457-2678

State Comptroller, Office of the
110 State St, 15th Fl
Albany, NY 12236-0001
518-474-4044 Fax: 518-473-3004
Web site: www.osc.state.ny.us

633 Third Ave, 31st Fl
New York, NY 10017-6754
212-681-4491
Fax: 212-681-4468

State Comptroller:
 Thomas P DiNapoli ....518-474-4040 or 212-681-4469

Operations
Executive Deputy Comptroller, Operations:
 Joan Sullivan.................................518-402-4103

 Payroll & Revenue Services Division
 Deputy Comptroller:
  Daniel Berry.................................518-408-4149
 Director, Unclaimed Funds:
  Lawrence Schantz.............................518-473-6438
 Director, State Payroll Services:
  Robin R Rabii................................518-474-3400

Executive Office
First Deputy Comptroller:
 Pete Grannis..................................518-474-2909
Chief of Staff:
 Shawn Thompson...............................518-474-4044
Deputy Comptroller & Chief Information Officer:
 Kevin Belden..................................518-486-4003

Retirement Services
Deputy Comptroller:
 Kevin Murray..................................518-474-2600
Asst Comptroller:
 Nancy Burton..................................518-474-4600

 Accounting Bureau
 Director:
  Michelle Camuglia............................518-474-3670

 Actuarial Bureau
 Actuary:
  Teri Landin..................................518-474-4537

 Benefit Calculations & Disbursements
 Director:
  James Normile 518-474-5556

 Disability Processing/Hearing Administration
 Director:
  Kathy Nowak 518-473-1347

 Member & Employee Services
 Director:
  Ginger Dame..................................518-474-1101

 Retirement Communications
 Director:
  Paul Kentoffio 518-474-7096

Offices and agencies generally appear in alphabetical order, except when specific order is requested by listee.

CORPORATIONS, AUTHORITIES AND COMMISSIONS

New York State Teachers' Retirement System
10 Corporate Woods Dr
Albany, NY 12211-2395
518-447-2900 or 800-348-7298 Fax: 518-447-2695
e-mail: media@nystrs.state.ny.us
Web site: www.nystrs.org

Executive Director:
   Thomas K Lee...................................518-447-2726
General Counsel:
   Joseph J. Indelicato, Jr........................518-447-2722
Actuary:
   Richard Young 518-447-2692
Managing Director Operations:
   Kevin Schaefer 518-447-2730
Director, Member Relations:
   Sheila Gardella 518-447-2684
Manager, Public Information:
   John Cardillo....................518-447-4743/fax: 518-447-2875
   e-mail: john.caradillo@nystrs.org
Managing Director Real Estate:
   David C. Gillian 518-447-2751
Managing Director, Private Equity:
   John W. Virtanen

NEW YORK STATE LEGISLATURE

See Legislative Branch in Section 1 for additional Standing Committee and Subcommittee information.

Assembly Standing Committees

Governmental Employees
Chair:
   Peter J Abbate, Jr (D) 518-455-3053
Ranking Minority Member:
   Nicole Malliotakis (R) 518-455-5716

Labor
Chair:
   Michele Titus (D) 518-455-5668
Ranking Minority Member:
   Karl Brabenec (R)...............................518-455-5991

Senate Standing Committees

Civil Service & Pensions
Chair:
   Martin J Golden (R) 518-455-2730
Ranking Minority Member:
   James Sanders, Jr. (D)...........................518-455-3531

Labor
Chair:
   Jack Martins (R) 518-455-3265
Ranking Minority Member:
   Jose R Peralta (D)...............................518-455-2529

Senate/Assembly Legislative Commissions

Government Administration, Legislative Commission on
Assembly Chair:
   Brian P. Kavanagh (D) 518-455-5506
Senate Vice Chair:
   Vacant..518-455-0000

U.S. GOVERNMENT

EXECUTIVE DEPARTMENTS AND RELATED AGENCIES

US Merit Systems Protection Board
Web site: www.mspb.gov

New York Field Office
   26 Federal Plaza, Room 3137A, New York, NY 10278-0022
Chief Administrative Judge:
   Arthur S. Joseph 212-264-9372/fax: 212-264-1417

US Office of Personnel Management
Web site: www.usajobs.opm.gov

PHILADELPHIA SERVICE CENTER (serving New York)
   William J Green Fed Bldg, Rm 3400, 600 Arch St, Philadelphia, PA 19106
Director:
   Joseph D Stix....................215-861-3031/fax: 215-861-3030
   e-mail: philadelphia@opm.gov

U.S. CONGRESS

See U.S. Congress Chapter for additional Standing Committee and Subcommittee information.

House of Representatives Standing Committees

Oversight and Government Reform
Chair:
   Darrell E. Issa (R-CA) 202-225-3906
Ranking Member:
   Elijah Cummings (D-MD) 202-225-4741
New York Delegate:
   Carolyn B Maloney (D) 202-225-7944
   Subcommittee
   Federal Workforce, Postal Service and the District of Columbia
      Chair:
         Blake Farenthold (R-TX)......................202-225-7742
      Ranking Member:
         Stephen F. Lynch (D-MA)....................202-225-8273

Senate Standing Committees

Homeland Security & Governmental Affairs
Chair:
   Thomas R. Carper (D-DE) 202-224-2441
Ranking Member:
   Tom Coburn (R-OK) 202-224-5754

PRIVATE SECTOR

AFSCME District Council 37
150 State St, Albany, NY 12207
518-436-0665 or 212-815-1550 Fax: 518-436-1066
NYC employees union
Wanda Williams, Director

American Federation of State, County and Municipal Employees (AFSCME)
212 Great Oaks Blvd, Albany, NY 12203
518-869-2245 Fax: 518-869-8649
e-mail: bmcdonnell@afscme.org
Web site: www.afscme.org
Union representing public service & healthcare workers; American Federation of State, County & Municipal Employees
Brian McDonnell, Legislative & Political Director

Offices and agencies generally appear in alphabetical order, except when specific order is requested by listee.

Civil Service Employees Assn of NY (CSEA), Local 1000, AFSCME, AFL-CIO
143 Washington Ave, Albany, NY 12210
518-257-1000 or 800-342-4146 Fax: 518-462-3639
Web site: www.csealocal1000.org
Public/private employees union
Danny Donohue, President

Cornell University, School of Industrial & Labor Relations
356 ILR Research Bldg, Ithaca, NY 14853-3901
607-255-7581 Fax: 607-255-0245
e-mail: klb23@cornell.edu
Web site: www.ilr.cornell.edu
Public sector organizations; leadership; temporary & contract workers; union organizing; & collective bargaining
Kate Bronfenbrenner, Director, Labor Education Research

District Council 37, AFSCME, AFL-CIO
125 Barclay St, New York, NY 10007
212-815-1000 Fax: 212-815-1402
e-mail: dsullivan@dc37.net
Web site: www.dc37.net
NYC employees union
Dennis Sullivan, Director, Research & Negotiations

NYC Board of Education Employees, Local 372/AFSCME, AFL-CIO
125 Barclay Street, 6th Floor, New York, NY 10007
212-815-1372 Fax: 212-815-1347
Web site: www.local372.com
Veronica Montgomery-Costa, President - District Council 37/372

NYS Association of Chiefs of Police Inc
2697 Hamburg Street, Schenectady, NY 12303-3783
518-355-3371 Fax: 518-356-5767
e-mail: nysacop@nycap.rr.com
Web site: www.nychiefs.org
Joseph S Dominelli, Executive Director

NYS Association of Fire Chiefs
1670 Columbia Turnpike, Box 328, East Schodack, NY 12063-0328
518-477-2631 Fax: 518-477-4430
e-mail: tlabelle@nysfirechiefs.com
Web site: www.nysfirechiefs.com
Thomas LaBelle, Executive Director

NYS Correctional Officers & Police Benevolent Association Inc
102 Hackett Blvd, Albany, NY 12209
518-427-1551 or 888-484-7279 Fax: 518-426-1635
e-mail: nyscopba@nyscopba.org
Web site: www.nyscopba.org
Mary Gulino,

NYS Court Clerks Association
170 Duane St, New York, NY 10013
212-941-5700 Fax: 212-941-5705
Kevin E Scanlon, Sr, President

NYS Deputies Association Inc
61 Laredo Dr, Rochester, NY 14624
585-247-9322 Fax: 585-247-6661
e-mail: tross1@rochester.rr.com
Web site: www.nysdeputy.org
Thomas H Ross, Executive Director

NYS Bar Assn, Attorneys in Public Service Cmte
NYS Health Department
433 River St, 5th Fl, Ste 330, Troy, NY 12180-2299
518-402-0748 Fax: 518-402-0751
e-mail: jfh01@health.state.ny.us
Advancing the interests of NY governmental & not-for-profit attorneys
Hon James F Horan, Chair

NYS Law Enforcement Officers Union, Council 82, AFSCME, AFL-CIO
Hollis V Chase Bldg, 63 Colvin Ave, Albany, NY 12206
518-489-8424 Fax: 518-489-8430
e-mail: c82@council82.org
Web site: www.council82.org
Daniel J Valente, Legislative Director

NYS Parole Officers Association
PO Box 5821, Albany, NY 12205-0821
518-393-6541 Fax: 518-393-6541
e-mail: hsj195@localnet.com
Professional association representing NYS parole officers
H Susan Jeffords, President

NYS Sheriffs' Association
27 Elk St, Albany, NY 12207
518-434-9091 Fax: 518-434-9093
e-mail: pkehoe@nysheriffs.org
Web site: www.nysheriffs.org
Peter R Kehoe, Executive Director

New York State Law Enforcement Council
One Hogan Place, New York, NY 10013
212-335-8927 Fax: 212-335-3808
Web site: www.nyslec.org
Founded in 1982 as a legislative advocate for NY's law enforcement community. The members represent leading law enforcement professionals throughout the state. An active voice and participant in improving the quality of justice and a safer NY.
Leroy Frazer, Jr, Coordinator

New York State Public Employees Federation (PEF)
1168-70 Troy-Schenectady Rd, PO Box 12414, Albany, NY 12212
518-785-1900 x211 Fax: 518-783-1117
e-mail: kbrynien@pef.org
Web site: www.nyspef.org
Professional, scientific & technical employees union
Kenneth D Brynien, President

New York State Supreme Court Officers Association
299 Broadway, Suite 1100, New York, NY 10007-1921
212-406-4292 or 212-406-4276 Fax: 212-791-8420
e-mail: lbroderick@nysscoa.org
Web site: www.nysscoa.org
Supreme Court Officers Union
John P McKillop, President

New York State United Teachers/AFT, AFL-CIO
800 Troy-Schenectady Road, Latham, NY 12110-2455
518-213-6000 or 800-342-9810
Web site: www.nysut.org
Richard Iannuzzi, President

Organization of NYS Management Confidential Employees
5 Pine West Plaza, Suite 513, Albany, NY 12205
518-456-5241 or 800-828-6623 Fax: 518-456-3838
e-mail: nysomce@gmail.com
Web site: www.nysomce.org
Professional organization of state management & confidential employees
Barbara Zaron, President

Patrolmen's Benevolent Association
40 Fulton St, 17th Fl, New York, NY 10038
212-233-5531 Fax: 212-233-3952
e-mail: union@nycpba.org
Web site: www.nycpba.org
NYC patrolmen's union
Patrick Lynch, President

Offices and agencies generally appear in alphabetical order, except when specific order is requested by listee.

Police Conference of NY Inc (PCNY)
112 State St, Ste 1120, Albany, NY 12207
518-463-3283 Fax: 518-463-2488
e-mail: pcnyinfo@pcny.org
Web site: www.pcny.org
Advocacy for law enforcement officers
Richard Wells, President

Professional Fire Fighters Association Inc (NYS)
111 Washington Ave, Suite 207, Albany, NY 12210-6511
518-436-8827 Fax: 518-436-8830
e-mail: suite207@nyspffa.org
Web site: www.nyspffa.org
Union representing city, village & town firefighters
Charles Morello, President

Retired Public Employees Association
435 New Karner Road, Albany, NY 12205-3833
518-869-2542 Fax: 518-869-0631
e-mail: mail@rpea.org
Web site: www.rpea.org
Advocacy for retired public employees & their families
Alan Dorn, Executive Director
Anthony Cantore, Legislative Representative

State Employees Federal Credit Union
1239 Washington Avenue, Albany, NY 12206-1067
518-452-8234 Fax: 518-464-5227
Web site: www.sefcu.com
John Gallagher, Director, Internal Audit

Syracuse University, Maxwell School of Citizenship & Public Affairs
215 Eggers Hall, Syracuse, NY 13244-1090
315-443-4000 Fax: 315-443-9721
e-mail: sibretsc@maxwell.syr.edu
Capital financing & debt management; public employee pensions; financial management

Stuart Bretschneider, Associate Dean & Chair, Professor of Public
  Administration

Trooper Foundation-State of New York Inc
3 Airport Park Blvd, Latham, NY 12110-1441
518-785-1002 Fax: 518-785-1003
e-mail: rmincher@nystf.org
Web site: www.nystrooperfoundation.org
Supports programs & services of the NYS Police
Rachael L Mincher, Foundation Administrator

Uniformed Fire Officers Association
225 Broadway, Suite 401, New York, NY 10007
212-293-9300 Fax: 212-292-1560
e-mail: administrator@ufoa.org
Web site: www.ufoa.org
NYC fire officers' union
John J McDonnell, President

United Transportation Union
35 Fuller Road, Suite 205, Albany, NY 12205
518-438-8403 Fax: 518-438-8404
e-mail: sjnasca@aol.com
Web site: www.utu.org
Federal government railroad, bus & airline employees; public employees
Samuel Nasca, Legislative Director

United University Professions
PO Box 15143, Albany, NY 12212-5143
518-640-6600 Fax: 518-640-6698
e-mail: feedback@uupmail.org
Web site: www.uupinfo.org
SUNY labor union of academic & other professional faculty
William E Scheuerman, President

Offices and agencies generally appear in alphabetical order, except when specific order is requested by listee.

REAL PROPERTY

NEW YORK STATE

GOVERNOR'S OFFICE

Governor's Office
Executive Chamber
State Capitol
Albany, NY 12224
518-474-8390 Fax: 518-474-1513
Web site: www.ny.gov

Governor:
Andrew M Cuomo 518-474-8390
Secretary to the Governor:
William Mulrow 518-474-4246
Counsel to the Governor:
Alphonso David 518-474-8343
Director, Communications:
Melissa DeRosa . . . . .518-474-8418 or 212-681-4640
First Assistant Counsel:
Sandi Toll 518-474-8434

EXECUTIVE DEPARTMENTS AND RELATED AGENCIES

General Services, Office of
Corning Tower, 41st Fl
Empire State Plaza
Albany, NY 12242
518-474-3899 Fax: 518-474-1546
Web site: www.ogs.state.ny.us

Commissioner:
RoAnn Destito 518-474-5991
First Deputy Commissioner:
Joseph J Rabito 518-473-6953
Director, Public Affairs:
Heather Groll 518-474-5987/fax: 518-474-3187
e-mail: heather.groll@ogs.ny.gov

Real Estate Planning & Development Group
Director, Real Estate Planning & Development:
James Sproat 518-474-4944
Asst Director, Real Estate Planning & Development:
Robert W Lazarou 518-486-7963
Bureau Chief, Land Management:
Charles Sheifer 518-474-2195
Bureau Chief, Real Estate Planning - Upstate:
Leah Nicholson 518-486-1484

Real Property Management Group
Executive Director:
Eric S McShane 518-474-6057/fax: 518-474-1523
Director, Downstate Regional Buildings:
Kevin Cahill 718-923-4448/fax: 718-923-4451
Assistant Regional Director, Empire State Plaza & Downtown Buildings:
Roger Fortune 518-474-8860/fax: 518-474-4182
Director, Upstate Harriman State Office Campus:
Louis Salerno 518-457-2290/fax: 518-457-8297
Director, Utilities Management:
Paul Cleveland 518-474-5585/fax: 518-485-1678

Law Department
120 Broadway
New York, NY 10271-0332

212-416-8000 or 800-771-7755
Web site: www.ag.ny.gov

State Capitol
Albany, NY 12224-0341
518-474-7330
Fax: 518-473-9909

Attorney General:
Eric T Schneiderman . . . . .212-416-8050 or 518-474-7330

Social Justice
Executive Deputy Attorney General:
Alvin L Braggs, Jr 212-416-8450/fax: 212-416-8942

Civil Rights Bureau
Bureau Chief:
Kristen Clarke 212-416-8250/fax: 212-416-8074

Investor Protection Bureau
Bureau Chief:
Chad Johnson 212-416-8225/fax: 212-416-8816

State Counsel
Chief Deputy Attorney General:
Harlan Levy 212-416-8525

Claims Bureau
Bureau Chief:
Katharine Brooks . . . . .518-776-2300 or 212-416-8913

Real Property Bureau
Bureau Chief:
Alison Crocker 518-776-2700

Real Property Tax Services, Office of
WA Harriman State Campus
Albany, NY 12227
518-474-2982 Fax: 518-474-9276
e-mail: nysorps@orps.state.ny.us
Web site: www.tax.ny.gov/about/orpts/

Acting Secretary of Board & Assistant Deputy Commissioner:
Susan Savage 518-474-6742
State Board Member (Chair):
Matthew Rand 518-474-3793
State Board Member:
John M. Bacheller 518-474-3793
State Board Member:
Edgar A. King 518-474-3793
Assistant to Board:
Darlene Maloney 518-474-3793
e-mail: darlene.maloney@tax.ny.gov

Research, Information & Policy Development
Director:
James Dunne 518-473-4532
e-mail: jim.dunne@orps.state.ny.us
Director:
David Williams 518-473-8743
e-mail: dave.williams@orps.state.ny.us

Albany (Northern Region)
WA Harriman State Campus, Bldg 8A, Albany, NY 12227
Regional Director:
Robert Aiken 518-486-4403/fax: 518-435-8573
e-mail: orpts.northern@tax.ny.gov

Batavia (Western Region)
Genesee County Bldg 2, 3837 W Main Rd, Batavia, NY 14020

Offices and agencies generally appear in alphabetical order, except when specific order is requested by listee.

Regional Director:
Christine Bannister 585-343-4363/fax: 518-435-8598
e-mail: orpts.western@tax.ny.gov

Long Island Satellite Office
250 Veterans Memorial Hgwy, Rm 4A-6, Hauppauge, NY 11788
Manager:
Steve Hartnett 631-595-4071/fax: 518-435-8572
e-mail: orpts.southern@tax.ny.gov

Newburgh (South)
263 Route 17K, Ste 2001, Newburgh, NY 12550
Regional Director:
John Wolham 845-567-2648/fax: 518-435-8498
e-mail: orpts.southern@tax.ny.gov

Ray Brook Satellite Office
884 NYS Rte 86, PO Box 309, Ray Brook, NY 12977
Regional Director:
Robert Aiken 518-891-1780/fax: 518-435-8593
e-mail: orpts.raybrook@tax.ny.gov

Syracuse (Central Region) . . . . fax: 315-471-3634
401 South Salina St, 5th Floor, Syracuse, NY 13202
Regional Director:
Teresa Frank 315-471-2347/fax: 518-435-8583
e-mail: internet.central@orps.state.ny.us

Transportation Department
50 Wolf Road
Albany, NY 12232
518-457-5100 or 518-457-6195 Fax: 518-457-5583
Web site: www.dot.ny.gov

Commissioner:
Joan McDonald 518-457-4422
Operations & Asset Management Division:
Roderic Sechrist 518-485-0887

Engineering Division
Acting Chief Engineer:
Joseph A Foglietta III 518-457-4430
Office of Design (Acting):
Richard Lee 518-457-6452
Office of Structures (Acting):
Richard Marchione 518-457-6827
Office of Environment:
Vacant 518-457-5672
Office of Major Projects:
Marie Corrado 518-4585-5025
Office of Technical Services:
Anthony Torre 518-457-4445
Office of Construction:
Jim Tynan 518-457-6472

NEW YORK STATE LEGISLATURE

See Legislative Branch in Section 1 for additional Standing Committee and Subcommittee information.

Assembly Standing Committees

Economic Development, Job Creation, Commerce & Industry
Chair:
Robin L Schimminger (D) 518-455-4767
Ranking Minority Member:
Raymond Walter (R). 518-455-54618

Housing
Chair:
Keith L.T. Wright (D). 518-455-4793

Ranking Minority Member:
Michael J Fitzpatrick (R) 518-455-5021

Real Property Taxation
Chair:
Sandra R Galef (D). 518-455-5348
Ranking Minority Member:
Kieran Michael Lalor (R) 518-455-5125

Senate Standing Committees

Commerce, Economic Development & Small Business
Chair:
Philip Boyle (R) 518-455-3411
Ranking Minority Member:
Timothy Kennedy (D). 518-455-2426

Housing Construction & Community Development
Chair:
Catharine M Young (R) 518-455-3563
Ranking Minority Member:
Adriano Espaillat (D) 518-455-2041

U.S. GOVERNMENT

EXECUTIVE DEPARTMENTS AND RELATED AGENCIES

US Department of Agriculture

Rural Development
Web site: www.rurdev.usda.gov/ny

New York State Office. . . . . fax: 315-477-6438
The Galleries of Syracuse, 441 S Salina St, Ste 357, Syracuse, NY
13202-2441
315-477-6400 Fax: 315-477-6438
State Director:
Stanley Telega 315-477-6437

US General Services Administration
Web site: www.gsa.gov

Region 2—New York
26 Federal Plaza, Rm 18-102, New York, NY 10278
212-264-9290
Regional Administrator:
Denise L. Pease. 212-264-2600
e-mail: denise.pease@gsa.gov
Special Assistant to the Regional Administrator:
Gita J. Stulberg 212-264-2600/fax: 212-264-3998
e-mail: guita.stulberg@gsa.gov

Administration
Director, Program Support & Human Resources:
Joseph J Giorgianni. 212-264-0780/fax: 212-264-6798
e-mail: joseph.giorgianni@gsa.gov

Federal Supply Service
Acting Asst Regional Administrator:
Charles B Weill. 212-264-3590/fax: 212-264-9759

Federal Technology Service
Asst Regional Administrator (Acting):
Steve Ruggiero 212-264-3590
e-mail: steve.ruggiero@gsa.gov

Inspector General's Office
Asst Regional Inspector, Investigations:
Daniel Walsh. 212-264-7300/fax: 212-264-7154
Regional Director, Audit:
Joseph Mastropietro 212-264-8620

Offices and agencies generally appear in alphabetical order, except when specific order is requested by listee.

Public Buildings Service
Regional Commissioner:
    Joanna Rosato 212-264-4282
    e-mail: joanna.rosato@gsa.gov
Deputy Asst Regional Administrator:
    Vacant 212-264-4285
Director, Property Management:
    David Segermeister 212-264-4273/fax: 212-264-2746
Director, Realty Services:
    Donald W Eigendorff 212-264-4210/fax: 212-264-9400

PRIVATE SECTOR

Appraisal Education Network School & Merrell Institute
1461 Lakeland Ave, Bohemia, NY 11716
631-563-7720 Fax: 631-563-7719
e-mail: bcm@doctor.com
Web site: www.merrellinstitute.com
Real estate sales, broker, appraiser, mortgage & property management education courses, paralegal, continuing education, home inspection
Bill C Merrell, Director

Brookfield Properties Corporation
Three World Financial Center, 200 Vesey Street, 11th Floor, New York, NY 10281
212-417-7000 Fax: 212-417-7214
e-mail: kkane@brookfieldproperties.com
Web site: www.brookfieldproperties.com
Commercial real estate
Kathleen G Kane, General Counsel

Building & Realty Institute
80 Business Park Dr, Armonk, NY 10504
914-273-0730 Fax: 914-273-7051
e-mail: aaaa@buildersinstitute.org
Web site: www.buildersinstitute.org
Building, realty & construction industry membership organization
Albert A Annunziata, Executive Director

Colliers ABR Inc
40 E 52nd St, New York, NY 10022
212-758-0800 Fax: 212-758-6190
Web site: www.colliersabr.com
Commercial real estate & property management
Mark P Boisi, Chairman

NYS Bar Assn, Real Property Law Section
D H Ferguson, Attorney, PLLC
141 Sully's Trail, Suite 12, Pittsford, NY 14534
585-586-0459 or 585-586-0450 Fax: 585-586-2297
e-mail: dhferguson@frontiernet.net
Dorothy H Ferguson, Chair

Ernst & Young
5 Times Square, New York, NY 10036-6350
212-773-4500 Fax: 212-773-4986
e-mail: dale.reiss@ey.com
Web site: www.ey.com
Dale Anne Reiss, Global & Americas Director Real Estate

FirstService Williams
380 Madison Ave, 3rd Floor, New York, NY 10017
212-716-3760 Fax: 212-716-3710
e-mail: jcaridi@fswre.com
Web site: www.fswre.com
Real estate brokerage, ownership, sales, leasing, management & consulting
Joseph J Caridi, Executive Managing Director

Fisher Brothers
299 Park Ave, New York, NY 10171
212-752-5000 Fax: 212-940-6879
Real estate investment & development
Arnold Fisher, Partner

Glenwood Management Corporation
1200 Union Turnpike, New Hyde Park, NY 11040
718-343-6400 Fax: 718-343-0009
Web site: www.glenwoodmanagement.com
Property management
Leonard Litwin, President

Greater Rochester Association of Realtors Inc
930 East Avenue, Rochester, NY 14607
585-292-5000 Fax: 585-292-5008
e-mail: karenw@grar.net
Web site: www.homesteadnet.com
Karen Wingender, Chief Executive Officer

Greater Syracuse Association of Realtors Inc
1020 Seventh North St, Ste 140, Liverpool, NY 13088
315-457-5979 Fax: 315-457-5884
e-mail: fetyko@cnyrealtor.com
Web site: www.cnyrealtor.com
Lynnore Fetyko, Chief Executive Officer

H J Kalikow & Co LLC
101 Park Ave, 25th Fl, New York, NY 10178
212-808-7000 Fax: 212-573-6380
Web site: www.hjkalikow.com
Real estate development
Peter S Kalikow, President

J J Higgins Properties Inc
20 North Main St, Pittsford, NY 14534
585-381-6030 Fax: 585-381-0571
e-mail: jjhigginsproperties@frontiernet.net
Web site: www.jjhigginsproperties.com
Residental properties, relocation, commercial properties, home sales & listings, buyer agency
John J Higgins, President

Landauer Realty Group Inc
1177 Avenue of the Americas, New York, NY 10036
212-759-9700 or 212-326-4752 Fax: 212-326-4802
e-mail: david.arena@grubb-ellis.com
Web site: www.landauer.com
Commercial real estate appraisers, analysts & transaction consultants
David Arena, President

MJ Peterson Corporation
501 Audubon Pkwy, Amherst, NY 14228
716-688-1234 Fax: 716-688-5463
e-mail: lpeterson@mjpeterson.com
Web site: www.mjpeterson.com
Residential, commercial, property management, development and new homes
Victor L Peterson, Jr, President

Mancuso Business Development Group
56 Harvester Ave, Batavia, NY 14020
585-343-2800 Fax: 585-343-7096
e-mail: tom@mancusogroup.com
Web site: www.mancusogroup.com
Improve operating performances of multi tenant industrial and office and business incubator properties
Tom Mancuso, President

Offices and agencies generally appear in alphabetical order, except when specific order is requested by listee.

Metro/Colvin Realty Inc
2211 Sheridan Dr, Kenmore, NY 14223
716-874-0110 Fax: 716-874-9015
e-mail: metrocolvin1@aol.com
Residential & commercial property
John Riordan, President

Metro/Horohoe-Leimbach
3199 Delaware Ave, Kenmore, NY 14217
716-873-5404 Fax: 716-873-8901
e-mail: whorohoe@aol.com
Web site: metrohorohoe.com
Residential real estate
William Horohoe, President

NY Commercial Association of Realtors
130 Washington Ave, Albany, NY 12210
518-463-0300 Fax: 518-462-5474
e-mail: nyscar@att.net
Web site: www.nyscarxchange.com
Commercial real estate
Maureen D Wilson, President

NYS Association of Realtors
130 Washington Ave, Albany, NY 12210-2298
518-463-0300 Fax: 518-462-5474
e-mail: admin@nysar.com
Web site: www.nysar.com
Duncan R MacKenzie, Chief Executive Officer

NYS Land Title Association
2 Rector St, Ste 901, New York, NY 10006-1819
212-964-3701 Fax: 212-964-7185
e-mail: rgt@nyslta.org
Web site: www.nyslta.org
Trade association for title insurance industry
Robert Treuber, Executive Vice President

NYS Society of Real Estate Appraisers
130 Washington Ave, Albany, NY 12210-2298
518-463-0300 Fax: 518-462-5474
e-mail: nyssrea@nysar.com
Web site: www.nyrealestateappraisers.com
Real estate appraisal
Wayne Feinberg, President

Community Bankers Assn of NY State, Mortgages & Real Estate Cmte
New York Community Bank
615 Merrick Ave, Westbury, NY 11590
516-683-4100 Fax: 516-683-8344
Web site: www.mynycb.com
James O'Donovan, Chair

New York Landmarks Conservancy
1 Whitehall St, 21 Fl, New York, NY 10004
212-995-5260 Fax: 212-995-5268
e-mail: nylandmarks@nylandmarks.org
Web site: www.nylandmarks.org
Technical & financial assistance for preservation & reuse of landmark buildings
Peg Breen, President

New York State Assessors' Association
PO Box 888, Middletown, NY 10940
845-344-0292 Fax: 845-343-8238
e-mail: nysaa@nyassessor.com
Web site: www.nyassessor.com
Real property tax issues
Thomas Frey, Executive Director

Pomeroy Appraisal Associates Inc
Pomeroy Pl, 225 W Jefferson St, Syracuse, NY 13202
315-422-7106 Fax: 315-476-1011
e-mail: dfisher@pomeroyappraisal.com
Web site: pomeroyappraisal.com
Real estate appraisal & consultation
Donald A Fisher, MAI, ARA

R W Bronstein Corporation
3666 Main St, Buffalo, NY 14226
716-835-7400 or 800-642-2500 Fax: 716-835-7419
e-mail: value@bronstein.net
Web site: www.bronstein.net
Real estate, appraisals & auctions; valuation & marketing of all types of realty and chattels
Richard W Bronstein, President

Real Estate Board of New York Inc
570 Lexington Ave, New York, NY 10022
212-532-3120 Fax: 212-481-0122
e-mail: stevenspinola@rebny.com
Web site: www.rebny.com
Representing real estate professionals & firms in New York City
Steven Spinola, President

Realty Advisory Board on Labor Relations
292 Madison Ave, New York, NY 10017
212-889-4100 Fax: 212-889-4105
e-mail: jberg@rabolr.com
Web site: www.rabolr.com
Labor negotiations for realtors & realty firms
James Berg, President

Realty USA
6505 E Quaker Rd, Orchard Park, NY 14127
716-662-2000 Fax: 716-662-3385
e-mail: mwhitehead@realtyusa.com
Web site: www.realtyusa.com
Residential real estate
Merle Whitehead, President & Chief Executive Officer

Red Barn Properties
Six Schoen Pl, Pittsford, NY 14534
585-381-2222 x11 Fax: 585-381-1854
e-mail: estelle@redbarnproperties.com
Web site: www.redbarnproperties.com
Specializing in local, national & global residential relocation
Estelle O'Connell, Relocation Director

Related Companies LP
60 Columbus Circle, 19th Fl, New York, NY 10023
212-421-5333 Fax: 212-801-1036
e-mail: bbeal@related.com
Web site: www.related.com
Residential & commercial real estate
Bruce A Beal, Jr, Executive Vice President, NY Development Group

Robert Schalkenbach Foundation
90 John Street, Suite 501, New York, NY 10038
212-683-6424 Fax: 212-683-6454
e-mail: msullivan@schalkenbach.org
Web site: www.schalkenbach.org
Land value taxation, real property & economic publications
Mark A Sullivan, Administrative Director

Roohan Realty
519 Broadway, Saratoga Springs, NY 12866-2208
518-587-4500 Fax: 518-587-4509
e-mail: troohan@roohanrealty.com
Web site: www.roohanrealty.com
Commercial & residential property
J Thomas Roohan, President

Offices and agencies generally appear in alphabetical order, except when specific order is requested by listee.

Silverstein Properties Inc
7 World Trade Center, 250 Greenwich Street, 38th Floor, New York, NY 10036
212-490-0666 Fax: 212-687-0067
NYC commercial real estate
Larry A Silverstein, President, Chief Executive Officer

Sonnenblick-Goldman Company
712 Fifth Ave, New York, NY 10019
212-841-9200 Fax: 212-262-4224
e-mail: asonnenblick@sonngold.com
Web site: www.sonngold.com
Real estate investment banking
Arthur I Sonnenblick, Senior Managing Director

Tishman Speyer Properties
Rockefeller Center, 45 Rockefeller Plaza, New York, NY 10111
212-715-0300 Fax: 212-319-1745
e-mail: jspeyer@tishmanspeyer.com
Web site: www.tishmanspeyer.com
Owners/builders
Jerry I Speyer, President

UJA-Federation of New York
130 E 59th St, New York, NY 10022
212-980-1000 Fax: 212-836-1653
e-mail: flynnc@ujafedny.org
Web site: www.ujafedny.org
Real property portfolio management
John S Ruskay, Executive Vice President & Chief Executive Officer

Policy Areas

SOCIAL SERVICES

NEW YORK STATE

GOVERNOR'S OFFICE

Governor's Office
Executive Chamber
State Capitol
Albany, NY 12224
518-474-8390 Fax: 518-474-1513
Web site: www.ny.gov

Governor:
  Andrew M Cuomo 518-474-8390
Secretary to the Governor:
  William Mulrow 518-474-4246
Counsel to the Governor:
  Alphonso David 518-474-8343
Director, Communications:
  Melissa DeRosa . . . . .518-474-8418 or 212-681-4640
Director, State Operations:
  James Malatras 518-486-9871

EXECUTIVE DEPARTMENTS AND RELATED AGENCIES

Aging, Office for the
2 Empire State Plaza
Albany, NY 12223
518-474-4425 or 800-342-9871 Fax: 518-474-0608
e-mail: nysofa@aging.ny.gov
Web site: www.aging.ny.gov

Director:
  Corinda Crossdale. 518-474-4425
Executive Deputy Director:
  Greg Olsen 518-474-7012
Counsel:
  Jennifer Seehase 518-474-0388
Public Information Officer:
  Reza Mizbani 518-474-7181
  e-mail: reza.mizbani@aging.ny.gov
Deputy Director, Agency Operations:
  John Cochran 518-486-3661
  e-mail: reza.mizbani@aging.ny.gov
Deputy Director, Division of Policy, Planning, Program & Outcomes:
  Laurie Pferr 518-474-7012

Federal Relations
Staff Liaison:
  Stephen Syzdek. 518-474-5041
Deputy Director:
  John J Lynch. 518-473-4808

Aging Projects
Director:
  Kelly Mateja 518-473-7424

Agriculture & Markets Department
10B Airline Dr
Albany, NY 12235
518-457-3880 Fax: 518-457-3087
e-mail: info@agriculture.ny.gov
Web site: www.agriculture.ny.gov

Commissioner:
  Richard Ball 518-457-8876

First Deputy Commissioner:
  Jen McCormick. 518-457-2771
  e-mail: jen.mccormick@agriculture.ny.gov
Public Information Officer:
  Jola Szubielski 518-485-7728/fax: 518-457-3087
  e-mail: jola.szubielski@agriculture.ny.gov

Agricultural Development Division
Director:
  Kevin King 518-457-7076
  e-mail: kevin.king@agriculture.ny.gov

Alcoholism & Substance Abuse Services, Office of
1450 Western Ave
Albany, NY 12203
518-473-3460 Fax: 518-457-5474
e-mail: communications@oasas.ny.gov
Web site: www.oasas.ny.gov

501 7th Ave
8th Fl
New York, NY 10018
646-728-4533

Commissioner:
  Arlene Gonzalez-Sanchez. 518-457-2061
Executive Deputy Commissioner:
  Sean M. Byrne 518-457-1758
Wellness & Medical Direction Office (Acting):
  Charles W Morgan, MD. 845-359-8500
Director, Office of Counsel & Internal Controls:
  Robert Kent. 518-485-2312
Director, Governmental Affairs, Grants Mgmt:
  Patricia Zuber-Wilson. 518-485-2317
Director, Bureau of Statewide Field Operations/NYC Operations:
  Manuel Mosquera 518-485-1758

Bureau of Public Information & Communications
Director:
  Susan A Craig, MPH. 518-457-8299/fax: 518-485-6014

Fiscal Administration Division
Associate Commissioner:
  P David Sawicki 518-457-5312
Director, Bureau of Budget Management:
  Tara Gabriel 518-485-2193
Director, Bureau of Capital Management:
  Jeff Emad 518-457-2545
Director, Bureau of Health Care Financing & Performance Improvement:
  Laurie Felter 518-457-2545

Outcome Management & System Information Division
Associate Commissioner:
  William F. Hogan 518-485-2322

Prevention, Housing & Management Services Division
Acting Associate Commissioner:
  Mary Ann DiChristopher 518-485-6022
Director, Bureau of Housing & Employment:
  Henri Williams 518-485-0498
Director, Bureau of Prevention Services:
  Scott Brady 518-457-4384
Director, Management Services:
  Vacant. 518-485-6689
Director, Bureau of Recovery Services:
  Susan Brandau 518-485-2107

Quality Assurance & Performance Improvement Division
Associate Commissioner:
  Charles W Monson 518-485-2257

Offices and agencies generally appear in alphabetical order, except when specific order is requested by listee.

Director, Bureau of Certification:
  Janet Paloski 518-485-2250
Director, Bureau of Standards Compliance:
  William Lanchanski 518-485-2255
Director, Bureau of Workforce Developement & Fiscal Evaluation:
  Douglas Rosenberry 518-485-2033

Treatment & Practice Innovation Division
Associate Commissioner:
  Steve Hanson 518-457-7077
Assistant Director, Bureau of Addiction Treatment Centers:
  Paula Bradwell . . . . .518-457-7077 or 585-461-0410

Children & Family Services, Office of
52 Washington St
Rensselaer, NY 12144
518-473-7793 Fax: 518-486-7550
Web site: www.ocfs.ny.gov

Acting Commissioner:
  Sheila Poole 518-402-3108
Ombudsman:
  Viola I Abbitt 518-486-7082
Executive Deputy Commissioner:
  Sheila Poole 518-402-3108
Executive Secretary:
  Nancy Degree 518-402-3108

Administration, Division of
Associate Commissioner:
  James Barron 518-486-6942
  Contract Management:
    Richard DiMezza 518-486-7224

Financial Management, Office of
Associate Commissioner:
  Derek Holtzclaw 518-486-7218
Director, Budget Management Bureau:
  Gabrielle Ares 518-474-1361
Director, Financial Operations:
  Susan A Costello 518-486-3848

Commission for the Blind & Visually Handicapped (CBVH)
Associate Commissioner:
  Brian S Daniels 518-474-7812
Director, Bureau of Program Evaluation,Support & Business Svcs:
  Roger Gray 518-474-7812
Director, Bureau of Field Operations & Implementation:
  Janice O'Connor 518-473-9685

Child Welfare and Community Services, Division of (CWCS)
Deputy Commissioner:
  Laura Velez 518-474-3377

Special Populations, Office of
Assistant Commissioner:
  Lisa Ghartey Ogundimu 518-473-9447
  State Central Registry
    Director:
      Linda A. Joyce 518-474-9607
  Native American Services
    Affairs Specialist:
      Vacant 716-847-3123

Prevention, Permanency & Program Support, Office of
Associate Commissioner:
  Renee Hallock 518-402-3181
  Adult Protective Services
    Director:
      Alan Lawitz 518-402-6782

Adoption Services
  Director:
    Brenda Rivers 518-473-1901

Child Care Services, Division of (DCCS)
Deputy Commissioner:
  Janice Molnar 518-486-6247

Information Technology, Division of
40 N Pearl Street, Albany, NY 12243
Business Solutions Director:
  John Birtwistle 518-408-3046
CIO:
  Rick Ryan 518-402-3194

Legal Affairs, Division of
Acting Deputy Commissioner & General Counsel:
  Lee Prochera 518-473-8418

Communications, Office of
Assistant Commissioner for Communications:
  Jennifer Givner 518-402-3130

Juvenile Justice & Opportunities for Youth, Division of (DJJOY)
Deputy Commissioner:
  Ines Neives 518-473-1786

Facility Management, Office of
Associate Commissioner:
  Vacant 518-473-4411
Facility Coordinator:
  Wendy Phillips 212-961-4121
Facility Coordinator:
  Dan Comins 607-538-1401
ACA Accreditation Coordinator:
  Kurt Pfisterer 518-408-3825
Supervisor, Facilities Fire Safety:
  Scott Hecox 518-473-5325
DOJ Settlement Coordinator:
  Edgardo Lopez 315-479-8356
Director, Management & Program Supprot, Bureau of:
  Merle Brandwene 518-486-7029

Community Partnerships, Office of
Associate Commissioner:
  Tim Roche 518-486-7170
Director, Upstate/Long Island:
  Daniel Maxwell 518-486-4018
Downstate Area Manager:
  Robert Ellis 212-961-4112
Director, Technical Support, IT, Office of:
  Jeff Evans 518-486-4335

Special Investigations Unit
Chief of Investigations:
  Larry Gravett 518-474-9478

Strategic Planning & Policy Development, Office of
Director:
  Vacant 518-473-1776
Bureau of Policy Analysis:
  Rayana Gonzales 518-473-6237
Bureau of Research, Evaluation & Performance Analytics:
  Rebecca Colman 518-474-9426
Director, Special Projects, Bureau of:
  Greg Owens 518-473-3990

Native American Services . . . . fax: 716-847-3812
716-847-3123 Fax: 716-847-3812
Director:
  Vacant 716-847-3123

Policy Areas

Offices and agencies generally appear in alphabetical order, except when specific order is requested by listee.

Youth Development, Office of . . . . fax: 518-473-6692
52 Washington Avenue, Room 1155, Rensselaer, NY 12144
Director:
Matt Beck 518-402-3296

Council on Children & Families (CCF)
52 Washington St, West Bldg, Ste 99, Rensselaer, NY 12144
Web site: www.ccf.ny.gov
Executive Director:
Deborah Benson 518-473-3652/fax: 518-473-2570
e-mail: debbie.benson@ccf.ny.gov
Deputy Director & Counsel:
Elana Marton. 518-473-3652
e-mail: elana.marton@ccf.ny.gov

Bureau of Policy, Research & Planning
Project Director, Head Start Collaboration:
Patricia Persell 518-473-3652
e-mail: patricia.persell@ccf.ny.gov

Bureau of Interagency Coordination & Case Resolution
Project Director, Kids Count:
Mary DeMasi 518-474-3652
e-mail: mary.demasi@ccf.ny.gov

Victim Services, Office of
80 South Swan Street
2nd Floor
Albany, NY 12210
518-457-8727 or 800-247-8035 Fax: 518-457-8658
Web site: www.ovs.ny.gov

55 Hanson Place
10th Fl
Brooklyn, NY 11217
718-923-4325
Fax: 718-923-4347

65 Court St
Rm 308
Buffalo, NY 14202
716-847-7992
Fax: 716-847-7995

Director:
Elizabeth Cronin Esq 518-485-5719
General Counsel/Legal Unit:
John Watson 518-457-8066/fax: 518-457-8658
Deputy Director for Administration:
Danny Morgan 518-457-8050
Director, MIS:
Susan Nardolillo 518-485-9299
Crime Victim Compensation Investigations (Brooklyn):
Claudette Christian Bullock 718-923-4348
Crime Victim Compensation Investigations (Albany & Buffalo):
Noreen Fyvie. 518-457-8176

Developmental Disabilities Planning Council
99 Washington Ave
12th Fl, Ste 1230
Albany, NY 12210
518-486-7505 or 800-395-3372 Fax: 518-402-3505
e-mail: ddpc@ddpc.ny.gov
Web site: www.ddpc.ny.gov

Chairperson:
Rose Marie Toscano 518-486-7505
Vice Chairperson:
Ansley Bacon, PhD. 518-486-7505

Executive Director:
Sheila M Carey 518-486-7505
e-mail: sheila.carey@ddpc.ny.gov
Deputy Director-Program Development Specialist:
Anna Lobosco 518-486-7505
e-mail: anna.lobosco@ddpc.ny.gov
Public Information Officer:
Thomas F Lee 518-486-7505/fax: 518-486-3505
e-mail: thomas.lee@ddpc.ny.gov

Education Department
State Education Bldg
89 Washington Ave
Albany, NY 12234
518-474-3852 Fax: 518-486-5631
Web site: www.nysed.gov

Commissioner, University President:
MaryEllen Elia 518-474-5844
Executive Deputy Commissioner:
Elizabeth Berlin 518-474-8381
Chief, External Affairs:
Dennis Tompkins 518-474-1201

Office of the Professions . . . . fax: 518-474-1449
89 Washington Ave, EB, 2nd Fl, West Mezz, Albany, NY 12234
Fax: 518-474-1449
Web site: www.op.nysed.gov
Deputy Commissioner:
Douglas Lentivech. 518-474-3817 x470
e-mail: opopr@mail.nysed.gov

Special Education
Assistant Commissioner:
James P. DeLorenzo 518-474-3817 x440
e-mail: opexdir@mail.nysed.gov
Coordinator, Special Education Policy & Professional Development:
Patricia J. Geary. 518-474-3817 x360
Supervisor, Program Development & Support:
Noel Granger 518-474-3817 x340

**Office of Adult Career & Continuing Education Services
(ACCES)** . . . . fax: 518-474-8802
One Commerce Plaza, Rm 1606, Albany, NY 12234
Fax: 518-474-8802
Web site: www.vesid.nysed.gov
Deputy Commissioner:
Kevin G. Smith 518-474-2714
e-mail: rcort@mail.nysed.gov

State School for the Blind at Batavia
2A Richmond Ave, Batavia, NY 14020
Superintendent:
Dr. Mathis A. Calvin, III 585-343-5384
e-mail: mcalvin@mail.nysed.gov

Vocational Rehabilitation Operations
Assitant Commissioner:
Debora Brown-Johnson 518-402-3955
e-mail: dbrowngr@mail.nysed.gov

Labor Department
Building 12, Room 500
Harriman State Office Campus
Albany, NY 12240
518-457-9000 Fax: 518-457-6908
e-mail: nysdol@labor.ny.gov
Web site: www.labor.ny.gov

Commissioner:
Peter M. Rivera 518-457-9000

Offices and agencies generally appear in alphabetical order, except when specific order is requested by listee.

Executive Deputy Commissioner:
Mario Musolino 518-457-4318
Acting Counsel:
Pico Ben-Amotz 518-457-7069
Director, Special Investigations:
John Dormin 518-457-7012
Director, Communications:
Leo Rosales 518-457-5519/fax: 518-485-1126
e-mail: leo.rosales@labor.ny.gov

Federal Programs
Deputy Commissioner, Federal Programs:
Bruce Herman 518-485-6410

Employment Services Division
Director:
Vacant 518-457-3584

Unemployment Insurance Division
Director:
Richard Marino 518-457-2878/fax: 518-485-8604

Workforce Development & Training Division
Acting Director:
Karen Coleman 518-457-0380/fax: 518-457-9526

Veterans Services
Program Coordinator:
Vacant 518-457-1343

Worker Protection
Deputy Commissioner, Workforce Development:
Karen A. Coleman 518-457-4317

Labor Standards Division
Director:
Carmine Ruberto 518-457-4256

Safety & Health Division
Director:
Eileen Franks 518-457-3518/fax: 518-457-1519

Prevention of Domestic Violence, Office for the
80 South Swan Street
11th Fl Rm 1157
Albany, NY 12210
518-457-5800 or 800-942-6906 Fax: 518-457-5810
Web site: www.opdv.ny.gov

Executive Director:
Gwen Wright. 518-457-5800
Director, NYC Program:
Sujata Warrier 212-417-4477
Counsel:
Johanna Sullivan 518-457-5800
Fiscal Officer:
Linda Cassidy 518-457-7995
Public Information Officer:
Suzanne Cecala. 518-457-5744
e-mail: suzanne.cecala@opdv.ny.gov

Temporary & Disability Assistance, Office of
40 N Pearl St
Albany, NY 12243
518-473-1090
e-mail: nyspio@otda.ny.gov
Web site: www.otda.ny.gov

Commissioner:
Kristin M. Proud 518-474-4152

Budget, Finance & Data Management
Director:
Nancy Maney 518-474-0183

Center for Child Well-Being
Deputy Commissioner & Director:
Eileen Stack 518-474-1078

Disability Determinations Division
Deputy Commissioner:
Gloria S Toal. 518-473-0070

Center for Employment & Economic Supports
Deputy Commissioner:
Phyllis Morris 518-474-9222/fax: 518-474-5281

Information Technology Services
Director:
Rick Ryan 518-486-1012

Legal Affairs Division
General Counsel:
Krista Rock. 518-474-9502

Operations & Program Support
Deputy Commissioner:
Wilma Brown Phillips 518-473-3912

Public Information
Director:
Kristi L. Berner 518-474-9516/fax: 518-486-6935
e-mail: nyspio@otda.ny.gov

Welfare Inspector General, Office of NYS
Chisholm State Office Building
55 Hanson Place
Room 650
Brooklyn, NY 11217
718-923-4290 or 800-682-4530 Fax: 718-923-4310
e-mail: owig@dfa.state.ny.us
Web site: www.owig.ny.gov

Acting Welfare Inspector General:
Catherine Leahy Scott. 718-923-4290
Chief Investigator:
Joseph Bucci 718-923-4290
Confidential Assitant to the Inspector General:
Joy Quiles 718-923-4290
e-mail: joy.quiles@owig.ny.gov

NEW YORK STATE LEGISLATURE

See Legislative Branch in Section 1 for additional Standing Committee and Subcommittee information.

Assembly Standing Committees

Aging
Chair:
Steven Cymbrowitz (D) 518-455-5214
Ranking Minority Member:
Angela M Wozniak (C). 518-455-5921

Alcoholism & Drug Abuse
Chair:
Linda Rosenthal (D) 518-455-5802
Ranking Minority Member:
Mark Johns (R) 518-455-5784

Offices and agencies generally appear in alphabetical order, except when specific order is requested by listee.

Children & Families
Chair:
Donna Lupardo (D)....................................518-455-5431
Ranking Minority Member:
Stevenr McLaughlin (R).............................518-455-5777

Social Services
Chair:
Andrew Hevesi (D)...................................518-455-4926
Ranking Minority Member:
Andrew Goodell (R)..................................518-455-4511

Assembly Task Forces

Puerto Rican/Hispanic Task Force
Chair:
Marcos Crespo (D) 518-455-5514
Executive Director:
Guillermo Martinez..................................518-455-3608

Women's Issues, Task Force on
Chair:
Aravella Simotas (D) 518-455-5014
Coordinator:
Christina Williams..........518-455-3632/fax: 518-455-4574

Senate Standing Committees

Aging
Chair:
Sue Serino (R)).....................................518-455-2945
Ranking Minority Member:
Ruben Diaz Sr (D) 518-455-2511

Children & Families
Chair:
Simcha Felder (D)...................................518-455-2754
Ranking Minority Member:
Velmanette Montgomery (D)...........................518-455-3451

Social Services
Chair:
David Carlucci (D) 518-455-2991

U.S. GOVERNMENT

EXECUTIVE DEPARTMENTS AND RELATED AGENCIES

Corporation for National & Community Service
Web site: www.cns.gov

New York Program Office
52 Washington Street, Room 228, North Building, Rensselaer, NY
12144-2796
Executive Director:
Mark J. Walter....................518-473-8882/fax: 518-402-3817
e-mail: mark.walter@newyorkersvolunteer.ny.gov

Social Security Administration
Web site: www.socialsecurity.gov

Region 2—New York ....fax: 212-264-6372
26 Federal Plz, Rm 3904, New York, NY 10278
Regional Commissioner:
Beatrice M Disman...................................212-264-3915
Deputy Regional Commissioner:
Paul M Doersam......................................212-264-3915
Employer Services Liaison Officer:
Tyrone S. Benefield 212-264-1117

Executive Officer:
Bernie Bowles.......................................212-264-4007

Office of Hearings & Appeals
Regional Chief Administrative Law Judge:
G Stephen Wright....................................212-264-4036

Office of Quality Assurance
Director:
Susan Pike 212-264-2827

Office of the General Counsel
Chief Counsel:
Lewis Spivak..212-264-3650

Program Operations Center
Director:
Janet Mullarkey 212-264-4004

Public Affairs
Public Affairs Director:
John E Shallman 212-264-2500/fax: 212-264-1444

US Department of Health & Human Services
Web site: www.os.dhhs.gov; www.hhs.gov/region2/

Administration for Children & Families ....fax: 212-264-4881
26 Federal Plaza, Rm 4114, New York, NY 10278
212-264-2890 Fax: 212-264-4881
Web site: www.acf.hhs.gov
Regional Administrator:
Joyce A. Thomas.....................................212-264-2890

Administration on Aging.......................fax: 212-264-0114
26 Federal Plaza, Rm 38-102, New York, NY 10278
212-264-2976 Fax: 212-264-0114
Web site: www.aoa.gov
Regional Administrator:
Kathleen Otte 212-264-2976
e-mail: kathleen.otte@aoa.hhs.gov

Centers for Disease Control & Prevention
Web site: www.cdc.gov

Agency for Toxic Substances & Disease Registry-EPA Region 2
290 Broadway, 20th Fl, New York, NY 10007
Web site: www.atsdr.cdc.gov
Director:
Leah Graziano, RS 212-637-4306/fax: 212-637-3253

New York Quarantine Station ....fax: 718-553-1524
Terminal 4E, Rm 219 016, JFK Airport, 2nd Floor, East Concourse,
Jamaica, NY 11430-1081
718-553-1685 Fax: 718-553-1524
Officer-in-Charge:
Margaret A Becker 718-553-1685/fax: 718-553-1524

Centers for Medicare & Medicaid Services
26 Federal Plaza, Rm 3811, New York, NY 10278
Web site: www.cms.hhs.gov
Consortium Administrator:
James T. Kerr....................212-616-2205/fax: 212-264-6189
e-mail: james.kerr@cms.hhs.gov
Regional Administrator:
Jay Weisman, MD.....................................212-616-2500

Medicaid and Children's Health (DMCH)
Associate Regional Administrator:
Michael Melendez

Medicare Financial Management (DMFM)
Associate Regional Administrator:
Vacant
e-mail: peter.reisman@cms.hhs.gov

Offices and agencies generally appear in alphabetical order, except when specific order is requested by listee.

Medicare Operations Division (DMO)
Associate Regional Administrator:
  Reginald Slaten...........................212-616-2300
  e-mail: jose.mirabal@cms.hhs.gov

Food & Drug Administration
888-463-6332
Web site: www.fda.gov

Northeast Region
158-15 Liberty Ave, Jamaica, NY 11433
Regional Director:
  Elizabeth O'Malley..............718-340-7000/fax: 718-662-5434
  New York District Office
    District Director:
      Ronald Pace 718-662-5447/fax: 718-662-5665
  Northeast Regional Laboratory
    158-15 Liberty Ave, Queens, NY 11433
    Director:
      Michael J Palmieri 718-662-5450/fax: 718-662-5439

Health Resources & Svcs Admin Office of Performance
Review ....fax: 212-264-2673
  26 Federal Plaza, Rm 3337, New York, NY 10278
Regional Division Director:
  Ron Moss 212-264-2664
  e-mail: robert.moss@hrsa.hhs.gov
Operations Director:
  Margaret Lee....................................212-264-2571
  e-mail: margaret.lee@hrsa.hhs.gov
Director, Ofc of Engineering Services:
  Emilio Pucillo..................................212-264-3600
  e-mail: emilio.pucillo@hrsa.hhs.gov

Indian Health Services-Area Office ....fax: 615-467-1501
  711 Stewarts Ferry Pike, Nashville, TN 37214-2634
Director:
  Martha Ketcher, MBA/HCM 615-467-1500

Office of Secretary's Regional Representative-Region 2-NY .. fax:
212-264-3620
  26 Federal Plaza, Rm 3835, New York, NY 10278
Regional Director:
  Deborah Konopko................................212-264-4600
  e-mail: deborah.konopko@hhs.gov
Sr Intergovernmental Affairs Specialist:
  Dennis Gonzalez................................212-264-4600
  e-mail: dennis.gonzalez@hhs.gov
Intergovernmental Affairs Specialist:
  Katherine Williams.............................212-264-4600
  e-mail: katherine.williams@hhs.gov

Office for Civil Rights.........................fax: 212-264-3039
  26 Federal Plaza, Rm 3312, New York, NY 10278
Fax: 212-264-3039
Web site: www.hhs.gov/ocr
Regional Manager:
  Michael Carter.................212-264-3313/fax: 212-264-3039
Deputy Regional Manager:
  Linda Colon 212-264-3313

Office of General Counsel
  26 Federal Plaza, Rm 3908, New York, NY 10278
Chief Counsel:
  Joel Lerner 212-264-6373

Office of Inspector General
Regional Inspector General, Audit:
  James P Edert...................................212-264-4620
Regional Inspector General & Regional Coordinator, Investigations:
  Gary Heuer......................................212-264-1691
Regional Inspector General, Evaluations & Inspections:
  Jodi Nudelman...................................212-264-1998

Office of Public Health & Science
26 Federal Plaza, Rm 3835, New York, NY 10278
Acting Regional Health Administrator:
  Robert Davidson.................................212-264-2560
  e-mail: rdavidson@osophs.dhhs.gov
Deputy Regional Health Administrator:
  Robert L Davidson...............................212-264-2560
  e-mail: rdavidson@osophs.dhhs.gov
Regional Family Planning Consultant:
  Robin Lane 212-264-3935
  e-mail: rlane@osophs.hhs.gov
Regional Minority Health Consultant:
  Claude Colimon..................................212-264-2560
Regional Women's Health Coordinator:
  Sandra Estepa...................................212-264-2560

U.S. CONGRESS

See U.S. Congress Chapter for additional Standing Committee and Subcommittee information.

House of Representatives Standing Committees

Ways & Means
Chair:
  Dave Kamp (R-MI)................................202-225-3561
New York Delegate:
  Charles B. Rangel (D)...........................202-225-4365
New York Delegate:
  Joseph Crowley (D)..............................202-225-3965
New York Delegate:
  Tom Reed (R)....................................202-225-3106

  Subcommittee
  Social Security
    Chair:
      Sam Johnson (R-TX)..........................202-225-4201
    Ranking Member:
      Xavier Becerra (D-CA) 202-225-6325

Senate Standing Committees

Health, Education, Labor & Pensions
Chair:
  Tom Harkin (D-IA)...............................202-224-3254
Ranking Member:
  Lamar Alexander (R-TN)..........................202-224-4944

Aging, Special Committee on
Chair:
  Bill Nelson (D-FL)..............................202-224-5274
Ranking Member:
  Susan Collins (R-ME)............................202-224-2523

PRIVATE SECTOR

AARP
780 3rd Ave, Fl 33, New York, NY 10017-2024
866-227-7442 Fax: 212-644-6390
Web site: www.aarp.org
AARP
Lois Aronstein, NY State Director

Offices and agencies generally appear in alphabetical order, except when specific order is requested by listee.

Abilities Inc, at Abilities!
201 IU Willets Rd, Albertson, NY 11507-1599
516-465-1490 or 516-747-5355 (TTY) Fax: 516-405-3757
e-mail: amuterspaw@abilitiesinc.org
Web site: www.abilitiesinc.org
Provides comprehensive services to help individuals with disabilities reach their employment goals; provides support services & technical assistance to employers who hire persons with disabilities.
Alice Muterspaw, Director of Consumer Services & Provider Relations

Action for a Better Community Inc
550 E Main St, Rochester, NY 14604
585-325-5116 or 585-295-1726 Fax: 585-325-9108
e-mail: fcaldwell@abcinfo.org
Web site: www.abcinfo.org
Advocacy for programs enabling the low-income to become self-sufficient; social services for the needy
Freddie Caldwell, Deputy Director

Agenda for Children Tomorrow
2 Washington St, 20th Floor, New York, NY 10004
212-487-8284 Fax: 212-487-8581
e-mail: actnet1@earthlink.net
Web site: www.actnyc.org
Public, private & community collaboration to identify, plan for & deliver social & community services to families
Deborah Rubien, Associate Executive Director (Acting)

American Red Cross in NYS
33 Everett Rd, Albany, NY 12205-1437
518-458-8111 x5113 Fax: 518-459-8262
e-mail: elizabeth.briand@redcross.org
Elizabeth H Briand, Director, State Government Relations

Asian American Federation
120 Wall St, 9th Floor, New York, NY 10005
212-344-5878 Fax: 212-344-5636
e-mail: info@aafederation.org
Web site: www.aafederation.org
Nonprofit leadership organization for member health & human services agencies serving the Asian American community
Cao K. O, Executive Director

Asian Americans for Equality
108 Norfolk Street, New York, NY 10002
212-979-8381 Fax: 212-979-8386
e-mail: info@aafe.org
Web site: www.aafe.org
Equal opportunities for minorities; affordable housing development, homeownership counseling, immigration services, housing rights
Christopher Kui, Executive Director

Berkshire Farm Center & Services for Youth
13640 Route 22, Canaan, NY 12029
518-781-4567 ext2211 Fax: 518-781-4577
e-mail: dharrington@berkshirefarm.org
Web site: www.berkshirefarm.org
Multi-function agency for troubled youth & families
Harith Flagg, Chief Executive Officer

Big Brothers Big Sisters of NYC
223 East 30th St, New York, NY 10016
212-686-2042 Fax: 212-779-1221
e-mail: help@bigsnyc.org
Web site: www.bigsnyc.org
Providing disadvantaged youth with one-to-one, long-term relationships with a trained volunteer
Hector Batista, Executive Director

CIDNY - Queens
137-02A Northern Blvd, Flushing, NY 11354
646-442-1520 or TTY 718-886-0427 Fax: 718-886-0428
Web site: www.cidny.org
Rights & advocacy for the disabled
Susan Dooha, Executive Director

CASA - Advocates for Children of NYS
911 Central Avenue, Suite 117, Albany, NY 12206
518-426-5354 Fax: 518-426-5348
e-mail: mail@casanys.org
Web site: www.casanys.org
Volunteer advocates appointed by family court judges to represent abused & neglected children in court
Penny Page, Executive Director

Camp Venture Inc
25 Smith Street, Suite 510, Nanuet, NY 10954
845-624-3860 Fax: 845-624-7064
Web site: www.campventure.org
Services for the developmentally disabled
Daniel Lukens, Executive Director

Catholic Charities of Onondaga County
1654 W Onondaga St, Syracuse, NY 13204
315-424-1800 Fax: 315-424-8262
Web site: www.ccoc.us
Eleanor Carr, Director, Elder Abuse Prevention Program

Center for Anti-Violence Education Inc
327 7th St, 2nd Fl, Brooklyn, NY 11215
718-788-1775 Fax: 718-499-2284
e-mail: info@caeny.org
Web site: www.caeny.org
Self-defense & violence prevention education for children, youth, women & LGBT people
Tracy Hobson, Executive Director

Center for Family & Youth (The)
Administrative Ofc, 135 Ontario St, PO Box 6240, Albany, NY 12206
518-462-4745 or 518-462-4630 Fax: 518-427-1464
e-mail: dbosworth@ctrfamyouth.com
Child welfare services, Project STRIVE
David A Bosworth, Executive Director

Center for Independence of the Disabled in NY (CIDNY)
841 Broadway, Ste 301, New York, NY 10003
212-674-2300 or TTY: 212-674-5619 Fax: 212-254-5953
Web site: www.cidny.org
Rights & advocacy for the disabled
Susan Dooha, Executive Director

Center for Urban Community Services
198 E 121st Street, New York, NY 10035
212-801-3300 Fax: 212-635-2191
e-mail: cucsinfo@cucs.org
Web site: www.cucs.org
Services to the homeless & low-income individuals, training & technical assistance to not-for-profit organizations
Anthony Hannigan, Executive Director

Center for Disability Services
314 S Manning Blvd, Albany, NY 12208
518-437-5700 Fax: 518-437-5705
Web site: www.cfdsny.org
Medical & dental services; education, adult & residential services & service coordination
Alan Krafchin, President & Chief Executive Officer

Offices and agencies generally appear in alphabetical order, except when specific order is requested by listee.

Cerebral Palsy Associations of New York State
90 State Street, Suite 929, Albany, NY 12207-1709
518-436-0178 Fax: 518-436-8619
e-mail: malvaro@cpofnys.org
Web site: www.cpofnys.org
Advocate and provide direct services with and for individuals with cerebral palsy and other significant disabilities and their families through a Statewide Affiliate network.
Michael Alvaro, Executive Vice President

Children's Aid Society (The)
105 E 22nd St, New York, NY 10010
212-949-4921 Fax: 212-460-5941
e-mail: pmoses@childrensaidsociety.org
Web site: www.childrensaidsociety.org
Child welfare, health, foster care/adoption, preventive services, community centers & public schools, camps
C Warren Moses, Chief Executive Officer

Children's Rights Inc
330 Seventh Ave, 4th Floor, New York, NY 10001
212-683-2210 Fax: 212-683-4015
e-mail: info@childrensrights.org
Web site: www.childrensrights.org
Advocacy & class action lawsuits on behalf of abused & neglected children
Marcia Robinson Lowry, Executive Director

Children's Village (The)
Echo Hills, Dobbs Ferry, NY 10522
914-693-0600 x1201 Fax: 914-674-9208
e-mail: jkohomban@childrensvillage.org
Web site: www.childrensvillage.org
Residential school, located 20 minutes outside of NYC. Treatment & prevention of behavioral problems for youth; residential & community-based services; mental health, education, employment & runaway shelter services
Jeremy Kohomban, PhD, President & Chief Executive Officer

Citizens' Committee for Children of New York Inc
105 E 22nd St, 7th Fl, New York, NY 10010
212-673-1800 Fax: 212-979-5063
e-mail: info@cccnewyork.org
Web site: www.cccnewyork.org
Public policy advocacy for children's rights & services; promoting improved quality of life for NYC children & families in need
Jennifer March-Joly, Executive Director

Coalition Against Domestic Violence, NYS
350 New Scotland Ave, Albany, NY 12208
518-482-5465 Fax: 518-482-3807
e-mail: vasquez@nyscadv.org
Web site: www.nyscadv.org
Jessica Vasquez, Executive Director

Coalition for Asian American Children & Families
50 Broad St, Rm 1701, New York, NY 10004
212-809-4675 Fax: 212-785-4601
e-mail: cacf@cacf.org
Web site: www.cacf.org
Advocacy for programs & policies supporting Asian American children & families; training & resources for service providers
Wayne H Ho, Executive Director

Coalition for the Homeless
129 Fulton St, 1st Flr, New York, NY 10038
212-776-2000 Fax: 212-964-1303
e-mail: info@cfthomeless.org
Web site: www.coalitionforthehomeless.org
Food, shelter, clothing assistance program, services for homeless New Yorkers
Mary Brosnahan Sullivan, Executive Director

Coalition of Animal Care Societies (The)
437 Old Albany Post Rd, Garrison, NY 10524
845-788-5070 Fax: 845-788-5071
e-mail: tzaleski@sprynet.com
Association of humane societies & animal welfare groups in NYS
Terence M Zaleski, Special Counsel

Coalition of Fathers & Families NY
PO Box 782, Clifton Park, NY 12065
518-383-8202
e-mail: fafny@fafny.org
Web site: www.fafny.org/fafnypac.htm
Working to keep fathers & families together
James Hays, President

Commission on Economic Opportunity for the Greater Capital Region
2331 Fifth Ave, Troy, NY 12180
518-272-6012 Fax: 518-272-0658
e-mail: kgordon@ceo-cap.org
Web site: www.ceo-cap.org
Preserve & advance the self-sufficiency, well-being & growth of individuals & families through education, guidance & resources
Karen E Gordon, Executive Director

Community Healthcare Network
79 Madison Avenue, Fl 6, New York, NY 10016-7802
212-366-4500 Fax: 212-463-8411
e-mail: cabate@chnnyc.org
Web site: www.chnnyc.org
Health & social services for low-income, ethnically diverse, medically underserved neighborhoods of NYC
Catherine Abate, President & Chief Executive Officer

Cornell Cooperative Extension, College of Human Ecology, Nutrition, Health
186 Martha Van Rensselaer Hall, Cornell University, Ithaca, NY 14853-4401
607-255-2247 Fax: 607-254-4403
e-mail: jas56@cornell.edu
Web site: www.cce.cornell.edu
Children, youth & family economic & social well-being
Josephine Swanson, Associate Director, Assistant Dean

Council of Community Services of NYS Inc
272 Broadway, Albany, NY 12204
518-434-9194 x103 Fax: 518-434-0392
e-mail: info@ccsnys.org
Web site: www.ccsnys.org
Build healthy, caring communities & human care delivery systems through a strong charitable nonprofit sector & quality community-based planning
Doug Sauer, Executive Director

Council of Family & Child Caring Agencies
254 West 31st Street, 5th Floor, New York, NY 10001
212-929-2626 Fax: 212-929-0870
e-mail: cofcca@cofcca.org
Web site: www.cofcca.org
Child welfare services membership organization
James F Purcell, Executive Director

EPIC-Every Person Influences Children Inc
1000 Main St, Buffalo, NY 14202
716-332-4100 Fax: 716-332-4101
Web site: www.epicforchildren.org
Uniting parents, teachers & community members to prevent child abuse & neglect, school dropout, juvenile crime, substance abuse & teenage pregnancy
Vito J Borrello, President

Policy Areas

Early Care & Learning Council
230 Washington Ave Ext, Albany, NY 12203-5390
518-690-4217 Fax: 518-690-2887
e-mail: mbasloe@earlycareandlearning.org
Web site: www.earlycareandlearning.org
Advocacy & education for the development of accessible and affordable, quality child care services
Marsha Basloe, Executive Director

Education & Assistance Corp Inc
50 Clinton St, Ste 107, Hempstead, NY 11550
516-539-0150 Fax: 516-539-0160
e-mail: lelder@eacinc.org
Web site: www.eacinc.org
Rehabilitation for nonviolent offenders; advocacy, education & counseling programs for youth, elderly & families
Lance W Elder, President & Chief Executive Officer

Empire Justice Center
119 Washington Ave, Albany, NY 12210
518-462-6831 Fax: 518-462-6687
e-mail: nkrupski@empirejustice.org
Web site: www.empirejustice.org
Empire Justice protects and strengthens the legal rights of people in New York State who are poor, disabled or disenfranchised.
Anne Erickson, President & Chief Executive Officer

Family Planning Advocates of New York State
17 Elk St, Albany, NY 12207
518-436-8408 Fax: 518-436-0004
e-mail: info@fpaofnys.org
Web site: www.fpaofnys.org
Reproductive rights
JoAnn M Smith, President/Chief Executive Officer

Federation Employment & Guidance Service (FEGS) Inc
315 Hudson St, 9th Fl, New York, NY 10013
212-366-8400 Fax: 212-366-8441
e-mail: info@fegs.org
Web site: www.fegs.org
Diversified health & human services system to help individuals achieve their potential at work, at home, at school and in the community
Gail Magaliff, Chief Executive Officer

Federation of Protestant Welfare Agencies Inc
281 Park Ave South, New York, NY 10010
212-777-4800 x322 Fax: 212-673-4085
e-mail: fgoldman@fpwa.org
Web site: www.fpwa.org
Childcare & child welfare, HIV/AIDS, elderly, income security
Fatima Goldman, Executive Director

Filipino American Human Services Inc (FAHSI)
185-14 Hillside Ave, Jamaica, NY 11432
718-883-1295 Fax: 718-523-9606
e-mail: admin@fahsi.org
Web site: www.fahsi.org
FAHSI is a community-based, non-profit organization dedicated to serving the Filipino and Filipino American community of New York City, particularly, marginalized sections such as youth, women, recent immigrants, and the elderly.
Johanna Martinez LMSW, Executive Director

Fordham University, Graduate School of Social Service
113 West 60th Street, Lincoln Center, New York, NY 10023
212-636-6616 Fax: 212-636-7876
e-mail: vaughan@fordham.edu
Web site: www.fordham.edu
Social work education, clinical social work, administration, client centered management
Peter B Vaughan, Dean

Friends & Relatives of Institutionalized Aged Inc (FRIA)
18 John St, Suite 905, New York, NY 10038
212-732-5667 or 212-732-4455 Fax: 212-732-6945
e-mail: fria@fria.org
Web site: www.fria.org
Free bilingual telephone helpline for information assistance and complaints about nursing homes, assisted living and other long-term care issues.
Betti Weimersheimer, Executive Director

Green Chimneys School-Green Chimneys Children's Services Inc
400 Doansburg Rd, Box 719, Brewster, NY 10509
845-279-2995 x119 Fax: 845-279-3077
Web site: www.greenchimneys.org
Residential treatment programs for emotionally troubled children & youths; therapeutic/educational Farm & Wildlife Conservation Center programs; therapeutic day school program
Joseph A Whalen, Executive Director

Guide Dog Foundation for the Blind Inc
371 East Jericho Turnpike, Smithtown, NY 11787-2976
631-930-9000 or 800-548-4337 Fax: 631-930-9009
e-mail: info@guidedog.org
Web site: www.guidedog.org
Provide guide dogs without charge to sight-impaired persons seeking enhanced mobility & independence
Wells B Jones, Chief Executive Officer

HeartShare Human Services of New York, Roman Catholic Diocese of Brooklyn
12 MetroTech Center, 29th Floor, Brooklyn, NY 11201
718-422-HEART Fax: 718-522-4506
e-mail: info@heartshare.org
Web site: www.heartshare.org
Service for the developmentally disabled children & family services & programs for people with HIV/AIDS
William R Guarinello, President & Chief Executive Officer

Helen Keller Services for the Blind
57 Willoughby Street, Brooklyn, NY 11201
718-522-2122 Fax: 718-935-9463
e-mail: info@helenkeller.org
Web site: www.helenkeller.org
Preschool, rehabilitation, employment & senior services, low vision & braille library services
Deborah Rodriguez-Samuelson, Director of Communications & Development

Hispanic Federation
55 Exchange Place, 5th Floor, New York, NY 10005
212-233-8955 Fax: 212-233-8996
Web site: www.hispanicfederation.org
Technical assistance, capacity building, grantmaking & advocacy for Latino nonprofit service providers
Lillian Rodriguez Lopez, President

Hispanic Outreach Services
40 North Main Ave, 5th Floor, Albany, NY 12010
518-453-6655 Fax: 518-641-6830
e-mail: elaine.escobales@reda.org
Web site: www.hispanicoutreachservices.org
Social service, youth guidance, language translation & immigration assistance programs
Elaine Escobales, Executive Director

Hospice & Palliative Care Association of NYS Inc
2 Computer Drive West, Suite 105, Albany, NY 12205
518-446-1483 Fax: 518-446-1484
e-mail: info@hpcanys.org
Web site: www.hpcanys.org
Hospice & palliative care information & referral service; educational programs; clinical, psychosocial & bereavement issues
Kathy A McMahon, President & Chief Executive Officer

Offices and agencies generally appear in alphabetical order, except when specific order is requested by listee.

Housing Works Inc
57 Willoughby Street, Brooklyn, NY 11201
347-473-7400 Fax: 347-473-7464
Web site: www.housingworks.org
Housing, health care, advocacy, job training & support services for homeless NY residents with HIV or AIDS
Michael Kink, Statewide Advocacy Coordinator & Legislative Counsel

Humane Society of the United States, Mid Atlantic Regional Office
270 US Hwy 206, Flanders, NJ 07836
973-927-5611 Fax: 973-927-5617
e-mail: maro@hsus.org
Web site: www.hsus.org
Nina Austenberg, Regional Director

Hunger Action Network of NYS (HANNYS)
275 State St, Albany, NY 12210
518-434-7371 Fax: 518-434-7390
e-mail: bhpham@hungeractionnys.org
Web site: www.hungeractionnys.org
Developing unified efforts to address the root causes of hunger & promote social justice
Bich Ha Pham, Executive Director

Hunter College, Brookdale Center for Healthy Aging and Longevity
425 E 25th St, New York, NY 10010
212-481-5420 or 212-481-4595 Fax: 212-481-3791
e-mail: mfahs@huntercuny.edu
Web site: www.brookdale.org
Policy research & development, training, publications & resources for institutions & community agencies
Marianne Fahs, Executive Director

Institute for Socio-Economic Studies
10 New King St, White Plains, NY 10604
914-686-7112 Fax: 914-686-0581
e-mail: info@socioeconomic.org
Web site: www.socioeconomic.org
Welfare reform, socioeconomic incentives, tax & healthcare reform
Leonard M Greene, President

Japanese American Social Services Inc
100 Gold St, Lower Level, New York, NY 10038
212-442-1541 Fax: 212-442-8627
e-mail: info@jassi.org
Web site: www.jassi.org
Bilingual/bicultural programs; assistance with government benefits, housing, immigration & legal rights
Margaret Fung, Executive Director

Korean Community Services of Metropolitan NY
149 West 24th St, 6th Fl, New York, NY 10011
212-463-9685 Fax: 212-463-8347
e-mail: kcskcsny.org
Web site: www.kcsny.org
Develop & deliver social services to support & assist members of the Korean & neighboring communities
Shin Son, Executive Director

NYS Bar Assn, Children & the Law Committee
Law Office of Anne Reynolds Copps
126 State St, 6th Fl, Albany, NY 12207
518-436-4170 Fax: 518-436-1456
e-mail: arcopps@nycap.rr.com
Anne Reynolds Copps, Chair

Lesbian, Gay, Bisexual & Transgender Community Ctr - Not For Profit
208 W 13th Street, New York, NY 10011-7702
212-620-7310 Fax: 212-924-2657
e-mail: info@gaycenter.org
Web site: www.gaycenter.org
Mental health counseling, out-patient chemical dependency treatment center, after-school youth services, HIV/AIDS services, advocacy, cultural programs, affordable meeting and conference services, and community-building.
Glennda Testone, Executive Director
Rob Wheeler, Director of Operations

Little Flower Children & Family Services
186 Joralemon St, Brooklyn, NY 11201-4326
718-875-3500 ext3650 or 631-929-6200 ext1123 Fax: 718-260-8863
e-mail: stupph@lfchild.org
Web site: www.littleflowerny.org
Foster care, adoption, child welfare, residential treatment services and residences for the developmentally disabled & day care; union free school district; corporate eldercare counseling services.
Hon. Herbert W. Stupp, Chief Executive Officer

Littman Krooks LLP
655 Third Ave, New York, NY 10017
212-490-2020 Fax: 212-490-2990
e-mail: bkrooks@littmankrooks.com
Web site: www.littmankrooks.com
Elder law and special needs planning
Bernard A Krooks, Partner

March of Dimes Birth Defects Foundation
1275 Mamaroneck Ave, White Plains, NY 10605
914-997-4641 Fax: 914-997-4662
e-mail: dstaples@marchofdimes.com
Web site: www.marchofdimes.com

New York Association for New Americans, Inc (NYANA)
2 Washington St, 9th Fl, New York, NY 10004-1102
212-425-2900 Fax: 212-344-1621
e-mail: jlazar@nyana.org
Web site: www.nyana.org
Social service referrals for immigrants
Joseph Lazar, CEO

NY Counseling Association Inc
PO Box 12636, Albany, NY 12212-2636
518-235-2026 Fax: 518-235-0910
e-mail: nycaoffice@nycounseling.org
Web site: www.nycounseling.org
Counseling professionals in education, mental health, career, employment, rehabilitation & adult development
Donald Newell, Executive Manager

NY Foundation for Senior Citizens Inc
11 Park Place, 14th Fl, New York, NY 10007-2801
212-962-7559 Fax: 212-227-2952
e-mail: nyfscinc@aol.com
Web site: www.nyfsc.org
Social services for seniors in New York City
Linda Hoffman, President

NYC Coalition Against Hunger
16 Beaver St, 3rd Fl, New York, NY 10004
212-825-0028 Fax: 212-825-0267
e-mail: jberg@nyccah.org
Web site: www.nyccah.org
Joel Berg, Executive Director

Policy Areas

Offices and agencies generally appear in alphabetical order, except when specific order is requested by listee.

NYS Association of Area Agencies on Aging
272 Broadway, Albany, NY 12204-2717
518-449-7080 Fax: 518-449-7055
e-mail: office@nysaaaa.org
Web site: www.nysaaaa.org
Agencies working to enhance effectiveness of programs for older persons
Laura A Cameron, Executive Director

NYS Corps Collaboration
24 Century Hill Drive, Ste 200, Latham, NY 12110
518-470-4995 Fax: 518-783-3577
e-mail: info@nyscc.net
Web site: www.nyscc.net
Statewide youth service & conservation corps addressing society's unmet needs & buiding self-esteem, a sense of civic responsibility & leadership skills
Linda J Cohen, Executive Director

NYS Industries for the Disabled (NYSID) Inc
11 Columbia Circle Drive, Albany, NY 12203
518-463-9706 or 800-221-5994 Fax: 518-463-9708
e-mail: administrator@nysid.org
Web site: www.nysid.org
Business development through 'preferred source' purchasing to increase employment opportunities for people with disabilities
Ronald P Romano, President & Chief Executive Officer

National Association of Social Workers, NYS Chapter
188 Washington Ave, Albany, NY 12210-2304
518-463-4741 or 800-724-6279 Fax: 518-463-6446
e-mail: info@naswnys.org
Web site: www.naswnys.org
Professional development & specialized training for professional social workers; standards for social work practice; advocacy for policies, services & programs that promote social justice
Jacqueline Melecio, Assistant Executive Director

National Council of Jewish Women
53 W 23rd St, 6th Fl, New York, NY 10010
212-645-4048 Fax: 212-645-7466
e-mail: action@ncjw.org
Web site: www.ncjw.org
Human rights & social service advocacy & education
Phyllis Snyder, President

National Urban League Inc (The)
120 Wall St, New York, NY 10005
212-558-5300 Fax: 212-344-5332
e-mail: info@nul.org
Web site: www.nul.org
Community-based movement devoted to empowering African Americans to enter the economic & social mainstream
Michele M Moore, Senior Vice President Communications & Marketing

Nelson A Rockefeller Inst of Govt, Federalism Research Grp
411 State St, Albany, NY 12203-1003
518-443-5522 Fax: 518-443-5788
e-mail: gaist@rockinst.org
Web site: www.rockinst.org
State management systems for social service programs
Thomas L Gais, Co-Director

New York Association of Homes & Services for the Aging
150 State St, Ste 301, Albany, NY 12207-1698
518-449-2707 Fax: 518-455-8908
e-mail: cyoung@nyahsa.org
Web site: www.nyahsa.org
Long term care
Carl Young, President

New York Community Trust (The)
909 Third Avenue, 22nd Fl, New York, NY 10022
212-686-0010 Fax: 212-532-8528
e-mail: info@nycommunitytrust.org
Web site: www.nycommunitytrust.org
Administrators of philanthropic funds
Lorie A Slutsky, President/Director

New York Public Welfare Association
130 Washington Ave, Albany, NY 12210
518-465-9305 Fax: 518-465-5633
e-mail: nypwa@nycap.rr.com
Web site: www.nypwa.com
Partnership of local social services districts dedicated to improve the quality & effectiveness of social welfare policy
Sheila Harrigan, Executive Director

New York Society for the Deaf
161 William St, 11th Fl, New York, NY 10038
646-278-8172 or TTY: 646-278-8171 Fax: 212-777-5740
Web site: www.nysd.org
Ensure full & equal access to appropriate, comprehensive clinical, residential & support services for deaf & deaf-blind persons
Kathleen Cox, Executive Director

New York State Association of Family Service Agencies Inc
29 North Hamilton Street, Suite 112, Poughkeepsie, NY 12601
845-790-5900 Fax: 845-790-5922
e-mail: info@nysafsa.org
Web site: www.nysafsa.org
Provides a forum for the exchange of information on issues relevant to children and families.
Allan Thomas, Executive Director

New York State Catholic Conference
465 State St, Albany, NY 12203-1004
518-434-6195 Fax: 518-434-9796
e-mail: info@nyscatholic.org
Web site: www.nyscatholic.org
Identify, formulate & implement public policy objectives of the NYS Bishops in health, education, welfare, human & civil rights
Richard E Barnes, Executive Director

New York State Citizens' Coalition for Children Inc
410 East Upland Road, Ithaca, NY 14850-2551
607-272-0034 Fax: 607-272-0035
e-mail: office@nysccc.org
Web site: www.nysccc.org
Adoption & foster care advocacy
Judith Ashton, Executive Director

New York State Community Action Association
2 Charles Blvd, Guilderland, NY 12084
518-690-0491 Fax: 518-690-0498
e-mail: dan@nyscaaonline.org
Web site: www.nyscaaonline.org
Dedicated to the growth & education of community action agencies in NYS to sustain their efforts in advocating & improving the lives of low-income New Yorkers
Daniel Maskin, Chief Executive Officer

New York State Rehabilitation Association
155 Washington Ave, Suite 410, Albany, NY 12210
518-449-2976 Fax: 518-426-4329
e-mail: nysra@nyrehab.org
Web site: www.nyrehab.org
Political advocacy, education, communications, networking & referral services for people with disabilities
Jeff Wise, JD, President

Offices and agencies generally appear in alphabetical order, except when specific order is requested by listee.

New York Urban League
204 W 136th St, New York, NY 10030
212-926-8000 Fax: 212-283-2736
Web site: www.nyul.org
Social services, job training, education & advocacy
Darwin M Davis, President & Chief Executive Officer

Nonprofit Coordinating Committee of New York
1350 Broadway, Rm 1801, New York, NY 10018-7802
212-502-4191 Fax: 212-502-4189
e-mail: mclark@npccny.org
Web site: www.npccny.org
Advocacy & government activities monitoring for NYC nonprofits
Michael Clark, Executive Director/President

North Shore Animal League America
25 Lewyt Street, Port Washington, NY 11050
516-883-7900 x257 Fax: 516-944-5732
e-mail: webmaster@nsalamerica.org
Web site: www.nsalamerica.org
Rescue, care & adoption services for orphaned companion animals
Perry Fina, Director, Marketing

Planned Parenthood of NYC, Inc
26 Bleecker St, New York, NY 10012
212-274-7292 Fax: 212-274-7276
e-mail: carla.goldstein@ppnyc.org
Web site: www.ppnyc.org
Carla Goldstein, Vice President, Public Affairs

Prevent Child Abuse New York
33 Elk Street, 2nd Floor, Albany, NY 12207
518-445-1273 or 800-CHILDREN Fax: 518-436-5889
e-mail: info@preventchildabuseny.org
Web site: www.preventchildabuseny.org
Child abuse prevention advocacy, education, technical assistance
Christine Deyss, Executive Director

ProLiteracy Worldwide
1320 Jamesville Ave, Syracuse, NY 13210-4224
315-422-9121 Fax: 315-422-6369
e-mail: info@proliteracy.org
Web site: www.proliteracy.org
Sponsors educational programs & services to empower adults & families through the acquisition of literacy skills & practices
Rochelle A Cassella, Director, Corporate Communications

Public/Private Ventures
The Chanin Building, 122 East 42nd St, 42nd Fl, New York, NY 10168
212-822-2400 Fax: 212-949-0439
e-mail: kfaulhaber@ppv.org
Web site: www.ppv.org
A national nonprofit, nonpartisan organization that tackles critical challenges facing low-income communities by seeking out and designing innovatove programs, rigorously testing them, and promoting the solutions proven to work.
Sheila Maguire, VP, Labor Market Initiatives

Resource Center for Independent Living (RCIL)
401-409 Columbia St, PO Box 210, Utica, NY 13503-0210
315-797-4642 or TTY 315-797-5837 Fax: 315-797-4747
e-mail: burt.danovitz@rcil.com
Web site: www.rcil.com
Services & advocacy for the disabled; public information & community education and awareness.
Burt Danovitz, Executive Director

Roman Catholic Diocese of Albany, Catholic Charities
40 N Main Ave, Albany, NY 12203
518-453-6650 Fax: 518-453-6792
Web site: www.ccrcda.org
Social & human services assistance: housing, shelters, day care, counseling, transportation, health & emergency
Sister Maureen Joyce, Chief Executive Officer

Rural & Migrant Ministry Inc
PO Box 4757, Poughkeepsie, NY 12602
845-485-8627 Fax: 845-485-1963
e-mail: hope@ruralmigrantministry.org
Web site: www.ruralmigrantministry.org
Working to end poverty & increase self-determination, education & economic resources for migrant farmworkers & the rural poor
Richard Witt, Executive Director

PathStone Corporation
400 East Ave, Rochester, NY 14607
585-340-3365 Fax: 585-340-3357
e-mail: jlewis@pathstone.org
Web site: www.pathstone.org
Advance self-sufficiency of farm workers, low-income & other disenfranchised people & communities through advocacy & programs including training & employment, housing child development, health & safety, & home ownership
Jeffrey Lewis, Senior VP Planning & Research

Salvation Army, Empire State Division
PO Box 148, Syracuse, NY 13206-0148
315-434-1300 x310 Fax: 315-434-1399
Web site: www.salvationarmy.org
Donald Lance, Divisional Commander

Springbrook NY, Inc
2705 State Highway 28, Oneonta, NY 13820
607-286-7171 Fax: 607-286-7166
e-mail: kennedyp@springbrookny.org
Web site: www.springbrookny.org
Patricia E Kennedy, Executive Director

Center for Policy Research
Syracuse University, Maxwell School of Citizenship & Public Affairs
200 Eggers Hall, Syracuse, NY 13244-1020
315-443-3114 Fax: 315-443-1081
e-mail: ctrpol@syr.edu
Web site: www.maxwell.syr.edu
Education, healthcare, entrepreneurship policies, social welfare, income distribution & comparative social policies
Christine L Himes, Professor of Sociology, Director

United Jewish Appeal-Federation of Jewish Philanthropies of NY
130 East 59th Street, New York, NY 10022
212-980-1000 Fax: 518-463-1266
e-mail: contact@ujafedny.org
Web site: www.ujafedny.org
Cares for those in need, rescues those in harm's way, and renews and strengthens the Jewish people in New York, in Israel , and around the world.
Jerry Levin, President

United Neighborhood Houses - Not For Profit
70 W 36th St, 5th Fl, New York, NY 10018
212-967-0322 Fax: 212-967-0792
e-mail: nwackstein@unhny.org
Web site: www.unhny.org
Federation of NYC settlement houses that provides issue advocacy & management assistance for member agencies' social, educational & cultural programs
Nancy Wackstein, Executive Director

Policy Areas

Offices and agencies generally appear in alphabetical order, except when specific order is requested by listee.

United Way of Central New York
518 James St, PO Box 2129, Syracuse, NY 13220-2227
315-428-2216
e-mail: ccollie@unitedway-cny.org
Web site: www.unitedway-cny.org
Fundraising & support to human & social services organizations
Craig E Collie, Vice President, Volunteer Resource Development

United Way of New York City
2 Park Ave, New York, NY 10016
212-251-2500 Fax: 212-696-1220
e-mail: lmandell@uwnyc.org
Web site: www.unitedwaynyc.org
Works with partners from all sectors to create, support, & execute strategic initiatives that seek to achieve measurable improvement in the lives of the city's most valuable residents and communities
Lawrence Mandell, President & Chief Executive Officer

Upstate Homes for Children & Adults Inc
2705 State Hwy 28, Oneonta, NY 13820
607-286-7171 Fax: 607-286-7166
e-mail: kennedyp@upstatehome.org
Web site: www.upstatehome.org
Education/mental hygiene
Patricia E Kennedy, Executive Director

Welfare Research Inc
112 State St, Suite 1340, Albany, NY 12207
518-432-2563 Fax: 518-432-2564
e-mail: administration@welfareresearch.org
Web site: www.welfareresearch.org
Contract research in social service & related policy areas
Virginia Hayes Sibbison, Executive Director

World Hunger Year Inc
505 Eighth Ave, Suite 2100, New York, NY 10018-6582
212-629-8850 Fax: 212-465-9274
e-mail: why@worldhungeryear.org
Web site: www.worldhungeryear.org
Addresses root causes of hunger & poverty by promoting effective & innovative community-based solutions
Bill Ayres, Executive Director

YAI/National Institute for People with Disabilities
460 W 34th St, New York, NY 10001-2382
212-273-6110 or 866-2-YAI-LINK Fax: 212-947-7524
e-mail: jmlcares@yai.org
Web site: www.yai.org
Programs, services & advocacy for people with autism, mental retardation & other developmental disabilities of all ages, and their families; special education & early learning programs
Joel M Levy, Chief Executive Officer

Offices and agencies generally appear in alphabetical order, except when specific order is requested by listee.

TAXATION & REVENUE

NEW YORK STATE

GOVERNOR'S OFFICE

Governor's Office
Executive Chamber
State Capitol
Albany, NY 12224
518-474-8390 Fax: 518-474-1513
Web site: www.ny.gov

Governor:
Andrew M Cuomo 518-474-8390
Secretary to the Governor:
William Mulrow 518-474-4246
Counsel to the Governor:
Alphonso David 518-474-8343
Director, Communications:
Melissa DeRosa .518-474-8418 or 212-681-4640

EXECUTIVE DEPARTMENTS AND RELATED AGENCIES

New York State Liquor Authority (Division of Alcoholic Beverage Control)
80 S Swan St
Ste 900
Albany, NY 12210-8002
518-474-3114 Fax: 518-402-4015
Web site: www.sla.ny.gov

317 Lenox Ave
New York, NY 10027
212-961-8300
Fax: 212-961-8299

Chair:
Vincent Bradley . . . . .212-961-8300 or 518-473-6559
Commissioner:
Jeanique Greene 212-961-8300
Counsel:
Jacqueline Flug 518-474-3114/fax: 518-402-2304

Administration
Secretary to the Authority:
Jacqueline Held. 518-473-6559
Deputy Commissioner, Administration:
Chad Loshbaugh 518-473-0365
Director, Public Affairs:
William Crowley . . . . .518-474-3114 or 518-474-4875
fax: 518-473-9565

Licensing & Enforcement

Albany (Zone II)
80 S Swan St, Ste 900, Albany, NY 12210-8002
CEO:
Kerri O'Brien 518-474-3114
Deputy Counsel:
Lisa Bonacci 518-474-3114
Director, Information Technology:
Michael Drake. 518-474-3114/fax: 518-473-7527

Buffalo (Zone III)
Iskalo Electric Tower, 535 Washington St, Ste 303, Buffalo, NY 14203
716-847-3035

Deputy Commissioner, Licensing:
David L Edmunds Jr. 716-847-3001
Supervising Beverage Control Investigator:
Gary Bartikofsky 716-847-3035

New York City (Zone I)
317 Lenox Avenue, New York, NY 10027
212-961-8385
Supervising Beverage Control Investigator:
Franklin Englander. 212-961-8376
Deputy Chief Executive Officer:
Michael Jones. 212-961-8300

Budget, Division of the
State Capitol
Albany, NY 12224
518-473-3885 Fax: 518-474-9041
Web site: www.budget.ny.gov

Director:
Mary Beth Labate 518-474-2300
First Deputy Director:
Dominic Colafati. 518-474-8282
Deputy Director:
Davaid Lara. 518-402-4246
Budget Services Head:
Bob Brondi 518-473-0580
Public Protrection Head:
Anne Bink 518-474-4313
Press Officer:
Morris Peters. 518-473-3885
e-mail: dob.sm.press@budget.ny.gov

Law Department
120 Broadway
New York, NY 10271-0332
212-416-8000 or 800-771-7755
Web site: www.ag.ny.gov

State Capitol
Albany, NY 12224-0341
518-474-7330
Fax: 518-473-9909

Attorney General:
Eric T Schneiderman . . . . .212-416-8050 or 518-474-7330

Social Justice
Executive Deputy Attorney General:
Alvin L Braggs, Jr. 212-416-8075/fax: 212-416-8942

Charities Bureau
Bureau Chief:
James G Sheehan 212-416-8410

Economic Justice
Executive Deputy Attorney General:
Karla Sanchez. 212-416-8050

Internet Bureau
Bureau Chief:
Kathleen McGee 212-416-8433/fax: 212-416-8369

Investor Protection Bureau
Bureau Chief:
Chad Johnson 212-416-8225/fax: 212-416-8816

State Counsel
Chief Deputy Attorney General & Counsel:
Harlan Levy 212-416-8525

Offices and agencies generally appear in alphabetical order, except when specific order is requested by listee.

Civil Recoveries Bureau
Bureau Chief:
    John Cremo 518-776-2173/fax: 518-915-7731

Litigation Bureau
Bureau Chief:
    Lisa Dell . . . . .518-776-2300 or 212-416-8610

New York State Gaming Commission

One Broadway Center
PO Box 7500
Schenectady, NY 12301-7500
518-388-3300 Fax: 518-388-3423
Web site: www.nylottery.ny.gov

Director:
    Robert Williams 518-388-3400
General Counsel:
    Ed Burns 518-388-3408
Deputy Director/COO:
    Gardner Gurney 518-388-3406
Director, Communications:
    Christy Calicchia 518-388-3415/fax: 518-388-3423
Director, Sales & Marketing:
    Randall Lex .518-388-3430/fax: 518-388-3433

Regional Offices

Eastern Region
One Broadway Center, Suite 700, Schenectady, NY 12301
Contact:
    Fred Chick 518-388-3428/fax: 518-388-3437

Central/Finger Lakes Regions
Rochester Office
    First Federal Plaza Bldg, 28 E Main St, Rochester, NY 14614
    Contact:
        Vacant 585-246-4200/fax: 585-246-4201
Syracuse Office
    Deys Centennial Bldg, 401 S Salina St, Syracuse, NY 13202
    Contact:
        Robin Sywulski 315-448-4300/fax: 315-448-4313

Hudson Valley Region
18 Westage Drive, Ste 6, Fishkill, NY 12524
Contact:
    Georgene Perlman 845-897-2412/fax: 845-897-3528

Long Island Region
1000 Zeckendorf Blvd, Garden City, NY 11530
Contact:
    Jim Benoit 516-222-8260/fax: 516-222-8279

New York City Region
15 Beaver St, New York, NY 10004
Contact:
    Thomas Breig 646-486-6100/fax: 646-486-6177

Western Region
165 Genesse St, Buffalo, NY 14203
Contact:
    Doug Bautz .716-847-3469/fax: 716-847-3479

Gaming Commission
Executive Director:
    Robert Williams 518-388-3400
Communications:
    Lee Park 518-388-3415

Real Property Tax Services, Office of

WA Harriman State Campus
Bldg. 8A
Albany, NY 12227
518-474-2982 Fax: 518-474-9276
e-mail: nysorps@orps.state.ny.us
Web site: www.tax.ny.gov/about/orpts

Acting Secretary of the Board & Assistant Deputy Commissioner:
    Susan Savage 518-474-6742
State Board Member:
    Darlene Maloney 518-474-3793
    e-mail: darlene.maloney@tax.ny.gov
State Board Member (Chair):
    Matthew Rand 518-474-3793
State Board Member:
    John M. Bacheller 518-474-3793
    e-mail: geoffrey.gloak@orps.state.ny.us
State Board Member:
    Edgar A King 518-474-3793
    e-mail: geoffrey.gloak@orps.state.ny.us

Albany (Northern Region)
WA Harriman State Campus, Bldg. 8A, Albany, NY 12227
Regional Director:
    Robert Aiken 518-486-4403/fax: 518-435-8593
    e-mail: orpts.northern@tax.ny.gov

Batavia (Western Region)
Genesee County Bldg 2, 3837 W Main Rd, Batavia, NY 14020
Regional Director:
    Christine Bannister 585-343-4363/fax: 585-435-8598
    e-mail: orpts.western@tax.ny.gov

Long Island Satellite Office
250 Veterans Memorial Hgwy, Rm 4A-6, Hauppauge, NY 11788
Manager:
    Steve Hartnett 631-595-4071/fax: 518-435-8572
    e-mail: orpts.southern@tax.ny.gov

South
44 S. Broadway, 6th Floor, White Plains, NY 10601
Regional Director:
    John Wolham 914-215-6300/fax: 518-435-8498
    e-mail: orpts.southern@tax.ny.gov

Ray Brook Satellite Office
884 NYS Rte 86, PO Box 309, Ray Brook, NY 12977
Regional Director:
    Robert Aiken 518-891-1780/fax: 518-435-8593
    e-mail: orpts.raybrook@tax.ny.gov

Syracuse (Central Region)
333 E. Washington ST, Syracuse, NY 13202
Regional Director:
    Teresa Frank 315-471-2347/fax: 518-435-8583
    e-mail: orpts.central@tax.ny.gov

Tax Appeals, Division of

Agency Building 1
Empire State Plaza
Albany, NY 12223
518-266-3000 Fax: 518-271-0886
e-mail: nysdota@nysdta.org
Web site: www.nysdta.org

Tax Appeals Tribunal
President & Commissioner:
    James H Tully Jr 518-266-3050
Commissioner:
    Charles H Nesbitt 518-266-3050

Offices and agencies generally appear in alphabetical order, except when specific order is requested by listee.

Commissioner:
   Vacant 518-266-3050
Counsel:
   Nicholas A. Behuniak 518-266-3052
Secretary to the Tribunal:
   Jean A McDonnell 518-266-3036

Administrative Law Judges & Officers
Supervising Administrative Law Judge:
   Daniel J Ranalli. 518-266-3000
Director, Administration:
   George J Cannon. 518-266-3041

Taxation & Finance Department
State Campus
Bldg 9, Rm 227
Albany, NY 12227
518-457-4242 Fax: 518-457-2486
Web site: www.tax.ny.gov

Commissioner:
   Thomas H Mattox 518-457-2244
Executive Deputy Commissioner:
   Nonie Manion 518-457-7358
Deputy Commissioner & Counsel:
   Amanda Hiller 518-457-3746/fax: 518-457-8247
Director, Conciliation & Mediation Services:
   Kevin Law. 518-485-8063
Director, Executive Correspondence & Legislative Affairs:
   Maryann Tucker 518-457-2398
Director, Public Information:
   Geoffrey Gloak 518-457-7377

Office of Processing & Taxpayer Services (OPTS)
Deputy Commissioner:
   Edward Chaszczewski 518-457-1000

Human Resources Management
Director:
   Gina Lysyczyn 518-457-2786

Operations Support Bureau
Director:
   Lisa Negus 518-457-4250

Office of Budget & Management Analysis
Chief Financial Officer:
   Eric Mostert 518-485-5080
Director:
   Eric Mostert 518-457-9559

Planning & Management Analysis Bureau
Director:
   Mary Ellen Nagengast 518-457-8660

Office of Information Technology Services
Chief Information Officer:
   Daniel Chan 518-292-7808

Office of Processing & Taxpayer Services
Director:
   Helen Pelersi. 518-591-1944

Office of State Treasury
Deputy Commissioner & Treasurer:
   Aida Brewer. .518-474-4250/fax: 518-402-4118

Office of Criminal Enforcement
Deputy Commissioner:
   Risa Sugarman 518-457-9692

Audit Division
Director, Tax Audits:
   Joe Carzo 518-451-8910

Collections & Civil Enforcement
Director:
   Patricia Coneys. 518-591-1980

Office of Tax Policy Analysis
Deputy Commissioner:
   Robert D Plattner 518-457-4357

CORPORATIONS, AUTHORITIES AND COMMISSIONS

New York State Financial Control Board
123 William St
23rd Fl
New York, NY 10038-3804
212-417-5046 Fax: 212-417-5055
e-mail: nysfcb@fcb.state.ny.us
Web site: www.fcb.state.ny.us

Acting Executive Director:
   Jeffrey Sommer 212-417-5066
Deputy Director, Expenditure & Covered Organization Analysis:
   Dennis DeLisle 212-417-5069
Deputy Director, Finance & Capital Analysis:
   Jewel A. Douglas
Acting Deputy Director, Economic & Revenue Analysis:
   Martin Fischman. 212-417-5068
Associate Director, Administration:
   Mattie W Taylor 212-417-5053

NEW YORK STATE LEGISLATURE

See Legislative Branch in Section 1 for additional Standing Committee and Subcommittee information.

Assembly Standing Committees

Racing & Wagering
Chair:
   James Gary Pretlow (D) 518-455-5291
Ranking Minority Member:
   Andrew Garbarino (R) 518-455-4611

Real Property Taxation
Chair:
   Sandra R Galef (D). 518-455-5348
Ranking Minority Member:
   Kieran Michael Lalor 518-455-5725

Ways & Means
Chair:
   Herman D Farrell, Jr (D). 518-455-5491
Ranking Minority Member:
   Bob Oaks (R) 518-455-5655

Senate Standing Committees

Finance
Chair:
   John A DeFrancisco (R) 518-455-3511
Ranking Minority Member:
   Liz Krueger (D). 518-455-2297

Racing, Gaming & Wagering
Chair:
   John J Bonacic (R) 518-455-3181

Offices and agencies generally appear in alphabetical order, except when specific order is requested by listee.

Policy Areas

Ranking Minority Member:
  Joseph Addabbo, Jr. (D) 518-455-2322

U.S. GOVERNMENT

EXECUTIVE DEPARTMENTS AND RELATED AGENCIES

US Department of Homeland Security (DHS)
Web site: www.dhs.gov

Bureau of Immigration & Customs Enforcement (ICE)
  Web site: www.ice.gov

  New York District Office
  601 W 26th St, Ste 700, New York, NY 10001
  Special Agent-in-Charge:
    Andrew M. McLees 646-230-3200
    Albany Sub Office
      1 Clinton Avenue, #746, Albany, NY 12207-2354
      Group Supervisor:
        LeRoy Tario 518-220-2100
      Resident Agent-in-Charge:
        Jack McQuade 518-220-2100

Customs & Border Protection (CBP)
  202-354-1000
  Web site: www.cbp.gov

  Buffalo Field Office
  300 Airborne Parkway, Suite 300, Buffalo, NY 14225
  716-626-0400
  Director:
    James T. Engelman 716-626-0400 x201/fax: 716-626-9281
    Albany, Port of
      445 Broadway, Room 216, Albany, NY 12207
      518-431-0200
      Port Director:
        Drew Wescott 518-431-0200/fax: 518-431-0203
    Buffalo, Port of
      Larkin at Exchange, 726 Exchange, Suite 400, Buffalo, NY 14210
      716-843-8300
      Area Port Director:
        Joseph Wilson 716-843-8300
    Champlain, Port of . . . . .fax: 518-298-8395
      237 W Service Rd, Champlain, NY 12919
      518-298-8311 Fax: 518-298-8395
      Area Port Director:
        Christopher Perry 518-298-8347/fax: 518-298-8314
    Ogdensburg, Port of
      104 Bridge Approach Rd, Ogdensburg, NY 13669
      Port Director:
        William Mitchell 315-393-1390/fax: 315-393-7472

  New York Field Office . . . . .fax: 646-733-3245
  1 Penn Plaza, 11th Fl, New York, NY 10119
  646-733-3100 Fax: 646-733-3245
  Director, Field Operations:
    Susan T Mitchell 646-733-3100
  Public Affairs Liaison:
    John Saleh 646-733-3215
    Field Counsel - New York
      Director, New York Field Operations:
        Robert Perez 646-733-3200
    Laboratory Division
      Director:
        Tom Governo 973-368-1901

US Justice Department
Web site: www.usdoj.gov

Bureau of Alcohol, Tobacco, Firearms & Explosives
Web site: www.atf.gov

  New York Field Division .fax: 646-335-9001
  32 Old Slip, Suite 3500, New York, NY 10005
  646-335-9000 Fax: 646-335-9001
  Spec Agent-in-Chg:
    Joseph Anarumo 646-335-9000
  Public Information Officer:
    Charles Mulham 718-650-4040

US Treasury Department
Web site: www.treasury.gov

Internal Revenue Service
  Web site: www.irs.gov

  Appeals Unit - Office of Directors
  290 Broadway, 13th Fl, New York, NY 10007
  Director, Appeals, Area 1 (Large Business & Specialty):
    Richard Guevara 212-298-2270/fax: 212-298-2282
  Director, Appeals, Area 1 (General):
    Raymond Wolff 212-298-2400/fax: 212-298-2648

  Criminal Investigation Unit - New York Field Office
  Spec Agent-in-Chg:
    Toni Weirauch

  Large & Mid-Size Business Division (LMSB)
  290 Broadway, 12th Fl, New York, NY 10007
  Director, Financial Services:
    Rosemary Sereti 212-298-2130/fax: 212-298-2124
    Office of Chief Counsel LMSB Area 1 . . . . .fax: 917-421-3937
      33 Maiden Ln, 12th Fl, New York, NY 10038
      Area Counsel:
        Roland Barral 917-421-4667
      Deputy Area Counsel:
        Peter J Graziano 917-421-4632

  Management Information Technology Services - Northeast Area
  290 Broadway, 12th Fl, New York, NY 10007
  Director, Information Technology:
    Vacant 212-298-2050/fax: 212-298-2595

  Office of Chief Counsel
  33 Maiden Ln, 14th Fl, New York, NY 10038
  Area Counsel for SBSE & W & I:
    Frances Regan 917-421-4737/fax: 917-421-3944
  Associate Area Counsel for SBSE & W & I:
    Janet F Appel 516-688-1707

  Small Business & Self-Employed Division (SBSE)
    New York SBSE Compliance Services
      290 Broadway, 14th Fl, New York, NY 10007
      Program Manager, Compliance Centers Document Matching
        Programs:
          Shirley Greene 212-298-2001/fax: 212-298-2062
    SBSE-Compliance Area 2/New York
      290 Broadway, 7th Fl, New York, NY 10007
      Director, Compliance Area 2:
        Michael Donovan 212-436-1886/fax: 212-436-1046
    SBSE-Taxpayer Education & Communication (TEC)
      10 Metro Tech Center, 625 Fulton St, 6th Fl, Brooklyn, NY 11201
      Area Director:
        Ellen Murphy 718-488-2000/fax: 718-488-2077

  Tax Exempt & Government Entities Div (TEGE)-Northeast Area
  10 Metro Tech Center, 625 Fulton St, PO Box 029162, Brooklyn, NY
  11201
  Area Manager, Employee Plans:
    Robert Henn 718-488-2014
    TEGE Area Counsel's Office
      1600 Stewart Ave, Ste 601, Westbury, NY 11590

Offices and agencies generally appear in alphabetical order, except when specific order is requested by listee.

Area Counsel:
Laurence Ziegler............516-688-1701/fax: 516-688-1750

Taxpayer Advocate Service (TAS)
Andover Campus Service Center
310 Lowell St, Stop 120, Andover, MA 1812
Taxpayer Advocate for Upstate NY:
Vicki L Coss...............973-474-5549/fax: 978-247-9034
Brookhaven Campus Service Center
1040 Waverly Ave, Stop 02, Holtsville, NY 11742
Taxpayer Advocate for Downstate NY:
Ed Safrey 631-654-6686/fax: 631-447-4879
Brooklyn Office
2 Metro Tech Center, 100 Myrtle Avenue, 7th Floor, Brooklyn, NY 11201
Taxpayer Advocate:
Anita Kitson 718-834-2200/fax: 718-834-6545
Manhattan Office
290 Broadway, 5th Fl, New York, NY 10007
Taxpayer Advocate:
Peter L Gorga, Jr............212-436-1011/fax: 212-436-1900
Office of Director, Area 1 (New York State & New England)
290 Broadway, 14th Fl, New York, NY 10007
Area Director:
Mary Ann Silvaggio.........212-298-2015/fax: 212-298-2016
Upstate New York Office
Leo O'Brien Federal Bldg, Rm 354, 1 Clinton Sq, Albany, NY 12207
Taxpayer Advocate:
Georgeann Smith 518-427-5413/fax: 518-427-5494
Western New York State Office
201 Como Park Blvd, Buffalo, NY 14227-1416
Taxpayer Advocate:
William Wirth.............716-686-4850/fax: 716-686-4851

Wage & Investmnt Div-Stakehldr Partnership Ed & Comm (SPEC)
Albany Territory
1 Clinton Ave, Rm 600, Albany, NY 12207
Territory Manager:
Amy Albee....................................518-427-5424
Area 1 Director's Office
135 High St, Hartford, CT 06103
Area Director:
Robert Nadeau.............................860-756-4566
Buffalo Territory
201 Como Park Blvd, Cheektowaga, NY 14227
Territory Manager:
Rick Pearl...................................716-961-5123
New York Territory
290 Broadway, 7th Fl, New York, NY 10007
Territory Mgr:
Susan Quackenbush.........................212-436-1517

US Mint ....fax: 845-446-6258
Rte 218, PO Box 37, West Point, NY 10996
Fax: 845-446-6258
Web site: www.usmint.gov
Plant Manager:
David Motl 800-872-6468

U.S. CONGRESS

See U.S. Congress Chapter for additional Standing Committee and Subcommittee information.

House of Representatives Standing Committees

Appropriations
Chair:
Harold Rogers (R-KY) 202-225-4601

Ranking Member:
Nita M. Lowey (D-NY) 202-225-6506
New York Delegate:
Bill Owens (D) 202-225-4611
New York Delegate:
Jose E Serrano (D) 202-225-4361

Budget
Chair:
Paul Ryan (R-WI)................................202-225-4601
Ranking Member:
Chris Van Hollen (D-MD) 202-225-5341
New York Delegate:
Hakeem Jeffries (D) 202-225-5936

Ways & Means
Chair:
Dave Camp (R-MI).................................202-225-3561
Ranking Member:
Sander Levin (D-MI) 202-225-3880
New York Delegate:
Joseph Crowley (D) 202-225-3965
New York Delegate:
Tom Reed (R)....................................202-225-3161
New York Delegate:
Charles B. Rangel (D)............................202-225-4365

Joint Senate & House Standing Committees

Joint Committee on Taxation
Chair:
Dave Camp (R-MI)................................202-224-3561
Vice Chair:
Max Baucus (D-MT) 202-225-2651

Senate Standing Committees

Appropriations
Chair:
Barbara A. Mikulski (D-MD).......................202-224-4654
Vice Chair:
Richard C. Shelby (R-AL) 202-224-5744

Budget
Chair:
Patty Murray (D-WA).............................202-224-2621
Ranking Member:
Jeff Sessions (R-AL)............................202-224-4124

Finance
Chair:
Max Baucus (R-MT)..............................202-224-2651
Ranking Member:
Orrin G. Hatch (R-UT)..........................202-224-5251

Subcommittee
Taxation & IRS Oversight
Chair:
Michael F. Bennet (D-CO) 202-224-5852
Ranking Member:
Michael B. Enzi (R-WY)......................202-224-3424

Homeland Security & Governmental Affairs
Chair:
Thomas R. Carper (D-DE) 202-224-2441
Ranking Member:
Tom Coburn (R-OK) 202-224-5754

Offices and agencies generally appear in alphabetical order, except when specific order is requested by listee.

PRIVATE SECTOR

NYS Bar Assn, Pension Simplification Cmte
Alvin D Lurie PC
13 Country Club Drive, Larchmont, NY 10538
914-834-6725 Fax: 914-834-6725
e-mail: allurie@optonline.net
First recipient of Lifetime Employee Benefits Achievement Award of
American Bar Association's Employee Benefits Committee of the Tax Section.
1st appointee of Assistant Commissioner in the Internal Revenue Service.
Alvin D Lurie, President

Association of Towns of the State of New York
150 State St, Albany, NY 12207
518-465-7933 Fax: 518-465-0724
e-mail: jhaber@nytowns.org
Web site: www.nytowns.org
Advocacy, education for local government
G Jeffrey Haber, Executive Director

Citizens Budget Commission
Two Penn Plaza, Fifth Floor, New York, NY 10121
212-279-2605 Fax: 212-868-4745
e-mail: cmb2@nyu.edu
Web site: www.cbcny.org
Nonpartisan, nonprofit civic organization devoted to influencing constructive
change in the finances and services of New York City and New York State
government
Charles Brecher, Consulting Research Director

Council of State Governments, Eastern Conference
100 Wall St, 20th Fl, New York, NY 10005
212-482-2320 Fax: 212-482-2344
e-mail: alan@csgeast.org
Web site: www.csgeast.org
Economic & fiscal programs
Alan V Sokolow, Regional Director

NYS Bar Assn, Tax Section
Sullivan & Cromwell LLP
125 Broad Street, New York, NY 10004
212-558-4000 Fax: 212-558-3588
Web site: www.sullcrom.com
David P Hariton, Chair

NYS Bar Assn, Trusts & Estates Law Section
Day Pitney LLP
7 Times Square, 41st & 42nd St, New York, NY 10036
212-297-5800 or 212-297-2468 Fax: 212-916-2940
e-mail: gwwhitaker@daypitney.com
Web site: www.daypitney.com
Domestic and international trusts and estates.
G Warren Whitaker,

Fiscal Policy Institute
1 Lear Jet Lane, Latham, NY 12110
518-786-3156
e-mail: mauro@fiscalpolicy.org
Web site: www.fiscalpolicy.org
Nonpartisan research & education; tax, budget, economic & related public
policy issues
Frank Mauro, Executive Director

Community Bankers Assn of NY State, Accounting & Taxation Cmte
North Fork Bank
275 Broadhollow Road, Melville, NY 11747
631-844-1004
Web site: www.greenpoint.com
Aurelie Campbell, Co-Chair

Hawkins Delafield & Wood LLP
One Chase Manhattan Plaza, 43rd Floor, New York, NY 10005
212-820-9434 Fax: 212-820-9666
e-mail: jprogers@hawkins.com
Web site: www.hawkins.com
Tax law; public finance & municipal contracts
Joseph P Rogers, Jr, Counsel

Manhattan Institute, Center for Civic Innovation
52 Vanderbilt Ave, 2nd Fl, New York, NY 10017
212-599-7000 Fax: 212-599-3494
Web site: www.manhattan-institute.org
NY city & state tax, fiscal policy
Lindsay Young, Executive Director, Communications

Moody's Investors Service, Public Finance Group
99 Church St, New York, NY 10007
212-553-7780 Fax: 212-298-7113
e-mail: dennis.farrell@moodys.com
Web site: www.moodys.com
Municipal debt ratings & analysis
Dennis M Farrell, Group Managing Director

NYS Conference of Mayors & Municipal Officials
119 Washington Ave, Albany, NY 12210
518-463-1185 Fax: 518-463-1190
e-mail: info@nycom.org
Web site: www.nycom.org
Legislative advocacy for NYS cities & villages
Peter A Baynes, Executive Director

National Federation of Independent Business
1 Commerce Plaza, Ste 1119, Albany, NY 12260-1000
518-434-1262 Fax: 518-426-8799
e-mail: mike.elmendorf@nfib.org
Web site: www.nfib.org
Small business advocacy; supporting pro-small business candidates at the
state & federal levels
Michael Elmendorf, State Director

Nelson A Rockefeller Institute of Government
411 State St, Albany, NY 12203-1003
518-443-5522 Fax: 518-443-5788
e-mail: nathanr@rockinst.org
Web site: www.rockinst.org
Management & finance of welfare, health & employment of state & local
governments nationally & especially in NY
Richard P Nathan, Director

New York State Assessors' Association
PO Box 888, Middletown, NY 10940
845-344-0292 Fax: 845-343-8238
e-mail: nysaa@nyassessor.com
Web site: www.nyassessor.com
Real property tax issues
Thomas Frey, Executive Secretary

New York State Government Finance Officers Association Inc
126 State St, 5th Fl, Albany, NY 12207
518-465-1512 Fax: 518-434-4640
e-mail: info@nysgfoa.org
Web site: www.nysgfoa.org
Membership organization dedicated to the professional management of
governmental resources
Brian Roulin CPA, President

New York State Society of Certified Public Accountants
3 Park Avenue, 18th Floor, New York, NY 10016-5991
212-719-8418 Fax: 212-719-3364
e-mail: doleary@nysscpa.org
Web site: www.nysscpa.org
Dennis O'Leary, Director, Government Relations

Offices and agencies generally appear in alphabetical order, except when specific order is requested by listee.

New York State Society of Enrolled Agents
Office of David J Silverman
866 UN Plaza, #415, New York, NY 10017
212-752-6983 Fax: 212-758-5478
e-mail: taxproblm@aol.com
Web site: www.nyssea.org
David J Silverman, Chair, Legislative/Government Relations Committee

Robert Schalkenbach Foundation
90 John Street, Suite 501, New York, NY 10038
212-683-6424 Fax: 212-683-6454
e-mail: msullivan@schalkenbach.org
Web site: www.schalkenbach.org
Land value taxation, real property & economic publications
Mark A Sullivan, Administrative Director

Urbanomics
115 Fifth Ave, 3rd Fl, New York, NY 10003
212-353-7462 Fax: 212-353-7494
e-mail: r.armstrong@urbanomics.org
Web site: www.urbanomics.org
Economic development planning studies, market studies, tax policy analyses, program evaluations, economic & demographic forecasts
Regina B Armstrong, Principal

Wachtell, Lipton, Rosen & Katz
51 W 52nd St, New York, NY 10019
212-403-1241 Fax: 212-403-2241
e-mail: pccanellos@wlrk.com
Web site: www.wlrk.com
Tax law
Peter C Canellos, Office of Counsel

Offices and agencies generally appear in alphabetical order, except when specific order is requested by listee.

TOURISM, ARTS & SPORTS

NEW YORK STATE

GOVERNOR'S OFFICE

Governor's Office
Executive Chamber
State Capitol
Albany, NY 12224
518-474-8390 Fax: 518-474-1513
Web site: www.ny.gov

Governor:
Andrew M Cuomo 518-474-8390
Secretary to the Governor:
William Mulrow 518-474-4246
Counsel to the Governor:
Alphonso David 518-474-8343
Director of Policy:
John Maggiore 518-408-2576
Director, Communications:
Melissa DeRosa . . . . .518-474-8418 or 212-681-4640
First Assistant Counsel:
Sandi Toll 518-474-8434

EXECUTIVE DEPARTMENTS AND RELATED AGENCIES

Council on the Arts
300 Park Avenue South
10th Floor
New York, NY 10010
212-459-8800 or 800-510-0021
e-mail: info@arts.ny.gov
Web site: www.nysca.org

Chair:
Aby Rosen. 212-459-8800
Vice Chair:
Dr Barbaralee Diamonstein-Spielvogel 212-459-8800
Executive Director:
Lisa Robb 212-459-8800
e-mail: executive.director@arts.ny.gov
Deputy Executive Director, Programs:
Megan White. 212-459-8806
e-mail: megan.white@arts.ny.gov
Director, Agency Operations:
Brenda Brown. 212-459-8827
e-mail: brenda.brown@arts.ny.gov

Administrative Services
Director:
Tracy Hamilton-Thompson. 212-459-8822
e-mail: tracy.hamilton@arts.ny.gov
Purchasing:
Judy Evans 212-459-8817
e-mail: judy.evans@arts.ny.gov

Fiscal Management
Associate Auditor:
Edward Leung. 212-459-8813
e-mail: edward.leung@arts.ny.gov

Information Technology
Manager:
Lenn Ditman 212-459-9910
e-mail: lenn.ditman@arts.ny.gov

Program Staff

Architecture & Design/Facilities/Museum
Director:
Kristen Herron 212-459-8825
e-mail: kristin.herron@arts.ny.gov

Arts Education/Literature
Director:
Kathleen Masterson 212-459-8826
e-mail: kathleen.masterson@arts.ny.gov

Dance/Theatre/Individual Artists
Director:
Robert Zuckerman 212-459-8831
e-mail: robert.zuckerman@arts.ny.gov

Electronic Media & Film/Visual Arts
Director:
Karen Helmerson 212-459-8824
e-mail: karen.helmerson@arts.ny.gov

Folk Arts/Music
Director:
Robert Baron 212-459-8821
e-mail: robert.baron@arts.ny.gov

Special Arts Services/Regional Economic Development
Director:
Susan Peirez. 212-459-8829
e-mail: susan.peirez@arts.ny.gov
Director:
Leanne Tintori Wells 212-459-8816
e-mail: leanne.wells@arts.ny.gov

Education Department
State Education Bldg
89 Washington Ave
Albany, NY 12234
518-474-3852 Fax: 518-486-5631
Web site: www.nysed.gov

Commissioner & University President:
MaryEllen Elia 518-474-5844
Assistant to the Commissioner:
Christopher J Halpin. 518-474-5845
Acting Counsel & Deputy Commissioner, Legal Affairs:
Erin O'Grady 518-474-6400
Chief of Staff & Deputy Commissioner, Innovation:
Allison Armour-Garb 518-486-1713

Cultural Education Office
10A 33 Cultural Education Center, Madison Ave, Albany, NY 12230
Web site: www.oce.nysed.gov
Deputy Commissioner:
Jeffrey Cannell. 518-474-5976/fax: 518-486-4850
e-mail: jcannell@mail.nysed.gov

State Museum Office
Assistant Commissioner & Director:
Clifford A Siegfried 518-474-5812
e-mail: csiegfri@mail.nysed.gov
Exhibits/Public Programs Director:
Mark Schaming. 518-486-2031
State Geologist:
William Kelly 518-474-5816

Research and Collections
Director:
Dr. John P. Hart 518-474-5813
Assistant Director:
Robert Daniels 518-474-5816

Offices and agencies generally appear in alphabetical order, except when specific order is requested by listee.

Empire State Development Corporation

633 Third Ave
New York, NY 10017
212-803-3100 Fax: 212-803-3131
Web site: www.esd.ny.gov

625 Broadway
Albany, NY 12207
518-292-5200

95 Perry Street
Ste 500
Buffalo, NY 14203
716-846-8200
Fax: 716-846-8260

President & CEO:
  Howard Zemsky 212-803-3700
Public Affairs:
  Kay Sarlin Wright 800-260-7313
  e-mail: esdpressoffice@esd.ny.gov

General Services, Office of

Corning Tower, 41st Fl
Empire State Plaza
Albany, NY 12242
518-474-3899 Fax: 518-474-1546
Web site: www.ogs.state.ny.us

Commissioner:
  RoAnn Destito 518-474-5991
First Deputy Commissioner:
  Joseph J Rabito 518-473-6953
Director, Public Affairs:
  Heather Groll .518-474-5987/fax: 518-474-3187
  e-mail: heather.groll@ogs.ny.gov

Empire State's Convention & Cultural Events Office

Director:
  Heather Flynn 518-474-0549
Manager, Convention Center:
  Vacant 518-474-0558/fax: 518-473-2190
Director, Marketing:
  Michael J Snyder 518-474-0538
Director, Curatorial & Tour Services:
  Dennis Anderson. 518-473-7521

Hudson River Valley Greenway

625 Broadway
4th Floor
Albany, NY 12207
518-473-3835 Fax: 518-473-4518
e-mail: hrvg@hudsongreenway.ny.gov
Web site: www.hudsongreenway.ny.gov

Greenway Conservancy for the Hudson River Valley

Acting Chair:
  Sara Griffen. 518-473-3835
Executive Director (Acting):
  Mark Castiglione. 518-473-3835

Hudson River Valley Greenway Communities Council

Board Chair:
  Barnabas McHenry 518-473-3835
Executive Director (Acting):
  Mark Castiglione. 518-473-3835

Parks, Recreation & Historic Preservation, NYS Office of

Empire State Plaza, Bldg 1
625 Broadway, 12207
Albany, NY 12238
518-486-0456 Fax: 518-486-2924
Web site: www.nysparks.com

Commissioner:
  Rose Harvey 518-474-0443
Executive Deputy Commissioner:
  Andrew Beers 518-474-0020
Deputy Commissioner, Finance & Administration:
  Melinda Scott 518-474-0414
Deputy Commissioner, Historic Preservation:
  Ruth Pierpont 518-237-8643 x3269
Secretary:
  Virginia Davis. 518-474-0443
Counsel:
  Patrick Bradford 518-474-0414
Deputy Commissioner, Natural Resources:
  Tom Alworth. 518-474-0414
Park Police/Director, Law Enforcement:
  Richard O'Donnell 518-474-4029/fax: 518-408-1032
Deputy Public Information Officer:
  Dan Keefe 518-486-1868
Chief Public Information Officer:
  Randy Simon. 518-486-1868

Concession Management

Director:
  Harold Hagemann 518-486-2932/fax: 518-486-2372

Historic Preservation

Field Services
Peebles Island, PO Box 189, Waterford, NY 12118
Deputy Commissioner:
  Ruth Pierpont 518-237-8643

Historic Sites Bureau
Peebles Island, Waterford, NY 12188
Acting Director:
  Mark Peckham 518-237-8643

Marine & Recreational Vehicles

Director:
  Brian Kempf 518-474-0445/fax: 518-408-1030

Regional Offices

Director, Regional Programs & Services:
  Debra Keville 518-474-8081

Central Region . . . . .fax: 315-492-3277
6105 E Seneca Turnpike, Jamesville, NY 13078-9516
315-492-1756 Fax: 315-492-3277
Regional Director:
  Robert Hiltbrand. 315-492-1756

Finger Lakes Region . . . . .fax: 607-387-3390
2221 Taughannock Park Rd, Box 1055, Trumansburg, NY 14886
607-387-7041 Fax: 607-387-3390
Regional Director:
  Tim Joseph 607-387-7041

Long Island Region . . . . .fax: 631-422-0638
625 Belmont Ave, Box 247, West Babylon, NY 11702-0247
631-669-1000 Fax: 631-422-0638
Acting Regional Director:
  George Gorman 631-321-3403

Palisades Region . . . . .fax: 845-786-2776
Administration Headquarters, Bear Mountain, NY 10911

Offices and agencies generally appear in alphabetical order, except when specific order is requested by listee.

Executive Director:
  Jim Hall. 845-786-2701

Saratoga/Capital District Region. . . . . fax: 518-584-5694
19 Roosevelt Drive, Saratoga Springs, NY 12866
518-584-2000 Fax: 518-584-5694
Regional Director:
  Alane Ball Chinian. 518-584-2000

Thousand Islands Region . . . . fax: 315-482-9413
Keewaydin State Park, 45165 NYS Rte 12, Alexandria Bay, NY 13607
315-482-2593 Fax: 315-482-9413
:
  Kevin Kieff. 315-482-2593

Regional Offices-Downstate District

New York City Region . . . . fax: 212-961-4382
A C Powell State Ofc Bldg, 163 W 125th St, New York, NY 10027
212-866-3100 Fax: 212-961-4382
Regional Director:
  Karen Phillips. 212-866-3100

Taconic Region. . . . . fax: 845-889-8217
9 Old Post Road, PO Box 308, Staatsburg, NY 12580
845-889-4100 Fax: 845-889-8217
Regional Director:
  Linda Cooper 845-889-4100

Regional Offices-Western District

Allegany Region. . . . . .fax: 716-354-6725
2373 Allegany State Park, Suite 3, Salamanca, NY 14779
716-354-9101 Fax: 716-354-6725
Acting Regional Director:
  Mark Whitecomb 716-354-9101

Genesee Region . . . . .fax: 585-493-5272
One Letchworth State Park, Castile, NY 14427-1124
585-493-3600 Fax: 585-493-5272
Regional Director:
  Richard Parker 585-493-3600

Niagara Region & Western District Office. . . . . fax: 716-278-1725
Niagara Frontier Park Region, Prospect P, PO Box 1132, Niagara Falls,
  NY 14303-0132
716-278-1770 Fax: 716-278-1725
:
  Mark Thomas 716-278-1770

Environmental Management
Director:
  Pamela Otis 518-474-0409/fax: 518-474-7013

New York State Gaming Commission
PO Box 7500
Schenectady, NY 12301-7500
518-395-5400 or 518-388-3445 Fax: 518-347-1250
e-mail: info@gaming.ny.gov
Web site: www.gaming.ny.gov

Chair:
  Vacant. 518-395-5400
Member:
  Vacant. 518-395-5400
Member:
  Vacant. 518-395-5400
Acting Executive Director:
  Robert Williams 518-395-5400
Public Information Officer:
  Vacant. 518-388-3415

Adirondack Park Agency
1133 NYS Route 86
PO Box 99
Ray Brook, NY 12977
518-891-4050 Fax: 518-891-3938
Web site: www.apa.ny.gov

Chair:
  Leilani Ulrich 518-891-4050
Executive Director:
  Terry Martino 518-891-4050
Counsel:
  James Townsend. 518-891-4050
Public Relations:
  Keith McKeever 518-891-4050
  e-mail: keith.mckeever@apa.ny.gov

Agriculture & NYS Horse Breeding Development Fund
1 Broadway Center
Suite 602
Schenectady, NY 12305
518-395-5484 Fax: 518-347-1483
e-mail: info@nysirestakes.com
Web site: www.nysirestakes.com

Executive Director:
  Mike Mullaney 518-395-5484
  e-mail: mike.mullaney@nysirestakes.com
Counsel:
  Mark Stuart 518-395-5484

Battery Park City Authority (Hugh L Carey)
One World Financial Center, 24th Fl
200 Liberty Street
New York, NY 10281
212-417-2000 Fax: 212-417-2001
e-mail: info@bpca.ny.gov
Web site: www.bpca.ny.gov

Chair & Chief Operating Officer:
  Dennis Mehiel. 212-417-2000
President & Chief Operating Officer:
  Shari Hyman 212-417-4205/fax: 212-417-4153
Vice Chair:
  Donald Cappocia. 212-417-2000
Member/Vice Chair:
  Frank J Branchini 212-417-2000
Member:
  Lester Petracca 212-417-2000
Member:
  Martha J Gallo. 212-417-2000
VP External Relations:
  Robin Forst 212-417-2276/fax: 212-417-2279
  e-mail: robin.forst@bpca.ny.gov

Capital District Regional Off-Track Betting Corporation
510 Smith St
Schenectady, NY 12305
518-344-5266 or 800-292-2387 Fax: 518-370-5460
e-mail: customerservice@capitalotb.com
Web site: www.capitalotb.com

Chair:
  Marcel Webb. 518-344-5225
Board Secretary & Director:
  F James Mumpton. 518-344-5225

Offices and agencies generally appear in alphabetical order, except when specific order is requested by listee.

President & Chief Executive Officer:
  John F Signor 518-344-5225
VP, Corporate Operations:
  Tod Grenci 518-344-5408
VP, Legal Affairs/General Counsel:
  Robert Hemsworth 518-344-5298
VP, Finance/Comptroller:
  Nancy Priputen-Madrian 518-344-5233
VP, Human Resources:
  Robert Dantz. 518-344-5301

Catskill Off-Track Betting Corporation
Park Place
Box 3000
Pomona, NY 10970
845-362-0407 Fax: 845-362-0419
e-mail: otb@interbets.com; customerservice@interbets.com
Web site: www.interbets.com

President:
  Donald J Groth 845-362-0400

Nassau Regional Off-Track Betting Corporation
139 Liberty Ave
Mineola, NY 11501
516-572-2800 Fax: 516-572-2840
e-mail: webmaster@nassauotb.com
Web site: www.nassauotb.com

President:
  Joseph G Cairo, Jr. 516-572-2800
Director, Facilities Development:
  John J Sparacio. 516-572-2800

New York Convention Center Operating Corporation
655 W 34th St
New York, NY 10001-1188
212-216-2000 Fax: 212-216-2588
e-mail: moreinfo@javitscenter.com
Web site: www.javitscenter.com

Chair:
  Henry Silverman. 212-216-2130
President & Chief Operating Officer:
  Alan Steel 212-216-2000
Senior Vice President & Chief Financial Officer:
  Edward B MacDonald Jr .212-216-2369
Senior Vice President & General Counsel:
  Elizabeth Bradford 212-216-2125
Senior Vice President, Sales & Marketing:
  Doreen Guerin. 212-216-2335

New York State Athletic Commission
123 William St
2nd Fl
New York, NY 10038
212-417-5700 Fax: 212-417-4987
e-mail: info@dos.ny.gov
Web site: www.dos.ny.gov/athletic

Chair:
  Melvina Lathan. 212-417-5700

New York State Commission on the Restoration of the Capitol
Corning Tower, 31st Fl
Empire State Plaza
Albany, NY 12242

518-473-0341 Fax: 518-486-5720

Executive Director:
  Andrea J Lazarski 518-473-0341
  e-mail: andrea.lazarski@ogs.ny.gov

New York State Olympic Regional Development Authority
Olympic Center
2634 Main St
Lake Placid, NY 12946
518-523-1655 Fax: 518-523-9275
e-mail: info@orda.org
Web site: www.orda.org/corporate

President & CEO:
  Ted Blazer 518-523-1655 x201
  e-mail: blazer@orda.org
Vice President:
  Jeffrey Byrne 518-523-1655 x203
  e-mail: byrne@orda.org
Olympic Center Manager:
  Dennis Allen 518-523-1655 x222
  e-mail: allen@orda.org
Director, Corporate Development:
  Jeff Potter 518-523-1655
  e-mail: jpotter@orda.org
Director, Events:
  Katie Million 518-523-1655 x212
  e-mail: kmillion@orda.org
Director, Finance:
  Padraig Power 518-523-1655 x217
  e-mail: ppower@orda.org
Communications Manager:
  Jon Lundin 518-523-1655
  e-mail: jlundin@orda.org

New York State Thoroughbred Breeding & Development Fund Corporation
One Broadway Center
Suite 601
Schenectady, NY 12305
518-388-0174 Fax: 518-395-5499
e-mail: nybreds@nybreds.com
Web site: www.nybreds.com

Executive Director:
  Tracy Egan 518-388-0174

New York State Thruway Authority
200 Southern Blvd
PO Box 189
Albany, NY 12201
518-436-2700 Fax: 518-436-2899
Web site: www.thruway.ny.gov

Chair:
  Joanne M Mahoney. 518-436-3000
Acting Executive Director:
  Robert Megna 518-436-2900
General Counsel:
  Gordon Cuffy 518-436-2840
Director, Media Relations & Communications:
  Dan Weiller 518-471-5300
Interim Director, Maintenance & Operations:
  Maria Lehman. 518-436-2840
Director, Administrative Services:
  John F. Barr. 518-436-2700

Offices and agencies generally appear in alphabetical order, except when specific order is requested by listee.

Policy Areas

New York State Canal Corporation
Web site: www.canals.ny.gov
Acting Executive Director:
Robert Megna 518-436-3055/fax: 518-471-5023

Roosevelt Island Operating Corporation (RIOC)
591 Main St
Roosevelt Island, NY 10044
212-832-4540 Fax: 212-832-4582
e-mail: information@rioc.ny.gov
Web site: www.rioc.ny.gov

President/CEO:
Charlene M Indelicato 212-832-4540 x319
Director Island Operations:
Cyril Opperman 212-832-4583
e-mail: cyril.opperman@rioc.ny.gov
VP/General Counsel:
Donald D. Lewis 212-832-4540 x311
e-mail: donald.lewis@rioc.ny.gov
VP/Chief Financial Officer:
Frances Walton 212-832-4540 x350
Interim Director Public Safety:
Captain Estrella Suarez. 212-832-4545
e-mail: keith.guerra@rioc.ny.gov

Suffolk Regional Off-Track Betting Corporation
5 Davids Dr
Hauppauge, NY 11788-2004
631-853-1000 Fax: 631-853-1086
e-mail: customerservice@suffolkotb.com
Web site: www.suffolkotb.com

President/CEO:
Philip C. Nolan 631-853-1000
Vice President:
Anthony Pancella 631-853-1000
General Counsel:
James McManmon 631-853-1000
Director Governmental & Public Affairs:
Debbie Pfeifer 631-853-1000

Western Regional Off-Track Betting Corp
8315 Park Road
Batavia, NY 14020
585-343-3750 Fax: 585-343-6873
e-mail: info@westernotb.com
Web site: www.westernotb.com

Chair:
Richard D Bianchi 585-343-3750
President & Chief Executive Officer:
Michael D Kane 585-343-3750
General Counsel & Secretary:
Henry Wojtaszek. 585-343-3750
Director, Video Gaming:
Mark Wolf. 585-343-3750
Director, Marketing:
Ryan Hasenauer 585-343-3750
Manager, Branch Operations:
Edward Merriman. 585-343-3750
VP-Administration:
William R White. 585-343-3750

Convention Centers & Visitors Bureaus

Albany County Convention & Visitors Bureau . . fax: 518-434-0887
25 Quackenbush Sq, Albany, NY 12207
800-258-3582 or 518-434-1217 Fax: 518-434-0887
Web site: www.albany.org
President & CEO:
Michele Vennard 518-434-1217 x300/fax: 518-434-0887
e-mail: mvennard@albany.org

Greater Binghamton New York Convention and Visitors Bureau
49 Court St, 2nd Floor, PO Box 995, Binghamton, NY 13902
800-836-6740 or 607-772-8860
Web site: www.binghamtoncvb.com; www.visitbinghamton.org
President:
Lou Santoni
e-mail: lou@visitbinghamton.org

Buffalo Niagara Convention & Visitors Bureau
617 Main St, Ste 200, Buffalo, NY 14203
800-283-3256
e-mail: info@visitbuffaloniagara.com
Web site: www.visitbuffaloniagara.com
President & CEO:
Patrick Kaler. 716-961-0200
e-mail: kaler@visitbuffaloniagara.com

Chautauqua County Visitors Bureau
Chautauqua Main Gate, Route 394, PO Box 1441, Chautauqua, NY 14722
866-908-4569
e-mail: info@tourchautauqua.com
Web site: www.tourchautauqua.com
Executive Director:
Andrew Nixon .716-357-4569/fax: 716-357-2284
e-mail: nixon@tourchautauqua.com

Greater Rochester Visitors Association
Visit Rochester, 45 East Ave, Ste 400, Rochester, NY 14604-2294
800-677-7282
Web site: www.visitrochester.com
Director:
Michael Hardy 585-279-8303
e-mail: michaelh@visitrochester.com

Ithaca/Tompkins County Convention & Visitors Bureau
904 E Shore Dr, Ithaca, NY 14850
800-28-ITHACA
e-mail: info@visitithaca.com
Web site: www.visitithaca.com
Director:
Fred Bonn .607-272-1313/fax: 607-272-7617
e-mail: fred@visitithaca.com

Lake Placid/Essex County Convention & Visitors Bureau
2608 Main St, Lake Placid, NY 12946
800-447-5224
Web site: www.lakeplacid.com
CEO:
James McKenna. 518-523-2445/fax: 518-523-2605
e-mail: james@lakeplacid.com

Long Island Convention & Visitors Bureau & Sports Commission
330 Motor Pkwy, Ste 203, Hauppauge, NY 11788
877-386-6654
e-mail: tourism@discoverlongisland.com
Web site: www.discoverlongisland.com
President:
R Moke McGowan. 631-951-3900 x305/fax: 631-951-3439
e-mail: mmcgowan@discoverlongisland.com

Offices and agencies generally appear in alphabetical order, except when specific order is requested by listee.

NYC & Company/Convention & Visitors Bureaufax: 212-245-5943
    810 Seventh Ave, 3 Fl, New York, NY 10019
    212-484-1200 Fax: 212-245-5943
    e-mail: visitorinfo@nycgo.com
    Web site: www.nycgo.com
CEO:
    George Fertitta. 212-484-1265/fax: 212-245-5943

Oneida County Convention & Visitors Bureau
    Oneida Cty Welcome Ctr, PO Box 551, dba: Oneida County Tourism,
        Utica, NY 13503-0551
    800-426-3132 or 888-999-6560
    Web site: www.oneidacountycvb.com
President:
    Kelly Blazosky 315-724-7221/fax: 315-724-7335
    e-mail: kelly@oneidacountytourism.com

Ontario County/Finger Lakes Visitors Connection
    25 Gorham St, Canandaigua, NY 14424
    877-386-4669
    e-mail: info@visitfingerlakes.com
    Web site: www.visitfingerlakes.com
President:
    Valerie Knoblauch. 585-394-3915/fax: 585-394-4067

Saratoga Convention & Tourism Bureau
    60 Railroad Pl, Ste 100, Saratoga Springs, NY 12866
    855-424-6073
    Web site: www.discoversaratoga.org
President:
    Todd Garofano 518-584-1531 x106/fax: 518-584-2969
    e-mail: todd@discoversaratoga.org

Steuben County Conference & Visitors Bureau
    1 West Market St, Corning, NY 14830
    866-946-3386
    e-mail: sccvb@corningfingerlakes.com
    Web site: www.corningfingerlakes.com
President:
    Peggy Coleman 607-936-6544/fax: 607-936-6575
    e-mail: pcoleman@corningfingerlakes.com

Sullivan County Visitors Association
    100 Sullivan Avenue, Suite 2, PO Box 248, Ferndale, NY 12734
    800-882-2287
    Web site: www.scva.net
President & CEO:
    Roberta Byron Lockwood 845-747-4449/fax: 845-747-4468
    e-mail: sctoursim@scva.net

Syracuse Convention & Vistors Bureau
    572 S Salina St, Syracuse, NY 13202
    800-234-4797
    e-mail: info@visitsyracuse.org
    Web site: www.visitsyracuse.org
President:
    David Holder. 315-470-1911/fax: 315-471-8545
    e-mail: dholder@visitsyracuse.org

Tourism Bureau of the Thousand Islands Region
    Box 400, Alexandria Bay, NY 13607
    800-847-5263
    Web site: www.visit1000islands.com
Director of Tourism:
    Gary DeYoung. 315-482-2520/fax: 315-482-5906
    e-mail: gary@visit1000islands.com

Westchester County Tourism & Film
    148 Martine Ave, Ste 104, White Plains, NY 10601
    800-833-9282
    e-mail: tourism@westchestergov.com
    Web site: www.thewestchesterway.com

Director of Tourism:
    Natasha Caputo. 914-995-8502
    e-mail: ncaputo@visitwestchesterny.com

NEW YORK STATE LEGISLATURE

See Legislative Branch in Section 1 for additional Standing Committee and Subcommittee information.

Assembly Standing Committees

Racing & Wagering
Chair:
    James Gary Pretlow (D) 518-455-5291
Ranking Minority Member:
    Andrew Garbarino (R) 518-455-4611

Tourism, Parks, Arts & Sports Development
Chair:
    Margaret Markey (D) 518-455-4755
Ranking Minority Member:
    John Ceretto (R) 518-455-5284

Senate Standing Committees

Cultural Affairs, Tourism, Parks & Recreation
Chair:
    Elizabeth O'C Little (R) 518-455-2811
Ranking Minority Member:
    Jose Serrano (D) 518-455-2795

Racing, Gaming & Wagering
Chair:
    John J Bonacic (R) 518-455-3181
Ranking Minority Member:
    Joseph Addabbo, Jr (D) 518-455-2322

U.S. GOVERNMENT

EXECUTIVE DEPARTMENTS AND RELATED AGENCIES

National Archives & Records Administration

Franklin D Roosevelt Presidential Library & Museum
    4079 Albany Post Rd, Hyde Park, NY 12538
    845-486-7770
    Web site: www.fdrlibrary.marist.edu
Director:
    Lynn A. Bassanese 845-486-7741
    e-mail: lynn.bassanese@nara.gov

Smithsonian Institution

Cooper-Hewitt National Design Museum
    2 East 91st St, New York, NY 10128
    212-849-8400
    Web site: www.cooperhewitt.org
Director:
    Caroline Bauman 212-849-8400

National Museum of the American Indian-George Gustav Heye Center
    US Custom House, One Bowling Green, New York, NY 10004
    212-514-3700
    Web site: www.nmai.si.edu
GGHC Director:
    Kevin Gouer 212-514-3700

Offices and agencies generally appear in alphabetical order, except when specific order is requested by listee.

Policy Areas

US Department of the Interior
202-208-3100
e-mail: webteam@ios.doi.gov
Web site: www.doi.gov

Fish & Wildlife Service-Northeast Region .... fax: 413-253-8308
300 Westgate Center Dr, Hadley, MA 01035-9589
413-253-8200 Fax: 413-253-8308
e-mail: northeast@fws.gov
Regional Director:
Wendi Weber 413-253-8300

National Park Service-Northeast Region
200 Chestnut St, US Custom House, 5th Floor, Philadelphia, PA 19106
Web site: www.nps.gov
Northeast Regional Director:
Dennis R. Reidenbach 215-597-5823
National Heritage Area Program Director:
Peter Samuel
e-mail: peter samuel@nps.gov

Fire Island National Seashore .... fax: 631-289-3010
120 Laurel St, Patchogue, NY 11772-3596
631-289-4750 Fax: 631-289-3010
Web site: www.nps.gov/fiis/
Superintendent:
Chris Soller 631-289-4750/fax: 631-289-3010

Fort Stanwix National Monument .... fax: 315-334-5051
112 E Park St, Rome, NY 13440
315-338-7730 Fax: 315-334-5051
Web site: www.nps.gov/fost/
Superintendent:
Deborah Conway 315-338-7730/fax: 315-334-5051

Gateway National Recreation Area
210 New York Ave, Staten Island, NY 10305
Web site: www.nps.gov/gate
General Superintendent:
Linda Canzanelli 718-354-4606/fax: 718-354-4764
Jamaica Bay Unit
Coordinator:
Dave Taft 718-338-3379
Sandy Hook Unit
Coordinator:
Pete McCarthy 732-872-5970
Staten Island Unit
Coordinator:
Brian Feeney 718-354-6970

Manhattan Sites
26 Wall St, New York, NY 10005
212-668-5180
Web site: www.nps.gov/masi
Commissioner:
Maria Burtes 212-668-2322

Martin Van Buren National Historic Site .... fax: 518-758-6986
1013 Old Post Rd, Kinderhook, NY 12106
518-758-9689 Fax: 518-758-6986
Web site: www.nps.gov/mava
Superintendent:
Daniel J Dattilio 518-758-9689/fax: 518-758-6986

Roosevelt-Vanderbilt National Historic Sites
4097 Albany Post Rd, Hyde Park, NY 12538
845-229-9115 x. 2010
Web site: www.nps.gov/hofr
Superintendent:
Sarah Olson 845-229-9115/fax: 845-229-0739

Sagamore Hill National Historic Site .... fax: 516-922-4792
20 Sagamore Hill Road, Oyster Bay, NY 11771
516-922-4788 Fax: 516-922-4792
Web site: www.nps.gov/sahi
Superintendent:
Tom Ross 516-922-4788/fax: 516-922-4792

Saratoga National Historical Park .... fax: 518-664-3349
648 Rt 32, Stillwater, NY 12170
518-664-9821 X224 Fax: 518-664-3349
Web site: www.nps.gov/sara
Superintendent:
Joe Finan .... 518-664-9821 ext 224/fax: 518-664-3349

Statue of Liberty National Monument & Ellis Island
Liberty Island, New York, NY 10004
TTY: 212-363-3211 or 212-363-3200
Web site: www.nps.gov/stli/
Superintendent:
David Luchsinger 212-363-3200

Theodore Roosevelt Inaugural National Historic Site fax: 716-884-0330
641 Delaware Ave, Buffalo, NY 14202
716-884-0095 Fax: 716-884-0330
Web site: www.nps.gov/thri/
Superintendent:
Molly Quackenbush 716-884-0095/fax: 716-884-0330

Women's Rights National Historical Park .... fax: 315-568-2141
136 Fall St, Seneca Falls, NY 13148
315-568-2991 Fax: 315-568-2141
Web site: www.nps.gov/wori
Superintendent:
Tammy Duchesne 315-568-2991/fax: 315-568-2141

U.S. CONGRESS

See U.S. Congress Chapter for additional Standing Committee and Subcommittee information.

House of Representatives Standing Committees

Natural Resources
Chair:
Doc Hastings (R-WA) 202-225-5816
Ranking Minority Member:
Edward J. Markey (D-MA) 202-225-2836

Subcommittee
Public Lands & Environmental Regulations
Chair:
Rob Bishop (R-UT) 202-225-0453
Ranking Minority Member:
Raul M. Grijalva (D-AZ) 202-225-2435

Senate Standing Committees

Energy & Natural Resources
Chair:
Ron Wyden (D-OR) 202-224-5244
Ranking Minority Member:
Lisa Murkowski (R-AK) 202-224-6665

Subcommittees
National Parks
Chair:
Mark Udall (D-CO) 202-224-4971
Public Lands, Forests & Mining
Chair:
Joe Manchin (D-WV) 202-224-3954

Offices and agencies generally appear in alphabetical order, except when specific order is requested by listee.

Ranking Minority Member:
    John Barrasso (R-WY) 202-224-6441

PRIVATE SECTOR

AAA Northway
1626 Union St, Schenectady, NY 12309
518-374-4575 Fax: 518-374-3140
Web site: www.aaanorthway.com
Capital region membership, travel & touring sales & services
Eric Stigberg, Marketing, Public & Government Affairs Manager

AAA Western and Central NY
100 International Dr, Buffalo, NY 14221
716-626-3225 Fax: 716-631-5925
e-mail: wsmith@nyaaa.com
Web site: www.AAA.com
Wallace Smith, Vice President

Adirondack Lakes Center for the Arts
Rte 28, PO Box 205, Blue Mountain Lake, NY 12812-0205
518-352-7715 Fax: 518-352-7333
e-mail: alca@frontiernet.net
Web site: www.adk-arts.org
Multi/Arts Center
Stephen Svoboda, Executive Director

Adirondack/Pine Hill/NY Trailways
499 Hurley Ave, Hurley, NY 12443-5119
845-339-4230 Fax: 845-853-7035
e-mail: info@trailwaysny.com
Web site: www.trailwaysny.com
Tour & charter service
Eugene J Berardi, Jr, President

Alliance for the Arts
330 W 42nd St, Ste 1701, New York, NY 10036
212-947-6340 Fax: 212-947-6416
e-mail: info@allianceforarts.org
Web site: www.allianceforarts.org
Advocacy, promotion, research, information, referrals & publications
Randall Bourscheidt, President

Alliance of Resident Theatres/New York (ART/New York)
520 Eighth Ave, Ste 319, New York, NY 10018
212-244-6667 Fax: 212-714-1918
Web site: www.art-newyork.org
Services & advocacy for New York City's not-for-profit theatre community
Virginia P Louloudes, Executive Director

American Museum of Natural History
Central Park West at 79th St, New York, NY 10024-5192
212-769-5100 Fax: 212-769-5018
e-mail: info@amnh.org
Web site: www.amnh.org
Education, exhibition & scientific research
Ellen V Futter, President

Art & Science Collaborations Inc
130 East End Ave 1A, New York, NY 10028
505-988-2994
e-mail: asci@asci.org
Web site: www.asci.org
Raising public awareness of art & artists using science & technology to explore new forms of creative expression
Cynthia Pannucci, Director

ArtsConnection Inc (The)
520 8th Ave, #321, New York, NY 10018
212-302-7433 Fax: 212-302-1132
e-mail: artsconnection@artsconnection.org
Web site: www.artsconnection.org
Arts-in-education programming & training for children, teachers & artists
Steven Tennen, Executive Director

Associated Musicians of Greater New York, Local 802 AFM, AFL-CIO
322 West 48th St, 5th Fl, New York, NY 10036
212-245-4802 Fax: 212-245-6255
e-mail: pmolloy@local802afm.org
Web site: www.local802afm.org
Paul Molloy, Political/Public Relations Director

Association of Independent Video & Filmmakers (AIVF), (The)
304 Hudson St, 6th Fl, New York, NY 10013
212-807-1400 Fax: 212-463-8519
e-mail: info@aivf.org
Web site: www.aivf.org
Membership service organization for independent producers & filmmakers
Beni Matias, Executive Director

Automobile Club of New York
1415 Kellum Place, Garden City, NY 11530
516-873-2252 Fax: 516-873-2375
Web site: www.aaany.com
Dennis J Crossley, President

Brooklyn Botanic Garden
1000 Washington Ave, Brooklyn, NY 11225-1009
718-623-7200 Fax: 718-857-2430
Web site: www.bbg.org
Comprehensive study of plant biodiversity in metropolitan New York; home gardener's resource center
Scot Medbury, President & CEO

Brooklyn Museum of Art
200 Eastern Pkwy, Brooklyn, NY 11238
718-638-5000 Fax: 718-501-6136
Web site: www.brooklynmuseum.org
Schawannah Wright, Manager, Community Involvement

Buffalo Bills
One Bills Drive, Orchard Park, NY 14127
716-648-1800 x8701 Fax: 716-648-3202
Web site: www.buffalobills.com
Scott Berchtold, Vice President-Communications

Buffalo Sabres
One Seymour H Knox III Plz, Buffalo, NY 14203
716-855-4100 x526 Fax: 716-855-4110
e-mail: michael.gilbert@sabres.com
Web site: www.sabres.com
Michael Gilbert, Director Public Relations

Buffalo Trotting Association Inc
5600 McKinley Parkway, Hamburg, NY 14075
716-649-1280 Fax: 716-649-0033
e-mail: mangoj@buffaloraceway.com
Web site: www.buffaloraceway.com
Harness horse racing
James Mango, General Manager

CUNY New York City College of Technology, Hospitality Mgmt
300 Jay St, Room 220, Brooklyn, NY 11201-2983
718-260-5630 Fax: 718-260-5997
Web site: www.nyct.cuny.edu
Hospitality & food service management; tourism
Jerry Van Loon, Professor & Chair

Offices and agencies generally appear in alphabetical order, except when specific order is requested by listee.

Campground Owners of New York
1 Grove Street, Suite 200, Pittsford, NY 14534
585-586-4360 Fax: 585-586-4360
e-mail: cony@frontiernet.net
Web site: www.nycampgrounds.com
Donald G Bennett Jr, Executive Administrator

Coalition of Living Museums
1000 Washington Ave, Brooklyn, NY 11225
718-623-7225 or 718-623-7373 Fax: 718-857-2430
e-mail: loiscarswell@bbg.org
Web site: www.livingmuseums.org
Advocacy organization for living museums (zoos, botanical gardens, aquaria, arboreta & nature centers) in NYS
Lois Carswell, Chair, Steering Committee

Cold Spring Harbor Fish Hatchery & Aquarium
1660 Route 25A, Cold Spring Harbor, NY 11724
516-692-6768 Fax: 516-692-6769
e-mail: cshfha@optonline.net
Web site: www.cshfha.org
Largest living collection of NYS freshwater fish, amphibians & turtles
Norman Soule, Director

Columbia University, School of the Arts
305 Dodge Hall, 2960 Broadway, MC1808, New York, NY 10027
212-854-2134 Fax: 212-854-7733
e-mail: bwf3@columbia.edu
Web site: www.columbia.edu/cu/arts
Bruce W Ferguson, Dean

Culinary Institute of America
1946 Campus Dr, Hyde Park, NY 12538-1499
845-451-1203 Fax: 845-451-1052
e-mail: N_Harvin@culinary.edu
Web site: www.ciachef.edu
Four-year regionally accredited college offering Associate and Occupational Studies and Bachelor of Professional Studies in culinary and baking/pastry arts management. Campuses in Hyde Park, New York, and St Helena, California.
Nancy Harvin, Vice President for Advancement

Darien Lake Theme Park Resort
9993 Allegheny Rd, PO Box 91, Darien Center, NY 14040
585-599-4641 Fax: 585-599-4053
e-mail: info@godarienlake.com
Web site: www.godarienlake.com
Darien Lake Theme Park Resort is New York State's largest theme park and resort, located between Buffalo and Rochester, NY and just a short drive from Niagara Falls.
Christopher Thorpe, Vice President & General Manager

Egg (The), Center for the Performing Arts
Empire State Plaza, PO Box 2065, Albany, NY 12220
518-473-1061 or 518-473-1845 Fax: 518-473-1848
e-mail: info@theegg.org
Web site: www.theegg.org
Dance, theatre, family entertainment, music, special events
Peter Lesser, Executive Director

NYS Bar Assn, Entertainment, Arts & Sports Law Section
Elissa D Hecker, Esq
90 Quail Close, Irvington, NY 10533
914-478-0457
e-mail: eheckeresq@yahoo.com
Elissa D Hecker, Chair

Empire State Restaurant & Tavern Association Inc
40 Sheridan Ave, Albany, NY 12210
518-436-8121 Fax: 518-436-7287
e-mail: esrta@verizon.net
Web site: www.esrta.org
Scott Wexler, Executive Director

Entertainment Software Association
317 Madison Ave, 22nd Fl, New York, NY 10017
917-522-3250 Fax: 917-522-3258
Web site: www.theesa.com
Michael D Gallagher, President/CEO

Exhibition Alliance Inc (The)
Route 12B South, PO Box 345, Hamilton, NY 13346
315-824-2510 Fax: 315-824-1683
e-mail: donnao@exhibitionalliance.org
Web site: www.exhibitionalliance.org
Exhibit-related services for museums in NYS & the surrounding region
Donna Ostraszewski Anderson, Executive Director

Farmer's Museum (The)
PO Box 30, Cooperstown, NY 13326
607-547-1400 Fax: 607-547-1404
e-mail: m.bruce@nysha.org
Web site: www.farmersmuseum.org
Historical & cultural exhibition, preservation and education
D Stephen Elliott, President

Film/Video Arts
270 W 96th St, New York, NY 10025
212-941-8787
e-mail: mariopaoli@fva.com
Web site: www.fva.com
Low cost training, postproduction suites, fiscal sponsorship, mentorship, internships
Chloe Kurabi, Programs Director, Fiscal Sponsorship and Filmmaker

Finger Lakes Racing Association
PO Box 25250, Farmington, NY 14425
585-924-3232 Fax: 585-924-3239
Web site: www.fingerlakesracetrack.com
Horse racing & video lottery gaming
Christian Riegle, General Manager

Finger Lakes Tourism Alliance
309 Lake St, Penn Yan, NY 14527
315-536-7488 Fax: 315-536-1237
e-mail: info@fingerlakes.org
Web site: www.fingerlakes.org
Regional tourism promotion
Cynthia Kimble, President

Gertrude Stein Repertory Theatre (The)
15 West 26th St, 2nd Fl, New York, NY 10010
212-725-0436 Fax: 212-725-7267
e-mail: info@gerstein.org
Web site: www.gertstein.org
Avant garde theater emphasizing international collaboration in experimental works incorporating new technologies
Liz Dreyer, General Manager

Great Escape Theme Park LLC (The)
PO Box 511, Lake George, NY 12845
518-792-3500 Fax: 518-792-3404
Web site: www.thegreatescape.com
John Collins, General Manager

Offices and agencies generally appear in alphabetical order, except when specific order is requested by listee.

Harvestworks
596 Broadway, Suite 602, New York, NY 10012
212-431-1130 Fax: 212-431-8473
e-mail: info@harvestworks.org
Web site: www.harvestworks.org
Nonprofit arts organization providing computer education & production studios for the digital media arts
Carol Parkinson, Director

Historic Hudson Valley
150 White Plains Rd, Tarrytown, NY 10591
914-631-8200 Fax: 914-631-0089
e-mail: mail@hudsonvalley.org
Web site: www.hudsonvalley.org
Tourism promotion
Waddell Stillman, President

Hotel Association of New York City Inc
320 Park Ave, 22nd Fl, New York, NY 10022-6838
212-754-6700 Fax: 212-688-2838
e-mail: jspinnato@hanyc.org
Web site: www.hanyc.org
Joseph E Spinnato, President

Hudson River Cruises
Rondout Landing, 1 East Strand Street, Kingston, NY 12401-3605
845-340-4700 or 800-843-7472 Fax: 845-340-4702
e-mail: hudsonrivercruises@hvc.rr.com
Web site: www.hudsonrivercruises.com
Sightseeing, music & dinner cruises and Private Charters
Sandra Henne, President

Hunter Mountain Ski Bowl
PO Box 295, Hunter, NY 12442
888-486-8376 or 518-263-4223 Fax: 518-263-3704
e-mail: info@huntermtn.com
Web site: www.huntermtn.com
Skiing, snowshoeing, snowboarding & snowtubing; coaching & race camps; summer & fall festivals; Kaatskill Mountain Club/Hotel, Loftside Village Condominiums, and other Four Season Mountain Resort activities.
Orville A Slutzky, General Manager

Jewish Museum (The)
1109 Fifth Ave, New York, NY 10128-0117
212-423-3271 Fax: 212-423-3233
e-mail: ascher@thejm.org
Web site: www.thejewishmuseum.org
Museum of art and Jewish culture
Anne Scher, Director, Communications

Lincoln Center for the Performing Arts Inc
70 Lincoln Center Plaza, New York, NY 10023-6583
212-875-5319 Fax: 212-875-5456
e-mail: jberry@lincolncenter.org
Web site: www.lincolncenter.org
Guided tours of Lincoln Center; Meet-the-Artist programs
Jennifer Berry, Director, Visitor Services

Lower Manhattan Cultural Council
125 Maiden Lane, 2nd Floor, New York, NY 10038
212-219-9401 Fax: 212-219-2058
e-mail: info@lmcc.net
Web site: www.lmcc.net
Supporting Manhattan arts organizations through funding assistance, support for creation & presentation of work & audience development
Mark Vevle, Director, Marketing & Communications

Madison Square Garden Corp
Two Penn Plaza, Madison Square Garden, New York, NY 10121
212-465-6000 Fax: 212-465-4423
Web site: www.thegarden.com
NY Knicks, NY Rangers, NY Liberty concerts, special events

Barry Watkins, Senior Vice President, Communications

Major League Baseball
245 Park Ave, New York, NY 10167
212-931-7800 Fax: 212-949-5654
Web site: www.mlb.com
Rich Levin, Senior Vice President, Public Relations

Metropolitan Museum of Art (The)
1000 Fifth Ave, New York, NY 10028
212-535-7710 Fax: 212-650-2102
Web site: www.metmuseum.org
Philippe de Montebello, Director;, Harold Holzer, Senior Vice President for External Affairs

Monticello Gaming & Raceway
204 Rte 17-B, PO Box 5013, Monticello, NY 12701
845-794-4100 Fax: 845-791-1402
Web site: www.monticelloraceway.com
Horse racing and video gaming machines.
Clifford Ehrlich, Senior Vice President/General Manager

Museum Association of New York
265 River St, Troy, NY 12180
518-273-3400 Fax: 518-273-3416
e-mail: info@manyonline.org
Web site: www.manyonline.org
An information and advocacy resource for the state's museum community.
Anne Ackerson, Director

NY Film Academy
100 East 17th St, New York, NY 10003-2160
212-674-4300 Fax: 212-477-1414
e-mail: film@nyfa.com
Web site: www.nyfa.com
Film making and acting for film.
Jerry Sherlock, President & Founder

NY State Historical Association/Fenimore Art Museum
PO Box 800, Cooperstown, NY 13326-0800
607-547-1400 Fax: 607-547-1404
e-mail: m.bruce@nysha.org
Web site: www.nysha.org; www.farmersmuseum.org
Historical & cultural exhibition, preservation & education
Paul S D'Ambroso, PhD, President/Chief Executive Officer

NYC Arts Coalition
351 West 54th St, New York, NY 10019
212-246-3788 Fax: 212-246-3366
e-mail: info@nycityartscoalition.org
Web site: www.nycityartscoalition.org
Develops public policy analysis, provides reports on arts policy & funding issues & acts as an advocacy vehicle for a united voice for the nonprofit arts sector
Norma P Munn, Chair

NYS Alliance for Arts Education
PO Box 2217, Albany, NY 12220-0217
800-ARTS-N-ED or 518-473-0823 Fax: 518-486-7329
e-mail: info@nysaae.org
Web site: www.nysaae.org
Advocacy, professional development, technical assistance & information for educators, organizations, artists, parents, policymakers
Jeremy Johannesen, Executive Director

NYS Arts
PO Box 96, Mattituck, NY 11952-0096
631-298-1234 Fax: 631-298-1101
e-mail: jkweiner@NYSARTS.org
Web site: www.nysarts.org
Technical assistance, professional development & advocacy services
Angela Lipfert, Office Manager

Offices and agencies generally appear in alphabetical order, except when specific order is requested by listee.

Policy Areas

NYS Outdoor Guides Association
1936 Saranac Ave, Suite 2 PO Box 150, Lake Placid, NY 12946-1402
866-469-7642 or 518-359-8194 Fax: 518-359-8194
e-mail: info@nysoga.org
Web site: www.nysoga.org
Provides information about member guide services & the profession of guiding through distribution of printed/electronic material and educational programs. Provides NYS licensed guides with support services, representation and sense of community
Sonny Young, President

NYS Passenger Vessel Association
PO Box 98, Brightwaters, NY 11718
631-321-9005
e-mail: info@cruisenewyork.com
Web site: www.cruisenewyork.com
Promote cruises on NYS's waterways
Mike Eagan, Treasurer

NYS Theatre Institute
37 First St, 1218 O, Troy, NY 12180
518-274-3200 Fax: 518-274-3815
e-mail: nysti@capital.net
Web site: www.nysti.org
Professional theater productions for family and school audiences; training & education, internships, community/school outreach & cultural exchange programs
Patricia Di Benedetto Snyder, Producing Artistic Director

NYS Turfgrass Association
PO Box 612, Latham, NY 12110
518-783-1229 Fax: 518-783-1258
e-mail: nysta@nysta.org
Web site: www.nysta.org
Grow & manage turf for golf courses, ball fields & landscape
Beth Same, Executive Director

National Basketball Association
645 5th Ave, New York, NY 10022
212-407-8000 Fax: 212-826-0579
Web site: www.nba.com
Brian McIntyre, Senior Vice President, Communications

National Football League
280 Park Ave, New York, NY 10017
212-450-2000 Fax: 212-681-7599
e-mail: aiellog@nfl.com
Web site: www.nfl.com
Greg Aiello, Vice President, Public Relations

National Hockey League
1185 Avenue of the Americas, New York, NY 10036
212-789-2000 Fax: 212-789-2020
e-mail: fbrown@nhl.com
Web site: www.nhl.com
Frank Brown, Vice President, Media Relations

National Women's Hall of Fame
PO Box 335, 76 Fall Street, Seneca Falls, NY 13148
315-568-8060 Fax: 315-568-2976
Web site: www.greatwomen.org
The hall celebrates outstanding American women & their achievements
Billie Luisi-Potts, Executive Director

New School University, Department of Sociology
65 Fifth Ave, New York, NY 10003
212-229-5782 or 212-229-5737 Fax: 212-229-5595
e-mail: zolbergv@newschool.edu
Web site: www.newschool/edu
Sociology of the arts; censorship; collective memory; outsider art
Vera Zolberg, Professor, Sociology & Liberal Studies

New York Academy of Art Inc
111 Franklin St, New York, NY 10013-2911
212-966-0300 Fax: 212-966-3217
e-mail: info@nyaa.edu
Web site: www.nyaa.edu
Wayne A Linker, Executive Director

New York Aquarium
Surf Ave at West 8th St, Brooklyn, NY 11224
718-265-3428 or 718-265-FISH Fax: 718-265-3400
e-mail: fhackett@wcs.org
Web site: www.nyaquarium.com
Conservation, education & research
Fran Hackett, Communications

New York Artists Equity Association Inc
498 Broome St, New York, NY 10013
212-941-0130 Fax: 212-941-0138
e-mail: reginas@tiac.net
Web site: www.anny.org
Web based advocacy for visual arts & cultural organizations; Call first to send fax
Regina Stewart, Executive Director

New York City Opera
20 Lincoln Center, New York, NY 10023
212-870-5600 Fax: 212-724-1120
Web site: www.nycopera.com
Susan Woelzl, Director, Press & Public Relations

New York Foundation for the Arts
155 Ave of the Americas, 14th Floor, New York, NY 10013-1507
212-366-6900 Fax: 212-366-1778
e-mail: nyfainfo@nyfa.org
Web site: www.nyfa.org
Advocacy, leadership, financial & resource support & collaborative relationships with those committed to the arts
Theodore S Berger, Executive Director

New York Giants
Giants Stadium, East Rutherford, NJ 07073
201-935-8111 Fax: 201-935-8493
Web site: www.giants.com
Pat Hanlon, Vice President, Communications

New York Hall of Science
4701 111th Street, Queens, NY 11368
718-699-0005 x323 Fax: 718-699-1341
e-mail: wbrez@nyscience.org
Web site: www.nysci.org
Hands-on science exhibits & education program
Mary Record, Director, Communications

New York Islanders
1535 Old Country Rd, Plainview, NY 11803
516-501-6700 Fax: 516-501-6762
e-mail: customerservice@newyorkislanders.com
Web site: www.newyorkislanders.com
Chris Botta, Vice President, Communications

New York Jets
1000 Fulton Ave, Hempstead, NY 11550
516-560-8100 Fax: 516-560-8197
e-mail: rcolangelo@jets.nfl.com
Web site: www.newyorkjets.com
Bruce Speight, Public Relations

Offices and agencies generally appear in alphabetical order, except when specific order is requested by listee.

New York Marine Trades Association
194 Park Ave, Suite B, Amityville, NY 11701
631-691-7050 Fax: 631-691-2724
e-mail: csqueri@aol.com
Web site: www.nymta.com
Promote & protect the marine & boating industry; own & operate two boat shows; monitor local, state & federal marine legislation
Christopher Squeri, Executive Director

New York Mets
Shea Stadium, 123-01 Roosevelt Ave, Flushing, NY 11368
718-507-6387 Fax: 718-639-3619
Web site: www.mets.com
Fred Wilpon, Chairman & Chief Executive Officer

New York Racing Association
PO Box 90, Jamaica, NY 11417
718-641-4700 Fax: 718-843-7673
e-mail: nyra@nyraing.com
Web site: www.nyra.com
Horse racing at Aqueduct, Belmont Park, and Saratoga.
Francis LaBelle, Jr, Director, Communications

New York State Hospitality & Tourism Association
80 Wolf Rd, Albany, NY 12205
800-642-5313 x13 or 518-465-2300 Fax: 518-465-4025
e-mail: dan@nyshta.org
Web site: www.nyshta.org
Hotels, motels, amusement parks & attractions
Daniel C Murphy, President

New York State Restaurant Association
409 New Karner Rd, Albany, NY 12205
518-452-4222 Fax: 518-452-4497
e-mail: ricks@nysra.org
Web site: www.nysra.org
Rick J Sampson, President & Chief Executive Officer

New York State School Music Association (NYSSMA)
718 The Plain Rd, Westbury, NY 11590-5931
516-997-7200 Fax: 516-997-1700
e-mail: executive@nyssma.org
Web site: www.nyssma.org
Advocacy for a quality school music education for every student
Steven Schopp, Executive Director

New York State Snowmobile Association
PO Box 612, Long Lake, NY 12847
518-624-3849 Fax: 518-624-2441
e-mail: jimjennings@nyssnowassoc.org
Web site: www.nyssnowassoc.org
Working to preserve & enhance snowmobiling & improve trails, facilities & services for participants
Jim Jennings, Executive Director

New York State Theatre Education Association
63 Hecla St, Buffalo, NY 14216
716-837-9434 Fax: 716-626-8207
e-mail: rogersouth@aol.com
Web site: www.nystea.org
Working to preserve & enhance drama & theater education & opportunities in NY schools & communities
Roger Paolini, President

New York State Travel & Vacation Association
PO Box 285, Akron, NY 14001
888-698-2970 or 716-542-1586 Fax: 716-542-1404
e-mail: info@nystva.org
Web site: www.nystva.org
The NYSTVA is the tourism industry's leader in communication, legislative awareness, professional development, and promotion.
Dawn L Borchert, Executive Director

New York University, Tisch School of the Arts
721 Broadway, 12th Floor, New York, NY 10003
212-998-1800 Fax: 212-995-4064
Web site: www.nyu.edu/tisch
Mary Schmidt Campbell, Dean, Tisch School of the Arts

New York Wine & Grape Foundation
800 S Main St, Ste 200, Canandaigua, NY 14424
585-394-3620 Fax: 585-394-3649
e-mail: info@newyorkwines.org
Web site: www.newyorkwines.org
Promotion of wine & grape products of New York; research for wine & grape related products & issues
James Trezise, President

New York Yankees
800 Ruppert Place, Bronx, NY 10451
718-293-4300 Fax: 718-293-8431
Web site: www.yankees.com
Randy Levine, President

Resources for Artists with Disabilities Inc
77 7th Ave, Suite PHH, New York, NY 10011-6644
212-691-5490 Fax: 212-691-5490
Organizes & promotes exhibition opportunities for visual artists with physical disabilities
Dr Lois Kaggen, President & Founder

Saratoga Gaming & Raceway
PO Box 356, Saratoga Springs, NY 12866
518-584-2110 or 518-581-5748 Fax: 518-583-1269
e-mail: info@saratogaraceway.com
Web site: www.saratogaraceway.com
Horse racing
John R Matarazzo, Director of Racing Operations

Seaway Trail Inc
401 West Main Street, Ray & West Main Streets, PO Box 660, Sackets Harbor, NY 13685
315-646-1000 or 800-SEAWAY-T Fax: 315-646-1004
e-mail: info@seawaytrail.com
Web site: www.seawaytrail.com
Promotes coastal recreation, economic development, resource management & heritage, cultural, agricultural & culinary tourism along a 454 mile NYS highway system
Teresa Mitchell, President

Ski Areas of New York Inc
PO Box 96, Glens Falls, NY 12801
518-792-5060 or 518-796-3601 Fax: 518-792-3970
e-mail: scottbrandi@iskiny.com
Web site: www.skiandrideny.com
Promote skiing in NYS
Patrick Dunn, Administrator

Solomon R Guggenheim Foundation
1071 5th Ave, New York, NY 10128
212-423-3680
e-mail: directorsoffice@guggenheim.org
Web site: www.guggenheim.org
Thomas Krens, Director

Special Olympics New York, Inc
504 Balltown Road, Schenectady, NY 12304-2290
518-388-0790 Fax: 518-388-0795
Web site: www.nyso.org
Not-for-profit organization provides year-round sports training & competition in Olympic-style sports for athletes with intellectual disabilities.
Neal J Johnson, President & Chief Executive Officer

Policy Areas

Offices and agencies generally appear in alphabetical order, except when specific order is requested by listee.

Sports & Arts in Schools Foundation
58-12 Queens Blvd, Suite 1 - 59th Entrance, Woodside, NY 11377
718-786-7110 Fax: 718-786-7635
e-mail: info@sasfny.org
Web site: www.sasfny.org
After-school, summer camps & clinics, winter-break festival
James R O'Neill, Executive Director

Staten Island Zoo
614 Broadway, Staten Island, NY 10310
718-442-3101 Fax: 718-981-8711
e-mail: kmithcell@statenislandzoo.org
Web site: www.statenislandzoo.org
Kenneth C. Mitchell, Interim Executive Director

Tribeca Film Institute
375 Greenwich St, New York, NY 10013
212-941-2400 Fax: 212-941-3892
Web site: www.tribecafilminstitute.org
Madeyln Wils, President & Chief Executive Officer

USA Track & Field, Adirondack Association Inc
233 Fourth St, Troy, NY 12180
518-273-5552 Fax: 518-273-0647
e-mail: info@usatfadir.org
Web site: www.usatfadir.org
Leadership & opportunities for athletes pursuing excellence in running, race walking & track & field
George Regan, President

Vernon Downs/Gaming-Racing-Entertainment
4229 Stuhlman Rd, PO Box 1040, Vernon Downs, NY 13476
315-829-2201 Fax: 315-829-3787
e-mail: vernonevents@vernondowns.com
Web site: www.vernondowns.com
Horse racing, concerts, motorcross, motorcycle, craft fairs & other entertainment
Ursula Hardin, President

Willow Mixed Media Inc
PO Box 194, Glenford, NY 12433
845-657-2914
e-mail: video@hvc.rr.com
Web site: www.willowmixedmedia.org
Not-for-profit specializing in documentary video & arts projects addressing social concerns
Tobe Carey, President

Yonkers Raceway
810 Central Park Ave, Yonkers, NY 10704
914-968-4200 Fax: 914-968-4479
Web site: www.yonkersraceway.com
Horse racing and video gaming entertainment
Timothy Rooney, President

Offices and agencies generally appear in alphabetical order, except when specific order is requested by listee.

TRANSPORTATION

NEW YORK STATE

GOVERNOR'S OFFICE

Governor's Office
Executive Chamber
State Capitol
Albany, NY 12224
518-474-8390 Fax: 518-474-1513
Web site: www.ny.gov

Governor:
  Andrew M Cuomo 518-474-8390
Secretary to the Governor:
  William Mulrow 518-474-4246
Counsel to the Governor:
  Alphonso David 518-474-8343
Director, Communications:
  Melissa DeRosa . . . . .518-474-8418 or 212-681-4640
Deputy Secretary, Transportation:
  Ron Thaniel. 518-408-2555
Deputy Secretary, Public Safety:
  Terrence O'Leary 518-474-3522

EXECUTIVE DEPARTMENTS AND RELATED AGENCIES

Motor Vehicles Department
6 Empire State Plaza
Albany, NY 12228
Web site: www.dmv.ny.gov

Commissioner:
  Barbara J Fiala. 518-486-9786/fax: 518-474-9578
Executive Deputy Commissioner:
  J David Sampson. 518-474-0846/fax: 518-474-0712
Associate Commissioner, Communications:
  Jackie McGinnis 518-473-7000/fax: 518-473-1930

Administration, Office for
Deputy Commissioner:
  Gregory J Kline 518-474-6876/fax: 518-474-0712
Director, Audit Services:
  Jannette Potera 518-474-0881
Director, Fiscal Management:
  Robert Simon 518-474-0990
Director, Human Resources:
  Steve France 518-474-7602
Director, Information Technology:
  Adam Gigandet. 518-474-0605
Labor Relations:
  Nancy Spenziero. 518-474-2902
Director, Program Analysis:
  Mary Bidell. 518-474-0623

Governor's Traffic Safety Committee
Web site: www.safeny.ny.gov
Assistant Commissioner:
  Chuck DeWeese 518-474-0972
Director, Traffic Safety Committee:
  Jim Allen. 518-474-5777

Legal Affairs, Office for
Deputy Commissioner, Legal Affairs:
  Neal Schoen. 518-473-1965/fax: 518-474-0712
Assistant Commissioner & Deputy General Counsel:
  Timothy Lennon 518-474-0871

Director, Legal:
  Ida Traschen 518-474-0871
Appeals Board:
  Deborah Dugan. 518-474-0645

Operations & Customer Service, Office for
Deputy Commissioner:
  Yomika Bennett 518-474-0846
Legislative Liaison:
  Meg Murray 518-474-7726
Director, Field Operations:
  Cheryl Wasley. 518-486-7400
Director, Field Operations:
  Joseph Crisafulli 518-473-7254
Director, Central Office Operations:
  Roseanne Kitchner 518-402-4746

Safety, Consumer Protection & Clean Air, Office for
Deputy Commissioner:
  Terri Egan 518-402-4860/fax: 518-474-0712
Director, Driver/Vehicle Safety:
  Jean Rosenthal 518-473-3347
Director, Field Investigation:
  Owen McShane. 518-474-8805
Director, Driver Safety Programs:
  Kathy McHale 518-474-0855
Vehicle Safety & Clean Air:
  Steve Cooper. 518-474-3785

Transportation Department
50 Wolf Road
Albany, NY 12232
518-457-5100 or 518-457-6195 Fax: 518-457-5583
Web site: www.dot.ny.gov

Commissioner:
  Joan McDonald. 518-457-4422
Executive Deputy Commissioner:
  Stanley Gee. 518-457-4422
CIO/Information Technology Division:
  Nancy Mulholland 518-485-8853
Director, Legal Affairs Division:
  Janice A McLachlan. 518-457-2411
Operations & Asset Management Division:
  Roderic Sechrist 518-485-0887
Acting Director, Policy & Planning Division:
  Ron Epstein. 518-457-2320
Chief Engineer/Engineering Division:
  Phillip Eng 518-457-4430
Director, Audit & Civil Rights Division:
  John Samaniuk 518-457-1590
Director, Communications Office:
  Beau Duffy 518-457-6400
  e-mail: beau.duffy@dot.ny.gov

Administrative Services Division
Director:
  Pete Snyder. 518-457-6300
Director, Human Resources:
  Beau Duffy 518-485-7043
  e-mail: beau.duffy@dot.ny.gov
Director, Contract Management Bureau:
  Bill Howe 518-457-2600
Director, Communications Office:
  William P Reynolds. 518-457-6400/fax: 518-457-6506
Director, Facilities Management:
  Mark Reuss 518-457-6445
Director, Purchase Unit:
  Christopher J Magin 518-457-4401

Policy Areas

Offices and agencies generally appear in alphabetical order, except when specific order is requested by listee.

Engineering Division
Chief Engineer & Assistant Commissioner:
  Phillip Eng 518-457-4430
Office of Design (Acting):
  Richard Lee. 518-457-6452
Office of Structures (Acting):
  Richard Marchione 518-457-6827
Office of Environment:
  Vacant. 518-457-5672
Office of Major Projects:
  Marie Corrado. 518-485-5025
Office of Technical Services:
  Anthony Torre. 518-457-4445
Office of Construction:
  James Tynan 518-457-6472

Legal Affairs Division
Director, Legal Affairs Division:
  Janice A McLachlan .518-457-2411

Information Technology Division
Director:
  Nancy Mulholland 518-485-8853
Business Solutions Bureau:
  Thomas Johnston 518-457-2800
Project Management Office:
  Susan Mardon 518-457-2800
Statewide Customer Support Bureau:
  Pat Bennison. 518-457-2800
Technical Services Bureau (Acting):
  Perry Taglienti 518-457-2800

Operations & Asset Management Division
Director:
  Roderic Sechrist 518-485-0887
Modal Safety & Security Office (Acting):
  Clifford A Thomas 518-457-6512
Fleet Administration & Support Office (Acting):
  Robert D Martz. 518-457-2875
Emergency Transportation Operations:
  Dawn Arnold. 518-457-1673
Transportation Maintenance Office (Acting):
  Bob Winans. 518-457-6435
Traffic Safety & Mobility Office (Acting):
  Todd B Westhuis 518-457-0271
Employee Health & Safety (Acting):
  Brian Gibney. 518-457-2420

Policy & Planning Division
Acting Deputy Commissioner:
  Ron Epstein. 518-457-2320
CFO/Finance Office:
  Ron Epstein. 518-457-2320
Policy, Planning & Performance Office (Acting):
  Lynn Weiskopf 518-457-2320
Integrated Modal Services:
  Jon Rondinaro. 518-457-2320
Regional Planning & Program Coordination:
  Dave Rettig. 518-457-2320

Audit & Civil Rights Division
Director:
  John Samaniuk. 518-457-1590
Office of Civil Rights (Acting):
  Mansour Aghili. 518-457-1129
  e-mail: maghili@dot.state.ny.us
Contract Audit Bureau:
  Joseph Stuhlman. 518-457-1590
Enterprise Risk Management (Acting):
  Kimberly Doran 518-457-1590
Internal Audit Bureau:
  Theresa Vottis. 518-457-4680

Investigations Bureau:
  Robert Keihm 518-457-6446

Office of Regional Affairs
Director:
  Vacant. 518-457-2470

Regional Offices
Region 1
328 State St, Schenectady, NY 12305
Director (Acting):
  Sam Zhou. 518-451-3522
Region 2
Utica State Ofc Bldg, 207 Genesee St, Utica, NY 13501
Director (Acting):
  Jack Williams. 607-721-8116
Region 3
State Ofc Bldg, 333 E Washington St, Syracuse, NY 13202
Director:
  Carl F Ford 315-428-4351/fax: 315-428-4834
Region 4
1530 Jefferson Rd, Rochester, NY 14623
Acting Director:
  Robert Traver 585-272-3310/fax: 585-427-8480
Region 5
100 Seneca Street, Buffalo, NY 14203
Director (Acting):
  Darrell F Kaminski. 716-847-3238/fax: 716-847-3961
Region 6
107 Broadway, Hornell, NY 14843
Acting Director:
  Brian Kelly 607-324-8404/fax: 607-324-0790
Region 7
Dulles State Ofc Bldg, 317 Washington St, Watertown, NY 13601
Acting Director:
  Mark Frechette 315-785-2333/fax: 315-785-2507
Region 8
Eleanor Roosevelt State Ofc Bldg, 4 Burnett Blvd, Poughkeepsie, NY 12603
Acting Director:
  William Gorton. 845-431-5750/fax: 845-431-5703
Region 9
44 Hawley St, Binghamton, NY 13901
Director:
  Jack Williams. 607-721-8116/fax: 607-721-8119
Region 10
State Ofc Bldg, 250 Veterans Memorial Hwy, Hauppauge, NY 11788
Director:
  Subi Chakraborti. 631-952-6632/fax: 631-952-6311
Region 11
One Hunters Point Plaza, 47-40 21st St, Long Island City, NY 11101
Director (Acting):
  Joseph Brown 718-482-4526/fax: 718-482-4525

CORPORATIONS, AUTHORITIES AND COMMISSIONS

Albany County Airport Authority
Albany International Airport
Administration Building
Second Floor
Albany, NY 12211
518-242-2222 x1 Fax: 518-242-2641
e-mail: info@albanyairport.com
Web site: www.albanyairport.com/airport_authority.php

Chief Executive Officer:
  John A O'Donnell PE .518-242-2222 x1
Chief Financial Officer:
  William O'Reilly. 518-242-2222 x1

Offices and agencies generally appear in alphabetical order, except when specific order is requested by listee.

Director, Public Affairs:
    Douglas I. Myers 518-242-2222 x1
Counsel:
    Peter F Stuto. 518-242-2222 x1
Airport Planner:
    Stephen A Iachetta. 518-242-2222 x1
Administrative Services:
    Liz Charland 518-242-2222 x1

Albany Port District Commission
106 Smith Blvd, Admin Bldg
Port of Albany
Albany, NY 12202
518-463-8763 Fax: 518-463-8767
e-mail: portofalbany@portofalbany.us
Web site: www.portofalbany.us

Chair:
    Georgette Steffens. 518-463-8763
General Manager:
    Richard Hendrick 518-463-8763
    e-mail: rhendrick@portofalbany.us
Counsel:
    Thomas Owens 518-694-0910

Buffalo & Fort Erie Public Bridge Authority (Peace Bridge Authority)
One Peace Bridge Plaza
Buffalo, NY 14213-2494
716-884-6744 Fax: 716-884-2089
Web site: www.peacebridge.com

Chair (US):
    William Hoyt. 716-884-6744/fax: 716-883-7246
Vice Chair (Canada):
    Anthony M Annunziata. 716-884-6744/fax: 716-883-7246
General Manager:
    Ron Rienas 716-884-6744

Capital District Transportation Authority
110 Watervliet Ave
Albany, NY 12206
518-437-8300 or 518-482-8822 Fax: 518-437-8318
Web site: www.cdta.org

Chair:
    David M Stackrow 518-437-8311
Vice Chair:
    Georgeanna Nugent Lussier 518-437-8311
CEO:
    Carm Basile 518-437-6840/fax: 518-437-8349
    e-mail: carmb@cdta.org
General Counsel:
    Amanda A Avery. 518-437-8315/fax: 518-473-8318
    e-mail: amandaa@cdta.org
VP, Finance & Administration:
    Michael P Collins 518-437-8380/fax: 518-437-8347
    e-mail: mikec@cdta.org
Director of Transportation:
    Gary Cook 518-437-8372/fax: 518-437-8328
    e-mail: garyc@cdta.org
VP, Planning & Infrastructure:
    Christopher G Desany. 518-437-8320/fax: 518-437-8328
    e-mail: chrisd@cdta.org

Central New York Regional Transportation Authority
200 Cortland Ave
PO Box 820
Syracuse, NY 13205-0820

315-442-3400 Fax: 315-442-3337
Web site: www.centro.org

Chair, Board of Directors:
    Brian M Schultz 315-442-3300
Executive Director:
    Frank Kobliski 315-442-3360
    e-mail: fkobliski@centro.org
VP, Finance:
    Christine LoCurto. 315-442-3355
Manager, Procurement & Grants Administration:
    EJ Moses. 315-442-3368

MTA Bridges & Tunnels
2 Broadway
22nd Floor
New York, NY 10004-2801
646-252-7000 Fax: 646-252-7408
Web site: www.mta.info/bandt

President:
    James Ferrara 212-360-3100
Chief Engineer:
    Joseph Keane 212-878-7200
Vice President, Labor Relations:
    Sharon Gallo-Kotcher. 212-360-3015
Vice President, Operations:
    James Fortunato 212-878-7200
Chief Procurement Officer:
    Anthony Koestler 646-252-7084
Vice President, Staff Services & Chief of Staff:
    Catherine T Sweeney 646-252-7421
Executive Vice President:
    David Moretti 646-252-7100
Chief Financial Officer:
    Don Spero 646-252-7132
Chief Technology Officer:
    Tariq Habib. 646-252-7230
General Counsel:
    M. Margaret Jerry 212-878-7200
Manager, Public Affairs:
    Judith Glave 646-252-7276

MTA Bus Company
2 Broadway
New York, NY 10004
212-878-7174 Fax: 2512-878-0205
Web site: www.mta.info/busco

President:
    Daryl Irick. 212-878-7174

MTA Capital Construction
2 Broadway
8th Fl
New York, NY 10002
646-252-4575
Web site: www.mta.info/capital

President:
    Dr Michael Horodniceanu .646-252-4277
Chief of Staff:
    Ayala Malinovitz 646-252-4011
Senior Director, Government & Community Affairs:
    Richard Mulieri. 646-252-4197
Executive Vice President:
    William Goldstein. 646-252-4277
Senior Vice President & General Counsel:
    Evan Eisland 646-252-4274

Offices and agencies generally appear in alphabetical order, except when specific order is requested by listee.

Senior Director & Chief Procurement Officer:
David Cannon 646-252-2321
Vice President & Chief Engineer:
Mike Kyriacou 646-252-4500
Senior Vice President & Program Executive, East Side Access:
Alan Paskoff 212-967-0118
Senior Vice President & Program Executive, 2nd Ave Subway:
William Goodrich 212-510-2661
VP & Program Executive, #7 Subway Line Extension:
Mark Schiffman 646-252-3723
Director, System Safety & Security:
Eric Osnes 646-252-4556
Vice President, Program Controls & Quality Safety:
Raymond Schaeffer 646-252-5393
Vice President, Planning, Development & External Relations:
Joseph Petrocelli 646-252-3813

MTA Long Island Rail Road
Jamaica Station
Jamaica, NY 11435
718-558-7400 Fax: 718-558-8212
Web site: www.mta.info/lirr

President:
Helena E Williams 718-558-8252
Executive Vice President:
Albert Cosenza 718-558-7993
e-mail: accosen@lirr.org
Chief Information Officer:
Scott Dieterich 718-588-8166
Vice President, General Counsel & Secretary:
Richard Gans 718-558-8264
Chief Engineer:
Kevin Tomlinson 718-558-7400
Vice President, Labor Relations:
Michael Chirillo 718-558-7405
Vice President, Market Development & Public Affairs:
Joseph Calderone 718-558-7301
Vice President, ESA/Special Projects:
John Coulter 718-558-7363
e-mail: jwcoult@lirr.org
Director, Safety System:
Frank Lo Presti 718-588-7711
General Manager, Public Affairs:
Susan McGowan 718-558-7400

MTA Metro-North Railroad
347 Madison Ave
New York, NY 10017
212-340-2677 Fax: 212-340-4995
Web site: www.mta.info/mnr

President:
Joseph Giulietti 212-340-2677
General Counsel:
Seth Cummins 212-340-4933
VP, Finanace & Informational Systems:
D. Kim Porcelain 212-340-2636
Senior VP, Operations:
Robert Lieblong 212-499-4300
Senior Director, Capital Planning & Program:
John Kennard 212-340-2500
Chief of Staff & Operations:
David Treasure 212-340-2677
Chief Safety & Security Officer:
Anne Kirsch 212-340-4913
Senior Director, Capital Programs:
Timothy McCartney 212-499-4403
Vice President, Business Operations:
Thomas Tendy 212-672-1251

Senior Director, Corporate & Public Affairs:
Mark Mannix 212-340-2142

MTA New York City Transit
2 Broadway
New York, NY 10004
718-330-3000 Fax: 718-596-2146
Web site: www.mta.info/nyct

Acting President:
Carmen Bianco 646-252-5800
Chief Transportation Officer:
Herbert Lambert 718-330-3000
Vice President, Labor Relations:
Christopher Johnson 718-330-3000
Vice President, Corporate Communications:
Paul Fleuranges 646-252-5873
Vice President, Technology & Information Services:
Sidney Gellineau 718-330-3000
Vice President & General Counsel:
Martin Schnabel 718-694-3900
Director, Labor Relations:
Andrew Paul 646-252-5880
Chief Officer, Staten Island Railway:
John Gaul 718-876-8239

MTA (Metropolitan Transportation Authority)
347 Madison Ave
New York, NY 10017
212-878-7000 Fax: 212-878-7264
Web site: www.mta.info

Chairman/CEO:
Thomas F. Prendergast 212-878-7200
Chief Operating Officer:
Nuria I. Fernandez 212-878-7274
Director of Security:
Raymond Diaz 212-878-7155
Deputy Executive Director, Government & Community Affairs:
Robert Brennan 212-878-7160
Senior Director, Human Resources:
Margaret M. Connor
Director, Labor Relations:
Anita Miller 212-878-7438
Auditor General:
Michael J Fucilli 212-878-7236
Chief Financial Officer:
Robert E Foran 212-878-7278
Chief Financial Officer:
Robert E. Foran
General Counsel:
Jerome F Page 212-878-7313/fax: 212-878-7050
Chief of Staff:
Catherine A. Rinaldi 212-878-1001
Director, External Communications:
Adam Lisberg 212-878-7440

MTA Office of the Inspector General
2 Penn Plaza, 5th Fl
New York, NY 10121
212-878-0000 or 800-682-4448 Fax: 212-878-0003
Web site: www.mtaig.state.ny.us

Inspector General:
Barry L Kluger 212-878-0000

New York Metropolitan Transportation Council
199 Water St, 22nd Fl
New York, NY 10038

Offices and agencies generally appear in alphabetical order, except when specific order is requested by listee.

212-383-7200 Fax: 212-383-2418
e-mail: nymtc-web@dot.ny.gov
Web site: www.nymtc.org

Executive Director:
Joel Ettinger 212-383-7236
Acting Director, Administration:
Anthony Gawrych. 212-383-7294
e-mail: anthony.gawrych@dot.ny.gov
Director, Planning:
Gerard J Bogacz 212-383-7260
e-mail: gerry.bogacz@dot.ny.gov
PIO:
Lisa Daglian 212-383-7241
e-mail: lisa.daglian@dot.ny.gov

New York State Bridge Authority
Mid-Hudson Bridge Plaza
PO Box 1010
Highland, NY 12528
845-691-7245 Fax: 845-691-3560
e-mail: info@nysba.ny.gov
Web site: www.nysba.ny.gov

Chair:
Richard A. Gerentine 845-691-7245
Vice Chair:
Joseph Ramaglia. 845-691-7245
Executive Director:
Joseph Ruggiero 845-691-7245
Director, IT:
Gregory J Herd 518-828-4107
Director, Toll Collections & Operations:
Wayne V Ferguson 845-691-7245

New York State Thruway Authority
200 Southern Blvd
PO Box 189
Albany, NY 12201
518-436-2700 Fax: 518-436-2899
Web site: www.thruway.ny.gov

Chair:
Joanne M Mahoney. 518-436-3000
Acting Executive Director:
Robert Megna 518-436-2900
General Counsel:
Gordon Cuffy 518-436-2840
Interim Director, Maintenance & Operations:
Maria Lehman. 518-436-2840
Director, Media Relations & Communications:
Dan Weiller 518-471-5300
e-mail: publicinfo@thruway.ny.gov
Director, Administrative Services:
John F. Barr
e-mail: publicinfo@thruway.ny.gov

New York State Canal Corporation
Web site: www.canals.ny.gov
Acting Executive Director:
Robert Megna 518-436-3055/fax: 518-471-5023

Niagara Falls Bridge Commission
5365 Military Rd
Lewiston, NY 14092
716-285-6322 Fax: 716-282-3292
e-mail: general_inquiries@niagarafallsbridges.com
Web site: www.niagarafallsbridges.com

Chair:
Kathleen L Neville 716-285-6322
Vice Chair:
Kenneth E Loucks. 716-285-6322
Treasurer:
Linda L McAusland 716-285-6322
Secretary:
Russell G Quarantello. 716-285-6322

Niagara Frontier Transportation Authority
181 Ellicott St
Buffalo, NY 14203
716-855-7300 or 800-622-1220 Fax: 716-855-6655
e-mail: info@nfta.com
Web site: www.nfta.com

Chair:
Howard Zemsky 716-855-7232
Executive Director:
Kimberley A Minkel. 716-855-7470
Chief Financial Officer:
John Cox 716-855-7300
General Counsel:
David J State. 716-855-7686
Director, Aviation:
William Vanecek 716-630-6030
Director, Human Resources:
Karen Novo. 716-855-7343
Director, Public Transit:
Thomas George. 716-855-7390
Director, Engineering:
Michael Bykowski 716-855-7389
Director, Public Affairs:
C Douglas Hartmayer 716-855-7420
Chief, NFTA Police:
George W. Gast. 716-855-7666

Ogdensburg Bridge & Port Authority
One Bridge Plaza
Ogdensburg, NY 13669
315-393-4080 Fax: 315-393-7068
e-mail: obpa@ogdensport.com
Web site: www.ogdensport.com

Chair:
Samuel J LaMacchia. 315-393-4080
Deputy Executive Director:
Wade A Davis. 315-393-4080
e-mail: wadavis@ogdensport.com

Port Authority of New York & New Jersey
225 Park Ave South
18th Fl
New York, NY 10003
212-435-7000 Fax: 212-435-4032
Web site: www.panynj.gov

Chair, New Jersey:
John J Degnan. 212-435-7000
Vice Chair, New York:
Scott H Rechler. 212-435-7000
Executive Director:
Patrick Foye 212-435-7271
Acting COO:
Stephanie E Dawson 212-435-7887
Director Government & Community Affairs - NJ:
Tina Lado 212-435-6903
General Counsel:
Darrell Buchbinder 212-435-3515

Offices and agencies generally appear in alphabetical order, except when specific order is requested by listee.

Chief Financial Officer:
Elizabeth McCarthy 212-435-7738
Acting Public Information Officer/Media Relations:
Steve Coleman. 212-435-7777/fax: 212-435-4032
Director, Public Safety/Superintendent of Police:
Michael A Fedorko. 212-435-7000
Chief Engineer:
Peter J Zipf 212-435-7449

Port of Oswego Authority
1 East Second St
Oswego, NY 13126
315-343-4503 Fax: 315-343-5498
e-mail: shipping@portoswego.com
Web site: www.portoswego.com

Chair:
Terrence Hammill. 315-343-4503
e-mail: chairman@portoswego.com
Executive Director & CEO:
Zelko N. Kirincich. 315-343-4503 x111
e-mail: zkirincich@portoswego.com
Manager, Administrative Services/Facility Security Officer:
William Scriber 315-343-4503 x108
e-mail: wscriber@portoswego.com
Supervisor of Marina Operations:
Bernie Bacon. 315-343-4503
e-mail: oswegomarina@yahoo.com

Rochester-Genesee Regional Transportation Authority-RTS
1372 E Main St
PO Box 90629
Rochester, NY 14609
585-654-0200 Fax: 585-654-0224
Web site: www.myrts.com

Chief Executive Officer:
Bill Carpenter 585-654-0200
Chief Operating Officer:
Miguel A Velazquez. 585-654-0200
Chief Financial Officer:
Scott Adair 585-654-0200
General Counsel/CAO:
Daniel DeLaus 585-654-0200
Media Contact:
Carole Dowling. 585-654-0730
e-mail: cdowling@myrts.com

Thousand Islands Bridge Authority
PO Box 428, Collins Landing
43530 Interstate 81
Alexandria Bay, NY 13607
315-482-2501 or 315-658-2281 Fax: 315-482-5925
e-mail: info@tibridge.com
Web site: www.tibridge.com

Chair:
Robert Barnard 315-482-2501
Executive Director:
Robert G Horr, III. 315-482-2501
e-mail: roberthorr@tibridge.com
Legal Counsel:
Dennis Whelpley. 315-482-2501

Waterfront Commission of New York Harbor
39 Broadway
4th Fl
New York, NY 10006
212-742-9280 Fax: 212-480-0587
Web site: www.wcnyh.org

Commissioner, New York:
Ronald Goldstock 212-742-9280
Commissioner, New Jersey:
Michael Murphy. 212-742-9280
Executive Director:
Walter M Arsenault 212-905-9201

NEW YORK STATE LEGISLATURE

See Legislative Branch in Section 1 for additional Standing Committee and Subcommittee information.

Assembly Standing Committees

Corporations, Authorities & Commissions
Chair:
James F Brennan (D) 518-455-5377
Ranking Minority Member:
Jane Corwin (R) 518-455-4601

Economic Development, Job Creation, Commerce & Industry
Chair:
Robin L Schimminger (D) 518-455-4767
Ranking Minority Member:
Raymond Walter (R). 518-455-4618

Transportation
Chair:
David F Gantt (D). 518-455-5606
Ranking Minority Member:
David G McDonough (R) 518-455-4633

Senate Standing Committees

Commerce, Economic Development & Small Business
Chair:
Philip Boyle (R) 518-455-3411
Ranking Minority Member:
Timothy Kennedy (D). 518-455-2426

Corporations, Authorities & Commissions
Chair:
Michael Ranzenhofer (R). 518-455-3161
Ranking Minority Member:
Bill Perkins (D). 518-455-2441

Transportation
Chair:
Joseph Robach (R) 518-455-2909
Ranking Minority Member:
Martin Malave Dilan (D) 518-455-2177

U.S. GOVERNMENT

EXECUTIVE DEPARTMENTS AND RELATED AGENCIES

Federal Maritime Commission
Web site: www.fmc.gov

New York Area Office
Bldg 75, Rm 205B, JFK Intl Airport, Jamaica, NY 11430

Offices and agencies generally appear in alphabetical order, except when specific order is requested by listee.

Area Rep:
   Emanuel J Mingione 718-553-2228/fax: 718-553-2229

National Transportation Safety Board
Web site: www.ntsb.gov

Aviation Division, Northeast Regional Office
2001 Route 46, Ste 203, Parsippany, NJ 07054
Regional Director:
   David Muzio

Office of Administrative Law Judges
490 L'Enfant Plaza, ESW, Washington, DC 20594
Chief Judge:
   Alfonso J. Montano 202-314-6151/fax: 202-314-8758

US Department of Homeland Security (DHS)
Web site: www.dhs.gov

Transportation Security Administration (TSA)
201 Varick St, Rm 1101, New York, NY 10014
Regional Spokesperson:
   Lisa Farbstein 212-620-3608

US Transportation Department
Web site: www.dot.gov

Federal Aviation Administration-Eastern Region
One Aviation Plaza, Jamaica, NY 11434-4809
718-553-3001
Web site: www.faa.gov
Regional Administrator:
   Carmine Gallo 718-553-3001
Deputy Regional Administrator:
   Diane Crean 718-553-3001

Accounting Division
Manager:
   Fred Glassberg .718-553-4190

Aerospace Medicine Division
Regional Flight Surgeon:
   Harriet Lester 718-553-3300

Air Traffic Division
Acting Area Director:
   John G McCartney 718-553-4500

Airports Division
Manager:
   Steve Urlass 516-227-3803

Aviation Information & Services Division
Manager:
   Alan Siperstein 718-553-3358

Engineering Services
Manager:
   Selin Haber 718-553-3400

Flight Standards Division
Manager:
   John M. Krepp . . . . .516-228-8029 x. 200

Human Resource Management Division
Manager:
   Gloria Quay 718-553-3132

Logistics Division
Manager:
   Vacant 718-553-3050

Military Liaison Officers to the Federal Aviation Admin (NYS)
12 New England Executive Park, Burlington, MA 1803

Air Force Regional Representatives
   Representative:
      Vacant 781-238-7901/fax: 781-238-7903
   Transportation Specialist:
      Cheryl W Carpenter 781-238-7910
      e-mail: cheryl.w.carpenter@faa.gov
Army Regional Representatives
   Liaison Officer:
      LTC Bill Walsh 781-238-7906
      e-mail: bill.walsh@faa.gov
   Liaison Officer:
      MSGT Jason Williams 781-238-7905
      e-mail: jason.williams@faa.gov
Navy Regional Representatives
   Liaison Officer:
      CDR Rick Perez 781-238-7907
      e-mail: rick.perez@faa.gov
   Liaison Officer:
      ACCS Mark Moon 781-238-7908/fax: 781-238-7902
      e-mail: mark.moon@faa.gov

Runway Safety Manager
Manager:
   Bill DeGraaff 718-553-3326

Federal Highway Administration-New York Division . . . . .fax: 518-431-4121
Leo W O'Brien Federal Bldg, Rm 719 Clinton Ave & N Pearl St, Albany, NY 12207
518-431-4125 Fax: 518-431-4121
Web site: www.fhwa.dot.gov
Division Administrator:
   John M. McDade 518-431-8897
   e-mail: john.mcdade@dot.gov
Acting Chief Operating Officer:
   Robert Clark 518-431-8879
   e-mail: robert.clark@dot.gov
NYC Federal Aid Liaison:
   John Formosa 212-668-2205
   e-mail: john.formosa@dot.gov
Engineer Coordinator:
   Joan P. Walters 518-431-8868
   e-mail: joan.walters@dot.gov

Federal Motor Carrier Safety Admin-New York Division . . . .fax: 518-431-4140
Leo O'Brien Federal Bldg, Rm 815, Clinton Avenue & North Pearl Street, Albany, NY 12207
518-431-4145 Fax: 518-431-4140
Web site: www.fmcsa.dot.gov
Division Administrator:
   Brian Temperine 518-431-4145 x311
Field Office Supervisor, Upstate:
   Pamela Noyes 518-431-4145 x316
State Program Specialist:
   Vacant
Manager, Intelligent Transportation Systems Commercial Vehicle Operati:
   Carolyn Temperine 518-431-4145 x270

Federal Railroad Administration-Field Offices
Web site: www.fra.dot.gov

Hazardous Material
1 Aviation Plaza, Jamaica, NY 11434-4089
Inspector:
   Steven Joseph 718-553-2596
   e-mail: steven.joseph@faa.gov

Highway-Rail Grade Crossing
PO Box 2144, Ballston Spa, NY 12020
Program Manager:
   Randall L Dickinson 518-899-5372/fax: 518-899-5372

Offices and agencies generally appear in alphabetical order, except when specific order is requested by listee.

Federal Transit Administration, Region II-New York
One Bowling Green, Rm 429, New York, NY 10004-1415
Web site: www.fta.dot.gov
Regional Admin:
Marilyn G. Shazor 212-668-2170/fax: 212-668-2136

Maritime Administration
Web site: www.marad.dot.gov

Great Lakes Region (includes part of New York State)
500 West Madison Street, Suite 1110, Chicago, IL 60661
312-353-1032
Regional Director:
Floyd Miras 312-353-1032/fax: 312-353-1036
e-mail: floyd.miras@dot.gov

North Atlantic Region
One Bowling Green, Rm 418, New York, NY 10004
Regional Director:
Jeffrey Flumignan 212-668-3330
e-mail: flumignan@dot.gov

US Merchant Marine Academy
300 Steamboat Rd, Kings Point, NY 11024-1699
516-726-5800
Web site: www.usmma.edu
Superintendent:
RADM James A. Helis 516-726-5800

National Highway Traffic Safety Administration, Reg II-NY
222 Mamaroneck Ave, Suite 204, White Plains, NY 10605
Web site: www.nhtsa.dot.gov
Team Leader:
Richard Simon .914-682-6162/fax: 914-682-6239
e-mail: region2@dot.gov

Office of Inspector General, Region II-New York
80 Madison Lane, New York, NY 10038
Web site: www.oig.dot.gov
Inspector General:
Debra Herlica .212-825-2413/fax: 212-825-3238
e-mail: dherlica@doi.nyc.gov

Saint Lawrence Seaway Development Corporation
180 Andrews St, Massena, NY 13662
Web site: www.greatlakes-seaway.com
Assoc Administrator:
Salvatore Pisani 315-764-3209/fax: 315-764-3235
e-mail: sal.pisani@sls.dot.gov

U.S. CONGRESS

See U.S. Congress Chapter for additional Standing Committee and Subcommittee information.

House of Representatives Standing Committees

Transportation & Infrastructure
Chair:
Bill Shuster (R-PA) 202-225-2431
Ranking Minority Member:
Nick J. Rahall II (D-WV) 202-225-3452
New York Delegate:
Sean Patrick Maloney (D) 202-225-5441
New York Delegate:
Timothy H Bishop (D) 202-225-3826
New York Delegate:
Richard L. Hanna 202-225-3665
New York Delegate:
Jerrold Nadler (D) 202-225-5635

Senate Standing Committees

Commerce, Science & Transportation
Chair:
John D Rockefeller IV (D-WV) 202-224-6472
Vice Chair:
John Thune (R-SD) 202-224-2321

Environment & Public Works
Chair:
Barbara Boxer (D-CA) 202-224-8832
Ranking Minority Member:
David Vitter (R-LA) 202-224-4623
New York Delegate:
Kirsten Gillibrand (D) 202-224-4451

Subcommittee
Transportation & Infrastructure
Chair:
Max Baucus (D-MT) 202-224-2651
Ranking Minority Member:
John Barrasso (R-WY) 202-224-6441

PRIVATE SECTOR

ALSTOM Transportation Inc
1 Transit Dr, Hornell, NY 14843
607-281-2487 Fax: 607-324-2641
e-mail: chuck.wochele@transport.alstom.com
Web site: www.transport.alstom.com
High-speed trains, rapid transit vehicles, commuter cars, AC propulsion & signaling, passenger locomotives
Wallace Smith, Vice President
Chuck Wochele, Vice President Business Development

A&W Architects and Engineers
Ammann & Whitney Consulting Engineers
96 Morton St, New York, NY 10014
212-462-8500 Fax: 212-929-5356
e-mail: nivanoff@ammann-whitney.com; asandor@ammann-whitney.com
Web site: www.ammann-whitney.com
Planning, engineering & construction mgmt for airport, transit, gov't, recreation & commercial facilities; highways; bridges
Nick Ivanoff, President & Chief Executive Officer

Automobile Club of New York
1415 Kellum Place, Garden City, NY 11530
516-873-2259 Fax: 516-873-2355
Web site: www.aaany.com
John Corlett, Director Government Affairs

Automotive Technology & Energy Group of Western NY
2568 Walden Avenue, Suite 103, Cheektowaga, NY 14225
716-651-4645 Fax: 716-651-4662
Garage & service station owners
Robert Gliss, Executive Director

British Airways PLC
75-20 Astoria Blvd, Jackson Heights, NY 11370
347-418-4729 Fax: 347-418-4204
e-mail: john.lampl@ba.com
Web site: www.ba.com
John Lampl, Vice President, Corporate Communications-Americas

CP Rail System
200 Clifton Corporate Parkway, PO Box 8002, Clifton Park, NY 12065
518-383-7200 Fax: 518-383-7222
Freight transport
Brent Szafron, Service Area Manager

Offices and agencies generally appear in alphabetical order, except when specific order is requested by listee.

DKI Engineering & Consulting USA, PC, Corporate World Headquarters
632 Plank Rd, Ste 208, Clifton Park, NY 12065
518-373-4999 Fax: 518-373-8989
e-mail: dki123@aol.com
Web site: www.dkitechnologies.com
Design, engineering, planning, construction management & program management oversight for airports, bridges, highways, railroads, transit, tunnels, water & wastewater facilities
D K Gupta, President & Chief Executive Officer

Empire State Passengers Association
PO Box 434, Syracuse, NY 13209
716-741-6384 Fax: 716-632-3044
e-mail: bbecker@esparail.org
Web site: www.esparail.org
Advocacy for improvement of rail passenger service
Bruce Becker, President

Ethan C Eldon Associates Inc
1350 Broadway, Ste 612, New York, NY 10018
212-967-5400 Fax: 212-967-2747
e-mail: eceaethan@aol.com
Environmental, EIS, traffic, hazardous & solid waste consulting
Ethan C Eldon, President

Gandhi Engineering Inc
111 John St, 3rd Fl, New York, NY 10038-3002
212-349-2900 Fax: 212-285-0205
e-mail: gandhi@gandhieng.com
Web site: www.gandhieng.com
Consulting architects & engineers; infrastructure projects & transportation facilities
Kirti Gandhi, President

General Contractors Association of NY
60 East 42nd St, Rm 3510, New York, NY 10165
212-687-3131 Fax: 212-808-5267
e-mail: felice@gca.gcany.net
Heavy construction, transportation
Felice Farber, Director, External Affairs

Jacobs Engineering
260 Madison Ave, 12th Floor, Suite 1200, New York, NY 10016
212-268-1500 Fax: 212-481-9484
Web site: www.jacobs.com
Multi-modal surface transportation planning, design, engineering, construction & inspection services
Vincent Mangieri, Vice President

Komanoff Energy Associates
636 Broadway, Rm 602, New York, NY 10012-2623
212-260-5237
e-mail: kea@igc.org
Energy, utilities & transportation consulting
Charles Komanoff, Director

Konheim & Ketcham Inc
175 Pacific St, Brooklyn, NY 11201
718-330-0550 Fax: 718-330-0582
e-mail: csk@konheimketcham.com
Web site: www.konheimketcham.com
Environmental impact analysis, traffic engineering, transportation planning & technical assistance to community groups
Carolyn Konheim, President

Kriss, Kriss, Brignola & Persing, LLP
350 Northern Blvd, Ste 306, Albany, NY 12204
518-449-2037 Fax: 518-449-7875
e-mail: office@krisslaw.com
Web site: www.krisslawoffice.com
Advocates for highway & auto safety

Mark C Kriss, Partner

Long Island Rail Road Commuter's Council
347 Madison Ave, 8th Fl, New York, NY 10017
212-878-7087 Fax: 212-878-7461
e-mail: mail@lirrcc.org
Web site: www.lirrcc.org
Represent interest of LIRR riders
Mark Epstein, Chair

Metro-North Railroad Commuter Council
347 Madison Ave, New York, NY 10017
212-878-7077 or 212-878-7087 Fax: 212-878-7461
e-mail: mail@pcac.org
Web site: www.pcac.org
Represent interests of MNR riders
William Henderson, Chair

NY Airport Service
15 Second Ave, Brooklyn, NY 11215
718-875-8200 Fax: 718-875-7056
Web site: www.nyairportservice.com
Airport shuttle bus services
Mark Marmurstein, Vice President

NY State Association of Town Superintendents of Highways Inc
119 Washington Avenue, Suite 300, Albany, NY 12210
518-694-9313 Fax: 518-694-9314
e-mail: info@nystownhwys.org
Web site: www.nystownhwys.org
Michael K Thompson, Communications Director

NYS Association of Service Stations & Repair Shops
6 Walker Way, Albany, NY 12205-4946
518-452-4367 Fax: 518-452-1955
e-mail: nysassn@together.net
Web site: www.nysassrs.com
Protect the interests of independent service stations & repair shops & the motoring public
Ralph Bombardiere, Executive Director

NYS County Hwy Super Assn / NY Aviation Mgt Assn / NY Public Transit Assn
119 Washington Ave, Ste 100, Albany, NY 12210
518-465-1694 Fax: 518-465-1942
e-mail: info@countyhwys.org; info@nyama.com; nypta@atdial.net
Web site: www.countyhwys.org; www.nyama.com; www.nytransit.org
County highways & bridges in NYS; aviation industry in NYS; public transit industry in NYS
Kathleen A Van De Loo, Communications Director

National Economic Research Associates
308 N Cayuga St, Ithaca, NY 14850
607-277-3007 Fax: 607-277-1581
e-mail: alfred.kahn@nera.com
Web site: www.nera.com
Utility & transportation regulation, deregulation & antitrust
Alfred E Kahn, Professor Emeritus & Special Consultant

New England Steamship Agents Inc
730 Downing St, Niskayuna, NY 12309
518-463-5749 Fax: 518-463-5751
e-mail: nesa0025@aol.com
Domestic transportation, vessel agency/husbandry, customs brokerage & vessel brokerage
Diane Delory, President

Offices and agencies generally appear in alphabetical order, except when specific order is requested by listee.

New York & Atlantic Railway (NYA)
68-01 Otto Rd, Glendale, NY 11385
7189497-3023 Fax: 718-497-3364
e-mail: pvictor@anacostia.com
Web site: www.anacostia.com
Freight transport
Paul Victor, President

New York Public Interest Research Group Straphangers Campaign
9 Murray St, 3rd Fl, New York, NY 10007
212-349-6460 Fax: 212-349-1366
e-mail: grussian@nypirg.org
Web site: www.straphangers.org; www.nypirg.org
Mass transit & government reform
Gene Russianoff, Senior Staff Attorney

New York Roadway Improvement Coalition (NYRIC)
629 Old White Plains Road, Tarrytown, NY 10591
914-631-6070 Fax: 914-631-5172
e-mail: cicwhv@cicnys.org
Heavy highway & bridge construction
Ross Pepe, President

New York Shipping Association Inc
100 Wood Ave South, Ste 304, Iselin, NJ 08830-2716
732-452-7800 Fax: 732-452-6312
e-mail: jcobb@nysanet.org
Web site: www.nysanet.org
*Maximizing the efficiency, cost competitiveness, safety & quality of marine
cargo operations in the Port of New York & New Jersey*
James H Cobb, Jr, Director, Governmental Affairs

New York State Auto Dealers Association
37 Elk St, Albany, NY 12207
518-463-1148 x204 Fax: 518-432-1309
e-mail: bob@nysada.com
Web site: www.nysada.com
Robert Vancavage, President

New York State Motor Truck Association
828 Washington Ave, Albany, NY 12203-1622
518-458-9696 Fax: 518-458-2525
e-mail: kadams@nytrucks.org
Web site: www.nytrucks.org
Safety & regulatory compliance
Kendra Adams, Executive Director

**New York State Transportation Engineering Alliance
(NYSTEA)**
99 Pine St, Ste 207, Albany, NY 12207
518-436-0786 Fax: 518-427-0452
e-mail: sdm@fwc-law.com
Transportation & infrastructure
Stephen D Morgan, Secretary

New York, Susquehanna & Western Railway Corporation, The
1 Railroad Ave, Cooperstown, NY 13326-1110
607-547-2555 Fax: 607-547-9834
e-mail: nfenno@nysw.com
Web site: www.nysw.com
Subsidiaries operate freight railroad systems
Nathan R Fenno, President

Parsons Brinckerhoff
One Penn Plaza, New York, NY 10119
212-465-5000 Fax: 212-465-5096
e-mail: bennett@pbworld.com
Web site: www.pbworld.com
*Engineering, planning, construction management & consulting for transit &
transportation, power & telecom projects*
Joel H Bennett, Senior Vice President

Regional Plan Association
4 Irving Place, 7th Fl, New York, NY 10003
212-253-2727 Fax: 212-253-5666
e-mail: jeff@rpa.org
Web site: www.rpa.org
Regional transportation planning & development issues
Jeffrey M Zupan, Senior Fellow, Transportation

Seneca Flight Operations
2262 Airport Dr, Penn Yan, NY 14527
315-536-4471 Fax: 315-536-4558
e-mail: rleppert@senecafoods.com
Web site: www.senecafoods.com
Executive air transportation
Richard Leppert, General Manager

Simmons-Boardman Publishing Corp
345 Hudson St, 12th Fl, New York, NY 10014-4590
212-620-7200 Fax: 212-633-1863
e-mail: sbrailgroup@sbpub.com
Web site: www.railwayage.com or www.rtands.com or www.railjournal.com
*Publisher of: Railway Age, International Railway Journal & Rapid Transit
Review, Railway Track & Structures*
Robert DeMarco, Publisher

Systra Consulting Inc
470 Seventh Ave, 10th Floor, New York, NY 10018
212-494-9111 Fax: 212-494-9112
Web site: www.systraconsulting.com
*Engineering consultants specializing in urban rail & transit systems,
passenger & freight railroads & high speed rail*
Peter Allibone, Executive Vice President

Transport Workers Union of America, AFL-CIO
1700 Broadway, 2nd Fl, New York, NY 10019
212-259-4900 Fax: 212-265-5704
Web site: www.twu.com
Bus, train, railroad & airline workers' union
James C Little, International President

Transportation Alternatives
127 W 26th Street, Suite 1002, New York, NY 10001
212-629-8080 Fax: 212-629-8334
e-mail: info@transalt.org
Web site: www.transalt.org
*NYC commute alternatives, traffic calming, pedestrian safety issues,
bicycling, public space*
Paul Steely White, Executive Director

Tri-State Transportation Campaign
350 W 31st St, Room 802, New York, NY 10001-2726
212-268-7474 Fax: 212-268-7333
e-mail: tstc@tstc.org
Web site: www.tstc.org
*Public interest, transit advocacy, planning & environmental organizations
working to reform transportation policies*
Kate Slevin, Executive Director

United Transportation Union
35 Fuller Road, Suite 205, Albany, NY 12205
518-438-8403 Fax: 518-438-8404
e-mail: sjnasca@aol.com
Web site: www.utu.org
Federal government railroad, bus & airline employees; public employees
Samuel Nasca, Legislative Director

Urbitran Group
71 West 23rd St, 11th Fl, New York, NY 10010
212-366-6200 Fax: 212-366-6214
e-mail: mhorodnicaenu@urbitran.com
Web site: www.urbitran.com
Engineering, architecture & planning
Michael Horodnicaenu, President & Chief Executive Officer

Offices and agencies generally appear in alphabetical order, except when specific order is requested by listee.

VETERANS AND MILITARY

NEW YORK STATE

GOVERNOR'S OFFICE

Governor's Office
Executive Chamber
State Capitol
Albany, NY 12224
518-474-8390 Fax: 518-474-1513
Web site: www.ny.gov

Governor:
 Andrew M Cuomo 518-474-8390
Secretary to the Governor:
 William Mulrow 518-474-4246
Counsel to the Governor:
 Alphonso David 518-474-8343
Director, Communications:
 Melissa DeRosa . . . . .518-474-8418 or 212-681-4640

EXECUTIVE DEPARTMENTS AND RELATED AGENCIES

Health Department
Corning Tower
Empire State Plaza
Albany, NY 12237
518-474-2011
Web site: www.health.ny.gov

Health Facilities Management
Director:
 David J Hernandez 518-474-2772/fax: 518-474-0611

Helen Hayes Hospital
Rte 9W, West Haverstraw, NY 10993-1195
845-786-4000
e-mail: info@helenhayeshospital.org
Web site: www.helenhayeshospital.org
CEO:
 Edmund Coletti 845-786-4202/fax: 845-947-0036
Chief Operating Officer:
 Kathleen Martucci 845-786-4201

New York State Veterans' Home at Batavia
220 Richmond Ave, Batavia, NY 14020
585-345-2000
Web site: www.nysvets.org
Administrator:
 Joanne I Hernick 585-345-2076/fax: 585-345-9030
Medical Director:
 Mary Obear MD 585-345-2042
Director, Nursing:
 Stephanie Sulyma 585-345-2000 x2041

New York State Veterans' Home at Montrose . . . . . . fax: 914-788-6100
2090 Albany Post Rd, Montrose, NY 10548
Fax: 914-788-6100
Web site: www.nysvets.org
Administrator:
 Nancy Baa-Danso 914-788-6003
Acting Medical Director:
 Ron Ammon, MD 914-788-6025
Director, Nursing:
 Christene St Paul Joseph 914-788-6021

New York State Veterans' Home at Oxford
4211 State Highway 220, Oxford, NY 13830
607-843-3100
Web site: www.nysvets.org
Administrator:
 James Wyzykowski 607-843-3129/fax: 607-843-3199
Medical Director:
 Philip Dzwonczyk MD 607-843-3140
Director, Nursing:
 Linda Winston 607-843-3165

New York State Veterans' Home at St Albans
178-50 Linden Blvd, Jamaica, NY 11434-1467
718-990-0300
Web site: www.nysvets.org
Administrator:
 Neville Goldson 718-990-0329
Medical Director:
 Thomas Bizarro MD 718-990-0328
Director, Nursing:
 Elaine Boyd-Brown 718-990-0316

Labor Department
Building 12, Room 500
Harriman State Office Campus
Albany, NY 12240
518-457-9000 Fax: 518-457-6908
e-mail: nysdol@labor.ny.gov
Web site: www.labor.ny.gov

Commissioner:
 Peter M. Rivera 518-457-9000
Executive Deputy Commissioner:
 Mario Musolino 518-457-4318

Federal Programs
Deputy Commissioner, Federal Programs:
 Bruce Herman 518-485-6410

Employment Services Division
Director:
 Vacant 518-457-3584
Assistant Director:
 Russell Oliver 518-457-3584

Veterans Services
Program Coordinator:
 Vacant 518-457-1343

Employer Services
Director:
 Vacant 518-457-6821
Rural Labor Services:
 Valerie Sewell 518-457-8539

Military & Naval Affairs, Division of
330 Old Niskayuna Rd
Latham, NY 12110
518-786-4786 or 518-489-6188 Fax: 518-786-4649
Web site: www.dmna.ny.gov

Adjutant General:
 Major Gen Patrick Murphy 518-786-4502
 e-mail: pat.murphy@us.army.mil
Assistant Adjutant General - Air:
 Anthony P. Gorman 518-786-4317
Executive Officer:
 Donald McKnight 518-786-4388
Legal Counsel:
 Robert G Conway, Jr 518-786-4541

Offices and agencies generally appear in alphabetical order, except when specific order is requested by listee.

Policy Areas

Director, Budget & Finance:
  Robert A Martin 518-786-4514
Director, Governmental & Community Affairs:
  James M Huelle 518-786-4580
Director, Public Affairs:
  Eric Durr 518-786-4581/fax: 518-786-4649
  e-mail: eric.d.durr.nfg@mail-mil

Veterans' Affairs, Division of
2 Empire State Plaza
17th Fl
Albany, NY 12223-1551
518-474-6114 or 888-838-7697 Fax: 518-473-0379
e-mail: dvainfo@veterans.ny.gov
Web site: www.veterans.ny.gov

Director:
  Eric J. Hesse 518-474-6114
  e-mail: ehesse@veterans.ny.gov
Executive Deputy Director:
  Vacant 518-474-6114
Secretary to the Director:
  Mary Quay 518-474-6114
  e-mail: m.quay@veterans.ny.gov
Deputy Director, Administration & Budget:
  Michelle LaRock 518-474-6114
  e-mail: mlarock@veterans.state.ny.us
Counsel:
  Samuel Spitzberg 518-474-6114
  e-mail: sspitzberg@veterans.ny.gov
Deputy Director, Programs, Operations & Training:
  Christine Tarnowski 518-474-6784
  e-mail: ctarnowski@veterans.state.ny.us
Assistant Director, Communications:
  Casey Lumbra 518-486-5251
  e-mail: clumbra@veterans.state.ny.us

Bureau of Veterans Education
Bureau Chief:
  James Bombard 518-474-5322
Supervisor:
  Craig Farley 518-474-7606

Counseling & Claims Service
  Web site: www.veterans.state.ny.us/ofcs.htm
State Veteran Counselor:
  Sue Doan 315-428-4046
State Veteran Counselor:
  Lloyd Collins 315-428-4046
State Veteran Counselor:
  Mark Tamkus 315-785-2468

Eastern Region
  55 Hanson Place, Brooklyn, NY 11217
Deputy Director:
  Andrew Roberts 718-722-2584

Western Region
  65 Court St, ste 310, Buffalo, NY 14202-3406
Deputy Director:
  Vacant 716-847-3414/fax: 716-847-3410

Veterans' Service Organizations

Albany Housing Coalition Inc . . . . fax: 518-465-6499
  278 Clinton Ave, Albany, NY 12210
  Fax: 518-465-6499
  e-mail: admin@ahcvets.org
  Web site: www.ahcvets.org
Executive Director:
  Joseph Sluszka 518-465-5251

Director, Veterans Svcs:
  Glenn E Read 518-465-5251

COPIN HOUSE (Homeless Veterans) . . . . fax: 716-283-5712
  5622 Buffalo Ave, Niagara Falls, NY 14304
Executive Director:
  Sharon McGrath 716-283-5622

Continuum of Care for Homeless Veterans in New York City

30th Street Shelter
  400-430 East 30th St, New York, NY 10016
Director:
  Yvonne Ballard 212-481-4730

Project TORCH, Veterans Health Care Center
  40 Flatbush Ave Ext, 8th Fl, Brooklyn, NY 11201
Program Coordinator:
  Julie Irwin 718-439-4345/fax: 718-439-4356

Hicksville Counseling Center, Veterans' Resource Center . . . fax: 516-935-2717
  385 West John St, Hicksville, NY 11801
Director, Substance Abuse Program & Veterans Resource Center:
  Geryl Pecora 516-935-6858

Saratoga Cnty Rural Preservation Co (Homeless Veterans)
  36 Church Ave, Ballston Spa, NY 12020
  Web site: www.vethome.org
Executive Director:
  A C Budd Mazurek 518-885-0091/fax: 518-885-0998

Suffolk County United Veterans Halfway House Project Inc
  PO Box 598, Patchogue, NY 11772
Executive Director:
  John Lynch 631-924-8088/fax: 631-924-0160

Veterans House (The) . . . . fax: 518-465-6499
  180 First St, Albany, NY 12210
House Manager:
  John Jacobie 518-449-8430

Veterans Outreach Center Inc . . . . fax: 585-546-5234
  459 South Ave, Rochester, NY 14620
  Fax: 585-546-5234
  Web site: www.veteransoutreachcenter.org
President & Chief Executive Officer:
  Thomas Cray 585-546-1081
  e-mail: info@veteransoutreachcenter.org

Veterans Services Center of the Southern Tier . . fax: 607-771-9395
  174 Clinton St, Binghamton, NY 13905
Executive Director:
  Patricia Gaven 607-771-8387

Veterans' Coalition of the Hudson Valley . . . . fax: 845-471-6113
  9 Vassar St, Poughkeepsie, NY 12601
  845-471-6113 Fax: 845-471-6113
Administrator:
  Marilyn Wickman 845-471-6113
  e-mail: vetcoal@aol.com

CORPORATIONS, AUTHORITIES AND COMMISSIONS

Brooklyn Navy Yard Development Corporation
63 Flushing Ave, Unit #300
Bldg 292, 3rd Fl
Brooklyn, NY 11205
718-907-5900 Fax: 718-643-9296
e-mail: info@brooklynnavyyard.org
Web site: www.brooklynnavyyard.org

Offices and agencies generally appear in alphabetical order, except when specific order is requested by listee.

Chair:
Henry Gutman 718-907-5900
President & Chief Executive Officer:
David Ehrenberg 718-907-5900
Executive Vice President & Chief Operating Officer:
Elliot S. Matz 718-907-5900
Senior Vice President, External Affairs:
Richard Drucker 718-907-5900
Chief of Staff:
Clare Newman 718-907-5900
Vice President/Deputy General Counsel:
Martin H. Baker 718-907-5900

NEW YORK STATE LEGISLATURE

See Legislative Branch in Section 1 for additional Standing Committee and Subcommittee information.

Assembly Standing Committees

Veterans Affairs
Chair:
Michael DenDekker (D) 518-455-4545
Ranking Minority Member:
Stephen Hawley (R) 518-455-5811

Senate Standing Committees

Veterans, Homeland Security & Military Affairs
Chair:
Thomas Croci (R) 518-455-3570
Ranking Minority Member:
Joseph P Addabbo, Jr (D) 518-455-2322

U.S. GOVERNMENT

EXECUTIVE DEPARTMENTS AND RELATED AGENCIES

US Defense Department
e-mail: www.defenselink.mil

AIR FORCE-National Media Outreach . . . . fax: 212-784-0149
805 Third Ave, 9th Fl, New York, NY 10022
Director:
Angela Billings 212-784-0147
e-mail: big.saf@us.af.mil
Public Relations Director:
Wesley Preston Miller 212-784-0147
e-mail: jason.medina@afnews.af.mil

Air National Guard

Francis S Gabreski Airport, 106th Rescue Wing . . . . fax: 631-723-7179
150 Old Riverhead Rd, Westhampton Beach, NY 11978
Commander:
Col. Thomas J. Owens II 631-723-7400
Public Affairs Officer:
Tech Sgt. Eric Miller 631-723-7470

Hancock Field, 174th Fighter Wing
6001 E Molloy Rd, Syracuse, NY 13211
315-454-6146
Commander:
Col. Greg A. Semmel 315-454-6146

Army

Fort Drum . . . . .fax: 315-772-8295
10012 South Riva Ridge Loop, Fort Drum, NY 13602-5028

315-772-5461 Fax: 315-772-8295
Web site: www.drum.army.mil
Commander:
Maj. Stephen J. Townsend 315-772-8295
Community Relations Officer:
Lori Haney 315-772-8295

Fort Hamilton . . . . .fax: 718-630-4709
Fort Hamilton, New York, NY 11252
Commander:
Col. Eluyn Gines 718-630-4101

Watervliet Arsenal
1 Buffington Street, Watervliet, NY 12189-4050
518-266-5111
Commander:
Mark F. Migaleddi 518-266-5111
Public Affairs Officer:
John Snyder 518-266-5055

Marine Corps

1st Marine Corps District
605 Stewart Ave, Garden City, NY 11530
Commander:
Col. J.J. Dill 516-228-5661
Executive Officer:
Lt. Col. Mark T. Donar 516-228-5661

Public Affairs Office . . . . .fax: 212-784-0169
805 Third Ave, 9th Fl, New York, NY 10022
Director:
Lt. Col. Christopher Perrine 347-292-8762

Navy

Saratoga Springs Naval Support Unit
19 JF King Dr, Saratoga Springs, NY 12866-9267
Commander:
CDR Vince D. Garcia 518-886-0200/fax: 518-886-0120

US Department of Veterans Affairs
Web site: www.va.gov

National Cemetery Administration
Web site: www.cem.va.gov

Bath National Cemetery
San Juan Ave, Bath, NY 14810
Director:
Walter Baroody 607-664-4853/fax: 607-664-4761

Calverton National Cemetery
210 Princeton Blvd, Calverton, NY 11933-1031
Director:
Michael G Picerno 631-727-5410

Cypress Hills National Cemetery . . . . fax: 631-694-5422
625 Jamaica Ave, Brooklyn, NY 11208
631-454-4949 Fax: 631-694-5422
Director:
Michael G Picerno 631-454-4949/fax: 631-694-5422

Gerald B.H. Solomon Saratoga National Cemetery
200 Duell Rd, Schuylerville, NY 12871-1721
Director:
Daniel Cassidy 518-581-9128/fax: 518-583-6975

Long Island National Cemetery . . . . fax: 631-694-5422
2040 Wellwood Ave, Farmingdale, NY 11735
631-454-4949 Fax: 631-694-5422
Director:
Michael G Picerno 631-454-4949/fax: 631-694-5422

Policy Areas

Offices and agencies generally appear in alphabetical order, except when specific order is requested by listee.

Woodlawn National Cemetery
1825 Davis St, Elmira, NY 14901
Director:
   Walter Baroody.................607-732-5411/fax: 607-742-1769

VA Regional Office of Public Affairs, Field Operations Svc
245 W Houston St, Ste 315B, New York, NY 10014
Regional Director:
   Lawrence M Devine...............212-807-3429/fax: 212-807-4030
Public Affairs Specialist:
   James A Blue.....................................212-807-3429
Public Affairs Specialist:
   Leo Marinacci....................................212-807-3429

Veterans Benefits Administration

Buffalo Regional Office
130 South Elmwood Avenue, Buffalo, NY 14202-2478
800-827-1000
Regional Director:
   Donna Ferrell.................716-857-3020/fax: 716-551-3072
Assistant Director:
   Lillie Jackson...................................800-827-1000
Veterans Service Center Manager:
   James Rogers...................................800-827-1000
Regional Counsel:
   Joseph Moreno..................................800-827-1000
Vocational Rehabilitation & Employment Division:
   Joseph Senulis..................................800-827-1000
Chief, Education Division:
   Robert Quall....................................800-827-1000

New York City Regional Office.................fax: 212-807-4024
245 West Houston St, New York, NY 10014-4085
Director:
   Patricia Amberg-Blyskal...........................212-807-3055
Veterans Benefits & Services Officer:
   Joseph Collorafi.................................212-807-3420
Vocational Rehabilitation & Counseling Division:
   Bernard Finger..................................212-807-3030

Veterans Health Admin Integrated Svc Network (VISN)

VA Healthcare Network Upstate New York (VISN2)
113 Holland Ave, Bldg 7, Albany, NY 12208
Web site: www.va.gov/visns/visn02
Acting Network Director:
   Michael Finegan.........................518-626-7317 x67317
Network Communications Manager:
   Kathleen Hider.................585-463-2642/fax: 585-463-2649
Albany VA Medical Center
   113 Holland Ave, Albany, NY 12208
   Director:
      Lisa W. Weiss, MS......................518-626-5000
   Patient Advocate:
      Bridgette Qualls........................518-626-7125
Batavia VA Medical Center....................fax: 585-344-3305
   222 Richmond Ave, Batavia, NY 14020
   716-343-7500 Fax: 585-344-3305
   Director:
      Brian G. Stiller.........................716-862-8529
   Patient Advocate:
      Tom Bligh..............................585-297-1257
Bath VA Medical Center
   76 Veterans Ave, Bath, NY 14810
   Director:
      Michael Swartz.........................607-664-4722
   Patient Advocate:
      Cheryl Mills
Buffalo VA Medical Center....................fax: 716-862-8759
   3495 Bailey Ave, Buffalo, NY 14215
   716-834-9200 Fax: 716-862-8759

Director:
   Brian G. Stiller.................................716-862-8529
Public Affairs Officer:
   Christine Krupski.................................716-862-8852
Canandaigua VA Medical Center
   400 Fort Hill Ave, Canandaigua, NY 14424
   Director:
      Michael Swartz.........................585-394-2000
   Patient Advocate:
      Laurie Guererri........................585-393-7612
      e-mail: robert.babcock2@med.va.gov
Syracuse VA Medical Center & Clinics
   800 Irving Ave, Syracuse, NY 13210
   Director:
      James Cody.............................315-425-4892
      e-mail: james.cody@med.va.gov
   Patient Advocate:
      Colleen Lancette.......................315-425-4345

VA NY/NJ Veterans Healthcare Network (VISN3)
Bldg 16, 130 W Kingsbridge Rd, Bronx, NY 10468
Web site: www.va.gov/visns/visn03
Network Director:
   Michael A. Sabo.................718-741-4143/fax: 718-741-4141
Chief Medical Officer:
   Joan McInerney, MD
James J. Peters VA Medical Center.............fax: 718-741-4269
   130 W Kingsbridge Rd, Bronx, NY 10468
   Director:
      MaryAnn Musumeci....................718-584-9000 x6512
   Director of Government/Community Relations:
      Jim Connell
Brooklyn Campus of the NY Harbor Healthcare System
   800 Poly Pl, Brooklyn, NY 11209
   718-836-6600
   Director:
      John J Donnellan, Jr.........718-630-3521/fax: 718-630-2840
   Associate Director:
      Veronica J Foy.........................718-630-3524
Castle Point Campus of the VA Hudson Vly Healthcare System..fax:
845-838-5193
   PO Box 100, 100 Rte 9D, Castle Point, NY 12511
   845-831-2000 Fax: 845-838-5193
   Executive Director:
      Michael A Sabo........................845-737-4400 x2460
Montrose Campus of the VA Hudson Valley Healthcare System..fax:
914-788-4244
   2094 Albany Post Rd, Montrose, NY 10548
   Director:
      Michael A. Sabo.......................914-737-4400
   Public Affairs:
      Nancy A Winter........................914-737-4400 x2255
New York Campus of the NY Harbor Healthcare System
   423 East 23rd St, New York, NY 10010
   212-686-7500
   Executive Chief of Staff:
      Michael S Simberkoff....................212-951-3417
   Associate Director:
      Martina A Parauda.....................212-951-3240
Northport VA Medical Center.................fax: 631-754-7933
   79 Middleville Rd, Northport, NY 11768
   Director:
      Robert Schuster........................631-261-4400 x2747
   Public Affairs Officer:
      Joe Sledge

US Labor Department
Web site: www.dol.gov/vets/

Offices and agencies generally appear in alphabetical order, except when specific order is requested by listee.

Field Offices

New York State Field Offices

Albany . . . . .fax: 518-435-0833
  Harriman State Campus, Bldg 12, Rm 518, Albany, NY 12240-0099
  518-457-7465 Fax: 518-435-0833
  Director:
    Barry Morgan 518-457-7465/fax: 518-435-0833
  Veteran's Program Assistant:
    Joan M Cramer. 518-457-7465
    e-mail: cramer.joan@dol.gov

Brooklyn
  9 Bond Street, Room 301/302, Brooklyn, NY 11201
  Assistant Director:
    Daniel A Friedman. 718-613-3676
    e-mail: friedman.daniel@dol.gov
  Veteran's Program Specialist:
    Edward L. Diaz 718-613-3676
    e-mail: diaz.edward.L@dol.gov

US State Department
Web site: www.state.gov

US Mission to the United Nations
  799 United Nations Plaza, New York, NY 10017
Permanent US Representative to the United Nations:
  Ambassador Susan E. Rice
Deputy Permanent US Representative to the United Nations:
  Ambassador Rosemary A. DiCarlo
Alternate Representative for Special Political Affairs to the United Nations:
  Ambassador Jeffrey DeLaurentis

U.S. CONGRESS

See U.S. Congress Chapter for additional Standing Committee and Subcommittee information.

House of Representatives Standing Committees

Armed Services
McKeon (R-CA):
  Howard P. Buck"" . . . . .Chair or 202-225-1956
Ranking Minority Member:
  Adam Smith (D-WA) 202-225-8901
New York Delegate:
  Dan Maffei (D) 202-225-3701
New York Delegate:
  Chris Gibson (R) 202-225-5614

Veterans' Affairs
Chair:
  Jeff Miller (R-FL) 202-225-4136
Ranking Minority Member:
  Michael H. Michaud (D-ME) 202-225-6306

Senate Standing Committees

Armed Services
Chair:
  Carl Levin (D-MI). 202-224-6221
Ranking Minority Member:
  James M. Inhofe (R-OK) 202-224-4721

Veterans' Affairs
Chair:
  Bernard Sanders (D-VT). 202-224-5141
Ranking Minority Member:
  Richard Burr (R-NC) 202-224-3154

PRIVATE SECTOR

369th Veterans Association Inc
PO Box 91, Lincolnton Station, New York, NY 10037
212-281-3308 Fax: 212-281-6308
e-mail: jamnat@earthlink.net
Web site: www.home.earthlink.net/~natlvets/
Assistance & referrals for all veterans
Nathaniel James, National President

Air Force Association (AFA)
1501 Lee Highway, Arlington, VA 22209-1198
703-247-5800 Fax: 703-247-5853
Web site: www.afa.org
Support & advance the interest & recognition of the US Air Force
Donald L Peterson, Executive Director

Air Force Sergeants Association (AFSA), Division 1
557 Sixth St, Dover, NH 3820
603-742-4844
e-mail: acaldwell557@comcast.net
Web site: www.afsahq.org
Protect rights & benefits of enlisted personnel-active, retired, National Guard, reserve & their families
Alfred B Caldwell, President Division 1

Air Force Women Officers Associated (AFWOA)
PO Box 780155, San Antonio, TX 78278
210-481-6383
e-mail: patriciamurphy@afwoa.com
Web site: www.afwoa.org
Represent interests of active duty, retired & former women officers of the Air Force; preserve the history & promote recognition of the role of military women
Col Patricia M Murphy, USAF Retired, President

Albany Housing Coalition Inc
278 Clinton Ave, Albany, NY 12210
518-465-5251 Fax: 518-465-6499
e-mail: admin@ahcvets.org
Web site: www.ahcvets.org
Providing a continuum of affordable housing for veterans & their families; rental housing referrals
Bryon Koshgarian, Phd, Director, Veterans Services

American Legion, Department of New York
112 State St, Suite 1300, Albany, NY 12207
518-463-2215 Fax: 518-427-8443
e-mail: info@nylegion.org
Web site: www.ny.legion.org
Advocate for veterans; entitlements for wartime veterans, their families & service to the community, children & youth of our nation
Richard M Pedro, New York State Adjutant

American Military Retirees Association Inc
5436 Peru St, Ste 1, Plattsburgh, NY 12901
800-424-2969 or 518-563-9479 Fax: 518-324-5204
e-mail: info@amra1973.org
Web site: www.amra1973.org
Works on behalf of military retirees aand their families to protect their rights and benefits under the law and to lobby on their behalf in Washington D.C. and elsewhere.
Peg Bergeron, Executive Director

Army Aviation Association of America (AAAA)
755 Main St, Ste 4D, Monroe, CT 06468-2830
203-268-2450 Fax: 203-268-5870
Advance the cause & recognition of US Army aviation; benefit all personnel, current, retired, families & survivors
William R Harris, Executive Director

Offices and agencies generally appear in alphabetical order, except when specific order is requested by listee.

Policy Areas

Army Aviation Association of America (AAAA), Empire Chapter
3 Glendale Dr, Clifton Park, NY 12065
518-786-4397 Fax: 518-786-4393
e-mail: mark.f.burke@us.army.mil
Advance the cause & recognition of US Army aviation; benefit all Army aviation personnel, current, retired, families & survivors
COL Mark F Burke, Chapter President

Association of Military Surgeons of the US (AMSUS), NY Chapter
105 Franklin Ave, Malverne, NY 11565-1926
516-542-0025 Fax: 516-593-3114
e-mail: amsusny@aol.com
Improve federal healthcare service; support & represent military & other health care professionals
Col John J Hassett, USAR, President NY Chapter

Association of the US Army (AUSA)
2425 Wilson Blvd, Arlington, VA 22201
703-841-4300 x639 or 800-336-4570 Fax: 703-525-9039
e-mail: wloper@ausa.org
Web site: www.ausa.org
Champion the cause & objectives of the US Army by public relations, communications & legislative action
William Loper, Director Government Affairs

Black Veterans for Social Justice Inc
665 Willoughby Street, Brooklyn, NY 11221
718-852-6004 Fax: 718-852-4805
e-mail: admin@bvsj.org; cfo@bvsj.org
Web site: www.bvsj.org
Assist all veterans in obtaining benefits, entitlements, employment & housing
Job Mashariki, President & Chief Executive Officer

Blinded Veterans Association New York Inc
245 W Houston St, 2nd Fl, Rm 208, New York, NY 10014
212-807-3173 Fax: 212-807-4022
Web site: www.bva.org
Jack Shapiro, Director

Catholic War Veterans of the United States of America
346 Broadway, Suite 812, New York, NY 10013
212-962-0988 Fax: 212-894-0517
e-mail: nyscwv@aol.com
Web site: www.nycatholicwarvets.org
Veterans & auxiliary of the Roman Catholic faith; assisting all veterans & their families
Richard Dogal, MA, State Commander

Commissioned Officers Assn of the US Public Health Svc Inc (COA)
8201 Corporate Dr, Ste 200, Landover, MD 20785
301-731-9080 Fax: 301-731-9084
e-mail: gfarrell@coausphs.org
Web site: www.coausphs.org
Committed to improving the public health of the US; supports corps officers & advocates for their interests through leadership, education & communication
Jerry Farrell, Executive Director

Disabled American Veterans, Department of New York
162 Atlantic Ave, Lynbrook, NY 11563-3597
516-887-7100 Fax: 516-887-7175
e-mail: davny@optonline.net
Web site: www.davny.org
Service, support & enhance healthcare & benefits for wartime disabled veterans
Sidney Siller, Adjutant

Fleet Reserve Association (FRA)
125 North West St, Alexandria, VA 22314
703-683-1400 Fax: 703-549-6610
e-mail: news-fra@fra.org
Web site: www.fra.org
Serving the interests of active duty, retired & reserve enlisted members of the US Navy, Marine Corps & Coast Guard
Joseph L Barnes, National Executive Secretary & Chief Lobbyist

Fleet Reserve Association (FRA), NE Region (NJ, NY, PA)
1118 West Jefferson Street, Philadelphia, PA 19122-3442
215-235-7796 Fax: 215-765-2671
e-mail: charlescrainey@post.com
Web site: www.fra.org
Serving the interests of active duty, retired & reserve enlisted members of the US Navy, Marine Corps & Coast Guard
Charles Rainey, Regional President

Gold Star Wives of America Inc
763B Blackberry Lane, Yorktown, NY 10598
914-962-8083
National nonprofit working to advance issues important to military service widows
Mary Dwyer, New York Contact

Jewish War Veterans of the USA
1811 R St NW, Washington, DC 20009
202-265-6280 Fax: 202-234-5662
e-mail: jwv@jwv.org
Web site: www.jwv.org
Honoring & supporting all Jewish war veterans, their benefits & rights; fight bigotry & discrimination; patriotic voice of American Jewry
Steve Zeitz, National Commander

Jewish War Veterans of the USA, State of NY
346 Broadway, Rm 817, New York, NY 10013
212-349-6640 Fax: 212-577-2575
e-mail: deptny.jwv@juno.com
Web site: www.jwv.org
Honoring & supporting Jewish war veterans
Saul Rosenberg, Department Commander

Korean War Veterans
54 Lyncrest Drive, Rochester, NY 14616-5238
518-865-0145
e-mail: kwvfn@aol.com
Web site: www.kwva.org
Ensuring that Korean war vets are remembered
Frank Nicalozzo, President

Marine Corps League
PO Box 505, White Plains, NY 10602
914-941-2118 Fax: 914-864-7129
e-mail: llc1@mclwestchester.com
Web site: www.mclwestchester.org
Marine Corps fraternal/veterans association
Lu Caldara, Coordinator

Marine Corps League (MCL)
PO Box 3070, Merrifield, VA 22116
703-207-9588 or 800-625-1775 Fax: 703-207-0047
e-mail: mcl@mcleague.org
Web site: www.mcleague.org
Support & promote the interests, history & tradition of the Marine Corps & all Marines
Michael Blum, Executive Director

Marine Corps League (MCL), Department of NY
46 Marine Corp Blvd, Staten Island, NY 10301
718-447-2306 Fax: 718-556-0590
Support & promote the interests, history & tradition of the Marine Corps & all Marines

---

Offices and agencies generally appear in alphabetical order, except when specific order is requested by listee.

Bob Powell, Commandant, Department of NY

Military Chaplains Association of the USA (MCA)
PO Box 7056, Arlington, VA 22207
703-533-5890
e-mail: chaplains@mca-usa.org
Web site: www.mca-usa-org
Promotes the recognition & interests of military, Civil Air Patrol & VA chaplains; develops & encourages candidates through national institutes, scholarships & outreach
David White, Executive Director

Military Officers Association of America
201 N Washington St, Alexandria, VA 22314-2539
703-549-2311 or 800-234-6622 Fax: 703-838-8173
Web site: www.moaa.org
Preserve earned entitlements of members of the uniformed services, their families & survivors; support of strong national defense; scholarship & support to members' families
Col Steve Strobridge, USAF Retired, Director Government Relations

Military Officers Association of America (MOAA), NYS Council
258 Randwood Dr, Williamsville, NY 14221
716-689-6295 Fax: 716-847-6405
e-mail: patc258@aol.com
Benefit members of uniformed services, active & retired, family & survivors; promote strong national defense
Col Patrick Cunningham, USA Retired, President, NYS Council of Chapters

Military Order of the Purple Heart
Syracuse Veterans Administration Medical, 800 Irving Ave, Room A176, Syracuse, NY 13210-2796
315-425-4685
e-mail: catherine.alexander@med.va.gov
Veterans' benefits & rehabilitation
Catherine Alexander, National Service Officer

Military Order of the Purple Heart (MOPH)
5413B Backlick Rd, Springfield, VA 22151
703-642-5360 Fax: 703-642-1841
e-mail: goberh@aol.com
Web site: www.purpleheart.org
Congressionally chartered organization representing the interests of America's combat-wounded veterans
Hershel Gober, National Legislative Director

Montford Point Marine Association
346 Broadway St, New York, NY 10013
212-267-3318 Fax: 212-566-4903
Web site: www.montfordpointmarines.com
James Maillard, Financial Secretary

National Amputation Foundation Inc
40 Church St, Malverne, NY 11565
516-887-3600 Fax: 516-887-3667
e-mail: amps76@aol.com
Web site: www.nationalamputation.org
Programs & services geared to help the amputee; donated medical equipment give-away program. Items must be picked up at the office-for anyone in need. Scholarship program for students with major limb amputation attending college full-time.
Paul Bernacchio, President

National Guard Association of the US (NGAUS)
One Massachusetts Ave NW, Washington, DC 20001
202-789-0031 Fax: 202-682-9358
e-mail: ngaus@ngaus.org
Web site: www.ngaus.org
Promote the interests of the Army National Guard through legislative action;
Bill Goss, Director, Legislative Affairs

National Military Family Association (NMFA)
2500 North Van Dorn St, Ste 102, Alexandria, VA 22302-1601
703-931-6632 or 800-260-0218 Fax: 703-931-4600
e-mail: families@nmfa.org
Web site: www.nmfa.org
Service to the families of active duty, retirees, reserve & National Guard uniformed personnel
Joyce Raezer, Director Government Relations

Naval Enlisted Reserve Association (NERA)
6703 Farragut Ave, Falls Church, VA 22042-2189
703-534-1329 or 800-776-9020
e-mail: members@nera.org
Web site: www.nera.org
Ensuring strong & well-trained Naval, Coast Guard & Marine Corps Reserves; improving reserve equipment, promotion, pay & retirement benefits through legislative action
Stephen R Sandy, Executive Director

Naval Reserve Association (NRA)
1619 King St, Alexandria, VA 22314-3647
703-548-5800 or 866-672-4968 Fax: 866-683-3647
e-mail: membership@navy-reserve.org
Web site: www.navy-reserve.org
Premier education & professional organization for Naval Reserve officers & the association voice of the Naval Reserve
Ike Puzon, USNR Retired, Director of Legislation

Navy League of the US (NLUS)
2300 Wilson Blvd, Arlington, VA 22201-3308
703-528-1775 or 800-356-5760 Fax: 703-528-2333
e-mail: jfleet@navyleague.org
Web site: www.navyleague.org
Citizens in support of the Sea Services
John Fleet, Director for Legislative Affairs

Navy League of the US (NLUS), New York Council
c/o US Coast Guard, Battery Park Bldg, 1 South St, Rm 318, New York, NY 10004
212-825-7333 Fax: 212-668-2138
e-mail: navyleaguenyc.aol.com
Web site: www.nynavyleague.org
Represent citizens in support of the Sea Services
J Robert Lunney, President

New Era Veterans, Inc
1150 Commonwealth Ave, Bronx, NY 10472
718-904-7036 Fax: 718-904-7024
e-mail: neweraveterans.yahoo.com
Web site: www.neweraveterans.org
Housing and services for homeless veterans.
Jason Ortiz, Associate Program Director

New York State Air Force Association
PO Box 539, Merrick, NY 11566-0539
516-623-5714
e-mail: brave3@aaahawk.com
Web site: www.nysafa.org
Support & advance the interest & recognition of the US Air Force
Robert Braverman, Vice President Government Relations

North Country Vietnam Veterans Association, Post 1
PO Box 1161, 27 Town Line Rd, Plattsburgh, NY 12901
518-563-3426
e-mail: kenhynes@charter.net; secretary@ncvva.org
Web site: www.ncvva.org
Peer counseling & referral
Ken Hynes, Contact

Policy Areas

Offices and agencies generally appear in alphabetical order, except when specific order is requested by listee.

Reserve Officers Association (ROA)
One Constitution Ave, NE, Washington, DC 20002
202-479-2200 or 800-809-9448 Fax: 202-547-1641
Web site: www.roa.org
Advance the cause of reserve officers through legislative action; promote the interests & recognition of ROTC & military academy students
Susan Lukas, Legislative Director

Office of Chief, Army Reserves
3 Wildwood Rd, Congers, NY 10920
845-638-5215 or 845-596-3494 Fax: 845-638-5035
e-mail: robert.j.winzinger@us.army.mil
Advance the cause of reserve officers of the US Armed Forces; promote the interests & recognition of ROTC & military academy students
Robert Winzinger, Army Reserve Ambassador - New York

United Spinal Association
75-20 Astoria Blvd, Jackson Heights, NY 11370
718-803-3782 Fax: 718-803-0414
e-mail: info@unitedspinal.org
Web site: www.unitedspinal.org
Managed & long-term care, disability assistance & benefits, advocacy & legislation
Linda Gutmann, Advocacy

Veterans of Foreign Wars
1044 Broadway, Albany, NY 12204
518-463-7427 Fax: 518-426-8904
Web site: www.vfwny.com
Art Koch III, State Adjutant

Veterans of Foreign Wars (VFW)
200 Maryland Ave, NE, Washington, DC 20002
202-543-2239 Fax: 202-543-0961
e-mail: dcullinan@vfw.org
Web site: www.vfw.org
Legislative action, community service & volunteerism in support of the nation's veterans, their families & survivors
Dennis Cullinan, Director National Legislative Affairs

Veterans' Widows International Network Inc (VWIN)
3657 E South Laredo, Aurora, CO 80013
303-693-4745
e-mail: vwin95@aol.com
Web site: www.vetsurvivors.com
Outreach to American veterans' survivors; assist with obtaining benefits; provide local contacts & support

Vietnam Veterans of America, NYS Council
8 Queen Dian Lane, Queensbury, NY 12804
518-293-7801
e-mail: nedvva@adelphia.net
Ned D Foote, President

Women Marines Association
59 Sawyer Ave, Dorchester, MA 02125-2040
617-265-1572
e-mail: sgtkwm@aol.com
Web site: www.womenmarines.org
Catherine Carpenter, Area 1 Director

Offices and agencies generally appear in alphabetical order, except when specific order is requested by listee.

Section 3:
STATE & LOCAL GOVERNMENT PUBLIC INFORMATION

PUBLIC INFORMATION OFFICES

This chapter includes state public information contacts with telephone and fax numbers as well as e-mail and Web site addresses, if available. For additional information, please refer to the related policy area or the indexes.

NEW YORK STATE

GOVERNOR'S OFFICE

Governor's Office
Web site: www.governor.ny.gov; www.ny.gov

Director, Communications:
Melissa DeRosa .518-474-8418 or 212-681-4640

Washington Office of the Governor
Director:
Alexander Cochran 202-434-7100

Lieutenant Governor's Office
Chief of Staff:
John Maggiore 518-402-2292

EXECUTIVE & ADMINISTRATIVE DEPARTMENTS & AGENCIES

Aging, Office for the
Web site: www.aging.ny.gov

Public Information Officer:
Reza Mizbani 518-474-7181
e-mail: reza.mizbani@aging.ny.gov

Agriculture & Markets Department
Web site: www.agriculture.ny.gov

Public Information Officer:
Jola Szubielski .518-485-7728/fax: 518-457-3087
e-mail: jola.szubielski@agriculture.ny.gov

New York State Liquor Authority (Division of Alcoholic Beverage Control)
Web site: www.sla.ny.gov

Director, Public Affairs:
William Crowley . . . . .518-474-3114 or 518-474-4875
fax: 518-473-9565
e-mail: press.office@sla.ny.gov

Alcoholism & Substance Abuse Services, Office of
Web site: www.oasas.ny.gov

Director, Public Information Office:
Susan A Craig, MPH 518-457-8299

Financial Services Department
Web site: www.dfs.ny.gov

Director, Public Affairs:
Andrew Mais .212-480-5257/fax: 212-480-6077
e-mail: public-affairs@dfs.ny.gov
Senior Public Information Specialist:
Ronald Klug 212-480-2285

Budget, Division of the
Web site: www.budget.ny.gov

Press Officer:
Morris Peters 518-473-3885/fax: 518-474-9041
e-mail: dob.sm.press@nysemail.state.ny.us

CIO & Office of Information Technology Services (ITS)
518-402-2537 or 866-789-4638 Fax: 518-474-1196
Web site: www.its.ny.gov

Director, Public Information:
Michelle McDonald . . . . .518-402-3899 or 518-473-9450

Children & Family Services, Office of
Web site: www.ocfs.state.ny.us

Council on Children & Families
Web site: www.ccf.state.ny.us
Executive Director:
Deborah Benson 518-473-3652/fax: 518-473-2570
e-mail: debbie.benson@ccf.ny.gov

Civil Service Department
e-mail: pio@cs.state.ny.us
Web site: www.cs.ny.gov

Public Information Officer:
Ed Walsh 518-457-9375/fax: 518-473-2372

Consumer Protection, Division of
Web site: www.dos.ny.gov/consumerprotection/

Executive Deputy Director:
Aiesha Battle. 518-474-2363

Corrections & Community Supervision Department
Web site: www.doccs.ny.gov

Director, Public Information:
Thomas Mailey 518-457-8182/fax: 518-457-7070

Council on the Arts
Web site: www.nysca.org

Manager, Information Technology:
Lenn Ditman 212-459-8810
e-mail: lenn.ditman@arts.ny.gov

Victim Services, Office of
Web site: www.ovs.ny.gov

General Counsel/Legal Unit:
John Watson .518-457-8066/fax: 518-457-8658

Criminal Justice Services, Division of
Web site: www.criminaljustice.ny.gov

Deputy Director, Public Information:
Janine Kava 518-457-8828/fax: 518-485-7715
e-mail: janine.kava@dcjs.ny.gov

Developmental Disabilities Planning Council
Web site: www.ddpc.ny.gov

Public Information Officer:
Thomas F Lee 518-486-7505
e-mail: thomas.lee@ddpc.ny.gov

Education Department
Web site: www.nysed.gov

Offices and agencies generally appear in alphabetical order, except when specific order is requested by listee.

Chief, External Affairs:
Dennis Tompkins 518-474-1201/fax: 518-473-2977
e-mail: aray@mail.nysed.gov
Secretary to the Board of Regents:
Anthony Lofrumento 518-474-5889
e-mail: djohnson@mail.nysed.gov

State Library
Web site: www.nysl.nysed.gov
Assistant Commissioner & State Librarian:
Bernard Margolis 518-474-5930

Elections, State Board of
e-mail: info@elections.ny.gov
Web site: www.elections.ny.gov

Director, Public Information:
John W Conklin 518-474-1953/fax: 518-473-8315

Homeland Security & Emergency Services, Division of
Web site: www.dhses.ny.gov

Public Information Officer:
Rachel McEneny 518-242-5133/fax: 518-322-4978

Empire State Development Corporation
Web site: www.esd.ny.gov

Public Affairs:
Kay Sarlin Wright 800-260-7313
e-mail: esdpressoffice@esd.ny.gov

Employee Relations, Governor's Office of
Web site: www.goer.ny.gov

Management/Confidential Affairs:
Lynda Scalzo 518-473-8317

Environmental Conservation Department
Web site: www.dec.ny.gov

Director, Public Information:
Michael Bopp 518-402-8000
Director, Public Affairs & Education Division:
Laurel Remus 518-402-8049/fax: 518-402-9036

General Services, Office of
Web site: www.ogs.ny.gov

Director, Public Affairs:
Heather Groll 518-474-5987/fax: 518-474-3187
e-mail: heather.groll@ogs.ny.gov

Health Department
Web site: www.health.ny.gov

Deputy Director, Public Affairs:
Marci Natale 518-474-7354 x1

Housing & Community Renewal, Division of
Web site: www.nyshcr.org

Director, Communications:
Charni Sochet 212-872-0681

Hudson River Valley Greenway
Web site: www.hudsongreenway.ny.gov

Acting Executive Director, Communities Council:
Mark Castiglione 518-473-3835/fax: 518-473-4518

Acting Executive Director, Greenway Conservancy:
Mark Castiglione 518-473-3835/fax: 518-473-4518

Human Rights, State Division of
Web site: www.dhr.ny.gov

Public Information Officer:
Leticia Greene 718-741-3223/fax: 718-741-3214
e-mail: lgreene@dhr.ny.gov

Inspector General (NYS), Office of the
Web site: www.ig.ny.gov

Director, Communications:
William Reynolds 518-474-1010/fax: 518-486-3745

Insurance Fund (NYS)
Web site: www.nysif.com

Public Information Officer:
Robert Lawson 518-437-3504/fax: 518-437-1849

Labor Department
Web site: www.labor.ny.gov

Director, Communications:
Leo Rosales 518-457-5519/fax: 518-485-1126
e-mail: leo.rosales@labor.ny.gov

Law Department
Web site: www.ag.ny.gov

Press Secretary:
Fernando Aquino 212-416-8060/fax: 212-416-6005

New York State Gaming Commission
Web site: www.nylottery.ny.gov; www.gaming.ny.gov

Director, Communications:
Christy Calicchia 518-388-3415/fax: 518-388-3423
Communications:
Lee Park 518-388-3415/fax: 518-388-3423

Mental Health, Office of
Web site: www.omh.ny.gov

Director, Public Affairs:
Benjamin Rosen 518-474-6540/fax: 518-473-3456

NYS Office for People with Developmental Disabilities
e-mail: communications.office@opwdd.ny.gov
Web site: www.opwdd.ny.gov

Director, Communications & PA:
Jennifer O'Sullivan 518-474-6601/fax: 518-473-1271
Director Public Information:
Dianne Henk 518-473-1997

Military & Naval Affairs, Division of
Web site: www.dmna.ny.gov

Director, Public Affairs:
Eric Durr 518-786-4581/fax: 518-786-4649
e-mail: eric.d.durr.nfg@mail.mil

Motor Vehicles Department
Web site: www.dmv.ny.gov

Associate Commissioner, Communications:
Jackie McGinnis 518-473-7000/fax: 518-473-1930

Offices and agencies generally appear in alphabetical order, except when specific order is requested by listee.

NYSTAR - Division of Science, Technology & Innovation
Web site: www.esd.ny.gov/nystar

Director, Communications/Government Affairs:
  Jannette Rondo 518-292-5700/fax: 518-292-5798
  e-mail: nystarsupport@esd.ny.gov

Parks, Recreation & Historic Preservation, NYS Office of
Web site: www.nysparks.com

Deputy Public Information Officer:
  Dan Keefe 518-486-1868/fax: 518-486-2924
Public Information Officer:
  Randy Simons 518-486-1868

Parole Board, The
Web site: www.parole.ny.gov; doccs.ny.gov

Administrative Assistant:
  Lorraine Morse 518-473-5424/fax: 518-473-6037

Prevention of Domestic Violence, Office for the
Web site: www.opdv.ny.gov

Public Information Officer:
  Suzanne Cecala 518-457-5744/fax: 518-457-5810
  e-mail: suzanne.cecala@opdv.ny.gov

Public Employment Relations Board
e-mail: perbinfo@perb.ny.gov
Web site: www.perb.ny.gov

Executive Director:
  Anthony Zumbolo 518-457-2676/fax: 518-457-2664

Public Service Commission
Web site: www.dps.ny.gov

Director, Telecommunications:
  Chad Hume 518-474-1668/fax: 518-474-5616
Director, Public Affairs:
  James Denn 518-474-7080/fax: 518-473-2838
  e-mail: james_denn@dps.ny.gov

Real Property Tax Services, Office of
Web site: www.tax.ny.gov/about/orpts

Director, Public Information:
  Vacant 518-486-3418/fax: 518-474-9276

State Comptroller, Office of the
Web site: www.osc.state.ny.us

Director, Communications:
  Jennifer Freeman . . . . 518-474-4015 or 212-681-4840
  fax: 518-473-8940

State Department
Web site: www.dos.state.ny.us

Deputy Secretary, Public Affairs:
  Vacant 518-474-4752/fax: 518-474-4597
  e-mail: info@dos.state.ny.us

State Police, Division of
Web site: www.troopers.ny.gov

Director, Public Information:
  Darcy Wells 518-457-2180/fax: 518-485-7818
  e-mail: pio@troopers.ny.gov

Tax Appeals, Division of
Web site: www.nysdta.org

Secretary to the Tribunal:
  Jean A McDonnell 518-266-3050

Taxation & Finance Department
Web site: www.tax.ny.gov

Director, Public Information:
  Geoffrey Gloak . . . . 518-457-4242 or 518-457-7377
  fax: 518-457-2486

Temporary & Disability Assistance, Office of
Web site: www.otda.ny.gov

Director, Public Information:
  Kristi L. Berner 518-474-9516/fax: 518-486-6935
  e-mail: nyspio@otda.ny.gov

Transportation Department
Web site: www.dot.ny.gov

Director, Communications Office:
  Beau Duffy 518-457-6400/fax: 518-457-6506
  e-mail: beau.duffy@dot.ny.gov
Public Information Officer:
  Jennifer Post 518-457-6400
  e-mail: jennifer.post@dot.ny.gov

Veterans' Affairs, Division of
e-mail: dvainfo@veterans.ny.gov
Web site: www.veterans.ny.gov

Counsel:
  Samuel Spitzberg 518-474-6114

Welfare Inspector General, Office of NYS
e-mail: owig@dfa.state.ny.us
Web site: www.owig.ny.gov

Chief Investigator:
  Anthony Jacaruso 212-417-2395/fax: 212-417-5849

Workers' Compensation Board
Web site: www.wcb.ny.gov

Director, Public Information:
  Rachel McEneny 518-408-5592/fax: 518-473-1415
  e-mail: publicinfo@wcb.ny.gov

JUDICIAL SYSTEM AND RELATED AGENCIES

Unified Court System
Web site: www.nycourts.gov

Director, Public Affairs:
  Gregory Murray 212-428-2116/fax: 212-428-2117
Director, Communications:
  David Bookstaver 212-428-2500/fax: 212-428-2507
  e-mail: dbooksta@courts.state.ny.us
Chief Law Librarian:
  Ellen Robinson 518-238-4373/fax: 518-238-2894

LEGISLATIVE BRANCH

Assembly
Press Secretary to the Speaker:
  Michael Winyland 518-455-3888/fax: 518-455-3858

Offices and agencies generally appear in alphabetical order, except when specific order is requested by listee.

State & Local
Government
Public Information

Director, Minority Communications:
    Michael Fraser .518-455-3751/fax: 518-455-3750
    e-mail: fraserm@assembly.state.ny.us
Public Information Officer:
    Robin Marilla. 518-455-4218/fax: 518-455-5175
Director, Communications:
    Michael Kane. 518-455-5767/fax: 518-455-4963
Director, Information Services:
    Vicki Chase 518-455-5767/fax: 518-455-4963

Legislative Library

Legislative Librarian:
    Ellen Breslin 518-455-2468/fax: 518-426-6901
Legislative Librarian:
    James Giliberto 518-455-2468
Law Librarian:
    Kate Balassie. 518-455-2468
Law Librarian:
    Stephen Gersztoff 518-455-2468

Senate

Director, Majority Communications:
    Kelly Cummings 518-455-2264/fax: 518-455-2260
Majority Press Secretary:
    Kris Thompson 518-455-3191/fax: 518-455-2448
Director, Minority Communications:
    Curtis Taylor 518-455-2415/fax: 518-426-6933
Minority Press Secretary:
    Vacant 518-455-2415/fax: 518-426-6955
Director, Student Programs Office:
    Krista Ketterer 518-455-2611/fax: 518-432-5470

CORPORATIONS, AUTHORITIES AND COMMISSIONS

Adirondack Park Agency

Web site: www.apa.ny.gov

Public Relations:
    Keith McKeever 518-891-4050/fax: 518-891-3938
    e-mail: keith.mckeever@apa.ny.gov

Agriculture & NYS Horse Breeding Development Fund

Web site: www.nysirestakes.com

Executive Director:
    Mike Mullaney 518-395-85484/fax: 518-347-1483
    e-mail: mike.mullaney@nysirestakes.com

Albany County Airport Authority

Web site: www.albanyairport.com/airport_authority.php

Director, Public Affairs:
    Douglas I. Myers 518-242-2222 x1/fax: 518-242-2641
    e-mail: info@albanyairport.com

Albany Port District Commission

Web site: www.portofalbany.us

General Manager:
    Richard Hendrick 518-463-8763/fax: 518-463-8767
    e-mail: rhendrick@portofalbany.us; portofalbany@portofalbany.us

Atlantic States Marine Fisheries Commission

Web site: www.asmfc.org

Director Communications:
    Tina Berger 703-842-0740/fax: 703-842-0741
    e-mail: tberger@asmfc.org

Battery Park City Authority (Hugh L Carey)

Web site: www.bpca.ny.gov

VP External Relations:
    Robin Forst 212-417-2276/fax: 212-417-2279
    e-mail: robin.forst@bpca.ny.gov

Brooklyn Navy Yard Development Corporation

e-mail: info@brooklynnavyyard.org
Web site: www.brooklynnavyyard.org

Senior Vice President, External Affairs:
    Richard Drucker 718-907-5900/fax: 718-643-9296

Buffalo & Fort Erie Public Bridge Authority (Peace Bridge Authority)

Web site: www.peacebridge.com

General Manager:
    Ron Rienas. 716-884-6744/fax: 716-884-2089

Capital District Regional Off-Track Betting Corporation

e-mail: customerservice@capitalotb.com
Web site: www.capitalotb.com

Secretary & Director:
    F James Mumpton 518-344-5225/fax: 518-370-5460

Capital District Regional Planning Commission

e-mail: cdrpc@cdrpc.org
Web site: www.cdrpc.org

Information Services:
    Tim Canty .518-453-0850/fax: 518-453-0856
    e-mail: dlwardle@cdrpc.org

Capital District Transportation Authority

Web site: www.cdta.org

VP, Planning & Infrastructure:
    Christopher G Desany 518-437-8320/fax: 518-437-8328
    e-mail: chrisd@cdta.org

Catskill Off-Track Betting Corporation

Web site: www.interbets.com

President:
    Donald J Groth 845-362-0400/fax: 845-362-0419
    e-mail: otb@interbets.com; customerservice@interbets.com

Central New York Regional Market Authority

Web site: cnyrma.com

Commissioner's Representative:
    Troy Waffner. 315-422-8647/fax: 315-442-6897
    e-mail: genedemos@gmail.com

Central New York Regional Transportation Authority

Web site: www.centro.org

Executive Director:
    Frank Kobliski 315-442-3360/fax: 315-422-3337
    e-mail: fkobliski@centro.org

Central Pine Barrens Joint Planning & Policy Commission

e-mail: info@pb.state.ny.us
Web site: www.pb.state.ny.us

Offices and agencies generally appear in alphabetical order, except when specific order is requested by listee.

Chair:
  Peter A Scully 631-288-1079/fax: 631-288-1367

City University Construction Fund
Counsel:
  Frederick Schaffer. 646-664-9210
  e-mail: frederick.schaffer@mail.cuny.edu

Delaware River Basin Commission
Web site: www.state.nj.us/drbc

Communications Manager:
  Clarke Rupert 609-883-9500 x260/fax: 609-883-9522
  e-mail: clarke.rupert@drbc.state.nj.us

Development Authority of the North Country
Web site: www.danc.org

Executive Director:
  James Wright 315-661-3200

Empire State Development Corporation
Web site: www.esd.ny.gov

Public Affairs:
  Kay Sarlin Wright 800-260-7313
  e-mail: esdpressoffice@esd.ny.gov

Great Lakes Commission
Web site: www.glc.org

Communications Director:
  Christine Manninen 734-971-9135/fax: 734-971-9150
  e-mail: manninen@glc.org

Hudson River-Black River Regulating District
Web site: www.hrbrrd.com

Executive Director:
  Michael A Clark 518-465-3491/fax: 518-432-2485
  e-mail: hrao@hrbrrd.com

Interest on Lawyer Account (IOLA) Fund of the State of NY
Web site: www.iola.org

Executive Director:
  Christopher O'Malley 646-865-1541/fax: 646-865-1545

Interstate Environmental Commission
Web site: www.iec-nynjct.org

Associate Director:
  Bill Shadel 212-967-1414/fax: 212-967-1430
  e-mail: iecmail@iec-nynjct.org

Interstate Oil & Gas Compact Commission
Web site: www.iogcc.ok.gov

Communications Manager:
  Carol Booth 405-525-3556/fax: 405-525-3592
  e-mail: iogcc@iogcc.state.ok.us

Lake George Park Commission
Web site: www.lgpc.state.ny.us

Executive Director:
  David Wick 518-668-9347/fax: 518-668-5001
  e-mail: info@lgpc.state.ny.us

Lawyers' Fund for Client Protection
Web site: www.nylawfund.org

Executive Director & Counsel:
  Timothy O'Sullivan. 518-434-1935/fax: 518-434-5641
  e-mail: info@nylawfund.org

Legislative Bill Drafting Commission
Commissioner:
  Randall G Bluth 518-455-7506/fax: 518-455-7598

MTA (Metropolitan Transportation Authority)
Web site: www.mta.info

Director, External Communications:
  Adam Lisberg 212-878-7440/fax: 212-878-7030

MTA Bridges & Tunnels
Web site: www.mta.info/bandt

Manager, Public Affairs:
  Judith Glave 646-252-7276

MTA Bus Company
Web site: www.mta.info/busco

Media Relations:
  Adam Lisberg 212-878-7440/fax: 212-878-7030

MTA Capital Construction
Web site: www.mta.info/capconstr

Senior Director/Chief Procurement Officer:
  David Cannon 646-252-2678

MTA Long Island Rail Road
Web site: www.mta.info/lirr

General Manager, Public Affairs:
  Susan McGowan 718-558-7301/fax: 718-558-8212

MTA Metro-North Railroad
Web site: www.mta.info/mnr

Senior Director, Corporate & Public Affairs:
  Mark Mannix 212-340-2142/fax: 212-340-3460
Vice President, Business Operations:
  Thomas Tendy 212-672-1251

MTA New York City Transit
Web site: www.mta.info/nyct

Corporate Communications:
  Paul Fleuranges 646-252-5873

MTA Office of the Inspector General
Web site: www.mtaig.state.ny.us

Inspector General:
  Barry L Kluger 212-878-0000/fax: 212-878-0003

Nassau Regional Off-Track Betting Corporation
Web site: www.nassauotb.com

Director, Public Affairs:
  Vacant. .516-572-2800 x124/fax: 516-572-2840

New England Interstate Water Pollution Control Commission
Web site: www.neiwpcc.org

Offices and agencies generally appear in alphabetical order, except when specific order is requested by listee.

Communications Manager:
Stephen Hochbrunn 978-349-2507
e-mail: shochbrunn@neiwpcc.org

New York City Housing Development Corporation
e-mail: info@nychdc.com
Web site: www.nychdc.com

Communications/Press Office:
Christina Sanchez...................212-227-2644/fax: B12-227-8580
e-mail: csanchez@nychdc.com

New York City School Construction Authority
Web site: www.nycsca.org

VP, Administration:
Craig Collins.......................................718-472-8149

New York Convention Center Operating Corporation
Web site: www.javitscenter.com

Public Affairs:
Leslie Buxton.....................212-216-2135/fax: 212-216-2588
e-mail: lbuxton@javitscenter.com

New York Metropolitan Transportation Council
Web site: www.nymtc.org

Public Information Officer:
Lisa Daglian.....................212-383-7241/fax: 212-383-2418
e-mail: lisa.daglian@dot.ny.gov

New York Power Authority
Web site: www.nypa.gov

Public Information Officer:
Connie Cullen.....................................914-390-8196
e-mail: connie.cullen@nypa.gov
Public Information Officer:
Paul DeMichele...................................914-390-8196
e-mail: paul.demichele@nypa.gov

New York State Assn of Fire Districts
Web site: www.firedistnys.com

Counsel:
William N Young...................800-349-2904 or 518-456-6767
fax: 518-456-4644
e-mail: byoung@yfkblaw.com

New York State Athletic Commission
Web site: www.dos.ny.gov/athletic

Chair:
Melvina Lathan 212-417-5700/fax: 212-417-4987
e-mail: info@dos.ny.gov

New York State Board of Law Examiners
Web site: www.nybarexam.org

Executive Director:
John J McAlary.....................518-453-5990/fax: 518-452-5729

New York State Bridge Authority
e-mail: info@nysba.ny.gov
Web site: www.nysba.ny.gov

Director, Toll Collections Operations:
Wayne V Ferguson...............................845-691-7245

New York State Commission of Correction
Web site: www.scoc.ny.gov

Deputy Director Public Information:
Walter McClure...................518-485-2346/fax: 518-485-2467
e-mail: infoscoc@scoc.ny.gov

New York State Commission on Judicial Nomination
Web site: www.nysegov.com/cjn/

Counsel:
Henry Greenberg...................518-689-1400/fax: 518-689-1499
e-mail: greenbergh@gtlaw.com

New York State Commission on the Restoration of the Capitol
Executive Director:
Andrea J Lazarski 518-473-0341/fax: 518-486-5720
e-mail: andrea.lazarski@ogs.ny.gov

New York State Disaster Preparedness Commission
Web site: www.dhses.ny.gov/oem/disaster-prep/

Chairman/Director:
Jerome M Hauer 518-292-2301/fax: 518-322-4978

New York State Dormitory Authority
Web site: www.dasny.org

Public Information Officer:
John Chirlin.......................518-257-3380/fax: 518-257-3387
e-mail: jchirlin@dasny.org

New York State Energy Research & Development Authority
Web site: www.nyserda.ny.gov

Director, Communications:
Kate Muller.................518-862-1090 x3582/fax: 518-862-1091
e-mail: ktm@nyserda.ny.gov

New York State Environmental Facilities Corp
Web site: www.nysefc.org

Director, PIO:
Jon Sorensen 518-402-6924/fax: 518-486-9323
e-mail: press@efc.ny.gov; jon.sorensen@efc.ny.gov

Joint Commission on Public Ethics (JCOPE)
Web site: www.jcope.ny.gov

Chief of Staff/Deputy Counsel:
Monica Stamm....................518-408-3976/fax: 518-408-3975

New York State Financial Control Board
Web site: www.fcb.state.ny.us

Acting Executive Director:
Jeffrey Sommer....................212-417-5066/fax: 212-417-5055

New York State Higher Education Services Corp (NYSHESC)
Web site: www.hesc.ny.gov

Senior Vice President, Communications:
Kathy Crowder 518-402-1448/fax: 518-474-5593
e-mail: kathy.crowder@hesc.ny.gov

New York State Judicial Conduct Commission
Web site: www.cjc.ny.gov

Offices and agencies generally appear in alphabetical order, except when specific order is requested by listee.

Administrator & Counsel:
Robert H Tembeckjian 646-386-4800
e-mail: cjc@cjc.ny.gov
Information Officer:
Amy Carpinello. 646-386-4800

New York State Law Reporting Bureau
Web site: www.courts.state.ny.us/reporter

State Reporter:
William J Hooks 518-453-6900
Deputy State Reporter:
Michael S Moran. 518-453-6900/fax: 518-426-1640
e-mail: Reporter@courts.state.ny.us

New York State Law Revision Commission
Web site: www.lawrevision.state.ny.us

Executive Director:
Rose Mary Bailly. 518-472-5858/fax: 518-445-2303

New York State Liquor Authority
Web site: www.sla.ny.gov

Director, Public Affairs:
William Crowley . . . . .518-474-3114 or 518-474-4875
fax: 518-473-9565
e-mail: press.office@sla.ny.gov

New York State Olympic Regional Development Authority
Web site: www.orda.org/corporate

Communications Manager:
Jon Lundin. 518-523-1655/fax: 518-523-9275
e-mail: jlundin@orda.org

New York State Teachers' Retirement System
Web site: www.nystrs.org

Manager, Public Information:
John Cardillo 518-447-4743/fax: 518-447-2875
e-mail: john.cardillo@nystrs.org

New York State Thoroughbred Breeding & Development Fund Corporation
Web site: www.nybreds.com

Executive Director:
Tracy Egan. 518-388-0174/fax: 518-395-5499

New York State Thruway Authority
Web site: www.thruway.ny.gov

Director, Media Relations & Communications:
Dan Weiller. 518-471-5300
e-mail: publicinfo@thruway.ny.gov

New York State Tug Hill Commission
Web site: www.tughill.org

Executive Director:
John K Bartow, Jr 315-785-2570/fax: 315-785-2574
e-mail: john@tughill.org

Niagara Falls Bridge Commission
Web site: www.niagarafallsbridges.com

General Manager:
Lew Holloway 716-285-6322 ext4151/fax: 716-282-3292

Niagara Frontier Transportation Authority
Web site: www.nfta.com

Director, Public Affairs:
C Douglas Hartmayer 716-855-7420/fax: 716-855-6655
e-mail: info@nfta.com

Northeastern Forest Fire Protection Commission
Web site: www.nffpc.org

Executive Director/Center Manager:
Thomas G Parent. 207-968-3782/fax: 207-968-3782
e-mail: necompact@fairpoint.net

Ogdensburg Bridge & Port Authority
Web site: www.ogdensport.com

Executive Director:
Wade A Davis 315-393-4080/fax: 315-393-7068
e-mail: wadavis@ogdensport.com

Ohio River Valley Water Sanitation Commission
Web site: www.orsanco.org

Communications Coordinator:
Lisa Cochran. . . . . .513-231-7719 ext 102/fax: 513-231-7761
e-mail: lcochran@orsanco.org

Port Authority of New York & New Jersey
Web site: www.panynj.gov

Acting Public Information Officer/Media Relations:
Steve Coleman. 212-435-7777/fax: 212-435-4032

Port of Oswego Authority
Web site: www.portoswego.com

Executive Director & CEO:
Zelko N. Kirincich 315-343-4503 x111/fax: 315-343-5498
e-mail: zkirincich@portoswego.com

Rochester-Genesee Regional Transportation Authority-RTS
Web site: www.myrts.com

Media Contact:
Carole Dowling 585-654-0730/fax: 585-654-0224
e-mail: cdowling@myrts.com

Roosevelt Island Operating Corporation (RIOC)
Web site: www.rioc.ny.gov

Community Relations:
Erica Spencer-El. 212-832-4540 x349/fax: 212-832-4582
e-mail: erica.spencer-el@rioc.ny.gov

State University Construction Fund
Web site: www.sucf.suny.edu

General Counsel/Director Legal Svcs:
William K Barczak 518-320-1746/fax: 518-443-1008

State of New York Mortgage Agency (SONYMA)
Web site: www.nyshcr.org

Director, Public Information:
Charni Sochet 212-872-0338
e-mail: plentz@nyhomes.org

Offices and agencies generally appear in alphabetical order, except when specific order is requested by listee.

State of New York Municipal Bond Bank Agency (MBBA)
e-mail: abergamo@nyhomes.org
Web site: www.nyhomes.org

Senior VP & Director of Communications:
   Philip Lentz 212-872-0679/fax: 212-872-0789
   e-mail: plentz@nyhomes.org

Suffolk Regional Off-Track Betting Corporation
Web site: www.suffolkotb.com

General Counsel:
   James McManmon 631-853-1000/fax: 631-853-1086
   e-mail: customerservice@suffolkotb.com

Thousand Islands Bridge Authority
Web site: www.tibridge.com

Executive Director:
   Robert G Horr, III 315-482-2501/fax: 315-482-6064
   e-mail: roberthorr@tibridge.com

Uniform State Laws Commission
Chair:
   Richard B Long 607-821-2202/fax: 607-723-1530
   e-mail: rlong@cglawoffices.com

United Nations Development Corporation
Web site: www.undc.org

Vice President:
   Kenneth Coopersmith 212-888-1618/fax: 212-588-0758

Waterfront Commission of New York Harbor
Web site: www.wcnyh.org

Executive Director:
   Walter M Arsenault 212-905-9201/fax: 212-480-0587

Western Regional Off-Track Betting Corp
Web site: www.westernotb.com

Communications/Mutuels Manager:
   James Haas 585-343-3750/fax: 585-344-6188

Offices and agencies generally appear in alphabetical order, except when specific order is requested by listee.

U.S. CONGRESS

U.S. SENATE: NEW YORK DELEGATION

Internet access, including e-mail addresses, is available at: www.senate.gov. Biographies of Senate Members appear in a separate section in the back of the book.

. . . .

,
Committees:

Kirsten E Gillibrand (D) . . . . (202) 224-4451/fax: 202-228-0282
478 Russell Senate Office Building, Washington, DC 20510
Committees: Foreign Relations;Agriculture; Environment and Public Works; Special Committee on Aging; Senate Armed Services

Charles E Schumer (D) 202-224-6542/fax: 202-228-3027
313 Hart Senate Office Building, Washington, DC 20510
Committees: Senate Finance; Joint Economic; Judiciary; Rules and Administration; Banking, Housing, and Urban Affairs

U.S. HOUSE OF REPRESENTATIVES: NEW YORK DELEGATION

Internet access, including e-mail addresses, is available at: www.house.gov. Biographies of House Members appear in a separate section in the back of the book.

. . . .

,
Congressional District:
Committees:

Gary L Ackerman (D) 202-225-2601/fax: 202-225-1589
2243 Rayburn House Office Bldg, Washington, DC 20515
Congressional District: 5
Committees: Foreign Affairs; Financial Services

Timothy H Bishop (D) 202-225-3826/fax: 202-225-3143
306 Canon House Office Building, Washington, DC 20515
Congressional District: 1
Committees: Education and Labor; Transportation and Infrastructure; Budget

Ann Marie Buerkle (D) 315-423-5657
1630 Longworth House Office Building, Washington, DC 20515
Congressional District: 25
Committees: Foreign Affairs; Oversight and Government Reform; Veterans Affairs

Yvette D Clarke (D) 202-225-6231/fax: 202-226-0112
1029 Longworth House Office Building, Washington, DC 20515
Congressional District: 11
Committees: Homeland Security; Small Business

Joseph Crowley (D) 202-225-3965
2404 Rayburn House Office Building, Washington, DC 20515
Congressional District: 7
Committees: Ways and Means; Foreign Affairs

Eliot L Engel (D) 202-225-2464/fax: 202-225-5513
2161 Rayburn House Office Building, Washington, DC 20515
Congressional District: 17
Committees: Energy and Commerce; Foreign Affairs

Chris Gibson (R) 202-225-5614/fax: 202-225-1168
120 Cannon HOB, Washington, DC 20515
Congressional District: 20
Committees: Agriculture; Armed Services

Michael Grimm (R) 202-225-3371/fax: 202-226-1272
323 Cannon House Office Building, Washington, DC 20515
Congressional District: 13
Committees: Financial Services

Richard Hanna (R) 607-756-2470
127 Cannon House Office Building, Washington, DC 20515
Congressional District: 24
Committees: Transportation and Infrastructure; Education and the Workforce

Nan Hayworth (R) 202-225-5441/fax: 202-225-3289
1217 Longworth House Office Building, Washington, DC 20515
Congressional District: 19
Committees: Financial Services

Brian Higgins (D) 202-225-3306/fax: 202-226-0347
431 Cannon House Office Building, Washington, DC 20515
Congressional District: 27
Committees: Foreign Affairs; Homeland Security

Maurice D Hinchey (D) 202-225-6335/fax: 202-226-0774
2431 Rayburn House Office Building, Washington, DC 20515
Congressional District: 22
Committees: Appropriations

Steve Israel (D) 202-225-3335/fax: 202-225-4669
2457 Rayburn House Office Building, Washington, DC 20515
Congressional District: 2
Committees: Appropriations

Pete King (R) 202-225-7896
339 Cannon House Office Building, Washington, DC 20515
Congressional District: 3
Committees: Homeland Security; Financial Services

Nita M Lowey (D) 202-225-6506/fax: 202-225-0546
2329 Rayburn House Office Building, Washington, DC 20515
Congressional District: 18
Committees: House Appropriations; Homeland Security

Carolyn B Maloney (D) 202-225-7944/fax: 202-225-4709
2332 Rayburn House Office Building, Washington, DC 20515
Congressional District: 14
Committees: Financial Services; Oversight and Government Reform

Carolyn McCarthy (D) 202-225-5516/fax: 202-225-5758
2346 Rayburn House Office Building, Washington, DC 20515
Congressional District: 4
Committees: Education and Labor; Financial Services

Gregory W Meeks (D) 202-225-3461/fax: 202-226-4169
2342 Rayburn House Office Building, Washington, DC 20515
Congressional District: 6
Committees: Financial Services; Foreign Affairs

Jerrold Nadler (D) 202-225-5635
2334 Rayburn House Office Building, Washington, DC 20515
Congressional District: 8
Committees: Judiciary; Transportation and Infrastructure

Bill Owens (R) 202-225-4611/fax: 202-226-0621
2366 Rayburn House Office Building, Washington, DC 20515-3223
Congressional District: 23
Committees: Agriculture; Armed Services; Small Business

Charles B Rangel (D) 202-225-4365/fax: 202-225-0816
2354 Rayburn House Office Building, Washington, DC 20515
Congressional District: 15
Committees: Ways and Means; Taxation

Tom Reed (R) 202-225-3161/fax: 202-226-6599
1208 Longworth House Office Building, Washington, DC 20515
Congressional District: 29
Committees: Rules

State & Local Government Public Information

Offices and agencies generally appear in alphabetical order, except when specific order is requested by listee.

Jose E Serrano (D)...................202-225-4361/fax: 202-225-6001
2227 Rayburn House Office Building, Washington, DC 20515
Congressional District: 16
Committees: Appropriations

Louise M Slaughter (D) 202-225-3615/fax: 202-225-7822
2469 Rayburn House Office Building, Washington, DC 20515
Congressional District: 28
Committees: Rules

Paul D Tonko (D)..................202-225-5076/fax: 202-225-5077
128 Cannon House Office Building, Washington, DC 20515
Congressional District: 21
Committees: Budget; Science and Technology

Edolphus Towns (D) 202-225-5936/fax: 202-225-1018
2232 Rayburn House Office Building, Washington, DC 20515
Congressional District: 10
Committees: Energy and Commerce; Oversight and Government

Nydia M Velazquez (D).............202-225-2361/fax: 202-226-0327
2466 Rayburn House Office Building, Washington, DC 20515
Congressional District: 12
Committees: Small Business; Financial Services

Anthony D Weiner (D).............................202-225-6616
2104 Rayburn House Office Building, Washington, DC 20515
Congressional District: 9
Committees: Homeland Security; Judiciary

U.S. SENATE STANDING COMMITTEES

Agriculture, Nutrition & Forestry
328A Senate Russell Office Building
Washington, DC 20510
202-224-2035
Web site: www.agriculture.senate.gov

Chair:
    Tom Harkin (D-IA)....................................202-224-3254
Ranking Republican Member:
    Saxby Chambliss (R-GA)..........................202-224-3521

Subcommittees

Domestic and Foreign Marketing, Inspection and Plant & Animal Health
Chair:
    Max Baucus (D-MT).................................202-224-2651
Ranking Member:
    Vacant

Energy, Science and Technology
Chair:
    Kent Conrad (D-ND)................................202-224-2043
Ranking Member:
    John Thune (R-SD)..................................202-224-2321

Nutrition & Food Assistance, Sustainable & Organic Agriculture & Gen Legis
Chair:
    Patrick J Leahy (D-VT)............................202-224-4242
Ranking Member:
    Norm Coleman (R-MN)...........................202-224-5641

Production, Income Protection and Price Support
Chair:
    Blanche L Lincoln (D-AR).........................202-224-4843
Ranking Member:
    Pat Roberts (R-KS).................................202-224-4774

Rural Revitalization, Conservation, Forestry and Credit
Chair:
    Debbie Stabenow (D-MI)..........................202-224-4822
Ranking Member:
    Mike Crapo (R-ID)..................................202-224-6142

Appropriations
The Capitol
S-128
Washington, DC 20510
202-224-7363
Web site: www.appropriations.senate.gov

Chair:
    Daniel K Inouye (D-HI).............................202-224-3934
Vice Chair:
    Thad Cochran (R-MS) 202-224-5054

Subcommittees

Agriculture, Rural Development, FDA, and Related Agencies
Chair:
    Herb Kohl (D-WI)...................................202-224-5653
Ranking Member:
    Sam Brownback (R-KS)...........................202-224-6521

Commerce, Justice, Science and Related Agencies
Chair:
    Barbara Mikulski (D-MD).........................202-224-4645
Ranking Member:
    Richard Shelby (R-AL) 202-224-5744

Defense
Chair:
    Daniel Inouye (D-HI)...............................202-224-3934
Ranking Member:
    Thad Cochran (R-MS).............................202-224-5054

Energy and Water Development
Chair:
    Byron Dorgan (D-ND).............................202-224-2551
Ranking Member:
    Robert Bennett (R-UT)............................202-224-5444

Financial Services and General Government
Chair:
    Richard Durbin (D-IL).............................202-224-2152
Ranking Member:
    Susan M Collins (R-ME) 202-224-2523

Homeland Security
Chair:
    Robert C Byrd (D-WV) 202-224-3954
Ranking Member:
    George V Voinovich (R-OH)......................202-224-3353

Interior, Environment and Related Agencies
Chair:
    Dianne Feinstein (D-CA)..........................202-224-3841
Ranking Member:
    Lamar Alexander (R-TN).........................202-224-4944

Labor, Health and Human Services, Education and Related Agencies
Chair:
    Tom Harkin (D-IA) 202-224-3254
Ranking Member:
    Arlen Specter (R-PA)..............................202-224-4254

Legislative Branch
Chair:
    Ben Nelson (D-NE) 202-224-6551
Ranking Member:
    Barbara Mikulsi (R-MD) 202-224-4645

Offices and agencies generally appear in alphabetical order, except when specific order is requested by listee.

Military Construction, Veterans Affairs and Related Agencies
Chair:
    Tim Johnson (D-SD) 202-224-5842
Ranking Member:
    Kay Bailey Hutchison (R-TX) 202-224-5922

State, Foreign Operations and Related Programs
Chair:
    Patrick Leahy (D-VT)............................202-224-4242
Ranking Member:
    Judd Gregg (D-NH) 202-224-3324

Transportation, Housing and Urban Development, and Related Agencies
Chair:
    Patty Murray (D-WA) 202-224-2621
Ranking Member:
    Christopher Bond (R-MO) 202-224-5721

Armed Services
Russell Senate Office Building
Room SR-228
Washington, DC 20510
202-224-3871
Web site: www.armed-services.senate.gov

Chair:
    Carl Levin (D-MI)..............................202-224-6221
Ranking Member:
    John McCain (R-AZ) 202-224-2235

Subcommittees

Airland
Chair:
    Joseph I Liberman (D-CT) 202-224-4041
Ranking Member:
    John Thune (R-SD) 202-224-2321

Emerging Threats & Capabilities
Chair:
    Jack Reed (D-RI) 202-224-4642
Ranking Member:
    Roger F Wicker (R-MS)........................202-224-6253

Personnel
Chair:
    Ben Nelson (D-FL)............................202-224-5274
Ranking Member:
    Lindsey O Graham (R-SC)......................202-224-5972

Readiness & Management Support
Chair:
    Evan Bayh (D-IN) 202-224-5623
Ranking Member:
    Richard Burr (R-NC) 202-224-3154

SeaPower
Chair:
    Edward M Kennedy (D-MA).....................202-224-4543
Ranking Member:
    Mel Martinez (R-FL) 202-224-3041

Strategic Forces
Chair:
    Bill Nelson (D-FL).............................202-224-5274
Ranking Member:
    Jeff Sessions (R-AL) 202-224-4124

Banking, Housing & Urban Affairs
534 Dirksen Seanate Office Building
Washington, DC 20510

202-224-7391
Web site: www.banking.senate.gov

Chair:
    Christopher J Dodd (D-CT) 202-224-2823
Ranking Member:
    Richard C Shelby (R-AL)........................202-224-5744

Subcommittees

Economic Policy
Chair:
    Sherrod Brown (D-OH) 202-224-2315
Ranking Member:
    Jim DeMint (R-SC) 202-224-6121

Financial Institutions
Chair:
    Tim Johnson (D-SD) 202-224-5842
Ranking Member:
    Mike Crapo (R-ID)............................202-224-6142

Housing, Transportation and Community Development
Chair:
    Robert Menendez (D-NJ)........................202-224-4744
Ranking Member:
    David Vitter (R-LA 202-224-4623

Securities, Insurance and Investment
Chair:
    Jack Reed (D-RI) 202-224-4642
Ranking Member:
    Jim Bunning (R-KY) 202-224-4343

Security and International Trade and Finance
Chair:
    Evan Bayh (D-IN) 202-224-5623
Ranking Member:
    Bob Corker (R-TN) 202-224-3344

Budget
624 Dirksen Senate Office Building
Washington, DC 20510
202-224-0642
Web site: www.budget.senate.gov

Chair:
    Kent Conrad (D-ND) 202-224-0642
Ranking Member:
    Judd Gregg (R-NH) 202-224-0642

Commerce, Science & Transportation
508 Dirksen Building
Washington, DC 20510
202-224-5115
Web site: www.commerce.senate.gov

Chair:
    John D Rockefeller, IV (D-WV) 202-224-6472
Ranking Member:
    Kay Bailey Hutchison (R-TX) 202-224-5922

Subcommittees

Aviation Operations, Safety & Security
Chair:
    Byron L Dorgan (D-ND) 202-224-9000
Ranking Member:
    Jim DeMint (R-SC) 202-224-5184

Communications, Technology, & the Internet
Chair:
    John Kerry (D-MA) 202-224-0415

Offices and agencies generally appear in alphabetical order, except when specific order is requested by listee.

State & Local Government Public Information

Ranking Member:
    John Ensign (R-NV)............................202-224-4852
Chair:
    Amy Klobuchar (R-MN) 202-224-1270
Ranking Member:
    Mel Martinez (R-FL) 202-224-5183

Consumer Protection, Product Safety, & Insurance
Chair:
    Mark Pryor (D-AR).............................202-224-1270
Ranking Member:
    Roger F Wicker (R-MS).........................202-224-5183

Oceans, Atmosphere, Fisheries and Coast Guard
Chair:
    Maria Cantwell (D-WA).........................202-224-4912
Ranking Member:
    Olympia J Snowe (R-ME) 202-224-8172

Science and Space
Chair:
    Bill Nelson (D-FL)............................202-224-0415
Ranking Member:
    David Vitter (R-LA)...........................202-224-4852

Surface Transportation & Merchant Marine Infrastructure, Safety & Security
Chair:
    Frank R Lautneberg (D-NJ).....................202-224-9000
Ranking Member:
    John Thune (R-SD) 202-224-4852

Energy & Natural Resources
304 Dirksen Senate Building
Washington, DC 20510
202-224-4971
Web site: energy.senate.gov

Chair:
    Jeff Bingaman (D-NM)..........................202-224-5521
Ranking Member:
    Lisa Murkowski (R-AK).........................202-224-6665

Subcommittees

Energy
Chair:
    Maria Cantwell (D-WA).........................202-224-4971
Ranking Member:
    James E Risch (R-ID)..........................202-224-0541

National Parks
Chair:
    Mark Udall (D-CO) 202-224-4971
Ranking Member:
    Richard Burr (R-NC) 202-224-0539

Public Lands & Forests
Chair:
    Ron Wyden (D-OR) 202-224-4971
Ranking Member:
    John Barrasso (R-WY)..........................202-224-7970

Water & Power
Chair:
    Debbie Stabenow (D-MI)........................202-224-4971
Ranking Member:
    Sam Brownback (R-KS)..........................202-224-7970

Environment & Public Works
410 Dirksen Senate Building
Washington, DC 20510

202-224-8832
Web site: http://epw.senate.gov

Chair:
    Barbara Boxer (D-CA) 202-224-8832
Ranking Minority Member:
    James M Inhofe (R-OK).........................202-224-6176
New York Delegate:
    Kisrten Gillibrand (D)........................202-224-4451

Subcommittees

Children's Health
Chair:
    Amy Klobuchar (D-MN) 202-224-3244
Ranking Member:
    Lamar Alexander (R-TN)........................202-224-4944

Clean Air and Nuclear Safety
Chair:
    Thomas R Carper (D-DE) 202-224-2441
Ranking Member:
    David Vitter (R-LA)...........................202-224-4623

Green Jobs and the New Economy
Chair:
    Bernard Sanders (D-VT) 202-224-5141
Ranking Member:
    Christopher S Bond (R-MO) 202-224-5721

Oversight
Chair:
    Sheldon Whitehouse (D-RI).....................202-224-2921
Ranking Member:
    John Barrasso (R-WY)..........................202-224-6441

Superfund, Toxics and Environmental Health
Chair:
    Frank R Lautenberg (D-NJ).....................202-224-3224
Ranking Member:
    Arlen Specter (R-PA)..........................202-224-4254

Transportation & Infrastructure
Chair:
    Max Baucus (D-MT).............................202-224-2651
Ranking Member:
    Johnny Isakson (R-GA) 202-224-3643

Water & Wildlife
Chair:
    Benjamin L Cardin (D-MD)......................202-224-4524
Ranking Member:
    Mike Crapo (R-ID).............................202-224-6142

Finance
219 Dirksen Senate Building
Washington, DC 20510
202-224-4515
Web site: www.finance.senate.gov

Chair:
    Max Baucus (D-MT) 202-224-2651
Ranking Member:
    Chuck Grassley (R-IA).........................202-224-3744

Subcommittees

Energy, Natural Resources and Infrastructure
Chair:
    Jeff Bingaman (D-NM) 202-224-5521
Ranking Member:
    Jim Bunning (R-KY)............................202-224-4343

Offices and agencies generally appear in alphabetical order, except when specific order is requested by listee.

Health Care
Chair:
    John D Rockefeller, IV (D-WV) 202-224-6472
Ranking Member:
    Orrin G Hatch (R-UT) 202-224-5251

International Trade, and Global Competitiveness
Chair:
    Ron Wyden (D-OR) 202-224-5244
Ranking Member:
    Mike Crapo (R-ID) 202-224-6142

Social Security, Pensions, and Family Policy
Chair:
    Blanche L Lincoln (D-AR) 202-224-1371
Ranking Member:
    Pat Roberts (R-KS) 202-224-4774

Taxation, IRS Oversight and Long-Term Growth
Chair:
    Kent Conrad (D-ND) 202-224-2043
Ranking Member:
    Jon Kyl (R-AZ) 202-224-4521

Foreign Relations
Dirksen Senate Building
Washington, DC 20510
202-224-4651
Web site: www.foreign.senate.gov

Chair:
    John F Kerry (D-MA) 202-224-2742
Ranking Member:
    Richard G Lugar (R-IN) 202-224-0360

Subcommittees

African Affairs
Chair:
    Russell D Feingold (D-WI) 202-224-5323
Ranking Minority Member:
    Johnny Isakson (R-GA) 202-224-3643

East Asian & Pacific Affairs
Chair:
    Jim Webb (D-VA) 202-224-4024
Ranking Member:
    Republican Leader Designee

European Affairs
Chair:
    Jeanne Shaheen (D-NH) 202-224-2841
Ranking Member:
    Jim DeMint (R-SC) 202-224-6121

International Development, Foreign Assist, Economic Affairs & Environment
Chair:
    Robert Menendez (D-NJ) 202-224-4744
Ranking Member:
    Bob Corker (R-TN) 202-224-3344

International Ops & Orgs, Human Rights, Democracy & Global Women's Issues
Chair:
    Barbara Boxer (D-CA) 202-224-3553
Ranking Member:
    Roger F Wicker (R-MS) 202-224-6253

Near Eastern and South and Central Asian Affairs
Chair:
    Robert P Casey, Jr (D-PA) 202-224-6324

Ranking Member:
    James E Risch (R-ID) 202-224-2752

Western Hemisphere, Peace Corps & Narcotics Affairs
Chair:
    Christopher J Dodd (D-CT) 202-224-2823
Ranking Member:
    John Barrasso (R-WY) 202-224-6441

Health, Education, Labor, & Pensions
428 Dirksen Senate Building
Washington, DC 20510
Web site: www.help.senate.gov

Chair:
    Edward M Kennedy (D-MA) 202-224-4543
Ranking Member:
    Michael B Enzi (R-WY) 202-224-3424
New York Delegate:
    Hillary Rodham Clinton (D) 202-224-4451

Subcommittees

Children and Families
Chair:
    Christopher J Dodd (D-CT) 202-224-2823
Ranking Member:
    Lamar Alexander (R-TN) 202-224-4944

Employment & Workplace Safety
Chair:
    Patty Murray (D-WA) 202-224-2621
Ranking Member:
    Johnny Isakson (R-GA) 202-224-3643

Retirement and Aging
Chair:
    Barbara Mikulski (D-MD) 202-224-4654
Ranking Member:
    Richard Burr (R-NC) 202-224-3154
New York Delegate:
    Hillary Rodham Clinton (D-NY) 202-224-4451

Homeland Security & Governmental Affairs
340 Dirksen Senate Building
Washington, DC 20510
202-224-2627
Web site: www.hsgac.senate.gov

Chair:
    Joseph I Lieberman (D-CT) 202-224-4041
Ranking Member:
    Susan Collins (R-ME) 202-224-2523

Subcommittees

Disaster Recovery
Chair:
    Mary L Landrieu (D-LA) 202-224-5824
Ranking Member:
    Lindsey O Graham (R-SC) 202-224-4751

Federal Financial Mgt, Govt Info, Federal Svcs, & International Security
Chair:
    Thomas R Carper (D-DE) 202-224-2441
Ranking Member:
    John Coburn (R-AZ) 202-224-2235

Oversight of Government Management, Federal Workforce & District of Columbia
Chair:
    Daniel K Akaka (D-HI) 202-224-6361

State & Local Government Public Information

Ranking Member:
George V Voinovich (R-OH).....................202-224-3353

Permanent Subcommittee on Investigations
Chair:
Carl Levin (D-MI).............................202-224-6221
Ranking Member:
Tom Coburn (R-OK).............................202-224-5754

State, Local, and Private Sector Preparedness and Integration
Chair:
Mark L Pryor (D-AR)...........................202-224-2353
Ranking Member:
John Ensign (R-NV)............................202-224-6244

Judiciary
226 Dirksen Senate Building
Washington, DC 20510
Web site: www.judiciary.senate.gov

Chair:
Patrick J Leahy (D-VT)........................202-224-4242
Ranking Member:
Arlen Specter (R-PA)..........................202-224-4254

Subcommittees

Administrative Oversight & the Courts
Chair:
Sheldon Whitehead (D-RI)......................202-224-2921
Ranking Member:
Jeff Sessions (R-AL)..........................202-224-4124

Antitrust, Competition Policy & Consumer Rights
Chair:
Herb Kohl (D-WI)..............................202-224-5653
Ranking Member:
Orrin G Hatch (R-UT)..........................202-224-5251

Constitution, The
Chair:
Russell D Feingold (D-WI).....................202-224-5323
Ranking Member:
Tom Coburn (R-OK).............................202-224-5754

Crime & Drugs
Chair:
Richard J Durbin (D-IL).......................202-224-2152
Ranking Member:
Lindsey O Graham (R-SC).......................202-224-5972

Immigration, Refugees and Border Security
Chair:
Charles E Schumer (D-NY)......................202-224-6542
Ranking Member:
John Cornyn (R-TX)............................202-224-2934
Chair:
Benjamin L Cardin (D-MD)......................202-224-4524
Ranking Member:
Jon Kyl (R-AZ)................................202-224-4521

Rules & Administration
305 Russell Senate Building
Washington, DC 20510
202-224-6352
Web site: www.rules.senate.gov

Chair:
Charles E Schumer (D-NY)......................202-224-6542
Ranking Member:
Bob Bennett (R-UT)............................202-224-5444

Small Business & Entrepreneurship
428A Russell Senate Building
Washington, DC 20510
202-224-5175
Web site: www.sbc.senate.gov

Chair:
Mary L Landrieu (D-LA)........................202-224-5824
Ranking Member:
Olympia J Snowe (R-ME)........................202-224-5344

Veterans' Affairs
412 Russell Senate Building
Washington, DC 20510
202-224-9126
Web site: www.veterans.senate.gov

Chair:
Daniel Akaka (D-HI)...........................202-224-6361
Ranking Member:
Richard Burr (R-NC)...........................202-224-3154

OTHER, SELECT & SPECIAL COMMITTEES

Aging, Special Committee on
G31 Dirksen Senate Building
Washington, DC 20510
202-224-5364
Web site: www.aging.senate.gov

Chair:
Herb Kohl (D-WI)..............................202-224-5653
Vice Chair:
Gordon Smith (R-OR)...........................202-224-3753

Ethics, Select Committee on
220 Hart Building
Washington, DC 20510
202-224-2981
Web site: www.ethics.senate.gov

Chair:
Barbara Boxer (D-CA)..........................202-224-3553
Vice Chair:
Johnny Isakson (R-GA).........................202-224-3643

Indian Affairs, Committee on
838 Hart Office Building
Washington, DC 20510
202-224-2251
Web site: indian.senate.gov

Chair:
Byron L Dorgan (D-ND).........................202-224-2251
Vice Chair:
John Barrasso (R-WY)..........................202-224-6641

Intelligence, Select Committee on
211 Hart Senate Building
Washington, DC 20510
202-224-1700
Web site: www.intelligence.senate.gov

Chair:
Dianne Feinstein (D-CA).......................202-224-3841
Vice Chair:
Christopher S Bond (R-MO).....................202-224-5721

Offices and agencies generally appear in alphabetical order, except when specific order is requested by listee.

U.S. HOUSE OF REPRESENTATIVES STANDING COMMITTEES

Agriculture
1301 Longworth House Office Building
Washington, DC 20515
202-225-2171
Web site: agriculture.house.gov

Chair:
Collin C Peterson (D-MN) 202-225-2165
Ranking Member:
Frank D Lucas (R-OK).............................202-225-5565

Subcommittees

Conservation, Credit, Energy, and Research
Chair:
Tim Holden (D-PA) 202-225-5546
Ranking Member:
Bob Goodlatte (D-VA).............................202-225-5431

Department Operations, Oversight, Nutrition, & Forestry
Chair:
Joe Baca (D-CA) 202-225-6161
Ranking Member:
Jeff Fortenberry (R-NE 202-225-4806

General Farm Commodities & Risk Management
Chair:
Leonard L Boswell (D-IA)..........................202-225-3806
Ranking Member:
Jerry Moran (R-KS) 202-225-2715

Horticulture and Organic Agriculture
Chair:
Dennis A Cardoza (D-CA)..........................202-225-6131
Ranking Member:
Jean Schmidt (R-OH)..............................202-225-3164

Livestock, Dairy, and Poultry
Chair:
David Scott (D-GA) 202-225-2939
Ranking Member:
Randy Neugebauer (R-TX) 202-225-4005

Specialty Crops, Rural Development and Foreign Agriculture
Chair:
Mike McIntyre (D-NC) 202-225-2731
Ranking Member:
K Michael Conaway (R-TX) 202-225-3605

Appropriations
H-218 US Capitol
Washington, DC 20515
202-225-2771
Web site: appropriations.house.gov

Chair:
David R Obey (D-WI) 202-225-3365
Ranking Member:
Jerry Lewis (R-CA)...............................202-225-5861
New York Delegate:
Maurice D Hinchey (D) 202-225-6335
New York Delegate:
Steve Israel (D)..................................202-225-3335
New York Delegate:
Nita M Lowey (D) 202-225-6506
New York Delegate:
Jose E Serrano (D) 202-225-4361

Subcommittees

Agriculture, Rural Development, FDA & Related Agencies
Chair:
Rosa DeLauro (D-CT) 202-225-3661
Ranking Member:
Jack Kingston (R-GA) 202-225-5831

Commerce, Justice, Science and Related Agencies
Chair:
Alan B Mollohan (D-WV) 202-225-4172
Ranking Member:
Frank R Wolf (R-VA) 202-225-5136

Defense
Chair:
John P Murtha (D-PA) 202-225-2847
Ranking Member:
C W Bill Young (R-FL) 202-225-5961

Energy and Water Development
Chair:
Peter J Visclosky (D-IN) 202-225-2461
Ranking Member:
Rodney P Frelinhuysen (R-NJ) 202-225-5034

Financial Services and General Government
Chair:
Jose Serrano (D-NY) 202-225-4361
Ranking Member:
Jo Ann Emerson (R-MO)..........................202-225-4404

Homeland Security
Chair:
David E Price (D-NC) 202-225-1784
Ranking Member:
Harold Rogers (R-KY) 202-225-4601

Interior, Environment and Related Agencies
Chair:
Norman D Dicks (D-WA) 202-225-5916
Ranking Member:
Michael K Simpson (R-ID) 202-225-5531

Labor, Health & Human Services, Education and Related Agencies
Chair:
David R Obey (D-WI) 202-225-3365
Ranking Member:
Todd Tiahrt (R-KS) 202-225-6216

Legislative Branch
Chair:
Debbie Wasserman Schultz (D-FL).................202-225-7931
Ranking Member:
Robert B Aderholt (R-AL).........................202-225-4876

Military Construction, Veterans Affairs and Related Agencies
Chair:
Chet Edwards (D-TX) 202-225-6105
Ranking Member:
Zach Wamp (R-TN) 202-225-3271

State, Foreign Operations and Related Programs
Chair:
Nita M Lowey (D-NY)..............................202-225-6506
Ranking Member:
Kay Granger (R-TX) 202-225-5071

Transportation, Housing and Urban Development, and Related Agencies
Chair:
John W Olver (D-MA)..............................202-225-5335
Ranking Member:
Tom Latham (R-IA) 202-225-5476

Offices and agencies generally appear in alphabetical order, except when specific order is requested by listee.

Armed Services
2120 Rayburn House Building
Washington, DC 20515
202-225-9077 Fax: 202-225-4151
Web site: www.house.gov/hasc/

Chair:
Ike Skelton (D-MO) 202-225-2876
Ranking Member:
John M McHugh (R-NY) 202-225-4611
New York Delegate:
Eric JJ Massa (D) 202-225-3161
New York Delegate:
Scott Murphy (D) 202-225-5614

Subcommittees

Air and Land Forces
Chair:
Neil Abercrombie (D-HI) 202-225-2726
Ranking Member:
Roscoe G Bartlett (R-MD) 202-225-2721

Military Personnel
Chair:
Susan A Davis (D-CA) 202-225-2040
Ranking Member:
Joe Wilson (R-SC) 202-225-2452

Oversight and Investigations
Chair:
Vic Snyder (D-AR) 202-225-2506
Ranking Member:
Rob Wittman (R-VA) 202-225-4261

Readiness
Chair:
Solomon P Ortiz (D-TX) 202-225-7742
Ranking Member:
J Randy Forbes (R-VA) 202-225-6365

Seapower and Expeditionary Forces
Chair:
Gene Taylor (D-MS) 202-225-5772
Ranking Member:
W Todd Akin (R-MO) 202-225-2561

Strategic Forces
Chair:
Ellen O Tauscher (D-CA) 202-225-1880
Ranking Member:
Michael Turner (R-OH) 202-225-6465

Terrorism, Unconventional Threats and Capabilities
Chair:
Adam Smith (D-WA) 202-225-8901
Ranking Member:
Jeff Miller (R-TX) 202-225-4136

Budget
207 Cannon House Building
Washington, DC 20515
202-226-7200 Fax: 202-225-9905
Web site: http://budget.house.gov

Chair:
John M Spratt, Jr (D-SC) 202-225-5501
Ranking Member:
Paul Ryan (R-WI) 202-225-3031
New York Delegate:
Tim Bishop (D) 202-225-3826

Education & Labor
2181 Rayburn House Building
Washington, DC 20515
202-225-3725
Web site: http://edworkforce.house.gov

Chair:
George Miller (D-CA) 202-225-2095
Ranking Member:
Howard P (Buck) McKeon (R-CA) 202-225-1956
New York Delegate:
Timothy H Bishop (D) 202-225-3826
New York Delegate:
Yvette Clarke (D) 202-225-6231
New York Delegate:
Carolyn McCarthy (D) 202-225-5516
New York Delegate:
Paul Tonko (D) 202-225-5076

Subcommittees

Early Childhood, Elementary and Secondary Education
Chair:
Dale E Kildee (D-MI) 202-225-3611
Ranking Member:
Michael N Castle (R-DE) 202-225-4165

Healthy Families and Communities
Chair:
Carolyn McCarthy (D-NY) 202-225-5516
Ranking Member:
Todd (Russell) Platts (R-PA) 202-225-5836

Higher Education, Lifelong Learning, and Competitiveness
Chair:
Rub‚n Hinojosa (D-TX) 202-225-2531
Ranking Member:
Brett Guthrie (R-KY) 202-225-3501

Health, Employment, Labor and Pensions
Chair:
Robert Andrews (D-NJ) 202-225-6501
Ranking Member:
John Kline (R-MN) 202-225-2271

Workforce Protections
Chair:
Lynn C Woolsey (D-CA) 202-225-5161
Ranking Member:
Tom Price (R-GA) 202-225-4501

Energy & Commerce
2125 Rayburn House Building
Washington, DC 20515
202-225-2927
Web site: energycommerce.house.gov

Chair:
Henry A Waxman (D-CA) 202-225-3976
Ranking Member:
Joe Barton (R-TX) 202-225-2002
New York Delegate:
Eliot L Engel (D) 202-225-2464
New York Delegate:
Anthony D Weiner (D) 202-225-6616

Subcommittees

Commerce, Trade & Consumer Protection
Chair:
Bobby L Rush (D-IL) 202-225-4372

Offices and agencies generally appear in alphabetical order, except when specific order is requested by listee.

Ranking Member:
George Radanovich (R-CA).........................202-225-4540

Communications, Technology & the Internet
Chair:
Rick Boucher (D-VA).........................202-225-3861
Ranking Member:
Cliff Stearns (R-FL).........................202-225-5744

Energy & the Environment
Chair:
Edward J Markey (D-MA).........................202-225-2836
Ranking Member:
Fred Upton (R-MI).........................202-225-3761

Health
Chair:
Frank J Pallone, Jr (D-NJ).........................202-225-4671
Ranking Member:
Nathan Deal (R-GA).........................202-225-5211

Oversight & Investigations
Chair:
Bart Stupak (D-MI).........................202-225-4735
Ranking Member:
Greg Walden (R-OR).........................202-225-6730

Financial Services
2129 Rayburn House Building
Washington, DC 20515
202-225-4247 Fax: 202-225-6952
Web site: http://financialservices.house.gov

Chair:
Barney Frank (D-MA).........................202-225-5931
Ranking Member:
Spencer Bachus (R-AL).........................202-225-4921
New York Delegate:
Gary L Ackerman (D).........................202-225-2601
New York Delegate:
Peter T King (R).........................202-225-7896
New York Delegate:
Christopher Lee (R).........................202-225-5265
New York Delegate:
Dan Maffei (D).........................202-225-3701
New York Delegate:
Carolyn B Maloney (D).........................202-225-7944
New York Delegate:
Carolyn McCarthy (D).........................202-225-5516
New York Delegate:
Gregory W Meeks (D).........................202-225-3461
New York Delegate:
Nydia M Velazquez (D).........................202-225-2361

Subcommittees

Capital Markets, Insurance & Government Sponsored Enterprises
Chair:
Paul E Kanjorski (D-PA).........................202-225-6511
Ranking Member:
Scott Garrett (R-NJ).........................202-225-4465
New York Delegate:
Gary L Ackerman (D).........................202-225-2601
New York Delegate:
Peter T King (R).........................202-225-7896
New York Delegate:
Carolyn McCarthy (D).........................202-225-5516
New York Delegate:
Carolyn B Maloney (D).........................202-225-7944
New York Delegate:
Nydia M Velazquez (D).........................202-225-2361

Domestic Monetary Policy & Technology
Chair:
Melvin L Watt (D-NC).........................202-225-1510
Ranking Member:
Ron Paul (R-TX).........................202-225-2831
New York Delegate:
Carolyn B Maloney (D).........................202-225-7944
New York Delegate:
Gregory W Meeks (D).........................202-225-3461

Financial Institutions & Consumer Credit
Chair:
Luis V Gutierrez (D-IL).........................202-225-8203
Ranking Member:
Jeb Hensarling (R-TX).........................202-225-3484
New York Delegate:
Gary L Ackerman (D).........................202-225-2601
New York Delegate:
Peter King (R).........................202-225-7896
New York Delegate:
Christopher Lee (R).........................202-225-5265
New York Delegate:
Carolyn B Maloney (D).........................202-225-7944
New York Delegate:
Carolyn McCarthy (D).........................202-225-5516
New York Delegate:
Gregory W Meeks (D).........................202-225-3461

Housing & Community Opportunity
Chair:
Maxine Waters (D-CA).........................202-225-2201
Ranking Member:
Shelley Moore Capito (R-WV).........................202-225-2711
New York Delegate:
Dan Maffei (D).........................202-225-3701
New York Delegate:
Nydia M Velazquez (D).........................202-225-2361

International Monetary Policy & Trade
Chair:
Gregory W Meeks (D-NY).........................202-225-3461
Ranking Member:
Gary Miller (R-CA).........................202-225-3201
New York Delegate:
Dan Maffei (D).........................202-225-3701

Oversight & Investigations
Chair:
Dennis Moore (D-KS).........................202-225-2865
Ranking Member:
Judy Biggert (R-IL).........................202-225-3515
New York Delegate:
Christopher Lee (R).........................202-225-5265

Foreign Affairs
2170 Rayburn House Building
Washington, DC 20515
202-225-5021
Web site: foreignaffairs.house.gov

Chair:
Howard L Berman (D-CA).........................202-225-3531
Ranking Member:
Ileana Ros- Lehtinen (R-FL).........................202-225-3931
New York Delegate:
Gary Ackerman (D).........................202-225-2601
New York Delegate:
Joseph Crowley (D).........................202-225-3965
New York Delegate:
Eliot L Engel (D).........................202-225-2464
New York Delegate:
Michael E McMahon (D).........................202-225-3371

Offices and agencies generally appear in alphabetical order, except when specific order is requested by listee.

321

New York Delegate:
  Gregory W Meeks (D) 202-225-3461

Subcommittees

Africa & Global Health
Chair:
  Donald M Payne (D-NJ)..........................202-225-3436
Ranking Member:
  Christopher H Smith (R-NJ)......................202-225-3765
New York Delegate:
  Gregory W Meeks (D) 202-225-3461

Asia, the Pacific and the Global Environment
Chair:
  Eni F H Faleomavaega (D-AS) 202-225-8577
Ranking Member:
  Donald A Manzullo (R-IL)........................202-225-5676
New York Delegate:
  Gary L Ackerman (D).............................202-225-2601
New York Delegate:
  Eliot L Engel (D) 202-225-2464
New York Delegate:
  Gregory W Meeks (D) 202-225-3461

Europe
Chair:
  Robert Wexler (D-FL) 202-225-3001
Ranking Member:
  Elton Gallegly (R-CA)...........................202-225-5811
New York Delegate:
  Michael E McMahon (D).........................202-225-3371

International Organizations, Human Rights and Oversight
Chair:
  Bill Delahunt (D-MA) 202-225-3111
Ranking Member:
  Dana Rohrabacher (R-CA)........................202-225-2415

Middle East and South Asia
Chair:
  Gary Ackerman (D-NY)..........................202-225-2601
Ranking Member:
  Dan Burton (R-IN) 202-225-2276
New York Delegate:
  Joseph Crowley (D) 202-225-3965
New York Delegate:
  Eliot L Engel (D) 202-225-2464
New York Delegate:
  Michael E McMahon (D).........................202-225-3371

Terrorism, Nonproliferation and Trade
Chair:
  Brad Sherman (D-CA) 202-225-5911
Ranking Member:
  Edward R Royce (R-CA) 202-225-4111

Western Hemisphere
Chair:
  Eliot Engel (D-NY) 202-225-2464
Ranking Member:
  Connie Mack (R-FL) 202-225-2536
New York Delegate:
  Joseph Crowley (D) 202-225-3965
New York Delegate:
  Gregory W Meeks (D) 202-225-3461

Homeland Security
176 Ford House Building
Washington, DC 20515
202-226-2616 Fax: 202-226-4499
Web site: www.hsc.house.gov

Chair:
  Bennie G Thompson (D-MS) 202-225-5876
Ranking Member:
  Peter T King (R-NY) 202-225-7896
New York Delegate:
  Yvette D Clarke (D) 202-225-6231
New York Delegate:
  Eric JJ Massa (D) 202-225-3161

Subcommittees

Border, Maritime and Global Counterterrorism
Chair:
  Loretta Sanchez (D-CA).........................202-225-2965
Ranking Member:
  Mark Souder (R-IN).............................202-225-4436

Emergency Communications, Preparedness and Response
Chair:
  Henry Cuellar (D-TX) 202-225-1640
Ranking Member:
  Mark Rogers (R-AL) 202-225-3261

Emerging Threats, Cybersecurity and Science and Technology
Chair:
  Yvette D Clark (D-NY) 202-225-6231
Ranking Member:
  Dan Lundgren (R-CA)...........................202-225-5716

Intelligence, Information Sharing and Terrorism Risk Assessment
Chair:
  Jane Harman (D-CA) 202-225-8220
Ranking Member:
  Michael McCall (R-TX)..........................202-225-2401

Management, Investigations and Oversight
Chair:
  Christopher P Carney (D-PA) 202-225-3731
Ranking Member:
  Gus Bilirakis (R-FL).............................202-225-5755

Transportation Security and Infrastructure Protection
Chair:
  Sheila Jackson- Lee (D-TX).......................202-225-3816
Ranking Member:
  Charlie Dent (R-PA).............................202-225-6411

House Administration
1309 Longworth Building
Washington, DC 20515
202-225-2061 Fax: 202-226-2774
Web site: http://cha.house.gov

Chair:
  Robert A Brady (D-PA) 202-225-4731
Ranking Member:
  Dan Lundgren (R-CA) 202-225-5671

Judiciary
2138 Rayburn House Building
Washington, DC 20515
Web site: www.judiciary.house.gov

Chair:
  John Conyers, Jr (D-MI)..........................202-225-5126
Ranking Member:
  Lamar S Smith (R-TX)...........................202-225-4236
New York Delegate:
  Dan Maffei (D).................................202-225-3701
New York Delegate:
  Jerrold Nadler (D)..............................202-225-5635

Offices and agencies generally appear in alphabetical order, except when specific order is requested by listee.

New York Delegate:
  Anthony D Weiner (D)..............................202-225-6616

Subcommittees

Commercial & Administrative Law
Chair:
  Steve Cohen (D-TN)..............................202-225-3265
Ranking Member:
  Trent Franks (R-AZ)............................202-225-4576

Constitution, Civil Rights and Civil Liberties
Chair:
  Jerrold Nadler (D-NY)..........................202-225-5635
Ranking Member:
  F James Sensenbrenner, Jr (R-WI)...............202-225-5101

Courts & Competition Policy
Chair:
  Hank Johnson (D-GA)............................202-225-1605
Ranking Member:
  Howard Coble (R-NC)............................202-225-3065

Crime, Terrorism and Homeland Security
Chair:
  Robert C Scott (D-VA)..........................202-225-8351
Ranking Member:
  Louie Gohmert (R-TX)...........................202-225-3035

Immigration, Citizenship, Refugees, Border Security and International Law
Chair:
  Zoe Lofgren (D-CA).............................202-225-3072
Ranking Member:
  Steve King (R-IA)..............................202-225-4426

Natural Resources
1324 Longworth Building
Washington, DC 20515
202-225-6065 Fax: 202-225-1931
Web site: resourcescommittee.house.gov

New York Delegate:
  Maurice D Hinchey (D)..........................202-225-6335
Chair:
  Nick J Rahall, II (D-WV).......................202-225-3452
Ranking Member:
  Doc Hastings (R-WA)............................202-225-5816

Office of Indian Affairs

Subcommittees

Energy & Mineral Resources
Chair:
  Jim Costa (D-CA)...............................202-225-3341
Ranking Member:
  Doug Lamborn (R-CO)............................202-225-4422

Insular Affairs, Oceans & Wildlife
Chair:
  Madelaine Z Bordallo (D-Guam)..................202-225-1188
Ranking Member:
  Henry E Brown, Jr (R-SC).......................202-225-3176

National Parks, Forests and Public Lands
Chair:
  Raul M Grijalva (R-AZ).........................202-225-2435
Ranking Member:
  Rob Bishop (R-UT)..............................202-225-0453

Water & Power
Chair:
  Grace F Napolitano (D-CA)......................202-225-5256

Ranking Member:
  Cathy McMorris Rodgers (R-WA)..................202-225-2006

Oversight and Government Reform
2157 Rayburn House Building
Washington, DC 20515
202-225-5051
Web site: oversight.house.gov

Chair:
  Edolphus Towns (D-NY)..........................202-225-5936
Ranking Member:
  Darrell E Issa (R-CA)..........................202-225-3906
New York Delegate:
  Carolyn B Maloney (D)..........................202-225-7944
New York Delegate:
  John M McHugh (R)..............................202-225-4611

Subcommittees

Domestic Policy
Chair:
  Dennis J Kucinich (D-OH).......................202-225-5871
Ranking Member:
  Jim Jordan (R-OH)..............................202-225-2676

Federal Workforce, Postal Service and the District of Columbia
Chair:
  Stephen F Lynch (D-MA).........................202-225-8273
Ranking Member:
  Jason Chaffetz (R-UT)..........................202-225-7751
New York Delegate:
  Carolyn D Maloney (D)..........................202-225-7944

Government Management, Organization and Procurement
Chair:
  Diane E Watson (D-CA)..........................202-225-7084
Ranking Member:
  Brian Bilbray (R-CA)...........................202-225-0508

Information Policy, Census and National Archives
Chair:
  William Lacy Clay (D-MO).......................202-225-2406
Ranking Member:
  Patrick McHenry (R-NC).........................202-225-2576
New York Delegate:
  Carolyn B Maloney (D)..........................202-225-7944

National Security and Foreign Affairs
Chair:
  John F Tierney (D-MA)..........................202-225-8020
Ranking Member:
  Jeff Flake (R-AZ)..............................202-225-2635
New York Delegate:
  Carolyn B Maloney (D)..........................202-225-7944

Rules
H-312 The Capitol
Washington, DC 20515
202-225-9091
Web site: www.rules.house.gov

Chair:
  Louise McIntosh Slaughter (D-NY)...............202-225-3615
Ranking Member:
  David Dreier (R-CA)............................202-225-2305

Subcommittees

Legislative & Budget Process
Chair:
  Alcee L Hastings (D-FL)........................202-225-1313

Offices and agencies generally appear in alphabetical order, except when specific order is requested by listee.

Ranking Member:
Lincoln Diaz-Balart (R-FL) 202-225-4211

Rules & Organization of the House
Chair:
James F McGovern (D-MA) 202-225-6101
Ranking Member:
Pete Sessions (R-TX) 202-225-2231

Science & Technology
2321 Rayburn Building
Washington, DC 20515
202-225-6375 Fax: 202-225-3895
Web site: www.house.gov/science

Chair:
Bart Gordon (D-TN) 202-225-4231
Ranking Member:
Ralph M Hall (R-TX) 202-225-6673
New York Delegate:
Paul D Tonko (D) 202-225-5076

Subcommittees

Energy & Environment
Chair:
Brian Baird (D-WA) 202-225-3536
Ranking Member:
Bob Inglis (R-SC) 202-225-6030

Investigations and Oversights
Chair:
Brad Miller (D-NC) 202-225-3032
Ranking Member:
Paul C Brown (R-GA) 202-225-4101

Research and Science Education
Chair:
Daniel Lipinski (D-IL) 202-225-5701
Ranking Member:
Vernon J Ehlers (R-MI) 202-225-3831

Space and Aeronautics
Chair:
Gabrielle Giffords (D-AZ) 202-225-2542
Ranking Member:
Pete Olson (R-TX) 202-225-5951

Technology and Innovation
Chair:
David Wu (D-OR) 202-225-0855
Ranking Member:
Adrian Smith (R-NE) 202-225-6435

Small Business
2361 Rayburn House Building
Washington, DC 20515
202-225-4038 Fax: 202-226-5276
Web site: www.house.gov/smbiz

Chair:
Nydia Velazquez (D-NY) .202-225-2361
Ranking Member:
Sam Graves (R-MO) 202-225-7041
New York Delegate:
Yvette D Clark (D) 202-225-6231

Subcommittees

Contracting and Technology
Chair:
Glenn C Nye III (D-IA) 202-225-4215

Ranking Member:
Aaron Schock (R-IL) 202-225-6201

Finance and Tax
Chair:
Kurt Schrader (D-OR) 202-225-5711
Ranking Member:
Vern Buchanan (R-FL) 202-225-5015

Investigations and Oversight
Chair:
Jason Altmire (D-PA) 202-225-2565
Ranking Member:
Mary Fallin (R-OK) 202-225-2132

Regulations and Health Care
Chair:
Kathy Dahlkemper (D-PA) 202-225-5406
Ranking Member:
Lynn Westmoreland (R-GA) 202-225-5901

Rural and Urban Entrepreneurship
Chair:
Heath Shuler (D-NC) 202-225-6401
Ranking Member:
Blaine Luetkemeyer (R-MO) 202-225-2956

Standards of Official Conduct
HT-2, The Capitol
Washington, DC 20515
202-225-7103 Fax: 202-225-7392
Web site: ethics.house.gov

Chair:
Zoe Lofgren (D-CA) 202-225-3072
Ranking Member:
Jo Bonner (R-AL) 202-225-4931

Transportation & Infrastructure
2165 Rayburn House Building
Washington, DC 20515
202-225-4472 Fax: 202-226-1270
Web site: www.transportation.house.gov

Chair:
James L Oberstar (D-MN) 202-225-4472
Ranking Member:
John L Mica (R-FL) 202-225-4035
New York Delegate:
Michael A Arcuri (D) 202-225-3665
New York Delegate:
Timothy H Bishop (D) 202-225-3826
New York Delegate:
John J Hall (D) 202-225-5441
New York Delegate:
Michael E McMahon (D) .202-225-3371
New York Delegate:
Jerrold Nadler (D) 202-225-5635

Subcommittees

Aviation
Chair:
Jerry F Costello (D-IL) 202-225-5661
Ranking Member:
Thomas E Petri (R-WI) 202-225-2476
New York Delegate:
John J Hall (D) 202-225-5441
New York Delegate:
Michael E McMahon (D) .202-225-3371

Offices and agencies generally appear in alphabetical order, except when specific order is requested by listee.

Coast Guard & Maritime Transportation
Chair:
  Elijah E Cummings (D-MD) 202-225-4741
Ranking Member:
  Frank LoBiondo (R-NJ) 202-225-6572
New York Delegate:
  Timothy H Bishop (D) 202-225-3826
New York Delegate:
  Michael E McMahon (D) 202-225-3371

Economic Development, Public Buildings & Emergency Management
Chair:
  Eleanor Holmes Norton (D-DC) .202-225-9961
Ranking Member:
  Mario Diaz-Balart (R-FL) 202-225-4211
New York Delegate:
  Michael A Arcuri (D) 202-225-3665

Highway and Transit
Chair:
  Peter A DeFazio (D-OR) 202-225-9989
Ranking Minority Member:
  John J Duncan, Jr (R-TN) 202-225-5435
New York Delegate:
  Michael A Arcuri (D) 202-225-3665
New York Delegate:
  Timothy H Bishop (D) 202-225-3826
New York Delegate:
  John J Hall (D) 202-225-5441
New York Delegate:
  Jerrold Nadler (D) 202-225-5635

Railroads, Pipelines and Hazardous Materials
Chair:
  Corrine Brown (D-FL) 202-225-3274
Ranking Member:
  Bill Schuster (PA) 202-225-2431
New York Delegate:
  Michael A Arcuri (D) 202-225-3665
New York Delegate:
  Michael E McMahon (D) 202-225-3371
New York Delegate:
  Jerrold Nadler (D) 202-225-5635

Water Resources & Environment
Chair:
  Eddie Bernice Johnson (D-TX) 202-225-0060
Ranking Member:
  John Boozman (R-AR) 202-225-4301
New York Delegate:
  Timothy H Bishop (D) 202-225-3826
New York Delegate:
  John J Hall (D) 202-225-5441

Veterans' Affairs

335 Cannon House Building
Washington, DC 20515
202-225-9756
Web site: www.veterans.house.gov

Chair:
  Bob Filner (D-CA) 202-225-8045
Ranking Member:
  Steve Buyer (D-IN) 202-225-5037
New York Delegate:
  John J Hall (D) 202-225-5441

Subcommittees

Disability Assistance & Memorial Affairs
Chair:
  John Hall (D-NY) 202-225-5441

Ranking Member:
  Doug Lamborn (R-CO) 202-225-4422

Economic Opportunity
Chair:
  Stephanie Herseth Sandlin (D-SD) 202-225-2801
Ranking Member:
  John Boozman (R-AR) 202-225-4301

Health
Chair:
  Mike Michaud (D-ME) 202-225-6306
Ranking Member:
  Henry E Brown, Jr (R-SC) 202-225-3176

Oversight & Investigations
Chair:
  Harry E Mitchell (D-AZ) 202-225-2190
Ranking Member:
  Phil Roe (R-TN) 202-225-6356

Ways & Means

1102 Longworth House Building
Washington, DC 20515
202-225-3625 Fax: 202-225-2610
Web site: waysandmeans.house.gov

Chair:
  Charles B Rangel (D-NY) 202-225-4365
Ranking Member:
  Dave Camp (R-MI) 202-225-3561
New York Delegate:
  Joseph Crowley (D) 202-225-3965
New York Delegate:
  Brian Higgins (D) 202-225-3306

Subcommittees

Health
Chair:
  Fortney Pete Stark (D-CA) 202-225-5065
Ranking Member:
  Wally Herger (D-CA) 202-225-3076

Income Security and Family Support
Chair:
  Jim McDermott (D-WA) 202-225-3106
Ranking Member:
  John Linder (R-GA) 202-225-

Oversight
Chair:
  John Lewis (D-GA) 202-225-3801
Ranking Member:
  Charles W Boustany, Jr (R-LA) 202-225-2031
New York Delegate:
  Brian Higgins (D) 202-225-3306

Select Revenue Measures
Chair:
  Richard E Neal (D-MA) 202-225-5601
Ranking Member:
  Pat Tiberi (R-OH) 202-225-5355
New York Delegate:
  Joseph Crowley (D) 202-225-3965

Social Security
Chair:
  John S Tanner (D-TN) 202-225-4714
Ranking Member:
  Sam Johnson (R-TX) 202-225-4201
New York Delegate:
  Joseph Crowley (D) 202-225-3965

Offices and agencies generally appear in alphabetical order, except when specific order is requested by listee.

Trade
Chair:
   Sander M Levin (MI) 202-225-4961
Ranking Member:
   Kevin Brady (R-TX). 202-225-4901

OTHER, SELECT & SPECIAL COMMITTEES

Energy Independence & Global Warming, House Select Committee on
B243 Longworth House Building
Washington, DC 20515
202-225-4012 Fax: 202-225-4092
Web site: globalwarming.house.gov

Chair:
   Ed Markey (D-MA) 202-225-2836
Ranking Member:
   James F Sensenbrenner, Jr (R-WI) 202-225-5101

Intelligence, House Permanent Select Committee on
Web site: intelligence.house.gov

Chair:
   Silvestre Reyes (D-TX) 202-225-4831
Ranking Member:
   Peter Hoekstra (R-MI) 202-225-4401

Subcommittees

Intelligence Community Management
Chair:
   Anna G Eshoo (D-CA). 202-225-8104
Ranking Member:
   Sue Myrick (R-NC) 202-225-1976

Oversight and Investigations
Chair:
   Jan Schakowsky (D-AL) .202-225-2111
Ranking Member:
   Jeff Miller (R-FL). 202-225-4136

Technical and Tactical Intelligence
Chair:
   C A Dutch Ruppersberger (D-MD) 202-225-3061
Ranking Member:
   Mack Thornberry (R-TX). 202-225-3706

Terrorism/HUMIT, Analysis and Counterintelligence
Chair:
   Mike Thompson (D-CA) .202-225-3311
Ranking Member:
   Mike Rogers (R-MI). 202-225-4872

JOINT SENATE AND HOUSE COMMITTEES

Economic Committee, Joint
Web site: www.house.gov/jec

Chair, House:
   Carolyn B Maloney (D-NY). 202-224-7944
Vice Chair, Senate:
   Charles E Schumer (D-NY) 202-224-6542
Ranking Member, House:
   Kevin Brady (R-TX). 202-225-4901
Ranking Member, Senate:
   Sam Brownback (R-KS). .202-225-6521
New York Delegate:
   Maurice D Hinchey (D) .202-224-6335

Library, Joint Committee on the
Chair:
   Charles E Schumer (D-NY) 202-224-6542
Ranking Member:
   Robert Bennett (R-UT). .202-224-5444

Printing, Joint Committee on
Web site: www.jcp.senate.gov

Chair:
   Charles E Schumer (D-NY 202-224-6542
Vice Chair:
   Robert F Bennett (R-UT) 202-224-5444

Taxation, Joint Committee on
1015 Longworth House Building
Washington, DC 20515
202-225-3621
Web site: www.house.gov/jct

Chair:
   Charles B Rangel (D-NY) 202-225-4365
Vice Chair:
   Max Baucus (D-MT) 202-224-2651

Offices and agencies generally appear in alphabetical order, except when specific order is requested by listee.

COUNTY GOVERNMENT

This section identifies senior government officials in all New York counties.

COUNTY GOVERNMENT

Albany County
112 State Street
Albany, NY 12207
518-447-7040 Fax: 518-447-5589
Web site: www.albanycounty.com

Chairman, County Legislature (D):
Shawn M. Morse 518-447-7168/fax: 518-447-5695
e-mail: shawn.morse@albanycounty.com
County Executive:
Daniel P. McCoy. 518-447-7040/fax: 518-447-5589
e-mail: county_executive@albanycounty.com
County Clerk:
Thomas G Clingan. 518-487-5100/fax: 518-487-5099
e-mail: countyclerk@albanycounty.com
County Attorney:
Thomas Marcelle. 518-447-7110/fax: 518-447-5564
District Attorney:
P David Soares 518-487-5460/fax: 518-487-5093
Sheriff:
Craig D. Apple, Sr. 518-487-5400/fax: 518-487-5037
Comptroller:
Michael F Conners, II 518-447-7130/fax: 518-433-1554
e-mail: mconners@albanycounty.com
General Services Commissioner:
John T. Evers. 518-447-7210/fax: 518-447-7747
Commissioner, Management & Budget:
David Friedfel 518-447-5525/fax: 518-447-5589
e-mail: budget@albanycounty.com

Allegany County
County Office Bldg, 7 Court St
Belmont, NY 14813
585-268-9222 Fax: 585-268-9446
Web site: www.alleganyco.com

Chairman, Board of Legislators (R):
Curtis W Crandall. 585-268-9222
Majority Leader (R):
Theodore L Hopkins. 585-268-9222
Minority Leader (D):
Vacant. 585-268-9222
Clerk, Board of Legislators:
Brenda A Rigby Riehle 585-268-9222/fax: 585-268-9446
e-mail: rigbyba@alleganyco.com
County Administrator:
John E Margeson. 585-268-9217/fax: 585-268-9623
e-mail: margesj@alleganyco.com
County Clerk:
Robert L Christman 585-268-9270/fax: 585-268-9659
e-mail: christr@alleganyco.com
District Attorney (Acting):
Keith Slep 585-268-9225/fax: 585-268-9727
e-mail: slepka@alleganyco.com
Public Defender:
Barbara J Kelley 585-268-9246/fax: 585-268-5888
e-mail: kelleybj@alleganyco.com
Sheriff:
Rick Whitney. 585-268-9200/fax: 585-268-9484
e-mail: whitneyrl@alleganyco.com

Treasurer:
Terri L Ross. .585-268-9289/fax: 585-268-7506
e-mail: rosstl@alleganyco.com
County Attorney:
Thomas A Miner 585-268-9410/fax: 585-268-9651
e-mail: minerta@alleganyco.com
Director, Emergency Management & Fire:
Jeff Luckey 585-268-5290
e-mail: luckeyj@alleganyco.com
Superintendent, Public Works:
Guy James 585-268-9230/fax: 585-268-9648
e-mail: roeskeds@alleganyco.com
Fire Coordinator:
Paul W Gallmann 585-268-5290/fax: 585-268-9695
e-mail: gallmapw@alleganyco.com
County Historian:
Craig R Braack 585-268-9293
e-mail: historian@alleganyco.com

Bronx County (NYC Borough of the Bronx)
851 Grand Concourse
Room 118
Bronx, NY 10451
866-797-7214 Fax: 718-590-8122
Web site: www.bronxcountyclerksoffice.com

Borough President:
Ruben Diaz Jr 718-590-3557/fax: 718-590-3537
Deputy Borough President:
Aurelia Greene 718-590-4036
County Clerk:
Luis M. Diaz .866-797-7214/fax: 718-590-8122
e-mail: hdiaz@courts.state.ny.us
District Attorney:
Robert T Johnson. 718-590-2000/fax: 718-590-2198

Broome County
County Office Bldg
60 Hawley St
PO Box 1766
Binghamton, NY 13902-1766
607-778-2109 Fax: 607-778-2044
e-mail: legclerk@co.broome.ny.us
Web site: www.gobroomecounty.com

Chairman, County Legislature (D):
Jerry F Marinich 607-778-2131/fax: 607-778-8869
e-mail: jmarinich@co.broome.ny.us
Majority Leader (D):
Wayne Howard 607-778-2131/fax: 607-778-8869
e-mail: whoward2@co.broome.ny.us
Minority Leader (R):
Mark R Whalen 607-778-2131/fax: 607-778-8869
e-mail: mwhalen2@co.broome.ny.us
County Executive:
Debra A. Preston 607-778-2109/fax: 607-778-2044
e-mail: bfiala@co.broome.ny.us
County Clerk:
Richard R Blythe 607-778-2255/fax: 607-778-2243
e-mail: clerkinfo@co.broome.ny.us
District Attorney:
Gerald F Mollen 607-778-2423/fax: 607-778-8870
e-mail: gmollen@co.broome.ny.us
Public Defender:
Jay L Wilber .607-778-2403/fax: 607-778-2432
e-mail: jwilber@co.broome.ny.us
Sheriff:
David E Harder 607-778-1911/fax: 607-778-2100
e-mail: bcsheriff@co.broome.ny.us

Offices and agencies generally appear in alphabetical order, except when specific order is requested by listee.

Director, Emergency Services:
    Brett B Chellis.....................607-778-2170/fax: 607-778-1150
    e-mail: bchellis@co.broome.ny.us
Office of Management & Budget:
    Marie F. Kalka....................607-778-2467/fax: 607-778-2044
    e-mail: jknebel@co.broome.ny.us
County Historian:
    Gerald R Smith 607-778-2076/fax: 607-778-6249
    e-mail: gsmith@co.broome.ny.us

Cattaraugus County

County Center
303 Court St
Little Valley, NY 14755
716-938-2577 Fax: 716-938-2760
Web site: www.cattco.org

Chair, County Legislature (R):
    Norman L. Marsh 716-938-6620/fax: 716-938-9698
Vice Chairman (R):
    Michael T O'Brien.............................716-938-9111 x2386
Majority Leader (R):
    James J Snyder...............................716-938-9111 x2333
Minority Leader (D):
    Linda Witte.................................716-938-9111 x2397
County Administrator & Clerk, Legislature:
    Jack Searles 716-938-9111 x2577/fax: 716-938-9306
    e-mail: jrsearles@cattco.org
County Clerk:
    James Griffith 716-938-2297/fax: 716-938-6009
    e-mail: jkgriffith@cattco.org
County Attorney:
    Thomas C. Brady..................716-938-2931/fax: 716-938-2763
District Attorney:
    Lori Pettit Rieman 716-938-2220/fax: 716-938-2763
Sheriff:
    Dennis B John 716-938-9111 x2204/fax: 716-938-6420
    e-mail: dbjohn@cattco.org
Treasurer:
    Joseph Keller.....................716-373-2290/fax: 716-938-2762
    e-mail: jgkeller@cattco.org
Public Defender:
    Mark S Williams.................716-373-0004 x11/fax: 716-373-3462
    e-mail: mswilliams@cattco.org
County Historian:
    Sharon Fellows 716-353-8200 x4721
    e-mail: scfellows@cattco.org

Cayuga County

160 Genesee St
Auburn, NY 13021
315-253-1525 Fax: 315-253-1586
Web site: www.cayugacounty.us

Chairman, County Legislature (R):
    Peter A Tortorici...............................315-253-1273
    e-mail: chairman@co.cayuga.ny.us
Clerk, Legislature:
    Sheila Smith 315-253-1498
    e-mail: lclerk@cayugacounty.us
County Manager:
    Wayne D Allen...................................315-253-1525
    e-mail: wallen@cayugacounty.us
County Clerk:
    Susan M Dwyer....................................315-253-1271
    e-mail: sdwyer@cayugacounty.us
County Attorney:
    Fredrick Westphal.................................315-253-1274
    e-mail: coatty@cayugacounty.us

District Attorney:
    Jon E Budelmann 315-253-1391
    e-mail: cayugada@cayugacounty.us
Director, Planning & Economic Development:
    Steve Lynch 315-253-1276
    e-mail: planning@cayugacounty.us
Emergency Management Director:
    Brian P Dahl 315-255-1161
    e-mail: ccoes@cayugacounty.us
Sheriff:
    David S Gould 315-253-1222
    e-mail: sheriff@cayugacounty.us
Treasurer:
    Jim H Orman.......................................315-253-1211
    e-mail: treasurer@cayugacounty.us
County Historian:
    Linda Frank.......................................315-253-1300
    e-mail: historian@cayugacounty.us

Chautauqua County

3 N Erie St
Mayville, NY 14757-1007
716-753-4241 Fax: 716-753-4756
Web site: www.co.chautauqua.ny.us

Majority Leader (D):
    Maria Kindberg.....................................716-753-4215
    e-mail: chuckcornell@hotmail.com
Gould, III:
    Frank Jay""..................Chairman, City Legis or 716-753-4215
Clerk, Legislature:
    Janet M. Jankowski.................................716-753-4215
    e-mail: cafliscj@co.chautauqua.ny.us
County Executive:
    Gregory J Edwards 716-753-4211
    e-mail: edwardsg@co.chautauqua.ny.us
County Clerk:
    Sandra K Sopak..................716-753-4331/fax: 716-753-4293
District Attorney:
    David Foley..716-753-4241
Public Defender:
    Nathaniel L. Barone, II.............................716-753-4376
Director, Emergency Services:
    Julius Leone 716-753-4341
Sheriff:
    Joseph A Gerace....................................716-753-2131
Finance Director:
    Susan Marsh 716-753-4223

Chemung County

John H Hazlett Bldg, 203 Lake St
PO Box 588
Elmira, NY 14902-0588
607-737-2912 Fax: 607-737-0351
e-mail: info@chemungcounty.com
Web site: www.chemungcounty.com

Chairman, County Legislature (R):
    Donna Draxler................607-737-2066/fax: 607-737-2851
    e-mail: cmilliken@co.chemung.ny.us
Majority Leader (R):
    Sidney S Graubard..................607-737-2066/fax: 607-737-2851
Minority Leader (D):
    Theodore A Bennett 607-737-2066/fax: 607-737-2851
    e-mail: ted.benn@verizon.net
Clerk, Legislature:
    Linda D Palmer 607-737-2066/fax: 607-737-2851
    e-mail: lpalmer@co.chemung.ny.us

Offices and agencies generally appear in alphabetical order, except when specific order is requested by listee.

County Executive:
  Thomas J Santulli 607-737-2912/fax: 607-737-0351
  e-mail: tsantulli@co.chemung.ny.us
County Clerk:
  Catherine K Hughes 607-737-2920/fax: 607-737-2897
  e-mail: chughes@co.chemung.ny.us
District Attorney:
  Weeden A Wetmore 607-737-2944/fax: 607-737-2965
  e-mail: wwetmore@co.chemung.ny.us
Public Defender:
  Scott N Fierro .607-737-2969/fax: 607-737-2853
Sheriff:
  Christopher J Moss 607-737-2987/fax: 607-737-2930
  e-mail: cmoss@co.chemung.ny.us

Chenango County
County Office Bldg
5 Court St
Norwich, NY 13815
607-337-1700 Fax: 607-334-8768
Web site: www.co.chenango.ny.us

Chairman, Board of Supervisors (R):
  Lawrence N Wilcox 607-337-1401
Clerk, Board of Supervisors:
  R C Woodford. 607-337-1430
County Clerk:
  Mary C Weidman 607-337-1450
Sheriff:
  Ernest R Cutting Jr 607-334-2000
Treasurer:
  William E Evans. 607-337-1414
Director, Public Works:
  Shawn Fry P.E., L.S.. 607-337-1710
County Historian:
  Patricia E. Evans. 607-337-1845

Clinton County
County Government Ctr
137 Margaret St, Ste 208
Plattsburgh, NY 12901
518-565-4600 Fax: 518-565-4616
e-mail: legislature@co.clinton.ny.us
Web site: www.clintoncountygov.com

Chairman (R):
  James R Langley, Jr. 518-643-9052/fax: 518-643-6640
  e-mail: langleyins@charter.net
Majority Leader (R):
  Samuel J Trombley 518-597-7742/fax: 518-594-7742
  e-mail: trombleyma@aol.com
Minority Leader (D):
  Dr John Gallagher. 518-561-0484
  e-mail: vze3gnnn@verizon.net
Clerk, Board of Legislators & County Administrator:
  Michael E Zurlo 518-565-4600/fax: 518-565-4616
  e-mail: legislature@co.clinton.ny.us
County Clerk:
  John H Zurlo 518-565-4700/fax: 518-565-4718
County Attorney:
  William Favreau 518-561-4400/fax: 518-561-4848
District Attorney:
  Andrew J Wylie. 518-565-4770/fax: 518-565-4777
  e-mail: da@co.clinton.ny.us
Director, Emergency Services:
  Eric Day. 518-565-4791/fax: 518-566-1202
  e-mail: e911@co.clinton.ny.us
Sheriff:
  David N Favro .518-565-4300/fax: 518-565-4333
  e-mail: sheriff@co.clinton.ny.us

Treasurer:
  Joseph W Giroux 518-565-4730/fax: 518-565-4516
  e-mail: treasurer@co.clinton.ny.us

Columbia County
401 State St
Hudson, NY 12534
518-828-1527 Fax: 518-822-0684
e-mail: dicosmo@govt.co.columbia.ny.us
Web site: www.columbiacountyny.com

Chairman, Board of Supervisors (R):
  Patrick M Gratton 518-828-1527/fax: 518-828-0684
  e-mail: pat.gratton@govt.co.columbia.ny.us
County Clerk:
  Holly C Tanner 518-828-3339/fax: 518-828-5299
  e-mail: htanner@govt.co.columbia.ny.us
County Attorney:
  Robert J Fitzsimmons 518-828-3303/fax: 518-828-9535
District Attorney:
  Paul Czajka 518-828-3414
Public Defender:
  Robert W. Linville. 518-828-3410/fax: 518-828-4076
Sheriff:
  David W Harrison Jr 518-828-0601/fax: 518-828-9088
Fire Coordinator:
  John Howe. 518-822-8610/fax: 518-828-1279
Director, Emergency Management:
  William Black .518-828-1212/fax: 518-828-1279
Treasurer:
  PJ Keeler 518-828-0513/fax: 518-822-1110
County Historian:
  Mary Howell 518-828-3442/fax: 518-828-2969
  e-mail: mhowell@govt.co.columbia.ny.us

Cortland County
County Office Bldg
60 Central Ave
Cortland, NY 13045
607-753-5048 Fax: 607-756-3492
Web site: www.cortland-co.org

Chairperson, County Legislature (D):
  Mike Park 607-753-5048
  e-mail: rjwilliams@cortland-co.org
Clerk, Legislature:
  Jeremy Boylan. 607-753-5049/fax: 607-756-3492
  e-mail: jboylan@cortland-co.org
County Clerk:
  Elizabeth P Larkin 607-753-5021
  e-mail: elarkin@cortland-co.org
County Attorney:
  Edward Purser. 607-753-5095
  e-mail: epurser@cortland-co.org
District Attorney:
  Mark Suben. 607-753-5008
Public Defender:
  Edward Goehler. 607-753-5046/fax: 607-753-0781
  e-mail: publicdefender@cortland-co.org
Sheriff:
  Lee A Price 607-753-5006
  e-mail: lprice@cortland-co.org
Fire/Emergency Management Coordinator:
  Scott Roman 607-753-5064/fax: 607-756-8457
  e-mail: grduell@cortland-co.org
Treasurer:
  Cynthia Monroe. 607-753-5070/fax: 607-758-5512
  e-mail: pomara@cortland-co.org

Offices and agencies generally appear in alphabetical order, except when specific order is requested by listee.

County Historian:
  Jeremy Boylan 607-753-5360
  e-mail: jboylan@cortland-co.org

Delaware County

County Office Bldg
111 Main St
Delhi, NY 13753
607-746-2603 Fax: 607-746-7012
Web site: www.co.delaware.ny.us

Chairman, Board of Supervisors (R):
  James E Eisel, Sr. 607-652-4350
Vice Chairman, Board of Supervisors (R):
  Tina Mole 607-832-4312
Clerk, Board of Supervisors:
  Christa M Schafer 607-832-5110/fax: 607-832-5111
  e-mail: cob@co.delaware.ny.us
County Clerk:
  Sharon O'Dell 607-746-2123
County Attorney:
  Richard B Spinney 607-652-3443/fax: 607-652-3334
District Attorney:
  Richard D Northrup, Jr 607-746-3557/fax: 607-746-2297
Sheriff:
  Thomas E Mills 607-746-2336/fax: 607-746-8151
County Treasurer:
  Beverly J Shields 607-832-5070/fax: 607-832-5077
  e-mail: treas@co.delaware.ny.us
Director, Emergency Services:
  Richard Bell 607-746-9600
Commissioner, Public Works:
  Wayne Reynolds 607-746-2128
County Historian:
  Gabrielle Price 607-746-8660
  e-mail: hist@co.delaware.ny.us

Dutchess County

County Office Bldg
22 Market St, 6th Fl
Poughkeepsie, NY 12601
845-486-2100 Fax: 845-486-2113
e-mail: internetsupport1@co.dutchess.ny.us
Web site: www.dutchessny.gov

Chairman, County Legislature (R):
  Robert Rolison 845-486-2100/fax: 845-486-2113
Majority Leader (D):
  Sandra Goldberg 845-297-76770
Minority Leader (R):
  Gary Cooper 845-297-8757/fax: 845-486-2113
County Executive:
  Marcus J. Molinaro 845-486-2000/fax: 845-486-2021
  e-mail: countyexec@co.dutchess.ny.us
Clerk, Legislature:
  Carolyn Morris 845-486-2100/fax: 845-486-2113
  e-mail: countylegislature@co.dutchess.ny.us
County Clerk:
  Bradford Kendall 845-486-2120/fax: 845-486-2138
County Attorney:
  James M Fedorchak 845-486-2110/fax: 845-486-2002
  e-mail: countyattorney@co.dutchess.ny.us
District Attorney:
  William V Grady 845-486-2300/fax: 845-486-2324
Public Defender (Acting):
  Thomas Angell 845-486-2280/fax: 845-486-2266
  e-mail: publicdefender@co.dutchess.ny.us
Sheriff:
  Adrian H Anderson 845-486-3800
  e-mail: sheriff@co.dutchess.ny.us

Comptroller:
  Jim Coughlan 845-486-2050/fax: 845-486-2055
  e-mail: comptroller@co.dutchess.ny.us
Finance Commissioner:
  Pamela Barrack 845-486-2025/fax: 845-486-2198
  e-mail: rptaxfinance@co.dutchess.ny.us
Emergency Response Coordinator:
  Dana Smith 845-486-2080/fax: 845-486-3998
  e-mail: response911@co.dutchess.ny.us
County Historian:
  William P. Tatum, III 845-486-2381
  e-mail: dchistory@co.dutchess.ny.us

Erie County

County Office Bldg
95 Franklin St
16th Fl
Buffalo, NY 14202
716-858-7500 Fax: 716-858-8895
e-mail: public_feedback@erie.gov
Web site: www2.erie.gov

Chair, County Legislature (D):
  Betty Jean Grant 716-894-0914/fax: 716-896-1463
  e-mail: bjg@erie.gov
Majority Leader, County Legislature (D):
  Thomas J. Mazur 716-893-4385/fax: 716-894-4539
  e-mail: mazurt@erie.gov
Minority Leader, County Legislature (R):
  John J Mills 716-858-8850/fax: 716-858-8818
  e-mail: jmills13@erie.gov
Clerk, Legislature:
  Robert M Graber 716-858-7500/fax: 716-858-8895
County Executive:
  Mark C Poloncarz 716-858-8500
County Clerk:
  Christopher L Jacobs 716-858-8785/fax: 716-858-6550
  e-mail: eriecountyclerk@erie.gov
District Attorney:
  Frank A Sedita III 716-858-2400/fax: 716-858-7425
Sheriff:
  Timothy B Howard 716-585-7618
Civil Defense/Disaster Preparedness Deputy Commissioner:
  Dean Messing .716-858-8477/fax: 716-858-7937
  e-mail: messingd@erie.gov
Comptroller:
  Stefan I. Mychajliw 716-858-8400/fax: 716-858-8507

Essex County

County Government Ctr
7551 Court St
PO Box 217
Elizabethtown, NY 12932
518-873-3350 Fax: 518-873-3356
Web site: www.co.essex.ny.us

Chairman, Board of Supervisors (D):
  Randall T Douglas
Vice Chairman, Board of Supervisors (R):
  Robert T Politi
  e-mail: super@northelba.org
Clerk, Board of Supervisors:
  Judith A. Garrison 518-873-3353/fax: 518-873-3356
  e-mail: dpalmer@co.essex.ny.us
County Manager:
  Daniel Palmer .518-873-3333/fax: 518-873-3339
  e-mail: danp@co.essex.ny.us

Offices and agencies generally appear in alphabetical order, except when specific order is requested by listee.

County Clerk:
Joseph A Provoncha 518-873-3601/fax: 518-873-3548
e-mail: jprovon@co.essex.ny.us
County Attorney:
Daniel Manning III 518-873-3380/fax: 518-873-3894
e-mail: dmanning@co.essex.ny.us
District Attorney:
Kristy Sprague. 518-873-3335/fax: 518-873-3788
e-mail: ksprague@co.essex.ny.us
Public Defender:
Brandon E Boutelle 518-873-3880/fax: 518-873-3888
Sheriff:
Richard C Cutting 518-873-6902/fax: 518-873-6949
Director, Emergency Services:
Donald Jaquish 518-873-3900/fax: 518-873-3963
e-mail: wwade@co.essex.ny.us
Treasurer:
Michael G Diskin 518-873-3317/fax: 518-873-3318
e-mail: mdiskin@co.essex.ny.us

Franklin County

Courthouse
355 W Main St
Malone, NY 12953
518-481-1641 or 800-397-8686 Fax: 518-483-0141
Web site: www.franklincony.org

Chairman, County Legislature (D):
D. Billy Jones. 518-353-1204/fax: 518-481-1639
Vice Chairman, County Legislature (D):
Gordan Crossman 518-483-5634/fax: 518-481-1639
Majority Leader, County Legislature (D):
Guy Smith 518-358-2592/fax: 518-481-1639
Minority Leader, County Legislature (R):
Paul A Maroun 518-359-3066/fax: 518-481-1639
e-mail: wawbeek@aol.com
Clerk, Legislature:
Gloria Valone 518-481-1640/fax: 518-481-1639
County Manager:
Thomas Leitz 518-481-1693
e-mail: jfeeley@co.franklin.ny.us
County Clerk:
Wanda D Murtagh 518-481-1681/fax: 518-483-9143
e-mail: wmurtagh@co.franklin.ny.us
County Attorney:
Jonathan J Miller 518-483-8400/fax: 518-483-2054
District Attorney:
Derek P Champagne 518-481-1544/fax: 518-481-1545
e-mail: da@co.franklin.ny.us
Public Defender:
Thomas G Soucia 518-481-1624
Sheriff:
Kevin Mulverhill. 518-483-3304
e-mail: jpelkey@co.franklin.ny.us
Director, Emergency Services:
Ricky Provost 518-483-2580
e-mail: rprovost@co.franklin.ny.us
Treasurer:
Byron A Varin. 518-481-1513/fax: 518-483-2326
e-mail: bvarin@co.franklin.ny.us
Conflict Defender:
Lorellei Miller. 518-481-1593
Assigned Counsel Coordinator:
Jill Dyer. 518-481-1423

Fulton County

County Office Bldg
223 W Main St
Johnstown, NY 12095

518-736-5540 Fax: 518-762-0224
e-mail: fultbos@co.fulton.ny.us
Web site: www.fultoncountyny.gov

Chairman, Board of Supervisors:
WIlliam H. Waldron. 518-736-5540
County Clerk:
William E Eschler 518-736-5555/fax: 518-762-9214
District Attorney:
Louise K. Sira 518-736-5511/fax: 518-762-2042
Public Defender:
J Gerard McAuliffe, Jr. 518-736-5820/fax: 518-762-0122
Sheriff:
Thomas J Lorey. 518-736-2100/fax: 518-736-2126
Treasurer:
Edgar T Blodgett 518-736-5580/fax: 518-736-1794
Fire Coordinator & Director, Civil Defense:
Allan Polmateer. 518-736-5858/fax: 518-762-4938
County Historian:
Peter Betz 518-736-5667

Genesee County

Old Courthouse, 7 Main Street
Batavia, NY 14020
585-344-2550 Fax: 585-344-8582
e-mail: legis@co.genesee.ny.us
Web site: www.co.genesee.ny.us

County Manager:
Jay Gsell 585-344-2550 x2204/fax: 585-344-8582
e-mail: comanager@co.genesee.ny.us
District Attorney:
Lawrence Friedman 585-344-2550 x2250/fax: 585-344-8544
Public Defender:
Gary Horton 585-344-2550 x2280/fax: 716-344-8553
e-mail: publicdefender@co.genesee.ny.us
Sheriff:
Gary T Maha. 585-345-3000
e-mail: sheriff@co.genesee.ny.us
Treasurer:
Scott D German 585-344-2550 x2210
e-mail: treas@co.genesee.ny.us
County Historian:
Susan L Conklin 585-344-2550 x2613
e-mail: history@co.genesee.ny.us

Greene County

411 Main St, 4th Fl
PO Box 467
Catskill, NY 12414
518-719-3270 Fax: 518-719-3793
e-mail: countyadministrator@discovergreene.com
Web site: www.greenegovernment.com

Chairman, County Legislature (R):
Wayne Speenburgh 518-929-1200/fax: 518-719-3793
e-mail: legislative@discovergreene.com
County Administrator (Acting):
Shaun S Groden. 518-719-3270/fax: 518-719-3793
e-mail: countyadministrator@discovergreene.com
County Clerk:
Michael Flynn 518-719-3255/fax: 518-719-3284
e-mail: countyclerk@discovergreene.com
County Attorney:
Carol D Stevens. 518-719-3540/fax: 518-719-3790
e-mail: cstevens@discovergreene.com
District Attorney:
Terry J Wilhelm. 518-719-3590/fax: 518-719-3792
e-mail: twilhelm@discovergreene.com

Offices and agencies generally appear in alphabetical order, except when specific order is requested by listee.

Public Defender:
  Angelo F. Scaturro 518-719-3220/fax: 518-719-3785
  e-mail: publicdefender@discovergreene.com
Sheriff:
  Gregory R Seeley 518-943-3300/fax: 518-943-6832
  e-mail: sheriff@discovergreene.com
Director, Emergency Services:
  John P Farrell Jr.................518-622-3643/fax: 518-622-0572
  e-mail: emergency@discovergreene.com
Treasurer:
  Peter Markov....................................518-719-3530
  e-mail: wvermilyea@discovergreene.com

Hamilton County
County Courthouse, Rte 8
PO Box 205
Lake Pleasant, NY 12108
518-548-6651 Fax: 518-548-7608
e-mail: hamcosup@klink.net
Web site: www.hamiltoncounty.com

Chairman, Board of Supervisors (R):
  William G Farber 518-548-6385
  e-mail: chairman@hamiltoncountyny.gov
Deputy Chairman, Board of Supervisors:
  Brian Towers...........................518-548-6385
  e-mail: inletsupervisor@eagle-wireless.com
Clerk, Board of Supervisors:
  Laura A Abrams 518-548-6651/fax: 518-548-7608
  e-mail: clerkofboard@hamiltoncountyny.gov
County Clerk:
  Jane S. Zarecki...............518-548-7111/fax: 518-548-9740
County Attorney:
  Charles Getty Jr...............315-336-3900/fax: 315-336-3902
  e-mail: cgetty@gettylaw.com
District Attorney:
  Marsha Purdue....................518-648-5113/fax: 518-648-5724
  e-mail: districtattorney@hamiltoncountyny.gov
Sheriff:
  Karl G Abrams.................518-548-3113/fax: 518-548-5704
  e-mail: sheriff@hamiltoncountyny.gov
Treasurer:
  Beth Hunt......................518-548-7911/fax: 518-548-4519
  e-mail: treasurer@hamiltoncountyny.gov

Herkimer County
109 Mary St, Ste 1204
Herkimer, NY 13350
315-867-1108 Fax: 315-867-1109
e-mail: hclegislature@herkimercounty.org
Web site: herkimercounty.org

Chairman, County Legislature (R):
  Vincent Bono...................315-867-1108/fax: 315-867-1109
Majority Leader (R):
  Patrick E Russell 315-867-1108/fax: 315-867-1109
Minority Leader (D):
  John L Brezinski 315-867-1108/fax: 315-867-1109
Clerk, Legislature:
  Carole L LaLonde 315-867-1108/fax: 315-867-1109
County Administrator:
  James W Wallace, Jr...........315-867-1112/fax: 315-867-1109
County Clerk:
  Sylvia M Rowan 315-867-1129
District Attorney:
  John H Crandall................315-867-1155/fax: 315-867-1348
Sheriff:
  Christopher P Farber 315-867-1167/fax: 315-867-1354

Director, Emergency Management:
  Robert Vandawalker 315-867-1212/fax: 315-867-5873
  e-mail: rvandawalker@herkimercounty.org
Treasurer:
  Kim Enea......................315-867-1145/fax: 315-867-1315
  e-mail: kenea@herkimercounty.org

Jefferson County
County Office Bldg
175 Arsenal St
Watertown, NY 13601
315-785-3075 Fax: 315-785-5070
Web site: www.co.jefferson.ny.us

Chairwoman, Board of Legislators (R):
  Carolyn D Fitzpatrick 315-785-3075
  e-mail: carolynf@co.jefferson.ny.us
County Administrator/Budget Officer & Clerk, Board:
  Robert F Hagemann, III..........315-785-3075/fax: 315-785-5070
Deputy County Administrator:
  Michael E Kaskan 315-785-3075/fax: 315-785-5070
County Clerk:
  Cheryl D Lane 315-785-3081/fax: 315-785-5145
County Attorney:
  David J Paulsen...............315-785-3088/fax: 315-785-5178
District Attorney:
  Cindy Intschert 315-785-3053/fax: 315-785-3371
Public Defender:
  Julie Hutchins 315-785-3152/fax: 315-785-5060
  e-mail: joannem@co.jefferson.ny.us
Sheriff:
  John P Burns
Director, Fire & Emergency Management (Acting):
  Joseph D Plummer 315-786-2654
Treasurer:
  Karen Christie 315-785-3055/fax: 315-785-7589

Kings County (NYC Borough of Brooklyn)
209 Joralemon St
Brooklyn, NY 11201
718-802-3700
Web site: www.brooklyn-usa.org

Borough President (D):
  Marty Markowitz 718-802-3700
  e-mail: askmarty@brooklynbp.nyc.gov
Deputy Borough President:
  Sandra Chapman................................718-802-3884
  e-mail: ygraham@brooklynbp.nyc.gov
County Clerk:
  Nancy T Sunshine..............................347-404-9772
District Attorney:
  Charles J Hynes 718-250-2000
  e-mail: schmj@brroklynda.org

Lewis County
Courthouse
7660 N State St
Lowville, NY 13367
315-377-2000 Fax: 315-376-5445
e-mail: it@lewiscountyny.org
Web site: www.lewiscountyny.org

Clerk, Board of Legislature:
  Terry Clark 315-376-5355/fax: 315-376-5445
  e-mail: legislature@lewiscountyny.org
County Clerk:
  Douglas P Hanno................315-376-5333/fax: 315-376-3768
  e-mail: clerk@lewiscountyny.org

Offices and agencies generally appear in alphabetical order, except when specific order is requested by listee.

County Attorney:
　　Richard Graham...................315-376-5282/fax: 315-376-3857
　　e-mail: rgraham@lewiscountyny.org
District Attorney:
　　Leanne Moser 315-376-5390/fax: 315-376-5873
　　e-mail: lmoser@lewiscountyny.org
Public Defender:
　　Lewis Defenders PLLC.............315-376-7543/fax: 315-376-8766
Sheriff:
　　Michael Carpinelli.................315-376-3511/fax: 315-376-5232
　　e-mail: LCSD@lewiscountyny.org
Treasurer:
　　Patricia O'Brien...................315-376-5325/fax: 315-376-8552
　　e-mail: treasurer@lewiscountyny.org
County Manager:
　　David Pendergast..................315-376-5354/fax: 315-376-5445
　　e-mail: county.manager@lewiscountyny.org
Fire & Emergency Management:
　　James Martin.....................315-376-5305/fax: 315-376-5293
County Historian:
　　Lewis County Historical Society 315-376-2825

Livingston County
Government Center
6 Court St, Rm 302
Geneseo, NY 14454
585-243-7030 Fax: 585-335-1701
e-mail: vamico@co.livingston.ny.us
Web site: www.co.livingston.state.ny.us

Chairman, Board of Supervisors (R):
　　James C Merrick.....................................585-243-7030
Vice Chairman, Board of Supervisors (R):
　　Gary D Moore.......................................585-243-7030
Clerk, Board of Supervisors:
　　Virginia O Amico....................................585-243-7030
　　e-mail: vamico@co.livingston.ny.us
County Administrator:
　　Ian M Coyle 585-243-7040
　　e-mail: icoyle@co.livingston.ny.us
County Clerk:
　　James A Culbertson 585-243-7010
　　e-mail: jculbertson@co.livingston.ny.us
County Attorney:
　　David J Morris 585-243-7033
　　e-mail: dmorris@co.livingston.ny.us
District Attorney:
　　Gregory J. McCaffrey................................585-243-7020
Public Defender:
　　Marcea Clark Tetamore.............585-243-7028/fax: 585-243-7193
　　e-mail: lcpd@co.livingston.ny.us
Emergency Management Services:
　　Kevin Niedermaier 585-243-7160
　　e-mail: kniedermaier@co.livingston.ny.us
Sheriff:
　　John M York 585-243-7120/fax: 585-243-7104
　　e-mail: lcso@co.livingston.ny.us
Treasurer:
　　Carolyn D Taylor..................585-243-7050/fax: 585-243-7597
　　e-mail: ctaylor@co.livingston.ny.us
Historian:
　　Amie Alden 585-243-7955/fax: 585-243-7956
　　e-mail: historian@co.livingston.ny.us

Madison County
County Office Bldg
138 N Court St
PO Box 635
Wampsville, NY 13163

315-366-2201 Fax: 315-366-2502
e-mail: supervisors@co.madison.ny.us
Web site: www.madisoncounty.gov

Chairman, Board of Supervisors (R):
　　John M Becker....................315-366-2201/fax: 315-366-2502
Clerk, Board of Supervisors:
　　Cindy Urtz......................315-366-2201/fax: 315-366-2502
County Clerk:
　　Kenneth J Kunkel Jr 315-366-2261
County Attorney:
　　S John Campanie..................315-366-2203/fax: 315-366-2502
District Attorney:
　　William G Gabor..................315-366-2236/fax: 315-366-2503
Public Defender Director:
　　Paul H Hadley 315-366-2585/fax: 315-366-2583
Fire Coordinator/Emergency Preparedness:
　　Joe DeFrancisco...................315-366-2258/fax: 315-366-2452
Sheriff:
　　Allen Riley.....................315-366-2318/fax: 315-366-2286
Treasurer:
　　Cindy Edick......................315-366-2371/fax: 315-366-2705
Public Information Officer:
　　Sharon A Driscoll................................315-366-2788

Monroe County
County Office Bldg
39 W Main St
Rochester, NY 14614
585-753-1950 Fax: 585-753-1932
Web site: www.monroecounty.gov

President, County Legislature (R):
　　Jeffrey R Adair 585-753-1950/fax: 585-753-1932
Majority Leader (R):
　　William W. Napier 585-753-1922/fax: 585-753-1960
Minority Leader (D):
　　Joe Rittler.......................585-753-1941/fax: 585-753-1946
Clerk, Legislature:
　　Cheryl Rozzi.......................................585-753-1950
　　e-mail: crozzi@monroecounty.gov
County Executive:
　　Maggie Brooks 585-753-1000/fax: 585-753-1014
　　e-mail: countyexecutive@monroecounty.gov
County Clerk:
　　Cheryl Dinolfo....................585-753-1600/fax: 585-753-1624
　　e-mail: mcclerk@monroecounty.gov
District Attorney:
　　Sandra Doorley 585-753-4500/fax: 585-753-4576
　　e-mail: districtattorney@monroecounty.gov
Sheriff:
　　Patrick M O'Flynn.................585-753-4178/fax: 585-753-4524
　　e-mail: sheriff@monroecountysheriff.info
Public Defender:
　　Tim Donaher......................585-753-4210/fax: 585-753-4234
　　e-mail: mcpublicdefender@monroecounty.gov
Chief Financial Officer:
　　Robert Franklin 585-753-1157/fax: 585-753-1133
　　e-mail: mcfinance@monroecounty.gov
Director, Communications:
　　Justin Feasel......................585-753-1080/fax: 585-753-1068
　　e-mail: communications@monroecounty.gov
County Historian:
　　Carolyn Vacca....................585-385-8244/fax: 585-428-8353

Montgomery County
County Annex Bldg
PO Box 1500
Fonda, NY 12068-1500

Offices and agencies generally appear in alphabetical order, except when specific order is requested by listee.

518-853-4304 Fax: 518-853-8220
Web site: www.co.montgomery.ny.us

Chairman, Board of Supervisors:
    John W. Thayer 518-853-4304/fax: 518-853-8220
Clerk, Board of Supervisors:
    Robin Loske. 518-853-4304/fax: 518-853-8220
County Clerk:
    Helen A Bartone 518-853-8111/fax: 518-853-8171
County Attorney:
    Douglas E Landon. 518-843-1300/fax: 518-842-5331
District Attorney:
    James E Conboy 518-853-8250/fax: 518-853-8212
Public Defender:
    William Martuscello 518-853-8305/fax: 518-853-8308
Sheriff:
    Michael J Amato 518-853-5500/fax: 518-853-4096
Director, Emergency Management/Fire Coordinator:
    Adam Schwabrow 518-853-4011/fax: 518-853-4714
Treasurer:
    Shawn J Bowerman. 518-853-8175/fax: 518-853-8344
County Historian:
    Kelly A. Farquhar 518-853-8187/fax: 518-853-8392

Nassau County
1550 Franklin Avenue
Mineola, NY 11501
516-571-3000 or 516-571-6200 Fax: 516-739-2636
Web site: www.nassaucountyny.gov

Presiding Officer of the Legislature (D):
    Peter J Schmitt 516-571-6212
Deputy Presiding Officer of the Legislature (R):
    John J Ciotti 516-571-6203
Minority Leader (R):
    Diane Yatauro 516-571-6218/fax: 516-571-6158
Clerk, Legislature:
    William J Muller. 516-571-4252
County Executive:
    Edward P Mangano. 516-571-3131
County Clerk:
    Maureen O'Connell 516-571-2664
County Attorney:
    John Ciampoli. 516-571-3056
District Attorney:
    Kathleen M Rice 516-571-3800
    e-mail: nassauda@nassauda.org
Emergency Management Commissioner:
    James J Callahan II 516-573-0636
Police Commissioner:
    Thomas V. Dale 516-573-8800
Comptroller:
    George Maragos 516-571-2386
    e-mail: nccomptroller@nassaucountyny.gov
Treasurer:
    John A Mastromarino. 516-571-2090

New York County (NYC Borough of Manhattan)
Municipal Bldg
One Centre St, 19th Fl
New York, NY 10007
212-669-8300 Fax: 212-669-4305
Web site: www.mbpo.org

Borough President:
    Scott M Stringer 212-669-8300
    e-mail: bp@manhattanbp.org
County Clerk:
    Norman Goodman. 646-386-5955

District Attorney:
    Cyrus Vance, Jr. 212-335-9000
Public Advocate:
    Betsy Gotbaum 212-669-7200/fax: 212-669-4091

Niagara County
County Courthouse
175 Hawley Street
1st Floor
Lockport, NY 14094
716-439-7000 Fax: 716-439-7124
Web site: www.niagaracounty.com

Chairman, County Legislature (R):
    William L Ross. 716-731-5949
    e-mail: william.ross@niagaracounty.com
Majority Leader (R):
    Richard Updegrove. .716-434-2140
    e-mail: richard.updegrove@niagaracounty.com
Minority Leader (D):
    Dennis F Virtuoso. 716-284-1582
    e-mail: dennis.virtuoso@niagaracounty.com
Clerk, Legislature:
    Mary Jo Tamburlin 716-439-7177/fax: 716-439-7124
County Manager:
    Jeffrey M Glatz 716-439-7006/fax: 716-439-7212
    e-mail: jeff.glatz@niagaracounty.com
County Clerk:
    Wayne F Jagow. 716-439-7022/fax: 716-439-7035
    e-mail: niagaracountyclerk@niagaracounty.com
County Attorney:
    Claude A Joerg 716-439-7105/fax: 716-439-7114
    e-mail: claude.joerg@niagaracounty.com
District Attorney:
    Michael J Violante. 716-439-7085/fax: 716-439-7102
    e-mail: ncda@niagaracounty.com
Public Defender:
    David J Farrugia 716-439-7071
Sheriff:
    James R Voutour 716-438-3393/fax: 716-438-3357
Emergency Services, Acting Director:
    John F Cecula III
    fax: 716-438-3173
Treasurer:
    Kyle R Andrews 716-439-7018/fax: 716-439-7021

Oneida County
County Office Bldg
800 Park Ave
Utica, NY 13501
315-798-5900 Fax: 315-798-5924
e-mail: bol@co.oneida.ny.us or bol@ocgov.net
Web site: www.co.oneida.ny.us or www.ocgov.net

Chairman, County Legislature (R):
    Gerald J Fiorini. 315-798-5900
    e-mail: gfiorini@ocgov.net
Majority Leader (R):
    David J Wood. 315-337-1989
    e-mail: dwood@ocgov.net
Minority Leader (D):
    Patricia A Hudak. 315-339-9960
    e-mail: phudak@ocgov.net
County Executive:
    Anthony J Picente Jr 315-798-5800/fax: 315-798-2390
    e-mail: ce@ocgov.net
County Clerk:
    Sandra J DePerno 315-798-5794
    e-mail: countyclerk@ocgov.net

Offices and agencies generally appear in alphabetical order, except when specific order is requested by listee.

County Attorney:
  Gregory J. Amoroso, Esq. 315-798-5910/fax: 315-798-5603
  e-mail: countyattorney@ocgov.net
District Attorney:
  Scott D McNamara 315-798-5766/fax: 315-798-5582
  e-mail: smcnamara@ocgov.net
Public Defender-Criminal Division:
  Frank J Nebush Jr 315-798-5870/fax: 315-734-0364
  e-mail: pubdef@ocgov.net
Public Defender-Civil Division:
  Frank J Furno 315-266-6100/fax: 315-266-6105
  e-mail: pdcivil@ocgov.net
Sheriff:
  Rob M. Maciol. 315-738-7804/fax: 315-765-2205
Finance Commissioner:
  Anthony R Carvelli 315-798-5750

Onondaga County

401 Montgomery Street
Room 407
Syracuse, NY 13202
315-435-2070 Fax: 315-435-8434
Web site: www.ongov.net

Chairman, County Legislature (R):
  J. Ryan McMahon II 315-435-2070/fax: 315-435-8434
County Executive:
  Joanne M Mahoney 315-435-3516/fax: 315-435-8582
Clerk, Legislature:
  Deborah L Maturo 315-435-2070/fax: 315-435-8434
  e-mail: debbiematuro@ongov.net
County Clerk:
  Sandra A. Schepp 315-435-2227/fax: 315-435-2229
County Attorney:
  Gordon J Cuffy
District Attorney:
  William J Fitzpatrick. 315-435-2470
Emergency Management Director:
  Peter P Alberti 315-435-2525/fax: 315-435-3309
  e-mail: emweb01@ongov.net
Sheriff:
  Kevin E Walsh 315-435-3044
Commissioner:
  Kevin Wisely 315-435-3044
Comptroller:
  Robert E Antonacci 315-435-2130/fax: 315-435-2250
  e-mail: bobantonacci@ongov.net
Chief Fiscal Officer:
  Steven Morgan. 315-435-2426/fax: 315-435-2421

Ontario County

Ontario Co Municipal Bldg
20 Ontario St
1st Fl Mezzanine
Canandaigua, NY 14424
585-396-4447 Fax: 585-396-8818
e-mail: bos@co.ontario.ny.us
Web site: www.co.ontario.ny.us

Chairman, Board of Supervisors (R):
  Theodore Fafinski 585-396-4447/fax: 585-396-8818
Vice Chairman, Board of Supervisors (R):
  Wayne F Houseman 585-396-4447
Clerk, Board of Supervisors:
  Karen R DeMay. 585-396-4447/fax: 585-396-8818
  e-mail: karen.demay@co.ontario.ny.us
County Administrator:
  John E. Garvey 585-396-4400
  e-mail: county.administrator@co.ontario.ny.us

County Clerk:
  Matthew J. Hoose 585-396-4200
Human Resources Director:
  Mary A. Krause . . . . .585-396-4465 or 315-719-0321
District Attorney:
  R Michael Tantillo. 585-396-4010/fax: 585-396-4860
  e-mail: michael.tantillo@co.ontario.ny.us
Emergency Management Director:
  Jeffrey R Harloff 585-396-4310/fax: 585-396-4583
Public Works Commissioner:
  Bill Wright. .585-396-4000/fax: 585-396-4283

Orange County

County Government Center
255 Main St
Goshen, NY 10924
845-291-4800
e-mail: legislature@co.orange.ny.us
Web site: www.co.orange.ny.us

Chairman, County Legislature (R):
  Michael R Pillmeier 845-651-7415
Majority Leader (R):
  Melissa Bonacic 845-858-2546
Minority Leader (D):
  Jeffrey D Berkman 845-342-6813
County Executive:
  Edward A Diana 845-291-2700/fax: 845-291-2724
County Clerk:
  Donna L Benson 845-291-2690/fax: 845-291-2691
County Attorney:
  David L Darwin 845-291-3150
District Attorney:
  Francis D Phillips 845-291-2050
Emergency Services Commissioner:
  Walter C Koury. 845-615-0400
Sheriff:
  Carl E DuBois 845-291-4033/fax: 845-294-1590
Finance Commissioner:
  Joel Kleiman 845-291-2485/fax: 845-291-2516
Historian:
  Cornelia W. Bush 845-291-2388/fax: 845-291-2027

Orleans County

Courthouse Sq
3 South Main St
Albion, NY 14411-1495
585-589-7053 Fax: 585-589-1618
Web site: www.orleansny.com

Chairman, County Legislature (R):
  David Callard 585-589-7053
Vice Chairman (R):
  George Bower 585-589-7053
Clerk, Legislature:
  Nadine P Hanlon 585-589-7053/fax: 585-589-1618
  e-mail: hanlonn@orleansny.com
Chief Administrative Officer:
  Charles H Nesbitt Jr 585-589-7053/fax: 585-589-1618
  e-mail: cnesbitt@orleansny.com
County Clerk:
  Karen Lake-Maynard. 585-589-5334/fax: 585-589-0181
  e-mail: lakemaynardk@orleansny.com
County Attorney:
  David C Schubel 585-798-2250/fax: 585-798-0776
  e-mail: occoa@orleansny.com
District Attorney:
  Joseph V Cardone 585-590-4130/fax: 585-590-4129
  e-mail: da@orleansny.com

Offices and agencies generally appear in alphabetical order, except when specific order is requested by listee.

Public Defender:
  Sanford A Church 585-589-7335/fax: 585-589-2592
Emergency Management Director:
  Paul Wagner .585-589-4414/fax: 585-589-7671
  e-mail: pwagner@orleansny.com
Sheriff:
  Scott D Hess 585-590-4142/fax: 585-590-4178
  e-mail: ocsher@orleansny.com
Treasurer:
  Susan M Heard 585-589-5353/fax: 585-589-9220
  e-mail: sheard@orleansny.com
County Historian:
  C W Lattin. 585-589-4174

Oswego County
46 E Bridge St
Oswego, NY 13126
315-349-8230 Fax: 315-349-8237
Web site: www.co.oswego.ny.us

Chairman, County Legislature (R):
  Fred Beardsley. 315-349-8230/fax: 315-349-8237
Majority Leader (R):
  James Oldenburg. 315-343-3744/fax: 315-668-3638
Minority Leader (D):
  Michael Kunzwiler 315-343-8358
  e-mail: mikekunzwiler@twcny.rr.com
Clerk, Legislature:
  Wendy Falls. .315-349-8230/fax: 315-349-8237
  e-mail: tjerrett@oswegocounty.com
County Administrator:
  Philip R Church. 315-349-8235/fax: 315-349-8237
  e-mail: pchurch@oswegocounty.com
County Clerk:
  Michael C. Backus 315-349-8621/fax: 315-349-8383
  e-mail: williamsg@oswegocounty.com
County Attorney:
  Richard C Mitchell 315-349-8296
  e-mail: rich@oswegocounty.com
District Attorney/Coroner:
  Gregory S. Oakes. 315-349-3200/fax: 315-349-3212
  e-mail: doddd@oswegocounty.com
Treasurer:
  Fred Beardsley. 315-349-8393/fax: 315-349-8255
  e-mail: cwolford@oswegocounty.com
Sheriff:
  Reuel A Todd 315-349-3302/fax: 315-349-3303
  e-mail: mtodd@oswegocounty.com
Vice Chairman:
  Kevin Gardner 315-349-8230/fax: 315-349-8237
  e-mail: mtodd@oswegocounty.com

Otsego County
County Office Bldg
197 Main St
Cooperstown, NY 13326-1129
607-547-4202 Fax: 607-547-4260
e-mail: childl@otsegocounty.com
Web site: www.otsegocounty.com

Chairman, Board of Representatives (R):
  Kathleen Clark 607-988-7844
  e-mail: dubbenf@otsegocounty.com
Vice Chairman, Board of Representatives (R):
  James V Johnson. 607-547-2095
  e-mail: johnsonjv@otsegocounty.com
Clerk, Board of Representatives:
  Carol McGovern 607-547-4202/fax: 607-547-4260
  e-mail: mcgovern@otsegocounty.com

County Clerk:
  Kathy Sinnott Gardner. 607-547-4276/fax: 607-547-7544
  e-mail: gardnerk@otsegocounty.com
County Attorney:
  Ellen Coccoma. 607-547-4208/fax: 607-547-7572
  e-mail: coccomae@otsegocounty.com
District Attorney:
  John M Muehl 607-547-4249/fax: 607-547-4373
  e-mail: distatty@otsegocounty.com
Public Defender:
  Richard A Rothermel 607-432-7410
Sheriff:
  Richard Devlin Jr . . . . .607-547-4271 or 607-547-4273
  fax: 607-547-6413
  e-mail: sheriff@otsegocounty.com
Coordinator, Emergency Services:
  Kevin N. Ritton. 607-547-4227
  e-mail: rittonk@otsegocounty.com
Treasurer:
  Dan Crowell. 607-547-4235/fax: 607-547-7579
  e-mail: crowelld@otsegocounty.com
County Historian:
  Vacant 607-397-9705

Putnam County
40 Gleneida Avenue
Carmel, NY 10512
845-225-8690 Fax: 845-225-0715
e-mail: putcoleg@putnamcountyny.com
Web site: www.putnamcountyny.com

Chairman, County Legislature (R):
  Richard T. Othmer, Jr. 845-808-1020/fax: 845-225-0715
Deputy Chair, County Legislature (R):
  Anthony DiCarlo 845-808-1020/fax: 845-225-0715
Clerk, Legislature:
  Diane Schonfeld 845-808-1020/fax: 845-808-1933
Legislative Counsel:
  Clement Van Ross 845-808-1020/fax: 845-808-1933
County Executive:
  Mary Ellen Odell. 845-808-1001/fax: 845-808-1901
County Clerk:
  Dennis J Sant 845-808-1142
County Attorney:
  Jennifer S Bumgarner 845-228-0480
District Attorney:
  Adam Levy 845-808-1050
Emergency Services Bureau Commissioner:
  Adam B. Stiebeling 845-808-4000/fax: 845-808-4010
  e-mail: administration@pcbes.org
Sheriff:
  Donald Blaine Smith 845-225-4300/fax: 845-225-4399
Finance Commissioner:
  William J Carlin, Jr. . . . . .845-808-1075 or 845-808-1910
  fax: 845-225-8290
County Historian:
  Vacant 845-808-1420/fax: 845-278-4865
  e-mail: putpast@bestweb.net

Queens County (NYC Borough of Queens)
120-55 Queens Blvd
Kew Gardens, NY 11424
718-286-3000 Fax: 718-286-2876
e-mail: info@queensbp.org
Web site: www.queensbp.org

Borough President:
  Helen M Marshall 718-286-3000/fax: 718-286-2876
Director of Community Boards:
  Barry Grodenchik 718-286-2900

Offices and agencies generally appear in alphabetical order, except when specific order is requested by listee.

Public Information Officer/Press Office:
    Daniel Andrews 718-286-2640
County Clerk:
    Gloria D'Amico . . . . .718-298-0605 or 718-520-3137
District Attorney:
    Richard A Brown 718-286-6000
Communications Director:
    Kevin R Ryan
    e-mail: krryan@queensda.org
Public Administrator:
    Lois M Rosenblatt . . . . .718-526-5037 or 718-520-3710
    fax: 718-526-5043
    e-mail: mail@queenscountypa.com
Counsel:
    Gerard J Sweeney 718-459-9000/fax: 718-459-3163

Rensselaer County
Ned Pattison Government Center
1600 Seventh Avenue
Troy, NY 12180
518-270-2880 Fax: 518-270-2983
Web site: www.rensco.com or www.rensselaercounty.org

Chairperson, County Legislature (R):
    Martin T Reid .518-270-2880/fax: 518-270-2983
    e-mail: mreid@rensco.com
Vice Chairman (R):
    Stan Brownell .518-270-2880/fax: 518-270-2983
    e-mail: sbrownell@rensco.com
Vice Chairman-Finance (R):
    Philip Danaher .518-270-2880/fax: 518-270-2983
    e-mail: pdanaher@rensco.com
Majority Leader (C):
    Kenneth H Herrington 518-270-2880/fax: 518-270-2983
    e-mail: kherrington@rensco.com
Minority Leader (D):
    Peter Grimm. 518-270-2890/fax: 518-270-2975
    e-mail: pryand3troy@rensco.com
Clerk, Legislature:
    JanŠt Marra
    e-mail: jallard@rensco.com
County Executive:
    Kathleen M Jimino 518-270-2900/fax: 518-270-2961
County Clerk:
    Frank Merola. 518-270-4080/fax: 518-271-7998
County Attorney:
    Stephen A Pechenik. 518-270-2950/fax: 518-270-2954
District Attorney:
    Richard J McNally Jr 518-270-4040
Public Defender:
    Jerome K Frost 518-270-4030
Sheriff:
    Jack Mahar. 518-266-1900/fax: 518-270-5447
Chief Fiscal Officer:
    Michael J Slawson. 518-270-2750/fax: 518-270-2728

Richmond County (NYC Borough of Staten Island)
Borough Hall
120 Borough Hall
Staten Island, NY 10301
718-816-2000 Fax: 718-876-2026
Web site: www.statenislandusa.com

Borough President:
    James P Molinaro 718-816-2000
County Clerk:
    Stephen J Fiala 718-675-7700
District Attorney:
    Daniel M Donovan Jr 718-876-6300
    e-mail: info@rcda.nyc.gov

Rockland County
County Office Bldg
11 New Hempstead Rd
New City, NY 10956
845-638-5100 Fax: 845-638-5675
Web site: rocklandgov.com

Chairwoman, County Legislature (D):
    Harriet D Cornell 845-638-5269
    e-mail: cornellh@co.rockland.ny.us
Majority Leader (D):
    Jay Hood, Jr. 845-638-5751
Minority Leader (R):
    Christopher J. Carey 845-638-5100
Clerk, Legislature:
    Laurence O Toole 845-638-5100/fax: 845-638-5675
    e-mail: toolel@co.rockland.ny.us
County Executive:
    C Scott Vanderhoef. 845-638-5122
County Clerk:
    Paul Piperato 845-638-5070/fax: 845-638-5647
    e-mail: rocklandcountyclerk@co.rockland.ny.us
Director Veterans Services:
    Gerald Donnellan 845-638-5244/fax: 845-638-5730
    e-mail: jerry@rockvets.com
District Attorney:
    Thomas P Zugibe. 845-638-5001/fax: 845-638-5298
Public Defender:
    James D Licata 845-638-5660
    e-mail: licataj@co.rockland.ny.us
Sheriff:
    Louis Falco, III 845-638-5400/fax: 845-638-5035
Finance/Budget Commissioner:
    Stephen F. DeGroat. 845-638-5131
    e-mail: kopfc@co.rockland.ny.us

Saratoga County
County Municipal Center
40 McMaster St
Ballston Spa, NY 12020
518-884-4742 Fax: 518-884-4723
Web site: www.saratogacountyny.gov

Chairman, Board of Supervisors (R):
    Alan Grattidge
County Administrator:
    Spencer P Hellwig. 518-884-4742/fax: 518-884-4723
Clerk, Board of Supervisors:
    Pamela A Hargrave 518-885-2240/fax: 518-884-4771
Deputy County Clerk:
    Charles Foehser, II. 518-885-2213/fax: 518-884-4726
County Attorney:
    Stephen M Dorsey 518-884-4770/fax: 518-884-4720
    e-mail: saracaty@govt.co.saratoga.ny.us
District Attorney:
    James A Murphy, III 518-885-2263/fax: 518-884-8627
Public Defender:
    John H Ciulla Jr. 518-884-4795/fax: 518-884-4789
    e-mail: sarpdinfo@govt.co.saratoga.ny.us
Veterans Services:
    Felipe Moon. .518-884-4115/fax: 518-884-4290
County Treasurer:
    Sam Pitcheralle 518-884-4724/fax: 518-884-4775

Schenectady County
County Legislature
620 State St
Schenectady, NY 12305

State & Local
Government
Public Information

Offices and agencies generally appear in alphabetical order, except when specific order is requested by listee.

518-388-4280 Fax: 518-388-4591
Web site: www.schenectadycounty.com

Chairperson, County Legislature (D):
    Judith Dagostino 518-388-4280/fax: 518-388-4591
Majority Leader (D):
    Gary Hughes 518-388-4280/fax: 518-388-4591
Minority Leader (R):
    James Buhrmaster 518-388-4280/fax: 518-388-4591
Clerk, Legislature:
    Goeffrey T Hall 518-388-4280/fax: 518-388-4591
County Clerk:
    John J Woodward 518-388-4220/fax: 518-388-4224
    e-mail: john.woodward@schenectadycounty.com
District Attorney:
    Robert M Carney 518-388-4364
    e-mail: districtattorney@schenectadycounty.com
Public Defender:
    Mark J Caruso. 518-386-2266
Sheriff:
    Dominic A. D'Agostino 518-388-4300/fax: 518-388-4593
Director, Emergency Management:
    Mark LaViolette . . . . .518-370-3113 ext. 1
Deputy Director, Emergency Management:
    Kyle Rudolph . . . . .518-370-3113 ext. 5

Schoharie County
Cty Office Bldg
284 Main Street, Rm 365
PO Box 429
Schoharie, NY 12157
518-295-8347 Fax: 518-295-8482
Web site: www.schohariecounty-ny.gov

Chairman, Board of Supervisors (R):
    Philip Skowfoe, Jr. 518-827-4896/fax: 518-827-7972
Clerk, Board of Supervisors:
    Sheryl Largeteau 518-295-8421/fax: 518-295-8482
    e-mail: millerk@co.schoharie.ny.us
County Clerk:
    M Indica Jaycox 518-295-8316/fax: 518-295-8338
County Attorney:
    Michael West. 518-296-8844/fax: 518-296-8855
District Attorney:
    James L Sacket 518-295-2272/fax: 518-295-2273
Sheriff:
    Anthony F Desmond 518-295-2266/fax: 518-295-2267
Director, Emergency Management:
    Kevin Neary. .518-295-2276/fax: 518-296-8632
Treasurer:
    William E Cherry. 518-295-8386/fax: 518-295-8364
Administrator Legal Defense:
    Raynor B Duncombe. 518-295-7515/fax: 518-295-7519

Schuyler County
County Bldg
105 Ninth St, Unit 6
Watkins Glen, NY 14891
607-535-8100 Fax: 607-535-8109
e-mail: legislature@co.schuyler.ny.us
Web site: www.schuylercounty.us

Chairman, County Legislature (R):
    Dennis A Fagan 607-535-8100
Clerk, Legislature:
    Stacey B Husted 607-535-8100
County Clerk:
    Linda M Compton 607-535-8133/fax: 607-535-8130
    e-mail: lcompton@co.schuyler.ny.us

County Administrator:
    Timothy M O'Hearn 607-535-8106/fax: 607-535-8108
    e-mail: tohearn@co.schuyler.ny.us
District Attorney:
    Joseph G Fazzary. 607-535-8383/fax: 607-535-8385
Public Defender:
    Wesley A. Rose, Esq. 607-535-6400/fax: 607-535-6404
Sheriff:
    William E Yessman Jr. 607-535-8222/fax: 607-535-8216
    e-mail: wyessman@co.schuyler.ny.us
Treasurer:
    Gary Whyman 607-535-8181/fax: 607-535-8187
County Historian:
    Marion M. Boyce 607-535-4730

Seneca County
County Office Bldg
1 DiPronio Dr
Waterloo, NY 13165
315-539-1700 Fax: 315-539-0207
e-mail: supervisors@co.seneca.ny.us
Web site: www.co.seneca.ny.us

Chairman, Board of Supervisors (R):
    Robert W Hayssen 315-539-1700/fax: 315-539-0207
Majority Leader (R):
    Robert Shipley 315-539-1700/fax: 315-539-0207
    e-mail: rshipley@co.seneca.ny.us
Minority Leader (D):
    Cindy Garlick Lorenzetti. 315-539-1700/fax: 315-539-0207
    e-mail: cindyl@rochester.rr.com
Clerk, Board of Supervisors:
    Margaret E Li. 315-539-1700/fax: 315-539-0207
County Clerk:
    Christina L Lotz 315-539-1771
    e-mail: clotz@co.seneca.ny.us
County Manager:
    C. Mitchell Rowe. 315-539-1701/fax: 315-539-0207
    e-mail: mrowe@co.seneca.ny.us
County Attorney:
    Frank R Fisher 315-539-1989/fax: 315-539-1657
    e-mail: ffisher@co.seneca.ny.us
District Attorney:
    Barry Porsch .315-539-1300/fax: 315-539-0531
    e-mail: da@co.seneca.ny.us
Sheriff:
    Jack S Stenberg 315-220-3200/fax: 315-220-3478
Public Defender:
    Michael J Mirras 315-568-4975
Treasurer:
    Nicholas A Sciotti 315-539-1735/fax: 315-539-1731
    e-mail: nsciotti@co.seneca.ny.us
County Historian:
    Walter Gable. 315-539-1785
    e-mail: wgable@co.seneca.ny.us

St Lawrence County
County Courthouse
48 Court St
Canton, NY 13617
315-379-2276 Fax: 315-379-2463
Web site: www.co.st-lawrence.ny.us

Chair, Board of Legislators (D):
    Jonathan S. Putney 315-379-2276/fax: 315-379-2463
    e-mail: jputney@stlawco.org
Vice Chair, Board of Legislators (R):
    Donald Peck. .315-379-2276/fax: 315-379-2463
    e-mail: peck_donald@yahoo.com

Offices and agencies generally appear in alphabetical order, except when specific order is requested by listee.

County Administrator:
   Karen St Hilaire. 315-379-2276/fax: 315-379-2463
   e-mail: ksth@co.st-lawrence.ny.us
County Clerk:
   MaryLou Rupp 315-379-2237/fax: 315-379-2302
Dept Head, County Attorney:
   Michael Crowe 315-379-2269/fax: 315-379-2254
District Attorney:
   Nicole M Duve 315-379-2225/fax: 315-379-2301
Public Defender:
   Stephen D. Button. 315-379-2115/fax: 315-386-8241
Emergency Services, Dept Head:
   Joseph M. Gilbert 315-379-2240/fax: 315-379-0681
   e-mail: thowie@co.st-lawrence.ny.us
Sheriff (Department Head):
   Kevin M Wells 315-379-2222/fax: 315-379-0335
   e-mail: kwells@stlawco.org
Treasurer:
   Kevin Felt .315-386-2234/fax: 315-379-5274
   e-mail: kfelt@co.st-lawrence.ny.us

Steuben County

County Office Bldg
3 East Pulteney Square
Bath, NY 14810
607-776-9631 Fax: 607-776-6926
e-mail: scplanning@co.steuben.ny.us
Web site: www.steubencony.org

Chairman, County Legislature (R):
   Joseph J Hauryski 607-664-2247
Vice Chair, County Legislature (R):
   Patrick McAllister. 607-664-2247
Clerk, County Legislature:
   Brenda Mori. 607-664-2247/fax: 607-664-2282
County Administrator:
   Mark R Alger. 607-664-2245/fax: 607-664-2282
County Clerk:
   Judith M Hunter 607-664-2563
District Attorney:
   Brooks Baker 607-664-2270
Public Defender:
   Philip J. Roche, Esq. 607-664-2413/fax: 607-664-2410
Acting Director:
   Timothy D. Marshall. 607-664-2700
Sheriff:
   David V. Cole. . . . . .607-622-3901 or 800-724-7777
Treasurer:
   Patrick F Donnelly. 607-664-2488/fax: 607-664-2188
   e-mail: treasurer@co.steuben.ny.us
Historian:
   Twila O'Dell. 607-664-2199
   e-mail: historian@co.steuben.ny.us

Suffolk County

William H Rogers Building
725 Veterans Memorial Hwy
North County Complex
Smithtown, NY 11787
631-853-4070 Fax: 631-853-4899
Web site: www.suffolkcountyny.gov

Presiding Officer, County Legislature (D):
   William J Lindsay 631-854-9611/fax: 631-854-9687
   e-mail: presidingofficer.legislature@suffolkcountyny.gov
Deputy Presiding Officer, County Legislature (D):
   Wayne R. Horsley 631-854-1100/fax: 631-854-1103
   e-mail: wayne.horsley@suffolkcountyny.gov

Majority Leader (D):
   Dwayne Gregory 631-854-1111/fax: 631-854-1114
   e-mail: dwayne.gregory@suffolkcountyny.gov
Minority Leader (R):
   John M. Kennedy, Jr.. . . . . .631-854-3735/ fax: 631-854-3744
   e-mail: john.kennedy@suffolkcountyny.gov
Clerk, County Legislature:
   Tim Laube 631-853-4074/fax: 631-853-4899
   e-mail: tim.laube@suffolkcountyny.gov
County Executive:
   Steven Bellone 631-853-4000
   e-mail: county.executive@suffolkcountyny.gov
County Clerk:
   Judith A Pascale 631-852-2000
   e-mail: countyclerk@suffolkcountyny.gov
County Attorney:
   Dennis M. Brown 631-853-4049/fax: 631-853-5169
District Attorney:
   Thomas J Spota. 631-853-4161
   e-mail: infoda@co.suffolkcountyny.gov
Director, Emergency Management:
   Joseph F Williams 631-852-4851/fax: 631-852-4861
   e-mail: scdfres@suffolkcountyny.gov
Sheriff:
   Vincent F DeMarco 631-852-2200
   e-mail: suffolk_sheriff@suffolkcountyny.gov
Comptroller:
   Joseph Sawicki Jr 631-853-5040
   e-mail: comptroller@suffolkcountyny.gov
Treasurer:
   Angie M Carpenter 631-852-1500/fax: 631-852-1507
   e-mail: treasurer@suffolkcountyny.gov

Sullivan County

County Gov't Center
100 North St
PO Box 5012
Monticello, NY 12701
845-807-0435 Fax: 845-807-0447
e-mail: info@co.sullivan.ny.us
Web site: www.co.sullivan.ny.us

Chairman (D):
   Scott B Samuelson 845-807-0443
   e-mail: scott.samuelson@co.sullivan.ny.us
Vice-Chairman (D):
   Eugene L. Benson. 845-807-0439
   e-mail: gene.benson@co.sullivan.ny.us
Majority Leader (D):
   Kathleen LaBuda 845-807-0442
   e-mail: kathy.labuda@co.sullivan.ny.us
Minority Leader (R):
   Alan J. Sorenson 845-807-0444
   e-mail: alan.sorensen@co.sullivan.ny.us
Acting County Manager:
   Joshua Potosek 845-807-0450/fax: 845-807-0460
County Clerk:
   Daniel Briggs. 845-807-0411/fax: 845-807-0434
County Attorney:
   Sam Yasgur 845-807-0560/fax: 845-807-0574
District Attorney:
   James R Farrell 845-794-3344/fax: 845-794-3646
Public Safety Commissioner:
   Richard A Martinkovic. 845-807-0512
Sheriff:
   Michael A Schiff 845-794-7100/fax: 845-794-7100
County Treasurer:
   Ira J Cohen. 845-807-0200/fax: 845-807-0220
   e-mail: ira.cohen@co.sullivan.ny.us

State & Local Government Public Information

Tioga County
County Office Bldg
56 Main St
Owego, NY 13827
607-687-8200 or 607-687-8240 Fax: 607-687-8232
Web site: www.tiogacountyny.com

Chair, County Legislature (R):
    Dale N Weston.....................607-687-8240/fax: 607-687-8232
    e-mail: westond@co.tioga.ny.us
Clerk, County Legislature:
    Maureen L Dougherty.............607-687-8240/fax: 607-687-8232
    e-mail: doughertym@co.tioga.ny.us
County Clerk:
    Robert L Woodburn................607-687-8660/fax: 607-687-8686
County Attorney:
    Judith M Quigley...................607-687-8253/fax: 607-223-7003
    e-mail: quigleyj@co.tioga.ny.us
Acting District Attorney:
    Irene Graven 607-687-8650/fax: 607-687-1614
Public Defender:
    George C Awad Jr...............................607-687-1000
Emergency Management:
    Richard LeCount.................................607-687-2023
    e-mail: steve.gorney@co.tioga.ny.us
Sheriff:
    Gary W Howard 607-687-1010
Treasurer:
    James P McFadden 607-687-8670/fax: 607-223-7035
    e-mail: mcfaddenj@co.tioga.ny.us

Tompkins County
125 E Court St
Ithaca, NY 14850
607-274-5551 Fax: 607-274-5558
Web site: www.tompkins-co.org

Chairman, County Legislature (D):
    Martha Robertson 607-274-5434/fax: 607-274-5430
    e-mail: mrobertson@tompkins-co.org
County Administrator:
    Joe Mareane.......................607-274-5551/fax: 607-274-5558
County Clerk:
    Aurora R Valenti..................607-274-5431/fax: 607-274-5445
    e-mail: countyclerkmail@tompkins-co.org
County Attorney:
    Jonathan Wood 607-274-5546/fax: 607-274-5547
    e-mail: countyattorney@tompkins-co.org
District Attorney:
    Gwen Wilkinson 607-274-5461/fax: 607-274-5429
Sheriff:
    Kenneth W Lansing................607-257-1345/fax: 607-266-5436
Finance Director:
    David Squires 607-274-5545
    e-mail: finance@tompkins-co.org
Historian:
    Vacant...607-274-5434
    e-mail: historian@tompkins-co.org

Ulster County
County Office Bldg
244 Fair Street
6th Floor
Kingston, NY 12401
845-340-3800 Fax: 845-334-5724
e-mail: exec@co.ulster.ny.us
Web site: www.co.ulster.ny.us

Chairman, County Legislature (D):
    Terry L Bernardo...................845-340-3900/fax: 845-340-3651
Majority Leader (D):
    Kenneth J. Ronk, Jr...............................845-340-3900
Minority Leader (R):
    David B. Donaldson 845-340-3900
Clerk of the County Legislature:
    Victoria Fabella...................845-340-3900/fax: 845-340-3651
County Executive:
    Michael P Hein 845-340-3800/fax: 845-334-5724
    e-mail: exec@co.ulster.ny.us
County Clerk:
    Nina Postupack 845-340-3288/fax: 845-340-3299
    e-mail: countyclerk@co.ulster.ny.us
County Attorney:
    Beatrice Havranek..................845-340-3685/fax: 845-340-3691
    e-mail: bhav@co.ulster.ny.us
District Attorney:
    D Holley Carnright.................845-340-3280/fax: 845-340-3185
Public Defender:
    Andrew Kossover 845-340-3232/fax: 845-340-3744
    e-mail: akos@co.ulster.ny.us
Director, Emergency Management:
    Arthur R Snyder 845-331-7000/fax: 845-331-1738
    e-mail: asny@co.ulster.ny.us
Sheriff:
    PJ Van Blarcum....................845-338-3640/fax: 845-331-2810
    e-mail: sheriff@co.ulster.ny.us
Commissioner of Finance:
    Burt Gulnick, Jr. 845-340-3460/fax: 845-340-3430
    e-mail: bgul@co.ulster.ny.us
Historian:
    Anne M Gordon 845-331-7380
    e-mail: pasaran@msn.com

Warren County
Municipal Center
1340 State Rte 9
Lake George, NY 12845
800-958-4748 x143 Fax: 518-761-6368
Web site: www.warrencountyny.gov

Chairman, Board of Supervisors (R):
    Kevin B. Geraghty 518-761-6536
Clerk, Board of Supervisors:
    Joan Sady 518-761-6563
Commissioner, Administrative & Fiscal Services:
    JoAnn McKinstry 518-761-7655
County Clerk:
    Pamela J Vogel.....................518-761-6427/fax: 518-761-6551
County Attorney:
    Martin D. Auffredov 518-761-6463/fax: 518-761-6377
District Attorney:
    Kathleen B Hogan...................518-761-6405/fax: 518-761-6254
Public Defender:
    John P M Wappett...................518-761-6207/fax: 518-761-6208
Treasurer:
    Michael R. Swan 518-761-6379/fax: 518-761-6470
Historian:
    Ann McCann........................518-761-6544/fax: 518-761-6551

Washington County
383 Broadway
Fort Edward, NY 12828
518-746-2100 Fax: 518-746-2108
Web site: www.co.washington.ny.us

Chairman, Board of Supervisors:
    John A. Rymph.................................518-746-2210

Offices and agencies generally appear in alphabetical order, except when specific order is requested by listee.

Clerk, Board of Supervisors:
    Debbie Prehoda....................................518-746-2210
County Administrator:
    Kevin G Hayes....................................518-746-2590
County Clerk:
    Dona Crandall...............518-746-2170/fax: 518-746-2177
County Attorney:
    Roger A Wickes....................................518-746-2216
District Attorney:
    Kevin C Kortright....................................518-746-2525
Public Defender:
    Vacant....................................518-747-2403
Sheriff:
    Jeff Murphy....................................518-746-2475
Fire Coordinator:
    Raymond Rathbun....................................518-746-2255
Treasurer:
    Albert Nolette....................................518-746-2220

Wayne County
Wayne County Courthouse
26 Church St
Lyons, NY 14489
315-946-5400 Fax: 315-946-5407
Web site: www.co.wayne.ny.us

Chairman, Board of Supervisors (R):
    James Hoffman....................315-946-5400/fax: 315-946-5407
    e-mail: jhoffman@co.wayne.ny.us
County Administrator:
    James Marquette...................315-946-5480/fax: 315-946-5407
County Clerk:
    Michael Jankowski.................315-946-7470/fax: 315-946-5978
    e-mail: mjankowski@co.wayne.ny.us
County Attorney:
    Daniel Connors....................................315-946-7442
District Attorney:
    Richard Healy...................315-946-5905/fax: 315-946-5911
Public Defender:
    Ronald C Valentine....................................315-946-7472
Director, Emergency Management:
    George Bastedo...................315-946-5663/fax: 315-946-9721
Sheriff:
    Barry Virts...................315-946-9711/fax: 315-946-5811
Treasurer:
    Thomas A Warnick.................315-946-7441/fax: 315-946-5949
    e-mail: warnicktreasurer@co.wayne.ny.us
County Historian:
    Peter Evans....................................315-946-5470
    e-mail: historian@co.wayne.ny.us

Westchester County
Board of Legislators
800 Michaelian Office Bldg
148 Martine Ave, 8th Fl
White Plains, NY 10601
914-995-2800 Fax: 914-995-3884
Web site: www.westchesterlegislators.com

Chair, Board of Legislators (D):
    Kenneth W Jenkins....................................914-995-2829
    e-mail: ryan@westchesterlegislators.com
Majority Leader (D):
    Peter Harckham....................................914-995-2810
    e-mail: rogowsky@westchesterlegislators.com
Minority Leader (R):
    James Maisano....................................914-995-2826
Clerk, Board of Legislature & Chief of Staff:
    Tina Seckerson....................................914-995-2823
    e-mail: tinas@westchesterlegislators.com

Westchester County
Administration
900 Michaelian Office Building
148 Martine Ave
White Plains, NY 10601
914-995-2900
Web site: www3.westchestergov.com

County Executive:
    Robert P. Astorino....................................914-995-2900
    e-mail: ce@westchestergov.com
Deputy County Executive:
    Kevin J. Plunkett...................914-995-2909/fax: 914-995-3372
County Clerk:
    Timothy C Idoni...................914-995-3080/fax: 914-995-4030
County Attorney:
    Robert Meehan....................................914-995-2690
    e-mail: rfm5@westchestergov.com
District Attorney:
    Janet Difiore....................................915-995-3414
Sheriff/Public Safety Commissioner:
    George Longworth....................................914-864-7710
    e-mail: gnl1@westchestergov.com
Finance Commissioner:
    Ann Marie Berg...................914-995-2757/fax: 914-995-3230
    e-mail: ppp7@westchestergov.com
Public Works Acting Commissioner:
    Jay T. Pisco...................914-995-2546/fax: 914-995-4479
    e-mail: jtp2@westchestergov.com
Emergency Management Office:
    John M. Cullen...................914-231-1851/fax: 914-231-1622
    e-mail: jmc5@westchestergov.com

Wyoming County
Gov't Center, 143 N Main St
Warsaw, NY 14569
585-786-8800 Fax: 585-786-8802
e-mail: CKetchum@wyomingco.net
Web site: www.wyomingco.net

Chairman, Board of Supervisors (R):
    A Berwanger...................585-786-8800/fax: 585-786-8802
    e-mail: abberwanger@wyomingco.net
Vice Chairman, Board of Supervisors (R):
    Douglas Patti....................................585-786-8800
Clerk, Board of Supervisors:
    Cheryl J Ketchum...................585-786-8800/fax: 585-786-8802
    e-mail: cketchum@wyomingco.net
County Clerk:
    Rhonda Pierce...................585-786-8810/fax: 585-786-3703
    e-mail: county.clerk@wyomingco.net
County Attorney:
    James Wvjcik....................585-591-1724/fax: 585-591-1722
District Attorney:
    Donald G O'Geen...................585-786-8822/fax: 585-786-8842
    e-mail: dogeen@wyomingco.net
Public Defender:
    Norman P Effman...................585-756-8450/fax: 585-786-8478
    e-mail: attlegal@yahoo.com
Director, Fire & Emergency Management:
    Anthony Santoro...................585-786-8867/fax: 585-786-8961
    e-mail: asantoro@wyomingco.net
Sheriff:
    Farris H Heimann...................585-786-2255/fax: 585-786-8961
    e-mail: fheimann@wyomingco.net
Treasurer:
    Cheryl Mayer...................585-786-8812/fax: 585-786-0466
    e-mail: cdmayer@wyomingco.net

State & Local Government Public Information

Offices and agencies generally appear in alphabetical order, except when specific order is requested by listee.

341

County Historian:
   Doris Bannister 585-786-8818

Yates County

417 Liberty St
Penn Yan, NY 14527
315-536-5150 Fax: 315-536-5166
Web site: www.yatescounty.org

Chairman, County Legislature (R):
   H Taylor Fitch .315-536-5150/fax: 315-536-5166
   e-mail: legislature@yatescounty.org
County Administrator:
   Sarah Purdy .315-536-5509/fax: 315-536-5118
   e-mail: ycadministrator@yatescounty.org
Clerk, County Legislature:
   Connie C Hayes 315-536-5150/fax: 315-536-5166
   e-mail: legislature@yatescounty.org
County Clerk:
   Julie D Betts .315-536-5120/fax: 315-536-5545
   e-mail: countyclerk@yatescounty.org

County Attorney:
   Scott P. Falvey .315-531-3233/fax: 315-531-3234
District Attorney:
   Jason Cook 315-536-5550/fax: 315-536-5556
Public Defender:
   Edward J Brockman . . . . .585-374-6439 or 315-536-0352
Sheriff:
   Ronald G Spike 315-536-4438/fax: 315-536-5191
   e-mail: sheriff@yatescounty.org
Treasurer:
   Winona B. Flynn 315-536-5192
   e-mail: treasurer@yatescounty.org
Emergency Management Director:
   Vacant 315-536-3000/fax: 315-536-5106
   e-mail: emergencymanagement@yatescounty.org
Historian:
   Frances Dumas 315-536-5147/fax: 315-531-3226
   e-mail: history@yatescounty.org

Offices and agencies generally appear in alphabetical order, except when specific order is requested by listee.

MUNICIPAL GOVERNMENT

This section identifies senior public officials for cities, towns and villages in New York State with populations greater than 20,000. New York City departments are included in the city listing.

MUNICIPAL GOVERNMENT

Albany, City of
City Hall
24 Eagle St
Albany, NY 12207
518-434-5175
e-mail: webmaster@ci.albany.ny.us
Web site: www.albanyny.gov

Mayor:
  Gerald D Jennings 518-434-5100/fax: 518-434-5013
  e-mail: mayor@ci.albany.ny.us
Deputy Mayor:
  Philip F Calderone. 518-434-5077/fax: 518-434-5074
President, Common Council:
  Carolyn McLaughlin. 518-462-1458
  e-mail: onlybelv@aol.com
City Clerk:
  Nala Woodward. 518-434-5090/fax: 518-434-5081
  e-mail: cityclerk@ci.albany.ny.us
Corporation Counsel:
  John Reilly. 518-434-5050/fax: 518-434-5070
City Deputy Auditor:
  Debra Perks. 518-434-5023
City Treasurer:
  Kathy Sheehan. 518-434-5036/fax: 518-434-5041
  e-mail: sheehank@ci.albanu.ny.us
Commissioner, General Services:
  Nicolas J D'Antonio 518-432-1144/fax: 518-427-7499
  e-mail: generalservices@ci.albany.ny.us
Commissioner, Assessment & Taxation:
  Keith McDonald 518-434-5155/fax: 518-434-5013
  e-mail: skrokoff@albany-ny.org
Police Chief:
  Steven Krokoff 518-462-8013
  e-mail: skrokoff@albany-ny.org
Fire Chief/Emergency Services:
  Robert Forezzi Sr. 518-447-7877/fax: 518-434-8675
Director, Community Development:
  Faye Andrews. 518-434-5265
Director, Building & Codes:
  Jeffrey Jamison 518-434-5165/fax: 518-434-6015

Amherst, Town of
5583 Main St
Williamsville, NY 14221
716-631-7000 Fax: 716-631-7146
e-mail: webmaster@amherst.ny.us
Web site: www.amherst.ny.us

Town Supervisor:
  Barry A Weinstein 716-631-7032
  e-mail: bweinstein@amherst.ny.us
Town Clerk:
  Marjory Jaeger 716-631-7021 x7010/fax: 716-631-7152
  e-mail: dbucki@amherst.ny.us
Town Attorney:
  E Thomas Jones 716-631-7164
  e-mail: tjones@amherst.ny.us

Comptroller:
  Darlene Carroll 716-631-7008
  e-mail: dcarroll@amherst.ny.us
Director Emergency Services & Safety:
  James J Zymanek 716-839-6707
  e-mail: jzymanek@amherst.ny.us
Police Chief:
  John C Askey. 716-689-1311/fax: 716-689-1310
  e-mail: jmoslow@apdny.org

Auburn, City of
Memorial City Hall
24 South Street
Auburn, NY 13021
315-255-4104 Fax: 315-253-8345
Web site: auburnny.gov

Mayor:
  Michael Quill. 315-255-4104/fax: 315-253-8345
  e-mail: mayorquill@ci.auburn.ny.us
City Manager:
  Doug Selby 315-255-4146/fax: 315-255-4735
  e-mail: citymanager@ci.auburn.ny.us
City Clerk:
  Debra A McCormick. 315-255-4100/fax: 315-255-4181
  e-mail: dmccormick@ci.auburn.ny.us
Corporation Counsel:
  John Rossi .315-255-4176/fax: 315-255-4735
  e-mail: jrossi@ci.auburn.ny.us
Planning & Economic Development Director:
  Jennifer Haines 315-255-4115/fax: 315-253-0282
  e-mail: jhaines@ci.auburn.ny.us
Comptroller:
  Lauren Poehlman. 315-255-4138/fax: 315-255-4727
Treasurer:
  Robert Gauthier 315-255-4143/fax: 315-255-4727
  e-mail: rgauthier@ci.auburn.ny.us
Police Chief:
  Brian Neagle 315-253-3235/fax: 315-255-2601
Fire Chief:
  Jeff Dygert. 315-253-4031/fax: 315-252-0318

Babylon, Town of
200 E Sunrise Highway
Lindenhurst, NY 11757-2598
631-957-3000 Fax: 631-957-7440
e-mail: info@townofbabylon.com
Web site: www.townofbabylon.com

Town Supervisor:
  Rich Schaffer. 631-957-3072/fax: 631-957-7440
Town Clerk:
  Carol Quirk 631-957-4291
Town Attorney:
  Joseph Wilson. 631-957-3029
Comptroller:
  Victoria Marotta 631-957-3179
Commissioner, Public Works:
  Tom Stay. 631-957-3161
Deputy Commissioner, Public Safety:
  Patrick Farrell 631-422-7600/fax: 631-893-1031
Commissioner, General Services:
  Theresa Sabatino. 631-957-3025

Bethlehem, Town of
445 Delaware Ave
Delmar, NY 12054

Offices and agencies generally appear in alphabetical order, except when specific order is requested by listee.

518-439-4955 Fax: 518-439-1699
e-mail: djacon@townofbethlehem.org
Web site: www.townofbethlehem.org

Town Supervisor:
    John Clarkson 518-439-4955 x1164
    e-mail: jclarkson@townofbethlehem.org
Town Clerk:
    Nanci Moquin. 518-439-4955 x1183/fax: 518-439-1699
    e-mail: nmoquin@townofbethlehem.org
Town Attorney:
    James Potter. 518-439-4955 x1164
    e-mail: jpotter@townofbethlehem.org
Comptroller:
    Michael E. Cohen .518-439-4955 x1123
    e-mail: mcohen@townofbethlehem.org
Police Chief:
    Louis G Corsi 518-439-9973/fax: 518-439-6965
Emergency Management Director:
    John E Brennan 518-439-4955 x1166
    e-mail: jbrennan@townofbethlehem.org
Historian:
    Susan E Leath 518-439-4955 x1160
    e-mail: sleath@townofbethlehem.org

Binghamton, City of
City Hall
38 Hawley St
Binghamton, NY 13901
607-772-7005 Fax: 607-772-0508
Web site: www.cityofbinghamton.com

Mayor:
    Matthew T Ryan 607-772-7001/fax: 607-772-7079
    e-mail: mayor@cityofbinghamton.com
Executive Assistant to the Mayor:
    Andrew Block 607-772-7001/fax: 607-772-7079
    e-mail: awblock@cityofbinghamton.com
City Clerk:
    Angela Holmes 607-772-7005/fax: 607-772-7155
    e-mail: clerk@cityofbinghamton.com
Corporation Counsel:
    Kenneth Frank. 607-772-7013
City Treasurer:
    Pauline Penrose 607-772-7027/fax: 607-772-7015
    e-mail: treasurer@cityofbinghamton.com
City Assessor:
    Scott Snyder. 607-772-7002/fax: 607-772-7106
    e-mail: assessor@cityofbinghamton.com
Commissioner, Public Works:
    Luke Day 607-772-7021/fax: 607-772-7023
    e-mail: dpw@cityofbinghamton.com
Police Chief:
    Joseph Zikuski. 607-772-7090/fax: 607-772-7996
    e-mail: police@cityofbinghamton.com
Acting Administrator, Civil Service:
    Judith Robb 607-772-7008/fax: 607-772-7066
    e-mail: cs@cityofbinghamton.com
Acting Director, Finance/Comptroller:
    Charles Pearsall 607-772-7011/fax: 607-772-7106
    e-mail: finance@cityofbinghamton.com
Director, Planning/Housing/Community Development:
    Tarik Abdelazim 607-772-7028/fax: 607-772-7063
    e-mail: tabdelazim@cityofbinghamton.com
Director, Economic Development:
    Merry Harris 607-772-7161/fax: 607-772-7244
    e-mail: maharris@cityofbinghamton.com

Brighton, Town of
2300 Elmwood Ave
Rochester, NY 14618
585-784-5250 Fax: 585-784-5373
Web site: www.townofbrighton.org

Town Supervisor:
    William W Moehle 585-784-5252
    e-mail: sandra.frankel@townofbrighton.org
Town Clerk:
    Dan Aman .585-784-5240/fax: 585-784-5374
Director, Finance:
    Suzanne Zaso. 585-784-5210/fax: 585-784-5396
    e-mail: suzanne.zaso@townofbrighton.org
Police Chief:
    Mark Henderson 585-784-5150/fax: 585-784-5151
Fire Marshal:
    Christopher Roth 585-784-5220/fax: 585-785-5207
    e-mail: christopher.roth@townofbrighton.org
Town Attorney:
    Kenneth W. Gordon 585-244-1070/fax: 585-244-1085
Commissioner, Public Works:
    Tim Keef 585-784-5250/fax: 585-784-5223
    e-mail: tim.keef@townofbrighton.org
Director, Communications:
    Douglas Clapp. 585-784-5253
    e-mail: doug.clapp@townofbrighton.org

Brookhaven, Town of
One Independence Hill
Farmingville, NY 11738
631-451-6655 Fax: 631-451-6677
Web site: www.brookhaven.org

Town Supervisor:
    Edward P. Romaine. 631-451-8696/fax: 631-451-6447
Town Clerk/Registrar:
    Patricia Eddington 631-451-9101/fax: 631-451-9264
Commissioner of Finance:
    Tamara Wright. 631-451-6680/fax: 631-451-6692
    e-mail: finance@brookhaven.org
Commissioner, Public Safety:
    Peter O'Leary 631-451-6291/fax: 631-451-6908

Buffalo, City of
City Hall
65 Niagara Square
Buffalo, NY 14202
716-851-4200 Fax: 716-851-4360
Web site: www.ci.buffalo.ny.us

Mayor:
    Byron W Brown
    e-mail: mayor@city-buffalo.com
Council President:
    Richard A. Fontana 716-851-5151/fax: 716-851-5141
    e-mail: rfontana@city-buffalo.com
City Clerk:
    Gerald Chwalinski. 716-851-5431/fax: 716-851-4845
    e-mail: gchwalinski@city-buffalo.com
Comptroller:
    Mark JF Schroeder 716-851-5255/fax: 716-851-4031
    e-mail: mschroeder@city-buffalo.com
Commissioner, Administration, Finance & Urban Affairs:
    Donna Estrich 716-851-5922
    e-mail: destrich@city-buffalo.com
Police Commissioner:
    Daniel Derenda. . . . . .716-851-4444 or 716-851-4571

Offices and agencies generally appear in alphabetical order, except when specific order is requested by listee.

Fire Commissioner:
  Garnell W Whitfield Jr 716-851-5333
  e-mail: gwhitfield@bfdny.org
Director Emergency Management:
  Garnell W. Whitfield, Jr. 716-851-5333/fax: 716-851-5341
  e-mail: gwhitfield@city-buffalo.com

Camillus, Town of
4600 W Genesee Street
Syracuse, NY 13219
315-488-1335 Fax: 315-488-8768
Web site: www.townofcamillus.com

Town Supervisor:
  Mary Ann Coogan 315-488-1335/fax: 315-488-8768
  e-mail: macoogan@townofcamillus.com
Town Clerk:
  Martha Dickson-McMahon 315-488-1234/fax: 315-488-8983
  e-mail: mdickson@townofcamillus.com
Comptroller:
  Catherine Albunio 315-488-2266/fax: 315-468-4179
  e-mail: calbunio@townofcamillus.com
Police Chief:
  Thomas Winn 315-487-0102/fax: 315-487-5572
  e-mail: twinn@townofcamillus.com

Carmel, Town of
Town Hall
60 McAlpin Ave
Mahopac, NY 10541
845-628-1500 Fax: 845-628-7434
Web site: www.ci.carmel.ny.us

Town Supervisor:
  Kenneth Schmitt 845-628-1500/fax: 845-628-6836
Town Clerk:
  Ann Spofford 845-628-1500/fax: 845-628-7434
Town Counsel:
  Gregory Folchetti 845-225-1900/fax: 845-228-4228
Police Chief:
  Michael R Johnson 845-628-1300/fax: 845-628-2597

Cheektowaga, Town of
Town Hall
3301 Broadway
Cheektowaga, NY 14227
716-686-3400 Fax: 716-686-3515
Web site: www.tocny.org

Town Supervisor:
  Mary F Holtz 716-686-3465/fax: 716-686-3551
Town Clerk:
  Alice Magierski 716-686-3434/fax: 716-686-3515
  e-mail: townclerkwebmail@tocny.org
Town Attorney:
  Kevin Schenk 716-686-3457/fax: 716-686-3997
  e-mail: lawweb@tocny.org
Emergency Services Manager:
  Earl Loder 716-893-0847/fax: 716-893-0835
  e-mail: eloder@tocny.org
Police Chief:
  David Zack 716-686-3500/fax: 716-685-1239

Chili, Town of
3235 Chili Avenue
Rochester, NY 14624

585-889-3550 Fax: 585-889-8710
e-mail: info@townofchili.org
Web site: www.townofchili.org

Town Supervisor:
  David Dunning 585-889-6111
Town Clerk:
  Richard J Brongo 585-889-6122
  e-mail: rbrongo@townofchili.org
Director of Finance:
  Dianne O'Meara 585-889-6120
Town Historian:
  Bonnie Moore 585-889-6123

Cicero, Town of
Town Hall
8236 S Main St
PO Box 1517
Cicero, NY 13039
315-699-1414 Fax: 315-699-0039
Web site: www.ciceronewyork.net

Town Supervisor:
  Jim Corl 315-699-1414
  e-mail: jcorl@ciceronewyork.net
Town Clerk:
  Tracy M Cosilmon 315-699-8109/fax: 315-699-0039
  e-mail: clerk@ciceronewyork.net
Comptroller:
  Shirlie Stuart 315-699-2759/fax: 315-698-0851
  e-mail: sstuart@ciceronewyork.net
Receiver of Taxes:
  Sharon Edick 315-699-2756/fax: 315-699-9562
  e-mail: sedick@ciceronewyork.net
Police Chief:
  Joseph F Snell Jr 315-699-3677/fax: 315-699-8128

Clarence, Town of
1 Town Place
Clarence, NY 14031
716-741-8930 Fax: 716-741-4715
Web site: www.clarence.ny.us

Town Supervisor:
  David C. Hartzell, Jr. 716-741-8930/fax: 716-741-4715
  e-mail: dhartzell@clarence.ny.us
Town Clerk:
  Nancy C Metzger 716-741-8938/fax: 716-407-2190
  e-mail: nmetzger@clarence.ny.us
Town Attorney:
  Lawrence M. Meckler 716-741-8935/fax: 716-741-4715
  e-mail: lmeckler@clarence.ny.us
Chief Security Officer:
  Joseph D Meacham 716-406-8928
  e-mail: jmeacham@clarence.ny.us

Clarkstown, Town of
10 Maple Ave
New City, NY 10956
845-639-2050 Fax: 845-639-2008
Web site: www.town.clarkstown.ny.us

Town Supervisor:
  Alexander J Gromack 845-639-2050/fax: 845-634-5456
  e-mail: a.gromack@town.clarkstown.org
Deputy Supervisor:
  Councilman Shirley Lasker 845-639-2050/fax: 845-634-5456
  e-mail: slasker@clarkstown.org

Offices and agencies generally appear in alphabetical order, except when specific order is requested by listee.

Town Clerk:
Justin Sweet.....................845-639-2010/fax: 845-639-2008
e-mail: clerk@clarkstown.org
Town Attorney:
Amy Mele.......................845-639-2060/fax: 845-639-2189
e-mail: legal@town.clarkstown.ny.us

Clay, Town of
4401 State Route 31
Clay, NY 13041
315-652-3800 Fax: 315-622-7259
Web site: www.townofclay.org

Town Supervisor:
Damian M Ulatowski...........315-652-3800 x114/fax: 315-622-7259
e-mail: supervisor@townofclay.org
Town Clerk:
Jill Hageman-Clark..........315-652-3800 ext 145/fax: 315-622-7259
e-mail: townclerk@townofclay.org
Town Attorney:
Robert M Germain.............315-652-3800 x151/fax: 315-622-7259
e-mail: legal@townofclay.org
Commissioner of Finance:
John Shehadi 315-652-3800 x121
Commissioner, Public Safety:
Mark Territo..............................315-622-7259
e-mail: planning@townofclay.org
Fire Chief:
Daniel L Ford 315-625-4242

Clifton Park, Town of
1 Town Hall Plaza
Clifton Park, NY 12065
518-371-6651 Fax: 518-371-1136
e-mail: info@cliftonpark.org
Web site: www.cliftonpark.org

Town Supervisor:
Philip Barrett.....................518-371-6651/fax: 518-371-1136
Town Administrator:
Michael Shahen..........................518-371-6651 ext243
Town Clerk:
Patricia O'Donnell.................518-371-6681/fax: 518-383-5088
e-mail: townclerk@cliftonpark.org
Comptroller:
Mark Heggen....................518-371-6651/fax: 518-371-1136
Historian:
John Scherer 518-371-2691/fax: 518-383-2668

Colonie, Town of
Memorial Town Hall
534 Loudon Rd
Newtonville, NY 12128
518-783-2700 Fax: 518-782-2360
e-mail: colonie@colonie.org
Web site: www.colonie.org

Town Supervisor:
Paula A Mahan 518-783-2700
Town Clerk:
Elizabeth A DelTorto 518-783-2734/fax: 518-783-3409
e-mail: deltortoe@colonie.org
Town Attorney:
Michael C Magguilli.................518-783-2704/fax: 518-786-7324
e-mail: attorney@colonie.org
Comptroller:
Craig Blair.......................518-783-2708/fax: 518-783-2877
e-mail: blairc@colonie.org

Emergency Management & Planning:
Michael Rayball 518-782-2609
e-mail: Rayballm@colonie.org
Police Chief:
Steven H Heider 518-783-2744/fax: 518-786-7326
e-mail: heiders@colonie.org
Public Works Commissioner:
John H Cunningham 518-783-6292/fax: 518-785-3529
e-mail: infodpw@colonie.org
Town Historian:
Kevin Franklin 518-782-2601
e-mail: historian@colonie.org

Cortlandt, Town of
1 Heady St
Cortlandt Manor, NY 10567-1224
914-734-1002 Fax: 914-734-1025
e-mail: townhall@townofcortlandt.com
Web site: www.townofcortlandt.com

Town Supervisor:
Linda D Puglisi 914-734-1002/fax: 914-734-1003
e-mail: lindap@townofcortlandt.com
Town Clerk:
Joann Dyckman...................914-734-1020/fax: 914-734-1102
Town Attorney:
Thomas F Wood 914-736-0930/fax: 914-736-9082
Comptroller:
Glenn Cestaro 914-734-1071/fax: 914-734-1077
e-mail: glennc@townofcortlandt.com
DES/Director:
Jeff Coleman 914-737-0100/fax: 914-862-3376
e-mail: jefft@townofcortlandt.com
Homeland Security:
Linda Puglisi.......................914-734-1001
e-mail: jefft@townofcortlandt.com

DeWitt, Town of
5400 Butternut Drive
East Syracuse, NY 13057-8509
315-446-3910 Fax: 315-449-2065
Web site: www.townofdewitt.com

Town Supervisor:
Edward M Michalenko 315-446-3910 ext5/fax: 315-449-0620
e-mail: supervisor@townofdewitt.com
Town Clerk:
Barbara K Klim ....315-446-3910 ext 2/fax: 315-449-2065
e-mail: clerk@townofdewitt.com
Police Chief:
Eugene J Conway 315-449-3640/fax: 315-449-3644
e-mail: police@townofdewitt.com
Comptroller:
Timothy Redmond ....315-446-3392 ext 6/fax: 315-449-2065
e-mail: comptroller@townofdewitt.com

East Fishkill, Town of
Town Hall
330 Route 376
Hopewell Junction, NY 12533
845-221-9191
Web site: www.eastfishkillny.org

Town Supervisor:
John L Hickman Jr 845-221-4303
e-mail: hickmanj@eastfishkillny.org
Town Clerk:
Carol Hurray 845-221-9191

Offices and agencies generally appear in alphabetical order, except when specific order is requested by listee.

Police Chief:
  Brian C Nichols 845-221-2111
Fire Inspector:
  William Stuart. 845-221-0378

East Hampton, Town of
159 Pantigo Rd
East Hampton, NY 11937
631-324-4140 Fax: 631-324-2789
e-mail: info@town.east-hampton.ny.us
Web site: www.town.east-hampton.ny.us

Town Supervisor:
  William J Wilkinson 631-324-4140/fax: 631-324-2789
Town Clerk:
  Fred Overton 631-324-4142/fax: 631-324-4128
  e-mail: Foverton@town.east-hampton.ny.us
Division of Finance/ Budget Officer:
  Len Bernard. 631-324-4141/fax: 631-324-2789
  e-mail: lbernard@town.east-hampton.ny.us
Town Attorney:
  John Jilnicki. 631-324-8787/fax: 631-329-5371
  e-mail: jjilnicki@town.east-hampton.ny.us
Police Chief:
  Edward V Ecker Jr. 631-537-7575/fax: 631-537-6833
Emergency Services:
  Bruce Bates 631-324-1736
Chief Fire Marshall:
  David Browne .631-329-3473/fax: 631-329-9403
  e-mail: dbrowne@town.east-hampton.ny.us

Eastchester, Town of
Town Hall
40 Mill Rd
Eastchester, NY 10709
914-771-3300 Fax: 914-771-3366
Web site: www.eastchester.org

Town Supervisor:
  Anthony S Colavita. 914-771-3301/fax: 914-793-2168
  e-mail: supervisor@eastchester.org
Town Clerk:
  Linda Doherty .914-771-3351/fax: 914-771-3366
  e-mail: townclerk@eastchester.org
Town Attorney:
  Louis J. Reda. .914-771-3325/fax: 914-771-3367
  e-mail: legal@eastchester.org
Comptroller:
  Dawn T Donovan 914-771-3330/fax: 914-771-9409
  e-mail: comptroller@eastchester.org

Elmira, City of
City Hall
317 E Church St
Elmira, NY 14901
607-737-5644 Fax: 607-737-5824
Web site: www.cityofelmira.net

Mayor:
  Susan J. Skidmore. 607-737-5644
City Manager:
  John J Burin 607-737-5644
City Clerk:
  Angela J Williams 607-737-5672/fax: 607-737-5783
Chamberlain:
  David Vandermark 607-737-5661/fax: 607-737-5783
Director, Public Works:
  Brian Beasley 607-737-5679

Police Chief:
  Michael Robertson 607-737-5811
Fire Chief:
  Patrick Bermingham. 607-737-5700

Fishkill, Town of
807 Route 52
Fishkill, NY 12524
845-831-7800 Fax: 845-831-6040
e-mail: tof@fishkill-ny.gov
Web site: www.fishkill-ny.gov

Town Supervisor:
  Robert LaColla. . . . . .845-831-7800 x. 3309
Town Clerk:
  Darlene Bellis . . . . .845-831-7800 x. 3329
  e-mail: dbellis@fishkill-ny.gov
Comptroller:
  Dawn H. Kertesz-Lee .845-831-7800 x3339
  e-mail: rwheeling@fishkill-ny.gov

Freeport, Village of
46 North Ocean Ave
Freeport, NY 11520
516-377-2200 Fax: 516-377-2323
e-mail: freeportmail1@freeportny.gov
Web site: www.freeportny.com

Village Mayor:
  Robert T. Kennedy 516-377-2252/fax: 516-377-2323
  e-mail: mayor@freeportny.gov
Village Clerk:
  Pamela Walsh Boening 516-377-2300/fax: 516-771-4127
Village Attorney:
  Howard E Colton. 516-377-2249/fax: 516-377-2366
  e-mail: hcolton@freeportny.gov
Treasurer:
  Ismaela Hernandez 516-377-2212/fax: 516-377-2255
  e-mail: vmontes@freeportny.gov
Superintendent, Public Works:
  Robert R. Fisenne, P.E. 516-377-2289
  e-mail: srichardson@freeportny.gov
Emergency Management Director:
  Richard E Holdener 516-377-2188
  e-mail: rholdener@freeportny.gov
Police Chief:
  Miguel Bermudez 516-377-2411/fax: 516-377-2432
  e-mail: mwoodword@freeportny.gov
Secretary to Fire Chief:
  Raymond Maguire 516-377-2190
  e-mail: rmaguire@freeportny.gov
Chief of the Fire Department:
  Stanley Kistela 516-377-2190
  e-mail: rmaguire@freeportny.gov

Garden City, Village of
351 Stewart Ave
Garden City, NY 11530
516-465-4000 Fax: 516-742-5223
Web site: www.gardencityny.net

Mayor:
  John J. Watras. 516-465-4051
  e-mail: mayor@gardencityny.net
Administrator:
  Robert L Schoelle, Jr 516-465-4051
  e-mail: rschoelle@gardencityny.net

Offices and agencies generally appear in alphabetical order, except when specific order is requested by listee.

Fire Chief:
William J Castoro 516-746-4130
e-mail: wcastoro@gardencityny.net
Director, Public Works:
Robert J Mangan 516-465-4004
e-mail: rmangan@gardencityny.net

Gates, Town of
1605 Buffalo Rd
Gates, NY 14624
585-247-6100 Fax: 585-247-0017
e-mail: admin@townofgates.org
Web site: www.townofgates.org

Town Supervisor:
Mark W Assini 585-247-6100
Town Clerk:
Richard A Warner 585-247-6100
e-mail: rwarner@townofgates.org
Finance Director:
Art Plewa 585-247-6100
Police Chief:
David R DiCaro 585-247-2262
Director, Building & Public Works:
John Lathrop 585-247-6100 x241
Town Historian:
Judy DeRooy 585-247-6100

Glen Cove, City of
9 Glen St
Glen Cove, NY 11542
516-676-2000 Fax: 516-676-0108
Web site: www.glencove-li.com

Mayor:
Ralph V Suozzi 516-676-2004/fax: 516-676-0108
e-mail: rsuozzi@cityofglencoveny.org
City Clerk:
Tina Pemberton . . . . .516-676-3345 or 516-676-3357
e-mail: tpemberton@cityofglencoveny.org
City Attorney:
Vincent Taranto 516-759-1111
e-mail: vtaranto@cityofglencoveny.org
Controller:
Sal Lombardi 516-676-2789
e-mail: slombardi@cityofglencoveny.org
Director, Public Works:
William Archambault 516-676-4402
e-mail: publicworks@cityofglencoveny.org
Police Chief:
William Whitton 516-676-1000
e-mail: wwhitton@cityofglencoveny.org

Glenville, Town of
18 Glenridge Rd
Glenville, NY 12302
518-688-1200 Fax: 518-384-0140
Web site: www.townofglenville.org

Town Supervisor:
Christopher A Koetzle 518-688-1202/fax: 518-384-0140
e-mail: ckoetzle@townofglenville.org
Town Clerk:
Linda Neals 518-688-1200x402/fax: 518-384-0140
e-mail: lneals@townofglenville.org
Town Attorney:
Michael R Cuevas 518-688-1200/fax: 518-384-0140

Town Planner:
Kevin Corcoran 518-688-1200x407/fax: 518-384-0140
e-mail: kcorcoran@townofglenville.org
Comptroller:
Jason Cuthbert 518-688-1200 ext306/fax: 518-384-0140
e-mail: gphillips@townofglenville.org
Highway Superintendent & Commissioner, Public Works:
Thomas Coppola 518-382-1406/fax: 518-382-3015
e-mail: tcoppola@townofglenville.org
Historian:
Joan Szablewski 518-982-0643/fax: 518-384-0140
Police Chief:
Michael Ranalli 518-384-3444/fax: 518-384-0141
e-mail: mranalli@townofglenville.org

Grand Island, Town of
Grand Island Town Hall
2255 Baseline Road
Grand Island, NY 14072
716-773-9618 Fax: 716-773-9618
e-mail: www.gigov.com

Town Supervisor:
Mary Cooke 716-773-9600/fax: 716-773-9618
e-mail: supervisor@grand-island.ny.us
Assistant/Deputy Supervisor:
Elizabeth Wilbert 716-773-9600/fax: 716-773-9618
e-mail: lwilbert@grand-island.ny.us
Town Clerk:
Pattie Frentzel .716-773-9600/fax: 716-773-9618
e-mail: pfrentzel@grand-island.ny.us
Town Attorney:
Peter Godfrey 716-773-9600/fax: 716-773-9618
e-mail: www.hodgsonruss.com
Town Accountant:
Pamela Barton .716-773-9600/fax: 716-773-9618
e-mail: pbarton@grand-island.ny.us
Town Assessor:
Judy M Tafelski 716-773-9600/fax: 716-773-9618
e-mail: assessor@grand-island.ny.us

Greece, Town of
1 Vince Tofany Blvd
Greece, NY 14612
585-225-2000 Fax: 585-225-1915
Web site: greeceny.gov

Town Supervisor:
John T Auberger 585-723-2311
Deputy Town Supervisor:
Jeffery McCann 585-723-2000
Director, Constituent Services:
Kathryn J Firkins 585-723-2000
Town Clerk:
Patricia Anthony 585-723-2341/fax: 585-723-2459
e-mail: panthony@townofgreece.ny.gov
Town Attorney:
Jeffery McCann .585-225-2000/fax: 585-225-1915
Director, Finance:
Rick Pellegrino 585-723-2335
Police Chief:
Todd Baxter 585-865-9200
Town Assessor:
Leo Carroll 585-723-2308

Greenburgh, Town of
177 Hillside Avenue
Greenburgh, NY 10607

Offices and agencies generally appear in alphabetical order, except when specific order is requested by listee.

914-993-1500 Fax: 914-993-1626
Web site: www.greenburghny.com

Town Supervisor:
Paul J Feiner 914-993-1540/fax: 914-993-1541
  e-mail: pfeiner@greenburghny.com
Town Clerk:
Judith A Beville. 914-993-1500/fax: 914-993-1626
  e-mail: townclerk@greenburghny.com
Historian:
Frank Jazzo 914-993-1641/fax: 914-993-1626
Chief of Police:
Joseph DiCarlo 914-682-5300/fax: 914-683-5342

Guilderland, Town of
Town Hall
5209 Western Turnpike
PO Box 339
Guilderland, NY 12084
518-356-1980 Fax: 518-356-3955
Web site: www.townofguilderland.org

Town Supervisor:
Kenneth Runion 518-356-1980 x1022/fax: 518-356-5514
  e-mail: runionk@townofguilderland.org
Town Clerk:
Rosemary Centi. 518-356-1980/fax: 518-356-3955
Police Chief:
Carol Lawlor .518-356-1980/fax: 518-356-4668
  e-mail: lawlorc@guilderlandpd.org
Town Historian:
Alice Begley 518-356-1980 x1050/fax: 518-356-3955
  e-mail: abegley27@aol.com

Hamburg, Town of
6100 South Park Ave
Hamburg, NY 14075
716-649-6111 Fax: 716-649-4087
Web site: www.townofhamburgny.com

Town Supervisor:
Steven J Walters 716-649-6111 x2381
  e-mail: supervisor@townofhamburgny.com
Town Clerk:
Catherine A Rybczynski 716-649-6111 x2360/fax: 716-646-1384
  e-mail: townclerk@townofhamburgny.com
Senior Public Safety Dispatcher:
Thomas E Taylor 716-649-6111 x2412
  e-mail: e911@townofhamburgny.com
Town Historian:
James Baker. . . . . .716-649-6111 x. 2400

Harrison, Town/Village of
11 Heineman Place
Harrison, NY 10528
914-670-3000 Fax: 914-835-8067
Web site: www.harrison-ny.gov

Supervisor/Mayor:
Ron Belmont .914-670-3005/fax: 914-835-8067
  e-mail: jwalsh@harrison-ny.gov
Town Clerk:
Jacqueline Greer 914-670-3030/fax: 914-835-2009
  e-mail: jgreer@harrison-ny.gov
Comptroller/Treasurer:
Maureen MacKenzie 914-670-3080/fax: 914-835-2759
  e-mail: comptroller@harrison-ny.gov
Police Chief:
Anthony Marraccini 914-967-5110

Commissioner, Public Works:
Anthony P Robinson 914-670-3229/fax: 914-835-2387
  e-mail: arobinson@harrison-ny.gov
Fire Marshal/Fire Prevention Dept:
Robert Fitzsimmons. 914-670-3051/fax: 914-670-3170

Haverstraw, Town of
1 Rosman Rd
Garnerville, NY 10923
845-429-2200 Fax: 845-429-4701
Web site: www.townofhaverstraw.us

Town Supervisor:
Howard T Phillips, Jr. 845-429-2200/fax: 845-429-4701
Town Clerk:
Karen L. Bulley . . . . .845-942-3727 or 845-942-3728
  fax: 845-942-4964
Town Attorney:
William Stein 845-429-2200
Finance Director:
Michael J Gamboli 845-429-2200

Hempstead, Town of
Town Hall Plaza
1 Washington St
Hempstead, NY 11550
516-489-5000 Fax: 516-538-2908
Web site: www.townofhempstead.org; www.toh.li

Town Supervisor:
Kate Murray. 516-489-6000 x3260
Town Clerk:
Mark A Bonilla 516-489-5000 x3046
  e-mail: markbon@hotmail.org

Hempstead, Village of
99 Nichols Court
Hempstead, NY 11550
516-489-3400 Fax: 516-489-4285
Web site: www.villageofhempstead.org

Mayor:
Wayne J Hall Sr 516-478-6200
Village Clerk:
Patricia Perez 516-478-6202
  e-mail: clerksoffice@villageofhempsteadny.gov
Public Works Director:
Frank Germinaro 516-489-3400 x270
Chief of Police:
Michael McGown. 516-483-6200

Henrietta, Town of
475 Calkins Rd
Henrietta, NY 14467
585-334-7700 Fax: 585-334-9667
Web site: www.henrietta.org

Town Supervisor:
Michael B Yudelson 585-359-7001/fax: 585-334-9667
  e-mail: supervisor@townofhenrietta.org
Town Clerk:
Leann Case .585-334-7700/fax: 585-334-9667
Sewer, Drainage, & Sidewalks Foreman:
Michael Catalano . . . . : 585-444-2211/fax: 585-359-7029
  e-mail: cmarshall@townofhenrietta.org

Huntington, Town of
100 Main St
Huntington, NY 11743

Offices and agencies generally appear in alphabetical order, except when specific order is requested by listee.

631-351-3000 Fax: 631-424-7856
Web site: http://huntingtonny.gov

Town Supervisor:
 Frank P Petrone 631-351-3030/fax: 631-424-7856
  e-mail: fpetrone@town.huntington.ny.us
Town Clerk:
 Jo-Ann Raia 631-351-3206/fax: 631-351-3205
  e-mail: jraia@town.huntington.ny.us
Town Attorney:
 Cindy Elan-Mangano 631-351-3042/fax: 631-351-3032
  e-mail: townattorney@town.huntington.ny.us
Public Safety Director:
 Vacant 631-351-3167/fax: 631-351-3169
  e-mail: publicsafety@town.huntington.ny.us
Director, General Services:
 Thomas J Boccard 631-351-3365/fax: 631-351-3337
  e-mail: genservices@town.huntington.ny.us
Historian:
 Robert C Hughes 631-351-3244/fax: 631-351-3245
  e-mail: huntingtonhistorial@verizon.net

Hyde Park, Town of
4383 Albany Post Rd
Hyde Park, NY 12538
845-229-5111 Fax: 845-229-0831
Web site: www.hydeparkny.us

Town Supervisor:
 Aileen Rohr 845-229-5111 x8/fax: 845-229-0831
  e-mail: supervisor@hydeparkny.us
Town Clerk:
 Donna McGrogan 845-229-5111 x5/fax: 845-229-7583
  e-mail: tcc-1@hydeparkny.us
Police Chief:
 Eric Paolilli 845-229-9340/fax: 845-229-6953
  e-mail: police@hydeparkny.us
Town Historian:
 Carey Rhinevault 845-229-8225

Irondequoit, Town of
Town Hall
1280 Titus Ave
Rochester, NY 14617
585-467-8840 Fax: 585-467-7294
e-mail: feedback@irondequoit.org
Web site: www.irondequoit.org

Town Supervisor:
 Mary Joyce D'Aurizio 585-336-6034
  e-mail: feedback@irondequoit.org
Town Clerk/Receiver of Taxes:
 Barbara Genier 585-336-6045
  e-mail: bgenier@irondequoit.org
Comptroller:
 Annie C Sealy 585-336-6010
  e-mail: asealy@irondequoit.org
Fire Marshal:
 Greg Merrick 585-336-6097
  e-mail: firemarshal@irondequoit.org
Town Historian:
 Patricia Wayne 585-336-7269
  e-mail: pwayne@irondequoit.org

Islip, Town of
Town Hall
655 Main St
Islip, NY 11751

631-224-5500 or 631-224-5691 Fax: 631-581-8424
Web site: www.townofislip-ny.gov

Town Supervisor:
 Tom Croci 631-224-5500
  e-mail: supervisorsoffice@townofislip-ny.gov
Town Clerk:
 Olga H. Murray 631-224-5490/fax: 631-224-5574
  e-mail: townclerk@townofislip-ny.gov
Town Attorney:
 Robert L. Cicale 631-224-5550/fax: 631-224-5573
  e-mail: townattorney@townofislip-ny.gov
Comptroller:
 Joseph Ludwig 631-595-3840/fax: 631-224-5701
  e-mail: comptroller@townofislip-ny.gov
Receiver of Taxes:
 Alexis Weik 631-224-5580
  e-mail: vallen@townofislip-ny.gov
Commissioner, Public Works:
 Thomas Owens 631-224-5600
  e-mail: commissioner-dpw@townofislip-ny.gov
Harbor Police Chief:
 Robert Sgroi 631-224-5656
  e-mail: harborpolice@townofislip-ny.gov

Ithaca, City of
City Hall
108 E Green St
Ithaca, NY 14850
607-274-6570 Fax: 307-274-6432
Web site: www.cityofithaca.org

Mayor:
 Svante Myrick 607-274-6501/fax: 607-274-6526
  e-mail: asherman@cityofithaca.org
City Clerk:
 Julie Conley Holcomb 607-274-6570/fax: 607-274-6432
  e-mail: julieh@cityofithaca.org
City Chamberlain:
 Debra Parsons 607-274-6580/fax: 607-272-7348
  e-mail: debrap@cityofithaca.org
City Attorney:
 Aaron O. Lavine 607-274-6504/fax: 607-274-6507
  e-mail: attorney@cityofithaca.org
Controller:
 Steven P Thayer 607-274-6576/fax: 607-274-6415
  e-mail: dredsicker@cityofithaca.org
Police Chief (Acting):
 John R. Barber 607-272-9973
  e-mail: edv@cityofithaca.org

Ithaca, Town of
Town Hall
215 North Tioga Street
Ithaca, NY 14850
607-273-1721
Web site: www.town.ithaca.ny.us

Town Supervisor:
 Herb Engman 607-273-1721 x125
  e-mail: Hengman@town.ithaca.ny.us
Town Clerk:
 Paulette Terwilliger 607-273-1721 x110
  e-mail: pterwilliger@town.ithaca.ny.us
Town Budget Officer:
 Al Carvill 607-273-1721 x113
  e-mail: acarvill@town.ithaca.ny.us
Town Historian:
 Laura Johnson-Kelly
  e-mail: lwjl@town.ithaca.ny.us

Offices and agencies generally appear in alphabetical order, except when specific order is requested by listee.

Jamestown, City of

Municipal Bldg
200 E Third St
Jamestown, NY 14701
716-483-7612 Fax: 716-483-7502
Web site: www.jamestownny.net

Mayor:
  Samuel Teresi 716-483-7600/fax: 716-483-7591
City Clerk:
  James Olson. .716-483-7612/fax: 716-483-7502
Corporation Counsel:
  Marilyn Fiore-Lehman 716-483-7540/fax: 716-483-7591
Comptroller:
  Joseph A Bellitto. 716-483-7538/fax: 716-483-7771
Director Financial Services:
  James Olson. .716-483-7512/fax: 716-483-7502
Police Chief/Director Public Safety:
  Harry Snellings 716-483-7536/fax: 716-483-7722

Kingston, City of

420 Broadway
Kingston, NY 12401
845-331-0080 Fax: 845-334-3904
Web site: www.ci.kingston.ny.us

Mayor:
  Shayne R Gallo 845-334-3902/fax: 845-334-3904
  e-mail: mayor@kingston-ny.gov
City Clerk:
  Carly Williams. 845-334-3915/fax: 845-334-3918
  e-mail: cwilliams@kingston-ny.gov
Corporation Counsel:
  Andrew Zweben 845-334-3947/fax: 845-334-3959
  e-mail: corpcounsel@kingston-ny.gov
Comptroller:
  John Tuey 845-334-3935/fax: 845-334-3944
  e-mail: comptroller@kingston-ny.gov
Executive Director, Community Development:
  Michael Murphy 845-334-3924/fax: 845-334-3932
  e-mail: mmurphy@kingston-ny.gov
Chief of Police/Commissioner:
  Egidio F. Tinti . . . . .845-331-1671 or 845-943-5720
  e-mail: gkeller@kingston-ny.gov
Fire Chief:
  John Reinhardt. 845-331-1326/fax: 845-331-3252
  e-mail: fire@kingston-ny.gov

Lancaster, Town of

21 Central Ave
Lancaster, NY 14086
716-683-1610 Fax: 716-683-0512
e-mail: lookatus@lancasterny.com
Web site: www.erie.gov/lancaster/depts

Town Supervisor:
  Dino J Fudoli. 716-683-1610/fax: 716-683-0512
Town Clerk:
  Johanna M Coleman 716-683-9028/fax: 716-683-2094
  e-mail: jcoleman@lancaster.ny.com
Town Attorney:
  John M Dudziak 716-684-3342/fax: 716-681-7475
  e-mail: jdudziak@lancasterny.com
Director, Administration & Finance:
  David J Brown 716-683-1610
Police Chief:
  Gerald Gill Jr. 716-683-2800/fax: 716-681-2352
Emergency Management/Nat'l Disaster Coordinator:
  Robert MacPeek 716-684-1232/fax: 716-684-1237

Town Assessor:
  Christine Fusco. 716-683-1311 x112/fax: 716-681-7054
  e-mail: assessor@lancasterny.com
Historian:
  Edward Mikula 716-683-6529

LeRay, Town of

8650 LeRay Street
Evans Mill, NY 13637-3191
315-629-4052 Fax: 315-629-4393
Web site: www.townofleray.org

Town Supervisor:
  Ronald C Taylor 315-629-5532/fax: 315-629-4393
  e-mail: lerayadmin@nnymail.com
Town Clerk/Receiver/Registrar:
  Mary C Smith 315-629-4052/fax: 315-629-4393
  e-mail: lerayclerk@nnymail.com

Lindenhurst, Village of

430 S Wellwood Ave
Lindenhurst, NY 11757
631-957-7500 Fax: 631-957-4605
e-mail: info@villageoflindenhurst.com
Web site: www.villageoflindenhurst.com

Village Mayor:
  Thomas A Brennan. 631-957-7500
Deputy Mayor:
  Kevin McCaffey 631-957-7500
Clerk/Treasurer:
  Shawn Cullinane
Deputy Clerk:
  Doug M Madlon
Fire Marshall:
  Richard Lyman 631-957-7514

Lockport, City of

Lockport Municipal Building
One Locks Plaza
Lockport, NY 14094
716-439-6665 Fax: 716-439-6668
Web site: www.elockport.com

Mayor:
  Michael W Tucker. 716-439-6665/fax: 716-439-6668
City Clerk:
  Richelle J. Pasceri 716-439-6676/fax: 716-439-6650
Treasurer:
  Michael White. 716-439-6744/fax: 716-439-6617
Police Chief:
  Lawrence Eggert. 716-439-6689
Fire Department Chief:
  Thomas J Passuite. 716-439-6724

Lockport, Town of

6560 Dysinger Rd
Lockport, NY 14094
716-439-9520 Fax: 716-439-0528
Web site: www.elockport.com

Town Supervisor:
  Marc Smith 716-439-9520/fax: 716-439-0528
Town Clerk:
  Nancy Brooks 716-439-9524/fax: 716-438-5465
Town Historian:
  Laurence Haseley 716-438-2159

Offices and agencies generally appear in alphabetical order, except when specific order is requested by listee.

351

Long Beach, City of

City Hall
1 West Chester St
Long Beach, NY 11561
516-431-1000 Fax: 516-431-1389
e-mail: info@longbeachny.org
Web site: www.longbeachny.org

City Manager:
    Jack Schnirman 516-431-1001
    e-mail: citymanager@longbeach.ny.org
City Clerk:
    David W Fraser 516-431-1002/fax: 516-431-2717
Corporation Counsel:
    Corey Klein 516-431-1003
Comptroller:
    Jeff Nogid 516-431-1004
Police Commissioner:
    Michael Tangney 516-431-1800
    e-mail: lbpd@longbeachny.org

Lysander, Town of

Town Hall
8220 Loop Rd
Baldwinsville, NY 13027
315-638-4264 Fax: 315-635-1515
Web site: www.townoflysander.org

Town Supervisor:
    John A Salisbury 315-857-0281/fax: 315-635-1515
    e-mail: supervisor@townoflysander.org
Town Clerk:
    Lisa Dell 315-638-0224/fax: 315-635-1515
    e-mail: townclerk@townoflysander.org
Comptroller:
    David J Rahrle 315-635-1443/fax: 315-635-1515
    e-mail: comptroller@townoflysander.org
Town Historian:
    Bonnie Kisselstein 315-638-0224/fax: 315-635-1515
    e-mail: bkissels@twcny.rr.com

Mamaroneck, Town of

Town Center
740 W Boston Post Rd
Mamaroneck, NY 10543
914-381-7805 Fax: 914-381-7809
e-mail: townclerk@townofmamaroneck.org
Web site: www.townofmamaroneck.org

Town Supervisor:
    Nancy Seligson
    e-mail: supervisor@townofmamaroneck.org
Town Administrator:
    Stephen Altieri 914-381-7810/fax: 914-381-7809
    e-mail: townadministrator@townofmamaroneck.org
Town Clerk:
    Christina Battalia 914-381-7870/fax: 914-381-7813
    e-mail: townclerk@townofmamaroneck.org
Police Chief:
    Richard Rivera 914-381-6100/fax: 914-381-7897
    e-mail: policechief@townofmamaroneck.org
Emergency Management Coordinator:
    Michael Liverzani 914-381-7838

Manlius, Town of

301 Brooklea Dr
Fayetteville, NY 13066

315-637-3521 Fax: 315-637-0713
Web site: www.townofmanlius.org

Town Supervisor:
    Edmond J Theobald 315-637-3414/fax: 315-637-0713
    e-mail: etheobald@townofmanlius.org
Town Clerk:
    Allison A Edsall 315-637-3521/fax: 315-637-0713
Receiver of Taxes:
    Laura Peschel 315-637-6481/fax: 315-637-0713
Police Chief:
    Francis Marlowe 315-682-2212/fax: 315-682-4527

Middletown, City of

City Hall
16 James St
Middletown, NY 10940
845-346-4100 Fax: 845-343-7439
Web site: www.middletown-ny.com

Mayor:
    Joseph M DeStefano 845-346-4100/fax: 845-343-7439
    e-mail: mayor@middletown-ny.com
Common Council President:
    J Miguel Rodrigues 845-742-8775
    e-mail: mrodrigues@middletown-ny.com
Common Council Clerk/Registrar:
    John Naumchik 845-346-4168/fax: 845-344-5428
City Attorney:
    Alex Smith 845-346-4140/fax: 845-346-4146
Treasurer:
    Donald Paris 845-346-4150/fax: 845-343-1101
Commissioner, Public Works:
    Jacob Tawil 845-343-3169/fax: 845-343-4014
Chief of Police:
    Ramon Bethencourt 845-343-3151/fax: 845-343-2660
    e-mail: rbethencourt@middletown-ny.com
Fire Chief:
    Tom Amodio 845-344-5003/fax: 845-344-5031
    e-mail: info@middletownfiredept.com

Monroe, Town of

11 Stage Road
Monroe, NY 10950
845-783-1900 Fax: 845-782-5597
Web site: www.monroeny.org

Town Supervisor:
    Sandy Leonard 845-783-1900 x227/fax: 845-782-5597
    e-mail: cathy@monroeny.org
Town Clerk:
    Mary Ellen Beams 845-783-1900 x221/fax: 845-782-5597
    e-mail: maryellen@monroeny.org
Tax Collector:
    Mary Ellen Beams 845-783-1990 x221/fax: 845-782-5597
Historian:
    James Nelson 845-783-3406
    e-mail: nelsonja@fastmail.fm

Montgomery, Town of

110 Bracken Rd
Montgomery, NY 12549
845-457-2660 Fax: 845-457-2613
Web site: www.townofmontgomery.com

Town Supervisor:
    Michael Hayes 845-457-2600
Town Clerk:
    Tara Stickles 845-457-2660/fax: 845-457-2613

Offices and agencies generally appear in alphabetical order, except when specific order is requested by listee.

Town Attorney:
  Charles T Bazydlo 845-361-3668
Receiver of Taxes:
  Janice A Cocks 845-457-2630/fax: 845-457-2613
  e-mail: tomtax@frontiernet.net
Police Chief:
  Arnold Amthor 845-457-9211
  e-mail: TMPDChief@frontiernet.net
Town Historian:
  Suzanne Isaksen 845-457-9098
  e-mail: tomhistorian@frontiernet.net

Mount Pleasant, Town of

One Town Hall Plaza
Valhalla, NY 10595
914-742-2360 Fax: 914-769-3155
Web site: www.mtpleasantny.com

Town Supervisor:
  Joan A Maybury 914-742-2301/fax: 914-769-3155
  e-mail: jmaybury@mtpleasantny.com
Town Clerk:
  Patricia June Scova 914-742-2312/fax: 914-747-6172
  e-mail: pscova@mtpleasantny.com
Deputy Town Attorney:
  Christopher W. McClure............914-742-2357/fax: 914-769-3155
Comptroller:
  Tina Peretti 914-742-2360
Police Chief:
  Louis Alagno....................914-769-1941/fax: 914-769-7199
  e-mail: lalagno@mtpleasantny.com

Mount Vernon, City of

City Hall
1 Roosevelt Square
Mount Vernon, NY 10550
914-665-2300 Fax: 914-665-2496
Web site: cmvny.com

Mayor:
  Ernest D. Davis...................................914-665-2360
  e-mail: mayor@cmvny.com
City Clerk/Registrar:
  George Brown....................................914-665-2348
Comptroller:
  Maureen Walker 914-665-2312
Police Commissioner:
  John Roland 914-665-2500
Police Chief:
  James Dumser....................................914-665-2500
Fire Chief:
  Edward Stephenson 914-665-2626
Deputy Public Works Commissioner:
  Curtis J Woods 914-665-2334

New Hartford, Town of

Butler Hall
48 Genesee Street
New Hartford, NY 13413
315-733-7500
Web site: www.newhartfordtown.com

Town Supervisor:
  Patrick M Tyksinski........................315-733-7500 x2332
  e-mail: nhsupervisor@town.new-hartford.ny.us
Town Clerk:
  Gail Wolanin Young 315-733-7500 x2322/fax: 315-797-9986
  e-mail: gyoung@town.new-hartford.ny.us

Receiver of Taxes:
  Gail Wolanin Young 315-733-7500 x2324/fax: 315-797-9986
  e-mail: hilarie@town.new-hartford.ny.us
Police Chief:
  Michael Inserra 315-724-7111/fax: 315-724-8618
  e-mail: mis108@town.new-hartford.ny.us

New Rochelle, City of

City Hall
515 North Ave
New Rochelle, NY 10801
914-654-2000 Fax: 914-654-2174
Web site: www.newrochelleny.com

Mayor:
  Noam Bramson 914-654-2150/fax: 914-654-2357
  e-mail: nbramson@newrochelleny.com
City Manager:
  Charles B Strome III 914-654-2140/fax: 914-654-2174
  e-mail: cstrome@newrochelleny.com
City Clerk:
  Bennie F Giles.....................914-654-2159/fax: 914-654-2158
  e-mail: bgiles@newrochellenewyork.com
Corporation Counsel:
  Kathleen Gill 914-654-2120/fax: 914-654-2345
Finance Commissioner:
  Howard Rattner 914-654-2062/fax: 914-654-2344
Public Works Commissioner:
  Alexander Tergis 914-654-2129/fax: 914-654-2195
  e-mail: atergis@newrochelleny.com
Police Commissioner:
  Patrick J Carroll 914-654-2228
Fire Chief:
  Louis DeMeglio.....................914-654-2212/fax: 914-632-2907
  e-mail: rkiernan@newrochelleny.com

New Windsor, Town of

555 Union Avenue
New Windsor, NY 12553
845-565-8800 Fax: 845-563-4693
e-mail: info@town.new-windsor.ny.us
Web site: http://town.new-windsor.ny.us

Town Supervisor/Chief Fiscal Officer:
  George A Green...................845-563-4610/fax: 845-563-4610
Town Clerk:
  Deborah Green.....................845-563-4611/fax: 845-563-4611
  e-mail: dgreen@town.new-windsor.ny.us
Town Attorney:
  Michael Blythe 845-563-4630/fax: 845-563-4630
  e-mail: mblythe@town.new-windsor.ny.us
Comptroller:
  Jack Finnegan 845-563-4623/fax: 845-563-4623
Police Chief:
  Michael C Biasotti.................845-565-7000/fax: 845-563-4694
  e-mail: pdadmin@town.new-windsor.ny.us
Fire Inspector & Department Head:
  Jennifer Gallagher 845-563-4618/fax: 845-563-4618
Town Historian:
  Glenn Marshall
  e-mail: historynw@aol.com

New York City

City Hall
New York, NY 10007
212-788-3000 Fax: 212-788-3247
Web site: www.nyc.gov

Offices and agencies generally appear in alphabetical order, except when specific order is requested by listee.

Mayor:
  Michael R Bloomberg . . . . 212-788-3000 or 212-639-9675
  fax: 212-312-0700
First Deputy Mayor:
  Patricia E Harris 212-788-3000/fax: 212-312-0700
Deputy Mayor, Economic Development:
  Robert K. Steel 212-788-3000/fax: 212-312-0700
Deputy Mayor, Government Affairs:
  Howard Wolfson 212-788-3000/fax: 212-312-0700
Deputy Mayor, Legal Affairs:
  Carol A Robles-Roman 212-788-3000/fax: 212-312-0700
Deputy Mayor, Operations:
  Cas Holloway 212-788-3000/fax: 212-312-0700
Deputy Mayor, Education & Community Development:
  Dennis M Walcott 212-788-3000/fax: 212-312-0700
Director, Communications:
  James Anderson 212-788-3000
Senior Advisor to Mayor:
  Shea Fink. 212-788-3000/fax: 212-312-0700
Press Secretary:
  Stu Loeser 212-788-3000/fax: 212-788-2460

Aging, Dept for the, NYC . . . . fax: 212-442-1095
  2 Lafayette St, New York, NY 10007
  212-442-1322 Fax: 212-442-1095
  Web site: www.nyc.gov/aging
Commissioner:
  Lilliam Barrios-Paoli
  e-mail: emendez@aging.nyc.gov
First Deputy Commissioner:
  Sally Renfro
  e-mail: srenfro@aging.nyc.gov
General Counsel:
  Steven Foo 212-442-3159
  e-mail: mamurphy@aging.nyc.gov
Deputy Commissioner, External Affairs:
  Caryn Resnick. 212-442-1277
  e-mail: cresnick@aging.nyc.gov
Executive Director, Aging in NY Fund:
  Ali Hodin-Baier 212-442-1375
Director, Public Affairs:
  Christopher Miller
  e-mail: cmiller@aging.nyc.gov

Public Design Commission, NYC . . . . fax: 212-788-3086
  City Hall, 3rd Fl, New York, NY 10007
  212-788-3071 Fax: 212-788-3086
  Web site: www.nyc.gov/artcommission
Executive Director:
  Jackie Snyder. 212-788-3071/fax: 212-788-3086
  e-mail: jsnyder@cityhall.nyc.gov
President:
  Signe Nielsen. 212-788-3071/fax: 212-788-3086
Project Manager:
  Rivka Weinstock 212-788-3071/fax: 212-788-3086
Special Projects Manager:
  Julianna Monjeau 212-788-3071/fax: 212-788-3086
Sculptor:
  Maria Elena-Gonzalez. 212-788-3071/fax: 212-788-3086
Painter:
  Byron Kim. 212-788-3071/fax: 212-788-3086
Architect:
  James Stewart Polshek 212-788-3071/fax: 212-788-3086
Director, Tour Programs:
  Joan H Bright. 212-788-3071/fax: 212-788-3086

Buildings, Department of, NYC. . . . . fax: 212-566-3784
  280 Broadway, 7th Fl, New York, NY 10007-1801
  212-566-5000 or TTY: 212-566-4769 Fax: 212-566-3784
  Web site: www.nyc.gov/buildings

Commissioner:
  Robert D LiMandri 212-566-0011
First Deputy Cmsr, Operations:
  Thomas Fariello, R.A.
Deputy Commissioner, Technology & Analysis:
  Marilyn King-Festa 212-566-4225/fax: 212-566-3865
Deputy Commissioner, Technical Affairs:
  Fatma Amer
General Counsel:
  Mona Sehgal 212-566-3291/fax: 212-566-3843

Campaign Finance Board, NYC . . . . fax: 212-306-7143
  40 Rector St, 7th Fl, New York, NY 10006
  212-306-7100 Fax: 212-306-7143
  e-mail: info@nyccfb.info
  Web site: www.nyccfb.info
Chair:
  Joseph P Parkes
Executive Director:
  Amy M Loprest
Chief of Administrative Services:
  Elizabeth Bauer
Director of External Affairs:
  Eric Friedman

City Council, NYC. . . . . fax: 212-788-7093
  250 Broadway, 18th Fl, New York, NY 10007
  212-788-7084 Fax: 212-788-7093
  Web site: council.nyc.gov
Speaker:
  Christine C Quinn. 212-788-7210
Minority Leader:
  James S Oddo 718-980-1017/fax: 718-980-1051
  e-mail: joddo@council.nyc.gov
Deputy Majority Leader:
  Leroy G Comrie. 718-766-3700/fax: 718-766-3798

City Planning, Department of, NYC . . . . fax: 212-720-3219
  22 Reade St, New York, NY 10007-1216
  212-720-3300 Fax: 212-720-3219
  Web site: www.nyc.gov
Chair:
  Amanda M Burden
Executive Director:
  Richard Barth
Director, Operations:
  David J Zagor 212-720-3650
Director, Public Affairs:
  Rachaele Raynoff 212-720-3471
General Counsel:
  David Karnovsky 212-720-3400

Citywide Administrative Services, Department of, NYC . . . . . fax:
212-669-8992
  One Centre St, 17th Fl S, New York, NY 10007
  212-669-7000 Fax: 212-669-8992
  Web site: www.nyc.gov/dcas
Commissioner:
  Edna Wells Handy
Chief Communication Officer:
  Julianne Cho 212-669-7140

Civil Service Commission, NYC
  1 Centre Street, 2300 N, New York, NY 10007
  212-669-2609
  e-mail: commission@nyc.csc.nyc.gov
  Web site: www.nyc.gov/html/csc
Chairwoman:
  Nancy G. Chaffetz
Acting Director & General Counsel:
  Norma I Lopez 212-669-2609

Offices and agencies generally appear in alphabetical order, except when specific order is requested by listee.

Office Manager:
Evelyn Horowitz...................................212-669-2608

Collective Bargaining, Office of, NYC..........fax: 212-306-7167
40 Rector St, 7th Fl, New York, NY 10006
212-306-7160 Fax: 212-306-7167
e-mail: nyc-ocb@ocb.nyc.gov
Web site: www.ocb-nyc.org
Director:
Marlene A Gold
Deputy Chair, Dispute Resolution:
Susan Panepento
General Counsel:
Philip Maier

Comptroller, NYC...........................fax: 212-669-2707
Municipal Bldg, One Centre St, Rm 530, New York, NY 10007
212-669-3500 Fax: 212-669-2707
Web site: www.comptroller.nyc.gov
Comptroller:
John C Liu
First Deputy Comptroller:
Ricardo E. Morales
Deputy Comptroller/General Counsel:
Valerie Budzik
Deputy Comptroller, Public Finance:
Carol Kostik
Deputy Comptroller, Budget and Public Affairs:
Ari Hoffnung

Conflicts of Interest Board, NYC..............fax: 212-442-1407
2 Lafayette St, Ste 1010, New York, NY 10007
212-442-1400 Fax: 212-442-1407
Web site: www.nyc.gov/ethics
Executive Director:
Mark Davies...................................212-442-1424
e-mail: davies@coib.nyc.gov
Deputy Exec Director/General Counsel:
Wayne G Hawley 212-442-1415
e-mail: hawley@coib.nyc.gov
Director, Enforcement:
Carolyn Lisa Miller............................212-442-1419
e-mail: miller@coib.nyc.gov
Director, Administration:
Ute O'Malley 212-442-1427
e-mail: omalley@coib.nyc.gov
Director, Information Technology:
Derick Yu 212-442-1605
e-mail: yu@coib.nyc.gov
Director, Training/Education Unit:
Alexander Kipp................................212-442-1421
e-mail: kipp@coib.nyc.gov
Director, Financial Disclosure/Special Counsel:
Felicia A. Mennin.............................212-442-1455
e-mail: mennin@coib.nyc.gov

Consumer Affairs, Department of, NYC ....fax: 212-487-4221
42 Broadway, New York, NY 10004
212-487-4401 Fax: 212-487-4221
Web site: www.nyc.gov/html/dca
Commissioner:
Jonathan Mintz
Deputy Director, Communications:
Vacant.......................................212-487-4283

Correction, Board of, NYC....................fax: 212-788-7860
51 Chambers St, Room 923, New York, NY 10007
212-788-7840 Fax: 212-788-7860
Web site: www.nyc.gov/boc
Chair:
Gerald Harris
e-mail: nycboc@earthlink.net

Executive Director:
Cathy Porter
Director, Field Operations:
Felix Martinez

Correction, Department of, NYC...............fax: 646-248-1219
60 Hudson St, 6th Fl, New York, NY 10013-4393
212-266-1500 Fax: 646-248-1219
Web site: www.nyc.gov/doc
Commissioner:
Dora B Schriro
Senior Dep Commissioner:
John J Antonelli

Cultural Affairs, Department of, NYC
31 Chambers St, New York, NY 10007
212-513-9300
Web site: www.nyc.gov/html/dcla
Commissioner:
Kate D Levin
Deputy Commissioner:
Margaret Morton
Chief of Staff:
Shirley Levy

Design & Construction, Dept of, NYC..........fax: 718-391-1608
30-30 Thomson Avenue, Long Island City, NY 11101
718-391-1000 Fax: 718-391-1608
Web site: www.nyc.gov/html/ddc
Commissioner:
David J Burney 718-391-1000
Chief of Staff:
Ana Barrio.......................718-391-2300/fax: 718-391-1893
Public Information:
Joe Soldevere....................718-391-1641/fax: 718-391-2600
Chief Contracting Officer:
Carol DiAgostino 718-391-1501/fax: 718-391-2600
General Counsel:
David Varoli 718-391-1721/fax: 718-391-2600

Disabilities, Mayor's Office, for People with.....fax: 212-341-9843
100 Gold Street, 2nd Floor, New York, NY 10038
212-788-2830 or TTY 212-504-4115 Fax: 212-341-9843
Web site: www.nyc.gov/html/mopd
Commissioner:
Matthew P Sapolin 212-788-2830

Economic Development Corp, NYC
110 William Street, New York, NY 10038
212-619-5000 or 888-692-0100
Web site: www.nycedc.com
President:
Seth W Pinsky................................212-312-3500
Senior VP, Budget:
Tom Jones....................................212-312-3877

Education, Dept of, NYC......................fax: 212-374-5588
52 Chambers St, New York, NY 10007
718-935-2000 Fax: 212-374-5588
Web site: www.nycenet.edu
Chancellor:
Dennis M Walcott
Deputy Chancellor, Finance/Admin:
Photeine Anagnostopoulos
Deputy Chancellor, Teaching/Learning:
Eric Nadelstern
Director, Strategic Partnerships:
Stephanie Dua
General Counsel & Legal Services Office:
Courtenaye Jackson-Chase
Executive Director, Intergovernmental Affairs:
Lenny Speiller

Offices and agencies generally appear in alphabetical order, except when specific order is requested by listee.

Communications & Media Relations:
  David Cantor

Elections, Board of, NYC.......................fax: 212-487-5349
  32 Broadway, 7th Fl, New York, NY 10004-1609
  212-487-5300 or TDD 212-487-5496 Fax: 212-487-5349
  Web site: www.vote.nyc.ny.us
President, Commissioners:
  Frederic M. Umane
  e-mail: fumane@boe.nyc.ny.us
Executive Director:
  Vacant
  e-mail: webmail_ravitzj@boe.nyc.ny.us
Deputy Executive Director:
  Dawn Sandow
  e-mail: webmail_sandow@boe.nyc.ny.us
Administrative Manager:
  Pamela Perkins
  e-mail: webmail_perkinsp@boe.nyc.ny.us
Director, Public Affairs & Communications:
  Valerie Vazquez
  e-mail: webmail_vazquezv@boe.nyc.ny.us

Environmental Protection, Department of, NYC
  59-17 Junction Blvd, 13th Fl, Flushing, NY 11373-5108
  212-639-6975
  Web site: www.nyc.gov/dep
Commissioner:
  Carter Strickland...............................718-595-6565
  e-mail: cward@dep.nyc.gov
First Dep Commissioner/Exec Dir Water Board:
  Steven Lawitts...................................718-595-6576
Chief of Staff:
  Kathryn Garcia
General Counsel:
  Mark D Hoffer 718-595-6528
Director, Public & Intergovernmental Affairs:
  Charles G Sturcken..............................718-595-6568

Equal Employment Practices Commission, NYC fax: 212-788-8652
  40 Rector Street, 14th Floor, New York, NY 10006
  212-788-8646 Fax: 212-788-8652
  Web site: www.nyc.gov/html/eepc
Executive Director:
  Charise L. Hendricks..............212-788-8646/fax: 212-788-8652
  e-mail: chendricks@eepc.nyc.gov
Deputy Director:
  Charise Hendricks................................212-788-8573
  e-mail: chendricks@eepc.nyc.gov
General Counsel:
  Judith Garcia Quinonez 212-788-8644
  e-mail: jquinonez@eepc.nyc.gov

Film, Theatre & Broadcasting, Mayor's Office of, NYC .....fax:
212-307-6237
  Ed Sullivan Theatre Bldg, 1697 Broadway, Ste 602, New York, NY 10019
  212-489-6710 Fax: 212-307-6237
  e-mail: info@film.nyc.gov
  Web site: www.nyc.gov/film
Commissioner:
  Katherine Oliver
Deputy Commissioner:
  John Battista 212-489-6710
Director, Production:
  Dean McCann....................................212-489-6710

Finance, Department of, NYC
  One Centre Street, 22nd Floor, New York, NY 10007
  212-639-9675
  e-mail: starkm@finance.nyc.gov
  Web site: www.nyc.gov/finance

Commissioner:
  David M Frankel
First Deputy Commissioner:
  Rochelle Patricof................................212-669-2525
Assistant Commissioner, Communications/Government Affairs:
  Sam Miller
Budget Director:
  Pat Mattera-Russell
Treasury Deputy Commissioner:
  Robert Lee

Fire Department, NYC.......................fax: 718-999-2582
  9 Metrotech Center, 8th Fl, Brooklyn, NY 11201
  718-999-2000 Fax: 718-999-2582
  Web site: www.nyc.gov/fdny
Commissioner:
  Salvatore J Cassano
First Deputy Commissioner:
  Daniel Shacknai
Chief of NYC Fire Department:
  Edward Kilduff
Deputy Commissioner, Administration:
  Douglas White
Deputy Commissioner, Technology & Support Services:
  Joel Golub
Deputy Commissioner, Intergovernmental Affairs:
  Daniel Shacknai 718-999-2013
Deputy Commissioner, Legal:
  Mylan Denerstein 718-999-2016
Deputy Commissioner, Public Information:
  Francis X Gribbon
Chief of Operations:
  James Esposito

Health & Hospitals Corporation, NYC..........fax: 212-788-0040
  125 Worth St, New York, NY 10013
  212-788-3321 Fax: 212-788-0040
  Web site: www.nyc.gov/hhc
President/CEO:
  Alan D Aviles
Senior VP, Corporate Planning/Community Health/Intergvt Relations:
  LaRay Brown
Senior VP, Operations:
  Frank J Cirillo
Senior VP/Chief Medical Officer, Medical & Professional Affairs:
  Ross Wilson 212-788-3648
Senior VP, Finance/Capital/CFO:
  Marlene Zurack 212-788-3494
General Counsel (Senior VP General Counsel):
  Salvatore J Russo
Senior VP Corporate Communications & Marketing:
  Ana Marengo

Health & Mental Hygiene, Dept of, NYC........fax: 212-964-0472
  125 Worth St, New York, NY 10013
  212-788-5290 or 212-825-5400 Fax: 212-964-0472
  Web site: www.nyc.gov/html/doh
Commissioner:
  Thomas Farley 212-219-5261
Executive Deputy Commissioner, Mental Hygiene:
  Adam Karpati
Chief of Staff:
  Emiko Otsubo
Deputy Commissioner, Administration:
  Julie Friesen
Deputy Commissioner, Disease Control:
  Jay Varma
Deputy Commissioner, Health Care Access/Improvement:
  Amanda Parsons
Deputy Commissioner, Epidemiology:
  Carolyn Greene

Offices and agencies generally appear in alphabetical order, except when specific order is requested by listee.

Deputy Commissioner, Environmental Health:
Daniel Kass
Deputy Commissioner, Health Promotion/Disease Prevention:
Andrew Goodman
General Counsel:
Thomas Merrill 212-788-5290

Homeless Services, Department of, NYC . . . . fax: 212-361-7950
33 Beaver St, 17th Fl, New York, NY 10004
212-361-8000 Fax: 212-361-7950
Web site: www.nyc.gov/dhs
Commissioner:
Seth Diamond
EEO Officer:
Mark Neal
Deputy Commissioner, Communications/External Affairs:
Barbara Brancaccio
General Counsel:
Michele Ovesey
Deputy Commissioner, Prevention, Policy & Planning:
Ellen Howard-Cooper
Deputy Commissioner, Adult Services:
Douglas C. James
Executive Deputy Commissioner, Family Services:
Anne Heller
Deputy Commissioner, Facility Maint/Development:
Yianna Pavlakos

Housing Authority, NYC . . . . fax: 212-306-8888
250 Broadway, New York, NY 10007
212-306-3000 Fax: 212-306-8888
Web site: www.nyc.gov/nycha
Chairman:
John B Rhea
General Manager:
Cecil House
Acting Executive Vice President, Legal Affairs & General Counsel:
K. MacNeal
Chief of Staff:
H. Morillo
Chief Information Officer & Executive Vice President:
A. Riazi
Deputy General Mgr, Finance:
Felix Lam
Executive Vice President, Operations:
C. Laboy-Diaz
Executive Vice President & Chief, Administration:
N. Rivers
Executive Vice President, Community Programs:
S. Myrie

Housing Preservation & Development, Dept of, NYC . . . . fax:
212-863-6302
100 Gold St, 5th Fl, New York, NY 10038
212-863-6300 Fax: 212-863-6302
Web site: www.nyc.gov/hpd
Commissioner:
Mathew M Wambua
Firsy Deputy Commissioner:
Douglas Apple
Deputy Commissioner/Legal Affairs:
Matthew Shafit
Senior Counsel, State & Legislative Affairs:
Joseph Rosenberg
Assistant Commissioner, Housing Supervision:
J. Walpert
Assistant Commissioner, Preservation Services:
E. Enderlin 212-863-7001
Assistant Commissioner, Administration:
J. Cucchiaro

Deputy Commissioner, Community Partnerships:
Kimberly D Hardy 212-863-5128/fax: 212-863-8907

Human Resources Administration, Dept of, NYC fax: 212-331-6214
180 Water St, 17th Fl, New York, NY 10038
212-331-6000 Fax: 212-331-6214
Web site: www.nyc.gov/html/hra
Commissioner:
Robert Doar. 212-331-6000
e-mail: egglestonv@hra.nyc.gov
First Deputy Commissioner:
Patricia M Smith 212-331-6230
Senior Exec Dep Commissioner:
Thomas DePippo. 212-331-6000
Exec Dep Commissioner, Medical Insur/Community Svcs Administration:
Mary Harper 212-273-0001
Executive Deputy Commissioner, Finance Office:
Jill Berry 212-331-3980
Agency Chief Contracting Officer:
Vincent Pullo 212-331-3434
Executive Deputy Commissioner, Family Independence Administration:
Matt Brune 212-331-6180
Deputy Commissioner, Data Reporting & Analysis:
Joe DeMartino. 212-331-6000
Executive Deputy Commissioner, Staff Resources:
Rachel Levine 212-331-3333
Executive Deputy Commissioner, Customized Assistance Services:
Frank R Lipton 212-495-2606
Deputy Commissioner, General Support Services:
Joseph Santino 212-274-5200
Deputy Commissioner, Constituency Services & Policy Improvement:
Jane Corbett
Executive Deputy Commissioner, Domestic Violence & Emergency
Intervention Office:
Cecile Noel 212-331-4500
Chief Integrity Officer, Ingestigation, Revenue & Enforcement:
James Sheehan 212-274-4740
First Deputy General Counsel, Legal Affairs:
Maureen Walsh. 212-331-6167
Chief of Staff:
Anne Heller. 212-331-6225
Deputy Commissioner, Communications & Marketing:
Connie Ress 212-331-6200

Human Rights Commission on, NYC . . . . fax: 212-306-7658
40 Rector St, 10th Fl, New York, NY 10006
212-306-5070 Fax: 212-306-7658
Web site: www.nyc.gov/cchr
Commissioner:
Patricia L Gatling 212-306-7560
Deputy Commissioner/General Counsel:
Cliff Mulqueen 212-306-7741
Executive Director, Law Enforcement:
Carlos Velez 212-306-7764
Deputy Commissioner, Public Affairs:
Dr Lee Hudson 212-306-7773
Director, Communications:
Betsy Herzog. 212-306-7530
Executive Director, Community Relations:
Alexander Korkhov 212-306-7423

**Information Technology & Telecommunications, Dept of,
NYC** . . . . fax: 212-788-8130
75 Park Place, 9th Fl, New York, NY 10007
212-788-6600 Fax: 212-788-8130
Web site: www.nyc.gov/doitt
Commissioner:
Rahul N. Merchant 212-788-6633
EEO Officer:
Emily Johnson. 212-788-6624

Offices and agencies generally appear in alphabetical order, except when specific order is requested by listee.

Chief of Staff/Governance & External Affairs:
 Evan Hines 718-403-8100
Executive Assistant, NYC 3-1-1:
 Jessica Diaz. 212-504-4421
General Counsel:
 Charles Fraser 212-788-6640
Deputy Commissioner, Finance/Admin:
 Brett Robinson 212-788-6616

Investigation, Department of, NYC . . . . fax: 212-825-2823
 80 Maiden Lane, New York, NY 10038
 212-825-5900 Fax: 212-825-2823
 Web site: www.nyc.gov/html/doi
Commissioner:
 Rose Gill Hearn 212-825-5913
 e-mail: rghearn@doi.nyc.gov
Chief of Staff:
 Michael Vitiello 212-825-2870
Deputy Commissioner, Investigations:
 Kim Berger 212-825-5979
General Counsel:
 Marjorie Landa 212-825-2404
Public Information Officer:
 Diane Struzzi. 212-825-3514

Juvenile Justice, Department of, NYC . . . . fax: 212-442-8546
 110th William St., 14th Floor, New York, NY 10038
 212-442-8000 or TTY/TDD:212-442-8578 Fax: 212-442-8546
 e-mail: nycdjj@djj.nyc.gov
 Web site: www.nyc.gov/html/acs
Commissioner:
 Ronald E. Richter 212-442-7630
First Deputy Commissioner:
 Judith Pincus 212-442-7510/fax: 212-442-8512
Deputy Commissioner, Operations & Detention:
 Jerome Davis 212-442-7245/fax: 212-442-8508
Deputy Commissioner, Administration:
 Donald Brosen 212-442-7840/fax: 212-442-8512
General Counsel:
 Joseph Cardieri 212-442-7530/fax: 212-442-8517
Deputy Commissioner, Communications and Community Affairs:
 Michael Fagan 212-442-7534/fax: 718-935-6454

Labor Relations, Office of, NYC . . . . fax: 212-306-7202
 40 Rector St, 4th Fl, New York, NY 10006
 212-306-7200 Fax: 212-306-7202
 Web site: www.nyc.gov/html/olr
Commissioner:
 James F Hanley 212-306-7200
Associate Commissioner:
 Jean N Brewer
General Counsel:
 Mayra Bell 212-306-7230/fax: 212-306-7223
Director, Employee Benefits Program:
 Dorothy A Wolfe 212-306-7200

Landmarks Preservation Commission, NYC . . . . fax: 212-669-7960
 One Centre Street, 9th Fl North, New York, NY 10007
 212-669-7817 Fax: 212-669-7960
 Web site: www.nyc.gov/html/lpc
Chair:
 Robert B Tierney 212-669-7888
 e-mail: rtierney@lpc.nyc.gov

Law, Department of, NYC . . . . fax: 212-788-0367
 100 Church St, New York, NY 10007-2601
 212-788-0303 Fax: 212-788-0367
 Web site: www.nyc.gov/html/law
Corporation Counsel:
 Michael A Cardozo 212-356-1000/fax: 212-356-1148
 e-mail: mcardozo@law.nyc.gov

Managing Attorney:
 G Foster Mills 212-356-2200/fax: 212-356-3585
 e-mail: gmills@law.nyc.gov
Chief of Operations:
 Kenneth J Majerus . . . . .212-356-4040 or 212-356-4049
 e-mail: kmajerus@lawny.gov
Director, Legal Recruitment:
 Stuart Smith 212-356-4070/fax: 212-227-6177
Inspector General:
 Michael Siller .212-825-0646 or 212-825-2505
 e-mail: cmorrick@doi.nyc.gov
Communications Director:
 Kate Ahlers . . . . .212-356-4001 or 212-788-8716
 fax: 212-788-8716
 e-mail: kahlers@law.nyc.gov

Legislative Affairs Office, NYC Mayor's City . . . fax: 212-788-2647
 253 Broadway, 14th Fl, New York, NY 10007
 212-788-3678 Fax: 212-788-2647
 e-mail: citylegislativeaffairs@cityhall.nyc.gov
 Web site: www.nyc.gov/html/moiga
Director:
 Patrick Wehle 212-788-3678/fax: 212-788-2647

Legislative Affairs Office, NYC Mayor's State . . fax: 518-462-5870
 119 Washington Ave, 3rd Fl, Albany, NY 12210
 518-447-5200 Fax: 518-462-5870
Director:
 Joseph N. Garba. 212-278-8820/fax: 212-278-1497

Library, Brooklyn Public . . . . .fax: 718-398-6798
 203 Arlington Avenue, Warwick St., Brooklyn, NY 11207
 718-277-6105 Fax: 718-398-6798
 Web site: www.bklynpubliclibrary.org
President & CEO:
 Linda E Johnson 718-230-2403
Chair, BPL Foundation:
 Anthony W Crowell 718-230-2158
Director, Public Affairs:
 Antonia Yuille Williams. 718-277-6105

Library, New York Public. . . . . .fax: 212-930-9299
 5th Ave & 42nd St, New York, NY 10018
 212-930-0800 or 212-340-0849 Fax: 212-930-9299
 Web site: www.nypl.org
President & CEO:
 Dr. Anthony W. Marx. 212-930-0736
 e-mail: president@nypl.org
Senior VP, External Affairs:
 Vacant 212-930-0611
Chief Operating Officer:
 David Offensend 212-930-0600
Vice President, Development:
 Jennifer Zaslow. 212-930-0692
 e-mail: hlubov@nypl.org
Director, Budget & Planning:
 Marjoel Montalbo 212-592-7400/fax: 212-592-7440
Vice President, Government & Community Affairs:
 George D. Mihaltses. 212-930-0051
VP, Communications & Marketing:
 Ken Weine 212-592-7700

Library, Queens Borough Public . . . . .fax: 718-291-8936
 89-11 Merrick Blvd, Jamaica, NY 11432
 718-990-0700 or TTY 718-990-0809 Fax: 718-291-8936
 Web site: www.queenslibrary.org
President & CEO:
 Thomas W Galante 718-990-0796
 e-mail: thomas.w.galante@queenslibrary.org
Director, Government & Community Affairs:
 James Van Bramer. 718-990-8585/fax: 718-990-5147

Offices and agencies generally appear in alphabetical order, except when specific order is requested by listee.

Director, Marketing & Communications:
Joanne King......................718-990-0704/fax: 718-291-2695
e-mail: joanne.king@queenslibrary.org

Loft Board, NYC ....fax: 212-788-7501
100 Gold St, 2nd Fl, New York, NY 10038
212-788-7610 Fax: 212-788-7501
Web site: www.nyc.gov/html/loft
Chairperson:
Robert D LiMandri......................212-788-7610
Executive Director:
Lanny R Alexander......................212-788-7619

Management & Budget, Office of, NYC.........fax: 212-788-6300
75 Park Place, 8th Fl, New York, NY 10007
212-788-5800 Fax: 212-788-6300
Web site: www.nyc.gov/omb
Director:
Mark Page......................212-788-5900
First Deputy Director:
Stuart Klein......................212-788-5904
Deputy Director/General Counsel:
Marjorie Henning......................212-788-5880
Deputy Director:
P V Anatharam......................212-788-5894
Deputy Director:
Michael Dardia......................212-788-5891

Medical Examiner, Office of Chief, NYC........fax: 212-447-2716
520 First Ave, New York, NY 10016
212-447-2030 Fax: 212-447-2716
Web site: www.nyc.gov/html/ocme
Acting Chief Medical Examiner:
Barbara A. Sampson......................212-447-2034
First Deputy Commissioner:
Barbara Sampson......................212-447-2335
Deputy Commissioner, Administration/Finance:
Janice English......................212-447-5351
Director, Medicolegal Investigations:
Barbara Butcher......................212-447-2036
Director, Public Affairs:
Ellen Borakove 212-447-2401/fax: 212-447-2755
General Counsel:
Jody Lipton......................212-447-2046

Parks & Recreation, Department of, NYC ......fax: 212-360-1329
The Arsenal, Central Park, 830 Fifth Ave, New York, NY 10065
212-360-8111 Fax: 212-360-1329
e-mail: commissioner@parks.nyc.gov
Web site: www.nyc.govparks.org
Commissioner:
Veronica M. White 212-360-1305/fax: 202-360-1345
First Deputy Commissioner, Operations:
Liam Kavanagh......................212-360-1307
Deputy Commissioner, Capital Projects:
Theresa Braddick......................718-760-6602
Assistant Commissioner, Public Programs:
Annika Holder......................212-360-1381
Deputy Commissioner, Management/Budget:
Robert L Garafola......................212-360-1302
Director, Public Affairs:
Vicki Karp......................212-360-1311

Police Department, NYC ....fax: 646-610-5865
One Police Plaza, New York, NY 10038
646-610-5000 Fax: 646-610-5865
Web site: www.nyc.gov/nypd
Police Commissioner:
Raymond W Kelly......................646-610-5410
First Dep Commissioner:
Rafael Pineiro......................646-610-5420

Deputy Commissioner, Strategic Initiatives:
Michael J Farrell......................646-610-8534
Deputy Commissioner, Counter Terrorism:
Richard A Daddario......................646-610-6169
Deputy Commissioner, Intelligence:
David Cohen......................646-610-5403
Deputy Commissioner, Equal Employment Opportunity:
Neldra M Zeigler......................646-610-5330
Deputy Commissioner, Labor Relations:
John P Beirne......................646-610-5060
Deputy Commissioner, Trials:
Martin G Karopkin......................646-610-5424
Deputy Commissioner, Training:
Dr. James O'Keefe......................646-610-4675
Deputy Commissioner, Legal Matters:
Douglas B. Maynard......................646-610-5336
Deputy Commissioner, Management & Budget:
Vincent Grippo......................646-610-6670
Deputy Commissioner, Operations:
John Bilich......................646-610-6100
Deputy Commissioner, Technological Development:
V James Onalfo......................646-610-6873
Deputy Commissioner, Public Information:
Paul J Browne......................646-610-6700

Probation, Department of, NYC.................fax: 212-361-0686
33 Beaver St, New York, NY 10004
212-361-8973 Fax: 212-361-0686
Web site: www.nyc.gov/html/prob
Commissioner:
Vincent N Schrialdi.................212-361-8977/fax: 212-361-8985
e-mail: mhorn@probation.nyc.gov
Senior Policy Advisor to the Commissioner:
Mark Ferrante......................212-361-8970
e-mail: mferrante@probation.nyc.gov
Director, Press & Public Information:
Ryan Dodge......................212-232-0684
e-mail: rdodge@probation.nyc.gov
Chief of Staff:
Michael Ognibene......................212-361-8973
General Counsel:
Wayne McKenzie......................212-232-0700
Deputy Commissioner, Administration:
Michael Forte......................212-361-8965
Deputy Commissioner, Family Court Services:
Patricia Brennan......................212-232-0486
Deputy Commssioner, Adult Services:
Clinton Lacey......................212-361-8982
Chief Information Officer:
Barry Abrams......................212-232-0455

Public Advocate, Office of the ....fax: 212-669-4701
Municipal Bldg, One Centre St, 15th Fl North, New York, NY 10007
212-669-7200 Fax: 212-669-4701
Web site: www.pubadvocate.nyc.gov
Public Advocate:
Bill de Blasio......................212-669-4102
e-mail: bgotbaum@pubadvocate.nyc.gov
General Counsel:
Steven Newmark......................212-669-4719
e-mail: snewmark@pubadvocate.nyc.gov
Chief of Staff:
Dominick Williams......................212-669-4743
e-mail: dwilliams@pubadvocate.nyc.gov
Director, Administration:
Elba Feliciano......................212-669-2179
e-mail: elba@pubadvocate.nyc.gov
Director, Intergovernmental Affairs:
Warren Gardiner......................212-669-4388
e-mail: wgardiner@pubadvocate.nyc.gov

Offices and agencies generally appear in alphabetical order, except when specific order is requested by listee.

Executive Assistant:
    Jane Schatz 212-669-4258
    e-mail: jschatz@pubadvocate.nyc.gov

Records & Information Services, Dept of, NYC . fax: 212-788-8614
    31 Chambers St, Rm 305, New York, NY 10007
    212-639-9675 or TTY: 212-788-8615 Fax: 212-788-8614
    Web site: www.nyc.gov/records
Deputy Commissioner:
    Eileen M Flannelly 212-788-8607
    e-mail: bgandersson@records.nyc.gov
Director, Administration:
    Vickie Moore 212-788-8622
Director, Municipal Archives:
    Leonora Gidlund 212-788-8585
Director, Municipal Records Management Division:
    Pearl L Boatswain 212-788-8550
Director, City Hall Library:
    Paul C Perkus 212-788-8596

Rent Guidelines Board, NYC .... fax: 212-385-2554
    51 Chambers St, Ste 202, New York, NY 10007
    212-385-2934 Fax: 212-385-2554
    e-mail: ask@housingnyc.com
    Web site: www.nycrgb.org
Chair:
    Jonathan L Kimmel..................................212-385-2934
    e-mail: chair@housingnyc.com
Executive Director:
    Andrew McLaughlin
Public Information Officer:
    Charmaine Superville
Senior Research Associate:
    Brian Hoberman 212-385-2934

Sanitation, Department of, NYC
    346 Broadway, 10th Floor, New York, NY 10013
    e-mail: comroffc@dsny.nyc.gov
    Web site: www.nyc.gov/html/dsny
Commissioner:
    John J Doherty 646-885-5020
First Deputy Commissioner:
    Bernard Sullivan....................................646-885-4727
Deputy Commissioner, of Public Info & Community Affairs:
    Vito A Turso 646-885-5020/fax: 212-791-3386

Small Business Services, Department of, NYC ... fax: 212-618-8991
    110 William St, 7th Fl, New York, NY 10038
    212-513-6300 Fax: 212-618-8991
    Web site: www.nyc.gov/html/sbs
Commissioner:
    Robert W Walsh 212-513-6350
First Deputy Commissioner, Financial Management/Administration:
    Andrew Schwartz 212-513-6428
Assistant Commissioner, Business Development & Recruitment:
    Katherine Janeski 212-618-6710
General Counsel:
    Deborah Buyer 212-442-6432
Assistant Commissioner, Finance & Administration:
    Shaazad Ali..212-618-8735
Chief of Staff:
    Sarah Krauss 212-513-6300

Sports Commission, NYC .... fax: 212-788-7514
    2 Washington Street, 15th Floor, New York, NY 10004
    877-692-7767 Fax: 212-788-7514
    Web site: www.nyc.gov/html/mail/html/mailsports.html
Commissioner:
    Kenneth J Podziba 212-487-5676
    e-mail: kpodziba@cityhall.nyc.gov

Standards & Appeals, Board of, NYC......... fax: 212-788-8769
    40 Rector Street, 9th Floor, New York, NY 10006
    212-788-8500 Fax: 212-788-8769
    e-mail: ppacific@dcas.nyc.gov
    Web site: www.nyc.gov/html/bsa
Chair:
    Meenakshi Srinivasan..............................212-788-8547
Vice Chair:
    Christopher Collins
Commissioner:
    Susan M Hinkson
Executive Director:
    Jeff Mulligan......................................212-788-8805

Tax Commission, NYC........................... fax: 212-669-8636
    Municipal Building, 1 Centre St, Rm 936, New York, NY 10007
    212-669-4410 Fax: 212-669-8636
    Web site: www.nyc.gov/html/taxcomm
President:
    Glenn Newman 212-669-4401
Director, Operations:
    Myrna Hall.......................212-669-4420/fax: 212-669-2003
Director, Information Technology:
    Iftikhar Ahmad 212-669-2954
Director, Appraisal & Hearings:
    Carlo Silvestri 212-669-4402
General Counsel:
    Vacant 212-669-4407

Taxi & Limousine Commission, NYC........... fax: 212-676-1100
    40 Rector St, New York, NY 10006
    212-639-9675 Fax: 212-676-1100
    Web site: www.nyc.gov/taxi
Commissioner/Chair/CEO:
    David Yassky 212-676-1003
Chief of Staff:
    Ira Goldstein 212-676-1017/fax: 212-676-2002
First Deputy Commissioner:
    Andrew Salkin ....212-676-1147 or 212-676-1148
Deputy Commissioner, Legal Affairs:
    Charles Fraser 212-676-1117
Deputy Commissioner, Licensing:
    Barbara Schechter.................718-391-5667 or 718-391-5666
Deputy Commissioner, Public Affairs:
    Allan J Fromberg..................212-676-1013/fax: 212-676-1101
Deputy Commissioner of Financial Management & Administration:
    Louis Tazzi 212-676-1035

Transportation, Department of, NYC
    55 Water Street, 9th Floor, New York, NY 10041
    212-639-9675 or TTY: 212-504-4115
    Web site: www.nyc.gov/dot
Commissioner:
    Janette Sadik-Khan 212-676-0868/fax: 212-442-7007
First Deputy Commissioner:
    Lori Ardito 212-839-6403
Deputy Commissioner, External Affairs:
    Seth Solomonow....................................212-839-4850
Deputy Commissioner, Sidewalks & Inspection Mgmt Division:
    Leon W Heyward 212-839-4300

Veterans' Affairs, Mayor's Office of, NYC ...... fax: 212-442-4170
    346 Broadway, 8 W, New York, NY 10007
    212-442-4171 Fax: 212-442-4170
    Web site: www.nyc.gov/html/vets
Commissioner:
    Terrance Holliday..................................212-442-4171
Deputy Commissioner:
    Clarice Joynes.....................................212-442-4171

Voter Assistance Commission (VAC), NYC ..... fax: 212-788-2527
    100 Gold Street, 2nd Floor, New York, NY 10038

Offices and agencies generally appear in alphabetical order, except when specific order is requested by listee.

212-788-8384 Fax: 212-788-2527
Web site: www.nyccfb.info
Chairman:
Joseph P. Parkes 212-306-7100/fax: 212-306-7143
Vice Chair:
Jane Kalmus 212-306-7100
Executive Director/Coordinator:
Amy M. Loprest 212-306-7100

Water Finance Authority, Municipal, NYC . . . . . fax: 212-788-9197
75 Park Place, 6th Fl, New York, NY 10007
212-788-5889 Fax: 212-788-9197
Web site: www.nyc.gov/html/nyw
Executive Director:
Thomas G Paolicelli 212-788-5889
e-mail: paolicellit@omb.nyc.gov
Comptroller:
Michele Mark Levine 212-788-5889
e-mail: levinem@omb.nyc.gov

Youth & Community Development, Department of, NYC . . . . fax:
212-442-5998
156 William St, New York, NY 10038
212-442-5900 or 800-246-4646 Fax: 212-442-5998
Web site: www.nyc.gov/dycd
Commissioner:
Jeanne B Mullgrav. 212-442-6006/fax: 212-442-5998
e-mail: jmullgrav@dycd.nyc.gov
General Counsel:
Everett Hughes 212-442-5980
Chief of Staff:
Heriberto Barbot 212-442-5989
Deputy Commissioner, Administration:
Carlos Cortes. 212-442-8573
e-mail: ccortes@dycd.nyc.gov
Deputy Commissioner, Community Development:
Suzanne M Lynn 212-442-6015

New York City Boroughs

Bronx (Bronx County) . . . . .fax: 718-590-3537
Executive Division, 851 Grand Concourse, 3rd Floor, Bronx, NY 10451
718-590-3500 Fax: 718-590-3537
e-mail: webmail@bronxbp.nyc.gov
Web site: bronxboropres.nyc.gov
Borough President:
Rueben Diaz Jr 718-590-3557
Deputy Borough President:
Aurelia Greene 718-590-4036
Director, Communications:
John DeSio 718-590-3543
e-mail: jdesio@bronxbg.ny.gov
Counsel:
Al Rodriguez. 718-590-8555
e-mail: arodriguez@bronxbp.ny.gov
Press Secretary:
Liseth Perez-Almeida 718-590-2509
e-mail: lalmeida@bronxbp.nyc.gov

Brooklyn (Kings County). . . . . .fax: 718-802-3805
Borough Hall, 209 Joralemon St, Brooklyn, NY 11201
718-802-3700 Fax: 718-802-3805
Web site: www.brooklyn-usa.org
Borough President:
Marty Markowitz 718-802-3700
e-mail: askmarty@brooklynbp.nyc.gov
Deputy Borough President:
Sandra Chapman 718-802-3884
e-mail: ygraham@brooklynbp.nyc.gov

Manhattan (New York County). . . . . .fax: 212-669-4305
Municipal Bldg, One Centre St, 19th Fl, New York, NY 10007

212-669-8300 Fax: 212-669-4305
Web site: www.mbpo.org
Borough President:
Scott M Stringer 212-669-8155
e-mail: bp@manhattanbp.org
Deputy Borough President:
Rose Pierre-Louis 212-669-8137
e-mail: rpierre-louis@manhattanbp.org
Chief of Staff:
Alaina Gilligo 212-669-2527
e-mail: agilligo@manhattanbp.org
General Counsel:
Jimmy Yan 212-669-8157
e-mail: jyan@manhattanbp.org
Director of Human Resources & Operations:
Lisa Kaufer 212-669-8300
e-mail: lkaufer@manhattanbp.org
Director, Policy & Research:
David Saltonstall. 212-669-8300
e-mail: dsaltonstall@manhattanbp.org
Director, Communications:
Josh Getlin 212-669-8139
e-mail: jgetlin@manhattanbp.org
Press Secretary:
Audrey Gelman 212-669-3882/fax: 212-669-3380
e-mail: agelman@manhattanbp.org

Queens (Queens County) .fax: 718-286-2876
Executive Division, 120-55 Queens Blvd, Kew Gardens, NY 11424
718-286-3000 Fax: 718-286-2876
e-mail: info@queensbp.org
Web site: www.queensbp.org
Borough President:
Helen M Marshall 718-286-3000/fax: 718-286-2876
Deputy Borough President:
Barry Grodenchik 718-286-2900
Chief of Staff:
Alexandra Rosa. 718-286-3000
General Counsel:
Hugh Weinberg. 718-286-3000
Director, Management & Budget:
Carol Ricci 718-286-2660
Director, Planning & Development:
Irving Poy 718-286-2860
Immigrant/Intercultural Affairs:
Susie Tanenbaum 718-286-2741
Press Office:
Daniel Andrews 718-286-2640

Staten Island (Richmond County) . . . . .fax: 718-816-2026
10 Richmond Terrace, Room 120, Staten Island, NY 10301
718-816-2000 Fax: 718-816-2026
Web site: www.statenislandusa.com
Borough President:
James P Molinaro 718-816-2200
Deputy Borough President:
Edward Burke 718-816-2231
Chief of Staff:
Joseph Sciortino 718-816-2058
Legal Counsel:
John Zaccone 718-816-2056
Borough Commissioner, DOT:
Thomas Cocola 718-816-2373

Newburgh, City of
83 Broadway
Newburgh, NY 12550
845-569-7300 Fax: 845-569-7370
e-mail: info@mail.cityofnewburgh-ny.gov
Web site: www.cityofnewburgh-ny.com

Mayor:
  Judy Kennedy 845-569-7303
City Manager:
  Richard F Herbeck 845-569-7301
Acting Director, Planning & Development:
  Ian MacDougall. 845-569-9400/fax: 845-569-9700
  e-mail: elynch@cityofnewburgh-ny.gov
City Clerk:
  Lorene Vitek 845-569-7311/fax: 845-569-7314
  e-mail: lvitek@cityofnewburgh-ny.gov
Corporation Counsel:
  Michelle Kelson. 845-569-7335/fax: 845-569-7338
Chief:
  Michael Ferrara 845-561-3131/fax: 845-565-5662
  e-mail: nfdchief@cityofnewburgh-ny.gov
Fire Chief:
  Michael Vatter. 845-569-7415/fax: 845-569-7435
Historian:
  Mary McTamaney. 845-569-8090
  e-mail: newburghhistory@usa.com

Newburgh, Town of
1496 Rte 300
Newburgh, NY 12550
845-564-4552 Fax: 845-566-9486
Web site: www.townofnewburgh.org

Town Supervisor:
  Wayne C Booth 845-564-4552/fax: 845-566-9486
  e-mail: townsupervisor@hvc.rr.com
Town Clerk:
  Andrew J Zarutskie 845-564-4554/fax: 945-564-8589
  e-mail: town-clerk@hvc.rr.com
Accountant:
  Jacqueline Calarco 845-564-5220
  e-mail: accountant@hvc.rr.com
Police Chief:
  Michael Clancy 845-564-1100/fax: 845-564-1870
  e-mail: jjmahoney@hvc.rr.com

Niagara Falls, City of
City Hall
745 Main St, PO Box 69
Niagara Falls, NY 14302-0069
716-286-4300 Fax: 716-286-4349
Web site: www.niagarafallsusa.org

Mayor:
  Paul Dyster 716-286-4310/fax: 716-286-4349
City Administrator:
  Donna D Owens 716-286-4320/fax: 716-286-4376
City Clerk:
  Carol Antonucci 716-286-4393
  e-mail: cantonucci@falls.niagara.ny.us
Corporate Counsel:
  Craig H Johnson 716-286-4422/fax: 716-286-4424
Controller:
  Maria C Brown 716-286-4340
Police Superintendent:
  John Chella. 716-286-4545
Director, Public Works & Parks:
  David L Kinney 716-286-4940/fax: 716-286-4877

Niskayuna, Town of
One Niskayuna Circle
Niskayuna, NY 12309
518-386-4500 Fax: 518-386-4592
Web site: www.niskayuna.org

Town Supervisor:
  Joe Landry 518-386-4503/fax: 518-386-4592
  e-mail: supervisor@niskayuna.org
Deputy Town Clerk:
  Barbara Nottke. 518-386-4511/fax: 518-386-4509
  e-mail: bnottke@niskayuna.org
Comptroller:
  Paul Sebesta. 518-386-4508/fax: 518-386-4592
  e-mail: psebesta@niskayuna.com
Town Attorney:
  Peter Scagnelli. 518-386-4503/fax: 518-386-4592
Police Chief:
  John Lubrant 518-386-4585/fax: 518-386-4594
  e-mail: jlubrant@niskayuna.com

North Hempstead, Town of
220 Plandome Rd
Manhasset, NY 11030
516-869-6311 Fax: 516-627-4204
e-mail: feedback@northhempstead.com
Web site: www.northhempstead.com

Town Supervisor:
  Jon Kaiman 516-869-6311
  e-mail: kaimanj@northhempstead.com
Town Clerk:
  Leslie Gross 516-869-6311
  e-mail: grossl@northhempstead.com
Town Attorney:
  Richard S Finkel 516-869-7600
  e-mail: finkelr@northhempstead.com
Director, Public Safety:
  Andrew DeMartin 516-869-6311
  e-mail: demartin@northhempstead.com
Commissioner, Public Works:
  Paul DiMaria. 516-739-6710
  e-mail: guineyj@northhempstead.com
Commissioner, Finance:
  JoAnne Taormina 516-869-6311
  e-mail: taorminaja@northhempstead.com
Comptroller:
  Kathleen Mitterway 516-869-7766
  e-mail: mitterwayk@northhempstead.com
Community Services:
  Kimberly Corcoran 516-869-6311
  e-mail: corcorank@northhempstead.com

North Tonawanda, City of
City Hall
216 Payne Ave
North Tonawanda, NY 14120
716-695-8555 Fax: 716-695-8557
Web site: www.northtonawanda.org

Mayor:
  Robert G Ortt. .716-695-8540/fax: 716-695-8541
  e-mail: robertort@northtonawanda.org
Common Council President:
  Richard L. Andres, Jr. 716-695-8555/fax: 716-695-8557
  e-mail: catherinesch@northtonawanda.org
City Clerk:
  Scott P Kiedrowski 716-695-8555/fax: 716-695-8557
  e-mail: scottkie@northtonawanda.org
City Attorney:
  Shawn P Nickerson 716-695-8590/fax: 716-695-8592
City Engineer:
  Dale W Marshall 716-695-8565/fax: 716-695-8568
  e-mail: dalemar@northtonawanda.org
Police Chief:
  William R. Hall 716-692-4325/fax: 716-692-4321

Offices and agencies generally appear in alphabetical order, except when specific order is requested by listee.

Fire Chief:
  Joseph L Krantz...................716-693-2201/fax: 716-693-2216

Onondaga, Town of
5020 Ball Road
Syracuse, NY 13215
315-469-3888 Fax: 315-498-6129
Web site: www.townofonondagany.com

Town Supervisor:
  Thomas Andino....................315-469-3888/fax: 315-498-6129
Town Clerk:
  Lisa Goodwin 315-469-1583/fax: 315-469-3461
  e-mail: lgoodwin@townofonondaga.com
Tax Receiver:
  Michele Kresser...................315-469-0483/fax: 315-469-3461
Town Attorney:
  Kevin Gilligan....................315-422-1152/fax: 315-422-1139
Town Historian:
  Mary Nowyj 315-214-2383

Orangetown, Town of
26 Orangeburg Rd
Orangeburg, NY 10962
845-359-5100 Fax: 845-359-2623
Web site: www.orangetown.com

Town Supervisor:
  Andy Stewart......................845-359-5100 x2261
  e-mail: supervisor@orangetown.com
Town Clerk:
  Charlotte E Madigan 845-359-5100 x5004/fax: 845-359-5126
  e-mail: townclerk@orangetown.com
Town Attorney:
  John S Edwards 845-359-5100 x2215/fax: 845-359-2715
  e-mail: townattorney@orangetown.com
Director, Finance:
  Jeffrey W. Bencik 845-359-5100 x2204
  e-mail: jbencik@orangetown.com
Police Chief:
  Kevin A Nulty....................845-359-3700
  e-mail: orangetownpd@yahoo.com

Orchard Park, Town of
4295 S Buffalo Rd
Orchard Park, NY 14127
716-662-6400 Fax: 716-662-6479
e-mail: colarussoj@orchardparkny.org
Web site: www.orchardparkny.org

Town Supervisor:
  Janis Colarusso...................716-662-6400
  e-mail: opsupervisor@orchardparkny.org
Town Clerk:
  Carol R Hutton 716-662-6410
  e-mail: optownclerk@orhardpark.ny.org
Receiver of Taxes:
  Carol R. Hutton 716-662-6405/fax: 716-662-6465
  e-mail: optax@orchardparkny.org

Ossining, Town of
16 Croton Ave
Ossining, NY 10562
914-762-6000 Fax: 914-762-7710
Web site: www.townofossining.com

Town Supervisor:
  Susanne Donnelly 914-762-6001/fax: 914-762-0833
  e-mail: sdonnelly@townofossining.com

Town Clerk:
  MaryAnn Roberts 914-762-8428/fax: 914-914-0627
  e-mail: townclerk@townofossining.com
Receiver of Taxes:
  Gloria Fried......................914-762-8790/fax: 914-762-0635
Police Chief:
  Mark E Busche 914-762-6007/fax: 914-762-6900
  e-mail: topd@ossiningtownpolice.com

Ossining, Village of
16 Croton Ave
Ossining, NY 10562
914-941-3554
Web site: www.villageofossining.org

Mayor:
  William R Hanauer..............................914-941-3554
Village Manager:
  Richard A Leins 914-941-3554
Village Clerk:
  Mary Ann Roberts................914-762-8428/fax: 914-762-7710
Corporation Counsel:
  Lori Lee Dickson.................914-941-3554/fax: 914-941-5940
Police Chief:
  Joseph Burton Jr 914-941-4099

Owego, Town of
2354 NYS Route 434
Apalachin, NY 13732
607-687-0123 Fax: 607-687-5191
Web site: www.townofowego.com

Town Supervisor:
  Donald Castellucci Jr...............607-687-0123/fax: 607-687-5191
  e-mail: dcastellucci@townofowego.com
Town Clerk/Receiver of Taxes:
  Michael E Zimmer..................607-687-0123 or 607-687-6381
  e-mail: owegotownclerk@gmail.com
Town Attorney:
  Eric Gartenman....................607-687-0123
Director, Water/Sewer:
  Michael Trivisonno................607-625-2197
  e-mail: mtrivisonno@townofowego.com
Town Historian:
  Vacant..........................607-687-1961

Oyster Bay, Town of
Town Hall East
54 Audrey Ave
Oyster Bay, NY 11771
516-624-6498 Fax: 516-624-6387
Web site: www.oysterbaytown.com

Town Supervisor:
  John Venditto 516-624-6350
Town Clerk:
  Steven L Labriola 516-624-6332
Attorney:
  Gregory J Giammalvo.................516-624-6150
Comptroller:
  Robert J McEvoy 516-624-6440

Peekskill, City of
City Hall
840 Main Street
Peekskill, NY 10566
914-737-3400
Web site: www.cityofpeekskill.com

Offices and agencies generally appear in alphabetical order, except when specific order is requested by listee.

State & Local Government Public Information

Mayor:
   Mary F Foster 914-734-4105
Acting City Manager:
   Brian Havranek 914-734-4246
   e-mail: rfinn@cityofpeekskill.com
City Clerk:
   Pamela Beach 914-737-3400
   e-mail: pbeach@cityofpeekskill.com
Comptroller:
   Charles Emberger 914-734-4118
   e-mail: cemberger@cityofpeekskill.com
Police Chief:
   Eric Johansen
   e-mail: ejohansen@police.com

Penfield, Town of
3100 Atlantic Ave
Penfield, NY 14526
585-340-8600 Fax: 585-340-8667
Web site: www.penfield.org

Town Supervisor:
   Tony LaFountain 585-340-8630/fax: 585-340-8762
   e-mail: supervisor@penfield.org
Town Clerk:
   Amy Steklof. 585-340-8629/fax: 585-340-8752
   e-mail: clerk@penfield.org
Fire Marshal:
   Wayne Cichetti 585-340-8643/fax: 585-340-8644
   e-mail: firemarshal@penfield.org
Town Historian:
   Kathy Kanauer. 585-340-8740/fax: 585-340-8748
   e-mail: historian@penfield.org

Perinton, Town of
1350 Turk Hill Rd
Fairport, NY 14450
585-223-0770 Fax: 585-223-3629
Web site: www.perinton.org

Town Supervisor:
   James E Smith. 585-223-0770
Town Clerk:
   Jennifer West 585-223-0770
Public Works:
   Thomas C Beck. 585-223-5115
Director, Finance:
   Kevin Spacher. 585-223-0770
Historian:
   Bill Poray 585-223-0770

Pittsford, Town of
11 S Main St
Pittsford, NY 14534
585-248-6200 Fax: 585-248-6247
Web site: www.townofpittsford.com

Town Supervisor:
   Sandra F. Zutes 585-248-6220/fax: 585-248-6247
   e-mail: szutes@townofpittsford.org
Town Clerk:
   Pat Chuhta 585-248-6210/fax: 585-248-6440
   e-mail: pchuhta@townofpittsford.org
Town Attorney:
   Richard T Williams II. 585-248-6216
   e-mail: rwilliams@townofpittsford.org
Director, Finance:
   Gregory J Duane 585-248-6225/fax: 585-248-6247
   e-mail: gduane@townofpittsford.org

Town Historian:
   Audrey M Johnson 585-248-6245/fax: 585-248-6247
   e-mail: ajohnson@townofpittsford.org

Port Chester, Village of
222 Grace Church St
Port Chester, NY 10573
914-939-5202 Fax: 914-937-3169
e-mail: krang@villageofportchester-ny.com
Web site: www.portchesterny.com

Mayor:
   Neil J. Pagano 914-939-5201
   e-mail: dpilla@portchesterny.com
Village Manager:
   Christopher Steers 914-939-2200/fax: 914-937-3169
Treasurer:
   Leonie Douglas 914-939-5205/fax: 914-305-2570
Village Attorney:
   Anthony Cerreto 914-939-5208/fax: 914-937-3169
Public Works General Foreman:
   Rocky Morabito 914-939-5207
Police Chief:
   Joseph Krzeminski. 914-939-1000/fax: 914-939-2303

Poughkeepsie, City of
62 Civic Center Plaza
Poughkeepsie, NY 12601
845-451-4072
e-mail: info@cityofpoughkeepsie.com
Web site: www.cityofpoughkeepsie.com

Mayor:
   John C Tkazyik 845-451-4073/fax: 845-451-4201
   e-mail: jtkazyik@cityofpoughkeepsie.com
City Administrator:
   Milo Bunyi. 845-451-4072/fax: 845-451-4013
   e-mail: mbunyi@cityofpoughkeepsie.com
City Chamberlain/Clerk:
   Deanne Flynn. 845-451-4276/fax: 845-451-4239
   e-mail: dflynn@cityofpoughkeepsie.com
Acting Finance Commissioner:
   Karen Sorrell .845-451-4027/fax: 845-451-4028
   e-mail: ksorrell@cityofpoughkeepsie.com
Police Chief:
   Ronald Knapp 845-451-4132

Poughkeepsie, Town of
One Overocker Rd
Poughkeepsie, NY 12603
845-485-3600 Fax: 845-485-3701
Web site: www.townofpoughkeepsie.com

Town Supervisor:
   Todd Taneredi 845-485-3607/fax: 845-485-3701
   e-mail: ttancredi@townofpoughkeepsie-ny.gov
Town Clerk:
   Susan Miller. .845-485-3620/fax: 845-485-8583
   e-mail: smiller@townofpoughkeepsie-ny.gov
Comptroller:
   Jim Wojtowicz. 845-485-3610/fax: 845-485-1130
   e-mail: jwojtowicz@townofpoughkeepsie-ny.gov
Police Chief:
   Thomas Mauro. 845-485-3666/fax: 845-485-3756
   e-mail: townpolice@hotmail.com

Queensbury, Town of
742 Bay Road
Queensbury, NY 12804

518-761-8200 Fax: 518-798-8359
Web site: www.queensbury.net

Town Supervisor:
  Dan Stec..........................518-761-8229/fax: 518-798-8359
  e-mail: supervisor@queensbury.net
Town Clerk/Receiver of Taxes:
  Darleen Dougher....................................518-761-8234
  e-mail: townclerk@queensbury.net
Town Counsel, Legal Assistant:
  Pamela Hunsinger 518-761-8251/fax: 518-745-4408
  e-mail: towncounsel@queensbury.net
Fire Marshal:
  Mike Palmer 518-761-8206/fax: 518-745-4437
  e-mail: firemarshal@queensbury.net
Historian:
  Dr Marilyn VanDyke 518-761-8252
  e-mail: historian@queensbury.net

Ramapo, Town of
Town Hall, 237 Route 59
Suffern, NY 10901
845-357-5100 Fax: 845-357-3877
e-mail: supervisor@ramapo-ny.org
Web site: www.ramapo.org

Town Supervisor:
  Christopher P St Lawrence 845-357-5100 x202
Town Clerk:
  Christian G Sampson 845-357-5100 x263/fax: 845-357-8513
  e-mail: townclerk@ramapo.org
Town Attorney:
  Michael L Klein...............................845-357-5100 x237
Director, Finance:
  Nathan Oberman 845-357-5100 x247
Director, Public Works:
  Ted Dzurinko................................845-357-0591 x112
Police Chief:
  Peter Brower 845-357-2400

Riverhead, Town of
200 Howell Avenue
Riverhead, NY 11901
631-727-3200 Fax: 631-727-6712
e-mail: info@riverheadli.com
Web site: www.townofriverheadny.gov

Town Supervisor:
  Sean Walter 631-727-3200 x251
  e-mail: pjc@riverheadli.com
Town Clerk:
  Diane M Wilhelm.............631-727-3200 x260/fax: 631-208-4034
  e-mail: wilhelm@riverheadli.com
Fire Marshal:
  Craig Zitek 631-727-3200 x209/fax: 631-727-3370
  e-mail: zitek@riverheadli.com
Town Attorney:
  Robert Kozakiewicz...........631-727-3200 x216/fax: 631-727-6712
  e-mail: rfk@riverheadli.com

Rochester, City of
City Hall
30 Church St
Rochester, NY 14614
585-428-5990 Fax: 585-428-6059
e-mail: info@cityofrochester.gov
Web site: www.cityofrochester.gov

Mayor:
  Thomas S Richards...............................585-428-7045
Deputy Mayor:
  Leonard E. Redon...............................585-428-7163
Council President:
  Lovely A Warren 585-428-7538
City Clerk:
  Daniel B Karin 585-428-7421
  e-mail: dan.karin@cityofrochester.gov
Corporation Counsel:
  Robert Bergin 585-428-6990
  e-mail: Richardt@cityofrochester.gov
City Treasurer:
  Charles A Benincasa.............................585-428-6705
  e-mail: charles.benincasa@cityofrochester.gov
Commissioner, Environmental Services:
  Paul Holahan...................................585-428-6855
  e-mail: paul.holahan@cityofrochester.gov
Police Chief:
  James Sheppard.................................585-428-7033
  e-mail: shepparj@cityofrochester.gov
Fire Chief:
  Salvatore Mitrano, III...........................585-428-7037
  e-mail: john.caufield@cityofrochester.gov
Director, Emergency Communications:
  John M Merklinger..............................585-528-2200
  e-mail: john.merklinger@cityofrochester.gov
Director, Finance:
  Brian L Roulin 585-428-7151
  e-mail: brian.roulin@cityofrochester.gov

Rockville Centre, Village of
1 College Place
Rockville Centre, NY 11571
516-678-9300 Fax: 516-678-9225
Web site: www.rvcny.us

Village Mayor:
  Francis X Murray 516-678-9260
Deputy Clerk Treasurer/Payroll:
  Mary Schmeling 516-678-9263
Village Attorney:
  Vacant.......................................516-678-9206
Comptroller:
  Michael Schussheim.............................516-678-9226
Police Commissioner:
  Charles Gennario 516-766-1500
Superintendent, Public Works:
  Harry Weed...................................516-678-9293

Rome, City of
City Hall
Liberty Plaza
198 N Washington St
Rome, NY 13440
315-339-7677 Fax: 315-339-7667
Web site: www.romenewyork.com

Mayor:
  Joseph R Fusco Jr 315-339-7677/fax: 315-339-7667
Common Council President:
  John J Mazzaferro...............................315-838-1731
City Clerk:
  Louise Glasso 315-339-7658/fax: 315-838-1160
  e-mail: jreid@romecitygov.com
Corporation Counsel:
  Timothy Benedict 315-339-7668/fax: 315-838-1166
Treasurer:
  David Nolan......................315-339-7690/fax: 315-838-1165

State & Local Government Public Information

Offices and agencies generally appear in alphabetical order, except when specific order is requested by listee.

Public Safety Commissioner:
Mike Grande 315-339-7676/fax: 315-339-7667
Commissioner, Public Works:
Frank Tallarino 315-339-7625/fax: 315-339-1167

Rotterdam, Town of
John F Kirvin Government Center
1100 Sunrise Blvd
Rotterdam, NY 12306
518-355-7575 x393 Fax: 518-355-7837
Web site: www.rotterdamny.org

Town Supervisor:
Harry C Buffardi .518-355-7575 x393
e-mail: fdelgallo@rotterdamny.org
Town Clerk:
Diane M. Marco 518-355-7575 x318
e-mail: eesposito@rotterdamny.org
Town Attorney:
Kate McGuirl 518-355-7575
Comptroller:
Jackie Every 518-355-7575 x394
e-mail: paragosa@rotterdamny.org
Police Chief:
James Hamilton 518-355-7331
e-mail: jhamilton@rotterdamny.org
Public Works Coordiantor:
Vince Romano 518-355-7575 x395/fax: 518-355-2725
e-mail: vromano@rotterdamny.org

Rye, Town of
10 Pearl St
Port Chester, NY 10573
914-939-3075 Fax: 914-939-1465
e-mail: super@townofryeny.com
Web site: www.townofryeny.com

Town Supervisor:
Joseph Carvin 914-939-3075
Town Clerk:
Hope B Vespia 914-939-3570
Town Attorney:
Paul Noto 914-698-9331
Comptroller:
David Byrnes 914-934-8489
Commissioner, Public Safety:
Richard Greenberg 914-939-3098

Salina, Town of
201 School Rd
Liverpool, NY 13088
315-457-6661 Fax: 315-457-4317
Web site: salina.ny.us

Town Supervisor:
Mark A Nicotra 315-457-6661/fax: 315-457-4476
e-mail: supervisor@salina.ny.us
Town Clerk:
Jeannie Ventre 315-457-2710/fax: 315-457-4317
Town Attorney:
Timothy A. Frateschi 315-475-6661
Comptroller:
Greg Maxwell 315-451-4210

Saratoga Springs, City of
City Hall
474 Broadway
Saratoga Springs, NY 12866

518-587-3550 Fax: 518-587-1688
e-mail: email@saratoga-springs.org
Web site: www.saratoga-springs.org

Mayor:
Scott Johnson 518-587-3550 x2514
Accounts Commissioner:
John Franck 518-587-3550 x2543
Finance Commissioner:
Michele Madigan 518-587-3550 x2571
Public Safety Commissioner:
Christian Mathiesen 518-587-3550 x2627
Public Works Commissioner:
Anthony Scirocco 518-587-3550 x2561

Saugerties, Town of
4 High Street
Saugerties, NY 12477
845-246-2800 Fax: 845-246-0355
Web site: www.saugerties.ny.us

Town Supervisor:
Kelly Myers 845-246-2800 x345/fax: 845-247-0355
e-mail: kmyers@saugerties.ny.us
Town Clerk:
Lisa Stanley 845-246-2800 x343/fax: 845-246-0127
e-mail: lstanley@saugerties.ny.us
Accounting Office:
Deborah Martino 845-246-2800 x348
e-mail: dmartino@saugerties.ny.us

Schenectady, City of
City Hall
105 Jay St
Schenectady, NY 12305
518-382-5000 Fax: 518-382-5272
Web site: www.cityofschenectady.com

Mayor:
Gary McCarthy 518-382-5000/fax: 518-382-5272
e-mail: mayor@nycap.rr.com
City Council President:
Margaret King 518-370-1885
City Clerk:
Chuck Thorne 518-382-5199 x5303
e-mail: cityclk1@nycap.rr.com
Finance Commissioner:
Deborah W. DeGenova 518-382-5010
Public Safety Commissioner:
Wayne Bennett 518-382-5201/fax: 518-382-5299
e-mail: wbennett@schenectadypd.com
Historian:
Don Rittner 518-788-1255
Police Chief:
Brian Kilcullen .518-382-5201/fax: 518-382-5299

Smithtown, Town of
99 W Main St
PO Box 9090
Smithtown, NY 11787
631-360-7600 Fax: 631-360-7668
Web site: www.smithtownny.gov

Town Supervisor:
Patrick R Vecchio 631-360-7600/fax: 631-360-7668
Town Clerk:
Vincent Puleo 631-360-7620/fax: 631-360-7692
e-mail: vpuleo@tosgov.com

Offices and agencies generally appear in alphabetical order, except when specific order is requested by listee.

Town Attorney:
John B. Zollo 631-360-7570/fax: 631-360-7719
e-mail: townattorney@tosgov.com
Comptroller:
Louis A. Necroto 631-360-7530/fax: 631-360-7625
Director, Public Safety:
Chief John Valentine 631-360-7553/fax: 631-360-7677
e-mail: publicsafety@tosgov.com

Southampton, Town of
116 Hampton Rd
Southampton, NY 11968
631-283-6000 Fax: 631-283-5606
e-mail: webmaster@southamptontownny.gov
Web site: www.southamptontownny.gov

Town Supervisor:
Anna Throne-Holst 631-283-6055/fax: 631-287-5708
e-mail: athrone-holst@southamptontownny.gov
Town Clerk:
Hon Sundy A Schermeyer. 631-287-5740/fax: 631-283-5606
e-mail: sschermeyer@southhamptontownny.gov
Town Attorney:
Michael C Sordi 631-287-3065
Comptroller:
Leonard J. Marchese 631-702-1887/fax: 631-287-5709
e-mail: lmarchese@southamptontownny.gov
Commissioner, Public Works/Highway Superintendent:
Alex D Gregor 631-728-3600/fax: 631-728-3605
e-mail: agregor@southamptontownny.gov
Police Chief:
Robert Pearce 631-728-5000
e-mail: rpearce@southamptontownny.gov
Town Historian:
Henry Moeller. 631-287-5740

Southold, Town of
53095 Route 25
PO Box 1179
Southold, NY 11971
631-765-1800 Fax: 631-765-6145
Web site: southoldtown.ny.gov

Town Supervisor & Emergency Coordinator:
Scott A Russell 631-765-1889/fax: 631-765-1823
e-mail: supervisor@town.southold.ny.us
Town Clerk/Registrar:
Elizabeth A Neville 631-765-1800/fax: 631-765-6145
e-mail: e.neville@town.southold.ny.us
Comptroller:
John Cushman .631-765-4333/fax: 631-765-1366
e-mail: accounting@town.southold.ny.us
Town Attorney:
Martin Finnegan 631-765-1939/fax: 631-765-6639
e-mail: martin.finnegan@town.southold.ny.us
Police Chief:
Martin Flatley .631-765-2600/fax: 631-734-2315
Historian:
Antonia Booth .631-765-1981/fax: 631-765-1366
e-mail: antonia.booth@town.southold.ny.us

Spring Valley, Village of
200 North Main Street
Spring Valley, NY 10977
845-352-1100 Fax: 845-352-1164
Web site: www.villagespringvalley.org

Mayor:
Noramie Jasmin. 845-573-5864

Village Clerk:
Sherry M Scott. 845-517-1128 x108
e-mail: sscott@villagespringvalley.org
Treasurer:
Kuruvilla Cherian 845-517-1121 x101
e-mail: kcherian@villagespringvalley.org
Superintendent:
Neil Vitiello 845-573-1198 x253/fax: 845-573-5802
Police Chief:
Paul J. Modica .845-573-5833 or 845-356-7400
fax: 845-573-5859

Syracuse, City of
233 East Washington St
203 City Hall
Syracuse, NY 13202
315-448-8005 Fax: 315-448-8067
e-mail: cityhall@ci.syracuse.ny.us
Web site: www.syracuse.ny.us

Mayor:
Stephanie A Miner. 315-448-8005/fax: 315-448-8067
e-mail: cityhall@syrgov.net
Common Council President:
Hon Van B Robinson 315-448-8466/fax: 315-448-8423
City Clerk:
John P Copanas 315-448-8216/fax: 315-448-8489
Commissioner, Assessment:
David Clifford .315-448-8280/fax: 315-448-8190
e-mail: assessment@syrgov.net
Commissioner, Neighborhood & Business Development:
Paul Driscoll 315-448-8100/fax: 315-488-8036
e-mail: cd@ci.syracuse.ny.us
Commissioner, Finance:
David DelVecchio 315-448-8279/fax: 315-448-8424
e-mail: finance@ci.syracuse.ny.us
Director, Administration & Budget Management:
Mary Vossler . . . . .315-448-8252 or 315-448-8116
e-mail: budget@syrgov.net
Police Chief:
Frank L Fowler 315-442-5111/fax: 315-442-5198
Fire Chief:
Paul Linnertz. .315-473-5525/fax: 315-422-7766

Tonawanda, Town of
2919 Delaware Ave
Kenmore, NY 14217
716-877-8800 Fax: 716-877-0578
Web site: www.tonawanda.ny.us

Town Supervisor:
Anthony F Caruana 716-877-8804/fax: 716-877-1261
e-mail: acaruana@tonawanda.ny.us
Town Clerk:
Marguerite Greco 716-877-8800 x810/fax: 716-877-0578
e-mail: mbrinson@tonawanda.ny.us
Town Attorney:
John J Flynn. 716-875-9947/fax: 716-875-9948
e-mail: jflynn@tonawanda.ny.us
Comptroller:
Edward D Mongold 716-877-8810/fax: 716-877-8236
e-mail: emongold@tonawanda.ny.us
Police Chief:
Anthony J Palombo 716-876-6607/fax: 716-876-6644

Troy, City of
City Hall
1776 Sixth Avenue
Troy, NY 12180

Offices and agencies generally appear in alphabetical order, except when specific order is requested by listee.

State & Local
Government
Public Information

518-270-4401 Fax: 518-270-4609
Web site: www.troyny.gov

Mayor:
Lou Rosamilia 518-279-7130/fax: 518-270-4609
  e-mail: mayorsoffice@troyny.gov
President, City Council:
Lynn Kopka. 518-279-7317/fax: 518-270-4639
  e-mail: citycouncil@troyny.gov
City Clerk:
William A McInerney. 518-279-7134
Chief of Police:
John Tedesco. 518-270-4421
Fire Chief:
Thomas O Garrett 518-270-4471

Union, Town of
3111 E Main St
Endwell, NY 13760
607-786-2900 Fax: 607-786-2998
Web site: www.townofunion.com

Town Supervisor:
Rose Sotak .607-786-2995/fax: 607-786-2998
  e-mail: rsotak@townofunion.com
Town Clerk:
Gail L Springer 607-786-2915/fax: 607-786-2913
  e-mail: townclerk@townofunion.com
Town Attorney:
Alan J Pope. 607-786-2910
  e-mail: attorney@townofunion.com
Comptroller/Finance:
Laura Lindsley. 607-786-2930/fax: 607-786-2998
  e-mail: llindsley@townofunion.com
Historian:
Suzanne Meredith 607-786-5786
  e-mail: historian@townofunion.com

Utica, City of
City Hall
One Kennedy Plz
Utica, NY 13502
315-797-5847 Fax: 315-734-9250
Web site: www.cityofutica.com

Mayor:
Robert Palmieri. 315-792-0100
  e-mail: mayor@cityofutica.com
Common Council President:
William C Morehouse 315-792-0113/fax: 315-792-0220
City Clerk:
Joan M Brenon 315-792-0113/fax: 315-792-0220
  e-mail: jbrenon@cityofutica.com
First Assistant Corporation Counsel:
Charles N Brown. 315-792-0171/fax: 315-792-0175
  e-mail: ulaw@cityofutica.com
Comptroller:
Michael T. Cerminaro 315-792-0133/fax: 315-797-5847
  e-mail: mcerminaro@cityofutica.com
City Assessor:
David H Williams 315-792-0125/fax: 315-792-9028
  e-mail: dwilliams@cityofutica.com
Commissioner, Parks & Public Works:
David Short. 315-738-0172
  e-mail: dshort@cityofutica.com
Deputy City Engineer:
Goran Smiljic. 315-792-0152/fax: 315-792-0236
  e-mail: engineering@cityofutica.com

Valley Stream, Village of
123 S Central Ave
Valley Stream, NY 11580
516-825-4200 Fax: 516-825-8316
Web site: www.vsvny.org

Mayor:
Edwin Fare 516-825-4200
Village Clerk/Administrator:
Robert Barra 516-825-4200
  e-mail: vsclerk@valleystream.govoffice.com
Treasurer:
Michael J. Fox. 516-825-4200

Vestal, Town of
605 Vestal Parkway West
Vestal, NY 13850
607-748-1514 Fax: 607-786-3631
Web site: www.vestalny.com

Town Supervisor:
W. John Schaffer 607-748-1514 x329
Town Clerk:
Emil Bielecki 607-748-1514 ext321
  e-mail: ebielecki@vestalny.com
Town Attorney:
David Berger. 607-748-1514 ext389
  e-mail: dbergerattorney@stny.rr.com
Comptroller:
Laura McKane 607-748-1514 ext324
  e-mail: lmckane@vestalny.com
Police Chief:
John Butler 607-754-2386 ext341
  e-mail: jbutler@vestalny.com
Fire Chief:
Pat McPherson 607-748-1514 x383
  e-mail: pmcpherson_vfd@vestalny.com
Historian:
Margaret Hadsell. 607-754-4243
  e-mail: mhadsell@vestalny.com

Wallkill, Town of
99 Tower Drive
Building A
Middletown, NY 10941
845-692-7800
Web site: www.townofwallkill.com

Town Supervisor:
Dan Depew 845-692-7832/fax: 845-692-2546
  e-mail: supervisor@townofwallkill.com
Town Clerk:
Louisa Ingrassia. 845-692-7826/fax: 845-692-6051
Chief of Police:
Robert Hertman. 845-692-7859/fax: 845-692-4166
  e-mail: chiefofpolice@townofwallkill.com

Wappinger, Town of
20 Middlebush Road
Wappinger Falls, NY 12590
845-297-5771 Fax: 845-298-1478
Web site: www.townofwappinger.us

Town Supervisor:
Barbara Gutzler. 845-297-2744
Town Clerk:
Christine Fulton. 845-297-5771/fax: 845-298-1478
Receiver of Taxes:
Patricia Maupin 845-297-4342/fax: 845-298-1478

Offices and agencies generally appear in alphabetical order, except when specific order is requested by listee.

Fire Inspector:
  Mark Liebermann 845-297-1373
Historian:
  Constance O Smith

Warwick, Town of

132 Kings Highway
Warwick, NY 10990
845-986-1124
e-mail: townhall@townofwarwick.org
Web site: www.townofwarwick.org

Town Supervisor:
  Michael Sweeton 845-986-1120 x240
Deputy Supervisor:
  James Gerstner. 845-986-1120 x241
Town Clerk:
  Marjorie Quackenbush 845-986-1124 x246
Public Works Commissioner:
  Jeffrey Feagles 845-986-3358
Police Chief:
  Thomas McGovern Jr. 845-986-3423

Watertown, City of

245 Washington St, Rm 302
Watertown, NY 13601
315-785-7730 Fax: 315-785-7796
Web site: www.watertown-ny.gov

Mayor:
  Jeffrey E Graham. 315-785-7720/fax: 315-782-9014
  e-mail: jgraham@watertown-ny.gov
City Manager:
  Sharon Addison .315-785-7730/fax: 315-782-9014
City Clerk:
  Ann Saunders. 315-785-7780/fax: 315-785-7796
Comptroller:
  James Mills 315-785-7754/fax: 315-785-7826
  e-mail: jmills@watertown-ny.gov
Fire Chief:
  Dale Herman 315-785-7800/fax: 315-785-7821
  e-mail: firechief@watertown-ny.gov

Webster, Town of

1000 Ridge Rd
Webster, NY 14580
585-872-1000 Fax: 585-872-1352
Web site: www.ci.webster.ny.us

Supervisor:
  Ronald Nesbitt 585-872-1000
  e-mail: supervisor@ci.webster.ny.us
Town Clerk:
  Barbara Ottenschot 585-872-1000/fax: 585-872-7058
  e-mail: townclerk@ci.webster.ny.us
Director, Finance:
  Kathy Tanea. 585-872-7067/fax: 585-872-7008
  e-mail: finance@ci.webster.ny.us
Public Works:
  Gary Kleist. 585-872-7025/fax: 585-872-1352
Police:
  Gerald Pickering. 585-872-1216 x240/fax: 585-872-7010
  e-mail: police@ci.webster.ny.us
Historian:
  Lynn Barton 585-265-3308

West Seneca, Town of

1250 Union Rd
West Seneca, NY 14224

716-674-5600 Fax: 716-677-4330
Web site: www.westseneca.net

Town Supervisor:
  Sheila Meegan . . . . .716-997-7200 or 716-558-3202
  e-mail: smeegan@twsny.org
Town Clerk:
  Jacqueline A. Felser 716-558-3215
  e-mail: jfelser@twsny.org
Town Attorney:
  Shawn P Martin 716-558-3240
  e-mail: shawn.martin@twsny.org
Comptroller:
  Robert J Bielecki. 716-558-3205
  e-mail: rbielecki@swccpas.com
Police Chief:
  Daniel Denz 716-674-2280
  e-mail: denz@wspolice.com

White Plains, City of

City Hall
255 Main St
White Plains, NY 10601
914-422-1200 Fax: 914-422-1395
e-mail: webpo@white-plains.ny.us
Web site: www.cityofwhiteplains.com

Mayor:
  Thomas M Roach 914-422-1411
Common Council President:
  Beth N. Smayda 914-419-6891
  e-mail: bsmayda@bethsmayda.com
Commissioner, Public Works:
  Joseph Nicoletti Jr. 914-422-1206
Chief of Police:
  James Bradley. 914-422-6230

Yonkers, City of

City Hall
40 S Broadway
Yonkers, NY 10701-3700
914-377-6000 Fax: 914-377-6048
Web site: www.cityofyonkers.com

Mayor:
  Mike Spano. 914-377-6300
Chief of Staff:
  Rachelle Richard. 914-377-6300
President, City Council:
  Chuck Lesnick 914-377-6060
  e-mail: chuck.lesnick@yonkersny.gov
Acting City Clerk:
  Vincent E. Spano 914-377-6020
Corporation Counsel:
  MIchael V. Curti. 914-377-6250
City Assessor:
  Mark Russell 914-377-6200
Acting Commissioner, Affordable Housing:
  William J. Schneider. 914-377-6501
Commissioner, Finance & Mgmt Services:
  James LaPerche. 914-377-6100
Commissioner, Parks, Recreation & Conservation:
  Yvette E. Hartsfield 914-377-6450
  e-mail: yvette.hartsfield@yonkersny.gov
Commissioner, Public Works:
  Thomas G. Meier 914-377-6270
Acting Commissioner, Planning & Development:
  Wilson Kimball. 914-377-6150
  e-mail: wilson.kimball@yonkersny.gov

Offices and agencies generally appear in alphabetical order, except when specific order is requested by listee.

Director, Public Affairs & Community Relations:
Richard Halevy 914-377-6053
Director Economic Development:
Louis C Kirven .914-377-6797/fax: 914-377-6003
e-mail: louis.kirven@yonkersny.gov
Emergency Management Director:
John Donaghy .914-377-7325/fax: 914-965-8430
Police Commissioner:
Charles Gardner 914-377-7900
Fire Commissioner:
Anthony Pagano 914-377-7500

Yorktown, Town of
363 Underhill Avenue
Yorktown Heights, NY 10598

914-962-5722 Fax: 914-962-1731
Web site: www.yorktownny.org

Town Supervisor:
Michael Grace 914-962-5722 x271/fax: 914-962-1004
e-mail: supervisor@yorktownny.org
Town Clerk:
Alice Roker. 914-962-5722 x209/fax: 914-962-6591
e-mail: townclerk@yorktownny.org
Comptroller:
Patricia Caporale 914-962-5722 x206/fax: 914-962-1004
Chief of Police:
Daniel McMahon. 914-962-4141/fax: 914-962-4458
e-mail: info@yorktownpd.org

Offices and agencies generally appear in alphabetical order, except when specific order is requested by listee.

Section 4:
POLITICAL PARTIES &
RELATED ORGANIZATIONS

NEW YORK POLITICAL PARTIES

NEW YORK STATE CONSERVATIVE PARTY

New York State Conservative Party
486 78th St
Suite 2
Brooklyn, NY 11209
718-921-2158 Fax: 718-921-5268
e-mail: cpnys@nycap.rr.com
Web site: www.cpnys.org

Capital District Office
325 Parkview Dr
Schenectady, NY 12303
518-356-7882
Fax: 518-356-3773

Statewide Party Officials

State Chairman:
Michael R. Long 718-921-2158/fax: 718-921-5268
486 78th St, Brooklyn, NY 11209
Executive Committee Member:
Carol Birkholz. 518-623-9151
1 Pucker St, Warrenburg, NY 12885
State Vice Chairman:
Gerard Kassar 718-748-9010
7520 10th Avenue, Brooklyn, NY 11228
Executive Director:
Shaun Marie. 518-356-7882/fax: 518-356-3773
325 Parkview Dr, Schenectady, NY 12303
Regional Vice Chairman:
Ralph C. Lorigo 716-675-8611
75 Rolling Woods, West Seneca, NY 14224
Secretary:
Howard Lim, Jr. 914-939-7180
83 Valley Terrace, Rye Brook, NY 10573-2137
Treasurer:
Frances Vella-Marrone 718-748-1797
7317 12th Avenue, Brooklyn, NY 11228
State Vice Chairman:
Allen Roth. 516-766-2784
255 Raymond Street, Rockville Centre, NY 11570

County Chairs

Albany
Richard M. Stack 518-465-5715
53 Nicholas Dr, Albany, NY 12205

Bronx
William Newmark. 718-822-0504
3252 Phillip Ave, Bronx, NY 10465

Broome
James M. Thomas 607-343-8767
25 Woodlawn Road, Binghamton, NY 13901-4454

Cattaraugus
Leonard C Caros 716-676-3965
7072 Route 16S, Franklinville, NY 14737-0000

Cayuga
Gregory S. Rigby 315-253-0736
124 Owasco St, Auburn, NY 13021-0000

Chautauqua
Anna M. Wilcox 716-672-8595
3105 Cable Road, Freedonia, NY 14063-0000

Chemung
Louis F. DeCicco 607-796-5129
4905 Hillview Road, Millport, NY 14864

Columbia
Matthew G. Torrey 518-392-9610
91 Nelson Avenue, Ghent, NY 12075

Delaware
John Bjorkander 845-676-4604
Wolf Hollow Road, Andes, NY 13731

Dutchess

Erie
Esquire:
Ralph C. Lorigo 716-675-8611
75 Rolling Woods, West Seneca, NY 14224

Essex
William McGahay. 518-369-3700
33 Greenwood Street, Lake Placid, NY 12946

Franklin
Esquire:
Robert E. White 518-327-3714
559 County Route 60, Rainbow Lake, NY 12976-0000

Fulton
Wayne Brooks. 518-725-1270
95 E Fulton St, Gloversville, NY 12078-3217

Genesee
Arthur R. Munger 585-762-9323
2753 Pearl St Rd, Batavia, NY 14020

Greene
Nicholas J. Passero 518-622-9407
264 Sweetwater Lane, Round Top, NY 12473

Herkimer
Daniel Pollak. 315-717-2789
124 Folts Rd, Herkimer, NY 13350

Jefferson
Kenneth H. Parks 315-786-2012
19520 Ball Rd, Black River, NY 13612

Kings
Gerard Kassar 718-748-9010
7521 10th Ave, Brooklyn, NY 11228

Livingston
Jason J. McGuire. 585-734-2199
1851 Livingston Street, Lima, NY 14485

Madison
Christopher J. Kendall 315-684-7810
6 Cedar Street, Morrisville, NY 13408

Monroe
Esquire:
Thomas D. Cook. 585-381-1988
29 Washington Avenue, Pittsford, NY 14534

Montgomery
Robert Mead 518-842-4345
1 Northhampton Road, Amsterdam, NY 12010

Nassau
Daniel F. Donovan Jr. 516-433-8568
1 Sydney Street, Plainview, NY 11803

New York
Stuart J. Avrick 212-912-0022
375 S End Avenue, New York, NY 10280

Offices and agencies generally appear in alphabetical order, except when specific order is requested by listee.

Niagara
Daniel Weiss 716-531-5332
1028 87th Street, Niagara Falls, NY 14304

Oneida
M. Julie Miller 315-735-7367
466 Tryon Rd, Utica, NY 13502

Onondaga
Austin W. Olmsted 315-696-8417
6519 Route 80, Apulia Station, NY 13020

Ontario
Michael Kloppel 585-393-9575
179 West Avenue, Canandaigua, NY 14424

Orange
John P. DeLessio 845-562-4963
7 Hill Street, Newburgh, NY 12550

Orleans
Lofthouse Allen 585-659-8382
2191 Center Road, Kendall, NY 14476

Oswego
Ronald K. Greenleaf .315-564-6427
879 Cayuga Street, Hannibal, NY 13074

Otsego
Sheila Ross 607-547-4037
32 Walnut Street, Cooperstown, NY 13326-0000

Putnam
James M. Maxwell 845-628-7716
117 Vista Terrace South, Mahopac, NY 10541

Queens
Thomas M. Long 718-474-3826
6 Beach 219th St, Rockaway Point, NY 11697

Rensselaer
William T. Fiacco 518-892-9273
3 Ruffinen Drive, Wynatskill, NY 12198

Richmond
Harold J. Wagner 718-720-7364
31 Longview Road, Staten Island, NY 10304

Rockland
Edward J. Lettre 845-624-8494
34 Auner Road, West Nyack, NY 10994

Saratoga
Robert D. Zordon 518-233-0121
1 Robin Lane, Waterford, NY 12188

Schenectady
Randy M. Pascarella .518-355-8753
610 Becker Crossing, Schenectady, NY 12306

Schoharie
William A. Hanson 607-588-6107
801 State Route 990 V, Gilboa, NY 12076

Schuyler
Linda D. Moore 607-535-7591
2485 Irelandville Rd, Watkins Glen, NY 14891

Seneca
William R. White 315-539-2534
19 Brookside Dr, Waterloo, NY 13165

St Lawrence
Henry Ford 315-262-2824
113 Stowe Bay Rd, Colton, NY 13625

Steuben
Donald E. Gwinner 607-329-6765
5582 Sanford Rd, Savona, NY 14879

Suffolk
Edward M. Walsh, Jr. 631-581-1781
211 Apex Lane, East Islip, NY 11730-3304

Sullivan
Steven J. Burke 845-434-2293
68 Cole Road, Hurleyville, NY 12747

Tioga
Bruce Ludwig 607-223-4173
652 Anderson Hill Road, Candor, NY 13743-2412

Ulster
Edward J. Gaddy 845-336-2020
176 Jocky Hill Rd, Kingston, NY 12401

Warren
Carol Birkholz 518-623-9151
1 Pucker St, Warrensburg, NY 12885

Washington
Beverly A. Jakway 518-260-3661
2092 County Road 43, Fort Ann, NY 12827

Wayne
James F. Quinn, Jr. 315-483-2240
8239 Lake St Ext, Sodus Point, NY 14555

Westchester
Hugh Fox Jr. 914-494-3306
262 Hoover Road, Yonkers, NY 10710

NEW YORK STATE DEMOCRATIC PARTY

New York State Democratic Committee
461 Park Ave. South
9th Floor
New York, NY 10016
212-725-8825 Fax: 212-725-8867
e-mail: nydems@nydems.org

Statewide Party Officials
State Chair:
Stephanie Miner 315-448-8005/fax: 315-448-8067
203 City Hall, Syracuse, NY 13202-1473
State Chair:
Keith L.T. Wright 212-866-5809
163 West 125th Street, New York, NY 10027
Executive Director:
Charlie King 212-725-8825 x235/fax: 212-725-8867
461 Park Ave. South, New York, NY 10016
Young Democrats:
Glenn Oldhoff
60 Madison Avenue, Ste 1201, New York, NY 10010
Executive Committee Chair:
Sheila Comar
29 Depot Street, Middle Granville, NY 12849
Treasurer:
David A Alpert 914-946-8300/fax: 914-946-8090
170 East Post Rd, White Plains, NY 10601

County Chairs

Albany
Matthew J. Clyne 518-438-8282
22 Colvin Ave, Albany, NY 12206

Allegany
Robert Christman

Offices and agencies generally appear in alphabetical order, except when specific order is requested by listee.

Bronx
Jeffrey Dinowitz 718-679-9000/fax: 347-281-5984
1640 Eastchester Rd, Bronx, NY 10461

Broome
Jim Testani 607-773-8369
PO Box 854, Binghamton, NY 13902

Cattaraugus
Joyce Melfi

Cayuga
Kate Lacey
144 Genesee Street, Auburn, NY 13021

Chautauqua
Norman Green

Chemung
Susan Skidmore 607-737-8261
518 West Third Street, Elmira, NY 14901

Chenango
Patrick McNeil
110 Fuller Road, Norwich, NY 13815

Clinton
Martin Mannix Jr.....................................518-569-5615
80 Rand Hill Road, Morissonville, NY 12962

Columbia
Cyndy Hall 518-851-7980
PO Box 507, Ghent, NY 12075

Cortland
Sandy Price
129 Port Watson Street, Cortland, NY 13045

Delaware
Tom Schimmerling
PO Box 366, New Kingston, NY 12459

Dutchess
Elisa Sumner
488 Freedom Plains Rd., Poughkeepsie, NY 12603

Erie
Jeremy Zellner.......................................716-853-2511
295 Main Street, Buffalo, NY 14203

Essex
Bethany A. Kosmider 518-597-9760
340 Buck Mountain Road, Crown Point, NY 12928-2021

Franklin
Joseph Pickreign 518-891-1174/fax: 518-891-1174
PO Box 6, Saranac Lake, NY 12983

Fulton
Edmund C. Jasewicz 518-736-5526/fax: 518-736-1612
2714 State Highway 29, Johnstown, NY 12095-9946

Genesee
Lorie Longhany......................................585-409-6373
8535 East Main Road, LeRoy, NY 14482

Greene
Doreen Davis 518-678-0317
PO Box 590, Palenville, NY 12463

Hamilton
Linda M Mitchell 518-648-5327
Tower Hill Rd, PO Box 163, Indian Lake, NY 12842

Herkimer
Richard Souza

Jefferson
Sean Hennessey 315-788-4590
95 Public Square, Watertown, NY 13601

Kings
Frank Seddio

Lewis
Ed Murphy 315-346-6473
PO Box 76, Beaver Falls, NY 13305

Livingston
Judith Hunter
39 South St, Geneseo, NY 14454

Madison
Marianne Simberg
433 Florence Ave, Oneida, NY 13421

Monroe
Joseph D Morelle...................585-232-2410/fax: 585-232-1223
1150 University Avenue, Rochester, NY 14607

Montgomery
Bethany Schumann....................................518-684-0236
286 Guy Park Avenue, Amsterdam, NY 12010

Nassau
Jay S. Jacobs 516-294-3366/fax: 516-873-0810
1 Old County Rd, Carle Place, NY 11514

New York
Keith L.T. Wright 212-687-6540/fax: 212-818-1723

Niagara
Nick J. Forster

Oneida
William Barry..315-736-3447

Onondaga
Mark English...315-422-0345
615 West Genesee Street, Syracuse, NY 13204

Ontario
Judith Baker

Orange
Jonathan G Jacobson................................845-567-6778
843 Union Ave, New Windsor, NY 12553

Orleans
Jeanne Crane...585-682-3089
13087 Hanlon Rd, Albion, NY 14411

Oswego
Michael Kunzwiler 315-422-0345
615 West Genesee Street, Syracuse, NY 13204

Otsego
Richard D. Abbate 607-544-5039

Putnam
Victor Grossman
PO Box 639, Carmel, NY 10512

Queens
Joseph Crowley 718-268-5100/fax: 718-268-7363

Rensselaer
Thomas W. Wade.....................................518-273-3367
PO Box 846, Troy, NY 12181

Richmond
John Gulino 718-983-5009/fax: 718-983-5541
35 New Dorp Plaza, Staten Island, NY 10306

Offices and agencies generally appear in alphabetical order, except when specific order is requested by listee.

Political Parties,
Lobbyists & PACs

Rockland
Kristen Zebrowski Stavisky 917-312-8939
106 Strawtown Road, West Nyack, NY 10994

Saratoga
Charley Brown
PO Box 124, Saratoga Springs, NY 12866

Schenectady
Brian Quail 518-388-9988

Schoharie
Cliff Hay 518-234-7165
337 Barnerville Rd., Cobleskill, NY 12043

Schuyler
Dale Walter

Seneca
Theodore H Young 315-539-9614/fax: 315-539-9614
PO Box 555, Seneca Falls, NY 13148

St Lawrence
Mark Bellardini...............................315-265-4023
645 River Road, Norwood, NY 13668

Steuben
Shawn D. Hogan 607-324-7421/fax: 607-324-3150
12 Mays Avenue, Hornell, NY 14843

Suffolk
Richard H. Schaffer...............631-439-0400/fax: 631-439-0404
1461 Lakeland Avenue, Bohemia, NY 11716

Sullivan
Steve Wilkinson 845-665-6152
PO Box 502, Kiamesha Lake, NY 12751

Tioga
Patricia Bence
3543 Bornt Hill Road, Endicott, NY 13760

Tompkins
Irene W. Stein 607-266-7579/fax: 607-266-7571
PO Box 6798, Ithaca, NY 14851

Ulster
Frank Cardinale.................845-512-1630/fax: 845-512-1630
32 John St, Kingston, NY 12401

Warren
Lynne Boecher

Washington
Sheila Comar....................................518-642-9566
29 Depot St, Middle Granville, NY 12849

Wayne
Mark H. Alquist 315-589-8864
4046 Wayne Street, Williamson, NY 14589

Westchester
Reginald A. LaFayette 914-995-5705
170 East Post Road, White Plains, NY 10601

Wyoming
Harold Bush Jr....................................585-786-8113

Yates
Carolyn Schaffer.................................315-536-0007
2997 Merritt Hill Rd, Penn Yan, NY 14527

NEW YORK STATE GREEN PARTY

New York State Green Party
365 Potomac Avenue
Buffalo, NY 14213
Web site: www.web.gpnys.com

Statewide Party Officials
Co-Chair:
Gloria Mattera....................................917-886-4538
Co-Chair:
Michael O'Neil....................................917-825-3562
Secretary:
Peter LaVenia
Treasurer:
Eric Jones
365 Potomac Avenue, Buffalo, NY 14213

NEW YORK STATE INDEPENDENCE PARTY

New York State Independence Party
225 Broadway
#2010
New York, NY 10007
Web site: www.ipnyc.org

County Chairs

Bronx
Nardo Reyes

Kings
Robert Conroy....................................718-415-0571
323 Putnam Avenue, Brooklyn, NY 11216

Manhattan
Cathy L. Stewart.................................212-962-1699
225 Broadway, New York, NY 10007

Queens
Nancy Hawkins

Richmond
Sarah D. Lyons...................................718-447-9689
36 Hamilton Ave, Staten Island, NY 10305

NEW YORK STATE REPUBLICAN PARTY

New York State Republican Party
315 State St
Albany, NY 12210
518-462-2601 Fax: 518-449-7443
e-mail: info@nygop.org
Web site: www.nygop.org

Statewide Party Officials
Chairman:
Edward F Cox....................................518-462-2601
315 State St, Albany, NY 12210
Executive Director:
Michael Lawler
315 State St, Albany, NY 12210
Secretary:
Rebecca Marino 315-866-2056
402 Prospect St, Herkimer, NY 13350
Treasurer:
John Riedman 518-462-2601
315 State St, Albany, NY 12210

Offices and agencies generally appear in alphabetical order, except when specific order is requested by listee.

First Vice Chairman:
Vincent D. Reda 518-462-2601/fax: 518-449-7443
315 State St, Albany, NY 12210
National Committeeman:
William D. Powers
National Committeewoman:
Jennifer Saul .516-334-5800/fax: 516-334-4406
164 Post Ave, Westbury, NY 11590

County Officials

Albany
Rachel Bledi
32 North Russell Road, Albany, NY 12206

Allegany
Mike Healy 585-268-5644
PO Box 23, Belmont, NY 14813

Bronx
Jay Savino 718-792-5800/fax: 718-863-2301
3029 Middletown Road, Bronx, NY 10461

Broome
Dave C. Hamlin 607-723-8201
59 Court Street, Binghamton, NY 13901

Cattaraugus
Paula Snyder 716-376-7569

Cayuga
Cherl Heary .315-255-1103/fax: 315-364-5164
PO Box 2, Auburn, NY 13021

Chautauqua
Allan Hendrickson 716-450-3813

Chemung
Mike Krusen .607-732-1245/fax: 607-739-4583
9 Longmeadow Dr, Elmira, NY 14905

Chenango
Thomas L Morrone 607-334-3234/fax: 607-334-4625
213 Randall Ave, Norwich, NY 13815-1613

Clinton
Don Lee. 518-569-9578
16 Ilene Drive, Morrisonville, NY 12962

Columbia
Greg Fingar. 518-329-1636
PO Box 1067, Hudson, NY 12534

Cortland
John Folmer 607-745-6207
PO Box 5522, Cortland, NY 13045

Delaware
Maria Kelso. 607-434-9483

Dutchess
Michael McCormack 914-475-5342
18 Beavers Edge Road, Rhinebeck, NY 12572

Erie
Nickolas Langworthy 716-856-8700/fax: 716-856-8703
715 Main Street, Buffalo, NY 14203

Essex
Ronald Jackson 518-963-7104

Franklin
Rolland Thomas 518-651-5225

Fulton
Susan McNeil 518-332-9722
2010 County Highway 107, Amsterdam, NY 12010

Genesee
Richard Siebert 585-343-5925/fax: 585-344-8521
8585 Seven Springs Rd, Batavia, NY 14020

Greene
Brent Bogardus 518-369-6098
7 Molly White Drive, Coxsackie, NY 12051

Hamilton
William Osborne. 518-775-3285

Herkimer
Sylvia Rowan 315-866-7884

Jefferson
Don Coon. 315-788-4120/fax: 315-786-1387
200 Washington Street, Watertown, NY 13601

Kings
Craig Eaton .718-332-7766/fax: 718-332-5898
1662 Sheepshead Bay Rd, Brooklyn, NY 11235

Lewis
Roscoe K. Fawcett Jr. 315-348-9991

Livingston
Lowell Conrad. 585-243-2665/fax: 585-243-2711
123 Main St, PO Box 123, Geneseo, NY 14454-1113

Madison
Ken Kunkel. 315-637-3663

Monroe
William Reilich 585-546-8040/fax: 585-546-8519
460 State Street, Rochester, NY 14608

Montgomery
Joe Emanuele 518-376-8084

Nassau
Joseph Mondello 516-334-5800/fax: 516-333-4406
164 Post Ave, Westbury, NY 11590

New York
Daniel Isaacs. 212-517-8444
122 East 83rd Street, New York, NY 10028

Niagara
Michael Norris. 716-946-5576/fax: 716-433-0032
PO Box 1127, Lockport, NY 14095

Oneida
Peter Sobel 315-327-8152

Onondaga
Tom Dadey .315-471-2020/fax: 315-471-2033
375 West Onondaga St, Syracuse, NY 13202-3207

Ontario
Doug Finch 585-329-7278

Orange
William L DeProspo 845-294-6467/fax: 845-294-7928
75 Main St, Goshen, NY 10924

Orleans
Edward Morgan. 585-638-5352/fax: 585-638-6214
3132 Hurlburton Rd, Holley, NY 14470

Oswego
Michael Backus. 315-342-0840
102 West Utica Street, Oswego, NY 13126

Otsego
Sheila Ross 607-547-8390
PO Box 55, Fly Creek, NY 13337

Offices and agencies generally appear in alphabetical order, except when specific order is requested by listee.

Political Parties,
Lobbyists & PACs

Putnam
James Dibella 917-703-6975

Queens
Philip Ragusa .718-690-3737/fax: 718-746-6356
24-55 Francis Lewis Blvd., Whitestone, NY 11357

Rensselear
John Rustin 518-470-4791

Richmond
Robert Scamardella 718-442-9000

Rockland
Vincent Reda .845-634-7100/fax: 845-634-2423
172 S Main St, PO Box 201, New City, NY 10956

Saratoga
John Herrick .518-462-2601/fax: 518-581-0748
517 Broadway, Saratoga Springs, NY 12866

Schenectady
Jim Buhrmaster 518-365-4809

Schoharie
Lewis Wilson 518-234-2534

Schuyler
Philip Barnes 607-535-4600
203 Lakeview Avenue, Watkins Glen, NY 14891

Seneca
Sue Ann Fisher 315-651-0381

St Lawrence
Tom Jenison 518-462-2601
PO Box 775, Canton, NY 13617

Steuben
Rusty Smith 607-329-9508

Suffolk
John Jay LaValle 631-580-1482/fax: 631-580-1490
1150 Portion Road, Holtsville, NY 11742

Sullivan
Richard Coomb 845-701-3342
PO Box 747, Monticello, NY 12701

Tioga
Don Leonard 607-589-4501/fax: 607-723-3246
PO Box 361, Spencer, NY 14883

Tompkins
James Drader 607-227-4503

Ulster
Roger Rascoe 845-338-6245
159 Green St, Kingston, NY 12402

Warren
Michael Grasso 518-656-9093/fax: 518-783-8754
23 Rapaport Drive, Lake George, NY 12845

Washington
John Patterson 518-692-7920

Wayne
Daniel Olson 315-946-4937/fax: 315-946-4937
12 William St, PO Box 200, Lyons, NY 14489

Westchester
Douglas Colety 914-949-3020/fax: 914-949-2275
214 Mamaroneck Ave, White Plains, NY 10601

Wyoming
Gordon Brown .716-675-8620/fax: 716-675-1619
PO Box 191, Warsaw, NY 14569

Yates
Sandra King 585-703-4714
4419 Italy Valley Road, Penn Yan, NY 14527

NEW YORK STATE RIGHT TO LIFE PARTY

New York State Right to Life Party
41 State Street
Suite M-100
Albany, NY 12207
518-434-1293
e-mail: admin@nysrighttolife.org
Web site: www.nysrighttolife.org

NEW YORK STATE WORKING FAMILIES PARTY

New York State Working Families Party
2 Nevins Street
3rd Floor
Brooklyn, NY 11217
718-222-3796 Fax: 718-246-3718
e-mail: wfp@workingfamiliesparty.org
Web site: www.workingfamiliesparty.org

Offices and agencies generally appear in alphabetical order, except when specific order is requested by listee.

LOBBYISTS

Each entry includes the name of the registered principal lobbyist, then lists names of additional lobbyists as well as all clients.

1199 SEIU United Healthcare Workers East (FKA 1199/SEIU New York's Health & Human Service Union)
330 West 42nd Street
7th Floor
New York, NY 10036
212-603-1735

Lobbyists:
Lillie Carino
Dick Farfaglia
Patrick Gaspard
George Gresham
Antonella Pechtel

1199/SEIU & GNYHA Healthcare Education Project
330 West 42nd Street
Room 739
New York, NY 10036
212-603-1741

Lobbyists:
Jessica Shearer

249 W 28th Street Properties, LLC
100 Washington Street
Newark, NJ 07102
973-643-7700

Lobbyists:
Jill Fink

92nd Street Young Men's and Young Women's Hebrew Association
1395 Lexington Avenue
New York, NY 10128
212-415-5470

Lobbyists:
Sol Adler

99 Solutions LLC
20 Jay Street
Suite 1006
Brooklyn, NY 11201

Clients:
American Racing and Entertainment, LLC
CSC Holdings, LLC (Cablevision)
Downtown Brooklyn Partnership, Inc.
L & M Development Partners, Inc.
Madison Realty Capital Advisors LLC (FKA Madison Realty Capital)
Putting New Yorkers to Work
Real Estate Board of New York
University (New York)
Urban Strategic Partners, LLC

Lobbyists:
Shevonn Howard
Jacquelyn Williams

Academy of Medicine (NY) (The)
1216 Fifth Avenue
New York, NY 10029
212-822-7222

Lobbyists:
Ruth Finkelstein
Ana Garcia
Simone-Marie Meeks

Accenture LLP
800 Coonecticut Ave NW
Ste 600
Washington, DC 20006
202-533-1140

Clients:
Accenture LLP

Lobbyists:
Ken Dircks
Steve Hurst
Sterling McCullough
Rick Webb

Ace Group - North America
436 Walnut St.
WA04P
Philadelphia, PA 19106
215-640-5741

Lobbyists:
Robert Diubaldo
Saraiya Kashyap

Acquard, Milissa
1170 Main St
Buffalo, NY 14209
716-882-1025

Clients:
Elizabeth Pierce Olmsted Medical Center for the Visually Impaired

Adams, Daniel J
47 Sweetbrier Dr
Ballston Lake, NY 12019
518-877-8225

Clients:
Brewers Association, Inc (NYS)
Illinois Tool Works Inc
Matt Brewing Co (The)

Adams, John
400 Calgon Carbon Drive
Pittsburgh, PA 15205
412-787-6662

Clients:
Calgon Carbon Corporation

Adirondack Council Inc (The)
PO Box D2
Elizabethtown, NY 12932
518-873-2240
e-mail: info@adirondackcouncil.org
Web site: www.adirondackcouncil.org

Offices and agencies generally appear in alphabetical order, except when specific order is requested by listee.

Clients:
Adirondack Council Inc (The)

Lobbyists:
Kevin Chlad
Diana Fish
Scott Lorey

Adolf, Jay
350 Broadway, Ste 900
New York, NY 10007
212-897-5848

Clients:
Physician's Reciprocal Insurers

Advance Group Inc (The)
481 Eighth Avenue
Suite 1202
New York, NY 10001
212-239-7323

Clients:
Children's Health Fund
Communication Workers of America Local 1180
Hotel and Motel Trades Council AFL-CIO (NY)

Lobbyists:
Katie Franger
Laura Kavanagh
Scott Levenson
Lindsey Melfi
Jonathan Yedin

Advocates for Children of New York, Inc. (FKA Sweet, Kim)
151 West 30th Street
5th Floor
New York, NY 10001
212-947-9779

Lobbyists:
Randi Levine
Kim Madden
Christian Villenas

Aetna
151 Farmington Ave
Hartford, CT 06156
518-451-3125

Clients:
Aetna

Lobbyists:
Maggie Moree
Susan Tully Abdo

After-School Corporation (The) (FKA Ford, Barry)
1440 Broadway
16th Floor
New York, NY 10018
646-943-8756

Clients:
After-School Corporation (The)

Lobbyists:
Lucy Friedman

Rachel Sabella
Saskia Traill

Ahern, Barbara J
One Commerce Plaza, Ste 400
Albany, NY 12210
518-463-0723
e-mail: bjahern@albany.net

Clients:
Croplife America
First Data Corporation & Subsidiaries
Hearing Healthcare Alliance of NY Inc (HHCANY)
Responsible Industry for a Sound Environment (RISE)

AIA New York State, Inc. (FKNA Rodriguez, Barbara J.)
AIA New York State, Inc.
52 South Pearl Street
Third Floor
Albany, NY 12207
518-449-3334

Lobbyists:
Edward C Farrell

AJ Consulting Services LLC
175 Swift Road
Voorheesville, NY 12186
518-439-6265

Clients:
Mercy College

Lobbyists:
Abe Lackman

Akerman Senterfitt LLP (FKA Stadtmauer Bailkin LLP)
850 Third Avenue, 19th Floor
New York, NY 10022
212-751-8600

Clients:
Azimuth Development Group, LLC
Macy's Retail Holdings, Inc. (FKA Macys East a Division of Macy's Retail Holdings, Inc.)

Lobbyists:
Richard Bowers
Jessica Loeser
Lance Michaels
Steven Polivy
Steven Sinacori
Calvin Wong
Howard Zipser

Albany Law School of Union University
80 New Scotland Avenue
Albany, NY 12208
518-445-2380

Lobbyists:
Helen Adams-Keane
Thomas Guernsey
Patricia Salkin

Albany-Colonie Regional Chamber of Commerce
5 Computer Drive South
Albany, NY 12205-1608

Offices and agencies generally appear in alphabetical order, except when specific order is requested by listee.

518-413-1417

Lobbyists:
Mark Eagan
Nicholas Vaughn

Allegue, Raul R
The Travelers Companies Inc & Subsidiary
1 Tower Square - 8MS
Hartford, CT 06183
860-277-4738

Clients:
Travelers Indemnity Company (The)

Lobbyists:
John D Miletti

Alliance for Donation, Inc. (New York) (FKA Stark, Lynette)
99 Troy Road, Suite 200
East Greenbush, NY 12061
518-533-7878

Lobbyists:
Melanie Evans
Aisha Tator

Alliance for Downtown New York, Inc.
120 Broadway
Suite 3340
New York, NY 10271
212-566-6700

Lobbyists:
Elizabeth Berger

Alliance for Quality Education (FKA Easton, Regina N)
94 Central Ave
Albany, NY 12206
518-432-5315

Clients:
Alliance for Quality Education

Lobbyists:
William Easton
Zakiyah Shaakir

Allinger, Stephen (FKA Nelson, Debra)
United Teachers (NYS)
800 Troy-Schenectady Rd
Latham, NY 12110-2455
518-213-6000

Clients:
Professional Staff Congress (The)
United Teachers (NYS)

Lobbyists:
Heather Barmore
Christopher Black
John Costello
John Green
Richard Iannuzzi
Daniel Kinley
Patrick Lyons
Maria Neira
Andrew Pallotta

Jacqueline Paredes
Melinda Persons
Charles Santelli
Peter Savage

Allocco, Carol
13 Sky Hollow Dr
Menands, NY 12204
518-432-8636
e-mail: callocco@corus.jnj.com

Clients:
Johnson & Johnson Services

Altman, Frederick M
6 Walker Way
Albany, NY 12205-4946
518-690-2828

Clients:
Associated Licensed Detectives of NYS, Inc

Altman, Robert S.
Robert S Altman, Esq., PLLC
27 Whitehall St
New York, NY 10004
212-232-8713

Clients:
Building Industry Assn of NY Inc
Queens & Bronx Building Assn

Altria Client Services Inc. and its Affiliates
101 Constitution Avenue, NW
Suite 400W
Washington, DC 20002
202-354-1500

Clients:
Altria Client Services Inc. and its Affiliates

Lobbyists:
Sven Bergmann
David Fernandez
Mary Margaret Marrin
Molly Slingerland
Michael Thorne-Begland

Alzheimer's Association, New York City Chapter
360 Lexington Avenue
4th Floor
New York, NY 10017
646-744-2900

Lobbyists:
Gail Allen
Lou-Ellen Barkan
Hillary Caceres
Ed Cisek
Patricia Dibenedetto
Elizabeth Hodges
Karen Holland
Fai Lin Lau
Anastasiya Lee
Sharon Lee
Jed Levine
Niurqui Maiano
Paula Rice
Elizabeth Santiago

Offices and agencies generally appear in alphabetical order, except when specific order is requested by listee.

Hillary Stuchin

Amanus Consulting Group
7 Sunrise Terrace
Clifton Park, NY 12065
518-424-4248

Clients:
Luther Forest Technology Campus Economic Development

Lobbyists:
Michael Relyea

AMDEC Foundation, Inc. (FKA AMDEC Policy Group, Inc.)
45 Rockefeller Plaza
Suite 1960
New York, NY 10111
212-218-5640
e-mail: info@amdec.org
Web site: www.amdec.org

Clients:
AMDEC Foundation

Lobbyists:
Maria K Mitchell

American Academy of Pediatrics District II (NYS)
1325 Franklin Avenue
Garden City, NY 11530
516-326-0310

Clients:
American Academy of Pediatrics District II (NYS)

Lobbyists:
Ellie Ward

American Beverage Association
1101 Sixteenth Street, NW
Washington, DC 20036
202-463-6732

Clients:
American Beverage Association

Lobbyists:
James McGreevy
Geena Gent
Sandra Grance

American Cancer Society Cancer Action Network
19 Dove St
Albany, NY 12210
518-449-5438

Clients:
American Cancer Society Cancer Action Network

Lobbyists:
Michele Bonan
Michael Burgess
Hillary Clark
Michael Davoli
Blair Horner
Theresa Tolokonsky

American Cancer Society, Inc.
One Penny Lane
Latham, NY 12110
518-454-4021

Clients:
American Cancer Society, Inc.

Lobbyists:
Don Boshart
Jan Chytilo
Peter Cittadino
Arianna De Felice
Danielle Heller
Nicole Larose
Susan Moranda
Michael Porpiglia
Martha Ryan
Carla Sterling
Joan Sterling
Jason Warchal

American Congress of Obstetricians & Gynecologists, Inc. District II
152 Washington Ave
Albany, NY 12210-2203
518-436-3461
e-mail: info@ny.acog.org
Web site: www.acog.org/goto/nys

Clients:
American Congress of Obstetricians & Gynecologists, Inc.

Lobbyists:
Kathryn Gordon
Donna Montalto
Sue Nigra

American Diabetes Association
330 Congress St, 5th Fl
Boston, MA 02210
617-482-4580

Clients:
American Diabetes Association

Lobbyists:
Stephen Habbe
Travis Heider

American Farmland Trust
112 Spring St
Suite 207
Saratoga Springs, NY 12866
518-581-0078

Clients:
Ameican Farmland Trust

Lobbyists:
David Haight
Diane Held
Laurie Ten Eyck

American Heart Assn/American Stroke Assn
440 New Karner Rd
Albany, NY 12205

Offices and agencies generally appear in alphabetical order, except when specific order is requested by listee.

518-869-4052
e-mail: paul.hartman@heart.org
Web site: www.americanheart.org; www.strokeassociation.org

Clients:
American Heart Assn/American Stroke Assn

Lobbyists:
Robert Collins
Jessica Dimeo
Maria Galarza
Julianne Hart
Mark Hurley
Brooks Lancaster
Zainab Magdon-Ismail
Katherine McCarthy
Jennifer Pratt
Kristy Smord
Carolyn Torella
Robin Vitale
Cathy Wilkins

American Institute of Architects New York Chapter
536 LaGuardia Place
New York, NY 10012
212-683-0023

Clients:
American Institute of Architects - New York Chapter

Lobbyists:
Fredric Bell
Jay Bond

American Insurance Assn
95 Columbia St
Albany, NY 12210-2707
518-462-1695
e-mail: ghenning@aiadc.org
Web site: www.aiadc.org

Clients:
American Insurance Assn

Lobbyists:
Gary Henning
John Murphy
Kenneth Stoller

AMGEN
601 13th Street, NW
12th Floor
Washington, DC 20005
202-585-9614

Lobbyists:
Lauren Novakowski

Anglin, Laura L.
17 Elk Street
PO Box 7289
Albany, NY 12224
518-436-4781

Clients:
Commission on Independent Colleges & Universities (CICU)

Lobbyists:
Susan Nesbitt Perez
Christopher Nolin

Sheila C Seery
Terri Standish-Kuon
Elizabeth Van Nest

ANHD, Inc.
50 Broad St, Ste 1125
New York, NY 10004
212-747-1117

Clients:
ANHD, Inc.

Lobbyists:
Benjamin Dulchin
Moses Gates
Bonnie Nesbitt
Ericka Stallings
Barika Williams

Anson, Joseph L.
10 Applewood Drive
Rexford, NY 12148-1601
518-371-0393

Clients:
Bayer Healthcare LLC

APAX Partners, LP
601 Lexington Ave
New York, NY 10022
212-753-6300

Clients:
APAX Partners, LP

Lobbyists:
Karla Garcia
David Kim

APICHA Community Health Center
400 Broadway
New York, NY 10013
212-334-7940

Clients:
Asian & Pacific Islander Coalition on HIV/AIDS, Inc.

Lobbyists:
David Boyd
Marcelito Custodio, M.D.
John Rafael Flores
Gertrudes Pajaron
Teresita Rodriguez

Apple Association, Inc. (NY)
7645 Main Street
PO Box 350
Fishers, NY 14453-0350
585-924-2171
e-mail: jimallen@nyapplecountry.com
Web site: www.nyapplecountry.com

Clients:
Apple Association, Inc. (NY)

Lobbyists:
James Allen

Offices and agencies generally appear in alphabetical order, except when specific order is requested by listee.

Apple Inc.
C/O 591 Redwood Highway
Bldg 4000
Mill Valley, CA 94941-3039
415-389-6800

Clients:
Apple Inc.

Lobbyists:
Scott Hughes
Jeffrey Lane
Fred Zeytoonjian

Arts Coalition (NYC)
809 West 181 Street
#1638
New York, NY 10033
212-246-3788

Clients:
Arts Coalition (NYC)

Lobbyists:
Norma Munn

Arvai, Joni
4 Westbrook Rd
West Hartford, CT 06107
860-206-9574

Clients:
Bristol-Meyers Squibb Company

Arzt, George Communications Inc
123 William Street
22nd Floor
New York, NY 10038
212-608-0333
e-mail: chief@arztcomm.com

Clients:
11 East 68th Street LLC
47th Street Business Improvement District
A.M Property Holding Corp.
Abax Incorporated
Age 680 Madison LLC
Blood Center (NY)
Broadway Trio
Concerned Physicians for Long Island College Hospital, Inc.
Cooper and 6th Property LLC
CPS Fee Company LLC
Crossroads Ventures, LLC
CRP/Extell Riverside LP
EXG 430W37 LLC
Extell 57th Tower LLC
Extell Development Company
Extell GT LLC
Generation 21 NY, Inc.
Gilbane Building Company
Glenwood POH LLC
Greater Jamaica Development Corporation
Henningson, Durham, & Richardson Architecture and Engineering, PC
Lend Lease (US) Construction LMB, Inc.
MP Liberty Development, LLC
New School (The)
PCV St Owner LP
RJM/EM 4 E 94th Street, LLC
SJP TS JV, LLC

Ska Marin
St. Barnabas Hospital
Structured Employment and Economic Development Corporation

Lobbyists:
George Arzt
Jane Crotty
Maya Gelfand
Fred Winters

Asciutto, Georgia M
74 Chapel Street
Albany, NY 12207
518-465-4274
e-mail: big5schools@mindspring.com

Clients:
Conference of Big 5 School Districts

Lobbyists:
Jennifer Pyle

Asian American Coalition for Children and Families, Inc.
50 Broad Street
18th Floor
New York, NY 10004
212-809-4675

Clients:
Asian American Coalition for Children and Families

Lobbyists:
Noilyn Abesamis-Mendoza
Wayne Ho
Elizabeth Lee
Vanessa Leung
Marissa Martin
Kim To
Mitchell Wu

Associated General Contractors of New York State, LLC
10 Airline Drive
Albany, NY 12205
518-452-1782

Lobbyists:
Michael Elmendorf
Joseph Hogan
Walter Pacholczak

Associated Medical Schools of New York
1270 Avenue of the Americas
Suite 606
New York, NY 10020
212-218-4610

Lobbyists:
Crystal Mainiero
Samuel Mott
Jo Wiederhorn

Assn for Community Living
632 Plank Rd, Ste 110
Clifton Park, NY 12065
518-688-1682

Clients:
Assn for Community Living

Offices and agencies generally appear in alphabetical order, except when specific order is requested by listee.

Lobbyists:
Antonia M Lasicki

Association of Chiefs of Police
2697 Hamburg St
Schenectady, NY 12303
518-355-3371

Clients:
Association of Chiefs of Police

Assn of Community & Residential Agencies (NYS)
99 Pine St, Ste C110
Albany, NY 12207
518-449-7551
Web site: www.nysacra.org

Clients:
Assn of Community & Residential Agencies (NYS)

Lobbyists:
Ann Hardiman
James Kosakoski
Kathleen Mayo

Assn of Counties & Its Affiliated Organizations (NYS)
540 Broadway 5th Floor
Albany, NY 12207
518-465-1473
Web site: www.nysac.org

Clients:
Assn of Counties & Its Affiliated Organizations (NYS)

Lobbyists:
Stephen Acquario
Patrick Cummings
Mark Lavigne
Dave Lucas
Melissa Tiberio
Kathryn Vescio

Association of County Health Officials (New York State)
One United Way
Pine West Plaza
Albany, NY 12205-5555
518-456-7905

Lobbyists:
Linda Wagner

Association of Legal Aid Attorneys UAW 2325 (AFL-CIO)
568 Broadway, 702A
New York, NY 10012-3225
212-343-0708

Lobbyists:
George Albro
Deborah Wright

Association of New York State Youth Bureaus
1653 Central Avenue
Albany, NY 12205
518-436-8712

Lobbyists:
Jacqueline Negri

Assn of PBAS, Inc (NYS)
111 Washington Ave
Albany, NY 11210-2207
518-465-1141

Clients:
Assn of PBAS, Inc (NYS)

Lobbyists:
James Carver
William Diebold
Lou Dini
Mickey Gilbride
James Hughes
Lou Matarazzo
Paul Nunziato
Michael Palladino
Peter B Paterson
Edward Perkins
William Plant
Vincent Provenzano
Fred Sales
Daniel Sisto
Gordon Warnock

Association of Realtors (New York State) (FKA-Mackenzie, Duncan)
Association of Realtors (NYS)
130 Washington Avenue
Albany, NY 12210-2220
518-463-0300

Lobbyists:
Blaise DiBernardo
Mackenzie Duncan
Anthony Gatto
Michael Kelly
Derick King

Association of Towns of the State of NY
150 State Street
Albany, NY 12207
518-465-7933

Lobbyists:
Chris Anderson
Sarah Brancatella
Gerry Geist
Mike Kenneally
Lori Mithen-Demasi

Association on Independent Living
99 Washington Avenue
Suite 806A
Albany, NY 12210
518-465-4650

Clients:
Association on Independent Living (NY)

Lobbyists:
Lindsey Miller
Melanie Shaw

Astellas Pharma US, Inc.
1 Astellas Way
Northbrook, IL 60062
224-205-8800

Offices and agencies generally appear in alphabetical order, except when specific order is requested by listee.

Clients:
Astellas Pharma

Lobbyists:
Paul Miller

AT&T Inc. and Its Affiliates (FKA Roos, David)
111 Washington Avenue
Suite 700
Albany, NY 12210-2213
518-463-3107
Web site: www.att.com

Lobbyists:
Anna Adams-Sarthou
Edward Bergstraesser
Deborah Bierbaum
Marry Burgess
Kevin Hanna
Amy Hines Kramer
Elizabeth Segal
Marissa Shorenstein

ATU NY State Legislative Conference Board
2115 Central Avenue
Box 15
Schenectady, NY 12304-4415
646-739-1121

Lobbyists:
Luis Alzate
Tom Carney
Daniel Cassella
Michael Cordiello
Vincent Crehan
Mark Guerling
James Hedge
Mark Henry
John Lyons
Ira Miller
Peter Schiraldi
Angelo Tanzi
Eric Wessell

Audubon New York
National Audubon Society
200 Trillium Lane
Albany, NY 12203
518-869-9731
Web site: www.ny.audubon.org

Lobbyists:
Albert Caccese
Graham Cox
Laura McCarthy

Automobile Dealers Assn (NYS)
37 Elk Street
PO Box 7347
Albany, NY 12224-0347
518-463-1148
Web site: www.nysada.com

Clients:
Automobile Dealers Assn (NYS)

Lobbyists:
Robert E Vancavage

AXA Real Estate Investment Managers US
1290 Avenue of the Americas
12th Floor
New York, NY 10104

Clients:
AXA Real Estate Investment Managers US

Lobbyists:
Charlene Behnke
Theo Dunoyer
Dennis Lopez
Isabelle Scemama

Baker & Hostetler LLP
1050 Connecticut Avenue
Suite 1100
Washington, DC 20036-5303

Clients:
Colgate-Palmolive Company

Lobbyists:
Nicole Jefferson
Tom McDonald

BALCONY-Business and Labor Coalition of New York
4 West 43rd Street
Suite 405
New York, NY 10036
212-219-7777

Lobbyists:
Louis Gordon

Bank of America Corporation and Subsidiaries
1 Bryant Park
NY1-100-12-01
New York, NY 10036
646-743-1359
Web site: www.bankofamerica.com

Lobbyists:
Holly Andreozzi
Maria Barry
Samuel Benigno
Mike Bowen
Karyn Brownell
Kathryn J. Busch
Peter Cunningham
Harry Curtis
Judi Cyr
Peter Forsgren
Craig Fowler
Allison Fresher
Todd Gomez
Brian Grip
Maragret Guarino
Eric Hanly
Matthew Harblin
Michael Hatfield
Matt Hoganbruen
Kyle Kincaid
Nicole Mancini
Pamela Opperman
Kelly Parden
David Petraglia
Debbie Phinney
Ed Powers

Offices and agencies generally appear in alphabetical order, except when specific order is requested by listee.

Eva Roldan
Joseph Santoro
Margaret Scopelianos
Sanjiv Shah
Daron Tubian
William Weir
Michele Wilson

Bankers Association, Inc.
C/O Bankers Association, Inc. (NY)
99 Park Avenue
4th Floor
New York, NY 10016-1502
212-297-1699

Lobbyists:
Karen Armstrong
Clare Cusack
Roberta Kotkin
Michael P. Smith

Banks, Steven
Legal Aid Society (The)
199 Water St
New York, NY 10038
212-577-3277
e-mail: sbanks@legal-aid.org

Clients:
Legal Aid Society (The)

Barclays Capital Inc.
745 Seventh Avenue
New York, NY 10019
212-526-4655

Lobbyists:
Jeff Anderson
Kym Arnone
William Bloom
Mohamed Elkordy
Jason Gans
Stephen Howard
Richard Rein
Johnny Wu

Barlette, Richard
10 Krey Boulevard
Rensselaer, NY 12144-9681
518-356-8883

Clients:
Independent System Operator, Inc. (New York)

Lobbyists:
Kimberly Ireland

Barnes, Richard E
C/O Catholic Conference (NYS)
465 State St
Albany, NY 12203-1004
518-434-6195
Web site: www.nyscatholic.org

Clients:
Catholic Conference (NYS)

Lobbyists:
James Cultrara

S Earl Eichelberger
Clayton Eichelberger
Kathleen M Gallagher
Dennis Poust

Barrett Associates
95 Columbia St
Albany, NY 12210-2707
518-465-5340

Clients:
Acadia Insurance Company
Ambrose Employer Group, LLC
America's Health Insurance Plans
Automobile Insurance Plan (NY)
Buckeye Partners, L.P
Capital One Financial Corporation
Care One Services, Inc. (National Strategies, LLC)
Central Mutual Fire Insurance Co. (NY)
Coventry
Ebay, Inc.
IAAC, Inc.
Independent Insurance Agents & Brokers of NY
Pitney Bowes, Inc.
Procter & Gamble
Property Insurance Underwriting Association
Travelers Indemnity Company (The)
United Services Automobile Association (USAA)

Lobbyists:
Michael V Barrett
Peter Carr
Jill Muratori

Bartimole, John E (FKA Western NY Healthcare Association) (FKA Larowe, Mary)
Western New York Healthcare Association
1876 Niagara Falls Blvd
Tonawanda, NY 14150-6439
716-695-0843

Lobbyists:
Paul Sweet

Bayview Asset Management
4425 Ponce De Leon Blvd
Coral Gables, FL 33146
305-341-3693

Lobbyists:
David Ertel
Howard Shoer

Beaudoin & Company (FKA Beaudoin, Heather)
275 7th Avenue, 18th Floor
New York, NY 10011
347-922-1074

Clients:
Building & Construction Trades Council of Greater New York
International Brotherhood of Teamsters Port Division
Joint Council #16, International Brotherhood of Teamsters
Major League Soccer

Lobbyists:
Heather Beaudoin
Rebecca Lynch

Offices and agencies generally appear in alphabetical order, except when specific order is requested by listee.

Bee Ready Fishbein Hatter & Donovan, LLP (FKA Bee, Peter A)
170 Old Country Road
Mineola, NY 11501
516-746-5599
Web site: www.beereadylaw.com

Clients:
Cablevision (CSC Holdings, Inc.)

Lobbyists:
Peter A Bee

Beha, Alyson
55 Broad St
23rd Floor
New York, NY 10004
212-838-9410

Clients:
New Yorkers for Parks

Lobbyists:
Alyson Beha
Jessica Feldman
Holly Leicht
Emily Walker
Edward Wallace
Robin Weinstein
James Yolles

Behan Communications, Inc.
83 Glen Street
PO Box 2077
Glens Falls, NY 12801
518-792-3856

Clients:
Catholic Conference Policy Group, Inc.
Finch Paper LLC

Lobbyists:
Mark Behan
John Brodt
William Callen
Patrick Dowd
Joan Gerhardt

Bender Cantone Consulting
1407 Broadway
Suite 1708
New York, NY 10018
347-328-1088

Clients:
Association of Car Wash Owners, Inc.
County of Suffolk Department of Economic Development and Planning
Genting NY
Lettire Construction Corp.
New York Yankees Partnership
Onexim Basketball, LLC
Virtu Financial LLC

Lobbyists:
Bruce Bender
Scott Cantone

Bennett Firm, Inc (The)
PO Box 38004
Albany, NY 12203
518-439-0077

Clients:
Coalition of Specialty Care Physicians
Society of Orthopaedic Surgeons (NYS)

Lobbyists:
Heather Bennett

Billig, Jacob
146 Rock Hill Dr
Rockhill, NY 12775
845-434-4780

Clients:
Trading Cove NY, LLC

Binghamton University
PO Box 6000
Binghamton, NY 13902-6000
607-777-5014

Lobbyists:
Terrence Kane
Mary Lou Sollis
Harvey Stenger

Blackstone Alternative Asset Management L.P
345 Park Avenue
New York, NY 10154
212-583-5000

Lobbyists:
J. Tomlinson Hill
John McCormick
Brian Schwartz

Bloom Energy Corporation
PO Box 1406
Princeton, NJ 08540
212-920-7151

Lobbyists:
Charles Fox

Boehringer Ingelheim Pharmaceuticals, Inc.
9660-138 Falls of Neuse Road
PO Box 188
Raleigh, NC 27615
919-556-6491

Lobbyists:
Gail Amato
Joseph Oros

Lobbyists:
Paul Fanikos

Bogdan Lasky & Frazier, LLC
111 Washington Avenue
Suite 750
Albany, NY 12210-2213
518-434-9000
e-mail: etricomi@blklobby.com
Web site: www.blklobby.com

Offices and agencies generally appear in alphabetical order, except when specific order is requested by listee.

Clients:
Alfred University
Anheuser-Busch Companies, Inc.
Association of Nurse Anesthetists, Inc. (NYS)
Astrazeneca Pharmaceuticals
Darden Restaurants, Inc.
Entertainment Software Association
International Council of Shopping Centers
International Game Technology
McLane Company, Inc.
Midland Credit Management, Inc.
Midtown Surgery Center, LLC
Motion Picture Association of America, Inc.
National Association of Theatre Owners of NYS
Providers Alliance
Sergeants Benevolent Association
Shell Energy North America
Society of New York Office Based Surgery Facilities
Sprint Nextel Corporation
Tecmar, LTD
Time Warner, Inc.
Toy Industry Association, Inc.
Wine Institute

Lobbyists:
Edward A Bogdan III
Kyle R. Christiansen
Diane E Frazier
Mary K Kopley
James A Lasky

Bolton St. Johns, Inc.

146 State St
Albany, NY 12207
518-462-4620
e-mail: mail@boltonstjohns.com
Web site: www.boltonstjohns.com

Clients:
1199 SEIU United Healthcare Workers East
AIDS Healthcare Foundation
AIRBNB, Inc.
Alliance of New York State YMCAs, Inc.
AMDEC Foundation, Inc.
American Council of Engineering Companies of NY (FKA Association of Consulting Engineers (NYS))
American Solar Partners
Amsterdam Nursing Home Corp.
Apple Valley Waste Conversions
Aquest South Park LLC
Baker Victory Services
Bluestone Gas Corporation of New York, Inc.
BMM Testlabs
Caesars Entertainment Operating Company, Inc.
Camp Dresser McKee & Smith
Care for the Homeless
City of Lackawanna
Clark Patterson Lee
Committee for Taxi Safety
Community Health Project, Inc.
Continuing Care Leadership Coalition
Corizon Health, Inc.
Correctional Officers and Police Benevolent Association, Inc. (NYS)
Elevator Industry Work Preservation Fund
Empire Education Corporation
Empire State Pride Agenda, Inc.
ENDO Pharmaceuticals, Inc.
Express Scripts, Inc.
Fashion Institute of Technology
Fifth Avenue Arcade, Inc.

Figure Skating in Harlem, Inc.
Financial Services Institute, Inc.
First Alert
Focused Technologies Imaging Services LLC
Gay & Lesbian Anti-Violence Project (NYC)
Gonzalez Saggio & Harlan LLP
Google, Inc.
Greater New York Hospital Association
Hailo Network USA, Inc.
Hartland Asset Management
Immigration Coalition, Inc.
Island Peer Review Organization, Inc. (IPRO)
IUOE Local 17
JPAY, Inc.
Kaleida Health
Keycorp & Subsidiaries
Kingsbrook Jewish Medical Center
Lackawanna School District
Lesbian & Gay Community Services Center, Inc.
Lifealike, LTD
Local 338 RWDSU
Long Island Federation of Labor, AFL-CIO
Major League Soccer, L.L.C.
Medical Answering Services, LLC
Medtronic, Inc.
Mehigan Bellone & Associates, Inc.
Mentoring Partnership Coalition
Metlife
Metropolitan Museum of Art (The)
MLOTTO, Inc.
Morphotrust USA, Inc.
NANOS Research
National Youth Recovery Foundation
New School (The)
Open View Consulting
Oracle America, Inc.
People, Inc.
Pfizer, Inc.
Phelps Dodge Refining Corporation (Subsidiary of Freeport-McMoran Corporation)
Pipe Trades Association
Pratt Holdings USA (FKA Visy Paper (NY))
RAI Services Company
Recording Industry Association of America, Inc.
Retail, Wholesale and Department Store Union (RWDSU)
Rocking the Boat, Inc.
Sacandaga Protection Company
Saratoga Hospital
Selective Staffing Solutions
Share Our Strength, Inc.
Shawanga Lodge, LLC
Siemens Industry, Inc.
St. Mary's Healthcare System For Children, Inc.
St. Regis Mohawk Tribe
Steamfitters Local 638 PAC
StoryCorps
Sysco Food Services of Albany, LLC
Transportation Alternatives, Inc.
Trustees of Columbia University in the City of NY (The)
Upstate New York Transplant Services
Verizon New York, Inc.
Vornado Realty L.P.
Western Union
WestField, LLC
Wholesale Beer Distributors Association (NYS)
Window Covering Manufacturers Association
Women's Housing & Economic Development Corporation
Yum! Brands, Inc.

Lobbyists:
Natasha Avanessians

Offices and agencies generally appear in alphabetical order, except when specific order is requested by listee.

Donald Baker
Brendan Baxter
David Beier
Tom Connolly
Georgio DeRosa
Edward Draves
Emily Giske
Michael Keogh
Julian Kline
Bill McCarthy
John McCarthy
John O'Donnell
Tweeps Phillips
Patricia Reilly

Boltz, John J Consulting
14 Linden Ct
Clifton Park, NY 12065
518-371-2790

Clients:
Altria Client Services, Inc.
First Data Corporation & its Subsidiaries (Barbara J. Ahern)
Kraft Foods Global, Inc,
Millercoors, LLC

Lobbyists:
Christina M. Bolton
John J Boltz

Bombardier Transit Corporation & Affiliates (FKA Bombardier Transit Corporation)
71 Wall Street
Plattsburgh, NY 12901
518-566-0150

Clients:
Bombardier Transit Corporation

Lobbyists:
Raymond Bachant
Robert E Furniss

Bombardiere, Ralph
C/O Assn of Svc. Stations & Repair Shops
6 Walker Way
Albany, NY 12205-4946
518-452-1979
e-mail: nysassn@together.net
Web site: www.nysassrs.com

Clients:
Assn of Service Stations & Repair Shops, Inc. (NYS)

Bonagura, David
5 Times Square
New York, NY 10036
212-773-7111

Clients:
Ernst & Young LLP

Lobbyists:
Mark Costello
Carmine Di Sibio
Michael Dings
Tom Griffith
Scott Halliday
Robert Jacobs

Samuel Johnson
Linda Lam
Peter Lease
Mark Manoff
Robert Marzziotti
David Milkosky
Kurt Neidhardt
Randy Nelson
Roger Savell

Bond, Schoeneck & King, PLLC
111 Washington Ave
Albany, NY 12210
518-533-3036

Clients:
Automobile Dealers Association (NYS)
Colgate University
Collectors Association, Inc. (NYS)
Financial Service Centers of New York, Inc.
Griffiss Local Development Corporation
Intuit, Inc.
Lowville Academy and Central School
Matt Brewing Company (The)
Ski Areas of NY, Inc.

Lobbyists:
Hermes Fernandez
Edwin Kelley
Raymond Meier
Richard L Smith

Bookman, Esq., Robert S
325 Broadway
Suite 501
New York, NY 10007
212-513-1988

Clients:
Hospitality Alliance, Inc.

Bopp, Linda
Nutrition Consortium of NYS, Inc.
14 Computer Drive East, 2nd Floor
Albany, NY 12205
518-436-8757

Clients:
Nutrition Consortium of NYS, Inc.

Lobbyists:
Gail Cooney
Casey Dinkin
Misha Marvel
Rachel Rupright
Rachel Rupright
Dawn Secor

Botanical Garden (The) (NY)
2900 Southern Boulevard
Bronx, NY 10458
718-817-8518

Clients:
Botanical Garden (NY) (The)

Lobbyists:
Aaron Bouska
J V Cossaboom
Elizabeth Figueroa

Offices and agencies generally appear in alphabetical order, except when specific order is requested by listee.

Todd Forrest
Carolyn Laney
Gregory Long
Michael Rivadeneyra

Bottlers Association (New York State)
99 Pine Street
Suite 207
Albany, NY 12207
518-436-0786

Lobbyists:
Tom Strahle
Phillip Swink
C. Thomas Tenney
Donald Thomas
Peter Wilcox
Bill Wilson

Boucher, Paul
1290 Avenue of the Americas
New York, NY 10104
212-314-3946

Clients:
AXA Equitable Life Insurance Company

Lobbyists:
Kermit Brooks

Brennan Center for Justice at New York
161 Avenue of the Americas
12th Floor
New York, NY 10013
646-292-8310

Lobbyists:
David Earley
Eliza Goitein
Mark Ladov
Larry Norden
Faiza Patel
Myrna Perez
Mike Price
Lee Rowland
Adam Skaggs
Ian Vandenwalker
Michael Waldman
Wendy Weiser
Kelly Williams

Brescia, Richard
321 Loudon Road
Loudonville, NY 12211
518-436-6733

Clients:
Propane Gas Association (NY)

Briand, Elizabeth H (FKA Striar, Gary)
American Red Cross-Greater NY
33 Everett Rd
Albany, NY 12205-1437
518-458-8111

Clients:
American Red Cross in Greater NY

Brickfield, Burchette, Ritts & Stone, P.C.
1025 Thomas Jefferson Street, NW
Suite 800
Washington, DC 20007-5201
202-342-0800

Clients:
Nucor Steel Auburn, Inc.

Lobbyists:
James Brew

Brighter Choice Foundation
4 Chelsea Place
2nd Floor
Clifton Park, NY 12065
518-383-2977

Clients:
Brighter Choice Foundation

Lobbyists:
Christian M. Bender
Wendy Berry
Maureen Blum
David Langdon

Broadcasters Association, Inc.
1805 Western Avenue
Albany, NY 12203
518-456-8888

Lobbyists:
David Donovan
Richard Novik

Bronx River Alliance, Inc.
One Bronx River Parkway
Bronx, NY 10462
718-430-4665

Lobbyists:
Linda Cox
Robin Kriesberg

Brookhaven Science Associates, LLC
Brookhaven National Laboratory
Building 400
Upton, NY 11973-5000
631-344-4747

Lobbyists:
Sam Aronson
Mike Bebon
Doon Gibbs
Marge Lynch
Mann Reinhold
Jim Misewich
Gerry Stokes

Brooklyn Museum
Terri Jackson
200 Eastern Parkway
Brooklyn, NY 11238
718-501-6332

Lobbyists:
Terri Jackson

Offices and agencies generally appear in alphabetical order, except when specific order is requested by listee.

Brooks, Helen M
590 Broadway
Menands, NY 12204
518-698-3422

Clients:
FedEx Corporation

Brown & Weinraub, PLLC
50 State Street
4th Floor
Albany, NY 12207
518-427-7350

Clients:
Accela, Inc.
Aeon Nexus Corporation
American International Group, Inc.
Applied Materials
Arnot-Ogden Medical Center
Association of Alcoholism & Substance Abuse Providers, Inc. (NY)
Astellas
Building & Construction Trades Council (NYS)
CAMBA (FKA Church Avenue Merchants Block Association, Inc.)
Catholic Health Services of Long Island
Catskill Regional Off-Track Betting Corporation
Center for Discovery
Charles T. Sitrin Network of Homes & Services, Inc.
Clearing House Association, LLC (The)
Community Health Care Association of New York State
DePaul
Ditmas Park Rehab Care Center
Dominion Voting Systems Inc.
Empire Generating Co., LLC
Entergy Nuclear Operations, Inc.
Extended Home Care
Finger Lakes Health Systems Agency
Government Employees Insurance Company (GEICO)
Hartland Asset Management
Hope Network
Hospitals Insurance Company, Inc.
Hudson Headwaters Health Network
Jewish Senior Life
KPMG, LLP
Living Essentials, LLC
LV Apartments LP
Merscorp, Inc.
MS Hospital
Nicholas Noyes Memorial Hospital
Novartis Pharmaceuticals Corporation
NTT Data, Inc.
NYU Langone Medical Center
ODA Primary Health Care Center
Oracle America, Inc.
Pacifica Ventures, LLC
Parsons Brinckerhoff, Inc.
Premium Finance Association
Proton Management, LLC
Psychotherapy & Counseling Center (New York)
Real Estate Tax Review Bar Association
Refuah Health Center
Richmond University Medical Center
Rochester Malls, LLC
Roswell Park Cancer Institute
Sibley Redevelopment Limited Partnership
Solar Energy Industries Association
Southampton Hospital
Stony Brook University Hospital
Sunrun, Inc.
Trading Cove New York, LLC

United Healthcare Services, Inc.
VNA of Albany, Inc.
Westmoreland Consulting, LLC
Whitney Capital LLC
William F. Ryan Health Center
Yahoo! Inc.
Young Adult Institute, Inc.
Zuffa LLC

Lobbyists:
Neil Benjamin
Michael Boxley
Patrick Brown
Jeffrey Buley
Justin Driscoll
John Harris
Carolyn Kerr
Ron Rock
David Weinraub

Brown, Arthur M.
16 Kensington Ct
Suite 3
Delmar, NY 12054
518-635-0556

Clients:
Accenture, LTD.
Computer Aid, Inc.
Unique Comp, Inc.

Browne, Brian
St John's University-Manhattan Campus
101 Murray St
New York, NY 10007
212-284-7005
Web site: www.stjohns.edu

Clients:
St John's University

Bryan Cave, LLP
1290 Avenue of the Americas
New York, NY 10104
212-541-2389

Clients:
390 Tower Associates LLC
Gerard Avenue LLC
MTM Associates, LLC
University (New York)

Lobbyists:
Phyllis Arnold
Frank Chaney
Robert Davis
Judith Gallent
Philip Karmel
Margery Perlmutter
Ivan Schonfeld
Stanley Santos

Buffalo State College
665 Main Street
Suite 200
Buffalo, NY 14203
716-878-4324

Offices and agencies generally appear in alphabetical order, except when specific order is requested by listee.

Lobbyists:
William Benfanti

Builders Association (NYS)
One Commerce Plaza
Suite 704
Albany, NY 12210
518-465-2492

Clients:
Builders Association (NYS)

Lobbyists:
Lewis Dubuque

Building & Construction Trades Council (NYS)
890 Third Street
Albany, NY 12206
518-435-9108

Clients:
Building & Construction Trades Council (NYS)

Lobbyists:
James Cahill
Tracy Connolly

Building & Construction Trades Council of Greater NY
71 West 23rd Street
Suite 501-03
New York, NY 10010
212-647-0700

Clients:
Building & Construction Trades Council of Greater NY

Lobbyists:
Paul Fernandes
Gary Labarbera

Burgos, Tonio & Associates
Trinity Centre
115 Broadway, Ste 1504
New York, NY 10006
212-566-5600

Clients:
American Airlines
Ben Barnes Group LP
Beverage Works NY, Inc. (The)
Broadway 4D Theater NY, LLC
Daytop Village, Inc.
Deepwater Wind,LLC
EmblemHealth Services Company, LLC
Genon Bowline, LLC
Greater New York Hospital Association
Jones Lang Lasalle
National Grid USA
Pfizer, Inc.
Shipping Association, Inc.
Union Community Health Center
United Water New York, Inc.
Univision Communications, Inc.
Verizon Corporate Resources Group LLC (FKA Verizon NY)
Williams Companies (The)

Lobbyists:
Jemine Burgos
Tonio Burgos
John Charlson

Francisco Diaz Jr.
Christopher Hahn
Seth Kaye
Ninfa Segarra

Business Council of NYS, Inc.
152 Washington Ave
Albany, NY 12210-2289
518-465-7511

Clients:
Business Council of NYS, Inc. (The)

Lobbyists:
Heather Briccetti
Marcus Ferguson
Lev Ginsberg
Catherine Jimenez
Heather Jung
Kenneth Pokalsky

Byrne, Elizabeth
One Orange Way
C1N
Windsor, CT 06095
860-580-2799

Clients:
ING America Insurance Holdings

Byrne, Kevin
200 Seaport Blvd
Boston, MA 02210-0000
617-563-4162

Clients:
Fidelity Capital Markets, a Division of National Financial Services

Lobbyists:
Kevin Byrne
Elizabeth Hanify
Suresh Perera

Caesars Entertainment Operating Company, Inc.
One Caesars Palace Drive
Las Vegas, NV 89109
702-407-6000

Lobbyists:
David Statz
Joseph Tyrrell
Thomas Minnick
Darren Suarez

Calvin, James S
C/O Assn of Convenience Stores (NY)
130 Washington Avenue
Suite 300
Albany, NY 12210
518-432-1400
e-mail: jim@nyacs.org
Web site: www.nyacs.org

Clients:
Assn of Convenience Stores (NY)

Offices and agencies generally appear in alphabetical order, except when specific order is requested by listee.

Camba, Inc. (FKA Church Avenue Merchants Block Association, Inc.)

1720 Church Avenue
Brooklyn, NY 11226
718-287-2600

Lobbyists:
Jeffrey Austin
Valerie Barton-Richardson
Tyesha Branch
Caitlyn Brazill
Kevin Coffey
Dany Cunningham
Sharon Daly-Browne
Thomas Dambakly
Kathy Dros
Kaida Edwards
Michael Erhard
Alison Goldberg
Claire Harding-Keefe
Stacy Ann Harris
Christie Hodgkins
Robin Landes
Mary Ann Lanzetta
Kathleen Masters
Janet Miller
Marjorie Momplaisir-Ellis
Joanne Oplustil
Jude Pierre
Patrick Pyronneau
Eileen Reilly
Rick Rodriguez
David Rowe
Matthew Schedler
Gary Sutnick
Frances Weinstock
David Zelamsky

Canisius College

2001 Main St
LY 209
Buffalo, NY 14208
716-888-2793

Lobbyists:
J. Patrick Greenwald
John J. Hurley
Debra Park
Patrick Richey
Melinda Sanderson

Cantore, Anthony S.

1073 Serafini Drive
Schenectady, NY 12303-5107
518-869-2542

Clients:
Retired Public Employees Association, Inc.

Capalino, James F & Associates Inc

233 Broadway
Suite 850
New York, NY 10279
212-616-5810
e-mail: james@capalino.com
Web site: www.capalino.com

Clients:
250 East 57th Street, LLC
328-36 West 53rd Street Redevelopment Company, LP
341-363 West 50th Street, LLC
3530 WPR LLC
39 West 23rd Street, LLC
414-24 West 48th Street Redevelopment Company, LP
444 Realty Company, LLC
Academy of Medicine (NY)
Acadia 161st Street, LLC
Albee Development, LLC
All Stars Project, Inc., The
American Institute of Architects - New York Chapter
American Youth Hostels, Inc.
Axis Group, Inc.
Axton Owner, LLC
Beth Israel Medical Center
BSDM Inc.
CBS Outdoor, Inc. (FKA Viacom Outdoor, Inc.)
Central United Talmudical Academy
Circle Entertainment, Inc.
Coach Farm Enterprises, Inc.
Computers for Youth
Douglaston Development LLC
Equality Charter School
Freeze Frame LLC
Gansevoort Market, Inc.
Healthcare Chaplaincy, The
HFZ Highline LLC
Hudson Eagle, LLC
Industry City Associates, LLC
Inwood House
ISJ Commercial Corp.
Jamestown Premier Chelsea Market, LP
Knic Partners LLC
Lands End Associates, LP
Langan Engineering & Environmental Services, Inc.
Leader House Associates, LP
Lower East Side District Management Association, Inc.
Madison Equities LLC
Manhattan by Sail Inc.
Manhattan School of Music
Media Metrica Ltd.
Metro Storage NY, LLC
Metropolitan Arts & Antiques Pavillion, LTD.
Midtown Trackage Ventures LLC
MPE Hotel I Tenant (Downtown NY) LLC
MTM Associates, LLC
National Media Services, Inc.
New Amsterdam Public Market Association, Inc.
Riverview Redevelopment Company LP
Rivington House- The Nicholas A. Rango Health Care Facility
Safe Space
Second Stage Theatre
Snowplow LLC
Solomon R. Guggenheim Museum
Stiles Properties, LLC
Sunnyside Community Services, Inc.
Trinity School
Two Bridges Associates, LP
Underground Development Foundation
Urban Muse LLC
Urban Space Holdings, Inc.
Wholeness of Life Center, Inc.
WW Acquisitions and Development LLC
Young Women's Leadership Network

Lobbyists:
James F Capalino
George Fontas
Ben Kleinbaum

Offices and agencies generally appear in alphabetical order, except when specific order is requested by listee.

Brooke Schafran
Travis Terry
Mark Thompson

Capital District Physicians' Health Plan Inc

500 Patroon Creek Blvd
Albany, NY 12206-1057
518-641-5211
Web site: www.cdphp.com

Clients:
Capital District Physicians' Health Plan Inc

Lobbyists:
John Bennett
Robert R Hinckley

Capital Public Affairs

111 Washington Ave, Rm 104
Albany, NY 12210
518-465-8760

Clients:
Pharmacists Society of the State of NY
Society of Oral and Maxillofacial Surgeons (NYS)

Lobbyists:
Elizabeth M Lasky
Roy E Lasky

Capitol Consultants Inc (NY)

130 Washington Ave, 3rd Floor
Albany, NY 12210
518-449-3333
e-mail: judith@nycapcon.com

Clients:
BP America Inc

Lobbyists:
Siobhan McGrath

Capitol Group, LLC

111 Washington Ave
Albany, NY 12210
518-463-4841
e-mail: nick@capitolgroupllc.com; tim@capitolgroupllc.com
Web site: www.capitolgroupllc.com

Clients:
American Safety Institute, Inc.
Association of Plumbing, Heating & Cooling Contractors, Inc. (NYS)
Clarity Imaging Technologies, Inc.
Clorox Company (The)
Consumer Healthcare Products Assn
Drexel Hamilton
Empire State Marine Trades Association
Envisage Information Systems, LLC
Grocery Manufacturers Assn (FKA Grocery Manufacturers of America)
Independent Health Association, Inc.
Long Island Forum for Technology
Morgan Construction Enterprises, Inc.
National Association of Professional Employer Organizations
National Shooting Sports Foundation, Inc.
Physicians Reciprocal Insurers
Rent A Center (Stateside Associates)
Rite Aid Corporation
Snowmobile Association (NYS)
Systech International

Tobacconist Association of NYS
TWC Administration LLC
Waste Management
Yonkers Raceway

Lobbyists:
Nicholas Barrella
Kathryn Holman
Timothy Sheridan

Capitol Hill Management Services Inc

1450 Western Avenue
Suite 101
Albany, NY 12203
518-463-8644
e-mail: chms@caphill.com
Web site: www.caphill.com

Clients:
Advocates for Adult Day Services
American Massage Therapy Assoc. - NY Chapter
Arcadis-US
Automotive Recyclers Association
Battery and Energy Storage Technology Consortium, Inc.
Capital Region Building Owners and Managers Association
Chamber Alliance of New York State
Council of Senior Centers and Services
Crossbow Coalition,Inc.
Custom Crews, Inc.
Dig Safely New York, Inc.
Epilepsy Foundation of Northeastern New York, Inc.
Maternity & Early Childhood Foundation, Inc.
Outdoor Advertising Council of NY, Inc.
Public Adjusters Association
Society of Opticians, Inc. (NYS)

Lobbyists:
John A Graziano, Jr
Rebecca Marino

Capitol Public Strategies, LLC (FKA McCulley & Associates, Inc.)

121 State Street
3rd Floor
Albany, NY 12207
518-432-3300

Clients:
Monroe County

Lobbyists:
David Catalfamo
Kelly MacMillan
Jeffrey Lovell
James McCulley
William McGahay
Ryan Moore
Ryan Moses
Robert Bulman

Capitol Strategies Group, LLC

30 S Pearl St
PO Box 445
Albany, NY 12207
518-432-3676

Clients:
Carahsoft Technology Corporation
Colt Refining and Recycling

Offices and agencies generally appear in alphabetical order, except when specific order is requested by listee.

Daw Systems, Inc.
Gartner Inc.
Hitachi Data Systems Corporation
Lexmark International, Inc.
Novell
Quest Public Sector, Inc.
Windstream Corporation

Lobbyists:
Robert Burdick
Christopher Cotrona

Capvest Partners LLP
677 Broadway
9th Floor
Albany, NY 12207
518-449-8893

Clients:
Capvest Partners LLP

Lobbyists:

Carey Group LLC
100 Wall Street
23rd Floor
New York, NY 10005
212-912-3661
Web site: www.careyllc.com

Clients:
125 MEC Center LLC
195 Broadway LLC
Cambridge Petroleum Corporation
Equity One, Inc.
Oliveira Contracting, Inc.
Proton Management LLC
Salmar Properties LLC
Triangle Equities

Lobbyists:
Michael Carey
Regina Demilia
Stephen Hayes

Carl Andrews & Associates, Inc.
111 Washington Avenue
Suite 750
Albany, NY 12210
518-810-0222

Clients:
Glenwood Management Corp
TD Bank, N.A.

Lobbyists:
Carl Andrews
Jahmila Joseph

Carnevale Consulting, LLC
Po Box 21
Wynantskill, NY 12198
518-326-4582

Clients:
Arista Networks
Avaya
BMC
GCOM
Salesforce.com, Inc.

Time Warner Cable

Lobbyists:
Carmella Carnevale

Carpino, Peter
United Way of Greater Rochester
75 College Ave
Rochester, NY 14607-1009
585-242-6400

Clients:
United Way of Greater Rochester

Lobbyists:
Dawn Borgeest
Patricia Davis
Jennifer Higgins

Carson, Martin
105 Fiddlers Elbow Rd
Middle Falls, NY 12848
518-692-3162

Clients:
Lorillard, Inc.

Casey Strategic Relations
518-331-8837

Clients:
American College of Occupational and Environmental Medicine
MedBox

Lobbyists:
Glen Casey

Casey, Teresa M.
Mackin & Casey
139 Lancaster Street
Albany, NY 12210-1903
518-449-4698

Clients:
Association of Financial Guarantee Insurers

Casey, William R.
65 East 55th St
30th Floor
New York, NY 10022
212-812-3100

Clients:
King Street Capital Management, L.P.

Lobbyists:
Brian Higgins
John Purcell

Catholic Community Relations Council of New York, Inc.
1011 First Avenue
16th Floor
New York, NY 10022
212-371-1011

Clients:
Catholic Community Relations Council of New York, Inc.

Lobbyists:
Joseph Rosenburg

Offices and agencies generally appear in alphabetical order, except when specific order is requested by listee.

Catskill Center for Conservation and Development, Inc.
P.O. Box 504
Route 28
Arkville, NY 12406
845-586-2611

Clients:
Catskill Center for Conservation and Development, Inc.

Lobbyists:
Peter Manning
Alan White

Center for Charter School Excellence (NYC)
111 Broadway
Suite 604
New York, NY 10006
212-437-8300
Web site: www.nyccchartercenter.org

Clients:
Center for Charter School Excellence (NYC)

Lobbyists:
Valerie Babb
David Golovner
James D. Merriman
Michael Reginer

Center for Children's Initiatives, Inc.
322 Eighth Avenue
New York, NY 10001
212-929-7686

Lobbyists:
Rhonda Carlos Smith
Betty Holcomb
Darius Charney

Center for Constitutional Rights (501C3 Organization With 501H Election)
666 Broadway
7th Floor
New York, NY 10012
212-614-6469

Clients:
Center for Constitutional Rights

Lobbyists:
Deborah Popowski
Annette Warren Dickerson
Qa'id Jacobs
Jennifer Nessel
Camilo Ramirez
Meejin Richart
Vincent Warren
An-Tuan Williams
Chauniqua Young
Nahal Zamani

Center for Disability Rights, Inc.
497 State Street
Rochester, NY 14608
585-546-7510

Clients:
Center for Disability Rights, Inc.

Lobbyists:
David Atias
Bruce Darling
Leah Farrell
Chris Hilderbrant
Lara Kassel

Center for Liver Transplantation
185 Jordan Rd
Troy, NY 12180
518-533-7877

Lobbyists:
Samantha Delair
Samantha Taylor

Centerstate Corporation for Economic Opportunity
572 S. Salina St
Syracuse, NY 13202
315-470-1800

Lobbyists:
Thomas Blanchard
David Holder
David Mankiewicz
Seth Mulligan
Mitchell Patterson
Dominic Robinson
Kevin Schwab
Robert Simpsons
Benjamin Sio
Deborah Warner

Central Hudson Gas & Electric Corporation (FKA Glusko, John)
C/O Central Hudson Gas & Electric Corp.
284 South Avenue
Poughkeepsie, NY 12601-4879
845-486-5201

Lobbyists:
Anthony Campagiorni
Steven Lant
James Laurito

Central New York School Boards Association
6390 Fly Road
East Syracuse, NY 13057
315-463-1904

Lobbyists:
Charles Borgognoni
Rick Timbs

Central Labor Council (NYC)
275 Seventh Avenue, 18th Floor
New York, NY 10001
212-604-9552

Lobbyists:
Sharada Polavarapu

Cetrino, Thomas
90 State Street
Suite 1029
Albany, NY 12207
518-432-4003

Offices and agencies generally appear in alphabetical order, except when specific order is requested by listee.

Clients:
Public Employees Federation

Lobbyists:
Wayne Bayer
Thomas Cetrino
Carlos Garcia
Susan Kent
Patricia Lavin
Christopher Leo
Musa Moore
John Murphy

Chadwick, Cindy
C/O Electric & Gas Corporation (NYS)
18 Link Dr, PO Box 5224
Binghamton, NY 13902-5224
607-762-7310
e-mail: ctchadwick@nyseg.com
Web site: www.nyseg.com

Clients:

Changaris, Steve
482 Southbridge St
Suite 373
Auburn, MA 01501
800-679-6263

Clients:
National Solid Wastes Management Association
Electric & Gas Corp (NYS)
Rochester Gas & Electric Corp

Chase Paymentech Solutions, LLC
14221 Dallas Parkway
Dallas, TX 75254-2942
614-865-3856

Lobbyists:
James P. Fleming
Dave Jimenez
Matthew P. Leman

Chesapeake Appalachia, LLC
6040 North Western Avenue
Oklahoma City, OK 73118
405-935-7888

Lobbyists:
Michael Atchie
Michael Brownell
William Freeman
Brian Grove
Paul Hartman
Jennifer Hoffman
Scott Rotruck
Matt Sheppard
David Spigelmyer

Chesterton, Jan Marie
1 Computer Drive S
Albany, NY 12205
518-465-2300

Clients:
Hospitality & Tourism NYS

Children's Aid Society (The)
105 East 22nd Street
New York, NY 10010
917-286-1554

Lobbyists:
Richard Buery
Adria Cruz
Katherine Eckstein
Lorena Jimenez
William Weisberg

Children's Health Fund (The)
215 West 125th Street
New York, NY 10027
212-535-9400

Lobbyists:
Deirdre Byrne
Dennis Johnson

Chin, Francis Y.
390 Greenwich Street
2nd Floor
New York, NY 10013
212-723-5576

Clients:
Citi Group Global Markets, Inc.

Lobbyists:
Douglas Auslander
Jay Bartlett
Matthew Bissonette
Daniel Cohen
Jennifer Conovitz
Benjamin Cooper
Paul Creedon
Robert DeMichiel
Andrew Ditton
Richard Gerwitz
Thomas Green
Steven Hall
Adam Halvorsen
Raymond High
Kristen Johanson
Michael Koessel
Barry Krinsky
Mike Leffler
David Livingstone
Bartley Livolsi
Ronald Marino
Shai Markowicz
Robert McMaster
Sandeep Satish
Matthew Tesseyman
Daniel Tomson
Miriam Wrobel
Tricia Yarger
William Yates

CitiGroup Management Corp.
1101 Pennsylvania Ave. NW
Suite 1000
Washington, DC 20004
202-879-6805

Lobbyists:
Mary Griffin

Offices and agencies generally appear in alphabetical order, except when specific order is requested by listee.

Citizens Campaign for the Environment

225A Main St
Farmingdale, NY 11735
516-390-7150
e-mail: ccefli@citizenscampaign.org
Web site: www.citizenscampaign.org

Clients:
Citizens Campaign for the Environment

Lobbyists:
William Cooke
Maureen Dolan
Sarah Eckle
Adrienne Esposito
Brian Smith

Citizens Committee for New York City

77 Water St
Suite 202
New York, NY 10005
212-989-0909

Lobbyists:
Peter Kostmayer

Citizens' Committee for Children of New York Inc

105 E 22nd St, 7th Fl
New York, NY 10010-5413
212-673-1800
Web site: www.cccnewyork.org

Clients:
Citizens' Committee for Children of New York Inc

Lobbyists:
Pamela Corbett
Louise Feld
Moira Flavin
Stephanie Gendell
Laura Jankstrom
Jennifer March-Joly
Elysia Murphy
Caroline Nagy
Phoebe Plagens
Courtney Wolf

City Harvest

6 East 32nd Street
New York, NY 10016
917-351-8700

Lobbyists:
Kate Mackenzie

City University of New York (CUNY)

111 Washington Ave
Suite 605
Albany, NY 12210
518-463-2177
Web site: www.cuny.edu

Clients:
City University of New York (CUNY)

Lobbyists:
Anthony Achille
Susan Agin
Michelle Anderson

Dean Balsamini
Peter Barbatis
Herb Berman
William Boone
Stephen Brier
Diane Call
Claudia Chan
Vincent Clark
Valli Cook
Ben Corpus
Mario Dellapina
Danielle Dimitrov
Allan Dobrin
Staci Emanuel
Scott Evenbeck
Ricardo R. Fernandez
Arthur Flung
William Fritz
Kathleen Galvez
Donna Gerstle
Eileen Goldmann
Matthew Goldstein
Karen Gould
Sumil Gupta
Sue Henderson
Jay Hershenson
Russell Holtzer
Kenichi Iwama
Howard Johnson
Marcia Keizs
MaryKaye Kellogg
William Kelly
Hugo Kijne
John Kotowski
Alexandra Logue
Eric Lugo
Ernesto Malave, Jr.
Felix Matos-Rodgriguez
Lavita McMath-Turner
Gail Mellow
John Mogulescu
James Muyskens
Moses Newsome
Gbubemi Okotieuro
Antonio Perez
Ira Persky
Regina Peruggi
Alice Pisciotta
William Pollard
F. Quintanilla
Jennifer J. Raab
Ana Garcia Reyes
Augie Rivera
Joshua Rivera
Chris Rosa
Jeff Rosenstock
Angela Sales
Frank Sanchez
Matt Sapienza
Frederick Schaffer
Stephen Schechter
Marc Shaw
Stephen Shepard
Maureen Shields
Pamela Silverblatt
Earl Simon
Gilian Small
Lisa Stoiano-Coico
Stuart Suss
Jeremy Travis
Carmen Vazquez

Offices and agencies generally appear in alphabetical order, except when specific order is requested by listee.

Mitchell Wallerstein
Iris Weinshall
Carol White
Karen Witherspoon
Paulette Zalduondo-Henriquez
Rosemary Zins

Civil Service Employees Assn, Inc
143 Washington Ave
Albany, NY 12210
518-257-1319

Clients:
Civil Service Employees Assn, Inc

Lobbyists:
Denise Berkley
Lester Crockett
Danny Donohue
Kathy Garrison
Nicholas Lamorte
Joseph McMullen
Billy Riccaldo
Mary Sullivan
Florence Tripi
Colleen Wheaton

Clarkson University (FKA Wood Jr., Robert H.)
8 Clarkson Ave
Potsdam, NY 13699-5537
315-268-6474

Clients:

Clean and Healthy New York, Inc.
62 Grand St.
Albany, NY 12207
518-708-3875

Lobbyists:
Roberta Chase
Kathleen Curtis
Clarkson University

Lobbyists:
Anthony G Collins
Robert H Wood, Jr

Clearing House Payments Company L.L.C.
1155 F Street NW
Suite 975
Washington, DC 20004
202-649-4600

Clients:
Clearing House Payments Company L.L.C.

Lobbyists:
Joe Alexander
Jill Hershey
David Wagner

Cleary, Kevin Government Relations, LLC
111 Washington Ave
6th Floor
Albany, NY 12210
518-210-7258

Clients:
Aetna
American Coatings Association, Inc.
Association on Independent Living, Inc. (NY)
Consumer Directed Personal Assistance Association of NYS
CVS Pharmacy, Inc.
Delta Dental of Pennsylvania
Fountain House
Institute for Community Living, Inc.
Magellan Health Services, Inc.
Reckitt Benckiser Pharmaceuticals, Inc.

Lobbyists:
Kevin J Cleary

CNA
CNA Plaza
43rd Fl
Chicago, IL 60685
312-822-1740

Clients:
CNA

Lobbyists:
Heather Davis
Christine Hanlon
Jon Kantor
Seth Lamont
Mike Warnick

Coalition Against Domestic Violence (NYS)
350 New Scotland Avenue
Albany, NY 12208
518-482-5465

Lobbyists:
Elizabeth Bliss
Connie Neal

Coalition Against Hunger (NYC)
16 Beaver Street
3rd Floor
New York, NY 10004
212-825-0028

Lobbyists:
Joel Berg

Coalition Against Sexual Assault (NYS)
C/O Coalition Against Sexual Assault
28 Essex Street
Albany, NY 12206
518-482-4222
Web site: www.nyscasa.org

Lobbyists:
Wendi Bazan Pazik
Joanne Zannoni

Coalition for Auto Repair Equality (CARE)
105 Oronoco Street
Suite 115
Alexandria, VA 22314
703-519-7555

Lobbyists:
Sandy Bass-Cors
Ray Pohlman

Offices and agencies generally appear in alphabetical order, except when specific order is requested by listee.

Coalition for Children's Mental Health Services (NYS)
PO Box 7124
Albany, NY 12224-0124
518-436-8715

Clients:
Coalition for Children's Mental Health Services (NYS)

Lobbyists:
Jacqueline Negri
Andrea Smyth

Coalition for Economic Justice
237 Main St
Suite 1200
Buffalo, NY 14203
716-892-5877

Lobbyists:
Jennifer Diagostino
Andrew Reynolds
Micaela Shapiro-Shellaby

Coalition for Education Reform & Accountability
4 Chelsea Place
2nd Floor
Clifton Park, NY 12065
518-383-1342

Clients:
Coalition for Education Reform & Accountability

Lobbyists:
Brian D Backstrom

Lobbyists:
Maureen Blum

Coalition for the Homeless
146 Washington Avenue
Albany, NY 12210
518-436-5612

Lobbyists:
Mary Brosnahan Sullivan
Patrick Markee
Ann Nortz
Giselle Routhier

Coalition for the Last Store on Main Street
99 Pine Street
Albany, NY 12207
518-436-0786

Lobbyists:
Michael Corera
Bob Fink
Mitchell Herman
Stefan Kalogrichs
Burt Natanus
Jeff Saunders
John Semmeles
Ed Wassner

Coalition of Institutionalized Aged and Disabled (FKA Lieberman, Geoff)
Coalition of Institutionalized Aged & Disabled

425 East 25th Street
New York, NY 10010
212-481-7572
Web site: www.ciadny.org

Lobbyists:
Judith K. Canepa
Gary Levin
Geoff Lieberman

Cobb Jr, James H
New York Shipping Association, Inc
333 Thornall Street
Suite 3A
Edison, NJ 08837
732-452-7808

Clients:
Shipping Association, Inc (NY)

Coca-Cola Refreshments USA, Inc.
One Coca-Cola Plaza
Atlanta, GA 30313
203-341-0687

Clients:
Coca-Cola Refershments USA, Inc.

Lobbyists:
Antonio Anaya
Donna Cirolia
Gary McElyea
Maria Pignataro
Lillian Rodriguez Lopez
Harriet Tolve

COFCCA Inc
254 West 31st St, 5th Fl
New York, NY 10001
212-929-2626

Clients:
COFCCA Inc

Lobbyists:
Sophine Charles
Mary Jane Dessables
Dianne Heggie
Edith Holzer
Meredith Lafave
Diane Leske
Lee Lounsbury
James Purcell

Coffin, Brian M.
C/O Empire State Pride Agenda
126 State Street
4th Floor
Albany, NY 12207
518-472-3330

Lobbyists:
Jonathan Lang
Nathan Schaefer

Offices and agencies generally appear in alphabetical order, except when specific order is requested by listee.

Coller Capital Limited and it's Affiliate Coller Capital, Inc.
33 Cavendish Square
London, NY

Clients:
Coller Capital, Inc.

Lobbyists:
Jeremy Coller
Susan Flynn
Tim Jones
Frank Morgan

Columbian Mutual Life Insurance Company
Vestal Parkway East
PO Box 1381
Binghamton, NY 13901-1381
607-724-2472

Lobbyists:
Patrick A. Mannion
Thomas Rattmann

Colwell Colwell & Petroccione, LLP (FKA Colwell Ferrentino & Petroccione, LLP)
20 Corporate Woods Blvd.
Albany, NY 12211
518-462-4242

Clients:
Empire State Petroleum Association, Inc.
Industries for the Blind of NYS, Inc.
Small Customer Marketer Coalition

Lobbyists:
Emilio Petroccione

Community Health Care Association of New York State
535 Eighth Avenue
8th Floor
New York, NY 10018
212-279-9686

Lobbyists:
Beverly Grossman
Lisa Perry Hellerstein
Elizabeth Swain
Kameron Wells

Community Preservation Corporation (The)
28 East 28th Street
9th Floor
New York, NY 10016-7943
212-869-5300

Lobbyists:
Rafael Cestero
Richard Conley
Richard Kumro
Sadie McKeown
Alexa Sewell

Community Research Initiative on AIDS, Inc.
230 West 38th Street
17th Floor
New York, NY 10018

212-924-3934
Web site: www.acria.org

Lobbyists:
Daniel Tietz

Comprehensive Health Management, Inc. (FKA Wellcare Health Plans, Inc.)
8735 Henderson Road
Ren 2
Tampa, FL 33634
813-206-1099

Lobbyists:
Elliott Shaw

Condon, Joseph M.
5 Hanover Square
Suite 1605
New York, NY 10004
212-838-7442

Clients:
Community Housing Improvement Program, Inc. (CHIP)

Conference of Local Mental Hygiene Directors (NYS)
41 State Street
Suite 505
Albany, NY 12207
518-462-9422
Web site: www.clmhd.org

Lobbyists:
Jeremy Darman
Kelly Hansen

Conference of Mayors & Municipal Officials (NYS)
119 Washington Ave
Albany, NY 12210
518-463-1185

Clients:
Conference of Mayors & Municipal Officials (NYS)

Lobbyists:
Peter Baynes
Wade Beltramo
John Mancini
Jennifer Purcell
Richard Sinnott
Jane Tsamardinos
Barbara Van Epps
Deanna Walker

Connelly Communications, Inc.
C/O Greenberg Traurig
54 State Street
6th Floor
Albany, NY 12207
518-689-1400

Clients:
Doctors Council

Lobbyists:
Maureen Connelly
Michael Woloz

Offices and agencies generally appear in alphabetical order, except when specific order is requested by listee.

Connelly McLaughlin & Woloz

C/O Greenberg Traurig
54 State Street, 6th Floor
Albany, NY 12207
518-689-1400

Clients:

Altria Client Services Inc. and its Affiliates
Balmar Parc LLC
Building Trades Employers Association
Chetrit Group (The)
CHIP-Community Housing Improvement Program, Inc
Clear Channel Outdoor
Creative Mobile Technology
Gansevoort Street Properties, LLC
Hunter College
International Code Council, Inc.
Metropolitan Parking Association, Inc.
Metropolitan Taxi Board of Trade
Museum of Modern Art (The)
Nightingale-Bamford School
Oil Heating Assn (NY)
One York Street Condominium
Park Avenue Armory
Toll Brothers, Inc.
Velodrome of New York City, Inc.
WB Stellar IP Owner LLC
William Gottlieb Management Co. LLC

Lobbyists:

Maureen Connelly
Kathy Cudahy
Martin McLaughlin
Michael Woloz

Consortium for Worker Education

275 Seventh Avenue
18th Floor
New York, NY 10001
212-647-1900
Web site: www.cwe.org

Lobbyists:

Heather Beaudoin

Consolidated Edison Company of New York, Inc.

4 Irving Place
Room 1650-S
New York, NY 10003
518-434-1193

Lobbyists:

John Banks
Karen Bourgeois
Thomas Brizzolara
Dan Brown
Kevin Burke
Kim Campbell
Larry Carbone
Rebecca Craft
Christine Cummings
Eric Dessen
David Gmach
Al Grillo
Philip Halliburton
Martin Heslin
Robert Hoglund
Stephen Ianello
Rolando Infante

Nick Inga
Mark Irving
Aseem Kapur
Kevin Lanahan
John Leo
William Longhi
John McMahon
Sandra Miller
Luke Mohaghan
John Mucci
Stuart Nachmias
Joseph Oates
Nelson Perez
Francis Peverly
Randolph Price
Jessica Reinhardt
Kenneth Reinhart
Frances Resheske
Marc Richter
Sara Schoenwetter
Steven Scotti
Joseph Segarra
William Slade
Colin Smart
Eric Soto
Greg Stephenson
Richard Struck
William Talbot
Joseph Tringali
Tom Tropea
Stephen Wemple
William White
Neil Winter

Constantinople & Vallone Consulting LLC (FKA Constantinople Consulting)

233 Broadway Suite 830
New York, NY 10279
212-393-6500
e-mail: constantinople@worldnet.att.net

Clients:

133 Greenwich Street Associates LLC
133 Greenwich Street Associates LLC
380 Development LLC
580 Park Avenue, Inc.
Applied Projects Company, Inc.
Bayonne Energy Center LLC
Bayrock Sapir Organization LLC
Bizzi & Partners Development LLC
Brooklyn Navy Yard Cogeneration Partners L.P.
Carmel Car and Limousine Service
Catapult Learning
Citizen Schools, Inc.
Coach USA Northeast, Inc.
College Board (The)
Dial 7 Car and Limousine Service, Inc.
Elmhurst Dairy, Inc.
Empire Office, Inc.
Forestdale, Inc.
H&M LLC
J.H. Reid, General Contractor
JC Penney Corporation, Inc.
Junior Tennis League, Inc.
McGrath Matter Associates, Inc.
Mega Contracting Group LLC
Premier Magnesia LLC
Prestige Properties and Development Co.
Prismatic Development Corporation
QSAC, Inc.

Offices and agencies generally appear in alphabetical order, except when specific order is requested by listee.

Quadlogic Controls Corporation
Shikibo LTD.
Solow Management Corp.
Sports and Arts in Schools Foundation
St. Michael's Cemetary
TA Ahern Contractors Corp.
TD Bank US Holding Company
Walgreen Co.
Waste Management of New York LLC
Yorkshire Towers
YYY 35th Street LLC

Lobbyists:
Robert Avaltroni
Francis Constantinople
Anthony Constantinople Jr.
Anthony Constantinople III
Irma Frier
Robert Kevin Jones
Keith Powers
Anthony Riccio
Melissa Rusinek
Paul Vallone
Perry Vallone
Peter Vallone Sr.

Consumers Union of US, Inc.
1535 Mission Street
San Francisco, CA 94103
415-431-6747

Lobbyists:
Chuck Bell
Elizabeth Foley
Norma Garcia
Jean Halloran
Michael Hansen
Michelle Jun
Suzanne Martindale
Elizabeth McGiffert
Chris Meyer
Kathy Mitchell
Minerva Novoa
Urvashi Rangan
Rob Schneider

Coppola, John
1 Columbia Place
Albany, NY 12207
518-426-3122
e-mail: jcoppola@asapnys.org
Web site: www.asapnys.org

Clients:
Assn of Alcoholism & Substance Abuse Providers Inc (NY)

Cordo & Company, LLC
100 State Street
Suite 400
Albany, NY 12207
518-445-2535

Clients:
1199 SEIU United Healthcare Workers East
1199 SEIU & GNYHA Healthcare Education Project
Amerigroup New York, LLC (DBA Amerigroup Community Care)
Beer Wholesalers Association, Inc. (NYS)
Camelot Global Services Limited
Cigar Association of America, Inc.

Commission on Independent Colleges & Universities (CICU)
CompPharma LLC
Consortium for Worker Education
Council for the Humanities (NY)
CVS Caremark Corporation
Elisa Seeger
Feld Entertainment, Inc.
Fig LLC
Genting New York LLC
Halmar International LLC
National Popular Vote, Inc.
New York English Schools Association (NYESA)
Oz Systems
Property Casualty Insurers Association of America (PCI)
Short Term Rental and Hospitality Association
Siemens Enterprise Communications, Inc.
Tracfone Wireless, Inc.
TripAdvisor Media Group
Visiting Nurse Service of NY

Lobbyists:
Michael Cinquanti
John Cordo
Kimberley Cutler
Steven Harris
Antoinette Heuber
Kristin Ruggles
Caley Taratus
Larisa Wick

Corlett, John A (FKA Marta Genovese)
1415 Kellum Place
Garden City, NY 11530-1690
516-873-2259

Clients:
AAA New York State, Inc.
Automobile Club of New York, Inc.

Lobbyists:
Jeffrey Frediani
Edward Welsh

Corning Place Consulting, LLC
121 State St
Albany, NY 12207-0693
518-689-7270

Clients:
4201 Schools Association
Association of Proprietary Colleges
Empire State Association of Assisted Living
Independent Oil and Gas Association of NY
LaSalle School
Literacy New York, Inc.
NYSCOP, Inc.
Police Benevolent Association of New York State
Professional Fire Fighters Association, Inc.
Unshackle Upstate (Rochester Business Alliance)
Viscardi Center, The

Lobbyists:
Deborah Fasser
Andrew Gregory
Paul Larrabee
James Smith

Offices and agencies generally appear in alphabetical order, except when specific order is requested by listee.

Correctional Officers & Police Benevolent Association, Inc. (NYS) (FKA Leo, Christopher)
102 Hackett Boulevard
Albany, NY 12209
518-427-1551

Lobbyists:
Chris Hickey
Donn Rowe
John Telisky
Daniel Valente

Couch White, LLP
540 Broadway
PO Box 22222
Albany, NY 12201
518-426-4600
e-mail: bbrenner@couchwhite.com
Web site: www.couchwhite.com

Clients:
Association of Realtors

Lobbyists:
Lawrence Malone
Leonard Singer
Michael Wallender

Council for Community Behavioral Healthcare (FKA Lupi, Virginia A.)
155 Washington Ave, 2nd Fl
Albany, NY 12210
518-445-2642

Clients:
Council for Community Behavioral Healthcare

Lobbyists:
Lauri Cole

Council for the Humanities
150 Broadway
Suite 1700
New York, NY 10038-4401
212-233-1131

Lobbyists:
Sara Ogger

Council of Nonprofits, Inc.
272 Broadway
Albany, NY 12204
518-434-9194

Lobbyists:
Melissa Currado
Kelly Mathews
William Sauer
Amber Vanderwarker
Valerie Venezia
David Watson
Mike West

Council of Senior Centers & Services of NYC, Inc.
49 West 45th Street
7th Floor
New York, NY 10036
212-398-6565

Lobbyists:
Igal Jellinek
Bobbie Sackman

Council of the City of New York (The)
111 Washington Ave, Ste 410
Albany, NY 12210-2208
518-462-5461
Web site: www.council.nyc.ny.us

Clients:
Council of the City of New York (The)

Lobbyists:
Natasha Kerry

County Medical Society New York (FKA Malone, Cheryl)
New York County Medical Society
12 East 41st Street, Fifteenth Floor
New York, NY 10017
212-684-4670

Clients:
County Medical Society (New York)

Lobbyists:
Lisa Joseph
Cheryl Malone
Natalie Ruoff
Susan Tucker

Covanta Energy Corporation
445 South St
Morristown, NJ 07960
862-435-5246
Web site: www.covantaholding.com

Lobbyists:
Bonny Betancourt
Ellie Booth
Michael Cavaliere
Daniel Dorlon
Paul Gilman
Scott Henderson
Rick Sandner
Paula Soos-Kobylski
Paul Stauder

Cozen O'Connor (FKA Wolfblock LLP)
277 Park Avenue
New York, NY 10172
212-297-2678

Clients:
Advocacy Association, Inc.
Air-Conditioning, Heating and Refridgeration Institute
American Council of Engineering Companies of New York
Greenpoint Industrial Center, Inc.
Houghton Mifflin Harcourt Publishing Company
ICONPLANS LLC
Rational Services Limited
Teacher's College, Columbia University

Lobbyists:
Kenneth Fisher
Vivien Krieger
Paul Proulx
Alan Rubin
Stuart Shorenstein

Offices and agencies generally appear in alphabetical order, except when specific order is requested by listee.

Clients:
Albany Information Technology Group, LLC
ARE-East River Science Park LLC
Cable Telecommunications Assn of NY, Inc (The)
Coastal Distribution, LLC
COMCAST
Delaware North Companies, Inc
Empire Racing Associates
Higher Education Initiative (New York State)
Institutional Life Markets Association, Inc
Judge Rotenberg Center
Library Association (NY)
Lift
Nestle Waters North America Inc.
Nucor Steel Aubrun, Inc.
Omni Childhood Center
PMSI
Roundabout Theatre Company
School Boards Association (NYS)
Stoneriver Pharmacy Solutions, Inc. (FKA Third Party Solutions)
Sunshine Development School, Inc.
United NY Ambulance Network
Zelle Hoffmann Voelbel & Mason LLP
Constance Crane
James B Crane
Andrea Debow
Christopher Duryea
George Penn
Steven Sanders

Crisis Program (The)
10 Airline Drive
Suite 203
Albany, NY 12205
518-456-1134

Lobbyists:
Michael Elmendorf II
Walter Pacholczak

Crosier, Barbara V
C/O United Cerebral Palsy Assn of NYS
90 State St, Ste 929
Albany, NY 12207
518-436-0178
e-mail: bcrosier@cerebralpalsynys.org
Web site: www.cerebralpalsynys.org

Clients:
United Cerebral Palsy Associations of NYS

Lobbyists:
Michael Alvaro
Susan Constantino

Curran, Brian F
C/O Public Employees Federation
100 State Street
Albany, NY 12207-1806
518-432-4003

Clients:
SEIU Local 200 United

Lobbyists:
Kenneth Brynien
Ryan Delgado
Musa Moore
John Murphy

Alan Schulkin

D'Ambrosio, John A
Orange County Chamber of Commerce
30 Scotts Corner Drive
Montgomery, NY 12549
845-457-9700

Clients:
Orange County Chamber of Commerce (The)

Lobbyists:
Carol Smith

D'Onofrio, Paul
67 Chestnut St
Albany, NY 12210
518-432-7393

Clients:
Assn of Electrical Workers (NYS)
Council of Sheet Metal Workers Int'l Assn (NYS)
Monticello Raceway Management Inc

Dadey, Dick (FKA Citizens Union of the City of New York)
Citizens Union of NYC
299 Broadway, Ste 700
New York, NY 10007
212-227-0342

Clients:
Citizens Union of the City of New York

Lobbyists:
Alex Camarda
Rachel Fauss

Dagnello, Vito
P.O. Box 706
St. James, NY 11780
631-208-1326

Clients:
United Correction Officers Coalition

Daiichi Sankyo, Inc.
1825 K Street NW
Suite 425
Washington, DC 20006
202-223-6575

Lobbyists:
Craig Nowacki

Dairylea Cooperative, Inc.
5001 Brittonfield Pkwy
P.O. Box 4844
Syracuse, NY 13221-4844
315-433-0100

Lobbyists:
William Beeman
Karen Cartier
Ed Gallagher
Leon Graves
John Siglow
Sanford Stauffer

Gregory Wickham

Dan Klores Communications, Inc. DBA DKC
Government Affairs
111 Washington Avenue
Albany, NY 12210
518-813-4832

Clients:
A. Servidone, Inc.
Alliant Insurance Services
Atlantic Auto Mall
Birchez Associates, LLC
Cable Telecommunications Association of NY, Inc. (The)
Central Life Sciences (Fleishman-Hillard, Inc.)
Consolidated Edison Company of New York, Inc.
CSC Holdings, Inc. FKA Cablevision Systems Corporation
D&D Power, Inc.
Dack Consulting Services, Inc.
Delta Air Lines, Inc.
Empire Resorts, Inc.
Farmingdale State College
Fidelity Investments
Friends of the High Line
Frontier Healthcare Management Services, Inc.
Gaming Association, Inc.
Home Care Association of NYS
Homeward Bound Adirondacks
Hudson Valley Fois Gras (HVFG, LLC)
Independent System Operator, Inc.
JP Morgan Chase & Co.
Linium LLC
Madison Square Garden
Major League Soccer
Professional Insurance Agents of New York
PSCH, Inc.
Southern Wine & Spirits of America, Inc.
Transmission Developers, Inc.
Trial Lawyers Association
TWC Administration LLC
WNET.org

Lobbyists:
Daniel Cain
Allison Lee
Andrew Marocco
Marie Ternes
Michelle Tuchman
Paul Zuber

Darwak, Stephanie
3 Independence Row
Stillwater, NY 12170
518-664-5880

Clients:
State Osteopathic Medical Society (NY)

Davidoff, Hutcher & Citron LLP
150 State Street
Suite 502
Albany, NY 12207
518-465-8230

Clients:
114 Kenmare Associates, LLC
212 LaFayette Associates, LLC
Abbott Laboratories
ABBVIE, Inc.
Adelphi University

Akwesasne Convenience Store Association
All Shows LLC
Association of Water & Sewer Excavators, Inc
Carpet and Rug Institute (The)
Castagna Realty
Center for Educational Innovation - Public Education Association (CEI-PEA)
Community Bancorp, Inc.
Coney Island Holdings LLC
Council of School Supervisors & Administrators
Court Reporters Association, Inc. (NYS)
Creditors Bar Association
DriversEd.com
Easy Choice Health Plan of New York
Fairmont Capital LLC
Figli Di San Gennaro, Inc.
Gateway College AS
Helen Keller Services for the Blind
Hunts Point Terminal Produce Cooperative Association, Inc.
IDT Energy
Local Control for Local Progress, Inc.
Looks Great Services, Inc.
Master Plumbers Council of the City of New York, Inc.
Metropolitan Package Store Association
Nassau County Village Officials Assn
National Insurance Crime Bureau
Nestle Waters North America Holdings Inc
New York Alliance of Library Systems
New York Cosmos LLC
New York Institute of Energy and Water
Northeast Kidney Foundation
O'Connor Capital Partners
Oxford Nursing Home, Inc.
Palladia Inc (Formerly Project Return Foundation Inc)
Penzim Produce Corp
Plyndirio LLC
Queens Borough Public Library
RCN Telecom Services, Inc.
Redvision Systems, Inc.
Reed Elsevier, Inc.
Staffing Assn (NY)
Taxicab Service Assn
Touro College
Town Hall Foundation, Inc.
United Hebrew of New Rochelle
Verde Electric Corporation
Vision Rehabilitation Assn (NYVRA) (NY)
Young Adult Institute, Inc.

Lobbyists:
Leslie Barbara
Charles Capetanakis
Jeff Citron
Peter R Crouse
Sean Crowley
Sid Davidoff
Arthur Goldstein
Anna Lisa Greco
John B Kiernan
Stephen A Malito
Howard Weiss
Derek Wolman
Michael Zapson

DCI Group AZ, LLC (FKA DCI Group, LLC)
2340 E Beardsley Road
Suite 100
Phoenix, AZ 85024
602-387-8000
Web site: www.dcigroup.com

Offices and agencies generally appear in alphabetical order, except when specific order is requested by listee.

Clients:
Altria Client Services Inc. and its Affiliates

Lobbyists:
Dan Combs
Charles Joslin IV

DDC Advocacy
174 Waterfront St
Suite 500
National Harbor, MD 20745
301-686-8000

Clients:
American Petroleum Institute

Lobbyists:
Bill Toye

Debevoise & Plimpton LLP
919 Third Avenue
New York, NY 10022
212-909-6000

Clients:
Columbian Mutual Life Insurance Comapny
Excess Line Association of NY

Lobbyists:
Eric R. Dinallo
Wolcott B. Dunham Jr.

Defenders Justice Fund, NYS
194 Washington Avenue
Suite 500
Albany, NY 12210
518-465-0519

Lobbyists:

Defoyd, Katherine
500 Summit Avenue
Maplewood, NJ 07040
973-650-5983

Clients:
Jonathan Gradess
Armory Foundation (The)
Mount Sanai Hospital (The)
Road Runners Foundation (NY)

Delbello Donnellan Weingarten Wise & Wiederkehr, LLP
One North Lexington Avenue
11th Floor
White Plains, NY 10601
914-681-0200

Clients:
Avalonbay Communities, Inc.
Cappelli Enterprises, Inc.
Fareri Associates
FC Yonkers Associates LLC
Forest City Residential Group, Inc.
Frontier Healthcare Management Services, Inc.
Wilder Balter Partners, Inc.

Lobbyists:
Ann Carson
Alfred Delbello

Alfred Donnellan
Janet Giris
Michael Schwarz
Mark Weingarten
Peter Wise

Deloitte & Touche LLP
30 Rockefeller Plaza
New York, NY 10112
973-602-4321

Lobbyists:
Doris Imperati
Henry Phillips
Gordon Sanit
Beth A. Schneider
Lisa Tracy Smith
Suzanne Whitworth

Deloitte Consulting
39 N. Pearl St.
3rd Floor
Albany, NY 12207
518-472-4990

Lobbyists:
Frank Pisciotta
Stewart Rog

Delta Air Lines, Inc.
112 West 34th Street
Suite 2104
New York, NY 10120
646-871-6985

Lobbyists:
Gail Grimmett

Desales Media Group, Inc.
1712 10th Ave
Brooklyn, NY 11215
718-499-9705

Lobbyists:
Vincent Levien

Destiny USA Management Company, LLC
4 Clinton Square
Syracuse, NY 13202
315-422-7000

Lobbyists:
David Aitken
Robert Congel
Bruce Kenan

Deutsch, Ronald
212 Great Oaks Blvd
Albany, NY 12203
518-452-2130

Clients:
New Yorkers for Fiscal Fairness

Deutsche Bank Trust Company
60 Wall Street
New York, NY 10005
212-250-2500

Offices and agencies generally appear in alphabetical order, except when specific order is requested by listee.

Lobbyists:
Willaim Baneky
Lucille Douglas
Elizabeth Zieglmeier

Clients:
Aflac New York
Association of Financial Guaranty Insurors
Equinox, Inc.
Excess Line Association of NY
International Underwriting Association of London
Lloyd's of London
Medical Liability Mutual Insurance Company
Mortgage Insurance Companies of America
State Farm Insurance Companies

Lobbyists:
H Michael Byrne
Thomas Dawson
Noelle M Kinsch
Jeffrey Mace
Jay B Martin
John Mulhern
Bradford Race
Edmond Valente

Dimaio, Mark
19 Longacre Court
Hockessin, DE 19707
302-437-4550

Clients:
Otsuka America Pharmaceutical, Inc.

Diageo
801 Main Avenue
Norwalk, CT 06851
203-229-4504

Clients:
Diageo, PLC

Lobbyists:
Dwayne Kratt

Diorio, L Todd
451 Little Britian Rd
Newburgh, NY 12550
845-565-2737

Clients:
Hudson Valley Building & Construction Trades Council
Laborers Int'l Union of North America AFL-CIO, Local 17

DirecTv
90 State Street
Suite 700
Albany, NY 122047
518-591-4639

Lobbyists:
Damon Stewart

Distilled Spirits Council of the US (FKA Wojnar, David E.)
C/O Distilled Spirits Council of the US
1250 I Street NW
Ste 400
Washington, DC 20005-3998

202-682-8836
Web site: www.discus.org

Lobbyists:
Jay Hibbard

Distinctive Public Affairs, LLC
2156 Cruger Avenue
Suite 45
Bronx, NY 10462
718-704-7039

Clients:
Coalition for Opportunity in Education, Inc.

Lobbyists:
Marysol Rodriguez

District Council 37, AFSCME
125 Barclay St
New York, NY 10007
212-815-1500
Web site: www.district37.net

Clients:
District Council 37, AFSCME

Lobbyists:
Oliver Gray
Ashton Matyi
Sybil McPherson
Wanda Williams

Dominion Resources
C/O Dominion Resources
701 E. Cary St.
21st Floor
Richmond, VA 23219
717-236-9261

Lobbyists:
Donald Houser

Donohue, Gavin J
Independent Power Producers of NY, Inc.
194 Washington Ave2
Suite 315
Albany, NY 12210
518-436-3749
e-mail: gavin@ippny.org
Web site: www.ippny.org

Lobbyists:
Radmila Miletich

Drexelius, Jr., John R.
PO Box 141
Buffalo, NY 14223
716-316-7552

Clients:
Developmental Disability Alliance of Western New York

Driscoll Group, Inc.
45-23 47th Street
Sunnyside, NY 11377
347-808-8614

Offices and agencies generally appear in alphabetical order, except when specific order is requested by listee.

Clients:
176 Woodward Owner LLC
Business Outreach Center Network, Inc.
Cement League
Child Center of New York
Edgestone Group LLC
Everyone Reading, Inc.
JMED Holding LLC
Lifeline Center for Child Development (The)
Queens College (Research Foundation of the City University of New York)
Queens Economic Development Corporation
S.W. Anderson Sales Corporation

Drug Policy Alliance
131 West 33rd Street
15th Floor
New York, NY 10001
212-613-8048

Lobbyists:
Kassandra Frederique
Evan Goldstein
Julie Netherland
Gabriel Sayegh

Dryfoos Group
45-02 Ditmars Blvd
Suite 1016
Astoria, NY 11105
347-642-5320

Clients:
Brooklyn Children's Museum
Community Works
Inside Broadway
Junior Tennis League (NY)
Literacy, Inc.
Midori and Friends
QSAC
Shareing & Careing Inc
Sports & Arts in School Foundation

Lobbyists:
Laura Jean Hawkins
Carol Swift

Duane Morris LLP
99 Washington Ave
Suite 803
Albany, NY 12210
518-598-1900

Clients:
Mortgage Insurance Companies of America
State Farm Insurance Companies

Lobbyists:
Edmond Valente

Duca, Anthony
5 Chelsea Court
Medford, NJ 08055
609-923-0577

Clients:
EISAI, Inc.

Duffy, Margaret
360 West 31st Street
5th Floor
New York, NY 10001
518-462-0787

Clients:
Amerigroup New York LLC

Dunne, John
225 Broadway
Suite 401
New York, NY 10007
212-293-9300

Clients:
Uniformed Fire Officers Association (NYC)

Lobbyists:
Marty Steadman

Durrani, Waqas
100 Motor Parkway
Suite 140
Hauppauge, NY 11788
634-233-6050

Clients:
Allstate Insurance Company

Lobbyists:
Vince Fusco
Bill Vainisi

Durst Development LLC
One Bryant Park
New York, NY 10036
212-257-6600

Lobbyists:
Jordan Barowitz

Durst Organization, Inc. (The)
One Bryant Park
New York, NY 10036
212-257-6600

Lobbyists:
Jordan Barowitz

E-3 Communications
551 Franklin Street
Buffalo, NY 14202
716-854-8182
Web site: www.e3communications.com

Clients:
Absolut Management Facilities, Inc.
Association of Ambulatory Surgery Centers
Beech-Nut Nutrition Corporation
Buffalo Police Benevolent Association, Inc.
Lawley Insurance
National Fuel Gas Company
Noco Energy Corporation
School Administrators Association of New York State
Vinyl Institute (The)

Lobbyists:
Kevin Banes

Offices and agencies generally appear in alphabetical order, except when specific order is requested by listee.

Earl Wells

Early Care and Learning Council
230 Washington Avenue Extension
Albany, NY 12203
518-690-4217

Lobbyists:
Marsha Basloe
Jessica Klos

Easter Seals New York
40 West 37th Street
New York, NY 10018
917-882-6460

Lobbyists:
Julie Bazan
Bradford Cook
Daniel Cooke
Kavan Desai
James DiBenedetto
Joseph Dichiara
Robin Doick
James Fahey
Kanti Gala
Neil Gala
Larry Gammon
John Hayes
Philip Laffey
Richard Lauricella
Mark Legaspi
John Mascialino
Gerald Mattimore
John McGrath
Heather Mills
Sylvia Ng
Aris Pavlides
Sam Scavone
Stanley Schlein
John Sheppard
Sue Silsby
Neil Sullivan
Angela Torres
Elin Trainor
Dave Vanblarcom
Lori Vanderhoof
Ed Vicinanza
Thomas Westle
Mick Wood

Eber, Lester
155 Paragon Drive
Rochester, NY 14624
585-317-1024

Clients:
Southern Wine & Spirits of America, Inc.

Economic Development Council Inc (NYS)
111 Washington Avenue 6th Floor
Albany, NY 12210
518-426-4058
e-mail: mcmahon@nysedc.org
Web site: www.nysedc.org

Clients:
Economic Development Council Inc (NYS)

Lobbyists:
Brian T McMahon

Edison Spring Street Company LLC
100 Washington St
Newark, NJ 07102
973-643-7700

Lobbyists:
Anthony Borelli

Education Reform Now Advocacy, Inc.
928 Broadway
New York, NY 10010
212-614-3213

Lobbyists:
Elisabeth Ling
Joe Williams

Education Reform Now, Inc.
928 Broadway
New York, NY 10010
212-614-3213

Lobbyists:
Elisabeth Ling
Joe Williams

Edward K. Flynn
520 Madison Avenue
8th Floor
New York, NY 10022
212-336-7029

Clients:
Jefferies LLC

Lobbyists:
Kojo Asiedu
Harold Bean
Roy Carlberg
Jeffrey Cohen
Neil Flanagan
Kenneth Gibbs
John Kearney
Joseph Nocerino
Shawn Sinel
William Torsiglieri

Egan, Paul (FKA Reiskin, Marvin)
C/O United Federation of Teachers
52 Broadway
New York, NY 10004
212-777-7500

Clients:
United Federation of Teachers

Lobbyists:
Jasaun Boone
Carol Gerstl
Jason Goldman
Jeremy Hoffman
Sandra March
Briget Rein

Offices and agencies generally appear in alphabetical order, except when specific order is requested by listee.

Eisland Strategies LLC
2600 Netherland Ave
Suite 811
Bronx, NY 10463
718-549-1950

Clients:
Marshall E. Bloomfield

Lobbyists:
June Eisland

Elk Street Group LLC
25 Elk Street
Albany, NY 12207
518-813-4383

Clients:
Beauty Schools Association
Catskill Off-Track Betting Corporation
Children's Institute
Exxon Mobil Corporation
Innocence Project (The)
Law School Admission Council
Norfolk Southern Corporation
Osborne Association
Partnership of Upstate Legal Services
Patrick F. Adams, P.C.
Pfizer, Inc.
PMSI
Ramapo Organized for Sustainability and a Safe Aquifer
Reckitt Benckiser, Inc.
Reenergy Holdings LLC
Stoneriver Pharmacy Solutions, Inc.
U.S Communities
United New York Ambulance Network
Williams Companies, Inc.

Lobbyists:
Andrea Debow
Diana Georgia
Pablo Rivera
Edward Wassermann

Emblemhealth Services Company, LLC
55 Water Street
New York, NY 10041
646-447-7091

Lobbyists:
David Abernethy
Frank Branchini
Arthur Byrd
Mohamed Diab
Dan Finke
William Gillespie
Jeff Goodwin
Nick Kambolis
William Lamoreaux
Charlene Maher
Edward Mailander
Bill Mastro
Eliza Ng
Jay Schoenfeld
Wanda Wareham
Tony Watson

EMD Serono, Inc.
975 F. Street NW
Suite 330
Washington, DC 20004
202-626-2596

Lobbyists:
Ethel Knighton

Empire Advocates LLC
50 Beaver Street
Albany, NY 12207
315-436-1352

Clients:
America's Natural Gas Alliance, Inc.

Lobbyists:
Paul B. Powers
Nancy Testani

Empire Consultants
580 Park Avenue
Suite 1B
New York, NY 10021
212-838-6600

Clients:
Dominican College
Empire City Labs
Rose Group Park Ave. LLC
Strike Force Protective Services, Inc.

Lobbyists:
Joseph Mirto

Empire Generating Co. LLC
100 Constitution Plaza
10th Floor
Hartford, CT 06095
860-656-0822

Lobbyists:
James Ginnetti

Empire Government Strategies
1425 RXR Plaza
East Tower - 15th Floor
Uniondale, NY 11556-1425
516-663-6688

Clients:
Bowling Proprietors Association
Caithness Long Island II LLC
Educational Houseing Servies, Inc.
Medical Staff Leadership Council
Plumbing Foundation City of New York, Inc.
USPLabs LLC

Lobbyists:
Anthony Figliola
Arthur Jerry Kremer

Empire Justice Center (FKA Greater Upstate Law Project)
1 West Main Street
Suite 200
Rochester, NY 14614

Offices and agencies generally appear in alphabetical order, except when specific order is requested by listee.

585-454-4060

Clients:
Empire Justice Center

Lobbyists:
Susan Antos
Linda Bennet-Rodriguez
Kristin Brown
Kate Callery
Robert Cisneros
Trilby Dejung
Anne Erickson
Rita Eygabroad Garretson
Don Friedman
Geoffrey Hale
Mike Hanley
Linda Hassberg
Bryan Hetherington
Kirsten Keefe
Cheryl Keshner
Ruhi Maker
Kevin Purcell
Reyna Remolete Hayashi
Cathy Roberts
Amy Schwartz
Lousie Tarantino
Barbara Van Kerkhove
Daniel Villena
Barbara Weiner
Tamara Wright

Empire State Association of Assisted Living (FKA Empire State Association of Adult Homes & Assisted)
646 Plank Road
Suite 207
Clifton Park, NY 12065
518-371-2573

Lobbyists:
James Kane
Lisa Newcomb

Empire State College, State University of NY
Empire State College
2 Union Avenue
Saratoga Springs, NY 12866-4931
518-587-2100
e-mail: marycaroline.powers@esc.edu
Web site: www.esc.edu

Clients:
Empire State College, State University of NY

Lobbyists:
Michael Mancini
Mary Powers

Empire State Forest Products Association
47 Van Alstyne Drive
Rensselaer, NY 12144
518-463-1297

Lobbyists:
Eric Carlson

Empire State Petroleum Association, Inc.
80 Wolf Rd
Suite 308
Albany, NY 12205
518-449-0702

Lobbyists:
Thomas Peters

Empire Strategic Planning, Inc.
111 Washington Avenue
Suite 103
Albany, NY 12210
518-701-2713

Clients:
ACS Home Care LLC
Bikepath Country
ECG Engineering P.C.
Glenwood Management Corporation
Grahel Associates LLC
Messenger & Courier Association
O'Connor Davies Munns & Dobbins LLP
Paraco Gas
Saint Joseph's Medical Center
Specialty Wine Retailers Association
Vista Developers Corp
Westchester County Correction Superior Officers Association
White Birch, LLC (FKA Camarda Realty Investments)
Zachy's Wine & Liquor Store, Inc.

Lobbyists:
James Cavanaugh
Maureen Kronau
John J. Spano

Employer Alliance for Affordable Health Care
PO Box 1412
Albany, NY 12201-1412
518-462-2296
Web site: employeralliance.com

Clients:
Employer Alliance for Affordable Health Care

Lobbyists:
Pamela Finch

Entergy Nuclear Operations, Inc
440 Hamilton Ave
White Plains, NY 10601
914-272-3350

Clients:
Entergy Nuclear Operations, Inc

Lobbyists:
Joanne Fernandez
Rick Smith
Kenneth Theobalds
Michael T. Twomey

Enterprise Holdings
1550 Route 23 North
Wayne, NJ 07470
973-709-2396

Clients:
Enterprise Holdings

Offices and agencies generally appear in alphabetical order, except when specific order is requested by listee.

Lobbyists:
Judson Church
Tomi Gerber
Todd Stockton
Dean Thompson

Entertainment Software Association
575 7th Street, NW
Suite 300
Washington, DC 20004
202-223-2400

Lobbyists:
Thomas Foulkes

Environmental Advocates of NY
353 Hamilton St
Albany, NY 12210
518-462-5526

Clients:
Environmental Advocates of NY

Lobbyists:
Melissa Andreychek
Saima Anjam
Ross Gould
Alison Jenkins
Robert J Moore
Katherine Nadeau
Travis Proulx
David Vanluven

Environmental Defense Fund
257 Park Avenue South
New York, NY 10010
212-505-2100

Lobbyists:
Mary Barber
Abbie Brown
Mark Brownstein
Andrew Darrell
Adam Peltz
Raya Salter
Isabelle Silverman
Elizabeth Stein
Jim Tripp

EPL/Environmental Advocates
353 Hamilton Street
Albany, NY 12210
518-462-5526

Lobbyists:
Melissa Andreychek
Saima Anjam
Ross Gould
Alison Jenkins
Robert J. Moore
Katherine Nadeau
Travis Proulx
David Vanluven

EQT Partners AB
677 Broadway
9th Floor
Albany, NY 12207
518-449-8893

Lobbyists:
Conni Jonsson
Jussi Saarinen
Jan Stahlberg
Marcus Wallinder

EQT Partner AS
677 Broadway
9th Floor
Albany, NY 12207
518-449-8893

Lobbyists:
Christian Sinding

EQT Partners Asia Limited
677 Broadway
9th Floor
Albany, NY 12207
518-449-8893

Lobbyists:
Wolfgang Gorny
Martin Mok

EQT Partners GMBH
677 Broadway
9th Floor
Albany, NY 12207
518-449-8893

Lobbyists:
Marcus Brennecke

EQT Partners, Inc.
1114 Avenue of the Americas
38th Floor
New York, NY 10036
917-281-0850

Lobbyists:
Erwin Thompson
James Wilson

EQT Partners UK Advisors LLP
677 Broadway
9th Floor
Albany, NY 12207
518-449-8893

Lobbyists:
Tequila Bone
Christian Broberg
Paul De Rome
Stephen Escudier
Paul Johnson
Cyril Konopelski
David Slade
Lloyd Thomas

Excelsior Advocates, LLC
403 Livingston Avenue
Albany, NY 12206
518-441-1884

Clients:
Coalition of Neighborhood Centers
General Motors Corporation

Offices and agencies generally appear in alphabetical order, except when specific order is requested by listee.

Rochester Genesee Regional Transportation Authority

Lobbyists:
Robert Gaddy

Exelon Generation Company LLC
300 Exelon Way
Kennett Square, PA 19348
610-765-6920

Lobbyists:
Daniel Allegretti
Christopher Wentlent

Express Scripts Holding Co.
300 New Jersey Avenue NW
Suite 600
Washington, DC 20001
202-383-7983

Lobbyists:
Jonah Houts

Extell Development Company
805 Third Ave
7th Floor
New York, NY 10022
212-712-6000
Web site: www.extelldev.com

Lobbyists:
Gary Barnett
Donna Gargano
Lela Goren
Raizy Haas
Anthony Mannarino
Jeff Torkin

Faist Government Affairs Group, LLC
54 Willett Street
Albany, NY 12210-1104
518-432-0599
e-mail: tfaist@aol.com

Clients:
American International Group, Inc.
Chemical Alliance (NYS)
Council of Insurance Brokers of Greater NY, Inc
E.I. Du Pont De Nemours and Company
Fashion Jewelry Trade Association
FMC Corporation
Guardian Life Insurance Co of America
Halogenated Solvents Industry Alliance, Inc.
National Assn of Health Underwriters
Palliatech, Inc.
Wine & Grape Foundation (NY)

Lobbyists:
Thomas W Faist

Families Together in NYS, Inc.
737 Madison Avenue
Albany, NY 12208
518-432-0333

Lobbyists:
Paige Pierce

Family Planning Advocates of New York State
17 Elk Street
Albany, NY 12207
518-436-8408

Lobbyists:
Carol Blowers
Tracey M. Brooks
Carolyn Ehrlich
Georgana Hanson
Kelli Owens
Dianne Patterson
Ronora Pawelko

Farber, Felice
60 East 42 Street, Suite 3510
New York, NY 10165
212-687-3131

Clients:
General Contractors Association of NY, Inc.

Lobbyists:
Denise Richardson

Farm Bureau, Inc. (NY)
159 Wolf Road
PO Box 5530
Albany, NY 12205-0330
518-436-8495

Lobbyists:
Steven Ammerman
Bambi Baehrel
Richard Ball
Timothy Bigham
William Hamilton
Marilyn Howard
T. Mark James
Donald Jensen
Amanda Krenning
Catherine Mural
Dean Norton
Eric Ooms
Fred Perrin
Jaclyn Sears
Julie Suarez
John Wagner
Lindsay Wickham
Jeffrey Williams
Nicole Willis
Kelly Young

Farmers Insurance Group
PO Box 201
Saratoga Springs, NY 12866
518-867-9255

Lobbyists:
Nicholas Masi

Fassler, Michael S
C/O Beth Abraham Family of Health Svcs
612 Allerton Ave
Bronx, NY 10467-7404
718-519-4001

Clients:
Centerlight Health Systems

Political Parties, Lobbyists & PACs

LOBBYISTS

Lobbyists:
Joseph Healy
Jacqueline Kennedy-Sadler
Paul Rosenfeld

Faucher, Jennifer
2790 Bragg Street
Apt 511
Brooklyn, NY 11235
917-687-0261

Clients:
Public Employees Federation

Featherstonhaugh, Wiley & Clyne, LLP
99 Pine St
Albany, NY 12207
518-436-0786

Clients:
AAA New York State, Inc.
Altria Client Services, Inc.
Association of Cemeteries (NYS)
Bottlers Association (NYS)
Building Congress (NY) (The)
Construction Industry Council of Westchester & Hudson Valley, Inc.
CVS Pharmacy, Inc.
Empire Merchants North, LLC
Empire Merchants, LLC
Entergy Nuclear Operations, Inc.
Estate of Marilyn Monroe LLC
Experience Hendrix LLC
Financial Service Centers of New York
Forest Lawn Cemetery/Cremation Group (The)
Friends of Democracy New York
Gaming Association, Inc.
General Contractors Association of NY, Inc. (The)
Goldman Sachs Group, Inc. (The) & Its Subsidiaries & Affiliates
Green-Wood Cemetary (The)
GTech Corporation
Just Energy New York Corporation (FKA Energy Savings)
Kohl Partners
Long Island Contractors Association
McKissack Group, Inc. (The)
Metropolitan Life Insurance Company
Nutrition Association
Park Outdoor Advertising of NY, Inc.
Roadway Imporvement Coalition (NY)
Society of Physician Assistants (NYS)
Thoroughbred Horsemens Association, Inc. (NY)
Tracfone Wireless, Inc.
UNISYS Corporation
United Healthcare Services, Inc.
Woodlawn Cemetery (The)
Yaddo

Lobbyists:
Elizabeth Clyne
James Featherstonhaugh
David Fleming
Dan Hallenbeck
John Hardy
Frank Hoare
Jonathan McCardle
Stephen Morgan
John Olsen

Federation of Mental Health Services, Inc. (The)
104-70 Queens Blvd.
Forest Hills
New York, NY 11375
718-275-6010

Lobbyists:
John Rossland

Federation of School Administrators (NYS) (FKA Gibbons, Brian)
40 Rector Street
12th Floor
New York, NY 10006-1729
212-823-2020

Lobbyists:
Crystal Boling-Barton
Dee Dee Goidel
Ernest Logan
Peter McNally
Steve Murphy
Alithia Rodriguez-Rolon

Feld Entertainment
8607 Westwood Center Dr
Vienna, VA 22182
703-749-5570

Clients:
Feld Entertainment, Inc

Lobbyists:
Thomas Albert
Sarah Lashford

Ferramosca, Joseph
189 Montague St
Suite 400
Brooklyn, NY 11201
718-243-0222

Clients:
Assistant Deputy Warden - Deputy Warden's Association
Correct Captain's Association, Dept. of Corrections, City of New York

Ferris, William E
AARP
One Commerce Plaza, Ste 706
Albany, NY 12260
518-434-4194
e-mail: wferris@aarp.org
Web site: www.aarp.org/ny

Clients:
AARP

Lobbyists:
William Armbuster
Chaunda Ball
Christine Deska
Lindsey Etringer
Beth Finkel
David Irwin
Stacy Kratz
Kristin Legere
Yvette Martinez
David McNally

Offices and agencies generally appear in alphabetical order, except when specific order is requested by listee.

416

Erin Mitchell
Laura Palmer
Dionne Polite
Will Stoner
Christopher Widelo

Finch Paper LLC
One Glen Street
Glens Falls, NY 12801
518-793-2541

Lobbyists:
Rob Baron
Kyle Brock
Sandra LaBarren
Michael McLarty
Joseph Raccuia

Fisher Development Strategies
21 Choir Lane
Westbury, NY 11590
516-238-0186

Clients:
Chamber Players International
Nassau Community College
Nassau County Firefighters Museum & Education Ctr

Lobbyists:
Daniel Fisher Jr.

Fitzgerald, Gary J
Iroquois Healthcare Alliance
17 Executive Park Drive
Clifton Park, NY 12065
518-383-5060
e-mail: gfitzgerald@iroquois.org
Web site: www.iroquois.org

Clients:
Iroquois Healthcare Alliance

Lobbyists:
Stacy Connors
Allan Filler

Fitzgerald, Kevin
11921 Freedom Dr
Reston, VA 20190
212-816-3656

Clients:
CitiBank, N.A.

Lobbyists:
Michael Casella
Ciara Imelda Deane
Joseph Imbro
Thomas C. Murphy
Gary Schneider

Fitzpatrick, Christine M
Adult Day Health Care Council
13 British American Blvd
Latham, NY 12110-1431
518-449-2707 x130
e-mail: cfitzpatrick@nyahsa.org
Web site: www.nyahsa.org

Clients:
Adult Day Health Care Council (ADHCC)

Lobbyists:
Anne Hille

FMR LLC
82 Devonshire Street, NSA
Boston, MA 02109
617-563-9891

Lobbyists:
Mark Gallagher
John Muggeridge
Maria Nieves

Focus Media Group, Inc.
10 Matthews Street
Goshen, NY 10924
845-294-3342

Clients:
Empire Resorts, Inc.

Lobbyists:
Joshua Cohen

Foley & Lardner LLP
90 Park Avenue
New York, NY 10016
212-338-3568

Clients:
Brookdale University Hospital and Medical Center
Jamaica Hospital Medical Center
Nassau Health Care Corporation

Lobbyists:
Jeffrey Thrope

Food & Water Watch
68 Jay St
Suite 713
Brooklyn, NY 11201
718-943-8068

Lobbyists:
Corinne Rosen
Eric Weltman

Food Bank for New York City
39 Broadway
10th Floor
New York, NY 10006
212-566-7855

Lobbyists:
Aine Duggan
Triada Stampas

Food Industry Alliance of NYS Inc
130 Washington Ave
Albany, NY 12210
518-434-1900

Clients:
New Yorkers for Real Recycling Reform (Food Industry Alliance of NYS Inc)

Offices and agencies generally appear in alphabetical order, except when specific order is requested by listee.

LOBBYISTS

Lobbyists:
Jay Peltz
James T Rogers
Michael E Rosen

Forest City Ratner Companies
1 Metrotech Center North
11th Floor
Brooklyn, NY 11201
718-923-8429

Lobbyists:
David Berliner
Ashley Cotton
Maryanne Gilmartin
Bruce Ratner
Katherine Welch

Forum Strategies & Communications
805 Third Avenue
14th Floor
New York, NY 10022
212-554-2160

Clients:
Altria Client Services, Inc.

Lobbyists:
David Laufer
Michelle Mitola
Andy Sands

Foundation for Opportunity in Education (The)
26 Century Hill Drive
Suite 203
Latham, NY 12110
518-640-8344

Lobbyists:
Thomas Carroll
Peter Murphy

Frack Action Fund, Inc.
107 South Albany St
Ithaca, NY 14850
518-322-2978

Lobbyists:
John Armstrong
Julia Walsh

Fried Frank Harris Shriver & Jacobson, LLP
One New York Plaza
New York, NY 10004-1980
212-859-8473

Clients:
117th Street Equities LLC
Archdiocese of New York
Cornell University
Durst Organization (The)
Greenpoint Landing Associates LLC
Jamestown Premier Chelsea Market, L.P.
Major League Soccer LLC
Rector, Church-Wardens and Vestrymen of Trinity Church in the City of
    New York (The)
Related Companies, L.P. (The)
Rudin Management Company, Inc.
SL Green Realty Company

TF Cornerstone, Inc.

Lobbyists:
David Badain
Adrienne Bernard
Zachary Bernstein
Holly Chen
Michele Chirco
Ilana Ettinger
David Geist
Tal Golumb
Hanna Gustafsson
Stephen Lefkowitz
Richard Leland
Jonathan Mechanic
Melanie Meyers
Carol Rosenthal

Friedlander Group (The)
120 Broadway
Suite 3300
New York, NY 10271
212-233-5555

Clients:
Community First Party
NYSHA Inc.
Shema Kolainu-Hear Our Voices
XChange Telecom Corp.

Lobbyists:
Ezra Friedlander

Friedman, John P
United Services Automobile Association
325 Columbia Tpk
Florham Park, NJ 07932
973-377-6662
e-mail: john.friedman@usaa.com

Clients:
United Services Automobile Assn (USAA)

Friends of the High Line, Inc.
529 West 20th Street
Suite 8W
New York, NY 10011
212-206-9922
Web site: www.thehighline.org

Lobbyists:
Joshua David
Robert Hammond
Peter Mullan
Maria Torres-Springer

Frost, Robert D.
853 Broadway
Suite 2014
New York, NY 10003
212-813-3575

Clients:
Industco Holdings, LLC

Lobbyists:
Alan Gifford Miller

Offices and agencies generally appear in alphabetical order, except when specific order is requested by listee.

Fund for the City of New York (FKA Employment & Training Coalition (NYC))
121 Avenue of the Americas
6th Floor
New York, NY 10013
212-925-6675

Lobbyists:
Anu Bhagwati
James Brodick
Haidee Cabusora
Michael Carey
Janet Carter
Samantha Clare
Michelle Del Guercio
Amy Ellenbogen
Carol Fisler
Mae Watson Grote
Richard Moses
Ambika Panday
Lindsay Pankok
John Raskin
Carolyn Ratcliffe
Susan Rodriguez
Gloria Searson
Alfred Siegel
DC Vito
Christopher Walter
Phillip Zielinski

Funeral Directors Association, Inc. (NYS)
426 New Karner Road
Albany, NY 12205
518-452-8230

Lobbyists:
Bonnie McCullough
Randy McCullough

Gallo, Richard J.
123 State Street
Albany, NY 12207-1622
518-465-3545

Clients:
Davita Inc.
Psychiatric Association, Inc. (NYS)

Gaming Association
99 Pine Street
Suite 210
Albany, NY 12207
518-436-1122

Lobbyists:
Matthew Cunningham
James Featherstonhaugh
Dan Sommer
Michael Wilton

Garfinkel, Neil
Abrams Garfinkel Margolis Bergson, LLP
237 West 35th Street, 4th Floor
New York, NY 10001
212-201-1173

Clients:
Real Estate Board of NY, Inc.

Gay Men's Health Crisis Inc
119 West 24th Street
New York, NY 10011-1995
212-367-1250
e-mail: ronaldj@gmhc.org
Web site: www.gmhc.org

Clients:
Gay Men's Health Crisis Inc

Lobbyists:
Elizabeth Lovinger
Nathan Schaefer
Lyndel Urbano
Robert Valadez
Janet Weinberg

Geiger, Bruce W & Associates
111 Washington Ave, Ste 606A
Albany, NY 12210
518-432-1607

Clients:
28 New York Masters of Foxhounds
Alzheimer's Disease Resource Center
Associated Dog Clubs of New York State, Inc.
Aviation Management Association (NY) (Association of Counties (NY))
County Highway Superintendents Assn (NYS) (Association of Counties (NYS))
Empire State Marine Trades Association (Capitol Group, LLC)
Long Island Gasoline Retailers Association (William A. Schnell & Associates, Inc.)
Pinelawn Cemetery
Rural Electric Cooperative Association, Inc. (NYS)
Snowmobile Association (NYS) (Capitol Group, LLC)

Lobbyists:
Bruce W Geiger

General Electric Company (FKA Farrell, Pamela)
1299 Pennsylvania Avenue
Suite 900
Washington, DC 2004
202-637-4455

Clients:
General Electric Company

Lobbyists:
James McGaugh
Scott Roberti

General Motors Corporation
25 Massachusetts Avenue, NW
Suite 400
Washington, DC 20001
202-775-5056

Clients:
General Motors Corporation

Lobbyists:
John Blanchard
Brian Lee
Jeffrey Perry
Bryan Roosa

Offices and agencies generally appear in alphabetical order, except when specific order is requested by listee.

Genovese, John

1095 Avenue of the Americas
New York, NY 10036-6769
212-578-6499

Clients:
Metropolitan Life Insurance Company

Lobbyists:
Timothy Ring
Michael Zarcone

Genworth Financial

700 12th Street, NW
Suite 710
Washington, DC 20005
202-662-2568

Lobbyists:
Samuel Morgante
David Sloane
John Taggart

George J. Hochbrueckner & Associates, Inc.

PO Box 637
Laurel, NY 11948
518-456-3629

Clients:
Town of Riverhead
Vision Quest Lighting

Lobbyists:
George Hochbrueckner

Gergela III, Joseph

C/O Long Island Farm Bureau
104 Edwards Avenue
Suite 3
Calverton, NY 11933
631-727-3777

Clients:
Long Island Farm Bureau

Geto & De Milly Inc

130 East 40th Street
16th Floor
New York, NY 10016-1726
212-686-4551
e-mail: pr@getodemilly.com
Web site: www.getodemilly.com

Clients:
Algin Management Co., LLC
Atlantic Yards Development Company, LLC
CAMBA, Inc.
Center Against Domestic Violence
Edwin Gould Services for Children & Families
FC Yonkers Associates LLC
Island Tennis LP D/B/A Sportime
Jewish Home Lifecare
Lightstone Bronx Venture LLC
Lightstone Real Estate Partners LLC
LM Legacy Group LLC
Local 802, American Federation of Musicians of Greater New York

Lobbyists:
Joyce Baumgarten

Michele De Milly
Laura Dolon
Ethan Geto
Julie Hendricks-Atkins
Daniel White
Westchester County PBA

Gilbane Building Company

3150 Brunswick Pike
Suite 300
Lawrenceville, NJ 08648
609-671-4385

Clients:
Gilbane Building Company

Lobbyists:
Denis Boylan
Sean Cahill
Dennis Cornick
William DeCamp III
Jon Dibiase
William Gilbane, III
Neil Heyman
John Larow
Nadera Persaud
Judith Pullar
Matthew Simone
Lee Sokloski

Gilberti Stinziano Heintz & Smith, PC (FKA) Devorsetz Stinziano Gilberti Heintz & Smith, PC

555 E Genesee St
Syracuse, NY 13202-2159
518-476-2001

Clients:
Catskill Off-Track Betting Corporation
Young Men's Christian Association and Women's Community Center of Rome, New York, Inc.

Lobbyists:
Thomas Kelly
Tarky Lombardi Jr.
Andrew Maniglia

Clients:
Nat'l Assn of Energy Service Companies

Glazer, Robert

560 White Plains Road
Suite 500
Tarrytown, NY 10591
914-333-5809

Clients:
ENT and Allergy Associates, LLP

Lobbyists:
Andrew Franklin
Phyllis Schaffer-Cohen

Glenwood Poh

159 Alexander St
Yonkers, NY 10701
917-362-2200

Clients:
Gelnwood Poh LLC

Offices and agencies generally appear in alphabetical order, except when specific order is requested by listee.

Lobbyists:
Ron Shemesh

Global Strategy Group
895 Broadway
5th Floor
New York, NY 10003
212-260-8813

Client:
Major League Soccer LLC

Lobbyists:
Justin Lapatine
Marcia Maxwell
Jon Silvan

Goens, Darin
11250 Waples Mill Road
Fairfax, VA 22030
703-267-1250

Clients:
National Rifle Association of America

Golden, Ben
NYSARC
393 Delaware Ave
Delmar, NY 12054-3094
518-439-8311

Clients:
Arc Inc (NYS)

Lobbyists:
Paul Kietzman
John Sherman

Golden Tree Asset Management LP
300 Park Avenue
21st Floor
New York, NY 10022
212-847-3500

Lobbyists:
Kevin McAdams
V. Theodore Roosevelt
Robert Zimardo

Goldman Harris LLC (FKA Law Offices of Howard Goldman, LLC)
475 Park Avenue South
28th Floor
New York, NY 10016
212-935-1622

Clients:
62 Wooster LLC
Metro Storage NY LLC
S.L. Green Realty Corporation

Lobbyists:
Howard Goldman
Caroline Harris
Keli Lin
Fred T. Milani
Ezra Moser
Eugene Travers

Goldman Sachs & Co.
200 West Street
New York, NY 10282
212-902-1000

Lobbyists:
Renee Beaumont
Michael Borys
Gregory Carey
Edward Droesch
Chris Elmore
Nikki Faison-Miller
Michael Marcus
Marvin Markus
Arthur Miller
Joseph Natoli
Robert O'Connor
Sandy Pae
Curtis Probst
Jeffrey Scruggs
Keith Shultis
Stacy Sonnenberg
Jill Toporek
David Utz
Freda Utz
Kevin Willens
Bervan Yeh

Golub, David
461 Nott Street
Schenectady, NY 12308
518-379-1421

Clients:
Golub Corporation (The)

Lobbyists:
Neil Golub
Jerel Golub
William Kenneally
Carrie Terraferma

Good Shepherd Services
305 Seventh Avenue
9th Floor
New York, NY 10001
212-243-7070

Lobbyists:
Amy Cohen
Sr. Paulette Lomonaco
Susan Singh
Michelle Yanche

Goode, Christian
110-00 Rockaway Blvd
Jamaica, NY 11420
718-215-2813

Clients:
Genting New York LLC

Google, Inc.
2350 Kerner Blvd
Suite 250
San Rafael, CA 94901
415-389-6800

Offices and agencies generally appear in alphabetical order, except when specific order is requested by listee.

Lobbyists:
William Floyd

Gordian Group, Inc. (The)
140 Bridges Road
Suite E
Mauldin, SC 29662
800-874-2291

Lobbyists:
David Plank
Paul Schreyer

Gotham Government Relations
1044 Northern Boulevard
Suite 302
Roslyn, NY 11576
516-880-8170

Clients:
Allstate Insurance Company
Association of Wholesale Marketers and Distributors (NYS)
AU Foundation, Inc.
Brooklyn Bar Association Volunteer Lawyers Project
Cam-Held Enterprise, Inc. DBA Just Kids
Family Residences & Essential Enterprises
First Equity Abstract Corporation
Flair Beverage Corp.
Florida Compass Group/Premier Pawn & Jewelry in New York
Old Westbury College Froundation, Inc.
Ovation LLC
Red Apple Group
School for Language and Communication Development
Talon Air, Inc.

Lobbyists:
Diane Cahill
Catherine Fee
Bradley Gerstman
David Schwartz

Gould, David (FKA Tallon Jr., James R.)
C/O United Hospital Fund
Empire State Building
350 5th Ave., 23rd Floor
New York, NY 10118-2399
212-494-0740

Clients:
United Hospital Fund

Governmental Insight LTD
379 Kenridge Rd
Lawrence, NY 11559
917-861-6776

Clients:
AFL-CIO
Injured Workers Alliance
Triad Group LLC
Union of Police Associations
Utility Workers of America Local 1-2

Lobbyists:
Arthur Wilcox

Grant Thornton LLP
2350 Kerner Blvd
Suite 250
San Rafael, CA 94901
415-389-6800

Lobbyists:
Tamara Anger
Anna Danegger
Terry Hastings
Douglas Lapham

Gray Media
1028 Boulevard
Suite 237
West Hartford, CT 06119
860-398-3916

Clients:
Pfizer Inc.

Lobbyists:
Jennifer Daly

Greater New York Health Care Facilities Association
519 8th Avenue
16th Floor
New York, NY 10018
212-643-2828

Lobbyists:
Michael Balboni

Greater NY Hospital Association, Subsidiaries & Affiliate (FKA Greater NY Hospital Association)
555 West 57th Street
Suite 1500
New York, NY 10019-2425
212-246-7100

Lobbyists:
Lloyd Bishop
Deborah Brown
Alison Burke
Karen Heller
Bridgett Ingraham-Roberts
Tim Johnson
Lee Perlman
Stewart Presser
Kenneth Raske
David Rich
Lorraine Ryan
Kathleen Shure
Zeynep Sumer
Susan Waltman
Elisabeth Wynn

Greenberg Traurig, LLP
54 State Street
6th Floor
Albany, NY 12207
518-689-1400
Web site: www.gtlaw.com

Clients:
13th Avenue Supermarket LLC
219-25 LLC
Ace Group- North America

Alliance for Children with Special Needs-School Age (NYS)
American Fair Credit Council
Argonaut Holdings LLC
Arker Diversified Companies
Association of Licensed Midwives
Association of School Psychologists
AT&T Services, Inc.
Auto Collision Technician's Association, Inc.
Bar Association
Barclays Capital, Inc.
Capital Region Council for Young Children with Special Needs
Certification Board for Nutrition Specialists
Child Resource Center, Inc.
Children's Day Treatment Coalition
Christie's
CNA
Coalition for Children With Special Needs
Coalition for Quality Assisted Living, Inc.
Coalition of Community Development Financial Institutions
Coalition of Ignition Interlock Manufacturers
Compliance Technologies Corporation, Inc.
Credit Union Association of New York
Daiichi Sankyo, Inc.
Direct Buy Holdings and it's Affiliates
Eastman Kodak Company
Empire State Water Well Drillers Association
Enterprise Holdings, Inc.
Forests Lots LLC
Geneva Worldwide, Inc.
GKC Industries, Inc.
Greater New York Health Care Facilities Association
H.W. Lochner, Inc.
Hartford Financial Services Group, Inc.
Health Plan Association
Healthplex, Inc.
Healthport Technologies, LLC
Honda North America, Inc.
Housing Association, Inc.
Hudson Alliance for Children with Special Needs
Hunts Point Cooperative Market, Inc.
IMS Health
Industco Holdings, LLC
International American University College of Medicine
Jewish Home Lifecare
Just Kids Diagnostic and Treatment Center
Just Kids Early Childhood Learning Center
Kaplan Higher Education
Lexington School for the Deaf/Center for the Deaf, Inc.
Liberty Mutual Group
Life Insurance Council of New York, Inc.
Logic Technology, Inc.
Long Island Coalition for Children with Special Needs
Maximus
Metropolitan Transportation Authority
MGM Resorts International
Microsoft Corporation
Momentive Performance Materials USA, Inc.
National Academy of Elder Law Attorneys New York Chapter
National Academy of Recording Arts & Sciences
National Conference of Commissioners in Uniform State Laws
News Corporation
North Shore Board of Education
NTT Data, Inc.
Nurse Practitioner Association NYS
NYSARC, Inc.
Partners Health Plan, Inc.
Phillips 66 Company
Podiatric Medical Association
Primerica Life Insurance Company
Prudential Financial, Inc.
Radar Associates, Inc.

Reed Elsevier, Inc.
Senior Care Pharmacy Alliance
Senior Whole Health
Servicemaster Company (The)
Sotheby's
Stop DWI Coordinators Association
Teva Pharmaceuticals USA, Inc.
Thrivent Financial for Lutherans
Tomra
Total Recall Corporation
Town of Huntington
Toys
Union College
Verax Biomedical Incorporated
Verifone, Inc.
Walter Kidde Portable Equipment, Inc.
Waterview at Greenpoint LLC
Wellcare of NY
Western Central Coalition for Children with Special Needs
Zurich

Lobbyists:
Michael Berlin
Lynelle Bosworth
Deidre Carson
Christopher Cernik
Diana Dellamere
James Dillon
Dan Egers
Mark Glaser
Robert Harding
Nick Hockens
Carla Hogan
Harold Iselin
Robert Ivanhoe
Warren Karp
Pamela Madeiros
John Mascialino
Michael Murphy
Joshua Oppenheimer
Jeffrey Pearlman
Jane Preston
Elizabeth Sacco
Jay Segal
Edward Wallace

Greenwich Village Society for Historic Preservation
232 East 11th St
New York, NY 10003
212-475-9585

Lobbyists:
Lloyd Andito
Amanda Davis
Andrew Durniak
Dana Schulz
Sheryl Woodruff

Greller, Matthew
75 Clinton Avenue
Millburn, NJ 07041
917-345-0005

Clients:
Liberty Natural Gas LLC
National Association of Theatre Owners, Inc.

Offices and agencies generally appear in alphabetical order, except when specific order is requested by listee.

Griffin Associates, LLC
600 Broadway
1st Floor - South
Albany, NY 12207
518-463-5949

Clients:
Explore Information Services, LLC
Millennium Pharmaceuticals, Inc.
Momentive Performance Materials (Plummer & Associates, LLC)

Lobbyists:
John Griffin

GSO Capital Partners LP
345 Park Avenue
31st Floor
New York, NY 10154
212-503-2157

Lobbyists:
John Cashwell
Beth Chartoff
Mary Lynn Eubanks
Doyle Queally
Matthew Quigley
Geoff Stockwell

Gtech Corporation
Gtech Center
8th Floor
10 Memorial Blvd
Providence, RI 02903
401-392-7459

Lobbyists:
Donald Sweitzer

Guardian Life Insurance Company
Seven Hanover Square
H23E
New York, NY 10004-2616
212-598-8956

Clients:
Guardian Life Insurance Company of America (The)

Lobbyists:
Ellie Jurado-Nieves
Ulysses Lee
Tracy Rich

Habitat for Humanity of New York State
911 E. Main Street
Endicott, NY 13760
607-748-4138

Lobbyists:
Judith Nelson

Hackensack University Medical Center
30 Prospect Avenue
Research Building, Room 240
Hackensack, NJ 07601

Lobbyists:
Erin Ihde

Hager, Susan
C/O United Way of NYS
155 Washington Ave
Albany, NY 12210
518-463-2522
e-mail: hagers@uwnys.org
Web site: www.uwnys.org

Clients:
United Way of NYS

Halpin Public Affairs
55 The Crescent
Babylon, NY 11702
516-848-0444

Clients:
Cablevision (CSC Holdings, Inc.)
Outlook Group, Inc.

Lobbyists:
Patrick Halpin

Hannan and O'Connell, Inc.
107 Washington Ave
Albany, NY 12210-2200
518-465-6550
e-mail: khannan401@aol.com
Web site: www.kthpa.com

Clients:
Campground Owners of New York, Inc.
Conpor Conference of Private Organizations (NYS)
Council of Professional Geologists NYS
Empire State Towing & Recovery Association
Firemen's Association of the State of NY
Hannaford Supermarkets
Millenium Laboratories
National Coalition of Pharmaceutical Distributors
Pest Management Coalition
VSweeps

Lobbyists:
Kirby T Hannan
Peter O'Connell

Hannesson, Paul (FKA McCormick, Lynde) (FKA Gaylord, Joan)
Christian Science Committee
51 East 42nd Street #600
New York, NY 10017
212-661-3838

Clients:
Chrsitian Science Committee on Publication for NY

Harlem United: Community AIDS Center, Inc.
306 Lenox Avenue
3rd Floor
New York, NY 10027
212-803-2850

Lobbyists:
Doug Berman
Soroya Elcock
Kimberleigh Smith

Harris, Steven W., LLC
90 State Street
Suite 1507
Albany, NY 12207
518-445-2535

Clients:
RAI Services Company

Lobbyists:
Steven Harris

Harter Secrest & Emery, LLP
1600 Bausch & Lomb Place
Rochester, NY 14604-2711
585-232-6500
e-mail: admin@hselaw.com
Web site: www.hartersecrest.com

Clients:
Alliance for Fine Wine Wholesalers, Ltd (NY)
Association of Safety Group Managers
ATU NY State Legislative Conference Board
Biotechnology Assn Inc (NY)
Buffalo & Pittsburgh Railroad Inc
Chiropractic Assn Inc (NYS)
Clinical Laboratory Assn Inc (NYS)
Cold Spring Harbor Laboratory
Empire State Petroleum Association, Inc.
Finger Lakes Horsemen's Benv & Protective Assn Inc
Genesee & Wyoming Railroad Company
Gershon & Company
GlaxoSmithKline, PLC
Hall of Science (NY)
Movers & Warehousemens Association Inc (NYS)
Municipal Electric Utilities Association
O-At-Ka Milk Products Cooperative, Inc.
Premier Exhibitions, Inc.
Roberts Wesleyan College
Rochester & Southern Railroad Inc
Rochester Technology & Manufacturing Association, Inc.
Rubber Manufacturers Association
South Buffalo Railway Company
Telecommunications Assn Inc (NYS)
Upstate Niagara Cooperative Inc (FKA Upstate Farms Cooperative Inc)

Lobbyists:
John Jennings
Amy Kellogg
Donald S Mazzulo
Richard E Scanlan

Hartford Financial Services Group, Inc. (The)
200 Hopmeadow Street
A4E-9
Simsbury, CT 06089
860-843-4587

Clients:
Hartford Financial Services Group, Inc. (The Hartford)

Lobbyists:
Thomas Bartell

Hawayek, Jonathan F
728 Main St
East Aurora, NY 14052
716-652-2038

Clients:
Allergan, Inc

Hawkins, Dennis (FKA Jockers, Ken)
351 West 54th Street
New York, NY 10019
212-541-6741

Clients:
Fund for Modern Courts

Lobbyists:
Dennis Hawkins
Denise Kronstadt

Health Facilities Association
33 Elk Stret
Suite 300
Albany, NY 12207-1010
518-462-4800

Lobbyists:
Gayle Farman
Stephen Hanes
Richard Herrick
Nancy Leveille
Karen Morris
Richard Patterson
Carl Pucci
Shelley Wagar Sabo

Health Plan Assn Inc (NY)
90 State Street
Suite 825
Albany, NY 12207-1717
518-462-2293
e-mail: info@nyhpa.org
Web site: www.nyhpa.org

Clients:
Health Plan Assn Inc (NY)

Lobbyists:
Rose Dunhan
Andrew Fogarty
Arlene Halpert
Paul F Macielak
Leslie S Moran
Sheila Nelson

Healthcare Association of New York State
One Empire Drive
Rensselear, NY 12144
518-431-7600

Clients:
Healthcare Association of New York State
Nassau-Suffolk Hospital Council, Inc.
Northern Metropolitan Hospital Association
Suburban Hospital Alliance of New York State

Lobbyists:
William Allison
Todd Ball
Sherry Chorost
Christa Christakis
Kathleen Ciccone
Eileen Clinton
Kevin Dahill

Offices and agencies generally appear in alphabetical order, except when specific order is requested by listee.

Wendy Darwell
Robin Frank
Christina Gahan
Sean Gemerek
Jeffrey Gold
Valerie Grey
Stephen Harwell
Frederick Heigel
Cara Henley
Nicholas Henley
Amy Jones
Steven Kroll
Nancy Landor
Debora LeBarron
Jennifer Lee
Cindy Levernois
Janine Logan
Melissa Mansfield
Edward McGill
Robert McLeod
Christina Miller-Foster
Molly Poleto
Karen Roach
Sara Rosenberger
Jerry Salkowe
Daniel Sisto
Angela Skretta
Christopher Smith
Mary Therriault
William Vanslyke
Shelby Wafer
Sue Ellen Wagner
Dennis Whalen

Healthcare Tort Reform Coalition (NY)
C/O Combined Coordinating Council, Inc.
14 Penn Plaza, Ste 720
New York, NY 10122
212-643-8100

Clients:
Healthcare Tort Reform Coalition (NY)

Lobbyists:
Terence Kelleher
Lisa Kramer
Christopher Smith

Henderson Global Investors (North America) Inc.
1 Financial Plaza
19th Floor
Hartford, CT 06103
860-723-8609

Lobbyists:
Daniel McDonough
Mark Toomey

Herrick, Feinstein LLP
2 Park Avenue
New York, NY 10016
212-592-1428

Clients:
Nissan North America, Inc.

Lobbyists:
Kevin Fullington
Michael McMahon

Heyman, Neil
C/O Southern NY Association
39 Broadway, Ste 1710
New York, NY 10006
212-425-5050
e-mail: njheyman@snya.com
Web site: www.snya.org

Clients:
Southern NY Assn

Higgins Roberts Beyerl & Coan, PC
1430 Balltown Rd
Niskayuna, NY 12309
518-374-3399

Clients:
Society of Anesthesiologists, Inc (NYS)

Lobbyists:
Charles J Assini Jr

Hill & Gosdeck
One Commerce Plaza
99 Washington Ave, Ste 400
Albany, NY 12210
518-463-5449
e-mail: nylobbyists@aol.com

Clients:
Alliance of Automobile Manufacturers
American Cleaning Institute
AOL, LLC
Arise, Inc.
Association of Marraige and Family Therapy, Inc.
AT&T, Inc.
Builders Exchange, Inc.
Concentra Health Services, Inc.
Consumer Data Industry Association
Facebook, Inc.
International Business Machine Corporation
International Paper
Lexmark International, Inc.
MillerCoors LLC
Monsanto Company
New York State Higher Education Initiative
Newspaper Publishers Association
Proctors Theater
SCA Tissue North America LLC
USA Training Company, Inc.
Veterinary Medical Society
Walgreen Co.

Lobbyists:
Thomas J Gosdeck
Jeffrey L Hill
Denise Murphy McGraw
Frank Nemeth

Hillside Family of Agencies
1183 Monroe Ave
Rochester, NY 14620
312-856-4836

Lobbyists:
Clyde Comstock
Dennis Richardson

Offices and agencies generally appear in alphabetical order, except when specific order is requested by listee.

Hinman Straub Advisors, LLC

121 State St
Albany, NY 12207-1693
518-436-0751
e-mail: reception@hspm.com
Web site: www.hspm.com

Clients:
4201 Schools Association
Academic Dental Centers (NYS)
Albert Einstein College of Medicine
Alliance of Boys & Girls Clubs, Inc. (NYS)
American Forest & Paper Association (Multistate Associates Incorporated)
American Safety Council
Americans United for Life
Associated Medical Schools of NY
Association for Superintendents of School Buildings & Grounds (NYS)
Association of Proprietary Colleges
Bard College
Boces Educational Consortium (The)
Capital District Physician's Health Plan
Caterpillar, Inc.
Centers for Specialty Care Group
Children's Aid Society (The)
Cigna Companies
Coalition of 853 Schools, Inc.
Coalition of Special Acts School Districts
COFCCA, Inc.
Computer Sciences Corporation
Consolidated Edison Company of NY, Inc.
Consumer Electronics Association
Contemporary Services Corporation
Dietetic Association
Education & Research Network, Inc.
Elizabeth Seton Pediatric Center
Empire State Association of Assisted Living
Equinox, Inc.
Estee Lauder Companies, Inc.
Excellus Health Plan, Inc.
Federation of Mental Health Services, Inc.
Federation of School Administrators
First Lincoln Holdings LLC
Foundling
Free Community Papers of New York
Fresenius Medical Care North America
H.O. Penn Caterpillar
HealthFirst
Hillside Family of Agencies
Hofstra University
HSBC North America
Hudson Center for Health Equity & Quality
Independent Oil & Gas Association of NY
Institute for Special Education
International Bottled Water Association
Iroquois Pipeline Operating Company
Island Harvest LTD
Jewish Home of Rochester (The)
Johnstown Fire Fighters Association Local 779
Le Moyne College
LeadingAge New York
Life Insurance Council of New York, Inc.
Literacy New York, Inc.
McGraw-Hill Education
Medical College (NY)
Mental Health Counselors Association (NY)
National Health Care Associates, Inc.
National Pork Producers Council
NationWide Mutual Insurance Company
Ophthalmological Society
Organization of NYS Management/Confidential Employees, Inc.

Parker Jewish Institute for Health Care & Rehabilitation
Police Benevolent Association of New York State
Professional Fire Fighters Association, Inc.
Public Health Solutions
Rescare, Inc.
Selfhelp Community Services, Inc.
Seneca Nation of Indians
Southworth-Milton
St. Anns of Greater Rochester, Inc.
State University of New York at Stony Brook
Stonehenge Capital Corporation
Support Services Alliance, Inc.
Supreme Court Justices Association of the City of New York
Tech Valley School Foundation
Tectonic Engineering & Surveying Consultants P.C.
To Life
Toyota Motor North America, Inc.
Treated Wood Council, Inc.
UCB, Inc.
Unshackle Upstate
Verizon NY
Wellpoint, Inc.
Wing of the Civil Air Patrol
X-Ray Optical Systems, Inc.

Lobbyists:
John Black
James Carr
Bartley J Costello, III
Terri Crowley
Caron Crummey
Sean M Doolan
Joseph Dougherty
Heather Evans
Michael Fallon
John Federman
Mara Ginsberg
Vincent Graber
Tracy Lloyd
Matthew O'Connor
Donald Robbins
Kelly Ryan
John Saccocio
Janet Silver

Hiscock & Barclay, LLP

Hiscock & Barclay, LLP
300 South Street
Syracuse, NY 13202-2078
315-425-2873

Clients:
Superfund Coalition, Inc. (NYS)

Lobbyists:
Angela M. Barry
David Burch
Maureen O. Helmer
Kevin R. McAuliffe
Michael McNulty
Thomas F Walsh
Jerry Weiss

Hodes & Landy

284 State St
Albany, NY 12210
518-465-8303
e-mail: nhodes@hodesassoc.org

Offices and agencies generally appear in alphabetical order, except when specific order is requested by listee.

Clients:
Assisted Living Federation of America (ALFA)
Benchmark Senior Living
Boehringer Ingelgheim Pharmaceuticals, Inc.
DentaQuest LLC
Dominican Village
Emeritus Senior Living
Insperity Services, L.P.
Lifetouch National School Studios, Inc.
Metropolitan College of New York
Public Consulting Group
Sony Pictures Entertainment
US BioLogic

Lobbyists:
Courtney David
Nancy L Hodes
Virginia Lynch-Landy
Michele O'Connor

Hofstra University
101 Hofstra University
Hempstead, NY 11549-1010
516-463-1800

Lobbyists:
Melissa Connolly
Dolores Fredrich
Stuart Rabinowitz

Holloway, Jr, Floyd
C/O State Farm Insurance Co
6 Hillman Drive
Suite 200
Chadds Ford, PA 19317-9039
610-361-4150
e-mail: floyd.holloway.clxm@statefarm.com

Clients:
State Farm Insurance Companies

Lobbyists:
Tim McFadden
Carolyn Schwadron
Joe Spicer

Home Care Assn of NYS Inc
194 Washington Ave, Ste 400
Albany, NY 12210
518-426-8764
e-mail: info@hcanys.org
Web site: www.hcanys.org

Clients:
Home Care Assn of NYS Inc

Lobbyists:
Alfredo Cardillo
Patrick Conole
Joanne Cunningham
Andrew Koski

Homeless Services United (FKA Council on Homeless Policies & Services)
207 East 2nd Street
Suite 1404
New York, NY 10018-2009
646-827-2270

Lobbyists:
Eric Lee
Christy Parque

Honeywell International, Inc.
101 Constitution Avenue NW
Suite 500 West
Washington, DC 20001
202-662-2612

Lobbyists:
Lawrence Kast

Horton, Dan J
C/O Nielsen, Merksamer, Et Al.
2350 Kerner Blvd., Suite 250
San Rafael, CA 94901
415-389-6800

Clients:
Exxon Mobil Corporation

Hotel & Motel Trades Council, AFL-CIO
707 Eighth Avenue
New York, NY 10036
212-492-2102

Lobbyists:
Josh Gold

Housing Conservation Coordinators
777 Tenth Ave
New York, NY 10019
212-541-5996

Clients:
Housing Conservation Coordinators

Lobbyists:
Bennett Baumer
Sarah Desmond
Rachel Jaffe
Robert Kalin
Matthew Klein

Howard Hughes Corporation (The)
13355 Noel Rd
22nd Floor
Dallas, TX 75240
214-741-7744

Lobbyists:
Christopher J. Curry
John DeWolf
Grant Herlitz
Adam Meister
David Weinreb

HR&A Advisors, Inc.
99 Hudson Street
3rd Floor
New York, NY 10013
212-977-5597

Clients:
Major League Soccer

Lobbyists:
John Alschuler
Cary Hirschstein

HSBC - North America Holdings, Inc.
30 South Pearl Street
Albany, NY 12207
518-432-2016

Lobbyists:
Lynne Brzezenski
Craig Lassen
Margaret McGovern
Faye Polayes
James Stiegel

Hudson Eagle LLC
435 Hudson St
Suite 402
New York, NY 10014
212-477-8008

Lobbyists:
Greg Carney

Hudson Valley Community College
80 Vandenburgh Avenue
Troy, NY 12180
518-629-8071

Lobbyists:
Joel Fatato
James Lagatta
Lucille Marion
Andrew Matonak
Kathryn Navarra Bradley
Karen Seward

Hunger Action Network of NYS
275 State Street
Albany, NY 12210
518-434-7371

Lobbyists:
Mark Dunlea

Hurley, Alicia D. (FKA Haberman, Michael)
70 Washington Square South
New York, NY 10012
212-998-6859

Clients:
University (NY)

Lobbyists:
Robert Berne
Kathleen Bernier
Lynne Brown
Gilda Ventresca Ecroyd
Robert Grossman
Steven Heuer
Sayar Lonial
Jennifer Pautz
John Sexton

Hutton & Solomon, LLP
475 Fifth Avenue
23rd Floor
New York, NY 10017
212-682-5702
Web site: www.hstax.com

Clients:
Eponymous Associates

Lobbyists:
Kenneth Moore
Stephen Solomon

Hynes, Daniel
200 E. Randolph Street
Chicago, IL 60601
312-726-0140

Clients:
Ariel Investments LLC

Ianno, Dominick
1 Walnut St.
Boston, MA 02108
617-201-9142

Clients:
Pfizer, Inc.

Immigration Coalition, Inc (NY)
137-139 W 25th St, 12th Fl
New York, NY 10001
212-627-2227

Clients:
Immigration Coalition, Inc (NY)

Lobbyists:
Jacqueline Esposito
Silvia Gonzales
Chung-Wha Hong
Karen Kaminsky
Melanie Reyes
Jacqueline Vimo
Jackie Wong

Independent Bankers Association of New York State
19 Dove Street
Albany, NY 12210
518-436-4646

Lobbyists:
Stephen Rice

Independent Health Association, Inc.
511 Farber Lakes Drive
Buffalo, NY 14221
716-635-3714

Lobbyists:
Scott Campbell
Michael Cropp
Don Gibson
Teresa Glanowski
David Naramore
Ann Pentkowski
Iris Schifeling
Julie St. Cyr

Offices and agencies generally appear in alphabetical order, except when specific order is requested by listee.

Dietra Steed
Jennifer Stoklosa
Robert Tracy

J Strategies, Inc.
8016 Bridgeport-Kirkville Road
Kirkville, NY 13082
315-382-6607

Clients:
Lilly USA
Pfizer, Inc.
Pharmaceutical Research and Manufacturers of America
Winn Companies

Lobbyists:
Jessica Johnson
Julie Miner
Jenna Peppenelli
Jaime Venditti

Institute of International Bankers
299 Park Avenue
17th Floor
New York, NY 10171
212-421-1611

Lobbyists:
Richard Coffman
Sarah Miller

Insurance Association, Inc. (NY)
130 Washington Avenue
Albany, NY 12210-2219
518-432-4227

Lobbyists:
Marc Craw
Ellen Melchionni

Inventiv Health, Inc.
C/O Nielsen Merksamer, Et Al.
2350 Kerner Blvd
Suite 250
San Rafael, CA 94901
415-389-6800

Clients:
Allergan, Inc.

Lobbyists:
Jack Quinn

Irving Place Capital Management L.P.
745 Fifth Avenue
7th Floor
New York, NY 10151
212-551-4520

Lobbyists:
Philip M. Carpenter III
Patricia Grad
John D. Howard
Robert Juneja
Douglas Korn
Eve Mongiardo
Richard L. Perkal

Island Peer Review Organization, Inc.
1979 Marcus Avenue
First Floor
Lake Success, NY 11042
516-209-5512

Lobbyists:
Harry Feder
Jaz-Michael King
Dan Schweitzer
Patti Weinberg
Marilyn Zumbo

Island Public Affairs
277 Indian Head Rd
Kings Park, NY 11754
631-724-0017

Clients:
Adelante of Suffolk County, Inc
Hands Across Long Island Inc
National Foundation for Human Potential Inc

Lobbyists:
Steven Moll

J.P. Morgan Securities Inc.
270 Park Avenue
38th Floor
New York, NY 10017
212-270-2428

Lobbyists:
Michael Altman
Brian Gonor
Peter McCarthy
Brian Middlebrook
Kyle Pulling

Janney Montgomery Scott LLC
575 Lexington Ave
35th Floor
New York, NY 10022
646-840-4616

Lobbyists:
Vivian Altman
Joseph Bosch
Elizabeth Caputo
Daniel Froehlich
Steve Nelson

JEM Associates NY, Inc.
224 Euclid Avenue
Albany, NY 12208
518-281-3322

Clients:
7-Eleven, Inc.
American Chemistry Council, Inc.
Chinese-American Planning Council, Inc.
Court Officers Benevolent Association of Nassau County, Inc.
Dr Pepper Snapple Group
Feld Entertainment
Good Shepherd Services
New Square Community Planning and Development Corporation
Pratt Institute
RAI Services Company
Reach Out and Read of Greater New York

Offices and agencies generally appear in alphabetical order, except when specific order is requested by listee.

WNET

Lobbyists:
James McMahon

Jenkins, Joanne E
C/O NY Life Insurance
111 Washington Ave
Albany, NY 12210
518-463-6649

Clients:
Life Insurance Co (NY)

Lobbyists:
Scott L. Berlin
Sheila Davidson
Tom English
Theodore Mathas
Carol Mayer
Joseph Muratore
George Nichols
Michael Oleske
Joel Steinberg
Rebecca Strutton
Maria Sullivan
Michael J Tobin
Gil Valdes
Douglas A. Wheeler

Jennison Associates LLC
466 Lexington Avenue
New York, NY 10017
973-367-3135
Web site: www.jennison.com

Lobbyists:
Peter H. Reinemann

Jerome, Stephen
121 State Street
Albany, NY 12207
518-437-1867

Clients:
Association of Proprietary Colleges

Jewish Association for Services for the Aged (FKA Saiger, Molly)
247 West 37th Street
9th Floor
New York, NY 10018
212-273-5260
Web site: www.jasa.org

Lobbyists:
Jolene Boden
Amy Chalfy
Donna Dougherty
Leah Ferster
Molly Krakowski
Donald Manning
Danielle Palmisano
Alla Pliss
Martha Pollack
Elaine Rockoff

Jewish Home and Hospital for Aged (The)
120 West 106th Street
New York, NY 10025
212-870-4600

Lobbyists:
Patricia Beilman
Kay Boonshoft
Rachel Fredman
Bridget Gallagher
Thomas Gilmartin
Bruce Nathanson
Judith Nicholson
Laura Radensky
Cara Unowsky
Audrey Weiner

JGN Associates LLC
190 Lape Rd
Nassau, NY 12123
518-766-7136

Clients:
Mutualink, Inc.

Lobbyists:
James Natoli

JJMH Consulting
90 State Street
Suite 700
Albany, NY 12207
518-591-4660

Clients:
Are-East Rive Science Park, LLC
Friedman & Moses
Omni Childhood Center
Stuyvesant Town-Peter Cooper Village Tenants Association

Lobbyists:
Steven Sanders

JLO Consultant, Inc.
139 Shear Hill Road
Mahopac, NY 10541
646-522-7914

Clients:
LaGuardia Community College

Lobbyists:
Jose Orengo

Jobs with Justice (NY)
50 Broadway
16th Floor
New York, NY 10004
212-631-0886

Lobbyists:
Nathalie Alegre
Matt Ryan

Jockey Club (The)
40 East 52nd Street
New York, NY 10022
212-521-5309

Political Parties,
Lobbyists & PACs

Offices and agencies generally appear in alphabetical order, except when specific order is requested by listee.

Lobbyists:
James L. Gagliano
Matt F. Juliano

John Hancock Life Insurance

601 Congress Street
Boston, MA 02210
617-663-2486

Lobbyists:
James Gallagher
Linda Watters

Johnson & Johnson Health Care Systems, Inc.

175 Hilltop Drive
Churchville, PA 18966
215-357-0495

Lobbyists:
Nick Rebholz

Johnson, Russ

8246 Ashington Drive
Baldwinsville, NY 13027-8715
415-389-6800

Clients:
Pfizer, Inc.

Johnston, Christine

C/O Association of Health Care Providers
20 Corporate Woods Blvd
2nd Floor
Albany, NY 12211
518-463-1118

Clients:
Association of Health Care Providers, Inc.

Lobbyists:
Nancy Erodes
Christine Johnston
Megan Tangjerd
Catherine Tully

Joint Industry Board of the Electrical Industry

58-11 Harry Van Arsdale Jr. Avenue
Flushing, NY 11365
718-591-2000

Lobbyists:
Robert McCormick
Humberto Restrepo

Jones, Jeff

55 Brookline Avenue
Albany, NY 12203-1804
518-265-0719

Clients:
Healthy Schools Network, Inc.
Land Trust Alliance Northeast Program
Natural Resources Defense Council
New Partners for Community Revitalization, Inc.

JPMorgan Chase Bank, National Association

270 Park Avenue
37th Floor
New York, NY 10017
212-270-0530

Lobbyists:
Martha Beard
Douglas A. Bennett
Steve Bernstein
Gerard J. Buchko
Michelle L. Buonfiglio
Wayne Burrell
Charles Callahan
Robin Chappelle Golston
Michelle Cipriani
Leonard T. Colica
Louis A. Constantino
Thomas P. Daly
Sandra T. Davis
Susan M. Farrell
Elizabeth French
John P. Gardell, Jr.
Michael S. Gardner
Debra B. Gentile
Peter Gibson
Robert W. Gibson
Scott M. Grossman
Peter D. Johnsen
Robert J. Kane
Craig M. Kantor
Tim Kemp
Karen P. Keogh
Jan Konigsberg
Marjorie V. Lauri
Angela L. Lavis
Alexander B. Leonard
Chad M. Levy
Carol B. Mark
Shirley McCoy
Nancy K. McDonnell
Ruth McMahon
Louise R. Meyer
Timothy Minahan
Edward J. Muendell
Lori A. Nelson
Michael James Nevins
Timothy G. Noble
Katy A. O'Donnell
Patricia A. O'Donnell
Lester J. Owens
Manny Patino
Jennifer A. Pegg
Michael Pressman
Chris Redvers
Robert J. Rehm
Susan M. Ridler
Alphonso Robinson
Lucas M. Ruglis
Matthew B. Sarson
Jeff Schor
John Simeone
Debbi M. Tholl
Pamela T. Thomson
Lisa A. Valle
Christopher Vavrina
Frederick Vosburgh

Offices and agencies generally appear in alphabetical order, except when specific order is requested by listee.

Justice, Lawrence P.

111 Washington Ave
Suite 203
Albany, NY 12210
518-368-7539

Clients:
Hudson River Pilots' Association
Industry AD HOC Committee on Pilotage

Justin McCarthy Consulting Services, Inc.

677 Broadway
12th Floor
Albany, NY 12207
518-424-7347

Clients:
Arista Power, Inc.
Capital District Regional Off-Track Betting Corporation
CDS Monarch
Correction Officers' Benevolent Association, City of New York, Inc.
Flaum Management Company, Inc.
Genessee County Economic Development Center
Monroe County Water Authority
Passero Associates
Seneca County IDA

Lobbyists:
Justin McCarthy

Kalanz, Edward

C/O Bridge & Tunnel Officers Benevolent
Association
1140 Bay Street, Suite A&B
Staten Island, NY 10305
718-727-7613

Kantor Davidoff Wolfe Mandelker Twomey & Gallanty, PC

51 East 42nd St
New York, NY 10017-5497
212-682-8383

Clients:
Metropolitan Retail Assn, LLC (NY)
Sports & Arts in School Foundation

Lobbyists:
Lawrence A Mandelker

Kaplan, Alden B.

83 Maiden Lane
New York, NY 10038
917-716-7111

Clients:
AHRC-NYC

Kasirer Consulting

321 Broadway, Ste 201
New York, NY 10007
212-285-1800
e-mail: skasirer@kasirerconsulting.com

Clients:
145 Americas Condominium
384 Bridge Street LLC
390 Tower LLC
50 Varick LLC
American Cancer Society, Inc.
Arcadis U.S., Inc.
Area Property Partners
Astoria Generating Company LP
ATCO Properties & Management, Inc.
Atlantic Yards Development Company
BCMUSA
Big Brothers Big Sisters of NYC
Brookfield Financial Properties, Inc.
Brooklyn Botanic Garden Corporation
CEMUSA, Inc.
City Meals-On-Wheels
Cooper Union for Advancement of Science and Art (The)
Cornell University
CSC Holdings LLC
Cubic Transportation Systems, Inc.
Delta Air Lines, Inc.
Eastern Region Helicopter Council
ELAD US Holding, Inc.
FCC Construction, Inc.
For the Benefit of Red Hook 100 LLC, Red Hook 212 LLC, and Red Hook 300 LLC
Foundling Hospital
GE Transportation Systems Global Signaling LLC
General Electric Company
Global Aerospace, Inc. and United States Aviation Underwriters, Inc
GT Forge, Inc. DBA GET Taxi
Hewlett Packard Company
Historical Society
Host Hotels and Resorts L.P.
KM Associates of NY, Inc.
Legal Assistance Group
Lend Lease Construction LMB, Inc.
Lincoln Center for the Performing Arts, Inc.
Looks Great Services, Inc.
Macerich
Macerich
Madison Square Garden L.P.
Metropolitan Realty Group LLC
MGM Resorts International Operations, Inc.
Mission Society (NYC)
Motion Picture Association of America, Inc.
Mount Sinai Hospital
Naftali Group (The)
NBC Universal
New Planet Energy LLC
New Visions for Public Schools, Inc.
Nontraditional Employment for Women
Northside Center for Child Development, Inc.
Paco Realty, LLC
Plumbing Foundation City of New York, Inc.
Project Renewal
Rainbow Media Holdings LLC
Rescare, Inc.
Restoration Project
Safe Horizon, Inc.
SDS Great Jones LLC
Silverite Construction
SL Green Realty Company
South Street Seaport Limited Partnership
Stahl York Avenue LLC
Steinway Child and Family Services
T&T Scrap LLC
Underground Utilities, Inc.
United American Land LLC

Lobbyists:
Omar Alvarellos
Julie Greenberg
Sara Kasirer

Offices and agencies generally appear in alphabetical order, except when specific order is requested by listee.

Peter Krokondelas

Katz, Arthur H
542 3rd Avenue
Brooklyn, NY 11220
718-439-9011

Clients:
Assn of Wholesale Marketers & Distributors (NYS)

Kaysen, Mary
104 Valley Street
Beverly Farms, MA 01915
978-232-1147

Clients:
Bristol-Myers Squibb Company

Kehoe, Clare
St. Joseph's College
245 Clinton Avenue
Brooklyn, NY 11205
718-940-5579

Clients:
St. Joseph's College

Lobbyists:
Michael Banach
Nancy Connors
James Graham
Elizabeth Hill

Kennedy, Ronald F.
C/O Bar Association (NYS)
One Elk Street
Albany, NY 12207
518-487-5652

Clients:
Bar Association (NYS)

Lobbyists:
Patricia K. Bucklin
Seymour W. James, Jr.
Kevin M. Kerwin
Richard Rifkin
David M. Schraver

Ketzer, Bill
P.O. Box 310
Glenmont, NY 12077
646-315-1416

Clients:
American Society for the Prevention of Cruelty to Animals (ASPCA)

Lobbyists:
Debora Bresch
Bill Ketzer
Cori Menkin
Edwin Sayres
Michelle Villagomez
Stacy Wolf

Keycorp & Subsidiaries
127 Public Square
Cleveland, OH 44114
216-689-3420

Clients:
Keycorp & Subsidiaries

Lobbyists:
Bonnie Bale
Tracy Barney
Patricia C. Barrett
Lyman A. Buck III
Lori Capron
James Carriero
Derek Chauvette
Robin J. Commerford
Thomas Coverick
James G Criniti
Kristy David
Jeffrey Eades
Amanda Earnshaw
Joseph Eicheldinger
Susan Facciola
Jason Fenwick
Greg Fertel
David Folcomer
Linda Freeman
Jeffrey Freese
Mike Garibaldi
Andrew C. Goff
Ken Gruber
Edward J. Hackett
Jose R. Herrera
Matthew Hunt
Shane Kranov
Victor Kunakowsky
Patrick J Lillo
Mitchell W Miller
Kathy Mizener
George Mohan
Susan Mooradian
Mark Morrison
Michael Moss
Steven M. Pierce
Christopher J. Puliese
Gary Quenneville
Tawana Smith
Jeffrey Stone
Brenda L. Stout
David J Sylvan
Gerhard O Voggel
Anne Marie Warren

Kiernan-Pagani, Kathleen
101 Constitution Ave
Suite 700
Washington, DC 20001
202-624-2463

Clients:
American Council of Life Insurers

King, Barbara
555 W 57th St, 5th Fl
New York, NY 10019
212-523-5367
e-mail: bking@chpnet.org
Web site: www.wehealnewyork.org

Clients:
Beth Israel Medical Ctr
St Luke's-Roosevelt Hospital Ctrs

Offices and agencies generally appear in alphabetical order, except when specific order is requested by listee.

Lobbyists:
Bradley Korn

Kramer Levin Naftalis & Frankel, LLP
1177 Ave of Americas
New York, NY 10036
212-715-7835
Web site: www.kramerlevin.com

Clients:
525 West 52nd Street Development LLC
AMV Unitel LLC
Broadway Trio LLC
Charlton Soho LLC
Columbus Square Management LLC
Hebrew Home at Riverdale Foundation
Jujamcyn Theaters LLC
Lenox Terrace Development Associates
Midtown Trackage Ventures LLC
MSG Holdings L.P.
Nederlander Organization, Inc.
Shubert Organization, Inc. (The)
South Street Seaport L.P.
Strategic 34th Street LLC

Lobbyists:
Valerie Campbell
Robert E Flahive
Albert Fredericks
James Greilsheimer
Marcie Kesner
Robin Kramer
Elizabeth Larsen
Samuel H Lindenbaum
Cynthia Lovinger
James P Powers
Sheila Pozon
Paul D Selver
Michael T Sillerman
Patrick Sullivan
Gary R Tarnoff
Adam Taubman
Elise Wagner

Kramer, Jason
NYSHEI
22 Corporate Woods
3rd Floor
Albany, NY 12211
518-443-5444

Clients:
Higher Education Initiative

Kriss Kriss & Brignola, LLP
350 Northern Blvd.
Suite 306
Albany, NY 12204
518-449-2037

Clients:
Society of Professional Engineers, Inc.

Lobbyists:
Mark Kriss

Kwan, Patrick
200 West 57th Street
Suite 705
New York, NY 10019
917-331-7187

Clients:
Humane Society of the United States (The)

Lackman, Abraham M.
Praxis Insights, Inc.
580 Broadway
Suite 1001
New York, NY 10012
518-605-6103

Clients:
Stony Brook Foundation

Lobbyists:
Abraham M. Lackman

Lambert, Linda A
C/O Am. College of Physicians
744 Broadway
Albany, NY 12207-1817
518-427-0366

Clients:
American College of Physicians Services, Inc. (NY)

Lobbyists:
Gary Babette

Land Title Association, Inc.
2 Rector Street
Suite 901
New York, NY 10006-1819
212-964-3701

Lobbyists:
Robert Treuber

Land Trust Alliance Northeast Program
112 Spring Street
Suite 205
Saratoga Springs, NY 12866
518-587-0774

Lobbyists:
Kevin Case
Katrina Howey
Ethan Winter

Langdon, David
491 State Street
3A
Albany, NY 12203-1019
518-432-5440

Clients:
Aetna, Inc.
Brighter Choice Foundation (The)
Charter School Association
Coalition for Opportunity in Education, Inc.
Community Service Society

Offices and agencies generally appear in alphabetical order, except when specific order is requested by listee.

Lanotte, Michael A.
1021 Watervliet-Shaker Rd
Albany, NY 12205
518-437-8236

Clients:
Credit Union Association

Lobbyists:
Leona Haberstro
Henry Meier
William Mellin

Lasky, Roy
111 Washington Ave
Albany, NY 12210
518-573-8647

Clients:
Dental Association
Medical Liability Mutual Insurance Company

Law Office of Usher Fogel
557 Central Ave
Suite 4A
Cedarhurst, NY 11516
516-967-3242

Clients:
Small Customer Marketer Coalition

Lobbyists:
Usher Fogel

LCI LLC
677 Broadway
Suite 1105
Albany, NY 12207
518-410-2024

Clients:
General Motors LLC

Lobbyists:
Christopher Grimaldi

League of Conservation Voters
30 Broad Street
30th Floor
New York, NY 10004
212-361-6350

Lobbyists:
Marcia Bystryn
Ricardo Gotla
Joshua Klainberg

League of Women Voters of New York State
62 Grand Street
Albany, NY 12207
518-465-4162

Clients:
League of Women Voters of New York State

Lobbyists:
Aimee Allaud
Janet Aram
Barbara Bartoletti

Laura Bierman
Ruth Bonn
Marian Bott
Ann Brandon
Lori Dawson
Georgia DeGregorio
Sally Dreslin
Cheryl Feldman
Gladys Gifford
Judie Gorenstein
Lois Haignere
Arlene Hinkemeyer
Anne Huberman
Ann Ingleman
Ellen Kotlow
Polly Kuhn
Carol Meller
Susan Multer
Suzanne Perry
Sarah Podber
Beth Radow
Sally Robinson
Helga Schroeter
Kay Sharp
Barbara Thomas
Therese Warden
Roberta Wiernak
Carly Wise

Lefebvre, Steve
6369 Collamer Drive
East Syracuse, NY 13057
315-463-7539

Clients:
Associated Builders and Contractors, Inc.

Lobbyists:
Marci Miller
Ruth Mulford
Joshua Reap

Legal Assistance Group (NY)
450 West 33rd Street
11th Floor
New York, NY 10001
212-613-5050

Lobbyists:
Julie Brandfield
Phyllis Brochestein
Laura Davis
Antoinette Delruelle
Ann Dibble
Irina Matiychenko
Richard Rand
Jeffrey Randal
Randye Retkin
Lisa Rivera
Alison Sclater
Jane Stevens
Kim Susser

Legal Information for Families Today (LIFT)
350 Broadway
Suite 501
New York, NY 10013
646-613-9633

Offices and agencies generally appear in alphabetical order, except when specific order is requested by listee.

Lobbyists:
Melanie Hart
Liv Johanson

Legal Services NYC
40 Worth Street
Suite 606
New York, NY 10013
646-442-3654

Lobbyists:
M. Audrey Carr
Jennifer Ching
Saba Debesu
Peggy Earisman
Meghan Faux
Tara Foster
Nancy Goldhill
Justin Haines
Jacob Inwald
Tyler Johnson
Edward Josephson
Peter Kempner
Pavita Krishnaswany
Jennifer Levy
Nelson Mar
Anne Nacinovich
Jose Quesada
Raun Rasmussen
Jennifer Sinton
Betty Staton
Tanya Wong

Lehrer, Sander
41 Madison Ave
41st Floor
New York, NY 10010
212-763-4150

Clients:
United Nations Development Corporation

Lesbian and Gay Community Services Center, Inc.
208 West 13th Street
New York, NY 10011
212-620-7310

Lobbyists:
Carrie Davis
Jefffrey Klein
Jose Lugaro
Glennda Testone
Robert Wheeler
Robert Woodworth

Levin, Brenda
301 East 48th Street #8E
New York, NY 10017-1741
212-755-7996

Levin, David
P.O. Box 25
New Baltimore, NY 12124
518-269-6830

Clients:
Capital Region Norml NY

Levine, Paul
Jewish Board of Family & Children Svcs
120 W 57th St
New York, NY 10019
212-632-4614

Clients:
Jewish Board of Family & Children's Services Inc

Lobbyists:
Carmen Collado
Lenny Rodriguez

Levy Ratner P.C.
80 Eighth Avenue
8th Floor
New York, NY 10011
212-627-8100

Lobbyists:
Kevin Finnegan

Levy, Norman P.C.
575 Madison Avenue
New York, NY 10022
212-605-0313

Lobbyists:
Norman Levy
Henry Sheinkopf

Library Assn (NY)
C/O Library Association (NY)
6021 State Farm Road
Guilderland, NY 12084-1802
518-432-6952
e-mail: nyladirector@pobox.com
Web site: www.nyla.org

Clients:
Library Assn (NY)

Lobbyists:
Michael J Borges

Lieberman, Mark L
900 Merchants Concourse, Ste 314
Westbury, NY 11590
516-228-4226

Clients:
American Lawyer Media
Court Clerks Assn (NYS)
EAC Inc
Forestcitydaly Housing
Glenwood Management Corp
Nassau Regional Off-Track Betting Corporation
Lockwood, Kessler & Bartlett Inc
Sanitary District No 6
Town of Hempstead

Lobbyists:
Rosemarie Garipoli
Reynold Levy
Maureen McCormick
Scott Noppe-Brandon
Melissa Thornton

Political Parties, Lobbyists & PACs

Offices and agencies generally appear in alphabetical order, except when specific order is requested by listee.

Lilly USA LLC
555 12th Street NW
Suite 650
Washington, DC 12210
518-434-8435

Lobbyists:
Tamara Atkins
John Ewashko
Anmari Hanrahan

Lincoln Center for the Performing Arts, Inc.
70 Lincoln Center Plaza
New York, NY 10023-6583
212-875-5000

Lobbyists:
Jennifer Berry
Russell Granet
Jessica Handrik
Hillary McAndrew-Plate
Tamar Podell
Levy Reynolds
Matthew Troy

LJM Rad, LLC
P.O. Box 38227
50 Beaver Street
Albany, NY 12203
518-677-2135

Lobbyists:
Michael McNulty
Louis R. Thompson
Jerry A. Weiss

Local 6, Hotel & Club Employees & Bartenders Union, AFL-CIO
709 Eighth Avenue
New York, NY 10036
212-492-2102

Lobbyists:
Jan Dunford
Neal Kwatra

LoCicero & Tan Inc
123 William St, 22nd Fl
New York, NY 10038
212-608-0888

Clients:
Bluestone Organization (The)
Covanta Energy Corp
Community Preservation Corporation (The)
Council of Senior Ctrs & Services of NYC Inc
Erie Basin Marine Associates (Kelly & Roth)
Fashion Institute of Technology
Flushing Commons
Forest City Ratner Companies
Gannett Fleming Engineers & Architects PC
Hospital for Special Surgery
Kingston Avenue Development LLC
Knickerbocker Plaza Associates
Millenium Partners
NYU School of Medicine
New York Botanical Garden (The)
Sequoia Community Initiatives (Consumer Info & Dispute Resolution)

SL Green Realty Corp
Snug Harbor Cultural Center
TDC Development & Construction Corp
TKGG LLC
Towers at Spring Creek
Village Care of NY Inc
Yonkers Contracting Co Inc
JBI International

Lobbyists:
John LoCicero
Eva Tan

Logan, Ernest
Council of School Supervs/Administrators
16 Court St
Brooklyn, NY 11241-1254
718-852-3000

Clients:
Council of School Supervisors & Administrators

Lobbyists:
Peter McNally
Rolon Alithia Rodriguez

Long Island Board of Realtors (FKA Kaplan, Randy L.)
Randy Kaplan C/O Long Island Board of Realtors
300 Sunrise Highway
West Babylon, NY 11704
631-661-4800

Lobbyists:
Philip Weiden

Long Island Contractors Association, Inc.
150 Motor Parkway
Suite 307
Hauppauge, NY 11788
631-231-5422

Lobbyists:
Marc Herbst

Long Term Care Community Coalition (FKA Nursing Home Community Coalition)
242 West 30th St, Ste 306
New York, NY 10001
212-385-0355
e-mail: crnhcc@aol.com
Web site: www.nhccnys.org

Clients:
Long Term Care Community Coalition (FKA Nursing Home Community Coalition)

Lobbyists:
Richard Mollot

Losquadro, Steven E.
649 Route 25A
Suite 4
Rocky Point, NY 11778
631-744-9070

Clients:
Caithness Long Island II, LLC

Offices and agencies generally appear in alphabetical order, except when specific order is requested by listee.

Louloudes, Virginia
520 Eighth Ave, Suite 319
New York, NY 10018-3011
212-244-6667
e-mail: questions@art-newyork.org
Web site: www.offbroadwayonline.com

Clients:
Alliance of Resident Theatres/New York

Luria, Robert S
12 Spruce Run
East Greenbush, NY 12061-9611
518-477-2581
e-mail: robert.s.luria@gsk.com

Clients:
GlaxoSmithKline, PLC

Lutheran Augustana Center for Extended Care and Rehabilitation
6434 2nd Avenue
Brooklyn, NY 11220
718-630-7335

Lobbyists:
David Rose

Lutheran Medical Center
150 55th Street
Brooklyn, NY 11220
718-630-7335

Lobbyists:
Claudia Caine
Wendy Goldstein
Richard Langfelder
Mary Quinones

Luthin Associates, Inc
15 Walling Place
Avon by the Sea, NJ 07717
732-774-0005

Clients:
Consumer Power Advocates

Lobbyists:
Catherine Luthin

Lutz, Jr., Alexander
520 West 48th Street
New York, NY 10019
212-875-2396

Lobbyists:
Theresa Bischoff
Denise Bloise
Jackie Dragone
Bonnie Fletcher
Scott Graham
Rosemary Mackey
Sonia Martinez
Alice Rivera
Corwin Smith
Olivier Szlos
Enrique Vega

Lynch, Bill Associates, LLC
308 Lenox Avenue
4th Floor
New York, NY 10027
212-283-7515

Clients:
CSC Holdings Inc
Downtown Brooklyn Partnership (The)
Industrial Technology Assistance Corp
Thor 280 Richards Street LLC
Trustees of Columbia University in the City of NY (The)

Lobbyists:
William Lynch
William Lynch, Jr.
Norman McConney
Luther Smith
Arelis Tavares
Kevin Wardally

Lynch, Patricia Associates
677 Broadway, Suite 1105
Albany, NY 12207
518-432-9220
e-mail: plynch@plynchassociates.com

Clients:
88 Greenwich Owner LLC
AHRC New York City
Albany Port District Commission
Alliance for Downtown New York, Inc.
Alliantgroup
American Chemistry Council
American Traffic Solutions
Association of Legal Aid Attorneys UAW 2325
Avis Budget Car Rental LLC
Buffalo Niagara Medical Campus, Inc.
Buffalo State College
Cablevision
Caramoor
Cathedral of the Immaculate Conception Restoration Committee
Catholic Conference Policy Group, Inc.
Catholic Health System
Champion Learning Center LLC
City of Buffalo
City of Yonkers
Coalition for the Homeless, Inc.
Coca-Cola Refreshments USA, Inc.
Columbia Development Companies
ConnectEdu, Inc.
Delbello Donnellan Weingarten Wise & Wiederkehr LLP
Destiny USA
Devon Capital LLP
Drum Route 11
Dunkin' Brands, Inc.
Eastern Paramedics, Inc.
Economic Development Council
Educational Housing Services, Inc.
Empire State Passengers Association
Fluor Enterprises, Inc.
Ford Gum & Machine Company, Inc.
Gaia Plant Based Medicine
Gaming Association
Gar Associates, Inc.
General Motors LLC
Genting New York LLC
Greater New York Hospital Association
Harlem Children Society
Henningson Durham & Richardson Architecture and Engineering P.C.

Honeywell International, Inc.
Integrated Medical Professionals PLLC
Interior Designers for Legislation in New York
JMA
John Mezzalingua Associates D/B/A PPC
Kulanu
LCO Buildings LLC
Legal Aid Society (The)
Lifespan of Greater Rochester, Inc.
Lightstone Group LLC
Maid of the Mist Corporation
Maritime Association
McKissack and McKissack
Medical Answering Services
Menorah Campus, Inc.
Mohawk Ambulance Service
Motor Truck Association
MSG Holdings L.P.
National Grid
Niagara University
Noble Environmental Power LLC
Pharmaceutical Research and Manufacturers of America
Polytechnic University of New York University
Prime LLC
Pyramid Management Group LLC
Related Companies L.P.
Rochester Genesee Regional Transportation Authority
Shephardic Heritage Museum
SHFL Entertainment, Inc.
Sorrento Lactalis, Inc.
Stony Brook Foundation, Inc.
Success Academy Charter Schools
Surf Manor Home for Adults
Suse and Peter Lowenstein
Tappan Zee Constructors, LLC
Taubman Company (The)
Technet
Transpro Consulting LLC
Trinet
US Digital Gaming, Inc.
Vornado Realty L.P.
Walt Disney Company (The)
Western Regional Off-Track Betting Corp.
Yeshiva University

Lobbyists:
Christopher Bombardier
Michelle Cummings
Danna Deblasio
Sam Gerrity
Christopher Grimaldi
Patricia Lynch
Patrick McCarthy
Mark Meyerhoffer
Jim Quent
Lisa Reid
Enrique Sosa
Paul Tokasz

M + R Strategic Services (FKA M & R Strategic Services)
80 Broad St.
17th Floor
New York, NY 10004
212-764-3878

Clients:
AIDS Service Center of NYC
Defenders Association (NYS)
Homeless Services United
Naral Pro-Choice NY

Pratt Center for Community Direct Marketing Association

Lobbyists:
Robert Liff
Ya-Ting Liu
Arthur Malkin
Kim Milbrath
Michael O'Loughlin
Rebecca Wallach

Madden, Susan (FKA Benson, Kathleen)
Museum of the City of New York
1220 Fifth Avenue
New York, NY 10029
917-492-3302

Lobbyists:
Martin McLaughlin
Ronay Menschel

Maher Jr., Daniel F.
C/O Excess Line Assn of NY
55 Broadway, 1 Exchange Plz, 29th Fl
New York, NY 10006-3728
646-292-5500
e-mail: dmaher@elany.org
Web site: www.elany.org

Clients:
Excess Line Assn of NY

Major League Soccer, LLC
420 Fifth Avenue
7th Floor
New York, NY 10018
212-450-1260

Lobbyists:
Mark Abbott
Don Garber
Brett Lashbrook

Malkin & Ross
80 State Street, 11th Floor
Albany, NY 12207-1801
518-449-3359
e-mail: amalkin@malkinross.com
Web site: www.malkinross.com

Clients:
Academy of Medicine (NY)
ALCOA, Inc.
Alliance for Clean Energy New York, Inc.
Alzheimer's Association, New York City Chapter
American Lung Association of New York
AmidaCare
Ascension Health
Assembly of the Association of Surgical Technologists
Association of Central Service Professionals
Barrier Free Living Family of Companies
Boyd Gaming
Brooklyn Botanic Garden
Brotherhood/Sister Sol
Business Outreach Center Network, Inc.
Camp Directors
Citizens Committee for Children of NY, Inc.
Coalition for the Homeless
Coalition of Behavioral Health Agencies, Inc.
Coalition of New York State Alzheimer's Association Chapters

Congregation of Yeshiva Machzikei Hadas
Court Appointed Special Advocates
Defenders Association
Direct Marketers and Publishers
Drug Policy Alliance
Elliott Management
Federation of Protestant Welfare Agencies
Food and Water Watch
Gay Men's Health Crisis, Inc.
Human Services Council
Judge Rotenberg Center
Learning Through an Expanded Arts Program
Legal Assistance Group
LI CSP-MSA Association
Lower Eastside Service Center, Inc.
Make the Road New York
Naral Pro-Choice New York
National Employment Lawyers Association
Nestle Waters North America Holdings, Inc.
New Yorkers for Fair Automobile Insurance Reform, Inc.
Nurses Association
Open Space Institute
Parent Child HOme Program, Inc.
Pharmacists Society
Police Benevolent Association of New York State
Regional Community Service Programs
Rehabilitation Association
Safe Horizon, Inc.
School Nutrition Association
Takeda Pharmaceuticals America
Therapeutic Communities Association of NY, Inc.
United Way of New York City
Village of Kiryas Joel
Visa, Inc.
Whitney M. Young Jr. Health Services
Yeled V'Yalda Early Childhood Center

Lobbyists:
Jay Adolf
Cynthia Dames
Laura Darman
Gene De Santis
Mary Ann Donnaruma
Arthur Malkin
Terry Pratt
Brendan Principato
Donald Ross
Jessica Schafroth
Christine Tramontano
Tracy Tress
Victoria Zwickel
Steven Sanders

Manatt, Phelps & Phillips, LLP

30 S Pearl Street
12th Fl
Albany, NY 12207
518-431-6700

Clients:
83-30 Austin Street LLC
Assn of Public Broadcasting Stations of NY
American Council of Life Insurers
Bayer Healthcare
Brain Trauma Foundation
Brooklyn Information & Culture
Callen-Lorde Coomunity Health Center
Coalition for Medically Fragile Children
Concepts of Independent Choices
Community Health Care Assoc of NYS

Corporation for Supportive Housing
Coalition of Voluntary Safety Net Hospitals (NYS)
Coalition of Prepaid Health Svcs Plans (NYS)
East Side Rezoning Alliance
El Paso Corporation
Federation of Protestant Welfare Agencies Inc
Glimmerglass Coalition
Group Health Incorporated
Health & Hospitals Corp (NYC)
Hewlett-Packard Company
Independent Care System (ICS)
Living Independently Inc
Memorial Sloan-Kettering Cancer Center
Montefiore Medical Ctr
NYS Council of Health-System Pharmacists
National Multiple Sclerosis Society, NY MS Coalition Action Netwo
Primary Care Development Corporation
Project Samaritan AIDS Services Inc
Ralph Lauren Center for Cancer Care & Prevention
Samaritan Village Inc
St Raymond Community Outreach
Structured Employment Economic Development Corp
Sephardic Bikur Holim
Structural Biology Center (NY)
Verizon Wireless
Visiting Nurse Service of NY

Lobbyists:
Robert Belfort
Karyn Bell
William Bernstein
Kalpana Bhandarkar
Patricia Boozang
Melinda Dutton
John Faso
Anthony Fiori
Paul Gangsei
Kerry Griffin
Susan Ingargiola
George Kalkines
Alice Lam
Emily Lee
David Oakley
Steve Polan
Helen Pfister
Jeremiah Sheehan
Joann Smith
Jeffrey Thrope
Mark Ustin
James Walsh
Vanessa Wisniewski
Marcia Alazraki
Melinda Dutton
Leah Griggs Pauly
Emily Lee
James Lytle
Elizabeth Mundinger
Helen Pfister

Manhattan Chamber of Commerce, Inc.

1375 Broadway
3rd Floor
New York, NY 10018
212-473-7875

Lobbyists:
Ronald Paltrowitz
Nancy Ploeger
Don Winter

Offices and agencies generally appear in alphabetical order, except when specific order is requested by listee.

Maniscalco, John D
14 Penn Plz, Ste 1102
New York, NY 10122
212-695-1380
e-mail: nyoilheating@nyoha.org
Web site: www.nyoha.org

Clients:
Oil Heating Assoc

Mannella, Peter F.
266 Hudson Ave
Albany, NY 12210
518-463-4937

Clients:
Association for Pupil Transportation (New York)

Manufacturers Assn of Central NY Inc
One Webster's Landing, 5th Fl
Syracuse, NY 13202-1044
315-474-4201

Clients:
Council of Industry of Southeastern NY
Manufacturers Assn of Central NY Inc

Lobbyists:
Karyn Burns
Randall Wolken

March of Dimes Birth Defects Foundation New York Chapter
515 Madison Avenue
20th Floor
New York, NY 10022
212-353-8353

Lobbyists:
Nelson Andino
Caitlin Conner
Frank Demeo
Susan Rose
Dennis Schrader

Marcus Attorneys
13 Greene Avenue
Brooklyn, NY 11238
718-643-6555

Lobbyists:
Katrice Clermont
Philip Lavender
Jed S. Marcus
Amy Mayer
Jennifer Payne
Guillermo Santiago

Maritato, Anna Maria
284 State Street, 2nd Floor
Albany, NY 12210
518-463-9133

Clients:
Pfizer Inc

Markee, Lionel
111 Washington Ave
Suite 404
Albany, NY 12210-2210
518-465-6294

Clients:
Association of PBAS, Inc.
International Longshoremen's Association, AFL-CIO
Sanitation Officer's Association
Vietnam Veterans of America, New York State Council

Lobbyists:
Louis Matarazzo

Marsh, Wassermann & McHugh, LLC
677 Broadway
Albany, NY 12207
518-436-6000
e-mail: marshpc@attglobal.net

Clients:
Amerigroup New York LLC/Amerigroup Community Care (FKA Care Plus
    Health Plan)
Assn of Independent Schools (NYS)
ATM Industry Association
Atomic Learning Inc
Auxilia
Canadian National Railway
Cardtronics LP
Chief Executives Network for Manufacturing
Education & Work Consortium (The)
Eyemed Vision Care LLC
Greater NY Health Care Facilities Assoc
Greene International Golf Assn
LB Furniture Industries LLC
Medstat
Metropolitan College of NY
Morton Grove Pharmaceuticals
National Safety Commission Inc
SSP Companies
Tier Technologies
Town Clerks Assn Inc (NYS)
UST Public Affairs Inc
Western Union

Lobbyists:
J. Scott Bonacic
Blaise S. Dibernardo
Darcy L. Green
Kerry D. Marsh
Juan A. Martinez
Patrick J. McHugh
Edward H Wassermann
Diana P. Georgia
Ryan V. Horstmyer

Martin Begun D/B/A Martin S. Begun Consulting
400 East 67th Street
Unit 22A
New York, NY 10065
212-308-2114

Clients:
NYU School of Medicine
NYU Hospitals Center

Lobbyists:
Martin Begun

Offices and agencies generally appear in alphabetical order, except when specific order is requested by listee.

Martin J. McLaughlin Communications, Inc.
54 State St
6th Floor
Albany, NY 12207
518-689-1436

Clients:
Verizon NY

Lobbyists:
Cathy Cudahy
Martin McLaughlin
Michael Woloz

Masiello, Martucci, Calabrese and Associates (FKA Government Action Professionals, Inc.)
Cathedral Place
298 Main Street
Suite 300
Buffalo, NY 14202-4005
716-923-4156

Clients:
Allergan USA, Inc.
Arcadis U.S., Inc.
Brennan Center for Justice
Buffalo City Cemetary, Inc.
Buffalo Zoo
CCS Oncology
Clarence Building Materials and Supplies/Ray-Gar Construction
County of Niagara
Delta Sonic
Fair Committee
Hamister Group, Inc.
Health Transportation Network
Insight Associates
John W. Danforth Company
Kaleida Health
Kissling Interests (The)
Mensch Capital Partners, Inc.
Mikhail Strut, MD.
Niagara Frontier Transpotation Authority
Norstar Development USA, LP
Palladian Health
Phillips Lytle LLP
Shea's Buffalo Theatre
St. John Fruit Belt Development Corporation
Try-It Distributing Company
Wendel LLC

Lobbyists:
Carl Calabrese
Victor Martucci
Anthony Masiello
Patricia Paul
Matthew J. Plunkett

Massachusetts Mutual Life Insurance Company
Massachusetts Mutual Life Insurance
Company
1295 State Street
Springfield, MA 01111
413-744-7204

Lobbyists:
Dennis Herchel

Master, Robert
C/O Communications Workers of America
80 Pine St, 37th Fl
New York, NY 10005
212-344-2515

Clients:
Communications Workers of America, District 1

Lobbyists:
Kenneth Peres
Peter Sikora

Matarazzo, Louis
36 Muirfield Rd
Rockville Centre, NY 11570
516-642-3900

Clients:
Captains Endowment Assn, NYC Police Department
Detectives Endowment Assn, Police Dept of NYC
Public Employee Conference (NYS)

Mathews, Dan
1123 Broadway, Suite 704
New York, NY 10010
212-226-8247

Lobbyists:
Karla Waples

Matusic, Karen
2350 Kerner Blvd
Suite 250
San Rafael, CA 94901
415-389-6800

Clients:
Exxon Mobil Corporation

MC Asset Management Americas, LTD.
655 Third Ave
2nd Floor
New York, NY 10017
212-644-1840

Clients:
MC Financial Services LTD.

Lobbyists:
John Dearing
Gregory Eudicone

McCormack, Jr., R. Christopher
111 Washington Avenue
Suite 200
Albany, NY 12210
518-436-4077

Clients:
Bank of America Corporation and Subsidiaries
RAI Services Company

McDonnell, Brian
212 Great Oaks Boulevard
Albany, NY 12203
518-869-2245

Offices and agencies generally appear in alphabetical order, except when specific order is requested by listee.

Lobbyists:
Jillian Matundan

McGrath Matter Associates
1500 Broadway
Suite 812
New York, NY 10036
212-354-5588
Web site: www.mcgrathmatter.com

Lobbyists:
Scott Matter
George McGrath

McGuire, Jason J.
P.O. Box 107
Spencerport, NY 14559-0107
585-225-2340

Clients:
New Yorkers for Constitutional Freedoms

Lobbyists:
Stephen Hayford, Esq.
Duane Motley

McGuire, Michael J
Mason Tenders Dist. Council of Grtr NY
266 W 37th St, 7th Fl
New York, NY 10018
212-452-9501

Clients:
Mason Tenders District Council Greater NY & Long Island PAC

Lobbyists:
Kris Kohler
James Hegarty
Peter Zarcone

McKenna Long & Aldridge, LLP
111 Washington Avenue
Albany, NY 12210
518-462-1800

Clients:
ALS Association of Greater New York (The)
Bellefaire JCB
Bombardier Transit Corporation
Brookhaven Memorial Hospital Medical Center
CBS Outdoor
Devry Incorporated
Fire Island Association, Inc.
Gilbane Building Company
Gordian Group, Inc. (The)
HealthPass
HNTB Corporation
Institute for International Bankers
Koch Companies Public Sector, LLC and it's Affiliates
OTG Management
Safelite Group, Inc.
Suffolk Regional Off-Track Betting Corporation
Talisman Energy USA, Inc.

Lobbyists:
Charles E. Dorkey III
Chris Graham
Michael Klein
Kathleen O'Connor
Timothy Plunkett

Frank Rapoport
Amy Solomon

McLean, Mary Ann
459 Mayfair Drive
Poinciana, FL 34759
863-427-3491

Clients:
Athletic Trainers' Association New York State
Society of Clinical Social Work, Inc. (NYS)

McMahon, Kathy A.
21 Aviation Rd
Suite 9
Albany, NY 12205
518-446-1483

Clients:
Hospice and Palliative Care Association of NYS

McManus, Michael T.
119 Washington Ave
#306
Albany, NY 12210
518-436-8827

Clients:
Professional Fire Fighters Association, Inc.

Lobbyists:
Samuel Fresina

Meara Avella Dickinson
111 Washington Avenue, Suite 305
Albany, NY 12210
518-472-2288

Lobbyists:
Michael Avella
Christina Dickinson
Brian Meara

Meara, Brian R, Public Relations Inc
321 Broadway
New York, NY 10007
518-472-2288

Clients:
ABC Inc
Altria Corporate Services Inc (ALCS)
American Lawyer Media Co
Assurant Solutions
Black Car Assistance Corporation
Black Car Operators' Injury Compensation Fund (NY)
Bus Association of NYS Inc
CBS Corporation
Delaware North Companies Gaming & Entertainment Inc
Court Officers Assn (NYS)
EAC Inc
Empire State Assn of Adult Homes & Assist Living Facilities
Finger Lakes Racing Association
Glenwood Management Corporation
Insurance Premium Finance Assn Inc
Long Island Power Authority
Nassau Regional Off-Track Betting Corporation
NBC Universal
Jets LLC (NY)
NYU School of Medicine

Offices and agencies generally appear in alphabetical order, except when specific order is requested by listee.

Parker Jewish Inst for Health Care & Rehab
Physicians' Reciprocal Insurers
Reliant Resources Inc
Retailers Alliance (The)
Solow Management Company
Simon Weisenthal Ctr Museum of Tolerance
Shinnecock Nation Gaming Authority
Silvercup Studios
Southern Tier Acquisition, LLC
Suffolk County Court Employees
Transit Alliance
Uniformed Fire Officers Assn (NYC)
Vanguard Car Rental USA Inc
Verizon
Wilmorite Holdings, LP
Yankees Partnership (NY)
Educational Housing Services (Regional Programs Inc)
Empire Resorts Inc
Guardian Life Insurance Company of America (The)
Lincoln Center for the Performing Arts Inc
New York Medical Staff Leadership Council
NYC & Company
NYC 2012

Lobbyists:
Michael Avella
Christina Dickinson
Brian R Meara

Medical Society of the State of New York
One Commerce Plaza
Suite 408
Albany, NY 12210
518-465-8085

Lobbyists:
Morris Auster, Esq.
Patricia F. Clancy
Barbara K. Ellman
Robert J. Hughes
Andrew Y. Kleinman
Philip Schuh
Sam L. Unterricht

Medtronic, Inc. (FKA Dena Scearce)
710 Medtronic Parkway
LS380
Minneapolis, MN 55432-5604
763-505-2597

Lobbyists:
William Fehrenbach
Dena Scearce

Memorial Sloan-Kettering Cancer Center
1275 York Avenue
New York, NY 10065
646-227-2788

Lobbyists:
James Gillson
Cynthia McCollum
Katherine Mikk
Paul Nelson

Mental Health Association in NYS
194 Washington Ave, Ste 415
Albany, NY 12210

518-434-0439
e-mail: mhapres@mhanys.org
Web site: www.mhanys.org

Clients:
Mental Health Association of NYC Inc

Lobbyists:
Glenn Liebman
John Richter

Mental Health Association of New York
50 Broadway
19th Floor
New York, NY 10012
212-964-5253
Web site: www.mhaofnyc.org

Lobbyists:
Michael B. Friedman
Giselle Stolper
Kimberly Williams
Carol Altieri

Merck Sharp & Dohme Corp. (Affiliates: Schering Corp and Merck Schering-Plough Pharmaceuticals)
351 North Sumneytown Pike
UG3A-94
North Wales, PA 19454
267-305-2384

Lobbyists:
Matthew Badalucco
Bindi Patel

Mercury Public Affairs LLC
250 Greenwich St
36th Floor
New York, NY 10007
212-681-1380

Clients:
Addiction Treatment Providers Association
Advanced Biohealing a Shire Company
AT&T
AutoDesk, Inc.
Centerlight Health Systems
Children's Hospital of Philadelphia
CWA Local 1182
Dart Container Corporation
FJC Security Services, Inc.
IBM Corporation
Intergraph Corporation
OHEL Children's Home & Family Services
Premier Kids Care, Inc.
Sallie Mae, Inc.
Shinnecock Nation Gaming Authority
Source Corp.
St. Johns Riverside Hospital
Twin America
United Ambulette Coalition
Van Wagner Communications LLC

Lobbyists:
Thomas Doherty
Fernando Ferrer
Jonathan Greenspun
Michael McKeon
Violet Moss

Offices and agencies generally appear in alphabetical order, except when specific order is requested by listee.

Merrill Lynch & Company, Inc.
222 Broadway
16th Floor
New York, NY 10038
212-670-2905

Lobbyists:
Maxine Awner
Robert Barber
William Bloom
James Calpin
Jeffrey Carey
Spencer Coker
Paul Critchlow
Mark Eidlin
Barbara Feldman
Christopher Fink
John Hallacy
Michael Jang
Susan Jun
John Keane
Richard Lasala
John Lawlor
Mark Liff
Brian Maier
David Notkin
James O'Connor
Rebecca Reape
Carol Rein
James Ryan
Garth Schulz
Chris Sebastian
David Stephens
Christopher Straub
Jeffrey Sula
Martha Wooding
Elvir Mujanovic

Metropolitan Jewish Health System (FKA Cross, Jeannie H.)
Metropolitan Jewish Health System
6323 Seventh Avenue
Brooklyn, NY 11220-4711
718-614-4183

Lobbyists:
Hany Abdelaal
Debra Boyce Martinez
Lurlene Buckley
Susan Caputo
Laurie Chichester
Jeannie Cross
Sandra Esner
Eli Feldman
Lydia Galeon
Diane Gallo
Barbara Hiney
Randall Klein
Shmuel Lefkowich
Joyce Little
Barbara Lyon
Ronald Milch
Derek Murray
David Nussbaum
Osarhiemen Okpeseyi
Tara Ragbir
Yeruchim Silber
Sandra Schau
Mary Wagner

Carol Altieri
Al Balko
Ron Chaffin
Gary Kleinberg
Robert Leamer
Emily Pring

Meyer Suozzi English & Klein, PC
One Commerce Plaza, Ste 1705
Albany, NY 12260
518-465-5551

Clients:
1199/SEIU New York's Health & Human Services Union
Actors Fund of America (The)
Brooklyn Public Library
City Works Foundation, (The)
Committee for Occupational Safety & Health (NY)
Committee for Workers' Compensation Reform
Conservation Service Group
Council for Unity
Consortium for Workers Education
Forest City Ratner Companies
Fractured Atlas
Friends of NY Racing Inc
Local 802, American Federation of Musicians of Greater NY
Int'l Brotherhood of Teamsters, AFL-CIO (Local 237)
Laborers' Political Action Committee (NYS)
Garment Industry Development Corporation
Local 1180, CWA, AFL-CIO
Mount Sinai Medical Center
Retail Wholesale Department Store Union
MFY Legal Services
Screen Actors Guild (National & Hollywood Offices)
Suffolk County Correction Officers Assn
Susquehanna & Western Railway Corp (NY)
Production Alliance (NY)
Unite Here
Utility Workers Union, Local 1-2, AFL-CIO
SEIU Local 200 United
Workers' Compensation Alliance
Working Today
SEIU, Local 300
Traffipax Inc

Lobbyists:
Deanne Braveman
Thomas Hartnett
Richard D Winsten

Michael Balboni, Esq.
50 Meritoria Drive
East Williston, NY 11596
516-567-0345

Clients:
1199 SEIU Greater New York Worker Participation Fund
Raytheon Company

Lobbyists:
Michael Balboni

Mid-Hudson Catskill Rural & Migrant Ministry Inc
360 Noxon Rd
PO Box 4757
Poughkeepsie, NY 12602
845-485-8627
e-mail: hope@ruralmigrantministry.org
Web site: www.ruralmigrantministry.org

Offices and agencies generally appear in alphabetical order, except when specific order is requested by listee.

Clients:
Mid-Hudson Catskill Rural & Migrant Ministry Inc

Lobbyists:
Jordan Wells
Richard Witt, Jr

Miller, Craig J.
137 Harrison St
Gloversville, NY 12078
518-773-7371

Clients:
Frontier Communications

Millman, Claude
7 World Trade Center
New York, NY 10007
212-808-8100

Clients:
Institute for Puerto Rican/Hispanic Elderly

Milroy, James
Erwin 218
SUNY Geneseo
Geneseo, NY 14454
585-245-5704

Clients:
SUNY Geneseo

Mirram Group, LLC (The)
895 Broadway, 5th Fl
New York, NY 10003
212-505-6633
e-mail: mirramgroup@aol.com

Clients:
Atlantic Development Co
Cable Telecommunications Association of NY
Coalition for the Homeless
First (NY)
Food Industry Alliance of NYS
Healthcare Education Project
Healthplex Inc
Monroe College
Morris Heights Health Center
New Visions for Public Schools
Protecting America.org
Transport Workers Union, Local 100
TVG Network
UBS Securities
Urban Health Plan Inc
World Trade Center Properties

Lobbyists:
Bernard Bryan
Luis A Miranda Jr
Gloria Mullen
Roberto Ramirez Sr
Kim Ramos
Catherine Torres

Mirrer, Louise
170 Central Park West
New York, NY 10024
212-873-3400

Clients:
Historical Society (NY)

Montalbano Initiatives Inc
64 Fulton St, Ste 603
New York, NY 10038
212-587-0587
Web site: www.nyclobbyist.com

Clients:
Covenant House NY
Teamsters Local 237
Trust for Public Land

Lobbyists:
Vincent Montalbano

Montefiore Medical Center
677 Broadway
Suite 1101
Albany, NY 12207
518-701-2713

Lobbyists:
Roberto Garcia
Deborah Konopko
Kate Rose

Moon Capital Management LP
499 Park Avenue
8th Floor
New York, NY 10022
212-652-4500

Lobbyists:
Ian Lindsay
Allyce O'Brien
Ramesh Parameswar
Veronica Wong

Mooney, William
1133 Westerchester Avenue
S-217
White Plains, NY 10604
914-948-6444

Lobbyists:
Amy Allen
Dorothy Forinca

Moreau, Karen
150 State St.
4th Floor
Albany, NY 12207-1675
518-465-3563

Clients:
American Petroleum Institute

Lobbyists:
Cathy Kenny
Maryann McCarthy

Morgan Stanley & Co. Incorporated
1585 Broadway
New York, NY 10036
212-761-4000
Web site: www.morganstanley.com

Offices and agencies generally appear in alphabetical order, except when specific order is requested by listee.

Lobbyists:
Randall Campbell
Michael Colton
Paula Dagen
Darryl Davis
Dennis Farrell
Grant Fraunfelder
David Hammer
Kent Hitchcock
Daniel Kelly
Melissa Labuda
Ben Langmead
Todd Lee
Richard McDermott
James McIntyre
Richard Molke
Edward Moulin
Lou Palladino
Geoff Proulx
Kevin Schwartz
Robert Shearer
R. Stratford Shields
Ira Smelkinson
Barbara Thomas
Charles Visconsi
Richard Weiss
Perry J. Offutt
Perry J. Offutt
David Rush

Morris, Mark
217 Great Oaks Blvd.
Albany, NY 12203-5964
518-862-0110

Clients:
Healthcare Professionals Insurance Company

Morse, Alan
Jewish Guild for the Blind (The)
15 W 65th St
New York, NY 10023
212-769-6215
e-mail: armorse@jgb.org
Web site: www.jgb.org

Clients:
Jewish Guild for the Blind (The)

Lobbyists:
Annemarie O'Hearn

Mosaic Federal Affairs LLC
One Park Place
300 South State Street
10th Floor
Syracuse, NY 13202
315-425-2839

Lobbyists:
Michael Brower

Motion Picture Association of America, Inc.
1600 Eye Street N.W.
Washington, DC 20006
202-293-1966
Web site: www.mpaa.org

Lobbyists:
Angela Miele
Vans Stevenson

Motorola, Inc.
1303 East Algonquin Road
7th Floor
Schaumburg, IL 60196
847-538-1955

Lobbyists:
Maureen Donovan

Mount Sinai Medical Center
One Gustave L Levy Pl
Box 1499
New York, NY 10029-6574
212-659-9011

Clients:
Mount Sinai Medical Center

Lobbyists:
Brad Beckstrom

Movement Group, LLC
1133 Broadway
Suite 416
New York, NY 10010
212-309-2863

Lobbyists:
Jan Feuerstadt
Charles King

MSG Holdings, L.P.
2 Penn Plaza
New York, NY 10121
212-465-6310

Lobbyists:
Irene Baker
Alex Diaz
Joel Fisher
Matthew Gorton
Annette Juriaco
Jeremiah O'Shea
Marc Schoenfeld
Hal Weidenfeld

Mueller, Tricia
91 Fieldcrest Avenue
Raritan Plaza II
2nd Floor
Edison, NJ 08037
914-592-0100

Clients:
Northeast Regional Council of Carpenters NY Political Education Committee

Lobbyists:
Tricia Brown

Muhs, Robert E.
c/o Avis Budget Group, Inc.
8 Sylvan Way
Parsippany, NY 07054
973-496-3532

Offices and agencies generally appear in alphabetical order, except when specific order is requested by listee.

Clients:
Avis Budget Group, Inc.

Municipal Art Society
457 Madison Ave
New York, NY 10022
212-935-3960

Clients:
Municipal Art Society

Lobbyists:
Melissa Baldock
Eve Baron
Micaela Birmingham
Vin Cipolla
Jasper Goldman
Vanessa Gruen
Lisa Kersavage
Frank Sanchis
David Schnakenberg
Lacey Tauber

Murray, Claire
1501 Twelfth Avenue
Watervliet, NY 12189-2402
518-273-1525

Clients:
New York Organization of Nurse Executives

MVP Health Insurance Co. and Its Affiliates (FKA MVP Service Corporation)
625 State Street
Schnectady, NY 12305
518-388-2235
Web site: www.mvphealthcare.com

Lobbyists:
Frank Fanshawe
David Oliker

MyWireless.org
MyWireless.org
1400 16th Street
NW Suite 600
Washington, DC 20036
202-736-3889
Web site: www.mywireless.org

Lobbyists:
Brian Johnston

NADAP
355 Lexington Avenue
New York, NY 10017
212-986-1170
Web site: www.nadap.org

Lobbyists:
John Darin
Elizabeth Madison
Sunita Manurekar
Karen Morton
Maria Pasceri
Lucy Redzeposki
Gary Stankowski

Nagel Law Office, PLLC
224 W 35th Street
Suite 508
New York, NY 10001
212-904-1139

Lobbyists:
William Nagel

NARAL Pro-Choice, New York
470 Park Ave S
7th Fl
New York, NY 10016
212-343-0114
e-mail: info@prochoiceny.org
Web site: www.prochoiceny.org

Clients:
NARAL Pro-Choice, New York

Lobbyists:
Emily Alexander
Myra Batchelder
Amy Boldesser
Mary Alice Carr
Kelli Conlin
Katherine Grainger
Angela Hooton
Lalena Howard
Debbie Johnson
Sabrina Shulman
Andrew Stern

Nasca, Samuel J
35 Fuller Road
Suite 205
Albany, NY 12205
518-438-8403
e-mail: sjnasca@aol.com

Clients:
United Transportation Union

Nassau Community College
One Education Drive
Garden City, NY 11530
516-572-7811
Web site: www.ncc.edu

Lobbyists:
Mary Adams
Frank (Chuck) Cutolo
John Durso
Carol Friedman
Alan Gurien
Joseph Muscarella
Reginald Tuggle
Donald Astrab
James Large
John LeBoutillier

National Assn of Chain Drug Stores
328 Still River Rd
Still River, MA 01467
978-456-9235
Web site: www.nacds.org

Offices and agencies generally appear in alphabetical order, except when specific order is requested by listee.

Clients:
National Assn of Chain Drug Stores

Lobbyists:
Anne Fellows

National Association of Mutual Insurance Companies (NAMIC)
3601 Vincennes Road
Indianapolis, IN 46268
317-875-5250

Lobbyists:
Paul Tetrault

National Assn of Social Workers (NYS Chapter) (FKA Paupini, Sara)
188 Washington Ave
Albany, NY 12210
518-463-4741

Clients:
National Assn of Social Workers (NYS Chapter)

Lobbyists:
Reinaldo Cardona
Kelley Martinson
Karin Moran

National Association of Social Workers - New York City Chapter
50 Broadway
Suite 1001
New York, NY 10004
212-668-0050

Lobbyists:
Launa Kliever
Harriet Putterman
Robert Schachter

National Employment Law Project
75 Maiden Lane, Suite 601
New York, NY 10038
212-285-3025

Lobbyists:
Annette Bernhardt
Tsedeye Gebreselassie
Sarah Leberstein
Sarah Leberstein
Paul Sonn
Andrew Stettner

National Federation of Independent Business
One Commerce Plaza
Suite 803
Albany, NY 12260
518-434-1262

Lobbyists:
Michael Elmendorf

National Fuel Gas Company (FKA Rose, Michael M.)
C/O National Fuel Gas Company
6363 Main Street
Williamsville, NY 14221-5887
716-857-7780

Lobbyists:
Patricia Paul
Michael Reville
David Smith

National Grid (FKA Crossett, Susan)
111 Washington Avenue
Albany, NY 12210
518-433-5213

Lobbyists:
Gary Ahern
Barry Allen
Janet Besser
Timothy Brennan
Edward Carr
Eileen Cifone
Anthony Curcio
Peter Flynn
William Flynn
Bart Franey
Vincent Frigeria
Cosmo Iannicco
Kim Ireland
Tom King
Roxane Maywalt
Belinda Pagdanganan
Marcy Reed
Joe Rende
Robert Teetz
Victor Vientos

National Multiple Sclerosis Society, New York City Chapter
733 3rd Avenue, 3rd Floor
New York, NY 10017-3288
212-463-7787

Lobbyists:
Debby Bennett
Robin Einbinder
Pamela Weiner

National Railroad Passenger Corporation
60 Massachusetts Avenue NE
Washington, DC 20002
202-906-4088

Clients:
AMTRAK

Lobbyists:
Frances Bourne
Clifford Cole
Alfred Fazio
Andrew Galloway
Stephen Gardner
William Hollister
Danielle Hunter
Marilyn Jamison
Robert Lacroix
Joseph McHugh
Tom Moritz
Dana Schaeffer
Petra Todorovich Messick

National Strategies, Inc.
95 Columbia Street
Albany, NY 12210

Offices and agencies generally appear in alphabetical order, except when specific order is requested by listee.

518-432-0488
Web site: www.nationalstrategiesinc.com

Lobbyists:
Arthur Brown
Roy Cales
Agostino Cangemi
Alfred Gordon
Gino Menchini
Susan Pedo
Ruth Walters

Natural Resources Defense Council (FKA Goldstein, Eric)
Natural Resources Defense Council
40 West 20th Street
New York, NY 10011
212-727-2700
Web site: nrdc.org

Lobbyists:
Rita Barol
Priscilla Bayley
Frances Beinecke
Dale Bryk
Pierre Bull
Lisa Catapano
Alison Chase
Sarah Chasis
Donna Decostanzo
Rick Duke
Eric Goldstein
Nathanael Greene
Ashok Gupta
David Hawkins
Mark Izeman
Richard Kassel
Robert Kennedy
Peter Lehner
Lawrence Levine
Ying Li
Luis Martinez
Robin Marx
Robin McCarthy
Yerina Mugica
Richard Schrader
Brad Sewell
Renata Silberblatt
Katherine Sinding
Katherine Slusark
Lisa Speer
Theodore Spencer
Luke Tonacle
Julie Truax-Glen
Joyce Wong

Nature Conservancy (The) (FKA Janeway, William C.)
195 New Karner Road
Suite 200
Albany, NY 12205
518-690-7873
Web site: www.nature.org

Lobbyists:
Colin Apse
Laura Bavaro
Marisa Biehl
Marci Bortman
Dirk Bryant
Michael Carr

Christopher Clapp
Sarah Clarkin
Katie Dolan
Neil Gifford
Wayne Grothe
Paul Hartman
Chris Hawver
David Higby
Kelly Hines
Jim Howe
Kara Jackson
Joseph Jannsen
Marilyn Jordan
Nancy Kelley
Meagan Kelly
Cara Lee
Stuart Lowrie
Nicole Maher
Patricia Manzi
Kevin McDonald
Patrick McGlew
Kathy Moser
Rita Murray
Zack Odell
Jessica Ottney Mahar
Alpa Pandya
Randy Parsons
Connie Prickett
Gregory Sargis
Michael Scheibel
George Schuler
Hilary Smith
Mark Smith
Timothy Tear
Bill Ulfelder
Troy Weldy
Alan White
Tony Wilkinson
Nathan Woiwode

NBCUniversal
30 Rockefeller Plaza
New York, NY 10112
212-664-2227

Lobbyists:
Brian O'Leary
Veronica Sullivan

Neidl, Michael
100 South Swan Street
Albany, NY 12210
518-436-8516

Clients:
AFL-CIO

Lobbyists:
Suzy Ballantyne
Joseph Canovas
Mario Cilento
Ryan Delgado
Michael Neidl

Neighborhood Family Services Coalition
120 Broadway
Suite 230
New York, NY 10271
212-619-1656

Offices and agencies generally appear in alphabetical order, except when specific order is requested by listee.

Lobbyists:
Kam Chi Li
Sierra Stoneman-Bell

Lobbyists:
Bernell Grier

New Yorkers Against Gun Violence
3 West 29th Street
Suite 1007
New York, NY 10001
212-679-2345

Lobbyists:
Mary Ellen Hilly
Barbaraen Hohlt

Newspaper Publishers Assn (NY)
50 Colvin Avenue
Albany, NY 12208
518-449-1667

Clients:
Newspaper Publishers Assn (NY)

Lobbyists:
Diane Kennedy

Nicholas & Lence Communications LLC
28 West 44th Street
Suite 1217
New York, NY 10036
212-938-0001
Web site: www.nicholaslence.com

Lobbyists:
Jennifer Landis
George Lence
Cristyne Nicholas
Jennifer Landis
Jessica Proud
Evlyn Tsimis

Nicolson, Karen
237 Main Street
Buffalo, NY 14226
716-853-3087

Clients:
Legal Services for the Elderly, Disabled or Disadvantaged of Western New York, Inc.

Nissan North America, Inc.
One Nissan Way
Franklin, TN 37067
615-725-1000

Lobbyists:
Joe Castelli
Mike Hobson
Timothy Slattery
Tracy Woodard

Nixon Peabody, LLP
677 Broadway
10th Floor
Albany, NY 12207
518-427-2650

Clients:
Assn of Laser Hair Removal Specialists, Inc (NYS)
Bellevue Women's Medical Center, Inc

Lobbyists:
Peter Millock
Robert Burgdorf
Thomas Reynolds

Nolan & Heller, LLP
39 North Pearl St
3rd Fl
Albany, NY 12207
518-449-3300
e-mail: tburke@nolanandheller.com

Clients:
Empire State Subcontractors Assn

Lobbyists:
Terence Burke
Brennan Francis

Norfolk Southern Corporation
4600 Deer Path Road
Harrisburg, PA 17110
717-541-2250

Lobbyists:
Michael Fesen

North Shore Land Alliance
151 Post Rd.
Old Westbury, NY 11568
516-626-0908
Web site: www.northshorelandalliance.org

Lobbyists:
Judith Goldsborough
Barbara Hoover
Jane Jackson
Lisa Ott
Carol Schmiddlapp

North Star Fund
520 8th Avenue
New York, NY 10018
212-620-9110

Clients:
Communities United for Police Reform

Lobbyists:
Priscilla Gonzalez
Joo-Hyun Kang

Northeast Government Consulting LLC
501 St Davids Lane
Niskayuna, NY 12309
518-469-8795
Web site: www.ngclobby.com

Lobbyists:
David Carroll
Gregory G. Podbielski

Northern Manhattan Improvement Corporation
76 Wadsworth Avenue
New York, NY 10033

Offices and agencies generally appear in alphabetical order, except when specific order is requested by listee.

212-822-8300

Lobbyists:
Matthew Chachere
Maria Lizardo
Barbara Lowry
Kenneth Rosenfeld

Northern Metropolitan Hospital Assn
400 Stony Brook Court
Newburgh, NY 12550-5162
845-562-7520
e-mail: awein@normet.org

Clients:
Northern Metropolitan Hospital Assn

Lobbyists:
Neil Abitabilo
Angela Skretta

Novartis Pharmaceuticals Corporation
One Health Plaza
East Hanover, NJ 07936
862-778-8421

Lobbyists:
Sara David

NP Associates, LLC
704 N. McBride Street
Syracuse, NY 13208
315-422-5311

Lobbyists:
Nicholas Pirro

Nurses Association (NYS)
c/o Nurses Association (NYS)
11 Cornell Road
Latham, NY 12110-1499
518-782-9400

Lobbyists:
Kristin Abrams
Eileen Avery
John Berry
Ellen Brickman
Nicole Burckard
Michael Chacon
Elaine Charpentier
Jay Dwyer
Camille Edwards
Deborah Elliott
Shaun Flynn
Renee Gecsedi
Tina Gerardi
Michelle Hart
Michael Hertz
Roberta Murphy
Carol Pitman
Roxanne Romney
Crystal Shipp
Kevin Smith
Lucille Sollazzo
Therese Wittner

Nyprocoa, Inc.
Trinity Centre
115 Broadway
Ste 1504
New York, NY 10006
212-566-5600

Lobbyists:
Tonio Burgos
Francisco Diaz Jr.
Joseph Fiordaliso
Matthew Greller
Ninfa Segarra
Michael Klein
Manuel Mirabal

NYSPIA Political Committee, Inc.
11 North Pearl Street
Suite 1202
Albany, NY 12207
518-436-0120

Lobbyists:
Jeffrey Kayser

O'Brien & Gere Limited
5000 Brittonfield Parkway
East Syracuse, NY 13057
315-437-6100
Web site: www.obg.com

Lobbyists:
Stephen Anagnost
Michelle Baines
Timothy Barry
Robert Bowers
Terry Brown
Christopher Calkins
Christopher Campbell
Gary Cannerelli
Richard Cawley
Stephen Commesso
Douglas Crawford
Paul Curran
R. Leland Davis
Stephen Delano
Robert Delorenzo
Marc Dent
Ricky Duff
Thomas Dumm
Thomas Dussing
Steven Eckler
Brian Edwards
James Evans
Stephen Fisher
George Fleming
James Fox
Robert Ganley
Richard Gell
Peter Gibbons
Mark Greene
Peter Grevelding
Scott Grieco
Ronald Harting
James Heckathorne
Christian Hine
Wayne Hoagland
Kevin Ignaszak
Kenneth Jones

Offices and agencies generally appear in alphabetical order, except when specific order is requested by listee.

Lowell Kachalsky
Swiatoslav Kaczmar
Robert Keyser
Michael Kolceski
James Kyles
Clare Leary
Dwight Macarthur
Terrence Madden
Maureen Markert
Michelle Mcentire
David Meixell
Stephen Mooney
Ralph Morse
Sami Nasr
Robert Neimeier
Jamie Dirk Newtown
Holly Nicholas
Jennifer Olivo
Lynette Paduano
Ronald Panek
Mark Parrish
George Rest
Steven Roland
John Rooney
Darcy Sachs
Scott Scheidelman
Hubert Schlientz
John Shaheen
Stuart Spiegel
Alan Steinhauer
Karen Storne
Guy Swenson
Matthew Traister
Douglas Warneck
Ralph Whedon
David Wilson
Cherylann Wiseman
Deborah Wright

O'Connell and Aronowitz
54 State Street
9th Floor
Albany, NY 12207-2501
518-462-5601

Lobbyists:
Peter Danzinger

O'Connell, Maurice J.
One Bell Crossing Road
Selkirk, NY 12158
518-767-6445

Lobbyists:
William Goetz

O'Malley, Michael
15 Mountain View Road
Warren, NJ 07059
908-903-7004

Clients:
Chubb & Son, a Division of Federal Insurance Company

Ohrenstein & Brown, LLP
1010 Franklin Ave, 2nd Fl
PO Box 9243
Garden City, NY 11530-9243

516-873-6334
Web site: www.oandb.com

Clients:
Jamaica Hospital Medical Center
Marsh USA Inc

Lobbyists:
Michael Brown
Manfred Ohrenstein

Open Space Institute
1350 Broadway
Suite 201
New York, NY 10018
212-629-3981

Lobbyists:
Christopher Ellman
Wes Gillingham
Jennifer Grossman
Joseph Martens

Ophthalmological Society (NYS)
408 Kenwood Avenue
Delmar, NY 12054
518-439-2020

Lobbyists:
Robin Pellegrino

Orange Regional Medical Center
Orange Regional Medical Center
Arden Hill Campus
4 Harriman Drive
Goshen, NY 10924
845-294-2205
Web site: www.ormc.org

Lobbyists:
Rosemary Frado

Organization of NYS Management/Confidential Employees Inc
3 Washington Square
Albany, NY 12205-5523
518-456-5241
e-mail: omce@aol.com
Web site: www.nysomce.org

Clients:
Org of NYS Mgmt/Confidential Employees, Inc

Lobbyists:
Joseph Sano
Barbara Zaron

Osteopathic Medical Society
1855 Broadway
New York, NY 10023
212-261-1784

Lobbyists:
Barbara Greenwald

Ostroff, Hiffa & Associates Inc
12 Sheridan Ave
Albany, NY 12207

Offices and agencies generally appear in alphabetical order, except when specific order is requested by listee.

518-436-6202
e-mail: ostroff_associates@msn.com
Web site: www.ostroff-hiffa.com

Clients:
380 Development LLC
Adirondack Pine Hill NY Trailways
Amerada Hess Corporation
Assn of Town Superintendents of Highways Inc (NYS)
CATS VLT, LLC (Canadian American Transportation Systems)
Catholic Family Center
Cemetery Employer Assn of Greater NY
Cephalon Inc
Courtroom Television Network
Creative Coalition (The)
Crisis Program (The)
Dreyfus Corporation (The)
Duke Energy Corporation
Empire State Restaurant & Tavern Assn
Fahs Construction Group (Fahs-Rolston Paving Corp)
FlexCare
Central NY Railroad
Greater NY Health Care Facilities Assn
Cross Harbor Railroad (NY)
Hubbell Galvanizing
International Imaging Technology Council (I-ITC)
Liquid Asphalt Distributors Assoc Inc of NY
Monument Builders Assn (NYS)
Mount St Mary's Hospital & Health Center
Cumberland Packing Corporation
Public Library (NY), Astor, Lenox & Tilden Foundations
Electric & Gas Corporation (NYS)
Eponymous Associates LLC (FKA Steiner Studios)
Pratt Institute
Riverside South Planning Corp
Rochester Gas & Electric Corp
Suit-Kote Corp
UST Public Affairs Inc
United Health Services
Washington Cemetery
Western NY Energy LLC

Lobbyists:
Megan Bailey
David Dudley
Frederick T Hiffa
Richard L Ostroff
Barbara Lee Steigerwald
Erin T Waterhouse
Scott Wexler
Lisa Wickens

P.S. 1 Contemporary Art Center
22-25 Jackson Avenue
Long Island City, NY 11101-5324
718-786-3098

Lobbyists:
Antoine Guerrero
Yun Joo Kang

Pace University
161 William Street
19th Floor
New York, NY 10038
212-346-1274

Lobbyists:
Jane Aoyama-Martin
Jessica Bacher

John Cronin
Stephen Friedman
Jeffrey Lejava
Franz Litz
Jackson Morris
Eric Morrissey
Jennie Nolon
John Nolon
Tiffany Zezula

Park Strategies, LLC
101 Park Ave, Ste 2506
New York, NY 10178
212-883-5608

Clients:
Aetna Inc
Concerned Home Care Providers
Cendant Car Rental Group Inc
Correction Officers & Police Benevolent Assn Inc
Covanta Energy Corp
Energy East Corporation
Health Care Subrogation Group
Canadian American Transportation Systems, LLC
Lilac Capital LLC
LS Power Associates LLC
Madison Square Garden LP
Manhattan Theatre Club
Magna Entertainment Corp
NYU Child Study Center
Sheriff Officers Assn
Subway Surface Supervisors Assn
Vector Group, Ltd

Lobbyists:
Anthony Cancellieri
Alfonse M D'Amato
Armand D'Amato
Christopher P D'Amato
Joel Giambra
Robert McBride
Melvin Miller
David Poleto
Gregory Serio
John Zagame
Peter Molinaro
Kraig Siracuse

Parks & Trails New York
29 Elk Street
Albany, NY 12207
518-434-1583

Lobbyists:
Martin Daley
Robin Dropkin
Wally Elton
Frances Gotcsik
Shawn McConnell

Parkside Group, LLC
132 Nassau St, Ste 400
New York, NY 10038
212-571-7717
Web site: www.theparksidegroup.com

Clients:
345 E 62nd Street Associate
AAFE Managment Co
AFSCME Local 2021

Offices and agencies generally appear in alphabetical order, except when specific order is requested by listee.

American Museum of the Moving Image Inc
Assn for the Advancement of Blind & Retarded Inc
Assn for Neurologically Impaired Brain Injured Children Inc
Brooklyn Public Library
Business Outreach Center Network Inc
Central Labor Council (NYC)
Coastal Communications Services Inc
Committee for Hispanic Children & Families
Communication Workers of America Local 1180
Community Bank (NY)
Council Management Inc
Communication Workers of America, Local 1182
Danaher Controls Inc
Flushing Commons LLC
Flushing Council on Culture & the Arts Inc
Fresh Direct, LLC
Gloria Wise Boys & Girls Club Inc
Hospital Medical Center of Queens (NY)
Jamaica Ctr for Arts & Learning Inc
Church Avenue Merchants Block Association Inc
Metropolitan Life Insurance Co
Mulvihill ICS Inc
New York Cares Inc
Plaza College
Queens Centers for Progress Inc
Queens Chamber of Commerce
Queens Child Guidance Center Inc
Queens Economic Development Corp
Queens Centers for Progress Inc
Queens Theatre in the Park
Queensborough Comm College Auxiliary Enterprise Assn Inc
Rockaway Development & Revitalization Corp
Service Employees International Union, Local 300
South Queens Boys & Girls Club Inc
Strive
Supershuttle NY Inc
Telebeam Telecommunications Corp
United Food & Commercial Workers Dist Cncl of NY & Northern NJ
Community Financial Services Association of America
Crystal Window & Door Systems, Ltd
Educational Assistance Corporation
Entergy Nuclear Operations Inc
Gaucho LLC
Gowanus Village 1 Inc
Jets (NY)
National Council to Prevent Delinquency Inc
Nextel Operations Inc
NYC & Company
Pratt Institute for Community & Environment Development
Queens College Foundation-Research of CUNY

Lobbyists:
William Driscoll
Jake Dilemani
Harry Giannoulis
Barry Grodenchik
Violet Moss
Tiffany Raspberry
Evan Stavisky
Damon Stewart
Cassandra Lovejoy

Partnership for NYC (FKA Mele, Don)
One Battery Park Plaza
New York, NY 10004-1479
212-493-7400
Web site: www.nycp.org

Lobbyists:
Maria Gotsch

Marysol Rodriguez
Michael Simas
Kathryn Wylde

Pastel & Rosen, LLP
130 Washington Ave
Albany, NY 12210
518-462-4715

Clients:
Carco Group Inc
Chubb & Son (Division of Federal Insurance Co)
Coalition for Mold Reform (State Farm Insurance Cos)
Fireman's Fund Insurance Co
Insurance Brokers' Association of the State of New York
Professional Insurance Wholesalers Assoc of NYS Inc
Progressive Insurance Companies

Lobbyists:
Robert S Pastel
Michael E Rosen

Patrolmen's Benevolent Association
40 Fulton Street
New York, NY 10038
212-298-9193

Lobbyists:
Frank Tramontano

Clients:
Bank Street College of Education
Trial Lawyers Association

Pepe, Ross J
CIC of Westchester
629 Old White Plains Rd
Tarrytown, NY 10591-5100
914-631-6070

Clients:
Construction Industry Cncl of Westchester & Hudson Valley Inc

Perry Capital LLC
767 Fifth Ave
19th Floor
New York, NY 10153
212-583-4000

Lobbyists:
Doreen Mochrie

Perry, Edmund F.
International Business Machines Corp.
1301 K Street N.W.
Suite 1200
Washington, DC 20005-3307
202-515-5039

Lobbyists:
Rodney Atkins
Michael Cadigan
Marianne Cooper
Kathleen Ginn
Ambuj Goyal
Phillip Guido
Bronwyn Guthrie
Robert E. Hanson, Jr.
John Kelly

Offices and agencies generally appear in alphabetical order, except when specific order is requested by listee.

David Lederbach
Tim Mann
Lisa Mativi
Steve Mills
Ed Perry
Linda Sanford
John Teltsch
Brian Whitfield

Perry, Robert
CLU-NY
125 Broad St, 19th Fl
New York, NY 10004
212-607-3323

Clients:
Civil Liberties Union (NY)

Lobbyists:
Linda Berns
Andrea Callan
Corinne Carey
John Curr
Gary Dudup
Christopher Dunn
Arthur Eisenberg
Matt Faiella
Barrie Gewanter
Angela Jones
Tara Keenan-Thomas
Donna Lieberman
Socheaita Meng
Johanna Miller
Udi Ofer
Fidelia Orozco
Ari Rosmarin
Ami Sanghvi
Rahul Saskena
Galen Sherwin
Melanie Trimble
Ed Wasserman
Katharine Brodoe
Erica Braudy
Lisa LaPlace
Adriana Pinon
Ariel Samach

Pershing Square Capital Management L.P.
888 7th Ave
42nd Floor
New York, NY 10019
212-813-3700

Lobbyists:
Steve Symonds

Persons, Eric
2-212 Center for Science and Technology
Syracuse, NY 13244-4100
315-443-3919

Clients:
Syracuse University

Lobbyists:
Joseph Alfieri
Eric Beattie
Doug Biklen
Edward Bogucz
Nancy Cantor

D. Chase Catalano
Thomas Dennison
Bradley Ellis
William Eppel
Theodore Hagelin
J. Michael Haynie
Marilyn Higgins
George Langford
Gina Lee-Glauser
Deborah Meyer
Michael Morris
Diana Napolitano
Mary Pagan
Eric Persons
Marsha Senior
Abbott Sherburne
James Spencer
Eric Spina
Michael Sponsler
Kevin Sweder
Timothy Sweet
Joey Tse
Mary Ann Tyszko
Laura Welch
Mark Weldon

PFM Asset Management, LLC
Two Logan Square
18th & Arch Streets
Philadelphia, PA 19103
215-567-6100

Lobbyists:
Stephen Faber
Sarah Underer

Phillips Lytle
437 Madison Ave
New York, NY 10022
212-508-0470

Clients:
Stealth Communications Services LLC

Lobbyists:
David Bronston

Phillips Nizer, LLP
666 Fifth Ave
New York, NY 10103-0084
212-977-9700

Clients:
CSC Holdings, Inc

Lobbyists:
Kevin McGrath

Pioneer Savings Bank
21 Second Street
Troy, NY 12180
518-284-4800

Lobbyists:
Eileen Bagnoli
James McGlynn
Frank C. Sarratori
John Scarchilli
Thomas Thouin
Fonza Wells

Offices and agencies generally appear in alphabetical order, except when specific order is requested by listee.

Pitta, Bishop, Del Giorno & Giblin, LLC

111 Washington Avenue
Albany, NY 12210
518-449-3320

Lobbyists:
Carlos Beato
Robert Bishop
Mickey Cekovic
Theresa Cosgrove
Jon Del Giorno
Gordon Forbes
Vincent Giblin
Matthew Mataraso
Vincent Pitta
Vito Pitta

Plummer & Associates, LLC (FKA Griffin, Plummer & Associates)

61 Columbia Street
4th Floor
Albany, NY 12210-2736
518-463-5949

Clients:
Direct Marketing Association
Delaware Engineering
Funeral Directors Association (NYS)
General Electric Company
Genworth Financial
Greene County Coalition for Economic Equality
Hunter Mountain Ski Bowl
Schenectady Metroplex Development Authority
Momentive Performance Materials
Mutualink Inc
Railroads of New York

Lobbyists:
Daniel Plummer
Neil Plummer
Barrett Russell
Clyne Paul
Norman Schneider
Scott Wigger

Podiatric Medical Association (NYS)

1255 5th Avenue
New York, NY 10029
212-996-4400

Lobbyists:
Leonard Thaler

Police Benevolent Association of New York State

11 North Pearl St
Suite 1200
Albany, NY 12207
518-433-5472

Lobbyists:
Peter Barry
Robert Cavanagh
Dan Defedericis
Gary Friedrich
Mike Mabee
Jim McCartney
Bernie Rivers
Thomas Smith
Manny Vilar

Police Benevolent Assn of the NYS Troopers Inc

120 State St
Albany, NY 12207
518-462-7448
e-mail: nystpba@capital.net
Web site: www.nystpba.org

Clients:
Police Benevolent Assn of the NYS Troopers Inc

Lobbyists:
Thomas Mungeer
Daniel Sisto
Gordon Warnock

Police Conference of NY, Inc.

112 State Street
Suite 1120
Albany, NY 12207
518-462-7448

Lobbyists:
Dixon Palmer
Richard Wells

Powers & Company

90 State St, Ste 1422
Albany, NY 12207
518-431-0720
Web site: www.powerscompany.com

Clients:
BearingPoint
Boulevard ALP Associates
Broadcasters Assn (NYS)
Building Contractors Assn Inc
Colony Liquor & Wine Distributors, LLC
Computer Associates
Empire State Liquor Store Assn
Funding Source (The)
Glenwood Management Corporation
Hodgson Russ LLP
Law Enforcement Officers Union, Distr Cncl 82 (NYS)
Lincoln Center for the Performing Arts
Laborers PAC (NYS)
Motorola Inc
Oneida Tribe of Indians of Wisconsin (Power Plant Entertainment NY)
Pollard Banknote Limited
Pro Tech Monitoring Inc
PSCH Inc
Racing and Gaming Services Inc
Shaker Museum (The)
Siena College
Stratford Business Corp
Susan O'Dell Taylor School for Children
Trustco Bank
Verizon
WelchAllyn Inc
Wilmorite Holdings
Yankees Partnership (NY)

Lobbyists:
Don Clarey
Matthew Dillon
Matthew Dillion
Thomas J Murphy
James Natoli
Jose Paulino
Jason A Powers

Offices and agencies generally appear in alphabetical order, except when specific order is requested by listee.

Matthew Powers
William Powers
Paul W Zuber

Powers Global Strategies, LLC
353 Lexington Avenue
17th Floor
New York, NY 10016
212-582-0833

Clients:
3M Company
ACS State & Local Solutions Inc
ADT Security Services Inc
American Continental Properties Inc
BearingPoint Inc
Beth Israel Medical Center
C/S 12th Avenue LLC
HNTB, New York
Juniper Networks Inc
Long Island College Hospital (The)
P&O Ports North America Inc
St Luke's-Roosevelt Hospital Centers
Simpson & Brown Inc
Site-Blauvelt Engineers
Tishman Speyer Properties
United Parcel Service
Valeray Real Estate Co Inc
Veolia Water
World Trade Center Properties, LLC

Lobbyists:
Seth Kaye
Sylvia Ng
Peter Powers

Praxiis Business Advisors
6 North Main Street
Suite 107
Fairport, NY 14450
585-313-8690

Lobbyists:
Charles Lattuca

Presbyterian Hospital (NY)
C/O Milstein Hospital Building
177 Ft Washington Ave, MHB1-HS214
New York, NY 10032
212-305-4223

Clients:
Presbyterian Hospital (NY)

Lobbyists:
Julio Batista
Willa Brody
Mary Hanrahan
David Liss
Helen Morik
Violet Moss
Wayne Osten
Herbert Pardes, MD
William A Polf, PhD
Phillip Wilner, MD

Preservation League of NYS (FKA DiLorenzo, Jay)
44 Central Avenue
Albany, NY 12206

518-462-5658
Web site: www.preservenys.org

Lobbyists:
Jay Dilorenzo
Daniel Mackay

PriceWaterhouseCoopers LLP
677 Broadway
Albany, NY 12207
518-427-4552

Lobbyists:
Gerard Bielak
Adam Bowman
Stephen Cairns
Brian Castelli
Joseph Devita
Brendan Dougher
Patricia Duffy
Steven Elek
Ann Filiault
Steven Gurtman
David Lee
Worth MacMurray
David Mandelbaum
Stephen Mark Moore
John Mattie
Doug Mears
Christopher O'Brien
Patrick Pilch
Lisa Preddice
William Reidy
Raveen Roa
Gary Ryan
Michael Tosh
Christopher Turner
Robert Valletta
Andrew Ward
Tim Weld
Bradley Williams

Primary Care Development Corporation
22 Cortlandt Street
12th Floor
New York, NY 10007
212-437-3926

Lobbyists:
Ronda Kotelchuck
Daniel Lowenstein
Michelle Shaljian

Professional Agencies for Children's Therapy Services
90 State Street
Suite 700
Albany, NY 12207
518-591-4659

Lobbyists:
Steven Sanders

Promontory Interfinancial Network LLC
1515 North Courthouse Road
Suite 1200
Arlington, VA 22201
703-292-3400

Offices and agencies generally appear in alphabetical order, except when specific order is requested by listee.

Lobbyists:
Jason Blair
Don Daily
Pam Denson
Ed Dunkelberger
Steve Kinner
Doug Phillips

Property Casualty Insurers Association of America (PCI) (FKA O'Brien, Frank)
90 South Swan Street
Albany, NY 12210
518-443-2200

Lobbyists:
Paul Blume, Jr.
Frank O'Brien

Prospect Park Alliance
95 Prospect Park West
Brooklyn, NY 11215
718-965-8953

Lobbyists:
Eric Landau

Prudential Financial, Inc. (Formerly Michael F. McCann)
751 Broad Street
Newark, NJ 07102
973-367-3135
Web site: www.prudential.com

Lobbyists:
Maureen E. Adolf
Riva F. Kinstlick
Robert Montellione
Michael McCann
Barbara Rothermel
Lee F. Wood

Prudential Insurance Company of America (The) (Formerly John J. Kalamarides)
280 Trumbull Street
Hartford, CT 06103
973-367-3135
Web site: www.prudential.com

Lobbyists:
John Barrasso
Gabriel D'Ulisse
Mark Grier
Karen Hilenski
Robert Katz
Michael Knowling
Robert Luciani
Robert Moore
Frank Mursko
Jennifer Nichols
Glenn O'Brien
Marc Pester
Lisa Powell
Raymond Sweetland
Anton Tansil
Carl Wagner
William Walsh
Andrew Shainberg

Prudential Investment Management, Inc. (Formerly Bernard B. Winograd)
100 Mulberry Street
Gateway Center Three
Newark, NJ 07102
973-367-3135
Web site: www.prudential.com

Lobbyists:
Charles F. Lowrey
James T. Murphy
Kevin Myers
Miguel C. Thames
Cliff Axelson
Sara Bonesteel
Mark Hoffmeister
Miguel C. Thames
Allen Weaver

Public Campaign Action Fund
1133 19th Street NW
Suite 900
Washington, DC 20036
202-640-5600

Lobbyists:
Betty Ahrens
Jeanette Galanis
Nick Nyhart
Johnny Papagiannis
Monica Rober
Adam Smith

Public Financial Management, Inc.
60 Broad Street
New York, NY 10004
212-809-4212

Lobbyists:
Randall Bauer
Stephanie Belcher
John Cape
Victor Chu
Thomas Egan
Tracey Keays
James Lanham
Brett Mateo
Charles Matthews
Michael Nadol
Christopher Pak
Robert Rich
Geoffrey Stewart
Michael Thomashow
Scott Trommer
Anton Voinov
John F. White
Nancy Winkler

Public Interest Research Group (NY)
9 Murray Street
New York, NY 10007
212-349-6460

Lobbyists:
Ariana Basco
Alicia Aimer
Brian Bishop
Cathleen Breen
Emily Boerner

Offices and agencies generally appear in alphabetical order, except when specific order is requested by listee.

Ryan Bullerdick
Jason Chinfatt
Fran Clark
Brenden Colling
Benjamin Deangelis
Roger Drew
Alicia Elmer
Alex Freundlich
Stanley Fritz
Laura Haight
Russ Haven
Blair Horner
Alexandra Jean
Roberto Lobianco
Melissa Lynch
William Mahoney
Sarah Moeller
Tishima Moore
James Munro
Michael O'Connor
Nicole Phister
Lynn Radle
Neal Rosenstein
Gene Russianoff
Tracy Shelton
Chia-Chia Song
Joseph Stelling
Daniel Tome
Corey Torreto

Public Interest Research Group Fund, Inc. (New York)
9 Murray Street
3rd Floor
New York, NY 10007
212-349-6460

Lobbyists:
Laura Haight
Russ Haven
Blair Horner
Jeremiah Makarowski
Michael Romeo
Joe Stelling

Public Library, Astor, Lenox & Tilden Foundations (NY) (The)
5th Ave & 42nd St
New York, NY 10018-2788
212-930-0611

Clients:
Public Library, Astor, Lenox & Tilden Foundations (NY)

Lobbyists:
Catherine Dunn
Paul Leclerc

Public Welfare Assn (NY)
130 Washington Ave
Albany, NY 12210
518-465-9305
e-mail: nypwa@nycap.rr.com
Web site: www.nypwa.com

Clients:
Public Welfare Assn (NY)

Lobbyists:
Sheila Harrigan

Andrea Smyth

Pujolas, Elizabeth
9 Bellair Road
Boston, MA 02132
617-323-1175

Clients:
Medimmune, Inc.

Pullium, Daniel
75 Gerber Road East
South Windsor, CT 06074
860-644-4000

Clients:
TicketNetwork, Inc.

Lobbyists:
Natalie Carpenter

Purdue Pharma L.P.
One Stamford Forum
201 Tresser Blvd.
Stamford, CT 06901
203-588-8121

Lobbyists:
Mike McGlinn
Melissa Petro

Pyle & Associates, Inc.
PO Box 25001
Georgetown Station
Washington, DC 20027-8001
202-333-8190

Lobbyists:
Nicholas Pyle

Quantitative Management Associates LLC
100 Mulberry Street
Gateway Center Two
Newark, NJ 07102
973-367-3135

Lobbyists:
Bradford J. Allinson
Margaret S. Stumpp

Queens Chamber of Commerce
75-20 Astoria Blvd.
Suite 140
Jackson Heights, NY 11370
718-898-8500

Lobbyists:
Carol Conslato
Jack Friedman

Racing Association, Inc.
110-00 Rockaway Boulevard
New York, NY 11420
718-641-4700

Lobbyists:
Charles J. Kruzansky
David J. Skorton

Offices and agencies generally appear in alphabetical order, except when specific order is requested by listee.

RAI Services Company (FKA Reynolds American, Inc.)
P.O. Box
Winston-Salem, NC 27102
336-741-4500

Lobbyists:
Cassie Folk
David Powers

Ravitz, John
108 Corporate Park Drive
Suite 101
White Plains, NY 10604
914-948-2110

Clients:
Business Council of Westchester (The)

Lobbyists:
Marsha Gordon

Raustiala, Margaret
428 River Rd
Nissequogue, NY 11780
631-724-7767

Clients:
Alliance of Long Island Agencies

RBC Capital Markets (FKA RBC Dain Rausher)
677 Broadway
Suite 305
Albany, NY 12207
518-432-5071

Lobbyists:
Michael Baumrin
Thomas Berger
Peter Brodie
Thomas Cullinan
Daniel Hemowitz
Andrew Mendelson
John Puig

Real Estate Board of NY Inc
570 Lexington Ave
New York, NY 10022
212-532-3100
e-mail: jdoyle@rebny.com
Web site: www.rebny.com

Clients:
Real Estate Board of NY Inc

Lobbyists:
Marolyn Davenport
John Doyle
Shannon Fales
Brian Klimas
Michael Slattery
Steven Spinola
Carol Van Guilder

Real Rent Reform Campaign
C/O Metropolitan Council on Housing
339 Lafayette Street
Suite 301
New York, NY 10012

917-669-2977

Lobbyists:
Michael McKee

Red Land Strategy, Inc.
50 Meritoria Drive
East Williston, NY 11596
516-567-0345

Clients:
TEI Group

Lobbyists:
Michael Balboni

Reenergy Holdings LLC
30 Century Hill Drive
Suite 101
Latham, NY 12110
518-810-0200

Lobbyists:
Sarah Boggess

Rehabilitation Assn Inc (NYS)
155 Washington Ave, Ste 410
Albany, NY 12210-2332
518-449-2976
e-mail: nysra@nyrehab.org
Web site: www.nyrehab.org

Clients:
Rehabilitation Assn Inc (NYS)

Lobbyists:
Patricia Dowse
Jeffrey Wise

Related Companies, LP (The)
60 Columbus Circle
New York, NY 10023
212-421-5333

Lobbyists:
Bruce A. Beal, Jr.
Jeff T. Blau
Jay Cross
Glenn Goldstein
Gregory Gushee
Jay Kriegel
Stephen M. Ross
Avi Kollenscher
Michael Samuelian
Dean Vanderwarker

Related Fund Management LLC
60 Columbus Circle
New York, NY 10023
212-801-3392

Lobbyists:
Justin Metz

Rensselaer Polytechnic Institute
110 8th Street
2021
Troy, NY 12180-3590

Offices and agencies generally appear in alphabetical order, except when specific order is requested by listee.

518-276-8432

Lobbyists:
Erin Crotty
Craig Dory
Kevin Duggan
Shirley Jackson
Eddie Knowles
Russ Leslie
Ray Lutzky
Robert Mayo
Allison Newman
Mark Rea
Wolf Von Maltzahn
John Wen

Rent Stabilization Assn of NYC Inc
123 William St, 14th Fl
New York, NY 10038
212-214-9266

Clients:
Rent Stabilization Assn of NYC Inc

Lobbyists:
Jack Freund
Jacqueline Monterosso
Mitchell Posilkin
Frank P Ricci
Joseph Strasburg

Repas, Peter G
33 Elk St
Albany, NY 12207
518-462-1590
e-mail: apbs@wxxi.org

Clients:
Assn of Public Broadcasting Stations of NY

Retired Public Employees Association, Inc.
435 New Karner Road
Albany, NY 12205-3858
618-869-2542

Lobbyists:
Michael Fitzgerald

RG Group
One Penn Plaza
36th Floor
New York, NY 10119
212-786-7627

Clients:
Benjamin Partners, Inc.
Building Owners and Managers Association of Greater New York, Inc.
Charleston Equities LLC
Computer Aid, Inc.
Dell Public Sector, Inc.
Edgewater Industrial Park LLC
Hunter College
PEC Group of NY, Inc.
Technology Enterprise Corporation
Triangle Enterprise Development Company LLC

Lobbyists:
Catherine Giuliani
Alan Rosenberg

Richardson Management
295 Main Street
Suite 214
Buffalo, NY 14203
716-854-2400

Lobbyists:
Richard Winter

Riddell Group, LLC (The)
119 Washington Avenue, 2nd Floor
Albany, NY 12210
518-434-7400

Lobbyists:
Michael Houseknecht
Glenn Riddell

Riddett Associates, Inc. (FKA Riddett, Kenneth E. Associates Inc.)
PO Box 7141
Albany, NY 12224
518-225-9986

Lobbyists:
Kenneth Riddett

Riddle, Gary
7 Willway Avenue
Richmond, VA 23226
804-450-0965

Clients:
EISAI, Inc.

Ridge Policy Group LLC
1140 Connecticut Avenue NW
Suite 510
Washington, DC 20036
202-480-8093

Clients:
Transcore

Lobbyists:
Mark Holman

Right to Life Committee Inc (NYS)
41 State St. M-100
Albany, NY 12207
518-434-1293
e-mail: lhougens1@aol.com
Web site: www.nysrighttolife.org

Clients:
Right to Life Committee Inc (NYS)

Lobbyists:
Debra J. Cody
Lori Kehoe

Roarke, Robert R.
Wilson Elser, Moskowitz,
Edelman and Dicker, LLP
150 East 42nd Street
New York, NY 10017
212-490-3000

Offices and agencies generally appear in alphabetical order, except when specific order is requested by listee.

Lobbyists:
Peter Lauricella
Theresa Marangas
Theresa Russo
Cynthia Shenker

Robinson & Cole LLP
885 Third Avenue
Suite 2800
New York, NY 10022-4944
212-451-2900

Lobbyists:
Andrew S. Roffe
Christine Rutigliano

Rochester Business Alliance, Inc.
150 State Street
Suite 400
Rochester, NY 14614-1308
585-256-4627

Lobbyists:
Colleen DiMartino
Brian Sampson
Chris West

Ronald Poppel
32 Regatta View Drive
Saratoga Springs, NY 12866
518-583-4986

Clients:
Bristol-Myers Squibb Company

Rooney, Timothy J.
C/O Yonkers Raceway
Yonkers & Central Aves.
Yonkers, NY 10704
914-968-4200

Lobbyists:
Robert J. Galterio
Wayne Smith

Rosenthal, Harvey
One Columbia Place
2nd Floor
Albany, NY 12207
518-436-0008

Clients:
Association of Psychiatric Rehabilitation Services

Royal Realty Corp.
One Bryant Park
New York, NY 10036
212-257-6600

Lobbyists:
Jordan Barowitz

Rreef America LLC
535 Anton Blvd
Suite 200
Costa Mesa, CA 92626
415-262-2003

Lobbyists:
Terry Doyle
Laura Gaylord
Todd Henderson

Rubin, Jamie Lyn
5001 Angel Canyon Road
Kanab, UT 84741
435-644-2001

Clients:
Best Friends Animal Society

Rubin, Kate
860 Courtlandt Ave
Bronx, NY 11230
718-838-7869

Clients:
Bronx Defenders

Lobbyists:
Kamau Butcher
Emma Ketteringham
Molly Kovel
Justine Olderman
Seann Riley
J. McGregor Smyth
Alexandra St. Charles
Robin Steinberg
Joanna Zuckerman-Bernstein

Runes, Richard
3 Kirby Ln N
Rye, NY 10580
212-457-9679
e-mail: rrunes@amlaw.com

Clients:
American Lawyer Media

Russo, Michael
107 Hermes Rd.
Suite 200
Malta, NY 12020
518-305-9023

Clients:
GlobalFoundries US, Inc.

Rutnik Law Firm (The)
80 State St, 9th Fl
Albany, NY 12207
518-436-9646

Clients:
DMJM & Harris Inc
Genentech Inc

Lobbyists:
Douglas P Rutnik

Ryan, Desmond
150 Motor Pkwy, Ste LL60
Hauppauge, NY 11772
631-951-2410

Clients:
Alliance of Long Island Agencies

Offices and agencies generally appear in alphabetical order, except when specific order is requested by listee.

Bethpage Federal Credit Union
Stop & Shop Supermarket Co (The)

Safe Horizon, Inc.
2 Lafayette Street
New York, NY 10007
212-577-7735

Lobbyists:
Nancy Arnow
Shonnie Ball
Pilar Bernabe
Christian W. Burgess
Cecilia Castelino
Lydia Colon-Fores
Marsha Genwright
Arthur Goodman
Bea Hanson
Alice Hawks
Jennifer Kob
Susan Loeb
Erika Miller
Lynn Neugebauer
J. Bukurije Pirane
Michael Polenberg
Myra Shapiro
Nancy Shea
Danny Stewart
Lac Tran
Michele Vigeant
Kathy Wickham
Michael Williams
Ariel Zwang

Sampson, Rick J
Restaurant Association (NYS)
409 New Karner Rd
Albany, NY 12205
518-452-4222
e-mail: ricks@nysra.org
Web site: www.nysra.org

Clients:
Restaurant Assn (NYS)

Lobbyists:
Melissa Fleischut
E Charles Hunt

Samuel A. Ramirez & Co., Inc.
61 Broadway
29th Floor
New York, NY 10006
212-248-0525

Lobbyists:
Amy Bartoletti
Ryan Donovan
Nicholas Fluehr
Robert Foran
Daniel Keating
Robert Pattison
Frederick Putnam
Samuel Ramirez
Theodore Sobel
Richard Tilghman
John Young

Sanctuary for Families
P.O. Box 1406
Wall Street Station
New York, NY 10268-1406
212-349-6009
Web site: www.sanctuaryforfamilies.org

Lobbyists:
Molly Bowen
Elizabeth Brownback
Yijen Scarlett Chang
Betty Chen
Elisandro De La Cruz
Julie Dinnerstein
Laurel W. Eisner
Helene Feldman
Jill Fernandez
Brett Figlewski
Carolien Hardenbol
Veronique Harvey
Colleen Hodgetts
Vivian Huelgo
Dorchen Leidholdt
Linda Lopez
Loretta McCarthy
Ted McCourtney
Sonia Monsoor
Krystle Montalvo
Avideh Moussavian
Lisa Mueller
Noreen Muhib
Romona Mukjerjee
Amanda Norejko
Sophia Pazos
Allison Rose
Catherine Shurgrue Dos Santos
Beth Silverman-Yam
Andrew Sta. Ana
Betsy Tsai
Diana Urquhart
Willie Werwaiss
John Wyeht

Sanzillo, Francis J. & Associates
130 Washington Avenue
Albany, NY 12203
914-448-0199

Lobbyists:
Francis Sanzillo

Saratoga Harness Racing, Inc.
P.O. Box 356
342 Jefferson Street
Saratoga Springs, NY 12866
518-584-2110

Clients:
Gaming Association, Inc.

Lobbyists:
George Carlson
Rita Cox
Daniel Gerrity
James Hartman

SAS Institute, Inc.
100 SAS Campus Drive
Cary, NC 27513

Offices and agencies generally appear in alphabetical order, except when specific order is requested by listee.

919-531-5865

Lobbyists:
Arielle Bernstein
Tim Finnegan
Jeremy Racine

Scenic Hudson Inc
One Civic Center Plaza
Ste 200
Poughkeepsie, NY 12601-3157
845-473-4440
e-mail: wreiss@scenichudson.org
Web site: www.scenichudson.org

Clients:
Scenic Hudson Inc

Lobbyists:
John Anzevino
Andrew Bicking
James Burgess
Raymond Curran
Margery Groten
Charles Laing
Donna Lenhart
Seth Martel
Maryanne McGovern
Seth McKee
Althea Mullarkey
Ivy Reeves
Warren Reiss
Steven Rosenberg
Rita Shaheen
James Slaughter
Reed Sparling
Sacha Spector
Edward O Sullivan
Jason Taylor
Cari Watkins-Bates

Schillo, John
14954 Madison Street NE
Ham Lake, MN 55304
763-413-5113

Clients:
Lundbeck Pharmaceutical Services LLC

Schlein, Stanley Esq.
481 King Ave
Bronx, NY 10464
917-359-3186

Clients:
Bronx Museum
Daimler Chrysler Corporation
Easton Bell Sports
Exxon Mobil Corporation
Hall of Sciences (NY)
SAS Institute Inc
Women's Housing & Economic Development Corporation

Schmidt, James A.
East River Realty Company, LLC
9 West 57th Street
New York, NY 10019
212-715-0293

Lobbyists:
James A. Schmidt

Schnell, William A & Associates Inc
51 E Main Street, 2nd Fl
Smithtown, NY 11787
631-724-6569
e-mail: wmasainc@earthlink.net

Clients:
Amusement & Music Owners Assn of NY
Federation of Organizations Inc
Long Island Gasoline Retailers Assn Inc
SDR Pharmaceuticals Inc
Securitas
Suffolk County Ambulance Chiefs Assoc
Suffolk County Deputy Sheriff's Police Benevolent Assn

Lobbyists:
William A Schnell

Schnur Associates, Inc.
1350 Avenue of the Americas
Suite 1200
New York, NY 10019
212-489-0600

Lobbyists:
Joel Schnur

Schomberg, Dora
P.O. Box 8832
Albany, NY 12208
518-478-9760

Clients:
Humane Society of the United States (The)

School Administrators Association of NYS
8 Airport Park Blvd
Latham, NY 12110
518-782-0600

Clients:
School Administrators Association of NYS

Lobbyists:
William Adam
Santo Barbarino
Paul Berkheimer
Roberto Calderin
Joyce Carr
Kevin Casey
Marystephanie Corsones
Paul Gasparini
Peter Griffin
Carrie Harvey-Zales
Shannon Karazuba
Lawrence King
Frederick Kirsch
Linda Klime
Elizabeth Mascitti-Miller
Frank McDermott
George Montone
Linda Mulvey
Don Nickson
Brian Nolan
Nancy Noonan
Tom O'Brien

Offices and agencies generally appear in alphabetical order, except when specific order is requested by listee.

Greg Paterniti
Maureen Patterson
Jennie Pennington
Deborah Price
Deborah Rider
Kevin Sheehan
Elisabeth Smith
Jeff Spiro
Jerry Tagliaferri
Robert Thomann
Richard Tomlinson
Bonnie Tryon
James Viola

School Boards Assn (NYS)
24 Century Hill Dr
Latham, NY 12110
518-783-0200
e-mail: nyssba@nyssba.org
Web site: www.nyssba.org

Lobbyists:
Francine Campbell
Michael Fox
Meghana Godambe
Timothy Kremer
David Little
Thomas Nespeca
Jay Worona

Schuh, Paul
35 George Karl Blvd
Suite 100
Amherst, NY 14221
716-632-1540

Clients:
UAW Region 9

Schuyler Center for Analysis & Advocacy
150 State Street
4th Floor
Albany, NY 12207
518-463-1896

Lobbyists:
Robin Christenson
Diane Mastin
Jenn O'Connor
Karen Schimke
Bridget Walsh

Scotts Miracle-Gro Company
14111 Scottslawn Road
Marysville, OH 43041
937-644-7606

Lobbyists:
Ann Aquillo
Jeff Garascia
Richard Shank
Chris Wible

Securities Industry & Financial Markets Association
120 Broadway
35th Floor
New York, NY 10271
212-313-1233

Lobbyists:
Marin Gibson
Nancy Lancia

Seneca Nation of Indians
12837 Route 438
Irving, NY 14801
716-532-4900

Lobbyists:
Mike John
Robert Porter
Peter Colavito

Shanahan Group
4019 County Rte 21
Schodack Landing, NY 12156
518-732-3312
e-mail: tom@shanahangroup.com
Web site: www.shanahangroup.com

Clients:
Guide Dog Foundation for the Blind Inc
Irrigation Assn of New York
Long Island Water Conference
Rural Water Assn (NY)
Suffolk County Water Authority

Lobbyists:
Thomas Shanahan

Shank, Suzanne
C/O Siebert Brandford Shank & Co., LLC
100 Wall St.
22nd Floor
New York, NY 10005
646-775-4841

Lobbyists:
Address Appolon
John Carter
Jonathan White
Sanna Wong-Chen
John Zurlo

Shapiro, Brian
P.O. Box 1111
Woodstock, NY 12498
845-707-5350

Clients:
Humane Society of the United States (The)

Sheehan Green Carraway Golderman & Jacques LLP
54 State Street
Suite 1001
Albany, NY 12207
518-462-0110

Lobbyists:
Jacques Keith

Sheinkopf, Ltd
152 Madison Ave
Ste 1603
New York, NY 10016
212-725-2378

Offices and agencies generally appear in alphabetical order, except when specific order is requested by listee.

Clients:
Committee to Save St Brigid's

Lobbyists:
Hank Sheinkopf
Henry A Sheinkopf

Shelter Rock Strategies, LLC
300 Garden City Plaza
4th Floor
Garden City, NY 11530
516-294-4000

Lobbyists:
Henry Berger
Douglas Forand
Thomas Garry
Marc Lapidus
Steven Schlesinger
Nathan Smith

Sherin, James R.
C/O Retail Council of NYS
258 State Street
PO Box 1992
Albany, NY 12210-1992
518-465-3586

Lobbyists:
Milissa Googas
Edward Potrikus

Lobbyists:
Lawrence Curtis
Joseph Eddy
Michael Putziger
Gilbert Winn

Siconolfi, Patrick
377 Broadway
3rd Floor
New York, NY 10013
212-838-7442

Siena College
515 Loudon Road
Office of Government Relations
Loudonville, NY 12211-1462
518-783-2307

Lobbyists:
Alfredo Medina Jr.
Fr. Kevin Mullen, OFM

Simons & Wright LLC
500 Fifth Avenue
Suite 1610
New York, NY 10110
646-370-3689

Clients:
Morgan B. Realty LLC

Lobbyists:
Emily Simons

Skybridge Capital II LLC
527 Madison Avenue
16th Floor
New York, NY 10022
212-485-3100

Lobbyists:
Peter Carey

Slippen, Daniel
Central Park West & 79th Street
New York, NY 10024-5192
212-769-5033

Clients:
American Museum of Natural History

Lobbyists:
Ellen Futter
Lisa Gugenheim

Smith, Joseph
38 Westbrook Road
Newburgh, NY 12550
845-522-0801

Clients:
Arent Fox LLP
Choice Self Insurance Trust
FCS Administrators, Inc.
Gardere Wynne Sewell LLP
Niagara Business Trust

Smith, Robert
Farm Credit East, ACA
2668 State Rte 7, Ste 21
Cobleskill, NY 12043-9707
518-296-8188

Clients:
First Pioneer Farm Credit ACA

Smyth, A Advocacy
130 Washington Ave, Ste A
Albany, NY 12210
518-426-8354
e-mail: asmyth@capital.net

Lobbyists:
Andrea Smyth

Sobol, Peter
328 A Wanser Avenue
Inwood, NY 11096
516-371-3882

Lobbyists:
Peter Sobol

Society of CPA's
3 Park Avenue
18th Floor
New York, NY 10016
212-719-8300

Lobbyists:
Joanne Barry
Ernest Markezin

Offices and agencies generally appear in alphabetical order, except when specific order is requested by listee.

Bradley Pryba

Solar Energy Industries Association
P.O. Box 534
Scituate, MA 02060
617-688-9417

Lobbyists:
Carrie Hitt

Solowan, Richard
GEICO
One Geico Plaza
Washington, DC 20076
301-986-3948
e-mail: rsolowan@geico.com

Clients:
Government Employees Insurance Co (GEICO)

Soloway, Ronald
155 Washington Ave
Albany, NY 12210
518-436-1091
e-mail: solowayr@ujafedny.org
Web site: www.ujafedny.org

Clients:
United Jewish Appeal Federation - Jewish Philanthropies NY

Lobbyists:
Anita Altman
Chantall Askins
Cara Berkowitz
Allison Grant
Edie Mesick
John Ruskay

Solus Alternative Asset Management LP
410 Park Ave
11th Floor
New York, NY 10022
212-284-4300

Lobbyists:
Janice Yu

Southern Tier Independence Center
135 East Frederick Street
Binghamton, NY 13904
607-724-2111

Lobbyists:
Thea Arnold
Danny Cullen
Robert Deemie
Ken Dibble
Maria Dibble
Darlene Dickinson
Jonathan Dollhopf
Kami Giglio
Sue Hoyt
Margret Hurlbert
Jody Kenyon
Charles Kramer
Susan Link
Jane Long
Cynthia Meredith
Joanne Novicky

Frank Pennisi
Jeff Rogers
Sue Ruff
Peg Schadt
Jennifer Watson

Starwood Capital LLC
591 West Putnam Avenue
Greenwich, CT 06830
203-422-7775

Lobbyists:
Jerome Silvey
Lanhee Yung

State & Broadway, Inc.
21 Elk Street
Albany, NY 12207
518-729-4555

Lobbyists:
Kristen Ruggles
Lawrence Scherer
Jacqueline Williams
John Wright

State Advisers, LLC
113 State Street
Albany, NY 12207
516-776-1500

Lobbyists:
Keith D. Sernick

State University of New York at Potsdam
44 Pierrepont Avenue
Potsdam, NY 13676-2294
315-267-2190

Lobbyists:
William Fisher
Sherry Paradis
Galen Pletcher
John Schwaller
Vicki Templeton-Cornell
Elizabeth Tuttle

State University of New York at Stony Brook
Administration Building
Room 310
Stony Brook, NY 11794-0701
631-632-6302

Lobbyists:
Peter Baigent
Bridget Baio
Henry Bokuniewicz
Ruth Brandwein
Helen Carrano
Marie Chandick
Barbara Chernow
Lisa Clark
Ellen Cohen
David Conover
Virginia Cover
Paul Edelson
Diane Fabel
Suzanne Fields
Chris Filstrup

Offices and agencies generally appear in alphabetical order, except when specific order is requested by listee.

Richard Fine
James Fiore
Deborah Firestone
Patricia Gilbert
Ray Goldstein
Mary Graves
Karol Gray
Gail Habicht
Gary Halada
Vanessa Herman
Mary Hotaling
Eric Kaler
Evonne Kaplan
Susan Katz
Theresa Leonard
John Lutterbie
Monica Mahaffey
Robert McGrath
Jennifer McMahon
Mario Mignone
Mary Pearl
John Pomeroy
Joe Puccio
Joseph Scaduto
Wolf Schaefer
Mark Sedler
Fred Sganga
Shetal Shah
Yacov Shamash
Denise Snow
Jonathan Spier
Samuel Stanley
Steven Strongwater
Larry Swanson
Bruce Teifer
Carlos Vidal
Lawrence Weber

State University of NY, System Administration

State University Plaza
Albany, NY 12246
518-443-5355

Lobbyists:
Pedro Caban
James Campbell
Johanna Duncan-Poitier
Dennis Golladay
Stacey Hengsterman
David Lavallee
Carlos Medina
John O'Connor
Monica Rimai
Nicholas Rostow
Michael Trunzo
Philip Wood
Nancy Zimpher

Stendardi, Deborah M

30 Lomb Memorial Dr
Rochester, NY 14534-5604
585-475-5040
e-mail: dmsgrl@rit.edu

Clients:
Rochester Institute of Technology

Lobbyists:
William Destler
Cynthia Gray

Nabil Nasr

Strategic Services, Inc

170 E Post Rd, Ste 207B
White Plains, NY 10601
914-946-8400

Clients:
City of Mount Vernon
Westchester Jewish Community Services

Lobbyists:
Arnold Linhardt

Stroock & Stroock & Lavan LLP

180 Maiden Lane
New York, NY 10038-4982
212-806-5400
Web site: www.strook.com

Lobbyists:
Glenn Borin
Leonard Boxer
Robert M. Fettman
Joseph B. Giminaro
Joon Kim
Penny Levine
Martin Minkowitz
Ross F. Moskowitz
Hon. Stanley Parness
Susan Shaw
Richard Siegler
E. Gail Suchman
Eva Talel

Stryker, Patricia

International Brotherhood of Teamsters
C/O Local 237
216 W 14th St.
New York, NY 10011
212-924-2000

Clients:
Teamsters Local 237

Stuto, Diane D

111 Washington Ave, Ste 300
Albany, NY 12210
518-436-8417
Web site: www.licony.org

Clients:
Life Insurance Council of NY Inc

Lobbyists:
John Kisson
Jana Lee Pruitt
Timothy A. Walsh
Thomas E Workman

SUNY College of Environmental Science and Forestry (FKA Micheal Brower)

C/O Suny College of Environmental
Science & Forestry
1 Forestry Drive
Syracuse, NY 13210-2778
315-470-6681

Offices and agencies generally appear in alphabetical order, except when specific order is requested by listee.

Lobbyists:
Maureen Fellows
Cornelius Murphy

SUNY Fredonia
272 Central Avenue
Fredonia, NY 14063
716-673-3321

Lobbyists:
Dennis Hefner
Timothy Murphy

SUNY Upstate Medical University
750 East Adams Street
Syracuse, NY 13210
315-464-4832
Web site: www.upstate.edu

Lobbyists:
Steven Brady
Daniel Hurley
Phillip Schaengold
David Smith

Supportive Housing Network of New York, Inc.
247 West 37th Street
18th Floor
New York, NY 10018
646-619-9640

Lobbyists:
Nicole Branca
Ted Houghton
Hilary Morgan
Stephen Piasecki

Taxpayers for Economic Justice, Inc. (NY)
P.O. Box 4543
New York, NY 10136
888-472-1555

Lobbyists:
Steven Day
Raymond Desposito
Richard Giliotti
Linda Isaacson
Robert Schmidlin
Sal Turano
John Welling
Charles Wimer

Technology Enterprise Corporation (NYS)
500 Avery Lane
Suite A
Griffis Industrial Park
Rome, NY 13441
315-338-5818

Lobbyists:
Jana Behe
Michael Donovan
William Pirillo
Michael Walsh

Thomson Strategies, LLC
61-23 190 Street
Suite 531
Fresh Meadows, NY 11365
718-487-3375

Lobbyists:
Terri Thomson

Time Warner Cable
120 East 23 Street
Att: Nina Facini (9th Floor)
New York, NY 10010
212-598-7223

Lobbyists:
Steve Arvan
Marion Boykin
Nickolas Darling
Thomas Doheny
Mark Dunford
John Fogarty
Sharon Hanson
John Keib
Brien Kelley
John Mucha
Chris Mueller
Harriet Novet
Brenda Parks
John Quigley
Terrence Rafferty
Whelan Rory
Howard Szarfarc
Peter Taubin
Jeff Unaitis
Roger Wells
David Whalen
Charles Williams III
Robin Wolfgang

Tishman Speyer Properties, L.P.
45 Rockefeller Plaza
New York, NY 10111
212-593-9480

Lobbyists:
George Hatzmann

TLM Associates LLC
233 Broadway, Suite 702
New York, NY 10007
646-467-8536

Lobbyists:
Jean Kim
Thomas McMahon
Ian Riley-Clendened

Tommasino, Nicholas
Deloitte & Touche LLP
1633 Broadway
New York, NY 10019
212-492-3746

Lobbyists:
Greg Durant
John Fogarty
Lawrence Kramer

Offices and agencies generally appear in alphabetical order, except when specific order is requested by listee.

Political Parties,
Lobbyists & PACs

Donal O'Callaghan
Kelly Saunders
Beth A. Schneider
Lisa Tracy Smith

Tourism Industry Coalition (TIC)
80 Wolf Road
Albany, NY 12205
518-465-2300

Lobbyists:
Daniel C. Murphy

Lobbyists:
Peter Goldwasser
Lindsey Lusher-Shute
Paul Steely White

Tranter Jr. G. Thomas
C/O Corning Incorporated
MP-BH-06
Corning, NY 14831
607-974-7818

Clients:
Corning Incorporated

Trial Lawyers Association (NYS) (FKA Feldman, Daniel)
C/O Trial Lawyers Association (NYS)
132 Nassau Street
New York, NY 10038
212-349-5890

Lobbyists:
Anna Adler
Joseph Awad
Richard Binko
David Golomb
Martin Edelman
Jeffrey Lichtman
Nicholas Papain
Lawrence Park
Tara Quinlan

Tribeca Film Institute
375 Greenwich Street
New York, NY 10013
212-941-2427

Lobbyists:
Beth Janson

Trustees of Columbia University in the City of NY (The)
535 West 116th St
302 Low Library
New York, NY 10027
212-854-3738

Clients:
Trustees of Columbia University in the City of NY (The)

Lobbyists:
Lee Bollinger
Alan Brinkley
Loftin Flowers
Ross Frommer
Lee Goldman
Lisa Hogarty
Maxine Griffith

Victoria Hamilton
Sandra Harris
David Hirsch
Lisa Hogarty
Joseph Ienuso
Howard Jacobson
Robert Kasdin
Dolores Kreisman
Ira Lamster
Jeffrey Lieberman
Victoria Mason-Ailey
Philip Pitruzzello
Jeffrey Sachs
Philip Silverman
Anne Sullivan
Marcelo Velez

Turner, Francine
Civil Service Employees PAC
143 Washington Ave
Albany, NY 12210
518-436-8622
e-mail: turner@cseainc.org

Clients:
Civil Service Employees Political Action Fund

Lobbyists:
Adam Acquario
John Belmont
Courtney Brunelle
Matthew D'Amico
Kelley Johnson
Bryan Miller
Ricky Noreault
Cody Peluso
Gretchen Penn
Robert Scholz
Joshua Terry
William Walsh

Tyson, Lisa
90 Pennsylvania Ave
Massapequa, NY 11758-4978
516-541-1006
e-mail: lisa@lipc.org
Web site: www.lipc.org

Clients:
Long Island Progressive Coalition

U.S. Green Building Council, New York Chapter
20 Broad Street
Suite 709
New York, NY 10005
212-514-9380

Lobbyists:
Richard Leigh
Jonah Cecil""
Russell Unger

UCB, Inc.
1950 Lake Park Drive
Smyrna, GA 30080
770-970-8949

Lobbyists:
Dale Aldrich

Offices and agencies generally appear in alphabetical order, except when specific order is requested by listee.

Ungar, Robert A Associates Inc

200 Garden City Plaza
Ste 201
Garden City, NY 11530
516-227-2400
e-mail: fireandems@aol.com

Clients:
Assn of Plumbing Heating Cooling Contractors Inc (NYS)
Building & Construction Trades Council (NYS)
Building & Construction Trades Council of Greater NY
Building Contractors' Assn, Inc
Building Trades Employers' Assn
Civil Svc Technical Guild, Local 375 DC-37, AFSCME AFL-CIO
Council of Administrators & Supervisors
Local 3, IBEW Communications Electricians
Local 246, SEIU
Nassau County PHCC
Plumbing Contractors Assn of Long Island Inc
Plumbing Foundation City of NY Inc
Purvis Systems Inc
Service Station Dealers of Greater NY, Inc
TBTA Maintenance Employees, Local 1931, DC-37, AFSCME
Uniformed EMT's & Paramedics, Local 2507-FDNY
Uniformed Fire Alarm Dispatchers Benevolent Assn-FDNY
Uniformed Firefighters Assn

Lobbyists:
Robert A Ungar

Uniformed Firefighters Association

204 E 23rd St.
New York, NY 10010
212-683-4832

Lobbyists:
Stephen Cassidy
James Slevin

United Healthcare Services, Inc.

UnitedHealth Group
284 State Street
Albany, NY 12210
518-432-0893

Clients:
United Healthcare Services, Inc

Lobbyists:
Jeffrey Alter
William Goldman
Carolyn Kerr
Carl Mattson
Judah Sommer

United Neighborhood Houses of NY

70 West 36th Street
5th Floor
New York, NY 10018-8007
212-967-0322

Lobbyists:
Clara Botstein
Gregory Brender
Anthony Ng
Susan Stamler
Carin Tinney
Nancy Wackstein

University at Albany (FKA Williams, Charlie)

C/O University at Albany
1400 Washington Avenue
UNH 302
Albany, NY 12222
518-956-8010
Web site: www.albany.edu

Lobbyists:
Stephen Beditz
Kristin Christodulu
Jose Cruz
Vincent Delio
James Diaz
Michael Fancher
Alain Kaloyeros
Brian Keough
Kim Clifford
George Phillip
Susan Phillips
Stephanie Wacholder

University of Rochester

601 Elmwood Avenue
Box 706
Rochester, NY 14642
585-273-5955

Lobbyists:
Nancy Bennett
Bradford Berk
Raffaella Borasi
Jonathan Burdick
Eric Caine
Rob Clark
Glenn Currier
Tony Dechario
Joshua Farrelman
Richard Fisher
Steven Goldstein
Michael Goonan
David Guzick
Amy Happ
Victoria Hines
Grant Holcomb
Allen Ibrisimovic
Katrina Korfmacher
Ralph Kuncl
Peter Lennie
Douglas Lowry
Theresa Mazzullo
Colleen McCarthy
Robert McCrory
Cyril Meyerowitz
Charles Murphy
Mark Noble
Ronald Paprocki
Kathy Parker
Kathy Parrinello
Douglas Phillips
Richard Pifer
Peter Robinson
Joel Seligman
Gaurav Sharma
Leonard Shute
Sue Stewart
Mary Tantillo
Mary Taubman
Barry Watkins

Offices and agencies generally appear in alphabetical order, except when specific order is requested by listee.

Upstate Consultants
80 Oakland Place
Buffalo, NY 14222
716-432-3602
e-mail: gregsehr@aol.com

Clients:
Catholic Health System
Gateway-Longview Inc
Kissling Interests, LLC

Lobbyists:
Gregory Sehr

Upstate Niagara Cooperative (FKA Upstate Farms Cooperative)
25 Anderson Rd
Buffalo, NY 14225
716-892-3156

Lobbyists:
Timothy Harner
Kimberly Pickard-Dudley
Thomas Rodak
William Young

Urban Justice Center
123 William Street
16th Floor
New York, NY 10012
646-602-5600

Lobbyists:
Sean Basinski
Madeline Garcia Bigelow
Molly Biklen
Jonathan Cohen
David Colodny
Jim Dike
Harvey Epstein
Shannon Ferguson
Susan Hazeldean
April Herms
Doug Lasdon
Bill Leinhard
Anya Mukarji-Connolly
Gerni Oster
Jennifer Parish
Thomas Renyak

Vantagepoint Management, Inc.
1001 Bayhill Drive
Suite 300
San Bruno, CA 94066
650-866-3100

Lobbyists:
J. Stephan Dolezalek
Stephen D. Gray
Robert F. Kennedy, Jr.
Patricia M. Roboostoff
Alan E. Salzman

Venable LLP
1270 Avenue of the Americas
24th Floor
New York, NY 10020
212-307-5500

Clients:
USTA/National Tennis Center, Inc.

Lobbyists:
Gordon Davis
Susan Golden

Vera Institute of Justice, Inc.
233 Broadway
12th Floor
New York, NY 10279
212-334-1300
Web site: www.vera.org

Lobbyists:
Adrienne Austin
Jean Callahan
Siobhan Carney
Jintana Chiu
Roohi Choudhry
Reagan Daly
Evan Elkin
Elizabeth Elston
Jennifer Fratello
Megan Golden
Karen Goldstein
Alexandra Hezir
Michael Jacobsen
Krista Larson
Peggy Ann McGarry
Joan Meyer
Sara Mogulescu
James Parsons
Celine Quashie
Oren Root
Timothy Ross
Ann Salsich
Danielle Sered
Susan Shah
Alison Shames
Andrea Snelson
Stacy Strongarone
Neil Weiner
Daniel Wilhelm
Michael Woodruff

Verizon
140 West Street
Floor 30
New York, NY 10007
518-396-1086

Clients:
Verizon

Lobbyists:
Richard Bozsik
John Butler
Sam Caldwell
Keefe Clemons
Catherine Gasteyer
April Horton
Andres Irlando
June Jee
Kathleen Kittrick
Czykanne Kowal
David Lamendola
Patrick Lespinasse
Eileen Mannion
Maureen Rasp-Glose

Offices and agencies generally appear in alphabetical order, except when specific order is requested by listee.

Sandra Wilson
Richard Windram
Susanna Zwerling

Vertex Pharmaceuticals, Inc.
130 Waverly Stret
Cambridge, MA 02139
617-444-6100

Lobbyists:
Gina Black
Mark Thomas O'Rourke

Vidal Group, LLC (The)
90 South Swan Street
Suite 112
Albany, NY 12210
518-434-5856

Clients:
ALM Medica Inc
American College of Occupational Environmental Medicine
Circulo De La Hispanidad
Earthwatch LTD
Hispanic Counseling Center Inc
Hispanic Federation
Hispanic Information Telecommunications Network
Latino Commission on AIDS
Glenwood Management Corporation
Oasis Children's Service LLC
Rain Inc
Partnership for NYC
Sepracor

Lobbyists:
Mary Briwa
Glen Casey
Jennifer Muthig
Alfredo Vidal

Village Care of New York, Inc.
154 Christopher Street
New York, NY 10014
212-337-5601

Lobbyists:
Emma Devito
Matthew Lesieur

Vista Equity Partners III LLC
150 California Street
19th Floor
San Francisco, CA 94111
415-765-6500

Lobbyists:
Brian Sheth
Robert Smith
Martin Taylor
John Warnken-Brill

Vornado Realty Trust
210 Route 4 East
Paramus, NJ 07652
201-587-1000

Lobbyists:
Kate Ascher

Michael Fascitelli
David Greenbaum
Barry Langer
Sandeep Mathrani
Myron Mauer
Steven Roth

Vose, Margie
500 Salem Street
Smithfield, RI 02917-0000
401-292-6515

Clients:
Fidelity Investments Institutional Services Company, Inc.

Lobbyists:
Marissa Hedge
Steve Johnson
Edward Schollmeyer

Wachtel & Masyr, LLP
110 East 59th Street
27th Floor
New York, NY 10022
212-909-9500
Web site: www.wmllp.com

Clients:
Ascent Real Estate Advisors
Blumenfeld Development Group
Botanical Garden (NY) (The)
Related Companies, LP (The)
Thor Properties, LLC (Acquisitions)

Lobbyists:
Ethan Goodman
Jerald Johnson
Raymond Levin
Jesse Masyr

Wal-Mart Stores, Inc.
702 SW 8th Street
MS 0350
Bentonville, AR 72716-0130
479-204-8119

Lobbyists:
Philip Serghini
Alexandra Serra

Walgreen Co.
104 Wilmot Rd
MS 1444
Deerfield, IL 60015
847-315-6829

Lobbyists:
Mike Altier

Walmart Free NYC
50 Broadway
29th Floor
New York, NY 10001
347-387-3549

Lobbyists:
Stephanie Yazgi

Offices and agencies generally appear in alphabetical order, except when specific order is requested by listee.

Walters Group (The)
95 Columbia Street
Albany, NY 12210
518-432-0488

Clients:
Accenture LLP
Annese and Associates, Inc.
Buckeye Partners, L.P.
CA, Inc.
Care One Services, Inc.
Computer Aid, Inc.
Light Tower Fiber LLC
Pitney Bowes, Inc.

Lobbyists:
Carrie Cody
Ruth Walters

Walton, Leigh
1 Elmcroft Road
Stamford, CT 06926-0700
203-351-6633

Lobbyists:
Alfie Charles

Weiss, Michael A.
15 Waldorf Court
Brooklyn, NY 11230
646-739-5391

Clients:
Marine Park Seaside Links LLC
Pennoni Engineering & Surveying of New York, PC

Wells Capital Management, Inc.
525 Market Street
10th Floor
San Francisco, CA 94105
414-577-7630

Lobbyists:
Meredith Ashwell
Rick Bisignano
Jeff Lang
Ann Larson
Frank Marckioni
Kathryn Schmidt

Wells Fargo and Company
301 South College Street
Charlotte, NC 28288
704-383-1554

Lobbyists:
Milton Aronowitz
Martin Bingham
Rick Bisignano
Jay Blanton
Todd Bleakney
Jennifer Bonita
Carrie Callahan
Felipe Comacho
Peter Cannava
John Caswell
Pam Clayton
Tom Clune
Sean Corrigan

Marie Day
Paul Digrado
Will Driver
Jennifer Ernest
Holger Ebert
Suanne Falvey
Nancy Feldman
Howard Forman
Scott Frail
Nick Gage
Elena Gallo
Dan George
Corbin Hankins
Rick Hartley
Angel Helm
Kevin Henson
Luke Hermann
Peter Hill
Rick Hollar
Jean Halloway
Craig Hrinkevich
Vanessa Hubbard
Steve Hudd
Glenn Johnson
Weldon Jones
Adam Joseph
Michael Karlosky
Bryan Kern
Robert Kinney
Jennifer Kirby
Vin Kurian
Ann Larson
Tommy Lawson
Tammy Leisen
Andrew Levenson
Robert Little
Monique Lopez
Zach Love
Robert Lubonski
Frank Marckioni
Matt Marone
Keziah McGuiness
Walker McQuage
John Menard
Richard Miller
Brian Mulligan
Mike Norman
William O'Conner
Shawn O'Sullivan
John Pedersen
Laurie Post
Bernardo Ramos
Larry Richardson
Casey Rogers
Patrick Russell
Mimi Sapp
Leela Scattum
Janelle Scheuer
Wayne Seaton
Phil Smith
Ronald Stack
Arthur Staub
Joseph Steniger
Karl Tourville
Michel Tram
Rick White
Janine Wilcox
Tim Wilk
Adam Woodard
John Wooten
Erin Young

Offices and agencies generally appear in alphabetical order, except when specific order is requested by listee.

West Firm PLLC (The)

677 Broadway
8th Floor
Albany, NY 12207-2990
518-641-0501

Clients:
American Natural Gas, LLC
Chesapeake Appalachia LLC
Deer & Elk Farmers Association
Independent Oil & Gas Association of NY

Lobbyists:
Amy Abbatti
Alita Giuda
Thomas S. West

West Harlem Environmental Action, Inc.

1638 Amsterdam Avenue
New York, NY 10031
347-488-8495

Lobbyists:
Yolande Cadore
Cecil Corbin-Mark
Peggy Shepard
James Sibbudhi
Stephanie Tyree

Westfield LLC

11604 Wilshire Blvd
11th Floor
Los Angeles, CA 90025
310-445-2405

Lobbyists:
John Genovese
George Giaquinto
Richard Steets

White and Williams LLP

One Penn Plaza
250 West 34th Street
Suite 4110
New York, NY 10119
212-244-9500

Clients:
American Insurance Association

Lobbyists:
John McCarrick
Maurice Pesso

Whiteman Osterman & Hanna LLP

One Commerce Plaza, 19th Fl
Albany, NY 12260
518-487-7741
Web site: www.woh.com

Clients:
American Express Co
AIA New York State Inc
Assn of Homes & Services for the Aging (NY)
Bristol-Myers Squibb Co
Central Boiler Inc
COFCCA Inc
Council of New York Cooperatives
Creosote Council III

Distilled Spirits Council of the US
Educational Testing Service
Empire State Petroleum Assn Inc
Gillen Brewer School (The)
Hertz Corporation (The)
Institute for Student Achievement
Johnson & Johnson
Long Island Life Sciences Initiative
MCI
Metropolitan Museum of Art (The)
NYS Coalition of 853 Schools Inc
NYS Funeral Directors Assn Inc
Physical Therapy Assn (NY)
Presbyterian Hospital (NY)
Preserve Associates LLC
Public Employer Risk Management Assn
Questar III
Quest Diagnostics Inc
Reinsurance Assn of America
Roundabout Theatre Co
SC Johnson & Son Inc
Society for Respiratory Care Inc (NYS)
Advantage Capital Partners
Syracuse University
Teachers Insurance & Annuity Assn/College Retirement Equities Fun
Thomson West
Haverstraw-Stony Point Central School District
Managed Funds Association
MBIA Insurance Corporation
Natural Resources Defense Council Inc
Sanofi Pasteur Inc
St Elizabeth Medical Center
Scotts Company (The)

Lobbyists:
William Y Crowell III
John Dunne
Philip Gitlen
Katherine Herlihy
Aggie Leahy
Richard E Leckerling
Brian J Lucey
Kevin Quinn
Daniel Ruzow
Michael Whiteman

Wiener, Judith R

2 Westchester Plaza
Elmsford, NY 10523
914-345-8737

Clients:
Lower Hudson Education Coalition

Wilder Balter Partners, Inc.

570 Taxter Road
6th Floor
Elmsford, NY 10523
914-610-3655
Web site: www.wbhomes.com

Lobbyists:
John Bainlardi
Robert Wilder

Wildlife Conservation Society

2300 Southern Blvd.
Bronx, NY 10460
718-220-7353

Offices and agencies generally appear in alphabetical order, except when specific order is requested by listee.

Lobbyists:
John Cavelli
Rosemary DeLuca
Nicole Robinson-Etienne
Janet Torres

Wilson Elser Moskowitz Edelman & Dicker

677 Broadway
Albany, NY 12207
518-449-8893
Web site: www.wemed.com

Clients:
1765 1st Associates LLC
250 E 57th Street, LLC
Albany Medical Ctr
Albert Lindley Lee Memorial Hospital
Alice Hyde Medical Center
American Insurance Assn
American International Group Inc (AIG)
Alliance of Resident Theatres (NY)
Assn of Professional Land Surveyors Inc (NYS)
Assn of Realtors Inc (NYS)
Athletic Trainers' Assn (NYS)
Assn of Independent Commercial Producers Inc
Asurion Corp & Subsidiaries (FKA Lock/Line LLC (DST Systems))
Ballet Theatre Foundation Inc/American Ballet Theatre
Bankers Assn (NY)
Barnes & Noble College Book Sellers (Dewey Square Group)
Brooklyn Adult Care Center
Brooklyn Hospital Center (The)
Canton-Potsdam Hospital
Carnegie Hall
Cathedral Church of St John the Devine (The)
Catholic Conference Policy Group Inc
College Board
Combined Coordinating Council Inc
Community Hospital Network of NY Eductl & Rsch Fund Inc
Community Service Society of NY
Consolidated Edison Co of NY Inc
Cortland Regional Medical Center (FKA Cortland Memorial Hospital)
Crouse Hospital
Center for Disability Services
CGI (FKA CGI Group)
Children's Institute
City of Syracuse Industrial Development Agency
Dell Inc
David B Kriser Dental Center of NY University
DeVry Incorporated
Deloitte & Touche, LLP
Education Management LLC
Elant, Inc
Elliott Management
Epilepsy Institute
Elizabethtown Community Hospital
Ernst & Young, LLP
Excelsior Racing Association (Powers & Company)
Family Planning Advocates
Forest City Ratner Companies
Glens Falls Hospital
Greater New York Automobile Dealers Assn
Groton Community Health Care Center
HANYS Services, Inc; D/B/A HANYS Solutions, Inc
Harbar Motors, Ltd
Healthcare Assn of NYS
Hebrew Home for the Aged at Riverdale (The)
Hedgewood Home for Adults
Henry Schein Inc
Hertz Corporation (The)
Hospitality & Tourism Assn (NYS)

Hospitals Insurance Company Inc
Hudson Valley Economic Development Corp
Hotel Assn of NYC Inc
IMG Models
Intrepid Museum Foundation
JXQ Holding Company, Inc
Jewish Guild for the Blind (The)
KPMG, LLP
Law School Admissions Council
League of American Theatres & Producers Inc
Lesbian Gay Bisexual & Transgender Community Center (The)
Jewish Museum (The)
John T Mather Memorial Hospital
Long Island Health Network
Long Island University
MCIC Vermont Inc
Marshals Assn (NYC)
Merchants Protective Co, Inc (NY)
Medtronic Inc (FKA Medtronic Sofamor Danek)
Taconic IPA Inc
Metropolitan Parking Assn
Morgan Stanley (Multistate Associates)
Nassau-Suffolk Hospital Association
New Brookhaven Town House for Adults
Norwegian Cruise Line
Niagara Mohawk Holdings, Inc., & NMPC DBA National Grid
New York University-College of Nursing
Nassau County Firefighter's Museum & Education Center
Northern Metropolitan Hospital Assn
Northern Westchester Hospital
North Country Healthcare Providers Eductl & Rsch Fund Inc (North Country
    Healthcare Providers, LLC)
Peconic Bay Medical Center
Phelps Memorial Hospital Center
Planned Parenthood of NYC Inc
Pricewaterhouse Coopers, LLP
Queens Adult Care Center
Queens-Long Island Medical Group, P.C.
Real Estate Board of NY
Rochester Institute of Technology
Samaritan Medical Center
Sanctuary for Families
School Bus Contractor's Coalition, Inc. (NY)
Segway Inc. (Multistate Associates)
Society for Clinical Social Work Inc (NYS)
St Luke's Cornwall Hospital
St Margaret's Center
St Mary's Healthcare System for Children Inc
T-Mobile USA Inc
To Life
Tanglewood Manor
United Hospital Fund
University (NY)
University School of Medicine (NY) & Hospitals (NY)
Viahealth

Lobbyists:
Nicholas Antenucci
Alexander L Betke
Martin Bienstock
Douglas Clark
Donna Clyne
Laurie T Cohen
Elizabeth Colombo
Victoria M Contino
Kathleen Corkery
Diana Georgia
John N Herring
Jerry S Hoffman
Darrell E Jeffers
Gerald J Jennings

Offices and agencies generally appear in alphabetical order, except when specific order is requested by listee.

Arnold Kideckel
Andrew Marocco
Lisa M Marrello
Mary Ann Mclean
Stuart Miller
Samir Nejame
Anthony Piscitelli
Peter A Piscitelli
Fred Pomerantz
Jessica Reinhardt
Philip Rosenberg
Theresa Russo
Jill Sandhaas
Kenneth L Shapiro
Cynthia D Shenker
Lester Shulklapper
Mark Thomas
Michael Weisberg
Jacob Wilkinson

Wilson, Alex
27 Elk Street
Albany, NY 12207
518-434-9091

Clients:
Sheriffs' Association

Wisneski, Jessica
c/o Citizen Action of New York
94 Central Avenue
Albany, NY 12206
518-465-4600

Lobbyists:
Pam Bennett
Kathleen Campbell
Diana Cihak
Mary Clark
Bob Cohen
Shanna Goldman
Tanika Jones
Chynel Lee
Karen Scharff
Lea Webb

Wladis Law Firm
P.O. Box 245
Syracuse, NY 13214
315-445-1700
Web site: www.wladislawfirm.com

Lobbyists:
Ryan Moses
Joe Rossi
Matthew Tynan

Worker Justice Center of New York, Inc.
1187 Culver Road
Rochester, NY 14609-5448
585-325-3050

Lobbyists:
Milan Bhatt
Emma Kreyche
Lewis Papenfuse

Working Assets Funding Service, Inc.
101 Market Street
Suite 700
San Francisco, CA 94105
415-369-2000

Lobbyists:
Leah Adler

Working Families Organization
2 Nevins Street
3rd Floor
Brooklyn, NY 11217
718-222-3796

Lobbyists:
Joseph Berry
Mike Boland
Emmanuel Caicedo
Dan Cantor
Bryan Collinsworth

Wright Group NY, Inc. (The)
151 West 30th Street
11th Floor
New York, NY 10001
212-216-0684

Clients:
Amigos Del Museo Del Barrio, Inc.
ANHD, Inc.
Botanical Garden (The)
Brooklyn Community Services
Carnegie Hall Corporation (The)
Coalition of Behavioral Health Agencies, Inc.
Connect, Inc.
Cool Culture, Inc.
Crenulated Company LTD DBA New Settlement Apartmens (The)
Cultural Institutions Group
Goddard Riverside Community Center
Greenwich House, Inc.
Hudson Guild
Lawyers for the Public Interest
LEAP
Learning Leaders
Legal Services for the Working Poor
Legal Services NYC
Legal Services NYC
MFY Legal Services, Inc.
New York City Ballet, Inc. and the David H. Koch Theater at Lincoln Center
Northern Manhattan Improvement Corporation
Powerplay NYC, Inc.
Sauti Yetu Center for African Women
Services & Advocacy for Gay, Lesbian, Bisexual & Transgender Elders
St. Ann's Warehouse
Union Theological Seminary

Lobbyists:
Lashaun Lesley
Barbara Martinez
Ayana Partee
Patricia Pulvirenti
Antonio Quesada
Larisa Wick
John Wright

Offices and agencies generally appear in alphabetical order, except when specific order is requested by listee.

Yankosky, Mary Ellen
146 Trenton Street
Suite 1
Boston, MA 02128
617-997-1551

Clients:
Dental Hygienists Association of the State of New York, Inc.

Yavornitzki, Mark L.
GR Initiatives LLC
125 State Street
3rd Floor
Albany, NY 12207
518-426-8178

Clients:
Association of Insurance & Financial Advisors, Inc.

Yeshiva University
500 West 18th Street
New York, NY 10033
212-960-5400

Lobbyists:
Gordon Earle
Michael Heller
Joshua Joseph
Andrew Lauer
Allison Liebman Rubin
Jeffrey Rosengarten

YMCA of Greater New York
5 West 3rd Street
6th Floor
New York, NY 10023
212-630-9600

Lobbyists:
Paul Custer
Sharon Levy
Jack Lund
Joshua Wojehowski

YMCAs of NYS, Inc.
33 Elk Street
Suite 200
Albany, NY 12207
518-462-8241

Lobbyists:
Kyle Stewart

Yockel, James
800 West Metro Park
Suite C
Rochester, NY 14623
585-341-2128

Clients:
Greater Rochester Association of Realtors, Inc.

York Group Associates
893 Myrtle Avenue
Suite 2B
Brooklyn, NY 11206
347-560-0139

Clients:
Bronx Community College
City University of New York
Greenetrack
Rocket Learning, Inc.

Yoswein New York Inc
150 Broadway
Ste 1300
New York, NY 10038
212-233-5700
e-mail: info@yosweinnewyork.com
Web site: www.yosweinnewyork.com

Clients:
40th Street Development LLC
Academy of Medicine (NY)
BA Cypress Bronx Holdings LLC
Bailey House Inc
Brooklyn Chamber of Commerce
Brooklyn Philharmonic
Brooklyn Technical High School Alumni Assn
Business Council of NYS, Inc (The)
Ceruzzi Holdings
College Community Services, Inc (DBA Brooklyn Center for the Performing Arts)
Flushing Commons, LLC
Gateway Center Properties Phase II, LLC
Groundwork, Inc
Keyspan Energy
Maimonides Medical Center
Metropolitan Funeral Directors Assn
Mt Sinai Hospital of Queens
New 42nd Street Inc (The)
Outward Bound Center (NYC)
Pfizer Inc
St Francis College
Standardbred Owners Assn of NY
Starwood Ceruzzi, LLC
SUNY Downstate Medical Center

Lobbyists:
Simone Hawkins
Melvin Norris
Jamie Van Bramer
Joni A Yoswein

Young Jr. William N.
1881 Western Avenue
Suite 140
Albany, NY 12203
518-456-6767

Clients:
Association of Fire Districts of the State of New York, Inc.

Zalcman, Fred
12500 Baltimore Ave
Beltsville, MD 20705
301-974-2721

Clients:
Sunedison LLC

Zaleski, Terence M
437 Old Albany Post Rd
Garrison, NY 10524
845-788-5070
e-mail: tzaleski@sprynet.com

Offices and agencies generally appear in alphabetical order, except when specific order is requested by listee.

Clients:
Coalition of NYS Career Schools
Green Chimneys Children's Services Inc

ZGA LLC
27 Elk Street
Albany, NY 12207
518-426-0214

Clients:
Association of Agricultural Fairs
Northeast Ag and Feed Alliance
Syngenta Crop Protection LLC

Lobbyists:
Rick Zimmerman

Zuffa LLC
P.O. Box 26959
Las Vegas, NV 89126
702-588-5509

Lobbyists:
Lawrence Epstein
Lorenzo Fertitta
Michael Mersch
Mark Ratner
Dana White

Offices and agencies generally appear in alphabetical order, except when specific order is requested by listee.

POLITICAL ACTION COMMITTEES

1199/SEIU New York State Political Action Fund
330 West 42nd Street, 7th Floor, New York, NY 10036
212-603-1737
George K. Gresham, Treasurer

2013 Committee to Elect Gwen Goodwin
152 East 100th Street, Suite 5E, New York, NY 10029
Gwen Goodwin, Treasurer

A Different Approach
19 East 213th Street, Suite 4C, Bronx, NY 10467
718-600-5054
Joseph Smith, Treasurer

ACEC New York City PAC
8 West 38th Street, Suite 1101, New York, 10018
212-682-6336
Raymond Daddazio, Chairman
Hannah O'Grady

Advertising Development Political Action Committee
PO Box 2269, New York, NY 10163
917-363-2323
Marty Judge, Chairman/Treasurer

AECOM US FEDERAL PAC
201 Wilson Boulevard, Suite 700, Arlington, VA 22201
703-465-5872
Nancy Butler, Chairwoman

Akiel Taylor For Council
186 Lefferts Place, Brooklyn, NY 11238
917-620-5725
Joseph N. Taylor, Treasurer

Albert 2013
427 Bronx Park Avenue, Bronx, NY 10460
347-427-8822
Luis C. Torres, Treasurer

Alex For NYC
10 Bethune Stret, Suite 3A, New York, NY 10014
305-992-6875
Ryan S. Reynolds, Treasurer

Alicia 4 Council 7
3333 Broadway, Suite D35A, New York, NY 10031
212-283-2019
Sandra Dawson, Treasurer

American Insurance Association New York City PAC
2101 L Street Northwest, Suite 400, Washington, DC 20037
202-828-7100
JS Zielezienski, Chairman

Andy King 2013
21 Riverdale Avenue, White Plains, NY 10607
646-644-9414
Katrina P. DeLa Cruz, Treasurer

AON Corporation Political Action Committee
200 East Randolph, Chicago, IL 60601
312-381-3352
Paul Hagy, Treasurer

Ari Kagan For City Council
330 Ocean Parkway, Suite C3, Brooklyn, NY 11218
347-556-4205
Alyona Badalova, Treasurer

Arroyo 2013
694 East 133rd Street, #2, Bronx, NY 10454
347-820-3723
Carmen M. Aquino, Treasurer

Asbestos Workers Local 12 Political Action Committee
25-19 43rd Avenue, Long Island City, NY 11101
718-784-3456
Nick Grgas, Chairman

AT&T PAC - New York
111 Washington Avenue, Albany, NY 12210
518-463-3092
Marissa J. Shorenstein, Chairwoman

ATU New York Cope Fund
5025 Wisconsin Avenue, Northwest, Washington, DC 20016
202-537-1645
Lawrence J. Hanley, Treasurer

Bank of America New York Political Action Committee
1100 North King Street, DE5-001-02-07, Wilmington, DE 19884
302-432-0956
Brian P. Grip, Chairman

Bendetto For Assembly
3280 Giegerich Place, Bronx, NY 10465
718-931-6675
Michael R. Bendetto, Chairman

Bill Thompson For Mayor
16 Court Street, 35th Floor, Brooklyn, NY 11241
718-855-2324
James F. Ross, Treasurer

Blishteyn For NYC
175-10 Jewel Avenue, Fresh Meadows, NY 11365
718-757-7389
Ross P. Weiner, Treasurer

Brab PAC, Inc.
850 Bronx River Road, Suite 105, Yonkers, NY 10708
914-966-2000
Michael Laub, Treasurer

Brad Lander 2013
256 13th Street, Brooklyn, NY 11215
917-822-4584
Margaret R. Barnette, Treasurer

Bricklayers & Allied Craftworkers Local 1 PAC
4 Court Square, Long Island City, NY 11108
718-392-0525
Jermiah Sullivan Jr., Chairman
Santo Lantzfamne, Treasurer

Bristol-Meyers Squibb Company Political Action Committee
345 Park Avenue, New York, NY 10154
609-252-5352
John E. Celentano, Chairman

Bryan Block 2013
120-43 219th Street, Cambria Heights, NY 11411
917-837-6102
Sanu K. Thomas, Treasurer

Building & Construction Trades Council PAC
71 West 23rd Street, Suite 501, New York, NY 10010
212-647-0700
Gary LaBarbera, Treasurer

Offices and agencies generally appear in alphabetical order, except when specific order is requested by listee.

Building Industry Association of NYC, Inc.
3130 Amboy Road, Staten Island, NY 10306
718-720-3070
Randy Lee, Chairman

Cablevision Systems New York PAC
1111 Stewart Avenue, Bethpage, NY 11714
516-803-2387
Thomas M. Rutledge, Chairman

Cabrera For City Council
2792 Sedgwick Avenue, 4A, Bronx, NY 10468
917-804-9298
Paul Susana, Treasurer

Captains Endowment Association
233 Broadway, Suite 1801, New York, NY 10279
212-791-8292
Roy T. Richter, Chairman

Carlo 2013
1275 81st Street, Brooklyn, NY 11228
917-622-4063
Camille Arezzo, Treasurer

Carlos For Council
215 Terrace Place, #3, Brooklyn, NY 11218
646-305-5224
Aimee Davis, Treasurer

Carolyn's PAC
24 East 93rd Street, Suite 1B, New York, NY 10128
212-987-5516
Carolyn B. Maloney, Chairwoman

Carrion 2013
1 Stuyvesant Oval, 11D, New York, NY 10009
917-952-1915
Loretta Class, Treasurer

Catholic Citizens Committee PAC
106 First Place, Brooklyn, NY 11231
917-685-5264
Martin Cottingham, Chairman

Central Brooklyn Independent Democrats
476 Tenth Street, Brooklyn, NY 11215
718-788-8698
Lucy Koteen, Chairwoman

CIR/SEIU Local 1957 Health Care Advocacy Fund
520 8th Avenue, Suite 1200, New York, NY 10018
212-356-8100
Eric Scherzer, Treasurer

CITIGROUP Inc. Political Action Committee - Federal/State
1101 Pennsylvania Avenue Northwest, #1000, Washington, DC 20004
202-879-6805
S. Colin Dowling, Chairman

Citizens For Sports & Arts, Inc.
58-12 Queens Boulevard, Suite 1, Woodside, NY 11377
718-786-7110
Lewis H. Hartman, Chairman

Civil Service Employees Political Action Fund
143 Washington Avenue, Albany, NY 12210
518-436-8622
Danny F. Donohue, Chairman

Cliff Stanton For Council
3861 Cannon Place, Bronx, NY 10463
917-699-5241
Joseph V. Kullhanek, Treasurer

Clifton Stanley Diaz For NYC Council
172-20 133rd Avenue, 2D, Jamaica, NY 11434
917-856-5454
David E. Diaz, Treasurer

Climate Action PAC
30 Broad Street, 30th Floor, New York, NY 10004
212-361-6350
Robert Hallman, Chairman

Cohen For Council
444 East 86th Street, 17H, New York, NY 10028
212-879-2971
Esther Fink-Sinovsky, Treasurer

Committee For Effective Leadership
63 Carriage Place, c/o William J. He, Edison, NJ 08820
732-744-1413
Lewis H. Goldstein, Chairman

Committee to Elect Abiodun Bello
PO Box 520843, Bronx, NY 10452
917-603-3553
Shakiru O. Kazeem, Treasurer

Committee to Elect Andy King
952 East 218th Street, PH, Bronx, NY 10469
718-515-5464
Winslow Luna, Treasurer

Committee to Elect Ariel Guerrero
411 East 118th Street, #35, New York, NY 10035
917-826-9661
Nicholas S. Burke, Treasurer

Committe to Elect Ceceilia Berkowitz for Mayor
143 East 30th Street, #402, New York, NY 10016
917-923-5760
Alex Castillo, Treasurer

Committee to Elect Charles A. Bilal 2010
121 03 Sutphin Boulevard, Jamaica, NY 11431
718-607-9119
Aziza N. Bilal, Treasurer

Committee to Elect Christopher Banks
669 Van Siclen Avenue, PH, Brooklyn, NY 11207
718-257-3050
Claudette Elliott, Treasurer

Committee to Elect Eric Adams
593 Vanderbilt Avenue, #305, Brooklyn, NY 11238
Eric Adams, Chairman

Committee to Elect Philip Marks For Mayor
1658 Ralph Avenue, 6C, Brooklyn, NY 11236
Philip A. Marks, Treasurer

Committee to Elect Robert E. Cornegy Jr.
653 Putnam Avenue, Brooklyn, NY 11221
917-586-7444
Michelle R. Cornegy, Treasurer

Committee to Elect Robert M. Waterman
207 Lewis Avenue, Brooklyn, NY 11221
Avis Jones, Treasurer

Offices and agencies generally appear in alphabetical order, except when specific order is requested by listee.

Committee to Elect Stephen S. Jones to City Council
107-52 139th Street, Jamaica, NY 11435
347-447-8148
Kenneth E. Nelson, Treasurer

Committee to Re-Elect Lawrence A. Warden
1103 East Gun Hill Road, Bronx, NY 10469
917-345-6860
Marcia E. McGann, Treasurer

Committee to Re-Elect Nydia M. Velazquez to Congress
315 Inspiration Lane, Gaithersburg, MD 20878
301-947-0278
Nydia M. Velazquez, Chairwoman

Committee to Re-Elect Mathieu Eugene
40 Argyle Road, C6, Brooklyn, NY 11218
347-725-6725
Delsie L. Lawson, Treasurer

Communications Workers of America Local 1180
6 Harrison Street, New York, NY 10013
212-226-6565
Arthur Cheliotes, Chairman

Community Campaign For Naaimat
10 Richman Plaza, 1K, Bronx, NY 10453
646-470-3436
Momodou S. Sawaneh, Treasurer

Community For Lynn Nunes
115-13 Jamaica Avenue, Richmond Hill, NY 11418
347-242-6600
George Parpas, Treasurer

Community Mental Health Political Action Committee, Inc.
52 Dublin Drive, Niskayuna, NY 12309
518-783-1417
Christopher Burke, Chairman

Comrie For NYC
115-03 Farmers Boulevard, St. Albans, NY 11412
718-772-3975
Tyrone A. Sellers, Treasurer

Conrad Tillard For Council
315 Flatbush Avenue, 521, Brooklyn, NY 11217
347-766-3628
Suedamay A. Monderson, Treasurer

Conservative Party Campaign Committee
32 Cunard Place, Staten Island, NY 10304
718-816-2237
Carmine Ragucci, Chairman

Consolidated Edison, Inc. Employees' Political Action Committee
4 Irving Place, New York, NY 10003
212-460-4202
Frances Resheske, Chairwoman

Correy For Council
777 Sixth Avenue, 6D, New York, NY 10001
917-750-5289
Mathew Bergman, Treasurer

Correction Captains Association - PAC
189 Montague Street, Suite 400, Brooklyn, NY 11201
718-243-0222
Patrick W. Ferraiuolo, Chairman

Correction Officers Benevolent Association
75 Broad Street, Suite 810, New York, NY 10004
212-274-8000
Norman Seabrook, Chairman

Council of School Supervisors and Administrators, Local 1 AFSA
16 Court Street, 4th Floor, Brooklyn, NY 11241
718-852-3000
Ernest Logan, Chairman

Cozen O'Connor Empire State PAC
1900 Market Street, Philadelphia, PA 19103
215-665-2000
Thomas A. Decker, Chairman

Craig Caruana 2013
7921 67 Drive, Middle Village, NY 11379
917-648-4787
Lawrence J. Caruana, Treasurer

Crowley For Congress
84-56 Grand Avenue, Elmhurst, NY 11373
718-639-7010
Joseph Crowley, Chairman

CWA District One PAC
80 Pine Street, 37th Floor, New York, NY 10005
212-344-2515
Christopher M. Shelton, Chairman

CWA SSF (NY)
80 Pine Street, 37th Floor, NY 10005
212-344-2515
Christopher M. Shelton, Chairman

Cynthia For Change
2375 Marion Avenue, 2C, Bronx, NY 10458
917-292-7015
Luana Malavolta, Treasurer

D & M P.A.C. LLC
605 Third Avenue, New York, NJ 10158
212-557-7200
Arthur Goldstein, Treasurer

David Kayode 2013
106-23 153rd Street, 1, Jamaica, NY 11433
Omolola Kayode, Treasurer

Davis 2013
459 Columbus Avenue, 365, New York, NY 10024
917-716-9236
Adam B. Karl, Treasurer

DC 37 Local 299
125 Barclay Street, New York, NY 10007
212-815-1299
Jackie Rowe-Adams, Chairwoman

DC 37 Political Action Committee
125 Barclay Street, New York, NY 10007
212-815-1550
Lillian Roberts, Chairwoman

Democracy For America - NYC
38 Eastwood Drive, Suite 300, South Burlington, VT 05403
802-651-3200
Arshad Hasan, Chairman

Offices and agencies generally appear in alphabetical order, except when specific order is requested by listee.

Democrat, Republican, Independent Voter Education
25 Louisiana Avenue Northwest, Washington, DC 20001
202-624-6821
James P. Hoffa, Chairman

Detectives Endowment Association - COPE
26 Thomas Street, New York, NY 10007
212-587-1000
Michael J. Palladino, Chairman

Diallo For Council 2013
3396 3rd Avenue, Suite 1A, Bronx, NY 10456
347-754-8239
Adama I. Barry, Treasurer

District Council 1707, AFSCME
101 Avenue of the Americas, 4th Floor, New York, NY 10013
212-219-0022
Raglan George Jr., Chairman

District Council No. 9 Political Action Committee
45 West 14th Street, New York, NY 10011
212-255-2950
Joseph Ramaglia, Chairman

DLA Piper New York Political Action Committee
1251 Avenue of the Americas, 29th Floor, New York, NY 10020
202-799-4349
John A. Merrigan, Chairman

Doctors Council SEIU COPE
50 Broadway, 11th Floor, Suite 1101, New York, NY 10004
212-532-7690
Barry L. Liebowitz, M.D., Chairman

Dodge Landesman For State Committee
4 Lexington Avenue, New York, NY 10010
917-453-1523
Dodge Landesman, Treasurer

Dromm For NYC
35-24 78th Street, B28, Jackson Heights, NY 11372
718-457-2928
Andrew P. Ronan, Treasurer

Duane For New York
43-07 Westmoreland Street, Little Neck, NY 11363
212-949-6720
Margaret M. McConnell, Treasurer

Duane Morris LLP Government Committee - New York Fund
30 South 17th Street, Philadelphia, PA 19103
215-979-1450
Lewis F. Gould Jr., Chairman

Educational Justice Political Action Committee
76 East 51st Street, 2F, Brooklyn, NY 11203
718-813-6229
Shelly L. Barrow, Treasurer

Effective Leadership Committee, Inc.
165 West End Avenue, 14R, New York, NY 10023
212-799-3312
Raymond Hodell, Chairman

EFO Jeffrey P. Gardner
124 Highview Terrace, Hawthorne, NJ 07506
973-951-7081
Jeffrey P. Gardner, Chairman

EISPAC
3 Park Avenue, 28th Floor, c/o Robe, New York, NY 10016
212-689-7744
Paul Eisland, Chairman

Elaine Nunes 2010
95-16 123rd Street, Richmond Hill, NY 11419
646-430-9067
Jaime Nunes, Treasurer

Eleanor Roosevelt Legacy Committee
PO Box 20293, New York, NY 10010
646-430-9067
Judith Hope, Chairwoman

Elect Newsome 2013
955 Sheridan Avenue, 5B, Bronx, NY 10456
347-913-3694
Chivona R. Newsome, Treasurer

Elizabeth Crowley 2013
77-24 83rd Street, Glendale, NY 11385
347-891-3973
Moira McDermott, Treasurer

Emily's List NY
1120 Connecticut Avenue Northwest, Suite 1100, Washington, DC 20036
202-326-1400
Amy Dacey, Treasurer

Empire Dental Political Action Committee
20 Corporate Woods Boulevard, Suite 602, Albany, NY 12211
518-465-0044
Lawrence E. Volland, Treasurer

Entergy Corporation Political Action Committee - New York
440 Hamilton Avenue, White Plains, NY 10601
914-272-3558
Michael Balduzzi, Chairman

Eric Adams 2013
PO Box 250-294, Brooklyn, NY 11225
917-327-3804
Emrod Martin, Treasurer

Eric Ulrich 2013
101-17 84th Street, Ozone Park, NY 11416
917-951-7251
Ronald Kulick, Treasurer

Ernst & Young Committee For Good Government
5 Times Square, New York, NY 10036
212-773-7111
David G. Bonagura, Chairman

Espinal For City Council
52 Hale Avenue, Brooklyn, NY 11208
347-967-9896
Wilson Rodriguez, Treasurer

Evergreen For City Council
41-34 Frame Place, 5K, Flushing, NY 11355
718-888-7412
Justin Lieu, Treasurer

Farrell 2012
31 Bleecker Place, Albany, NY 12202
Herman D. Farrell, Jr., Chairman

Federal Express New York State Political Action Committee
942 South Shady Grove Road, 1st Floor, Memphis, TN 38120
901-818-7407
Gina F. Adams, Chairwoman

Offices and agencies generally appear in alphabetical order, except when specific order is requested by listee.

Flowers For NYC
226-16 139th Avenue, Laurelton, NY 11413
718-928-5511
Raymond Baynard Jr., Treasurer

Food Industry Political Action Committee - NYC
130 Washington Avenue, Albany, NY 12210
914-220-8347
Jay M. Peltz, Chairman

Frank's Friends
9306 Flatlands Avenue, Suite A, Brooklyn, NY 11236
Jaime Rivas-Williams, Treasurer

Freelancers Union Political Action Committee
20 Jay Street, Suite 700, Brooklyn, NY 11201
718-532-1515
Ann Boger, Chairwoman

Friends For Peter Koo
133-24A 41st Avenue, Flushing, NY 11355
718-961-2931
Xiao Yun M. Yu, Treasurer

Friends For Ryan Wright
3025 Kingsland Avenue, PH, Bronx, NY 10469
Daphne C. Lewis, Treasurer

Friends of Alfonso Quiroz
76-10 34th Avenue, 2P, Jackson Heights, NY 11372
212-460-1372
Matthew Baker, Treasurer

Friends of Angel Molina
411 East 139th Street, Bronx, NY 10454
718-930-9712
Angel D. Molina, Treasurer

Friends of Antonio Reynoso
359 South 2nd Street, 3D, Brooklyn, NY 11211
718-909-3888
Pedro Pena, Treasurer

Friends of Assembly Speaker Joe Roberts
PO Box 1326, Bellmawr, NJ 08099
609-575-8893
Joe Roberts, Chairman

Friends of Assemblyman Jeffrey Dinowitz
c/o Heidi Schwartz, 3050 Fairfiel, Bronx, NY 10463
718-549-1729
Jeffrey Dinowitz, Chairman

Friends of Audrey Pheffer
8800 Shore Front Parkway, 10E, Rockaway Beach, NY 11693
917-501-5489
Stacey G. Amato, Treasurer

Friends of Austin Shafran
14-23 209th Street, 2F, Bayside, NY 11360
917-838-2404
Jennifer B. Krinsky, Treasurer

Friends of Balboni
9 Legends Circle, Melville, NY 11747
631-242-0548
Michael A. Balboni, Chairman

Friends of Benjamin Kallos
535 East 88th Street, 5A, New York, NY 10128
212-600-4960
David Kogelman, Treasurer

Friends of Bill Suggs
929 Lincoln Place, Brooklyn, NY 11213
646-596-1527
Elizabeth N. Suggs, Treasurer

Friends of Bola Omotosho
146 Morton Place, Bronx, NY 10453
718-644-0108
Anthony K. Adjei, Treasurer

Friends of Breina Payne
121-02 Sutphin Boulevard, E103, Jamaica, NY 11434
347-894-1287
Nadja M. Taffe, Treasurer

Friends of Brodie Enoch 2013
247 West 145th Street, 6A, New York, NY 10039
347-476-9057
Donna L. Linzy, Treasurer

Friends of Carl E. Heastie
PO Box 840, Bronx, NY 10469
718-570-1881
Carl E. Heastie, Chairman

Friends of Catherine Nolan
6464 229th Street, Oakland Gardens, NY 11364
718-229-4201
Catherine T. Nolan, Chairwoman

Friends of Costa Constantinides
24-60 28th Street, Astoria, NY 11102
917-716-4540
Leah A. Carter, Treasurer

Friends of Cultural Institutions
540 Broadway, 7th Floor, Albany, NY 12207
518-426-8111
Richard J. Miller, Treasurer

Friends of Dara Adams
171 East 77th Street, 2B, New York, NY 10017
646-543-9166
Marilyn Feuer, Treasurer

Friends of David Kayode For Council
106-23 153rd Street, #1, Jamaica, Queens, NY 11433
917-747-0837
Alfred Oyewole, Treasurer

Friends of DeMeo
2023 73rd Street, Brooklyn, NY 11204
917-913-9111
Claudio DeMeo, Chairman

Friends of Donovan Richards 2013
1526 Central Avenue, Far Rockaway, NY 11691
718-471-1117
Carol Richards, Treasurer

Friends of Dorothy Phelan
35-53 82nd Street, 1C, Jackson Heights, NY 11372
718-424-2162
Dorothy A. Phelan, Chairwoman

Friends of Ed Hartzog
300 East 75th Street, 12J, New York, NY 10021
917-705-6126
Cabot J. Marks, Treasurer

Offices and agencies generally appear in alphabetical order, except when specific order is requested by listee.

Friends of Ede Fox
315 Saint Johns Place, 4E, Brooklyn, NY 11238
347-262-7977
Judith T. Pierce, Treasurer

Friends of Erick Salgado
2502 86th Street, 3rd Floor, Brooklyn, NY 11214
718-266-4778
Yury S. Rozel, Treasurer

Friends of F. Richard Hurley 2013
150 Crown Street, C4, Brooklyn, NY 11225
917-297-9429
Dwayne A. Nicholson, Treasurer

Friends of Felipe de Los Santos
2446 University Avenue, 4A, Bronx, NY 10468
718-825-7037
Carlos J. De La Cruz, Treasurer

Friends of Gale Brewer - 2013
29 West 95th Street, New York, NY 10025
917-881-3375
Adele Bartlett, Treasurer

Friends of Harpreet
79-19 257th Street, Floral Park, NY 11004
718-343-9146
Manjit King, Treasurer

Friends of I. Daneek Miller
1078 Clyde Road, Baldwin, NY 11510
516-369-8735
Mark A. Henry, Treasurer

Friends of Inez Barron
744 Bradford Street, 2nd Floor, Brooklyn, NY 11207
917-853-9615
Rosalyn C. McIntosh, Treasurer

Friends of James Vacca
PO Box 562, Bronx, NY 10461
646-269-8414
Jonathan D. Conte, Treasurer

Friends of Jean Similien
3420 Avenue H, 3C, Brooklyn, NY 11210
347-709-5326
Antoine C. Coq, Treasurer

Friends of Joe Lazar
1430 East 24th Street, Brooklyn, NY 11210
917-968-5250
Aaron Biderman, Treasurer

Friends of Joe Marthone
116-37 227th Street, Cambria Heights, NY 11411
347-722-1126
Henry Derenoncourt, Treasurer

Friends of Joel R. Rivera
209 East 165th Street, 1B, Bronx, NY 10456
646-345-4263
Dion J. Powell, Treasurer

Friens of John Calvelli
11 Island View Place, New Rochelle, NY 10801
914-636-4045
John F. Calvelli, Chairman

Friends of John Lisyanskiy
155 Bay 20th Street, 2-D, Brooklyn, NY 11214
718-996-4609
Bella Waldman, Treasurer

Friends of John Liu
PO Box 520631, Flushing, NY 11352
917-501-6781
Shiang Liu, Treasurer

Friends of Johnnie Goff
2952 Laconia Avenue, Bronx, NY 10469
917-797-1771
Deborah Wilkerson, Treasurer

Friends of Jonathan J. Judge
345 Webster Avenue, 2N, Brooklyn, NY 11230
718-853-1932
Victoria A. Judge, Treasurer

Friends of Joseph Nwachukwu
1416 East Gunhill Road, Bronx, NY 10469
917-705-2478
Henrietta U. Ilomudio, Treasurer

Friends of Joyce Johnson
733 Amsterdam Avenue, 28B, New York, NY 10025
646-244-8630
Manuel Casanova, Treasurer

Friends of JR
321 West 89th Street, 6, New York, NY 10024
646-337-7700
Darrell L. Paster, Treasurer

Friends of Julio Pabon
143 East 150th Street, Bronx, NY 10451
718-402-9310
Blanca Canino-Vigo, Treasurer

Friends of Kevin P. Coenen Jr. Inc.
417 East 60th Street, 21, New York, NY 10022
917-603-9330
Kevin P. Coenen Jr., Treasurer

Friends of Kimberly Council
102 Etna Street, Brooklyn, NY 11208
347-645-1877
Trevor A. Hyde Jr., Treasurer

Friends of Kirsten John Foy
215 East 23rd Street, Brooklyn, NY 11226
James Sanon, Treasurer

Friends of Larry Hirsch 2010
321 West 89th Street, 6, New York, NY 10024
646-337-7700
Larry Hirsch, Chairman

Friends of Luis Tejada
157-10 Riverside Drive, New York, NY 10032
646-399-6163
Aydee Martinez, Treasurer

Friends of Manny Caughman Committee
115-05 179th Street, Saint Albans, NY 11412
718-809-6354
Andrea C. Scarborough, Treasurer

Friends of Marie Adam-Ovide For Council 31
121-12 234th Street, Laurelton, NY 11422
718-723-0645
Robinson Ovide, Treasurer

Offices and agencies generally appear in alphabetical order, except when specific order is requested by listee.

POLITICAL ACTION COMMITTEES

Friends of Mark Thompson
77 West 55th Street, 12B, New York, NY 10019
212-616-5810
Joseph G. Hagelmann III, Treasurer

Friends of Mark Weprin 2013
80-15 233rd Street, Queens Village, NY 11427
718-898-8500
Jack M. Friedman, Treasurer

Friends of Mark Winston Griffith
1238 Dean Street, Brooklyn, NY 11216
917-837-1587
Sharon M. Griffith, Treasurer

Friends of Martha Taylor
175-14 Mayfield Road, Jamaica, NY 11432
718-300-7308
Robert P. Miraglia, Treasurer

Friends of Martha Taylor Butler
133-02 133rd Avenue, South Ozone Park, NY 11420
917-364-7097
Martha T. Butler, Treasurer

Friends of Martin For City Council
292 Martin Avenue, Staten Island, NY 10314
718-698-1776
Martin S. Krongold, Treasurer

Friends of Menegon
31 East 92nd Street, 2B, New York, NY 10128
Karl Seidenwurm, Treasurer

Friends of Michael A. Alvarez
6120 North Kirkwood, Chicago, IL 60646
847-791-4105
Michael A. Alvarez, Chairman

Friends of Michael Duncan 2013
130-05 235th Street, Rosedale, NY 11422
347-528-4479
Tahisha Salmon, Treasurer

Friends of Michael Simanowitz
137-31 71st Avenue, Flushing, NY 11367
646-235-5095
Simon Pelman, Treasurer

Friends of Mike Gianaris
17 Canterbury Road South, Harrison, NY 10528
917-322-9212
Michael N. Gianaris, Treasurer

Friends of Mike Treybich
2925 West 5th Street, 23B, Brooklyn, NY 11224
718-288-3625
Daniel Dugan, Treasurer

Friends of Nicole Paultre Bell
129-10 Liberty Avenue, Floor 2, Richmond Hill, NY 11419
347-355-2324
Laura A. Harper, Treasurer

Friends of Olanike Alabi
PO Box 380075, Brooklyn, NY 11238
718-398-0750
Olanike T. Alabi, Chairman

Friends of Osina
1092 Beach 12th Street, Far Rockaway, NY 11691
718-868-2720
Eli Shapiro, Treasurer

Friends of Paul Drucker
PO Box 393, Paoli, PA 19301
480-275-1876
Paul Drucker, Chairman

Friends of Pedro Alvarez
1411 Townsend Avenue, A3, Bronx, NY 10452
917-775-9865
Jerson R. Mezquita, Treasurer

Friends of Randy Credico
4712 Vernon Boulevard, Long Island City, NY 11101
212-924-6980
Melchior Leone, Treasurer

Friends of Richard del Rio
208 East Broadway, J604, New York, NY 10002
646-257-9062
Stephanie D. Curry, Treasurer

Friends of Ruben Wills
194-19 115th Drive, St. Albans, NY 11412
516-663-0630
Sharon Carnegie-Hall, Treasurer

Friends of Sean K. Henry 2013
659 Ashford Street, 2, Brooklyn, NY 11207
718-216-6188
Sean K. Henry, Treasurer

Friends of Selvena Brooks
PO Box 130379, Springfield Gardens, NY 11413
347-564-0730
Nyoka Dada, Treasurer

Friends of Seymour Lachman
1207 Avenue N, Brooklyn, NY 11230
718-887-6449
Seymour P. Lachman, Chairman

Friends of Steve Cohn
16 Court Street, Brooklyn, NY 11241
718-875-7057
Steven Cohn, Chairman

Friends of Theresa Scavo
2626 Homecrest Avenue, 7T, Brooklyn, NY 11235
347-668-4548
Anthony Scavo, Treasurer

Friends of Todd Dobrin
4216 Manhattan Avenue, Brooklyn, NY 11224
917-667-2139
Deena L. Venezia-Dobrin, Treasurer

Friends of Tommy Torres
401 Morgan Avenue, Brooklyn, NY 11211
718-812-0515
Samuel Rodriguez, Treasurer

Friends of Torres
PO Box 670192, Bronx, NY 10467
718-635-2827
Marjorie Velazquez, Treasurer

Friends of Yetta
350 Broadway, Suite 701, New York, NY 10013
718-852-3710
Leo Glickman, Treasurer

Offices and agencies generally appear in alphabetical order, except when specific order is requested by listee.

Garodnick 2013
132 East 43rd Street, #560, New York, NY 10017
212-210-9362
Andrew J. Ehrlich, Treasurer

Gay and Lesbian Victory Fund
1133 15th Street, Northwest, Suite 350, Washington, DC 20005
202-842-8679
Charles A. Wolfe, Chairman

Gentile For the Future
8901 Shore Road, 7E, Brooklyn, NY 11209
347-272-9734
Mary Brannan, Treasurer

Gibson For Assembly
190 West Burnside Avenue, 2D, Bronx, NY 10453
917-309-7854
Vanessa L. Gibson, Chairwoman

Gibson For City Council
21 Riverdale Avenue, White Plains, NY 10607
646-644-9414
Katrina De La Cruz, Treasurer

Gibson, Dunn & Crutcher LLP PAC
333 South Grand Avenue, Suite 5208, Los Angeles, CA 90071
213-229-7252
Kenneth M. Doran, Treasurer

Gonzalez 2013
349 Bleecker Street, 1, Brooklyn, NY 11237
347-743-8322
Julissa G. Santiago, Treasurer

Gotlieb For City Council
2930 West 5th Street, 12G, Brooklyn, NY 11224
718-996-5668
Ira Spodek, Treasurer

Gramercy Stuyvesant Independent Democrats
145 East 15th Street, 4U, New York, NY 10003
917-445-3370
Sam Albert, Chairman

Grassy Sprain PAC
51 Pondfield Road, Bronxville, NY 10708
914-961-6100
William E. Griffin, Chairman

Greenberg Traurig PA PAC
101 East College Avenue, Tallahassee, FL 32301
850-222-6891
Mark F. Glaser, Chairman

Greenfield 2010
1011 East 3rd Avenue, Brooklyn, NY 11230
347-985-1135
Jeffrey Leb, Treasurer

Grodenchik For Queens 2013
125-28 Queens Boulevard, 504, Kew Gardens Hill, NY 11415
718-670-0720
Simon Pelman, Treasurer

Gronowicz For Mayor
2267 Haviland Avenue, 11, Bronx, NY 10462
347-920-1606
Carl L. Lundgren, Treasurer

Guerriero For Advocate
PO Box 20105, New York, NY 10014
347-709-5406
Ray Guerriero, Chairman

Hakeem Jeffries For Assembly
28 Sterling Street, Brooklyn, NY 11225
212-239-7323
Hakeem Jeffries, Chairman

Halloran 2013
166-06 24th Road, Whitestone, NY 11357
Chrissy Voskerichian, Treasurer

Harlem Charter School Parents PAC
PO Box 1930, New York, NY 10025
646-363-9047
Thomas A. Lopez-Pierre, Treasurer

HCA PAC
433 Delaware Avenue, Delmar, NY 12054
518-810-0664
Joanne Cunningham, Treasurer

HDR, Inc. Political Action Committee - NY
8404 Indian Hills Drive, Omaha, NE 68114
248-371-7268
Elwin M. Larson, Treasurer

He Gin Lee Committee to Elect For Mayor
34-16 149th Street, 2, Flushing, NY 11354
718-461-2917
Nick Polyzogopouos, Treasurer

Healthcare Association of New York State PAC
1 Empire Drive, Rensselaer, NY 12144
518-431-7600
Daniel Sisto, Chairman

Helal A. Sheikh 2013
190 Forbell Street, 1, Brooklyn, NY 11208
917-415-5681
Hifzur Rahman, Treasurer

Helen Rosenthal For City Council
225 West 83rd Street, 4K, New York, NY 10024
917-923-1019
Patricia Craddick, Treasurer

HF Responsibility Fund
2 Park Avenue, New York, NY 10016
212-592-1400
George J. Wolf, Treasurer

Hill 2013
509 East 81st Street, 10, New York, NY 10028
917-596-2432
Marianne P. Peterson, Treasurer

Hoffnung 2013
646 West 227th Street, Bronx, NY 10463
917-687-6106
Jay Horowitz, Treasurer

Holland and Knight Committee For Responsible Government
31 West 52nd Street, 12th Floor, New York, NY 10019
212-513-3562
Frank G. Sinatra, Chairman

Hotel Association of New York City, Inc.
320 Park Avenue, 22nd Floor, New York, NY 10022
212-754-6700
Joseph E. Spinnato, Chairman

Offices and agencies generally appear in alphabetical order, except when specific order is requested by listee.

Housing New York Political Action Committee
5 Hanover Square, Suite 1605, New York, NY 10004
212-838-7442
Andrew K. Hoffman, Chairman

Hoylman For Senate
80 Eighth Avenue, Suite 1802, New York, NY 10011
212-206-0033
Brad Hoylman, Chairman

HSBC North America Political Action Committee
1401 Eye Street Northwest, Suite 520, Washington, DC 20005
202-466-3561
Kevin Fromer, Chairman

Human Rights Campaign New York PAC
1640 Rhode Island Avenue, Northwest, Washington, DC 20036
202-628-4160
Susanne Salkind, Chairwoman

Humberto Soto For New York City Council 2013
268 Jefferson Street, 2B, Brooklyn, NY 11237
917-651-5595
Humberto Soto Jr., Treasurer

Hunts Point Produce Redevelopment PAC - Corporate Contribution Account
464 NYC Terminal Market, Bronx, NY 10474
718-589-4095
Jeffrey Haas, Chairman

Hunts Point Produce Redevelopment PAC - Personal Contribution Account
464 NYC Terminal Market, Bronx, NY 10474
718-589-4095
Jeffrey Haas, Chairman

IAFF FIREPAC New York Non-Federal
1750 New York Avenue, Washington, DC 20006
202-737-8484
Harold Schaitberger, Chairman

IBT Joint Council No. 16 PAC
265 West 14th Street, Suite 1201, New York, NY 10011
212-924-0002
George Miranda, Chairman

Ignizio 2013
265 Barbara Street, Staten Island, NY 10306
917-763-0951
Susan LaForgia, Treasurer

Igor 2013
2928 West 5th Street, 2R, Brooklyn, NY 11224
718-648-9186
Dan U. Levitt, Treasurer

Int'l Longshoremen's Ass'n, AFL-CIO Committee on Political Education
17 Battery Place, Suite 930, New York, NY 10004
212-425-1200
Richard P. Hughes Jr., Chairman

International Brotherhood of Electrical Workers Political Action Committee
900 Seventh Street N.W., Washington, DC 20001
202-728-6046
Edwin D. Hill, Chairman

International Union of Operating Engineers Local 14-14B Voluntary Political Action Committee
141-57 Northern Boulevard, Flushing, NY 11354
718-939-0600
Edwin L. Christian, Treasurer

International Union of Operating Engineers Local 15 A B C D
265 West 14th Street, Room 505, New York, NY 10011
212-929-5327
James T. Callahan, Chairman

International Union of Painters and Allied Trades Political Action Committee
7234 Parkway Drive, Hanover, MD 21706
410-564-5880
James Williams, Chairman

Ironworkers Local 46 PAC
1322 3rd Avenue, New York, NY 10021
347-461-6300
Terrence Moore, Treasurer

Ironworkers Political Action League
1750 New York Avenue, NW, Washington, DC 20006
202-383-4881
Joseph J. Hunt, Chairman

IUOE Local 15 Political Action Fund
44-40 11th Street, Long Island City, NY 11101
212-929-5327
Daniel J. Schneider, Chairman

Iwachiw 4 Mayor
48-35 41st Street, PH, Sunnyside, NY 11104
347-239-0965
Walter Iwachiw, Treasurer

Jacques Leandre For New York
232-06A Merrick Boulevard, Laurelton, NY 11413
347-613-2315
John M. Hogan, Treasurer

Jennings NYC
130-35 126th Street, South Ozone Park, NY 11420
718-529-5339
Donovan O. Folkes, Treasurer

Jesse Hamilton 2013
910 Lincoln Place, Brooklyn, NY 11213
917-553-7953
Denise F. Mann, Treasurer

Jim Owles Liberal Democratic Club
450 West 17th Street, 2405, New York, NY 10011
212-741-3677
Allen Roskoff, Chairman

Joan Flowers For the 27th District
173-35 113th Avenue, Addisleigh Park, NY 11433
917-723-5713
Leon P. Hart Esq., Treasurer

Joe Lhota For Mayor, Inc.
132 East 43rd Street, New York, NY 10017
212-681-0055
Vincent A. Lapadula, Treasurer

Joel Bauza For City Council
PO Box 709, Bronx, NY 10460
917-349-2596
Rafael E. Abreu, Treasurer

John Catsimatidis For Mayor 2013 Committee, Inc.
823 Eleventh Avenue, New York, NY 10019
Deborah A. Heinichen, Treasurer

John Quaglione For City Council
449 81st Street, Brooklyn, NY 11209
347-560-4555
Georgea C. Kontzamanis, Treasurer

Johnson 2013
3856 Bronx Boulevard, 7H, Bronx, NY 10467
347-762-8683
Geneva A. Johnson, Treasurer

Johnson NYC 2013
1426 Morris Avenue, Bronx, NY 10456
718-930-5030
Geoffrey Longmore, Treasurer

JPMorgan Chase & Co. PAC
10 South Dearborn, IL 1-0520, Chicago, IL 60603
312-732-5852
Peter L. Scher, Chairman

JuanPagan2013
1225 FDR Drive, 4B, New York, NY 10009
646-730-6037
Lillian Rivera, Treasurer

Judge Analisa Torres For Supreme Court 2011
321 West 89th Street, #6, New York, NY 10024
646-337-7700
Analisa Torres, Chairwoman

Julie Menin 2013
PO Box 1261, New York, NY 10013
646-415-2050
Michael Connolly, Treasurer

Julissa 2013
104-01 Roosevelt Avenue, Suite 1, Corona, NY 11368
800-829-7059
Guiyermo DeJesus, Treasurer

Jumaane 2013
PO Box 100323, Brooklyn, NY 11210
Joan M. Alexandre-Bakiriddin, Treasurer

Keeling Campaign 2013
3614 Johnson Avenue,
Charles K. LaSister, Treasurer

Kellner Campaign 2013
135 East 61st Street, 4C, New York, NY 10065
917-558-3198
Cory A. Evans, Treasurer

Ken 2013
54 West 76th Street, 4R, New York, NY 10023
703-593-0608
Andrew W. Kalish, Treasurer

Kesselly For Council
353 Beach 57th Street, 2F, Arverne, NY 11692
718-233-2590
Hanif Russell, Treasurer

Khari Edwards 2013
463 Lincoln Place, Box 121, Brooklyn, NY 11238
347-915-6362
Tyieast S. Lloyd, Treasurer

Kings County Conservative Party Campaign Committee
486 78th Street, Brooklyn, NY 11209
718-921-2158
Gerard Kassar, Chairman

Lancman 2013
76-21 172nd Street, Hillcrest, NY 11366
917-363-9004
Stephanie Goldstone, Treasurer

Landis For New York
400 Central Park West, 6B, New York, NY 10025
917-338-6415
Audrey J. Isaacs, Treasurer

Lantigua 2013
230 West 103rd Street, 6G, New York, NY 10025
914-384-5062
Julio C. Negron, Treasurer

Laurie Cumbo 2013
2146 Canarsie Road, Brooklyn, NY 11236
917-518-6610
Shante L. Cozier, Treasurer

Lee New York Political Action Committee
1413 K Street, NW, 3rd Floor, Washington, DC 20005
202-552-2400
Mike Buman, Chairman

Lesbian & Gay Democratic Club of Queens
PO Box 857, Jackson Heights, NY 11372
Bruce I. Friedman, Chairman

Letitia James 2013
371 Utica Avenue, Brooklyn, NY 11213
347-470-8813
Latrice M. Walker, Treasurer

Levin 2013
576 Morgan Avenue, 3L, Brooklyn, NY 11222
908-380-7626
William J. Harris, Treasurer

Levine 2013
900 West 190th Street, 4K, New York, NY 10040
646-382-8992
Janet A. McDowell, Treasurer

Liutenants Benevolent Association NY Police Department PAC
233 Broadway, Suite 850, New York, NY 10279
646-610-8682
Dennis Gannon, Chairman

Lisa G For NY
45 Grymes Hill Road, Staten Island, NY 10301
718-448-1600
Michael J. Kuharski, Treasurer

Local 1182 Political Action Fund
108-18 Queens Boulevard, 7th Floor, Forest Hills, NY 11375
718-793-7755
James S. Huntley, Chairman

Local 1407 AFSCME Political Committee
125 Barclay Street, New York, NY 10007
212-815-1933
Maf M. Uddin, Chairman

Local 147 Political Action Committee
4332 Katonah Avenue, Bronx, NY 10470
718-994-6664
Christopher Fitzsimmons, Chairman

Offices and agencies generally appear in alphabetical order, except when specific order is requested by listee.

Local 1500 Political Candidates and Education Fund
425 Merrick Avenue, Westbury, NY 11590
516-214-1300
Bruce W. Both, Chairman

Local 1814 ILA AFL-CIO Political Action and Education Fund
70 20th Street, Brooklyn, NY 11232
718-499-9600
Raul Vasquez Jr., Chairman

Local 2021 AFSCME Political Action Account
125 Barclay Street, 7th, New York, NY 10007
212-815-1977
Leonard Allen, Chairman

Local 23-25 Unite State & Local Campaign Committee
33 West 14th Street, New York, NY 10011
212-929-2600
Edgar Romney, Chairman

Local 30 IUOE PAC
115-06 Myrtle Hill, Richmond Hill, NY 11418
718-847-8484
John T. Ahern, Chairman

Local 32BJ SEIU NY/NJ American Dream Fund
101 Avenue of the Americas, New York, NY 10013
212-388-2171
Hector J. Figueroa, Chairman

Local 372 Political Action
125 Barclay Street, New York, NY 10007
212-815-1960
Veronica Montgomery-Costa, Chairwoman

Local 4 Action Fund
2917 Glennwood Road, Brooklyn, NY 11210
718-252-8777
Lewis Resnick, Chairman

Local 6 Committee on Political Education
709 8th Avenue, New York, NY 10036
212-957-8000
Peter Ward, Chairman

Local 891 IUOE Political Education Committee
63 Flushing Avenue, Building 292, Suite 401, Brooklyn, NY 11205
718-455-9731
Margaret McMahon, Chairwoman

Local 891 IUOE State Engineers Political Education Committee
63 Flushing Avenue, Building 292, Suite 401, Brooklyn, NY 11205
718-455-9731
Margaret McMahon, Chairwoman

Local 94-94A-94B IUOE Political Action Committee
331-337 West 44th Street, New York, NY 10036
212-245-7040
Kuba Brown, Chairman

Lotovsky For City Council 2013
1318 Gravesend Neck Road, Brooklyn, NY 11229
718-554-1741
Alina G. Krasovskaya, Treasurer

Lundgren For Council
290 West 234th Street, Bronx, NY 10463
718-510-4926
John H. Reynolds, Treasurer

Lynn Sanchez For City Council
1505 Walton Avenue, 3J, Bronx, NY 10452
646-696-4056
Ronnette Summers, Treasurer

Mailman For Council
037 East 44th Street, 1403, New York, NY 10017
718-598-0609
Jessica A. Mailman, Treasurer

Maisel For Council
1757 Coleman Street, Brooklyn, NY 11234
Reeves Eisen, Treasurer

Mancuso For Council
41 Challenger Drive, Staten Island, NY 10312
718-701-3416
Nick Popolo, Treasurer

Margaret Chin 2013
3 Hanover Square, 7H, New York, NY 10004
917-582-1845
Yee S. Shau, Treasurer

Mark Gjonaj 2012
970 Morris Park Avenue, Bronx, NY 10462
917-731-6850
Mark Gjonaj, Chairman

Mark Otto For City Council
474 West 150 Street, 3D, New York, NY 10031
856-981-3656
Cavol Forbes, Treasurer

Mark Treyger For Council
2733 Mill Avenue, Brooklyn, NY 11234
917-434-5684
Elina Gofman, Treasurer

Mark Weprin For New York PAC
5 Peter Cooper Road, ME c/o E.A.S., New York, NY 10010
212-475-7389
Mark Weprin, Chairman

Markowitz/Brooklyn
15 Waldorf Court, Brooklyn, NY 11230
718-434-8430
Marty Markowitz, Chairman

Marthone For City Council
179-18 135th Avenue, Jamaica Avenue, NY 11434
917-504-4687
Joseph R. Marthone, Treasurer

Mason Tenders District Council of Greater New York Political Action Committee
266 West 37th Street, 7th Floor, New York, NY 10018
212-452-9552
Robert Bonanza, Chairman

Mateo 2013
2817 Fulton Street, Brooklyn, NY 11207
Crystal J. Flores, Treasurer

Matteo For Council
256 Wardwell Avenue, Staten Island, NY 10314
917-975-5541
Angela M. Thornton, Treasurer

Maximus Inc. Political Action Committee
1891 Metro Center Drive, Reston, VA 20190
703-251-8500
David Casey, Chairman

Offices and agencies generally appear in alphabetical order, except when specific order is requested by listee.

McDonald 2013
52 Main Street, c/o Parker, Bedford Hills, NY 10507
914-242-2090
Craig R. Parker, Treasurer

McKenna Long & Aldridge LLP NY PAC
303 Peachtree Street, Suite 5300, Atlanta, GA 30308
404-527-8527
Eric Tanenblatt, Chairman

Mel 2013
10 West 87th Street, 3B, New York, NY 10024
Ken Coughlin, Treasurer

Melinda Katz 2013
220 East 23rd Street, Suite 809, New York, NY 10010
212-231-9753
Jennie Berger, Treasurer

Meloni NYCC
21-17 23rd Avenue, Astoria, NY 11105
718-626-9514
Angela A. Meloni, Treasurer

Mercedes For Council
105-18 Avenue L, Brooklyn, NY 11236
347-731-5091
Lystra Moore-Besson, Treasurer

METLIFE, Inc. Employees' Political Participation Fund A
1095 Avenue of the Americas, New York, NY 10036
212-578-4133
Heather Wingate, Chairwoman

METRET PAC Inc.
51 East 42nd Street, 17th Floor, New York, NY 10017
212-682-8383
Thomas R. Zapf, Chairman

Metropolitan Funeral Directors PAC
322 8th Avenue, New York, NY 10001
800-763-8332
Peter DeLuca, Treasurer

Michael 2013
666 East 233 Street, 1C, Bronx, NY 10466
718-231-8003
Michael Welch, Treasurer

Middle Village Republican Club
64-82 83rd Street, Middle Village, NY 11379
718-326-8616
Rosemarie Toomey, Treasurer

Mike Duvalle 4 City Council
127-16 Liberty Avenue, Richmond Hill, NY 11419
718-323-1100
Michael Duvalle, Treasurer

Minerva For City Council
1755 York Avenue, 17D, New York, NY 10128
917-657-8184
Brian T. Carney, Treasurer

Molinari Republican Club
1010 Forest Avenue, Staten Island, NY 10310
718-442-0900
Robert J. Scamardella, Treasurer

Moore 2013
PO Box 927, Bronx, NY 10451
347-989-2013
Lynette A. Taylor, Treasurer

Morris & McVeigh NYS PAC
19 Dove Street, Albany, NY 12210
518-426-8111
Richard Miller, Jr., Treasurer

Moustafa For NYC
34-23 Steinway Street, Astoria, NY 11101
718-679-7959
Foseph E. Botros, Treasurer

MPAC
137 Fifth Avenue, 3rd Floor, New York, NY 10010
212-681-1380
Heather Swift, Treasurer

N.S.A. Inc. Action Fund
30-50 Whitestone Expressway, Suite 301, Whitestone, NY 11354
718-747-2860
Nelson Eusebio, Chairman

Nachman Caller Community First
4309 13th Avenue, Brooklyn, NY 11219
718-513-2055
Pesach Osina, Treasurer

Nadler For Congress
PO Box 40, Village Station, NY 10014
212-352-0370
Jerrold L. Nadler, Chairman

NARAL/NY Multcandidate Political Action Committee
470 Park Avenue South, 7th Floor South, New York, NY 10016
212-343-0114
Lorna Brett Howard, Chairwoman

National Grid Voluntary New York State Political Action Committee
40 Sylvan Road, Waltham, MA 02451
781-907-1764
Marcy L. Reed, Chairwoman

Ndigo For City Council
PO Box 820, New York, NY 10027
212-726-2063
Lylburn K. Downing, Treasurer

Neighborhood Preservation Political Action Fund
123 William Street, 14th Floor, New York, NY 10038
212-214-9266
Sandra K. Paul, Treasurer

Neighbors For Kenneth Rice
1345 East 4th Street, 6F, Brooklyn, NY 11230
516-817-0716
Eileen Flaherty, Treasurer

Neil Grimaldi For New York City Mayor
2860 Buhre Avenue, New York, NY 10461
646-229-7974
John Tamburri, Chairman

New Visions Democratic Club
PO Box 55, Jackson Heights, NY 11372
Yonel Letellier, Chairman

New York Bankers Political Action Committee
99 Park Avenue, 4th Floor, New York, NY 10016
212-297-1635
James J. Landy, Chairman

POLITICAL ACTION COMMITTEES

New York Building Congress State PAC
44 West 28th Street, 12th Floor, New York, NY 10038
212-481-1911
Richard T. Anderson, Treasurer

New York Check P.A.C., Inc.
286 Madison Avenue, Suite 907, New York, NY 10017
212-268-1911
Henry F. Shyne, Treasurer

New York City Central Labor Council Political Committee
275 7th Avenue, 18th Floor, New York, NY 10001
212-604-9552
Jinella Hinds, Treasurer

New York City Justice Political Action Committee
132 Nassau Street, Room 200, New York, NY 10038
212-349-5890
Jeffrey A. Lichtman, Treasurer

New York City Partnership State PAC
One Battery Park Plaza, 5th Floor, New York, NY 10004
212-493-7400
Barry M. Gosin, Chairman

New York County Dental Society Political Action Committee
6 East 43rd Street, New York, NY 10017
212-573-8500
Elliot Davis, Chairman

New York Hotel & Motel Trades Council Committee
707 Eighth Avenue, New York, NY 10036
212-245-8100
Christopher K. Cusack, Chairman

New York Professional Nurses Union Political Action Committee
1104 Lexington Avenue, New York, NY 10075
212-988-5565
Maureen McCarthy, Chairwoman

New York State AFL-CIO COPE
100 South Swan Street, Albany, NY 12210
518-436-8516
Mario Cilento, Chairman

New York State Association of PBA's PAC
23 Reynolds Road, Glen Cove, NY 11542
Thomas Willidigg, Chairman

New York State Council of Machinists PAC Fund
652 4th Avenue, Brooklyn, NY 11232
718-422-0090
James Conigliaro, Chairman

New York State Higher Education - PAC
3210 Avenue H, 6C, Brooklyn, NY 11210
646-331-4612
Robert Ramos, Chairman

New York State Laborers' Political Action Committee
18 Corporate Woods Boulevard, Albany, NY 12211
518-449-1715
George S. Truicko, Chairman

New York State Nurses Association Political Action Committee
11 Cornell Road, Latham, NY 12110
518-782-9400
Linda O'Brien, Chairwoman

New Yorkers For Affordable Housing
15 Verbena Avenue, Suite 100, Floral Park, NY 11001
516-277-9317
Sol Arker, Treasurer

New Yorkers For De Blasio
65 Broadway, 803, New York, NY 10006
917-558-1390
Mark Peters, Treasurer

New Yorkers For Katz
219-12 74th Avenue, Bayside, NY 11364
718-465-7839
Melinda R. Katz, Chairwoman

New Yorkers For Putting Students First
345 7th Avenue, Suite 501, New York, NY 10001
212-257-4411
Enoch Woodhouse, Treasurer

New Yorkers For Robert Jackson
499 Fort Washington Avenue, 3A, New York, NY 10033
917-733-0439
Nan Beer, Treasurer

Nikki Lucas 2013
566 Essex Street, 2nd Floor, Brooklyn, NY 11208
347-457-8556
Aysha J. Gourdine, Treasurer

Nixon Peabody LLP PAC
1300 Clinton Square, Rochester, NY 14604
585-263-1000
Stephen J. Wallace, Chairman

Noah E. Gotbaum 2013
330 West 87th Street, New York, NY 10024
212-799-7291
Jeffrey D. Ravetz, Treasurer

NY CCR Nonpartisan PAC For Good Government
1 Coca-Cola Plaza NW, Atlanta, GA 30313
404-676-2121
William Hawkins, Chairman

NY Region 9A UAW PAC Council
111 South Road, Farmington, CT 06032
860-674-0143
Julie Kushner, Chairwoman

NYC District Council of Carpenters PAC
395 Hudson Street, 9th Floor, New York, NY 10014
212-366-3388
Stephen C. McInnis, Treasurer

NYC Greenfield
1011 East 3rd Street, Brooklyn, NY 11230
347-985-1135
Jeffrey Leb, Treasurer

NYS Democratic Senate Campaign Committee
1275 Scotch Church Road, Pattersonville, NY 12137
Jeffrey Klein, Chairman

NYSAFAH PAC
450 7th Avenue, Suite 2401, New York, NY 10123
646-473-1207
Frank J. Anelante, Jr., Treasurer

NYSRPA-PVF
90 South Swan Street, Suite 395, Albany, NY 12210
518-272-2654
Thomas H. King, Chairman

Oddo For Staten Island
131 Old Town Road, Staten Island, NY 10304
917-533-8241
Marie Carmody-LaFrancesca, Treasurer

Offices and agencies generally appear in alphabetical order, except when specific order is requested by listee.

Olanike Alabi 2013
PO Box 380075, Brooklyn, NY 10304
718-398-0750
Sharon J. Pierre, Treasurer

Organization of Staff Analysts PAC
220 East 23 Street, Suite 707, New York, NY 10010
212-686-1229
Robert J. Croghan, Chairman

Otano 2013
367 South 5th Street, 2B, Brooklyn, NY 11211
917-566-7542
Emily E. Gallagher, Treasurer

PAC L375 CSTG
125 Barclay Street, New York, NY 10013
212-815-1375
Claude Fort, Chairman

PAC of the Patrolmen's Benevolent Association of NYC
125 Broad Street, 11th Floor, New York, NY 10004
212-233-5531
Joseph A. Alejandro, Chairman

Palma 2013
1510 UnionPort Road, 11F, Bronx, NY 10462
347-733-5145
Ricky Pizarro, Treasurer

Pamela Johnson For NYC Council
3856 Bronx Boulevard, 7H, Bronx, NY 10467
347-762-8683
Geneva Johnson, Treasurer

Paul Graziano 2013
146-24 32nd Avenue, Flushing, NY 11354
718-358-2535
Stephen Garza, Treasurer

People For Albert Baldeo
106-11 Liberty Avenue, Ozone Park, NY 11417
718-323-8260
Mandrawattie Singh, Treasurer

People For Bing
132 East 43rd Street, New York, NY 10022
646-228-9111
Jonathan L. Bing, Chairman

People For Brodsky
2121 Saw Mill River Road, White Plains, NY 10607
914-720-5206
Richard L. Brodsky, Chairman

People For Carlton Berkley
4555 Carpenter Avenue, PH, New York, NY 10470
917-468-8461
Alexander Williams, Treasurer

People For Cheryl
585 West 214 Street, 4C, New York, NY 10034
646-314-3079
Cheryl A. Pahaham, Treasurer

People For Debra Cooper
290 West End Avenue, 9A, New York, NY 10024
212-362-7788
Darrell L. Paster, Treasurer

People For Diaz
840 Grand Concourse, 1A, Bronx, NY 10451
718-731-2009
Kalman Yeger, Treasurer

People For Jelani
83 Lefferts Place, Brooklyn, NY 11238
718-753-3302
Kuzaliwa Campbell, Treasurer

People For Jerome Rice
1505 Metropolitan Avenue, MG, Bronx, NY 10462
347-631-4489
Dawn Jeffrey, Treasurer

People For John C. Whitehead
903 Drew Street, 410, Brooklyn, NY 11208
718-216-2169
Leslie A. Murray, Treasurer

People For Lappin
333 East 55th Street, New York, NY 10022
718-541-3278
Andrew W. Wuertele, Treasurer

People For Leroy Gadsen
87-60 113th, 3C, Richmond Hills, NY 11418
917-297-7824
Candace Prince, Treasurer

People For Miguel Estrella
3716 10th Avenue, 13L, New York, NY 10034
347-664-7147
Aria Vargas, Treasurer

People For Pu-Folkes
78-27 37th Avenue, Suite 4, Jackson Heights, NY 11372
718-595-2045
Bryan R. Pu-Folkes, Chairman

People For Ydanis
475 Atlantic Avenue, 3rd Floor, Brooklyn, NY 11217
917-582-1405
Roberto A. Cruz, Treasurer

People For Yudelka Tapia
1941 Mulliner Avenue, Bronx, NY 10462
917-685-7810
Juan Mora, Treasurer

Peralta 2013
635 Hicksville Road, Far Rockaway, NY 11691
917-723-2097
Monique Renaud, Treasurer

Peralta For Senate
635 Hicksville Road, Far Rockaway, NY 11691
718-471-2475
Jose Peralta, Chairman

Peterson 2013
25-10 30th Road, Astoria, NY 11102
David Haywood, Treasurer

Pfizer Inc. PAC
235 East 42nd Street, New York, NY 10017
212-573-1265
Sally Susman, Chairman

Plumbers & Steamfitters Local No. 73 State & Local PAC Fund
705 East Seneca Street, PO Box 911, Oswego, NY 13126
315-343-4037
Eric M. Saunders, Chairman

Offices and agencies generally appear in alphabetical order, except when specific order is requested by listee.

Plumbers Local Union No. 1 NYC - Political Action Committee
158-29 George Meany Boulevard, Howard Beach, NY 11414
718-738-7500
John J. Murphy, Treasurer

Port Authority PBA of NY PAC
611 Palisade Avenue, Englewood Cliffs, NJ 07632
201-871-2100
Paul Nunziato, Chairman

Port Authority Police DEA NY PAC
Po Box 300406, JFK Station, Jamaica, NY 11430
201-216-6549
Patrick McNerney, Chairman

Powell 2013
134-35 166th Place, 4B, Jamaica, NY 11434
Dawn P. Martin, Treasurer

PSC PAC
61 Broadway, 15th Floor, New York, NY 10006
212-354-1252
Steven London, Chairman

Queens County Republican Committee
24-55 Francis Lewis Boulevard, Whitestone, NY 11357
718-690-3737
Phil Ragusa, Chairman

Quinn For New York
30 Vesey Street, 1st Floor, New York, NY 10007
917-438-7063
Kenneth T. Monteiro, Treasurer

Ralina Cardona 2013
286 Alexander Avenue, Bronx, NY 10454
Wilfred Renta, Treasurer

Rangel For Congress NY State
193 Lenox Avenue, Suite 1, New York, NY 10023
212-862-4990
James E. Capel, Chairman

Raquel Batista 2013
2104 Clinton Avenue, 2, Bronx, NY 10457
Katiuska M. Lopez, Treasurer

Re-Elect Eric Ulrich
101-17 84th Street, Ozone Park, NY 11416
917-951-7251
Ronald Kulick, Treasurer

Re-Elect Koslowitz 2013
6940 108th Street, c/o R. Croce, 3A, Forest Hills, NY 11375
718-268-3626
Ronnie Croce, Treasurer

Re-Elect Mealy
800 Hancock Street, 2A, Brooklyn, NY 11233
Marjorie Parker, Treasurer

Recchia For New York
172 Gravesend Neck Road, Brooklyn, NY 11223
718-336-3441
Marianna Wilen, Treasurer

Regina Powell 2013
675 Lincoln Avenue, 16F, Brooklyn, NY 11208
917-285-4894
Barrington Rodney, Treasurer

Reginald Boddie For Supreme Court
387 Halsey Street, Brooklyn, NY 11233
917-660-1487
Reginald A. Boddie, Chairman

Rego Hills Republican Club
85-32 65th Road, c/o Dolores Maddis, Rego Park, NY 11374
718-275-6005
Thomas Hoar, Chairman

Republican Majority For Choice NF PAC
2417 Jericho Turnpike, Suite 303, Garden City Park, NY 11040
516-316-6982
Kellie R. Ferguson, Chairman

Rescare Inc. Advocacy Fund
9901 Linn Station Road, Louisville, KY 40223
502-394-2335
Roger LaPoint, Chairman

Reshma For New York
240 West 23rd Street, 3C, New York, NY 10011
646-386-6398
Sumana Setty, Treasurer

Retail Wholesale and Department Store Union C.O.P.E.
30 East 29th Street, New York, NY 10016
212-684-5300
Stuart Appelbaum, Chairman

Rhonda F. Joseph 2013
910 Lenox Road, Brooklyn, NY 11203
917-751-7516
Basil A. Davidson, Treasurer

Rivera 2013
601 Pelham Parkway North, 501, Bronx, NY 10467
347-601-1551
Joel Rivera, Treasurer

Rivera 2013
1936 Haviland Avenue, Bronx, NY 10472
646-533-5228
Kenneth J. Thomas, Treasurer

Rosenthal For Assembly
321 West 89th Street, 6, New York, NY 10024
646-337-7700
Linda B. Rosenthal, Chairwoman

Rosie Mendez 2013
52 East 1st Street, c/o Kaplan, 2A, New York, NY 10003
646-229-6127
Lisa M. Kaplan, Treasurer

RPAC of New York
130 Washington Avenue, Albany, NY 12210
518-463-0300
Harding Mason, Chairman

RSA PAC City Account
123 Williams Street, 14th Floor, New York, NY 10038
212-214-9266
Frank P. Ricci, Treasurer

Ruben Wills 2013
194-19 115 Drive, St. Albans, NY 11412
516-663-0630
Sharon Carnegie-Hall, Treasurer

Offices and agencies generally appear in alphabetical order, except when specific order is requested by listee.

RWDSU Local 338 Political Action Committee
1505 Kellum Place, Mineola, NY 11501
516-294-1338
John R. Durso, Chairman

Sal 2013
957 78th Street, Brooklyn, NY 11228
917-992-1693
John H. O'Donnell, Treasurer

Sanders For Senate
1526 Central Avenue, 3rd Floor, Far Rockaway, NY 11691
718-471-7111
Donovan J. Richards, Treasurer

Sanitation Officers Association Volunteer Political Action COPE Account
8510 Bay 16th Street, 2nd Floor, Brooklyn, NY 11214
718-837-9832
Joseph Mannion, Chairman

Santiago NYC 2013
50 Manhattan Avenue, 4H, Brooklyn, NY 11206
Juan C. Pocasangre, Treasurer

Santos 2013
420 East 21st Street, Brooklyn, NY 11226
307-340-1074
Luke L. Frye, Treasurer

Sarah M. Gonzalez 2013
512 83rd Street, Brooklyn, NY 11209
307-340-1074
Sonia Rodriguez, Treasurer

Sasson For NYC
43-70 Kissena Boulevard, 14H, Flushing, NY 11355
718-461-9338
Amul Mehta, Treasurer

Saundra Thomas 2013
490 Stratford Road, Brooklyn, NY 11218
718-282-5595
Gary M. Singer, Treasurer

Savino For New York
481 8th Avenue, Suite 1202, New York, NY 10001
212-239-7323
Diane J. Savino, Chairwoman

SEIU Political Education and State Action Fund
1800 Massachusetts Avenue, N.W., Washington, DC 20036
202-730-7000
Mary Kay Henry, Chairwoman

Semper Fi NYS PAC Inc.
17 Christopher Street, New York, NY 10014
212-269-7308
Christopher Johnson, Chairman

Sergeants Benevolent Association
35 Worth Street, New York, NY 10013
212-226-2180
Robert Ganley, Chairman

Service Corporation International Political Association Committee
1929 Allen Parkway, Houston, TX 77019
713-525-9062
Caressa F. Hughes, Chairwoman

Sidique Wai For Public Advocate
770 Empire Boulevard, 2N, Brooklyn, NY 11213
201-526-1422
Fritzner L. Altidor, Treasurer

Sierra 2013
1581 Fulton Avenue, 1B, Bronx, NY 10457
201-526-1422
Jonathan Vizcaino, Treasurer

Silverstein 2013
211-40 18th Avenue, 3K, Bayside, NY 11360
718-644-0791
Gary Jacobowitz, Treasurer

Simcha NY
475 Atlantic Avenue, 3rd Floor, Brooklyn, NY 11217
718-852-3710
Simcha Felder, Chairman

Simmons-Oliver For City Council
4120 Hutchinson River Parkway East, 15A, Bronx, NY 10475
917-596-7251
Rafael Paulino, Treasurer

SMWIA Local 28 Political Action Committee
500 Greenwich Street, New York, NY 10013
212-941-7700
Frederick Buckheit, Treasurer

SMWIA Political Action League Local 137
21-42 44th Drive, Long Island City, NY 11101
718-937-4514
Paul Collins, Jr., Chairman

Soft Drink and Brewery Workers Political Action Committee
445 Northern Boulevard, Great Neck, NY 11021
516-303-1455
John O'Neill, Chairman

Sondra Peeden 2013
40 Memorial Highway, 33F, New Rochelle, NY 10801
914-355-4197
Katrina De La Cruz, Treasurer

South Asians United For a Better America PAC
333 East 30th Street, 2D, New York, NY 10016
571-228-6925
Prince Agarwal, Chairman

Squadron For New York
219 West 81st Street, 8D, New York, NY 10024
212-228-5222
Anne S. Squadron, Treasurer

SSL Political Action Committee
180 Maiden Lane, 34th Floor, New York, NY 10038
212-806-5851
Leonard S. Boxer, Chairman

Staten Island PAC
32 Cunard Place, Staten Island, NY 10304
718-816-2237
James P. Molinaro, Chairman

Steamfitters Local 638 PAC
32-32 48th Avenue, Long Island City, NY 11101
718-392-3420
John J. Torpey, Chairman

Offices and agencies generally appear in alphabetical order, except when specific order is requested by listee.

Stringer 2013
40 Worth Street, Suite 812, New York, NY 10013
212-349-2013
Peter Frank, Treasurer

STV Engineers Inc. Political Action Committee
205 West Welsh Drive, Douglassville, PA 19518
610-385-8294
Dominick M. Servedio, Chairman

Suffolk County Association of Municipal Employees, Inc -
Political Action Committee
30 Orville Drive, Suite A, Bohemia, NY 11716
631-589-8400
Cheryl A. Felice, Chairwoman

Sullivan For NYC
138 71st Street, 9F, Brooklyn, NY 11209
516-522-4033
Maureen J. Daly, Treasurer

Sunny Hahn For City Council
137-60 45th Avenue, 4N, Flushing, NY 11355
718-888-9420
Stuart Garmise, Treasurer

Tamika For City Council 2013
342 East 119th Street, 5B, New York, NY 10035
516-782-9339
Monisha R. Mapp, Treasurer

Taxpayers For an Affordable New York Political Action
Committee
570 Lexington Avenue, 2nd Floor, New York, NY 10022
212-616-5224
Steven Spinola, Chairman

Team Greenfield
1011 East 3rd Street, Brooklyn, NY 11230
347-985-1135
Jeffrey Leb, Treasurer

Teamsters Local 813 PAC
45-18 Court Square, Suite 600, Long Island City, NY 11101
718-937-7010
Anthony Marino, Chairman

Tempo 802
322 West 48th Street, New York, NY 10036
John O'Connor, Chairman

The Committee to Re-Elect Inez E. Dickens 2013
2153 Adam Calyton Powell Jr. Boulevard, New York, NY 10027
212-749-3615
Delores Richards, Treasurer

The Debi Rose Campaign Committee
1300 Richmond Avenue, 23A, Staten Island, NY 10314
646-675-7617
Emanuel Braxton, Treasurer

The General Contractors Association of New York PAC
60 East 42nd Street, New York, NY 10165
212-687-3131
Denise M. Richardson, Chairwoman

The High-Need Hospital PAC, Inc.
12 Stuyvesant Oval, 9A, New York, NY 10009
212-674-6122
Mark Pollack, Chairman

The N.Y. Public Library Guild, Local 1930
125 Barclay Street, Room 701PAC, New York, NJ 10007
212-815-1930
Valentin Colon, Chairman

The NYS Economic Growth PAC
60 Columbus Circle, New York, NY 10023
212-801-1162
Eugene Angelo, Treasurer

Theatrical Teamsters Local 817 PAC Fund
127 Cutter Mill Road, Great Neck, NY 11021
516-365-3470
Thomas I. O'Donnell, Chairman

Thomas Lopez-Pierre For City Council 2013
927 Columbus Avenue, 5S, New York, NY 10025
646-363-9047
Thomas Lopez-Pierre, Treasurer

Tile, Marble & Terrazzo BAC Union Local 7 PAC Fund
45-34 Court Square, Long Island City, NY 11101
718-786-7648
Thomas W. Lane, Chairman

Toll Bros., Inc. PAC
250 Gibraltar Road, Horsham, PA 19044
215-938-8000
Zvi Barzilay, Chairman

Tom Allon 2013
17 east 17th Street, 4th Floor, New York, NY 10003
347-960-2399
Charles Platkin, Treasurer

Tom Duane For Senate
80 8th Avenue, #1802, New York, NY 10011
646-265-7082
Thomas K. Duane, Chairman

Tony Avella For Queens
PO Box 570052, Whitestone, NY 11357
718-762-0235
Rocco F. D'Erasmo, Treasurer

Torodash For Truth
12325 82nd Avenue, 5T, Kew Gardens, NY 11415
646-318-1426
Meredith Helfenbein, Treasurer

TPU Local One IATSE NYC
20 West 46th Street, New York, NY 10036
212-333-2500
James J. Claffey, Jr., Chairman

Transport Workers Union Local 100
80 West End Avenue, New York, NY 10023
212-873-6000
John Samuelsen, Chairman

Ullico Inc. Political Action Committee
1625 Eye Street, NW, Washington, DC 20006
Edward M. Smith, Chairman

Uniformed Fire Officers 527 Account
225 Broadway, Suite 401, New York, NY 10007
212-293-9300
Alexander Hagan, Chairman

Uniformed Firefighters Association State FIREPAC
204 East 23rd Street, New York, NY 10010
212-683-4832
James Slevin, Chairman

Offices and agencies generally appear in alphabetical order, except when specific order is requested by listee.

Unite Here Local 2 PAC
209 Golden Gate Avenue, San Francisco, CA 94102
415-864-8770
Michael Casey, Treasurer

Unite Here Local 26 Political Committee
33 Harrison Avenue, 4th Floor, Boston, MA 02111
617-426-1515
Brian Lang, Chairman

Unite Here Local 5 PAC Fund
1516 South King Street, Honolulu, HI 96826
808-941-2141
Godfrey T. Maeshiro, Chairman

Unite Here Local 54 PAC Committee
203-205 North Sovereign Avenue, Atlantic City, NJ 08401
609-344-5400
Charles R. McDevitt, Chairman

Unite Here Tip State and Local Fund
275 Seventh Avenue, 11th Floor, New York, NY 10001
212-265-7000
Donald Taylor, Chairman

United Federation of Teachers (UFT) on Political Education
52 Broadway, New York, NY 10004
212-598-7744
Paul Egan, Chairman

United Food & Commercial Workers Active Ballot Club
1775 K Street, NW, Washington, DC 20006
202-223-3111
Joseph T. Hansen, Chairman

United Neighbors for Neville Mitchell
888 East 233rd Street, Bronx, NY 10469
347-224-9880
Derrick L. Shippy, Treasurer

United Parcel Service Inc. Political Action Committee - New York
55 Glenlake Parkway, NE, Atlanta, GA 30328
404-828-6012
Teri P. McClure, Chairwoman

UWUA Local 1-2 Non Federal PAC
5 West 37th Street, New York, NY 10018
212-575-4400
Lucia Pagano, Treasurer

Vallone For New York
22-45 31st Street, Suite 6, Astoria, NY 11105
718-274-0007
Albana Haxhia, Treasurer

Van Bramer 2013
39-19 46th Street, Sunnyside, NY 11104
718-786-1324
Phillip L. Velez, Treasurer

Vargas 2013
105 West 104th Street, 3A, New York, NY 10025
646-330-5411
Ruben Vargas, Sr., Treasurer

Veras For Council 2013
141-60 84th Road, 5C, Briarwood, NY 11435
917-589-1459
Zlata Akilova, Treasurer

Verizon Communications Good Government Club PAC
140 West Street, Floor 30, New York, NY 10007
212-321-8110
James J. Gerace, Chairman

Victor Babb For N.Y.C. Council
106-03 Liberty Avenue, Ozone Park, NY 11417
917-324-8071
Henderson Kinch, Treasurer

Vince Morgan 2013
130 Lenox Avenue, 1003, New York, NY 10026
347-602-0908
RD Snyden, Treasurer

Vish Mahadeo 2010
130-10 109th Avenue, South Ozone Park, NY 11420
646-918-0334
Videsh A. Persaud, Treasurer

Vito Lopez For City Council
1704 Decatur Street, Ridgewood, NY 11385
347-744-8632
Andy J. Marte, Treasurer

Viverito 2013
211 East 111th Street, 2, New York, NY 10029
212-426-7552
Randolph Mark, Treasurer

Vote Vallone 2013
25-59 Francis Lewis Boulevard, Flushing, NY 11358
718-428-7285
Vito Tautonico, Treasurer

VoteBhusan2013
2793 Brighton 8th Street, Brooklyn, NY 11235
646-295-0629
Leonard H. Sturner, Treasurer

Weiner For Mayor
254 Park Avenue South, 12A, New York, NY 10010
212-777-7755
Nelson Braff, Treasurer

Wilson Elser Moskowitz Edelman & Dicker LLP, PAC
677 Broadway, Albany, NY 12207
518-449-8893
Cynthia D. Shenker, Chairwoman

Win With Winslow
162-10 South Road, Jamaica, NY 11433
347-423-4233
Shannell T. Harper, Treasurer

WM NY PAC
701 Pennsylvania Avenue, NW, Suite 590, Washington, DC 20004
202-639-1221
Barry Caldwell, Chairman

Women's Democratic Club of NYC
100 West 12th Street, 4M, New York, NY 10113
646-657-8040
Patricia S. Rudden, Chairwoman

Wright 2013
297 Hancock Street, Brooklyn, NY 11216
718-399-3807
Kimberly B. Berry, Treasurer

Political Parties, Lobbyists & PACs

Offices and agencies generally appear in alphabetical order, except when specific order is requested by listee.

Zead Ramadan 2013
5900 Arlington Avenue, 22V, Bronx, NY 10471
212-882-1520
Rasul H. Miller, Treasurer

ZETEPAC
PO Box 75021, Washington, DC 20013
202-210-5431
Dan Backer, Chairman

Section 5:
BUSINESS

CHAMBERS OF COMMERCE and ECONOMIC & INDUSTRIAL DEVELOPMENT ORGANIZATIONS

Provides a combined listing of public and private organizations involved in regional economic development.

Adirondack Economic Development Corporation
67 Main St, Ste 300, PO Box 747, Saranac Lake, NY 12983-0747
518-891-5523 or 888-243-2332 Fax: 518-891-9820
e-mail: nwright@aedconline.com
Web site: www.aedconline.com

Adirondack Regional Chambers of Commerce
136 Glen Street, Ste 3, Glens Falls, NY 12801
518-798-1761 Fax: 518-792-4147
e-mail: paust@adirondackchamber.org
Web site: www.adirondackchamber.org
Peter Aust, President & CEO

Adirondacks Speculator Region Chamber of Commerce
PO Box 184, Rts 30 & 8, Speculator, NY 12164
518-548-4521 Fax: 518-548-4905
e-mail: info@speculatorchamber.com
Web site: www.speculatorchamber.com
Cathleen Connolly, President

African American Chamber of Commerce of Westchester & Rockland Counties
100 Stevens Ave, Ste 202, Mount Vernon, NY 10550
914-699-9050 Fax: 914-699-6279
e-mail: robinlisadouglas@cs.com
Web site: www.aaccnys.org
Robin L Douglas, Founder & CEO & President

Albany County Industrial Development Agency
112 State St, Room 825, Albany, NY 12207-2017
518-447-7040 Fax: 518-447-5589
e-mail: county_executive@albanycounty.com
Web site: www.albanycounty.com
Daniel McCoy, County Executive

Albany-Colonie Regional Chamber of Commerce
5 Computer Drive South, Albany, NY 12205-1631
518-431-1400 Fax: 518-431-1402
e-mail: info@acchamber.org
Web site: www.acchamber.org
Mark Egan, CEO

Alden Chamber of Commerce
13500 Broadway, PO Box 149, Alden, NY 14004
716-937-6177 Fax: 716-937-4106
e-mail: secretary@aldenny.org
Web site: www.aldenny.org
Christopher Gust, President

Alexandria Bay Chamber of Commerce
7 Market St, Alexandria Bay, NY 13607
315-482-9531 or 800-541-2110 Fax: 315-482-5434
e-mail: info@alexbay.org
Web site: www.visitalexbay.org
Susan Boyer, Executive Director

Allegany County Office of Development & Industrial Development Agency (IDA)
Crossroads Commerce Center, 6087 NYS Rte 19 North, Suite 100, Belmont, NY 14813
585-268-5500 or 800-836-1869 Fax: 585-268-7473
e-mail: tourism@alleganyco.com
Web site: www.discoveralleganycounty.com
John E Foels, Director of Development & IDA

American Indonesian Chamber of Commerce
317 Madison Ave, Suite 1619, New York, NY 10017
212-687-4505
Web site: www.aiccusa.org
Wayne Forrest, President

Amherst Chamber of Commerce
Centerpointe Corporate Park, 350 Essjay Road, Suite 200, Williamsville, NY 14221
716-632-6905 Fax: 716-632-0548
e-mail: cdipirro@amherst.org
Web site: www.amherst.org
Colleen C DiPirro, CEO & President

Amherst Industrial Development Agency (Town of)
4287 Main Street, Amherst, NY 14226
716-688-9000 Fax: 716-688-0205
e-mail: jallen@amherstida.com
Web site: www.amherstida.com
James Allen, Executive Director

Amsterdam Industrial Development Agency
City Hall, 61 Church St, Amsterdam, NY 12010
518-841-4305 Fax: 518-841-4300
e-mail: fvaliante@amsterdamida.com
Web site: www.amsterdamida.com
Frank Valiante, Executive Director

Arcade Area Chamber of Commerce
684 W. Main St., Arcade, NY 14009
585-492-2114 Fax: 585-492-5103
e-mail: aacc278@verizon.net
Web site: www.arcadechamber.org
Dorie Clinch, Executive Secretary

Babylon Industrial Development Agency
47 West Main St, Ste 3, Babylon, NY 11702
631-587-3679 Fax: 631-587-3675
e-mail: info@babylonida.org
Web site: www.babylonida.org
Robert Stricoff, CEO

Bainbridge Chamber of Commerce
PO Box 2, Bainbridge, NY 13733
607-967-8700
e-mail: bainbridge.chamber@yahoo.com
Web site: www.bainbridgeny.org
Barb Mulkins, President

Baldwin Chamber of Commerce
PO Box 804, Baldwin, NY 11510
516-223-8080
e-mail: info@baldwinchamber.com
Web site: baldwinchamber.com
Eric Mahlar, Co-President; Ralph Rose, Co-President

Baldwinsville Chamber of Commerce (Greater Baldwinsville)
27 Marble Street, Baldwinsville, NY 13027
315-638-0550 Fax: 315-720-1450
e-mail: baldwinsvillechamger@gmail.com
Web site: www.baldwinsvillechamber.com
Anthony Saraceni, President

Bath Area Chamber of Commerce (Greater Bath Area)
10 Pulteney Square W, Bath, NY 14810
607-776-7122 Fax: 607-776-7122
e-mail: email@bathnychamber.com
Web site: www.americantowns.com
Jim Maglione, Co-President
Ed Panian, Co-President

Offices and agencies generally appear in alphabetical order, except when specific order is requested by listee.

Bayshore Chamber of Commerce
77 East Main St, PO Box 5110, Bayshore, NY 11706
631-665-7003 Fax: 631-665-5204
e-mail: bayshorecofcbid@optonline.net
Web site: www.bayshorecommerce.com
Donna Periconi, President

Bellmores Chamber of Commerce
2700 Pettit Avenue, N Bellmore, NY 11710
516-679-1875 Fax: 516-409-0544
e-mail: info@bellmorechamber.com
Web site: www.bellmorechamber.com
Debbie Izzo, President

Bethlehem Chamber of Commerce
184 Greenwood Avenue, Delmar, NY 12054
518-439-0512 Fax: 518-475-0910
e-mail: info@bethlehemchamber.com
Web site: www.bethlehemchamber.com
Lorraine Schrameck, Co-President
Lisa Whitmore, Co-President

Bethlehem Industrial Development Agency (Town of)
445 Delaware Ave, Delmar, NY 12054
518-439-4955 Fax: 518-439-5808
e-mail: mmorelli@townofbethlehem.org
Web site: www.bethlehemida.com
Michael Morellia, Executive Director & CEO

Bethpage Chamber of Commerce
PO Box 636, Bethpage, NY 11714
516-433-0010
Dennis Brady, President/CEO

Binghamton Chamber of Commerce (Greater Binghamton)
49 Court Street, PO Box 995, Binghamton, NY 13902
607-772-8860 Fax: 607-722-4513
e-mail: chamber@greaterbinghamtonchamber.com
Web site: www.greaterbinghamtonchamber.com
Lou Santoni, President & CEO

Black Lake Chamber of Commerce
PO Box 12, Hammond, NY 13646
315-375-8640
e-mail: info@blacklake.com
Web site: www.blacklakeny.com
William Dashnshaw, President
Carole McCann, President

Blue Mountain Lake Association
PO Box 724, Indian Lake, NY 12842
518-642-5112 Fax: 518-648-5489
Web site: indian-lake.com
Christine Pouch, President

Bolton Landing Chamber of Commerce
4928 Lake Shore Drive, Bolton Landing, NY 12814-0368
518-644-3831 Fax: 518-644-5951
e-mail: mail@boltonchamber.com
Web site: www.boltonchamber.com
Dave Forshay, President

Boonville Area Chamber of Commerce
122 Main St, PO Box 163, Boonville, NY 13309
315-942-5112 Fax: 315-942-6823
e-mail: info@boonvillechamber.com
Web site: www.boonvillechamber.com
Melinda Wittwer, Executive Secretary

Brewster Chamber of Commerce
16 Mount Ebo Road S, Ste 12A, Brewster, NY 10509
845-279-2477 Fax: 845-278-8349
e-mail: info@brewsterchamber.com
Web site: www.brewsterchamber.com
Rose Z. Aglieco, Executive Director

Brockport Chamber of Commerce (Greater Brockport)
PO Box 119, Brockport, NY 14420
585-234-1512
Web site: brockportchamber.org
Marie Bell, President

Bronx Chamber of Commerce
Hutchinson Metro Center, 1200 Waters Place, Suite 106, Bronx, NY 10461
718-828-3900 Fax: 718-409-3748
e-mail: info@bronxchamber.com
Web site: www.bronxchamber.org
Lenny Caro, President

Bronxville Chamber of Commerce
81 Pondfield Rd, Suite 7, Bronxville, NY 10708
914-337-6040 Fax: 914-337-6040
e-mail: bronxvillechamber@verizon.net
Web site: www.bronxvillechamber.com
Susan Miele, Executive Director

Town of Brookhaven Industrial Development Agency
1 Independence Hill, Farmingville, NY 11738
631-451-6563 Fax: 631-451-6925
e-mail: lmulligan@brookhaven.org
Web site: www.brookhavenida.org
Lisa Mulligan, CEO

Brooklyn Chamber of Commerce
25 Elm Place, Suite 200, 2nd Floor, Brooklyn, NY 11201
718-875-1000 Fax: 718-222-0781
e-mail: info@brooklynchamber.com
Web site: www.ibrooklyn.com
Veronica Harris, Director/HR/Administration/Operations

Brooklyn Economic Development Corporation
2001 Oriental Blvd, Rm T-4162, Brooklyn, NY 11235
718-368-6790 Fax: 718-368-6788
e-mail: info@bedc.org
Web site: www.bedc.org
Joan G Bartolomeo, President

Broome County Industrial Development Agency
PO Box 1510, Binghamton, NY 13902-1510
607-584-9000 Fax: 607-584-9009
e-mail: info@bcida.com
Web site: www.bcida.com
Richard D'Attilio, Executive Director

Buffalo Economic Renaissance Corporation
Office of Strategic Planning, City of Buffalo, 920 City Hall, Buffalo, NY 14202-3309
716-851-5035 Fax: 716-842-6942
e-mail: contact@berc.org
Web site: www.berc.org
Timothy E Wanamaker, Interim President

Buffalo Niagara Partnership
665 Main Street, Suite 200, Buffalo, NY 14203-1487
716-852-7100 Fax: 716-852-2761
e-mail: arudnick@thepartnership.org
Web site: www.thepartnership.org
Andrew J Rudnick, President & CEO

Offices and agencies generally appear in alphabetical order, except when specific order is requested by listee.

Business Council of Westchester, The
108 Corporate Park Drive, Suite 101, White Plains, NY 10604
914-948-2110 Fax: 914-948-0122
Web site: www.westchesterny.org
Dr Marsha Gordon, President/CEO

Canandaigua Area Chamber of Commerce
113 S Main St, Canandaigua, NY 14424
585-394-4400 Fax: 585-394-4546
e-mail: chamber@canandaiguachamber.com
Web site: www.canandaiguachamber.com
Alison Grems, President & CEO

Canastota Chamber of Commerce
222 S Peterboro St, PO Box 206, Canastota, NY 13032
315-697-3677
Web site: www.canastota.org
Rick Stevens, President

Canton Chamber of Commerce
PO Box 369, 60 Main Street, Canton, NY 13617
315-386-8255 Fax: 315-386-8255
e-mail: cantoncc@northnet.org
Web site: www.cantonnychamber.org
Sally Hill, Executive Director

Cape Vincent Chamber of Commerce
PO Box 482, 173 N James Street, Cape Vincent, NY 13618
315-654-2481 Fax: 315-654-4141
e-mail: thecape@tds.net
Web site: www.capevincent.org
501C (6) organization supported by over 200 mebers including businesses,
organizations, and individuals.
Shelley Higgins, Executive Director

Capitalize Albany Corporation
21 Lodge St, Albany, NY 12207
518-434-2532 Fax: 518-434-9846
e-mail: info@capitalizealbany.com
Web site: www.capitalizealbany.com
Michael Yevoli, CEO

Carthage Area Chamber of Commerce
120 S. Mechanic Street, Carthage, NY 13619
315-493-3590 Fax: 315-493-3590
e-mail: carthagechamber@centralny.twcbc.com
Web site: www.carthageny.com
Lori Borland, Executive Director

Cattaraugus Empire Zone Corporation
120 N Union St, Olean, NY 14760
716-373-9260 Fax: 716-372-7912
e-mail: meme@oleanny.com
Web site: www.cattempirezone.org
James Snyder, President

Cayuga County Chamber of Commerce
2 State Street, Auburn, NY 13021
315-252-7291 Fax: 315-255-3077
e-mail: admin@cayugacountychamber.com
Web site: www.cayugacountychamber.com
Andrew Fish, Executive Director

Cazenovia Area Chamber of Commerce (Greater Cazenovia Area)
59 Albany St, Cazenovia, NY 13035
315-655-9243 or 888-218-6305 Fax: 315-655-9244
e-mail: info@cazenovia.com
Web site: www.cazenoviachamber.com
Gene Gissin, Chairman

Central Adirondack Association
PO Box 68, Old Forge, NY 13420
315-369-6983 or 877-653-3674 Fax: 315-369-2676
e-mail: lbarkauskas@visitmyadirondacks.com
Web site: www.visitmyadirondacks.com
Laurie Barkauskas, Events Coordinator

Central Catskills Chamber of Commerce
PO Box 605, Margaretville, NY 12455
845-586-3300 Fax: 845-586-3161
e-mail: chamber@centralcatskills.com
Web site: www.centralcatskills.com
John Tufillaro, President

Chamber of Commerce of the Tonawandas
15 Webster Street, North Tonawanda, NY 14120
716-692-5120 Fax: 716-692-1867
e-mail: chamber@the-tonawandas.com
Web site: www.thetonawandas.com
Joyce M Santiago, Executive Director

Chaumont-Three Mile Bay Chamber of Commerce
PO Box 24, Three Mile Bay, NY 13693
315-694-3404
e-mail: chaumontchamber@yahoo.com
Web site: www.chaumontchamber.com
Amanda Miller, President

Chautauqua County Chamber of Commerce
512 Falconer St, Jamestown, NY 14701
716-484-1101 Fax: 716-487-0785
e-mail: cccc@chautauquachamber.org
Web site: www.chautauquachamber.org
Todd Tranum, President/CEO

Chautauqua County Chamber of Commerce, Dunkirk Branch
10785 Bennett Road, Dunkirk, NY 14048
716-366-6200 Fax: 761-366-4276
e-mail: cccc@chautauquachamber.org
Web site: www.chautauquachamber.org

Chautauqua County Industrial Development Agency
200 Harrison St, Jamestown, NY 14701
716-661-8900 Fax: 716-664-4515
e-mail: ccida@ccida.com
Web site: www.ccida.com
William Daly, CEO

Cheektowaga Chamber of Commerce
AppleTree Business Park, 2875 Union Road, Ste 50, Cheektowaga, NY 14227
716-684-5838 Fax: 716-684-5571
e-mail: chamber@cheektowaga.org
Web site: www.cheektowaga.org
Debra S Liegl, President & CEO

Chemung County Chamber of Commerce
400 E Church St, Elmira, NY 14901-2803
607-734-5137 Fax: 607-734-4490
e-mail: info@chemungchamber.org
Web site: www.chemungchamber.org
Kevin D Keeley, President & CEO

Chemung County Industrial Development Agency
400 Church Street, Elmira, NY 14901
607-733-6513 Fax: 607-734-2698
e-mail: gminer@steg.com
Web site: www.steg.com
George Miner, President

Offices and agencies generally appear in alphabetical order, except when specific order is requested by listee.

Chambers of Commerce

Chenango County Chamber of Commerce
15 South Broad Street, Norwich, NY 13815
607-334-1400 or 877-243-6264 Fax: 607-336-6963
e-mail: info@chenangony.org
Web site: www.chenangony.org
Steve Craig, President/CEO

Clarence Chamber of Commerce
8899 Main Street, Suite 4, Clarence, NY 14031
716-631-3888 Fax: 716-631-3946
e-mail: info@clarence.org
Web site: www.clarencechamber.org
Judy Sirianni, President

Clarence Industrial Development Agency (Town of)
1 Town Place, Clarence, NY 14031
716-741-8930 Fax: 716-741-4715
Web site: www.clarence.ny.us
David Hartzell, Chairman

Clayton Chamber of Commerce
517 Riverside Dr, Clayton, NY 13624
315-686-3771 or 800-252-9806 Fax: 315-686-5564
e-mail: info@1000islands-clayton.com
Web site: www.1000islands-clayton.com
Tricia Bannister, Executive Director

Clifton Springs Area Chamber of Commerce
2 E Main St, PO Box 86, Clifton Springs, NY 14432
315-462-8200 Fax: 315-548-6429
e-mail: info@cliftonspringschamber.com
Web site: www.cliftonspringschamber.com
Jeff Criblear, President

Clinton Chamber of Commerce Inc
PO Box 142, Clinton, NY 13323
315-853-1735 Fax: 315-853-1735
e-mail: info@clintonnychamber.org
Web site: www.clintonnychamber.org
Ferris J Betrus, Executive Vice President

Clinton County, The Development Corporation
190 Banker Rd, Suite 500, Plattsburgh, NY 12901
518-563-3100 or 888-699-6757 Fax: 518-562-2232
e-mail: tdc@thedevelopcorp.com
Web site: www.thedevelopcorp.com
Paul Grasso, President/CEO

Clyde Chamber of Commerce
24 Park Street, PO Box 69, Clyde, NY 14433
315-923-4862 Fax: 315-923-9862
e-mail: info@clydeontheerie.com
Web site: www.co.wayne.ny.us
Rudolph A DeLisio, President

Clyde Industrial Development Corporation
PO Box 92, Clyde, NY 14433
315-923-7238 Fax: 315-923-9863
e-mail: info@clydeontheerie.com
Web site: www.clydeontheerie.com
Kenneth DiSanto, President

Cohoes Industrial Development Agency (City of)
97 Mohawk Street, Cohoes, NY 12047
518-233-2117 Fax: 518-233-2168
e-mail: mayor@ci.cohoes.ny.us
Web site: www.cohoesida.org
Adam Hotaling, Chairman

Colonie Chamber of Commerce
950 New Loudon Rd, Latham, NY 12110
518-785-6995 Fax: 518-785-7173
e-mail: info@coloniechamber.org
Web site: www.coloniechamber.org
Tom Nolte, President

Columbia County Chamber of Commerce
1 North Front Street, Hudson, NY 12534
518-828-4417 Fax: 518-822-9539
e-mail: mail@columbiachamber-ny.com
Web site: www.columbiachamber-ny.com
David B Colby, President

Columbia Hudson Partnership
4303 Rte 9, Hudson, NY 12534-2415
518-828-4718 Fax: 518-828-0901
e-mail: kenneth.flood@columbiacountyny.com
Web site: www.chpartnership.com
Kenneth J Flood, Executive Director

Coney Island Chamber of Commerce
1015 Surf Ave, Brooklyn, NY 11224
718-266-1234 Fax: 718-714-0379
Norman Kaufman, President

Cooperstown Chamber of Commerce
31 Chestnut St, Cooperstown, NY 13326
607-547-9983 Fax: 607-547-6006
e-mail: info1@cooperstownchamber.org
Web site: www.cooperstownchamber.org
Susan O'Handley, Executive Director

Copiague Chamber of Commerce
PO Box 8, Copiague, NY 11726
631-226-2956
e-mail: info@copiaguechamber.org
Web site: copiaguechamber.org
Sharon Fattoruso, Board President

Corinth Industrial Development Agency (Town of)
600 Palmer Ave, Corinth, NY 12822
518-654-9232 Fax: 518-654-7615
e-mail: rlucia@townofcorinthny.com
Web site: www.townofcorinthny.com
Richard B Lucia, Chairman

Corning Area Chamber of Commerce
1 West Market Street, Suite 202, Corning, NY 14830
607-936-4686 or 866-463-6264 Fax: 607-936-4685
e-mail: info@corningny.com
Web site: www.corningny.com
Denise Ackley, President

Cortland County Chamber of Commerce
37 Church St, Cortland, NY 13045
607-756-2814 Fax: 607-756-4698
e-mail: info@cortlareachamber.com
Web site: www.cortlandareachamber.com
Bob Haight, Executive Director
Bradley Totman, President
Debbie Thayer, Manager of Member Services

Coxsackie Area Chamber of Commerce
PO Box 251, Coxsackie, NY 12051
518-731-7300
e-mail: info@coxsackieregionalchamber.com
Web site: www.coxsackieareachamber.com
Bradley Totman, President

Offices and agencies generally appear in alphabetical order, except when specific order is requested by listee.

Cutchogue-New Suffolk Chamber of Commerce
PO Box 610, Cutchogue, NY 11935
631-734-2335 Fax: 631-734-5050
Richard Noncarrow, President

Dansville Chamber of Commerce
126 Main St, PO Box 105, Dansville, NY 14437
585-335-6290 or 800-949-0174 Fax: 585-335-6296
e-mail: dansvillechamber@hotmail.com
Web site: www.dansvilleny.net
William Bacon, President

Delaware County Chamber of Commerce
5 1/2 Main Street, Delhi, NY 13753
607-746-2281 Fax: 607-746-3571
e-mail: info@delawarecounty.org
Web site: www.delawarecounty.org
Mary Beth Silano, Executive Director

Delaware County Planning Department
PO Box 367, Delhi, NY 13753
607-746-2944 Fax: 607-746-8479
e-mail: pln@co.delaware.ny.us
Web site: www.delawarecountyplanning.com
Nicole Franzese, Director of Planning

Deposit Chamber of Commerce
PO Box 222, Deposit, NY 13754
Web site: www.depositchamber.com
Nick Barone, President

Development Authority of the North Country
317 Washington Street, Watertown, NY 13601
315-661-3200 or 800-662-1220 Fax: 315-785-2591
e-mail: info@danc.org
Web site: www.danc.org
James Wright, Executive Director

Dover-Wingdale Chamber of Commerce
PO Box 643, Dover Plains, NY 12522
845-877-9800
Melanie Ryder, President

Downtown-Lower Manhattan Association
120 Broadway, Rm 3340, New York, NY 10271
212-566-6700 Fax: 212-566-6707
e-mail: contactus@downtownny.com
Web site: downtownny.com
Elizabeth Berger, President

Dutchess County Economic Development Corporation
3 Neptune Rd, Poughkeepsie, NY 12601
845-463-5400 or 845-463-5407 Fax: 845-463-5401
e-mail: pbalga@dcedc.com
Web site: http://thinkdutchess.com
Pamela J Balga, Administrative Services Manager

East Aurora Chamber of Commerce (Greater East Aurora)
652 Main Street, East Aurora, NY 14052-1783
716-652-8444 Fax: 716-652-8384
e-mail: eanycc@verizon.net
Web site: www.eanycc.com
Gary D Grote, Executive Director

East Hampton Chamber of Commerce
42 Gingerbread Lane, East Hampton, NY 11937
631-324-0362 Fax: 631-329-1642
e-mail: info@easthamptonchamber.com
Web site: www.easthamptonchamber.com
Marina Van, Executive Director

East Islip Chamber of Commerce
PO Box 88, East Islip, NY 11730
631-859-5000
Web site: www.isliplife.com/eastislipchamber
Tony Fanni, President

East Meadow Chamber of Commerce
PO Box 77, East Meadow, NY 11554
516-794-3727 Fax: 516-794-3729
Web site: www.eastmeadowchamber.com
Dolloras Rome, President

East Northport Chamber of Commerce
24 Larkfield Road, East Northport, NY 11731
631-261-3573 Fax: 631-261-9885
e-mail: enptcc@aol.com
Web site: www.eastnorthport.com
Brian Valeri, President
Jill Bergman, Vice President

Eastchester-Tuckahoe Chamber of Commerce
65 Main Street, Suite 202, Tuckahoe, NY 10707
914-779-7344
e-mail: cetcoc@aol.com
Web site: www.eastchestertuckahoechamberofcommerce.com
Mariam Janusz, Executive Director

Ellenville/Wawarsing Chamber of Commerce
PO Box 227, 124 Canal St, Ellenville, NY 12428
845-647-4620
e-mail: info@ewcoc.com
Web site: ewcoc.com
Dr. Mark Craft, President

Ellicottville Chamber of Commerce
9 W Washington St, PO Box 456, Ellicottville, NY 14731
716-699-5046 or 800-349-9099 Fax: 716-699-5636
e-mail: info@ellicottvilleny.com
Web site: www.ellicottvilleny.com
Heather Snyder, Administrative Assistant

Erie County Industrial Development Agency
143 Genesee Street, Buffalo, NY 14203
716-858-8500 Fax: 716-858-6679
e-mail: info@ecidany.com
Web site: www.ecidany.com
Mark Poloncarz, County Executive

Erie County Planning & Economic Development
95 Franklin St, 10th Floor, Buffalo, NY 14202
716-858-6170 Fax: 716-858-7248
Web site: www.erie.gov
Kathy Konst, Commissioner

Erwin Industrial Development Agency (Town of)
Three Rivers Dev Corp Inc, 114 Pine St Suite 201, Corning, NY 14830
607-962-4693 Fax: 607-936-9132
e-mail: info@3riverscorp.com
Web site: www.threeriversdevelopment.com
Jack Benjamin, President

Essex County Industrial Development Agency
7566 Court Street, PO Box 217, Elizabethtown, NY 12932
518-873-9114 Fax: 518-873-2011
e-mail: info@essexcountyida.com
Web site: www.essexcountyida.com
Carol Calabrese; Jody Olcott, Co-Executive Directors

Chambers of Commerce

Offices and agencies generally appear in alphabetical order, except when specific order is requested by listee.

Evans-Brant Chamber of Commerce
70 North Main Street, Angola, NY 14006
716-549-3221 Fax: 716-549-3475
e-mail: chamber@ebccny.org
Web site: www.ebccny.org
Michelle Parker, President

Fair Haven Area Chamber of Commerce
PO Box 13, Fair Haven, NY 13064
315-947-6037
e-mail: fairhaveninfo@fairhavenny.com
Web site: www.fairhavenny.com
Dan Larson, President

Farmington Chamber of Commerce
1000 County Rd, #8, Farmington, NY 14425
585-398-2861 Fax: 315-986-4377
Web site: www.farmingtoncofc.com
Cal Cobb, President

Farmingville/Holtsville Chamber of Commerce
PO Box 66, Holtsville, NY 11742
631-926-8259
James V Marciante, President

Fayetteville Chamber of Commerce
PO Box 712, Fayetteville, NY 13066
315-637-5544
e-mail: fayettevillechamber@twcny.rr.com
Web site: www.fayettevillechamber.org

Findley Lake Area Chamber of Commerce
PO Box 211, Findley Lake, NY 14736
716-769-7609 or 888-769-7609 Fax: 716-769-7609
e-mail: chamber@findleylakeinfo.org
Web site: www.findleylakeinfo.org

Fort Brewerton/Greater Oneida Lake Chamber
PO Box 655, Brewerton, NY 13029
315-668-3408 Fax: 315-668-3408
e-mail: info@oneidalakechamber.com
Web site: www.oneidalakechamber.com
Don Deval, President

Fort Edward Chamber of Commerce
PO Box 267, Fort Edward, NY 12828
518-747-3000 Fax: 518-747-0622
Web site: www.fortedwardchamber.com
Larry Moffitt, President

Franklin County Industrial Development Agency
10 Elm Street, Suite 2, Malone, NY 12953
518-483-9472 Fax: 518-483-2900
e-mail: jtubbs@franklinida.org
Web site: www.franklinida.org
John Tubbs, CEO

Franklin Square Chamber of Commerce
PO Box 11, Franklin Square, NY 11010
516-775-0001 Fax: 516-292-0930
Web site: www.fschamberofcommerce.com
Joseph Ardito, President

Fredonia Chamber of Commerce
5 East Main St, Fredonia, NY 14063
716-679-1565 Fax: 716-672-5240
e-mail: fredcham@netsync.net
Web site: www.fredoniachamber.org
Mary Beth Fagan, Executive Director

French-American Chamber of Commerce
1350 Broadway, Suite 2101, New York, NY 10018
212-867-0123 Fax: 212-867-9050
e-mail: info@faccnyc.org
Web site: www.faccnyc.org
Martin Biscoff, Director

Fulton County Economic Development Corporation
55 East Main Street, Suite 110, Johnstown, NY 12095
518-773-8700 Fax: 518-773-8701
e-mail: fccrg.org
Web site: www.sites4u.org
Mike Reese, President/CEO

Fulton County Industrial Development Agency
One East Montgomery St, Johnstown, NY 12095
518-736-5660 Fax: 518-762-4597
Web site: ida.fultoncountyny.gov
James Mraz, Director

Fulton County Reg Chamber of Commerce & Ind
2 N Main St, Gloversville, NY 12078
518-725-0641 or 800-676-3858 Fax: 518-725-0643
e-mail: info@fultoncountyny.org
Web site: fultoncountyny.org
Mark Kilmer, President

Garden City Chamber of Commerce
230 Seventh Street, Garden City, NY 11530
516-746-7724 Fax: 516-746-7725
e-mail: gcchamber@verizon.net
Web site: www.gardencitychamber.org
Althea Robinson, Executive Director

Genesee County Chamber of Commerce
210 E Main St, Batavia, NY 14020
585-343-7440 Fax: 585-343-7487
e-mail: chamber@geneseeny.com
Web site: www.geneseeny.com
Lynn Freeman, President

Genesee County Economic Development Center
99 MedTech Drive, Suite 106, Batavia, NY 14020
585-343-4866 or 877-343-4866 Fax: 585-343-0848
e-mail: gcedc@gcedc.com
Web site: www.gcedc.com
Steven G Hyde, CEO

Geneva Area Chamber of Commerce
41 Lake Street, PO Box 587, Geneva, NY 14456
315-789-1776 or 877-543-6382 Fax: 315-789-3993
e-mail: info@genevany.com
Web site: www.genevany.com
Elizabeth Winter, President/CEO

Geneva Industrial Development Agency (City of)
47 Castle St, Geneva, NY 14456
315-828-6550 Fax: 315-789-0604
e-mail: vbassett@geneva.ny.us
Web site: www.geneva.ny.us
Valerie Bassett, Executive Director

Glen Cove Chamber of Commerce
19 Village Square, 2nd Floor, Glen Cove, NY 11542
516-676-6666 Fax: 516-676-5490
e-mail: info@glencovechamber.org
Web site: www.glencovechamber.org
Phyllis Gorham, Executive Director

Offices and agencies generally appear in alphabetical order, except when specific order is requested by listee.

Gore Mountain Region Chamber of Commerce
228 Main Street, PO Box 84, North Creek, NY 12853
518-251-2612 Fax: 518-251-5317
e-mail: info@gorechamber.com
Web site: www.gorechamber.com
Ed Milner, President

Goshen Chamber of Commerce
223 Main Street, PO Box 506, Goshen, NY 10924
845-294-7741 Fax: 845-294-7746
e-mail: info@goshennychamber.com
Web site: www.goshennychamber.com
Lynn A Cione, Executive Director

Gouverneur Chamber of Commerce
214 East Main St, Gouverneur, NY 13642
315-287-0331 Fax: 315-287-3694
e-mail: info@governcurchamber.net
Web site: www.gouverneurchamber.net
Donna Lawrence, Executive Director

Gowanda Area Chamber of Commerce
49 W Main Street, PO Box 45, Gowanda, NY 14070
716-532-2834 Fax: 716-532-2834
e-mail: gowandachamber@yahoo.com
Web site: gowandachamber.com
Mary Pankow, President

Grand Island Chamber of Commerce
2257 Grand Island Blvd, Grand Island, NY 14072
716-773-3651 Fax: 716-773-3316
e-mail: info@gichamber.org
Web site: www.gichamber.org
Eric Fiebelkorn, President

Granville Chamber of Commerce
One Main St, PO Box 13, Granville, NY 12832
518-642-2815 Fax: 518-642-2772
e-mail: info@granvillechamber.com
Web site: www.granvillechamber.com
Charles King, President

Great Neck Chamber of Commerce
Kiosk Information Center, 1 Middle Neck Road, PO Box 220432, Great Neck, NY 11022
516-487-2000 Fax: 516-829-5472
e-mail: greatneckinfo@gmail.com
Web site: www.greatneckchamber.org
Hooshang Nematzadeh, President

Greater Cicero Chamber of Commerce
5701 East Circle Drive, #302, Cicero, NY 13039
315-699-1358
e-mail: info@cicerochamber.com
Web site: www.cicerochamber.com
John Annable, President

Greater Jamaica Development Corporation
90-04 161st Street, Jamaica, NY 11432
718-291-0282 Fax: 718-658-1405
Web site: www.gjdc.org
Carlisle Towery, President

The Greater Mahopac-Carmel Chamber of Commerce
953 South Lake Blvd, PO Box 160, Mahopac, NY 10541-0160
845-628-5553 Fax: 845-628-5962
e-mail: info@mahopaccarmelchamber.com
Web site: www.mahopaccarmelonline.com
Laurie Lee Ford, Chairwoman

The Greater Manlius Chamber of Commerce
425 E Genesee Street, Fayetteville, NY 13066
315-637-4760 Fax: 315-637-4762
e-mail: greatermanlius@windstream.net
Web site: www.manliuschamber.com
Kim Kutzer, President

Greater Massena Chamber of Commerce
16 Church Street, Massena, NY 13662
315-769-3525 Fax: 315-769-5295
e-mail: chamber@massenachamber.com
Web site: www.massenachamber.com
Michael Gleason, Executive Director

Greater Mexico Chamber of Commerce
3236 Main Street, Mexico, NY 13114
315-963-1042
e-mail: secretary@mexico-cofc.org
Web site: www.mexicocofc.net
Adam Judware, President

Greater New York Chamber of Commerce
20 W 44th Street, 4th Floor, New York, NY 10036
212-686-1772 Fax: 212-686-7232
e-mail: info@ny-chamber.com
Web site: www.ny-chamber.com
Mark Jaffe, President & CEO

Greater Oneida Chamber of Commerce
136 Lenox Ave, Oneida, NY 13421
315-363-4300 Fax: 315-361-4558
e-mail: oneidachamber@cnymail.com
Web site: www.oneidachamberny.org
Rebecca Halstrom-O'Bierne, President
Tari Timmer, Executive Assistant

Greater Ossining Chamber of Commerce, The
2 Church Street, Suite 205, Ossining, NY 10562
914-941-0009 or 914-941-0812
e-mail: info@ossiningchamber.org
Web site: www.ossiningchamber.org
Kay Hawley, Administrator

Greater Port Jefferson Chamber of Commerce
118 W Broadway, Port Jefferson, NY 11777-1314
631-473-1414 Fax: 631-474-4540
e-mail: info@portjeffchamber.com
Web site: www.portjeffchamber.com
Suzanne Velazquez, President

Greece Chamber of Commerce
2402 West Ridge Rd, Suite 201, Rochester, NY 14626-3053
585-227-7272 Fax: 585-227-7275
e-mail: info@greecechamber.org
Web site: www.greecechamber.org
Jodie Perry, President

Green Island Industrial Development Agency (Village of)
20 Clinton St, Green Island, NY 12183
518-273-2201 Fax: 518-273-2235
Web site: www.villageofgreenisland.com
Local government, Industrial Development Agency
Kristen Swinton, Chief Executive Officer

Greene County Department of Planning & Economic Development
411 Main Street, Catskill, NY 12414
518-719-3290 Fax: 518-719-3789
e-mail: business@discovergreene.com
Web site: www.greenebusiness.com
Warren Hart, AICP Director

Offices and agencies generally appear in alphabetical order, except when specific order is requested by listee.

Greene County Tourism Promotion
700 Rte 23B, Leeds, NY 12451
518-943-3223 or 800-355-CATS Fax: 518-943-2296
e-mail: tourism@discovergreene.com
Web site: www.greenetourism.com
Warren Hart, Director

Greenport-Southold Chamber of Commerce
PO Box 1415, Southold, NY 11971
631-765-3161
e-mail: info@northforkchamber.org
Web site: www.greenportsoutholdchamber.org
Andy Binkowski, President

Greenvale Chamber of Commerce
PO Box 123, Greenvale, NY 11548
516-621-6545
Web site: www.greenvalechamber.com
Ken White, Board President

Greenwich Chamber of Commerce (Greater Greenwich)
6 Academy St, Greenwich, NY 12834
518-692-7979 Fax: 518-692-7979
e-mail: info@greenwichchamber.org
Web site: www.greenwichchamber.org
Kathy Nichols-Tomkins, Secretary

Greenwich Village-Chelsea Chamber of Commerce
129 West 27th Street, 6th Floor, New York, NY 10001
646-470-1773 Fax: 212-924-0714
e-mail: info@villagechamber.com
Web site: www.villagechelsea.com
Lauren Danziger, Executive Director

Greenwood Lake Chamber of Commerce
PO Box 36, Greenwood Lake, NY 10925
845-477-0112 Fax: 914-477-2798
Joyce Monti, Contact

Guilderland Chamber of Commerce
2050 Western Ave, Guilderland, NY 12084
518-456-6611 Fax: 518-456-6690
e-mail: kburbank@guilderlandchamber.com
Web site: www.guilderlandchamber.com
Kathy Burbank, Executive Director

Guilderland Industrial Development Agency (Town of)
Town Hall, PO Box 339, Guilderland, NY 12084
518-356-1980 Fax: 518-356-5514
Web site: www.townofguilderland.org
William N Young, Jr., Chairman

Hague on Lake George Chamber of Commerce
PO Box 615, Hague, NY 12836
518-543-6441 Fax: 518-585-9890
e-mail: haguechamberofcommerce@yahoo.com
Web site: www.visithague.com

Hamburg Chamber of Commerce
6122 S Park Ave, Hamburg, NY 14075
716-649-7917 or 877-322-6890 Fax: 716-649-6362
e-mail: mailhcc@hamburg-chamber.org
Web site: www.hamburg-chamber.org
Cindy Galley, Executive Director

Hamburg Industrial Development Agency
S6100 South Park Avenue, Hamburg, NY 14075
716-648-4145 Fax: 716-648-0151
Web site: www.hamburgida.com
Michael J Bartlett, Executive Director

Hammondsport Chamber of Commerce
47 Shethar Street, Hammondsport, NY 14840
607-569-2989
e-mail: info@hammondsport.org
Web site: www.hammondsport.org

Hampton Bays Chamber of Commerce
140 West Main St, Hampton Bays, NY 11946
631-728-2211
Web site: www.hamptonbayschamber.com
Stan Glinka, President

Hancock Area Chamber of Commerce
Box 525, Hancock, NY 13783-0525
607-637-4756 or 800-668-7624 Fax: 607-637-4756
e-mail: hancockchamber@hancock.net
Web site: www.hancockareachamber.com
Lori Ray, President

Harlem Chamber of Commerce (Greater Harlem)
200 A West 136th St, New York, NY 10030
212-862-7200 or 877-427-5364 Fax: 212-862-8745
e-mail: info@harlemdiscover.com
Web site: www.greaterharlemchamber.com
Lloyd Williams, President

Hastings-on-Hudson Chamber of Commerce
PO Box 405, Hastings-on-Hudson, NY 10706
914-478-0900 Fax: 914-478-1720
Web site: www.hohchamber.com
Joseph R LoCascio, Jr, President

Hempstead Industrial Development Agency (Town of)
350 Front St, Rm 234-A, Hempstead, NY 11550
516-489-5000 x4200 or 800-593-3870 Fax: 516-489-3179
e-mail: fparola@tohmail.org
Web site: www.tohida.org
Frederick Parola, Executive Director

Henderson Harbor Area Chamber of Commerce
PO Box 468, Henderson Harbor, NY 13651
315-938-5568 or 888-938-5568
e-mail: thechambertreasure@gmail.com
Web site: www.hendersonharborny.com

Herkimer County Chamber of Commerce
420 East German Street, Herkimer, NY 13350
315-866-7820 or 877-984-4636 Fax: 315-866-7833
e-mail: jscarano@herkimercountychamber.com
Web site: www.herkimercountychamber.com
John Scarano, Executive Director

Herkimer County Industrial Development Agency
320 N Prospect Street, PO Box 390, Herkimer, NY 13350
315-867-1373 Fax: 315-867-1515
e-mail: markfeane@herkimercounty.org
Web site: www.herkimercountyida.com
Mark Feane, Executive Director

Hicksville Chamber of Commerce
10 W Marie St, Hicksville, NY 11801
516-931-7170 Fax: 516-931-8546
Web site: www.hicksvillechamber.com
Lionel Chitty, President

Holbrook Chamber of Commerce, The
PO Box 565, Holbrook, NY 11741
631-471-2725 Fax: 631-343-4816
e-mail: info@holbrookchamber.com
Web site: www.4holbrook.com
Rick Ammirati, President

Offices and agencies generally appear in alphabetical order, except when specific order is requested by listee.

Hornell Area Chamber of Commerce/Hornell Industrial Development Agency (City of)
40 Main St, Hornell, NY 14843
607-324-0310 or 877-HORNELL Fax: 607-324-3776
e-mail: margie@hornellny.com
Web site: www.hornellny.com
James W Griffin, President & Executive Director

Hudson Valley Gateway Chamber of Commerce
One S Division St, Peekskill, NY 10566
914-737-3600 Fax: 914-737-0541
e-mail: info@hvgatewaychamber.com
Web site: www.hvgatewaychamber.com
Deborah Milone, Executive Director

Hunter Chamber of Commerce (Town of)
PO Box 177, Hunter, NY 12442
518-263-4900 Fax: 518-589-0117
e-mail: chamberinfo@hunterchamber.org
Web site: www.hunterchamber.org
Michael McCrary, President

Huntington Township Chamber of Commerce
164 Main St, Huntington, NY 11743
631-423-6100 Fax: 631-351-8276
e-mail: info@huntingtonchamber.com
Web site: www.huntingtonchamber.com
Ellen O' Brien, Executive Director

Hyde Park Chamber of Commerce
PO Box 17, Hyde Park, NY 12538
845-229-8612 Fax: 845-229-8638
e-mail: info@hydeparkchamber.org
Web site: www.hydeparkchamber.org
Dave Stewart, President

Indian Lake Chamber of Commerce
PO Box 724, Indian Lake, NY 12842
518-648-5112 or 800-328-5253 Fax: 518-648-5489
e-mail: info@indian-lake.com
Web site: www.indian-lake.com
Christine Pouch, President

Inlet Information Office
160 State Route 28 at Arrowhead Park, Inlet, NY 13360
315-357-5501 or 866-GOINLET Fax: 315-357-3570
e-mail: info@inletny.com
Web site: www.inletny.com
Adele Burnett, Director of Information & Tourism

Irvington-on-Hudson Chamber of Commerce
PO Box 161, Irvington, NY 10533
914-473-4819
e-mail: bettylaurenson@gmail.com
Web site: www.irvingtonnychamber.com
Eric Spino; Betty Laurenson, Presidents

Islip Chamber of Commerce
PO Box 112, Islip, NY 11751-0112
631-581-2720 Fax: 631-581-2720
e-mail: info@islipchamberofcommerce.com
Web site: www.islipchamberofcommerce.org
Jim Guariglia, President

Islip Economic Development Division & Industrial Development Agency (Town of)
40 Nassau Ave, Islip, NY 11751
631-224-5512 Fax: 631-224-5532
e-mail: ecodev@townofislip-ny.gov
Web site: www.islipida.com
Tom Croci, Supervisor

Islip Industrial Development Agency (Town of)
40 Nassau Ave, Islip, NY 11751
631-224-5512 Fax: 631-224-5532
e-mail: ecodev@townofislip-ny.gov
Web site: www.townofislip-ny.gov
Phil Nolan, Chairman

Jamaica Chamber of Commerce
157-11 Rockaway Boulevard, Jamaica, NY 11432
718-413-7182 Fax: 718-413-2325
Robert M Richards, President

Jeffersonville Area Chamber of Commerce, The
PO Box 463, Jeffersonville, NY 12748
845-482-3652
Web site: www.jeffersonvilleny.com

Japanese Chamber of Commerce
145 W 57th St, New York, NY 10019
212-246-8001 Fax: 212-246-8002
e-mail: info@jcciny.org
Web site: www.jcciny.org
Seiei Ono, President

Katonah Chamber of Commerce
PO Box 389, Katonah, NY 10536
914-232-2668
e-mail: info@katonahchamber.org
Web site: www.katonahchamber.org
Edris Scherer; Christopher Roberts, Presidents

Kenmore-Town of Tonawanda Chamber of Commerce
3411 Delaware Ave, Kenmore, NY 14217
716-874-1202 Fax: 716-874-3151
e-mail: info@ken-ton.org
Web site: www.ken-ton.org
Tracey M Lukasik, Executive Director

Kings Park Chamber of Commerce
3 Main St, PO Box 322, Kings Park, NY 11754
631-269-7678 Fax: 631-269-5575
e-mail: info@kingsparkli.com
Web site: www.kingsparkli.com
Dee Grasso, Executive Director

Lackawanna Area Chamber of Commerce
638 Ridge Rd, Lackawanna, NY 14218
716-823-8841 Fax: 716-823-8848
e-mail: info@lackawannachamber.com
Web site: www.lackawannachamber.com
Michael J Sobaszek, Executive Director

Lake George Regional Chamber of Commerce
PO Box 272, Lake George, NY 12845
518-668-5755 or 800-705-0059 Fax: 518-668-4286
e-mail: info@lakegeorgechamber.com
Web site: www.lakegeorgechamber.com
Janice Bartkowski-Fox, President

Lake Luzerne Chamber of Commerce
PO Box 222, Lake Luzerne, NY 12846-0222
518-696-3500 Fax: 518-696-6122
Web site: www.lakeluzernechamber.org
George Beagle, President

Lake Placid Chamber of Commerce
2608 Main Street, Lake Placid, NY 12946-1592
518-523-2445 or 800-447-5224 Fax: 518-523-2605
Web site: www.lakeplacid.com
James McKenna, CEO

Chambers of Commerce

Offices and agencies generally appear in alphabetical order, except when specific order is requested by listee.

Lancaster Area Chamber of Commerce
11 W Main Street, Suite 100, PO Box 284, Lancaster, NY 14086
716-681-9755 Fax: 716-684-3385
e-mail: info@laccny.org
Web site: www.laccny.org
Megan Burns-Moran, Executive Director

Lancaster Industrial Development Agency (Town of)
21 Central Avenue, Lancaster, NY 14086
716-683-1610 Fax: 716-683-0512
e-mail: lida@lancasterny.com
Web site: www.lancasterny.com
Dino J Fudoli, Chairman

Lewis County Chamber of Commerce
7576 South State Street, Lowville, NY 13367
315-376-2213 or 800-724-0242 Fax: 315-376-0326
e-mail: info@lewiscountychamber.org
Web site: www.lewiscountychamber.org
Anne Merrill, Executive Director

Lewis County Industrial Development Agency
7642 State St, PO Box 106, Lowville, NY 13367
315-376-3014
e-mail: lcida@lcida.org
Web site: www.lcida.org
Richard Porter, Executive Director

Lindenhurst Chamber of Commerce
101 Montauk Hwy, Lindenhurst, NY 11757
631-226-4641
Web site: lindenhurstchamber.org
Jo-Ann Boettcher, President

Liverpool Chamber of Commerce (Greater Liverpool)
314 Second St, Liverpool, NY 13088
315-457-3895 Fax: 315-234-3226
e-mail: chamber@liverpoolchamber.com
Web site: www.liverpoolchamber.com
Dennis Hebert, President

Livingston County Chamber of Commerce
4635 Millennium Dr, Geneseo, NY 14454-1134
585-243-2222 Fax: 585-243-4824
e-mail: llane@livingstoncountychamber.com
Web site: www.livingstoncountychamber.com
Laura Lane, President

Livingston County Economic Development Office & Industrial Development Agency
6 Court St, Room 306, Geneseo, NY 14454-1043
585-243-7124 Fax: 585-243-7126
e-mail: info@build-here.com
Web site: www.build-here.com
Julie Marshall, Executive Director

Lockport Industrial Development Agency (Town of)
6560 Dysinger Rd, Lockport, NY 14094
716-439-9535 Fax: 719-439-9715
e-mail: LES@elockport.com
Web site: www.lockporteconomicdevelopment.com
David Kinyon, Administrative Director

Locust Valley Chamber of Commerce
PO Box 178, Locust Valley, NY 11560
516-671-1310
Web site: www.locustvalleychamber.com
Len Margolis, President

Long Beach Chamber of Commerce
350 National Blvd, Long Beach, NY 11561-3312
516-432-6000 Fax: 516-432-0273
Web site: www.thelongbeachchamber.com
Michael J Kerr, President

Long Island Association
300 Broadhollow Road, Suite 110 W, Melville, NY 11747-4840
631-493-3000 Fax: 631-499-2194
e-mail: perlkamer@hotmail.com
Web site: www.liaonline.org
Pearl M Kamer, Chief Economist

Long Island Council of Dedicated Merchants Chamber of Commerce
PO Box 512, Miller Place, Long Island, NY 11764
631-821-1313
Web site: www.cdmlongisland.com
Dr Tom Ianniello, President

Long Island Development Corporation
400 Post Avenue, Suite 201A, Westbury, NY 11590
866-433-5432 Fax: 516-433-5046
e-mail: info@lidc.org
Web site: www.lidc.org
Roslyn D Goldmacher, President & CEO

Lynbrook Chamber of Commerce
PO Box 624, Lynbrook, NY 11563
516-599-5946
e-mail: info@lynbrookusa.com
Web site: www.lynbrookusa.com
Denise Rogers, President

Madison County Industrial Development Agency
3215 Seneca Turnpike, Canastota, NY 13032
315-697-9817 Fax: 315-697-8169
e-mail: direector@madisoncountyida.com
Web site: www.madisoncountyida.com
Kipp Hicks, Director

Malone Chamber of Commerce
497 East Main Street, Malone, NY 12953
518-483-3760 or 877-625-6631 Fax: 518-483-3172
Web site: www.visitmalone.com
Dene Savage, President

Mamaroneck Chamber of Commerce
430 Center Ave, Mamaroneck, NY 10543
914-698-4400
e-mail: chamber10543@optonline.net
Web site: www.mamaroneckchamberofcommerce.org
Rose Silvestro, President

Manhasset Chamber of Commerce
PO Box 754, Manhasset, NY 11030
516-627-8688
e-mail: limanhassetcc@aol.com
Web site: www.manhassetny.org
Les Forrai, President

Manhattan Chamber of Commerce Inc
1375 Broadway, Third Floor, New York, NY 10018
212-479-7772 Fax: 212-473-8074
e-mail: info@manhattancc.org
Web site: www.manhattancc.org
Nancy Ploeger, President

Offices and agencies generally appear in alphabetical order, except when specific order is requested by listee.

Marcy Chamber of Commerce
PO Box 429, Marcy, NY 13403
315-725-3294 Fax: 315-865-6144
e-mail: marcycofc@gmail.com
Web site: www.marcychamber.com
Lesley Grogan, Board President

Massapequa Chamber of Commerce
674 Broadway, Massapequa, NY 11758
516-541-1443 Fax: 516-541-8625
e-mail: masscoc@aol.com
Web site: www.massapequachamber.com
Patricia Orzano, President

Mastics/Shirley Chamber of Commerce
PO Box 4, Mastic, NY 11950
631-399-2228
e-mail: admin@masticsshirleychamber.com
Web site: masticsshirleychamber.com
Mark Smothergill, President

Mattituck Chamber of Commerce
PO Box 1056, Mattituck, NY 11952
631-298-5757
e-mail: info@mattituckchamber.org
Web site: www.mattituckchamber.org
Donielle Cardinale, President

Mayville/Chautauqua Chamber of Commerce
PO Box 22, Mayville, NY 14757
716-753-3113 Fax: 716-753-3113
e-mail: maychautcham@yahoo.com
Web site: www.chautaquachamber.org
Deborah Marsala, Coordinator

Mechanicville Area Chamber of Commerce
312 N 3rd Ave, Mechanicville, NY 12118
518-664-7791 Fax: 518-664-0826
Web site: www.mechancvilleareachamber.com
Barbara Corsale, President

Mechanicville/Stillwater Industrial Development Agency
City Hall, 36 North Main Street, Mechanicville, NY 12118
518-664-8331
Web site: www.mechanicville-stillwater-ida.org
Barbara Zecca Corsale, Chair

Merrick Chamber of Commerce
124 Merrick Ave, PO box 53, Merrick, NY 11566
516-771-1171 Fax: 516-868-6692
e-mail: merrickchamber@aol.com
Web site: www.merrickchamber.org
Randy Shotland, President

Mid-Hudson Pattern for Progress
Desmond Campus, 6 Albany Post Rd, Newburgh, NY 12550
845-565-4900 Fax: 845-565-4918
e-mail: jdrapkin@pfprogress.org
Web site: www.pattern-for-progress.org
Jonathan Drapkin, President

Miller Place/Mt Sinai/Sound Beach/Rocky Point Chamber of Commerce
5507-10 Nesconet Highway, #410, Mount Sinai, NY 11766
631-821-1313
Web site: www.northbrookhavenchamber.org
Dr Tom Ianniello, President

Mineola Chamber of Commerce
PO Box 62, Mineola, NY 11501
516-408-3554 Fax: 516-408-3554
Web site: www.mineolachamber.com
Ray Sikorski, President

Mohawk Valley Chamber of Commerce
Radisson Hotel, Suite 1, 200 Genessee St, Utica, NY 13502
315-724-3151 Fax: 315-724-3177
e-mail: info@mvchamber.org
Web site: www.mvchamber.org
Thomas Bashant, President

Mohawk Valley Economic Development District
26 W Main St, PO Box 69, Mohawk, NY 13407-0106
315-866-4671 Fax: 315-866-9862
e-mail: info@mvedd.org
Web site: www.mvedd.org
Regional Economic Development Activities
Stephen Smith, Director

Mohawk Valley Economic Development Growth Enterprises
584 Phoenix Drive, Rome, NY 13441-4105
315-338-0393 or 800-765-4990 Fax: 315-338-5694
e-mail: mrizzo@mvedge.org
Web site: www.mvedge.org
Laura Casamento, President

Monroe County Industrial Development Agency (COMIDA)
CityPlace, 50 W Main St, Suite 8100, Rochester, NY 14614
585-753-2000 Fax: 585-753-2002
Web site: www.growmonroe.org
Theresa Mazzullo, Chairman

Montauk Chamber of Commerce, The
742 Montauk Hwy, Montauk, NY 11954-5338
631-668-2428 Fax: 631-668-9363
e-mail: info@montaukchamber.com
Web site: www.montaukchamber.com

Montgomery County Chamber of Commerce/Montgomery County Partnership
1166 Riverfront Center, Amsterdam, NY 12010
518-842-8200 Fax: 518-684-0111
e-mail: chamber@montgomerycountyny.com
Web site: www.montgomerycountyny.com
Peter Capobianco, President

Moravia Chamber of Commerce
PO Box 647, Moravia, NY 13118
315-497-1431 Fax: 315-497-9319
Web site: www.moravia-lockeny.com
Dennis Bilow, President

Mount Kisco Chamber of Commerce
3 N Moger Ave, Mount Kisco, NY 10549
914-666-7525 Fax: 914-666-7663
e-mail: mtkiscochamber@aol.com
Web site: www.mtkiscochamber.com
Phil Bronzi, President

Mount Vernon Chamber of Commerce
65 Haven Ave, PO Box 351, Mount Vernon, NY 10550
914-667-7500 or 888-716-2460 Fax: 914-699-0139
e-mail: info@mtvernonchamber.org
Web site: www.mtvernonchamber.org
Frank T Fraley, President

Mount Vernon Industrial Development Agency (City of)
City Hall, Roosevelt Square, Mount Vernon, NY 10550
914-665-2300 Fax: 914-665-2496
Web site: www.cmvny.com
Yolanda Robinson, Chief of Staff

Nassau Council of Chambers
PO Box 365, Bellmore, NY 11710
516-248-1112 Fax: 516-663-6715
Web site: www.ncchambers.org
Julie Marchesella, President

Offices and agencies generally appear in alphabetical order, except when specific order is requested by listee.

Nassau County Industrial Development Agency
1550 Franklin Avenue, Suite 235, Mineola, NY 11501
516-571-1945 Fax: 516-571-1076
e-mail: cpereira@nassauida.com
Web site: www.nassauida.com
Colleen Pereira, Administrative Director

New City Chamber of Commerce
65 N Main St, New City, NY 10956
845-638-1395 Fax: 845-638-1395
e-mail: info@newcitychamber.com
Web site: www.newcitychamberofcommerce.org
Gary Oteri, President

New Hyde Park Chamber of Commerce
PO Box 247, New Hyde Park, NY 11040
888-400-0311
e-mail: info@nhpchamber.com
Web site: www.nhpchamber.com
Mark Laytin, President

New Paltz Regional Chamber of Commerce
257 Main St, New Paltz, NY 12561-1525
845-255-0243 Fax: 845-255-5189
e-mail: info@newpaltzchamber.org
Web site: www.newpaltzchamber.org
Michael Smith, President

New Rochelle, Chamber of Commerce, Inc
459 Main St, PO Box 140, New Rochelle, NY 10801-6412
914-632-5700 Fax: 914-632-0708
e-mail: info@newrochellechamber.com
Web site: www.newrochellechamber.org
Rosemary McLaughlin, President

New York Chamber of Commerce (Greater New York)
20 West 44th Street, 4th fl, New York, NY 10036
212-686-7220 Fax: 212-686-7232
e-mail: info@chamber.com
Web site: www.ny-chamber.com
Mark S Jaffe, President & CEO

New York City, Partnership for
One Battery Park Plaza, 5th Floor, New York, NY 10004
212-493-7400 Fax: 212-344-3344
e-mail: info@pfnyc.org
Web site: www.pfnyc.org
Kathryn S Wylde, President & CEO

New Yorktown Chamber of Commerce (The)
Parkside Corner, PO Box 632, Suite 203, Yorktown Heights, NY 10598
914-245-4599 Fax: 914-734-7171
e-mail: info@yorktownchamber.org
Web site: www.yorktownchamber.org
Arlette Rossignol, Operations Director

Newark Chamber of Commerce
199 Van Buren St, Newark, NY 14513
315-331-2705 Fax: 315-331-2705
e-mail: supportnewarknychamber.com
Web site: www.newarknychamber.org
Tammra Schiller, President

Niagara County Center for Economic Development
6311 Inducon Corporate Dr, Ste 1, Sanborn, NY 14132-9099
716-278-8750 Fax: 716-278-8757
e-mail: info@niagaracountybusiness.com
Web site: www.nccedev.com
Samuel M Ferraro, Commissioner

Niagara Falls Chamber of Commerce
6311 Inducon Corporate Drive, Sanborn, NY 14132
716-285-9141 Fax: 716-285-0941
e-mail: dalteriobrennen@niagarachamber.org
Web site: niagarachamber.org
Deanna Alterio Brennen, President/CEO

Niagara USA Chamber of Commerce
6311 Inducon Corporate Dr, Sanborn, NY 14132
716-285-9141 Fax: 716-285-0941
e-mail: dalteriobrennen@niagarachamber.org
Web site: niagarachamber.org
Deanna Alterio Brennen, President

North Fork Chamber of Commerce
PO Box 1415, Southold, NY 11971
631-765-3161 Fax: 631-765-3161
e-mail: info@northforkchamber.org
Web site: www.northforkchamber.org
Andy Binkowski, President

North Greenbush IDA
2 Douglas Street, Wynantskill, NY 12198-7561
518-283-5313 Fax: 518-283-5345
e-mail: ashworth@townofng.com
Web site: www.townofng.com
James Flanigan, Chairman

Northport Chamber of Commerce
PO Box 33, Northport, NY 11768
631-754-3905
Web site: www.northportny.com

North Warren Chamber of Commerce
PO Box 490, 3 Dynamite Hill, Chestertown, NY 12817
518-494-2722 Fax: 518-494-2722
e-mail: info@northwarrenchamber.com
Web site: www.northwarren.com
Promoting local business Sponsors Tourist Information Center on route 8 in Chestertown.
Barbara Thomas, President

Nyack Chamber of Commerce
PO Box 677, Nyack, NY 10960
845-353-2221 Fax: 845-353-4204
Web site: www.nyackchamber.com
Carlo Pelligrini, President

Oceanside Chamber of Commerce
PO Box 1, Oceanside, NY 11572
516-763-9177 Fax: 516-766-4575
Web site: www.oceansidechamber.org
Gail Carlin, President

Ogdensburg Chamber of Commerce (Greater Ogdensburg)
1 Bridge Plaza, Ogdensburg, NY 13669
315-393-3620 Fax: 315-393-1380
e-mail: chamber@gisco.net
Web site: www.ogdensburgny.com
Sandra Porter, President

Olean Area Chamber of Commerce (Greater Olean)
120 N Union Street, Olean, NY 14760
716-372-4433 Fax: 716-372-7912
e-mail: info@oleanny.com
Web site: www.oleanny.com
Jim Stitt Jr, President

Offices and agencies generally appear in alphabetical order, except when specific order is requested by listee.

Oneida Industrial Development Agency (City of)
584 Phoenix Drive, Rome, NY 13441
315-338-0393 or 800-765-4990 Fax: 315-338-5694
e-mail: info@mvedge.org
Web site: www.oniedacountyida.org
David C Grow, Chairman

Onondaga County Industrial Development Agency
333 West Washington Street, Suite 130, Syracuse, NY 13202
315-435-3770 or 877-797-8222 Fax: 315-435-3669
e-mail: info@syracusecentral.com
Web site: www.syracusecentral.com
Marth Beth Primo, Director of Economic Development

Ontario Chamber of Commerce
PO Box 100, Ontario, NY 14519-0100
315-524-5886
e-mail: ontarionychamber.org
Web site: www.ontariotown.org
Donna Burolla, Chamber Board of Directors

Ontario County Industrial Development Agency & Economic Development
20 Ontario Street, Suite 106-B, Canandaigua, NY 14424
585-396-4460 Fax: 585-396-4594
e-mail: info@ontariocountydev.org
Web site: www.ontariocountydev.org
Michael J Manikowski, Executive Director

Orange County Chamber of Commerce Inc
30 Scott's Corners Drive, Montgomery, NY 12549
845-457-9700 Fax: 845-457-8799
e-mail: info@orangeny.com
Web site: www.orangeny.com
Dr John A D'Ambrosio, President

Orange County Partnership
40 Matthews St, Suite 108, Goshen, NY 10924
845-294-2323 Fax: 845-294-8023
e-mail: maureen@ocpartnership.org
Web site: www.ocpartnership.org
Scott Batulis, President & CEO

Orchard Park Chamber of Commerce
4211 N Buffalo St, Ste 14, Orchard Park, NY 14127-2401
716-662-3366 Fax: 716-662-5946
e-mail: opcc@orchardparkchamber.com
Web site: www.orchardparkchamber.com
Nancy L Conley, Executive Director

Orleans County Chamber of Commerce
102 N Main St, Albion, NY 14411
585-589-7727 Fax: 585-589-7326
e-mail: ckelly@orleanschamber.com
Web site: www.orleanschamber.com
Cindy Robinson, President

Orleans Economic Development Agency (OEDA)
121 N Main St, Albion, NY 14411
585-589-7060 Fax: 585-589-5258
e-mail: jwhipple@orleansdevelopment.org
Web site: www.orleansdevelopment.org
James Whipple, CEO & CFO

Oswego-Fulton Chamber of Commerce
44 East Bridge Street, Oswego, NY 13126
315-343-7681 Fax: 315-342-0831
e-mail: gofcc@oswegofultonchamber.com
Web site: www.oswegofultonchamber.com
Beth A Hilton, Executive Director

Oswego County, Operation/Oswego County Industrial Development Agency
44 West Bridge St, Oswego, NY 13126
315-343-1545 Fax: 315-343-1546
e-mail: ooc@oswegocounty.org
Web site: www.oswegocounty.org
L Michael Treadwell, Executive Director

Otsego County Chamber (The)
189 Main Street, Suite 201, Oneonta, NY 13820
607-432-4500 or 877-5-OTSEGO Fax: 607-432-4506
e-mail: info@otsegocountychamber.com
Web site: www.otsegocountychamber.com
Barbara Ann Heegan, Executive Director

Otsego County Economic Development Department & Industrial Development Agency
242 Main St, Oneonta, NY 13820
607-432-8871 Fax: 607-432-5117
e-mail: info@otsegoeconomicdevelopment.com
Web site: www.otsegoeconomicdevelopment.com
Joseph A Bernier, Chair

Oyster Bay Chamber of Commerce
PO Box 21, Oyster Bay, NY 11771
516-922-6464 Fax: 516-624-8082
e-mail: obenchamber@gmail.com
Web site: www.visitoysterbay.com
Dottie Simmons, President

Painted Post Area Board of Trade
304 South Hamilton Street, PO Box 128, Painted Post, NY 14870
607-937-6162
e-mail: info@paintedpostny.com
Web site: www.paintedpostny.com
Jean Wise-Wicks, President

Patchogue Chamber of Commerce (Greater Patchogue)
15 N Ocean Ave, Patchogue, NY 11772
631-207-1000 or 631-475-0121 Fax: 631-475-1599
e-mail: info@patchoguechamber.com
Web site: www.patchoguechamber.com
Gail Hoag, Executive Director

Patterson Chamber of Commerce
PO Box 316, Patterson, NY 12563
845-363-6304 Fax: 845-363-6304
e-mail: info@pcofc.org
Web site: www.pcofc.org
Debra Boccarossa, President

Peekskill Industrial Development Agency (City of)
840 Main Street, Room 31, Peekskill, NY 10566-2016
914-737-3400 Fax: 914-737-2688
Web site: www.cityofpeekskill.com
Brian Havranek, Executive Director

Perry Area Chamber of Commerce
102 N Center St, PO Box 35, Perry, NY 14530
585-237-5040
e-mail: joinus@perrychamber.com
Web site: www.perrychamber.com
Lorraine Sturm, Secretary

Offices and agencies generally appear in alphabetical order, except when specific order is requested by listee.

CHAMBERS OF COMMERCE/ECONOMIC DEVELOPMENT ORGANIZATIONS

Phelps Chamber of Commerce
PO Box 1, Phelps, NY 14532
315-548-5481
e-mail: chamber@phelpsny.com
Web site: www.phelpsny.com

Plainview-Old Bethpage Chamber of Commerce
PO Box 577, Plainview, NY 11803
516-937-5646
e-mail: chamber@pobcoc.com
Web site: www.plainview-oldbethpage.org
Gary Epstein, President

Plattsburgh-North Country Chamber of Commerce
7061 Route 9, PO Box 310, Plattsburgh, NY 12901
518-563-1000 Fax: 516-563-1028
e-mail: chamber@northcountrychamber.com
Web site: www.northcountrychamber.com
Garry Douglas, CEO & President

Port Chester-Rye Brook Rye Town Chamber of Commerce
222 Grace Church Street, Port Chester, NY 10573
914-939-1900 Fax: 914-437-7779
e-mail: pcrbchamber@gmail.com
Web site: www.pcrbchamber.com
Ken Manning, President

Port Jefferson Chamber of Commerce
118 W Broadway, Port Jefferson, NY 11777
631-473-1414 Fax: 631-474-4540
e-mail: info@portjeffchamber.com
Web site: www.portjeffchamber.com
Suzanne Velazquez, President

South Bronx Overall Economic Development Corporation
555 Bergen Ave, Bronx, NY 10455
718-292-3113 Fax: 718-292-3115
e-mail: info@sobro.org
Web site: www.sobro.org
Phillip Morrow, President/CEO

Port Washington Chamber of Commerce
PO Box 121, Port Washington, NY 11050
516-883-6566 Fax: 516-883-6591
e-mail: pwcoc@optonline.net
Web site: pwguide.com
Bobbie Polay, Executive Director

Potsdam Chamber of Commerce
One Market Street, Potsdam, NY 13676
315-274-9000 Fax: 315-274-9222
e-mail: potsdam@slic.com
Web site: www.potsdamchamber.com
Marylee Ballou, Executive Director

Dutchess County Regional Chamber of Commerce
One Civic Center Plaza, Suite 400, Poughkeepsie, NY 12601
845-454-1700 Fax: 845-454-1702
e-mail: info@dcrcoc.org
Web site: www.dcrcoc.org
Charles S North, President & CEO

Pulaski-Eastern Shore Chamber of Commerce
3044 State Route 13, PO Box 34, Pulaski, NY 13142-0034
315-298-2213
Web site: www.pulaskinychamber.com
Nancy Farrell, President

Putnam County Economic Development Corporation
34 Gleneida Ave, Carmel, NY 10512
845-228-8066 Fax: 845-225-0311
e-mail: meghan.taylor@putnamcountyny.gov
Web site: www.putnamedc.org
Kevin Bailey, President

Queens Chamber of Commerce (Borough of)
75-20 Astoria Blvd, Suite 140, Jackson Heights, NY 11370
718-898-8500 Fax: 718-898-8599
e-mail: info@queenschamber.org
Web site: www.queenschamber.org
Carol Consiato, President

Red Hook Area Chamber of Commerce
PO Box 254, Red Hook, NY 12571-0254
845-758-0824 Fax: 845-758-0824
e-mail: info@redhookchamber.org
Web site: www.redhookchamber.org
Ray Amater, President

Rensselaer County Regional Chamber of Commerce
255 River St, Troy, NY 12180
518-274-7020 Fax: 518-272-7729
e-mail: info@renscochamber.com
Web site: www.renscochamber.com
Linda Hillman, President

Rhinebeck Area Chamber of Commerce
PO Box 42, 23F E Market Street, Rhinebeck, NY 12572
845-876-5904 Fax: 845-876-8624
e-mail: info@rhinebeckchamber.com
Web site: www.rhinebeckchamber.com
Colleen Cruishank, Executive Director

Richfield Springs Area Chamber of Commerce
PO Box 909, Richfield Springs, NY 13439-0909
315-858-7028
e-mail: elbudro@aol.com
Web site: www.richfieldspringschamber.org
E Lawrence Budro, Executive Director

Riverhead Chamber of Commerce
542 E Main St, Suite 2, Riverhead, NY 11901
631-727-7600 Fax: 631-727-7946
e-mail: info@riverheadchamber.com
Web site: www.riverheadchamber.com
Tracy Stark James, President
Mary Hughes, Executive Director

Rochester Business Alliance Inc
150 State St, Ste 400, Rochester, NY 14614-1308
585-244-1800 Fax: 585-263-3679
e-mail: sandyp@rballiance.com
Web site: www.rochesterbusinessalliance.com
Sandra Parker, President & CEO

Rochester Downtown Development Corporation
One HSBC Plaza, 100 Chestnut Street, Suite 1910, Rochester, NY 14604
585-546-6920 Fax: 585-546-4784
e-mail: rddc@rddc.org
Web site: www.rochesterdowntown.com
Heidi N Zimmer-Meyer, President

Rochester Economic Development Corporation
30 Church Street, Room 223B, Rochester, NY 14614
585-428-8801 Fax: 585-428-6042
e-mail: carballc@cityofrochester.gov
Web site: www.cityofrochester.gov
R Carlos Carballada, President

Offices and agencies generally appear in alphabetical order, except when specific order is requested by listee.

Rockaway Development & Revitalization Corporation
1920 Mott Ave, 2nd Fl, Far Rockaway, NY 11691
718-327-5300 Fax: 718-327-4990
e-mail: info@rdrc.org
Web site: www.rdrc.org
Kevin W Alexander, Executive Director

Rockaways, Chamber of Commerce, Inc
253 Beach 116th St, Rockaway Park, NY 11694
718-634-1300 Fax: 718-634-9623
e-mail: rockawaychamberofcommerce@gmail.com
Web site: www.rockawaychamberofcommerce.com

Rockland Chamber of Commerce
PO Box 2001, New City, NY 10956
914-634-4646 Fax: 914-353-5533
e-mail: martreal@aol.com
Martin Bernstein, President

Rockland Economic Development Corporation
2 Blue Hill Plaza, PO Box 1575, Pearl River, NY 10965-1575
845-735-7040 Fax: 845-735-5736
e-mail: stevenp@redc.org
Web site: www.redc.org
Michael DiTullo, President & CEO

Rockville Centre Chamber of Commerce
PO Box 226, Rockville Centre, NY 11571
516-766-0666 Fax: 516-706-1550
e-mail: info@rockvillecentrechamber.com
Web site: www.rvcchamber.com
Lawrence G Siegel, President

Rome Area Chamber of Commerce
139 West Dominick St, Rome, NY 13440-5809
315-337-1700 Fax: 315-337-1715
e-mail: info@romechamber.com
Web site: www.romechamber.com
William K Guglielmo, President

Rome Industrial Development Corporation
584 Phoenix Drive, Rome, NY 13441
315-338-0393 Fax: 315-338-5694
e-mail: mkaucher@mvedge.org
Web site: www.romeny.org
Mark Kaucher, Executive Director

Ronkonkoma Chamber of Commerce
PO Box 2546, Ronkonkoma, NY 11779
631-963-2796
e-mail: info@ronkonkomachamber.com
Web site: www.ronkonkomachamber.com
Denise Schwartz, President

Sackets Harbor Chamber of Commerce
PO Box 17, 301 W Main Street, Sackets Harbor, NY 13685
315-646-1700 Fax: 315-646-2160
e-mail: shvisit@gisco.net
Web site: www.visitsackets.com
Anita Prather Harvell, President

Sag Harbor Chamber of Commerce
PO Box 2810, Sag Harbor, NY 11963
631-725-0011 Fax: 631-919-1662
e-mail: info@sagharborchamber.com
Web site: www.sagharborchamber.com
Kelly Connaughton, President

Salamanca Area Chamber of Commerce
26 Main St, Salamanca, NY 14779
716-945-2034 Fax: 716-945-2034
e-mail: info@salmun.com
Web site: www.salamancachamber.org
Jayne L Fenton, President

Salamanca Industrial Development Agency
225 Wildwood Ave, Salamanca, NY 14779-1547
716-945-3230 Fax: 716-945-8289
e-mail: pwelch1@salmun.com
Web site: www.salmun.com
Patrick Welch, Office Manager

Saranac Lake Area Chamber of Commerce
193 River St, Saranac Lake, NY 12983
518-891-1990 or 800-347-1992 Fax: 518-891-7042
e-mail: info@saranaclake.com
Web site: www.saranaclake.com
Katy Van Anden, Executive Director

Saratoga County Chamber of Commerce
28 Clinton St, Saratoga Springs, NY 12866
518-584-3255 Fax: 518-587-0318
e-mail: info@saratoga.org
Web site: www.saratoga.org
Todd Shimkus, President

Saratoga County Industrial Development Agency
50 W High St, Ballston Spa, NY 12020
518-884-4705 Fax: 518-884-4780
e-mail: larrybeuton61@msn.com
Web site: www.saratogacountyida.org
Raymond F Callanan, Chairman

Saratoga Economic Development Corporation
28 Clinton St, Saratoga Springs, NY 12866
518-587-0945 Fax: 518-587-5855
Web site: www.saratogaedc.com
Dennis Brobston, President

Sayville Chamber of Commerce (Greater Sayville)
Bud Van Wyen Memorial BUilding, PO Box 235, Sayville, NY 11782-0235
631-567-5257 Fax: 631-218-0881
e-mail: info@sayvillechamber.com
Web site: www.greatersayvillechamber.com
Bill Etts, President

Scarsdale Chamber of Commerce
PO Box 635, Scarsdale, NY 10583
914-620-2426
Web site: www.scarsdalechamber.org
Lewis Arlt, President

Schenectady County Chamber of Commerce
306 State St, Schenectady, NY 12305-2302
518-372-5656 or 800-962-8007 Fax: 518-370-3217
e-mail: info@schenectadychamber.org
Web site: www.schenectadychamber.org
Charles P Steiner, President

Schenectady County Industrial Development Agency/Economic Development Corporation
Center City Plaza, Schenectady, NY 12305
518-377-1109 Fax: 518-382-2575
Web site: www.schenectadycounty.com
Jayme Lahut, President

Offices and agencies generally appear in alphabetical order, except when specific order is requested by listee.

Schoharie County Chamber of Commerce
143 Caverns Road, Howes Cave, NY 12092
518-296-8820 Fax: 518-296-8825
e-mail: info@schohariechamber.com
Web site: www.schohariechamber.com
Georgia Van Dyke, Interim Executive Director

Schoharie County Industrial Development Agency
349 Mineral Springs Rd, Cobleskill, NY 12043
518-234-7604 Fax: 518-234-4346
e-mail: rfscrpc@nycap.rr.com
Web site: www.growscny.com
Ronald Filmer, Director

Schroon Lake Area Chamber of Commerce
1075 US Rte 9, PO Box 726, Schroon Lake, NY 12870-0726
518-532-7675 or 888-SCHROON
e-mail: chamber@schroonlakeregion.com
Web site: www.schroonlakechamber.com
Mike Bush, President

Schuyler County Industrial Development Agency
2 N Franklin St, Ste 330, Watkins Glen, NY 14891
607-535-4341 Fax: 607-535-7221
e-mail: kelsey@scoped.biz
Web site: www.scoped.biz
J. Kelsey Jones, Executive Director

Schuyler County Partnership for Economic Development
2 N Franklin St, Ste 330, Watkins Glen, NY 14891
607-535-4341 Fax: 607-535-7221
e-mail: brian@scoped.biz
Web site: www.scoped.biz
Brian Williams, Economic & Community Development Specialist

Seaford Chamber of Commerce
2479 Jackson Avenue, PO Box 1634, Seaford, NY 11783
516-221-2888 Fax: 516-221-8683
e-mail: likoub@gmail.com
Web site: www.seafordchamberofcommerce.com
Kenneth Jacobsen, President

Seneca County Chamber of Commerce
2020 Rtes 5 & 20 West, Seneca Falls, NY 13148
315-568-2906 or 800-732-1848 Fax: 315-568-1730
e-mail: info@senecachamber.org
Web site: www.senecachamber.org
Jeff Shipley, Executive Director

Seneca County Industrial Development Agency
One Di Pronio Dr, Waterloo, NY 13165
315-539-1725 Fax: 315-539-4340
e-mail: raronson@co.seneca.ny.us
Web site: www.senecacountyida.org
Robert J Aronson, Executive Director

Sidney Chamber of Commerce
24 River St, PO Box 2295, Sidney, NY 13838
607-561-2642 Fax: 607-561-2644
e-mail: office@sidneychamber.org
Web site: www.sidneychamber.org
Kerri Green, President

Skaneateles Area Chamber of Commerce
22 Jordan St., PO Box 199, Skaneateles, NY 13152
315-685-0552 Fax: 315-685-0552
e-mail: info@skaneateles.com
Web site: www.skaneateles.com
Susan Dove, Executive Director

Sleepy Hollow Chamber of Commerce
1 Neperan Rd, Tarrytown, NY 10591-3660
914-631-1705 Fax: 914-366-4291
e-mail: info@sleepyhollowchamber.com
Web site: www.sleepyhollowchamber.com
John Sardy, Executive Director

Slovak American Chamber of Commerce
10 E 40th Street, New York, NY 10016
212-532-4920

Smithtown Chamber of Commerce
79 E Main Street, Suite E, PO Box 1216, Smithtown, NY 11787
631-979-8069 Fax: 631-979-2206
e-mail: info@smithtownchamber.com
Web site: www.smithtownchamber.com
Barbara Franco, Executive Director

South Jefferson Chamber of Commerce
PO Box 73, Adams, NY 13605
315-232-4215 or 888-476-5333 Fax: 315-232-3967
Web site: www.1000islands.com

Southampton Chamber of Commerce
76 Main St, Southampton, NY 11968
631-283-0402 Fax: 631-283-8707
e-mail: info@southamptonchamber.com
Web site: www.southamptonchamber.com
Micah Schlendorf, President

Southeastern New York, Council of Industry of
6 Albany Post Rd, Newburgh, NY 12550
845-565-1355 Fax: 845-565-1427
e-mail: hking@councilofindustry.org
Web site: www.councilofindustry.org
Robert Miniger, President

Southern Dutchess Chamber of Commerce (Greater Southern Dutchess)
Nussbickel Building, 2582 S Ave (Route 9D), Wappingers Falls, NY 12590
845-296-0001 Fax: 845-296-0006
e-mail: webmaster@gsdcc.org
Web site: www.gsdcc.org
Ann M Meagher, President/CEO

Southern Madison County Chamber of Commerce
10 Utica Street, 2nd Floor, PO Box 3, Hamilton, NY 13346
315-824-8213 or 315-824-0002 Fax: 315-824-0086
Web site: www.hamiltonny.com

Southern Saratoga County Chamber of Commerce
15 Park Avenue, Suite 7, Clifton Park, NY 12065
518-371-7748 Fax: 518-371-5025
e-mail: info@southernsaratoga.org
Web site: www.southernsaratoga.org
Southern Saratoga Countys premier local business advocate with over 1025 members.
Pete Bardunias, President & CEO
Loretta Rigney, Vice President

Southern Tier Economic Growth Inc
400 Church St, Elmira, NY 14901
607-733-6513 Fax: 607-734-2698
e-mail: info@steg.com
Web site: www.steg.com
George Miner, President

Southern Ulster County Chamber of Commerce
3553 Route 9W, PO Box 320, Highland, NY 12528
845-691-6070 Fax: 845-691-9194
e-mail: info@southernulsterchamber.org
Web site: www.southernulsterchamber.org
William Farrell, President

Offices and agencies generally appear in alphabetical order, except when specific order is requested by listee.

Springville Area Chamber of Commerce
23 N Buffalo St, PO Box 310, Springville, NY 14141-0310
716-592-4746 Fax: 716-592-4746
e-mail: info@springvillechamber.com
Web site: www.springvillechamber.com
Duane W Fischer, Executive Director

St James Chamber of Commerce
PO Box 286, St James, NY 11780
631-584-8510 Fax: 631-862-9839
e-mail: info@stjameschamber.org
Web site: www.stjameschamber.org
Ryan McKenna, President

St Lawrence County Chamber of Commerce
101 Main Street, Canton, NY 13617-1248
315-386-4000 or 877-228-7810 Fax: 315-379-0134
e-mail: pmck123@aol.com
Web site: www.northcountryguide.com
Patricia McKeown, Executive Director

St Lawrence County Industrial Development Agency
19 Commerce Lane, Suite 1, Canton, NY 13617-1496
315-379-9806 Fax: 315-386-2573
e-mail: info@slcida.com
Web site: www.slcida.com
Patrick Kelly, Chief Executive Officer

Staten Island Chamber of Commerce
130 Bay St, Staten Island, NY 10301
718-727-1900 Fax: 718-727-2295
e-mail: info@sichamber.com
Web site: www.sichamber.com
Linda M Baran, President & CEO

Staten Island Economic Development Corporation
900 South Ave, Ste 402, Staten Island, NY 10314
718-477-1400 Fax: 718-477-0681
e-mail: newsinfo@siedc.net
Web site: www.siedc.org
Cesar J Claro, President & CEO

Steuben County Industrial Development Agency
7234 Rte 54, PO Box 393, Bath, NY 14810-0390
607-776-3316 Fax: 607-776-5039
e-mail: scida@steubencountyida.com
Web site: www.steubencountyida.com
James Johnson, Executive Director

Suffern Chamber of Commerce
PO Box 291, 71 Lafayette Avenue, Suffern, NY 10901
845-357-8424
e-mail: suffernchamberofcommerce@yahoo.com
Web site: www.suffernchamberofcommerce.com

Sullivan County Chamber of Commerce
PO Box 405, Mongaup Valley, NY 12762
845-791-4200 Fax: 845-791-4220
e-mail: chamber@catskills.com
Web site: www.catskills.com
Terri Ward, President & CEO

Sullivan County Industrial Development Agency
1 Cablevision Ctr, Ferndale, NY 12734
845-295-2603 Fax: 845-295-2604
e-mail: scida@hvc.rr.com
Web site: www.sullivanida.com
Jennifer C S Brylinski, Executive Director & COO

Syracuse & Central NY, Metropolitan Development Association of
572 South Salina Street, Syracuse, NY 13202
315-422-8284 Fax: 315-471-4503
e-mail: ceo@centerstateceo.com
Web site: www.centerstateceo.com
Robert Simpson, President & CEO

Syracuse Chamber of Commerce (Greater Syracuse)
572 S Salina St, Syracuse, NY 13202-3320
315-470-1800 Fax: 315-471-8545
e-mail: ceo@centerstateceo.com
Web site: www.centerstateceo.com
Robert Simpson, President

Syracuse Economic Development
333 Washington Street, Suite 130, Syracuse, NY 13202
315-435-3770 Fax: 315-435-3669
e-mail: info@syracusecentral.com
Web site: www.syracusecentral.com
Mary Beth Primo, Director of Economic Development

Syracuse Industrial Development Agency
City Hall, 233 E Washington St, Syracuse, NY 13202
315-448-8100 Fax: 315-448-8036
e-mail: bwalsh@ci.syracuse.ny.us
Web site: www.syracuse.ny.us
William M Ryan, Chair

Three Rivers Development Foundation Inc
114 Pine St, Suite 201, Corning, NY 14830
607-962-4693 Fax: 607-936-9132
e-mail: info@3riverscorp.com
Web site: www.3riverscorp.com
Jack Benjamin, President

Ticonderoga Area Chamber of Commerce
94 Montcalm Street, Suite 1, Ticonderoga, NY 12883
518-585-6619 Fax: 518-585-9184
e-mail: chamberinfo@ticonderogany.com
Web site: www.ticonderogany.com
Pamela Nolan, Executive Director

Tioga County Chamber of Commerce
80 North Avenue, Owego, NY 13827
607-687-8255 Fax: 607-687-1435
e-mail: business@tiogachamber.com
Web site: www.tiogachamber.com
Douglas Barton, Director

Tioga County Industrial Development Agency
County Office Bldg, 56 Main Street, Owego, NY 13827
607-687-8259 Fax: 607-687-8282
e-mail: ida@developtioga.com
Web site: www.developtioga.com
Aaron Gowan, Chairman

Tompkins County Area Development
400 East State Street/East MLK Jr. St., Suite 402B, Ithaca, NY 14850
607-273-0005 Fax: 607-273-8964
e-mail: info@tcad.org
Web site: www.tcad.org
Michael Stamm, President

Tompkins County Chamber of Commerce
904 E Shore Drive, Ithaca, NY 14850
607-273-7080 Fax: 607-272-7617
e-mail: marilyn@tompkinschamber.org
Web site: www.tompkinschamber.org
Jean McPheeters, President

Chambers of Commerce

Offices and agencies generally appear in alphabetical order, except when specific order is requested by listee.

CHAMBERS OF COMMERCE/ECONOMIC DEVELOPMENT ORGANIZATIONS

Tonawanda (Town Of) Development Corporation
169 Sheridan Parkside Dr, Tonawanda, NY 14150
716-871-8847 Fax: 716-871-8857
e-mail: ttdc@tonawanda.ny.us
Web site: www.tonawanda.com
James Hartz, Director

Tonawandas, Chamber of Commerce of the
15 Webster St, North Tonawanda, NY 14120
716-692-5120 Fax: 716-692-1867
e-mail: chamber@the-tonawandas.com
Web site: www.the-tonawandas.com
Joyce M Santiago, President

Tri-State Chamber of Commerce
PO Box 386, Lakeville, CT 06039-0386
860-435-0740
e-mail: info@tristatechamber.com
Web site: www.tristatechamber.com
Susan Dickinson, President
Cheryl Reynolds, President

Tupper Lake Chamber of Commerce
121 Park Street, PO Box 987, Tupper Lake, NY 12986
518-359-3328 Fax: 518-359-2434
e-mail: chamber@tupper-lake.com
Web site: www.tupper-lake.com
David Tomerlin, President

Ulster County Chamber of Commerce
214 Fair Street, Kingston, NY 12401
845-338-5100 Fax: 845-338-0968
e-mail: info@ulsterchamber.org
Web site: www.ulsterchamber.org
Ward Todd, President

Ulster County Development Corporation/Ulster County Industrial Development Agency
5 Development Court, Kingston, NY 12401
845-338-8840 or 800-7-ULSTER Fax: 845-338-0409
e-mail: develop@ulsterny.com
Web site: www.ulsterny.com
Lance Matteson, President

Union Local Development Corporation (Town of)
3111 E Main St, Endwell, NY 13760
607-786-2900 Fax: 607-786-2998
e-mail: economicdevelopment@townofunion.com
Web site: www.townofunion.com
Joseph M Moody, Director of Economic Development

Utica Industrial Development Agency (City of)
One Kennedy Plz, Utica, NY 13501
315-792-0195 Fax: 315-792-9819
e-mail: jspaeth@cityofutica.com
Web site: www.cityofutica.com
Jack N Spaeth, Executive Director

Valley Stream Chamber of Commerce
PO Box 1016, Valley Stream, NY 11580-1016
516-825-1741
e-mail: valleystreamcc@gmail.com
Web site: www.valleystreamchamber.org

Victor Chamber of Commerce
37 East Main Street, Victor, NY 14564
585-742-1476 Fax: 585-924-0523
e-mail: info@victorchamber.com
Web site: www.victorchamber.com
Mitch Donovan, President

Waddington Chamber of Commerce
PO Box 291, Waddington, NY 13694
315-388-4765 or 315-388-5576
e-mail: waddingtonchamber@gmail.com
Web site: www.waddingtonny.us/chamber
Alicia Murphy, President

Walton Chamber of Commerce
129 North Street, Walton, NY 13856-1217
607-865-6656
e-mail: waltonchamber@yahoo.com
Web site: www.waltonchamber.com
Maureen Wacha, President

Wantagh Chamber of Commerce
Pond Rd, PO Box 660, Wantagh, NY 11793
516-679-0100 or 516-781-6145
e-mail: denise@langweberlaw.com
Web site: www.wcc.li
Denise Langweber, President

Warren & Washington Industrial Development Agency
5 Warren St, Suite 210, Glens Falls, NY 12801
518-792-1312 Fax: 518-792-4147
e-mail: info@warren-washingtonida.com
Web site: www.warren-washingtonida.com
Harold Taylor, Chairman

Warren County Economic Development Corporation
234 Glen Street, Glens Falls, NY 12801
518-761-6007 Fax: 518-761-9053
e-mail: info@edcwc.org
Web site: www.edcwc.org
Leonard Fosbrook, President

Warrensburg Chamber of Commerce
3728 Main St, Warrensburg, NY 12885
518-623-2161 Fax: 518-623-2184
e-mail: info@warrensburgchamber.com
Web site: www.warrensburgchamber.com
Lynn Smith, President

Warsaw Chamber of Commerce (Greater Warsaw)
PO Box 221, Warsaw, NY 14569
585-786-3989 Fax: 585-786-3083
e-mail: info@warsawchamber.com
Web site: warsawchamber.com
Becky Ryan, President

Warwick Valley Chamber of Commerce
South St, Caboose, PO Box 202, Warwick, NY 10990
845-986-2720 Fax: 914-986-6982
e-mail: info@warwickcc.org
Web site: www.warwickcc.org
Michael Johndrow, Executive Director

Washington County Local Development Corporation
383 Broadway, Building A, Fort Edward, NY 12828
518-746-2292 Fax: 518-746-2293
e-mail: info@wcldc.org
Web site: www.wcldc.org
Tori J.E. Riley, President

Watertown Empire Zone
PO Box 3367, Saratoga Springs, NY 12866
315-782-1167 Fax: 518-899-9642
e-mail: michael@camoinassociates.com
Web site: www.watertownempirezone.com
R Michael N'dolo, Zone Coodinator

Offices and agencies generally appear in alphabetical order, except when specific order is requested by listee.

Watertown-North Country Chamber of Commerce (Greater Watertown)
1241 Coffeen St, Watertown, NY 13601
315-788-4400 Fax: 315-788-3369
e-mail: chamber@watertownny.com
Web site: www.watertownny.com
Lynn Pietroski, President & CEO

Watkins Glen Area Chamber of Commerce
214 N Franklin St, St Rte 14, Watkins Glen, NY 14891
607-535-4300 or 800-607-4552 Fax: 607-535-6243
e-mail: info@watkinsglenchamber.com
Web site: www.watkinsglenchamber.com
Rebekah LaMoreaux, President/CEO

Wayne County Industrial Development Agency & Economic Development
16 William St, Lyons, NY 14489
315-946-5917 or 888-219-2963 Fax: 315-946-5918
e-mail: wedcny@co.wayne.ny.us
Web site: www.wedcny.org
Peg Churchill, Executive Director

Webster Chamber of Commerce
1110 Crosspointe Lane, Ste C, Webster, NY 14580-3280
585-265-3960 Fax: 585-265-3702
e-mail: info@websterchamber.com
Web site: www.websterchamber.com
Barry Howard, President/CEO

Weedsport Area Chamber of Commerce
PO Box 973, Weedsport, NY 13166
315-834-2280
e-mail: weedsportchamber@yahoo.com
Web site: www.weedsportchamber.org
Penny Fay, President

Wellsville Area Chamber of Commerce
114 N Main St, Wellsville, NY 14895
585-593-5080 Fax: 585-593-5088
e-mail: info@wellsvilleareachamber.com
Web site: www.wellsvilleareachamber.com
Steven Havey, Executive Director

Westbury-Carle Place Chamber of Commerce
PO Box 474, Westbury, NY 11590
516-997-3966
e-mail: info@wcpchamber.com
Web site: www.wcpchamber.com
Frank Frisone, President

West Manhattan Chamber of Commerce
150 W 88 St, PO Box 1028, New York, NY 10024
212-787-1112 Fax: 212-787-1115
e-mail: mail@westmanhattanchamber.org
Web site: www.westmanhattanchamber.org
Andrew Albert, Executive Director

West Seneca Chamber of Commerce
950A Union Rd, Suite 5, West Seneca, NY 14224
716-674-4900 Fax: 716-674-5846
e-mail: director@westseneca.org
Web site: www.westseneca.org
Frank Calieri, Executive Director

Westchester County Association Inc (The)
1133 Westchester Ave, Suite S-217, White Plains, NY 10604
914-948-6444 Fax: 914-948-6913
e-mail: wmooney@westchester.org
Web site: www.westchester.org
William M Mooney, Jr, President

Westchester County Chamber of Commerce
108 Corporate Park Dr, Ste 101, White Plains, NY 10604
914-948-2110 Fax: 914-948-0122
e-mail: mpgordon@westchesterny.org
Web site: www.westchesterny.org
Dr Marsha Gordon, President & CEO

Westchester County Industrial Development Agency
Room 903, Michaelian Office Building, 148 Martine Avenue, White Plains, NY 10601
914-995-2963 Fax: 914-995-3044
e-mail: jcoleman@westchestergov.com
Web site: www.thinkingwestchester.com
Jim Coleman, Executive Director

Westfield/Barcelona Chamber of Commerce
27 East Main St, PO Box 125, Westfield, NY 14787-1319
716-326-4000 Fax: 716-326-2299
Tony Pisicoli, President

Westhampton Chamber of Commerce (Greater Westhampton)
PO Box 1228, 7 Glovers Lane, Westhampton Beach, NY 11978
631-288-3337 Fax: 631-288-3322
e-mail: info@whbcc.org
Web site: www.whbcc.org
Dwayne Wagner, President

Whiteface Mountain Regional Visitor's Bureau
PO Box 277, Wilmington, NY 12997
518-946-2255 or 888-Whiteface Fax: 518-946-2683
e-mail: info@whitefaceregion.com
Web site: www.whitefaceregion.com
Diane Buckley, Office Manager

Whitehall Area Chamber of Commerce
130 Main Street, PO Box 97, Whitehall, NY 12887
518-499-2292
Web site: www.whitehall-chamber.org

Williamson Chamber of Commerce
PO Box 907, Williamson, NY 14589
315-589-2020 Fax: 315-589-9682
e-mail: williamsoncofc@aol.com
Web site: www.williamsonchamberofcommerceny.org
TBA, President

Willistons Chamber of Commerce
PO Box 207, Williston Park, NY 11596
516-739-1943 Fax: 516-294-1444
e-mail: info@chamberofthewillistons.org
Web site: www.chamberofthewillistons.org
Bobby Shannon, President

Woodstock Chamber of Commerce & Arts
PO Box 36, Woodstock, NY 12498
845-679-6234
e-mail: info@woodstockchamber.com
Web site: www.woodstockchamber.com
Nick Altomare, President

Wurtsboro Board of Trade
PO Box 907, Wurtsboro, NY 12790
845-888-4884
Web site: www.wurtsboro.org
James Arnott, President

Wyoming County Chamber of Commerce
6470 Route 20A, Suite 2, Perry, NY 14530-9798
585-237-0230 or 800-839-3919 Fax: 585-237-0231
e-mail: info@wycochamber.org
Web site: www.wycochamber.org
Laura Lane, President/CEO

Chambers of Commerce

Offices and agencies generally appear in alphabetical order, except when specific order is requested by listee.

Yates County Chamber of Commerce
2375 Rte 14A, Penn Yan, NY 14527
800-868-YATES Fax: 315-536-3791
e-mail: info@yatesny.com
Web site: www.yatesny.com
Michael Linehan, President/CEO

Finger Lakes Economic Development Center
One Keuka Business Park, Penn Yan, NY 14527
315-536-7328 Fax: 315-536-2389
e-mail: info@fingerlakesedc.com
Web site: www.fingerlakesedc.com
Steve Griffin, CEO

Yonkers Chamber of Commerce
55 Main Street, Yonkers, NY 10701
914-963-0332 Fax: 914-963-0451
e-mail: info@yonkerschamber.com
Web site: www.yonkerschamber.com
Kevin T Cacace, President

Yonkers Economic Development/Yonkers Industrial Development Agency (City of)
470 Nepperhan Ave, Suite 200, Yonkers, NY 10701
914-509-8651 Fax: 914-509-8651
e-mail: info@yonkersida.com
Web site: www.cityofyonkersida.com
Melvina Carter, President/CEO

Section 6:
NEWS MEDIA

NEWS MEDIA

This chapter identifies key journalists and editorial management for daily and weekly newspapers in New York State, major news services with reporters assigned to cover State government, radio stations with a news format and television stations with news staff.

NEWSPAPERS

Newspapers included in this chapter employ reporters who cover state and regional news. The newspapers are listed alphabetically by primary city served.

ALBANY

Legislative Gazette *Weekly Circulation: 13,222*

Legislative Gazette
Empire State Plaza, Concourse Level, PO Box 7329, Room 106, Albany, NY 12224
518-473-9739 Fax: 518-486-6609
e-mail: editor@legislativegazette.com
Web site: www.legislativegazette.com
Executive Publisher/Project Director . . . . Professor Alan S Chartock
Editor. . . . . .James Gormley
    e-mail: editor@legislativegazette.com
Assistant General Manager / Circulation / Production Manager . . . Beth Rider
    e-mail: ads@legislativegazette.com

American City Business Journals *Weekly Circulation: 4,000,000*

The Business Review
40 British American Blvd, Latham, NY 12210
518-640-6800 Fax: 518-640-6801
e-mail: albany@bizjournals.com
Web site: www.albany.bizjournals.com
Publisher . . . . .Carolyn M Jones
    e-mail: cmjones@bizjournals.com
Editor-in-Chief . . . . .Michael Hendricks
    e-mail: mhendricks@bizjournals.com
Managing Editor . . . . .Robin E Cooper
    e-mail: rcooper@bizjournals.com

Times Union *Weekday Circulation: 96,974*

Times Union
645 Albany Shaker Road, Albany, NY 12211
518-454-5694 Fax: 518-454-5628
e-mail: tubusiness@timesunion.com
Web site: www.timesunion.com
Publisher/CEO . . . . .George R Hearst III
    e-mail: rsmith@timesunion.com
VP/Editor. . . . . .Rex Smith
    e-mail: rsmith@timesunion.com
Associate Editor. . . . . .Michael V Spain
    e-mail: mspain@timesunion.com
Director of Circulation . . . . .Mark Vinciguerra
    e-mail: mvinciguerra@timesunion.com
Senior Editor/Features. . . . . .Tracy Ormsbee
    e-mail: tormsbee@timesunion.com
Senior News Editor. . . . . .Teresa Buckley
    e-mail: tbuckley@timesunion.com
Senior News Editor/Information Services . . . . .Tena Tyler
    e-mail: ttyler@timesunion.com

AMSTERDAM

Recorder (The) *Weekly Circulation: 8,000*

Recorder (The)
One Venner Rd, Amsterdam, NY 12010
518-843-1100 or 800-453-6397 Fax: 518-843-6580
e-mail: news@recordernews.com
Web site: www.recordernews.com
Publisher . . . . .Kevin McClary
    e-mail: kevin@recordernews.com
Associate Publisher . . . . .Geoff Dylong
    e-mail: geoff@recordernews.com
Executive Editor . . . . .Kevin Mattison
    e-mail: kmattison@recordernews.com
Advertising/Marketing Director . . . . .Brian Krohn
    e-mail: briankrohn@recordernews.com
Editor . . . . .Charlie Kraebel
    e-mail: ckraebel@recordernews.com
Business Manager . . . . .Bill Brzezicki
    e-mail: bbrzezicki@recordernews.com

AUBURN

Citizen (The) *Circulation: Daily 11,770; Sunday 13,600*

Auburn Publishers Inc
25 Dill St, Auburn, NY 13201-3605
315-253-3700 Fax: 315-253-6031
e-mail: newsroom@tds.net
Web site: www.auburnpub.com
Publisher . . . . .Michael Rifanburg
    e-mail: michael.rifanburg@lee.net
Executive Editor . . . . .Jeremy Boyer
    e-mail: jeremy.boyer@lee.net
Managing Editor . . . . .Michael Dowd
    e-mail: michael.dowd@lee.net
Advertising Director . . . . .Sarah Dunham
    e-mail: sarah.dunham@lee.net
Circulation Directory. . . . . .Todd Ackerman
    e-mail: todd.ackerman@lee.net
Asst News Editor . . . . .Chris Sciria
    e-mail: chris.sciria@lee.net

BINGHAMTON

Press & Sun Bulletin *Weekday Circulation: 37,915*

Gannet Co Inc
33 Lewis Rd, Binghamton, NY 13905-1044
607-798-1234 Fax: 607-352-2645
e-mail: bgm-newsroom@gannett.com
Web site: www.pressconnects.com
Publisher. . . . . .Sherman M Bodner
    e-mail: sbodner@gannett.com
Executive Editor . . . . .Calvin Stovall
    e-mail: cstovall@binghamt.gannett.com
Assistant Managing Editor . . . . .Al Vieira
    e-mail: avieira@binghamt.gannett.com
Circulation Director . . . . .Anthony Rapczynski
    e-mail: arapczyn@binghamt.gannett.com
Advertising Director . . . . .Jodie Riesbeck
    e-mail: jriesbec@binghamt.gannett.com

News Media

Offices and agencies generally appear in alphabetical order, except when specific order is requested by listee.

BRONXVILLE-EASTCHESTER

Review *Weekly Circulation: 35,000*

Journal News (The)/Gannett Co Inc
5910 Firestone Drive, Syracuse, NY 13206
315-434-8889 Fax: 315-434-8883
e-mail: newsroom@cnylink.com
Web site: www.cnylink.com/about/review.php
Publisher . . . . .David Tyler
    e-mail: dtyler@eaglenewsonline.com
Editor. . . . . .Sarah Hall
    e-mail: editor@eaglestarreview.com

BROOKLYN

Brooklyn Daily Eagle *Weekly Circulation: 13,000*

Brooklyn Daily Eagle
16 Court St, Ste 1208, Brooklyn, NY 11241
718-422-7400
e-mail: editor@brooklyneagle.net
Web site: www.brooklyneagle.net
Publisher . . . . .J Dozier Hasty
    e-mail: publisher@brooklyneagle.net

Canarsie Courier Publications, Inc. *Weekly Circulation: 10,000*

Canarsie Courier
1142 East 92nd Street, Brooklyn, NY 11236
718-257-0600 Fax: 718-272-0870
e-mail: canarsiec@aol.com
Web site: www.canarsiecourier.com
Associate Editor . . . . .Dara Mormile
    e-mail: canarsiec@aol.com
Publisher. . . . . .Donna M Marra
Managing Editor . . . . .Charles Rogers
Associate Editor . . . . .Neil Friedman
Business Manager . . . . .Catherine Rosa

New York Daily Challenge (The) *Weekday Circulation: 81,000*

New York Daily Challenge (The)
1195 Atlantic Ave, Brooklyn, NY 11216
718-636-9500 Fax: 718-857-9115
Publisher. . . . . .Thomas H Watkins, Jr
    e-mail: t.watkins@challenge-group.net
Managing Editor . . . . .Duwad Philip

BUFFALO

Buffalo Business First *Weekly Circulation: 10,000*

Buffalo Business First
465 Main Street, Buffalo, NY 14203-1793
716-854-5822 Fax: 716-854-7960
e-mail: buffalo@bizjournals.com
Web site: www.bizjournals.com/buffalo
Publisher. . . . . .Jack Connors
Editor. . . . . .Tim O'Shei
Advertising Director . . . . .Shelley Rohaurer
Circulation Marketing Director. . . . . .Karen Schiffmacher

Buffalo News (The) *Weekday Circulation: 191,000*

Buffalo News (The)
1 News Plaza, Buffalo, NY 14240-0100
716-849-4444 Fax: 716-856-5150
e-mail: citydesk@buffnews.com
Web site: www.buffalonews.com
Editor . . . . .Mike Connelly
    e-mail: editor@buffnews.com
Managing Editor . . . . .Brian Connolly
    e-mail: bconnolly@buffnews.com
Deputy Managing Editor . . . . .Stan L Evans
    e-mail: sevans@buffnews.com
Assistant Managing Editor . . . . .Margaret Kenny
    e-mail: mkenny@buffnews.com
Editorial Page Editor. . . . . .John Neville
    e-mail: jneville@buffnews.com
City Editor . . . . .William Flynn
    e-mail: wflynn@buffnews.com

CANANDAIGUA

Daily Messenger (The) *Weekly Circulation: 400,000*

Messenger Post Newspapers
73 Buffalo St, Canandaigua, NY 14424
585-394-0770 Fax: 585-394-1675
e-mail: messenger@mpnewspapers.com
Web site: www.mpnnow.com
Publisher. . . . . .Richard Procida
General Manager/Advertising Director . . . . .Beth Kesel
    e-mail: bkesel@messengerpostmedia.com
Regional Editor . . . . .Allison Cooper
    e-mail: acooper@messengerpostmedia.com
Local Editor/Wayne County . . . . .Steve Buchiere
    e-mail: sbuchiere@messengerpostmedia.com
Local Editor/Ontario County. . . . . .Nora Hicks
    e-mail: nhicks@messengerpostmedia.com

CATSKILL

Daily Mail (The) *Weekday Circulation: 3,524*

Hudson Valley Newspapers Inc
414 Main St, PO Box 484, Catskill, NY 12414
518-943-2100 Fax: 518-943-2063
e-mail: editorial@thedailymail.net
Web site: www.thedailymail.net
Publisher . . . . .Roger F Coleman
    e-mail: rpignone@thedailymail.net
Managing Editor . . . . .Ray Pignone
    e-mail: rpignone@thedailymail.net
Executive Editor. . . . . .Theresa Hyland
    e-mail: thyland@thedailymail.net
Advertising Director . . . . .Pamela Geskie
    e-mail: pgeskie@registerstar.net

CORNING

Corning Leader (The) *Weekday Circulation: 13,585*

GateHouse Media
34 W Pulteney St, Corning, NY 14830
607-936-4651
Web site: www.the-leader.com
Publisher . . . . .Fred Benson
    e-mail: fbenson@the-leader.com
News Editor . . . . .Stella Dupree
    e-mail: sdupree@the-leader.com

Offices and agencies generally appear in alphabetical order, except when specific order is requested by listee.

Circulation Manager . . . . Elmer Kuehner
    e-mail: ejkuehner@the-leader.com

CORTLAND

Cortland Standard Printing Co Inc *Weekday Circulation: 10,500*

Cortland Standard
110 Main St, Cortland, NY 13045
607-756-5665 Fax: 607-756-5665
e-mail: news@cortlandstandard.net
Web site: www.cortland.org/news
Publisher. . . . . .Kevin R Howe
Managing/News Editor . . . . .Kevin Conlon
Editorial Page Editor . . . . .Skip Chapman

DUNKIRK-FREDONIA

Observer Today *Weekday Circulation: 11,648*

Observer (The)
10 E Second st, PO Box 391, Dunkirk, NY 14048-0391
716-366-3000 Fax: 716-366-3005
e-mail: editorial@observertoday.com
Web site: www.observertoday.com
Publisher. . . . . .John D'Agostino
    e-mail: jdagostino@observertoday.com
Managing Editor. . . . . .Greg Bacon
    e-mail: gbacon@observertoday.com
News Editor . . . . .Bill Hammond
    e-mail: bhammond@observertoday.com
City Editor . . . . .Gib Snyder
    e-mail: gsnyder@observertoday.com

CHEMUNG

Star-Gazette *Weekday Circulation: 73,000*

Gannett Co Inc
201 Bladwin Street, Elmira, NY 14901
607-734-5151 Fax: 607-732-3786
e-mail: news@stargazette.com
Web site: www.stargazette.com
Publisher. . . . . .Sherman M Bodner
    e-mail: sbodner@gannett.com
Managing Editor & General Manager .Lois Wilson
    e-mail: lowilson@elmira.gannett.com
Circulation Director . . . . .Anthony Rapczynski
    e-mail: arapczyn@binghamt.gannett.com

GENEVA

Finger Lakes Times *Circulation: Sunday: 19,102; Daily: 16,185*

Finger Lakes Printing Co
218 Genesee St, Geneva, NY 14456
315-789-3333 or 800-388-6652 Fax: 315-789-4077
e-mail: fltimes@fltimes.com
Web site: www.fltimes.com
President/Publisher. . . . . .William L McLean III
Executive Editor . . . . .Michael J. Cutillo
Managing Editor . . . . .Chuck Schading
    e-mail: cschading@fltimes.com
News Editor . . . . .Alan Brignall

GLENS FALLS

Post-Star (The) *Weekday Circulation: 29,000*

Lee Enterprises Inc
76 Lawrence St, Glens Falls, NY 12801
518-792-3131 ext3220 or 800-724-2543 Fax: 518-761-1255
e-mail: obits@poststar.com
Web site: www.poststar.com
Publisher. . . . . .Rick Emanuel
    e-mail: emanuel@poststar.com
City Editor . . . . .Bob Condon
    e-mail: condon@poststar.com
News Editor . . . . .Rhonda Triller
    e-mail: rtriller@poststar.com
Sunday Editor. . . . . .Todd Kehoe
    e-mail: tkehoe@poststar.com
Online News Editor . . . . .Lindsey Hollenbaugh
    e-mail: lhollenbaugh@poststar.com
Circulation Director. . . . . .Michelle Giorgianni
    e-mail: giorgianni@poststar.com
Editor . . . . .Ken Tingley
    e-mail: tingley@poststar.com
News Editor. . . . . .Mary Serkalow
    e-mail: serkalow@poststar.com
News Editor . . . . .Paul Tackett
    e-mail: tackett@poststar.com

GLOVERSVILLE-JOHNSTOWN

Leader-Herald (The) *Weekday Circulation: 11,500*

William B Collins Co
8 E Fulton St, PO Box 1280, Gloversville, NY 12078
518-725-8616 Fax: 518-725-7407
e-mail: news@leaderherald.com
Web site: www.leaderherald.com
Publisher . . . . .Patricia Beck
    e-mail: pbeck@leaderherald.com
Managing Editor. . . . . .Tim Fonda
    e-mail: tfonda@leaderherald.com
Sr. News Editor . . . . .Rodney Minor
    e-mail: rminor@leaderherald.com
Sunday Editor. . . . . .Bill Ackerbauer
Circulation Manager . . . . .Toni Mosconi

HERKIMER

Telegram (The) *Weekday Circulation: 6,000*

GateHouse Media Inc.
111 Green St, Herkimer, NY 13350
315-866-2220 Fax: 315-866-5913
e-mail: news@herkimertelegram.com
Web site: www.herkimertelegram.com
Publisher & Advertising Director .Beth A Brewer
    e-mail: beth@herkimertelegram.com
Features Editor . . . . .Donna Thompson
Managing Editor . . . . .Todd Dewan
    e-mail: tdewan@littlefallstimes.com

Offices and agencies generally appear in alphabetical order, except when specific order is requested by listee.

HORNELL

Evening Tribune (The) *Weekday Circulation: 7,562*

GateHouse Media Inc.
85 Canisteo St, Hornell, NY 14843
607-324-1425 Fax: 607-324-2317
Web site: www.eveningtribune.com
Publisher . . . . Tom Connors
   e-mail: tomconnors@eveningtribune.com
Marketing Director . . . . John Frungillo
   e-mail: john@eveningtribune.com
Managing Editor . . . . Andrew Thompson
   e-mail: andythompson@eveningtribune.com
Circulation . . . . Gary Shaver
   e-mail: garyshaver@eveningtribune.com

HUDSON

Register-Star *Weekday Circulation: 6,100*

Johnson Newspaper Corporation
One Hudson City Centre, Hudson, NY 12534
518-828-1616 Fax: 518-828-3870
e-mail: editorial@registerstar.com
Web site: www.registerstar.com
Publisher . . . . Harold B Johnson II
   e-mail: publisher@registerstar.com
Executive Editor . . . . Theresa Hyland
   e-mail: thyland@registerstar.com
City Editor . . . . Mary Dempsey
   e-mail: mdempsey@registerstar.com
Editor . . . . Lori Anander
Editor . . . . Karrie Allen

ITHACA

Ithaca Journal (The) *Weekday Circulation: 10,371*

Gannett Co Inc
123 W State St, Ithaca, NY 14850
607-272-2321 Fax: 607-272-4248
Web site: www.theithacajournal.com
Publisher . . . . Sherman M Bodner
   e-mail: sbodner@gannett.com
Managing Editor/General Manager . . . . Bruce Estes
   e-mail: bestes@ithaca.gannett.com
News Editor . . . . Steve Gattine
   e-mail: sgattine@ithaca.gannett.com
Assistant Managing Editor . . . . Dave Bohrer
   e-mail: dbohrer@ithacajournal.com

JAMESTOWN

Post-Journal, The *Weekday Circulation: 20,000*

Post-Journal, The
PO Box 3386, Jamestown, NY 14702-3386
716-487-1111 or 866-756-9600 Fax: 716-664-3119
e-mail: editorial@post-journal.com
Web site: www.post-journal.com
Publisher . . . . Michael Bird
   e-mail: mbird@post-journal.com
Editor . . . . John Whittaker
   e-mail: jwhittaker@post-journal.com
Editor . . . . Matt Spielman
   e-mail: mspielman@post-journal.com
News/Wire Editor . . . . Mike Rukavina
   e-mail: mrukavina@post-journal.com

Circulation Director . . . . Andrew Gee
   e-mail: agee@post-journal.com

KINGSTON

Daily Freeman *Weekday Circulation: 20,391*

Journal Register Company
79 Hurley Ave, Kingston, NY 12401
845-331-5000 Fax: 845-331-3557
e-mail: jdewey@journalregister.com
Web site: www.dailyfreeman.com
Publisher . . . . Jan Dewey
   e-mail: jdewey@journalregister.com
Managing Editor . . . . Tony Adamis
   e-mail: tadamis@freemanonline.com
City Editor . . . . Jeremy Schiffres
   e-mail: jschiffres@freemanonline.com
Regional Circualtion Director . . . . Jim Collier
   e-mail: jcollier@journalregister.com

LITTLE FALLS

Times (The) *Weekday Circulation: 5,042*

GateHouse Media Inc.
347 S 2nd St, Little Falls, NY 13365
315-823-3680 Fax: 315-823-4086
e-mail: news@littlefallstimes.com
Web site: www.littlefallstimes.com
Publisher . . . . Beth Brewer
   e-mail: bethtimes@twcny.rr.com
Production Manager . . . . Wayne Galt
News Editor . . . . Todd Dewan
   e-mail: news@littlefallstimes.com

LOCKPORT

Journal-Register, The *Weekday Circulation: 3,500*

Greater Niagara Newspapers
170 East Ave, Medina, NY 14094
585-798-1400 Fax: 585-798-0290
e-mail: jr@gnnewspaper.com
Web site: www.journal-register.com
Publisher . . . . Diane Crowe
Managing Editor . . . . John Hopkins
   e-mail: john.hopkins@journal-register.com
Circulation Manager . . . . Beth Podgers
   e-mail: elizabeth.podgers@lockportjournal.com

Lockport Union-Sun & Journal *Weekday Circulation: 12,300*

Greater Niagara Newspapers
170 East Ave, Lockport, NY 14094
716-439-9222 Fax: 716-439-9249
Web site: www.lockportjournal.com
Publisher . . . . Diane Crowe
   e-mail: diane.crowe@lockportjournal.com
Managing Editor . . . . John Hopkins
   e-mail: john.hopkins@lockportjournal.com
Night/City Editor . . . . Scott Leffler
   e-mail: scott.leffler@lockportjournal.com
Circulation Manager . . . . Elizabeth Podgers
   e-mail: elizabeth.podgers@lockportjournal.com

Offices and agencies generally appear in alphabetical order, except when specific order is requested by listee.

LONG ISLAND

Newsday *Weekday Circulation: 470,316*

Newsday Inc
235 Pinelawn Rd, Melville, NY 11747-4250
631-843-2700 or 800-639-7329 Fax: 631-843-2953
e-mail: web@newsday.com
Web site: www.newsday.com
Publisher . . . . .Fred Groser
    e-mail: publisher@newsday.com
Editor-in-Chief. . . . . .Theresa Mills
    e-mail: editor@newsday.com
Editor . . . . .Howard Schneider
Editor . . . . .Ronald Roel
Editor . . . . .Valerie Kellogg
Circulation Manager. :. . .Sandy Elder

Queens Gazette *Weekly Circulation: 160,000*

Queens Gazette
42-16 34th Avenue, Long Island City, NY 11101
718-361-6161 Fax: 718-784-7552
e-mail: qgazette@aol.com
Web site: www.qgazette.com
Publisher/Editor. . . . . .Tony Barsamian
Associate Editor. . . . . .Jason D. Antos
Contibuting Editor . . . . .Linda Wilson

MALONE

Malone Telegram, The *Weekday Circulation: 6,000*

Johnson Newspaper Corporation
469 E Main St, Malone, NY 12953
518-483-2000 Fax: 518-483-8579
e-mail: news@mtelegram.com
Web site: www.mtelegram.com
Publisher . . . . .Russell Webster
Editor . . . . .Doug Buchanan
    e-mail: dbuchanan@mtelegram.com
Managing Editor . . . . .Connie Jenkins

MASSENA

Daily Courier-Observer *Weekday Circulation: 7,800*

Johnson Newspaper Corporation
1 Harrowgate Commons, PO Box 300, Massena, NY 13662
315-265-6000 Fax: 315-265-6001
e-mail: rmartin@ogd.com
Web site: www.mpcourier.com
Publisher . . . . .Charles Kelly
    e-mail: ckelly@ogd.com
Managing Editor . . . . .Ryne Martin
    e-mail: rmartin@ogd.com
Editor . . . . .Bob Beckstead
    e-mail: bbeckstead@ogd.com
District Circulation Manager . . . . .Cris Pitts

MEDINA

Journal-Register, The *Weekday Circulation: 3,500*

Greater Niagara Newspapers
541-543 Main St, Medina, NY 14103
585-798-1400 Fax: 585-798-0290
e-mail: jr@gnnewspaper.com
Web site: www.journal-register.com
Publisher . . . . .Diane Crowe

Managing Editor . . . . .John Hopkins
Circulation Manager. . . . . .Beth Podgers

MIDDLETOWN

Times Herald-Record *Weekday Circulation: 80,000*

Times Herald-Record
40 Mulberry St, PO Æ Box 2046, Middletown, NY 10940-6357
845-343-2181 or 800-620-1700 Fax: 845-343-2170
e-mail: readeradvocate@th-recordonline.com
Web site: www.recordonline.com
Executive Editor . . . . .Derek Osenenko
    e-mail: dosenenko@th-record.com
Senior Editor/Local News . . . . .Adrianne Reilly
Editor/Local News . . . . .Mike Carey
Editor/Night Publications. . . . . .Robert Berczuk
Editor/Community News. . . . . .Eric Stutz

NEW YORK CITY

AM Law Daily, The *Weekday Circulation: 16,000*

American Lawyer Media
120 Broadway, 5th Fl, New York, NY 10271
800-888-8300 Fax: 646-822-5146
Web site: www.alm.com
Editor-in-Chief . . . . .Robin Sparkman
    e-mail: rsparkman@alm.com
VP/Group Publisher . . . . .Scott Pierce
    e-mail: spierce@alm.com
Executive Editor . . . . .Emily Barker
Managing Editor .Maryann Saltser
Editor/New Media .Jonathan Hayter
. . . .
    e-mail: news@joc.com
SVP/Strategy. .Peter M Tirschwell
    e-mail: ptirschwell@joc.com
Executive Editor . . . . .Chris Brooks
    e-mail: jbonney@joc.com
Publisher. . . . . .Tony Stein
    e-mail: tstein@joc.com
Managing Editor . . . . .Barbara Wyker
    e-mail: bwyker@joc.com
Senior Editor . . . . .Joseph Bonney
    e-mail: jbonney@joc.com

Wall Street Journal (The) *Daily Circulation: 2,000,000*

Dow Jones & Company
1211 Avenue of the Americas, New York, NY 10036
212-416-2000 or 800-568-7625 Fax: 212-416-2653
e-mail: nywireroom@dowjones.com
Web site: www.wsj.com
Publisher . . . . .Lex Fenwick
Managing Editor. . . . . .Gerard Baker
Managing Editor/Newswires . . . . .Neal Lipschutz
Editor-in-Chief/Dow Jones . . . . .Gerard Baker
Managing Director/Dow Jones . . . . .Kelly E. Leach

People's World *Weekly Circulation: 27,000*

Long View Publishing Co
235 W 23rd St, New York, NY 10011
212-924-2523 Fax: 212-229-1713
e-mail: ny@peoplesworld.org
Web site: www.peoplesworld.org
Co-editor. . . . . .Teresa Albano
    e-mail: talbano@peoplesworld.org
Managing Editor . . . . .Dan Margolis
    e-mail: dmargolis@peoplesworld.org

Offices and agencies generally appear in alphabetical order, except when specific order is requested by listee.

Labor Editor. . . . . .John Wojcik
    e-mail: jwojcik@peoplesworld.org

New York Post *Weekday Circulation: 686,207*

NYP Holdings Inc
1211 Ave of the Americas, New York, NY 10036-8790
212-930-8000 Fax: 212-930-8005
e-mail: letters@nypost.com
Web site: www.nypost.com
Publisher . . . . .Paul Carlucci
Managing Editor . . . . .Frank Zini
Editor. . . . . .Debra Birnbaum
Editor. . . . . .Muhammad Cohen

New York Daily News *Weekday Circulation: 688,584*

New York Daily News
4 New York Plaza, New York, NY 10004
212-210-2100 Fax: 212-643-7831
e-mail: news@edit.nydailynews.com
Web site: www.nydailynews.com
Publisher . . . . .Mortimer Zuckerman
    e-mail: mzuckerman@edit.nydailynews.com
Editor-in-Chief. . . . . .Kevin R. Coney
News Editor. . . . . .John Oswald
Managing Editor . . . . .Robert Sapio
    e-mail: rsapio@edit.nydailynews.com
Editor . . . . .Arthur Browne

The Independent News *Weekly Circulation: 50,000*

The Independent News
74 Montauk Highway, Suite 16, East Hampton, NY 11937
631-324-2500 Fax: 631-324-2544
e-mail: news@indyeastend.com
Web site: www.indyeastend.com
Editor-in-Chief. . . . . .Rick Murphy
    e-mail: rmurphy@indyeastend.com
Publisher . . . . .James J. Mackin
    e-mail: jim@indyeastend.com
News Editor. . . . . .Kitty Merrill
    e-mail: kmerrill@indyeastend.com

New York Observer (The) *Weekday Circulation: 50,000*

The New York Observer
321 W. 44th St, 6th Floor, New York, NY 10036
212-755-2400 or 800-542-0420 Fax: 212-980-2087
e-mail: editorial@observer.com
Web site: www.observer.com
Publisher . . . . .Jared Kushner
Editor-in-Chief. . . . . .Peter Feld
Editor . . . . .Elizabeth Spiers
City Editor . . . . .Terry Golway

The New York Times *Weekday Circulation: 1,121,057*

The New York Times
620 Eighth Avenue, New York, NY 10018
212-556-1234 Fax: 212-556-3815
e-mail: letters@nytimes.com
Web site: www.nytimes.com
Publisher . . . . .Arthur O. Sulzberger, Jr
    e-mail: publisher@nytimes.com
Executive Editor . . . . .Jill Abramson
    e-mail: abramson@nytimes.com
Editorial Page Editor . . . . .Andrew M. Rosenthal
    e-mail: rosenthal@nytimes.com

The Putnam County News and Recorder *Weekly Circulation: 4,000*

The Putnam County News and Recorder
144 Main Street, Cold Spring, NY 10516
845-265-2468 Fax: 845-265-2144
e-mail: editor@pcnr.com
Web site: www.pcnr.com
Publisher . . . . .Elizabeth Ailes
Associate Publisher/Editor-in-Chief. . . . . .Douglas Cunningham
    e-mail: doug@pcner.com

Village Voice (The) *Weekly Circulation: 250,000*

Village Voice Media, Inc
36 Cooper Sq, New York, NY 10003
212-475-3333 Fax: 212-475-8944
e-mail: editor@villagevoice.com
Web site: www.villagevoice.com
Editor-in-Chief. . . . . .Will Bourne
Deputy Editor . . . . .Jessica Lustig
Senior Associate Editor . . . . .Angela Ashman
Senior Associate Editor. .Araceli Cruz

Wave Publishing Co. *Weekly Circulation: 12,300*

The Wave
88-08 Rockaway Beach Blvd, PO Box 930097, Rockaway Beach, NY 11693-0097
718-634-4000 Fax: 718-945-0913
e-mail: editor@rockawave.com
Web site: www.rockawave.com
Publisher . . . . .Susan B. Locke
    e-mail: sbl@rockawave.com
General Manager. .Sanford M. Bernstein
    e-mail: smb@rockawave.com
Associate Editor . . . . .Dan Guarino
Contributing Editor . . . . .Miriam Rosenberg
    e-mail: miriamsue18@aol.com

NIAGARA FALLS

Niagara Gazette *Weekday Circulation: 20,268*

Greater Niagara Newspapers
310 Niagara St, PO Box 549, Niagara Falls, NY 14302-0549
716-282-2311 Fax: 716-286-3895
e-mail: bevacquad@gnnewspaper.com
Web site: www.niagara-gazette.com
Publisher . . . . .Peter Mio
    e-mail: peter.mio@niagara-gazette.com
Managing Editor . . . . .Matt Winterhalter
    e-mail: matt.winterhalter@niagara-gazette.com
City Editor . . . . .Mark Scheer
    e-mail: scheerm@gnnewspaper.com

NORWICH

Evening Sun *Weekday Circulation: 5,200*

Snyder Communications Corp
29 Lackawanna Ave, PO Box 151, Norwich, NY 13815
607-334-3276 Fax: 607-334-8273
e-mail: news@evesun.com
Web site: www.evesun.com
Publisher . . . . .Richard Snyder
    e-mail: dsnyder@evesun.com
Managing Editor. . . . . .Brian Golden
    e-mail: bgolden@evesun.com
Circulation Manager . . . . .Lori Chmieliowiec
    e-mail: lchmieliowiec@evesun.com

Offices and agencies generally appear in alphabetical order, except when specific order is requested by listee.

OGDENSBURG

The Journal *Weekday Circulation: 5,200*

St Lawrence County Newspapers
308 Isabella St, PO Box 409, Ogdensburg, NY 13669
315-393-1003 Fax: 315-393-5108
Web site: www.ogd.com
City Editor . . . . .Elizabeth Lyons
    e-mail: egraham@wdt.net
District Circulation Manager . . . . .Michael Eldridge
    e-mail: meldridge@ogd.com

OLEAN

Olean Times Herald *Weekday Circulation: 15,000*

Bradford Publications Inc
639 Norton Dr, Olean, NY 14760
716-372-3121 Fax: 716-373-6397
e-mail: news@oleantimesherald.com
Web site: www.oleantimesherald.com
Publisher/General Manager . . . . .Bill Fitzpatrick
Managing Editor . . . . .Jim Eckstrom
    e-mail: jeckstrom@oleantimesherald.com
City Editor . . . . .Brian Lothridge
    e-mail: blothridge@oleantimesherald.com

ONEIDA

Oneida Daily Dispatch *Weekday Circulation: 6,818*

Journal Register Co
130 Broad Street, Oneida, NY 13421
315-363-5100 Fax: 315-363-9832
e-mail: newsroom@oneidadispatch.com
Web site: www.oneidadispatch.com
Publisher . . . . .Jan Dewey
    e-mail: jdewey@journalregister.com
News Editor . . . . .Kurt W Wanfried
    e-mail: kwanfried@oneidadispatch.com
General Manager . . . . .Karen Alvord
    e-mail: kalvord@journalregister.com
Circulation Manager . . . . .Sabrina Sharkey
    e-mail: ssharkey@oneidadispatch.com

ONEONTA

Daily Star (The) *Weekday Circulation: 21,000*

Ottaway Newspapers Inc
102 Chestnut St, Oneonta, NY 13820
607-432-1000 Fax: 607-432-5847
e-mail: webmaster@thedailystar.com
Web site: www.thedailystar.com
Publisher . . . . .Mitchell D. Lynch
    e-mail: mlynch@thedailystar.com
Editor . . . . .Sam Pollak
    e-mail: spollak@thedailystar.com
Editor . . . . .Mark Boshnack
    e-mail: mboshnack@thedailystar.com
News Editor . . . . .Denise Richardson
    e-mail: drichardson@thedailystar.com

OSWEGO-FULTON

Palladium-Times (The) *Weekday Circulation: 8,500*

The Palladium-Times
140 W First St, Oswego, NY 13126
315-343-3800 Fax: 315-343-0273
e-mail: editor@palltimes.com
Web site: www.pall-times.com
Publisher . . . . .Jon Spaulding
    e-mail: jspaulding@palltimes.com
Editor . . . . .Sarah McCrobie
    e-mail: smccrobie@palltimes.com
Advertising Manager . . . . .Kate Percival
    e-mail: kpercival@palltimes.com
Circulation . . . . .Tom Van Schaack
    e-mail: tvanschaack@palltimes.com

PLATTSBURGH

Press-Republican *Weekday Circulation: 20,210*

Press-Republican
PO Box 459, Plattsburgh, NY 12901
518-565-4131 Fax: 518-561-3362
e-mail: news@pressrepublican.com
Web site: www.pressrepublican.com
Publisher . . . . .Robert W. Parks
Editor . . . . .Lois M. Clermont
News Editor . . . . .Suzanne Moore
Managing Editor . . . . .Nathan Ovalle

POUGHKEEPSIE

Poughkeepsie Journal *Weekday Circulation: 40,202*

Gannett Co Inc
PO Box 1231, Poughkeepsie, NY 12602
845-437-4800 Fax: 845-437-4921
e-mail: newsroom@poughkee.gannett.com
Web site: www.poughkeepsiejournal.com
Publisher/President . . . . .Barry Rothfeld
    e-mail: brothfeld@gannett.com
Executive Editor . . . . .Stuart Shinske
    e-mail: sshinske@poughkeepsie.gannett.com
Local Editor . . . . .Kevin Lenihan
    e-mail: klenihan@poughkeepsie.gannett.com
Circulation Manager . . . . .Bill Farrell
    e-mail: farrellb@poughkeepsie.gannett.com
Editorial Page Editor . . . . .John Penney
    e-mail: jpenney@poughkeepsie.gannett.com

ROCHESTER

Daily Record (The) *Weekly Circulation: 4,500*

The Dolan Company
16 W Main St, Rochester, NY 14614
585-232-6920 Fax: 585-232-2740
Web site: www.nydailyrecord.com
Publisher . . . . .Kevin Momot
    e-mail: kevin.momot@nydailyrecord.com
Associate Editor . . . . .Kristy O'Malley
    e-mail: kristy.omalley@nydailyrecord.com
News Reporter . . . . .Denise Champagne
    e-mail: denise.champagne@nydailyrecord.com

News Media

Offices and agencies generally appear in alphabetical order, except when specific order is requested by listee.

Democrat and Chronicle *Weekday Circulation: 170,000*

Gannett Co Inc
55 Exchange Blvd, Rochester, NY 14614
585-232-7100 Fax: 585-258-2237
e-mail: webmaster@democratandchronicle.com
Web site: www.democratandchronicle.com
President/Publisher . . . . .Michael Kane
    e-mail: mgkane@democratandchronicle.com
Vice President/Editor . . . . .Karen Magnuson
    e-mail: kmagnuso@democratandchronicle.com
Local Editor . . . . .Catherine Roberts
    e-mail: cathyr@democratandchronicle.com
Editorial Page Editor . . . . .James Lawrence
    e-mail: jlawrenc@democratandchronicle.com

Suburban News & Hamlin Clarkson Herald *Weekly Circulation: 32,000*

Westside News Inc
1776 hilton-Parma Corners Road, PO Box 106, Spencerport, NY 14559
585-352-3411 Fax: 585-352-4811
e-mail: editor@westsidenewsny
Web site: www.westsidenewsny.com
Publisher . . . . .Keith Ryan
Editor . . . . .Evelyn Dow
    e-mail: ediotr@westsidenewsny.com
Circulation Manager . . . . .Don Griffin
    e-mail: circulation@westsidenewsny.com

ROME

Daily Sentinel *Weekday Circulation: 16,500*

Rome Sentinel Co
333 W Dominick St, Rome, NY 13440-5701
315-337-4000 Fax: 315-337-4704
e-mail: sentinel@rny.com
Web site: www.romesentinel.com
Publisher . . . . .Stephen Waters
    e-mail: dswanson@rny.com
Managing Editor . . . . .David C Swanson
Editor . . . . .Thomas Merz
    e-mail: editor@rny.com
News Editor . . . . .Kathleen Twellman Haley
    e-mail: editor@rny.com

SALAMANCA

Salamanca Press *Weekday Circulation: 2,200*

Bradford Publishing Co
36 River St, Salamanca, NY 14779
716-945-1644 Fax: 716-945-4285
e-mail: salpressnews@verizon.net
Web site: www.salamancapress.com
Managing Editor . . . . .Rich Place
    e-mail: salpressnews@verizon.net

SARANAC LAKE

Adirondack Daily Enterprise *Weekday Circulation: 5,000*

Adirondack Publishing Co Inc
54 Broadway, PO Box 318, Saranac Lake, NY 12983
518-891-2600 Fax: 518-891-2756
e-mail: adenews@adirondackdailyenterprise.com
Web site: www.adirondackdailyenterprise.com
Publisher . . . . .Catherine Moore
    e-mail: cmoore@adirondackdailyenterprise.com

Managing Editor . . . . .Peter Crowley
    e-mail: pcrowley@adirondackdailyenterprise.com
News Editor . . . . .Brittany Proulx
    e-mail: adenews@adirondackdailyenterprise.com
Circulation Manager . . . . .Trinity Bushey
    e-mail: circulation@adirondackdailyenterprise.com

SARATOGA SPRINGS

Saratogian (The) *Weekday Circulation: 10,000*

Journal Register Company
20 Lake Ave, Saratoga Springs, NY 12866
518-584-4242 Fax: 518-587-7750
e-mail: news@saratogian.com
Web site: www.saratogian.com
Publisher . . . . .Michael F. O'Sullivan
    e-mail: mosullivan@journalregister.com
Managing Editor . . . . .Barbara A Lombardo
    e-mail: blombardo@journalregister.com
Editor . . . . .Donna Bell
    e-mail: cnews@saratogian.com
Regional Circulation Director .Jim Collier
    e-mail: jcollier@journalregister.com

SCHENECTADY

Daily Gazette (The) *Weekday Circulation: 53,800*

Daily Gazette Co
2345 Maxon Road Extension, Schenectady, NY 12308
518-374-4141 Fax: 518-395-3089
e-mail: news@dailygazette.com
Web site: www.dailygazette.com
Publisher . . . . .John E N Hume, III
City Editor . . . . .Irv Dean
News Editor . . . . .William Finelli
Online Editor . . . . .Jeffrey Haff
Day City Editor . . . . .Miles Reed
Circulation Supervisor . . . . .Brian Zarelli

STATEN ISLAND

Staten Island Advance *Circulation: Monday, Tuesday, Wednesday, Friday: 59,000; Thursday: 67,000; Sunday: 77,000*

Advance Publications Inc
950 Fingerboard Rd, Staten Island, NY 10305
718-981-1234 Fax: 718-981-5679
e-mail: editor@siadvance.com
Web site: www.silive.com
Publisher . . . . .Caroline Diamond Harrison
Circulation Manager . . . . .Richard Salemo
    e-mail: salemo@siadvance.com
Editor . . . . .Brian J. Laline
    e-mail: laline@siadvance.com
Managing Editor . . . . .William A. Huus
    e-mail: bhuus@siadvance.com
Editorial Page Editor . . . . .Mark Hanley
    e-mail: hanley@siadvance.com
City Editor . . . . .Tom Checchi
    e-mail: checchi@siadvance.com
News Editor . . . . .Richard Ryan
    e-mail: ryan@siadvance.com

Offices and agencies generally appear in alphabetical order, except when specific order is requested by listee.

SYRACUSE

Post-Standard (The) *Weekday Circulation: 115,000*

Syracuse Newspapers Inc
PO Box 4915, Syracuse, NY 13221
315-470-0011 Fax: 315-470-3081
e-mail: business@syracuse.com
Web site: www.syracusemediagroup.com
Vice President of Content . . . . .Michael J Connor
    e-mail: mconnor@syracuse.com
Director of Content . . . . .John Lammers
    e-mail: jlammers@syracuse.com
Director of Publications . . . . .Stan Linhorst
    e-mail: slinhorst@syracuse.com
Managing Producer/Editor . . . . .Steven M. Billmeyer
    e-mail: sbillmeyer@syracuse.com

TONAWANDA

Tonawanda News *Weekday Circulation: 9,000*

Greater Niagara Newspapers
435 River Road, PO Box 668, North Tonawanda, NY 14120-6809
716-693-1000 Fax: 716-693-0124
e-mail: newsroom@tonawanda-news.com
Web site: www.tonawanda-news.com
Managing Editor . . . . .Eric DuVall
    e-mail: duvalle@gnnewspaper.com
Circulation Director . . . . .Ken Skryp
Advertising Director . . . . .John Brundo
Publisher . . . . .Peter Mio

TROY

Record (The) *Weekday Circulation: 16,872*

Journal Register Co
501 Broadway, Troy, NY 12180
518-270-1200 Fax: 518-270-1202
e-mail: letters@troyrecord.com
Web site: www.troyrecord.com
Publisher . . . . .Michael F. O'Sullivan
    e-mail: mosullivan@journalregister.com
Editor . . . . .Lisa Robert Lewis
    e-mail: llewis@troyrecord.com
City Editor . . . . .James V. Franco
    e-mail: jfranco@troyrecord.com
Regional Circulation Director . . . . .Jim Collier
    e-mail: jcollier@journalregister.com

UTICA

Observer-Dispatch *Weekday Circulation: 45,956*

GateHouse Media
221 Oriskany Plz, Utica, NY 13501
315-792-5000 Fax: 315-792-5033
e-mail: news@uticaod.com
Web site: www.uticaod.com
President/Publisher . . . . .Donna Donovan
    e-mail: ddonovan@uticaod.com
Editor . . . . .Kris Worrell
    e-mail: kworrell@uticaod.com
Managing Editor . . . . .Ron Johns
    e-mail: rjohns1@uticaod.com
News Editor . . . . .Fran Perritano
    e-mail: fperrita@utica.gannett.com

WATERTOWN

Watertown Daily Times *Weekday Circulation: 27,020*

Johnson Newspaper Corp
260 Washington St, Watertown, NY 13601
315-782-1000 Fax: 315-661-2523
e-mail: news@wdt.net
Web site: www.watertowndailytimes.com
Executive Editor . . . . .Bert Gault
    e-mail: bgault@wdt.net
Managing Editor . . . . .Robert Gorman
    e-mail: bgorman@wdt.net
Editorial Page Editor . . . . .Francis Pound
    e-mail: fpound@wdt.net
Editor (Sunday) . . . . .Mary Kaskan
    e-mail: mkaskan@wdt.net

WELLSVILLE

Wellsville Daily Reporter/Spectator *Weekday Circulation: 4,400*

Gate House Media
159 N Main St, Wellsville, NY 14895
585-593-5300 Fax: 585-593-5303
e-mail: editor@wellsvilledaily.com
Web site: www.wellsvilledaily.com
Publisher . . . . .Oak Duke
Editor . . . . .John Anderson
Reporter . . . . .Kathryn Ross
Sports . . . . .Heather Matta

NEWS SERVICES/MAGAZINES

ABC News (New York Bureau)
47 W 66th St, New York, NY 10023
212-456-7777 Fax: 212-456-2795
e-mail: netavdr@abc.com
Web site: www.abcnews.go.com
President & Publisher . . . . .Ellen Archer
Bureau Chief . . . . .Amy Brenholts
Director/Domestic News . . . . .Wendy Fisher

American Metal Market
225 Park Avenue South, 6th Floor, New York, NY 10003
212-213-6202 Fax: 212-213-6617
e-mail: helpdesk@amm.com
Web site: www.amm.com
President . . . . .Raju Daswani
    e-mail: rdaswani@amm.com
Editor . . . . .Jo Isenberg-O'Loughlin
    e-mail: jisenberg@amm.com
Senior Vice President . . . . .David Brooks
    e-mail: dbrooks@amm.com
Deputy Managing Editor . . . . .Josephine Mason
    e-mail: jmason@amm.com
Chief Correspondent, Steel . . . . .Scott Robertson
    e-mail: srobertson@amm.com

Associated Press (New York/Metro)
450 West 33rd St, New York, NY 10001
212-621-1500 or 212-621-5447 Fax: 212-621-1679
e-mail: info@ap.org
Web site: www.ap.org
Bureau Chief . . . . .Howard Goldberg
    e-mail: hgoldberg@ap.org
Executive Editor . . . . .Kathleen Carroll
Editor/West Region . . . . .Traci Carl
Editor/Asia Pacific . . . . .Brian Carovillano
Editor/South Region . . . . .Lisa Pane

Offices and agencies generally appear in alphabetical order, except when specific order is requested by listee.

Editor/Central Region . . . . David Scott

BNA (formerly Bureau of National Affairs)
PO Box 7169, Albany, NY 12224
518-399-8414 Fax: 518-399-8403
Web site: www.bna.com
NYS Correspondent . . . . Gerald Silverman

Business Review
40 British American Blvd, Latham, NY 12110
518-640-6800 Fax: 518-640-6801
e-mail: albany@bizjournals.com
Web site: www.bizjournals.com/albany
Publisher . . . . Carolyn Jones
    e-mail: cjones@bizjournals.com
Managing Editor . . . . Neil Springer
    e-mail: nspringer@bizjournals.com

CBS News (New York)
51 West 52nd St, New York, NY 10019-6188
212-975-4321 Fax: 212-975-9387
Web site: www.cbsnews.com
Editor-in-Chief . . . . Jeremy Murphy
Executive Editor . . . . Jack Otter
Executive Story Editor . . . . Victoria M. Gordon
Executive News Producer . . . . Peter Wilgoren
News Planning Editor . . . . Abby Lawing
News Planning Editor . . . . Gretchen White
News Writer . . . . Arlene Lebe
News Director . . . . Jeff Hatthorn

Central New York Business Journal
231 Walton Street, Syracuse, NY 13202
315-472-3104 Fax: 315-472-3644
e-mail: info@cnybj.com
Web site: www.cnybj.com
Publisher . . . . Norman Poltenson
    e-mail: npoltenson@cnybj.com
Editor-in-Chief . . . . Adam Rombel
    e-mail: arombel@cnybj.com

City Journal (Manhattan Institute for Policy Research)
52 Vanderbilt Ave, 3rd Floor, New York, NY 10017
212-599-7000 Fax: 212-599-0371
e-mail: cj@city-journal.org
Web site: www.city-journal.org
Editor . . . . Brian C Anderson
    e-mail: banderson@city-journal.org
Managing Editor . . . . Benjamin Plotinsky

Crain's New York Business
711 Third Ave, New York, NY 10017
212-210-0100 Fax: 212-210-0799
e-mail: ecordova@crainsnewyork.com
Web site: www.crainsnewyork.com
Publisher & Vice President . . . . Jill Kaplan
    e-mail: jkaplan@crainsnewyork.com
Editor . . . . Glenn Coleman
    e-mail: gcoleman@crainsnewyork.com
Managing Editor . . . . Jeremy Smerd
    e-mail: jsmerd@crainsnewyork.com
Deputy Managing Editor . . . . Valerie Block
    e-mail: vblock@crainsnewyork.com
Copy Chief . . . . Stephen Noveck
    e-mail: snoveck@crainsnewyork.com

Cuyler News Service
PO Box 7205, State Capitol, Albany, NY 12224
518-465-1745 Fax: 518-465-6849
e-mail: efmnews@aol.com
Owner . . . . Elizabeth G Flood
Contact . . . . Janet Sanders

Contact . . . . Amy Despirito

Dow Jones Newswires (Dow Jones & Company)
1155 Ave of the Americas, 7th Fl, New York, NY 10036
201-938-5400 Fax: 201-938-5600
Web site: www.dowjonesnews.com
Editor-in-Chief . . . . Gerard Baker
Managing Editor . . . . Neal Lipschutz

Empire State Report (CINN Worldwide Inc)
PO Box 9001, Mount Vernon, NY 10553
914-966-3180 Fax: 914-966-3264
e-mail: empire@cinn.com
Web site: www.empirestatereport.com
Associate Publisher/Editor . . . . Maria Chiulli
Head of Circulation . . . . Jennifer Jehn

Gannett News Service
150 State St, 2nd Fl, Albany, NY 12207
518-436-9781 Fax: 518-436-0130
e-mail: gannett@albany.net
Web site: www.gannett.com
Bureau Chief . . . . Joseph Spector
    e-mail: spector@gannett.com
Correspondent . . . . Jon Campbell
Correspondent . . . . Cara Matthews
    e-mail: clmatthe@gannett.com

Hudson Valley Business Journal
86 East Main Street, Wappingers Falls, NY 12590
845-298-6236 Fax: 845-298-6238
e-mail: debhvbj@gmail.com
Web site: www.hvbj.com
Publisher . . . . Debbie Kwiatoski
    e-mail: debhvbj@gmail.com

ITAR-TASS News Agency
780 Third Ave, 19th Fl, New York, NY 10017
212-245-4250 Fax: 212-245-4258
e-mail: info@itar-tass.com
Web site: www.itar-tass.com
Bureau Chief . . . . Vladimir Kikilo

Legislative Correspondents Association
PO Box 7340, State Capitol, 3rd Fl, Albany, NY 12224
518-455-2388
Web site: www.lgapressroom.blogspot.com
Press Room Supervisor . . . . Jean Gutbtodt
President . . . . Brendan Scott

Long Island Business News
2150 Smithtown Avenue, Ronkonkoma, NY 11779
631-737-1700 Fax: 631-737-1890
e-mail: editor@libn.com
Web site: www.libn.com
Managing Editor . . . . Andrea Jones
    e-mail: andrea.jones@libn.com
Publisher . . . . John Kominicki
    e-mail: andrea.jones@libn.com

Mid-Hudson News Network
42 Marcy Lane, Middletown, NY 10941
845-537-1500 or 845-695-2923 Fax: 845-692-2921
e-mail: news@midhudsonnews.com
Web site: www.midhudsonnews.com
Managing Director/Publisher . . . . Hank Gross
. . . .
President/NBC News . . . . Steve Capus
SVP/News Marketing and Communications . . . . Lauren Kapp

Offices and agencies generally appear in alphabetical order, except when specific order is requested by listee.

NY Capitolwire
172 W State St, Trenton, NJ 08608
717-986-0225
e-mail: info@capitolwire.com
Web site: www.capitolwire.com
President/Publisher....................................Craig Leach

New York Magazine (New York Media, LLC)
75 Varick Street, 4th Floor, New York, NY 10013
212-508-0700 Fax: 212-221-9195
e-mail: nyletters@nymag.com
Web site: www.nymag.com
Editor-in-Chief..Adam Moss
    e-mail: adam_moss@newyorkmag.com
Executive Editor.....................................John Homans
    e-mail: john_homans@newyorkmag.com
Managing Editor......................................Ann Clarke
    e-mail: ann_clarke@newyorkmag.com
Publisher ....Lawrence Burstein
    e-mail: larry_burstein@newyorkmag.com
....Jared Hohlt

Newsweek/The Daily Beast
7 Hanover Sq, New York, NY 10004
212-445-4600 Fax: 212-445-4425
e-mail: editors@newsweek.com
Web site: www.newsweek.com
Publisher ....Rhona Murphy
    e-mail: rhona.murphy@newsweek.com
Editor/Newsweek International ....Fareed Zakaria
Executive Editor ....Justine A. Rosenthal
Editor-at-Large ....Kyle Pope

Ottaway News Service (NYS only)
N State Capitol, 3rd Fl, Albany, NY 12224
518-463-1157 Fax: 518-463-7486
Legislative Correspondent...........................John Milgrim
    e-mail: jmottaway@aol.com

Reuters (Thomson Reuters Markets LLC)
3 Times Square, New York, NY 10036
646-223-4000 Fax: 646-223-4001
Web site: www.reuters.com
Bureau Chief..Matthew Bigg
Editor-in-Chief..................................Stephen J. Adler
Chief White House Correspondent....................Steve Holland
Correspondent.......................................Scott Malone
Correspondent...Sam Nelson

Rochester Business Journal
45 E Avenue, Suite 500, Rochester, NY 14604
585-546-8303 Fax: 585-546-3398
e-mail: rbj@rbj.net
Web site: www.rbjdaily.com
Editor/Vice President................................Paul Ericson
    e-mail: pericson@rbj.net
Associate Editor....................................Smriti Jacob
    e-mail: sjacob@rbj.net
Managing Editor ....Michael Dickinson
    e-mail: mdickinson@rbj.net
President/Publisher.................................Susan Holliday
    e-mail: mdickinson@rbj.net

Scripps Howard News Service
1090 Vermont Ave NW, Ste 1000, Washington, DC 20005
202-408-1484 Fax: 202-408-2062
Web site: www.shns.com
Desk Editor......................................Carol Guensburg
Photo Editor......................................Sheila Person
    e-mail: persons@shns.com
Content Editor.....................................Carolyn Cerbin
National Correspondent ....Thomas Hargrove

RADIO

Stations included in this chapter produce news and/or public affairs programming and are listed alphabetically by primary service area.

ALBANY

WAMC (90.3 FM)
WAMC, Northeast Public Radio, PO Box 66600, Albany, NY 12206
518-465-5233 or 800-323-9262 Fax: 518-432-6974
e-mail: mail@wamc.org
Web site: www.wamc.org
President & CEO ....Alan Chartock
    e-mail: alan@wamc.org
Associate News Director.............................Joe Donahue
    e-mail: jcd@wamc.org
News Director ....Ian Pickus
    e-mail: ipick@wamc.org

BALDWINSVILLE

WSEN (92.1 FM)
8456 Smokey Hollow Road, PO Box 1050, Baldwinsville, NY 13027-1050
315-635-3971 Fax: 315-635-3490
e-mail: webmaster@wsenfm.com
Web site: www.wsenfm.com
General Manager ....Judy Kelly
    e-mail: jkelly@lmgiradio.com

BATH

WCIK (103.1 FM)
7634 Campbell Creek Rd, PO Box 506, Bath, NY 14810-0506
607-776-4151 Fax: 607-776-6929
e-mail: mail@fln.org
Web site: www.fln.org
President/General Manager ....Rick Snavely
Program Director ....John Owens
VP/CFO ....Dick Snavely

BEACON

WSPK (104.7 FM)
715 Rte 52, PO Box 310, Beacon, NY 12508
845-838-6000 Fax: 845-838-2109
Web site: www.k104online.com
General Manager ....Jason Finkelberg
    e-mail: jfinkelberg@pamal.com
Promotions Director ....Megan Denaut
    e-mail: mdenaut@pamal.com
News Director......................................Allison Dunne
News Director...Brian Jones

BINGHAMTON

WINR (680 AM)
320 N Jensen Road, Vestal, NY 13850
607-584-5800 Fax: 607-584-5900
e-mail: www.680winr.com
General Manager ....Tom Barney
News Director ....Dave Lozzi

WNBF (1290 AM)
PO Box 414, Binghamton, NY 13902-0414
607-772-8400 Fax: 607-772-9806
Web site: www.wnbf.com
News Director ....Bernie Fionte
Program Director....................................Roger Neal

Offices and agencies generally appear in alphabetical order, except when specific order is requested by listee.

Talk Show Host . . . . .Tony Russell
    e-mail: roger@wnbf.com

WSKG (89.3 FM), WSQX (91.5 FM)
PO Box 3000, Binghamton, NY 13902
607-729-0100 Fax: 607-729-7328
e-mail: wskg_mail@wskg.pbs.org
Web site: www.wskg.com
Program Director . . . . .Ken Campbell
    e-mail: ken_campbell@wskg.pb.org
Music Director. . . . . .Bill Snyder
President. . . . . .Brian Sickora

BRONX

WFUV (90.7 FM)
441 East Fordham Road, Fordham University, Bronx, NY 10458-5149
718-817-4550 Fax: 718-365-9815
e-mail: thefolks@wfuv.org
Web site: www.wfuv.org
General Manager . . . . .Dr Ralph Jennings
News & Public Affairs Director . . . . .George Bodarky
Program Director. . . . . .Chuck Singleton
    e-mail: chucksingleton@wfuv.org

BUFFALO

WBEN (930 AM/FM)
800 Corporate Parkway, Suite 200, Buffalo, NY 14226
716-803-0930 or 716-843-0600 Fax: 716-832-3080
Web site: www.wben.com
Operations Manager. . . . . .Tim Wenger
Anchor/Reporter/Editor. . . . . .Dave Debo
Sales Director . . . . .Tim Holly

WBLK (93.7 FM), WJYE (96.1 FM)
14 Lafayette Sq, Ste 1300, Buffalo, NY 14203
716-852-9393 or 800-828-2191 Fax: 716-852-9390
Web site: www.wjye.com; www.wblk.com
General Manager. . . . . .Jeff Silver
Production & Program Director . . . . .Chris Reynolds
Production Director. . . . . .Frank Dawkins
Program Director (WJYE). .Joe Chille

WDCX (99.5 FM)
625 Delaware Avenue, Suite 308, Buffalo, NY 14202
716-883-3010 Fax: 716-883-3606
e-mail: wcdxinfo@crawfordbroadcastin.com
Web site: www.wdcxfm.com
General Manager. . . . . .Nev Larson
Writer/Producer . . . . .Keri Cardinale
Chief Engineer. . . . . .Brian Cunningham

WHTT (104.1 FM)
50 James Casey Drive, Buffalo, NY 14206
716-881-4555 Fax: 716-884-2931
Web site: www.whtt.com
Regional President . . . . .Kevin LeGrett
    e-mail: wedg@wedg.com
General Manager . . . . .Chet Osadchey
Program Director . . . . .Joe Siragusa
    e-mail: joe.siragusa@citcomm.com

WNED (94.5 FM)
140 Lower Terr., PO Box 1263, Buffalo, NY 14240-1263
716-845-7000 Fax: 716-845-7043
Web site: www.wned.org
Program Director. . . . . .Al Wallack
News Director. . . . . .Jim Ranney
    e-mail: jranney@wned.org

WYRK (106.5 FM), WBUF (92.9 FM)
14 Lafayette Sq., Suite 1200, Buffalo, NY 14203
716-852-9292 Fax: 716-852-9290
General Manager . . . . .Jeff Silver
Program Director (WYRK). . . . . .RW Smith
Program Director (WBUF) . . . . .Joe Russo
Sales Manager (WYRK) . . . . .Mark Plimpton
General Sales Manager (WBUF) . . . . .Rose Vecchiarelli

CHAMPLAIN

WCHP (760 AM)
137 Rapids Road, PO Box 888, Champlain, NY 12919
518-298-2800 Fax: 518-298-2604
e-mail: wchp@wchp.com
Web site: www.wchp.com
General Manager . . . . .Teri Billiter
    e-mail: teri@wchp.com
Program Director . . . . .Brandi Lloyd
    e-mail: brandi@wchp.com
Operations Manager . . . . .Tonya Billiter
    e-mail: tonya@wchp.com

CORTLAND

WKRT (920 AM), WIII (99.9 or 100.3 FM)
277 Tompkins Street, Cortland, NY 13045
607-257-6400 Fax: 607-257-6497
e-mail: i100@wiii.com
Web site: www.i100rocks.com
General Manager . . . . .Susan Johnston
Operations Manager . . . . .Chris Allinger
    e-mail: mark.vanness@citcomm.com
Director of Sales. . . . . .Margaret Tollner
    e-mail: margaret.tollner@citcomm.com

ELMIRA

WPGI (100.9 FM), WWLZ (820 AM)
2205 College Avenue, Elmira, NY 14903-1201
607-732-4400 Fax: 607-732-7774
General Manager (WWLZ). . . . . .Kevin White
Program Director (WWLZ). . . . . .Scott Free
    e-mail: scott.free@bybradio.com
Program Director (WWLZ). . . . . .James Poteat
    e-mail: vinny@bybradio.com

HORNELL

WKPQ (105.3 FM)
1484 Beech St, PO Box 726, Hornell, NY 14843-9404
607-654-0322 Fax: 877-575-1320
e-mail: news@hornellradio.com
Web site: www.wkpq.com
General Manager . . . . .Kevin White
Station Manager. .Richard O Stevenson

HORSEHEADS

WMTT (94.7 FM)
734 Chemung Street, Horseheads, NY 14845
607-795-0795 Fax: 607-795-1095
e-mail: bob@themetrocks.com
Web site: www.themetrocks.com
General Manager. . . . . .George Hawras
Opertions Manager. . . . . .Steve Shimer
Station Manager . . . . .Bob Smith

Offices and agencies generally appear in alphabetical order, except when specific order is requested by listee.

ITHACA

WHCU (870 AM)
1751 Hanshaw Road, Ithaca, NY 14850
607-257-6400 Fax: 607-257-6497
e-mail: info@whcu870.com
Web site: www.whcu870.com
General Manager . . . . .Susan Johnston
   e-mail: sjohnston@cyradiogroup.com
BPD/News Director/Program Director. . . . . .Geoff Dunn
   e-mail: gdunn@cyradiogroup.com

JAMESTOWN

WKZA (106.9 FM)
106 West 3rd Street, Suite 106, Jamestown, NY 14701
716-487-1106 or 866-367-1069 Fax: 716-488-2169
e-mail: morningshow@1069kissfm.com
Web site: www.1069kissfm.com
Sales Manager . . . . .Sherrie Brookmire
Program Director . . . . .Steve Rockford

LATHAM

WROW (590 AM)
6 Johnson Road, Latham, NY 12110-5641
518-786-6600 Fax: 518-786-6695
e-mail: wrownews@albanybroadcasting.com
Web site: www.wrow.com
General Manager . . . . .Dan Austin
   e-mail: DAustin@albanybroadcasting.com
News Director . . . . .Mike Carey
   e-mail: mcarey@albanybroadcasting.com
Public Affairs Director . . . . .Joe Condon
   e-mail: jcondon@albanyradio.net
Program Director . . . . .Scott Miller

WPYX (106.5 FM), WRVE (99.5 FM)
1203 Troy Schenectady Road, Latham, NY 12110
518-452-4800 Fax: 518-452-4813
e-mail: feedback@pyx106.com
Web site: www.pyx106.com
Operations Manager & Program Director (WPYX) . . . . .John Cooper
   e-mail: johncooper@clearchannel.com
VP/General Manager . . . . .Kristen Delaney

NEW ROCHELLE

WVOX (1460 AM)
1 Broadcast Forum, New Rochelle, NY 10801-2094
914-636-1460 Fax: 914-636-2900
e-mail: don@wvox.com
Web site: www.wvox.com
Editorial Director/President/CEO. . . . . .William O'Shaughnessy
Operations Manager . . . . .Don Stevens

NEW YORK CITY

WABC (770 AM)
2 Penn Plaza, 17th Floor, New York, NY 10121
212-613-3800 Fax: 212-613-3823
e-mail: info@wabc.com
Web site: www.wabcradio.com
Program Director/News Director . . . . .Phil Boyce
   e-mail: phil.boyce@abc.com
General Manager . . . . .Mitch Dolan
Promotions Director . . . . .Eric Lemieux
   e-mail: ericlemieux@clearchannel.com
Promotions Director/Public Affairs . . . . .Russ King

Music Director . . . . .Eric Wellman
   e-mail: ericwellman@clearchannel.com

WBBR (1130 AM) Bloomberg News
499 Park Avenue, New York, NY 10022-1240
212-318-2300 or 800-955-4003 Fax: 917-369-5000
e-mail: mwomack4@bloomberg.net
Web site: www.bloomberg.com/radio
Editor-in-Chief. . . . . .Matthew Winkler
Managing Editor. . . . . .Michael Clancy
Press Contact. . . . . .Amanda Cowie
   e-mail: acowie@bloomberg.net

WCBS (880 AM)
345 Hudson Street, New York, NY 10014
212-975-4321 Fax: 212-975-4675
e-mail: wcbsamdesk@wcbs880.com
Web site: www.wcbs880.com
General Manager/VP. . . . . .Chad Brown
Director of News & Programming . . . . .Tim Scheld
   e-mail: tscheld@wcbs880.com

WINS (1010 AM)
345 Hudson Street, 10th Floor, New York, NY 10014
212-315-7000 Fax: 212-315-7015
e-mail: mevorach@wins.com
Web site: www.1010wins.com
News Director. . . . . .Ben Mevorach
   e-mail: mevorach@wins.com
News Editor . . . . .Ralph Saro
   e-mail: saro@wins.com

WLTW (106.7 FM)
32 Avenue of the Americas, New York, NY 10013
212-377-7900 Fax: 212-603-4602
e-mail: info@wltw.com
Web site: www.1067litefm.com
Program Director . . . . .Jim Ryan
Marketing Director. . . . . .Susan Bacich

WOR (710 AM)
32 Avenue of the Americas, New York, NY 10013
212-337-7900
e-mail: news@wor710.com
Web site: www.wor710.com
General Manager . . . . .Jerry Crowley
News Director . . . . .Joe Bartlett

OLEAN

WPIG (95.7 FM), WHDL (1450 AM)
3163 NYS Route 417, Olean, NY 14760-1853
716-372-0161 or 800-877-9749 Fax: 716-372-0164
e-mail: wpig.production@bybradio.com
Web site: www.wpig.com
General Manager . . . . .John Morton
   e-mail: john.morton@bybradio.com
Program Manager . . . . .Mark Thompson
   e-mail: mark.thompson@bybradio.com

PEEKSKILL

WHUD (100.7 FM)
715 Rte 52, Box 310, Beacon, NY 12508
845-838-6000 Fax: 845-838-2109
e-mail: newsroom@pamal.com
Web site: www.whud.com
General Manager . . . . .Jason Finkelberg
   e-mail: jfinkelberg@pamal.com
Program Director . . . . .Steve Petrone
   e-mail: spetrone@pamal.com

Offices and agencies generally appear in alphabetical order, except when specific order is requested by listee.

News Media

News Director . . . . .Brian Jones
    e-mail: newsroom@pamal.com

MIDDLETOWN

WRRV (92.7 FM)
2 Pendell Road, Poughkeepsie, NY 12601
845-471-1500 Fax: 845-454-1204
Web site: www.wrrv.com
Business Manager . . . . .Kathy Butsko
    e-mail: kathy.butsko@cumulus.com
Program Directory. . . . . .Andrew Boris
    e-mail: andrew.boris@cumulus.com

POUGHKEEPSIE

WPDH (101.5 FM)
2 Pendell Road, Poughkeepsie, NY 12601
845-471-1500 Fax: 845-454-1204
Web site: www.wpdh.com
Business Manager . . . . .Kathy Butsko
    e-mail: kathy.butsko@cumulus.com
Program Director. . . . . .Andrew Boris
    e-mail: andrew.boris@cumulus.com
Branch Manager . . . . .Chuck Benfer
    e-mail: chuck.benfer@cumulus.com
Promotions Manager. . . . . .Anthony Verano
    e-mail: anthony.verano@cumulus.com

ROCHESTER

WHAM (1180 AM)
1700 HSBC Plaza, 100 Chestnut Street, Rochester, NY 14604-2016
585-454-4884 Fax: 585-454-5081
e-mail: whamnews@wham1180.com
Web site: www.wham1180.com
Station Manager . . . . .Jeff Howlett
    e-mail: jeffhowlett@wham1180.com
Promotions Director . . . . .Brian Guck
    e-mail: brianguck@clearchannel.com
News Director . . . . .Randy Gorbman
    e-mail: randygorbman@wham1180.com

SCHENECTADY

WGNA (107.7 FM)
1241 Kings Road, Suite 4200, Schenectady, NY 12303
518-881-1515 or 800-476-1077 Fax: 518-881-1516
e-mail: john.hirsch@regentcomm.com
Web site: www.wgna.com
Regional Vice President/General Manager. . . . . .Robert Ausfeld
    e-mail: robert.ausfeld@regentcomm.com
Operations Manager/Program Director . . . . .Tom Jacobsen
    e-mail: bbrindle@wgna.com
Station Manager . . . . .John Hirsh
    e-mail: johnhirsch@regentcomm.com
Music Director . . . . .Bill Earley
    e-mail: bearley@wgna.com

SYRACUSE

WNTQ (93.1 FM), WAQX (95.7 FM)
1064 James St, Syracuse, NY 13203
315-472-0200 Fax: 315-478-5625
Web site: www.93Q.com; www.95x.com
General Manager. . . . . .Dan Austin
Program Director (WNTQ). . . . . .Janice Cole
Program Director (WAQX). . . . . .Hunter Scott

WVOA (103.9 FM)
7095 Myers Road, East Syracuse, NY 13057-9748
315-656-2231 Fax: 315-656-2259
e-mail: programming@wvoaradio.com
Web site: www.wvoaradio.com
General Manager . . . . .Sam Furco
Public Service Coordinator . . . . .Susan Anderson
Music Director . . . . .Allen Elson

WYYY (94.5 FM)
500 Plum St, Suite 100, Syracuse, NY 13204
315-472-9797 Fax: 315-472-1904
Web site: www.sybercuse.com
Program Director. . . . . .Kathy Rowe
Operations Manager. . . . . .Rich Lauber
    e-mail: richlauber@clearchannel.com

UTICA

WOUR (96.9 FM)
39 Kellogg Rd, New Hartford, NY 13413
315-797-0803 Fax: 315-738-1073
e-mail: ask@wour.com
Web site: www.wour.com
General Manager/Sales Manager . . . . .Brian Delaney
    e-mail: brianelany@clearchannel.com
Program Director. . . . . .Tom Starr
    e-mail: tomstarr@clearchannel.com

WATERTOWN

WFRY (97.5 FM)
134 Mullin Street, Watertown, NY 13601
315-788-0790 Fax: 315-788-4379
e-mail: eliva.gaines@smgny.com
Web site: www.froggy97.com
General Manager. . . . . .Don Wagner
Program Director. . . . . .Matt Raisman

TELEVISION

*Stations included in this chapter produce news and/or public affairs pro-
gramming and are listed alphabetically by primary service area.*

ALBANY

WMHT (17) Public Broadcasting-NY Capitol Region
4 Global View Road, Troy, NY 12180
518-880-3400 Fax: 518-880-3409
e-mail: email@wmht.org
Web site: www.wmht.org
Production Manager . . . . .Dominick Figliomeni
    e-mail: dfigliomeni@wmht.org
Producer/Director. . . . . .Joanne Durfee
    e-mail: jdurfee@wmht.org
Senior Producer/Director . . . . .Dave Povero
    e-mail: dpovero@wmht.org
President/CEO . . . . .Robert Altman
    e-mail: raltman@wmht.org
Chief Technology Officer. . . . . .Anthony Tassarotti
    e-mail: atassarotti@wmht.org

WNYT (12)
715 N Pearl Street, PO Box 4035, Albany, NY 12204
518-486-4991 or 518-207-4700 Fax: 518-434-0659
e-mail: comments@wnyt.com
Web site: www.wnyt.com
General Manager . . . . .Steve Baboulis
    e-mail: sbaboulis@wnyt.com

Offices and agencies generally appear in alphabetical order, except when specific order is requested by listee.

Director Public Affairs/Programming . . . . Maryann Ryan
    e-mail: maryan@wnyt.com
News Director . . . . Paul Lewis
General Sales Manager. . . . . Tony McManus
Engineering Director. . . . . Richard Klein

WRGB (6)

1400 Balltown Rd, Schenectady, NY 12309
518-346-6666 or 800-666-3355 Fax: 518-381-3736
e-mail: news@cbs6albany.com
Web site: www.cbs6albany.com
General Manager. . . . . Bob Furlong
    e-mail: bfurlong@wrgb.com
News Director/Station Manager . . . . Lisa Jackson
    e-mail: ljackson@wrgb.com
Production Manager. . . . . Bill Brandt
Producer. . . . . Jessica Harrison

WTEN (10)

341 Northern Blvd, Albany, NY 12204
518-436-4822 or 800-888-9836 Fax: 518-462-6065
e-mail: news@news10.com
Web site: www.news10.com
Senior Producer. . . . . Jeanne Beatty
    e-mail: jeanne.beatty@wten.com
Programming Coordinator . . . . Chris Terwilliger
    e-mail: cterwilliger@wten.com
President & General Manager. . . . . Rene LaSpina
    e-mail: cterwilliger@wten.com

WXXA (23)

28 Corporate Circle, Albany, NY 12203
518-862-2323 or 518-862-0995 Fax: 518-862-0865
e-mail: news@fox23news.com
Web site: www.fox23news.com
General Manager. . . . . Bill Sally
News Director . . . . Gene Ross
CEO & President . . . . Sandy DiPasquale
Program Director . . . . Paul Pelliccia

WYPX DT-50

1 Charles Blvd, Guilderland, NY 12084
518-464-0143 or 800-646-7296 Fax: 518-464-0633
Web site: www.ionline.tv
Station Manager . . . . Renee Osterlitz
Public Service Director. . . . . Chris Iorio

BINGHAMTON

WBNG-TV (7)

560 Columbia Dr, Johnson City, NY 13790
607-729-8812 Fax: 607-797-6211
e-mail: wbng@wbngtv.com
Web site: www.wbng.com
News Director . . . . Greg Catlin
    e-mail: catlin@wbngtv.com
President/General Manager. . . . . Matt Rosenfeld
    e-mail: chapman@wbngtv.com

WICZ (40)

4600 Vestal Pkwy E, Vestal, NY 13850
607-770-4040 Fax: 607-798-7950
e-mail: fox40@wicz.com
Web site: www.wicz.com
General Manager . . . . John Leet
    e-mail: wicztv@aol.com
News Director . . . . Suh Neubauer
    e-mail: fox40suh@wicz.com
Program Director . . . . Vernon Rowlands
News Director . . . . Kent Garrett

WIVT (34)

203 Ingraham Hill Rd, Binghamton, NY 13903
607-771-3434 Fax: 607-723-1034
e-mail: newschannel34@newschannel34.com
Web site: www.newschannel34.com
News Director . . . . Jim Ehmke
Promotions Manager. . . . . Jim La Vasser

WSKG (46) Public Broadcasting

601 Gates Road, Vestal, NY 13850
607-729-0100 Fax: 607-729-7328
e-mail: mail@wskg.org
Web site: www.wskg.org
President/CEO/General Mgr . . . . Brian Sicora
Station Manager . . . . Juan Martinez
Operations Director/General Sales Mgr . . . . Nancy Christensen

BUFFALO

WGRZ (33)

259 Delaware Ave, Buffalo, NY 14202
716-849-2222 or 716-849-2200 Fax: 716-849-7602
e-mail: newsdesk@wgrz.com
Web site: www.wgrz.com
News Director . . . . Jeff Woodard
    e-mail: ecrookge@wgrz.gannett.com
Assignment Editor . . . . Maria Sisti
General Manager/President . . . . Jim Toellner
    e-mail: james.toellner@wgrz.com

WIVB-TV (39)

2077 Elmwood Ave, Buffalo, NY 14207
716-874-4410 Fax: 716-879-4896
e-mail: newsroom@wivb.com
Web site: www.wivb.com
News Director. . . . . Joseph Schlaerth
Senior Producer . . . . Vic Baker
Producer . . . . Mary Czopp
    e-mail: mary.czopp@wivb.com
News Producer . . . . Lynne Donley
    e-mail: lynne.donley@wivb.com
Executive Producer . . . . Jeff Sabato
    e-mail: jeff.sabato@wivb.com
Producer . . . . Andrew Tamutus

WKBW-TV (38)

7 Broadcast Plaza, Buffalo, NY 14202
716-845-6100 Fax: 716-842-1855
e-mail: news@wkbw.com
Web site: www.wkbw.com
News Director. . . . . Glen Horn
Station Manager . . . . Michael Nurse
Senior Producer. . . . . Paula D'Amico

WNED (43) Western NY Public Broadcasting

Horizon's Plaza, 140 Lower Terr., PO Box 1263, Buffalo, NY 14202
716-845-7000 Fax: 716-845-7036
Web site: www.wned.org
Station Manager . . . . Ron Santora
    e-mail: rdaly@wned.org
VP TV Production . . . . David Rotterman
    e-mail: drotterman@wned.org

WETM (18)

101 E Water Street, Box 1207, Elmira, NY 14901
607-733-5518 Fax: 607-734-1176
e-mail: info@wetmtv.com
Web site: www.wetmtv.com
General Manager. . . . . Randy Reid
News Director. . . . . Scott Nichols
    e-mail: snichols@wetmtv.com

Offices and agencies generally appear in alphabetical order, except when specific order is requested by listee.

Chief Managing Editor . . . . .Jeff Stone
    e-mail: jstone@wetmtv.com

HORSEHEADS

WENY (36)
474 Old Ithaca Rd, Horseheads, NY 14845
607-739-3636 Fax: 607-739-1418
e-mail: info@weny.com
Web site: www.weny.com
Anchor . . . . .Sarah Sheridan
Executive Producer. . . . . .Renata Stiehl
News Director . . . . .Scott Cook
President & CEO . . . . .Kevin Lilly

KINGSTON

WRNN (48)
800 Westchester Avenue, Suite S-640, Rye Brook, NY 10573
914-417-2700 Fax: 914-696-0279
e-mail: comments@rnntv.com
Web site: www.rnntv.com
General Manager . . . . .Richard French
Executive Producer . . . . .Don Dudley

LONG ISLAND

WLIW (21) Public Broadcasting
Box 21, Plainview, NY 11803
516-367-2100 Fax: 516-692-7629
e-mail: programming@wliw.org
Web site: www.wliw.org
General Manager . . . . .Terrel Cass
    e-mail: terrel_cass@wliw.pbs.org
Executive Producer . . . . .Tom Casciato
President . . . . .Neal Shapiro

MELVILLE

WLNY (47)
270 S Service Road, Suite 55, Melville, NY 11747
631-777-8855 Fax: 631-777-8180
e-mail: ny55news@aol.com
Web site: www.wlnytv.com
Sales VP . . . . .Elliot Simmons
News Director. . . . . .Richard Rose

NEW YORK CITY

Bloomberg Television
499 Park Avenue, New York, NY 10022
212-318-2300 Fax: 917-617-5999
e-mail: mwomack@bloomberg.net
Web site: www.bloomberg.com/tv/
Editor-in-Chief. . . . . .Matthew Winkler
Managing Editor. . . . . .Michael Clancy
    e-mail: mclancy@bloomberg.net
Press Contact. . . . . .Amanda Cowie
    e-mail: acowie@bloomberg.net

Fox News Channel
1211 Ave of the Americas, 2nd Floor, New York, NY 10036
212-301-3000 or 888-369-4762 Fax: 212-301-8274
e-mail: newsmanager@foxnews.com
Web site: www.foxnews.com
SVP/News Operations. . . . . .Sharri Berg
EVP/Executive Editor . . . . .John Moody
EVP/News . . . . .Michael Clemente

New York 1 News (1)
75 Ninth Avenue, New York, NY 10011
212-691-6397 Fax: 212-379-3575
e-mail: ny1news@ny1.com
Web site: www.ny1.com
Albany Reporter . . . . .Erin Billups
Geeral Assignment Reporter . . . . .Roger Clark
Anchor . . . . .Lewis Dodley
Politcal Reporter . . . . .Bobby Cuza

WABC (7)
7 Lincoln Sq, New York, NY 10023
917-260-7697 Fax: 212-456-2290
e-mail: iwitness@wabc.com
Web site: www.7online.com
News Director. . . . . .Ken Plotnik
VP of Programming . . . . .Art Moore
    e-mail: art.moore@abc.com
Executive Producer . . . . .Nancy Kennedy
. . . .
    e-mail: cbsnewyork@cbs.com
News Director . . . . .David M. Friend
Executive Producer . . . . .Byron Harmon
    e-mail: bharmon@cbs.com

WNBC (4)
30 Rockefeller Plaza, New York, NY 10112
212-664-4444 Fax: 212-664-2994
e-mail: newstips@wnbc.com
Web site: www.wnbc.com
Executive Editor. . . . . .Richard Wolfe
VP/News & Product . . . . .Gregory Gittrich
Editor. . . . . .Erica Tilles
Senior Editor . . . . .John Baiata

WNYW (44)
205 E 67th St, New York, NY 10021
212-452-5555 Fax: 212-452-5750
Web site: www.myfoxny.com
Executive Producer . . . . .Byron Harmon
News Writer . . . . .Donielle Stanton

WPIX (11)
220 East 42nd St, 2nd Fl, New York, NY 10017
212-210-2411 Fax: 212-210-2591
e-mail: news@pix11.com
Web site: www.pix11.com
Executive Producer. . . . . .Monica Zack
Editor. . . . . .Brian Waizel
Editor . . . . .Reynaldo Meno
Senior Editor . . . . .Jennifer Tanaka

WWOR (UPN 9)
205 E 67th Street, New York, NY 10065-6050
212-852-7000 Fax: 212-852-7145
Web site: www.my9tv.com
President & Editor . . . . .Edwin A. Finn, Jr.
Managing Editor . . . . .Richard Rescigno
Senior Deputy Managing Editor . . . . .Jonathan Krim

PLATTSBURGH

WPTZ (5) NBC
5 Television Dr, Plattsburgh, NY 12901
518-561-5555 Fax: 518-561-5940
e-mail: newstips@wptz.com
Web site: www.wptz.com
President/General Manager . . . . .Paul Sands
News Director . . . . .Kyle Grimes
Assignment Editor. . . . . .Matt Morin
    e-mail: mmorin@herst.com

Offices and agencies generally appear in alphabetical order, except when specific order is requested by listee.

ROCHESTER

WHEC (10)
191 East Ave, Rochester, NY 14604
585-546-5670 Fax: 585-546-5688
e-mail: news1@whec.com
Web site: www.10nbc.com
News Director. . . . . .Mike Goldrick
Producer . . . . .Carla Hanlon
 e-mail: chanlon@whec.com
Executive Producer . . . . .Ray Sullivan
 e-mail: news1@whec.com

WHAM (13)
4225 W Henrietta Road, Box 20555, Rochester, NY 14623
585-334-8700 Fax: 585-359-1570
e-mail: feedback@13wham.com
Web site: www.13wham.com
General Manager. . . . . .Chuck Samuels
 e-mail: csamuels@13wham.com
TV Community Affairs Director. . . . . .Charlotte Clarke
News Director . . . . .Matt Malyn
General Manager . . . . .Kent Beckwith
 e-mail: kbeckwith@13wham.com
Executive Producer . . . . .Brad Smith
 e-mail: bsmith@13wham.com

WXXI (16) Public Broadcasting
280 State St, PO Box 30021, Rochester, NY 14603
585-325-7500 Fax: 585-258-0335
Web site: www.wxxi.org
Executive Producer/Assistant VP . . . . .Todd Mccammon
 e-mail: wxxi@wxxi.org
Vice President, Television . . . . .Elissa Orlando
 e-mail: emarra@wxxi.org
News Director. . . . . .Peter Iglinksi
 e-mail: newsroom@wxxi.org

SYRACUSE

WCNY (25)
506 Old Liverpool Road, PO Box 2400, Syracuse, NY 13220
315-453-2424 Fax: 315-451-8824
e-mail: wcny-online@wcny.org
Web site: www.wcny.org
Program Manager . . . . .Peter McElvein
President/CEO . . . . .Robert Daino
 e-mail: robert_diano@wcny.org
News/Public Affairs Director .Susan Arbetter
 e-mail: robert_diano@wcny.org

WSYR (17)
5904 Bridge St, Box 699, East Syracuse, NY 13057
315-446-9999 Fax: 315-446-9283
e-mail: newschannel9@9wsyr.com
Web site: www.9wsyr.com
News Director . . . . .Jim Tortora
VP/General Manager. . . . . .Theresa Underwood

WSTM (24)
1030 James St, Syracuse, NY 13203
315-477-9400 Fax: 315-474-5082
Web site: www.wstm.com
Anchor . . . . .Matt Mulcahy

Chief Investigative Reporter . . . . .Jim Kenyon
 e-mail: pphillip@wstm.com
Chief Engineer . . . . .Kevin Tubbs
 e-mail: pphillip@wstm.com
News Director. . . . . .Peggy Phillip
 e-mail: pphillip@wstm.com

WSYT (19)
1000 James St, Syracuse, NY 13203
315-472-6800 Fax: 315-471-8889
e-mail: info@wsyt68.com
Web site: www.wsyt68.com
Program Coordinator . . . . .Becky Walsh

WTVH (47)
980 James St, Syracuse, NY 13203
315-425-5555 Fax: 315-425-5513
e-mail: wtvh@wtvh.com
Web site: www.wtvh.com
Executive Producer . . . . .Megan Tennyson
 e-mail: mtennyson@wtvh.com
General Manager/President. . . . . .Matt Rosenfeld
News Director. . . . . .Frank Kracher

UTICA

WKTV (29)
5936 Smith Hill Rd, PO Box 2, Utica, NY 13503
315-733-0404 Fax: 315-793-3498
e-mail: newslink2@wktv.com
Web site: www.wktv.com
Program Director. . . . . .Tom Coyne
 e-mail: tcoyne@wktv.com
News Director. . . . . .Steve McMurray
 e-mail: smcmurray@wktv.com
Vice President/General Manager. . . . . .Vic Vetters
 e-mail: vvetter@wktv.com

WATERTOWN

WWNY (7)
120 Arcade St, Watertown, NY 13601
315-788-3800 Fax: 315-788-3787
e-mail: wwny@wwnytv.net
Web site: www.wwnytv.net
General Manager . . . . .Cathy Pircsuk
 e-mail: cpircsuk@wwnytv.net
News Director . . . . .Scott Atkinson
 e-mail: satkinsn@wwnytv.net
Producer/Assistant News Director . . . . .Anne Richter

WWTI (21)
Box 6250, 1222 Arsenal St, Watertown, NY 13601
315-785-8850 Fax: 315-785-0127
e-mail: news@myabc50.com
Web site: www.newswatch50.com
General Mgr/Sales Mgr . . . . .David J Males
News Director. . . . . .John Moore
 e-mail: johnmoore@clearchannel.com

News Media

Offices and agencies generally appear in alphabetical order, except when specific order is requested by listee.

Section 7:
EDUCATION

COLLEGES AND UNIVERSITIES

STATE UNIVERSITY OF NEW YORK

SUNY Board of Trustees
State University of New York
State University Plz
353 Broadway
Albany, NY 12246
518-320-1157 or 800-342-3811 Fax: 518-443-5131
e-mail: trustees@suny.edu
Web site: www.suny.edu

Chair:
  H. Carl McCall 212-239-2362
Member:
  Joseph Belluck 315-320-1157
Member:
  Henrik Dullea 518-320-1157
Member:
  Ronald Ehrenberg 518-320-1157
Member:
  Angelo Fatta 518-320-1157
Member:
  Tina Good 518-320-1256
Member:
  Stephen Hunt. 914-232-6259
Member:
  Eunice A. Lewin 518-320-1157
Member:
  Marshall Lichtman 518-320-1157
Member:
  John Murad 518-320-1157
Member:
  Kenneth O'Brien 518-443-5326
Member:
  Kevin Rea 518-320-1157
Member:
  Linda Sanford 914-766-3800
Member:
  Richard Socarides 518-320-1157
Member:
  Carl Spielvogel 212-641-6522
Member:
  Cary Staller 518-320-1157
Member:
  Gerri Warren-Merrick 212-694-4933

SUNY System Administration & Executive Council
State University Plz
353 Broadway
Albany, NY 12246
518-443-5555
Web site: www.suny.edu

Chancellor:
  Nancy L. Zimpher. 518-320-1355
  e-mail: Nancy.Zimpher@suny.edu
Executive Vice Chancellor & Provost:
  David K. Lavallee. 518-320-1251
Senior Vice Chancellor for Community Colleges & the Education Pipeline:
  Johanna Duncan-Poitier 518-320-1276
Senior Vice Chancellor & General Counsel, Secretary of the University:
  William F. Howard
Vice Chancellor for Academic Programs and Planning & Vice Provost:
  Elizabeth L. Bringsjord. 518-320-1356

Vice Chancellor for Capital Facilities & General Manager/Construction Fund:
  Robert Haelen 518-320-1502
Vice Chancellor for Financial Services & CFO:
  Brian Hutzley 518-320-1497
Vice Chancellor for Global Affairs:
  Mitch Leventhal 212-317-3546
Vice Chancellor for Human Resources:
  Curtis L. Lloyd 518-320-1192
Vice Chancellor for Research & President of the Research Foundation:
  Timothy Killeen
Associate Vice Chancellor for Health Affairs:
  Lora Lefebvre 518-320-1193
Assistant Vice Chancellor for External Affairs:
  Jennifer LoTurco. 518-320-1805
Assistant Vice Chancellor for Government Relations:
  Stacey Hengsterman 518-320-1148
Assistant Vice Chancellor for Strategic Planning & University Advancement:
  Kaitlin Gambrill 212-364-5789
Associate Provost & Associate Vice Chancellor for Diversity, Equity & Inclusion:
  Carlos Medina. 518-320-1176
Director of Communications:
  David Doyle 518-320-1311
President, Student Assembly:
  Kevin Rea
President, University Faculty Senate:
  Kenneth O'Brien
President, Faculty Council of Community Colleges:
  Tina Good. 518-320-1256

New York Network . . . . .fax: 518-426-4198
Suite 146, South Concourse, Empire State Plaza, Albany, NY 12223
518-443-5333 Fax: 518-426-4198
e-mail: mscinfo@ogs.ny.gov
Web site: www.nyn.suny.edu
Executive Director:
  Neil Satterly. 518-443-5333/fax: 518-426-4198
Production Manager:
  Sara Hill
Senior Producer:
  Chris Conto. 518-443-5333
Supervising Television Engineer:
  Patrick Roche 518-443-5333

Rockefeller Institute of Government . . . . .fax: 518-443-5788
411 State St, Albany, NY 12203-1003
518-443-5522 Fax: 518-443-5788
e-mail: info@rockinst.org
Web site: www.rockinst.org
Director:
  Thomas Gais 518-443-5238
  e-mail: gaist@rockinst.org
Deputy Director of Research:
  Jason E. Lane 518-443-5825
  e-mail: jlane@albany.edu
Deputy Director for Operations:
  Robert E. Bullock
  e-mail: rbullock@albany.edu
Senior Policy Analyst:
  Lucy Dadayan 518-443-5828
  e-mail: dadayanl@rockinst.org

SUNY Center for Student Recruitment . . . . .fax: 518-320-1573
33 W 42nd St (across from Bryant Park), New York, NY 10036
212-364-5821 Fax: 518-320-1573
e-mail: csr@suny.edu
Web site: www.suny.edu/student/mrc.cfm
Director:
  Beryl S. Jeffers

Offices and agencies generally appear in alphabetical order, except when specific order is requested by listee.

Associate Director for Financial Aid Services:
  Julieta Schiffino
Assistant to the Director for Special Programs:
  Gail Reilly
Admissions Recruitment Advisor:
  Cynthia Marino
Admissions Recruitment Advisor:
  Beverly Santos

Small Business Development Center
  State University Plaza, Administration Office, 22 Corporate Woods Bldg,
    3rd Fl, Albany, NY 12246
  518-443-5398 or 800-732-7232
  Web site: www.nyssbdc.org
State Director:
  James L King 518-443-5398 x166/fax: 518-443-5275
  e-mail: j.king@nyssbdc.org

State University Construction Fund
  353 Broadway, Albany, NY 12246
  518-320-3200
  Web site: www.sucf.suny.edu
General Manager:
  Robert Haelen 518-320-1502
Counsel:
  William K Barczak 518-320-1746

UNIVERSITY CENTERS

Binghamton University, State University of New York
4400 Vestal Parkway East
PO Box 6000
Binghamton, NY 13902
607-777-2000
e-mail: info@binghamton.edu
Web site: www.binghamton.edu

President:
  Harvey G. Stenger 607-777-2131/fax: 607-777-2533

College of Agriculture & Life Sciences at Cornell University
177 Roberts Hall
Ithaca, NY 14853
607-255-2241 Fax: 607-255-3803
Web site: www.cals.cornell.edu

Dean:
  Kathryn Boor 607-255-2241
  e-mail: kjb4@cornell.edu

College of Human Ecology at Cornell University
170 Martha Van Rensselaer Hall
Ithaca, NY 14853-4401
607-255-5471 Fax: 607-255-2293
e-mail: humec_admissions@cornell.edu
Web site: www.human.cornell.edu

Dean:
  Alan Mathios 607-255-2138
  e-mail: adm5@cornell.edu

College of Veterinary Medicine at Cornell University
Cornell University
Ithaca, NY 14853
607-253-3000 Fax: 607-253-3701
Web site: www.vet.cornell.edu

Dean:
  Michael I Kotlikoff 607-253-3771

NYS College of Ceramics at Alfred University
2 Pine St
Alfred, NY 14802
607-871-2137 Fax: 607-871-2339
e-mail: mastin@alfred.edu
Web site: nyscc.alfred.edu

Provost:
  Suzanne Buckley 607-871-2137

SUNY Downstate Medical Center
450 Clarkson Ave
Brooklyn, NY 11203
718-270-1000 Fax: 718-270-7592
Web site: www.downstate.edu

President:
  John C LaRosa 718-270-2611
  e-mail: jclarosa@downstate.edu

SUNY State College of Optometry
33 West 42nd St
New York, NY 10036-8003
212-938-4000 or 212-938-4001
Web site: www.sunyopt.edu

President:
  Dr David A Heath 212-938-5650
  e-mail: dheath@sunyopt.edu

SUNY Upstate Medical University
750 E Adams St
Syracuse, NY 13210
315-464-5540 Fax: 315-464-4838
Web site: www.upstate.edu

President:
  David R Smith 315-464-5540
  e-mail: smith@upstate.edu

School of Industrial & Labor Relations at Cornell University (ILR School)
309 Ives Hall
Ithaca, NY 14853
607-255-2762 Fax: 607-255-7774
e-mail: info@ilr.cornell.edu
Web site: www.ilr.cornell.edu

Dean:
  Harry C Katz 607-255-2185
  e-mail: hck2@cornell.edu

State University of New York at Albany
1400 Washington Ave
Albany, NY 12222
518-442-3300
Web site: www.albany.edu

President:
  George Philip 518-956-8010
  e-mail: presmail@uamail.albany.edu

Offices and agencies generally appear in alphabetical order, except when specific order is requested by listee.

State University of New York College of Environmental Science & Forestry

One Forestry Dr
Syracuse, NY 13210
315-470-6500 or TDD: 315-470-6966 Fax: 315-470-6933
e-mail: esfinfo@esf.edu
Web site: www.esf.edu

President:
   Cornelius B Murphy Jr 315-470-6681/fax: 315-470-6977
   e-mail: cbmurphy@esf.edu

Stony Brook University, SUNY

118 Administration Bldg
Stony Brook, NY 11794
631-632-6000
Web site: www.sunysb.edu

President:
   Samuel L Stanley. 631-632-6265/fax: 631-632-6621
   e-mail: samuel.stanley@stonybrook.edu

University at Buffalo, State University of New York

12 Capen Hall
Buffalo, NY 14260
716-645-2000
Web site: www.buffalo.edu

President:
   John B Simpson. 716-645-2901/fax: 716-645-3728
   e-mail: simpson@buffalo.edu

UNIVERSITY COLLEGES

Buffalo State College

1300 Elmwood Ave
Buffalo, NY 14222-1095
716-878-4000 or TTD 716-878-3182 Fax: 716-878-3039
e-mail: webadmin@buffalostate.edu
Web site: www.buffalostate.edu

President:
   Aaron Podolefsky 716-878-4101/fax: 716-878-6527
   e-mail: president@buffalostate.edu

College at Brockport

350 New Campus Dr
Brockport, NY 14420
585-395-2211 or 585-395-2796 Fax: 585-395-2401
Web site: www.brockport.edu

President:
   John R Halstead 585-395-2361
   e-mail: halstead@brockport.edu

Purchase College, State University of New York

735 Anderson Hill Rd
Purchase, NY 10577
914-251-6000
Web site: www.purchase.edu

President:
   Thomas J Schwarz. 914-251-6010/fax: 914-251-6014
   e-mail: thomas.schwarz@purchase.edu

State University at Old Westbury

223 Store Hill Rd
PO Box 210
Old Westbury, NY 11568-0210
516-876-3000
Web site: www.oldwestbury.edu

President:
   Calvin O Butts, III. 516-876-3160/fax: 516-876-3347
   e-mail: buttsc@oldwestbury.edu

State University at Potsdam

44 Pierrepont Ave
Potsdam, NY 13676
315-267-2000 or 877-768-7326
Web site: www.potsdam.edu

President:
   John Schwaller 315-267-2100
   e-mail: schwaljf@potsdam.edu

State University College at Cortland

Graham Ave
PO Box 2000
Cortland, NY 13045
607-753-2011 Fax: 607-753-5688
Web site: www.cortland.edu

President:
   Erik J Bitterbaum. 607-753-2201/fax: 607-753-5993
   e-mail: bitterbaume@cortland.edu

State University College at Geneseo

1 College Circle
Geneseo, NY 14454-1450
585-245-5000 Fax: 585-245-5005
e-mail: web@geneseo.edu
Web site: www.geneseo.edu

President:
   Christopher Dahl. 585-245-5501
   e-mail: cdahl@geneseo.edu

State University College at New Paltz

1 Hawk Drive
New Paltz, NY 12561
845-257-7869 or 877-696-7411 Fax: 845-257-3009
Web site: www.newpaltz.edu

Interim President:
   Donald Christian 845-257-3288/fax: 845-257-3389
   e-mail: poskanzer@newpaltz.edu

State University Empire State College

One Union Ave
Saratoga Springs, NY 12866
518-587-2100 Fax: 518-587-3033
Web site: www.esc.edu

President:
   Alan Davis 518-587-2100 x2260/fax: 518-587-2886
   e-mail: president@esc.edu

State University of New York, Fredonia

280 Central Ave
Fredonia, NY 14063-1136

Offices and agencies generally appear in alphabetical order, except when specific order is requested by listee.

716-673-3111 Fax: 716-673-3156
Web site: www.fredonia.edu

President:
Dennis L Hefner 716-673-3456
e-mail: dennis.hefner@fredonia.edu

State University of New York at Oneonta
108 Ravine Pkwy
Oneonta, NY 13820
607-436-3500
Web site: www.oneonta.edu

President:
Nancy Kleniewski 607-436-2500/fax: 607-436-3089
e-mail: klenien@oneonta.edu

State University of New York at Oswego
7060 Route 104
Oswego, NY 13126
315-312-2500 Fax: 315-312-2863
e-mail: proffice@oswego.edu
Web site: www.oswego.edu

President:
Deborah F Stanley 315-312-2211
e-mail: stanley@oswego.edu

State University of New York at Plattsburgh
101 Broad St
Plattsburgh, NY 12901
518-564-2000 Fax: 518-564-2094
Web site: www.plattsburgh.edu

President:
John Ettling 518-564-2010/fax: 518-564-3932
e-mail: president_office@plattsburgh.edu

COLLEGES OF TECHNOLOGY

Alfred State College of Technology
10 Upper College Dr
Alfred, NY 14802
607-587-4215 or 800-425-3733 Fax: 607-587-4299
Web site: www.alfredstate.edu

President:
John M Anderson 607-587-4010/fax: 607-587-4209
e-mail: presidentsoffice@alfredstate.edu

Farmingdale State College of Technology
2350 Broadhollow Rd
Farmingdale, NY 11735-1021
631-420-2000 Fax: 631-420-2633
e-mail: regoff@farmingdale.edu
Web site: www.farmingdale.edu

President:
W Hubert Keen 631-420-2239/fax: 631-420-2753
e-mail: keenhu@farmingdale.edu

Morrisville State College
Administration Bldg, South St
PO Box 901
Morrisville, NY 13408
315-684-6000 or 800-258-0111 Fax: 315-684-6116
Web site: www.morrisville.edu

President:
Raymond W Cross. 315-684-6044/fax: 315-684-6109
e-mail: crossrw@morrisville.edu

SUNY College of Agriculture & Technology at Cobleskill
State Route 7
Cobleskill, NY 12043
518-255-5700 or 800-295-8988 Fax: 518-255-6769
Web site: www.cobleskill.edu

President:
Donald Zingdale 518-255-5111

State University College of Technology at Canton
34 Cornell Drive
Canton, NY 13617
315-386-7011 or 800-388-7123 Fax: 315-386-7929
e-mail: admissions@canton.edu
Web site: www.canton.edu

President:
Joseph L Kennedy 315-386-7204/fax: 315-386-7934
e-mail: president@canton.edu

State University College of Technology at Delhi
2 Main St
Delhi, NY 13753
607-746-4550 or 800-963-3544 Fax: 607-746-4104
Web site: www.delhi.edu

President:
Candace S Vancko. 607-746-4090/fax: 607-746-4346
e-mail: vanckocs@delhi.org

State University Institute of Technology
Horatio St, Marcy Campus
100 Seymour Road
Utica, NY 13502
315-792-7500 Fax: 315-792-7837
Web site: www.sunyit.edu

Interim President:
Wolf Yeigh 315-792-7400/fax: 315-792-7407
e-mail: yeighw@sunyuit.edu

State University of New York Maritime College
6 Pennyfield Ave
Throgs Neck, NY 10465
718-409-7200 or 800-642-1874 Fax: 718-409-7465
Web site: www.sunymaritime.edu

President:
John W Craine Jr. 718-409-7271

COMMUNITY COLLEGES

Adirondack Community College
640 Bay Rd
Queensbury, NY 12804
518-743-2200 Fax: 518-745-1433
e-mail: info@sunyacc.edu
Web site: www.sunyacc.edu

President:
Ronald Heacock 518-743-2237/fax: 518-743-2262
e-mail: heacockr@sunyacc.edu

Offices and agencies generally appear in alphabetical order, except when specific order is requested by listee.

Broome Community College
PO Box 1017
Binghamton, NY 13902
607-778-5000 Fax: 607-778-5310
Web site: www.sunybroome.edu

Interim President:
Kevin E Drumm 607-778-5100
e-mail: oday-p@sunybroome.edu

Cayuga Community College
197 Franklin St
Auburn, NY 13021
315-255-1743 Fax: 315-255-2117
Web site: www.cayuga-cc.edu

President:
Daniel Paul Larson 315-255-1743 x2208
e-mail: daniel.larson@cayuga-cc.edu

Clinton Community College
136 Clinton Point Dr
Plattsburgh, NY 12901
518-562-4200 Fax: 518-562-4159
Web site: www.clinton.edu

Clinton Community College
518-562-4100

Columbia-Greene Community College
4400 Route 23
Hudson, NY 12534-0327
518-828-4181 Fax: 518-828-8543
e-mail: info@sunycgcc.edu
Web site: www.sunycgcc.edu

President:
James R Campion 518-828-4181x3325/fax: 518-822-2006
e-mail: campion@sunycgcc.edu

Corning Community College
1 Academic Dr
Corning, NY 14830
607-962-9222 or 800-358-7171 Fax: 607-962-9456
Web site: www.corning-cc.edu

President:
Floyd F Amann. 607-962-9232 x9232/fax: 607-962-9485
e-mail: amann@corning-cc.edu

Dutchess Community College
53 Pendell Rd
Poughkeepsie, NY 12601-1595
845-431-8000 Fax: 845-431-8984
e-mail: communityrelations@sunydutchess.edu
Web site: www.sunydutchess.edu

President:
D David Conklin. 845-431-8980
e-mail: conklin@sunydutchess.edu

Erie Community College
121 Ellicott St
Buffalo, NY 14203-2698
716-851-1322
e-mail: info@ecc.edu
Web site: www.ecc.edu

President:
Jack Quinn 716-851-1200
e-mail: jquinn@ecc.edu

Fashion Institute of Technology
7th Ave at 27th St
New York, NY 10001-5992
212-217-7999
e-mail: fitinfo@fitnyc.edu
Web site: www.fitnyc.edu

President:
Joyce F Brown. 212-217-4000/fax: 212-217-7639

Finger Lakes Community College
3325 Marvin Sands Drive
Canandaigua, NY 14424
585-394-3500 or 585-394-3522 Fax: 585-394-5017
e-mail: admissions@flcc.edu
Web site: www.fingerlakes.edu

President:
Dr. Barbara Risser 585-394-3500 x7201
e-mail: risserbg@flcc.edu

Fulton-Montgomery Community College
2805 State Hwy 67
Johnstown, NY 12095-3790
518-762-4651 Fax: 518-762-4334
e-mail: geninfo@fmcc.suny.edu
Web site: www.fmcc.suny.edu

President:
Dustin Swanger. . . . . .518-762-9651 x 8000

Genesee Community College
One College Rd
Batavia, NY 14020-9704
585-343-0055 Fax: 585-343-4541
Web site: www.genesee.edu

President:
Stuart Steiner 585-343-0055 x6201
e-mail: ssteiner@genesee.edu

Herkimer County Community College
100 Reservoir Rd
Herkimer, NY 13350-9987
315-866-0300 or 888-464-4222 Fax: 315-866-7253
Web site: www.herkimer.edu

President:
Ann Marie Murray 315-866-0300 x8261/fax: 315-866-5539
e-mail: president@herkimer.edu

Hudson Valley Community College
80 Vandenburgh Ave
Troy, NY 12180
518-629-4822 or 877-325-4822 Fax: 518-629-8070
e-mail: input@hvcc.edu
Web site: www.hvcc.edu

President:
Andrew Matonak 518-629-4530
e-mail: a.matonak@hvcc.edu

Offices and agencies generally appear in alphabetical order, except when specific order is requested by listee.

Jamestown Community College

525 Falconer St
PO Box 20
Jamestown, NY 14702-0020
716-338-1000 or 800-388-8557 Fax: 716-338-1466
Web site: www.sunyjcc.edu

President:
Gregory T DeCinque 716-665-5220 x2315
e-mail: gregdecinque@mail.sunyjcc.edu

Jefferson Community College

1220 Coffeen St
Watertown, NY 13601
315-786-2200 Fax: 315-786-0158
e-mail: webmaster@sunyjefferson.edu
Web site: www.sunyjefferson.edu

President:
Carole A McCoy. 315-786-2230
e-mail: cmccoy@sunyjefferson.edu

Mohawk Valley Community College

1101 Sherman Dr
Utica, NY 13501-5394
315-792-5400 Fax: 315-792-5666
Web site: www.mvcc.edu

President:
Randall S Van Wagoner 315-792-5333/fax: 315-792-5678
e-mail: rvanwagoner@mvcc.edu

Monroe Community College

1000 E Henrietta Rd
Rochester, NY 14623-5780
585-292-2000 Fax: 585-292-3060
e-mail: collcommrelations@monroecc.edu
Web site: www.monroecc.edu

President:
Anne M Kress PhD 585-292-2100/fax: 585-292-3870
e-mail: akress@monroecc.edu

Nassau Community College

1 Education Dr
Garden City, NY 11530-6793
516-572-7501 Fax: 516-572-8118
e-mail: info@ncc.edu
Web site: www.ncc.edu

President:
Donald P Astrab 516-572-7205
e-mail: presidentsoffice@ncc.edu

Niagara County Community College

3111 Saunders Settlement Rd
Sanborn, NY 14132
716-614-6222 Fax: 716-614-6700
Web site: www.niagaracc.suny.edu

President:
James P Klyczek 716-614-5901
e-mail: klyczek@niagaracc.suny.edu

North Country Community College

23 Santanoni Ave
PO Box 89
Saranac Lake, NY 12983-0089
518-891-2915 or 888-879-6222 Fax: 518-891-6562
e-mail: helpdesk@nccc.edu
Web site: www.nccc.edu

President:
Carol Brown 518-891-2915 x201/fax: 518-891-5029
e-mail: president@nccc.edu

Onondaga Community College

4585 West Seneca Turnpike
Syracuse, NY 13215
315-498-2622 Fax: 315-469-4475
e-mail: occinfo@sunyocc.edu
Web site: www.sunyocc.edu

President:
Debbie L Sydow 315-498-2211
e-mail: sydowd@sunyocc.edu

Orange County Community College

115 South St
Middletown, NY 10940
845-344-6222 Fax: 845-343-1228
Web site: www.sunyorange.edu

President:
William Richards 845-341-4701
e-mail: president@sunyorange.edu

Rockland Community College

145 College Rd
Suffern, NY 10901
845-574-4000
Web site: www.sunyrockland.edu

President:
Cliff L Wood. 845-574-4214
e-mail: cwood@sunyrockland.edu

Schenectady County Community College

78 Washington Ave
Schenectady, NY 12305
518-381-1200 Fax: 518-346-0379
Web site: www.sunysccc.edu

President:
Dr Quintin B Bullock 518-381-1304/fax: 518-346-8680
e-mail: bullocqb@sunysccc.edu

Suffolk County Community College

533 College Rd
Selden, NY 11784
631-451-4000 Fax: 631-451-4090
Web site: www3.sunysuffolk.edu

President:
Shaun L McKay 631-451-4736
e-mail: mckays@sunysuffolk.edu

Sullivan County Community College

112 College Rd
PO Box 4002
Loch Sheldrake, NY 12759

Offices and agencies generally appear in alphabetical order, except when specific order is requested by listee.

845-434-5750 or 800-577-5243 Fax: 845-434-4806
e-mail: sccc@sullivan.suny.edu
Web site: www.sullivan.suny.edu

President:
   Mamie Howard Golladay 845-434-5750 x4261/fax: 845-434-9308
   e-mail: mgollada@sullivan.suny.edu

Tompkins Cortland Community College

170 North St
PO Box 139
Dryden, NY 13053
607-844-8211 or 888-567-8211 Fax: 607-844-9665
Web site: www.tc3.edu

President:
   Carl E Haynes 607-844-8222 x4368/fax: 607-844-6545
   e-mail: haynesc@tc3.edu

Ulster County Community College

491 Cottekill Rd
Stone Ridge, NY 12484
845-687-5000 or 800-724-0833 Fax: 845-687-5083
Web site: www.sunyulster.edu

President:
   Donald C Katt 845-687-5050/fax: 845-687-5292
   e-mail: kattd@sunyulster.edu

Westchester Community College

75 Grasslands Rd
Valhalla, NY 10595-1693
914-606-6600 Fax: 914-785-6565
e-mail: info@sunywcc.edu
Web site: www.sunywcc.edu

President:
   Joseph N Hankin 914-606-6707/fax: 914-785-6780
   e-mail: joseph.hankin@sunywcc.edu

EDUCATIONAL OPPORTUNITY CENTERS

Bronx Educational Opportunity Center

1666 Bathgate Ave
Bronx, NY 10457
718-530-7000 Fax: 718-530-7047
Web site: www.brx.eoc.suny.edu

Executive Director:
   Stephen H Adolphus 718-530-7040

Brooklyn Educational Opportunity Center

111 Livingston St
Brooklyn, NY 11201
718-802-3300 Fax: 718-802-3381
e-mail: admissions@beoc.suny.edu
Web site: www.bkl.eoc.suny.edu

Executive Director/Dean:
   Lois Blades-Rosado 718-246-2057
   e-mail: rosadol@bklyn.eoc.cuny.edu

Buffalo Educational Opportunity Center

465 Washington St
Buffalo, NY 14203

716-849-6727 x500 Fax: 716-849-6738
e-mail: eoc465@buffalo.edu
Web site: www.bfl.eoc.suny.edu

Director:
   Sherryl D Weems 716-849-6727 x125
   e-mail: weems@buffalo.edu

Capital District Educational Opportunity Center

145 Congress St
Troy, NY 12180
518-273-1900 Fax: 518-273-1919
e-mail: eocinfo@hvcc.edu
Web site: www.hvcc.edu/eoc/

Executive Director/VP:
   Lucille A Marion 518-273-1900 x2212
   e-mail: l.marion@hvcc.edu

Educational Opportunity Center of Westchester

26 S Broadway
Yonkers, NY 10701
914-606-7600 Fax: 914-606-7640
Web site: www.ynk.eoc.suny.edu

Director/Associate Dean:
   Renee Guy 914-606-7612
   e-mail: renee.guy@sunywcc.edu

Long Island Educational Opportunity Center

269 Fulton Ave
Hempstead, NY 11550
516-489-8705
Web site: www.li.sunyeoc.org

Dean/Executive Director:
   Veronica Henry 631-420-2507
   e-mail: henryv@farmingdale.edu

Manhattan Educational Opportunity Center

163 W 125th St
New York, NY 10027
212-961-4400 Fax: 212-961-4343
e-mail: info@meoc.suny.edu
Web site: www.man.eoc.suny.edu

Executive Director/Dean:
   Rodney Alexander 212-961-4320
   e-mail: rodney.alexander@man.eoc.suny.edu

North Bronx Career Counseling & Outreach Center

2901 White Plains Road
Bronx, NY 10467
718-547-1001 Fax: 718-547-1973
Web site: www.nbx.eoc.suny.edu

Director:
   Mitch Duren 718-547-1001 x210
   e-mail: mmduren@sunyeoc.org

Queens Educational Opportunity Center

SUNY
158-29 Archer Ave
Jamaica, NY 11433
718-725-3300 Fax: 718-658-5604
Web site: www.qns.eoc.suny.edu

Offices and agencies generally appear in alphabetical order, except when specific order is requested by listee.

Director:
Khayriyyah Ali 718-725-3403
e-mail: ali_29@eoc.suny.edu

Rochester Educational Opportunity Center

305 Andrews St
Rochester, NY 14604
585-232-2730 Fax: 585-546-7824
Web site: www.reoc.brockport.edu

Dean/Executive Director:
Melva L Brown 585-232-2730 x269/fax: 585-232-8154
e-mail: mebrown@brockport.edu

SUNY College & Career Counseling Center

120 Emmons St
Schenectady, NY 12304
518-370-2654 Fax: 518-370-2661

Director:
Lois M Tripp 518-370-2654
e-mail: sunyccc@nycap.rr.com

Syracuse Educational Opportunity Center

100 New St
Syracuse, NY 13202
315-472-0130 Fax: 315-472-1241
e-mail: wallam@morrisville.edu
Web site: www.syracuseeoc.com

Vice President:
Tim Penix 315-472-0130/fax: 315-472-1241

THE CITY UNIVERSITY OF NEW YORK

CUNY Board of Trustees

535 E 80th St
New York, NY 10021
212-794-5450 Fax: 212-794-5678
Web site: www.cuny.edu

Chair:
Benno C. Schmidt Jr. 212-794-5450
Vice Chair:
Philip Alfonso Berry 212-794-5450
Member:
Valerie Lancaster Beal 212-794-5450
Member:
Wellington Z. Chen. 212-794-5450
Member:
Rita DiMartino 212-794-5450
Member:
Freida Foster 212-794-5450
Member:
Judah Gribetz 212-794-5450
Member:
Joseph J. Lhota 212-794-5450
Member:
Hugo M. Morales 212-794-5450
Member:
Brian D. Obergfell 212-794-5450
Member:
Peter S. Pantaleo 212-794-5450
Member:
Kathleen M. Pesile 212-794-5450
Member:
Carol A. Robles-Roman 212-794-5450

Member:
Charles A. Shorter. 212-794-5450
Member:
Jeffrey A. Weisenfeld 212-794-5450
Member:
Kafui Kouakou 212-794-5450
Member:
Terrence F. Martell 212-794-5450

CUNY Central Administration

535 E 80th St
New York, NY 10021
212-794-5555
Web site: www.cuny.edu

Chancellor:
Matthew Goldstein 212-794-5311/fax: 212-794-5671
Executive Vice Chancellor & COO:
Allan H. Dobrin 212-794-5305
Executive Vice Chancellor & University Provost:
Alexandra W. Logue. 212-794-5414
Senior Vice Chancellor, University Relations & Secretary of the Board:
Jay Hershenson 212-794-5317
Senior Vice Chancellor, Legal Affairs & General Counsel:
Frederick P. Schaffer 212-794-5506
Vice Chancellor, Budget & Finance:
Marc Shaw 212-794-5403
Vice Chancellor for Student Affairs:
Frank D. Sanchez 212-794-5775
Vice Chancellor, Labor Relations:
Pamela S. Silverblatt. 212-794-5568
Vice Chancellor, Research:
Gillian Small 212-794-5417
Vice Chancellor, Human Resources Management:
Gloriana Waters 212-794-5353
Vice Chancellor, Facilities Planning, Construction & Management:
Iris Weinshall 212-794-5315
Associate Vice Chancellor & University CIO:
Brian Cohen 212-541-0365

City University Construction Fund . . . . .fax: 212-541-0175

555 W 57th St, 10th Fl, New York, NY 10019
212-541-0171 Fax: 212-541-0175
Acting Chairman:
Philip Berry 212-541-0171
Member:
Wellington Z. Chen. 212-541-5315
Member:
Noel N. Hankin
Executive Director:
Iris Weinshall 212-794-5315
Counsel:
Frederick P. Schaffer 212-794-5506
Deputy Executive Director:
Howard Alschuler. 212-541-0999
Administrative Officer:
Denise Philips 212-541-0190
Special Assistant:
Nancy Nichols. 212-541-0442

Bernard M Baruch College

One Bernard Baruch Way
New York, NY 10010
646-312-1000 Fax: 646-312-1362
Web site: www.baruch.cuny.edu

President:
Mitchel Wallerstein 646-312-3310/fax: 646-312-3311

Offices and agencies generally appear in alphabetical order, except when specific order is requested by listee.

Borough of Manhattan Community College
199 Chambers St
New York, NY 10007
212-220-8000 Fax: 212-220-1244
Web site: www.bmcc.cuny.edu

President:
Antonio Perez 212-220-1230 x1234
e-mail: aperez@bmcc.cuny.edu

Bronx Community College
2155 University Ave
Bronx, NY 10453
718-289-5100
e-mail: webmaster@bcc.cuny.edu
Web site: www.bcc.cuny.edu

Senior VP:
Carolyn Williams 718-289-5151

Brooklyn College
2900 Bedford Ave
Brooklyn, NY 11210
718-951-5000
Web site: www.brooklyn.cuny.edu

President:
Karen L Gould....................718-951-5671/fax: 718-951-4872
e-mail: klgould@brooklyn.cuny.edu

City College of New York, The
160 Covent Ave
New York, NY 10031
212-650-7000
Web site: www1.ccny.cuny.edu

Interim President:
Lisa Staiano-Coico 212-650-7285
e-mail: president@ccny.cuny.edu

College of Staten Island
2800 Victory Blvd
Staten Island, NY 10314
718-982-2000
Web site: www.csi.cuny.edu

President:
Tomas Morales 718-982-2000 x2400
e-mail: president@csi.cuny.edu

Graduate Center
365 Fifth Ave
New York, NY 10016-4309
212-817-7000 or 877-428-6942
Web site: www.gc.cuny.edu

President:
William P Kelly...................212-817-7100/fax: 212-817-1606
e-mail: pres@gc.cuny.edu

Graduate School of Journalism
219 W 40th St
New York, NY 10018
646-758-7800
Web site: www.journalism.cuny.edu

Dean:
Steve Shepard 646-758-7816/fax: 646-758-7809
e-mail: steve.shepard@journalism.cuny.edu

Hostos Community College
500 Grand Concourse
Bronx, NY 10451
718-518-4444 or 718-518-4100
Web site: www.hostos.cuny.edu

President:
Felix V Matos Rodriguez 718-518-4300
e-mail: president@hostos.cuny.edu

Hunter College
695 Park Ave
New York, NY 10021
212-772-4000
Web site: www.hunter.cuny.edu

President:
Jennifer J Raab 212-772-4242/fax: 212-772-4724
e-mail: jennifer.raab@hunter.cuny.edu

John Jay College of Criminal Justice
899 Tenth Ave
New York, NY 10019
212-237-8000 Fax: 212-237-8607
Web site: www.jjay.cuny.edu

President:
Jeremy Travis 212-237-8600
e-mail: jtravis@jjay.cuny.edu

Kingsborough Community College
2001 Oriental Blvd
Brooklyn, NY 11235-2398
718-265-5343
e-mail: info@kbcc.cuny.edu
Web site: www.kbcc.cuny.edu

President:
Regina S Peruggi 718-368-5100
e-mail: president@kingsborough.edu

LaGuardia Community College
31-10 Thomson Ave
Long Island City, NY 11101
718-482-7200
Web site: www.lagcc.cuny.edu

President:
Gail O Mellow 718-482-5050
e-mail: gmellow@lagcc.cuny.edu

Lehman College
250 Bedford Park Blvd West
Bronx, NY 10468
718-960-8000 or 877-534-6261
Web site: www.lehman.edu

President:
Ricardo R Fernandez...............718-960-8111/fax: 718-584-1765
e-mail: president@lehman.cuny.edu

Medgar Evers College
1650 Bedford St
Brooklyn, NY 11225

Offices and agencies generally appear in alphabetical order, except when specific order is requested by listee.

718-270-4900
Web site: www.mec.cuny.edu

President:
William Pollard .718-270-5000/fax: 718-270-5126
e-mail: wlpollard@mec.cuny.edu

New York City College of Technology
300 Jay St
Brooklyn, NY 11201
718-260-5000
e-mail: connect@citytech.cuny.edu
Web site: www.citytech.cuny.edu

President:
Russell K Hotzler 718-260-5400
e-mail: rhotzler@citytech.cuny.edu

Queens College
65-30 Kissena Blvd
Flushing, NY 11367-1597
718-997-5000
Web site: www.qc.cuny.edu

President:
James L Muyskens 718-997-5550/fax: 718-793-8044
e-mail: james.muyskens@qc.cuny.edu

Queensborough Community College
222-05 56th Ave
Bayside, NY 11364-1497
718-631-6262
Web site: www.qcc.cuny.edu

President:
Diane Call 718-631-6222/fax: 718-281-5588

School of Law at Queens College
65-21 Main St
Flushing, NY 11367
718-340-4200 Fax: 718-340-4435
Web site: www.law.cuny.edu

Dean:
Michelle J Anderson 718-340-4201
e-mail: anderson@mail.law.cuny.edu

School of Professional Studies
101 West 31st St
New York, NY 10001
212-652-2869
Web site: sps.cuny.edu

Dean:
John Mogulescu 212-794-5429
e-mail: john.mogulescu@mail.cuny.edu

Sophie Davis School of Biomedical Education
160 Convent Ave
New York, NY 10031
212-650-7000 Fax: 212-650-6696
Web site: med.cuny.edu

Dean:
Eitan Friedman 212-650-5275/fax: 212-650-6696
e-mail: friedman@med.cuny.edu

York College
94-20 Guy R Brewer Blvd
Jamaica, NY 11451
718-262-2000
Web site: york.cuny.edu

President:
Marcia Keizs 718-262-2350/fax: 718-262-2352
e-mail: president@york.cuny.edu

INDEPENDENT COLLEGES & UNIVERSITIES

Adelphi University
1 South Ave
PO Box 701
Garden City, NY 11530
516-877-3050 or 800-233-5744 Fax: 516-877-3090
Web site: www.adelphi.edu

President:
Robert A Scott .516-877-3838/fax: 516-877-3845

Albany College of Pharmacy
106 New Scotland Ave
Albany, NY 12208-3492
518-694-7200 or 888-203-8010 Fax: 518-694-7202
e-mail: info@acphs.edu
Web site: www.acphs.edu

President:
James J Gozzo 518-694-7255
e-mail: gozzoj@acphs.edu

Albany Law School
80 New Scotland Ave
Albany, NY 12208-3494
518-445-2311 Fax: 518-445-2315
e-mail: info@albanylaw.edu
Web site: www.albanylaw.edu

President/Dean:
Thomas F Guernsey 518-445-2380/fax: 518-472-5865
e-mail: tguer@albanylaw.edu

Albany Medical College
43 New Scotland Ave
Albany, NY 12208
518-262-3125 Fax: 518-262-6515
e-mail: webmaster@mail.amc.edu
Web site: www.amc.edu

Dean:
Vincent P Verdile 518-262-6008
e-mail: verdilv@mail.amc.edu

Alfred University
1 Saxon Dr
Alfred, NY 14802-1205
800-541-9229 or 607-871-2175 Fax: 607-871-2339
Web site: www.alfred.edu

President:
Charles M Edmondson 607-871-2101
e-mail: edmondson@alfred.edu

Offices and agencies generally appear in alphabetical order, except when specific order is requested by listee.

American Academy McAllister Institute of Funeral Service
619 West 54th St, 2nd Fl
New York, NY 10019
212-757-1190 Fax: 212-765-5923
e-mail: info@funeraleducation.org
Web site: www.funeraleducation.org

President/CEO:
Meg Dunn 212-757-1190

American Academy of Dramatic Arts
120 Madison Ave
New York, NY 10016-7004
212-686-9244 or 800-463-8990
Web site: www.aada.org

Acting President:
Susan Zech 212-686-9244

Bank Street College of Education/Graduate School
610 West 112th St
New York, NY 10025-1898
212-875-4400 Fax: 212-875-4678
e-mail: collegepubs@bankstreet.edu
Web site: www.bankstreet.edu

President:
Elizabeth D Dickey 212-875-4595/fax: 212-875-4594
e-mail: presidentoffice@bankstreet.edu
Dean, Graduate School:
Virginia Roach 212-875-4466
e-mail: vroach@bankstreet.edu

Bard College
PO Box 5000
Annandale-on-Hudson, NY 12504-5000
845-758-6822 Fax: 845-758-5208
Web site: www.bard.edu

President:
Leon Botstein 845-758-7423
e-mail: president@bard.edu

Barnard College
3009 Broadway
New York, NY 10027
212-854-5262 Fax: 212-854-6220
Web site: www.barnard.edu

President:
Deborah L Spar 212-854-2021
e-mail: dspar@barnard.edu

Boricua College
3755 Broadway
New York, NY 10032
212-694-1000 Fax: 212-694-1015
e-mail: acruz@boricuacollege.edu
Web site: www.boricuacollege.edu

President:
Victor G Alicea 212-694-1000
e-mail: valicea@boricuacollege.edu

Bramson ORT College
69-30 Austin St
Forest Hills, NY 11375-4239
718-261-5800 Fax: 718-575-5118
Web site: www.bramsonort.org

Director:
Ephraim Buhks 718-261-5800 x102
e-mail: ebuhks@bramsonort.edu

Brooklyn Law School
250 Joralemon St
Brooklyn, NY 11201-3798
718-625-2200 Fax: 718-780-0393
Web site: www.brooklaw.edu

President:
Joan G Wexler 718-780-7900
e-mail: joan.wexler@brooklaw.edu

Canisius College
2001 Main St
Buffalo, NY 14208-1098
716-883-7000 Fax: 716-888-2525
Web site: www.canisius.edu

President:
John J Huxley 716-888-2100/fax: 716-888-3220

Cazenovia College
22 Sullivan St
Cazenovia, NY 13035
315-655-7000 or 800-654-3210 Fax: 315-655-4143
e-mail: admissions@cazenovia.edu
Web site: www.cazenovia.edu

President:
Mark John Tierno 315-655-7116
e-mail: mtierno@cazenovia.edu

Christ the King Seminary
711 Knox Rd
East Aurora, NY 14052-0607
716-652-8900 Fax: 716-652-8903
e-mail: cksacad@cks.edu
Web site: www.cks.edu

President/Rector:
Rev Peter J Drilling 716-652-8900
e-mail: pdrilling@cks.edu

Clarkson University
8 Clarkson Ave
Potsdam, NY 13699
315-268-6400 or 800-527-6577 Fax: 315-268-7993
Web site: www.clarkson.edu

President:
Anthony G Collins 315-268-6444
e-mail: collins@clarkson.edu

Cochran School of Nursing
St John's Riverside Hospital
967 N Broadway, Andrus Pavilion
Yonkers, NY 10701

Offices and agencies generally appear in alphabetical order, except when specific order is requested by listee.

914-964-4296 Fax: 914-964-4266
e-mail: admissions@cochranschoolofnursing.us
Web site: www.cochranschoolofnursing.us

Vice President & Dean:
  Kathleen Dirschel 914-964-4280
  e-mail: kdirschel@riversidehealth.org
Director, Administration:
  David T George 914-964-4296
  e-mail: dgeorge@riversidehealth.org

Colgate Rochester Crozer Divinity School
1100 S Goodman St
Rochester, NY 14620-2589
585-271-1320 Fax: 585-271-8013
Web site: www.crcds.edu

President:
  Rev. Jack McKelvey 585-340-9680

Colgate University
13 Oak Dr
Hamilton, NY 13346
315-228-1000 Fax: 315-228-7798
Web site: www.colgate.edu

President:
  Jeffrey Herbst 315-228-7444/fax: 315-228-6010
  e-mail: jherbst@colgate.edu

College of Mount Saint Vincent
6301 Riverdale Ave
Riverdale, NY 10471-1093
800-665-2678 or 718-405-3267
Web site: www.mountsaintvincent.edu

President:
  Charles L Flynn Jr. 718-405-3233
  e-mail: president@mountsaintvincent.edu

College of New Rochelle (The)
Brooklyn Campus
29 Castle Pl
New Rochelle, NY 10805-2339
914-654-5000 or 800-211-7077 Fax: 914-654-5833
e-mail: info@cnr.edu
Web site: www.cnr.edu

President:
  Stephen J Sweeny 914-654-5430
  e-mail: ssweeny@cnr.edu

College of Saint Rose (The)
432 Western Ave
Albany, NY 12203-1490
800-637-8556
Web site: www.strose.edu

President:
  R Mark Sullivan 518-454-5120
  e-mail: sullivan@strose.edu

Columbia University
2960 Broadway
New York, NY 10027
212-854-1754 Fax: 212-854-9973
Web site: www.columbia.edu

President:
  Lee C Bollinger 212-854-9970/fax: 212-854-9973
  e-mail: officeofthepresident@columbia.edu

Concordia College
171 White Plains Rd
Bronxville, NY 10708
914-337-9300 Fax: 914-395-4500
Web site: www.concordia-ny.edu

President:
  Viji D George 914-337-9300 x2111
  e-mail: viji.george@concordia-ny.edu

Cooper Union for the Advancement of Science & Art
30 Cooper Sq, 8th floor
New York, NY 10003-7120
212-353-4100 Fax: 212-353-4327
e-mail: webmaster@cooper.edu
Web site: www.cooper.edu

President:
  Jamshed Bhurucha 212-353-4195

Cornell University
300 Day Hall
Ithaca, NY 14853
607-254-4636 Fax: 607-254-5175
e-mail: info@cornell.edu
Web site: www.cornell.edu

President:
  David J Skorton .607-255-5201/fax: 607-255-9924
  e-mail: president@cornell.edu

Crouse Hospital School of Nursing
736 Irving Ave
Syracuse, NY 13210
315-470-7481 Fax: 315-470-7232
e-mail: crouseson@crouse.org
Web site: www.crouse.org/nursing

Director:
  Ann Sedore 315-470-7932

Culinary Institute of America
1946 Campus Dr
Hyde Park, NY 12538-1499
845-452-9600 or 800-285-4627 Fax: 845-451-1068
e-mail: admissions@culinary.edu
Web site: www.ciachef.edu

President:
  Tim Ryan. 845-451-1352

D'Youville College
320 Porter Ave
Buffalo, NY 14201
716-829-8000 or 800-777-3921 Fax: 716-881-7790
Web site: www.dyc.edu

President:
  Sister Denise A Roche 716-829-7673
  e-mail: roche@dyc.edu

Daemen College
4380 Main St
Amherst, NY 14226

Offices and agencies generally appear in alphabetical order, except when specific order is requested by listee.

716-839-3600 or 800-462-7652 Fax: 716-839-8516
Web site: www.daemen.edu

President:
   Martin J Anisman 716-839-8210/fax: 716-839-8279
   e-mail: manisman@daemen.edu

Davis College
400 Riverside Dr
Johnson City, NY 13790
607-729-1581 or 877-949-3248 Fax: 607-729-2962
e-mail: info@davisny.edu
Web site: www.davisny.edu

President:
   Dino Pedrone 607-729-1581 x316/fax: 607-729-1581
   e-mail: president@davisny.edu

Dominican College
470 Western Highway
Orangeburg, NY 10962
845-359-7800 Fax: 845-359-2313
Web site: www.dc.edu

President:
   Sister Mary Eileen O'Brien 845-848-7801/fax: 845-359-7988
   e-mail: mary.eileen.obrien@dc.edu

Dorothea Hopfer School of Nursing at Mount Vernon Hospital
53 Valentine St
Mount Vernon, NY 10550
914-361-6221 Fax: 914-665-7047
e-mail: hopferadmissions@sshsw.org
Web site: www.hopfer.org

Dean of Nursing Education:
   Joanna Scalabrini 914-361-6220
   e-mail: hopfer@sshsw.org

Dowling College
150 Idle Hour Blvd
Oakdale, NY 11769
800-369-5464 Fax: 631-589-6644
Web site: www.dowling.edu

President:
   Jeremy Brown 631-244-3200

Ellis Hospital School of Nursing
1101 Nott St
Schenectady, NY 12308
518-243-4471 Fax: 518-243-4470
Web site: www.ehson.org

Director:
   Marilyn Stapleton 518-243-4471
CEO:
   Jim Connolly 518-243-4000

Elmira College
One Park Pl
Elmira, NY 14901
607-735-1800 or 800-935-6472
e-mail: admissions@elmira.edu
Web site: www.elmira.edu

President:
   Thomas K Meier 607-735-1790
   e-mail: tmeier@elmira.edu

Excelsior College
7 Columbia Cir
Albany, NY 12203-5159
518-464-8500 or 888-647-2388 Fax: 518-464-8777
e-mail: info@excelsior.edu
Web site: www.excelsior.edu

President:
   John F Ebersole 518-464-8500

Fordham University
Rose Hill
441 East Fordham Rd
Bronx, NY 10458
718-817-1000
Web site: www.fordham.edu

President:
   Joseph M McShane 718-817-3000/fax: 718-817-3005

General Theological Seminary of the Episcopal Church
175 Ninth Ave
Chelsea Sq
New York, NY 10011-4977
212-243-5150 Fax: 212-727-3907
Web site: www.gts.edu

Interim President/Dean:
   Lang Lowrey 212-243-5150 x302

Hamilton College
198 College Hill Rd
Clinton, NY 13323
315-859-4421 or 800-843-2655 Fax: 315-859-4457
Web site: www.hamilton.edu

President:
   Joan Hinde Stewart 315-859-4104
   e-mail: jstewart@hamilton.edu

Hartwick College
PO Box 4020
Oneonta, NY 13820-4020
800-427-8942 or 607-431-4000 Fax: 607-431-4102
Web site: www.hartwick.edu

President:
   Dr Margaret L Drugovich 607-431-4990
   e-mail: president@hartwick.edu

Hebrew Union College - Jewish Institute of Religion
The Brookdale Center
One W 4th St
New York, NY 10012
212-674-5300 Fax: 212-388-1720
Web site: www.huc.edu

President:
   David Ellenson 800-424-1336 x2201/fax: 212-979-0853
   e-mail: presoff@huc.edu

Helene Fuld College of Nursing North General Hospital
24 East 120th St
New York, NY 10035

Offices and agencies generally appear in alphabetical order, except when specific order is requested by listee.

212-616-7200
Web site: www.helenefuld.edu

President:
  Margaret Wines.....................................212-423-2750

Hilbert College
5200 South Park Ave
Hamburg, NY 14075
716-649-7900 Fax: 716-649-0702
e-mail: info@hilbert.edu
Web site: www.hilbert.edu

President:
  Cynthia Zane 716-649-7900 x200
  e-mail: czane@hilbert.edu

Hobart & William Smith Colleges
300 Pulteney Street
Geneva, NY 14456
315-781-3000 or 800-852-2256
Web site: www.hws.edu

President:
  Mark D Gearan 315-781-3309
  e-mail: gearan@hws.edu

Hofstra University
100 Fulton Ave
Hempstead, NY 11550
800-463-7872 or 516-463-6600 Fax: 516-463-4867
Web site: www.hofstra.edu

President:
  Stuart Rabinowitz 516-463-6800/fax: 516-463-6096
  e-mail: president@hofstra.edu

Houghton College
1 Willard Ave
Houghton, NY 14744-0128
800-777-2556 Fax: 585-567-9572
Web site: www.houghton.edu

President:
  Shirley Mullen 585-567-9526
  e-mail: cindy.lastoria@houghton.edu

Institute of Design & Construction
141 Willoughby St
Brooklyn, NY 11201
718-855-3661 Fax: 718-852-5889
e-mail: info@idc.edu
Web site: www.idc.edu

Executive Director:
  Vincent C Battista...............................718-855-3661
  e-mail: vcbattista@idc.edu

Iona College
715 North Ave
New Rochelle, NY 10801
914-633-2000 or 800-231-4662 Fax: 914-633-2018
Web site: www.iona.edu

President:
  Joseph Nyre.......................................914-633-2203

Ithaca College
953 Danby Rd
Ithaca, NY 14850
607-274-3011 Fax: 607-274-1900
e-mail: thurston@ithaca.edu
Web site: www.ithaca.edu

President:
  Thomas R Rochon.................607-274-3111/fax: 607-274-3064
  e-mail: president@ithaca.edu

Jewish Theological Seminary
3080 Broadway
New York, NY 10027-4649
212-678-8000 Fax: 212-678-8947
Web site: www.jtsa.edu

Chancellor/President of Faculties:
  Arnold Eisen......................................212-678-8072
  e-mail: arreisen@jtsa.edu

Juilliard School (The)
60 Lincoln Center Plz
New York, NY 10023-6588
212-799-5000 Fax: 212-724-0263
Web site: www.juilliard.edu

President:
  Joseph W Polisi............................212-799-5000 X207
Dean & Provost:
  Ara Guzalimian 212-799-5000 x204

Keuka College
141 Central Ave
Keuka Park, NY 14478
315-279-5000 or 800-335-3852 Fax: 315-279-5216
Web site: www.keuka.edu

President:
  Joseph Burke.....................315-279-5201/fax: 315-279-5335
  e-mail: president@keuka.edu

King's College (The)
Empire State Bldg
350 Fifth Ave, Ste 1500
New York, NY 10118
888-969-7200 or 212-659-7200 Fax: 212-659-7210
e-mail: information@tkc.edu
Web site: www.tkc.edu

President:
  Dinesh D'Souza 212-659-7200

Le Moyne College
1419 Salt Springs Rd
Syracuse, NY 13214-1301
315-445-4100 Fax: 315-445-4540
Web site: www.lemoyne.edu

President:
  Dr. Fred Pestello.................................315-445-4120
  e-mail: president@lemoyne.edu

Long Island College Hospital School of Nursing
340 Court St
Brooklyn, NY 11231

Offices and agencies generally appear in alphabetical order, except when specific order is requested by listee.

718-780-1953 Fax: 718-780-1936
Web site: www.futurenurselich.org

Dean:
  Nancy Dimauro...................................718-780-1998

Long Island University
700 Northern Blvd
Brookville, NY 11548
516-299-2000 Fax: 516-299-2072
Web site: www.liu.edu

President:
  David J Steinberg 516-299-2501/fax: 516-229-2590
  e-mail: president@liu.edu

Manhattan College
4513 Manhattan College Pkwy
Riverdale, NY 10471
718-862-8000 or 800-622-9235
Web site: www.manhattan.edu

President:
  Brother Brennan O'Donnell 718-862-7301/fax: 718-862-8030
  e-mail: brennan.odonnell@manhattan.edu

Manhattan School of Music
120 Claremont Ave
New York, NY 10027
212-749-2802 Fax: 212-749-5471
Web site: www.msmnyc.edu

President:
  Robert Sirota 212-749-2802 x4477
  e-mail: officeofthepresident@msmnyc.edu

Manhattanville College
2900 Purchase St
Purchase, NY 10577
914-694-2200 Fax: 914-694-2386
Web site: www.manhattanville.edu

President:
  Molly E Smith....................914-323-5230/fax: 914-694-6234
  e-mail: president@mville.edu

Maria College of Albany
700 New Scotland Ave
Albany, NY 12208
518-438-3111 Fax: 518-453-1366
Web site: www.mariacollege.edu

President:
  Sister Laureen A Fitzgerald.....................518-438-3111 x213
  e-mail: lfitz@mariacollege.edu

Marist College
3399 North Rd
Poughkeepsie, NY 12601
845-575-3000
e-mail: timmian.massie@marist.edu
Web site: www.marist.edu

President:
  Dennis J Murray 845-575-3600
  e-mail: dennis.murray@marist.edu

Marymount Manhattan College
221 East 71st St
New York, NY 10021
800-627-9668 or 212-517-0400 Fax: 212-517-0567
Web site: www.mmm.edu

President:
  Judson R Shaver 212-517-0560
  e-mail: jshaver@mmm.edu

Medaille College
18 Agassiz Cir
Buffalo, NY 14214
716-880-2000 or 800-292-1582
Web site: www.medaille.edu

President:
  Richard Jurasek..................................716-880-2201
  e-mail: richard.t.jurasek@medaille.edu

Memorial Hospital School of Nursing
600 Northern Blvd
Albany, NY 12204
518-471-3221 Fax: 518-447-3559
e-mail: dorseyp@nehealth.com
Web site: www.nehealth.com

Director:
  Mary-Jane Araldi 518-471-3260
  e-mail: martinm@nehealth.com

Mercy College
Main Campus
555 Broadway
Dobbs Ferry, NY 10522
877-637-2946 Fax: 914-674-7382
e-mail: admissions@mercy.edu
Web site: www.mercy.edu

President:
  Kimberly Cline 914-674-7307/fax: 914-674-5978
  e-mail: Kcline@mercy.edu

Metropolitan College of New York
431 Canal St
New York, NY 10013
212-343-1234 or 800-338-4465 Fax: 212-343-7399
Web site: www.metropolitan.edu

President:
  Vinton Thompson 212-343-1234 x3301
  e-mail: vthompson@metropolitan.edu

Mid-America Baptist Theological Seminary Northeast Branch
2810 Curry Rd
Schenectady, NY 12303
518-355-4000 or 800-209-3447 Fax: 518-355-8298
e-mail: mjohn@mabtsne.edu
Web site: www.mabts.edu

Director:
  Shawn Buice.....................................518-355-4000
  e-mail: sbuice@mabtsne.edu

Offices and agencies generally appear in alphabetical order, except when specific order is requested by listee.

Molloy College
1000 Hempstead Ave
PO Box 5002
Rockville Centre, NY 11571-5002
516-678-5000 or 888-466-5569
Web site: www.molloy.edu

President:
   Drew Bogner 516-678-5000 x6200/fax: 516-678-5321
   e-mail: presidentdrew@molloy.edu

Mount Saint Mary College
330 Powell Ave
Newburgh, NY 12550
845-561-0800 Fax: 845-562-6762
Web site: www.msmc.edu

President:
   Fr Kevin E Mackin OFM 845-569-3202
   e-mail: mackin@msmc.edu

Mount Sinai School of Medicine of NYU
One Gustave L Levy Pl
New York, NY 10029-6574
212-241-6500
Web site: www.mssm.edu

President/CEO/Dean:
   Kenneth L Davis 212-659-8888/fax: 212-659-9800
   e-mail: kenneth.davis@mssm.edu

Nazareth College of Rochester
4245 East Ave
Rochester, NY 14618-7390
585-389-2525 Fax: 585-586-2452
Web site: www.naz.edu

President:
   Daan Braveman .585-389-2004/fax: 585-389-2015
   e-mail: dbravem7@naz.edu

New School University (The)
66 West 12th St
New York, NY 10011
212-229-5600 Fax: 212-229-5937
e-mail: kerreyb@newschool.edu
Web site: www.newschool.edu

President:
   David VanZandt 212-229-5656
Dean:
   Linda Dunne 212-229-5613
   e-mail: dunnel@newschool.edu

New York Academy of Art Inc
111 Franklin St
New York, NY 10013
212-966-0300 Fax: 212-966-3217
e-mail: info@nyaa.edu
Web site: www.nyaa.edu

President:
   David Kratz 212-966-0300
Dean:
   Peter Drake 212-966-0300

New York Chiropractic College
2360 Route 89
Seneca Falls, NY 13148
315-568-3000 or 800-234-6922 Fax: 315-568-3012
Web site: www.nycc.edu

President:
   Frank J Nicchi 315-568-3100
   e-mail: fnicchi@nycc.edu

New York College of Health Professions
6801 Jericho Tpke
Suite 300
Syosset, NY 11791
516-364-0808 or 800-922-7337 Fax: 516-364-0989
e-mail: info@nycollege.edu
Web site: www.nycollege.edu

President:
   Lisa E Pamintuan 516-364-0808
   e-mail: pamintuan@nycollege.edu

New York College of Podiatric Medicine
53 East 124th St.
New York, NY 10035-1940
212-410-8000 Fax: 212-722-4918
e-mail: admissions@nycpm.edu
Web site: www.nycpm.edu

President/CEO:
   Louis L Levine .212-410-8024/fax: 212-876-7670
   e-mail: llevine@nycpm.edu

New York College of Traditional Chinese Medicine
155 First St.
Mineola, NY 11501
516-739-1545
Web site: www.nyctcm.edu

President:
   Yemeng Chen 212-685-0888

New York Institute of Technology
Northern Blvd
PO Box 8000
Old Westbury, NY 11568-8000
516-686-1000 or 800-345-6948 Fax: 516-686-7613
e-mail: asknyit@nyit.edu
Web site: www.nyit.edu

President/CEO:
   Edward Guiliano 516-686-7650
   e-mail: president@nyit.edu

New York Law School
185 W Broadway
New York, NY 10013
212-431-2872 or 212-431-2100 Fax: 212-406-0103
e-mail: alevat@nyls.edu
Web site: www.nyls.edu

President/Dean:
   Richard A Matasar 212-431-2840/fax: 212-219-3752
   e-mail: ddean@nyls.edu

Offices and agencies generally appear in alphabetical order, except when specific order is requested by listee.

New York Medical College
Administration Bldg
40 Sunshine Cottage Rd
Valhalla, NY 10595
914-594-4000
Web site: www.nymc.edu

President/CEO:
Karl P Adler, M.D. 914-594-4600

New York School of Interior Design
170 East 70th St
New York, NY 10021
212-472-1500 or 800-336-9743 Fax: 212-472-3800
e-mail: info@nysid.edu
Web site: www.nysid.edu

President:
Christopher Cyphers. 212-472-1500 x401/fax: 212-472-1952

New York Theological Seminary
475 Riverside Dr, Ste 500
New York, NY 10115-0083
212-870-1211 Fax: 212-870-1236
e-mail: online@nyts.edu
Web site: www.nyts.edu

President:
Dale T Irvin. 212-870-1223
e-mail: dirvin@nyts.edu

New York University
70 Washington Square South
New York, NY 10012
212-998-1212
Web site: www.nyu.edu

President:
John Sexton .212-998-2345/fax: 212-995-4790
e-mail: john.sexton@nyu.edu

Niagara University
Lewiston Rd
Niagara University, NY 14109
716-285-1212 or 800-778-3450 Fax: 716-286-8710
Web site: www.niagara.edu

President:
Rev Joseph L Levesque. 716-286-8350/fax: 716-286-8350
e-mail: jll@niagara.edu

Northeastern Seminary
2265 Westside Dr
Rochester, NY 14624
585-594-6802 or 800-777-4792 Fax: 585-594-6801
e-mail: seminary@roberts.edu
Web site: www.nes.edu

President:
John A Martin. 585-594-6100
e-mail: martinj@roberts.edu

Nyack College
1 South Blvd
Nyack, NY 10960-3698

845-358-1710 Fax: 845-358-1751
e-mail: president@nyack.edu
Web site: www.nyack.edu

President:
Michael Scales. 845-358-1710 x310

Pace University
1 Pace Plz
New York, NY 10038
212-346-1200 or 800-722-3338 Fax: 212-346-1933
Web site: www.pace.edu

President:
Stephen J Friedman 212-346-1097/fax: 212-346-1384
e-mail: sfriedman@pace.edu

Paul Smith's College
Routes 86 & 30
PO Box 265
Paul Smiths, NY 12970-0265
518-327-6227 or 800-421-2605 Fax: 518-327-6016
e-mail: kaaron@paulsmiths.edu
Web site: www.paulsmiths.edu

President/Acting Provost:
John W Mills 518-327-6223/fax: 518-327-6060
e-mail: millsj@paulsmiths.edu

Phillips Beth Israel School of Nursing
776 Ave of Americas
4th Fl
New York, NY 10001-6354
212-614-6110 Fax: 212-614-6109
Web site: www.futurenursebi.org

Dean:
Janet MacKin 212-614-6107
e-mail: jmackin@chpnet.org

Polytechnic University
Main Campus
6 MetroTech Ctr
Brooklyn, NY 11201-2999
718-260-3600 Fax: 718-260-3136
e-mail: inquiry@poly.edu
Web site: www.poly.edu

President:
Jerry MacArthur Hultin 718-260-3500/fax: 718-260-3755
e-mail: hultin@poly.edu

Pratt Institute
200 Willoughby Ave
Brooklyn, NY 11205
718-636-3600 Fax: 718-636-3785
e-mail: info@pratt.edu
Web site: www.pratt.edu

President:
Thomas F Schutte 718-636-3646
e-mail: tschutte@pratt.edu

Professional Business College
125 Canal St
New York, NY 10002

Offices and agencies generally appear in alphabetical order, except when specific order is requested by listee.

212-226-7300
Web site: www.pbcny.edu

President:
Leon Y Lee 212-226-7300

Rensselaer Polytechnic Institute
110 8th St
Troy, NY 12180
518-276-6000
Web site: www.rpi.edu

President:
Shirley Ann Jackson 518-276-6211/fax: 518-276-8702
e-mail: president@rpi.edu

Roberts Wesleyan College
2301 Westside Dr
Rochester, NY 14624-1997
585-594-6000 or 800-777-4792 Fax: 585-594-6371
e-mail: admissions@roberts.edu
Web site: www.roberts.edu

President:
John A Martin .585-594-6100/fax: 585-594-6780
e-mail: presidentsoffice@roberts.edu

Rochester Institute of Technology
One Lomb Memorial Dr
Rochester, NY 14623-5603
585-475-2411 Fax: 585-475-5700
Web site: www.rit.edu

President:
William W Destler 585-475-2394
e-mail: bill.destler@rit.edu

Rochester, University of
Wallis Hall
Administration
Rochester, NY 14627
585-275-2121 Fax: 585-275-0359
Web site: www.rochester.edu

President:
Joel Seligman. 585-275-8356/fax: 585-256-2473
e-mail: seligman@rochester.edu

Rockefeller University
1230 York Ave
New York, NY 10065
212-327-8000 Fax: 212-327-7974
e-mail: pubinfo@rockefeller.edu
Web site: www.rockefeller.edu

President:
Marc Tessier-Lavigne. 212-327-8000
e-mail: marc.tessier-lavigne@rockefeller.edu

Sage Colleges (The)
65 1st Street
Troy, NY 12180
518-244-2000 or 888-837-9724 Fax: 518-244-2470
Web site: www.sage.edu

President:
Susan Scrimshaw 518-244-2214
e-mail: scrims@sage.edu

Salvation Army School for Officer Training
201 Lafayette Ave
Suffern, NY 10901
845-368-7200 Fax: 845-357-6644
Web site: www.use.salvationarmy.org

Director of Business:
Major Ivan Rock 845-244-2214
e-mail: Ivan.Rock@use.salvationarmy.org

Samaritan Hospital School of Nursing
2215 Burdett Ave
Troy, NY 12180
518-271-3300 Fax: 518-271-3303
e-mail: dorseyp@nehealth.com
Web site: www.nehealth.com

Director:
Susan Birkhead 518-271-3285

Sarah Lawrence College
1 Mead Way
Bronxville, NY 10708-5999
914-337-0700 Fax: 914-395-2515
e-mail: slcadmit@slc.edu
Web site: www.slc.edu

President:
Karen Lawrence. 914-395-2201/fax: 914-395-2668
e-mail: president@sarahlawrence.edu
Dean:
Jerrilynne Dodds 914-395-2303
e-mail: jdodds@sarahlawrence.edu

Seminary of the Immaculate Conception
440 West Neck Rd
Huntington, NY 11743
631-423-0483 Fax: 631-423-2346
e-mail: info@icseminary.edu
Web site: www.icseminary.edu

Rector:
Rev Msgr Peter Vaccari 631-423-0483
e-mail: pvaccari@icseminary.edu

Siena College
515 Loudon Rd
Loudonville, NY 12211-1462
518-783-2300 or 888-287-4362 Fax: 518-783-4293
Web site: www.siena.edu

President:
Fr Kevin Mullen 518-783-2302
e-mail: kmullen@siena.edu

Skidmore College
815 N Broadway
Saratoga Springs, NY 12866-1632
518-580-5000 Fax: 518-580-5699
e-mail: info@skidmore.edu
Web site: www.skidmore.edu

President:
Philip A Glotzbach 518-580-5700/fax: 518-580-5699
e-mail: pglotzba@skidmore.edu

Offices and agencies generally appear in alphabetical order, except when specific order is requested by listee.

St Bernard's School of Theology & Ministry
120 French Rd
Rochester, NY 14618
585-271-3657 Fax: 585-271-2045
Web site: www.stbernards.edu

President:
Patricia A Schoelles............................585-271-3657 x298
e-mail: pschoelles@stbernards.edu

St Bonaventure University
3261 W State Rd
St Bonaventure, NY 14778-2284
716-375-2000 or 800-462-5050
Web site: www.sbu.edu

President:
Sister Margaret Carney............................716-375-2222
e-mail: mcarney@sbu.edu

St Elizabeth College of Nursing
2215 Genesee St
Utica, NY 13501
315-798-8144 Fax: 315-798-8271
e-mail: conadmin@secon.edu
Web site: www.secon.edu

Interim President:
Marian Kovatchitch 315-798-8125
e-mail: mkovatch@secon.edu

St Francis College
180 Remsen St
Brooklyn Heights, NY 11201
718-489-5200 or 718-522-2300 Fax: 718-237-8964
Web site: www.stfranciscollege.edu

President:
Brendan J Dugan................................718-489-5416
e-mail: bdugan@stfranciscollege.edu

St John Fisher College
3690 East Ave
Rochester, NY 14618
585-385-8000 Fax: 585-385-8289
Web site: www.sjfc.edu

President:
Donald E Bain...................................585-385-8010
e-mail: dbain@sjfc.edu

St John's University
Queens Campus
8000 Utopia Pkwy
Queens, NY 11439
718-990-2000 or 888-978-5646 Fax: 718-990-5723
e-mail: admhelp@stjohns.edu
Web site: www.stjohns.edu

President:
Rev Donald J Harrington 718-990-6301
e-mail: pres@stjohns.edu

St Joseph's College
Main Campus
245 Clinton Ave
Brooklyn, NY 11205-3688

718-940-5300 Fax: 718-636-7242
Web site: www.sjcny.edu

President:
Elizabeth A Hill....................718-940-5989/fax: 718-636-6102
e-mail: ehill@sjcny.edu

St Joseph's Seminary Institute of Religious Studies
201 Seminary Ave
Yonkers, NY 10704-1896
914-968-6200 Fax: 914-376-2019
e-mail: vocations@archny.org
Web site: www.ny-archdiocese.org/seminary

Dean:
Kevin P O'Reilly 914-968-6200

St Lawrence University
23 Romoda Dr
Canton, NY 13617
315-229-5011 or 800-285-1856 Fax: 315-229-7422
Web site: www.stlawu.edu

President:
William L Fox....................................315-229-5892
e-mail: wfox@stlawu.edu

St Thomas Aquinas College
125 Route 340
Sparkill, NY 10976-1050
845-398-4100
Web site: www.stac.edu

President/CEO:
Margaret M Fitzpatrick 845-398-4012/fax: 845-359-8136
e-mail: mfitzpat@stac.edu

St Vladimir's Orthodox Theological Seminary
575 Scarsdale Rd
Yonkers, NY 10707
914-961-8313 Fax: 914-961-4507
e-mail: info@svots.edu
Web site: www.svots.edu

Dean:
Very Rev John Behr 914-961-8313 X326
e-mail: jbehr@svots.edu

Sunbridge College
285 Hungry Hollow Rd
Chesnut Ridge, NY 10977
845-425-0055 Fax: 845-425-1413
e-mail: info@sunbridge.edu
Web site: www.sunbridge.edu

Executive Director:
Jessica H Ziegler 845-425-0055 x23
e-mail: jziegler@sunbridge.edu

Syracuse University
Skytop Office Building
Syracuse, NY 13244-1100
315-443-1870 Fax: 315-443-3503
Web site: www.syr.edu

Chancellor & President:
Nancy Cantor 315-443-2235
e-mail: ncantor@syr.edu

Offices and agencies generally appear in alphabetical order, except when specific order is requested by listee.

Teachers College, Columbia University
525 W 120th St
New York, NY 10027
212-678-3000
Web site: www.tc.columbia.edu

President:
Dr Susan H Fuhrman 212-678-3131/fax: 212-678-3205
e-mail: susanf@exchange.tc.columbia.edu

Touro College
27-33 W 23rd St
New York, NY 10010
212-463-0400 Fax: 212-627-9144
Web site: www.touro.edu

President/CEO:
Alan Kadish 718-820-4900

Trocaire College
360 Choate Ave
Buffalo, NY 14220-2094
716-826-1200 Fax: 716-828-6109
e-mail: info@trocaire.edu
Web site: www.trocaire.edu

President:
Paul B Hurley, Jr. 716-826-1200
e-mail: hurleyp@trocaire.edu

Unification Theological Seminary
30 Seminary Dr
Barrytown, NY 12507
845-752-3000 Fax: 845-752-3014
e-mail: registrar@uts.edu
Web site: www.uts.edu

President:
Richard Panzer 212-563-6647 x110

Union College
807 Union St
Schenectady, NY 12308-3107
518-388-6000 Fax: 518-388-6006
Web site: www.union.edu

President-Elect:
Stephen C Ainlay 518-388-6101
e-mail: ainlays@union.edu
Dean:
Steve Leavitt 518-388-6116/fax: 518-388-6648
e-mail: leavitts@union.edu

Union Theological Seminary
3041 Broadway at 121st St
New York, NY 10027
212-662-7100 Fax: 212-280-1416
e-mail: contactus@uts.columbia.edu
Web site: www.utsnyc.edu

President:
Serene Jones 212-280-1403
e-mail: sjones@uts.columbia.edu

Utica College
1600 Burrstone Rd
Utica, NY 13502-5159

315-792-3006 Fax: 315-792-3003
Web site: www.utica.edu

President:
Todd S Hutton 315-792-3222
e-mail: thutton@utica.edu

Vassar College
124 Raymond Ave
Poughkeepsie, NY 12604
845-437-7000 Fax: 845-437-7187
Web site: www.vassar.edu

President:
Catharine B Hill 845-437-7200

Vaughn College of Aeronautics & Technology
86-01 23rd Ave
Flushing, NY 11369
718-429-6600 or 866-682-8446 Fax: 718-779-2231
Web site: www.vaughn.edu

President:
John C Fitzpatrick 718-429-6600 x104/fax: 718-429-4020
e-mail: john.fitzpatrick@vaughn.edu

Villa Maria College of Buffalo
240 Pine Ridge Rd
Buffalo, NY 14225
716-896-0700 Fax: 716-961-1871
e-mail: admissions@villa.edu
Web site: www.villa.edu

President:
Sr Marcella Marie Garus 716-961-1868
e-mail: smgarus@villa.edu

Wagner College
1 Campus Rd
Staten Island, NY 10301
718-390-3100 or 800-221-1010 Fax: 718-390-3105
Web site: www.wagner.edu

President:
Richard Guarasci 718-390-3131/fax: 718-390-3170
e-mail: guarasci@wagner.edu

Watson School of Biological Sciences at Cold Spring Harbor Laboratory
One Bungtown Rd
Cold Spring Harbor, NY 11724
516-367-8800 Fax: 516-367-6919
e-mail: gradschool@cshl.edu
Web site: www.cshl.edu/gradschool

President/CEO:
Bruce Stillman 516-367-6890

Webb Institute
298 Crescent Beach Rd
Glen Cove, NY 11542-1398
516-671-2213 or 866-708-9322 Fax: 516-674-9838
Web site: www.webb-institute.edu

President:
Admiral Robert Olsen 516-671-2213 x102
e-mail: rolsen@webb-institute.edu

Offices and agencies generally appear in alphabetical order, except when specific order is requested by listee.

Wells College
170 Main St
Aurora, NY 13026-0500
315-364-3266
Web site: www.wells.edu

President:
Lisa Marsh Ryerson. 315-364-3265/fax: 315-364-3335
e-mail: president@wells.edu

Yeshiva University
Wilf Campus
500 W 185th St
New York, NY 10033-3201
212-960-5400
e-mail: administration@yu.edu
Web site: www.yu.edu

President:
Richard M Joel 212-960-5300
e-mail: president@yu.edu

PROPRIETARY COLLEGES

ASA Institute of Business & Computer Technology
81 Willoughby St
Brooklyn, NY 11201
877-679-8772
Web site: www.asa.edu

President:
Alex Shchegol. 877-679-8772

Art Institue of New York City (The)
11 Beach St
New York, NY 10013
212-226-5500 or 800-654-2433 Fax: 212-818-1079
e-mail: ainycadm@aii.edu
Web site: www.artinstitutes.edu/newyork/

President:
David Warren

Berkeley College, New York City Campus
3 East 43rd St
New York, NY 10017
212-986-4343 or 800-446-5400 Fax: 212-697-3371
e-mail: info@berkeleycollege.edu
Web site: www.berkeleycollege.edu

President:
Darlo A Cortes. 973-278-5400 x1102
e-mail: president@berkeleycollege.edu

Berkeley College, Westchester Campus
99 Church St
White Plains, NY 10601
914-694-1122 Fax: 914-328-9469
e-mail: info@berkeleycollege.edu
Web site: www.berkeleycollege.edu

SVP, Administration:
Cynthia Rubino. 914-694-1122

Briarcliffe College-Bethpage
1055 Stewart Ave
Bethpage, NY 11714
516-918-3600 or 88-348-4999 Fax: 516-470-6020
e-mail: info@bcl.edu
Web site: www.bcbeth.com

President:
George Santiago, Jr. 516-918-3603
e-mail: gsantiago@bcl.edu

Briarcliffe College-Patchogue
225 West Main St
Patchogue, NY 11772
631-654-5300
Web site: www.bcpat.com

President:
George Santiago, Jr. 631-654-5300

Bryant & Stratton College-Albany Campus
1259 Central Ave
Albany, NY 12205
518-437-1802
e-mail: rpferrell@bryantstratton.edu
Web site: www.bryantstratton.edu

Campus Director:
Michael Gutierrez. 518-437-1802
e-mail: magutierrez@bryantstratton.edu

Bryant & Stratton College-Amherst Campus
3650 Millersport Highway
Getzville, NY 14068
716-625-6300
e-mail: amherst@brayntstratton.edu
Web site: www.bryantstratton.edu

Campus Director:
Michael Mariani 716-625-6300

Bryant & Stratton College-Buffalo Campus
465 Main St, Ste 400
Buffalo, NY 14203
716-884-9120
e-mail: buffalo@bryantstratton.edu
Web site: www.bryantstratton.edu

Campus Director:
Marvel Ross-Jones 716-884-9120

Bryant & Stratton College-Greece Campus
150 Bellwood Dr
Rochester, NY 14606
585-720-0660
e-mail: bjdinell@bryantstratton.edu
Web site: www.bryantstratton.edu

Campus Director:
Marc Ambrosi. 585-720-0660

Bryant & Stratton College-Henrietta Campus
1225 Jefferson Rd
Rochester, NY 14623
585-292-5627
e-mail: djprofita@bryantstratton.edu
Web site: www.bryantstratton.edu

Offices and agencies generally appear in alphabetical order, except when specific order is requested by listee.

Director of Rochester Colleges:
  Jeffrey Moore 585-292-5627

Bryant & Stratton College-Southtowns Campus

200 Red Tail
Orchard Park, NY 14127
716-677-9500
e-mail: southtowns@bryantstratton.edu
Web site: www.bryantstratton.edu

Campus Director:
  Paul Bahr. 716-677-9500

Bryant & Stratton College-Syracuse Campus

953 James St
Syracuse, NY 13203-2502
315-472-6603
e-mail: syracusedt@bryantstratton.edu
Web site: www.bryantstratton.edu

Campus Director:
  Michael Sattler 315-472-6603

Bryant & Stratton College-Syracuse North Campus

8687 Carling Rd
Liverpool, NY 13090
315-652-6500
e-mail: sninfo@bryantstratton.edu
Web site: www.bryantstratton.edu

Campus Director:
  Susan Cumoletti 315-652-6500

Business Informatics Center

134 S Central Ave
Valley Stream, NY 11580
516-561-0050 Fax: 516-561-0074
e-mail: info@thecollegeforbusiness.com
Web site: www.thecollegeforbusiness.com

President:
  Constance Brown 516-561-0050

Christie's Education Inc

11 W 42 St
8th Fl
New York, NY 10036
212-355-1501 Fax: 212-355-7370
e-mail: christieseducataion@christies.com
Web site: www.christieseducation.com

Director of Studies:
  Veronique Chagnon-Burke. 212-355-1501
  e-mail: vchagnon-burke@christies.com

College of Westchester (The)

325 Central Park Ave
PO Box 710
White Plains, NY 10606
914-831-0200 or 800-660-7093 Fax: 914-948-5441
Web site: www.cw.edu

President:
  Karen J Smith 914-831-0200

DeVry Institute of Technology, College of New York

180 Madison Av., Suite 900
New York, NY 10016
212-312-4301
Web site: www.ny.devry.edu

Director:
  Newton Myvett 212-312-4301

Elmira Business Institute

Langdon Plaza
303 N Main St
Elmira, NY 14901-2731
607-733-7177 or 800-843-1812 Fax: 607-733-7178
e-mail: info@ebi-college.com
Web site: www.ebi-college.com

President:
  Brad C Phillips. 607-733-7177 x202

Elmira Business Institute-Vestal

Vestal Executive Pk
4100 Vestal Rd
Vestal, NY 13850
607-729-8915 or 866-703-7550 Fax: 607-729-8916
e-mail: info@ebi-college.com
Web site: www.ebi-college.com

Campus Director:
  Bob Williams. 607-729-8915 x202

Everest Institute

1630 Portland Ave
Rochester, NY 14621-3007
585-266-0430 or 888-741-4270 Fax: 585-266-8243
Web site: www.everest.edu

Five Towns College

305 N Service Rd
Dix Hills, NY 11746-5871
631-656-2110 Fax: 631-424-7008
e-mail: info@ftc.edu
Web site: www.ftc.edu

President:
  Stanley G Cohen 631-424-7000/fax: 631-656-2172

Globe Institute of Technology

500 7th Ave
New York, NY 10018
212-349-4330 Fax: 212-227-5920
Web site: www.globe.edu

President:
  Martin Oliner 212-349-4330
  e-mail: moliner@globe.edu

ITT Technical Institute

13 Airline Dr
Albany, NY 12205
518-452-9300 or 800-489-1191 Fax: 518-452-9393
Web site: www.itt-tech.edu

Director:
  Michael Mariani 518-452-9300
  e-mail: mmariani@itt-tech.edu

Offices and agencies generally appear in alphabetical order, except when specific order is requested by listee.

Island Drafting & Technical Institute

128 Broadway, Route 110
Amityville, NY 11701-2704
631-691-8733 Fax: 631-691-8738
e-mail: info@idti.edu
Web site: www.idti.edu

President:
James G DiLiberto 631-691-8733
e-mail: dilibertoj@idti.edu

Jamestown Business College

7 Fairmount Ave
Jamestown, NY 14701
716-664-5100 Fax: 716-664-3144
Web site: www.jbcny.org

President:
David Conklin. 716-664-5100
e-mail: davidconklin@jamestownbusinesscollege.edu

Laboratory Institute of Merchandising

12 E 53 St
New York, NY 10022
212-752-1530 or 800-677-1323 Fax: 212-750-3432
e-mail: info@limcollege.edu
Web site: www.limcollege.edu

President:
Elizabeth S Marcuse 212-752-1530
e-mail: execs@limcollege.edu

Long Island Business Institute-Commack

6500 Jericho Tpke
Commack, NY 11725
631-499-7100 Fax: 631-499-7114
e-mail: info@libi.edu
Web site: www.libi.edu

President:
Monica Foote 631-499-7100

Long Island Business Institute-Flushing

136-18 39 Ave
Flushing, NY 11354
718-939-5100 Fax: 718-939-9235
Web site: www.libi.edu

President:
Monica Foote 718-939-5100

Mandl School

254 W 54th St
New York, NY 10019
212-247-3434
Web site: www.mandlschool.com

Mildred Elley

855 Central Ave
Albany, NY 12206
518-786-0855 or 800-622-6327 Fax: 518-786-0898
e-mail: admissions@mildred-elley.edu
Web site: www.mildred-elley.edu

President:
Faith A Takes 518-786-0855 x1213/fax: 518-785-7560
e-mail: faith.takes@mildred-elley.edu

Monroe College-Bronx

2501 Jerome Ave
Bronx, NY 10468
718-933-6700 or 800-556-6676 Fax: 718-364-3552
Web site: www.monroecollege.edu

President:
Stephen J Jerome 718-933-6700 x8252

Monroe College-New Rochelle

434 Main St
New Rochelle, NY 10801
914-632-5400 Fax: 914-632-5462
Web site: www.monroecollege.edu

President:
Stephen J Jerome

New York Career Institute

11 Park Place
4th Fl
New York, NY 10007
212-962-0002 Fax: 212-385-7574
e-mail: info@nyci.com
Web site: www.nyci.com

CEO:
Ivan Londa 212-962-0002

Olean Business Institute

301 North Union St
Olean, NY 14760
716-372-7978 Fax: 716-372-2120
e-mail: admin@obi.edu
Web site: www.obi.edu

President:
Jennifer L Madison 716-372-7978

Pacific College of Oriental Medicine

915 Broadway 2nd Floor
New York, NY 10010
212-982-3456 or 800-729-3468 Fax: 212-982-6514
Web site: www.pacificcollege.edu

President:
Jack Miller 212-982-3456
e-mail: jmiller@pacificcollege.edu

Plaza College

74-09 37th Ave
Jackson Heights, NY 11372
718-779-1430 Fax: 718-779-7423
e-mail: info@plazacollege.edu
Web site: www.plazacollege.edu

President:
Charles E Callahan 718-779-1430

School of Visual Arts

209 East 23rd St
New York, NY 10010
212-592-2000 or 888-220-5782 Fax: 212-725-3587
e-mail: admissions@sva.edu
Web site: www.schoolofvisualarts.edu

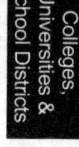

Colleges,
Universities &
School Districts

Offices and agencies generally appear in alphabetical order, except when specific order is requested by listee.

President:
  David John Rhodes 212-592-2350

Simmons Institute of Funeral Service Inc
1828 South Ave at West Brighton Ave
Syracuse, NY 13207
315-475-5142 or 800-727-3536 Fax: 315-475-3817
e-mail: info@simmonsinstitute.com
Web site: www.simmonsinstitute.com

President/CEO:
  Maurice C Wightman 315-475-5142

Swedish Institute
226 W 26th St
New York, NY 10001
212-924-5900 Fax: 212-924-7600
Web site: www.swedishinstitute.org

President:
  William C Ehrhardt

Technical Career Institutes Inc
320 W 31st St
New York, NY 10001
212-594-4000 or 800-878-8246
e-mail: admissions@tcicollege.edu
Web site: www.tcicollege.edu

President:
  James Melville 212-594-4000
  e-mail: jmelville@tcicollege.edu

Tri-State College of Acupuncture
80th Ave, Ste 400
New York, NY 10011
212-242-2255 Fax: 212-242-2920
Web site: www.tsca.edu

CEO:
  Mark D Seem 212-496-7514

US Merchant Marine Academy
300 Steamboat Road
Kings Point, NY 11024
516-773-5000 Fax: 516-773-5774
Web site: www.usmma.edu

Superintendent & Dean:
  Phillip Greene, Jr.

US Military Academy at West Point
626 Swift Road
West Point, NY 10996
845-938-4041 or 800-367-2884 Fax: 845-938-2363
Web site: www.usma.edu

Superintendent:
  LTG Franklin L Hagenbeck 845-938-2610

Utica School of Commerce
201 Bleecker St
Utica, NY 13501
315-733-2300 or 800-321-4872 Fax: 315-733-9281
Web site: www.uscny.edu

President:
  Philip M Williams 315-733-2309 x2214
  e-mail: pwilliams@uscny.edu

Wood Tobe-Coburn
8 E 40th St
New York, NY 10016
212-686-9040 or 800-394-9663 Fax: 212-686-9171
Web site: www.woodtobecoburn.edu

President:
  Sandi Gruninger 212-686-9040
  e-mail: sgruninger@woodtobecoburn.edu

Offices and agencies generally appear in alphabetical order, except when specific order is requested by listee.

PUBLIC SCHOOL DISTRICTS

SCHOOL DISTRICT ADMINISTRATORS

ALBANY

Albany City SD
Academy Park, Albany, NY 12207-1099
518-475-6010 Fax: 518-475-7295
e-mail: rcolucciello@albany.k12.ny.us
Web site: www.albanyschools.org
Raymond Colucciello, Superintendent

Berne-Knox-Westerlo CSD
1738 Helderberg Trl, Berne, NY 12023-2926
518-872-1293 Fax: 518-872-0341
e-mail: pdorward@bkwcsd.k12.ny.us
Web site: www.bkwcsd.k12.ny.us
Paul Dorward, Superintendent

Bethlehem CSD
90 Adams Place, Delmar, NY 12054
518-439-7098 Fax: 518-475-0352
e-mail: mtebbano@bcsd.neric.org
Web site: bcsd.k12.ny.us
Dr Michael D Tebbano, Superintendent

Cohoes City SD
7 Bevan Street, Cohoes, NY 12047-3299
518-237-0100 Fax: 518-237-2912
e-mail: rlibby@cohoes.org
Web site: www.cohoes.org
Robert K Libby, Superintendent

Green Island UFSD
171 Hudson Ave, Green Island, NY 12183-1293
518-273-1422 Fax: 518-270-0818
e-mail: mmugits@greenisland.org
Web site: www.greenisland.org
Michael Mugits, Superintendent

Guilderland CSD
6076 State Farm Rd, Guilderland, NY 12084-9533
518-456-6200 Fax: 518-456-1152
e-mail: wilesm@guilderlandschools.org
Web site: www.guilderlandschools.org
Marie Wiles, Superintendent

Menands UFSD
19 Wards Ln, Menands, NY 12204-2197
518-465-4561 Fax: 518-465-4572
e-mail: kmeany@nycap.rr.com
Web site: www.menandsschool.nycap.rr.com
Kathleen Meany, Interim Superintendent

North Colonie CSD
91 Fiddler's Ln, Latham, NY 12110-5349
518-785-8591 Fax: 518-785-8502
e-mail: dcorr@ncolonie.org
Web site: www.northcolonie.org
Joseph Corr, Superintendent

Ravena-Coeymans-Selkirk CSD
26 Thatcher St, Selkirk, NY 12158-0097
518-756-5200 Fax: 518-767-2644
e-mail: dteplesky@rcscsd.org
Web site: www.rcscsd.org
Daniel Teplesky, Superintendent

South Colonie CSD
102 Loralee Dr, Albany, NY 12205-2298
518-869-3576 Fax: 518-869-6481
Web site: www.southcolonieschools.org
Jonathan Buhner, Superintendent

Voorheesville CSD
432 New Salem Rd, Voorheesville, NY 12186-0498
518-765-3313 Fax: 518-765-2751
e-mail: tsnyder@vcsdk12.org
Web site: vcsd.neric.org
Teresa T Snyder, Superintendent

Watervliet City SD
1245 Hillside Dr, Watervliet, NY 12189
518-629-3200 Fax: 518-629-3265
e-mail: ppadalin@vliet.neric.org
Web site: www.watervlietcityschools.org
Paul Padalino, Superintendent

ALLEGANY

Alfred-Almond CSD
6795 Rt 21, Almond, NY 14804-9716
607-276-6500 Fax: 607-276-6304
e-mail: rcalkins@aacs.wnyric.org
Web site: www.aacs.org
Richard Calkins, Superintendent

Andover CSD
31-35 Elm St, PO Box G, Andover, NY 14806-0508
607-478-8491 x222 Fax: 607-478-8833
e-mail: wberg@andovercsd.org
Web site: www.andovercsd.org
William C Berg, Superintendent

Belfast CSD
1 King St, Belfast, NY 14711
585-365-9940
e-mail: jmay@belf.wnyric.org
Web site: www.belfast.wnyric.org
Judy May, Superintendent

Bolivar-Richburg CSD
100 School St, Bolivar, NY 14715
585-928-2561 Fax: 585-928-1368
e-mail: mcapawan@brcs.wnyric.org
Web site: www.brcs.wnyric.org
Marilyn Capawan, Superintendent

Canaseraga CSD
4-8 Main St, PO Box 230, Canaseraga, NY 14822-0230
607-545-6421 Fax: 607-545-6265
e-mail: mblum@ccsdny.org
Web site: www.ccsdny.org
Marie Blum, Superintendent

Cuba-Rushford CSD
5476 Rt 305, Cuba, NY 14727-1014
585-968-2650 x4426
e-mail: kshanley@crcs.wnyric.org
Web site: www.crcs.wnyric.org
Kevin Shanley, Superintendent

Fillmore CSD
104 W. Main St, Fillmore, NY 14735-0177
585-567-2251
e-mail: mcox@fillmore.wnyric.org
Web site: www.fillmorecsd.org
Martin D Cox, Superintendent

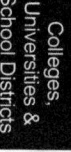
Colleges, Universities & School Districts

Offices and agencies generally appear in alphabetical order, except when specific order is requested by listee.

Friendship CSD
46 W Main St, Friendship, NY 14739-9702
716-973-3311 Fax: 716-973-2023
Web site: www.friendship.wnyric.org
Maureen Donahue, Superintendent

Genesee Valley CSD
1 Jaguar Dr, Belmont, NY 14813-9788
585-268-7900
Web site: www.genvalley.org
Ralph Wilson, Superintendent

Scio CSD
3968 Washington St, Scio, NY 14880-9507
716-593-5510 Fax: 716-593-3468
e-mail: tpreston@scio.wnyric.org
Web site: scio.schooltools.us
Tracie Preston, Superintendent

Wellsville CSD
126 W State St, Wellsville, NY 14895
585-596-2170 Fax: 585-596-2177
Web site: www.wellsville.wnyric.org
Kimberly Mueller, Superintendent

Whitesville CSD
692 Main St, Whitesville, NY 14897
607-356-3301 Fax: 607-356-3598
Web site: www.whitesville.wnyric.org
Douglas H Wyant, Superintendent

BROOME

Binghamton City SD
164 Hawley St, Binghamton, NY 13901-2126
607-762-8100 x318
e-mail: wozniakp@binghamtonschools.org
Web site: www.binghamtonschools.org
Peggy J Wozniak, Superintendent

Chenango Forks CSD
One Gordon Dr, Binghamton, NY 13901-5614
607-648-7543 Fax: 607-48-7560
e-mail: bundyr@cforks.org
Web site: www.cforks.org
Robert Bundy, Superintendent

Chenango Valley CSD
221 Chenango Bridge Road, Binghamton, NY 13901-1653
607-762-6800 Fax: 607-762-6890
e-mail: tdouglas@cvcsd.stier.org
Web site: www.cvcsd.stier.org
Dr Thomas Douglas, Superintendent

Deposit CSD
171 Second St, Deposit, NY 13754-1397
607-467-5380 Fax: 607-467-5535
e-mail: bhauber@deposit.stier.org
Web site: www.depositcsd.org
Bonnie Hauber, Superintendent

Harpursville CSD
54 Main St, Harpursville, NY 13787-0147
607-693-8101
Web site: www.hcs.stier.org
Kathleen M Wood, Superintendent

Johnson City CSD
666 Reynolds Rd, Johnson City, NY 13790-1398
607-763-1230 Fax: 607-729-2767
e-mail: mfrys@jcschools.stier.org
Web site: www.jcschools.com
Mary Kay Frys, Superintendent
Joseph F Stoner, Superintendent

Susquehanna Valley CSD
1040 Conklin Rd, Conklin, NY 13748-0200
607-775-0170
Web site: www.svsabers.org
Gerardo Tagliaferri, Acting Superintendent

Union-Endicott CSD
1100 E Main St, Endicott, NY 13760-5271
607-757-2103 Fax: 607-757-2809
Web site: www.uek12.org
Suzanne McLeod, Superintendent

Vestal CSD
201 Main St, Vestal, NY 13850-1599
607-757-2241
e-mail: mdlaroach@vcs.stier.org
Web site: www.vestal.stier.org
Mark LaRoach, Superintendent

Whitney Point CSD
10 Keibel Rd, Whitney Point, NY 13862-0249
607-692-8202 Fax: 607-692-4434
e-mail: mhibbard@wpcsd.org
Web site: www.wpcsd.org
Mary Hibbard, Superintendent

Windsor CSD
1191 NY Route 79, Windsor, NY 13865-4134
607-655-8216 Fax: 607-655-3553
e-mail: jandrews@windsor-csd.org
Web site: www.windsor-csd.org
Jason A Andrews, Superintendent

CATTARAUGUS

Allegany - Limestone CSD
3131 Five Mile Rd, Allegany, NY 14706-9627
716-375-6600 x2006
e-mail: dmunro@alli.wnyric.org
Web site: www.alli.wnyric.org
Diane M Munro, Superintendent

Cattaraugus-Little Valley CSD
207 Rock City St, Little Valley, NY 14755-1298
716-938-9155 x2210 Fax: 716-938-9367
Web site: www.cattlv.wnyric.org
Jon W Peterson, Superintendent

Ellicottville CSD
5873 Route 219, Ellicottville, NY 14731-9719
716-699-2368 Fax: 716-699-6017
e-mail: mward@eville.wnyric.org
Web site: www.ellicottvilecentral.com
Mark Ward, Superintendent

Franklinville CSD
31 N Main St, Franklinville, NY 14737-1096
716-676-8029 Fax: 716-676-3779
e-mail: mspasiano@frkl.wnyric.org
Web site: www.tbafcs.org/franklinville/
Michael Spasiano, Superintendent

Offices and agencies generally appear in alphabetical order, except when specific order is requested by listee.

Gowanda CSD
10674 Prospect St, Gowanda, NY 14070
716-532-3325 Fax: 716-995-2156
e-mail: crinaldi@gowcsd.org
Web site: www.gowcsd.org
Charles J Rinaldi, Superintendent

Hinsdale CSD
3701 Main St, Hinsdale, NY 14743-0278
716-557-2227 x401
e-mail: jmccarthy@hinsdale.wnyric.org
Judy McCarthy, Superintendent

Olean City SD
410 W Sullivan St, Olean, NY 14760-2596
716-375-8001
e-mail: ctaggerty@olean.wnyric.org
Web site: www.oleanschools.org
Colleen Taggerty, Superintendent

Yorkshire-Pioneer CSD
12125 County Line Rd, Yorkshire, NY 14173-0579
716-492-9300 Fax: 716-492-9360
e-mail: jbowen@pioneercsd.org
Jeffrey Bowen, Superintendent

Portville CSD
500 Elm Street, Portville, NY 14770-9791
716-933-6000 Fax: 716-933-7124
Web site: www.portville.wnyric.org
Thomas J Simon, Superintendent

Randolph Academy UFSD
336 Main Street ER, Randolph, NY 14772-9696
716-358-6866 Fax: 716-358-9076
Web site: www.randoplhacademy.org
Lori DeCarlo, Superintendent

Randolph CSD
18 Main St, Randolph, NY 14772-1188
716-358-7005 or 716-358-6161 Fax: 716-358-7072
e-mail: kmortiz@rand.wnyric.org
Web site: www.randolphcsd.org
Kimberly Moritz, Superintendent

Salamanca City SD
50 Iroquois Dr, Salamanca, NY 14779-1398
716-945-2403 Fax: 716-945-3964
e-mail: dhay@salamancany.org
Web site: www.salamancany.org
J Douglas Hay, Superintendent

West Valley CSD
5359 School St, West Valley, NY 14171
716-942-3293 Fax: 716-942-3440
e-mail: hbowen@wvalley.wnyric.org
Web site: www.wvalley.wnyric.org
Hillary W Bowen, Superintendent

CAYUGA

Auburn Enlarged City SD
78 Thornton Ave, Auburn, NY 13021-4698
315-255-8835
Joseph D Pabis, Superintendent

Cato-Meridian CSD
2851 NYS Rt 370, Cato, NY 13033-0100
315-626-3439 Fax: 315-626-2888
W Noel Patterson, Superintendent

Moravia CSD
68 S Main St, Moravia, NY 13118-1189
315-497-2670 Fax: 315-497-2260
Michelle Brantner, Superintendent

Port Byron CSD
30 Maple Ave, Port Byron, NY 13140-9647
315-776-5728 Fax: 315-776-4050
e-mail: nobrien@portbyron.cnyric.org
Web site: www.portbyron.cnyric.org
Neil F O'Brien, Superintendent

Southern Cayuga CSD
2384 State Rt 34B, Aurora, NY 13026-9771
315-364-7211 Fax: 315-364-7863
e-mail: worthmk@southerncayuga.org
Web site: www.southerncayuga.org
Mary Kay Worth, Superintendent

Union Springs CSD
239 Cayuga St, Union Springs, NY 13160
315-889-4101
e-mail: lrice@unionspringscsd.org
Web site: www.uscsd.info
Linda Rice, Superintendent

Weedsport CSD
2821 E Brutus St, Weedsport, NY 13166-9105
315-834-6637
Shaun A O'Connor, Superintendent

CHAUTAUQUA

Bemus Point CSD
3980 Dutch Hollow Rd, Bemus Point, NY 14712
716-386-2375
Web site: www.bemusptcsd.org
Albert D'Attilio, Superintendent

Brocton CSD
138 W Main St, Brocton, NY 14716
716-792-2121 Fax: 716-792-7944
e-mail: jhertlein@broc.wynric.org
Web site: www.broctoncsd.org
John Hertlein, Superintendent

Cassadaga Valley CSD
5935 Route 60, PO Box 540, Sinclairville, NY 14782-0540
716-962-5155
e-mail: JBrown@cvcs.wnyric.org
John Brown, Superintendent

Chautauqua Lake CSD
100 N Erie St, Mayville, NY 14757
716-753-5808 Fax: 716-753-5813
e-mail: bspitzer@clake.org
Web site: www.clake.org
Benjamin B Spitzer, Superintendent

Clymer CSD
8672 E Main St, Clymer, NY 14724-0580
716-355-4444
Web site: www.clymercsd.org
Scott D Smith, Superintendent

Dunkirk City SD
620 Marauder Dr, Dunkirk, NY 14048-1396
716-366-9300
Web site: www.dunkirkcsd.org
Gary Cerne, Superintendent

Offices and agencies generally appear in alphabetical order, except when specific order is requested by listee.

Falconer CSD
2 East Ave N, Falconer, NY 14733
716-665-6624 x4101 Fax: 716-665-9265
e-mail: spenhollow@falcon.wynric.org
Web site: wwwfalconerschools.org
Stephen Penhollow, Superintendent

Forestville CSD
12 Water St, Forestville, NY 14062-9674
716-965-2742 Fax: 716-965-2265
e-mail: jconnor@forestville.wnyric.org
Web site: www.forestville.com
John O'Connor, Superintendent

Fredonia CSD
425 E Main St, Fredonia, NY 14063
716-679-1581
Web site: www.fredonia.wnyric.org
Paul Di Fonzo, Superintendent

Frewsburg CSD
26 Institute St, Frewsburg, NY 14738
716-569-9241
Web site: www.frewsburgcsd.org
Stephen Vanstrom, Superintendent

Jamestown City SD
197 Martin Road, Jamestown, NY 14701
716-483-4350
Web site: www.jamestownpublicschools.org
Daniel E Kathman, Superintendent

Panama CSD
41 North St, Panama, NY 14767-9775
716-782-2455 Fax: 716-782-4674
e-mail: blictus@mx.pancent.org
Web site: www.pancent.org
Bert Lictus, Superintendent

Pine Valley CSD (South Dayton)
7755 Rt 83, South Dayton, NY 14138
716-988-3293 Fax: 716-988-3864
Web site: www.pval.org
Peter Morgante, Superintendent

Ripley CSD
12 N State St, Ripley, NY 14775
716-736-6201 Fax: 716-736-6226
Web site: ripleycsd.wnyric.org
Karen Krause, Interim Superintendent

Sherman CSD
127 Park St, PO Box 950, Sherman, NY 14781-0950
716-761-6122 x1289 Fax: 716-761-6119
e-mail: tschmidt@sherman.wnyric.org
Web site: www.sherman.wnyric.org
Thomas Schmidt, Superintendent

Silver Creek CSD
1 Dickinson St, PO Box 270, Silver Creek, NY 14136
716-934-2603 Fax: 716-934-7983
Web site: www.silvercreek.wnyric.org
David O'Rourke, Superintendent

Southwestern CSD at Jamestown
600 Hunt Rd, Jamestown, NY 14701
716-484-1136
Web site: swcs.wnyric.org
Daniel A George, Superintendent

Westfield CSD
203 E Main St, Westfield, NY 14787
716-326-2151
Web site: www.wacs.wnyric.org
Mark Sissel, Superintendent

CHEMUNG

Elmira City SD
951 Hoffman St, Elmira, NY 14905-1715
607-735-3000 Fax: 607-735-3002
Web site: www.elmiracityschools.com
Joseph E Hochreiter, Superintendent

Elmira Heights CSD
2083 College Ave, Elmira Heights, NY 14903-1598
607-734-7114 Fax: 607-734-7134
e-mail: mbfiore@gstboces.org
Web site: www.heightsschools.com
Mary Beth Fiore, Superintendent

Horseheads CSD
One Raider Ln, Horseheads, NY 14845-2398
607-739-5601 x4200
e-mail: hcsdinfo@horseheadsdistrict.com
Web site: www.horseheadsdistrict.com
Ralph Marino, Superintendent

CHENANGO

Afton CSD
29 Academy St, PO Box 5, Afton, NY 13730-0005
607-639-8229
Web site: www.afton.stier.org
Elizabeth A Briggs, Superintendent

Bainbridge-Guilford CSD
18 Juliand St, Bainbridge, NY 13733
607-967-6321 Fax: 607-967-4231
Web site: www.bgcsd.org
Karl Brown, Superintendent

Greene CSD
40 S Canal St, Greene, NY 13778
607-656-4161
Web site: www.greenecsd.org
Jonathan R Rietz, Superintendent

Norwich City SD
89 Midland Drive, Norwich, NY 13815
607-334-1600 X5523 Fax: 607-336-8652
e-mail: gosulliv@norwich.stier.org
Web site: www.norwichcsd.org
Gerard M O'Sullivan, Superintendent

Georgetown-South Otselic CSD
125 County Rd 13A, South Otselic, NY 13155-0161
315-653-7591 Fax: 315-653-7500
Web site: www.ovcs.org
Richard Hughes, Superintendent

Oxford Academy & CSD
12 Fort Hill Park, PO Box 192, Oxford, NY 13830-0192
607-843-2025 x4041 Fax: 607-843-3241
Web site: www.oxac.org
Randall Squier, Superintendent

Offices and agencies generally appear in alphabetical order, except when specific order is requested by listee.

Sherburne-Earlville CSD
15 School St, Sherburne, NY 13460-0725
607-674-7300 Fax: 607-674-7386
Web site: www.secsd.org
Gayle H Hellert, Superintendent

Unadilla Valley CSD
4238 State Hwy 8, New Berlin, NY 13411
607-847-7500 Fax: 607-847-9194
Web site: www.uvstorm.org
Robert J Mackey, Superintendent

CLINTON

Ausable Valley CSD
1273 Rt 9N, Clintonville, NY 12924-4244
518-834-2845 Fax: 518-834-2843
e-mail: psavage@avcsk12.org
Web site: avcs.org
Paul D Savage, Superintendent

Beekmantown CSD
37 Eagle Way, West Chazy, NY 12992-2577
518-563-8250 x5501 Fax: 518-563-8132
e-mail: amo.scott@bcsdk12.org
Web site: www.bcsdk12.org
Scott A Amo, Superintendent

Chazy Central RSD
609 Miner Farm Rd, Chazy, NY 12921-0327
518-846-7135 Fax: 518-846-8322
e-mail: jfairchild@chazy.org
Web site: www.chazy.org
John Fairchild, Superintendent

Northeastern Clinton CSD
103 Route 276, Champlain, NY 12919
518-298-8242 Fax: 518-298-4293
Web site: www.nccscougars.org
Peter J Turner, Superintendent

Northern Adirondack CSD
5572 Rt 11, Ellenburg Depot, NY 12935-0164
518-594-7060
Web site: www.nacs1.org
Laura Marlow, Superintendent

Peru CSD
17 School St, PO Box 68, Peru, NY 12972-0068
518-643-6000
Web site: www.perucsd.org
A Paul Scott, Superintendent

Plattsburgh City SD
49 Broad St, Plattsburgh, NY 12901-3396
518-957-6002 Fax: 518-957-6026
e-mail: jshort@plattscsd.org
Web site: www.plattscsd.org
James Short, Superintendent

Saranac CSD
32 Emmons St, Dannemora, NY 12929
518-565-5600
e-mail: kcringle@saranac.org
Web site: www.saranac.org
Kenneth O Cringle, Superintendent

COLUMBIA

Berkshire UFSD
13640 Rt 22, Canaan, NY 12029-0370
518-781-3500 X3545
e-mail: jgaudette@berkshireufsd.k12.ny.us
James G Gaudette, Superintendent

Chatham CSD
50 Woodbridge Ave, Chatham, NY 12037-1397
518-392-2400
Web site: www.chathamcentralschools.com
Cheryl Nuciforo, Superintendent

Germantown CSD
123 Main St, Germantown, NY 12526
518-537-6280 Fax: 518-537-3284
Web site: germantowncsd.org
Patrick Gabriel, Superintendent

Hudson City SD
215 Harry Howard Ave, Hudson, NY 12534-4011
518-828-4360 x2101
Web site: www.hudsoncityschooldistrict.com
John F Howe, Superintendent

Ichabod Crane CSD
2910 Rt 9, Valatie, NY 12184-0137
518-758-7575 x3002 Fax: 518-758-7579
e-mail: lbordick@ichabodcrane.org
Web site: www.ichabodcrane.org
Lee Bordick, Superintendent

New Lebanon CSD
14665 Route 22, New Lebanon, NY 12125-2307
518-794-9016 Fax: 518-766-5574
e-mail: kmcgraw@newlebanoncsd.org
Web site: www.newlebanoncsd.org
Karen McGraw, Superintendent

Taconic Hills CSD
73 County Rt 11A, PO Box 482, Craryville, NY 12521
518-325-0313 Fax: 518-325-3557
e-mail: info@taconichills.k12.ny.us
Web site: www.taconichills.k12.ny.us
Mark A Sposato, Superintendent

CORTLAND

Cincinnatus CSD
2809 Cincinnatus Rd, Cincinnatus, NY 13040-9698
607-863-3200 Fax: 607-863-4109
e-mail: shubbard@cc.cnyric.orgic.org
Web site: www.cc.cnyric.org
Steven V Hubbard, Superintendent

Cortland Enlarged City SD
1 Valley View Dr, Cortland, NY 13045-3297
607-758-4100 Fax: 607-758-4128
e-mail: superintendent@cortlandschools.org
Web site: www.cortlandschools.org
Larry Spring, Superintendent

Homer CSD
Route 281, PO Box 500, Homer, NY 13077-0500
607-749-7241
Web site: www.homercentral.org
Nancy Ruscio, Superintendent

Offices and agencies generally appear in alphabetical order, except when specific order is requested by listee.

Marathon CSD
1 E Main St, PO Box 339, Marathon, NY 13803-0339
607-849-3251 Fax: 607-849-3305
e-mail: turecekt@marathon.cnyric.org
Web site: www.marathonschools.org
Timothy Turecek, Superintendent

McGraw CSD
W Academy St, PO Box 556, McGraw, NY 13101-0556
607-836-3636 Fax: 607-836-3635
e-mail: mcurcio@mcgrawschools.org
Web site: www.mcgrawschools.org
Mary Curcio, Superintendent

DELAWARE

Andes CSD
85 Delaware Ave, PO Box 248, Andes, NY 13731-0248
845-676-3167 Fax: 845-676-3181
e-mail: rchakar@andescentralschool.org
Web site: www.andescentralschool.org
Robert Chakar, Superintendent

Charlotte Valley CSD
15611 St Hwy 23, Davenport, NY 13750-0202
607-278-5511 Fax: 607-278-5900
e-mail: dupra.mark@charlottevalley.org
Mark R Dupra, Superintendent

Delhi CSD
2 Sheldon Dr, Delhi, NY 13753-1276
607-746-1300 Fax: 607-746-6028
Web site: www.delhischools.org
Roger W Adams, Superintendent

Downsville CSD
Maple St, Po Box J, Downsville, NY 13755
607-363-2101 Fax: 607-363-2105
Web site: www.dcseagles.org
James F Abrams, Superintendent

Franklin CSD
26 Institute St, Franklin, NY 13775-0888
607-829-3551 x309 Fax: 607-829-2101
Web site: www.franklincsd.org
Gordon Daniels, Superintendent

Hancock CSD
67 Education Ln, Hancock, NY 13783
607-637-1301
Web site: hancock.stier.org
Terrance Dougherty, Superintendent

Margaretville CSD
415 Main St, Margaretville, NY 12455-0319
845-586-2647 Fax: 845-586-2949
e-mail: talbanese@margaretvillecs.org
Web site: www.margaretvillecs.org
Anthony R Albanese, Superintendent

Roxbury CSD
53729 NYS Route 30, Roxbury, NY 12474-0207
607-326-4151 Fax: 607-326-4154
e-mail: tobrien@roxburycs.org
Thomas J O'Brien, Superintendent

Sidney CSD
95 W Main St, Sidney, NY 13838-1699
607-563-2135 Fax: 607-563-4275
Web site: www.sidneycsd.org
William Christensen, Superintendent

South Kortright CSD
58200 State Hwy 10, South Kortright, NY 13842-0113
607-538-9111 Fax: 607-538-9205
Web site: www.skcs.org
Patricia Norton-White, Superintendent

Stamford CSD
1 River St, Stamford, NY 12167-1098
607-652-7301 Fax: 607-652-3446
Web site: www.stamfordcs.org
Tonda Dunbar, Superintendent

Walton CSD
47-49 Stockton Ave, Walton, NY 13856
607-865-4116 Fax: 607-865-8568
Web site: www.waltoncsd.org
Thomas P Austin, Superintendent

DUTCHESS

Arlington CSD
696 Dutchess Tpke, Poughkeepsie, NY 12603
845-486-4460
Web site: www.arlingtonschools.org
Geoffrey Hicks, Superintendent

Beacon City SD
10 Education Dr, Beacon, NY 12508
845-838-6900 x2010
e-mail: aefsky.f@beaconcityk12.org
Web site: www.beaconcityk12.org
Fern Aefsky, Superintendent

Dover UFSD
2368 Rt 22, Dover Plains, NY 12522
845-832-4500 Fax: 845-832-4511
e-mail: mike.tierney@doverschools.org
Web site: www.doverschools.org
Michael Tierney, Superintendent

Hyde Park CSD
11 Boice Rd, PO Box 2033, Hyde Park, NY 12538-1632
845-229-4000 Fax: 845-229-4056
Web site: www.hydeparkschools.org
Greer Fischer, Superintendent

Millbrook CSD
PO Box AA-3323 Franklin, Millbrook, NY 12545
845-677-4200 x101
e-mail: lloyd.jaeger@millbrookcsd.org
Web site: www.millbrookcsd.org
Lloyd Jaeger, Superintendent

Pawling CSD
515 Route 22, Pawling, NY 12564
845-855-4600
Web site: www.pawlingschools.org
Joseph Sciortino, Superintendent

Pine Plains CSD
2829 Church St, Pine Plains, NY 12567-5504
518-398-7181 Fax: 518-398-6592
Web site: www.pineplainsschools.org
Linda Kaumeyer, Superintendent

Poughkeepsie City SD
11 College Ave, Poughkeepsie, NY 12603-3313
845-451-4950 Fax: 845-451-4954
e-mail: lwilson@poughkeepsieschools.org
Web site: www.poughkeepsieschools.org
Laval S Wilson, Superintendent

Offices and agencies generally appear in alphabetical order, except when specific order is requested by listee.

Red Hook CSD
7401 South Broadway, Red Hook, NY 12571-9446
845-758-2241 Fax: 845-758-4720
e-mail: pfinch@rhcsd.org
Web site: www.redhookcentralschools.org
Paul Finch, Superintendent

Rhinebeck CSD
North Park Rd, Rhinebeck, NY 12572
845-871-5520 Fax: 845-876-4276
e-mail: jphelan@rhinebeckcsd.org
Web site: www.rhinebeckcsd.org
Joseph L Phelan, Superintendent

Spackenkill UFSD
15 Croft Rd, Poughkeepsie, NY 12603-5028
845-463-7800 Fax: 845-463-7804
Web site: www.spackenkillschools.org
Lois Powell, Superintendent

Wappingers CSD
167 Meyers Corners Rd, Wappingers Falls, NY 12590-3296
845-298-5000
Web site: www.wappingersschools.org
James Parla, Superintendent
David Paciencia, Superintendent

ERIE

Akron CSD
47 Bloomingdale Ave, Akron, NY 14001-1197
716-542-5010 Fax: 716-542-5018
e-mail: rzymroz@akronschools.org
Web site: www.akronschools.org
Robin B Zymroz, Superintendent of Schools

Alden CSD
13190 Park St, Alden, NY 14004
716-937-9116
Web site: aldenschools.org
Lynn Marie Fusco, Superintendent

Amherst CSD
55 Kings Hwy, Amherst, NY 14226
716-362-3051 Fax: 716-836-2537
Web site: www.amherstschools.org
Laura Chabe, Superintendent

Buffalo SD
712 City Hall, Buffalo, NY 14202-3375
716-816-3500 Fax: 716-816-3600
Web site: www.buffaloschools.org
James A Williams, Superintendent

Cheektowaga CSD
3600 Union Rd, Cheektowaga, NY 14225-5170
716-686-3606 Fax: 716-681-5232
Web site: www.cheektowagaschools.org
Dennis Kane, Superintendent

Cheektowaga-Sloan UFSD
166 Halstead Ave, Sloan, NY 14212
716-891-6402
Web site: www.sloanschools.org
James P Mazgajewski, Superintendent

Clarence CSD
9625 Main St, Clarence, NY 14031-2083
716-407-9102
e-mail: tcoseo@clar.wnyric.org
Web site: www.clarenceschools.org
Thomas G Coseo, Superintendent

Cleveland Hill UFSD
105 Mapleview Rd, Cheektowaga, NY 14225-1599
716-836-7200
Web site: www.clevehill.wnyric.org
Sharon Huff, Superintendent

Depew UFSD
591 Terrace Blvd, Depew, NY 14043-4535
716-686-5105 Fax: 716-686-2269
e-mail: jrabey@depew.wnyric.org
Web site: www.depewschools.org
Jeffrey Rabey, Superintendent

East Aurora UFSD
430 Main St, East Aurora, NY 14052
716-687-2302
Web site: www.eaur.wnyric.org
Brian Russ, Superintendent

Eden CSD
3150 Schoolview Rd, Eden, NY 14057
716-992-3629
Web site: www.edencentral.org
Ronald Buggs, Superintendent

Evans-Brant CSD (Lake Shore)
959 Beach Rd, Angola, NY 14006
716-549-2300 or 716-926-2201 Fax: 716-549-6407
e-mail: jprzepasniak@lakeshore.wnyric.org
Web site: www.lakeshore.wnyric.org
James Przepasniak, Superintendent

Frontier CSD
5120 Orchard Ave, Hamburg, NY 14075-5657
716-926-1700 Fax: 716-926-1776
Web site: www.frontier.wnyric.org
James Bodziak, Superintendent

Grand Island CSD
1100 Ransom Rd, Grand Island, NY 14072-1460
716-773-8801
e-mail: robertchristmann@k12.ginet.org
Web site: www.k12.ginet.org
Robert W Christmann, Superintendent

Hamburg CSD
5305 Abbott Rd, Hamburg, NY 14075
716-646-3220 Fax: 716-646-3209
Web site: www.hamburgschools.org
Steven Achramovitch, Superintendent

Holland CSD
103 Canada St, Holland, NY 14080
716-537-8222
e-mail: djohnson@holland.wnyric.org
Web site: www.hlnd.wnyric.org
Dennis Johnson, Superintendent

Hopevale UFSD at Hamburg
3780 Howard Rd, Hamburg, NY 14075-2252
716-648-1930 Fax: 716-648-2361
Web site: www.hopevale.com
Cynthia Stachowski, Superintendent

Iroquois CSD
2111 Girdle Rd, Elma, NY 14059-0032
716-652-3000
Web site: www.iroquoiscds.org
Bruce Fraser, Superintendent

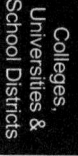

Colleges,
Universities &
School Districts

Offices and agencies generally appear in alphabetical order, except when specific order is requested by listee.

Kenmore-Tonawanda UFSD
1500 Colvin Blvd, Buffalo, NY 14223-1196
716-874-8400 Fax: 716-874-8624
Web site: www.kenton.k12.ny.us
Mark P Mondanaro, Superintendent

Lackawanna City SD
245 South Shore Blvd, Lackawanna, NY 14218
716-827-6767 Fax: 716-827-6710
Web site: www.lackawannaschools.org
Nicholas Korach, Superintendent

Lancaster CSD
177 Central Ave, Lancaster, NY 14086-1897
716-686-3200
Web site: www.lancasterschools.org
Edward Myszka, Interim Superintendent

Cheektowaga-Maryvale CSD
1050 Maryvale Dr, Cheektowaga, NY 14225-2386
716-631-0300 Fax: 716-635-4699
Web site: www.maryvale.wnyric.org
Deborah Ziolkowski, Superintendent

North Collins CSD
2045 School St, North Collins, NY 14111
716-337-0101
Web site: www.northcollins.com
Benjamin A Halsey, Superintendent

Orchard Park CSD
3330 Baker Rd, Orchard Park, NY 14127
716-209-6280 Fax: 716-209-6353
Web site: www.opschools.org
Matthew McGarrity, Superintendent

Springville-Griffith Inst CSD
307 Newman St, Springville, NY 14141
716-592-3200 or 716-592-3412
Web site: www.spingvillegi.org
Paul Hashem, Superintendent

Sweet Home CSD
1901 Sweet Home Rd, Amherst, NY 14228
716-250-1402 Fax: 716-250-1374
e-mail: aday@shs.k12.ny.us
Web site: www.sweethomeschools.com
Anthony Day, Superintendent

Tonawanda City SD
100 Hinds St, Tonawanda, NY 14150
716-694-7690
Web site: www.tonawandacsd.org
Whitney K Vantine, Superintendent

West Seneca CSD
1397 Orchard Park Rd, West Seneca, NY 14224-4098
716-677-3101
Web site: www.wscschools.org
Mark Crawford, Superintendent

Williamsville CSD
105 Casey Rd, PO Box 5000, East Amherst, NY 14051-5000
716-626-8005 Fax: 716-626-8089
Web site: www.williamsvillek12.org
Howard S Smith, Superintendent

Crown Point CSD
2758 Main St, Crown Point, NY 12928-0035
518-597-4200 Fax: 518-597-4121
Web site: www.cpcsteam.org
Shari L Brannock, Superintendent

Elizabethtown-Lewis CSD
7530 Court St, Elizabethtown, NY 12932-0158
518-873-6371 Fax: 518-873-9552
Web site: elcs.neric.org
Gail J Else, Superintendent

Keene CSD
33 Market St, PO Box 67, Keene Valley, NY 12943-0067
518-576-4555 Fax: 518-576-4599
e-mail: cfjkcs@yahoo.com
Web site: www.keenecentralschool.org
Cynthia Ford-Johnston, Superintendent

Lake Placid CSD
23 Cummings Rd, Lake Placid, NY 12946-1500
518-523-2475
Randy Richards, Superintendent

Minerva CSD
1466 County Rt 29, Olmstedville, NY 12857-0039
518-251-2000 Fax: 518-251-2395
e-mail: farrellt@minervasd.org
Web site: www.minervasd.org
Timothy Farrell, Superintendent

Moriah CSD
39 Viking Ln, Port Henry, NY 12974
518-546-3301 Fax: 518-546-7895
Web site: www.moriahk12.org
William Larrow, Superintendent

Newcomb CSD
5535 Rt 28 N, Newcomb, NY 12852-0418
518-582-3341 Fax: 518-582-2163
Web site: www.newcombcsd.org
Clark Hults, Superintendent

Schroon Lake CSD
1125 US Rt 9, PO Box 338, Schroon Lake, NY 12870-0338
518-532-7164 Fax: 518-532-0284
Web site: www.schroonschool.org
Gerald Blair, Superintendent

Ticonderoga CSD
5 Calkins Place, Ticonderoga, NY 12883
518-585-9158
Web site: www.ticonderogak12.org
John C McDonald Jr, Superintendent

Westport CSD
25 Sisco St, Westport, NY 12993
518-962-8244 Fax: 518-962-4571
Web site: www.westportcs.org
John W Gallagher, Superintendent

Willsboro CSD
29 School Lane, Willsboro, NY 12996-0180
518-963-4456 Fax: 518-963-7577
Web site: www.willsborocsd.org
Stephen Broadwell, Superintendent

Offices and agencies generally appear in alphabetical order, except when specific order is requested by listee.

FRANKLIN

Brushton-Moira CSD
758 County Rt 7, Brushton, NY 12916
518-529-7342 Fax: 518-529-6062
e-mail: district@bmcsd.org
Web site: www.bmcsd.org
Steven Grenville, Superintendent

Chateaugay CSD
42 River St, PO Box 904, Chateaugay, NY 12920-0904
518-497-6611 Fax: 518-497-3170
e-mail: dbreault@mail.fehb.org
Web site: www.chateaugay.org
Dale L Breault, Superintendent

Malone CSD
42 Huskie Ln, PO Box 847, Malone, NY 12953-1118
518-483-7800 Fax: 518-483-3071
Web site: www.malone.k12.ny.us
Wayne C Walbridge, Superintendent

Salmon River CSD
637 County Rt 1, Fort Covington, NY 12937-9722
518-358-6600 Fax: 518-358-3492
e-mail: jcollins@srk12.org
Web site: www.srk12.org
Jane A Collins, Superintendent

Saranac Lake CSD
79 Canaras Ave, Saranac Lake, NY 12983-1500
518-891-5460
Gerald A Goldman, Superintendent

St Regis Falls CSD
92 N Main St, PO Box 309, St Regis Falls, NY 12980-0309
518-856-9421
Web site: www.stregisfallscsd.org
Beverly Ouderkirk, Superintendent

Tupper Lake CSD
294 Hosley Ave, Tupper Lake, NY 12986-1899
518-359-3371 Fax: 518-359-7862
Seth McGowan, Superintendent

FULTON

Broadalbin-Perth CSD
20 Pine St, Broadalbin, NY 12025-9997
518-954-2500 Fax: 51-954-2509
Web site: www.bpcsd.org
Stephen M Tomlinson, Superintendent

Gloversville Enlarged SD
243 Lincoln St, PO Box 593, Gloversville, NY 12078
518-775-5700 Fax: 518-725-8793
Robert DeLilli, Superintendent

Greater Johnstown SD
1 Sir Bills Circle, Ste 101, Johnstown, NY 12095
518-762-4611 Fax: 518-726-6379
Web site: www.johnstownschools.org
Katherine A Sullivan, Superintendent

Mayfield CSD
27 School Street, Mayfield, NY 12117-0216
518-661-8207 Fax: 518-661-7666
e-mail: williamson.paul@mayfieldcsd.org
Web site: www.mayfieldk12.com
Paul G Williamson, Superintendent

Northville CSD
131 S Third St, PO Box 608, Northville, NY 12134-0608
518-863-7000 x4121
Web site: northvillecsd.k12.ny.us
Kathy Dougherty, Superintendent

Oppenheim-Ephratah CSD
6486 State Hwy 29, St Johnsville, NY 13452-9309
518-568-2014 Fax: 518-568-2941
e-mail: dmrussom@oecs.k12.ny.us
Web site: www.oecs.k12.ny.us
Dan M Russom, Superintendent

Wheelerville UFSD
PO Box 756, Caroga Lake, NY 12032
518-835-2171 Fax: 518-835-3551
Web site: www.wufselementary.k12.ny.us
David D Carr, Superintendent

GENESEE

Alexander CSD
3314 Buffalo St, Alexander, NY 14005-9769
585-591-1551 Fax: 585-591-2257
Web site: www.alexandercsd.org
Kathleen Maerten, Superintendent

Batavia City SD
39 Washington Ave, Batavia, NY 14020
585-343-2480 Fax: 585-344-8204
e-mail: mpuzio@bataviacsd.org
Web site: www.bataviacsd.org
Margaret L Puzio, Superintendent

Byron-Bergen CSD
6917 W Bergen Rd, Bergen, NY 14416
585-494-1220 Fax: 585-494-2613
Web site: www.bbschools.org
Scott G Martzloff, Superintendent

Elba CSD
57 S Main St, Elba, NY 14058
585-757-9967 x1034
Web site: www.elbacsd.org
Jerome Piwko Jr, Superintendent

Le Roy CSD
2-6 Trigon Park, Le Roy, NY 14482
585-768-8133
Web site: www.leroycsd.org
Kim Cox, Superintendent

Oakfield-Alabama CSD
7001 Lewiston Rd, Oakfield, NY 14125
585-948-5211 Fax: 585-948-9362
Web site: www.oacs.k12.ny.us
Christopher Todd, Superintendent

Pavilion CSD
7014 Big Tree Rd, Pavilion, NY 14525
585-584-3115
Web site: www.pavilioncsd.org
Kenneth J Ellison, Superintendent

Pembroke CSD
Rt 5 & 77, PO Box 308, Corfu, NY 14036
585-599-4525 Fax: 585-762-9993
Web site: www.pembroke.k12.ny.us
Gary T Mix Sr, Superintendent

Colleges,
Universities &
School Districts

Offices and agencies generally appear in alphabetical order, except when specific order is requested by listee.

GREENE

Cairo-Durham CSD
424 Main St, Cairo, NY 12413-0780
518-622-8534
e-mail: ssharkey@cairodurham.org
Web site: www.cairodurham.org
Sally Sharkey, Superintendent

Catskill CSD
343 W Main St, Catskill, NY 12414-1699
518-943-4696 Fax: 518-943-7116
Web site: www.catskillcsd.org
Kathleen Farrell, Superintendent

Coxsackie-Athens CSD
24 Sunset Blvd, Coxsackie, NY 12051-1132
518-731-1700 Fax: 518-731-1729
Web site: www.coxsackie-athens.org
Annemarie Barkman, Interim Superintendent

Greenville CSD
4976 Route 81, Greenville, NY 12083-0129
518-966-5070
Web site: www.greenville.k12.ny.us
Cheryl Dudley, Superintendent

Hunter-Tannersville CSD
6094 Main St, Tannersville, NY 12485-1018
518-589-5400 Fax: 518-589-5403
e-mail: psweeney@htcsd.org
Web site: www.htcsd.org
Patrick Darfler-Sweeney, Superintendent

Windham-Ashland-Jewett CSD
5411 State Route 23, PO Box 429, Windham, NY 12496-0429
518-734-3403 Fax: 518-734-6050
e-mail: jwiktorko@wajcs.org
John Wiktorko, Superintendent

HAMILTON

Indian Lake CSD
28 W Main St, Indian Lake, NY 12842-9716
518-648-5024 Fax: 518-648-6346
e-mail: brandm@ilcsd.org
Web site: www.ilcsd.org
Mark T Brand, Superintendent

Inlet Common School
3002 Rt 28, Old Forge, NY 13420
315-369-3222 Fax: 315-369-6216
e-mail: dgooley@tows.moric.org
Donald Gooley, Superintendent

Lake Pleasant CSD
120 Elm Lake Rd, PO Box 140, Speculator, NY 12164-0140
518-548-7571 Fax: 518-548-3230
Web site: www.lpschools.com
Ernest D Virgil, Superintendent

Long Lake CSD
20 School Lane, PO Box 217, Long Lake, NY 12847-0217
518-624-2221 Fax: 518-624-3896
Web site: www.longlakecsd.org
Mary Jo Dickerson, Acting Superintendent

Piseco Common SD
Rt 8, Piseco, NY 12139
518-548-7555 Fax: 518-548-5310
Peter J Hallock, Superintendent

Raquette Lake UFSD
PO Box 10, Raquette Lake, NY 13436-0010
315-354-4733
Peter J Hallock, Superintendent

Wells CSD
1571 Route 30, PO Box 300, Wells, NY 12190-0300
518-924-6000
Web site: www.wellscsd.com
John Zeis, Superintendent

HERKIMER

Dolgeville CSD
38 Slawson St, Dolgeville, NY 13329
315-429-3155 x3500 Fax: 315-429-8473
e-mail: creynolds@dolgeville.org
Web site: www.dolgeville.org
Christine Reynolds, Superintendent

Frankfort-Schuyler CSD
605 Palmer St, Frankfort, NY 13340
315-894-5083 Fax: 315-895-7011
e-mail: rreina@frankfort-schuyler.org
Web site: www.frankfort-schuyler.org
Robert Reina, Superintendent

Herkimer CSD
801 W German St, Herkimer, NY 13350-2199
315-866-2230
Web site: www.herkimercsd.org
Carol Zygo, Superintendent

Ilion CSD
1 Golden Bomber Dr, PO Box 480, Ilion, NY 13357-0480
315-894-9934 Fax: 315-894-2716
e-mail: ctangorra@ilioncsd.org
Web site: www.ilioncsd.org
Cosimo Tangorra, Superintendent

Little Falls City SD
15 Petrie St, Little Falls, NY 13365
315-823-1470
Web site: www.lfcsd.com
Louis J Patrei, Superintendent

Mohawk CSD
28 Grove St, Mohawk, NY 13407-1782
315-867-2904
e-mail: jcaputo@mohawkcsd.org
Joyce M Caputo, Superintendent

Mount Markham CSD
500 Fairground Rd, West Winfield, NY 13491-0500
315-822-2800
Web site: www.mmcsd.org
Casey Barduhn, Superintendent

Poland CSD
74 Cold Brook St, Poland, NY 13431
315-826-0203 Fax: 315-826-7516
Web site: www.polandcs.com
Laura Dutton, Superintendent

Town of Webb UFSD
3002 State Route 28, PO Box 38, Old Forge, NY 13420-0038
315-369-3222 Fax: 315-369-6216
Web site: www.towschool.org
Donald Gooley, Superintendent

Offices and agencies generally appear in alphabetical order, except when specific order is requested by listee.

Van Hornesville-Owen D Young CSD
2316 State Rt 80, PO Box 125, Van Hornesville, NY 13475-0125
315-858-0729 Fax: 315-858-2019
Web site: www.odyoungcsd.org
Virginia Keegan, Superintendent

West Canada Valley CSD
5447 State Rt 28, Newport, NY 13416-0360
315-845-6800 Fax: 315-845-8652
e-mail: jbanek@westcanada.org
Web site: www.westcanada.org
John Banek, Superintendent

JEFFERSON

Alexandria CSD
34 Bolton Ave, Alexandria Bay, NY 13607-1699
315-482-9971
Web site: www.alexandriacentral.org
Robert Wagoner, Superintendent

Belleville Henderson CSD
8372 County Rt 75, Belleville, NY 13611-0158
315-846-5826
e-mail: rmoore@bhpanthers.org
Web site: www.bhpanthers.org
Rick T Moore, Superintendent

Carthage CSD
25059 County Rt 197, Carthage, NY 13619-9527
315-493-5000
Web site: www.carthagecsd.org
Joseph Catanzaro, Superintendent

General Brown CSD
PO Box 500, Dexter, NY 13634
315-639-5100 Fax: 315-639-6916
e-mail: svigliotti@gblions.org
Web site: www.gblions.org
Stephan J Vigliotti Sr, Superintendent

Indian River CSD
32735-B County Rt 29, Philadelphia, NY 13673-0308
315-642-3441
Web site: www.ircsd.org
James Kettrick, Superintendent

La Fargeville CSD
20414 Sunrise Ave, PO Box 138, La Fargeville, NY 13656
315-658-2241 Fax: 315-658-4223
Web site: www.lafargevillecsd.org
Susan Whitney, Superintendent

Lyme CSD
11868 Academy St, PO Box 219, Chaumont, NY 13622-0219
315-649-2417 Fax: 315-649-2663
Web site: www.lymecsd.org
Karen M Donahue, Superintendent

Sackets Harbor Central School
215 S Broad St, Sackets Harbor, NY 13685
315-646-3575 Fax: 315-646-1038
e-mail: fhall@sacketspatriots.org
Web site: www.sacketspatriots.org
Frederick E Hall, Superintendent

South Jefferson CSD
PO Box 10, Adams, NY 13605
315-583-6104
e-mail: jmoese@spartanpride.org
Web site: www.spartanpride.org
Jamie A Moesel, Superintendent

Thousand Islands CSD
8483 County Rt 9, PO Box 1000, Clayton, NY 13624-1000
315-686-5594 Fax: 315-686-5511
Web site: www.1000islandschools.org
Joseph Menard, Superintendent

Watertown City SD
1351 Washington St, PO Box 586, Watertown, NY 13601
315-785-3700 Fax: 315-785-6855
e-mail: tfralick@watertowncsd.org
Web site: www.watertowncsd.org
Terry N Fralick, Superintendent

LEWIS

Beaver River CSD
9508 Artz Rd, Beaver Falls, NY 13305-0179
315-346-1211 Fax: 315-346-6775
Web site: www.brcsd.org
Leueen Smithing, Interim Superintendent

Copenhagen CSD
3020 Mechanic St, Copenhagen, NY 13626-0030
315-688-4411 Fax: 315-688-2001
Web site: www.ccsknights.org
Scott Connell, Superintendent

Harrisville CSD
14371 Pirate Lane, PO Box 200, Harrisville, NY 13648
315-543-2707
Web site: www.hcsk12.org
Rolf A Waters, Superintendent

Lowville Academy & CSD
7668 State St, Lowville, NY 13367
315-376-9000 Fax: 315-376-1933
Web site: www.lacs-ny.org
Kenneth J McAuliffe, Superintendent

South Lewis CSD
PO Box 10, Turin, NY 13473-0010
315-348-2500
Web site: www.southlewis.org
Douglas E Premo, Superintendent

LIVINGSTON

Avon CSD
191 Clinton St, Avon, NY 14414
585-226-2455 x1318 Fax: 585-226-8202
e-mail: bamey@avoncsd.org
Web site: www.avoncsd.org
Bruce Amey, Superintendent

Caledonia-Mumford CSD
99 North St, Caledonia, NY 14423
585-538-3400
e-mail: ddinolfo@cal-mum.org
Web site: www.cal-mum.org
David V Dinolfo, Superintendent

Dansville CSD
284 Main St, Dansville, NY 14437-9798
585-335-4000 Fax: 585-335-4002
Web site: www.dansvillecsd.org
Alioto Paul, Superintendent

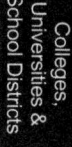

Colleges, Universities & School Districts

Offices and agencies generally appear in alphabetical order, except when specific order is requested by listee.

Geneseo CSD
4050 Avon Rd, Geneseo, NY 14454
585-243-3450 Fax: 585-243-9481
e-mail: timhayes@geneseocsd.org
Web site: www.geneseocsd.org
Timothy Hayes, Superintendent

Dalton-Nunda CSD (Keshequa)
13 Mill St, Nunda, NY 14517
585-468-2541 x1105 Fax: 585-468-3814
e-mail: jallman@keshequa.org
Web site: www.keshequa.org
John Allman, Superintendent

Livonia CSD
6 Puppy Lane, PO Box E, Livonia, NY 14487
585-346-4000 Fax: 585-346-6145
e-mail: sbischoping@livoniacsd.org
Web site: www.livoniacsd.org
Scott Bischoping, Superintendent

Mt Morris CSD
30 Bonadonna Ave, Mount Morris, NY 14510
585-658-2568 Fax: 585-658-4814
Web site: www.mtmorriscsd.org
Ed Orman, Superintendent

York CSD
2578 Genesee St, PO Box 102, Retsof, NY 14539-0102
585-243-1730 x2223 Fax: 585-243-5269
Web site: www.yorkcsd.org
Daniel Murray, Superintendent

MADISON

Brookfield CSD
1910 Fairground Rd, Brookfield, NY 13314-0060
315-899-3323 x200
Web site: www.bcsbeavers.org
Steve Szatko, Interim Superintendent

Canastota CSD
120 Roberts St, Canastota, NY 13032-1198
315-697-2025
Web site: www.canastotacsd.org
Frederick J Bragan, Superintendent

Cazenovia CSD
31 Emory Ave, Cazenovia, NY 13035-1098
315-655-1317 Fax: 315-655-1375
e-mail: rdubik@caz.cnyric.org
Web site: www.caz.cnyric.org
Robert Dubik, Superintendent

Chittenango CSD
1732 Fyler Rd, Chittenango, NY 13037-9520
315-687-2840 Fax: 315-687-2841
Web site: www.chittenangoschools.org
Thomas E Marzeski, Superintendent

De Ruyter CSD
711 Railroad St, Deruyter, NY 13052-0000
315-852-3410 Fax: 315-852-9600
Web site: www.deruyter.k12.ny.us
Charles W Walters, Superintendent

Hamilton CSD
47 W Kendrick Ave, Hamilton, NY 13346-1299
315-824-6310
e-mail: dbowers@hamiltoncentral.org
Web site: hamiltoncentral.org
Diana Bowers, Superintendent

Madison CSD
7303 State Route 20, Madison, NY 13402
315-893-1878
e-mail: cdedominick@madisoncentralny.org
Web site: www.madisoncentralny.org
Cynthia DeDominick, Superintendent

Morrisville-Eaton CSD
PO Box 990, Morrisville, NY 13408-0990
315-684-9300 Fax: 315-684-9399
e-mail: mdrahos@m-ecs.org
Web site: www.m-ecs.org
Michael Drahos, Superintendent

Oneida City SD
565 Sayles St, Oneida, NY 13421-0327
315-363-2550
e-mail: rspadafora@oneidacsd.org
Web site: www.oneida.org
Ronald R Spadafora Jr, Superintendent

Stockbridge Valley CSD
6011 Williams Rd, Munnsville, NY 13409-0732
315-495-4400 Fax: 315-495-4492
e-mail: cchafee@stockbridgevalley.org
Web site: www.stockbridgevalley.org
Chuck Chafee, Superintendent

MONROE

Brighton CSD
2035 Monroe Ave, Rochester, NY 14618-2027
585-242-5080 Fax: 585-242-5212
Web site: www.bcsd.org
Kevin McGowan, Superintendent

Brockport CSD
40 Allen St, Brockport, NY 14420-2296
585-637-1810
Web site: www.brockport.k12.ny.us
Garry Stone, Superintendent

Churchville-Chili CSD
139 Fairbanks Rd, Churchville, NY 14428-9797
585-293-1800 Fax: 585-293-1013
Web site: www.cccsd.org
Pam Kissel, Superintendent

East Irondequoit CSD
600 Pardee Rd, Rochester, NY 14609
585-339-1210 Fax: 585-288-0713
Web site: www.eicsd.k12.ny.us
Susan K Allen, Superintendent

East Rochester UFSD
222 Woodbine Ave, East Rochester, NY 14445
585-248-6302 Fax: 585-586-3254
Web site: www.erschools.org
Ray Giamartino, Jr, Superintendent

Fairport CSD
38 W Church St, Fairport, NY 14450-2130
585-421-2004 Fax: 585-421-3421
e-mail: jon_hunter@fairport.monroe.edu
Web site: www.fairport.org
Jon Hunter, Superintendent

Gates-Chili CSD
3 Spartan Way, Rochester, NY 14624
585-247-5050 x1217
Web site: www.gateschili.org
Mark C Davey, Superintendent

Offices and agencies generally appear in alphabetical order, except when specific order is requested by listee.

Greece CSD
PO Box 300, N Greece, NY 14515-0300
585-966-2000 Fax: 585-581-8203
Web site: www.greece.k12.ny.us
John O'Rourke, Interim Superintendent

Hilton CSD
225 West Ave, Hilton, NY 14468-1283
585-392-1000 Fax: 585-392-1038
Web site: www.hilton.k12.ny.us
David Dimbleby, Superintendent

Honeoye Falls-Lima CSD
20 Church St, Honeoye Falls, NY 14472-1294
585-624-7010
e-mail: michelle_kavanaugh@hflcsd.org
Web site: www.hflcsd.org
Michelle Kavanaugh, Superintendent

Penfield CSD
PO Box 900, Penfield, NY 14526-0900
585-249-5700 Fax: 585-248-8412
Web site: penfield.edu
John D Carlevatti, Superintendent

Pittsford CSD
75 Barker Road, Pittsford, NY 14534
585-267-1000 Fax: 585-381-2105
e-mail: maryalice_price@pittsford.monroe.edu
Web site: www.pittsfordschools.com
Mary Alice Price, Superintendent

Rochester City SD
131 W Broad St, Rochester, NY 14614
585-262-8100
Web site: www.rcsdk12.org
Jean Claude Brizard, Superintendent

Rush-Henrietta CSD
2034 Lehigh Station Rd, Henrietta, NY 14467-9692
585-359-5012 Fax: 585-359-5045
e-mail: kgraham@rhnet.org
Web site: www.rhnet.org
Kenneth Graham, Superintendent

Spencerport CSD
71 Lyell Ave, Spencerport, NY 14559-1899
585-349-5000 Fax: 585-349-5011
e-mail: bseaburn@spencerportschools.org
Web site: www.spencerportschools.org
Bonnie Seaburn, Superintendent

Webster CSD
119 South Ave, Webster, NY 14580-3594
585-216-0001 Fax: 585-265-6561
Web site: www.websterschools.org
Adele Bovard, Superintendent

West Irondequoit CSD
321 List Ave, Rochester, NY 14617-3125
585-336-2983 Fax: 585-266-1556
e-mail: marykay_herman@westiron.monroe.edu
Web site: www.westirondequoit.org
Jeffrey B Crane, Superintendent

Wheatland-Chili CSD
13 Beckwith Ave, Scottsville, NY 14546
585-889-4500 Fax: 585-889-6284
Web site: www.wheatland.k12.ny.us
Thomas Gallagher, Superintendent

MONTGOMERY

Canajoharie CSD
136 Scholastic Way, Canajoharie, NY 13317
518-673-6302 Fax: 518-673-3177
e-mail: richard.rose@canjo.org
Web site: www.canajoharieschools.org
Richard Rose, Superintendent

Fonda-Fultonville CSD
112 Old Johnstown Rd, Fonda, NY 12068-1501
518-853-4415 Fax: 518-853-4461
e-mail: jhoffman@ffcsd.org
Web site: www.ffcsd.org
James Hoffman, Superintendent

Fort Plain CSD
25 High St, Fort Plain, NY 13339-1218
518-993-4000 Fax: 518-993-3393
e-mail: fpcsss@hotmail.com
Web site: www.fortplain.org
Douglas C Burton, Superintendent

Greater Amsterdam SD
11 Liberty St, Amsterdam, NY 12010
518-843-3180 Fax: 518-842-0012
e-mail: tperillo@gasd.org
Web site: gasd.org
Thomas F Perillo, Superintendent

St Johnsville CSD
44 Center St, St Johnsville, NY 13452
518-568-7024 Fax: 518-568-5407
Web site: www.sjcsd.org
Ralph Acquaro, Superintendent

NASSAU

Baldwin UFSD
960 Hastings St, Baldwin, NY 11510
516-377-9200 Fax: 516-377-9421
Web site: www.baldwin.k12.ny.us
James Mapes, Superintendent

Bellmore UFSD
580 Winthrop Ave, Bellmore, NY 11710-5099
516-679-2909 Fax: 516-679-3027
Web site: www.bellmore.k12.ny.us
Joseph S Famularo, Superintendent

Bellmore-Merrick Central HS District
1260 Meadowbrook Rd, North Merrick, NY 11566
516-992-1000
Web site: www.bellmore-merrick.k12.ny.us
Henry Kiernan, Superintendent

Bethpage UFSD
10 Cherry Ave, Bethpage, NY 11714
516-644-4001
e-mail: tclark@bethpage.ws
Web site: wwwbethpagecommunity.com/Schools
Terrence Clark, Superintendent

Carle Place UFSD
168 Cherry Ln, Carle Place, NY 11514
516-622-6575
Web site: www.cps.k12.ny.us
David Flatley, Superintendent

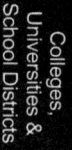

Colleges,
Universities &
School Districts

Offices and agencies generally appear in alphabetical order, except when specific order is requested by listee.

East Meadow UFSD
718 The Plain Road, Westbury, NY 11590
516-478-5776
Web site: www.eastmeadow.k12.ny.us
Louis R DeAngelo, Superintendent

East Rockaway UFSD
443 Ocean Ave, East Rockaway, NY 11518
516-887-8300
Web site: www.eastrockawayschools.org
Dr. Roseanne Melucci, Superintendent

East Williston UFSD
11 Bacon Rd, Old Westbury, NY 11568
516-333-3758 Fax: 516-333-1937
Web site: www.ewsdonline.org
Lorna R Lewis, Superintendent

Elmont UFSD
135 Elmont Rd, Elmont, NY 11003-1609
516-326-5500 Fax: 516-326-5574
Web site: www.elmontschools.org
Al Harper, Superintendent

Farmingdale UFSD
50 Van Cott Ave, Farmingdale, NY 11735
516-752-6510
Web site: www.farmingdaleschools.org
John Lorentz, Superintendent

Floral Park-Bellerose UFSD
One Poppy Pl, Floral Park, NY 11001
516-327-9300 Fax: 516-327-9304
Web site: www.floralpark.k12.ny.us
Lynn Pombonyo, Superintendent

Franklin Square UFSD
760 Washington St, Franklin Square, NY 11010
516-481-4100
e-mail: info@franklinsquare.k12.ny.us
Web site: franklinsquare.k12.ny.us
Patrick Manley, Superintendent

Freeport UFSD
235 N Ocean Ave, Freeport, NY 11520
516-867-5205 Fax: 516-623-4759
e-mail: kkuncham@freeportschools.org
Web site: www.freeportschools.org
Dr. Kishore Kunchan, Superintendent

Garden City UFSD
56 Cathedral Ave, PO Box 216, Garden City, NY 11530-0216
516-478-1000
Web site: www.gardencity.k12.ny.us
Robert Feirsen, Superintendent

Glen Cove City SD
150 Dosoris Ln, Glen Cove, NY 11542
516-801-7001
Web site: www.glencove.k12.ny.us
Joseph Laria, Superintendent

Great Neck UFSD
345 Lakeville Rd, Great Neck, NY 11020
516-441-4001 Fax: 516-773-6685
e-mail: tdolan@greatneck.k12.ny.us
Web site: www.greatneck.k12.ny.us
Dr Thomas P Dolan, Superintendent

Hempstead UFSD
185 Peninsula Blvd, Hempstead, NY 11550
516-292-7111 x1001
Web site: www.hempsteadschools.org
Patricia Watkins, Superintendent

Herricks UFSD
999 B Herricks Rd, New Hyde Park, NY 11040
516-305-8901
e-mail: jbierwirth@herricks.org
Web site: www.herricks.org
John E Bierwirth, Superintendent

Hewlett-Woodmere UFSD
1 Johnson Pl, Woodmere, NY 11598
516-374-8100 Fax: 516-374-8101
Web site: www.hewlett-woodmere.net
Joyce Bisso, Superintendent

Hicksville UFSD
200 Division Ave-Adm, Hicksville, NY 11801-4800
516-733-2110
Web site: www.hicksvillepublicschools.org
Maureen K Bright, Superintendent

Island Park UFSD
150 Trafalgar Blvd, Island Park, NY 11558
516-431-8100 Fax: 516-431-7550
Web site: www.ips.k12.ny.us
Rosmarie Bovino, Superintendent

Island Trees UFSD
74 Farmedge Rd, Levittown, NY 11756
516-520-2100
e-mail: cmurphy@islandtrees.org
Web site: www.islandtrees.org
Charles J Murphy, Superintendent

Jericho UFSD
99 Cedar Swamp Rd, Jericho, NY 11753
516-203-3600 x3201
e-mail: hgrishman@jerichoschools.org
Web site: www.bestschools.org
Henry L Grishman, Superintendent

Lawrence UFSD
195 Broadway, Lawrence, NY 11559
516-295-8000
Web site: www.lawrence.org
John T Fitzsimons, Superintendent

Levittown UFSD
150 Abbey Ln, Levittown, NY 11756
516-520-8300 Fax: 516-520-8314
Web site: www.levittownschools.com
Herman A Sirois, Superintendent

Locust Valley CSD
22 Horse Hollow Rd, Locust Valley, NY 11560
516-277-5001
e-mail: ahunderfund@lvcsd.k12.ny.us
Web site: www.lvcsd.k12.ny.us
Anna Hunderfund, Superintendent

Long Beach City SD
235 Lido Blvd, Long Beach, NY 11561-5093
516-897-2104
Web site: www.lbeach.org
Robert Greenberg, Superintendent

Lynbrook UFSD
111 Atlantic Ave, Lynbrook, NY 11563
516-887-0253
Web site: www.lynbrook.k12.ny.us
Santo Barbarino, Superintendent

Malverne UFSD
301 Wicks Ln, Malverne, NY 11565-2244
516-887-6400
Web site: www.malverne.k12.ny.us
James H Hunderfund, Superintendent

Manhasset UFSD
200 Memorial Pl, Manhasset, NY 11030
516-267-7705 Fax: 516-627-8158
e-mail: ccardillo@manhasset.k12.ny.us
Web site: www.manhasset.k12.ny.us
Charles S Cardillo, Superintendent

Massapequa UFSD
4925 Merrick Rd, Massapequa, NY 11758
516-308-5001
Web site: www.msd.k12.ny.us
Charles Sulc, Superintendent

Merrick UFSD
21 Babylon Rd, Merrick, NY 11566
516-992-7240
Web site: www.merrick-k6.org
Ranier W Melucci, Superintendent

Mineola UFSD
121 Jackson Ave, Mineola, NY 11501
516-237-2001 Fax: 516-237-2008
e-mail: mnagler@mineola.k12.ny.ua
Web site: www.mineola.k12.ny,us
Michael Nagler, Superintendent

New Hyde Park-Garden City Park UFSD
1950 Hillside Ave, New Hyde Park, NY 11040
516-352-6257 x221
e-mail: rkatulak@nhp-gcp.org
Web site: www.nhp-gcp.org
Robert Katulak, Superintendent

North Bellmore UFSD
2616 Martin Ave, Bellmore, NY 11710
516-992-3000 x4001
Web site: www.northbellmoreschools.org
Arnold Goldstein, Superintendent

North Merrick UFSD
1057 Merrick Ave, Merrick, NY 11566
516-292-3694 Fax: 516-292-3097
Web site: www.nmerrickschools.org
David S Feller, Superintendent

North Shore CSD
112 Franklin Ave, Sea Cliff, NY 11579
516-277-7800 or 516-277-7801
Web site: www.northshore.k12.ny.us
Edward K Melnick, Superintendent

Oceanside UFSD
145 Merle Ave, Oceanside, NY 11572-2206
516-678-1215
e-mail: hbrown@oceanside.k12.ny.us
Web site: www.oceanside.k12.ny.us
Herb R Brown, Superintendent

Oyster Bay-East Norwich CSD
1 McCouns Ln, Oyster Bay, NY 11771-3105
516-624-6505
e-mail: pharrington@obenschools.org
Web site: obenschools.org
Phyllis Harrington, Superintendent

Plainedge UFSD
241 Wyngate Dr, PO Box 1669, North Massapequa, NY 11758
516-992-7455 Fax: 516-992-7446
Web site: www.plainedgeschools.org
Christine P'Simer, Superintendent

Plainview-Old Bethpage CSD
106 Washington Ave, Plainview, NY 11803-3612
516-937-6301
Web site: www.pob.k12.ny.us
Gerald W Dempsey, Superintendent

Port Washington UFSD
100 Campus Dr, Port Washington, NY 11050
516-767-5005 Fax: 516-767-5007
e-mail: gng@portnet.k12.ny.us
Web site: www.portnet.k12.ny.us
Geoffrey N Gordon, Superintendent

Rockville Centre UFSD
128 Shepherd St, Rockville Centre, NY 11570-2298
516-255-8920
Web site: www.rvcschools.org
William H Johnson, Superintendent

Roosevelt UFSD
240 Denton Pl, Roosevelt, NY 11575-1539
516-345-7001 Fax: 516-379-0178
e-mail: rwharris@rooseveltufsd.com
Web site: www.rooseveltufsd.com

Roslyn UFSD
300 Harbor Hill Rd, Roslyn, NY 11576-1531
516-625-6303 Fax: 516-625-6336
e-mail: roslynsd@roslynschools.org
Web site: www.roslynschools.org
Daniel Brenner, Superintendent

Seaford UFSD
1600 Washington Ave, Seaford, NY 11783
516-592-4002
e-mail: bconboy@mail.seaford.k12.ny.us
Web site: www.seaford.k12.ny.us
Brian Conboy, Superintendent

Sewanhaka Central HS District
77 Landau Ave, Floral Park, NY 11001
516-488-9800 Fax: 516-488-9899
Web site: www.sewanhaka.k12.ny.us
Warren A Meierdiercks, Superintendent

Syosset CSD
99 Pell Ln, PO Box 9029, Syosset, NY 11791
516-364-5605
Web site: www.syosett.k12.ny.us
Carole G Hankin, Superintendent

Uniondale UFSD
933 Goodrich St, Uniondale, NY 11553-2499
516-560-8824 Fax: 516-292-2659
e-mail: wlloyd@uniondaleschools.org
Web site: district.uniondaleschools.org
William K Lloyd, Superintendent

Colleges,
Universities &
School Districts

Offices and agencies generally appear in alphabetical order, except when specific order is requested by listee.

Valley Stream 13 UFSD
585 N Corona Ave, Valley Stream, NY 11580
516-568-6100 Fax: 516-825-2537
e-mail: elison@valleystream13.com
Web site: www.valleystream13.com
Elizabeth Lison, Superintendent

Valley Stream 24 UFSD
75 Horton Ave, Valley Stream, NY 11581-1420
516-256-0153
Web site: www.valleystreamdistrict24.com
Edward M Fale, Superintendent

Valley Stream 30 UFSD
175 N Central Ave, Valley Stream, NY 11580-3801
516-285-9881
Web site: www.valleystream30.com
Elaine Kanas, Superintendent

Valley Stream Central HS District
One Kent Rd, Valley Stream, NY 11580-3398
516-872-5601 Fax: 516-872-5658
Web site: www.vschsd.org
Richard Marsh, Superintendent

Wantagh UFSD
3301 Beltagh Ave, Wantagh, NY 11793-3395
516-679-6300
e-mail: wantaghinfo@wantaghschools.org
Web site: www.wantaghschools.org
Lydia Begley, Superintendent

West Hempstead UFSD
252 Chestnut St, West Hempstead, NY 11552-2455
516-390-3107 Fax: 516-489-1776
Web site: www.whufsd.com
John J Hogan, Superintendent

Westbury UFSD
2 Hitchcock Ln, Old Westbury, NY 11568-1624
516-876-5016 Fax: 516-876-5187
e-mail: cclark-snead@westburyschools.org
Web site: www.westburyschools.org
Constance R Clark-Snead, Superintendent

NEW YORK CITY

NYC Chancellor's Office
52 Chambers St, New York, NY 10007
212-374-6000 Fax: 212-374-5763
Cathie Black, Chancellor

NYC Citywide Alternative HS District & Programs
9027 Sutphin Blvd, Jamaica, NY 11435
718-557-2681
Cami Anderson, Senior Superintendent

NYC Citywide Special Ed District 75
400 First Ave, New York, NY 10010
212-802-1500
Web site: schools.nycenet.edu/d75/
Gary Hecht, Superintendent

NYC Region 1
1 Fordham Plz, Rm 81, Bronx, NY 10458
718-741-7030
Yvonne Torres, Superintendent

NYC Region 2
1230 Zerega Ave, Bronx, NY 10462
718-828-2440
Timothy Behr, Superintendent

NYC Region 3
30-48 Linden Pl, Flushing, NY 11354
718-281-7575
Anita Saunder, Superintendent

NYC Region 4
28-11 Queens Plz N, Long Island City, NY 11101
718-391-8300
Madeline Chan, Superintendent

NYC Region 5
82-01 Rockaway Blvd, Queens, NY 11416
718-270-5800 or 718-922-4960
Kathleen M Cashin, Superintendent

NYC Region 6
5619 Flatlands Ave, Brooklyn, NY 11234
718-968-6100
Jean Claude Brizard, Superintendent

NYC Region 7
715 Ocean Terr, Building 1, Staten Island, NY 10301
718-556-8350
Margaret Schultz, Superintendent

NYC Region 8
131 Livingston St, Brooklyn, NY 11201
718-935-3900
Anita Scop, Superintendent

NYC Region 9
333 7th Ave & 28th St, Room 712, New York, NY 10001
212-356-7500
Luz Cortazzo, Superintendent

NYC Region 10
4360 Broadway, Rm 52, New York, NY 10033
917-521-3700
Gale Reeves, Superintendent

NIAGARA

Barker CSD
1628 Quaker Rd, Barker, NY 14012-0328
716-795-3832
Dr Roger J Klatt, Superintendent

Lewiston-Porter CSD
4061 Creek Rd, Youngstown, NY 14174-9799
716-286-7266
e-mail: rappoldd@lew-port.com
Web site: www.lew-port.com
R Christopher Roser, Superintendent

Lockport City SD
130 Beattie Ave, Lockport, NY 14094-5099
716-478-4835 Fax: 716-478-4863
e-mail: tacarbone@lockport.wnyric.org
Web site: www.lockportschools.wnyric.org
Terry Ann Carbone, Superintendent

Newfane CSD
6273 Charlotteville Rd, Newfane, NY 14108
716-778-6850 Fax: 716-778-6852
Web site: www.newfane.wnyric.org
Christine Tibbetts, Superintendent

Offices and agencies generally appear in alphabetical order, except when specific order is requested by listee.

Niagara Falls City SD
630-66th Street, Niagara Falls, NY 14304
716-286-4205 Fax: 716-286-4283
e-mail: cbianco@nfschools.net
Web site: www.nfschools.net
Cynthia A Bianco, Superintendent

Niagara-Wheatfield CSD
6700 Schultz St, Niagara Falls, NY 14304
716-215-3003 Fax: 716-215-3039
e-mail: jhoward@nwcsd.wnyric.org
Web site: www.nwcsd.k12.ny.us
Carl H Militello, Superintendent

North Tonawanda City SD
175 Humphrey St, North Tonawanda, NY 14120-4097
716-807-3500
Web site: www.ntschools.org
Gregory Woytila, Superintendent

Royalton-Hartland CSD
54 State St, Middleport, NY 14105-1199
716-735-3031 Fax: 716-735-3660
e-mail: macdonaldk@royhart.org
Web site: www.royhart.org
Kevin MacDonald, Superintendent

Starpoint CSD
4363 Mapleton Rd, Lockport, NY 14094
716-210-2342
e-mail: dwhelan@starpointcsd.org
Web site: www.starpointcsd.org
C Douglas Whelan, Superintendent

Wilson CSD
412 Lake St, Wilson, NY 14172
716-751-9341
Web site: www.wilson.wnyric.org
Michael Wendt, Superintendent

ONEIDA

Adirondack CSD
110 Ford St, Boonville, NY 13309-1200
315-942-9200 Fax: 315-942-5522
Web site: www.adirondackcsd.org
David Hubman, Superintendent

Camden CSD
51 Third St, Camden, NY 13316-1114
315-245-4075
Web site: www.camdenschools.org
Dr Jeffrey K Bryant, Superintendent

Clinton CSD
75 Chenango Ave, Clinton, NY 13323
315-557-2253 Fax: 315-853-8727
e-mail: mreilly@ccs.edu
Web site: www.ccs.edu
Matthew Reilly, Superintendent

Holland Patent CSD
9601 Main St, Holland Patent, NY 13354-4610
315-865-7221
Web site: www.hpschools.org
Kathleen M Davis, Superintendent

NY Mills UFSD
1 Marauder Blvd, New York Mills, NY 13417-1566
315-768-8127 Fax: 315-768-3521
Web site: www.newyorkmills.org
Kathy Houghton, Superintendent

New Hartford CSD
33 Oxford Rd, New Hartford, NY 13413
315-624-1218
Web site: www.newhartfordschools.org
Robert J Nole, Superintendent

Oriskany CSD
1313 Utica St, Oriskany, NY 13424-0539
315-768-2058 Fax: 315-768-2057
Web site: www.oriskanycsd.org
Gregory Kelahan, Superintendent

Remsen CSD
9733 Davis Dr, PO Box 406, Remsen, NY 13438
315-831-3797
Web site: www.remsencsd.org
Joanne Shelmidine, Superintendent

Rome City SD
409 Bell Rd, Rome, NY 13440
315-338-6500 Fax: 315-334-7409
Web site: www.romecsd.org
Jeffrey Simons, Superintendent

Sauquoit Valley CSD
2601 Oneida St, Sauquoit, NY 13456-1000
315-839-6311
Web site: www.svcsd.org
Ronald J Wheelock, Superintendent

Sherrill City SD
5275 State Route 31, PO Box 128, Verona, NY 13478-0128
315-829-2520 Fax: 315-829-4949
Web site: www.vvsschools.org
Norman Reed, Superintendent

Utica City SD
106 Memorial Parkway, Utica, NY 13501-3709
315-792-2222
Web site: www.uticaschools.org
James Willis, Superintendent

Vernon-Verona-Sherrill CSD
5275 State Rt 31, Verona, NY 13478-0128
315-829-2520 Fax: 315-829-4949
Web site: www.vvscentralschools.org
Norman Reed, Superintendent

Waterville CSD
381 Madison St, Waterville, NY 13480-1100
315-841-3900
e-mail: districtoffice@watervilleschools.org
Web site: www.watervilleschools.org
Gary Lonczak, Superintendent

Westmoreland CSD
5176 Rt 233, Westmoreland, NY 13490-0430
315-557-2601
e-mail: tkulak@westmorelandschool.org
Web site: www.westmorelandschool.org
Rocco Migliori, Superintendent

Whitesboro CSD
67 Whitesboro St, PO Box 304, Yorkville, NY 13495-0304
315-266-3303 Fax: 315-768-9723
Web site: www.wboro.org
Dave Langone, Superintendent

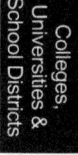

Colleges,
Universities &
School Districts

Offices and agencies generally appear in alphabetical order, except when specific order is requested by listee.

ONONDAGA

Baldwinsville CSD
29 E Oneida St, Baldwinsville, NY 13027-2480
315-638-6043 Fax: 315-638-6041
e-mail: jdangle@bville.org
Web site: www.bville.org
Jeanne M Dangle, Superintendent

East Syracuse-Minoa CSD
407 Fremont Rd, East Syracuse, NY 13057-2631
315-434-3012 Fax: 315-434-3020
e-mail: mvasiloff@esmschools.org
Web site: www.esmschools.org
Dr Donna J DeSiato, Superintendent

Fabius-Pompey CSD
1211 Mill St, Fabius, NY 13063-8719
315-683-5301 Fax: 315-683-5827
e-mail: tryan@fabius.cnyric.org
Web site: www.fabiuspompey.org
Timothy P Ryan, Superintendent

Fayetteville-Manlius CSD
8199 E Seneca Tpke, Manlius, NY 13104-2140
315-692-1200 Fax: 315-692-1227
e-mail: ckaiser@fmschools.org
Web site: www.fmschools.org
Corliss Kaiser, Superintendent

Jamesville-Dewitt CSD
6845 Edinger Dr, PO Box 606, Dewitt, NY 13214-0606
315-445-8304 Fax: 315-445-8477
e-mail: ckendrick@jd.cnyric.org
Web site: www.jamesvilledewitt.org
Alice Kendrick, Superintendent

Jordan-Elbridge CSD
9 N Chappell St, Jordan, NY 13080
315-689-8500 or 315-689-0084
e-mail: mdominick@jecsd.org
Web site: www.jecsd.org
Lawrence Zacher, Superintendent

LaFayette CSD
5955 Rt 20 W, Lafayette, NY 13084-9701
315-677-9728 Fax: 315-677-3372
e-mail: ptigh@lafcs.cnyric.org
Web site: www.lafayetteschools.org
Peter A Tigh, Superintendent

Liverpool CSD
195 Blackberry Rd, Liverpool, NY 13090
315-622-7125 Fax: 315-622-7115
e-mail: jan@liverpool.k12.ny.us
Web site: www.liverpool.k12.ny.us
Dr Richard N Johns, Superintendent

Lyncourt UFSD
2707-2709 Court St, Syracuse, NY 13208
315-455-7571 Fax: 315-455-7573
e-mail: msandore@lyncourt.cnyric.org
Web site: www.lyncourt.cnyric.org
Michael Schiedo, Superintendent

Marcellus CSD
2 Reed Pkwy, Marcellus, NY 13108-1199
315-673-0201 Fax: 315-673-0329
e-mail: ctice@mcs.cnyric.org
Web site: marcellusschools.org
Craig J Tice, Superintendent

North Syracuse CSD
5355 W Taft Rd, North Syracuse, NY 13212-2796
315-218-2151
e-mail: jmelvin@nscsd.org
Web site: www.nscsd.org
Jerome F Melvin, Superintendent

Onondaga CSD
4466 S Onondaga Rd, Nedrow, NY 13120-9715
315-552-5000
Web site: www.ocs.cnyric.org
Joseph Rotella, Superintendent

Skaneateles CSD
45 E Elizabeth St, Skaneateles, NY 13152
315-685-8361 Fax: 315-685-0347
Web site: www.skanschools.org
Philip D D'Angelo, Superintendent

Solvay UFSD
103 3rd St, Solvay, NY 13209-1532
315-468-1111 Fax: 315-468-2755
e-mail: manningj@solvay.cnyric.org
Web site: www.solvayschools.org
J Francis Manning, Superintendent

Syracuse City SD
725 Harrison St, Syracuse, NY 13210
315-435-4161 Fax: 315-435-4015
e-mail: dlowengard@scsd.org
Web site: www.syracusecityschools.com
Daniel G Lowengard, Superintendent

Tully CSD
20 State St, PO Box 628, Tully, NY 13159-0628
315-696-6204
e-mail: kraig@pobox.com
Web site: www.tullyschools.org
Kraig D Pritts, Superintendent

West Genesee CSD
300 Sanderson Dr, Camillus, NY 13031-1655
315-487-4562 Fax: 315-487-2999
e-mail: rrubeis@wgmail.cnyric.org
Web site: www.westgenesee.org
Dr Christopher R Brown, Superintendent

Westhill CSD
400 Walberta Rd, Syracuse, NY 13219-2214
315-426-3000 Fax: 315-488-6411
e-mail: sbocciolatt@westhillschools.org
Web site: www.westhillschools.org
Stephen A Bocciolatt, Superintendent

ONTARIO

Thomas Striving, Interim Superintendent

Canandaigua City SD
143 N Pearl St, Canandaigua, NY 14424-1496
585-396-3700
e-mail: rawd@canandaiguaschools.org
Web site: www.canandaiguaschools.org
Ronald Raw Jr, Superintendent

East Bloomfield CSD
1 Oakmont Avenue, East Bloomfield, NY 14443
585-657-6121
Web site: www.bloomfieldcsd.org
Michael J Midey, Superintendent

Offices and agencies generally appear in alphabetical order, except when specific order is requested by listee.

Geneva City SD
400 W North St, Geneva, NY 14456
315-781-0400 Fax: 315-781-4128
e-mail: ryoung@genevacsd.org
Web site: www.genevacsd.org
Robert C Young Jr, Superintendent

Gorham-Middlesex CSD (Marcus Whitman)
4100 Baldwin Road, Rushville, NY 14544
585-554-4848 X1805
Web site: www.mwcsd.org
Michael Chirco, Superintendent

Honeoye CSD
8523 Main St, Honeoye, NY 14471-0170
585-229-4125
Web site: www.honeoye.org
David C Bills, Superintendent

Manchester-Shortsville CSD
1506 Rt 21, Shortsville, NY 14548-9502
585-289-3964 Fax: 585-289-6660
e-mail: rleiby@redjacket.org
Web site: www.redjacket.org
Robert E Leiby, Superintendent

Marcus Whitman CSD
4100 Baldwin Rd, Rushville, NY 14544-9799
585-554-4848
e-mail: mchirco@mwcsd.org
Web site: www.mwcsd.org
Michael Chirco, Superintendent

Naples CSD
136 N Main St, Naples, NY 14512-9201
585-374-7901
e-mail: kward@naples.k12.ny.us
Web site: www.naples.k12.ny.us
Kimberle Ward, Superintendent

Phelps-Clifton Springs CSD
1490 Rt 488, Clifton Springs, NY 14432-9334
315-548-6420
Web site: www.midlakes.org
Michael J Ford, Superintendent

Victor CSD
953 High St, Victor, NY 14564-1167
585-924-3252 x1400 Fax: 585-742-7090
e-mail: santiago-marullod@victorschools.org
Web site: www.victorschools.org
Dawn A Santiago-Marullo, Superintendent

ORANGE

Chester UFSD
64 Hambletonian Ave, Chester, NY 10918
845-469-5052
Sean Michel, Superintendent

Cornwall CSD
24 Idlewild Ave, Cornwall on Hudson, NY 12520
845-534-8000 Fax: 845-534-4231
e-mail: trehm@cornwallschools.com
Web site: www.cornwallschools.com
Timothy J Rehm, Superintendent

Florida UFSD
51 N Main St, PO Box 7, Florida, NY 10921-0757
845-651-3095
e-mail: dburnside@floridaufsd.org
Web site: www.floridaufsd.org
Douglas Burnside, Superintendent

Goshen CSD
227 Main St, Goshen, NY 10924
845-615-6720 Fax: 845-615-6725
Web site: www.goshenschoolsny.org
Daniel T Connor, Superintendent of Schools

Greenwood Lake UFSD
PO Box 8, Greenwood Lake, NY 10925
845-782-8678
e-mail: rbrockel@gwlufsd.org
Web site: www.gwlufsd.org
Dr Richard J Brockel, Superintendent

Highland Falls CSD
PO Box 287, Highland Falls, NY 10928
845-446-9575 Fax: 845-446-3321
Web site: www.hffmcsd.org
Dr Debra Jackson, Superintendent

Kiryas Joel Village UFSD
48 Bakertown Rd- Ste 401, Monroe, NY 10950-0398
845-782-2300
Joel Petlin, Superintendent

Middletown City SD
223 Wisner Ave Ext, Middletown, NY 10940-3240
845-326-51158 Fax: 845-343-9938
e-mail: keastwood@ecsdm.org
Web site: middletowncityschools.org
Kenneth Eastwood, Superintendent

Minisink Valley CSD
Rt 6, PO Box 217, Slate Hill, NY 10973-0217
845-355-5110
Web site: www.minisink.com
John Latini, Superintendent

Monroe-Woodbury CSD
278 Rte 32, Educ Ctr, Central Valley, NY 10917-1001
845-460-6200 Fax: 845-460-6080
Web site: www.mw.k12.ny.us
Edward Mehrhof, Superintendent

Newburgh Enlarged City SD
124 Grand St, Newburgh, NY 12550-4600
845-563-3400 Fax: 845-563-3501
e-mail: rpizzo1@necsd.net
Web site: www.newburghschools.org
Ralph A Pizzo, Superintendent

Pine Bush CSD
156 State Rt 302, PO Box 700, Pine Bush, NY 12566-0700
845-744-2031
Web site: www.pinebushschools.org
Philip G Steinberg, Superintendent

Port Jervis City SD
9 Thompson St, Port Jervis, NY 12771-3058
845-858-3100 Fax: 845-856-1885
e-mail: jxanthis@pjschools.org
Web site: www.pjschools.org
John P Xanthis, Superintendent

Colleges,
Universities &
School Districts

Offices and agencies generally appear in alphabetical order, except when specific order is requested by listee.

Tuxedo UFSD
Route 17, Box 2002, Tuxedo Park, NY 10987
845-351-2296 Fax: 845-351-5296
e-mail: clomascolo@tuxedoschooldistrict.com
Web site: www.tuxedoschooldistrict.com
Carol Lomascolo, Superintendent

Valley CSD (Montgomery)
944 State Rt 17k, Montgomery, NY 12549-2240
845-457-2400
Web site: www.vcsd.k12.ny.us
Richard M Hooley, Superintendent

Warwick Valley CSD
PO Box 595, Warwick, NY 10990-0595
845-987-3010
e-mail: fbryant@wvcsd.org
Web site: www.warwickvalleyschools.org
Dr Raymond W Bryant, Superintendent

Washingtonville CSD
52 W Main St, Washingtonville, NY 10992-1492
845-497-4000 Fax: 845-496-4031
Roberta Green, Superintendent

ORLEANS

Albion CSD
324 East Ave, Albion, NY 14411
585-589-2056
Web site: www.albionk12.org
Michael Bonnewell, Superintendent

Holley CSD
3800 N Main St, Holley, NY 14470-9330
585-638-6316
Web site: www.holleycsd.org
Robert C D'Angelo, Superintendent

Kendall CSD
1932 Kendall Rd, Kendall, NY 14476-0777
585-659-2741
e-mail: kcsd@kendallschools.org
Web site: www.kendallschools.org
Julie Christensen, Interim Superintendent

Lyndonville CSD
25 Housel Ave, Lyndonville, NY 14098-0540
585-765-2251 x3101
e-mail: bdeane-williams@lyndonville.wnyric.org
Web site: www.lyndonvillecsd.org
Barbara Deane-Williams, Superintendent

Medina CSD
One Mustang Dr, Medina, NY 14103-1845
585-798-2700
e-mail: rgalante@medinacsd.org
Web site: www.medinacsd.org
Neal S Miller, Superintendent

OSWEGO

Altmar-Parish-Williamstown CSD
639 County Rt 22, Parish, NY 13131
315-625-5251
e-mail: dhaab@apw.cnyric.org
Gerry D Hudson, Superintendent

Central Square CSD
642 S Main St, Central Square, NY 13036-3511
315-668-4220
e-mail: ccostello@cssd.org
Carolyn Costello, Superintendent

Fulton City SD
167 S Fourth St, Fulton, NY 13069-1859
315-593-5510
e-mail: blynch@fulton.cnyric.org
William R Lynch, Superintendent

Hannibal CSD
928 Cayuga St, Hannibal, NY 13074
315-564-7900
e-mail: mdifabio@hannibal.cnyric.org
Michael J DiFabio, Superintendent

Mexico CSD
40 Academy St, Mexico, NY 13114-3432
315-963-8400
Robert Pritchard, Superintendent

Oswego City SD
120 E 1st St, Oswego, NY 13126-2114
315-341-2001
e-mail: wcrist@oswego.org
Web site: www.oswego.org
William Crist, Superintendent

Phoenix CSD
116 Volney St, Phoenix, NY 13135-9778
315-695-1555
Web site: www.phoenixcsd.org
Judy Belfield, Superintendent

Pulaski CSD
2 Hinman Rd, Pulaski, NY 13142-2201
315-298-5188
e-mail: mmarshal@pacs.cnyric.org
Marshall Marshall, Superintendent

Sandy Creek CSD
124 Salisbury St, Sandy Creek, NY 13145-0248
315-387-3445
e-mail: samell@sccs.cnyric.org
Stewart R Amell, Superintendent

OTSEGO

Cherry Valley-Springfield CSD
597 County Hwy 54, Cherry Valley, NY 13320-0485
607-264-3265 Fax: 607-264-3458
e-mail: info@cvscs.org
Web site: www.cvscs.org
Robert Miller, Superintendent

Cooperstown CSD
39 Linden Ave, Cooperstown, NY 13326-1496
607-547-5364 Fax: 607-547-1000
Web site: www.cooperstowncs.org
Clifton Hebert, Superintendent

Edmeston CSD
11 North St, PO Box 5129, Edmeston, NY 13335-0529
607-965-8931 Fax: 607-965-8942
e-mail: drowley@edmeston.net
David Rowley, Superintendent

Offices and agencies generally appear in alphabetical order, except when specific order is requested by listee.

Gilbertsville-Mount Upton CSD
693 State Hwy 51, Gilbertsville, NY 13776
607-783-2207
e-mail: gmu@gmucsd.org
Web site: www.gmucsd.org
Glenn R Hamilton, Superintendent

Laurens CSD
PO Box 301, Laurens, NY 13796-0301
607-432-2050 Fax: 607-432-4388
e-mail: rwenck@laurenscs.org
Romona N Wenck, Superintendent

Milford CSD
42 W Main St, Milford, NY 13807-0237
607-286-3341 Fax: 607-286-7879
Peter N Livshin, Superintendent

Morris CSD
65 Main St, Morris, NY 13808-0040
607-263-6100 Fax: 607-263-2483
e-mail: mvigil@morriscs.org
Matthew Sheldon, Superintendent

Oneonta City SD
189 Main St, Ste 302, Oneonta, NY 13820-1142
607-433-8232 Fax: 607-433-3641
e-mail: mshea@oneontacsd.org
Web site: www.oneontacsd.org
Michael P Shea, Superintendent

Otego-Unadilla CSD
2641 State Hwy 7, Otego, NY 13825
607-988-5038 Fax: 607-988-1039
Web site: www.unatego.org
Charles Molloy, Superintendent

Richfield Springs CSD
93 Main St, PO Box 631, Richfield Springs, NY 13439-0631
315-858-0610
Web site: www.richfieldcsd.org
Robert Barraco, Superintendent

Schenevus CSD
159 Main St, Schenevus, NY 12155-0008
607-638-5530 Fax: 607-638-5600
e-mail: lbooknard@schenevuscs.org
Lynda Booknard, Superintendent

Unatego CSD
2641 State Hwy 7, Otego, NY 13825
607-988-5000 Fax: 607-988-1039
Web site: www.unatego.org
Charles Molloy, Superintendent

Worcester CSD
198 Main St, Worcester, NY 12197
607-397-8785 Fax: 607-397-9454
e-mail: seloverj@worcestercs.org
Gary M Kuch, Superintendent

PUTNAM

Brewster CSD
30 Farm-to-Market Rd, Brewster, NY 10509-9956
845-279-8000
e-mail: jsandbank@brewsterschools.org
Web site: www.brewsterschools.org
Jane Sandbank, Superintendent

Carmel CSD
81 South St, PO Box 296, Patterson, NY 12563-0296
845-878-2094 Fax: 845-878-4337
e-mail: info@ccsd.k12.ny.us
Web site: www.ccsd.k12.ny.us or www.carmelschools.com
James M Ryan, Superintendent

Garrison UFSD
1100 Rt 9 D, Garrison, NY 10524-0193
845-424-3689 Fax: 845-424-4733
e-mail: gcolucci@gufs.org
Web site: www.gufs.org
Gloria J Colucci, Superintendent

Haldane CSD
15 Craigside Dr, Cold Spring, NY 10516-1899
845-265-9254
Web site: www.haldaneschool.org
Mark Villanti, Superintendent

Mahopac CSD
179 East Lake Blvd, Mahopac, NY 10541-1666
845-628-3415 ext 326 Fax: 845-628-5502
Web site: www.mahopac.k12.ny.us
Thomas J Manko, Superintendent

Putnam Valley CSD
146 Peekskill Hollow Rd, Putnam Valley, NY 10579-3238
845-528-8143 Fax: 845-528-0274
e-mail: bfuchs@pvcsd.org
Web site: www.pvcsd.org
Barbara Fuchs, Superintendent

RENSSELAER

Averill Park CSD
146 Gettle Rd, Averill Park, NY 12018-9798
518-674-7055 Fax: 518-674-3802
e-mail: mocciaj@averillpark.k12.ny.us
Web site: www.averillpark.k12.ny.us
Josephine Moccia, Superintendent

Berlin CSD
53 School St, PO Box 259, Berlin, NY 12022-0259
518-658-2690 Fax: 518-658-3822
e-mail: tdiamond@berlincentral.org
Web site: www.berlincentral.org
Brian Howard, Acting Superintendent

Brunswick CSD (Brittonkill)
3992 NY Rt 2, Troy, NY 12180-9034
518-279-4600 x602 Fax: 518-279-1918
e-mail: dburnham@brittonkill.k12.ny.us
Louis C McIntosh, Superintendent

East Greenbush CSD
29 Englewood Ave, East Greenbush, NY 12061
518-207-2500
Web site: www.egcsd.org
Dr Angela M Guptill, Superintendent

Hoosic Valley CSD
2 Pleasant Ave, Schaghticoke, NY 12154
518-753-4450
Web site: www.hoosickvalley.k12.ny.us
Douglas Kelley, Superintendent

Hoosick Falls CSD
21187 NY Rt 22, PO Box 192, Hoosick Falls, NY 12090-0192
518-686-7012 Fax: 518-686-9060
Kenneth A Facin, Superintendent

Colleges,
Universities &
School Districts

Offices and agencies generally appear in alphabetical order, except when specific order is requested by listee.

Lansingburgh CSD
576 Fifth Ave, Troy, NY 12182-3295
518-233-6850
George Goodwin, Superintendent

North Greenbush Common SD (Williams)
476 N Greenbush Rd, Rensselaer, NY 12144
518-283-6748
Mary Ann Taylor, Superintendent

Rensselaer City SD
25 Van Rensselaer Dr, Rensselaer, NY 12144-2694
518-465-7509
Web site: www.rcsd.k12.ny.us
Sally Ann Shields, Superintendent

Schodack CSD
1216 Maple Hill Rd, Castleton, NY 12033-1699
518-732-2297 Fax: 518-732-7710
Web site: www.schodack.k12.ny.us
Robert Horan, Superintendent

Troy City Enlarged SD
2920 5th Ave, Troy, NY 12180
518-328-5052
Fadhilika Atiba-Weza, Superintendent

Wynantskill UFSD
East Ave, PO Box 345, Wynantskill, NY 12198-0345
518-283-4679 Fax: 518-283-3799
e-mail: chamill@wynantskillufsd.org
Web site: www.wynantskillufsd.org
Christine Hamill, Superintendent

ROCKLAND

Clarkstown CSD
62 Old Middletown Rd, New City, NY 10956
845-639-6419 Fax: 845-639-6488
e-mail: mkeller@ccsd.edu
Web site: www.ccsd.edu
Margaret Keller-Cogan, Superintendent

East Ramapo CSD (Spring Valley)
105 S Madison Ave, Spring Valley, NY 10977
845-577-6011
e-mail: mschwartz@ercsd.k12.ny.us
Web site: www.eram.k12.ny.us
Ira E Oustatcher, Superintendent

Haverstraw-Stony Point CSD
65 Chapel Street, Garnerville, NY 10923
845-942-3002
Web site: www.nrcsd.org
Ileana Eckert

Nanuet UFSD
101 Church St, Nanuet, NY 10954-3000
845-627-9890
e-mail: mmcneil@nufsd.lhric.org
Web site: nanunet.lhric.org
Mark S McNeill, Superintendent

North Rockland CSD
65 Chapel St, Garnerville, NY 10923
845-942-3000 Fax: 845-942-3047
e-mail: ieckert@nrcsd.org
Web site: www.nrcsd.org
Ileana Eckert, Superintendent

Nyack UFSD
13A Dickinson Ave, Nyack, NY 10960-2914
845-353-7015 Fax: 845-353-7019
Web site: www.nyackschools.org
Jason Friedman, Acting Superintendent

Pearl River UFSD
275 E Central Ave, Pearl River, NY 10965-2799
845-620-3900 Fax: 845-620-3927
e-mail: auriemmaf@pearlriver.org
Web site: www.pearlriver.k12.ny.us
Frank V Auriemma, Superintendent

Ramapo CSD (Suffern)
45 Mountain Ave, Hillburn, NY 10931-0935
845-357-7783 Fax: 845-357-5707
e-mail: rmacnaughton@ramapocentral.org
Web site: www.ramapocentral.org
Robert B MacNaughton, Superintendent

South Orangetown CSD
160 Van Wyck Rd, Blauvelt, NY 10913-1299
845-680-1050
Web site: www.socsd.org
Kenneth Mitchell, Superintendent

SARATOGA

Ballston Spa CSD
70 Malta Ave, Ballston Spa, NY 12020-1599
518-884-7195 Fax: 518-885-3201
e-mail: jdragone@bscsd.org
Web site: www.bscsd.org
Joseph P Dragone, Superintendent

Burnt Hills-Ballston Lake CSD
50 Cypress Dr, Glenville, NY 12302
518-399-9141 x5002
e-mail: jschultz@bhbl.org
Web site: www.bhbl.org
James Schultz, Superintendent

Corinth CSD
105 Oak St, Corinth, NY 12822-1295
518-654-2601 Fax: 518-654-6266
Web site: www.corinthcsd.org
Daniel Starr, Superintendent

Edinburg Common SD
4 Johnson Rd, Edinburg, NY 12134-5390
518-863-8412
Randy W Teetz, Superintendent

Galway CSD
5317 Sacandaga Rd, Galway, NY 12074-0130
518-882-1033 Fax: 518-882-5250
Web site: www.galwaycsd.org
Kimberly Labelle, Superintendent

Mechanicville City SD
25 Kniskern Ave, Mechanicville, NY 12118-1995
518-664-5727
Web site: www.mechanicville.org
Michael J McCarthy, Superintendent

Saratoga Springs City SD
3 Blue Streak Blvd, Saratoga Springs, NY 12866-5967
518-583-4709
Web site: www.saratogaschools.org
Janice M White, Superintendent

Offices and agencies generally appear in alphabetical order, except when specific order is requested by listee.

Schuylerville CSD
14 Spring St, Schuylerville, NY 12871-1098
518-695-3255 Fax: 518-695-6491
e-mail: administration@scuylerville.org
Web site: www.schuylervilleschools.org
Ryan C Sherman, Superintendent

Shenendehowa CSD
5 Chelsea Pl, Clifton Park, NY 12065-3240
518-881-0600
e-mail: robioliv@shenet.org
Web site: www.shenet.org
L Oliver Robinson, Superintendent

South Glens Falls CSD
6 Bluebird Rd, South Glens Falls, NY 12803-5704
518-793-9617
Web site: www.sgfallssd.org
Gregory J Aidala, Superintendent

Stillwater CSD
1068 N Hudson Ave, Stillwater, NY 12170-0490
518-373-6100
e-mail: smaziejka@scsd.org
Web site: www.scsd.org
Stanley Maziejka, Superintendent

Waterford-Halfmoon UFSD
125 Middletown Rd, Waterford, NY 12188-1590
518-237-0800 Fax: 518-237-7335
e-mail: tlange@whufsd.org
Web site: www.whufsd.org
Timothy Lange, Superintendent

SCHENECTADY

Duanesburg CSD
133 School Dr, Delanson, NY 12053-0129
518-895-2279 Fax: 518-895-2626
Web site: duanesburg.org
Christine Crowley, Superintendent

Mohonasen CSD
2072 Curry Rd, Schenectady, NY 12303-4400
518-356-8200 Fax: 518-356-8247
e-mail: kspring@mohonasen.org
Web site: www.mohonasen.org
Kathleen A Spring, Superintendent

Niskayuna CSD
1239 Van Antwerp Rd, Schenectady, NY 12309-5317
518-377-4666 x206 Fax: 518-377-4074
e-mail: baughman.k@nisk.k12.ny.us
Web site: www.niskayunaschools.org
Kevin S Baughman, Superintendent

Rotterdam-Mohonasen CSD
2072 Curry Road, Schenectady, NY 12303
518-356-8200
e-mail: kspring@mohonasen.org
Web site: www.mohonasen.org
Kathleen A Spring

Schalmont CSD
4 Sabre Dr, Schenectady, NY 12306-1981
518-355-9200 Fax: 518-355-9203
e-mail: vkelsey@sabrenet.net
Web site: www.schalmont.org
Valerie Kelsey, Superintendent

Schenectady City SD
108 Education Dr, Schenectady, NY 12303-3442
518-370-8100 Fax: 518-370-8173
Web site: www.schenectady.k12.ny.us
John Yagielski, Superintendent

Scotia-Glenville CSD
900 Preddice Pkwy, Scotia, NY 12302-1049
518-382-1215 Fax: 518-386-4336
e-mail: sshwartz@sgcsd.net
Web site: www.sgcsd.neric.org
Susan M Swartz, Superintendent

SCHOHARIE

Cobleskill-Richmondville CSD
155 Washington Ave, Cobleskill, NY 12043-1099
518-234-4032 Fax: 518-234-7721
e-mail: macanl@crcs.k12.ny.us
Web site: www.crcs.k12.ny.us
Lynn Macan, Superintendent

Gilboa-Conesville CSD
132 Wyckoff Rd, Gilboa, NY 12076-9703
607-588-7541 Fax: 607-588-6820
Web site: www.gilboa-conesville.k12.ny.us
Ruth Reeve, Superintendent

Jefferson CSD
1332 St Rt 10, Jefferson, NY 12093-0039
607-652-7821 Fax: 607-652-7806
e-mail: c.mummenthey@jeffersoncs.org
Web site: www.jeffersoncs.org
Carl J Mummenthey, Superintendent

Middleburgh CSD
168 Main St, Middleburgh, NY 12122
518-827-5567 Fax: 518-827-6632
e-mail: michele.weaver@middleburghcsd.org
Web site: www.middleburghcsd.org
Michele R Weaver, Superintendent

Schoharie CSD
136 Academy Drive, PO Box 430, Schoharie, NY 12157-0430
518-295-6679 Fax: 518-295-8178
e-mail: bsherman@schoharie.k12.ny.us
Web site: www.schoharieschools.org
Brian Sherman, Superintendent

Sharon Springs CSD
514 State Rt 20, PO Box 218, Sharon Springs, NY 13459-0218
518-284-2266 Fax: 518-284-9033
e-mail: pgreen@sharonsprings.org
Web site: www.sharonsprings.org
Patterson Green, Superintendent

SCHUYLER

Odessa-Montour CSD
300 College Ave, PO Box 430, Odessa, NY 14869-0430
607-594-3341 Fax: 607-594-3976
e-mail: jframe@gstboces.org
Web site: www.omschools.org
James R Frame, Superintendent

Watkins Glen CSD
303 12th St, Watkins Glen, NY 14891-1699
607-535-3219
e-mail: tphillips@watkinsglenschools.com
Web site: www.watkinsglenschools.com
Tom Phillips, Superintendent

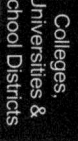

Colleges,
Universities &
School Districts

Offices and agencies generally appear in alphabetical order, except when specific order is requested by listee.

SENECA

Romulus CSD
5705 Rt 96, Romulus, NY 14541-9551
866-810-0345 x399
e-mail: mmidey@rcs.k12.ny.us
Web site: www.rcs.k12.ny.us
Michael J Hoose, Superintendent

Seneca Falls CSD
98 Clinton St, Seneca Falls, NY 13148-1090
315-568-5500 Fax: 315-568-0535
e-mail: gmacaluso@sfcs.k12.ny.us
Web site: www.sfcs.k12.ny.us
Robert McKeveny, Superintendent

South Seneca CSD
7263 Main St, Ovid, NY 14521-9586
607-869-9636
e-mail: jnusser@southseneca.k12.ny.us
Web site: www.southseneca.com
Janie L Nusser, Superintendent

Waterloo CSD
109 Washington St, Waterloo, NY 13165
315-539-1500
Web site: www.waterloocsd.org
Terry MacNabb, Superintendent

ST. LAWRENCE

Brasher Falls CSD
1039 State Hwy 11C, Brasher Falls, NY 13613-0307
315-389-5131 Fax: 315-389-5245
e-mail: sputnam@bfcsd.org
Web site: www.bfcsd.org
Stephen Putman, Superintendent

Canton CSD
99 State St, Canton, NY 13617-1099
315-386-8561
Web site: www.ccsdk12.org
William A Gregory, Superintendent

Clifton-Fine CSD
11 Hall Ave, PO Box 75, Star Lake, NY 13690-0075
315-848-3335 x190
Web site: www.cfeagles.org
Denise Dzikowski, Superintendent

Colton-Pierrepont CSD
4921 State Hwy 56, Colton, NY 13625-0005
315-262-2100 Fax: 315-262-2644
e-mail: bregg@cpcs.us
Web site: www.cpcs.k12.ny.us
Martin Bregg, Superintendent

Edwards-Knox CSD
2512 County Hwy 24, PO Box 630, Russell, NY 13684-0630
315-562-8130 Fax: 315-562-2477
Web site: www.ekcsk12.org
Suzanne Kelly, Superintendent

Gouverneur CSD
133 E Barney St, Gouverneur, NY 13642-1100
315-287-4870
e-mail: clarose@gcs.neric.org
Christine J Larose, Superintendent

Hammond CSD
51 S Main St, PO Box 185, Hammond, NY 13646-0185
315-324-5931 x811
Web site: hammond.sllboces.org
Douglas McQueer, Superintendent

Hermon-Dekalb CSD
709 E DeKalb Rd, DeKalb Junction, NY 13630-0213
315-347-3442 Fax: 315-347-3817
e-mail: aadams@mum.neric.org
Web site: www.hdcsk12.org
Ann M Adams, Superintendent

Heuvelton CSD
87 Washington St, PO Box 375, Heuvelton, NY 13654-0375
315-344-2414 Fax: 315-344-2349
e-mail: stodd@heuvelton.k12.ny.us
Web site: www.heuvelton.schoolfusion.us
Susan E Todd, Superintendent

Lisbon CSD
6866 County Rt 10, PO Box 39, Lisbon, NY 13668
315-393-4951 Fax: 315-393-7666
e-mail: woodse@lisbon.k12.ny.us
Web site: lisboncs.schoolwires.com
Erin E Woods, Superintendent

Madrid-Waddington CSD
2582 State Hwy 345, Madrid, NY 13660-0067
315-322-5746
e-mail: lroy@mwcsk12.org
Web site: www.mwcsk12.org
Lynn Roy, Superintendent

Massena CSD
84 Nightengale Ave, Massena, NY 13662-1999
315-764-3700 x3005 Fax: 315-764-3701
e-mail: dhuntley@mcs.k12.ny.us
Web site: www.mcs.k12.ny.us
Roger B Clough, Superintendent

Morristown CSD
408 Gouverneur St, Morristown, NY 13664-0217
315-375-8814
Web site: mcsd.schoolfusion.us
David J Glover, Superintendent

Norwood-Norfolk CSD
PO Box 194, 7852 State Hwy 56, Norwood, NY 13668-0194
315-353-9951
Web site: www.nncsk12.org
Elizabeth Kirnie, Superintendent

Ogdensburg City SD
1100 State St, Ogdensburg, NY 13669-3398
315-393-0900 Fax: 315-393-2767
Web site: www.ogdensburg12.org
Timothy M Vernsey, Superintendent

Parishville-Hopkinton CSD
12 County Rt 47, Parishville, NY 13672-0187
315-265-4642 Fax: 315-268-1309
Web site: phcs.neric.org
Darin P Saiff, Superintendent

Potsdam CSD
29 Leroy St, Potsdam, NY 13676-1787
315-265-2000 Fax: 315-265-2048
e-mail: pbrady@potsdam.k12.ny.us
Web site: www.potsdam.k12.ny.us
Patrick Brady, Superintendent

Offices and agencies generally appear in alphabetical order, except when specific order is requested by listee.

STEUBEN

Addison CSD
7787 State Rt 417, Addison, NY 14801
607-359-2244 Fax: 607-359-2246
e-mail: bstiker@addison.wnyric.org
Betsey A Stiker, Superintendent

Arkport CSD
35 East Ave, PO Box 70, Arkport, NY 14807-0070
607-295-7471 Fax: 607-295-7473
Web site: www.acs.stev.net
Glenn Niles, Superintendent

Avoca CSD
17-29 Oliver St, Avoca, NY 14809-0517
607-566-2221 Fax: 607-566-2398
e-mail: ryochem@avocacsd.org
Richard Yochem, Superintendent

Bath CSD
25 Ellas Ave, Bath, NY 14810-1107
607-776-3301 Fax: 607-776-5021
Web site: www.bathcsd.org
Patrick Kelley, Superintendent

Bradford CSD
2820 Rt 226, Bradford, NY 14815-9602
607-583-4616 Fax: 607-583-4013
e-mail: wfield@bradfordcsd.org
Wendy S Field, Superintendent

Campbell-Savona CSD
8455 County Rt 125, Campbell, NY 14821-9518
607-527-9800 Fax: 607-527-8363
e-mail: khagen@cscsd.org
Web site: www.cscsd.org
Kathy Hagenbuch, Superintendent

Canisteo-Greenwood CSD
84 Greenwood St, Canisteo, NY 14823-1299
607-698-4225 Fax: 607-698-2833
e-mail: jmatteson@cgcsd.org
Web site: www.cgcsd.org
Jeffrey A Matteson, Superintendent

Corning-Painted Post Area SD
165 Charles St, Painted Post, NY 14870-1199
607-936-3704 Fax: 607-654-2735
Michael Ginalski, Superintendent

Hammondsport CSD
PO Box 368, Hammondsport, NY 14840-0368
607-569-5200 Fax: 607-569-5212
e-mail: kbower@hport.wnyric.org
Kyle C Bower, Superintendent

Hornell City SD
25 Pearl St, Hornell, NY 14843-1504
607-324-1302 Fax: 607-324-4060
e-mail: george.kiley@hornellcsd.org
Web site: www.hornellcityschools.com
George Kiley, Superintendent

Jasper-Troupsburg CSD
3769 N Main St, Jasper, NY 14855
607-792-3675 Fax: 607-792-3749
e-mail: chadgroff@jt.wnyric.org
Chad C Groff, Superintendent

Prattsburgh CSD
1 Academy St, Prattsburgh, NY 14873-0249
607-522-3795 Fax: 607-522-6221
e-mail: jrumsey@pratts.wnyric.org
Joseph L Rumsey, Superintendent

Wayland-Cohocton CSD
2350 Rt 63, Wayland, NY 14572
585-728-2211
e-mail: mwetherbee@wccsk12.org
Web site: www.wccsk12.org
Michael J Wetherbee, Superintendent

SUFFOLK

Amagansett UFSD
320 Main St, PO Box 7062, Amagansett, NY 11930-7062
631-267-3572 Fax: 631-267-7504
Web site: www.amagansettschool.org
Eleanor Tritt, Superintendent

Amityville UFSD
150 Park Ave, Amityville, NY 11701-3195
631-598-6520 Fax: 631-598-6516
e-mail: jwilliams@amityvilleufsd.org
Web site: www.amityville.k12.ny.us
John R Williams, Superintendent

Babylon UFSD
50 Railroad Ave, Babylon, NY 11702-2221
631-893-7925
Web site: www.babylon.k12.ny.us
Ellen Best-Laimit, Superintendent

Bay Shore UFSD
75 W Perkal St, Bayshore, NY 11706-6696
631-968-1117 Fax: 631-968-1129
Web site: www.bayshore.k12.ny.us
Evelyn B Holman, Superintendent

Bayport-Blue Point UFSD
189 Academy St, Bayport, NY 11705
631-472-7860 Fax: 631-472-7873
Web site: www.bbpschools.org
Anthony J Annunziato, Superintendent

Brentwood UFSD
52 Third Ave, Brentwood, NY 11717-6198
631-434-2325 Fax: 631-434-6575
Web site: www.brentwood.k12.ny.us
Joseph Bond, Superintendent

Bridgehampton UFSD
2685 Montauk Hwy, PO Box 3021, Bridgehampton, NY 11932-3021
631-537-0271 Fax: 631-537-1030
Web site: www.bridgehampton.k12.ny.us
Lois Favre, Superintendent

Brookhaven-Comsewogue UFSD
290 Norwood Ave, Port Jefferson, NY 11776-2999
631-474-8105 Fax: 631-474-8399
Joseph Rella, Superintendent

Center Moriches UFSD
529 Main Street, Center Moriches, NY 11934
631-878-0052 Fax: 631-878-4326
Web site: www.centermoriches.k12.ny.us
Russell Stewart

Colleges,
Universities &
School Districts

Offices and agencies generally appear in alphabetical order, except when specific order is requested by listee.

Central Islip UFSD
50 Wheeler Road, Central Islip, NY 11722-9027
631-348-5112 Fax: 631-348-0366
Web site: www.centralislip.k12.ny.us
Craig Carr, Superintendent

Cold Spring Harbor CSD
75 Goose Hill Rd, Cold Spring Harbor, NY 11724-9813
631-367-5931
Web site: www.csh.k12.ny.us
Judith A Wilansky, Superintendent

Commack UFSD
480 Clay Pitts Rd, East Northport, NY 11731-3828
631-912-2010
e-mail: djames@commack.k12.ny.us
Web site: www.commack.k12.ny.us
Donald James, Superintendent

Connetquot CSD
780 Ocean Ave, Bohemia, NY 11716
631-244-2215 Fax: 631-589-0683
Web site: www.connetquot.k12.ny.us
Alan B Groveman, Superintendent

Copiague UFSD
2650 Great Neck Rd, Copiague, NY 11726-1699
631-842-4015 x501
Web site: www.copiague.k12.ny.us
Charles A Leunig, Superintendent

Deer Park UFSD
1881 Deer Park Ave, Deer Park, NY 11729-4326
631-274-4010
Web site: www.deerparkschools.org
Eva J Demyen, Superintendent

East Hampton UFSD
4 Long Ln, East Hampton, NY 11937
631-329-4100 Fax: 631-329-0109
Web site: www.easthampton.k12.ny.us
Raymond D Gualtieri, Superintendent

East Islip UFSD
1 Craig B Gariepy Ave, Islip Terrace, NY 11752
631-224-2000 Fax: 631-581-1617
e-mail: wchu@eischools.org
Web site: www.eischools.org
Wendell Chu, Superintendent

East Moriches UFSD
9 Adelaide Ave, East Moriches, NY 11940-1320
631-878-0162 Fax: 631-878-0186
e-mail: crusso@emo.ny.k12us.com
Web site: www.eastmoriches.k12.ny.us
Charles Russo, Superintendent

East Quogue UFSD
6 Central Ave, East Quogue, NY 11942
631-653-5210 Fax: 631-653-8644
Web site: www.eastquogue.k12.ny.us
Les Black, Acting Superintendent

Eastport-South Manor CSD
149 Dayton Ave, Manorville, NY 11949
631-874-6720 Fax: 631-878-6308
e-mail: nocero@esmonline.org
Web site: www.esmonline.org
Mark A Nocero, Superintendent

Elwood UFSD
100 Kenneth Ave, Greenlawn, NY 11740-2900
631-266-5402
e-mail: superintendent@elwood.k12.ny.us
Web site: www.elwood.k12.ny.us
Peter C Scordo, Superintendent

Fire Island UFSD
Surf Rd, PO Box 428, Ocean Beach, NY 11770-0428
631-583-5626 Fax: 631-583-5167
e-mail: wchu@fi.k12.ny.us
Web site: www.fi.k12.ny.us
Loretta Ferraro, Superintendent

Fishers Island UFSD
PO Drawer A, Fishers Island, NY 06390
631-788-7444 Fax: 631-788-5532
Web site: www.fischool.com
Charles Meyers, Superintendent

Greenport UFSD
720 Front St, Greenport, NY 11944
631-477-1950 Fax: 631-477-2164
Web site: www.greenport.k12.ny.us
Micahel Comanda, Superintendent

Half Hollow Hills CSD
525 Half Hollow Rd, Dix Hills, NY 11746-5899
631-592-3008
e-mail: superintendent@hhh.k12.ny.us
Web site: www.halfhollowhills.k12.ny.us
Sheldon Karnilow, Superintendent

Hampton Bays UFSD
86 E Argonne Rd, Hampton Bays, NY 11946
631-723-2100 Fax: 631-723-2109
Web site: www.hbschools.us
Lars Clemensen, Superintendent

Harborfields CSD
2 Oldfield Rd, Greenlawn, NY 11740
631-754-5320 x321
e-mail: carasitif@harborfieldscsd.net
Web site: www.harborfieldscsd.net
Frank J Carasiti, Superintendent

Hauppauge UFSD
495 Hoffman Ln, PO Box 6006, Hauppauge, NY 11788
631-761-8208 Fax: 631-265-3649
Web site: www.hauppauge.k12.ny.us
Patricia Sullivan-Kriss, Superintendent

Huntington UFSD
50 Tower St, Huntington Station, NY 11746
631-673-2038
e-mail: jfinello@hufsd.edu
Web site: www.hufsd.edu
John J Finello, Superintendent

Islip UFSD
215 Main St, Islip, NY 11751-3435
631-650-8200 Fax: 631-650-8218
Web site: www.islipufsd.org
Susan Schnebel, Superintendent

Kings Park CSD
101 Church St, Kings Park, NY 11754-1769
631-269-3310
Web site: www.kpcsd.k12.ny.us
Susan Agruso, Superintendent

Offices and agencies generally appear in alphabetical order, except when specific order is requested by listee.

Lindenhurst UFSD
350 Daniel St, Lindenhurst, NY 11757-0621
631-867-3001
Web site: www.lindenhurstschools.org
Richard Nathan, Superintendent

Little Flower UFSD
2460 N Wading River Rd, Wading River, NY 11792
631-929-4300 Fax: 631-929-0303
Web site: www.littleflowerufsd.org
George Grigg, Superintendent

Longwood CSD
35 Yaphank-Mid Isl Rd, Middle Island, NY 11953-2369
631-345-2172 Fax: 631-345-2166
Web site: www.longwood.k12.ny.us
Allan Gerstenlauer, Superintendent

Mattituck-Cutchogue UFSD
385 Depot Ln, PO Box 1438, Cutchogue, NY 11935
631-298-4242 Fax: 631-298-8520
Web site: www.mufsd.com
James McKenna, Superintendent

Middle Country CSD
Eight 43rd St, Centereach, NY 11720-2325
631-285-8005
Web site: www.middlecountry.k12.ny.us
Roberta Gerold, Superintendent

Miller Place UFSD
275 Route 25A, Miller Place, NY 11764-2036
631-474-2700 Fax: 631-331-8832
Web site: www.millerplace.k12.ny.us
Susan Hodun, Superintendent

Montauk UFSD
50 S Dorset Rd, Montauk, NY 11954
631-668-2474 Fax: 631-668-1107
Web site: www.montaukschool.org
J Philip Perna, Superintendent

Mt Sinai UFSD
148 N Country Rd, Mount Sinai, NY 11766-0397
631-870-2554 Fax: 631-473-0905
e-mail: mts@mtsinai.k12.ny.us
Web site: www.mtsinai.k12.ny.us
Dr Anthony J Bonasera, Superintendent

New Suffolk Common SD
7605 New Suffolk Rd, PO Box 111, New Suffolk, NY 11956-0111
631-734-6940 Fax: 631-734-6940
e-mail: superintendent@newsuffolkschool.com
Web site: www.newsuffolkschool.com
Robert Feger, Superintendent

North Babylon UFSD
5 Jardine Pl, North Babylon, NY 11703-4203
631-321-3226
Web site: www.northbabylonschools.net
Patricia Godek, Superintendent

Northport-East Northport UFSD
158 Laurel Ave, Northport, NY 11768-3455
631-262-6604
e-mail: mmcdermott@northport.k12.ny.us
Web site: www.northport.k12.ny.us
Marylou McDermott, Superintendent

Oysterponds UFSD
23405 Main Rd, PO Box 98, Orient, NY 11957
631-323-2410 Fax: 631-323-3713
Web site: www.oysterponds.org
Joan Frisicano, Superintendent

Patchogue-Medford UFSD
241 S Ocean Ave, Patchogue, NY 11772-3787
631-687-6380
e-mail: mmostow@pmschools.org
Web site: www.pmschools.org
Michael Mostow, Superintendent

Port Jefferson UFSD
550 Scraggy Hill Rd, Port Jefferson, NY 11777-1969
631-476-4404
Web site: www.portjeff.k12.ny.us
Max Riley, Superintendent

Quogue UFSD
10 Edgewood Rd, PO Box 957, Quogue, NY 11959-0957
631-653-4285 Fax: 631-653-4864
e-mail: super@quogueschool.com
Web site: www.quogue.k12.ny.us
Richard J Benson, Superintendent

Remsenburg-Speonk UFSD
11 Mill Rd, PO Box 900, Remsenburg, NY 11960-0900
631-325-0203 Fax: 631-325-8439
Web site: www.rsufsd.org
Ronald Masera, Superintendent

Riverhead CSD
700 Osborne Ave, Riverhead, NY 11901
631-369-6717 Fax: 631-369-6718
Web site: www.riverhead.net
Nancy Carney, Superintendent

Rocky Point UFSD
170 Rt 25A, Rocky Point, NY 11778-8401
631-744-1600
Web site: www.rockypointschools.org
Michael Ring, Superintendent

Sachem CSD
245 Union Ave, Holbrook, NY 11741
631-471-1300 Fax: 631-471-1341
Web site: www.sachem.edu
James Nolan, Superintendent

Sag Harbor UFSD
200 Jermain Ave, Sag Harbor, NY 11963-3549
631-725-5300 Fax: 631-725-5330
e-mail: jgratto@sagharborschools.org
Web site: www.sagharborschools.org

Sagaponack Common SD
Main St, PO Box 1500, Sagaponack, NY 11962-1500
631-537-0651 Fax: 631-537-2342
Lee Ellwood, Superintendent

Sayville UFSD
99 Greeley Ave, Sayville, NY 11782
631-244-6510 Fax: 631-244-6504
Web site: www.sayville.k12.ny.us
Walter F Schartner, Superintendent

Shelter Island UFSD
33 North Ferry Rd, PO Box 2015, Shelter Island, NY 11964-2015
631-749-0302 Fax: 631-749-1262
Web site: www.shelterisland.k12.ny.us
Robert Parry, Superintendent

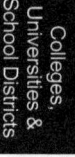

Colleges,
Universities &
School Districts

Offices and agencies generally appear in alphabetical order, except when specific order is requested by listee.

Shoreham-Wading River CSD
250B Rt 25A, Shoreham, NY 11786
631-821-8105 Fax: 631-929-3001
Web site: www.swrcsd.org
Harriet Copel, Superintendent

Smithtown CSD
26 New York Ave, Smithtown, NY 11787-3435
631-382-2005 Fax: 631-382-2010
Web site: www.smithtown.k12.ny.us
Edward Ehmann, Superintendent

South Country CSD
189 Dunton Ave, East Patchogue, NY 11772
631-730-1510 Fax: 631-286-6394
Web site: www.southcountry.org
Joseph Cipp Jr, Superintendent

South Huntington UFSD
60 Weston St, Huntington Station, NY 11746-4098
631-812-3070 Fax: 631-425-5362
e-mail: tshea@shufsd.org
Web site: www.shuntington.k12.ny.us
Thomas C Shea, Superintendent

Southampton UFSD
70 Leland Ln, Southampton, NY 11968
631-591-4510 Fax: 631-287-2870
Web site: www.southhampton.k12.ny.us
Richard Boyes, Superintendent

Southold UFSD
420 Oaklawn Ave, PO Box 470, Southold, NY 11971-0470
631-765-5400 Fax: 631-765-5086
Web site: www.southoldufsd.net
David A Gamberg, Superintendent

Springs UFSD
48 School St, East Hampton, NY 11937
631-324-0144 Fax: 631-324-0269
Web site: www.springs.k12.ny.us
Michael Hartner, Superintendent

Three Village CSD
100 Suffolk Ave, Stony Brook, NY 11790
631-730-4010 Fax: 631-474-7784
e-mail: nlederer@3villagecsd.org
Web site: www.threevillagecsd.org
Neil Lederer, Superintendent

Tuckahoe Common SD
468 Magee St, Southampton, NY 11968-3216
631-283-3550 Fax: 631-283-3469
Web site: www.tuckahoe.k12.ny.us
Chris Dyer, Superintendent

Wainscott Common SD
PO Box 79, Wainscott, NY 11975-0079
631-537-1080 Fax: 631-537-6977
Stuart Rachlin, Superintendent

West Babylon UFSD
10 Farmingdale Rd, West Babylon, NY 11704-6289
631-321-3142 Fax: 631-661-5166
Web site: www.wbschools.org
Anthony Cacciola, Superintendent

West Islip UFSD
100 Sherman Ave, West Islip, NY 11795-3237
631-893-3200 Fax: 631-893-3217
Web site: www.wi.k12.ny.us
Richard Simon, Superintendent

Westhampton Beach UFSD
340 Mill Rd, Westhampton Beach, NY 11978
631-288-3800 Fax: 631-288-8351
Web site: www.westhamptonbeach.k12.ny.us
Lynn Schwartz, Superintendent

William Floyd UFSD
240 Mastic Beach Rd, Mastic Beach, NY 11951
631-874-1201 Fax: 631-281-3047
Web site: www.wfsd.k12.ny.us
Paul Casciano, Superintendent

Wyandanch UFSD
1445 MLK Jr Blvd, Wyandanch, NY 11798-3997
631-870-0400 Fax: 631-491-3032
Web site: www.wyandanch.k12.ny.us
Pless Dickerson, Superintendent

SULLIVAN

Eldred CSD
600 Rt 55, Eldred, NY 12732-0249
845-456-1100 Fax: 845-557-3672
e-mail: dufourr@eldred.k12.ny.us
Web site: www.eldredschools.org
Robert Dufour, Superintendent

Fallsburg CSD
115 Brickman Rd, PO Box 124, Fallsburg, NY 12733-0124
845-434-5884 x1215
e-mail: ikatz@fallsburgcsd.net
Web site: www.fallsburg.net
Ivan J Katz, Interim Superintendent

Liberty CSD
115 Buckley St, Liberty, NY 12754-1600
845-292-6990 Fax: 845-292-1164
e-mail: vanyomic@libertyk12.org
Web site: www.libertyk12.org
Michael B Vanyo, Superintendent

Livingston Manor CSD
19 School St, Livingston Manor, NY 12758-0947
845-439-4400 Fax: 845-439-4717
Web site: lmcs.k12.ny.us
Deborah Fox, Superintendent

Monticello CSD
237 Forestburgh Rd, Monticello, NY 12701
845-794-7700 Fax: 845-794-7710
Web site: www.monticelloschools.org
Edward Rhine, Acting Superintendent

Roscoe CSD
6 Academy St, Roscoe, NY 12776-0429
607-498-4126
Web site: roscoe.k12.ny.us
John P Evans, Superintendent

Sullivan West CSD
33 Schoolhouse Rd, Jeffersonville, NY 12748
845-482-4610 x3000
Web site: www.swcsd.org
Kenneth H Hilton, Superintendent

Tri-Valley CSD
34 Moore Hill Rd, Grahamsville, NY 12740-5609
845-985-2296 x5101
Web site: tvcs.k12.ny.us
Thomas W Palmer, Superintendent

Offices and agencies generally appear in alphabetical order, except when specific order is requested by listee.

TIOGA

Candor CSD
1 Academy St, PO Box 145, Candor, NY 13743-0145
607-659-5010
e-mail: jkisloski@candor.org
Web site: www.candor.org
Jeffrey J Kisloski, Superintendent

Newark Valley CSD
79 Whig St, Newark Valley, NY 13811-0547
607-642-3221
Web site: www.nvcs.stier.org
Ryan Dougherty, Superintendent

Owego-Apalachin CSD
36 Talcott St, Owego, NY 13827-9965
607-687-6224
e-mail: russellw@oacsd.org
Web site: www.oacsd.org
Bill Russell, Superintendent

Spencer-Van Etten CSD
16 Dartts Crossroad, PO Box 307, Spencer, NY 14883
607-589-7100 Fax: 607-589-3010
Web site: www.svecsd.org
Joseph Morgan, Superintendent

Tioga CSD
27 Fifth Ave, Tioga Center, NY 13845-0241
607-687-8001
Web site: www.tiogacentral.org
Scot Taylor, Superintendent

Waverly CSD
15 Frederick St, Waverly, NY 14892-1294
607-565-2841 Fax: 607-565-4997
e-mail: mmcmahon@gstboces.org
Web site: www.waverlyschools.com
Michael W McMahon, Superintendent

TOMPKINS

Dryden CSD
118 Freeville Road, PO Box 88, Dryden, NY 13053
607-844-8694 x601
Web site: www.dryden.k12.ny.us
Sandra R Sherwood, Superintendent

George Junior Republic UFSD
24 McDonald Rd, Freeville, NY 13068-9699
607-844-6343
Web site: www.georgejuniorrepublic.com
J Brad Herman, Superintendent

Groton CSD
400 Peru Rd, Groton, NY 13073-1297
607-898-5301 Fax: 607-898-4647
e-mail: jabrams@groton.cnyric.org
Web site: www.grotoncs.org
James Abrams, Superintendent

Ithaca City SD
400 Lake St, Ithaca, NY 14851-0549
607-274-2101
Web site: www.icsd.k12.ny.us
Luvelle Brown, Superintendent

Lansing CSD
284 Ridge Rd, Lansing, NY 14882
607-533-4294 Fax: 607-533-3602
e-mail: stephen.grimm@lcsd.k12.ny.us
Web site: www.lcsd.k12.ny.us
Stephen L Grimm, Superintendent

Newfield CSD
247 Main St, Newfield, NY 14867-9313
607-564-9955
Web site: www.newfieldschools.org
Cheryl Thomas, Superintendent

Trumansburg CSD
100 Whig St, Trumansburg, NY 14886-9179
607-387-7551 x421
Web site: www.tburg.k12.ny.us
Paula Hurley, Superintendent

ULSTER

Ellenville CSD
28 Maple Ave, Ellenville, NY 12428
845-647-0100 Fax: 845-647-0105
Web site: www.ecs.k12.ny.us
Lisa A Wiles, Superintendent

Highland CSD
320 Pancake Hollow Rd, Highland, NY 12528-2317
845-691-1012 Fax: 845-691-3904
Web site: www.highland-k12.org
Deborah A Haab, Superintendent

Kingston City SD
61 Crown St, Kingston, NY 12401-3833
845-339-3000
Web site: www.kingstoncityschools.org
Gerard M Gretzinger, Superintendent

Marlboro CSD
1510 Route 9W, Suite 201, Marlboro, NY 12542
845-236-5804 Fax: 848-236-5817
Web site: marlboroschools.org
Raymond Castellani, Superintendent

New Paltz CSD
196 Main St, New Paltz, NY 12561-1200
845-256-4020 Fax: 845-256-4025
Web site: www.newpaltz.k12.ny.us
Maria Rice, Superintendent

Onteora CSD
PO Box 300, Boiceville, NY 12412-0300
845-657-6383 Fax: 845-657-9687
e-mail: pmcgill@onteora.k12.ny.us
Web site: onteora.k12.ny.us
Phyllis Spiegel McGill, Superintendent

Rondout Valley CSD
122 Kyserike Rd, PO Box 9, Accord, NY 12404-0009
845-687-2400 Fax: 845-687-9577
Web site: www.rondout.k12.ny.us
Rosario Agostaro, Superintendent

Saugerties CSD
Call Box A, Saugerties, NY 12477
845-247-6500 Fax: 845-246-8364
Seth Turner, Superintendent

Offices and agencies generally appear in alphabetical order, except when specific order is requested by listee.

Wallkill CSD
19 Main St, Wallkill, NY 12589
845-895-7101
Web site: www.wallkillcsd.k12.ny.us
William J Hecht, Superintendent

West Park UFSD
2112 Rt 9W, West Park, NY 12493-0010
845-384-6710
Joyce Mucci, Superintendent

WARREN

Bolton CSD
26 Horicon Ave, Bolton Landing, NY 12814-0120
518-644-2400
e-mail: info@boltoncsd.org
Web site: www.boltoncsd.org
Raymond Ciccarelli Jr, Superintendent

Glens Falls City SD
15 Quade St, Glens Falls, NY 12801-2725
518-792-1212
e-mail: tmcgowan@gfsd.org
Web site: www.gfsd.org
Thomas F McGowan, Superintendent

Glens Falls Common SD
120 Lawrence St, Glens Falls, NY 12801-3758
518-792-3231 Fax: 518-792-2557
Ella W Collins, Superintendent

Hadley-Luzerne CSD
273 Lake Ave, Lake Luzerne, NY 12846
518-696-2112 x134
Web site: www.hlcsd.org
Irwin H Sussman, Superintendent

Johnsburg CSD
165 Main St, North Creek, NY 12853-0380
518-251-2921 Fax: 518-251-2562
Web site: www.johnsburgcsd.org
Michael Markwica, Superintendent

Lake George CSD
381 Canada St, Lake George, NY 12845-1197
518-668-5456 Fax: 518-668-2285
Web site: www.lkgeorge.org
Patrick Dee, Superintendent

North Warren CSD
6110 State Rt 8, Chestertown, NY 12817
518-494-3015
Web site: www.northwarren.k12.ny.us
Joseph R Murphy, Superintendent

Queensbury UFSD
429 Aviation Rd, Queensbury, NY 12804-2914
518-824-5602 Fax: 518-793-4476
Web site: www.queensburyschool.org
Douglas W Huntley, Superintendent

Warrensburg CSD
103 Schroon River Rd, Warrensburg, NY 12885-4803
518-623-2861
e-mail: lawsont@wcsd.org
Web site: www.wcsd.org
Timothy D Lawson, Superintendent

WASHINGTON

Argyle CSD
5023 State Rt 40, Argyle, NY 12809-0067
518-638-8243 Fax: 518-638-6373
e-mail: jehring_j@argylecsd.org
Web site: www.argylecsd.org
Jan Jehring, Superintendent

Cambridge CSD
58 S Park St, Cambridge, NY 12816
518-677-8527 Fax: 518-677-3889
Web site: www.cambridgecsd.org
Vincent Canini, Superintendent

Fort Ann CSD
One Catherine St, Fort Ann, NY 12827-5039
518-639-5594 Fax: 518-639-8911
e-mail: mvanburen@fortannschool.org
Web site: www.fortannschool.org
Maureen VanBuren, Superintendent

Fort Edward UFSD
220 Broadway, Fort Edward, NY 12828-1598
518-747-4594 x100
Web site: www.fortedward.org
Jeffery Ziegler, Superintendent

Granville CSD
58 Quaker St, Granville, NY 12832-1596
518-642-1051 Fax: 518-642-2491
Web site: www.granvillecsd.org
Mark Bessen, Superintendent

Greenwich CSD
10 Gray Ave, Greenwich, NY 12834-1107
518-692-9542
Web site: www.greenwichcsd.org
Matthias Donnelly, Superintendent

Hartford CSD
4704 State Rt 149, Hartford, NY 12838-0079
518-632-5931
Web site: www.hartfordcsd.org
Thomas W Abraham, Administrator

Hudson Falls CSD
1153 Burgoyne Ave, Hudson Falls, NY 12839-0710
518-747-2121
e-mail: mdoody@hfcsd.org
Web site: www.hfcsd.org
Mark E Doody, Superintendent

Putnam CSD
126 County Rt 2, PO Box 91, Putnam Station, NY 12861
518-547-8266 Fax: 518-547-9567
e-mail: matthew.boucher@putnamcsd.org
Web site: putnamcsd.org
Matthew Boucher, Superintendent

Salem CSD
41 E Broadway, Salem, NY 12865-0517
518-854-7855
Web site: www.salemcsdnyk-12.org
Kerri Erin Piemme, Superintendent

Whitehall CSD
87 Buckley Rd, Whitehall, NY 12887-3633
518-499-1772
e-mail: jwatson@railroaders.net
Web site: www.railroaders.net
James Watson, Superintendent

Offices and agencies generally appear in alphabetical order, except when specific order is requested by listee.

WAYNE

Clyde-Savannah CSD
215 Glasgow St, Clyde, NY 14433-1222
315-902-3000
Web site: www.clydesavannah.org
Theresa Pulos, Superintendent

Gananda CSD
1500 Dayspring Ridge, Walworth, NY 14568
315-986-3521
Web site: www.gananda.org
Shawn Van Scoy, Superintendent

Lyons CSD
10 Clyde Rd, Lyons, NY 14489-9371
315-946-2200
e-mail: ramundson@lyonscsd.org
Web site: www.lyonscsd.org
Richard Amundson, Superintendent

Marion CSD
4034 Warner Rd, Marion, NY 14505-0999
315-926-4228
Web site: www.marioncs.org
Kathryn A Wegman, Superintendent

Newark CSD
100 E Miller St, Newark, NY 14513-1599
315-332-3217
e-mail: hhann@newark.k12.ny.us
Web site: www.newark.k12.ny.us
Henry Hann, Acting Superintendent

North Rose-Wolcott CSD
11669 Salter-Colvin Rd, Wolcott, NY 14590-9398
315-594-3141 Fax: 315-594-2352
Web site: www.nrwcs.org
John C Walker, Superintendent

Palmyra-Macedon CSD
151 Hyde Pkwy, Palmyra, NY 14522-1297
315-597-3401
Web site: www.palmac.k12.ny.us
Robert Ike, Superintendent

Red Creek CSD
6815 Church St, PO Box 190, Red Creek, NY 13143-0190
315-754-2010 Fax: 315-754-8169
e-mail: dsholes@rccsd.org
Web site: www.rccsd.org
David G Sholes, Superintendent

Sodus CSD
PO Box 220, Sodus, NY 14551-0220
315-483-5201 Fax: 315-483-4755
e-mail: ssalvaggio@soduscsd.org
Web site: www.soduscsd.org
Susan Kay Salvaggio, Superintendent

Wayne CSD
6076 Ontario Ctr Rd, Ontario Center, NY 14520-0155
315-524-1001
Web site: www.wayne.k12.ny.us
Renee Garrett, Superintendent

Williamson CSD
PO Box 900, Williamson, NY 14589-0900
315-589-9661
e-mail: mehresman@williamsoncentral.org
Web site: www.williamsoncentral.org
Maria Ehresman, Superintendent

WESTCHESTER

Abbott UFSD
100 N Broadway, Irvington, NY 10533-1254
914-591-7428
Web site: www.abbottufsd.org
Harold A Coles, Superintendent

Ardsley UFSD
500 Farm Rd, Ardsley, NY 10502-1410
914-693-6300
Web site: www.ardsleyschools.k12.ny.us
Lauren Allan, Superintendent

Bedford CSD
Fox Lane Campus, PO Box 180, Mt. Kisco, NY 10549
914-241-6010
Web site: www.bedford.k12.ny.us
Jere Hochman, Superintendent

Blind Brook-Rye UFSD
390 North Ridge St, Rye Brook, NY 10573-1105
914-937-3600
Web site: www.blindbrook.org
William J Stark, Superintendent

Briarcliff Manor UFSD
45 Ingham Rd, Briarcliff Manor, NY 10510-2221
914-941-8880 x303
Web site: www.briarcliffschools.org
Jerry Cicchelli, Superintendent

Bronxville UFSD
177 Pondfield Rd, Bronxville, NY 10708-4829
914-395-0500
e-mail: quattrod@bronxville.k12.ny.us
Web site: www.bronxville.lhric.org
David Quattrone, Superintendent

Byram Hills CSD
10 Tripp Ln, Armonk, NY 10504-2512
914-273-4082
e-mail: jtaylor@byramhills.org
Web site: www.byramhills.org
Jacquelyn Taylor, Superintendent

Chappaqua CSD
66 Roaring Brook Rd, Chappaqua, NY 10514-1703
914-238-7200 Fax: 914-238-7231
Web site: www.chappaqua.k12.ny.us/ccsd/
John Chambers, Superintendent

Croton-Harmon UFSD
10 Gerstein St, Croton-on-Hudson, NY 10520-2303
914-271-4793 or 914-271-4713 Fax: 914-271-8685
e-mail: efuhrman@croton-harmonschools.org
Web site: www.croton-harmonschools.org
Edward R Fuhrman Jr, Superintendent

Dobbs Ferry UFSD
505 Broadway, Dobbs Ferry, NY 10522-1118
914-693-1506 Fax: 914-693-1787
e-mail: kapland@dfsd.org
Web site: www.dfsd.org
Debra Kaplan, Superintendent

Eastchester UFSD
580 White Plains Rd, Eastchester, NY 10709
914-793-6130 Fax: 914-793-9006
Web site: www.eastchester.k12.ny.us
Marilyn Terranova, Superintendent

Colleges, Universities & School Districts

Offices and agencies generally appear in alphabetical order, except when specific order is requested by listee.

Edgemont UFSD
300 White Oak Ln, Scarsdale, NY 10583-1725
914-472-7768 Fax: 914-472-6846
Web site: www.edgemont.org
Nancy L Taddiken, Superintendent

Elmsford UFSD
98 South Goodwin Ave, Elmsford, NY 10523
914-592-6632
Web site: www.elmsd.org
Barbara Peters, Superintendent

Greenburgh 7 CSD
475 W Hartsdale Ave, Hartsdale, NY 10530-1398
914-761-6000 x3103
Web site: www.greenburgh.k12.ny.us
Ronald L Smalls, Superintendent

Greenburgh Eleven UFSD
Children's Vlg Campus-W, PO Box 501, Dobbs Ferry, NY 10522-0501
914-693-8500
Sandra G Mallah, Superintendent

Greenburgh-Graham UFSD
One S Broadway, Hastings-on-Hudson, NY 10706-3809
914-478-1106
Amy J Goodman, Superintendent

Greenburgh-North Castle UFSD
71 S Broadway, Dobbs Ferry, NY 10522-2834
914-693-4309
Edward Placke, Superintendent

Harrison CSD
50 Union Ave, Harrison, NY 10528-2032
914-630-3021
Web site: www.harrisoncsd.org
Louis N Wool, Superintendent

Hastings-On-Hudson UFSD
27 Farragut Ave, Hastings-on-Hudson, NY 10706-2395
914-478-6200
Web site: www.hastings.k12.ny.us
Timothy P Connors, Acting Superintendent

Hawthorne-Cedar Knolls UFSD
226 Linda Ave, Hawthorne, NY 10532-2099
914-749-2903 Fax: 914-749-2904
Web site: www.hcks.org
Mark K Silverstein, Superintendent

Hendrick Hudson CSD
61 Trolley Rd, Montrose, NY 10548-1199
914-257-5100 Fax: 914-257-5101
e-mail: dmccann@henhudschools.org
Web site: www.henhudschools.org
Daniel McCann, Superintendent

Irvington UFSD
6 Dows Ln, Irvington, NY 10533-1328
914-591-8501
e-mail: kmatusiak@irvingtonschools.k12.ny.us
Web site: www.irvingtonschools.org
Kathleen Matusiak, Superintendent

Katonah-Lewisboro UFSD
PO Box 387, Katonah, NY 10536
914-763-7003 Fax: 914-763-7033
Web site: www.klschools.org
Michael Jumper, Superintendent

Lakeland CSD
1086 Main St, Shrub Oak, NY 10588-1507
914-245-1700
Web site: www.lakelandschools.org
George Stone, Superintendent

Mamaroneck UFSD
1000 W Boston Post Rd, Mamaroneck, NY 10543-3399
914-220-3005
Web site: www.mamkschools.org
Robert Shaps, Superintendent

Mt Pleasant CSD
Westlake Drive, Thornwood, NY 10594
914-769-5500 Fax: 914-769-3733
e-mail: sguiney@mtplcsd.org
Web site: www.mtplcsd.org
Susan Guiney, Acting Superintendent

Mt Pleasant-Blythedale UFSD
95 Bradhurst Ave, Valhalla, NY 10595-1697
914-347-1800 Fax: 914-592-5484
e-mail: ebergman@mpbschools.org
Web site: www.mpbschools.org
Ellen Bergman, Superintendent

Mt Pleasant-Cottage UFSD
1075 Broadway, Pleasantville, NY 10570-0008
914-769-0456 Fax: 914-769-7853
e-mail: nfreimark@mail.mpcsny.org
Web site: www.mpcsny.org
Norman Freimark, Superintendent

Mt Vernon City SD
165 N Columbus Ave, Mount Vernon, NY 10553-1199
914-665-5000
Web site: mtvernoncsd.org
Welton L Sawyer, Superintendent

New Rochelle City SD
515 North Ave, New Rochelle, NY 10801-3416
914-576-4200 Fax: 914-632-4144
e-mail: rorganisciak@nred.org
Web site: www.nred.org
Richard Organisciak, Superintendent

North Salem CSD
230 June Rd, North Salem, NY 10560-1211
914-669-5414
Web site: www.northsalemschools.org
Kenneth Freeston, Superintendent

Ossining UFSD
190 Croton Ave, Ossining, NY 10562
914-941-7700 Fax: 914-941-2794
Web site: www.ossiningufsd.org
Phyllis Glassman, Superintendent

Peekskill City SD
1031 Elm St, Peekskill, NY 10566-3499
914-737-3300 Fax: 914-737-3912
Web site: www.peekskillcsd.org
Lorenzo Licopoli, Superintendent

Pelham UFSD
18 Franklin Pl, Pelham, NY 10803
914-738-3434
Web site: www.pelhamschools.org
Dennis Lauro, Superintendent

Offices and agencies generally appear in alphabetical order, except when specific order is requested by listee.

Pleasantville UFSD
60 Romer Ave, Pleasantville, NY 10570-3157
914-741-1400 Fax: 914-741-1499
Web site: www.pleasantvilleschools.com
Mary Fox-Alter, Superintendent

Pocantico Hills CSD
599 Bedford Rd, Sleepy Hollow, NY 10591-1215
914-631-2440 Fax: 914-631-3280
e-mail: vdouglas@pocanticohills.org
Web site: www.pocanticohills.org
Valencia Douglas, Superintendent

Port Chester SD
113 Bowman Ave, Port Chester, NY 10573-2851
914-934-7901 Fax: 914-934-0727
Web site: www.portchesterschools.org
Thomas Elliott, Superintendent

Rye City SD
411 Theodore Fremd Ave, South Lobby, Rye, NY 10580-3899
914-967-6100 Fax: 914-967-6957
e-mail: shinee@ryeschools.org
Web site: www.ryeschools.org
Edward J Shine, Superintendent

Rye Neck UFSD
310 Hornidge Rd, Mamaroneck, NY 10543-3898
914-777-5200
e-mail: pmustich@ryeneck.k12.ny.us
Web site: www.ryeneck.k12.ny.us
Peter J Mustich, Superintendent

Scarsdale UFSD
2 Brewster Rd, Scarsdale, NY 10583-3049
914-721-2410
e-mail: mmcgill@scarsdaleschools.k12.ny.us
Web site: www.scarsdaleschools.k12.ny.us
Michael V McGill, Superintendent

Somers CSD
334 Route 202, PO Box 620, Somers, NY 10589
914-277-2400
Web site: www.somers.k12.ny.us
Raymond Blanch, Superintendent

Tarrytown UFSD
200 N Broadway, Sleepy Hollow, NY 10591-2696
914-332-6241 Fax: 914-332-4690
e-mail: hwsmith@tufsd.org
Web site: www.tufsd.org
Howard W Smith, Superintendent

Tuckahoe UFSD
29 Elm St, Tuckahoe, NY 10707
914-337-6600
Web site: www.tuckahoeschools.org
Michael Yazurlo, Superintendent

Valhalla UFSD
316 Columbus Ave, Valhalla, NY 10595-1300
914-683-5040 Fax: 914-683-5075
Web site: valhalla.k12.ny.us
Brenda Myers, Superintendent

White Plains City SD
5 Homeside Ln, White Plains, NY 10605-4299
914-422-2019 or 914-422-2029 Fax: 914-422-2024
Web site: www.wpcsd.k12.ny.us
Dr Christopher P Clouet, Superintendent

Yonkers City SD
1 Larkin Center, Yonkers, NY 10701
914-376-8100
Web site: www.yonkerspublicschools.org
Bernard P Pierorazio, Superintendent

Yorktown CSD
2725 Crompond Rd, Yorktown Heights, NY 10598
914-243-8001
e-mail: rnapolitano@yorktown.org
Web site: www.yorktowncsd.org
Ralph Napolitano, Superintendent

WYOMING

Attica CSD
3338 E Main St, Attica, NY 14011
585-591-2173
Web site: www.atticacs.k12.ny.us
Bryce L Thompson, Superintendent

Letchworth CSD
5550 School Rd, Gainesville, NY 14066
585-493-5450
Web site: www.letchworth.k12.ny.us
Joseph W Backer, Superintendent

Perry CSD
33 Watkins Ave, Perry, NY 14530
585-237-0270 x1000 Fax: 585-237-6172
e-mail: dwhite@perry.k12.ny.us
Web site: www.perry.k12.ny.us
William Stavisky, Superintendent

Warsaw CSD
153 W Buffalo St, Warsaw, NY 14569
585-786-8000 Fax: 585-786-8008
Web site: www.warsaw.k12.ny.us
Valerie K Burke, Superintendent

Wyoming CSD
Route 19, PO Box 244, Wyoming, NY 14591-0244
585-495-6222 Fax: 585-495-6341
Web site: www.wyoming.k12.ny.us
Sandra B Duckworth, Superintendent

YATES

Dundee CSD
55 Water St, Dundee, NY 14837-1099
607-243-5533 Fax: 607-243-7912
Web site: www.dundeecs.org
Kathy Ring, Superintendent

Penn Yan CSD
One School Dr, Penn Yan, NY 14527-1099
315-536-3371
Web site: www.pycsd.org
Thomas A Cox, Acting Superintendent

BOCES DISTRICT SUPERINTENDENTS

Broome-Delaware-Tioga BOCES
435 Glenwood Rd, Binghamton, NY 13905-1699
607-766-3802 Fax: 607-763-3691
e-mail: abuyck@btboces.org
Web site: www.btboces.org
Allen D Buyck

Colleges,
Universities &
School Districts

Offices and agencies generally appear in alphabetical order, except when specific order is requested by listee.

Capital Region (Albany-Schoharie-Schenectady) BOCES
900 Watervliet-Shaker Rd, Albany, NY 12205-2106
518-862-4901 Fax: 518-862-4903
Web site: www.capregboces.org
Charles Dedrick, District Superintendent

Cattaraugus-Allegany-Erie-Wyoming BOCES
Olean Center, 1825 Windfall Rd, Olean, NY 14760-9303
716-376-8246 or 716-376-8200 Fax: 716-376-8452
Web site: www.caboces.org
Tim Cox

Cayuga-Onondaga BOCES
1879 West Genesee Street Road, Auburn, NY 13021-9430
315-253-0361 Fax: 315-252-6493
e-mail: bspeck@cayboces.org
Web site: www.cayboces.org
William S Speck

Champlain Valley Educational Svcs
(Clinton-Essex-Warren-Washington)
1585 Military Tpk, PO Box 455, Plattsburgh, NY 12901-0455
518-536-7340
Web site: www.cves.org
Craig L King

Delaware-Chenango-Madison-Otsego BOCES
6678 County Rd #32, Norwich, NY 13815-3554
607-335-1233 Fax: 607-334-9848
Web site: www.dcmoboces.com
Bill Tammaro

Dutchess BOCES
5 Boces Rd, Poughkeepsie, NY 12601-6599
845-486-4800 Fax: 845-486-4981
e-mail: john.pennoyer@dcboces.org
Web site: www.dcboces.org
John C Pennoyer

Eastern Suffolk BOCES
James Hines Administration Ctr, 201 Sunrise Hwy, Patchogue, NY 11772-1868
631-687-3006 Fax: 631-289-2529
e-mail: ezero@esboces.org
Web site: www.esboces.org
Edward J Zero

Erie 1 BOCES
355 Harlem Rd, West Seneca, NY 14224-1892
716-821-7001 Fax: 716-821-7452
Web site: www.e1b.org
Donald A Ogilvie, District Superintendent

Erie 2-Chautauqua-Cattaraugus BOCES
8685 Erie Rd, Angola, NY 14006-9620
716-549-4454 or 800-228-1184 Fax: 716-549-5181
Web site: e2ccb.org
Robert S Guiffreda

Franklin-Essex-Hamilton BOCES
23 Huskie Lane, PO Box 28, Malone, NY 12953-0028
518-483-6420 Fax: 518-483-2178
Web site: www.fehb.org
Stephen T Shafer

Genesee-Livingston-Steuben-Wyoming BOCES
80 Munson St, LeRoy, NY 14482-8933
585-658-7903 Fax: 585-344-7903
Web site: www.gvboces.org
Michael A Glover

Greater Southern Tier BOCES
(Schuyler-Chemung-Tioga-Allegany-Steuben)
9579 Vocational Dr, Painted Post, NY 14870
607-654-2283 or 607-962-3175 Fax: 607-962-1579
Web site: www.gstboces.org
Horst Graefe

Hamilton-Fulton-Montgomery BOCES
2755 St Hwy 67, Johnstown, NY 12095
518-736-4300 Fax: 518-736-4301
Web site: www.hfmboces.org
Patrick Michel

Herkimer-Fulton-Hamilton-Otsego BOCES
352 Gros Blvd, Herkimer, NY 13350-1499
315-867-2000 Fax: 315-867-2024
e-mail: ssimpson@herkimer-boces.org
Web site: www.herkimer-boces.org
Sandra A Simpson

Jefferson-Lewis-Hamilton-Herkimer-Oneida BOCES
20104 State Rte 3, Watertown, NY 13601-5560
315-779-7010 Fax: 315-779-7009
e-mail: jboak@mail.boces.com
Web site: www.boces.com
Jack J Boak Jr

Madison-Oneida BOCES
4937 Spring Rd, PO Box 168, Verona, NY 13478-0168
315-361-5510 Fax: 315-361-5595
e-mail: districtsuperintendent@moboces.org
Web site: www.moboces.org
Jacklin G Starks

Monroe 1 BOCES
41 O'Connor Rd, Fairport, NY 14450-1390
585-388-2200 Fax: 585-383-6404
Web site: www.monroe.edu
Frederick A Wille

Monroe 2-Orleans BOCES
3599 Big Ridge Rd, Spencerport, NY 14559-1799
585-352-2400 Fax: 585-352-2442
Web site: www.monroe2boces.org
Jo Anne Antonacci

Nassau BOCES
71 Clinton Rd, PO Box 9195, Garden City, NY 11530-9196
516-396-2500 or 516-396-2200 Fax: 516-997-8742
Web site: www.nassauboces.org
James D Mapes

Oneida-Herkimer-Madison BOCES
PO Box 70, 4747 Middle Settlement Rd, New Hartford, NY 13413-0070
315-793-8561 Fax: 315-793-8541
e-mail: tdorr@oneida-boces.org
Web site: www.oneida-boces.org
Thomas Dorr

Onondaga-Cortland-Madison BOCES
6820 Thompson Rd, PO Box 4754, Syracuse, NY 13221-4754
315-433-2602 Fax: 315-437-4816
e-mail: jcohen@ocmboces.org
Web site: ocmboces.org
Jessica F Cohen

Orange-Ulster BOCES
53 Gibson Rd, Goshen, NY 10924-9777
845-291-0100 Fax: 845-291-0118
e-mail: jpennoyer@ouboces.org
Web site: www.ouboces.org
John Pennoyer

Offices and agencies generally appear in alphabetical order, except when specific order is requested by listee.

Orleans-Niagara BOCES
4232 Shelby Basin Rd, Medina, NY 14103-9515
585-344-7903 Fax: 585-798-1317
Web site: www.onboces.org
Clark J Godshall

Oswego BOCES
179 County Rte 64, Mexico, NY 13114-4498
315-963-4222 Fax: 315-963-7131
Web site: www.oswegoboces.org
Joseph P Camerino

Otsego Northern Catskills BOCES
(Otsego-Delaware-Schoharie-Greene)
159 W Main St, Frank W Cyr Center, Stamford, NY 12167-1027
607-652-1209 Fax: 607-652-1215
Web site: www.oncboces.org
Nicholas Savin, District Superintendent

Putnam-Northern Westchester BOCES
200 Boces Dr, Yorktown Heights, NY 10598-4399
914-245-2700 or 914-248-2302 Fax: 914-248-2308
e-mail: jlanglois@pnwboces.org
Web site: www.pnwboces.org
James T Langlois

Rensselaer-Columbia-Greene (Questar III) BOCES
10 Empire State Blvd, 2nd Fl, Castleton, NY 12033-2692
518-477-8771 Fax: 518-477-9833
Web site: www.questar.org
Charles Dedrick

Rockland BOCES
65 Parrott Rd, West Nyack, NY 10994-0607
845-627-4700 or 845-627-4702 Fax: 845-624-1764
e-mail: mmarsico@rboces.org
Web site: www.rocklandboces.org
Dr. Mary Jean Marsico, Superintendent

Southern Westchester BOCES
17 Berkeley Dr, Rye Brook, NY 10573-1422
914-937-3820 x535 Fax: 914-937-7850
Web site: www.swboces.org
James T Langlois, Superintendent

St Lawrence-Lewis BOCES
139 State Street Rd, PO Box 231, Canton, NY 13617
315-386-4504 Fax: 315-386-3395
e-mail: tburns@sllboces.org
Web site: www.sllboces.org
Thomas R Burns

Sullivan BOCES
6 Wierk Ave, Liberty, NY 12754-2151
845-295-4000 Fax: 845-292-8694
e-mail: lthomas@scboces.org
Web site: www.scboces.org
Lawrence Thomas

Tompkins-Seneca-Tioga BOCES
555 Warren Rd, Ithaca, NY 14850-1833
607-257-1551 x201 Fax: 607-257-2825
e-mail: eodonnell@mail.tstboces.org
Web site: www.tstboces.org
Ellen O'Donnell

Ulster BOCES
175 Rte 32 North, New Paltz, NY 12561-1034
845-255-1400 or 845-255-3040 Fax: 845-255-7942
e-mail: lthomas@scboces.org
Web site: www.ulsterboces.org
Lawrence Thomas

Washington-Saratoga-Warren-Hamilton-Essex BOCES
1153 Burgoyne Ave, Ste 2, Fort Edward, NY 12828-1134
518-746-3310 or 518-581-3310 Fax: 518-746-3319
e-mail: jdexter@wswheboces.org
Web site: www.wswheboces.org
James P Dexter

Wayne-Finger Lakes BOCES
131 Drumlin Ct, Newark, NY 14513-1863
315-332-7284 Fax: 315-332-7425
e-mail: cmurray@wflboces.org
Web site: www.wflboces.org
Joseph J Marinelli, District Superintendent

Western Suffolk BOCES
507 Deer Park Rd, PO Box 8007, Huntington Station, NY 11746-9007
631-549-4900 x222 Fax: 631-623-4996
e-mail: centraladmin@wsboces.org
Web site: www.wsboces.org
Thomas Rogers, Interim Superintendent

Offices and agencies generally appear in alphabetical order, except when specific order is requested by listee.

Section 8:
BIOGRAPHIES

BIOGRAPHIES

EXECUTIVE BRANCH

ANDREW M CUOMO (D)

Andrew M Cuomo was elected New York's 56th governor in 2010, and was re-elected on November 4, 2014. As governor, Cuomo has presided over passage of the state's first ever property tax cap, signed the marriage equality law that legalized gay marriage, and banned hydraulic fracturing, also called fracking, in New York. Prior to his election as governor, Cuomo served four years as New York's Attorney General, bringing national reform to the student loan industry, uncovering health insurance fraud, and making the Internet safer for children. His investigations ended decades of government corruption in New York's pension system. In 1997, President Clinton appointed Cuomo as Secretary of Housing and Urban Development (HUD). Under Cuomo's leadership, HUD earned the 'Innovations in American Government Award' from Harvard University's Kennedy's School of Government and the Ford Foundation three times. While in office, he brought over 2,000 anti-discrimination cases across the country. Cuomo established Housing Enterprise for Less Privileged (HELP) in 1986, which became the nation's largest private provider of transitional and low-income housing. Based on his pioneering work, he was appointed in 1991 by New York City Mayor David Dinkins to lead the New York City Commission on the Homeless. Cuomo worked as an assistant district attorney in Manhattan and at a NYC law firm after graduating from Fordham University in 1979 and Albany Law School in 1982. He is the son of former New York Gov. Mario Cuomo, and has three daughters, twins Mariah and Cara, and Michaela.

LT. GOV. KATHLEEN C HOCHUL, (D)

Kathleen C. Hochul was elected New York's 77th Lieutenant Governor on November 4, 2014, and inaugurated January 1, 2015. She previously served as a Group Vice President for Strategic Relationships at M&T Bank, and was a liaison for community issues and key economic development projects. She served two years in Congress, from 2011 to 2013, elected from New York's 26th Congressional District. Prior to that time, she was the Erie County Clerk from 2007 to 2011. Her public service also includes 14 years as a Hamburg Town Councilmember. An attorney by training, she was in private practice early in her career, working for a large Washington D.C. firm as well as a major corporation. She then served as legal counsel and legislative assistant to Congressmen John LaFalce (D-NY) and NY Sen. Daniel Patrick Moynihan. With her mother and aunt, she established a transitional home for victims of domestic violence called Kathleen Mary House, and also co-founded the Village Action Coalition to help local business compete with big box stores. She and her husband, Bill, are parents to a daughter and son.

THOMAS P DINAPOLI (D)

New York State Comptroller Thomas P DiNapoli became New York State's 54th Comptroller in 2007. DiNapoli has instilled reforms to make government more effective, efficient and ethical, and has pushed for increased transparency and accountability. As trustee of New York State's $176.8 billion pension fund, DiNapoli has imposed controls including new reporting requirements on investments, fees and other information; barring investment firms contributing to his campaign from doing business with the state pension; and creating opportunities for minority and women fund managers. He has completed a five-year school accountability project that audited all 733 school districts, and launched a fiscal monitoring system to rate communities on their fiscal condition and sending an early warning to those in trouble. Prior to becoming State Comptroller, DiNapoli represented northwestern Nassau County in the New York State Assembly for nearly 20 years. At age 18, he was elected to the Mineola Board of Education He is a lifelong resident of Nassau County, and graduated from Hofstra University and holds a master's degree in management and urban policy from The New School University.

ERIC T SCHNEIDERMAN (D)

Eric T Schneiderman was elected the 65th Attorney General of New York State on November 2, 2010. A key priority is ensuring one set of rules applies to all, regardless of wealth or power. He used funds recovered from drug traffickers to pay for bulletproof vests for local police officers when federal funding was cut. He created the Homeownership Protection Program, which has served 24,000 homeowners at risk of foreclosure. He was active in securing a $13 billion settlement with JP Morgan Chase for their role in the housing crisis. In addition, Attorney General Schneiderman created the Community Overdose Prevention program, a $5 million plan to equip law enforcement agencies with naloxone, which can immediately stop a heroin overdose. Before becoming Attorney General, Schneiderman served in the New York State Senate as a reformer, which included chairing the committee to expel a corrupt senator for the first time in modern history. Prior to that time he was an attorney in private practice. He is a graduate of Amherst College and Harvard Law School, and the father of one.

NEW YORK STATE SENATE

JOSEPH P ADDABBO JR (D)
15th - Part of Queens County

159-53 102nd Street, Howard Beach, NY 11414
718-738-1111/addabbo@nysenate.gov

66-85 73rd Place, Middle Village, NY 11379
718-497-1630

88-08 Rockaway Beach Blvd. Room 311, Rockaway Beachn, NY 11693
718-318-0194

188 State Street Room 613, Legislative Office Building, Albany, NY 12247
518-455-2322

Joseph Addabbo Jr. was most recently elected to the New York Senate in 2014, having first been elected in 2008. He carries on the tradition of public service of his father, Congressman Joseph P. Addabbo, Sr. Addabbo's district includes all or part of the following communities: Broad Channel, Elmhurst, Forest Hills, Glendale, Hamilton Beach, Kew Gardens, Kew Gardens Hills, Maspeth, Middle Village, Ozone Park, Rego Park, Richmond Hill, Ridgewood, South Ozone Park, Woodhaven, Woodside, and the Rockaways. Addabbo, a lifelong resident of Queens, is the ranking member of the standing committee on racing, gaming and wagering, as well as veterans, homeland security and military affairs. He also sits on the following standing committees: aging; civil service; environmental conservation; and labor. He sat on the Senate Bipartisan Task Force on Hurricane Sandy, which impacted his district, to help the community recover from the devastating storm. In addition to his legislative duties, Addabbo sponsors and organizes events for his constituency ranging from job fairs to health screenings. He formerly chaired the Senate Elections Committee and worked to pass ethics reform and to force large companies to disclose their information about money they spend to influence elections. In addition, Addabbo opposes hydraulic fracking. Addabbo practiced law for 10 years at Addabbo and Greenberg. In 2001, he was elected to the New York City Council and served for eight years and secured millions of dollars in funding for improvements in infrastructure, school technology, and senior and youth services. Joseph Addabbo graduated from St. John's University and Touro Law School. He is married with two daughters.

GEORGE AMEDORE (R)
46 - Montgomery, Ulster, Greene

42 Crown St., Kingston, NY 12401
518-455-2350/Amedore@nysenate.gov

20 Park Street Room 121, Fonda, NY 12068
518-853-3401

George Amedore was elected to the New York State Senate in 2014. He chairs the Committee on Alcoholism and Drug Abuse and the Heroin Task Force. In addition, he sits on the following standing committees: banks; consumer protection; elections; judiciary; social services; and veterans, homeland security and military affairs. Sen. Amedore previously served in the New York State Assembly, where he worked to create a property tax cap and also aided communities impacted by the floods that followed Tropical Storms Irene and Lee. His family business is Amedore Homes, which has built more than 3,500 homes around the Capital Region. He is the married father of three.

TONY AVELLA (D-WF)
11th - Part of Queens County

38-50 Bell Boulevard Suite C, Bayside, NY 11361
718-357-3094/avella@nysenate.gov

Tony Avella was first elected to the New York State Senate in 2010. In 2014, he joined the Independent Democratic Conference, five Democratic senators working toward efficiency and bipartisanship in the Senate. He chairs the Ethics Committee and vice-chairs the environmental conservation committee. He sits on the following committees: banks; cultural affairs, tourism, parks and recreation; education; housing, construction and community development; insurance; judiciary; and transportation. The former chair of the Social Services Committee, Avella now chairs the Senate Task Force on the Delivery of Social Services to New York City, aimed at improving access to social services programs. In 2015, he spearheaded legislation to bring transparency to the budgetary process at the Queens Public Library, as well as changes to its leadership and organization. Avella is also a noted opponent of hydraulic fracking, and is fighting against increased airplane noise in Queens and the city.

Prior to being elected to the Senate, Avella served as an aide to New York City Council Member Peter Vallone, Sr., to Mayors Koch and Dinkins and as Chief of Staff to the late State Senator Leonard Stavisky and to State Senator Toby Stavisky. In 2001, he was elected to Council, where he served as Chair of the Zoning and Franchises Committee. He was also the founder and Chair of the first Italian-American Caucus of the City Council. Avella graduated from Hunter College and is married. He resides in Whitestone, Queens.

JOHN J BONACIC (R-C-IP)
42nd - Sullivan County, Parts of Delaware, Orange and Ulster counties

201 Dolson Avenue, Suite F, Middletown, NY 10940
845-344-3311/bonacic@nysenate.gov

111 Main Street, Delhi, NY 13753
607-746-6675

John Bonacic was first elected to the New York State Senate in 1998 and was most recently re-elected in 2014. He chairs the Senate Judiciary Committee, as well as the Racing, Gaming and Wagering Committee. In addition he serves on the following standing committees: alcoholism and drug abuse; banks; children and families; cultural affairs, tourism, parks and recreation; finance; housing, construction and community development, and rules. Prior to his election to the Senate, he served seventeen years as an Orange County Legislator, including as Chairman. In addition, he served as Assistant District Attorney for Orange County. In 1990, Bonacic was elected to the New York State Assembly, where he served until his election to the Senate. His Senate legislative achievements include sponsoring the Women's Health and Wellness Act, which grants women equality in healthcare services covered by insurance. He also has negotiated agreements that kept two rural hospitals in his district open, and negotiated the re-opening of Tri-Town Regional Hospital. He also led the effort to affiliate Catskill Regional Medical Center with the Orange Regional Medical Center, and created a public-private partnership to the Catskill Regional Medical Center's emergency room services. In a prior role as chairman of the Senate Committee on Housing, Construction, and Community Development he sponsored legislation that allowed for the creation of thousands of new housing opportunities. Bonacic holds an undergraduate degree from Iona College and a JD from Fordham Law School. He and his wife have two children and three grandchildren.

PHILIP M. BOYLE (R)
4th - Part of Suffolk County

69 W Main Street Suite B, Bay Shore, NY 11706
631-665-2311
/pboyle@nysenate.gov

Philip Boyle was elected to the New York State Senate in 2012. He is chairman of the Commerce, Economic Development and Small Business Committee. In addition, he is a member of the following standing committees: codes; consumer protection; housing, construction and community development; local government; and racing, gaming and wagering. Prior to his election to the Senate, Boyle served in the New York State Assembly from 1994-2002, and again starting in 2006. He also served many years as a senior congressional aide in Washington, D.C. to the late U.S. Rep. Frank Horton as legislative director, then as campaign manager and chief of staff to former U.S. Rep. Frank Lazio. He is a founding partner in the law firm of Steinberg & Boyle LLC, and is now an attorney with the law firm of Cronin, Cronin, Harris and O'Brien, PC. He is active in his community, including as a volunteer firefighter for the Great River Fire Department. He holds a B.A. from the University of North Carolina/Chapel Hill, a JD from Albany Law School, and a MPA from the Rockefeller College of Public Affairs and Policy at the University of Albany. He is married and the stepfather to two.

NEIL D BRESLIN (D-IP-WF)
44th - Parts of Albany and Rensselaer counties

172 State Street, Room 414, Capitol, Albany, NY 12247
518-455-2225/breslin@nysenate.gov

Neil Breslin was first elected to the New York State Senate in 1996. He sits on the following standing committees: banks; education; finance; higher education; insurance; judiciary; and rules. Breslin has been an associate or partner in law firms, and currently is of counsel to the firm of Hiscock & Barclay. He is an active member of the New York State Bar Association, as well as the National Conference of Insurance Legislators (NCOIL), where he is President of the Executive Committee and former chair of the State/Federal Relations Committee. His civic involvement includes serving for many years on the board of Arbor House, a women's residence facility, including seven years as its president. In addition, he has been the attorney for St Anne's Institute in Albany. The Albany native graduated from Fordham University with a BS degree in Political Science. He received his JD from the University of Toledo in Toledo, Ohio. His is married with three children.

DAVID CARLUCCI (D-WF)
38th - Parts of Rockland and Westchester counties

95 South Middletown Road, Nanuet, NY 10954
845-623-3627/carlucci@nysenate.gov

David Carlucci was first elected to the New York State Senate 2010. He is the Independent Democratic Conference Whip, and chairs the Senate Committee on Social Services. In addition, he sits on the following committees: alcoholism and drug abuse; energy and telecommunications; infrastructure and capital investment; insurance; investigations and government operations; mental health and developmental disabilities; racing, gaming and wagering; rules, transportation; and veterans, homeland security and military affairs. He formerly co-chaired the Administrative Regulations Review Commission. He formerly chaired the Senate Mental Health and Developmental Disabilities Committee, where he worked to restore key funding to provide services and assistance to this population. Prior to being elected to the Senate, Carlucci served three terms as Town Clerk of Clarkstown in Rockland County where he digitized hundreds of thousands of records and created a mobile office that took town clerk services to residents. He graduated from Rockland Community College and holds a B.S. from Cornell University. He is the married father to one child and resides in Clarkstown.

LEROY COMRIE (D)
14th- Southeast Queens

205-20 Jamaica Avenue 2nd Floor, Hollis, NY 11423
718-454-0162/ Comrie@nysenate.gov

Leroy Comrie was elected to the New York State Assembly in 2014 to represent a Queens district that includes portions of Jamaica, Cambria Heights, Queens Village, Hollis, St. Albans, Laurelton, Jamaica Estates, Briarwood, and Kew Gardens. He is Ranking Minority Member of the

Consumer Protection Committee and the Elections Committee. He also sits on the following committees: civil service and pensions; judiciary; racing, gaming & wagering; veterans, homeland security & military affairs.

Prior to his election, he was Deputy Majority Leader of the New York City Council and Chairman of the Queens Delegation, where his legislative achievements include increasing tax and property exemptions for seniors and instituting the city's first foreclosure prevention program. He was also President of his local Community School Board.

The South Queens native attended the University of Bridgeport and is the married father of two.

THOMAS D CROCI (R)
3rd - Part of Suffolk County

250 Veterans Memorial Highway NYS Office Building, Room 2a-1
Hauppauge, NY 11788
631-361-3356
/croci@nysenate.gov

Tom Croci was elected to the New York State Senate in 2014. He chairs the Committee on Veterans, Homeland Security and Military Affairs, and sits on the following committees: alcoholism and drug abuse; civil service and pensions; energy and telecommunications; higher education; and infrastructure and capital investment. The former Islip Town Supervisor is himself a veteran, having received a commission from the Navy Officer Candidate School in Pensacola, Fla., and having spent more than eight years on active duty. He rose to the rank of Commander and served active duty tours in the Arabian Gulf, Afghanistan, and in the Office of Naval Intelligence. He ended his active duty as Senior Duty Office in the White House Situation Room, National Security Council, Executive Office of the President where he supported the President and National Security Advisor. He then was appointed by President Bush to serve on the Homeland Security Council Staff and the Obama Administration requested that he stay on the Presidential Transition Team. He went back to active duty to Afghanistan with a Navy SEAL team. In 2013 he was mobilized again to active duty. He returned home to Long Island in 2014. He and his family support local charitable causes and the Senator is President of the Tom & Jo-Ann Croci Foundation - named in memory of his parents - to provide educational scholarships and grants to support youth. Sen. Croci holds a BS from James Madison University, and graduated from the The New York Law School.

JOHN A DEFRANCISCO (R)
50th - Most of Onondaga County

333 East Washington St, 800 State Office Bldg, Syracuse, NY 13202
315-428-7632/jdefranc@senate.state.ny.us

416 Capitol; Albany, NY 12247
518-455-3511

John A DeFrancisco was elected to the New York State Senate in 1992 and is the Chairman of the Senate Finance Committee, a position that gives him a key role in reviewing the governor's budget proposals and developing Senate budget priorities. He formerly chaired the Senate Judiciary Committee, of which he remains a member. He is also a member of the following standing committees: banks; cities; codes; crime victims, crime and correction; and labor. His long Senate career includes advocating for constituents in areas such as limiting the use of eminent domain, and creating a residential property tax exemption for Syracuse in an effort to alleviate the problem of vacant homes in the city. In 2014, his "Vince's Law" legislation, named for a constituent killed by a drunk driver with multiple prior DWI-related convictions, became law. It strengthened the law by allowing stronger penalties for people with multiple DWI convictions. He also backed legislation to provide for the Amber Alert System in New York. An attorney by profession, DeFrancisco worked in a New York City law firm, an Assistant District Attorney in

Biographies

Onondaga County and a Judge Advocate in the U.S. Air Force before going into private practice for good. He was an adjunct professor of law from 1978-1990 at Syracuse University College of Law and currently is of counsel to the DeFrancisco & Falgitano Law Firm. Prior to his election to the Senate, he served eleven years on the Syracuse Common Council. He holds a B.S. from Syracuse University's College of Engineering and a J.D. from Duke University. He is married with three children and eight grandchildren.

RUBÉN DÍAZ, SR (D)
32nd - Part of Bronx County

900 Rogers Place, Bronx, NY 10459
718-991-3161/diaz@nysenate.gov

188 State Street Room 606, LOB, Albany, NY 12247
518-455-2511

Reverend Rubén Díaz was elected to the New York State Senate in 2002 in the South Bronx, including the communities of Castle Hill, Longwood, Melrose, Morrisania, Parkchester, West Farms and Concourse Village. He sits on the following standing committees: aging; banks; finance, investigations and government operations; judiciary; and transportation. As State Senator, Reverend Díaz continues to work hard to improve economic opportunities, housing, health care, and education for the people of the Bronx. Prior to his election, he served on the New York City Council. Born in Bayamón, Puerto Rico, he served in the US Army before moving to New York City in 1965. In 1978, he became an ordained Minister of the Church of God. In 1977, Díaz founded, and until 2001 served as the Executive Director for, the Christian Community Benevolent Association Inc. He is also founder and pastor of the Christian Community Neighborhood Church. Díaz holds a B.A. from Herbert H. Lehman College, and a theological degree from Damascus Bible Institute. He is married with three children; one of his children is Bronx Borough President Rubén Díaz, Jr. He also has six grandchildren.

MARTIN M DILAN (D)
18th - Part of Kings County

786 Knickerbocker Ave, Brooklyn, NY 11207
718-573-1726/dilan@senate.state.ny.us

188 State Street Room 711B, LOB, Albany, NY 12247
518-455-2177

Martin M Dilan was first elected to the New York State Senate in 2002. His North Brooklyn district includes the communities of Bushwick, Williamsburg, Greenpoint, Cypress Hills, City-Line, East New York, Bedford-Stuyvesant, and Brownsville. Senator Dilan is the Assistant Minority Leader for Policy and Administration in the Senate's Democratic Conference. He sits on the following standing committees: civil service and pensions; elections; energy and telecommunications; finance; infrastructure and capital investment; judiciary; labor; rules; and transportation. He is the former Assistant Minority Leader of Conference Operations, Chairman of the Minority Conference, and Senior Assistant Majority Leader. His legislative achievements include fighting to form a non-partisan redistricting process as part of his membership on the Legislative Task Force on Demographic Research and Reapportionment, which he formerly co-chaired.

Prior to his election to the Senate, Dilan was a member of the New York City Council for ten years. He also served as a member of Community School Board #32 for fourteen years, seven as the Chair. He served as a Legislative Assistant for the US House of Representatives, as a Democratic District Leader, and as a Democratic State Committeeman. He attended a special baccalaureate degree program at Brooklyn College, and married with three children and two grandchildren. His son, Erik, is a state Assemblyman.

ADRIANO ESPAILLAT (D-WF)
31st - Part of New York County

5030 Broadway Suites 701 and 702, New York, NY 10034
212-544-0173/espailla@nysenate.gov

Room 513 LOB, Albany, NY 12247
518-455-2041

Andriano Espaillat was elected to the Senate in November 2010, where he represents a district that stretches from Manhattan's Upper West Side through Washington Heights and includes Riverdale, Marble Hill, and Hamilton Heights. He serves on the following committees: codes; environmental conservation; finance; higher education; housing, construction, and community development; insurance; judiciary; and rules. He is the top-ranking Democrat on the Senate Housing Committee, formerly chaired the Veterans Affairs Committee and the Small Businesses Committee, and chairs the Senate Puerto Rican/Latino Caucus. In addition, he is a member of Gov. Cuomo's Minority and Women-Owned Business Enterprise Team. Espaillat's legislative accomplishments include enacting legislation supporting over 40,000 livery drivers by extending protections from violent crimes and inclusion of the drivers in the Workers' Compensation benefits program. He also endorsed legislation allowing 35,000 daycare providers to organize and collectively bargain.

The Dominican Republic-born Espillat became the first Dominican-American elected to a state legislature when he was elected to the New York State Assembly in 1996. He formerly worked as the Director of Project Right Start, a Robert Woods Johnson Foundation-funded program to educate the parents of pre-school children to combat substance abuse, and as Director of the Washington Heights Victims Services Community Office. He also was a Manhattan Court Services Coordinator for the NYC Criminal Justice Agency, a subcontractor to the city. He holds a B.S. from Queens College and has completed post graduate courses in public administration at NYU and the Rutgers University Leadership for Urban Executives Institute. He is the married father of two.

HUGH T FARLEY (R-C-I)
49th - St. Lawrence, Hamilton, Clinton County, Fulton Counties, Saratoga County

199 Milton Avenue Suite 4, Ballston Spa, NY 12020
518-885-1829/farley@nysenate.gov

33-41 East Main Street City Hall, Johnstown, NY 12095
518-762-3733

188 State Street Room 711, LOB, Albany, NY 12247
518-455-2181

Senator Farley was elected to the New York State Senate in 1976 and is Vice President Pro Tempore. He is vice-chair of the Senate Committee on Banks and a member of the following committees: education; ethics; health; finance; rules; and social services. He has previously held a number of leadership positions, including Majority Whip, and has chaired the Aging, Banks, and Environmental Conservation committees. He has also been the Senate Chair of the General Government/Local Assistance budget conference committee, and Chair of the Senate Majority Program Development Committee. He also served as Chair of the Senate Subcommittee on Libraries, thereby sponsoring nearly every piece of significant library legislation from 1978 through 2008. He has backed legislation that defends personal privacy rights, and developed the Schenectady Metroplex law to help the renewal of industrial cities through public and private cooperation. He was a faculty member in the School of Business of the University of Albany and was named a professor emeritus of business law in 2000. First elected to public office in 1970, Senator Farley originally served as a Councilman and, later, Majority Leader in the Town of Niskayuna. He served in the U.S. Army in Germany. He graduated from Mohawk Valley Community College, holds a B.S. from the University of Albany; and holds a J.D. from the

American University School of Law. He is married and the father of three.

SIMCHA FELDER (D)
17th - Parts of Brooklyn

1412 Avenue J, Suite. 2E, Brooklyn, NY 11230
718-253-2015

Simcha Felder was first elected to the New York State Senate in 2012. His Brooklyn district includes the neighborhoods of Midwood, Flatbush, Borough Park, Kensington, Sunset Park, Madison and Bensonhurst. He chairs the Children and Families Committee, as well as the Taskforce on the Delivery of Social Services for New York City. In addition, he is a member of the following committees: aging; commerce, economic development and small business; health; infrastructure and capital investment; and mental health and developmental disabilities. His legislative achievements include legislation that allows parents of special education children to more easily receive funding for their child's schooling. Professionally, he is a CPA and has been a professor of management at Touro College and CUNY's Brooklyn College. He was Deputy Comptroller for Budget, Accounting, Administration and Information Technology in the New York City Comptroller's Office. He also has worked for the New York State Assembly and as a tax auditor for the New York City Dept. of Finance. He also held previous elective office as a member of the New York City Council, where he chaired two committees. Felder holds an MBA from Baruch College. He and his family live close to the home where Felder was raised.

JOHN J FLANAGAN (R-C-I)
2nd - Part of Suffolk County

260 Middle Country Rd, Suite. 102, Smithtown, NY 11787
631-361-2154/flanagan@nysenate.gov

John J Flanagan was first elected to the New York State Senate in 2002 to a district that includes the town of Smithtown and portions of the towns of Brookhaven and Huntington. On May 11, 2015, he was elected Temporary President and Majority Leader of the Senate. He chaired the Committee on Education, and also serves on the following committees: codes; corporations, authorities and commissions; energy and telecommunications; finance; higher education; insurance; judiciary; rules; and veterans, homeland security and military affairs. In his role on the education committee, he has supported the Safe Schools Against Violence in Education Act, and worked to permanently extend the Child Safety Zone law that gives otherwise ineligible children access to bus service. He recently was instrumental in securing nearly a billion dollars in additional aid for New York school districts. He also sponsored a bill, signed into law in 2012, that ensures that mammography reports tell women their breast density so they may pursue other screening options. He served in the New York State Assembly for 16 years prior to his election to the senate, and was Deputy Minority Whip for one year. The Hamilton-raised Flanagan holds a B.A. from the College of William and Mary and a J.D. from the Touro Law School. He and his wife are parents to three. Flanagan is the son of the late New York State Assemblyman John Flanagan.

RICH FUNKE (R)
55th District - Monroe County, Ontario County

230 Packett's Landing, Fairport, NY 14450
585-223-2800
/Funke@nysenate.gov.

Rich Funke was first elected to the New York State Senate in 2014. He is Chair of the Committee on Elections, and also sits on the following committees: aging; cities; commerce, economic development and small business; consumer protection; environmental conservation; and higher education. He is a well-known broadcaster in the area, having retired in

2012 after a 44-year career that included many years at NEWS10 NBC where he went from the sports desk to the anchor chair. The Batavia native started out in local radio and then went to Miami, Fl., before returning to Rochester. He also has done play by play for the Rochester Knighthawks and Amerks, as well as local college and high school football and basketball games. His civic work includes co-hosting the annual telethon for Golisano Children's Hospital at Strong, serving on the boards of Cancer Action and Ronald McDonald House, and hosting a monthly radio show for Camp Good Days and Special Times. He holds a bachelor's degree in business from Adelphi University and has been married to his wife, Patricia, for 43 years.

PATRICK M GALLIVAN (R-C-IP)
59th - Wyoming, Livingston and Ontario Counties and Part of Erie County

2721 Transit Rd, Suite 116, Elma, NY 14059
716-656-8544
gallivan@nysenate.gov

143 North Main Street Room 103, Warsaw, NY 14569
585-786-2187

Livingston County Government Center, 6 Court Street, Rm 304, Geneseo, NY 14454
585-243-6929

900 Jefferson Rd., Ste 202, Henrietta, NY 14623
585-272-1032

Patrick M Gallivan was elected to the New York State Senate in 2010. He chairs the Crime Victims, Crime and Correction Committee, and also sits on the following committees: agriculture; codes; commerce, economic development and small business; elections; finance; higher education; housing, construction, and community development; infrastructure and capital investment; labor; and transportation. During his first term in the Senate, Gallivan drafted and introduced more than 20 bills that were signed into law by Governor Andrew Cuomo. His legislative achievements include a piece of Medicaid reform legislation to eliminate Medicaid's mandate burden on local governments. Prior to representing the citizens of Western New York in the Senate, Sen. Gallivan was twice-elected Sheriff of Erie County, Upstate New York's most populous county. Prior to that, he spent 15 years in the New York State Police, rising to the rank of captain. He is a former member of the New York State Executive Committee on Counter-terrorism, as well as a member of the New York State Board of Parole. He founded and operates a professional investigation and security firm. He holds an undergraduate degree from Canisius College and a Master's degree in criminal justice from SUNY-Albany. He is the married father of two.

MICHAEL GIANARIS (D-WF)
12th - Part of Queens County

21-77 31st Street, Astoria, NY 11105
718-728-0960/gianaris@nysenate.gov

Michael Gianaris was elected to the State Senate in 2010 is Deputy Minority Leader. He sits on Ethics Committee and the Rules Committee. Prior to being elected to the Senate, he served for ten years in the New York State Assembly. He backed same-sex marriage throughout his public service career, and advocates against dysfunction in state government. His legislative achievements also include authorship of the Clean Energy Law. Prior to seeking elective office, he was an aide to Congressman Thomas Manton, Gov. Mario Cuomo's Queens County Regional Representative, and Counsel to the Speaker of the Assembly. He has also litigated cases in private practice. He holds an undergraduate degree from Fordham University and a J.D. from Harvard Law School.

MARTIN J GOLDEN (R-C-I)
22nd - Part of Kings County

7408 5th Avenue, 1st Floor, Brooklyn, NY 11209
718-238-6044/golden@nysenate.gov

3604 Quentin Rd., Brooklyn, NY 11234

Martin J Golden was first elected to New York State Senate in November 2002. He represents a Brooklyn district that includes the neighborhoods of Bay Ridge, Dyker Heights, Bensonhurst, Marine Park, Gerritsen Beach, Gravesend and parts of Sheepshead Bay, Borough Park and Midwood. He chairs the Civil Service and Pensions Committee, and is also a member of the following committees: aging; banks; codes; finance; health; insurance; investigations and government operations; and veterans, homeland security and military affairs. He is Chairman of the Republican Conference Steering Committee. He has held numerous leadership positions in the past, including service as the former Assistant Majority Whip and Chairman of the Republican Conference Steering Committee. His legislative output includes authorship over more than 222 laws with a focus on public safety, tax cuts, economic development, and issues of interest to senior citizens. As the former Chairman of the Senate Aging Committee, he was credited by nationally recognized advocacy groups for championing the rights of senior citizens through the Assisted Living Law of 2004. Under his leadership, a number of significant bills affecting older Americans were enacted, including a new elder law, the Senior Bill of Rights; Long Term Care Reform; internet posting of retail prescription drug prices; and a single EPIC/Medicare prescription drug card. Prior to his election, he served on the New York City Council. He is a former New York City police officer who retired after suffering a serious on-the-job injury. He is a graduate of St. John's University and is the married father of two.

JOSEPH A GRIFFO (R-C-I)
47th - Oneida, Lewis, and St. Lawrence counties

207 Genesee St, Room 408, Utica, NY 13501
315-793-9072/griffo@nysenate.gov

Joseph A. Griffo was elected to the New York State Senate in 2006. He is Chairman of the Energy and Telecommunications Committee. He also sits on the following committees: codes; commerce, economic development and small business; crime victims, crime and correction; cultural affairs, tourism, parks and recreation; finance; higher education; racing, gaming and wagering; and veterans, homeland security and military affairs. Prior to his election, Griffo held a number of public service positions including Oneida County executive for over three years. In that position, he played a key role in boosting the local economy by over 600 jobs by taking the principal role in efforts to protect U.S. Dept. of Defense-related jobs at the nearby Griffiss Air Force Base. He also served on the Board of Directors of the New York State Association of Counties. Griffo also served for 11 years as Mayor of his hometown of Rome, NY, an Oneida County legislator, director of community relations for the City of Rome, and as an administrative assistant to the Rome mayor. He holds a B.A. in Political Science from the State University of New York at Brockport. He is married and lives in Rome.

JESSE HAMILTON (D)
20 - Part of Kings County

1669 Bedford Avenue, 2nd Floor & Mezzanine, Brooklyn, NY 11225
718-284-4700/Hamilton@nysenate.gov

Jesse Hamilton was first elected to the New York State Senate in 2014. He sits on the following committees: agriculture; banks; codes; commerce, economic development and small business; education; energy and telecommunications; and mental health and developmental disabilities. Prior to his election he served as President of Community School Board 17 in Crown Heights and as District Leader of the 43rd Assembly District. He was Vice President of Community Board 8. He also spent 28

years conducting small claims hearings in the New York City Dept. of Finance. He holds an undergraduate degree from Ithaca College, an MBA from Long Island University and a JD from Seton Hall University. He is the married father of two children.

KEMP HANNON (R-C-IP)
6th - Part of Nassau County

595 Stewart Ave. Suite 540, Garden City, NY 11530
516-739-1700/hannon@nysenate.gov

Kemp Hannon was first elected to the New York State Senate in November 1989. He is Chairman of the Health Committee, and also sits on the following committees: finance; judiciary; labor; mental health and developmental disabilities; and rules. His interest and advocacy on behalf of health care been a hallmark of his legislative career. He was deeply involved with the reauthorization of the Health Care Reform Act and the development of New York's Assisted Living Program. During his Senate tenure, he also has served as Chairman of the Committee for Housing and Community Development, Assistant Majority Whip, as well as Chair of the National Conference of State Legislators' Health Committee. Hannon was a New York State Assemblyman for 12 years until his election to the Senate. An attorney by profession, Hannon holds a BA from Boston College and a JD from Fordham Law School. He is the married father of two.

RUTH HASSELL-THOMPSON (D-WF)
36th - Parts of Bronx and Westchester Counties

959 E. 233rd St, Bronx, NY 10466
718-547-8854/hassellt@senate.state.ny.us

First elected to the New York State Senate in 2000, Hassell-Thompson sits on the following committees: alcoholism and drug abuse; commerce, economic development and small business; crime victims, crime and correction; finance; health; judiciary; and rules. Her previous elective office was to the Mount Vernon City Council in 1993, where she served as both Council President and Acting Mayor. Prior to her election, Hassell-Thompson was the Executive Director of the Westchester Minority Contractors Association (WMCA). In this position, she became well versed in economic development issues that affect women and people of color. Among her many achievements was her ability to spearhead bank loans for financing minority and women-owned business activities. She also was CEO of Whart Development Company, Inc., a real estate development company. In addition, Hassell-Thompson is a retired nurse and counselor at Mount Vernon Hospital for 35 years, specializing in pediatrics and helping women with substance abuse issues. She has served as President and CEO of The Gathering, a volunteer-staffed women's center in Mount Vernon that provides counseling and support services. She graduated from Bronx Community College and holds two honorary doctorates. She is the widowed mother of two children and two grandchildren.

BRAD HOYLMAN (D)
27th - Part of New York County

322 Eighth Avenue, Suite 1700, New York, NY 10001
212-633-8052

Brad Hoylman was elected to the New York State Senate in 2012. His Manhattan district includes Clinton/Hell's Kitchen, Chelsea, Greenwich Village, and parts of the Upper West Side, Midtown/East Midtown, the East Village, and the Lower East Side. He sits on the following committees: aging; cultural affairs, tourism, parks and recreation; environmental conservation; investigations and government operations; judiciary; and local government. Prior to being elected to the Senate, Hoylman was a three-term chair of Manhattan Community Board 2. In addition, he was a trustee of the Community Service Society, a board member of the Empire State Pride Agenda, Tenants & Neighborhoods, Class Size Matters and Citizen Action. He also served as general counsel of the Partnership for New York City, a non-profit business and civic organization. Hoylman holds an undergraduate degree from West Virginia University, a master's in politics from Oxford University, and a J.D. from Harvard Law School. He and his husband are parents to one.

TIMOTHY M KENNEDY (D-IP-WF)
58th - Part of Erie County

2239 South Park Ave, Buffalo, NY 14220
716-826-2683/kennedy@nysenate.gov

Timothy M. Kennedy was elected to the New York State Senate in 2010, to a district comprised Cheektowaga, Lackawanna and most of the city of Buffalo. He is the Assistant Democratic Whip and sits on the following committees: banks; commerce, economic development and small business; cultural affairs, tourism, parks and recreation; energy and telecommunications; finance; infrastructure and capital investment; insurance; and transportation. His legislative achievements include sponsoring legislation to develop a green workforce for emerging clean technology industries. He also played a significant role in helping to strengthen state law against texting while driving. His prior public service includes service on the Erie County Legislature, Second District, where he chaired the Economic Development Committed and sat on the Board of Directors of the Erie County Industrial Development Agency. He spearheaded a push to include Buffalo Public School No. 84 in the school districts renovation program. As a result, children with the most severe disabilities in Erie County continue to receive good care and education. The licensed occupational therapist has worked with geriatric and pediatric populations. He holds both a bachelor's and a master's degree in occupational therapy from D'Youville College. He is the married father of three.

JEFFREY D KLEIN (D)
34th - Parts of Bronx and Westchester Counties

1250 Waters Place, Suite 1202, Bronx, New York 10461
718-822-2049/jdklein@senate.state.ny.us

Jeffrey Klein was first elected to the New York State Senate in 2004. He is the Senate Coalition Leader and Independent Democrat Conference Leader, a conference he co-founded in 2011. His previous leadership positions include Senate President Pro Tempore for two years, and Deputy Majority Leader for two years. He also formerly chaired the Senate Committee on Alcohol and Substance Abuse. Klein's legislative achievements include being the prime sponsor of the New York SAFE Act, major legislation that gave New York the nation's toughest gun laws. He has also worked to expand access to key programs and services such as fully-funded universal pre-kindergarten and increased eligibility for major senior support programs. Prior to his election to the Senate, Klein sat in the New York State Assembly for ten years. He holds a B.A. from Queens College, an M.P.A. from Columbia University, and a J.D. from the City of New York Law School and has lived in the northeast Bronx his entire life.

LIZ KRUEGER (D)
28th - Part of New York County, including the Upper East Side

1850 Second Ave, New York, NY 10128
212-490-9535/lkrueger@senate.state.ny.us

First elected to the New York State Senate in a Special Election in February 2002, Sen. Krueger is currently the Ranking Member of Senate Finance Committee. She is also a member of the following committees: codes; elections; higher education; housing, construction, and community development; mental health and developmental disabilities; and rules. She is also a founding co-chair of the New York State Bipartisan Legislative Pro-Choice Caucus and has been highly active in the area of women's health. She helped to lead the successful fight to pass the Women's Health and Wellness Act. Senator Krueger's legislative initia-

tives also efforts to expand and protect affordable housing, opposing hydofracking, and expanding access to food stamps and safety net assistance for those in need. She has chaired the New York City Food Stamp Task Force and has sat on the board of the City-Wide Task Force on Housing Court. She also served as Co-facilitator of the New York City Welfare Reform Network. Prior to being elected to the Senate, Krueger was Associate Director of the Community Food Resource Center for 15 years. She also was the founding Director of the New York City Food Bank. She holds a B.A. from Northwestern University and a Master's degree from the University of Chicago's Harris Graduate School of Public Policy. She and her husband live on Manhattan's East Side.

ANDREW J LANZA (R)
24th - Part of Richmond County

3845 Richmond Ave, Suite 2A, Staten Island, NY 10312
718-984-4073/lanza@senate.state.ny.us

Senator Lanza was elected to the New York State Senate in November 2006. He chairs the Cities Committee, and is Vice Chair of the Codes Committee. He also sits on the following committees: civil service and pensions; education; ethics; finance; insurance; and judiciary. His legislative achievements include authoring legislation to create an online database to allow doctors and pharmacists to report and track controlled narcotics in real time, an effort to combat prescription drug abuse. He also backed efforts to force New York City to restore bus service to Staten Island's 7th and 8th graders. In addition, Sen. Lanza passed legislation that created the 13th Judicial District in the State of New York, comprised solely of Richmond County, allowing Staten Island to have its own judicial district. Prior to being elected to the Senate, Lanza sat on the New York City Council and also served as a prosecutor. He holds a B.S. from St. John's University and a JD from Fordham University Law School. He and his wife have three children and reside in Great Kills.

WILLIAM J LARKIN, JR (R-C)
39th - Parts of Orange, Ulster and Rockland Counties

1093 Little Britain Road, New Windsor, NY 12553
845-567-1270/larkin@senate.state.ny.us

Senator Larkin was first elected to the New York State Senate in 1990 to a district that includes, in Orange County, the city of Newburgh and the Towns of Blooming Grove, Chester, Cornwall, Crawford, Highlands, Monroe, Montgomery, New Windsor, Newburgh, and Woodbury, and in Ulster County, the city of Kingston and the Towns of Plattekill and Marlborough, and Haverstraw and Stony Point in Rockland County. Sen. Larkin is Assistant Majority Leader for House Operations, and also serves on the new Senate Task Force on Workforce Development. He also serves on the following committees: corporations, authorities and commissions; finance; health; insurance; rules; transportation; and veterans, homeland security and military affairs.

Senator Larkin was Majority Whip from 2011 to 2015, and has served in other leadership positions during his Senate tenure. His legislative achievements include authoring a new law to change the operations and procedures of local Industrial Development Agencies (IDAs). The law increased the public accountability of IDAs while giving IDAs more flexibility to create jobs. As chair of the veterans' committee, he sponsored changes in veteran's benefits that increased the financial protections for families of U.S. servicemen fighting in the Persian Gulf War, as well as conflicts in Lebanon, Panama and Grenada. In addition, he is recognized for his expertise relating to the insurance industry; he is past president of the National Conference of Insurance Legislators (NCOIL). Senator Larkin is a veteran of 23 years of active military duty including combat assignments during World War II and the Korean War. He retired from the United States Army in 1967 with the rank of Lieutenant Colonel. Following his military service, Senator Larkin served as an Executive Assistant in the New York State Senate and as Supervisor of the Town of New Windsor in Orange County. The Troy native graduated

Biographies

613

from LaSalle Institute. He and his wife, between them, have eight children and 17 grandchildren.

GEORGE S. LATIMER (D)
37th - Part of Westchester County

222 Grace Church St., Port Chester, NY 10572
914-934-5256/latimer@nysenate.gov

George S. Latimer was first elected to the New York State Senate in 2012, and represents Bedford, Bronxville, Eastchester, Harrison, Larchmont, Mamaroneck, New Rochelle, Port Chester, Rye, Rye Brook, Tuckahoe, White Plains, and Yonkers. He sits on the following committees: banks; consumer protection; education; environmental conservation; insurance; local government; and racing, gaming and wagering. Latimer previously served in the New York State Assembly, where he authored more than 20 new laws, and on the Westchester County Board of Legislators, including as Chairman and Minority Leader. During his chairmanship, the board oversaw the creation of smoke free workplace laws and the creation of a Human Rights Commission, among other accomplishments. Latimer also served on the Rye City Council for four years. He is a marketing executive by profession with project experience at major corporations. He holds a BA from Fordham University and an MPA from New York University's Wagner School. He is the married father of one.

KENNETH P LAVALLE (R)
1st - Part of Suffolk County

29 North Country Road, Suite 203, Mt. Sinai, NY 11766
631-473-1461/lavalle@nysenate.gov

Kenneth P LaValle was first elected to the New York State Senate in 1976. He is Chairman of the Senate Majority Conference, Chair of the Senate Committee on Higher Education. In addition, he sits on the following committees: aging; education; environmental conservation; finance; insurance; judiciary; rules; and social services. In his many years chairing the higher education committee, LaValle has helped shape higher education policy in New York State. In 2007, the governor appointed Senator LaValle to the New York State Commission on Higher Education that was charged with identifying ways of improving the quality of higher education. LaValle also served on the National Council of State Legislatures' Blue Ribbon Commission on Higher Education that sought to create awareness among state legislatures of their role in providing accessible and affordable public higher education. He has also been active in the healthcare arena, including work to establish a burn unit at Stony Brook University Medical Center. An attorney by profession, LaValle holds an undergraduate degree from Adelphi College, an education degree from SUNY New Paltz, and a J.D. from Touro College Jacob D. Fuchsberg Law Center. He has also completed graduate student in government and international relations at NYU. He is married and the father of two and grandfather to four.

THOMAS W LIBOUS (R-C-I)
52nd - Broome, Tioga, Chenango and Delaware counties

44 Hawley Street, Room 1607, Binghamton, NY 13901
607-773-8771/http://www.nysenate.gov/senator/tom-libous

Senator Thomas W Libous was first elected to the New York State Senate in 1988. He is Deputy Majority Coalition Leader. He formerly chaired the Transportation Committee, as well as the Mental Health and Developmental Disabilities Committee, and the Alcoholism and Drug Abuse Committee. As Chair of the Select Committee on the Disabled, he authored legislation giving tax credits to those who hire people with disabilities. The Senator, who was diagnosed with prostate cancer in 2009, founded I Turned Pro to encourage men over the age of 50 to talk to their doctors about their prostate cancer risk. Prior to his election he served on the Binghamton City Council. He graduated from Broome Community

College and the State University of New York at Utica. Libous lives with his wife in Binghamton and they have two children. On July 1, 2014, *The New York Times* reported that Sen. Libous had been indicted on a charge of giving a false statement to the FBI. It was reported on May 18, 2015, that he was scheduled to go on trial that summer.

ELIZABETH "BETTY" LITTLE (R-C-I)
45th - Clinton, Essex, Franklin, Warren and parts of St. Lawrence and Washington counties.

Betty Little was first elected to the New York State Senate in 2002. She serves as Deputy Majority Whip, and formerly served as Assistant Majority Whip. She chairs the Committee on Cultural Affairs, Tourism, Parks and Recreation, and also sits on the following committees: crime victims, crime and correction; education; energy and telecommunications; environmental conservation; finance; health; and rules. Her legislative achievements include creating the Adirondack Community Housing Trust and passing the Timber Theft Law. Prior to being elected to the Senate, she served in the New York State Assembly for seven years. She also served as an At-Large Supervisor to the Warren County Board of Supervisors for the Town of Queensbury. She holds a degree from the College of Saint Rose, and is the mother of six and grandmother of 14.

CARL LOUIS MARCELLINO (R)
5th - Parts of Nassau and Suffolk Counties

250 Townsend Square, Oyster Bay, NY 11771
516-922-1811/marcelli@senate.state.ny.us

Senator Carl Louis Marcellino was elected to the New York Senate in 1995. He is the Vice Chairman of the Senate Majority Conference, and also chairs the Committee on Infrastructure and Capital Investment, as well as the Committee on Investigations and Government Operations. In addition, Sen. Marcellino also serves on the Senate committees on banks; cultural affairs, tourism, parks and recreation; education; environmental conservation; finance; labor; and rules. He is Vice-Chair of the Transportation Committee. His legislative achievements include authorship of more than 100 environmental laws during his 1995 to 2008 chairmanship of the Senate Environmental Conservation Committee. Among them was his primary sponsorship of the Brownfield/Superfund Reform Law, the Pesticide Notification Law, and the first law in the county to phase out the groundwater contaminate MTBE from gasoline. He also focuses on health and safety issues, including efforts such as banning the use of handheld cell phones while driving in New York. In addition, he was the prime sponsor of the "Stephanie's Law" which made it a felony to engage in video voyeurism, the Unpaid Wages Prohibition Act, the disability registry that provides vital information to aid in rescues and evacuations, and the permanent COLA bill, granting retirees from state service annual cost-of-living adjustments. He is Chairman of the Oyster Bay Western Waterfront Committee and Chairman of the Council of State Governments. Prior to being elected to the Senate, Sen. Marcellino was a science teacher and administrator in the New York City School System, as well as the elected Oyster Bay Town Clerk. The Brooklyn-born Marcellino holds a B.S. and a M.S. from New York University and a Professional Diploma in Administration and Supervision from St. John's University. He and his wife are parents of two.

KATHLEEN A MARCHIONE (R-C)
43rd - Columbia County and Parts of Rensselaer, Saratoga and Washington Counties

2 Halfmoon Town Plaza, Halfmoon, NY
12065/marchione@nysenate.gov

560 Warren St., 2nd Floor, Hudson, NY 12534
518-828-5947

Kathleen A. Marchione was first elected to the New York State Senate in 2012. She chairs the Local Government Committee, and also sits on the following committees: aging; banks; consumer protection; cultural affairs, tourism, parks and recreation; elections; labor; and racing, gaming and wagering. Prior to her election to the Senate, Marchione was the Saratoga County Clerk for many years. She previously served as the Halfmoon Town Clerk and as a Halfmoon Town Supervisor. She is the former President of the New York State Association of County Clerks, former Chairwoman of the Capital District Regional District Planning Commission, and, for a decade, the chair of the New York State Regional Records Advisory Committee. She also sat on the New York State Local Government Records Committee. She has been deeply involved in her regional Republican clubs, and she has received numerous awards including the highest distinction that a record management professional can receive, the Wheeler B. Melius Award from the New York Association of Local Government Records Officers. She is the married mother of two, stepmother of one, and grandmother to four.

JACK M MARTINS (R)
7th - Part of Nassau County

252 Mineola Blvd., Mineola, NY 11501
516-746-5924/martins@nysenate.gov

Jack M. Martins was first elected to the New York State Senate in 2010. He chairs the Labor Committee, and sits on the following committees: banks; civil service and pensions; corporations, authorities and commissions; finance; health; insurance; social services; and transportation. His legislative achievements include working to cut middle class income tax rates and repealing the MTA Payroll Tax on counties, towns, villages, and libraries. He also authored the law that created the state's Homeless Veterans Assistance Fund, as well as the law to create the statewide Financial Restructuring Board for local governments, on which he serves. Prior to his election to the Senate, Martins served as Mayor of the Village of Mineola. He holds an undergraduate degree from American University and a J.D. from St. John's University School of Law. He and his wife and four children live in his hometown of Mineola.

VELMANETTE MONTGOMERY (D-WF)
25th - Part of Kings County

30 3rd Ave, Brooklyn, NY 11217
718-643-6140/montgome@senate.state.ny.us

Velmanette Montgomery was first elected to the New York State Senate in 1984. She is Ranking Democrat on the Committee on Children and Families, and also serves on the following committees: agriculture; children and families; crime victims, crime and correction; education; finance; health; rules; social services; and finance. She previously served as Assistant Majority Whip. She advocates on behalf of school-based health care for delivery of comprehensive primary and mental health services to school children. She backed a measure that prevents the NYS Office of Children and Families from posting the home address or personal information of day care providers on the Internet. She is also the sponsor of the 2012 law that supports agriculture by requiring the state's Procurement Council to include a member of a non-profit organization that represents farming communities. Professionally, she has been a teacher, and she is former President of Community School Board 13 and co-founder of the Day Care Forum of New York City. She holds a BA and MS from NYU; she also attended the University of Accra in Ghana.

TERRENCE P MURPHY (R)
40 (Putnam, Dutchess, and Westchester counties)

Putnam County Office Bldg., 3rd Floor, 40 Gleneida Avenue, Carmel, NY 10512
845-225-3025

691 E. Main St, 1st Floor, Shrub Oak, NY 10588
914-962-2624
/murphy@nysenate.gov

Terrence Murphy was elected to the New York State Senate in 2014. He sits on the following committees: banks; ethics; health; investigations and government operations; labor; local government; and mental health and developmental disabilities. A chiropractor by training, he opened the Yorktown Health and Wellness Center in 1999, and opened Murphy's Irish Restaurant in Yorktown in 2006, along with his mother and siblings. The lifelong Hudson Valley resident was elected to the Yorktown Town Board in 2009, where his achievements included back-to-back tax cuts and $250 million in economic development. He is the married father of three.

MICHAEL F NOZZOLIO (R-IP-C)
54th - Seneca and Wayne Counties, Parts of Cayuga, Monroe, Ontario, and Tompkins Counties

119 Fall Street, Seneca Falls, NY 13148
1-888-568-9816/nozzolio@nysenate.gov

Michael F Nozzolio was first elected to the New York State Senate in 1992. He is Majority Whip and Chair of the Codes Committee. In the latter position, he guides the committee as it considers issues and legislation relating to New York's criminal and civil justice system. In addition, Sen. Nozzolio sits on the following committees: crime victims, crime and correction; elections; finance; housing, construction, and community development; investigations and government operations; judiciary; racing, gaming and wagering; rules; and transportation. Prior to his election to the New York State Senate, Nozzolio served for 10 years in the New York State Assembly, where he served as Deputy Minority Leader. He also served in the U.S. Naval Reserve as a JAG officer, and is a Commander in the New York Naval Militia. The Seneca Falls born-and-raised Nozzolio holds a bachelor's degree in labor relations and a Master's degree in public administration and agricultural economics from Cornell University. He holds a JD from Syracuse University College of Law. He and his wife reside in Seneca Falls.

THOMAS F O'MARA (R-C)
58th - Chemung, Schuyler, Steuben and Yates counties, and part of Tompkins County including the city and town of Ithaca, and the towns of Enfield, Newfield and Ulysses

333 East Water Street, 3rd Floor, Suite 301, Elmira, NY 14901
607-735-9671/omara@nysenate.gov

105 East Steuben Street, Bath, NY 14810
607-776-3201

Thomas F O'Mara was elected to the New York State Senate on November 2, 2010. He is Chair of the Environmental Conservation Committee, and also sits on the following committees: agriculture; banks; codes; energy and telecommunications; finance; insurance; investigations and government operations; judiciary; and transportation. He also is one of five senators sitting on the joint bipartisan Legislative Commission on the Development of Rural Resources. He has been a strong advocate of revitalizing Upstate New York's manufacturing sector. Prior to his election to the Senate, O'Mara sat in the New York State Assembly for three terms, where he rose to the rank of Assistant Minority Leader Pro Tempore. He is a former Chemung County District Attorney, Chemung County Attorney, and an Assistant District Attorney in both Manhattan and Chemung County. He remains active in his community, including as counsel to the Chemung County Industrial Development Agency. He holds a B.A. from the Catholic University of America and a J.D. from Syracuse University College of Law. He is married with three children and resides in Big Flats.

ROBERT ORTT (R)
62nd - Niagara, Orleans and Monroe Counties

175 Walnut Street, Suite 6, Lockport, NY 14094
716-434-0680/Ortt@nysenate.gov

Robert Ortt was first elected to the New York State Senate in 2014. He chairs the Committee on Mental Health and Developmental Disabilities, and also sits on the following committees: cities; civil service and pensions; corporations, authorities and commissions; environmental conservation; higher education; local government; and veterans, homeland security and military affairs. He is the former Mayor of North Tonawanda, where he served for four years and developed executive expertise. He was the City Treasurer and Clerk Treasurer from 2007-2010. He enlisted in the NY Army National Guard following the 9/11 attacks, and served in Afghanistan as the Executive Officer/Unit Movement Officer for an infantry company. His awards included the Bronze Star. He is a former independent personal financial analyst and lives in North Tonawanda with his wife.

MARC PANEPINTO (D)
60th - Erie County

65 Court Street, Rm. 213 (Mahoney State Office Building), Buffalo, NY 14202
(716) 854-8705/Panepinto@nysenate.gov

Marc Panepinto was elected to the New York State Senate in 2014 from a Western New York district that includes parts of the City of Buffalo, the City of Tonawanda, and the Towns of Grand Island, Tonawanda, Hamburg, Orchard Park, Evans, and Brant. He is Ranking Member on the Committee on Local Government and the Agriculture Committee. He also sits on the following committees: codes; health; housing, construction and community development; insurance; local government; transportation; veterans, homeland security and military affairs. He opposes the Gap Elimination Adjustment (GEA) and advocates to reform the education systems testing culture. He also backs the Jobs Protection Act, and increased funding for Erie County infrastructure. The Town of Tonawanda native graduated from the University of Buffalo, and went on to study Labor and Industrial Relations at the University of Illinois and become a union organizer. He received a law degree from the University of Buffalo and is principal in the law firm of Dolce Panepinto P.C. He is the married father of three.

KEVIN S PARKER (D-WF)
21st - Part of Kings County

55 Hansen Place Shirley A. Chisholm SOB, Suite 605, Brooklyn, NY 11217
718-629-6401/parker@senate.state.ny.us

Kevin S Parker was first elected to the New York State Senate in 2002. He represents an ethnically diverse district that includes Flatbush, East Flatbush, Midwood, Ditmas Park, Kensington, Windsor Terrace and Park Slope. The Brooklyn-born Parker is currently a member of the following committees: alcoholism and drug abuse; banks; cultural affairs, tourism, parks and recreation; energy and telecommunications; finance; higher education; insurance; and rules. He is former Majority Whip and a member of the New American Task Force. He is also Parliamentarian of the NY State Association of Black and Puerto Rican Legislators, Inc. Sen Parker was Special Assistant to former New York State Comptroller H. Carl McCall and managed intergovernmental relations in New York City, and also was liaison between the Comptroller and city, state and federal elected officials. He also was a New York City Urban Fellow and also served as a Special Assistant to former Manhattan Borough President Ruth Messinger; Legislative Aide to former New York City Councilmember Una Clarke and Special Assistant to Assemblyman Nick Perry. He has worked as a project manager with the New York State Urban Development Corporation, and on government affairs issues within the chairman's office of UBS PaineWebber. Parker previously served as 2nd vice-chairman and chair of Community Board 17's Education Committee. He has been a professor of African-American studies and political science at Baruch College-CUNY, SUNY Old Westbury, John Jay College, and Brooklyn College. Parker earned a B.S. from Penn State and an M.S. from the New School for Social Research Graduate School

of Management and Urban Study. He is pursuing a doctorate in political science from CUNY's Graduate School and University Center.

JOSE PERALTA (D-WF)
13th - Part of Queens County

32-37 Junction Boulevard, East Elmhurst, NY 11369
718-205-3881/jperalta@nysenate.gov

Jose Peralta was first elected to the senate in a 2010 special election to a district that includes Corona, East Elmhurst, Elmhurst, Jackson Heights and parts of Woodside and Astoria. He is the Minority Whip, and also serves on the following committees: cities, consumer protection; crime victims, crime and correction; finance; higher education; and labor. Prior to his election to the senate, Peralta served in the New York State Assembly from 2002-2010. His legislative goals include efforts to bring economic development to Willets Point and neighboring communities, as well as a drive to rejuvenate Roosevelt Avenue. He holds a BA from Queens College and is the married father of two.

BILL PERKINS (D-WF)
30th - Part of New York County

163 West 125th Street, Harlem State Office Bldg., Suite 912, New York, NY 10027
212-222-7315/perkins@senate.state.ny.us

Bill Perkins was first elected to the New York State Senate in 2006 and represents a district that encompasses Harlem, the Upper West Side, and Washington Heights. He is the Senate's Deputy Minority Whip. He sits on the following committees: codes; corporations, authorities and commissions; crime victims, crime and correction; finance; judiciary; labor; rules; and transportation. A life-long resident of Harlem, Sen. Perkins started his political career as a community activist. Prior to his election to the Senate, he spent eight years on the New York City Council where he served as the Deputy Majority Leader. In this position, he was prime sponsor of the Childhood Lead Paint Poisoning Prevention Act of 2004. He holds a B.A. in political science from Brown University, and is the married father of four.

MICHAEL RANZENHOFER (R-C-IP)
61st - Genesee County and Parts of Erie and Monroe Counties

8203 Main Street, Suite 4, Williamsville, NY 14221
716-631-8695/ranz@senate.state.ny.us

Michael Ranzenhofer was first elected to the New York Senate in 2008. His district includes the towns of Amherst, Clarence and Newstead, and the villages of Akron and Williamsville in Erie County, the towns of Chili and Riga, the village of Churchville, and part of the city of Rochester in Monroe County, and all of Genesee County. He chairs the Corporations, Authorities and Commissions Committee, and also sits on the following committees: agriculture; education; finance; judiciary; racing, gaming and wagering; and transportation. His legislative achievements include working with non-profit organizations and the New York State Bar Association to pass legislation to overall the state's not-for-profit laws. Prior to his election, he served in the Erie County Legislature and was both Majority and Minority Leader. A lawyer by profession, Ranzenhofer is a partner at Friedman & Ranzenhofer, P.C. He holds a BA from SUNY-Albany and a JD from SUNY at Buffalo Law School. He and his wife have two children.

PATTY RITCHIE (R-C-IP)
48th - Oswego, Jefferson and St. Lawrence Counties

Dulles State Office Building, Room 418, Watertown, NY 13601
315-782-3418/ritchie@nysenate.gov

46 East Bridge St., 1st floor, Oswego, NY 13126
315-342-2057

330 Ford St. (basement of City Hall), Ogdensburg, NY 13669
315-393-3024

Patty Ritchie was elected to the State Senate in 2010. She is Deputy Majority Leader for Senate and Assembly Relations, as well as Chair of the Agriculture Committee. She also sits on the following committees: alcoholism and drug abuse; civil service and pensions; crime victims, crime and correction; cultural affairs, tourism, parks and recreation; energy and telecommunications; finance; higher education; local government; and transportation. Her legislative achievements include working to strengthen family farms, including authoring a new 2% cap on farmland assessments, and proposing the Young Farmers NY program to provide incentives to help new farmers. Prior to her election to the Senate, Sen. Ritchie served as St. Lawrence County Clerk for over a decade. As County Clerk, she made the County Clerk's Office more accessible and user-friendly for residents of her sprawling county; and established four local DMV offices that eliminated long lines, improved efficiency, and increased revenue for the county. She graduated from Mater Dei College and SUNY Potsdam, and lives in Oswegatchie with her husband. They have three children and three grandchildren.

GUSTAVO RIVERA (D-WF)
33rd - Part of Bronx County

2432 Grand Concourse, Suite 506, Bronx, NY 10458
718-933-2034/grivera@nysenate.gov

In 2010, Gustavo Rivera was elected to the New York State Senate. His district, from Northwest Bronx to parts of the East Bronx, includes Kingsbridge Heights, East Tremont, Crotona Park, Fordham, Belmont, Van Nest, Claremont, High Bridge, and Morris Park. He is the Ranking Minority Member on the Health Committee, and also sits on the following committees: crime victims, crime and correction; ethics; finance; higher education; labor; and mental health and developmental disabilities. Rivera had early success in the Senate: he introduced legislation that proposed making it mandatory for public officials to disclose all sources of income they receive apart from their government salary. This provision was included in Gov. Andrew Cuomo's ethics package that was signed into law. In addition, Rivera introduced and passed legislation that will allow charitable organizations throughout the state to post bail bonds for individuals who cannot afford to do so themselves. He is an adjunct professor at Pace University, and a former community organizer for candidates running for state senate and the NYC mayor's seats. SEIU hired Rivera to manage their activities on behalf of presidential candidate Barack Obama in a number of key states in 2008. He has also been Director of Community Outreach for U.S. Sen. Kirsten Gillibrand. The Santurce, Puerto Rico-born Rivera graduated from the University of Puerto Rico. He came to New York to attend a doctoral program at the CUNY's Graduate Center.

JOSEPH E ROBACH (R-C-IP)
56th - Part of Monroe County

2300 W. Ridge Road, Rochester, NY 14626
585-225-3650/robach@nysenate.gov

Joseph Robach was first elected to the New York State Senate in 2002. His district includes the Towns of Greece, Brighton, Parma, Clarkson, Gates, Hamlin, and parts of the City of Rochester. He chairs the Transportation Committee and sits on the following committees: commerce, economic development and small business; consumer protection; education; finance; higher education; infrastructure and capital investment, and labor. In addition, he chairs the Majority Steering Committee. Before his election to the Senate, Robach served as an Assemblyman for 11 years filling the seat vacated by the passing of his father, Roger Robach. He is also a member of the Finger Lakes Regional Economic Development Council. Sen. Robach holds both B.S. and M.P.A. degrees from the State University of New York College at Brockport. He is also a graduate of Aquinas Institute. He is the married father of three.

JOHN L SAMPSON (D-WF)
19th - Part of Kings County

1222 East 96th St, Brooklyn, NY 11236
718-649-7653/http://www.nysenate.gov/senator/john-l-sampson

John L Sampson was first elected to the New York State Senate in 1996. He represents a district that encompasses Canarsie, East New York, Parts of Brownsville, Spring Creek, Georgetown, Bergen Beach, Mill Basin, Mill Island, Flatlands, Marine Park, and Sheepshead Bay. Sen. Sampson is the first African American to serve as the Chairman of the Senate Judiciary Committee. He formerly served as Democratic Conference Leader, State Senate Minority Leader, and Deputy Majority Leader. He has also chaired the Senate Ethics Committee and the Senate Administrative Regulations Review Commission. While Chair of the Judiciary Committee, Senator Sampson called for more hiring of minorities and women for judgeships. Prior to his election, Senator Sampson worked as a staff attorney for the Legal Aid Society of New York, as well as an attorney in private practice. He holds a BA from CUNY's Brooklyn College and a J.D. from Albany Law School. On May 6, 2013, Sampson was arraigned on federal embezzlement charges according to the *New York Times*. A federal judge dropped two of the charges in 2014, and Sampson was scheduled to go to trial in June 2015, according to the *Buffalo News*.

JAMES SANDERS, JR. (D)
10th - Parts of Queens County

142-01 Rockaway Blvd., South Ozone Park, NY 11436
718-523-3069/sanders@nysenate.gov

1931 Mott Avenue, Suite 305, Far Rockaway, NY 11691
718-327-7017

James Sanders Jr. was elected to represent the New York State Senate in 2012 to a district that includes South Jamaica, Rochdale Village, Rosedale, Richmond Hill, South Ozone Park, Springfield Gardens and most of the Rockaways.. He is the ranking Democrat on the Civil Services & Pensions Committee, and also sits on the following committees: banks; commerce, economic development and small business; cultural affairs, tourism, parks and recreation; insurance; labor, racing, gaming and wagering; and veterans, homeland security and military affairs. He has advocated on behalf of higher wages for working people, including helping to lead the fight for higher pay for airport food servers employed by the Port Authority of New York and New Jersey. Prior to being elected to the senate, Sen. Sanders was a member of the New York City Council for 12 years. He also sat on Queens School Board District 27 for a decade, including seven years as president, having been the first African-American who ascended to that post. He also served in the United States Marine Corps for three years, and holds an undergraduate degree from Brooklyn College. Sen. Sanders is the married father of two.

DIANE J SAVINO (D-IP-WF)
23rd District - Parts of Kings and Richmond Counties

36 Richmond Terrace, Suite 112, Staten Island, New York 10301
718-727-9406/savino@senate.state.ny.us

2872 West 15th Street, Brooklyn, NY 11224
718-333-0311

Diane J Savino was first elected to the New York State Senate in 2004 to represent a district that encompasses the North and East Shore of Staten Island and portions of Southern Brooklyn, including Borough Park, Brighton Beach, Dyker Heights, Gravesend, Coney Island, Bensonhurst, and Sunset Park. She is Chairman of the Banks Committee, as well as a member of the following committees: children and families; civil service and pensions; consumer protection; elections; finance; health; higher education; and judiciary. Sen. Savino is co-founder of the Independent Democratic Conference and its liaison to the executive branch. Her many legislative successes include the nation's first Domestic Workers' Bill of

Rights that expands basic worker protection rights to domestic workers; the Prompt Pay Bill that ensures prompt payment to construction contractors and their employees, and the Wage Theft Prevention Act that assesses preventative and punitive measures to employers who steal income from their employees. Professionally, she worked as a caseworker for the New York City's Child Welfare Administration, and she has been active in her local labor union, where she rose through the ranks. She holds a BA from St. John's University and also graduated from Cornell School of Industrial and Labor Relations.

SUE SERINO (R)
41st - Dutchess County

Susan J. Serino was elected to the New York State Senate in 2014 and chairs the Aging Committee. In addition, she sits on the following committees: children and families; cultural affairs, tourism, parks and recreation; education; higher education; judiciary; mental health and development disabilities. Her previous public service was as a member of the Hyde Park Town Board for a year, and then the Dutchess County Legislature where she advocated on behalf of holding the line on taxes and fees. She operates a Hyde Park-based real estate business. She is mother to one.

JOSE M SERRANO (D-WF)
29th - Parts of Bronx and New York Counties

1916 Park Ave., Suite 202, New York, NY 10037
212-828-5829/serrano@senate.state.ny.us

Senator Jose M Serrano was first elected to the New York State Senate in 2004 and represents the 29th Senate District which includes neighborhoods in the South and West Bronx, East Harlem, Upper Yorkville, Roosevelt Island, Central Park, and the Upper West Side. He is Chair of the Senate Democratic Conference and serves as the Ranking Member of the Committee on Cultural Affairs, Tourism, Parks and Recreation. He also sits on the following committees: aging, agriculture; children and families; consumer protection; environmental conservation; mental health and developmental disorders; and veterans, homeland security, and military affairs. His legislative achievements include Senate passage of bills that: require the Department of Environmental Conservation to publish a list of areas in the state that are most adversely affected by existing environmental hazards; to incentivize affordable development on vacant properties in Northern Manhattan; and to mandate the New York State Dept. of Health to conduct an intensive study on the high rates of asthma in the Bronx. Prior to his election to the Senate, Serrano was a member of Community Board 4 in the Bronx, Chairman of the Board for the Institute for Urban Family health, and, in 2001, he was elected to the New York City Council, where he chaired the Committee on Cultural Affairs. Serrano holds a BA from Manhattan College and lives with his wife and two children in the South Bronx.

JAMES L SEWARD (R-C-IP)
51st - Clinton, Cortland, Delaware, Herkimer, Otsego Ulster, and Schoharie counties

41 S Main Street, Oneonta, NY 13820
607-432-5524/seward@nysenate.gov

235 N. Prospect St., Herkimer, NY 13350
315-866-1632

4030 West Rd., Cortland, NY 13045
607-758-9005

James L Seward was first elected to the New York State Senate in 1986. He chairs the Majority Program Development Committee, as well as the Senate's Insurance Committee, and has held numerous leadership positions during his Senate tenure. He also sits on the following committees: agriculture; education; finance; health; higher education; mental health and developmental disabilities; and rules. In his role on the insurance committee, Seward's legislative successes include passage of legislation in 2002 that extends group health insurance offered by chambers of commerce to sole proprietors of businesses, and in 2008 Sen. Seward secured legislative approval of a bill to provide short-term health insurance policies to young adults and college students. In addition, he has advocated on behalf of education, jobs, and business growth. Seward is a former Milford town justice, and remains active in his community, including in such posts as trustee of Glimmerglass Opera. He holds a B.A. from Hartwick College, and also studied at the Nelson Rockefeller Institute of SUNY Albany. He is the married father of two.

DEAN G SKELOS (R-C-IP)
9th - Part of Nassau County

55 Front Street, Rockville Centre, NY 11570
516-766-8383/http://www.nysenate.gov/senator/dean-g-skelos

Dean G. Skelos was first elected to the New York State Senate in 1984. He is the former Majority Leader, having served from 2011-2015. In 2013, Skelos was co-President Pro Tempore as Majority Coalition Leader, a bipartisan power-sharing arrangement. Before becoming Majority Leader, Skelos was Senate Republican Leader. Skelos's legislative successes include a property tax cap, and laws eliminating the statute-of-limitations in cases of rape and violent assault. He also wrote the law eliminating a New York City "Commuter Tax." As the author of Megan's Law, Skelos created the New York State Sex Offender Registry and authored numerous measures to strengthen the statute, including the Workplace and Campus Registration acts and laws establishing lifetime registration for dangerous sexual predators and posting information and photos about more sex offenders on the internet. Prior to being elected to the Senate, Skelos sat in the New York General Assembly for two years. He holds a BA from Washington College and a JD from Fordham University School of Law. He and his wife are parents to one and grandparents to one. On May 4, 2015, *The New York Times* reported that Sen. Skelos and his son were arrested on federal extortion, fraud and bribe solicitation charges. On June 1, 2015, *Capital New York* reported that the pair pleaded not guilty to federal corruption charges.

DANIEL L SQUADRON (D-WF)
26th - Parts of Kings and New York Counties

250 Broadway, Suite 2011, New York, NY 10007
212-298-5565/squadron@nysenate.gov

209 Joralemon Street, Suite 310 Brooklyn, NY 11201
718-875-1517

Elected to the New York State Senate in 2008, Daniel Squadron's district includes the Brooklyn neighborhoods of Greenpoint, Williamsburg, Vinegar Hill, DUMBO, Fulton Ferry, Brooklyn Heights, Downtown Brooklyn, Boerum Hill, Cobble Hill, Carroll Gardens, and Columbia Waterfront, and the Manhattan neighborhoods of Tribeca, Battery Park City, the Lower East Side, Chinatown, the Financial District, Little Italy, SoHo, and the East Village. He sits on the following committees: cities; codes; corporations, authorities and commissions; finance; investigations and government operations; social services; and transportation. Among his legislative achievements is passage into law of his bill to allow more than $1 billion in federal funds for New York City public housing over 15 years, as well as backing a bill to create benefit corporations, which are a new type of business that can pursue both profit and social good. Prior to his election to the Senate, Squadron was a top aide to U.S. Sen. Chuck Schumer. Squadron holds an undergraduate degree from Yale University and resides in Carroll Gardens with his wife and two children.

TOBY ANN STAVISKY (D)
16th - Part of Queens County

142-29 37th Ave Suite 1, Flushing, NY 11354
718-445-0004/stavisky@nysenate.gov.

Toby Ann Stavisky was first elected to the Senate in 1999 and is the first woman from Queens County elected to the State Senate and the first woman to chair the Senate Committee on Higher Education. Currently, Stavisky is the Ranking Minority Member of the Higher Education Committee, and also sits on the following committees: education; finance; health; judiciary; and transportation. She is Leader for Conference Operations and previously served as Assistant Minority Whip. Prior to entering public life, Stavisky worked in the actuarial department of a major insurance company and taught social studies in the New York City high schools, and served as district manager in Northeast Queens for the U.S. Census. She holds an undergraduate degree from Syracuse University, and two M.A. degrees: one from Hunter College, and one from Queens College.

ANDREA STEWART-COUSINS (D-IP-WF)
35th - Part of Westchester County

28 Wells Ave, Bldg 3, Yonkers, NY 10701
914-423-4031/scousins@senate.state.ny.us

Andrea Stewart-Cousins was first elected to the New York State Senate in 2006 and her district includes Greenburgh, and parts of White Plains, New Rochelle, Yonkers and Scarsdale. She is the Leader of the Senate Democratic Conference, becoming the state's first female leader of a legislative conference. Stewart-Cousins also sits on the Rules Committee. Her legislative achievements include sponsoring and passing the Government Reorganization and Citizen Empowerment Act, which empowers communities to consolidate local governments, which reduces overlap of municipal services and saves taxpayer dollars. She also sponsored and passed Jimmy Nolan's law in 2009, which extends the time by which 9/11 responders can file compensation claims for injuries sustained from the World Trade Center rescue, recovery or cleanup operations. Finally, she sponsored and passed the Child Health Plus and School Meal Enrollment Coordination Law, the 2010 law that allows families to use their proof of eligibility for Free or Reduced Price School Meal Programs as proof of income to enroll their child in Medicaid and Child Health Plus. Stewart-Cousins previously served as Westchester County Legislator, and was the first African American Director of Community Affairs for the City of Yonkers. She holds a BS from Pace University, earned her teaching credentials from Lehman College, and holds a MPA from Pace University. She is the widowed mother of three and grandmother of two.

DAVID J VALESKY (D-IP)
53rd - Madison County and Parts of Oneida County and Onondaga County including the city of Syracuse

333 East Washington St, 805 State Office Building, Syracuse, NY 13202
315-478-8745/valesky@nysenate.gov

Senator David J Valesky was elected to the New York State Senate in 2004. He is the Deputy Independent Democratic Conference Leader for Legislative Operations and also is Vice Chair of the Health Committee. In addition, he sits on the following committees: aging; agriculture; commerce, economic development and small business; education; finance; higher education; local government, and transportation. Valesky has

sponsored several laws that promote investment in communities and make it easier for businesses to locate and stay in New York State. Prior to his election, Valesky served as an aide to former State Assembly Majority Leader Michael Bragman. He then became Vice President of Communications at WCNY, the public television and radio station of Central New York, a post he occupied from 1995 to 2004. There, he hosted the midday talk show HOUR CNY. The Oneida native holds an undergraduate degree from SUNY Potsdam and a Master's degree from the University of Connecticut. He is the married father of three.

MICHAEL VENDITTO (R-C-I)
8th - Nassau County and part of Suffolk County

5550 Merrick Road, Suite 205, Massapequa, NY 11758
516-882-0630/Venditto@nysenate.gov

Michael Venditto was elected to the New York State Senate in 2014 from a district that includes the Towns of Hempstead and Oyster Bay, and the Town of Babylon. He chairs the Consumer Protection Committee and also is a member of the following committees: crime victims, crime and correction; insurance; judiciary; and labor. The lifelong resident of the South Shore was a Nassau County Legislator who is concerned about the middle class and champions small businesses. He holds a B.A. from Hofstra University and a J.D. from St. John's University School of Law. He and his wife are parents to one.

CATHARINE M YOUNG (R-C-IP)
57th - Allegany, Cattaraugus, Chautauqua County

Westgate Plaza, 700 West State Street, Olean, NY 14760
716-372-4901/cyoung@senate.state.ny.us

2-6 East 2nd Street Fenton Building, Suite 302, Jamestown, NY 14701
716-664-4603

Catharine Young was first elected to the New York Senate in 2005. She is Assistant Senate Majority Whip, chairs the Legislative Commission on Rural Resources, and chairs the Housing, Construction, and Community Development Committee. She also sits on the following committees: agriculture; children and families; environmental conservation; finance; health; insurance; rules and transportation. She also founded the Legislative Wine and Grape Caucus to boost the industry-sponsored legislation that formed the New York State Council on Food Policy. She previously served in the New York State Assembly, where she helped pass Penny's Law, which ensures that violent killers are not released prematurely. She also served on the Cattaraugus County Legislature including a leadership post as Majority Whip, and was a member of the Cattaraugus County Board of Health. She graduated from St. Bonaventure University and is a major in the Civil Air Patrol. She is the married mother of three.

NEW YORK STATE ASSEMBLY

PETER J ABBATE, JR (D)
49th - Part of Kings County

6605 Fort Hamilton Parkway, Brooklyn, NY 11219
718-236-1764/abbatep@assembly.state.ny.us

Peter Abbate was first elected to the New York State Assembly in 1986. His district includes Dyker Heights, Bath Beach, Bensonhurst, and Borough Park in Brooklyn. He is chair of the Governmental Employees Committee, a position he first assumed in 2002. He is also a member of the following committees: aging; banks; consumer affairs and protection; and labor. In addition, he chairs the Subcommittee on Safety in the Workplace. Abbate is also treasurer of the New York Conference of Italian American State Legislators. Abbate has sponsored legislation creating a wide range of laws, including laws to stop unscrupulous prize award schemes by providing for mandatory disclosure, requiring that school bus lights be illuminated while students are being transported, and allowing civil servants union representation during investigation reviews. In addition, he is responsible for a number of laws relating to real taxes, including one to allow a property tax exemption for improvements made to comply with the Americans with Disabilities Act. Rep. Abbate worked as a legislative assistant to then-Assemblyman Stephen J. Solarz; when Solarz was elected to Congress Abbate became his district representative. Abbate has received numerous awards from a range of community groups, including Man of the Year by the Federation of Italian American Organizations of Brooklyn and the Council of Neighborhood Organizations. The lifelong resident of Bensonhurst earned an undergraduate degree in political science from St. John's University.

THOMAS J ABINANTI (D)
92nd - Parts of Westchester and New York Counties

303 South Broadway, Suite 229, Tarrytown, NY 10591
914-631-1605/abinantit@assembly.state.ny.us

Thomas J. Abinanti was first elected to the New York State Assembly in 2010. His District includes the Towns of Greenburgh and Mount Pleasant. He is Chair of the Libraries and Education Technology Committee, and is a member of the following committees: codes; corporations, authorities and commissions, election law, environmental conservation, and health. Prior to his election to the Assembly, Abinanti spent ten terms in the Westchester County Legislature where he served three times as Majority Leader. He was instrumental in establishing the Westchester Medical Center as an independent public benefit corporation. In addition, Abinanti sat on the Greenburgh Town Council for two terms. Prior to his election, he worked as legislative counsel to Congresswoman Nita Lowey and as staff counsel to the New York State Assembly. He also served as prosecuting attorney for the Villages of Ardsley and Dobbs Ferry, and has taught at Pace Law School and Mercy College of Dobbs Ferry. Abinanti received his undergraduate degree from Fordham College and his JD from New York University School of Law. He is married and has two children.

CARMEN E ARROYO (D)
84th - Part of Bronx County

384 E 149th St, Suite 301, Bronx, NY 10455
718-292-2901/arroyoc@assembly.state.ny.us

In a special election in February 1994, Carmen E. Arroyo became the first and only Puerto Rican/Hispanic woman elected to the New York State Assembly. She is chair of the Majority Program. In addition, she is a member of the following standing committees: aging, alcoholism & drug abuse; children and families; and education.

Assemblywoman Arroyo was born, raised, and educated in Corozal, Puerto Rico. She came to the mainland U.S. in 1964 and worked in a factory in New York, and sent for her seven children in 1965. Her experience during this time, which included receiving public assistance for nine months, led her to found the South Bronx Action Group, where she served as executive director and advocated on behalf of tenant needs such as employment, health, adult education and welfare. She also served as a member and President of Community School Board 7 for 20 years, and was the state's first Puerto Rican housing developer in the state, and has served on a number of boards. She also writes poetry. She earned an associate's degree from Eugenio Maria de Hostos Community College, and an undergraduate degree from the College of New Rochelle. In addition to her seven children, she has 13 grandchildren.

JEFFRION L AUBRY (D-L)
35th - Part of Queens County

98-09 Northern Blvd, Corona, NY 11368
718-457-3615/aubryj@assembly.state.ny.us

Jeffrion Aubry was first elected to the New York State Assembly in 1992. Assemblyman Aubry is the New York State Speaker Pro Tempore, and is a member of the following committees: ways and means, rules, social services and governmental employees. He also chairs the Board of Justice Center, a national organization which provides technical assistance to states to develop data-driven consensus-supported criminal justice policies to reduce crime and decrease the cost of incarceration nationwide. Assemblyman Aubry is a member of the Council of State Governments and is a "Toll Fellow," a distinguished association of state legislators from across the country. His legislative achievements include backing a 2009 measure that that significantly reformed the Rockefeller Drug Laws in New York State by returning discretion to judges to sentence drug-addicted offenders to treatment as an alternative to prison. He also led the fight to ensure that prisoners suffering from serious mental illness receive needed treatment, and are not confined under inhumane conditions through the enactment of the Special Housing Unit Exclusion Law. Professionally, Assemblyman Aubrey has been the Director of Economic Development for the Borough President's Office of Queens, Executive Director of Elmcor Youth and Adult Activities, and Director of the North Shore Fair Housing Center. He has received numerous awards and holds an undergraduate degree from the College of Santa Fe. He is the married father of five.

WILLIAM A BARCLAY (R)
120th - Parts of Onondaga, Oswego and Jefferson Counties, the cities of Oswego and Fulton

200 N Second St, Fulton, NY 13069
315-598-5185/ barclaw@assembly.state.ny.us

William A Barclay was first elected to the New York State Assembly in 2002. He State Assembly Deputy Minority Leader. He is Ranking Minority Member of the Assembly Insurance Committee, and also sits on the following committees: energy; judiciary; rules; and ways and means. He is a partner in the Syracuse law firm of Hiscock and Barclay, specializing in business law, and he serves as a board member of Pathfinder Bank and Countryway Insurance Company. Assemblyman Barclay served as a clerk for Judge Roger Miner of the US Court of Appeals, Second Circuit, in Albany and New York City. His civic activity has included membership on the boards of directors for the Friends of the Rosamond Gifford Zoo at Burnet Park, the Everson Museum of Art, and Northern Oswego County Health Services. He is a graduate of St. Lawrence University and Syracuse University College of Law. Assemblyman Barclay represents the eighth generation of his family to live n Pulaski, Oswego County, where he resides with his wife and two sons.

DIDI BARRETT (D-WP)
106th - Parts of Columbia and Dutchess Counties

12 Raymond Ave. Suite 105, Poughkeepsie, NY 12603
845-454-2408
/BarrettD@assembly.state.ny.us

751 Warren St., Hudson, NY 12534
518-828-1961

Didi Barrett was elected to the New York State Assembly on March 20, 2012. She serves on the following committees: aging; veterans' affairs; agriculture; mental health; economic development, job creation, commerce and industry; and tourism, parks, arts and sports development. In addition, Barrett is a member of the Task Force on Legislative Women's Caucus. Barrett has long been active among not-for-profit organizations throughout the Hudson Valley. She helped create and serves on the board of the North East Dutchess Fund (NED) of the Berkshire Taconic Community Foundation, an initiative that focuses on improving life in several towns in northeastern Dutchess County. Additionally, she helped pioneer NED Corps alongside the Dutchess Community Action Partnership and serves on its affiliated Latino Roundtable, working to provide social services to this region's communities that are more rural. She is a member of the board of Spout Creek Farm, an educational farm, and led the creation of the Dutchess Girls Collaborative to support young women and girls. She is the founding chair of Girls Incorporated of NYC, a former board member of NARAL Pro-Choice New York, and a trustee emeritus of the American Folk Art Museum. Barrett holds an undergraduate degree in speech communications from UCLA and a MA in Folk Art Studies from NYU. She and her husband have two children.

CHARLES BARRON (D)
60 - Part of Kings County

669 Vermont St., Brooklyn, NY 11207
718-257-5824/barronc@assembly.state.ny.us

Charles Barron was elected to the New York State Assembly in 2014. He sits on the following committees: aging; alcoholism and drug abuse; economic development, job creation, commerce and industry; energy; small business; and social services. He previously served on the New York City Council for 13 years, where he chaired the Committee on Higher Education and secured funding for parks, schools, and funding for the Black Male Initiative for City University of New York. A community activist for more than 45 years, Assemblyman Barron is a founding member of Operation POWER (People Organizing and Working for Empowerment and Respect), the founding chairperson of the National Black United Front's Harlem Chapter, Chief of Staff to the Chair of the National Black United Front, and Secretary General of African Peoples Christian Organization, operated by Re. Dr. Herbert Daughtry, Chair of the NBUF. Assemblyman Barron holds an associate's degree from New York Technical College and a B.A. from Hunter College. He is the married father to two children.

MICHAEL R BENEDETTO (D)
82nd - Part of Bronx County

177 Dreiser Loop, Rm 12, Bronx, NY 10475
718-320-2220

3602 E. Tremont Ave, Suite 201, Bronx, NY 10465
718-892-2235/benedettom@assembly.state.ny.us

Michael R Benedetto was first elected to the New York State Assembly in 2004. He chairs the Committee on Cities, and also sits on the following committees: agriculture; education; governmental operations; labor; and ways and means. The Bronx native spent 35 years teaching elementary and secondary school students. In 1974, he joined the New York City public school system as a teacher of mentally and physically challenged students; in 1977 he was assigned to PS 160, the Walt Disney School, and in 1988 became coordinator of the special education unit. He is currently an adjunct instructor at Mercy College. While with the NYC schools, Assemblyman Benedetto ran the first "very special" Olympics for multiply handicapped children. In addition, he established the Throggs Neck Community Players Community Theater and served as member of Community Planning Board #10. Assemblyman Benedetto also started the Bronx Times Reporter, which became the largest com-

munity paper in the Bronx. He has received numerous awards. He holds an undergraduate degree in history and education from Iona College, and also earned a MA in social studies and education.

RODNEYSE BICHOTTE (D)
42 - Part of King's County

1414 Cortelyou Road, Brooklyn, NY 11226
718-940-0428/bichotter@assembly.state.ny.us

Rodneyse Bichotte was elected to the New York State Assembly in 2014. She sits on the following committees: banks; economic development, job creation, commerce and industry; housing; mental health; small business; and social services. She was elected District Leader in 2010, and in that position has sponsored events in Flatbush such as a Voter's Forum; a mayoral debate; and annual senior luncheons. Professionally, she has been a public school teacher, an engineer, and a finance manager. Of Haitian descent, she has traveled the world, including for work. She is also active in her community, including as a Community Board 17 member and Scholarship Chair of Chicago Urban League Metroboard Scholarship. She holds an MBA from Northwestern University's Kellogg School of Management, an MS in Electrical Engineering from Illinois Institute of Technology, a BS in Electrical Engineering from SUNY Buffalo, a BS in Mathematics in Secondary Education, and a BT in Electrical Engineering, both from Buffalo State College. She was born and raised in Brooklyn.

MICHAEL BLAKE (D)
79 - Part of Bronx County

780 Concourse Village West, Ground Fl. Professional, Bronx, NY 10451
718-538-3829/BlakeM@assembly.state.ny.us

Michael Blake was elected to the New York State Assembly in 2014 and sits on the following committees: banks; correction; election law; housing; and veterans' affairs. His district includes parts of Concourse Village, Morrisania, Melrose, Claremont and East Tremont. He is the Founding Principal of Atlas Strategy Group, which focuses on political and economic empowerment for communities of color. He also served as Director of Public Policy & External Affairs for Green For All, and a Senior Advisor for Operation Hope. Assemblyman Blake joined the Obama Campaign's "Yes We Can" political training program in 2006, and went on to successfully co-organize three state house campaigns. He worked in the Obama campaign in Iowa, and went on to work for the Presidential Inaugural Committee, and then joined the White House staff where he created the White House Urban Entrepreneurship Summit Series. He also worked for President Obama's 2012 re-election campaign. He is a graduate of the Medill School of Journalism at Northwestern University.

KEN BLANKENBUSH (R)
117th - Lewis County, Parts of St. Lawrence, Jefferson and Oswego Counties

40 Franklin St., Suite 2, Carthage, NY 13619
315-493-3909/blankenbushk@assembly.state.ny.us

Ken Blankenbush was first elected to the New York State Assembly in 2010. His district includes Lewis County and parts of Oneida, Saint Lawrence, and Jefferson counties. He sits on the following committees: agriculture; corporations, authorities and commissions; insurance; and tourism, parks, arts and sports development. The longtime Black River resident is a U.S. Air Force veteran of the Vietnam War who was stationed at Plattsburg Air Force Base upon his return. He worked at Metropolitan Life Insurance Company prior to launching BEL Associates, his Watertown-based insurance and financial services business. Blankenbush's public service includes eight years as a councilman in LeRay, and two terms as chair of the Jefferson County Board of Legislators. His memberships include the Association of the United States Army, the Greater Watertown Chamber, Watertown Elks, Black River

American Legion, and National Assoc. of Insurance and Financial Advisers. He holds a B.S. from SUNY Plattsburg, and also finished two years at Monroe Community College. He is married with two children and six grandchildren.

JOSEPH BORELLI (R-C-I)
62nd - Part of Staten Island

101 Tyrellan Ave., Suite 200, Staten Island, NY 10309
718-967-5194/BorelliJ@assembly.state.ny.us

Joseph Borelli was elected to the New York State Assembly in 2012. He sits on the following committees: cities, energy; health; and housing. The native Staten Islander worked as Chief of Staff to New York City Councilman Vincent Ignizio from 2005 to 2012, as well as in other capacities. He has been active in a number of his community's initiatives, including helping to form the South Shore Local Development Corporation. He has also helped coordinate a number of Park and Rides on Staten Island, as well as helped to secure funding to install a Smartboard in almost every South Shore classroom. He sits on the Development Board of St. Joseph by the Sea High School and the Friends of the College of Staten Island. Borelli is an adjunct professor of Political Science at the College of Staten Island. He holds an undergraduate degree from Marist College and an M.A. from the College of Staten Island.

KARL A BRABENEC (R)
98 - Orange and Rockland counties

123 Rt. 94 South, Suite 2, Warwick, NY 10990,
845-544-7551/brabeneck@assembly.state.ny.us

Karl Brabenec was elected to the New York State Assembly in 2014 from a district that includes the City of Port Jervis and the towns of Deerpark, Greenville, Minisink, Warwick, Monroe, Tuxedo, and portions of Ramapo. He sits on the following committees: aging; cities; election law; labor; and local governments. His priorities include alleviating residents' tax burden, and cutting red tape to create jobs and business growth. Prior to his election, he was Deerpark Town Supervisor, an assistant to the former Orange County Executive, a member of the Deerpark Town Council, and the Deerpark Zoning Board. He holds an undergraduate degree from Mount Saint Mary College and an MPA from the John Jay College of Criminal Justice. He is the married father of two.

EDWARD C BRAUNSTEIN (D)
26th - Part of Queens County

213-33 39th Ave, Suite 238, Bayside, NY 11361
718-357-3588/braunsteine@assembly.state.ny.us

Assemblyman Edward C. Braunstein was elected to the New York State Assembly in November, 2010. His Northeast Queens district that includes the neighborhoods of Auburndale, Bay Terrace, Bayside, Bayside Hills, Broadway-Flushing, Douglaston, Floral Park, Glen Oaks, Little Neck, New Hyde Park, North Shore Towers, Oakland Gardens, and Whitestone. Assemblyman Braunstein chairs the Subcommittee on Trust and Estates, and is a member of the following committees: Aging; Cities; Health; Insurance, Judiciary, Small Business, and Transportation. His legislative achievements include leading the effort to ban so-called "bath salts," and also protecting New Yorkers from fraudulent attorneys by making it a felony to practice law without a license. Assemblyman Braunstein's professional background includes serving as a legislative assistant in Assembly Speaker Sheldon Silver's New York City office. He also served on Community Board 11. He holds a BS in Finance from the University at Albany, a law degree from New York Law School, and lives in Whitestone with his wife.

JAMES F BRENNAN (D-WF)
44th - Part of Kings County

416 Seventh Ave, Brooklyn, NY 11215
718-788-7221

1414 Cortelyou Road, Brooklyn, NY 11226
718-940-0641/brennanj@assembly.state.ny.us

James Brennan was first elected to the New York State Assembly in 1984, and his Brooklyn district includes sections of Park Slope, Flatbush, Kensington, Midwood, and Windsor Terrace. Assemblyman Brennan chairs the Committee on Corporations, Authorities and Commissions and is a member of the committees on Codes; Education; and Real Property Taxation. His legislative successes including funding 5,000 units of housing and allowing half-fare on the MTA system for people with mental illness; exposing - via a report called Delaying Necessities, Denying Needs - the shortcomings and delays of the New York State Dept. of Health's program to provide durable medical equipment to people with disabilities; and creating a $300 million urban revitalization fund known as Restoring New York Communities. He holds an undergraduate degree from Yale University and a JD from Brooklyn Law School.

ANTHONY J BRINDISI (D)
119th - Part of Oneida County

207 Genessee St, Rm 401, Utica, NY 13501
315-732-1055/brindisia@assembly.state.ny.us

Anthony J. Brindisi was elected to the New York State Assembly in a special election in 2011. His Mohawk Valley district includes the cities of Utica and Rome and the towns of Floyd, Frankfort, Marcy, and Whitestown. He is chair of the Subcommittee on Volunteer Emergency Services, and sits on the following committees: aging; economic development, job creation, commerce and industry; energy; higher education; transportation; and veterans' affairs. Among the initiatives Assemblyman Brindisi has backed are efforts to create a Career and Technical Education diploma pathway for high school students, as well as bipartisan efforts to revitalize the economy in the Mohawk Valley. He has been instrumental in helping to secure millions of dollars, including $108 million for the Nano Utica project on the SUNY Polytechnic Institute campus in Marcy, and millions for cyber-security and unmanned aerial vehicle research and development at Griffiss Business and Technology Park in Rome.

Assemblyman Brindisi is a former Utica School Board member, and a partner in the law firm of Bridisi, Murad, Brindisi, Pearlman, Julian & Pertz. He graduated from Siena College and Albany Law School, and is married with two children.

HARRY B BRONSON (D)
138th - Part of Monroe County

840 University Ave, Rochester, NY 14607
585-244-5255/bronsonh@assembly.state.ny.us

Harry Bronson was first elected to the New York State Assembly in 2010. His district includes parts of the City of Rochester and the towns and villages of Chili and Henrietta. He sits on the following committees: agriculture; economic development, job creation, commerce and industry; labor; local governments; transportation. In addition, he chairs the Commission on Skills Development and Career Education. He is a former law partner at Blitman and King. He currently co-owns Equal=Grounds, a coffeehouse noted as a neighborhood meeting place in the Southwedge part of the 138th Assembly District. His public service resume includes service as Assistant Minority Leader and Minority Leader of the Monroe County Legislature. He holds an undergraduate degree in public justice from SUNY Oswego and a JD from the University of Buffalo.

ALEC BROOK-KRASNY (D)
46th - Part of Kings County

2823 West 12 St, Suite 1F, Brooklyn, NY 11224
718-266-0267

8018 5th Avenue, Brooklyn, NY 11209
718-680-2845/BrookKrasnyA@assembly.state.ny.us

Alec Brook-Krasny was first elected to the New York State Assembly in 2006, and serves on the following committees: aging, cities, election law, governmental employees, housing, and social services. He also serves as vice chair of the majority steering committee. His recent legislative achievements include backing a series of bills that passed the Assembly that would help prevent human trafficking, strengthen protections for victims, and increase penalties on traffickers. Assemblyman Brook-Krasny emigrated to the U.S. from the former Soviet Union in 1989 and became a business owner, operating the 14,000-square foot "Fun-O-Rama" cultural, educational and entertainment center in Brooklyn. He became the first Russian-speaking American to run for political office during an unsuccessful 2000 campaign for the New York State Assembly. In 2001, Assemblyman Brook-Krasny became the founding Executive Director of The Council of Émigré Community Organizations (COJECO), a coordinating body for 42 community-based Russian-speaking émigré organizations in New York. He holds an undergraduate degree in economics and engineering from Moscow Technological Institute, and graduated from the Institute for Not-for-Profit Management at Columbia University Graduate School of Business. He is married with three children.

DAVID BUCHWALD (D)
93rd - Parts of Westchester County

125-131 East Main St., Suite 204, Mount Kisco, NY 10549
914-244-4450/BuckwaldD@assembly.state.ny.us

David Buchwald was elected to the New York State Assembly in 2012, and sits on the following committees: consumer affairs and protection; corporations, authorities and commissions; election law; governmental operations, judiciary; and local governments. His legislative advocacy includes efforts to increase state aid to local school districts. In addition, he is lead sponsor of a bill to strip public officials of their state pensions if they commit a felony involving a violation of the public trust. He is a former member of the White Plains Common Council, where he authored legislation to strengthen the city's code of ethics, improve sidewalk snow removal, combat illegal dumping, and allow council members to have unpaid interns. He also chaired the White Plains Traffic Commission. Buchwald also served as a Westchester representative to the Metro-North Railroad Commuter Council, a position he was appointed to by then-Gov. David Patterson. Buchwald went on to chair the MNRCC. His resume also includes three years in the Manhattan offices of economics research firm NERA, and he worked for the law firm of Paul Weiss, Rifkind, Wharton & Garrison, representing business and pro bono clients on tax cases. Buckwald is a former board member of the White Plains Historical Society and the White Plains Downtown Residents Association. The Larchmont native holds a BS in physics from Yale University and a JD from Harvard Law School. In addition, he holds a Master's of Public Policy from the John F. Kennedy School of Government.

MARC W BUTLER (R-C-I)
118th - Fulton and Herkimer counties and parts of Otsego County

33-41 East Main St, Johnstown, NY 12095
518-762-6486

235 North Prospect St, Herkimer, NY 13350
315-866-1632/butlerm@assembly.state.ny.us

Marc W. Butler was first elected to the New York State Assembly in 1995. He is the Ranking Minority Member on the Economic Develop-

ment, Job Creation, Commerce and Industry Committee, and also sits on the following committees: agriculture; environmental conservation; higher education, insurance, and rules. As a freshman legislator in Albany, he joined with several other legislators in developing the legislation that ultimately resulted in the STAR Tax Exemption Program. Prior to his election to the Assembly, his political career included service as a Newport Village Trustee and Deputy Mayor and two terms in the Herkimer County Legislature, where he was elected Majority Leader in 1993.He is a former reporter for the Utica Observer-Dispatch and also worked as a corporate communications specialist for Utica National Insurance. He holds a bachelor's degree in English from SUNY Potsdam and is married with two children.

KEVIN A CAHILL (D)
103rd - Parts of Dutchess and Ulster Counties

Gov Clinton Bldg, Suite G-4, 1 Albany Ave, Kingston, NY 12401
845-338-9610/ cahillk@assembly.state.ny.us

Kevin Cahill was first elected to the New York State Assembly in from 1993 to 1995, and was re-elected in 1998. He chairs the Committee on Insurance, and also sits on the following committees: economic development, job creation, commerce and industry; ethics and guidance; health; higher education; and ways and means. He has backed legislation to place a moratorium on fracking. He formerly chaired the Committee on Energy, which allowed him to focus on issues surrounding energy efficiency. Legislation was passed to take proceeds from RGGI, the carbon emission cap and trade program, and direct the funding toward communities and small businesses to create a workforce aimed at improving building energy efficiency. He also helped to increase investments in energy efficiency and renewable power, green the state's facilities and vehicle fleet, and make New York's net-metering law one of the most expansive in the country. In addition, he has backed education, helping to secure $100 million to modernize the campuses of Ulster County Community College and SUNY New Paltz. He formerly served as minority leader of the Ulster County Legislature, and has worked as an attorney and director of a Medicare health plan. He has an undergraduate degree from SUNY New Paltz, a law degree from Albany Law School, is father to two daughters, and is a lifelong resident of Kingston.

JOHN D CERETTO (R-I)
145th - Part of Niagara County and Erie County

800 Main Street, Suite 2C, Niagara Falls, NY 14301
716-282-6062/cerettoj@assembly.state.ny.us

John D. Ceretto was first elected to the New York State Assembly in 2010. His district includes the city of Niagara Falls and the towns of Cambria, Niagara, Lewiston and Wheatfield, as well as portions of the City of North Tonawanda and the town of Grand Island in Erie County. He is Ranking Minority Member on the Tourism, Parks, Arts and Sports Development Committee, and a member of the following committees: cities; education; energy; and labor. His legislative achievements include backing bi-partisan measures such as the property tax cap. Assemblyman Ceretto's elected public service career began in 1995 when he became a councilman on the Lewiston Town Board, a post he held for ten years. In 2005, Ceretto was elected Niagara County Legislator in the 12th District. In addition, he was vice chairman of the Niagara County Economic Development Committee and chaired the Niagara County Refuse Department. Ceretto is active in his local community of Lewiston, and is married with four children. He holds bachelors and master's degrees in education and administration from Niagara University.

BARBARA M CLARK (D)
33rd - Part of Queens County

97-01 Springfield Blvd, Queens Village, NY 11429
718-479-2333/clarkb@assembly.state.ny.us

Barbara Clark was first elected to the New York State Assembly in 1986. Clark is the Assembly's Deputy Majority Whip and a member of the Majority Steering Committee, and sits on the following standing committees: children and families; education; health; labor; libraries and education technology; and rules. During her long Assembly tenure, Assemblywoman Clark has backed numerous initiatives to improve schools, including authoring legislation (based on the New York State Board of Regents) to require children to attend school full-time at age 6. She also led the conversion of 3,500-student Andrew Jackson High School in Queens into a campus of four small magnet high schools. She is a former chair of the Assembly's Committee on Aging, and Committee on State and Federal Relations. She is also former chair of the New York State Legislative Women's Caucus, as well as the Education Committee of the NYS Black, Puerto Rican, Hispanic and Asian Legislative Caucus. Nationally, she was vice-chair of the National Conference of State Legislators' (NCSL) Education, Labor and Job Training Committee, and is a member of the NCSL's policy group called the Education Partners. She served as Vice Chair of the Education Commission of the States (ECS). She and her husband Thomas live in Queens Village and have four children and two grandchildren.

WILLIAM COLTON (D-WF)
47th - Part of Kings County

155 Kings Highway, Brooklyn, NY 11223
718-236-1598/coltonw@assembly.state.ny.us

William Colton was elected to the New York State Assembly in November 1996 to a district that includes the neighborhoods of Bensonhurst, Gravesend, Bath Beach, Dyker Heights, and Midwood. He is the Assembly's Majority Whip and sits on the following committees: correction; environmental conservation; government employees; labor; rules; and ways and means. Prior to running for the Assembly, Colton was co-founder and organizer of the Bensonhurst Tenants Council, and also was the attorney in a successful lawsuit to halt the opening of the Southwest Brooklyn Incinerator. In the Assembly, he also was appointed Chair of the Legislative Commission on Solid Waste Management, and currently serves as Chair of the Majority Conference. Colton has remained active in his community, including sitting on the Board of Trustees of the Verrazano Lodge of the Order of the Sons of Italy and the Board of Directors of the Cardinal Stritch Knights Corporation of the Cardinal Stritch Knights of Columbus Council. He has received numerous awards for teaching and for community service. He is a former school teacher, is married with two stepchildren, and holds an undergraduate degree in urban education from St. John's University, an M.S. in Urban Education from Brooklyn College, and a J.D. from St. John's School of Law.

VIVIAN E COOK (D)
32nd - Part of Queens County

142-15 Rockaway Blvd, Jamaica, NY 11436
718-322-3975/cookv@assembly.state.ny.us

Vivian Cook was elected to the New York State Assembly in 1990. She sits on the following standing committees: codes; corporations, authorities and commissions; housing; insurance; rules; and ways and means. Her previous leadership posts include former service as the Assembly's former Majority Whip. She also chaired the Task Force on Food, Farm and Nutrition Policy. The Rock Hill, South Carolina native has served as District Leader of Queens County for more than 25 years. She founded the Rockaway Boulevard Local Development Corporation. She has supported community housing programs that provide residents with affordable homes, as well as projects to improve senior services and recreational facilities. She is the recipient of many awards for her community and civic service. She is a graduate of the DeFrans Business Institute.

JANE L CORWIN (R-C-I)
144th - Parts of Erie, Niagara, and Orleans counties

8180 Main St, Clarence, NY 14221
716-839-4691/CorwinJ@assembly.state.ny.us

Jane Corwin was elected to the New York State Assembly in 2008, and currently serves as Minority Leader Pro Tempore. She is the Ranking Minority member of the Corporations, Authorities and Commissions Committee, and also serves on the following standing committees: education; environmental conservation; mental health; ways and means. She is a strong backer of small businesses in Western New York, and led efforts to call for an overhaul of the New York State Thruway Authority's fiscal management while successfully opposing a 45 percent toll increase. Professionally, Corwin was Director of Research at Henry Ansbacher, Inc. on Wall Street, and Vice President at the Talking Book in Western New York. In addition to her Assembly duties, she is a full-time mother and active in her community where she is president and founder of the Philip M. and Jane Lewis Corwin Foundation, which funds educational, medical and religious charities to benefit children. She holds an undergraduate degree from the State University of New York at Albany and a Master's in business administration from Pace University. Corwin lives in Clarence with her husband and three children.

MARCOS A CRESPO (D-WF)
85th - Part of Bronx County

1163 Manor Avenue, Bronx, NY 10472
718-893-0202/crespom@assembly.state.ny.us

Marcos A. Crespo was first elected to the New York State Assembly in 2009 and is Chair of the Peurto Rican/Hispanic Task Force. He also sits on the following standing committees: alcoholism and drug abuse; cities; energy; environmental conservation; insurance; and transportation. In his role as Chairman of the Assembly Task Force on New Americans, he worked to address major issues for New York's 4.3 million immigrants, as well as to highlight their major economic contributions. In addition to fighting on behalf of his constituency, Crespo has backed such proposals as a new law to create an emergency energy backup system for critical state health and safety infrastructure during a natural disaster. Crespo was born in Puerto Rico and moved with his family to New York as a young age. He also lived in Lima, Peru during his early years, and returned to Puerto Rico where he finished high school. After that, he returned to New York City. He holds a BA from John Jay College of Criminal justice and is the married father of two.

CLIFFORD W CROUCH (R)
122nd - Parts of Broome, Chenango, Delaware and Otsego Counties

1 Kattelville Rd, Suite 1, Binghamton, NY 13901
607-648-6080/crouchc@assembly.state.ny.us

Clifford Crouch was first elected to the New York State Assembly in 1995. He chairs the Minority Conference, and sits on the following standing committees: agriculture; economic development, job creation, commerce and industry; labor, rules, and ways and means. He advocates on behalf of budget reform and mandate relief, as well as education funding, common core reform, and responsible teacher evaluation. Prior to serving in the Assembly, Crouch was a Town Councilman for the Town of Bainbridge from 1982 to 1986, and then a town Supervisor until he was elected to the Assembly. He also served from 1993 until 1995 as Chairman of the Board of Supervisors in Chenango County. His efforts on behalf of his community include leading the siting of the Chenango County landfill and the implementation of the county recycling program in his position as chair of the Chenango County Solid Waste Committee. He has been a member of the Bainbridge Local Development Corporation, the Board of Directors of the Broome Cooperative Fire Insurance Company, and other civic and community organizations. Crouch holds an AAS in Dairy Science from Cornell University and owned and operated a 180-head dairy farm on 350 acres from 1967 to 1989. He and his wife live in Bainbridge and have three children and seven grandchildren.

BRIAN F. CURRAN (R)
21st - Part of Nassau County

108 Merrick Road, Lynbrook, NY 11563
516-561-8216/curranb@assembly.state.ny.us

Brian Curran was elected to the New York State Assembly in 2010 to a Long Island district that includes Lynbrook, Rockville Centre, and parts of the towns of South Hempstead, West Hemmpstead, Baldwin, Oceanside, East Rockaway, Malverne, Franklin Square, Freeport, and Hewlett.He is Ranking Minority Member on the Ethics and Guidance Committee, and also serves on the following standing committees: banks; insurance; labor; and veterans' affairs. At the time he was elected to the Assembly, Curran was Lynbrook's mayor. Curran's professional resume includes service as a legislative counsel to the Assembly. He was also the Nassau Deputy County Attorney in the Litigation Bureau and Municipal Contracts and the Assistant Village Prosecutor of Lynbrook. He is currently a partner in the private law firm of Nicolini, Paradise, Ferretti, and Sabella. He graduated from Wilkes University and holds a JD from CUNY Law School. Curran is involved in a number of community organizations in his hometown, where he lives with his wife and four children.

MICHAEL J CUSICK (D)
63rd - Part of Richmond County

1911 Richmond Ave, Staten Island, NY 10314
718-370-1384/cusickm@assembly.state.ny.us

Michael Cusick was first elected to the New York State Assembly in 2002. He currently chairs the Election Law Committee. Cusick is also a member of the following standing committees in the Assembly: governmental employees; higher education; mental health; transportation; veterans' affairs; and ways and means. Prior to launching his own elective bid, Cusick was Director of Constituent Services for U.S. Sen. Charles E. Schumer, and managed the day-to-day operations for Schumer's New York City office. Prior to that, he was chief of staff to former Staten Island Assemblyman Eric N. Vitaliano and Special Assistant to former President of the City Council Andrew J Stein. Among his legislative achievements since taking office are authoring a law to set a building moratorium that paved the way for the Mid-Island Blue Belt and requiring notice to neighborhood landowners of an application to build on wetland areas. He also created "Total Fitness Challenge" in 2008 to boost youth reading and exercising during summer break. Cusick has sat on the boards of the Staten Island Board of Directors of the Catholic Youth Organization and the Boy Scouts of America. He received his undergraduate degree from Villanova University and is married and lives in his native Staten Island.

STEVEN H CYMBROWITZ (D)
45th - Part of Kings County

1800 Sheepshead Bay Rd, Brooklyn, NY 11235
718-743-4078/cymbros@assembly.state.ny.us

Steven Cymbrowitz was first elected to the New York State Assembly in November 2000. He represents the 45th Assembly District in Brooklyn that includes parts of Sheepshead Bay, Midwood, Manhattan Beach, Gravesend, and Brighton Beach. Cymbrowitz is Chair of the Committee on Aging, and also sits on the following committees: codes; environmental conservation; health; and insurance. His was among the districts hard-hit by Hurricane Sandy and has actively worked to help his constituents through the recovery. He also has worked to open the Lena Cymbrowitz Pavilion of the Maimonides Cancer Center in tribute to his late wife, Assemblywoman Lena Cymbrowitz. Before his election to the Assembly, he served as Executive Director of the North Brooklyn Devel-

opment Corporation, Director of Housing and Community Development for the Metropolitan New York Coordinating Council on Jewish Poverty, Assistant Commissioner of the Division of Homeless Housing Development for the New York City Department of Housing Preservation and Development (HPD), Assistant Commissioner of the Division of Housing Production and Finance for HPD, and Deputy Commissioner of Development at HPD. He also served as the New York City Housing Authority's Director of Intergovernmental Relations. He holds a bachelor's degree from C.W. Post College, a master's degree in social work from Adelphi University and a law degree from Brooklyn Law School.

MARITZA DAVILA (D)
53rd - Parts of Kings County

249 Wilson Avenue, Brooklyn, NY 11237
718-443-1205/DavilaM@assembly.state.ny.us

Maritza Davila was elected to the New York State assembly on November 5, 2013. She is Chair of the Subcommittee on Retention of Homeownership and Stabilization of Affordable Housing, and also sits on the following committees: housing; alcoholism and drug abuse; children and families; correction; economic development, job creation, commerce and industry; and social services. Prior to her election, she served as President of the Community School Board of Education of District 32, and also as the Director of a state-wide program to raise awareness for the dangers of lead-based paint. In addition, she advocates for women's rights; as a founding member of the North Brooklyn Coalition Against Domestic Violence she served on its Board for two years. Assemblywoman Davila founded the Northern Brooklyn Residents Association to advocate on behalf of affordable housing and community development. Originally a native of Catano, Puerto Rico, she moved to Bushwick, Brooklyn as a young girl and has lived there ever since. She holds an AA in Political Science from Long Island University and is mother to three children.

MICHAEL G DENDEKKER (D-WF)
34th - Part of Queens County

75-35 31st Avenue Suite 206B (2nd Floor), East Elmhurst, NY 11370/DenDekkerM@assembly.state.ny.us

Michael DenDekker was elected to the New York State Assembly in 2008 and his district, where he has lived his whole life, includes Jackson Heights, East Elmhurst and Woodside. He is Chair of the Committee on Veterans' Affairs, and a member of the following committees: aging; alcoholism and drug abuse; governmental employees; labor; and transportation. His legislative efforts include establishing a voluntary state database for video camera surveillance. He was also instrumental in bringing the retired space shuttle Enterprise to New York City as part of the Intrepid Sea, Air & Space Museum. Professionally, DenDekker has worked as facilities manager for the New York City Council, responsible for day-to-day operations for city council offices, as well as assisting with city hall operations. Previously, he was Supervisor in the New York City Department of Sanitation. He was a member of the Bureau of Public Information and Community Affairs and, after 9/11, served as a public information officer in the Joint Information Center of the Mayor's Office of Emergency Management. DenDekker is also a member of the Screen Actors Guild, with movie and TV credits. His community involvement has included serving on Community Board #3, and as Deputy Chief for the Jackson Heights-Elmhurst Volunteer Ambulance Corp. He majored in Automotive Technology at SUNY Farmington, and lives in Jackson Heights with his wife. They have four children and two grandchildren.

ERIC M DILAN (D)
54 - Part of King's County

366 Cornelia St, Brooklyn, NY 11237
718-386-4576/DilanE@assembly.state.ny.us

Erik Dilan was elected to the New York State Assembly in 2014 from a district that includes parts of Bedford Stuyvesant, Bushwick, Cypress-Hills, and East New York. He sits on the following committees: cities; consumer affairs and protection; corporations, authorities and commissions; governmental operations; housing; and insurance. Prior to his election, Assemblyman Dilan served 12 years on the New York City Council, where his leadership posts included chairing the housing and building committee; the Brooklyn Delegation, and as a member of the budget negotiating team. The lifelong resident of North Brooklyn holds an A.S. degree in business administration from St. John's University and lives with his wife and two children in Cypress-Hills.

JEFFREY DINOWITZ (D-L-WF)
81st - Part of Bronx County

3107 Kingsbridge Ave, Bronx, NY 10463
718-796-5345/dinowij@assembly.state.ny.us

Jeffrey Dinowitz was first elected to the New York State Assembly in 1994. The district includes Riverdale, Kingsbridge, Van Cortlandt Village, Norwood, Woodlawn, and Wakefield. Dinowitz chairs the Committee on Consumer Affairs and Protection and serves on the following standing committees: election law; health; rules; and judiciary. Dinowitz previously chaired the Committee on Aging, the Committee on Alcoholism and Drug Abuse, and the Legislative Commission on Government Administration, as well as others. His legislative interests focus on senior issues, education reform, housing, the environment, and increased education aid for New York City. Assemblyman Dinowitz's professional resume prior to holding elective office includes a decade spent as an Administrative Law Judge for the State of New York for 10 years. In addition, he has served in numerous community organizations, including Vice President of the Riverdale Community Council, member of Bronx Area Policy Board #7, and member of the Boards of Directors for the Bronx High School of Science Foundation and for the Bronx Council for Environmental Quality. His extensive community activity also includes service on the Executive Committee of the Riverdale-Hudson Chapter of B'nai B'rith. In addition, he has been a member of District Council 37 and the Public Employees Federation. The Bronx native is married with two children. He earned a BA from Herbert Lehman College of City University of New York and a JD from Brooklyn Law School.

DAVID DIPIETRO (R)
147th - Parts of Erie County and Wyoming County

411 Main Street, East Aurora, NY 14052
716-655-0951/DiPietroD@assembly.state.ny.us

David DiPietro was elected to serve the constituents of the 147th Assembly District on November 6, 2012. His district includes the southern portion of Erie County and all of Wyoming County. He sits on the following committees: alcoholism and drug abuse; economic development, job creation, commerce and industry; labor; small business; and transportation. He previously served as Trustee and Mayor of the Village of East Aurora and was recognized at the State of the County of Erie conference as the leader in New York State in mergers and consolidations of government departments and services. As Mayor of East Aurora, DiPietro cut taxes for three consecutive years, and reduced the overall size of the government. His private sector experience includes positions at M&T Bank in Buffalo, Trust Division, and computer and accounting consultant to small businesses in Western New York. He received his B.S. degree in Business Administration from Wittenberg University. He is married and has three children.

JANET L DUPREY (R-I)
115th - Clinton and Franklin Counties and Part of St. Lawrence County

202 U.S. Oval, Plattsburg, NY 12903
518-562-1986/DupreyJ@assembly.state.ny.us

Janet L Duprey was first elected to the New York State Assembly in November 2006 to represent her district that includes all of Clinton and Franklin counties, as well as four towns in St. Lawrence County. She is Ranking Minority member on the Governmental Operations Committee, and also sits on the following committees: correction; higher education; rules; and ways and means. In addition, she is Vice Chairman of the Minority Program Committee. Prior to being elected to the Assembly, Duprey was Clinton County Treasurer from 1986-2006. She the first woman elected to the Clinton County Legislature, where she served for ten years, including two as chair. The Assemblywoman has been active for many years in her community and has received numerous honors. She has served on the boards of directors of the Champlain Valley Physicians Hospital Medical Center, the Clinton-Northern Essex Chapter American Red Cross and others. Assemblywoman Duprey is married with two children and four grandchildren

STEVEN C ENGLEBRIGHT (D)
4th - Part of Suffolk County

149 Main Street, E Setauket, NY 11733
631-751-3094/engles@assembly.state.ny.us

Steve Englebright was elected to the New York State Assembly in 1992. His north shore, Long Island district includes Port Jefferson Station and sections of Coram, Centereach, Selden and Lake Grove as well as the historic maritime communities that developed around the harbors of Stony Brook, Setauket, Port Jefferson and Mt. Sinai. Englebright chairs the Assembly's Committee on Environmental Conservation, and sits on the following standing committees: education, energy, higher education, and rules. Trained as a geologist and biologist, his scientific background informs his legislative approach, such as his successful advocacy on behalf of a state ban on the sale of baby bottles and other childcare products containing BPA, bisphenol-A which disrupts estrogen. He also has pushed successfully for the NYS Pine Barrens Protection Act., authored New York's solar and wind net-metering laws in the 1990s and successfully pushed in 2008 for the expansion of solar net-metering to include all utility customer classes. He has advocated on behalf of advancing the NY-SUNY2020 Challenge Grant Program in an effort to expand research and economic development, as well as increase access to education at Stony Brook. Assemblyman Englebright's previous elective office includes service in the Suffolk County Legislature from 1983-1992. The Georgia-born Englebright holds a B.S. from the University of Tennessee, and a M.S. in Paleontology/Sedimentology from SUNY Stony Brook. The father of two children lives in Setauket.

PATRICIA FAHY (D)
109th - City of Albany and Towns of Bethlehem, Guilderland and New Scotland

LOB 452, Albany, NY 12248
518-455-4178/FahyP@assembly.state.ny.us

Patricia Fahy was first elected to the New York State Assembly in 2012. She chairs the Subcommittee on Oversight of the Department of Environmental Conservation. She also sits on the following standing committees: banks; children and families; environmental conservation; higher education; and tourism, parks, arts and sports development. Prior to running for the Assembly, Fahy served as President of the Albany City School Board for one of her four years on the board. Professionally, Fahy boasts an extensive background in labor-related, legislative issues. She was Associate Commissioner of Intergovernmental Affairs and Federal Policy at the NYS Department of Labor for five years. She co-chaired the Disconnected Youth Work Group of Gov. Paterson's Children's Cabinet. Prior to moving to Albany in 1997, she was Executive Director of the Chicago Workforce Board. Prior to that time, she worked as both a legislative assistant and a legislative analyst on Capitol Hill in Washington, DC, then went on to become the Associate Director for Employment and Training in the U.S. Dept. of Labor Congressional Affairs Office. The Chicago-area native has been active within her community, including service on the Boys and Girls Club of Albany's board of directors since 2005. She earned a B.S. from Northern Illinois University and a Masters of Public Administration from the University of Illinois at Chicago. She is married to RPI professor Dr. B. Wayne Bequette. The couple has two children.

HERMAN D FARRELL, JR (D)
71st - Part of New York City

2541-55 Adam Clayton Powell Jr. Blvd, New York, NY 10039
212-234-1430/farrelh@assembly.state.ny.us

751 W 183rd St, New York, NY 10033
212-568-2828/farrelh@assembly.state.ny.us

Herman Farrell was first elected to the New York State Assembly in 1974. He represents the district that encompasses West Harlem, Washington Heights and Inwood. He has chaired the powerful Ways and Means Committee since 1994. In addition, he is a member of the Rules Committee. He formerly chaired the Banks Committee from 1979-1994 and has held other leadership positions. Farrell has been highly active in Democratic politics, serving in numerous capacities, and also has been honored by numerous organizations. For nearly two decades he served as the leader of the New York County Democratic Committee, finally stepping down in 2009. Within the Assembly, Farrell is known for his banking legislation, notably the passage of the Omnibus Consumer Protection and Banking Legislation Act with consumer protections in the auto leasing industry; the establishment of a toll-free number at the New York State Banking Department to enable consumers to receive free information on credit card interest rates, fees and grace periods; and a requirement that banks provide low-cost lifeline checking accounts. In addition, the bill prohibits discrimination based on residency in the opening of bank accounts, and requires banks to make annual reports of the number and amount of small business and small farm loans. His other legislative achievements include the Neighborhood Preservation Companies Act that enables the state to fund community groups to provide tenant advocacy and fight housing abandonment in their neighborhoods. Prior to his election, he served as Assistant Director of the Mayor's Office in Washington Heights, and also served as a Confidential Aide to a state Supreme Court Justice. Farrell grew up 20 blocks from where he now resides, in Washington Heights. He has three children and two grandchildren and has been recognized by numerous organizations.

GARY D FINCH (R-I)
126th - Parts of Cayuga, Chenango, Cortland and Onandaga Counties

69 South Street, Auburn, NY 13021
315-255-3045/ finchg@assembly.state.ny.us

Gary Finch was first elected to the New York State Assembly in 1999 to represent a large Upstate New York district and currently serves as Assistant Minority Leader. He sits on the following committees: agriculture; banks; correction; insurance; and rules. He previously served as ranking minority member of the Assembly's Corrections Committee and continues to advocate on behalf of correction officers, their families and correction issues. Professionally, Finch for 35 years has been owner and COO of Brew-Finch Funeral Homes, Inc., operating in northern, central, and southern New York. He was first elected to public office in 1979 as a Village of Aurora Trustee, and in 1982, he was elected mayor, a post he held for eight years. His extensive community service includes chairing the Board of Trustees at his alma mater, Cayuga Community College. He also has served as Cayuga County United Way's president and campaign chair and as a member of its executive and finance committees. He is a past member of Leadership Cayuga's Curriculum Program; former chair of the membership committee for the Cayuga County Chamber of Commerce; and a charter member, past president, and big brother for Big Brothers and Big Sisters. He and his wife are parents to two children, and live in Springport.

MICHAEL J FITZPATRICK (R)
8th - Part of Suffolk County

50 Rte 111, Suite 202, Smithtown, NY 11787
631-724-2929/fitzpatrickm@assembly.state.ny.us

Michael J. Fitzpatrick was elected to the New York State Assembly representing the 7th Assembly District in November 2002. His district includes the town of Smithtown and parts of Islip and Brookhaven townships. He is the Ranking Minority Member of the Housing Committee, and also sits on the following committees: higher education; labor; and ways and means. Professionally, Fitzpatrick is an investment associate in with Morgan Stanley in the firm's Port Jefferson branch office. Prior to his election to the Assembly, Fitzpatrick was an elected member of the Smithtown Town Council for 15 years, from 1988 through 2003. Fitzpatrick is secretary of the New York State American-Irish Legislators Society, and active in his local community. Born in Jamaica, Queens and raised in Hauppauge, Fitzpatrick received his B.A. in business administration from St. Michael's College in Vermont. He and his wife live in St. James, in Smithtown, and are parents to two children.

CHRISTOPHER S FRIEND (R)
124th - Tioga County and parts of Broome and Chemung Counties.

476 Maple Street, PO Box 441, Big Flats, NY 14814
607-562-3602/friendc@assembly.state.ny.us

Christopher Friend was elected to the New York State Assembly in 2011. His district includes all of Tioga County; the Town of Maine in Broome County; the city of Elmira; the towns of Ashland, Baldwin, Big Flats, Chemung, Elmira, Horseheads, Southport, and the villages of Elmira Heights, Horseheads, and Wellsburg in Chemung County. He is the Ranking Minority Member on the Committee on Children and Families and the Committee on Local Governments, and also sits on the following committees: aging; corporations, authorities and commissions; and housing. A chemist by traning, he has published more than 20 scientific papers and symposiums. Friend's public service began with work on advisory boards and commissions for the Town of Big Flats starting in 2004. He moved on to the Chemung County Legislature, to which he was elected in 2004. Assemblyman Friend holds a B.S. in chemistry from the University of New Hampshire, as well as a Master's and Ph.D. in chemistry from the State University of New York at Buffalo. He and his wife live in Big Flats with their four children.

SANDRA R GALEF (D)
95th - Parts of Westchester County

2 Church Street, Ossining, NY 10562
914-941-1111/galefs@assembly.state.ny.us

Sandy Galef was first elected to the Assembly in 1992. Her district covers the Towns of Cortlandt, Ossining, Kent, Philipstown, and the City of Peekskill. She chairs the Real Property Tax Committee and also serves on the following committees: corporations, authorities, and commissions; election law; government operations; and health. She has held previous leadership positions, including chair of the Libraries and Education Technology Committee. Her recent legislative successes include Assembly passage of legislation to end sexual harassment in smaller businesses and work environments. Before her election to the Assembly, Galef sat on the Westchester County Legislature for 13 years, including eight as the Board of Legislator's minority leader. Galef also serves on the Assembly Majority Steering Committee and the Hudson Valley Greenway Communities Council. Galef is a former teacher in the Scarsdale school system and has been deeply active in Westchester community affairs for many years. Nationally, she chaired the National Association of Counties' Labor and Employee Benefits Steering Committee, and received an Eastern Leadership Academy fellowship from the University of Pennsylvania Fels Institute Of Government. Galef has sat on the boards of directors of numerous health or educational organizations in the Westchester region, and has received numerous awards. She also hosts two TV shows, called "Dear Sandy" and "Speakout with Sandy Galef."She holds a B.S. from Purdue University and an M.Ed from the University of Virginia. Galef, a widow, resides in Ossining and has two children.

DAVID F GANTT (D)
137th - Part of Monroe County

74 University Ave, Rochester, NY 14605
585-454-3670/ganttd@assembly.state.ny.us

David F. Gantt was first elected to the Assembly in 1982. His district includes the northeastern and southwestern sections of the City of Rochester and the suburban town of Gates. He chairs the Committee on Transportation, and is a member of the following committees: economic development, job creation, commerce and industry; local governments; rules; and ways and means. Among his many legislative achievements, he has advocated on behalf of affordable housing development, health care and services for the young and elderly; maintaining transportation infrastructure safety; laws extending and expanding the 65 mph speed limit; and numerous laws to ensure voters equal access to their local polling places. His professional experience includes serving as the administrator of the Anthony L. Jordan Health Center; a working member of the Lithographers and Photoengravers International Union Local 230, and as a youth counselor to the City of Rochester. Prior to joining the Assembly, Gantt served nine years in the Monroe County Legislature, where he was Assistant Majority leader among other leadership positions. He became Monroe County's first elected African-American to hold a statewide office. Gantt attended Roberts Wesleyan College and the Rochester Institute of Technology.

ANDREW R. GARBARINO (R-C-I)
7th - Parts of Suffolk County

859 Montauk Hwy, Suite 1, Bayport, NY 11705
631-589-0348/GarbarinoA@assembly.state.ny.us

Andrew Garbarino was first elected to the New York State Assembly in 2012. His district includes much of the South Shore and Fire Island. He is a member of the following committees: banks; environmental conservation; health; higher education; and racing and wagering. His legislative achievements include the recent passage of legislation he co-sponsored to establish greater protections for women who become sex trafficking victims. Professionally, Garbarino is an attorney and works in his family's Sayville law firm. He is active in his local community, and serves as counsel to the Captain Merrill H. Masin and Graham D. Masin Foundation, which annually awards over $25,000 in local scholarships to high school students. The Sayville native holds a B.A. from the George Washington University in Washington, D.C. and a law degree from Hofstra University School of Law.

JOSEPH M GIGLIO (R-C-I)
148th - Cattaraugus County, Allegany County and parts of Steuben County

700 West State St, Olean, NY 14760
716-373-7103/GiglioJ@assembly.state.ny.us

Joseph Giglio was first elected to the Assembly in 2005.His district includes all of Cattaraugus and Allegany counties, as well as the towns of Greenwood, Jasper, Troupsburg and West Union in Steuben County. The district also includes parts of three Seneca Nation of Indians reservations. He chairs the Assembly Minority Conference's Steering Committee and is Ranking Minority Member of the Corrections Committee. His other committee memberships are as follows: aging; children and families; codes; ethics and guidance. Within the Assembly, Giglio co-chaired the Minority Statewide Forum on Workforce Issues in the Correctional System. Giglio is a former State Deputy Inspector General, focused on investigating criminal and corruption in state agencies and those who do business with the state within the Western New York area. He also previ-

ously worked as a special assistant in the State Attorney General's office, and he also worked for both the Cattaraugus and Erie County sheriff's departments. His many awards include one from the New York State Farm Bureau as a member of their "circle of friends" for his perfect voting record in support of agricultural issues. He holds a bachelor's degree from the State University of New York at Buffalo. He is married, the father of four, and lives in Gowanda.

MARK GJONAJ (D)
80th - Part of Bronx County

1126 Pelham Parkway South, Bronx, NY 10461
718-409-0109/GjonajM@assembly.state.ny.us

Mark Gjonaj was elected to represent New York's 80th Assembly District in 2012. His district encompasses the neighborhoods of Allerton, Bedford Park, Morris Park, Mosholu Parkway, Norwood, Pelham Gardens, Pelham Parkway, and Van Nest in the Bronx. Gjonaj has devoted significant efforts to community activities and organizations, including the Illyria Clinic at Jacobi Medical Center, Einstein College of Medicine Community Advisory Council, and Westchester School for Special Children. Previously he served as Commissioner of the NYC Taxi and Limousine Commission, a volunteer board that regulates the taxi, livery and black car industry.. He has served as president of M.P. Realty Group Corporation, and holds a bachelor's degree from St. John's University. He and his wife have two sons.

DEBORAH J GLICK (D)
66th - Part of New York County

853 Broadway, Suite 1518, New York, NY 10003
212-674-5153/glickd@assembly.state.ny.us

Deborah Glick was first elected to the Assembly in 1990, and is the first openly lesbian or gay member of the New York State Legislature. She chairs the Higher Education Committee, and also sits on the following committees: environmental conservation; governmental operations; rules; and ways and means. Prior to being elected to the Assembly, Glick owned and managed a small TriBeCa printing business, and later became Deputy Director of General Services for the City Department of Housing, Preservation and Development. Her legislative achievements include passage of the Sexual Orientation Non-Discrimination Act (SONDA), which was signed into law in 2002, as well as the Women's Health and Wellness Act, which became law in 2003. She saw her Hospital Visitation Bill, which gives domestic partners the same rights as spouses and next-of-kin when the loved one is in a hospital or nursing facility, became law in 2004. She also backed the Loft Law, which brings former commercial buildings up to residential code and protects current tenants, many of them artists, from eviction. She graduated from the City University of New York's Queens College and holds an MBA from Fordham University.

PHILLIP GOLDFEDER (R)
23rd - Part of Queens County

95-16 Rockaway Beach Blvd., Rockaway Beach, NY 11693
718-945-9550
/goldfederp@assembly.state.ny.us.

162-38 Crossbay Blvd., Howard Beach, NY 11414
718-641-8755

Phillip Goldfeder was elected to the New York State Assembly in September 2011. His district includes Ozone Park, Lindenwood, Howard Beach, Hamilton Beach, Broad Channel and the Rockaways in Southwest Queens. Sandy. He is Chair of the Subcommittee on Autism Retention, and sits on the following committees: aging; corporations, authorities and commissions; governmental employees; insurance; mental health; racing and wagering. His career in public service began as a community liaison for the New York City Council. He also worked in the Mayor's Office as the representative to the borough of Queens, and for Senator Charles E. Schumer, where he worked as Director of Intergovernmental Affairs. His district was severely impacted by Superstorm Sandy and Assemblyman Goldfeder has been instrumental in helping his constituents recover. The Far Rockaway native graduated from CUNY Brooklyn College, and he lives in his hometown with his wife and two children.

ANDREW W. "ANDY" GOODELL (R-C-I)
150th - Chatauqua County

Fenton Bldg, 2 E. 2nd St, Suite 320, Jamestown, NY 14701
716-664-7773/goodella@assembly.state.ny.us

Andy Goodell was elected to the New York State Assembly in 2010. He sits on the following committees: governmental operations; health; judiciary; and social services. He is managing partner at the law firm of Goodell & Rankin. Goodell's public service includes eight years as County Executive for Chautauqua County. As County Executive, he cut the tax rate six years in a row. In the community, he is founding member and former officer of the Chautauqua Leadership Network, past president of the Jamestown Rotary, treasurer for Bemus Bay Pops, and former co-chair of the United Way Professional Division. Goodell has earned numerous awards, including the Ed Crawford Award, the highest honor bestowed by the New York State Association of Counties. He holds an undergraduate degree from Williams College and his law degree from Cornell Law School, where he was a member of the Cornell Law Review. He is married with three daughters, a stepson, and several grandchildren.

RICHARD N GOTTFRIED (D-WF)
75th - Part of New York County

242 W 27th Street, New York, NY 10001
212-807-7900/GottfriedR@assembly.state.ny.us

Richard N. Gottfried was first elected to the New York State Assembly in 1971 and represents a district that includes Chelsea, Hell's Kitchen, Murray Hill, Midtown and part of the Lincoln Center area in Manhattan. He has chaired the Assembly Committee on Health since 1987. In addition, Gottfried sits on the higher education and rules committees. He is the former Deputy Majority Leader and Assistant Majority Leader, and has chaired major committees. Gottfried's achievements in his long tenure helming the health committee are numerous; he was a major architect of New York's landmark managed care reforms. His legislative achievements include the passage of the Prenatal Care Assistance Program for low-income women; the Child Health Plus Program that allows low- and moderate-income parents to get free or low-cost health insurance for their children; Family Health Plus that provides free health coverage for low-income adults; and the Health Care Proxy Law. He has advocated on behalf of patient autonomy, especially in end-of-life care, and reproductive freedom. Gottfried introduced the first same-sex marriage bill in the Assembly in 2003, and was a co-sponsor of the bill that became law in 2011. He also sponsors the Gender Non-Discrimination Act (GENDA), to prohibit discrimination based on gender identity (transgender); a bill to prohibit NY-licensed health professionals from cooperating in the torture or improper treatment of prisoners; and the bill to legalize the use of medical marijuana. He is a fellow of the New York Academy of Medicine, holds an undergraduate degree from Cornell University and a JD from Columbia Law School. He lives in Manhattan with his wife. They have one child and a grandchild.

AL GRAF (R)
5th - Part of Suffolk County

991 Main Street, Suite 202, Holbrook, NY 11741
631-585-0310
/grafa@assembly.state.ny.us

Al Graf was elected to the New York State Assembly in 2010. His district includes parts of the towns of Brookhaven and Islip, including Holbrook, Lake Ronkonkoma, Ronkonkoma, Holtsville, Centereach, as well as parts of Farmingville, Islandia, North Patchogue and Stony Brook. He sits on the following committees: codes; education; housing; and judiciary. Graf has worked on behalf of bringing lower cost hydropower to Long Island during his Assembly tenure. Professionally, Graf is a practicing attorney who began his career by enlisting in the U.S. Navy. He rose to the rank of Operations Specialist Third Class Petty Officer, then joined the New York City Police Department and worked his way up to a plainclothes unit prior to retiring due to an on-the-job injury. His public service has included two terms as a Town of Brighton Supervisor, and he remains active in his community. Graf earned an undergraduate degree in elementary education from SUNY Plattsburg and a JD from Touro Law School. He and his wife live in Holbrook and have three children.

AILEEN M GUNTHER (D-I-WF)
100th - Sullivan and Orange counties

Middletown City Hall, 3rd Floor, 16 James Street, Middletown, NY 10940
845-342-9304

18 Anawana Lake Road, Monticello, NY 12701
845-794-5807 GuntheA@assembly.state.ny.us

Aileen Gunther was first elected to the Assembly in 2003 to fill the vacancy created by the untimely death of her husband, Assemblyman Jake Gunther. She chairs the Mental Health Committee and also sits on the following committees: agriculture; environmental conservation; health; racing and wagering; and real property taxation. Gunther is a registered nurse and worked many years at Catskill Regional Medical Center, where she rose to Director of Performance Improvement and Risk Management. Among the legislation she has introduced are measures to enact the New York state nursing shortage correction act; establish the nurse loan repayment program; and create a rural home health flexibility program. She holds a nursing degree from Orange County Community College. Gunther.

STEPHEN HAWLEY (R-I-C)
139th - Genesee County, parts of Monroe and Orleans counties

121 N Main Street, Suite 100, Albion, NY 14411
585-589-5780/hawleys@assembly.state.ny.us

Stephen Hawley was elected to the New York State Assembly during a special election in 2006. His district includes all of Genesee County; the Towns of Clarkson, Hamlin, Sweden and Riga in Monroe County; and all of Orleans County except the town of Shelby. He is Assistant Minority Leader, Minority Whip, and formerly served as Deputy Minority Whip. He is a member of the following committees: agriculture; insurance; veterans' affairs; and ways and means. Professionally, Hawley owned and operated Hawley Farms, and now owns The Insurance Center in his hometown of Batavia. In addition, Hawley sells residential and commercial property in the region. He also served in the Ohio Army National Guard, and the U.S. Army Reserves. Hawley has been highly involved in his community, and his involvement includes former service on the Genesee County Legislature, the Board of Directors of the Genesee Community College Foundation, as president of the Genessee County Empire Zone Development Board, Cornell Cooperative Extension of Genesee County, and many other local organizations. During his Assembly tenure, Hawley has helped develop substantial legislation that prevents registered level two or three sex offenders from working in amusement parks and requires that certain sex offenders' addresses be reported to the Division of Criminal Justice Services. He authored several pieces of legislation that would assist the agricultural industry including exempting owners of farms and the owners of multiple dwellings from the Scaffold Law. He holds a B.S. in education from the University of Toledo and is father to two sons.

CARL E HEASTIE (D)
83rd - Part of Bronx County

1446 E Gun Hill Road, Bronx, NY 10469
718-654-6539/Speaker@assembly.state.ny.us

Carl E Heastie was first elected to the New York State Assembly in 2000 and, in February 2015, was elected to the position of Speaker of the Assembly. He is the first African America to hold the post. His first budget as Speaker makes a $1.8 billion investment in education; addresses homelessness; and gives working families resources to achieve financial independence. He retains a seat on the Rules Committee., which he chairs. His legislative achievements prior to ascending to the Speaker position include being a principal negotiator to secure a minimum wage increase that took effect January 1, 2014. He has also advocated on behalf of increases in unemployment insurance benefits. Professionally, Heastie was a budget analyst in the New York City comptroller's office prior to his election to the Assembly. He holds a BS in applied mathematics and statistics from SUNY Stony Brook, and an MBA from Bernard M. Baruch College.

ANDREW HEVESI (D)
28th - Parts of Queens County

70-50 Austin St, Suite 110, Forest Hills, NY 11375
718-263-5595/hevesia@assembly.state.ny.us

Andrew Hevesi was first elected to the New York State Assembly in May 2005. His district includes Forest Hills, Rego Park, Ridgewood, Richmond Hill, Middle Village, Glendale, and Kew Gardens. He chairs the Committee on Social Services, and also sits on the following standing committees: energy; health; insurance; and labor. In his role on the social services committee, he has started initiatives that seek to assist individuals on the verge of homelessness to remain sheltered in their communities. His legislative achievements also include laws to enhance renewable energy generation in New York State. He is the former Chairman of the Assembly's Oversight, Analysis, and Investigations Committee. Professionally, Hevesi was Director of Community Affairs for the New York City Public Advocate, as well as Chief of Staff to former Assemblyman Jeff Klein, who is now a state senator. He also worked for the Queens County District Attorney's office. He holds a bachelor's degree in political science from Queens College and is married with one child.

DOV HIKIND (D)
48th - Part of Kings County

1310 48th St, Brooklyn, NY 11219
718-853-9616/hikindd@assembly.state.ny.us

Dov Hikind was first elected to the New York State Assembly in 1982. His district includes Borough Park, Dyker Heights, and sections of Flatbush in Brooklyn. In the Assembly, he serves as Assistant Majority Leader. Assemblyman Hikind formerly chaired the Subcommittee on Human Rights. He is a strong proponent of Israel, and provided funds for closed-circuit cameras in nine subway stations on the N, D, and F lines following terrorism concerns. The son of Holocaust survivors, he has traveled widely to fight anti-Semitism. He has been married for over three decades and is father to three children.

EARLENE HOOPER (D-L)
18th - Part of Nassau County

33 Front St, Suite 104, Hempstead, NY 11550
516-489-6610

Earlene Hooper was elected to the New York State Assembly in 1988. She serves as Deputy Speaker, the first woman to hold the office and therefore the highest-ranking female in the New York State legislature. She is a member of the following committees: education; rules; and ways and means. Her legislative priorities include increased funding for local school districts and strengthening economic development. Professionally, Hooper is a social worker who has worked as an administrator in the New York State Department of Social Services, Division of Children and Family Services. She is an adjunct professor at Adelphi University's Graduate School of Social Work. She is widely active in her community. As legislative chair of the Nassau County Chapter of Jack and Jill of America, she established the DEALS project (Developing and Expanding Adult Life Skills). She is an active member of the NAACP, the Central Nassau Chapter of the Negro Business and Professional Women's Association and Delta Sigma Theta Sorority. She holds a BA in English from Norfolk State College and a MSW from Adelphi University. She also holds a Doctor of Humane Letters from Five Towns College. She is married.

ELLEN JAFFEE (D)
97th - Part of Rockland County

1 Blue Hill Plaza, Suite 1116, PO Box 1549, Pearl River, NY 10965
845-624-4601/JaffeeE@assembly.state.ny.us

Ellen Jaffee was first elected to the New York State Assembly in November 2006. Her district includes Orangetown, the Ramapo Villages of Spring Valley, Suffern, Airmont, Chestnut Ridge, Hillburn, parts of Montebello, New Square, and areas in unincorporated Ramapo including sections of Monsey. She chairs the Committee on Oversight, Analysis and Investigation, and is a member of the following committees: children and families; economic development, job creation, commerce and industry; environmental conservation; health; higher education; and mental health. Her legislative achievements include the Breast Density Inform Law that helps to increase early detection standards in breast cancer screenings; banning smoking outside on hospital and residential health care facility grounds; and prohibiting over-the-counter sales of medicines that contain DXM to people under 18 without a prescription. Prior to her election to the Assembly, Jaffee served as Rockland County Legislator and a trustee for the Village of Suffern. She has received numerous awards. The Brooklyn native has lived in Rockland County since 1978, and holds a B.A. from Brooklyn College and an M.S. in Special Education from Fordham University. She and her husband are parents to two children and grandparents to three.

KIMBERLY JEAN-PIERRE (D)
11 - Suffolk County

640 West Montauk Highway, Lindenhurst, NY 11757-5538
631-957-2087/jeanpierrek@assembly.state.ny.us

Kimberly Jean-Pierre was first elected to the New York State Assembly in 2014. She sits on the following committees: banks; economic development, job creation, commerce and industry; local governments; mental health; and transportation. Prior to her election she served as Vice President of Properties for the Town of Babylon's Industrial Development Agency. Prior to that, she was a legislative aide to Congressman Steve Israel - as Community Outreach Coordinator - and to Suffolk County legislator DuWayne Gregory. She holds an undergraduate degree from Brooklyn College and an MS in Public Policy.

MARK JOHNS (R)
135th - Part of Monroe County

268 Fairport Village Landing, Fairport, NY 14450
585-223-9130/johnsm@assembly.state.ny.us

Mark Johns was elected to the New York State Assembly in 2010 to a district that includes the Monroe County communities of Webster, Penfield, Fairport/Perinton and East Rochester, and currently sits on the following committees: aging; alcoholism and drug abuse; governmental employees; governmental operations; and housing. He backs lower taxes, including the property tax cap. Professionally, he worked for the Monroe County Department of Public Education for more than 30 years. His public service includes membership on the Webster Conservation Board. In addition, he served two years on Webster's Town Board. He serves as Government Liaison to the Fairport-Perinton Chemical Advisory Prevention Committee, and volunteers for the Eastside and Bay View YMCA branches in Penfield. An Eagle Scout by age 14, he holds a bachelor's degree from St. John Fisher College.

LATOYA JOYNER (D)
77th - Bronx County

910 Grand Concourse, Suite 1JK, Bronx, NY 10451
718-538-2000/joynerl@assembly.state.ny.us

Latoya Joyner was first elected to the New York State Assembly in 2014 from a Bronx district that includes Claremont, Concourse, Highbridge, Mount Eden and Morris Heights. She sits on the following committees: aging; consumer affairs and protection; housing; insurance; and social services. Prior to her election, she was a member of Community Board 4 and the Neighborhood Advisory Board. She interned with Assemblywoman Aurelia Green, then became a community liaison in her district office. She holds an undergraduate degree from SUNY Stoney Brook, as well as a J.D. from the University at Buffalo Law School.

TODD KAMISKY (D)
20th - Nassau County

20 W Park Ave Suite 301, Long Beach, NY 11561,
516-431-0500/kaminskyt@assembly.state.ny.us

Todd Kaminsky was first elected to the New York State Assembly in 2014 from a district that includes Long Beach, Atlantic Beach, East Atlantic Beach, Point Lookout, Lido Beach, Oceanside, Island Park, Lawrence, Cedarhurst, Hewlett, Woodmere, Inwood, and portions of East Rockaway. He sits on the following committees: consumer affairs and protection; environmental conservation; judiciary; transportation; and veterans' affairs. Prior to his election he was an Assistant U.S. Attorney for the Eastern District of New York and served as acting deputy chief of the Public Integrity Section. In addition, he was an Assistant District Attorney for the Queens County DA's office. In his community, he organized free legal clinics for people impacted by Hurricane Sandy. He holds an undergraduate degree from the University of Michigan and a law degree from the New York University School of Law. He is the married father of one.

STEVE KATZ (R-C-I)
94th - Parts of Dutchess, Putnam, and Westchester Counties

947 S. Lake Blvd., Ste 1C, Mahopac, NY 10541
845-628-3781/katzs@assembly.state.ny.us

Steve Katz was first elected to the New York State Assembly in 2010. He sits on the following committees: aging; alcoholism and drug abuse; economic development, job creation, commerce and industry; housing; and mental health. He has advocated against the Common Core curriculum in the legislature. Assemblyman Katz, a veterinarian, spearheaded construction of a million-dollar veterinary hospital in the Bronx. He holds a B.S. in animal science from Cornell University; his studies included field research in French Guiana and Galapagos for the World Wildlife Fund. He earned his Doctor of Veterinary Medicine from the University of Pennsylvania. He is married with four children.

BRIAN P KAVANAGH (D)
74th - Part of New York County

237 1st Avenue (14th Street), Room 407, New York, NY 10003
212-979-9696/KavanaughB@assembly.state.ny.us

Brian P Kavanaugh was first elected to the New York State Assembly in November 2006; his district includes the Lower East Side, Stuyvesant Town, Peter Cooper Village, Union Square, Gramercy, East Midtown

Plaza, Waterside Plaza, Kips Bay, Murray Hill, and Tudor City.. He chairs the Commission on Government Administration and sits on the following committees: cities; corporations, authorities and commissions; election law; environmental conservation; housing; and labor. He also chairs American State Legislators for Gun Violence Prevention among other leadership posts. His legislative successes include legislation to increase New York's commitment to energy efficiency, green energy and alternative to fossil fuels, and ensure equality in civil service laws. Professionally, Kavanagh in an attorney and has served as a Chief of Staff ,and as an aide to three New York City Mayors. Assemblyman Kavanagh has introduced well over 200 bills in the Assembly. He holds an undergraduate degree from Princeton University and a JD from New York University Law School.

MICHAEL P KEARNS (D)
142nd - Erie County

1074 Union Rd., West Seneca, NY 14224
716-608-6099/kearnsm@assembly.state.ny.us

Michael P. Kearns was first elected to the New York Assembly in a special election in March 2012. He sits on the following committees: banks; cities; housing; oversight, analysis and investigation. His public service career began in 2005 when he was elected to the South District Common Council Member for the City of Buffalo. His legislation includes sponsoring a Volunteer Tax Credit Bill to incentivize volunteering. Professionally, he worked as a sanitation worker for the City of Buffalo after college, and then worked for the Law Offices of Hiscock & Barclay while studying to become a paralegal. Then he went on to Kearns & Associations, where he worked his way up from fundraising consultant to vice president. The Buffalo native holds degrees from Erie Community College and Canisius College. He is married and has one child.

RONALD T KIM (D)
40 - Part of Queens County

136-20 38th Ave., Suite 10A, Flushing, NY 11354
718-939-0195/KimR@assembly.state.ny.us

Ron Kim was first elected to the New York State Senate in 2012. He sits on the following committees: children and families; corporations, authorities and commissions; education; governmental operations; housing; social services. Prior to his election, he most recently worked for The Parkside Group, which he joined after serving as a Regional Director for Government and Community Affairs in the administrations of Governors Eliot Spitzer and David A. Paterson. His other public service positions have included: working for then-Councilmember John C. Liu; as an aide to then-Assemblyman Mark Weprin; and working for the New York City Dept. of Buildings and the Dept. of Small Business Services. He became a National Urban Fellow, where he advised the Chief Education Office of the Chicago Public Schools while earning and Masters in Public Administration from Baruch College. He also holds a B.A. from Hamilton College. Assemblyman Kim lives in Flushing with his wife.

BRIAN M KOLB (R-C-I)
131st - Ontario County and Parts of Seneca County

607 W Washington St, Ste 2, Geneva, NY 14456
315-781-2030/ kolbb@assembly.state.ny.us

Brian Kolb was elected to the Assembly in 2000. He has served as Minority Leader since 2009, and serves on the Committee on Rules. He advocates on behalf of improved education, reduced taxes, sound health care, economic development, and reforming state government. Kolb - a business consultant, entrepreneur, COO, and notary public - formerly served as president of Refractron Technologies, and he co-founded the North American Filter Corporation. He also served as an adjunct professor in adult and graduate education at Roberts Wesleyan College. Within his community, with which he has been deeply involved, he chaired the

Finger Lakes Community College Foundation and served on a variety of regional boards. His public service background includes service as Supervisor for the Town of Richmond, and as a member of the Ontario County Board of Supervisors and the New York State Public Authorities Control Board. He is also a member of numerous organizations. He both a B.S. and an M.S. from Roberts Wesleyan College. The Canadaigua resident is married with three children and one grandchild.

KIERAN MICHAEL LALOR (R)
105th - Parts of Dutchess County

North Hopewell Plaza, Ste 1, 1075 Rt. 82, Hopewell Junction, NY 12533
845-221-2202
lalork@assembly.state.ny.us

Kieran Michael Lalor was first elected to the Assembly in 2012 to a district that includes Beekman, Dover, East Fishkill, Fishkill, LaGrange, Pawling, Union Vale, Wappinger and Washington. He serves on the following committees: banks; governmental operations; real property taxation; small business and veterans' affairs. Professionally, he is the founder of KML Strategies, LLC, a business development and research services consulting firm working with companies that make safety products for military and law enforcement. He served as an infantryman in the Marine Corps Reserve and his unit was twice activated, including in Nasiriya, Iraq. He also helped rescue Gulf Coast residents impacted by Hurricane Katrina. Lalor is involved in numerous local and veteran's organizations. He holds a B.A. from Providence College and a J.D. from Pace Law School. The Fishkill resident is married and has four children.

CHARLES D LAVINE (D)
13th - Part of Nassau County

1 School Street, Suite 303-B, Glen Cove, NY 11542
516-676-0050/lavinec@assembly.state.ny.us

Charles D Lavine was elected to the New York State Assembly in 2004.

He chairs the Committee on Ethics and Guidance, and is a member of the following committees: codes; health; higher education; insurance; and judiciary. He also co- chairs the New York State Ethical Commission. He has sponsored legislation to increase penalties for those who use high-capacity magazines, as well as legislation to help halt illegal gun trafficking into New York. He is President of the New York Chapter of the National Association of Jewish Legislators. Prior to being elected to the Assembly, Lavine was appointed to the Glen Cove Planning Board. He later was appointed to a vacancy on the Glen Cove City Council and was subsequently elected.

Professionally, Lavine worked as an attorney in the Legal Aid Society of the City of New York, as well as his own private practice in Queens County and lower Manhattan. However, he has been a full-time legislator since becoming an Assembly member.

He holds a B.A. in English Literature from the University of Wisconsin and a J.D. from New York Law School. He and his wife have two children.

PETER A LAWRENCE (R-C-IP)
134 - Parts of Monroe County

2496 West Ridge Rd., Rochester, NY 14626
585-225-4190/lawrencep@assembly.state.ny.us

Peter Lawrence was first elected to the New York State Assembly in 2014 from a district that includes the towns of Greece, Ogden and Parma in western Monroe County. He serves on the following committees: ethics and guidance; higher education; oversight, analysis and investigation; racing and wagering; and small business. Prior to his election, Assemblyman Lawrence served nearly 29 years with the New York State Police, rising to the rank of Staff Inspector assigned to the International Affairs Division Headquarters. He retired in 2002 to become U.S. Marshal for

the Western District of New York, appointed by President George W. Bush. He served in that post until 2010. His civic involvement includes serving as a board member of New York Law Enforcement, Inc., and founding an ALS golf tournament that has raised over $1.75 million to benefit patients who are receiving treatment at the University of Rochester Medical Center.

JOSEPH R LENTOL (D)
50th - Part of Kings County

619 Lorimer Street, Brooklyn, NY 11211
718-383-7474/ lentolj@assembly.state.ny.us

Joseph R. Lentol was first elected to the New York State Assembly in 1972. Both his father and grandfather served in the New York State Legislature as well. He chairs the Committee on Codes and also sits on the following committees: election law; rules; ways and means. In the past, he has been Chair of the Committee on Governmental Employees, which oversees the State's pension and employee benefits. In that capacity, Lentol presided over the state's divestiture of its pension fund's investments in South Africa. He also former Chair of the Committee on Governmental Operations. He co-sponsored the NY SAFE Act, the landmark gun control legislation passed and signed into law in 2013. Lentol, an attorney and lifelong resident of New York City, formerly served as Assistant District Attorney in Kings County. He holds a B.A. from the University of Dayton and a J.D. from Baltimore University School of Law.

BARBARA LIFTON (D-WF)
125th - Tompkins County and Part of Cortland County

106 E Court St, Ithaca, NY 14850
607-277-8030/liftonb@assembly.state.ny.us

Barbara Lifton was first elected to the New York State Assembly in 2002 and serves on the following standing committees: agriculture; education; election law; environmental conservation, higher education and rural resources. She has advocated on behalf of education and issues of importance to women. Prior to her election to the Assembly, she served as Chief of Staff to Assemblyman Marty Luster. She also was a public school teacher at Genesee Central School and in Ithaca schools for many years. Her civic and professional activities include membership on the steering committee of the Tompkins County Nuclear Weapons Freeze Campaign. In addition, she co-founded the Coalition for Community Unity and served two years on the Cornell/Community Waste Management Committee. She holds a B.A. and an M.A. in English from SUNY Genesee. She resides in Ithaca and has two children and two grandchildren.

GUILLERMO LINARES (D)
72 - New York County

210 Sherman Ave, Ste A&C, New York, NY 10034
212-544-2278/linaresg@assembly.state.ny.us

Guillermo Linares was elected to the New York State Assembly in 2014 from a district that includes Washington Heights, Inwood and Marble Hill in Northern Manhattan, having previously served in the chamber from 2011-2012. He sits on the following committees: aging; banks; cities; housing; and mental health. He previously served as Commissioner of the Mayor's Office of Immigrant Affairs from 2004-2009, on the New York City Council where he was Co-President of the council's Black and Latino Legislative Caucus, and Chair of the White House Initiative for Educational Excellence for Hispanic Americans. He also sat on the board of the National Council of La Raza. At the time Assemblyman Linares was elected to the City Council, in 1991, he was the first Dominican-born person to be elected to public office in the United States. He immigrated to the Bronx in 1966, drove a taxi, and pursued his education. He was instrumental in founding the CUNY Dominican Students

Institute and the Center for Latin American and Latino Studies at the CUNY Graduate Center. He has been deeply involved in the community for decades as he seeks to improve public education and champion immigrant issues. He holds a BA and an MS from City College and a Professional Diploma in Administration and Supervision from Fordham University. In addition, he holds a Doctorate in Education - recently achieved - from Teachers College, Columbia University. He is the married father of two and grandparent to three.

PETER D LOPEZ (R)
102nd - Schoharie and Green counties, and parts of Delaware, Otsego, Columbia, Albany and Ulster counties.

45 Five Mile Woods Rd., Ste. 3, Catskill, NY 12414
518-943-1371

113 Park Place, Ste. 6, Schoharie, NY 12157
518-295-7250/lopezp@assembly.state.ny.us

Peter D. Lopez was first elected to the New York State Assembly in 2006. He is a member of the following committees: agriculture; alcoholism and drug abuse; corporations, authorities and commissions; education; and environmental conservation. His extensive background in public service includes serving as Schoharie County Clerk. Prior to his election to the Assembly, he spent 21 years on the staff of the New York State Legislature, where his duties included service as Associate Director of the Senate Agriculture Committee, Assistant Director of the Legislative Commission on Rural Resources, and District Office Director for Assembly Minority Leader John J. Faso. He was also Executive Assistant to Senator John J. Bonacic. In his community, he has also been village trustee, town Councilman, and a member of the Schoharie County Board of Supervisors. His extensive volunteer service ranges from Red Cross water safety instructor to founding member of a local Habitat for Humanity chapter. He graduated from the State University College at Cobleskill and holds a Master of Public Administration degree from the University at Albany. He and his wife have four children.

DONNA LUPARDO (D)
123rd - Part of Broome County

State Office Building, 17th Fl; 44 Hawley St, Binghamton, NY 13901
607-723-9047/lupardod@assembly.state.ny.us

Donna A Lupardo was elected to the New York State Assembly in 2004 to represent a district that includes the City of Binghamton and the Towns of Vestal and Union. She chairs the Committee on Children and Families and also sits on the following committees: economic development, job creation, commerce and industry; environmental conservation; higher education; and transportation. Her legislative achievements include backing the State Green Building Construction Act, tenant notification of environmental testing results, and authorship of the Contract Disclosure Act, which reformed the way state resources are allocated. Prior to being elected to the Assembly, she was an adjunct lecturer at SUNY Binghamton. She served on the Broome County Legislature from 1999 to 2000. She holds an undergraduate degree from Wagner College and a Master's degree in philosophy from SUNY Binghamton. She is married.

CHAD A LUPINACCI (R-C-I-WP)
10th - Part of Suffolk County

630 New York Avenue, Suite D, Huntington Station, NY 11746
631-271-8025/LupinacciC@assembly.state.ny.us

Chad A. Lupinacci was elected to the New York State Assembly in 2012 to a district that includes parts of the towns of Huntington and Babylon. He sits on the following committees: election law; higher education; judiciary; tourism, parks, arts and sports development; and transportation. His prior public service includes serving three terms as a Trustee for the South Huntington Union Free District, home of his high school alma ma-

ter, Walt Whitman High School. He is an attorney specializing in real estate and estate planning, and an adjunct professor of political science at St. Joseph's College and Hofstra University. He holds a BA, a JD, and a MBA, all from Hofstra University.

WILLIAM MAGEE (D)
121st - Madison County, Parts of Oneida and Otsego Counties

214 Farrier Ave, Oneida, NY 13421
315-361-4125, 607-432-1484/ mageew@assembly.state.ny.us

William Magee was elected to the New York State Assembly in 1990. He chairs the Committee on Agriculture, a post he has held since 1999. He is also a member of the following committees: aging; banks; higher education; and local governments. Prior to being elected to the Assembly, Magee served 19 years on the Madison County Board of Supervisors. In addition, he worked for the New York State Fair as manager of agriculture and livestock, equestrian events manager, and coordinator of special projects. He is also an auctioneer. As a member of the Assembly, Magee has sponsored numerous proposals to reduce state taxes, energy costs and bureaucracy. Assemblyman Magee's legislative achievements include the Agricultural Land Tax Cap, Farmland Viability Act, Farm to School Program, and authorship of laws that helped to bring back farm breweries and cideries - spurring new markets for apple growers and helping to revitalize the hops industry. He is a member of a variety of community organizations, and holds a bachelor's degree from Cornell University. He is married.

WILLIAM B MAGNARELLI (D)
129th - Parts of the City of Syracuse plus Geddes and Van Buren

Room 840, 333 East Washington St. Syracuse, NY 13202
315-428-9651/ magnarw@assembly.state.ny.us

William Magnarelli was first elected to the New York State Assembly in 1998. He is Chair of the Local Governments Committee. In addition, he sits on the following committees: economic development, job creation, commerce and industry; education; oversight, analysis and investigation; and rules. Prior to being elected to the Assembly, Magnarelli was Majority Leader of the Syracuse Common Council. By profession, he is a practicing attorney, and was a member of the U.S. Army Reserves where he rose to the rank of Captain. He backed the statewide Amber Plan law, and supported Family Health Plus that provides health care coverage to one million uninsured New Yorkers. In addition, he has secured funding for a variety of Central New York resources, such as $37 million for the Syracuse Center of Excellence, to boost the region's economic development. His community involvement includes serving on the board of the Arthritis Foundation and as president of Our Lady of Pompeii Church Parish Council. He attended Syracuse University and Syracuse University College of Law, where he received his law degree. He is married and the father of three children.

NICOLE MALLIOTAKIS (R-C)
64th - Parts of Richmond and Kings Counties

7408 Fifth Avenue, Brooklyn, NY 11209
718-987-0197

11 Maplewood Place, Staten Island, NY 10306
718-987-0197/malliotakisn@assembly.state.ny.us

Nicole Malliotakis was first elected to the New York State Assembly in 2010. She sits on the following committees: banks; corporations, authorities and commissions; governmental employees; transportation; and ways and means. Her public service background includes stints as a liaison for the late Sen. John Marchi and former Gov. George Pataki. More recently, she was public affairs manager for Consolidated Edison. In the Assembly, she has been active on behalf of those impacted by Hurricane Sandy. She also has backed efforts to restore and expand transit service in Brooklyn and Staten Island. She earned an undergraduate degree from

633

Seton Hall University in South Orange, NJ, and an MBA from Wagner College on Staten Island.

MARGARET M MARKEY (D)
30th - Part of Queens County

55-19 69th St, Maspeth, NY 11378
718-651-3185/ markeym@assembly.state.ny.us

Margaret Markey was first elected to the New York State Assembly in 1998. Her district is comprised of the Queens neighborhoods of Maspeth, Woodside and parts of Long Island City, Middle Village, Astoria and Sunnyside. She chairs the Tourism, Parks, Arts, and Sports Committee. In addition, she sits on the following committees: governmental operations; labor; racing and wagering; and ways and means. Her legislative goals include growing the state's tourism industry, which generates more than $50 billion each year.Prior to joining the Assembly, she was Director of Marketing and Tourism for the Borough of Queens; and Assistant Director of Economic Development, Office of Queens Borough President Claire Shulman. She has long been active in her community and served as a member of Community Boards 2 and 5 and is the founder of Maspeth Town Hall, Inc., a community center that serves over 1000 families. She graduated from Berkeley Business School. The Queens-born Markey is the married mother of three children.

SHELLEY MAYER (D-WP-I)
90th - Part of Nassau County

35 E Grassy Sprain Rd, 406B, Yonkers, NY 10710
914-779-8805/MayerS@assembly.state.ny.us

Shelley Mayer was first elected to the New York State Assembly in 2012 to represent her hometown district comprised of Yonkers. She chairs the Subcommittee on Students with Special Needs, and sits on the following committees: children and families; cities; education; health; labor; and social services. Mayer brings a strong professional background to her elected position. Prior to joining the Assembly, she was a Senior Counsel at the National State Attorney General Program at Columbia Law School focusing on health care and labor law rights. Prior to that, she was Vice President of Government and Community Affairs at Continuum Health Partners, one of New York City's largest teaching hospital systems. From 1982 to 1994, she was an Assistant Attorney General in the office of New York Attorney General Bob Abrams. Mayer served in the Civil Rights Bureau, as Chief of the Westchester Regional Office, as the legislative liaison for the Attorney General and finally as a senior advisor to the Attorney General. She remains active in her community, and has served as a member of the Yonkers NAACP, Yonkers YWCA, Westchester Women's Bar Association, and Westchester Women's Agenda. She also served on the boards of the Jewish Council of Yonkers/Westchester Community Partners and the Board of the Yonkers Public Library. She holds an undergraduate degree from UCLA and a JD from SUNY Buffalo School of Law. Mayer is the married mother of three.

JOHN T MCDONALD III (D)
108th - Parts of Albany, Rensselaer and Saratoga Counties

LOB 417, Albany, NY 12248
518-455-4474/McDonaldJ@assembly.state.ny.us

John T. McDonald III was elected to the New York State Assembly in 2012 to a district that includes sections of Albany, Troy and the communities of Green Island, North Greenbush, Rensselaer, Waterford and Watervliet. He chairs the Subcommittee on Effective Treatment, and sits on the following committees: aging; alcoholism and drug abuse; cities; insurance; mental health; and real property taxation. He is President of his family-owned Marra's Pharmacy in his hometown of Cohoes. Prior to being elected to the Assembly, McDonald spent 13 years as Mayor of Cohoes. In this role, he focused on economic development and revitalization or developments in key areas. As a result, 2,000 new residential

units arrived in the city, downtown revitalization is underway, and improvements to the Cohoes Falls have helped to make it a regional attraction. McDonald was also actively involved in the New York State Conference of Mayors, including serving as president of the state-wide organization. He also has been actively involved on numerous boards, including chairing the Capital District Transportation Committee, and the Cohoes Industrial Development Agency, as well as sitting on boards such as the State Comptroller's Local Advisory Team. He holds a BS in pharmacy science from Albany College of Pharmacy, as well as a Doctorate of Humanity, and is the married father of three.

DAVID G MCDONOUGH (R)
14th - Part of Nassau County

404 Bedford Ave, Bellmore, NY 11710
516-409-2070/mcdonoughd@assembly.state.ny.us

David McDonough was first elected to the New York State Assembly in 2002, and sits on the following committees: consumer affairs and protection; education; health; transportation; and veterans' affairs. McDonough is past president of the Nassau County Council of Chambers of Commerce, a member of the Committee for the Merrick Downtown Revitalization Project, and four-term President for the Merrick Chamber of Commerce. In this role, his achievements included growing the membership ranks by 35 percent. In addition, he is a founding member and former board member of the Bellmore-Merrick Community Wellness Council and a member and past president of the Kiwanis Club of Merrick. In addition, McDonough served in both the U.S. Coast Guard and the U.S. Air Force. He holds a B.A. in economics from Columbia University, and is a graduate of the American Academy of Dramatic Arts. The Merrick resident is married with three children and four grandchildren.

TOM MCKEVITT (R)
17th - Part of Nassau County

1975 Hempstead Trnpke, Ste. 202, East Meadow, NY 11554
516-228-4960/mckevit@assembly.state.ny.us

Tom McKevitt was elected to the New York State Assembly in a special election in 2006. He is Assistant Minority Leader Pro Tempore, which means he holds the third ranking position in the Minority Conference and is responsible for assisting in the management of all floor activity and debates. He also serves on the following standing committees: codes; consumer affairs and protection; election law; and local governments. Prior to joining the Assembly, McKevitt worked in the offices of state Senator Kemp Hannon and U.S. Senator Alfonse D'Amato. He also was the Deputy Town Attorney for the Town of Hempstead, and he has been an attorney in private law firms in Nassau County, where he has lived all his life. He remains active in professional and civic organizations, including as past chair of the Nassau County Bar Association's Municipal Law Committee. He is a member of the East Meadow Chamber of Commerce and the East Meadow Kiwanis Club. He holds both an undergraduate degree and a JD from Hofstra University. The East Meadow resident is married and the father of two.

STEVEN F MCLAUGHLIN (R-C)
107th - Parts of Columbia, Washington, and Rensselaer Counties

258 Hoosick St., Ste 109, Troy, NY 12180
518-272-6149/ mclaughlins@assembly.state.ny.us

Steve McLaughlin was elected to the New York State Assembly in 2010 to his Upstate district in the Capital Region. He is a member of the following committees: children and families; economic development, job creation, commerce and industry; education; and social services. As an Assemblyman, his focus is on putting New Yorkers back to work, reducing spending and cleaning up corruption in Albany. In addition, he backs substantive ethics reform, including requiring the full disclosure of officials' outside income and imposing term limits on the legislative leadership. He received his commercial and instrument airplane ratings from Florida Institute of Technology, and earned his bachelor's degree from USNY and an MBA from the University of Phoenix. He has flown for both corporate and commercial airlines, and was a mortgage loan officer for Citizens Bank. Currently, he is works for Monolith Solar. He and his wife have two children.

MICHAEL G MILLER (D)
38th - Part of Queens County

83-91 Woodhaven Blvd, Woodhaven, NY 11421
718-805-0950/millermg@assembly.state.ny.us

Michael G. Miller was elected in September 2009 to a Queens County district that includes the neighborhoods of Woodhaven, Ridgewood, Richmond Hill, Ozone Park and Glendale. He is Chair of the Committee on House Operations, and also sits on the following committees: aging; banks; education; labor; racing and wagering; and veterans' affairs. Assemblyman Miller's achievements include authoring a law that requires level two sex offenders to register their employment address. He also has backed the $9 minimum wage increase, as well as a freight locomotive engine upgrade to reduce air pollution. Prior to his election, Miller sat on Community Board 5 and advocated for affordable housing, expansion of services for seniors and additional after-school programs. He was Capital Campaign Director for the Greater Ridgewood Youth Council, and he founded the Forest Park Aktion Club, which supports adults with mental disabilities. Professionally, Miller managed the New York office of Tiger Federal Credit Union. He attended both Queens College and the University of Georgia CUNA Management School.

MICHAEL A MONTESANO (R-I-C)
15th - Part of Nassau County

111 Levittown Parkway, Hicksville NY 11801
516-937-3571/montesanom@assembly.state.ny.us

Michael Montesano was elected to the New York State Assembly in 2010. He sits on the following committees: codes; corporations, authorities and commissions; ethics and guidance; judiciary; and oversight, analysis and investigation. Prior to his election, he was a police officer and detective for the NYPD for a decade and served as an EMT supervisor and investigator for the NYC Emergency Medical Service. In 1990 he started his own private practice law firm and served as Acting Village Justice in Roslyn Harbor. He also was a Village Prosecutor for Roslyn Harbor and adjunct professor at the New York Institute of Technology. He has served as a President, Vice-President and Trustee of the North Shore School District Board of Education. He holds an associate degree from Nassau County Community College, a bachelor's degree in Criminal Justice from St. John's University, and law degree from CUNY Law School at Queens College. He is married, resides in Glen Head, and has two children and two stepchildren.

JOSEPH D MORELLE (D)
136th - Cities of Irondequoit, Brighton, and Rochester

1945 E Ridge Rd, Rochester, NY 14622
585-467-0410/morellej@assembly.state.ny.us

Joseph Morelle was elected to the Assembly in 1990. He became the Assembly's Majority Leader in 2013, which makes him responsible for the day-to-day operations in the Assembly chamber, including running the floor during debates. He also sits on the Committee on Rules, and formerly chaired the Committee on Insurance. His legislative achievements include working with state and local leaders to bring 250 new, well-paying jobs to the Rochester region. He also sponsored New York's autism health insurance law, which requires carriers to cover the cost of autism screening and treatment. He has served on the Finger Lakes Regional Economic Development Council. Prior to his election to the Assembly,

he served in the Monroe County Legislature. Morelle lives in Irondequoit, the Rochester suburb where he grew up, and holds a bachelor's degree in political science from SUNY Geneseo. He and his wife have three children.

WALTER T. MOSLEY (D)
57th - Part of Queens County

55 Hanson Place, Brooklyn, NY 11217
718-596-0100/MosleyW@assembly.state.ny.us

Walter T. Mosley was elected to the New York State Assembly in 2012 to a Brooklyn district that includes Clinton Hill, Fort Greene, Prospect Heights, and parts of Crown Heights, and Bed-Stuy. He chairs the subcommittee on regulated mortgage lenders, and sits on the following committees: banks; codes; correction; education; and housing. His first vote was on behalf of the NY Safe Act, the landmark gun control act signed into law in 2013. He also has introduced the Retail Anti-Profiling Act calling for more transparency regarding NYPD personnel in private businesses, and legislation to prohibit smoking on all State University of New York campuses. Prior to his election, Mosley was special advisor and external relations specialist for the New York State Senate Minority Conference and Director of Contract Compliance and Government & Community Relations for Spectrum Personal Communications. He holds a bachelor's degree from Pennsylvania State University at University Park, and a law degree from Howard University. He and his wife have two children.

FRANCISCO P MOYA (D-WF)
39th - Part of Queens County

82-11 37th Avenue, Ste 607, Jackson Heights, NY 11372
718-458-5367

Francisco P. Moya was elected to the New York State Assembly in 2010, which made the lifelong resident of Corona the first Ecuadorian-American elected to public office in the United States. He chairs the Commission on Science and Technology and the Subcommittee on Workplace Safety. In addition, he sits on the following committees: corporations, authorities and commissions; energy; housing; insurance; labor; and ways and means. Prior to his election, he worked for the Queens Health Network at Elmhurst Hospital, and served as Secretary to the Senate for former Senate Minority Leader David A. Patterson. After the 2008 beating death of Ecuadorian immigrant Jose Sucuzhanay, Moya acted as spokesperson for the family, and helped to organize community rallies and vigils. Long active in his community, he helped to start the after-school sports program at St. Leo's school. He holds an undergraduate degree from St. John's University and was selected a National Urban Fellow to get his master's degree in public administration.

DEAN MURRAY (R)
3 - Part of Suffolk County

1735 N. Ocean Ave., Ste. A, Medford, NY 11763
631-207-0073/murrayd@assembly.state.ny.us

Dean Murray was elected to the New York State Assembly in 2014 from a Suffolk County district that includes Medford and Mastic Beach. He previously represented the district from 2010-2013. He currently sits on the following committees: aging; education; small business; tourism, parks, arts and sports development; and transportation. He advocates on behalf of reduced property taxes and bi-partisan solutions to high taxes. He owns D & S Advertising Inc., a Long-Island based advertising agency that publishes publications such as the Long Island Job Finder and the Long Island Fugitive Finder. He previously worked in regional sales for TCI Cable, and prior to that was a radio and television news reporter in New York, Delaware, Maryland and Pennsylvania, where he covered the state capital for more than 100 radio stations. He is involved in his local community, graduated from the Broadcast Institute of Maryland, and is the married father of one.

BILL NOJAY (R)
133rd - Livingston County and Parts of Monroe and Steuben Counties

3011 Rochester Road, Ste 3, Lakeville, NY 14480
585-346-0002/NojayW@assembly.state.ny.us

Bill Nojay was elected to his upstate district in the New York State Assembly in 2012 and sits on the following committees: consumer affairs and protection; election law; mental health; and transportation. Nojay is an attorney by profession, and hosts a daily radio show on stations in Upstate New York. He is a small business owner. He is focused on improving the Upstate economy via cutting state spending and regulations, as well as reducing property taxes. Prior to his election to the Assembly, Nojay served as President of the International Business Council of the Greater Rochester Chamber of Commerce and Commissioner of the Rochester Genesee Regional Transportation Authority, including service as chairman. He chaired the Regional Trails Initiative Steering Committee for the Rochester Region. He was COO of Detroit's transportation system under Detroit Mayor David Bing. The Rochester native has been deeply involved in his community, formerly serving as director and treasurer of the Al Sigl Center for the Developmentally Disabled; Chairman of the Monroe County Sports Commission and Chairman of the U.S. Army's Community Advisory Board in the Rochester region. He has served as an election monitor for the International Republican Institute in Ukraine and Afghanistan and supported other democracy movements around the globe. He holds a JD from Columbia University, as well as an MBA, also from Columbia. He also received a certificate in international and comparative law from the Parker School of Columbia University and was a research fellow at Tribhuvan University in Kathmandu, Nepal when he lived there as a Thomas J. Watson Fellow. He and his wife live in Pittsford and are parents to three children.

CATHERINE T NOLAN (D)
37th - Part of Queens County

41-02 Queens Blvd, Ste 2B, Sunnyside, NY 11104
718-784-3194

61-08 Linden Street, Ridgewood, NY 11385
718-456-9492/nolanc@assembly.state.ny.us

Catherine Nolan was elected to the New York State Assembly in 1984 and represents a district that includes the neighborhoods of Sunnyside, Ridgewood, Long Island City, Queensbridge, Ravenswood, Astoria, Woodside, Maspeth, Dutch Kills and Blissville. She has chaired the Assembly's Committee on Education since 2006 and in that capacity has spearheaded efforts to achieve class size reduction, universal pre-K, middle school initiatives, and improve high school graduation rates. She also sits on the following committees: corporations, authorities and commissions; rules; veterans' affairs; and ways and means. She has previously chaired the Committee on Banks, the Committee on Labor, the Real Property Taxation Committee, and the Assembly's Commission on State-Federal Relations. She also represented the Assembly on the MTA Capital Program Review Board. She also serves on the Assembly Majority Steering Committee. She holds a B.A. from NYU and resides in Ridgewood with her husband and son.

DANIEL J O'DONNELL (D)
69th - Part of New York County

245 W 104th Street, New York, NY 10025
212-866-3970/odonnelld@assembly.state.ny.us

Daniel J O'Donnell was first elected to the New York State Assembly in 2002 and represents a district that includes Manhattan Valley, Morningside Heights, and parts of the Upper West Side. He chairs the Committee on Correction, as well as the Subcommittee on Criminal Procedure. In

addition, he sits on the following committees: codes; education; environmental conservation; and tourism, parks, arts and sports development. O'Donnell is the first openly gay man elected to the New York State Assembly. During his tenure in the Assembly, he has been the prime sponsor of major legislation including the Marriage Equality Act, a bill O'Donnell led to passage in the Assembly five times; it was finally signed into law in June 2011. He also backed the Dignity for All Students Act, which requires public schools in New York to combat bias-based bullying and harassment. Prior to joining the Assembly, O'Donnell was a public defender in the Brooklyn office of the Legal Aid Society; he then opened his own public interest law firm. He earned a B.A from George Washington University and his J.D. from CUNY Law School. Born in Queens and raised in Commack, O'Donnell lives with his husband in Morningside Heights.

ROBERT C OAKS (R-C)
130th - Wayne County, Parts of Cayuga, and Oswego Counties

10 Leach Rd, Lyons, NY 14489
315-946-5166/oaksr@assembly.state.ny.us

Robert C. Oaks was first elected to the New York State Assembly in 1992; his district includes Wayne County, the towns of Aurelius, Brutus, Cato, Conquest, Ira, Mentz, Montezuma, Sennett, Sterling and Victory in Cayuga County, and the towns of Hannibal, Minetto, and Oswego in Oswego County. He sits on the Rules Committee and the powerful Ways and Means Committee, where he is the Ranking Minority Member. He previously served as the Deputy Minority Leader. Prior to his election to the Assembly, he was elected to three terms as Wayne County Clerk. Professionally, Oaks served as Assistant Director of the Continuing Education for the Greece Central School District, and Director of the Wayne County Youth Bureau. Oakes remains deeply involved with his community, including serving on the boards of directors for the Seneca Waterways Council, the Boy Scouts of America, and the Wayne County Community Endowment Advisory Board. He holds an undergraduate degree from Colgate University and a master's degree in recreational administration from the University of Montana. He and his wife reside in Macedon and are parents to two children.

FÉLIX ORTIZ (D)
51st - Part of Kings County

404 55th St, Brooklyn, NY 11220
718-492-6334/ortizf@assembly.state.ny.us

Félix Ortiz was elected to the New York State Assembly in 1994. He is Assistant Speaker of the New York State Assembly. He is a member of the following committees: correction; labor; rules; ways and means. His legislative achievements include backing a $2 billion bond act to repair the state's aging infrastructure, as well as a fight to create the state's first Child Obesity Education Program. He formerly chaired the Puerto Rican/Hispanic Task Force, as well as the cities; mental health, alcohol and substance abuse, and veterans' affairs committees. Assemblyman Ortiz was born and raised in La Playa De Salinas, Puerto Rico, and became the first member of his family to move to the U.S. mainland in 1980. He served in the U.S. Army for two years. Ortiz is also Vice President of the Parliamentary Confederation of the Americas; Executive Board member of the National Conference of State Legislatures, and also co-founded and served as President of the National Hispanic Caucus of State Legislatures, among other organizations. He holds a BS from Boricua College, and a Master's in Public Administration from New York University. He is married and father to three.

STEVEN OTIS (D)
91st - Part of Westchester County

222 Grace Church Street Suite 305, Port Chester, NY 10573
914-939-7167/OtisS@assembly.state.ny.us

Steven Otis was first elected in 2012 to the New York State Assembly to represent a district that includes the Sound Shore communities of Larchmont, Mamaroneck, New Rochelle, Port Chester, Rye and Rye Brook. He chairs the Commission on Solid Waste Management, and sits on the following committees: agriculture; corporations, authorities and commissions; environmental conservation; libraries and education technology; local governments; and tourism, parks, arts and sports development. Otis is the former Mayor of Rye, a post he held for 12 years, the longest in the city's history. He also served for many years as counsel and chief of staff to Sen. Suzi Oppenheimer from 1985 until his election to the Assembly. Prior to that, he was a Senate Fellow and legislative director to State Senator Jeremy S. Weinstein. He has been deeply involved in his community's civic life - particularly focusing on environment and water-related issues - for many years, including serving as chair of the City of Rye Conservation Commission, and Vice Chair of the Long Island Sound Watershed Intermunicipal Council. He graduated from Hobart & William Smith Colleges and holds a Master's degree in public administration from New York University and a JD from Hofstra University School of Law. He is married and lives with his wife in Rye.

PHILIP A PALMESANO (R-C-I)
132nd - Schuyler and Yates Counties, Parts of Steuben, Chemung, and Seneca Counties

105 E. Steuben St, Bath, NY 14810
607-776-9691/palmesanop@assembly.state.ny.us

Assemblyman Phil Palmesano was first elected to the Assembly in 2010. His district includes most of Steuben County, Schuyler and Yates counties, and the following towns in Chemung and Seneca counties: Catlin, Erin, Van Etten, Veteran, Covert, Lodi, Ovid and Romulus. He is Ranking Minority Member on the Energy Committee, and sits on the following Assembly committees: corporations, authorities and commissions; energy; libraries and education technology; real property taxation; and tourism, parks, arts and sports development.

His public service background includes stints as a legislative aide to former State Assemblyman Donald Davidsen; former State Assemblyman Jim Bacalles, and district director to former Congressman Randy Kuhl, Jr. In addition, Assemblyman Palmesano was the district director for New York State Senator George Winner, and represented the city of Corning in the Steuben County Legislature. He is active in community organizations such as the marketing committee of Catholic Charities of Steuben County. He holds a B.A. in political science from St. Bonaventure University, and resides in Corning with his wife and two children.

ANTHONY H PALUMBO (R-C)
2nd - Parts of Suffolk County

400 W. Main St., Suite 201, Riverhead, NY 11901
631-727-0204/palumboa@assembly.state.ny.us

Anthony H. Palumbo was elected to serve the residents of the 2nd Assembly District in a Special Election held on November 5, 2013. His district includes the North Fork of Long Island in Suffolk County. His legislative achievemets include sponsoring a tax-cut bill that would save the average Suffolk County resident over $2,500 per year. Prior to his election to the Assembly, he served as an assistant district attorney for the Suffolk County District Attorney's Office, where he prosecuted hundreds of cases on misdemeanor and felony levels. He served as Trial Supervisor to the five Eastern Suffolk Towns and he has also been in private practice. His community involvement includes serving as the Vice President of the Cutchogue-New Suffolk Library Board of Trustees. Palumbo received a degree in Government and Law from Lafayette College in Easton, Pennsylvania, and graduated from St. John's Law School in Jamaica, New York. He currently resides in New Suffolk with his wife Tracy and their two children.

AMY R PAULIN (D)
88th - Part of Westchester County

700 White Plains Rd, Ste 252, Scarsdale, NY 10583
914-723-1115/paulina@assembly.state.ny.us

Assemblywoman Amy Paulin was elected to the New York State Assembly in November 2000 and represents a district that includes Bronxville, Pelham, Pelham Manor, Scarsdale, Tuckahoe, Eastchester, and parts of New Rochelle and White Plains. She currently chairs the Assembly's Energy Committee, also serves on the following committees: education; health; and higher education. Her work in the energy committee is focused on encouraging renewable energy and ensuring a reliable electricity grid. Prior to joining the Assembly, she served as Executive Director of My Sisters' Place and as a member of the Scarsdale Village Board. She also was Founder and Chairwoman of the Westchester Women's Agenda.. She is the recipient of numerous awards. The Brooklyn-born Paulin graduated from SUNY-Albany, holds a Master's degree from SUNY-Albany and has completed doctoral coursework in Criminal Justice from the same school. She and her husband reside in Scarsdale and have three children.

CRYSTAL D PEOPLES-STOKES (D)
141st - Part of Erie County

792 E Delavan Ave, Buffalo, NY 14215
716-897-9714/peoplec@assembly.state.ny.us

Crystal Davis Peoples-Stokes was first elected to the New York State Assembly in 2002. She is Chair of the Committee on Governmental Operations. In addition, she sits on the following standing committees: alcoholism and drug abuse; environmental conservation; health; higher education; and insurance. She has been actively involved in making sure that minority and women-owned businesses have a fair chance at obtaining state contracts, including being appointed by Gov. Cuomo to sit on the Minority and Women Owned Business Enterprise Teach Task Force. She also has backed major funding for a number of Western New York projects such as funds for a new home for the Community Health Center of Buffalo and the city's Educational Opportunity Center's new facility. She holds an undergraduate degree from Buffalo State College, as well as a M.S. in student personnel training from the same school. She is married and lives in Buffalo, her hometown.

N NICK PERRY (D)
58th - Part of Kings County

903 Utica Avenue, Brooklyn, NY 11203
718-385-3336/ perryn@assembly.state.ny.us

N Nick Perry was elected to the New York State Assembly in 1992 to represent his Brooklyn district. He is the Assistant Speaker Pro Tempore also sits on the following committees: banks; codes; labor; transportation; and ways and means. He also is the Chairman of the New York State Association of Black and Puerto Rican Legislators and the Regional Chairman (for NY and PA) of the National Black Caucus of State Legislators. Perry, who emigrated from his native Jamaica, volunteered for the U.S. Army, where he served two years' active duty and four years' reserve. He has long been active in local public service, serving on his local Community Board as chair. He also served on the Brooklyn Borough Board. In the Assembly, Perry achieved two recent, significant victories with the Cyber Crime Youth Rescue Act and the Taxpayer Refund Choice Act. He holds a B.A. in political science from Brooklyn College and an M.A. in public policy and administration from the same school. He is the married father to two.

ROXANNE PERSAUD (D)
59 - Part of King's County

5318 Avenue N, 1st Floor Store, Brooklyn, NY 11234
718-252-2124/PersaudR@assembly.state.ny.us

Biographies

Roxanne Persaud was elected to the New York State Assembly in 2014. She sits on the following committees: children and families; higher education; libraries and education technology; real property taxation; and social services. She is former President of the 69th Precinct Community Council in Canarsie, and a Commissioner on the New York City Districting Commission. She was also a member of Community Board 18 and numerous other community organizations. Professionally she has worked in institutions of higher education, including as the registrar at St. Francis College and the Director of Student Accounts and Registrar Service at Pace University. Born in Guyana, Assemblywoman Persaud holds a B.S. and M.S. in Education Administration from Pace University.

VICTOR M PICHARDO (D)
86th - Parts of New York County

2175C Jerome Ave., Bronx, NY 10453
718-933-6909/pichardov@assembly.state.ny.us

Victor M. Pichardo was elected to the represent New York Assembly District 86 during a special election held on November 5, 2013. His district includes University Heights and areas of West Bronx. He formerly served as Staff Assistant to Senator Chuck Schumer, and was promoted to Community Outreach Coordinator/Latino Liaison. He has also held the position of Associate Director of Public Relations at Mercy College, and the Director of Community Affairs for State Senator Gustavo Rivera in the Bronx. He holds a degree in Communications with double minors in English and Sociology from the University of Buffalo.

J. GARY PRETLOW (D)
89th - Part of Westchester County

6 Gramatan Ave, Mt Vernon, NY 10550
914-667-0127/pretlowj@assembly.state.ny.us

J Gary Pretlow was elected to the New York State Assembly in 1992 to represent a district that includes Mount Vernon and Yonkers. He chairs the Committee on Racing and Wagering, and also sits on the following standing committees: codes; insurance; rules; and ways and means. Assemblyman Pretlow is responsible for Cynthia's Law, a provision of which makes reckless assault of a child a class D felony. In addition, he has worked to stabilize the finances of the New York City Off Track Betting Corporation; he backs a state takeover. Professionally, he is financial planner with Moncur-Pretlow and Co. His previous public service includes the Mount Vernon City Council, where he chaired the Finance and Planning Committee, and the Capital Projects Board. He remains active in his local community and has received numerous awards. He holds a B.B.A. from Baruch College, and is the married father to one child.

DAN QUART (R)
73rd - Part of New York County

360 E 57th St, Mezzanine, New York, NY 10022
212-605-0937/quartd@assembly.state.ny.us

Assemblyman Dan Quart was elected in November 2011 to represent a district that encompasses the Upper East Side, Midtown East, Turtle Bay and Sutton Place. He is Chair of the Subcommittee on Museums & Cultural Institutions, and sits on the following standing committees: alcoholism and drug abuse; consumer affairs and protection; corporations, authorities and commissions; insurance; judiciary; and tourism, parks, arts and sports development. His previous public office was on Community Board 8, where he co-chaired the Transportation Committee and chaired the 2nd Avenue Subway Task Force. An attorney, Quart has been heavily involved in doing pro bono work for many years. He has served as a volunteer for the Housing Division of the Legal Aid Society, providing free representation for low-income tenants in eviction proceedings, since 2002. In 2003, New York State Chief Judge Judith Kaye awarded him the Pro Bono Publico Award as one of New York City's top pro bono attorneys. He also has been the pro bono attorney for the

tenants in the Eastwood Housing complex on Roosevelt Island; and for the Disabled Veterans Consortium, representing a disabled veteran who was denied benefits. Beginning in 2009, Dan has partnered with Eviction Intervention Services to organize and lead a pro bono clinic representing tenants on the East Side who fall just above the monetary threshold for free legal services, but cannot afford an attorney of their own. He holds an undergraduate degree from SUNY Binghamton and a JD from St. John's Law School. He is the married father of one.

EDWARD P RA (R)
19th - Part of Nassau County

825 East Gate Blvd, Suite 207, Garden City, NY 11530
516-535-4095
rae@assembly.state.ny.us

Ed Ra was elected to the New York State Assembly in 2010 to a district on his native Long Island that includes parts of the Towns of Hempstead, North Hempstead, and Oyster Bay. He Ranking Minority member on the Education Committee and also sits on the following committees: codes; education; health; higher education; and transportation. He is also Vice-Chairman of the Minority Steering Committee. Ra has served as the Deputy Town Attorney for the Town of Hempstead and as a legal aide in the Office of the New York State Attorney General. He holds an undergraduate degree from Loyola College of Maryland, and a J.D. from St. John's University School of Law. Ra also holds an LL.M in Intellectual Property Law from Benjamin N. Cardozo School of Law. He and his wife live in Garden City South.

ANDREW P RAIA (R-I-C-WF)
12th - Part of Suffolk County

75 Woodbine Ave, Northport, NY 11768
631-261-4151/ raiaa@assembly.state.ny.us

Andrew P Raia was first elected to the New York State Assembly in 2002. He has been Deputy Minority Whip since 2014, and also serves as the Ranking Minority member on the Health Committee. He also sits on the following committees: banks; environmental conservation; health; housing; and rules. He is the former Ranking Minority Member of the Committee on Banks where he co-sponsored the Home Equity Theft Prevention Act. He also focuses on health care policy, senior issues, and efforts to rein in unfunded mandates that he believes stifle economic growth on Long Island and otherwise impose burdens on schools and governments there. Prior to being elected to the Assembly, Raia spent 12 years on the staffs of legislative offices in the State Assembly, State Senate, and the Suffolk County Legislature. He continues to be active within his community, including serving as a director of the Huntington Boys and Girls Club, the Huntington Freedom Day Care Center, and the Huntington Station Enrichment Center. Raia holds a bachelor's degree in political science from SUNY-New Paltz.

PHILIP R RAMOS (D-WF)
6th - Part of Suffolk County

1010 Suffolk Ave, Brentwood, NY 11717
631-435-3214/ ramosp@assembly.state.ny.us

Phil Ramos was first elected to the New York State Assembly in 2002 to a district that includes portions of the hamlets of Brentwood, Central Islip, Bay Shore, North Bay Shore, and Islandia. He is Deputy Majority Leader, and sits on the following standing committees: aging; economic development, job creation, commerce and industry; education; and local governments. Assemblyman Ramos is retired detective who rose through the ranks of the Suffolk County Police Department. During his two decades in law enforcement, Assemblyman Ramos worked undercover in the Narcotics Unit for eight years, then went on to become a detective. He joined with other Latino police officers to found the Suffolk County Police Hispanic Society to address Latino issues in the community, and he also helped organize the Long Island Latino Elected Officials Association. He began his working career as a therapy aide and Emergency Medical Technician. He is father to two.

DIANA C RICHARDSON (D-WF-G)
43 - Part of Kings County

1216 Union Street. Brooklyn, NY 11225
718-771-3105/richardsond@assembly.state.ny.us

Diana C. Richardson was first elected to the New York State Assembly in a special election on May 5, 2015 from a district that includes Crown Heights, Lefferts Gardens, Wingate and East Flatbush. She sits on the following committees: banks; corporations, authorities and commissions; economic development, job creation, commerce and industry; mental health; and small business. She was Director of Constituent Affairs for NYS Senator Kevin Parker, and has been Executive Member of Brooklyn's Community Board 9. She holds an undergraduate degree from CUNY Medgar Evers, and a Master's of Public Administration from CUNY Baruch College. She is mother of one.

JOSÉ RIVERA (D)
78th - Part of Bronx County

One Fordham Plaza, Ste 1008, 10th Fl, Bronx, NY 10458
718-933-2204/riveraj@assembly.state.ny.us

José Rivera was first elected to the New York State Assembly in 1982, where he served for five years. He then left office and was re-elected in 2000. He is Assistant Majority Whip, and a member of the following committees: aging; agriculture; insurance; and small business. He formerly chaired the Task Force on Food, Farm and Nutrition Policy. During his previous stint in the Assembly, he served as Treasurer, Vice Chair and Chairman of the Black and Puerto Rican Caucus. As the Chair of this committee, he was instrumental in establishing the Martin Luther King holiday in the state of New York. Rivera also has served on the New York City Council.

SAMUEL D. ROBERTS (D-WF)
128th - Part of Onondaga County

711 E Genesee St, Ste 2, Syracuse, NY 13210
315-449-9536/robertsS@assembly.state.ny.us

Samuel D. Roberts was elected to the New York State Assembly in 2010. He chairs the Task Force on University-Industry Cooperation, and also sits on the following committees: aging; labor; libraries and education technology; small business; tourism, parks, arts and sports development; and transportation. Roberts also served as an Onondaga County Legislator from 1990-1999. The former journeyman tool/die maker retired from General Motors after 30 years. A member of the United Auto Workers Union, Roberts was elected Recording Secretary of UAW Local Union #465 and Chair of Local Union #854's Education and Civil Rights Committees. The Syracuse native is a 6th degree black belt in American Shotokan Karate who competed for several years, winning major championships.

ANNETTE M ROBINSON (D)
56th - Part of Kings County

1360 Fulton Street, Rm 417, Brooklyn, NY 11216
718-399-7630/ RobinsonA@assembly.state.ny.us

Annette M Robinson was first elected to the New York State Assembly in 2002. She chairs the Committee on Banks, and also is a member of the following committees: aging; children and families; housing; oversight, analysis and investigation; real property taxation; and small business. She has long been involved in public service, having been elected to the first of three terms to the District 16 Community School Board in 1977, and then elected to the New York City Council in 1991. She is a District

leader/State Committeewoman in the 56th A.D., has served as coordinator and liaison for former New York City Comptroller Harrison J. Goldin, and has been District Director for U.S. Congressman Major R. Owens. She earned both her bachelor's and Master's degrees from New Hampshire College. Now a widow, she and her husband William were married more than 50 years. She is the mother to six, and is also a grandmother and great-grandmother.

ROBERT J RODRIGUEZ (D)
68th - Part of New York County

55 E 115th St, New York, NY 10029
212-828-3953/rodriguezrj@assembly.state.us

Robert J. Rodriguez was elected to the New York State Assembly in 2010. He chairs the subcommittee on infrastructure, and is a member of the following standing committees: banks; corporations, authorities and commissions; housing; labor; mental health; and ways and means. His professional experience includes work as vice president of a minority-owned public finance firm. He served on Community Board 11, including as chair. In addition, he sat on the board of directors of the Upper Manhattan Empowerment Zone. Other community service includes sitting on the boards of the Terrence Cardinal Cooke Community Advisory Board, Catholic Charities Community Services of New York, and SCANNY, a youth and family services organization. Professionally, he was vice president of a minority-owned public finance firm prior to being elected to the Assembly. The East Harlem native holds an undergraduate degree from Yale University and an MBA from New York University.

LINDA B ROSENTHAL (D)
67th - Part of New York County

230 West 72nd St, Ste 2F, New York, NY 10023
212-873-6368/RosentL@assembly.state.ny.us

Linda B Rosenthal was first elected to the New York State Assembly in 2006. Her district includes the Upper West Side and parts of Clinton/Hell's Kitchen in Manhattan. She chairs the Committee on Alcoholism and Drug Abuse, and sits the following standing committees: agriculture; education; energy; health; housing; tourism, parks, arts and sports development. Among her legislative achievements is passage more than 40 laws, including laws that extend orders of protection to companion animals; allowing same sex couples to adopt non-biological children together in New York State, and banning the sale of electronic cigarettes to minors.. Prior to joining the legislature, Rosenthal served as Manhattan District Director and Director of Special Projects to Congressman Jerrold Nadler. She holds a B.A. from the University of Rochester, and is a lifelong resident of the Upper West Side.

NILY ROZIC (D)
25th - Part of Queens County

159-16 Union Turnpike, Flushing, NY 11366
718-820-0214/RozicN@assembly.state.ny.us

Nily Rozic was first elected to the New York State Assembly in 2012 to a district that includes northeast Queens neighborhoods including Flushing, Queensboro Hill, Hillcrest, Fresh Meadows, Oakland Gardens, Bayside and Douglaston. She chairs the Subcommittee on Emerging Workforce, and sits on the following committees: children and families; corporations, authorities and commissions; correction; environmental conservation; and labor. She is the former Chief of Staff to Assemblyman Brian Kavanaugh. Within her community, she served on Community Board 8. The Fresh Meadows resident, who was born in Jerusalem and raised in Queens, holds an undergraduate degree from New York University.

ADDIE J RUSSELL (D)
116th - Parts of Oswego, Jefferson and Saint Lawrence counties

Dulles State Office Bldg, Ste 210, 317 Washington Street, Watertown, NY 13601
315-786-0284

3 Remington Ave., Suite 1, Canton, NY 13617
315-386-2037/ RussellA@assembly.state.ny.us

Addie Jenne Russell was elected to the New York State Assembly in 2008 from a district that follows the shore of the St. Lawrence River from the northeast corner of Lake Ontario to the manufacturing town of Massena and borders Fort Drum and the Black River to the east. She chairs the Task Force on Food, Farm & Nutrition Policy and the Subcommittee on Women Veterans. She is also a member of the following standing committees: agriculture; corporations, authorities and commissions; economic development, job creation, commerce and industry; energy; local governments; and veterans' affairs. Prior to her election, she was an attorney at the law firm of Conboy, McKay, Bachman & Kendal, LLP. In addition, she served on the Jefferson County Board of Legislators from 2006-2009. She has been highly active in the community, serving as past President of the Jefferson County Branch of the American Association of University Women, on the Board of Directors of the Volunteer Transportation Center; and serving on Jefferson County's Community Services Board. She holds a B.A. from the University at Albany and a J.D. with a Certificate in Family Law and Social Policy from Syracuse University College of Law. The seventh generation of her family to live in the North Country, she and her husband reside in Theresa with their two children.

SEAN RYAN (D)
149th - Part of Erie County

936 Delaware Ave, Buffalo NY 14209
716-885-9630/RyanS@assembly.state.ny.us

Sean Ryan was first elected to the New York State Assembly in 2011. He chairs the Commission on State-Local Relations, and sits on the following standing committees: banks; energy; education; environmental conservation; local governments; and veterans' affairs. Prior to his election, Ryan worked with People United for Sustainable Housing, Inc. to create a non-profit development entity called the Buffalo Neighborhood Stabilization Company, Inc. (BNSC). He served as the Executive Director and General Counsel of BNSC, which secured more than $3 million in funding for construction projects to turn vacant houses into affordable housing. He has also worked for Neighborhood Legal Services, as well as sitting on the boards of directors and providing legal representation to non-profits including Buffalo Niagara River Keeper, Autistic Services Inc., and the City of Buffalo's Living Wage Commission. He received his undergraduate degree from SUNY College at Fredonia and his J.D. from Brooklyn Law School. He is married with two children and resides in Buffalo.

JOSEPH S SALADINO (R)
9th - Part of Nassau County

512 Park Blvd., Massapequa Park, NY 11762
516-541-4598/saladij@assembly.state.ny.us

Assemblyman Joseph Saladino was elected in a special election held in 2004. He is Chairman of the Minority Conference's Program Committee, and sits on the following standing committees: environmental conservation; governmental employees; labor; libraries and education technology; and ways and means. His legislative achievements include helping to sponsor and pass the current civil confinement law and fought for a newer and stronger Megan's Law. Prior to joining the Assembly, he had a career as a news anchor and reporter with Long Island's largest television and radio stations, was the Director of Operations for the Town of Oyster Bay and served as Executive Assistant for the Town of

Hempstead. He has been a member of the area Kiwanis Club for many years, where he has served as President, as well as numerous other community organizations. He attended Tulane University in New Orleans, LA and holds a master's degree from the New York Institute of Technology.

ANGELO SANTABARBARA (D-WP-I)
111th - Montgomery, Schenectady and Albany counties

2550 Riverfront Center, Amsterdam, NY 12010
518-843-0227/SantabarbaraA@assembly.state.ny.us

433 State Street, Schenectady, NY 12305
518-381-2941

Angelo Santabarbara was first elected to the New York State Assembly in 2012. He chairs the Subcommittee on Agriculture Economic Development and Farmland Protection, and also sits on the following committees: agriculture; energy; governmental employees; racing and wagering; small business; veterans' affairs. Professionally, he is an engineer. He was previously elected to the Schenectady County Legislature where he chaired the transportation committee. In addition, he sits on the Board of Directors for the Autism Society of the Greater Capital Region. He started a cheese-making company and donates all profits to local children's charities. Santabarbara, a lifelong resident of Schenectady County, served in the US Army Reserves and is commander of AMVETS Post 35. He holds a bachelor's degree from SUNY Albany and lives in Rotterdam with his wife and two children.

MICHELLE SCHIMEL (D)
16th - Part of Nassau County

45 N Station Plaza, Suite 203, Great Neck, NY 11021
516-482-6966/scmimelm@assembly.state.ny.us

Michelle Schimel was first elected to the New York State Assembly in 2007 to represent her Long Island district. She is Majority Conference Chair, and sits on the following committees: environmental conservation; governmental operations; local governments; transportation; and veterans' affairs. The full-time legislator is focused on preventing gun violence and protecting the environment. She has served on the board of New Yorkers Against Gun Violence for 20 years, co-chairs State Legislators Against Illegal Guns, and is a member of American State Legislators for Gun Violence. She helped to assemble -after the Newtown massacre - a broad coalition to create an eight-point plan against gun violence, many of which were part of the NY SAFE Act, considered one of the country's toughest gun-safety acts. Prior to her election to the Assembly, she served eight years as North Hempstead Town Clerk. She also is the former vice president of a Manhattan-based fashion accessories company, and she also worked as a physical therapist at North Shore University Hospital. She holds an undergraduate degree from the University of Pennsylvania. She is mother to two children.

ROBIN L SCHIMMINGER (D-I-C)
140th - Parts of Erie and Niagara Counties

3514 Delaware Ave, Kenmore, NY 14217
716-873-2540/ schimmr@assembly.state.ny.us

Robin Schimminger was elected to the New York State Assembly in 1976. He is chair of the Economic Development, Job Creation, Commerce and Industry committee. In addition, he sits on the following committees: codes; health; and ways and means. During his long tenure in the Assembly he has been the first Chair of the Committee on Small Business; chaired the Committee on Economic Development, Job Creation, Commerce and Industry, and also served on the joint Legislative Commission on Government Administration. His numerous legislative accomplishments - nearly 400 laws - include his Omnibus Procurement Act, which maximizes the opportunity for in-state firms to do business with New York State. Prior to his election to the Assembly, he was twice elected to the Erie County Legislature, in 1973 and 1975 where he chaired the Public Health Committee. He has served on the boards of numerous civic organizations. He is a co-founder of the Buffalo Dortmund Sister City Committee. Schimminger holds a B.A. from Canisius College, and also studied at the William Butler Yeats International School of Literature and the University College, Dublin. He holds a J.D. from NYU School of Law. He is married and lives in Kenmore.

REBECCA A SEAWRIGHT (D)
76th - Part of New York County

1365 First Ave., New York, NY 10021
212-288-4607/SeawrightR@assembly.state.ny.us

Rebecca Seawright was elected to the New York State Assembly in 2014 from a district that includes Manhattan's Upper East Side, Yorkville, and Roosevelt Island. She sits on the following committees: banks; consumer affairs and protection; corporations, authorities and commissions; judiciary; and tourism, parks, arts and sports development. She is former Assistant District Attorney in the Brooklyn DA's office and legal counselor to small business owners and entrepreneurs. She is also a former member of Community Planning Board 8. In addition, she is Chair of the Board of Visitors of CUNY School of Law, and Chair of the Board of Directors for the Feminist Press. Originally from Texas, Assemblywoman Seawright was state director of the National Women's Political Caucus, and Chief of Staff for Texas legislator Bob Melton. She also worked in Washington, DC for former U.S. Sen. Lloyd Bensten, and Congressmen Charles Stenholm and the late Marvin Leath. An Upper East Side resident for more than 20 years, she holds a law degree from CUNY Law School. She is the married mother of one.

LUIS R SEPÚLVEDA (D-WF)
87th - Part of Bronx County

1973 Westchester Avenue, Bronx, NY 10462
718-931-2620/SepulvedaL@assembly.state.ny.us

Luis R. Sepulveda was first elected to the New York State Assembly in 2012. He chairs the Subcommittee on Transitional Services, and sits on the following committees: aging; agriculture; banks; correction; and housing. His legislative efforts include protecting privacy, including legislation to restrain the use of drones, and developing a workforce education bill to help unemployed workers transition to new fields. An attorney by training, he has a community law practice in the Bronx's Parkchester area. He has been appointed counsel to several New York State Senators and to the New York State Senate Majority Counsel's office. Previously, he ran a pro bono project to provide free legal assistance to Bronx residents. He and State Sen. Ruben Diaz co-founded the Parkchester Public Initiative, the Castle Hill Community Public Safety Project, and the West Farms/Lambert House Public Safety Office. He holds a B.A. from Hofstra University and a J.D., also from Hofstra. He entered his law program after a fellowship with the Council on Legal Educational Opportunities. He is married with two children.

SHELDON SILVER (D)
65th - Part of New York County

250 Broadway, Ste 2234, New York, NY 10007
212-312-1420/http://assembly.state.ny.us/mem/?ad=065

Sheldon Silver was elected to the New York State Assembly in 1976. He served as Speaker of the New York State Assembly from 1994-2015. Among his legislative achievements was a 2011 effort, made in concert with the governor and Senate, to revamp the state tax code. In addition, through a comprehensive education initiative called LADDER, (Learning, Achieving, Developing By Directing Educational Resources), New York State established the nation's first pre-kindergarten program for all four-year olds. Silver also staved off efforts to end rent control, and successfully fought for passage of the Clinic Access and Anti-Stalking Act,

which ensures access to women's reproductive services and cracks down on violence against clinic workers. He saw the enactment of the Bias Crime Law, which combats violence associated with hatred, bigotry and prejudice. He holds a B.A. from Yeshiva University, and a J.D. from Brooklyn Law School. He resides on Manhattan's Lower East Side and is married with four children. He also has several grandchildren.

According to the *New York Times,* Silver was arrested on January 21, 2015 on extortion charges. On February 24, 2015, the *New York Observer* reported that Silver pleaded not guilty.

MICHAEL SIMANOWITZ (D)
27th - Part of Queens County

159-06 71st Ave, Flushing, NY 11365
718-969-1508/simanowitzm@assembly.state.ny.us

Michael Simanowitz was elected to the New York State Assembly in 2011 to a district that includes College Point, Forest Hills, Kew Gardens Hills, Electchester, Pomonok, Briarwood, Kew Gardens, and Richmond Hill. He chairs the Commission on Toxic Substances and Hazardous Wastes, and sits on the following committees: aging; agriculture; consumer affairs and protection; economic development, job creation, commerce and industry; higher education; and small business. His legislative successes include passing legislation that requires children under 18 to receive written parental consent prior to obtaining a body piercing. Prior to his election, he served as the Chief of Staff to Assemblywoman Nettie Mayersohn for over 15 years until her retirement. Professionally, Simanowitz also was a Planner and Community Liaison at New York City Housing Preservation and Development where he worked on several major developments in Brooklyn including the completion of MetroTech Center and Atlantic Terminal. During his tenure with Mayersohn, Assemblyman Simanowitz worked closely with the Assemblywoman Mayersohn and the New York State Department of Health to develop development of a pilot program establishing stroke centers in Queens and Brooklyn. The success of the program prompted an expansion to 110 hospitals across New York State. He holds a B.A. from Queens College and lives in Electchester Housing Cooperative with his wife and four children.

JO ANNE SIMON
52nd - Part of Kings County

341 Smith Street, Brooklyn, NY 11231
718-246-4889/simonj@assembly.state.ny.us

Jo Anne Simon was elected to the New York State Assembly in 2014 and sits on the following committees: consumer affairs and protection; higher education; judiciary; labor, and transportation. She established a disability civil rights firm following positions such as teaching in Hofstra University School of Law's clinical program, and is a nationally-recognized expert in her field. She is also an adjust Assistant Professor of Law at Fordham University. She is highly active in area Democratic, civic and community affairs, including as President of the Boerum Hill Association, and has founded or co-founded organizations such as Council of Brooklyn Neighborhoods, the Downtown Brooklyn Traffic Calming Task Force, and the Association on Higher Education and Disability, of which she is general counsel. She also chaired the Gowanus Community Stakeholder Group and Gowanus Expressway Community Coalition. She holds a B.A. in Communication Sciences from Iona College, a Master's Degree in Education of the Deaf from Gallaudet University; and a law degree from Fordham University School of Law. A Brooklyn resident since 1981, the Yonkers native lives in Boerum Hill, Brooklyn, with her husband.

Biographies

ARAVELLA SIMOTAS (D-WC)
36th - Part of Queens County

31-19 Newtown Avenue, Suite 401, Astoria, NY 11102
718-545-3889/simotasa@assembly.state.ny.us

Aravella Simotas was elected to the New York State Assembly in 2010, becoming the first woman elected to office in her district. She chairs the Task Force on Women's Issues and sits on the following standing committees: banks; corporations, authorities and commissions; consumer affairs and protection; and energy. Her legislative efforts have been aimed at promoting a revitalized New York economy, protecting neglected consumers, and strengthening the criminal justice system. Prior to her election to the New York State Assembly, Assemblywoman Simotas worked a as a district representative for New York City Council Speaker Peter F. Vallone, Sr. and Councilmember Peter F. Vallone, Jr. In addition, she worked for the New York State Department of Environmental Conservation during law school and collaborated with her predecessor, New York State Senator Michael Gianaris, in a battle to curb construction of additional power plants in western Queens. Professionally, she is an attorney who worked with the firm of Bickel & Brower and contributed her time to providing legal representation to those who could not afford it. She formerly served on the Queens Community Planning Board 1, as well as the boards of United Community Civic Association and the Hellenic Times Scholarship Fund. She holds a B.A. from Fordham University and a J.D. from Fordham Law School. She and her husband live in Astoria.

FRANK SKARTADOS (D)
104th - Dutchess and Orange counties

154 North Plank Road, Ste 2, Newburgh, NY 12550
845-562-0888/skartadosf@assembly.state.ny.us

Frank Skartados first served in the New York State Assembly from 2008-2010 then was elected again in a March 2012 special election. He sits on the following standing committees: agriculture; economic development, job creation, commerce and industry; local governments; small business; tourism, parks, arts and sports development; and transportation. Professionally, Skartados was a teacher and department chair at the New York Military Academy, and then focused on buying and renovating properties in downtown Poughkeepsie. He is founder and president of the Academy Street Business Association. In addition, he owns a small farm in Milton, NY. Assemblyman Skartados holds a bachelor's degree from SUNY New Paltz and a Master's degree in international studies from the State University of California at Sacramento. He was born in Greece and moved to the U.S. with his mother when he was 14.

JAMES SKOUFIS (D-I-WF)
99th - Orange and Rockland Counties

11 Main Street, Chester, NY 10918
845-469-6929/SkoufisJ@assembly.state.ny.us

James Skoufis was first elected to the New York State Assembly in 2012. He chairs the Subcommittee on Catastrophic Natural Disasters, and sits on the following standing committees: agriculture; local governments; insurance; labor; and transportation; and veterans' affairs. His legislative priorities include raising the minimum wage to $9 and creating tax penalties for corporations that ship jobs overseas. Prior to his election to the Assembly, Skoufis sat on the Woodbury Town Council, where he led the local relief effort for those impacted by Hurricane Irene. He also worked as a project manager for Amerigard Alarm and Security Corporation. He holds a B.A. from the George Washington University and an M.A. from Columbia University.

MICHAELLE C SOLAGES (D)
22nd - Parts of Nassau County

1690 Central Court, Valley Streanm BT 11580
516-599-2972/SolagesM@assembly.state.ny.us

Michaelle Solages was first elected to the New York State Assembly in 2012. Her Long Island district includes North Valley Stream, Valley Stream, South Floral Park, Floral Park, Bellarose Terrace, North Woodmere, Elmont, Stewart Manor, and parts of Franklin Square. She chairs the Subcommittee on Product Safety, and sits on the following standing committees: consumer affairs and protection; governmental employees; libraries and education technology; racing and wagering; and social services. Professionally, she has worked in libraries as a supervisor of access services at her alma mater, Hofstra University, from which she holds a bachelor's degree. She and her husband live in Elmont.

DAN STEC (R-C-I)
114th - Essex and Warren Counties, Parts of Saratoga and Washington Counties

140 Glen St., Glens Falls, NY 12801
518-792-4546/StecD@assembly.state.ny.us

7559 Court St., Rm. 203, PO Box 217, Elizabethtown, NY 12932
518-873-3803

Dan Stec was elected to the New York State Assembly in 2012. He is Ranking Minority member on the Committee on Environmental Conservation, and also sits on the following committees: banks; local governments; social services; and tourism, parks, arts and sports development. Assemblyman Stec has been outspoken on behalf of pension forfeiture for corrupt legislators. Prior to his election, Stec was Queensbury Town Supervisor - where he returned nearly $10 million to local taxpayers in rebates - and Chairman of the Warren County Board of Supervisors. He also sat on the Queensbury town council and zoning board. The Navy veteran served for eight years as a nuclear engineer aboard the USS Truxtun and was stationed in the Persian Gulf during Operation Desert Storm. He holds a BS from Clarkson University and an MBA from the University of Rhode Island. The married father of one lives in his hometown of Queensbury.

PHIL STECK (D)
110th - Parts of Schenectady and Albany Counties

1609 Union St., Schenectady, NY 12309
518-377-0902/SteckP@assembly.state.ny.us

Phil Steck was first elected to the New York State Assembly in 2012. He chairs the Subcommittee on Insurer Investments and Market Practices and also sits on the following committees: children and families; health; insurance; judiciary; and transportation. In the legislature, among the issues he backs are single-payer health insurance and raising revenue through the stock transfer tax to pay for rebuilding the infrastructure of Upstate New York. Prior to his election to the Assembly, Steck served on the Albany County Legislature for four terms. An attorney by profession, he is a civil rights and employment law specialist in the firm of Cooper, Erving and Savage LLP. He also spent two years as Assistant District Attorney in Rensselaer and New York counties. He holds an undergraduate degree from Harvard University and a JD from the University of Pennsylvania Law School. The married father of two lives in Loudonville.

AL STIRPE (D)
127th - Part of Onondaga County

7293 Buckley Rd., Ste. 201, N. Syracuse, NY 13212
315-452-1115/StirpeA@assembly.state.ny.us

Al Stirpe was elected to the New York State Assembly in 2012. He previously served in the Assembly from 2007-2010. He chairs the Subcommittee on Export Trade, and sits on the following standing committees: agriculture; alcoholism and drug abuse; economic development, job creation, commerce and industry; higher education; tourism, parks, arts and sports development. Prior to his most recent election, Stirpe served as Executive Director of Synapse Sustainability Trust, an environmental non-profit that Stirpe's leadership. Professionally, he worked for General Electric, then spun off a GE operation to form CID Technologies and became its CFO until the company was sold. Stirpe then formed a new venture, Qube Software Inc., and took it from startup to multi-million dollar business. He has received awards including the first SUNY Empire State College Excellence in Environmental Sustainability Awards. He holds an undergraduate degree from the University of Notre Dame and is the married father of one and stepfather to two.

JAMES N TEDISCO (R-I-C)
112th - Parts of Schenectady and Saratoga Counties

636 Plank Rd, Ste 101, Clifton Park, NY 12065
518-370-2812/tediscj@assembly.state.ny.us

James Tedisco was first elected to the Assembly in 1982 and served as Minority Leader from 2005 to 2009. He currently sits on the following committees: banks; economic development, job creation, commerce and industry; racing and wagering; and rules. Tedisco's legislative successes include ensuring the passage of Buster's Law to make animal cruelty - often a bridge crime - a felony; legislation to make the state go digital with communications - thereby reducing paper waste - and authoring the property tax cap bill, the Property Taxpayers Protection Act. Assemblyman Tedisco worked in education from 1973 to 1982 as a guidance counselor, varsity basketball coach and athletic director, special education teacher, and resource room instructor. He went on to become a Schenectady City Councilman. He is active in his community, and holds a B.A. from Union College and an MA in special education from the College of Saint Rose. He is the married father to a son.

CLAUDIA TENNEY (R-C-I)
101st - Parts of Oneida, Herkimer, Otsego, Delaware, Ulster, Sullivan and Orange counties

4747 Middle Settlement Road, Po Box 627, New Hartford, NY 13413
315-736-3879
/tenneyc@assembly.state.ny.us

Claudia Tenney was elected to the New York State Assembly in 2010. She sits on the following committees: banks; codes; education; social services; and veteran's affairs. Prior to her election, she served as legal counsel and chief of staff to former District 115 Assemblyman David Townsend. She is also co-owner and legal counsel for her family's printing and manufacturing business, Mid-York Press. She served as publisher and corporate counsel to Tenney Media Group that she established, which published free community newspapers founded by her parents and grandparents. She also has been a radio and television host in the area. In addition, she has worked for the Consulate General of Yugoslavia and was a partner in the firm of Groben, Gilroy, Oster, and Saunders. Her community service includes stints on boards such as the Mohawk Valley Community College Foundation Board. Her father was is the late Hon. John R. Tenney, Justice of the Supreme Court of New York in the Fifth Judicial District for more than 30 years. She holds an undergraduate degree from Colgate University and a J.D. from the Taft College of law at the University of Cincinnati and is mother to one.

FRED W THIELE, JR (D-I-WF)
1st - Part of Suffolk County

2302 Main Street, Box 3062, Bridgehampton, NY 11932
631-537-2583/thielef@assembly.state.ny.us

Fred Thiele was elected to the New York State Assembly in 1995 and represents a district at the end of Long Island.. He chairs the Committee on Small Business, and sits on the following committees: education; election law; environmental conservation; oversight, analysis and investigation; transportation; and ways and means. His legislative successes include drafting and sponsoring legislation that created the Peconic Bay Community Preservation Fund Act which authorized the five towns in

the region to establish dedicated funds, financed by a 2% real estate transfer tax, for land acquisition for open space, farmland, and historic preservation, as well as recreational purposes. This program was overwhelmingly approved in a public referendum in 1998 and has generated more than $150 million for land preservation efforts and has resulted in the preservation of thousands of acres of sensitive lands. He also has backed efforts to create Peconic County from Long Island's five easternmost towns, and has supported efforts to ensure fiscal responsibility at all levels of government. Prior to joining the Assembly, Theile was counsel to Assemblyman John Behan, then Southampton Town Attorney. In 1987 he served in the Suffolk County Legislature, and in 1991 he went on to become Southampton Town Supervisor. Thiele has been widely involved in legislative issues during his long tenure in the Assembly. For instance, he drafted and was a prime sponsor of legislation, which created the Peconic Bay Community Preservation Fund Act, Theile holds a B.A. from Long Island University, Southampton College, and a J.D. from Albany Law School. He is father to three and has lived in Sag Harbor for his entire life.

MATTHEW TITONE (D)
61st - Part of Richmond County

853 Forest Avenue, Staten Island, NY 10310
718-442-9932/ TitoneM@assembly.state.ny.us

Matthew Titone was first elected to the New York State Assembly during a special election in 2007. He chairs the Office of State-Federal Relations, and sits on the following standing committees: education; environmental conservation; health; judiciary; social services; and tourism, parks, arts and sports development. An attorney by profession, Titone has worked as a senior trial associate and managed the labor law litigation department for the Wall Street firm of Morgan, Melhuish, Monahan, Arvidson, Abrutyn & Lisowski. He left the firm in 1998 to open his own practice. He has provided pro bono services for many years. He serves on the Board of Directors of Community Health Action of Staten Island - formerly known as the Staten Island AIDS Task Force - and has also served on the Board of Trustees for Legal Services of New York. He also sits on the Board of Trustees for the Snug Harbor Cultural Center. He is the son of the Hon. Vito J. Titone and holds a law degree from St. John's University School of Law.

MICHELE R TITUS (D)
31st - Part of Queens County

131-17 Rockaway Blvd, South Ozone Park, NY 11420
718-322-4958

19-31 Mott Avenue, Far Rockaway, NY 11691
718-327-1845/titusm@state.ny.us

Michele Titus was elected to the New York State Assembly in 2002. She represents the communities of South Ozone Park, Springfield Gardens, Rosedale, Far Rockaway and Laurelton. Titus chairs the Committee on Labor, as well as the Legislative Women's Caucus. She also sits on the following standing committees: children and families; codes; education; ethics and guidance; and judiciary. Her legislative achievements include policy that would mandate after-school programs in every public school, expand early childhood education, and lower senior prescription costs. Prior to her election, Titus served as Chief of Staff to State Sen. Ada L. Smith, and then was Executive Director for the New York State Black and Puerto Rican Legislative Caucus. She also has been an attorney for the New York City Board of Education, the New York State Attorney General's Frauds Bureau, and the Integrity Bureau of the Queens County District Attorney's Office. She holds a B.A. from SUNY-Binghamton and a J.D. from Albany Law School. She lives in Queens with her husband and two children.

LATRICE MONIQUE WALKER (D)
55 - Part of Kings County

400 Rockaway Avenue, Brooklyn, NY 11212
718-498-8681/WalkerL@assembly.state.ny.us

Latrice Walker was elected to the New York State Assembly in 2014. She sits on the following committees: correction; economic development, job creation, commerce and industry; election law; energy; and housing. She previously served as Counsel to U.S. Rep. Yvette D. Clarke. She supports affordable housing while preserving and advocating on behalf of residents of the New York City Housing Authority. She is a founding member of the Ocean Hill-Brownsville Coalition of Young Professionals. She holds an undergraduate degree from SUNY Purchase College and a J.D. from Pace University, and is mother to one.

RAYMOND WALTER (R)
146th - Part of Erie County

5555 Main St, Williamsville, NY 14221
716-634-1895/ walterr@assembly.state.ny.us

Raymond Walter was elected to the New York State Assembly in 2011. His district includes the Towns of Amherst and Pendleton, and the Village of Williamsville. He sits on the following committees: economic development, job creation, commerce and industry; health; housing; insurance; and ways and means. An attorney by profession, Walter has worked for the law firm of Magavern Magavern Grimm LLP since 2007. While still in law school, he clerked for the US Attorney's Office and the Erie County District Attorney's Office. Assemblyman Walter also has a prior public service record; he was appointed and later elected to the Erie County Legislature. He remains active in his community, including sitting on the board for the Amherst Senior Citizens Foundation. He holds a B.A. from the University of New York College, Geneseo, and a J.D. from the SUNY School of Law, Buffalo. He lives in East Amherst with his wife and two children.

HELENE E WEINSTEIN (D)
41st - Part of Kings County

3520 Nostrand Ave, Brooklyn, NY 11229
718-648-4700/ weinsth@assembly.state.ny.us

Helene Weinstein was first elected to the New York State Assembly in 1980. Her district includes the Sheepshead Bay, Midwood, Flatlands, Canarsie, and East Flatbush communities in Brooklyn. She chairs the Committee on Judiciary - the first woman in the state to hold the position - and also sits on the following standing committees: aging; codes; rules; and ways and means. She has sponsored major reforms in the state's jury system and is the leading proponent of ensuring civil legal services for low-income New Yorkers. She is also a leading advocate for women, having chaired the Task Force on Women's Issues, and sponsored the Family Court Fair Access law of 2008, a reform measure that expanded access to civil orders of protection to domestic violence victims in dating and intimate relationships. Other major state laws she has sponsored include a law declaring surrogate parenting contracts void and against public policy and a rape shield extension law to protect crime victims. She has held a number of significant posts and has received numerous awards. Her civic involvement includes sitting on the board of the Center for Women in Government. She holds a B.A. from American University and a J.D. from New England School of Law.

DAVID I WEPRIN (D)
24th - Part of Queens County

185-06 Union Turnpike, Fresh Meadows, NY11366
718-454-3027/weprind@assembly.state.ny.us

111-12 Atlantic Avenue, #5, Richmond Hill, NY 11419
718-805-2384

David Weprin was elected to the New York State Assembly in 2010 and now represents the same district his father, the late Assembly Speaker Saul Weprin, represented for 23 years. His brother Mark Weprin spent more than 15 years in the same seat. Weprin chairs the Task Force for People With Disabilities and sits on the following committees: banks; cities; codes; election law; judiciary; and ways and means. Professionally, Weprin spent many years in the financial services industry. From 1983 to 1987, he was Deputy Superintendent of Banks and Secretary of the Banking Board for New York State, an appointment made by former Gov. Mario Cuomo. As Deputy Superintendent, he advised the Banking Department on the formulation of banking standards, and exercised power to approve or disapprove the issuance of bank charters and licenses and the establishment of branch banks. His elected public service began when he was elected to the New York City Council in 2001. He holds a BA from SUNY-Albany and a JD from Hofstra University. He and his wife are parents to five children.

CARRIE WOERNER (D)
113 - Saratoga and Washington counties.

112 Spring Street, Suite 109; Saratoga Springs, NY 12866;
518-584-5493/woernerc@assembly.state.ny.us

Carrie Woerner was elected to the New York State Assembly in 2014. She sits on the following committees: agriculture; local governments; racing and watering; small business; and tourism, parks, arts and sports development. She is Vice President and General Manager of MeetMax Conference Software, a division of The Wall Street Transcript, and established the software division in Saratoga Springs in 2008. She has also worked for Dell/Perot systems and IMB. She is the former Executive Director of the Saratoga Springs Preservation Foundation, where she expanded the organization, published a walking tour guide, and secured $130 in state funding to restore historic buildings in the Beekman Street Arts District. She also founded the Historic Saratoga Race Track Preservation Coalition. She served as a Round Lake Village Trustee for three terms, and is a member of the Town of Malta Planning Board. She holds a bachelor's degree from Carnegie Mellon University and a master's degree from Santa Clara University.

ANGELA M WOZNIAK (R)
143 - Erie County

2562 Walden Avenue, Suite 102, Cheektowaga, NY 14225
716-686-0080/wozniaka@assembly.state.ny.us

Angela M. Wozniak was first elected to the New York State Assembly in 2014 from a district that includes the Towns of Cheektowaga and Lancaster and the Village of Depew. She sits on the following committees: aging; children and families; cities; labor; and local governments. Prior to her election, she sat on the Town Council for the Town of Cheektowaga starting in 2011, where she advocated on behalf of tax and ethics reform, as well as term limits and school board consolidation. She operates The Angela Wozniak Insurance Agency. She holds a degree in business management from D'Youville College. She and her husband are parents to one.

KEITH L T WRIGHT (D)
70th - Part of New York County

163 W 125th St, Ste 911, Adam Clayton Powell Jr Bldg, New York, NY 10027
212-866-5809/wrightk@assembly.state.ny.us

Keith Wright was first elected to the Assembly in 1992. He currently chairs the Committee on Housing. He served as Assistant Majority Whip from 1998-2012, and is also the former chair of the Committee on Labor. He also sits on the following committees: codes; correction; rules; and ways and means. He has held previous committee chairmanships, including the election law, social services, and labor committees. In his current capacity, he has authored numerous pieces of legislation to strengthen the rights of tenants against unscrupulous landlords. Prior to his election to the Assembly, the lifelong Harlem resident held positions in the New York City Human Resources Administration, the Manhattan Borough President's Office, and the New York City Transit Authority. Wright holds a MA from Tufts University, and a JD from Rutgers University. He is the married father of two children and the son of the late New York Supreme Court Justice Bruce Wright.

KENNETH ZEBROWSKI (D)
96th - Rockland County

67 North Main St, New City, NY 10956
845-634-9791/zebrowskik@assembly.state.ny.us

Ken Zebrowski was first elected to the New York State Assembly on May 1, 2007 during a special election held to fill the seat of his late father, Assemblyman Kenneth P Zebrowski. He currently chairs the Commission on Administrative Regulations Review, and he sits on the following standing committees: codes; environmental conservation; ethics and guidance; governmental employees; judiciary; and labor. His legislative efforts have been aimed at recuing unfunded mandates, cutting government waste, fostering business and job growth, keeping seniors' prescription costs down, and protecting youth athletes from concussions. Prior to his election, Zebrowski served in the Rockland County Legislature. He founded the law firm of Zebrowski & Zebrowski with his father, and is currently of counsel to the New City law firm of Braunfotel & Frendel, LLC. He holds a B.A. from SUNY-Albany and a JD from Seton Hall University School of Law.

US SENATE: NEW YORK DELEGATION

KIRSTEN E GILLIBRAND (D)

478 Russell Senate Office Building, Washington, DC 20510
202-224-4451/fax: 202-228-0282/www.gillibrand.senate.gov

780 Third Avenue, Suite 2601, New York, NY 10017
212-688-6262/fax: 866-824-6340

P.O. Box 893, Mahopac, NY 10541
845-875-4585/fax: 845-875-9099

Kenneth B. Keating Federal Building, 100 State Street, Room 4195,
Rochester, NY 14614
585-263-6250/fax: 585-263-6247

James M. Hanley Federal Building, 100 S. Clinton Street, Room 1470,
PO Box 7378, Syracuse, NY 13261
315-448-0470/fax: 315-448-0476

155 Pinelawn Road, Suite 250 North, Melville, NY 11747
631-249-2825/fax: 631-249-2847

P.O. Box 273, Lowville, NY 13367
315-376-6118/fax: 315-376-6118

Leo W. O'Brien Federal Building, 11A Clinton Square, Room 821, Albany, NY 12207
518-431-0120/fax: 518-431-0128

Larkin at Exchange, 726 Exchange Street, Suite 511, Buffalo, NY, 14210
716-854-9725/fax: 716-854-9731

Kirsten E. Gillibrand was sworn in as United States Senator from New York in January 2009, filling the seat that opened up when former Secretary of State, Hillary Rodham Clinton, first took the diplomatic post. Gillibrand was subsequently re-elected in 2012. In the Senate, Gillibrand has focused on transparency, even posting her personal tax returns online, and worked to repeal "Don't Ask Don't Tell," the policy that bans gays from serving openly in the military. She sits on the Agriculture, Nutrition and Forestry Committee - New York's first senator to do so in almost 40 years - and also sits on the Senate Armed Services Committee, the Committee on Environment and Public Works, and the Special Committee on Aging. Her legislative agenda puts middle class and working families first, and her FAMILY Act would create a national paid leave program for all workers. Prior to her service in the Senate, Gillibrand served in the United States House of Representatives, representing New York's 20th Congressional District, after being elected to the post in 2006. An attorney by profession, she served as Special Counsel to then-U.S. Secretary of Housing and Urban Development, current New York Gov. Andrew Cuomo. She received her undergraduate degree from Dartmouth College, and earned her law degree from the UCLA School of Law and clerked in the Second Circuit Court of Appeals. The Upstate native is married with two children and lives in Brunswick.

CHARLES E SCHUMER (D)

322 Hart Senate Office Bldg, Washington, DC 20510
202-224-6542/http:// schumer.senate.gov

780 3rd Ave, Ste 2301, New York, NY 10017
212-486-4430

Leo O'Brien Bldg, Rm 420, Albany, NY 12207
518-431-4070

15 Henry St, Rm 100 A-F, Binghamton, NY 13901
607-772-6792

130 S Elmwood Ave, #660, Buffalo, NY 14202
716-846-4111

One Park Place, Ste 100, Peekskill, NY 10566
914-734-1532

145 Pine Lawn Road, #300, Melville, NY 11747
631-753-0978

100 State St, Rm 3040, Rochester, NY 14614
585-263-5866

100 S. Clinton St, Rm 841, Syracuse, NY 13261
315-423-5471

In 1998, Charles E. Schumer was elected to the U.S. Senate; he became New York's senior senator when Senator Daniel Patrick Moynihan retired in 2000. Senator Schumer is the Ranking Member of the Senate Rules Committee, which oversees federal elections, voting rights, campaign finance, and the operation of the Senate complex. In addition, Senator Schumer sits on the following committees: banking, housing and urban affairs; finance; judiciary; and the Joint Committee on the Library. Senator Schumer also sits on the Joint Committee on the Library, Joint Committee on Printing, and the U.S. Senate Caucus on International Narcotics Control. Senator Schumer continues the tradition he began in his first term: visiting each of New York's 62 counties each year. His achievements have included bringing affordable air service to Upstate New York and the Hudson Valley and securing over $20 billion in aid to New York City following the attacks on September 11, 2001. He authored legislation that eliminated barriers that delay low-cost generic medications from entering the marketplace. In the Senate, he is the Chairman of the Democratic Policy and Communications Center. Prior to serving in the Senate, the Brooklyn-born Schumer was elected to the U.S. House of Representatives where he served from 1980-1998 and represented Brooklyn and Queens. He also served six years in the New York State Assembly. He holds both a BA and a JD from Harvard University, and is the married father of two children.

US HOUSE OF REPRESENTATIVES: NEW YORK DELEGATION

YVETTE D CLARKE (D)
9th - Part of Kings County

2351 Rayburn House Office Building, Washington, DC 20515
202-225-6231/clarke.house.gov

123 Linden Boulevard, 4th Floor, Brooklyn, NY 11226
718-287-1142

Yvette D Clarke was first elected to the US House of Representatives in 2006. She represents the 9th Congressional District which includes the communities of Brownsville, Crown Heights, East Flatbush, Flatbush, Gerritsen Beach, Madison, Midwood, Ocean Hill, Park Slope and Flatlands, Prospect Heights, Prospect-Lefferts Gardens, Sheepshead Bay, and Windsor Terrace. She sits on the following committees: energy and commerce - including three of its subcommittees - and the Ethics Committee. In Congress, Clarke has secured funding for major Brooklyn institutions including the Brooklyn Botanic Garden and the Brooklyn Public Library. Prior to being elected to Congress, she served three terms in the New York City Council and chaired the Contracts Committee and co-chaired the New York City Women's Caucus. Professionally, her positions included Director of Business Development for the Bronx Empowerment Zone. The Brooklyn native is a graduate of Oberlin College.

CHRIS COLLINS (R)
27th - Parts of Erie, Niagara, Orleans, Genesee, Wyoming, Monroe, Livingston and Ontario Counties

1117 Longworth House Office Building, Washington, DC 20515
202-225-5265/chriscollins.house.gov

128 Main St., Geneseo, NY 14454
585-519-4002

2813 Wehrle Dr., Ste 13, Williamsville, NY 14221
716-634-2324

Chris Collins was first elected to the U.S. House of Representatives in 2012 and represents a large Western New York/Finger Lakes district. He sits on the Energy and Commerce Committee and three of its subcommittees. Prior to his election to Congress, Collins was elected Erie County Executive at a time the county was in dire fiscal shape and operated under a state-imposed control board. In four years, the county's saw its debt reduced by more than $120 million, a cash surplus created of more than $100 million, the infrastructure and recreational facilities were reopened; the county workforce was reduced by 22 %, and the control board was gone within 18 months. He began his career with Westinghouse Electric. He holds a BS in mechanical engineering from NC State and an MBA in Finance from the University of Alabama - Birmingham. He is the married father of three, and grandfather of three.

JOSEPH CROWLEY (D)
14th - Parts of Bronx and Queens Counties

1436 Longworth House Office Building, Washington, DC 20515
202-225-3965/Crowley.house.gov

82-11 37th Avenue, Ste 402, Queens, NY 11372
718-779-1400

2800 Bruckner Blvd, Ste 201, Bronx, NY 10465
718-931-1400

Joseph Crowley was first elected to the US House of Representatives in November 1998.. He sits on the powerful Ways and Means Committee, as well as two of its subcommittees, and is the Vice Chair of the Democratic Caucus. In Congress, Rep. Crowley has focused on building strong communities, creating jobs, protecting senior benefits, and increasing educational opportunities for working families. Rep. Crowley, who lost a cousin who was a first responder on 9/11, authored the 9/11 Heroes Medal of Valor Act, passed unanimously in the House and Senate, which calls for a special Public Safety Office Medal of Valor, honored rescue workers who died while responding to the terrorist attacks. Congressman Crowley also has advocated for New York City's Homeland Security requirements, and led the creation of the Urban Area Security Initiative that targets homeland security funding to at-risk urban centers. Prior to his election to Congress, Crowley ran a successful small business and sat in the New York State Assembly for 12 years. He holds an undergraduate degree from Queens College. He is the married father of three.

DANIEL DONOVAN, JR (R)
11th - Richmond County

1725 Longworth HOB, Washington, DC 20515
(202) 225-3371/https://Donovan.house.gov

Daniel M. Donovan Jr. was elected to the U.S. House of Representatives on May 5, 2015, and was sworn in to office one week later. Prior to his election, he was District Attorney for Richmond County for 12 years, and, prior to that, he was Deputy Borough President for Staten Island. He began his professional career an assistant to longtime New York District Attorney Robert M. Morgenthau in Manhattan for a number of years after he graduated from law school. Then, Rep. Donovan became Chief of Staff to then-Richmond County Borough President Guy V. Molinari prior to being appointed Deputy Borough President. He is active in professional circles, having been elected President of the New York State District Attorney's Association, as well as the New York State Director for the National District Attorneys Association. He holds a B.A. from St. John's University and a J.D. from Fordham University School of Law.

ELIOT L ENGEL (D)
16th - Parts of Bronx and Westchester Counties

2162 Rayburn House Office Bldg, Washington, DC 20515
202-225-2464/engle.house.gov

3655 Johnson Ave, Bronx, NY 10463
718-796-9700

177 Dreiser Loop, Room 3, Bronx, NY 10475
718-320-2314

6 Gramatan Ave, Ste 205, Mt Vernon, NY 10550
914-699-4100

Eliot Engel was first elected to the US House of Representatives in 1988. He is the Ranking Member of the House Foreign Affairs Committee. In addition, he serves on the Energy and Commerce Committee including the Subcommittee on Health, and the Subcommittee on Energy and Power. He founded and co-chairs the House Oil and National Security Caucus, focused on clean and energy-efficient alternatives to oil, and he serves on the Commission on Human Rights. He created the Dependence Reduction through Innovation in Vehicles and Energy (DRIVE) Act to help reduce American dependence on imported oil, and saw many of its provisions signed into law as part of the energy bill signed in 2007. In addition, he authored the ALS Registry Act to establish a national registry for the collection and storage of data on people suffering from ALS. Prior to his election to Congress, Engel was a teacher and guidance counselor in the New York City public school system and then served twelve years in the New York State Assembly (1977-1988). He holds an undergraduate degree from Hunter College and a Master's degree from Herman H. Lehman College of the City University of New York. He also holds a JD from New York Law School. He and his wife have three children.

CHRIS GIBSON (R)
19th - Delaware, Columbia, Greene, Otsego, Rensselaer, Sullivan, Schoharie, Ulster, and Dutchess Counties

1708 Longworth House Office Bldg, Washington, DC 20515
202-225-5614/http://gibson.house.gov/

721 Broadway, Kingston, NY 12401
845-514-2322

2 Hudson St, PO Box 775, Kinderhook, NY 12106
518-610-8133

92 Sullivan Avenue, PO Box 578, Ferndale, NY 12754
845-747-9261

111 Main Street, Delhi, NY 13753
607-746-9537

25 Chestnut Street; Cooperstown, NY 13326
(607) 282-4002

92 Sullivan Avenue, PO Box 578, Ferndale, NY 12754
(845) 747-9261

4328 Albany Post Road, Hyde Park, NY 12538
845-698-0132

Chris Gibson was elected to the US House of Representatives in 2010. He sits on the House Armed Services Committee (Subcommittees on Readiness and Emerging Threats and Capabilities), the House Agriculture Committee and the House Small Business Committee. Prior to being elected to Congress, Gibson served in the U.S. Army for 24 years, rising to the rank of Colonel. He was deployed seven times, including four combat tours to Iraq, and separate deployments to Kosovo, and the Southwestern U.S. for a counter-drug operation. Most recently, he was deployed to Haiti where he commanded the 82nd Airborne Division's 2nd Brigade Combat Team during the opening month of a humanitarian relief operation. Other key assignments included tours teaching American Politics at the United States Military Academy at West Point, serving as a Congressional Fellow with US Representative Jerry Lewis (R-CA), the Chairman of the Defense Appropriations Subcommittee, and completing a Hoover National Security Affairs Fellowship at Stanford University. He holds an undergraduate degree from Siena College, an MPA and a PhD from Cornell University. In addition, he is the author of Securing the State, a 2008 book on national security decision-making. He and his wife are parents to three.

RICHARD HANNA (R)
22nd - Broome, Chenango, Cortland, Herkimer, Madison, Oneida, Ontario, Otsego, and Tioga Counties

319 Cannon House Office Bldg, Washington, DC 20515
202-225-3665/http://hanna.house.gov/

258 Genesee St, Utica, NY 13502
315-724-9740

49 Court St., Ste. 230, Binghamton, NY 13901
607-723-0212

Congressman Richard Hanna was elected to the US House of Representatives in 2010. He sits on the Transportation and Infrastructure Committee, as well as the Committee on Small Business. He is also a member of a number of subcommittees, including the Subcommittee on Railroads, Pipelines, and Hazardous Material, the Subcommittee on Highways and Transit, and the Subcommittee on Aviation. Prior to his election, he was president of Hanna Construction, which has grown from the small company Hanna founded to one that employed more than 450 people and handled multi-million dollar commercial and municipal projects in Upstate New York. Hanna is a licensed pilot with high performance and seaplane certifications. He has been deeply involved in his community, including ten years of service on the board of The Community Founda-

tion of Herkimer and Oneida Counties, Inc., including two years as the board chairperson. He graduated from Reed College in Portland, Oregon, and is the married father of two.

Hanna holds an undergraduate degree from Reed College and is the married father of two.

BRIAN M. HIGGINS (D)
27th - Parts of Niagara and Erie Counties

2459 Rayburn House Office Bldg, Washington, DC 20515
202-225-3306

726 Exchange St., Ste. 601, Buffalo, NY 14210
716-852-3501

640 Park Place, Niagara Falls, NY 14301
716-282-1274

Brian Higgins was first elected to the US House of Representatives in 2004. His district includes most or all of the cities of Buffalo, Lackawanna, Niagara Falls, North Tonawanda and Tonawanda, as well as a number of towns and villages in the area. He serves on the Committee on Homeland Security - where he is Ranking Member of the Subcommittee on Counterterrorism and Intelligence - and the Committee on Foreign Affairs. He formerly sat on the powerful Ways and Means Committee but stepped down due to a realignment of seats. He will re-join the committee when a seat opens up. In Congress, Higgins was instrumental in securing at $279 million settlement from the New York Power Authority that is earmarked for development along Buffalo's inner and outer harbor fronts. Prior to his election, Higgins sat on the New York State Assembly for four years, and prior to that he was a member of the Buffalo Common Council. He was an instructor at Buffalo State College, where he earned an undergraduate degree. He also holds a MA in public policy and administration from Harvard University's Kennedy School. He and his wife have two children.

STEVE ISRAEL (D)
3rd - Parts of Nassau, Suffolk, and Queens Counties

2457 Rayburn House Office Bldg, Washington, DC 20515
202-225-3335/http://www.house.gov/israel

534 Broad Hollow Road, Ste 302, Melville, NY 11747
631-777-7391/Suffolk
516-505-1448/Nassau/718-875-1675/Queens

Steve Israel was first elected to the US House of Representatives in November 2000. His district includes northeast Queens and the townships of, North Hempstead, Oyster Bay, Huntington and Smithtown. He sits on the Appropriations Committee and two of its subcommittees: defense; and interior, environment, and related agencies. He is the sixth ranking member of the House Democratic Leadership, serving as Chair of Policy & Communications where he focuses on middle-class economic security and opportunity. He served as the Chairman of the Democratic Congressional Campaign Committee from 2011-2015. Among his achievements is funding the U.S.-Israel Energy Cooperation Act and the Advanced Research Projects Agency for Energy; launching an initiative to require full ingredient labeling on household cleaning products; and an advocate of tax code revisions to reflect regional variations in cost-of-living. Prior to his election to Congress, Israel was an elected member of the Huntington Town Board and Congressional aide. He holds an undergraduate degree from George Washington University and an AA from Nassau Community College. He and his wife have two children.

HAKEEM JEFFRIES (D)
8th - Parts of Kings County and Southwest Queens

1607 Longworth HOB, Washington, DC 20515
202-225-5936/Jeffries.house.gov

56 Hanson Place, Ste 603, Brooklyn, NY 11217
718-237-2211

445 Neptune Ave, First Floor, Brooklyn, NY 11224
718-373-0033

Hakeem Jeffries was first elected to the U.S. House of Representatives in 2012 and sits on the Education and the Workforce Committee and the Judiciary Committee, a two subcommittees of each Senate committee. In addition, he is Congressional Black Caucus Whip, and a member of the Democratic Caucus Steering and Policy Committee. He opposes turning Social Security and Medicare cuts and backed measures to help those impacted by Superstorm Sandy. Prior to his election to Congress, Jeffries spent six years in the New York State Assembly. His legislative successes there included a 2010 law that prohibits the New York Police Department from keeping electronic data on people stopped, questioned and frisked - but not charged - during an encounter with police.. An attorney by profession, Jeffries clerked for Hon. Harold Baer Jr. of the U.S. District Court for the Southern District of New York, and then entered private practice, including as counsel in the litigation departments for Viacom Inc. and CBS. He holds a BA from SUNY-Binghamton, a master's in public policy from Georgetown University, and a JD from New York University Law School. He is married with two children.

JOHN KATKO (R)
24th - Onondaga, Cayuga, Wayne and Oswego counties

1123 Longworth House Office Building, Washington, DC 20515, (202) 225-3701/https://katko.house.gov

71 Genesee St., Auburn, NY 13021, (315) 253-4068

7376 State Route 31, Lyons, NY 14489

13 W. Oneida St., 2nd Floor, Oswego, NY 13126

440 South Warren St., 7th Floor Suite 711, Syracuse, NY 13202, (315) 423-5657

John Katko was elected to the US House of Representatives in 2014. He sits on the Homeland Security Committee and two of its subcommittees, including the Subcommittee on Transportation Security of which is he chair. In addition, he sits on the Transportation and Infrastructure Committee and three of its subcommittees. Professionally, he served as Assistant District Attorney. He began his professional career in Washington, DC, where he worked in private practice, then joined the US Securities and Exchange Commission as a Senior Trial Attorney. He went on to become an Assistant U.S. Attorney at the U.S. Dept. of Justice for 20 years, practicing in Virginia, Texas, and Puerto Rico early in his career as a federal prosecutor with the Dept. of Justice's Criminal Division, Narcotics & Dangerous Drug Section. He went on to move back to his upstate New York roots with his family, and prosecuted organized crime in the Northern District of New York for 15 years. He has lectured at Syracuse University College of Law and at Cornell Law School, and has led attorney trainings for criminal investigations and prosecutions around the world. He holds an undergraduate degree from Niagara University and a J.D. from Syracuse University College of Law. He remains active in his community, and he and his wife are parents to three children.

PETER T KING (R)
2nd - Parts of Nassau and Suffolk counties

339 Cannon House Office Bldg, Washington, DC 20515
202-225-7896/peteking.house,gov

1003 Park Blvd, Massapequa Park, NY 11762
516-541-4225

Peter King was first elected to the US House of Representatives in 1992. His Long Island district includes the Townships of Hempstead, Oyster Bay, Baylon, Islip, and much of Fire Island National Seashore. He sits on the Homeland Security Committee, which he previously chaired, as well

as its subcommittee on counterterrorism and intelligence, which he chairs. He also serves on the Financial Services Committee and the Permanent Select Committee on Intelligence. King successfully fought to secure $60.4 million emergency funding for Hurricane Sandy victims. He began his political career in November 1977 by winning election to the Hempstead Town Council. Subsequently, he was elected to three terms as Comptroller of Nassau County. Prior to entering public service, he was a practicing attorney. He holds an undergraduate degree from St. Francis College in Brooklyn and a JD from the University of Notre Dame Law School. He and his wife have two children and two grandchildren.

NITA M LOWEY (D)
17th - Parts of Rockland and Westchester Counties

2365 Rayburn House Office Bldg, Washington, DC 20515
202-225-6506/http://lowey.house.gov

222 Mamaroneck Ave, Ste 310, White Plains, NY 10605
914-428-1707

67 North Main St., Ste 101, New City, NY 10956
845-639-3485

Nita Lowey was first elected to the US House of Representatives in 1988. She is the Ranking Democrat on the powerful House Appropriations Committee, the first woman to lead either party on the committee. She is also Ranking Democrat on the State and Foreign Operations Subcommittee. . During her long tenure in Congress, Lowey has had numerous successes, from helping to secure $20 billion recovery money after the 9/11 terrorist attacks to helping to obtain $68 million in federal funding to develop local bioterrorism response plans and equip first responders. She has defended the National Endowment for the Arts, and authored the first-ever bill to mandate clear and concise food allergen labeling. On the Appropriations Committee, she advocates on behalf of increased federal funding for biomedical research into diseases such as cancer, diabetes and Alzheimer's at the National Institute of Health. She is the former Chair of the Congressional Women's Caucus. Prior to her election to Congress, she was the State of New York's Assistant Secretary of State. She holds an undergraduate degree from Mount Holyoke College, and is the married mother of three children and eight grandchildren.

CAROLYN B MALONEY (D)
12th = Manhattan, Queens, Brooklyn

Carolyn B. Maloney was first elected to the US House of Representatives in 1992. She sits on the House Financial Services Committee and the House Oversight and Government Reform Committee. In addition, she is Vice Chair of the House Democrats' Steering and Policy Committee, and former Chair of the Joint Economic Committee. Her legislative achievements include the Credit Cardholders' Bill of Rights, signed by President Obama in 2009. She co-founded the House 9/11 Commission Caucus, working to write and pass legislation to implement the 9/11 Commission's recommendations for improved intelligence gathering, as well as the James Zadroga 9/11 Health Care and Compensation Act, signed in 2011, to provide health care and compensation for 9/11 first responders. She has also helped pass legislation to target the 'demand' side of sex trafficking and increased funding for law enforcement to process DNA rape kids, among other strong efforts on behalf of women and women's health. She began her professional career as a community affairs coordinator for the New York City board of education welfare education program, and went on to work for the New York State Assembly and Senate, and sit on the New York City Council. She holds an undergraduate degree from Greensboro College.

SEAN P MALONEY (D)
18th - Orange, Rockland, Putnam, Dutchess and Westchester Counties

1529 Longworth House Office Building, Washington, DC 20515
202-225-5441/seanmaloney.house.gov

123 Grand St., 2nd Floor, Newburgh, NY 12550
845-561-12550

Sean Maloney was first elected to the U.S. House of Representatives in 2012 from his Hudson Valley district. He serves on the House Agriculture Committee, the Transportation and Infrastructure Committee and three of its subcommittees. Prior to his election he was a senior advisor to President Bill Clinton, a post he left to build a high-tech startup. He also has been a senior staff member to two Democratic governors from New York. He holds both a BA and a JD from the University of Virginia and is the married father of three.

GREGORY W MEEKS (D)
5th - Part of Queens County

2324 Rayburn House Office Bldg, Washington, DC 20515
202-225-3461/ http://meeks.house.gov/

153-01 Jamaica Avenue, 2nd Floor, Jamaica, NY 11432
718-725-6000

67-12, Far Rockaway, Rockaway Beach Blvd., Arverne, NY 11692
347-230-4032

Gregory W Meeks was first elected to the US House of Representatives in 1998. He is a senior member of the House Financial Services Committee and serves on two of its committees. He also serves on the House Foreign Affairs Committee where he is Ranking Member of the Subcommittee on Europe and Eurasia and Emerging Threats, and also sits on the Subcommittee on the Western Hemisphere. He works to promote policies that strengthen the United States's economic and national security and build relationships with other nations in an increasingly globalized world, and co-chairs the Brazil Caucus and Columbia Caucus in the House of Representatives, as well as the Organization of American States Caucus. He holds undergraduate degrees from Adelphi University and a JD from Howard University Law School. He is the married father of three.

GRACE MENG (D)
6th - Part of Queens County

1317 Longworth HOB, Washington, DC 20515
202-225-2601
meng.house.gov

40-13 159th Street, Flushing, NY 11358
718-358-MENG

118-35 Queens Boulevard, 17th Floor, Forest Hills, NY 11375
718-358-MENG

Grace Meng was first elected to the U.S. House of Representatives in 2012, New York's first Asian American member of Congress. She sits on two standing legislative committees, the House Foreign Affairs Committee and the House Small Business Committee and two of its subcommittees, Agriculture, Energy and Trade, and Contracting and Workforce, where she is the Ranking Member. In the former committee's subcommittee structure, she sits on the Subcommittee on Asia and the Pacific, and the Subcommittee on The Middle East and North Africa. She also founded and co-chairs the bipartisan Kids' Safety Caucus. Prior to her election to Congress, Meng served in the New York State Assembly. Prior to entering elective office, she was a public interest attorney. She holds an undergraduate degree from the University of Michigan and a JD from Yeshiva University's Benjamin Cardozo School of Law. She is the married mother of two.

JERROLD L NADLER (D)
10th - Parts of New York and Kings Counties

2109 Rayburn House Office Bldg, Washington, DC 20515
202-225-5635/ http://nadler.house.gov

445 6605 Fort Hamilton Pkwy, Brooklyn, NY 11219
718-373-3198

201 Varick St, Ste 669, New York, NY 10014
212-367-7350

Jerrold "Jerry" Nadler was first elected to the U.S. House of Representatives in 1992. His district includes much of the West Side of Manhattan, the Financial District as well as a diverse group of Brooklyn neighborhoods. He is a member of the powerful Judiciary Committee, and also the Transportation and Infrastructure Committee. He sits on two subcommittees of the each standing committee, and has been either Chair or Ranking Member of the Judiciary Subcommittee on the Constitution and Civil Justice. He is also the Ranking Democrat on the Subcommittee on Courts, Intellectual Property and the Internet. He is an Assistant Democrat Whip. Nadler's district includes Ground Zero, the site where the World Trade Center towers collapsed during the 9/11 terrorist attacks. After the attacks, he was instrumental in securing $20 billion in federal funds to rebuild Lower Manhattan. He has also been instrumental in addressing the health and environmental impacts of the collapse on first responders and area residents, workers and students. He also has advocated on behalf of increased funding for New York's mass transit system. Prior to becoming a Congressman, Nadler was a member of the New York State Assembly for 16 years. He also was a member of Community Planning Board 7 in Manhattan. He graduated from Columbia University and holds a JD from Fordham University Law School. He is the married father of one.

CHARLES B RANGEL (D)
13th - Part of New York and Bronx counties

2354 Rayburn House Office Bldg, Washington, DC 20515
202-225-4365/ http://rangel.house.gov/

163 W 125th St, Ste 737, New York, NY 10027
212-663-3900

Charles Rangel was first elected to the U.S. House of Representatives in 1970. His district includes Central and East Harlem, Manhattanville, Morningside Heights, Hamilton Heights, Washington Heights, Inwood, Marble Hill and the Bronx neighborhoods of Kingsbridge, Norwood, Bedford Park, Fordham, and University Heights. He is currently senior member of the powerful Ways and Means Committee, a committee he formerly chaired starting in 2007. At that time, he was the first African American to chair the committee. In addition, he is a founding member of the Congressional Black Caucus. Rep. Rangel's Congressional achievements are many over the years, and examples include authoring the Empowerment Zone program that provides $3.5 billion for urban and rural development; expanding the earned income tax credit; spearheading a program that generates investment in low- and moderate-income housing construction and rehabilitation; and numerous programs investing in the arts, healthcare facilities, and community programs. He also led efforts to award a Congressional Gold Medal on behalf of the Tuskegee Airmen. He served in the US Army from 1948 to 1952 in Korea, earned a BS from New York University School of Commerce in 1957 and a JD from St John's University School of Law. He served as assistant US Attorney in the Southern District of New York, and later served as General Counsel to the National Advisory Commission on Selective Service. In 1967, he was elected to the New York State Assembly. He is the married father of two.

TOM REED III (R)

23rd - Allegany, Cattaraugus, Chatauqua, Chemung, Ontario, Schuyler, Seneca, Steuben, Tioga, Tompkins, and Yates Counties

2437 Rayburn House Office Building, Washington, DC 20515
202-225-3161/http://reed.house.gov/

89 W. Market Street, Corning, NY 14830
607-654-7566

One Bluebird Square, Olean, NY 14760
716-379-8434

433 Exchange St., Geneva, NY 14456
315-759-5229

2 East 2nd St, Suite 300, Jamestown, NY 14701
716-379-8434

401 E. State St. Suite 304-1, Ithacan, NY 14850
607-222-2027

Congressman Tom Reed was elected to the U.S. House of Representatives in 2010. Since 2011, he has sat on the powerful Committee on Ways and Means and three of its subcommittees: Human Resources; Select Revenue Measures; and Social Security. He also co-chairs the House Manufacturing Caucus and the Congressional Natural Gas Caucus, and is Vice Chair of the Congressional Diabetes Caucus. An attorney by profession, he opened a private practice as well as other real estate and mortgage brokerage businesses. He served one term as Mayor of Corning. He graduated from Alfred University and holds a JD from the Ohio Northern University College of Law. He is the married father of two.

KATHLEEN M RICE (D)

4th - Nassau County

1508 Longworth H.O.B., Washington, DC 20515
(202) 225-5516/https://kathleenrice.house.gov

300 Garden City Plaza Suite 200, Garden City, NY 11530
(516) 739-3008

Kathleen M. Rice was elected to the U.S. House of Representatives in 2014. She serves on the Homeland Security Committee and is Ranking Member on the Subcommittee on Transportation Security, one of the Committee's three subcommittees on which she sits. She also sits on the Veterans' Affairs Committee and two of its subcommittees. Prior to being elected to Congress, she was Nassau County District Attorney from 2006-2014, becoming Long Island's first DA and focusing on combatting drunk driving. Her professional life began as an Assistant District Attorney in Brooklyn, and she also served as Assistant U.S. Attorney in Philadelphia. She holds a J.D. from Touro Law Center and a B.A. from Catholic University.

JOSÉ E SERRANO (D)

15th - Part of Bronx County

2227 Rayburn House Office Bldg, Washington, DC 20515
202-225-4361/Serrano.house.gov

1231 Lafayette Ave, 4th Fl, Bronx, NY 10474
718-620-0084

José E Serrano was first elected to the U.S. House of Representatives in 1990. His Bronx district includes the neighborhoods of Mott Haven, Hunts Point, Melrose, High Bridge, Morrisania, East Tremont, Tremont, Morris Heights, University Heights, Belmont, Fordham, Bedford Park, West Farms, the Longwood Avenue Historic District, and parts of Soundview. He sits on the House Appropriations Committee and three of its subcommittees; he is Ranking Member of the Subcommittee on Financial Services and General Government. He is Senior Whip for the Majority Whip operation, and an active member of the Congressional

Hispanic Caucus, which he formerly chaired. As an appropriator, Serrano has secured millions of dollars in federal funding for his Bronx district; perhaps the most significant project has been the environmental restoration of the Bronx River. He also proposed the bill, signed into law as part of a larger bill, which grants posthumous citizenship to non-citizens who died because of the 9/11 attack and who had already initiated the process to become US citizens. He served in the New York State Assembly from 1975-1990 1990, and also served on the New York City Board of Education. He served in the US Army Medical Corps. The Mayaguez, Puerto Rico-born Serrano holds an undergraduate degree from Lehman College of CUNY and is married with five children.

LOUISE MCINTOSH SLAUGHTER (D)

25th - Monroe County

2469 Rayburn House Office Bldg, Washington, DC 20515
202-225-3615/ louise.house.gov

3120 Federal Bldg, 100 State St, Rochester, NY 14614
585-232-4850

Louise McIntosh Slaughter was first elected to the U.S. House of Representatives in 1986, the first woman to represent western New York, and serves as the Ranking Member of the Rules Committee, which she formerly chaired - also the first woman to do so. As chair of this committee, she helped shepherd legislation such as the Affordable Care Act. Her legislative achievements also include establishing the Office of Research on Women's Health at NIH, as well as allocating the first $500 million in federal funding at NIH. She co-authored the Violence Against Women Act in 1994. She opposes free trade agreements, believing those have caused Rochester business serious harm and led to widespread hardship in local communities. She successfully passed the STOCK Act, which outlawed insider trading by members of Congress and their staffs. She served in the Monroe County Legislature from 1976 to 1979 and in the New York State Assembly from 1982 to 1986. She attended the University of Kentucky, where she received a BS degree in Microbiology and a Master of Science degree in Public Health; she is the only microbiologist in Congress. She was married for 57 years to the late Robert Bruce Slaughter, Jr.; they are parents to three children and grandparents to seven.

ELISE STEFANIK (R)

21 - Jefferson, Lewis, St. Lawrence, Franklin, Hamilton, Herkimer, Fulton, Saratoga, Washington, Warren, Essex, Clinton and Franklin counties

512 Cannon House Office Building, Washington, DC 20515, (202) 225-4611/https://stefanik.house.gov

136 Glen Street, Glens Falls, NY 12801
518-743-0964

23 Durkee Street Suite C, Plattsburgh, NY 12901
518-561-2324

120 Washington St. Suite 200, Watertown, NY 13601
(315) 782-3150

Elise Stefanik was first elected to the U.S. House of Representatives in 2014; at the time of her swearing she was the youngest Congresswoman in history. She serves on the Armed Services Committee and three of its subcommittees, and on the Education and the Workforce Committee, and two of its subcommittees. She also served as the Freshman Representative to the Policy Committee.

She served on President George W. Bush's Domestic Police Council staff and in the Chief of Staff's office. She has served in a number of positions such as Vice President of Debate Prep for candidate Paul Ryan, and Director of Communications for the Foreign Policy Initiative which launched Defending Defense, a coalition of think tanks warning of the dangers of the sequester. Prior to being elected to Congress, she worked for Premium Plywood Products, Inc., her family business. She graduated from Harvard University.

PAUL TONKO (D)
20th - Albany, Montgomery, Rensselaer, Saratoga and Schenectady Counties

2463 Rayburn House Office Building, Washington, DC 20515
202-225-5076/ tonko.house.gov

61 Columbia St, 4th Fl, Albany, NY 12210
518-465-0700

105 Jay Street, Rm 15, Schenectady, NY 12305
518-374-4547

61 Church St, Room 309, Amsterdam, NY 12010
518-843-3400

Paul Tonko was elected to his first term in the U.S. House of Representatives in 2008. His district includes the communities of Albany, Schenectady, Troy, Saratoga Springs, and Amsterdam. He sits on the Energy and Commerce Committee and three of its subcommittees including the Subcommittee on Environment and the Economy of which he is Ranking Member. He also sits on the Science, Space and Technology Committee and one of its subcommittees. Among his recent legislation is a proposal to ask the Energy Dept. to carry out a research, development, and technology demonstration program to improve the efficiency of gas turbines used in power generation systems and to identify the technologies that will lead to gas turbine combined cycle efficiency of 65 percent or simple cycle efficiency of 50 percent. He holds a BA in mechanical and industrial engineering from Clarkson University.

NYDIA M VELAZQUEZ (D)
7th - Parts of New York, Queens and Kings Counties

2302 Rayburn House Office Bldg, Washington, DC 20515
202-225-2361/velazquez.house.gov

266 Broadway, Ste 201, Brooklyn, NY 11211
718-599-3658

500 Pearl Street, Ste 973, New York, NY 10007
212-619-2606

16 Court Street, Ste 1006, Brooklyn, NY 11241
718-222-5819

Nydia Velazquez was first elected to the U.S. House of Representatives in 1992. She is the Ranking Member of the House Small Business Committee and a senior member of the Financial Services Committee; she sits on two of the latter committee's subcommittees. The Yabucoa, Puerto Rico-born Velazquez was the first Puerto Rican woman elected to the U.S. House of Representatives, the first Hispanic woman to serve as Ranking Member of a full House Committee, and the first Latina to chair a full Congressional committee, the latter achievement coming in 2006 when she chaired the House Small Business Committee. She is a former teacher of Puerto Rican Studies at CUNY's Hunter College, former Special Assistant to Congressman Edolphus Towns, and the New York City Council's first Latina member. She also was the Director of the Department of Puerto Rican Community Affairs in the U.S. She holds a degree from the University of Puerto Rico in Rio Piedras, and a master's degree from NYU. She is married.

LEE M. ZELDIN (R)
1st - Suffolk County

1517 Longworth House Office Building, Washington, DC 20515
(202) 225-3826/https://zeldin.house.gove

31 Oak Street Suite 20, Patchogue, NY 11772, (631) 289-1097

Lee Zeldin was first elected to the U.S. House of Representatives in 2014 from a district at the east end of Long Island. He sits on the Foreign Affairs Committee and three of its subcommittees; the Transportation and Infrastructure Committee and three of its subcommittees; the Veterans' Affairs Committee, and two of its subcommittees; and the Transportation & Infrastructure Committee. He served in the New York State Senate from 2010-2014, where he chaired the Consumer Protection Committee. His legislative achievements included securing funding for the PFC Joseph Dwyer Program, a state-wide program that helps veterans cope with post-traumatic stress disorder, or PTSD, and traumatic brain injury (TBI). He also wrote the law to protect fallen veterans and their families from protests and military burials. Rep. Zeldin spent four years on active duty in the US Army, including a 2006 deployment to Iraq. He is a major in the US Army Reserves, an attorney by profession, and holds a BA from SUNY-Albany and a JD from Albany Law School. He is the married father of two.

APPENDICES

CASH DISBURSEMENTS BY FUNCTION
ALL GOVERNMENTAL FUNDS
(thousands of dollars)

	FY 2014 Actuals	FY 2015 Current	FY 2016 Proposed	FY 2017 Projected	FY 2018 Projected	FY 2019 Projected
ECONOMIC DEVELOPMENT AND GOVERNMENT OVERSIGHT						
Agriculture and Markets, Department of	93,470	108,556	96,248	95,697	96,075	96,142
Alcoholic Beverage Control, Division of	17,986	17,537	17,394	17,551	17,728	17,728
Economic Development Capital	11,358	14,000	14,000	23,000	23,000	23,000
Economic Development, Department of	88,537	118,310	102,421	88,219	87,419	87,419
Empire State Development Corporation	553,490	563,042	776,623	875,311	834,199	844,628
Energy Research and Development Authority	34,463	30,458	22,600	25,000	13,500	13,000
Financial Services, Department of	504,094	508,165	376,585	377,233	379,038	379,170
Olympic Regional Development Authority	4,134	10,061	10,661	3,161	3,161	3,161
Public Service Department	70,481	74,639	75,248	76,134	77,514	78,913
Regional Economic Development Program	172	1,500	1,500	1,500	1,500	1,500
Strategic Investment Program	1,899	5,000	5,000	5,000	5,000	5,000
Functional Total	1,380,084	1,451,268	1,498,280	1,587,806	1,538,134	1,549,661
PARKS AND THE ENVIRONMENT						
Adirondack Park Agency	4,294	4,642	4,680	4,680	4,680	4,680
Environmental Conservation, Department of	1,016,286	887,132	898,490	867,557	821,298	778,607
Hudson River Park Trust	10,008	0	0	0	0	0
Parks, Recreation and Historic Preservation, Office of	341,451	292,325	319,797	331,929	329,104	324,104
Functional Total	1,372,039	1,184,099	1,222,967	1,204,166	1,155,082	1,107,391
TRANSPORTATION						
Metropolitan Transportation Authority	62,519	183,229	559,651	395,440	254,400	335,440
Motor Vehicles, Department of	305,726	309,282	305,144	306,686	307,028	309,635
Thruway Authority, New York State	22,497	25,800	23,300	23,300	23,300	23,300
Transportation, Department of	8,562,904	9,033,521	9,151,742	9,559,476	9,869,248	9,790,638
Functional Total	8,953,646	9,551,832	10,039,837	10,284,902	10,453,976	10,459,013
HEALTH						
Aging, Office for the	217,583	222,045	227,339	233,014	238,087	243,287
Health, Department of	46,197,507	49,022,314	54,396,330	56,924,989	59,939,713	61,725,894
Medical Assistance	39,971,486	43,580,643	46,978,635	48,327,280	51,166,674	52,811,464
Basic Health Plan	0	0	1,678,851	2,659,379	2,730,314	2,809,542
Medicaid Administration	1,259,009	1,382,902	1,315,767	1,350,640	1,388,960	1,403,360
Public Health	4,967,012	4,058,769	4,423,077	4,587,690	4,653,765	4,701,528
Medicaid Inspector General, Office of the	53,441	56,702	53,702	53,486	53,486	53,486
Stem Cell and Innovation	32,571	31,785	29,785	37,390	37,390	37,390
Functional Total	46,501,102	49,332,846	54,707,156	57,248,879	60,268,676	62,060,057
SOCIAL WELFARE						
Children and Family Services, Office of	2,856,400	3,122,317	3,236,552	3,294,342	3,591,936	3,594,861
OCFS	2,768,218	3,037,020	3,149,778	3,206,168	3,502,367	3,505,463
OCFS - Other	88,182	85,297	86,774	88,174	89,569	89,398
Housing and Community Renewal, Division of	237,170	238,735	247,973	280,798	287,541	292,707
Human Rights, Division of	15,592	13,620	14,266	14,266	14,329	14,383
Labor, Department of	666,793	606,839	566,955	570,589	576,755	576,755
National and Community Service	19,619	14,909	14,909	14,909	16,029	16,335
Temporary and Disability Assistance, Office of	5,671,389	5,422,963	5,026,891	5,077,999	5,085,488	5,103,459
Welfare Assistance	4,414,284	4,159,039	3,735,199	3,745,199	3,754,699	3,763,699
All Other	1,257,105	1,263,924	1,291,692	1,332,800	1,330,789	1,339,760
Functional Total	9,466,963	9,419,383	9,107,546	9,252,903	9,572,078	9,598,500
MENTAL HYGIENE						
Alcoholism and Substance Abuse Services, Office of	559,538	578,143	600,592	618,922	640,646	654,675
OASAS	477,011	495,925	515,736	536,147	556,760	569,164
OASAS - Other	82,527	82,218	84,856	82,775	83,886	85,511
Developmental Disabilities Planning Council	3,148	4,200	4,200	4,200	4,200	4,200
Justice Center	32,264	38,553	42,590	43,836	45,233	46,842
Mental Health, Office of	3,259,553	3,336,368	3,349,484	3,469,140	3,619,884	3,748,530
OMH	1,454,842	1,491,713	1,562,405	1,639,374	1,727,693	1,793,693
OMH - Other	1,804,711	1,844,655	1,787,079	1,829,766	1,892,191	1,954,837
Mental Hygiene, Department of	312	0	0	0	0	0
People with Developmental Disabilities, Office for	3,450,583	3,509,832	3,155,585	3,158,613	3,538,975	3,723,507
OPWDD	496,778	510,315	272,667	467,667	417,667	417,667
OPWDD - Other	2,953,805	2,999,517	2,882,918	2,690,946	3,121,308	3,305,840
Quality of Care and Advocacy for Persons With Disabilities, Commission on	4,333	0	0	0	0	0
Functional Total	7,309,731	7,467,096	7,152,451	7,294,711	7,848,938	8,177,754
PUBLIC PROTECTION/CRIMINAL JUSTICE						
Correction, Commission of	2,101	2,651	2,651	2,651	2,651	2,651
Correctional Services, Department of	2,838,898	2,893,649	2,934,494	2,885,173	2,897,177	2,897,177
Criminal Justice Services, Division of	227,237	254,215	226,095	226,396	226,396	226,396
Disaster Assistance	33,106	(22,580)	0	0	0	0
Homeland Security and Emergency Services, Division of	1,983,938	2,615,197	2,368,337	1,603,675	1,066,007	752,927
Indigent Legal Services, Office of	54,584	51,917	67,917	105,867	104,467	104,467
Judicial Conduct, Commission on	5,165	5,484	5,484	5,484	5,484	5,543
Judicial Nomination, Commission on	45	30	30	30	30	30

CASH DISBURSEMENTS BY FUNCTION
ALL GOVERNMENTAL FUNDS
(thousands of dollars)

	FY 2014 Actuals	FY 2015 Current	FY 2016 Proposed	FY 2017 Projected	FY 2018 Projected	FY 2019 Projected
Judicial Screening Committees, New York State	50	38	38	38	38	38
Military and Naval Affairs, Division of	83,405	134,083	111,249	104,750	89,559	90,030
State Police, Division of	685,293	690,170	713,192	709,670	698,362	699,962
Statewide Financial System	52,390	32,396	30,137	29,711	29,717	29,717
Victim Services, Office of	63,881	66,908	68,820	68,830	68,830	68,830
Functional Total	6,030,093	6,724,158	6,528,444	5,742,275	5,188,718	4,877,768
HIGHER EDUCATION						
City University of New York	1,471,374	1,538,424	1,542,341	1,548,335	1,581,345	1,625,339
Higher Education - Miscellaneous	366	1,300	1,300	1,300	1,300	1,300
Higher Education Facilities Capital Matching Grants Program	8,353	7,000	15,000	25,000	35,000	37,900
Higher Education Services Corporation, New York State	1,064,910	1,091,710	1,144,875	1,202,482	1,236,290	1,253,290
State University of New York	8,128,157	8,135,806	7,908,377	7,955,703	8,010,639	8,121,557
Functional Total	10,673,160	10,774,240	10,611,893	10,732,820	10,864,574	11,039,386
EDUCATION						
Arts, Council on the	27,009	61,053	45,953	45,953	45,953	45,953
Education, Department of	29,895,193	31,232,351	32,856,537	33,959,507	35,208,126	36,596,010
School Aid	23,001,609	24,282,603	26,066,280	27,220,069	28,349,278	29,655,515
STAR Property Tax Relief	3,356,792	3,374,375	3,230,679	3,216,244	3,157,192	3,097,632
Special Education Categorical Programs	2,210,604	2,292,500	2,279,650	2,378,500	2,500,400	2,630,800
All Other	1,326,188	1,282,873	1,279,928	1,144,694	1,201,256	1,212,063
Functional Total	29,922,202	31,293,404	32,902,490	34,005,460	35,254,079	36,641,963
GENERAL GOVERNMENT						
Budget, Division of the	30,760	30,905	30,393	30,495	30,596	30,596
Civil Service, Department of	13,275	12,980	13,395	13,381	13,381	13,507
Deferred Compensation Board	689	854	855	866	866	866
Elections, State Board of	10,614	29,584	9,484	12,404	13,404	137,509
Employee Relations, Office of	2,282	2,581	2,581	2,581	2,581	2,601
Gaming Commission, New York State	151,546	175,552	206,934	177,943	232,841	232,841
General Services, Office of	249,445	277,590	280,160	275,484	297,799	248,729
Inspector General, Office of the	6,434	6,917	6,917	6,917	6,917	6,977
Labor Management Committees	19,637	25,356	35,356	45,356	35,356	35,356
Prevention of Domestic Violence, Office for	2,076	2,281	2,281	2,281	2,281	2,281
Public Employment Relations Board	3,333	3,731	3,731	3,572	3,573	3,604
Public Integrity, Commission on	3,610	4,331	4,331	4,331	4,331	4,376
State, Department of	136,090	139,662	130,230	127,211	126,161	126,161
Tax Appeals, Division of	2,818	3,040	3,040	3,040	3,040	3,040
Taxation and Finance, Department of	368,773	363,537	357,323	358,476	358,778	358,778
Technology, Office for	238,467	461,955	652,562	565,891	552,861	541,022
Veterans' Affairs, Division of	13,084	15,824	15,713	15,546	15,546	15,631
Welfare Inspector General, Office of	355	972	972	972	972	986
Workers' Compensation Board	200,986	197,474	198,558	205,278	212,232	214,015
Functional Total	1,454,274	1,755,126	1,954,816	1,852,025	1,913,516	1,978,876
ELECTED OFFICIALS						
Audit and Control, Department of	171,989	175,086	174,968	174,511	174,622	174,683
Executive Chamber	13,673	13,578	13,578	13,578	13,578	13,578
Judiciary	2,598,591	2,707,603	2,783,379	2,839,053	2,887,153	2,922,153
Law, Department of	212,783	222,236	228,778	232,320	233,374	235,116
Legislature	207,984	218,795	218,795	218,795	218,795	218,795
Lieutenant Governor, Office of the	427	614	614	614	614	614
Functional Total	3,205,447	3,337,912	3,420,112	3,478,871	3,528,136	3,564,939
LOCAL GOVERNMENT ASSISTANCE						
Aid and Incentives for Municipalities	718,950	737,009	738,161	757,428	762,608	763,430
Efficiency Incentive Grants Program	4,987	3,230	0	0	0	0
Miscellaneous Financial Assistance	4,873	7,798	400	800	0	0
Municipalities with VLT Facilities	27,246	29,331	27,246	27,246	27,246	27,246
Small Government Assistance	217	218	218	218	218	218
Functional Total	756,273	777,586	766,025	785,692	790,072	790,894
ALL OTHER CATEGORIES						
General State Charges	4,045,490	4,120,307	4,484,431	4,990,847	5,265,170	5,547,141
Long-Term Debt Service	6,437,053	5,876,109	5,573,037	6,330,436	6,771,258	7,033,601
Miscellaneous	18,931	(63,494)	26,983	69,132	351,863	592,036
Functional Total	10,501,474	9,932,922	10,084,451	11,390,415	12,388,291	13,172,778
TOTAL ALL GOVERNMENTAL FUNDS SPENDING	137,526,488	143,001,872	149,996,468	154,860,925	160,764,270	165,018,980

GSC: Agency disbursements include grants to local governments, state operations and general state charges, which is a departure from prior Financial plan publications. In prior reports, general state charges were excluded from agency spending totals.

Note: This information is excerpted from the New York State FY 2016 Executive Budget Financial Plan. All Governmental Funds combines activity in the four governmental fund types: General Fund; Special Revenue Funds; Capital Projects Funds; and Debt Service Funds.

Name Index

Aaron, Merik A., 55
Aaron, Stewart D, 218
Aarons, Sharon, 48
Abate, Catherine, 183, 259
Abbate, Jr, Peter J, 28, 36, 38, 40, 244, 620
Abbate, Jr., Peter, 35
Abbate, Richard D, 135
Abbate, Richard D., 375
Abbatti, Amy, 477
Abbitt, Viola I, 253
Abbott, Mark, 440
Abdallah, Jill, 30
Abdelaal, Hany, 446
Abdelazim, Tarik, 344
Abdus-Salaam, Sheila, 45
Abercrombie, Neil, 320
Abernethy, David, 412
Abernethy, Samuel F, 93
Abesamis-Mendoza, Noilyn, 384
Abinanti, Thomas, 28, 36, 37, 38, 39, 40, 125
Abinanti, Thomas J, 620
Abitabilo, Neil, 453
Abraham, Thomas W, 598
Abram, Brian C, 132
Abrams, Barry, 359
Abrams, James, 597
Abrams, James F, 574
Abrams, Karl G, 332
Abrams, Kristin, 453
Abrams, Laura A, 332
Abrams, William, 206
Abramson, Jill, 530
Abreu, Rafael E., 490
Acampora, Patricia L, 12
Accetta, Joseph, 60
Achille, Anthony, 399
Achramovitch, Steven, 575
Acker, Ruth, 140
Ackerbauer, Bill, 527
Ackerman, Gary, 321, 322
Ackerman, Gary L, 313, 321, 322
Ackerman, Todd, 525
Ackerson, Anne, 128, 281
Ackley, Denise, 506
Acosta, Rolando T, 45
Acquario, Adam, 472
Acquario, Stephen, 385
Acquario, Stephen J, 172, 240
Acquaro, Ralph, 581
Adabbo, Joseph, 22
Adair, Jeffrey R, 333
Adair, Scott, 107, 290
Adam, William, 466
Adamis, Tony, 528
Adams, Ann M, 592
Adams, Christopher, 181, 225

Adams, Diane, 179
Adams, Eric, 483
Adams, Eric R, 53
Adams, Gina F., 485
Adams, Kendra, 294
Adams, Kenneth, 92
Adams, Mary, 58, 449
Adams, Michelle, 91, 193
Adams, Rachel A., 46
Adams, Rachel Amy, 49
Adams, Roger W, 574
Adams, Thomas, 212
Adams, Thomas A., 47
Adams, Toby, 74
Adams-Keane, Helen, 380
Adams-Sarthou, Anna, 386
Addabbo Jr, Joseph P, 16, 20, 22, 24, 25, 608
Addabbo Jr., Joseph, 21, 25
Addabbo, Jr, Joseph, 277
Addabbo, Jr, Joseph P, 297
Addabbo, Jr., Joseph, 268
Addepalli, Raj, 142
Addison, Sharon, 369
Aderholt, Robert, 73
Aderholt, Robert B, 319
Adjei, Anthony K., 486
Adler, Anna, 472
Adler, Harold, 49
Adler, Leah, 479
Adler, Lester B, 47
Adler, M.D., Karl P, 561
Adler, Sol, 379
Adler, Stephen J., 535
Adolf, Jay, 441
Adolf, Maureen E., 460
Adolphus, Stephen H, 551
Aefsky, Fern, 574
Affronti, Francis A, 47
Agans, Barbara, 64
Agard, Michele D, 99, 212
Agarwal, Prince, 497
Agate, Augustus C, 47
Aghili, Mansour, 286
Agin, Susan, 399
Agins, Bruce D, 175
Aglieco, Rose Z., 504
Agostaro, Rosario, 597
Agostine, Jr, Joseph A, 194
Agostino, Aprilanne, 45
Agostino, Tom, 204, 223
Agrawal, Rajendra, 177
Agruso, Susan, 594
Ahern, Gary, 450
Ahern, John T., 492
Ahl, Caroline, 6, 236, 242
Ahlers, Kate, 358

Ahmad, Iftikhar, 360
Ahrens, Betty, 460
Aidala, Gregory J, 591
Aiello, Greg, 282
Aiello, Kathleen, 56
Aiken, Doris, 119
Aiken, Robert, 237, 247, 248, 266
Aikens, Patricia, 118, 219
Ailes, Elizabeth, 530
Aimer, Alicia, 460
Aina, Eileen, 135
Aini, Cheryl, 78, 178
Ainlay, Stephen C, 564
Aison, Howard M, 61
Aitken, David, 408
Ajemian, Peter, 18
Akaka, Daniel, 318
Akaka, Daniel K, 317
Akilova, Zlata, 499
Akin, W Todd, 320
Alabi, Olanike T., 488
Alagno, Louis, 353
Alazraki, Marcia, 441
Albanese, Anthony R, 574
Albano, Teresa, 529
Albee, Amy, 269
Albert, Andrew, 521
Albert, John P, 127
Albert, Patricia, 203, 221
Albert, Sam, 489
Albert, Thomas, 416
Alberti, Peter P, 335
Albrecht, Greg, 70
Albrecht, Kathy, 30
Albro, George, 385
Albunio, Catherine, 345
Alch, Bruce, 142
Alden, Amie, 333
Aldous, Ken, 149, 177
Aldrich, Dale, 472
Alegre, Nathalie, 431
Alejandro, Joseph A., 495
Alessandrino, Daniel M., 46
Alessandro, Francis M, 49
Alexander, Catherine, 301
Alexander, Emily, 449
Alexander, Joe, 400
Alexander, Kevin W, 517
Alexander, Lamar, 126, 144, 181, 226, 257, 314, 316, 317
Alexander, Lanny R, 359
Alexander, Louis, 8, 148
Alexander, Paul, 21, 22
Alexander, Rodney, 551
Alexander, Valerie, 60
Alexandre-Bakiriddin, Joan M., 491
Alfieri, Joseph, 457

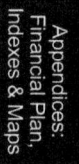

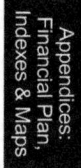

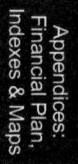

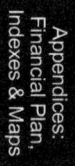

Name Index

Higgins, Christopher, 22, 24
Higgins, Jennifer, 396
Higgins, John J, 249
Higgins, Marilyn, 457
Higgins, Mark D, 204, 223
Higgins, Shelley, 505
High, Raymond, 398
Hikind, Dov, 27, 31, 630
Hilchey, Duncan, 74
Hild, Amy M, 136
Hilderbrant, Chris, 397
Hilenski, Karen, 460
Hill, Catharine B, 564
Hill, Edwin D., 490
Hill, Elizabeth, 434
Hill, Elizabeth A, 563
Hill, J. Tomlinson, 388
Hill, Jeffrey L, 426
Hill, Michael T., 215
Hill, Peter, 476
Hill, Sally, 505
Hill, Sara, 545
Hille, Anne, 417
Hiller, Amanda, 13, 87, 267
Hiller, Edward, 202, 221
Hillerman, Stephen, 12, 164, 238
Hillman, Hilary, 132
Hillman, Linda, 516
Hilly, Mary Ellen, 452
Hiltbrand, Robert, 273
Hilton, Beth A, 515
Hilton, Kenneth H, 596
Himes, Christine L, 130, 263
Hinchey, Maurice D, 313, 319, 323, 326
Hinckley, Robert R, 395
Hinds, Jinella, 494
Hinds-Radix, Sylvia C., 45
Hine, Christian, 453
Hines Kramer, Amy, 386
Hines, Evan, 358
Hines, Kelly, 451
Hines, Mary, 8, 242
Hines, Victoria, 473
Hiney, Barbara, 446
Hinkemeyer, Arlene, 436
Hinkson, Susan M, 360
Hinojosa, Rub,n, 320
Hinrichs, C. Randall, 47
Hinrichs, C.ÆRandall, 212
Hirsch Riback, Melanie, 29
Hirsch, David, 472
Hirsch, Fred J., 60
Hirsch, Larry, 487
Hirsch, Michelle, 204, 223
Hirschstein, Cary, 429
Hirsh, John, 538
Historical Society, Lewis County, 333
Hitchcock, Kent, 448
Hitt, Carrie, 469
Ho, Wayne, 384
Ho, Wayne H, 259

Hoag, Bonnie, 157
Hoag, Gail, 515
Hoagland, Wayne, 453
Hoar, Thomas, 496
Hoare, Frank, 416
Hobbs, Gary C, 62
Hoberman, Brian, 360
Hobson, Mike, 452
Hobson, Tracy, 258
Hochbrueckner, George, 420
Hochbrunn, Stephen, 310
Hochman, Jere, 599
Hochreiter, Joseph E, 572
Hochul, Jr., William J., 116, 215
Hochul, Kathleen C, 3, 162, 607
Hockens, Nick, 423
Hodell, Raymond, 485
Hodes, Nancy L, 428
Hodges, Elizabeth, 381
Hodges, Mary C, 59
Hodgetts, Colleen, 465
Hodgkins, Christie, 394
Hodin-Baier, Ali, 354
Hodun, Susan, 595
Hoekstra, Peter, 326
Hofer, Andrew P, 80
Hoffa, James P., 485
Hoffer, Mark D, 356
Hoffman, Andrew K., 490
Hoffman, Diana, 71
Hoffman, Douglas, 50
Hoffman, Douglas E., 46, 50
Hoffman, James, 341, 581
Hoffman, Jennifer, 398
Hoffman, Jeremy, 411
Hoffman, Jerry S, 478
Hoffman, Linda, 261
Hoffman, Maria, 30
Hoffman, Peter, 35
Hoffman, Richard, 58
Hoffman, Robert W, 65
Hoffmeister, Mark, 460
Hoffnung, Ari, 355
Hogan, Carla, 423
Hogan, Elizabeth C, 7
Hogan, John J, 584
Hogan, John M., 490
Hogan, Joseph, 384
Hogan, Kathleen B, 340
Hogan, Shawn D., 376
Hogan, William F., 4, 174, 229, 252
Hoganbruen, Matt, 386
Hogarty, Lisa, 472
Hoglund, Robert, 403
Hohlt, Barbaraen, 452
Hohlt, Jared, 535
Holahan, Paul, 365
Holbrook, Elizabeth, 56
Holcomb, Betty, 397
Holcomb, Grant, 473
Holcomb, Julie Conley, 350

Holden, Maria, 121
Holden, Ross J, 101, 124
Holden, Tim, 319
Holdener, Richard E, 347
Holder, Annika, 359
Holder, David, 277, 397
Holdorf, Armin, 202, 221
Holford, Donald, 199
Holland, Karen, 381
Holland, Steve, 535
Hollar, Rick, 476
Hollenbaugh, Lindsey, 527
Hollenbeck, Lee A, 133
Holliday, Susan, 535
Holliday, Terrance, 360
Hollie, Ronald D, 48
Hollis, Richard, 131
Hollister, William, 450
Hollmen, Linda, 111
Holloway, Cas, 354
Holloway, Lew, 311
Holly, Tim, 536
Hollyer, A Rene, 218
Holman, Evelyn B, 593
Holman, Kathryn, 395
Holman, Marcia, 235
Holman, Mark, 463
Holmes Norton, Eleanor, 192, 325
Holmes, Angela, 344
Holmes, Grace, 182
Holmes, M Frances, 169, 198
Holmes, Steve, 201, 235
Holst, Stephen L, 187
Holt, Rush, 144
Holtby, Tammey, 156
Holtby, Tammy, 73
Holtz, Mary F, 345
Holtzclaw, Derek, 253
Holtzer, Russell, 399
Holzer, Edith, 401
Hom, Vincent, 192
Homans, John, 535
Hong, Chung-Wha, 201, 429
Honorof, Alan L, 48
Hood, Elizabeth, 121
Hood, Jr., Jay, 337
Hood, Kelley S, 134
Hooker, Patrick, 3, 69
Hooks, William J, 105, 166, 213, 311
Hooley, Richard M, 588
Hooper, Earlene, 27, 31, 37, 41, 43, 630
Hoose, Matthew J., 335
Hoose, Michael J, 592
Hooton, Angela, 449
Hoover, Barbara, 452
Hope Davis, Tracy, 216
Hope, Judith, 485
Hopkins, John, 528, 529
Hopkins, Kathryn D, 55
Hopkins, Theodore L, 327
Horan, Allison, 31

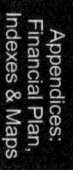

Organization Index

Includes the names of the top three levels in all New York State executive departments and agencies; public corporations; authorities; commissions; all organizations listed in the Private Sector sources segment of each policy chapter; lobbyist organizations; political action committees; chambers of commerce; newspapers; news services; radio and television stations; SUNY and CUNY locations; and private colleges.

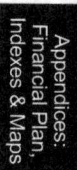

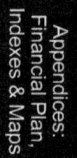

Geographic Index

Includes the names of the top three levels in all New York State executive departments and agencies; public corporations; authorities; commissions; all organizations listed in the Private Sector sources segment of each policy chapter; lobbyist organizations; political action committees; chambers of commerce; newspapers; news services; radio and television stations; SUNY and CUNY locations; and private colleges.

Alabama

Montgomery
US Department of Agriculture
Agricultural Marketing Service, 71

Arizona

Phoenix
DCI Group AZ, LLC (FKA DCI Group, LLC), 407

Arkansas

Bentonville
Wal-Mart Stores, Inc., 475

California

Costa Mesa
Rreef America LLC, 464

Los Angeles
Gibson, Dunn & Crutcher LLP PAC, 489
Westfield LLC, 477

Mill Valley
Apple Inc., 384

San Bruno
Vantagepoint Management, Inc., 474

San Francisco
Consumers Union of US, Inc., 404
Unite Here Local 2 PAC, 499
Vista Equity Partners III LLC, 475
Wells Capital Management, Inc., 476
Working Assets Funding Service, Inc., 479

San Rafael
Google, Inc., 421
Grant Thornton LLP, 422
Horton, Dan J, 428
Inventiv Health, Inc., 430
Matusic, Karen, 443

Colorado

Aurora
Veterans' Widows International Network Inc (VWIN), 302

Connecticut

Fairfield
Kudlow & Company LLC, 81

Farmington
NY Region 9A UAW PAC Council, 494

Greenwich
Starwood Capital LLC, 469

Hartford
Aetna, 380
Allegue, Raul R, 381
Empire Generating Co. LLC, 412
Henderson Global Investors (North America) Inc., 426
Prudential Insurance Company of America (The) (Form, 460
US Treasury Department
Area 1 Director's Office, 269

Lakeville
Tri-State Chamber of Commerce, 520

Monroe
Army Aviation Association of America (AAAA), 299

Norwalk
Diageo, 409

Simsbury
Hartford Financial Services Group, Inc. (The), 425

South Windsor
Pullium, Daniel, 461

Stamford
Purdue Pharma L.P., 461
Walton, Leigh, 476

West Hartford
Arvai, Joni, 384
Gray Media, 422

Windsor
Byrne, Elizabeth, 393
US Postal Service
NORTHEAST AREA (Includes part of New York State), 170

Delaware

Hockessin
Dimaio, Mark, 409

Wilmington
Bank of America New York Political Action Committee, 482

District of Columbia

Washington
AMGEN, 383
ATU New York Cope Fund, 482
Accenture LLP, 379
Aging, Special Committee on, 318
Agriculture, 319
Agriculture, Nutrition & Forestry, 314
Altria Client Services Inc. and its Affiliates, 381
American Beverage Association, 382
American Federation of Teachers, 226
American Insurance Association New York City PAC, 482
Appropriations, 314, 319
Armed Services, 315, 320
Baker & Hostetler LLP, 386
Banking, Housing & Urban Affairs, 315
Brickfield, Burchette, Ritts & Stone, P.C., 391
Budget, 315, 320
CITIGROUP Inc. Political Action Committee - Federal/State, 483
CitiGroup Management Corp., 398
Clearing House Payments Company L.L.C., 400
Commerce, Science & Transportation, 315
Commodity Futures Trading Commission, 70
Daiichi Sankyo, Inc., 406
Democrat, Republican, Independent Voter Education, 485

Florida

Georgia

Hawaii

Illinois

Indiana

Listings appear in alphabetical order by state, then city.

Listings appear in alphabetical order by state, then city.

Mueller, Tricia, 448
US Environmental Protection Agency
Division of Environmental Science & Assessment (DESA), 155

Englewood Cliffs
Port Authority PBA of NY PAC, 496

Flanders
Humane Society of the United States, Mid Atlantic Regional Office, 75, 261

Florham Park
Friedman, John P, 418

Hackensack
Hackensack University Medical Center, 424

Hawthorne
EFO Jeffrey P. Gardner, 485

Iselin
New York Shipping Association Inc, 294

Lawrenceville
Gilbane Building Company, 420

Lyndhurst
US Department of Homeland Security (DHS)
Newark Asylum Offc-Including NYS not served by New York City, 169, 198

Maplewood
Defoyd, Katherine, 408

Medford
Duca, Anthony, 410

Millburn
Greller, Matthew, 423

Morristown
Covanta Energy Corporation, 405

New York
D & M P.A.C. LLC, 484
The N.Y. Public Library Guild, Local 1930, 498

Newark
249 W 28th Street Properties, LLC, 379
Edison Spring Street Company LLC, 411
Federal Mediation & Conciliation Service
Northeastern Region, 224
Prudential Financial, Inc. (Formerly Michael F. McCann), 460
Prudential Investment Management, Inc. (Formerly Bernard B. Winograd, 460
Quantitative Management Associates LLC, 461
Small Business Administration
New Jersey, 89

Paramus
Hartman & Winnicki, PC, 93, 218

NYS Bar Assn, Intellectual Property Law Section, 93, 218
Vornado Realty Trust, 475

Parsippany
National Transportation Safety Board
Aviation Division, Northeast Regional Office, 291

Princeton
Bloom Energy Corporation, 388

Trenton
NY Capitolwire, 535

Warren
O'Malley, Michael, 454

Wayne
Enterprise Holdings, 413
Valley National Bank, 82

West Trenton
Delaware River Basin Commission, 98, 151

New York

Accord
Rondout Valley CSD, 597

Adams
South Jefferson CSD, 579
South Jefferson Chamber of Commerce, 518

Addisleigh Park
Joan Flowers For the 27th District, 490

Addison
Addison CSD, 593

Afton
Afton CSD, 572

Akron
Akron CSD, 575
Bank of Akron, 80
New York State Travel & Vacation Association, 283

Akwesasne
St Regis Mohawk Tribe, 168

Albany, 247
3rd Department, 45
AFSCME District Council 37, 244
AIA New York State, Inc. (FKNA Rodriguez, Barbara J.), 380
AIDS Council of Northeastern New York, 181
AT&T Inc. and Its Affiliates (FKA Roos, David), 386
AT&T PAC - New York, 482
AeA New York Council, 91, 144
Aging, Office for the, 4, 252

Agriculture & Markets Department, 4, 69, 252
Albany, 70
Soil & Water Conservation Committee, 70
Ahern, Barbara J, 380
Albany
Civil Court, 61
Criminal Court, 61
Traffic Court, 61
Albany City SD, 569
Albany College of Pharmacy, 554
Albany County, 327
County Court, 50
Family, 50
Supreme Court & Surrogate, 50
Albany County Airport Authority, 96, 286
Albany County Industrial Development Agency, 503
Albany Housing Coalition Inc, 299
Albany Law School, 554
Albany Law School of Union University, 380
Albany Law School, Government Law Center, 171
Albany Medical College, 554
Albany Port District Commission, 96, 287
Albany, City of, 343
Albany-Colonie Regional Chamber of Commerce, 380, 503
Alcoholism & Substance Abuse Services, Office of, 4, 174, 229, 252
Alliance for Quality Education (FKA Easton, Regina N), 381
Altman, Frederick M, 381
Alzheimer's Association, Northeastern NY, 182
American Cancer Society Cancer Action Network, 382
American Cancer Society-Eastern Division, 182
American Chemistry/American Plastics Council, 91
American College of Physicians, New York Chapter, 182
American Congress of Obstetricians & Gynecologists, Inc. District II, 382
American Congress of Obstetricians & Gynecologists/NYS, 182
American Council of Engineering Companies of NY (ACEC New York), 91
American Federation of State, County and Municipal Employees (AFSCME), 244
American Heart Assn/American Stroke Assn, 382
American Institute of Architects (AIA) New York State Inc, 91, 192
American Insurance Assn, 383
American Legion, Department of New York, 299
American Lung Association of NYS Inc, 182
American Red Cross in NYS, 258

Listings appear in alphabetical order by state, then city.

Listings appear in alphabetical order by state, then city.

Listings appear in alphabetical order by state, then city.

Appendices:
Financial Plan,
Indexes & Maps

Listings appear in alphabetical order by state, then city.

Listings appear in alphabetical order by state, then city.

Listings appear in alphabetical order by state, then city.

Listings appear in alphabetical order by state, then city.

Listings appear in alphabetical order by state, then city.

Listings appear in alphabetical order by state, then city.

Listings appear in alphabetical order by state, then city.

Geographic Index

Elections, State Board of
  Chemung, 132
Elmira
  Civil & Criminal Courts, 62
Elmira Business Institute, 566
Elmira City SD, 572
Elmira College, 557
Elmira, City of, 347
Gannett Co Inc, 527
Mental Health, Office of
  Elmira Psychiatric Center, 230
Southern Tier Economic Growth Inc, 518
Star-Gazette, 527
US Department of Veterans Affairs
  Woodlawn National Cemetery, 298
WETM (18), 539
WPGI (100.9 FM), WWLZ (820 AM), 536

Elmira Heights
Elmira Heights CSD, 572

Elmont
Elmont UFSD, 582

Elmsford
Elmsford UFSD, 600
Radon Testing Corp of America Inc, 160, 187
Wiener, Judith R, 477
Wilder Balter Partners, Inc., 477

Endicott
Habitat for Humanity of New York State, 424
Insurance Fund (NYS)
  Binghamton, 203, 221
Labor Department
  Southern Tier, 222
Union-Endicott CSD, 570

Endwell
Union Local Development Corporation (Town of), 520
Union, Town of, 368

Evans Mill
LeRay, Town of, 351

Fabius
Fabius-Pompey CSD, 586

Fair Haven
Fair Haven Area Chamber of Commerce, 508

Fairport
Fairport CSD, 580
Monroe 1 BOCES, 602
Perinton, Town of, 364
Praxiis Business Advisors, 459

Falconer
Falconer CSD, 572

Fallsburg
Corrections & Community Supervision Department
  Sullivan Correctional Facility, 111
Fallsburg CSD, 596

Far Rockaway
Friends of Donovan Richards 2013, 486
Friends of Osina, 488
Peralta 2013, 495
Peralta For Senate, 495
Rockaway Development & Revitalization Corporation, 517
Sanders For Senate, 497

Farmingdale
Citizens Campaign for the Environment, 399
Farmingdale State College of Technology, 548
Farmingdale UFSD, 582
Long Island Nursery & Landscape Association Inc, 75
US Department of Veterans Affairs
  Long Island National Cemetery, 297

Farmington
Farmington Chamber of Commerce, 508
Finger Lakes Racing Association, 280

Farmingville
Brookhaven, Town of, 344
Town of Brookhaven Industrial Development Agency, 504

Fayetteville
Fayetteville Chamber of Commerce, 508
Manlius, Town of, 352
The Greater Manlius Chamber of Commerce, 509

Ferndale
Convention Centers & Visitors Bureaus
  Sullivan County Visitors Association, 277
Sullivan County Industrial Development Agency, 519

Fillmore
Fillmore CSD, 569

Findley Lake
Findley Lake Area Chamber of Commerce, 508

Fishers
Apple Association, Inc. (NY), 383
New York Apple Association Inc, 76

Fishers Island
Fishers Island UFSD, 594

Fishkill
Corrections & Community Supervision Department
  Downstate Correctional Facility, 110
Fishkill, Town of, 347

New York State Gaming Commission
  Hudson Valley Region, 266

Floral Park
Floral Park-Bellerose UFSD, 582
Friends of Harpreet, 487
New Yorkers For Affordable Housing, 494
Sewanhaka Central HS District, 583

Florida
Florida UFSD, 587

Flushing
CIDNY - Queens, 199, 258
Evergreen For City Council, 485
Friends For Peter Koo, 486
Friends of John Liu, 487
Friends of Michael Simanowitz, 488
He Gin Lee Committee to Elect For Mayor, 489
International Union o, 490
Joint Industry Board of the Electrical Industry, 432
Long Island Business Institute-Flushing, 567
NYC Region 3, 584
New York City
  Environmental Protection, Department of, NYC, 356
New York Mets, 283
Paul Graziano 2013, 495
Queens College, 554
Sasson For NYC, 497
School of Law at Queens College, 554
Sunny Hahn For City Council, 498
Vaughn College of Aeronautics & Technology, 564
Vote Vallone 2013, 499

Fonda
Elections, State Board of
  Montgomery, 134
Fonda-Fultonville CSD, 581
Montgomery County, 333
  Supreme, County, Family & Surrogate's Courts, 55

Forest Hills
Bramson ORT College, 555
Local 1182 Political Action Fund, 491
Re-Elect Koslowitz 2013, 496

Forestville
Forestville CSD, 572

Fort Ann
Fort Ann CSD, 598

Fort Covington
Salmon River CSD, 577

Fort Drum
US Defense Department
  Fort Drum, 297

Listings appear in alphabetical order by state, then city.

824

Listings appear in alphabetical order by state, then city.

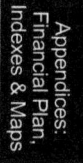

Listings appear in alphabetical order by state, then city.

Appendices:
Financial Plan,
Indexes & Maps

Listings appear in alphabetical order by state, then city.

Listings appear in alphabetical order by state, then city.

Listings appear in alphabetical order by state, then city.

Listings appear in alphabetical order by state, then city.

Listings appear in alphabetical order by state, then city.

Listings appear in alphabetical order by state, then city.

Listings appear in alphabetical order by state, then city.

Listings appear in alphabetical order by state, then city.

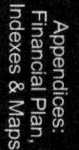

Listings appear in alphabetical order by state, then city.

Listings appear in alphabetical order by state, then city.

Listings appear in alphabetical order by state, then city.

Listings appear in alphabetical order by state, then city.

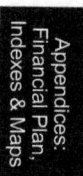

Listings appear in alphabetical order by state, then city.

Listings appear in alphabetical order by state, then city.

Listings appear in alphabetical order by state, then city.

Listings appear in alphabetical order by state, then city.

Listings appear in alphabetical order by state, then city.

Appendices:
Financial Plan,
Indexes & Maps

Listings appear in alphabetical order by state, then city.

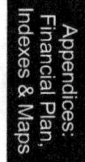

Listings appear in alphabetical order by state, then city.

North Carolina

Ohio

Oklahoma

Listings appear in alphabetical order by state, then city.

Listings appear in alphabetical order by state, then city.

Demographic and Reference Maps

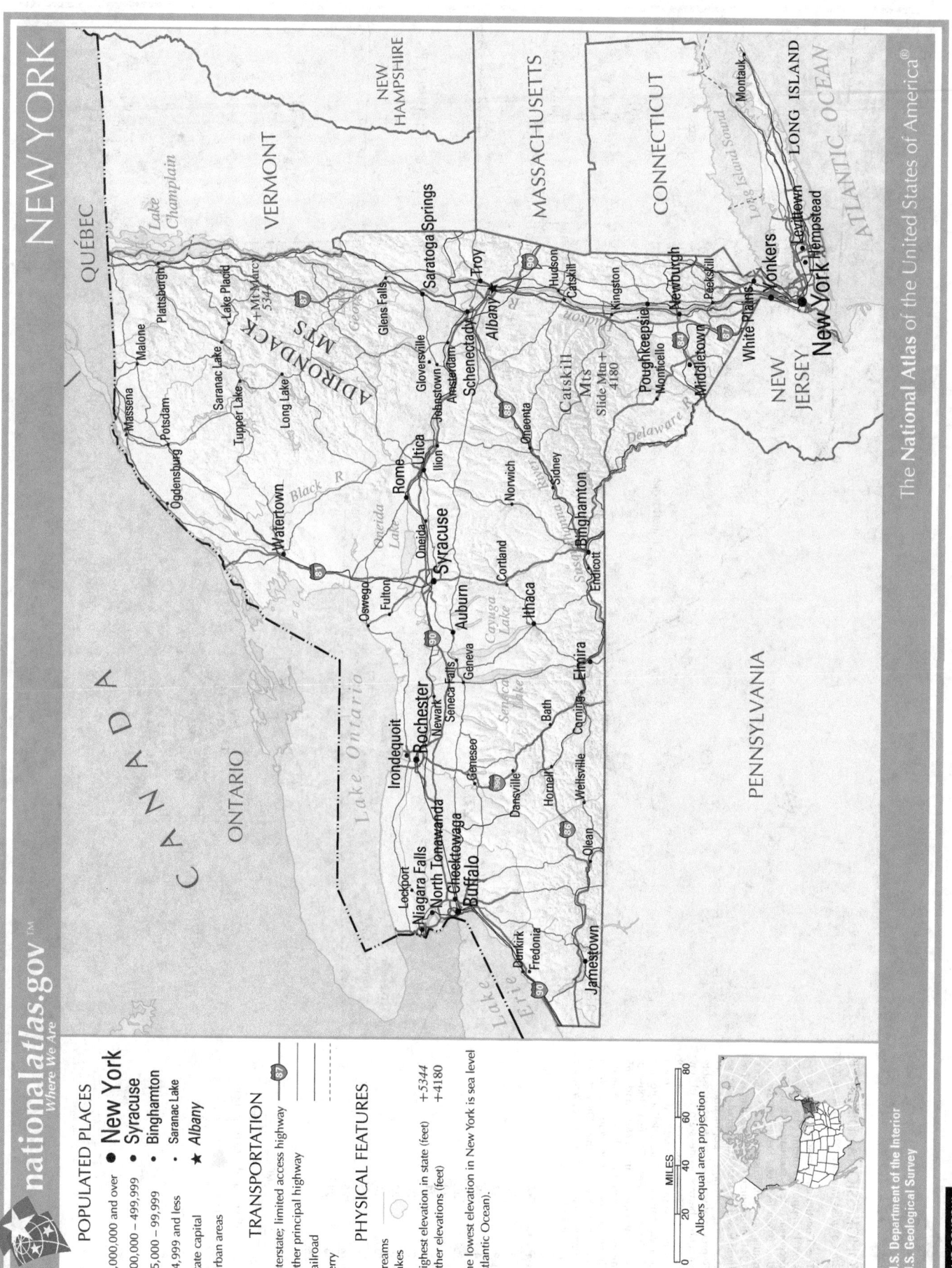

NEW YORK

nationalatlas.gov ™
Where We Are

POPULATED PLACES

● **New York** 1,000,000 and over

● **Syracuse** 100,000 – 499,999

● **Binghamton** 25,000 – 99,999

· **Saranac Lake** 24,999 and less

★ *Albany* State capital

Urban areas

TRANSPORTATION

⎯〔87〕⎯ Interstate; limited access highway

⎯⎯⎯ Other principal highway

⎯⎯⎯ Railroad

----- Ferry

PHYSICAL FEATURES

Streams

Lakes

Highest elevation in state (feet) +5344

Other elevations (feet) +4180

The lowest elevation in New York is sea level (Atlantic Ocean).

MILES
0 20 40 60 80

Albers equal area projection

U.S. Department of the Interior
U.S. Geological Survey

QUÉBEC

CANADA

ONTARIO

NEW HAMPSHIRE

VERMONT

MASSACHUSETTS

CONNECTICUT

NEW JERSEY

PENNSYLVANIA

LONG ISLAND

ATLANTIC OCEAN

Lake Ontario

Lake Erie

Lake Champlain

ADIRONDACK MTS

+Mt Marcy 5344

Catskill Mts

Slide Mtn +4180

Long Island Sound

Black R

Delaware R

Hudson R

Niagara Falls

North Tonawanda

Cheektowaga

Buffalo

Lockport

Dunkirk

Fredonia

Jamestown

Olean

Wellsville

Hornell

Dansville

Bath

Corning

Elmira

Geneseo

Newark

Rochester

Irondequoit

Seneca Falls

Geneva

Ithaca

Cortland

Auburn

Oswego

Fulton

Oneida

Syracuse

Rome

Utica

Ilion

Watertown

Ogdensburg

Potsdam

Massena

Malone

Plattsburgh

Saranac Lake

Lake Placid

Tupper Lake

Long Lake

Saratoga Springs

Glens Falls

Gloversville

Johnstown

Amsterdam

Schenectady

Troy

Albany

Hudson

Catskill

Kingston

Oneonta

Sidney

Norwich

Binghamton

Endicott

Monticello

Poughkeepsie

Newburgh

Middletown

Peekskill

White Plains

Yonkers

Levittown

Hempstead

New York

Montauk

Oneida Lake

Seneca Lake

Cayuga Lake

Lake George

Susquehanna River

Mohawk R

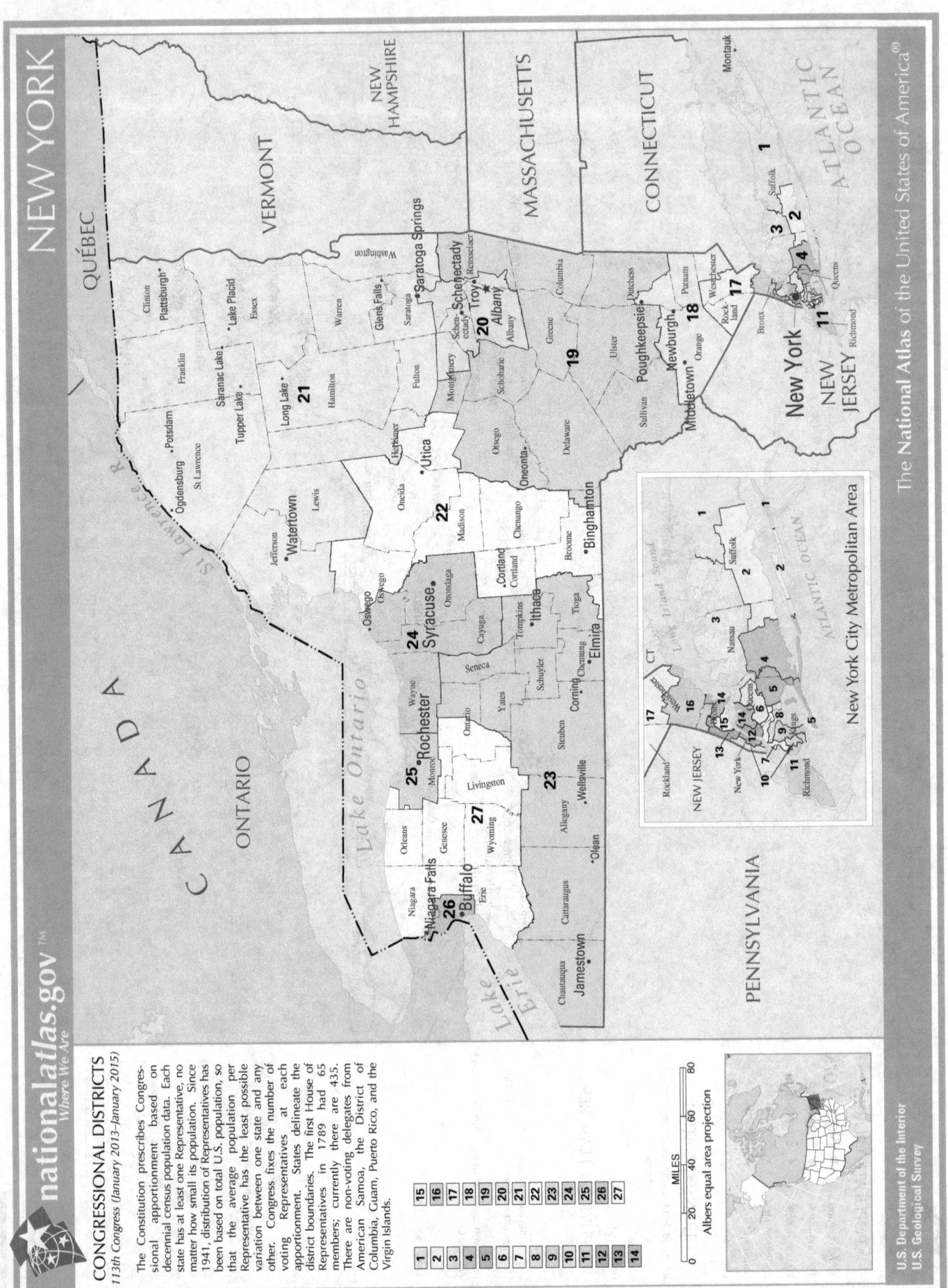

NEW YORK

The National Atlas of the United States of America®

nationalatlas.gov™
Where We Are

CONGRESSIONAL DISTRICTS
113th Congress (January 2013–January 2015)

The Constitution prescribes Congressional apportionment based on decennial census population data. Each state has at least one Representative, no matter how small its population. Since 1941, distribution of Representatives has been based on total U.S. population, so that the average population per Representative has the least possible variation between one state and any other. Congress fixes the number of voting Representatives at each apportionment. States delineate the district boundaries. The first House of Representatives in 1789 had 65 members; currently there are 435. There are non-voting delegates from American Samoa, the District of Columbia, Guam, Puerto Rico, and the Virgin Islands.

New York City Metropolitan Area

MILES
0   20   40   60   80

Albers equal area projection

U.S. Department of the Interior
U.S. Geological Survey

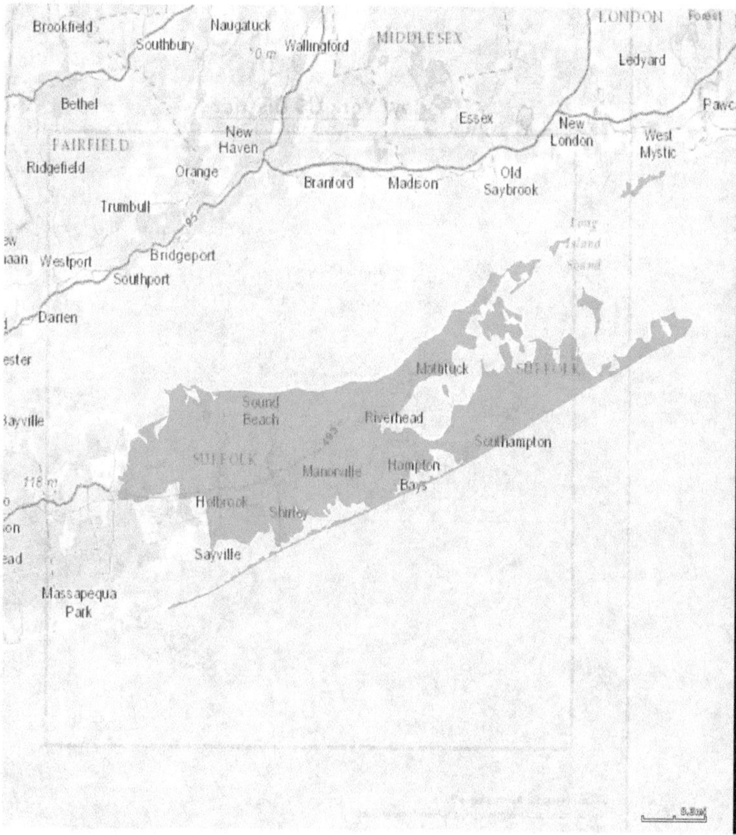

New York US District 1

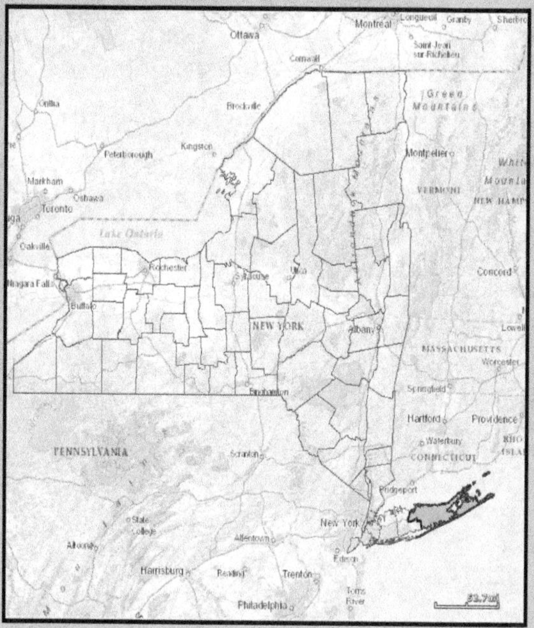

US Congressional districts since 2013
Source: http://nationalatlas.gov, 1 Million Scale project.

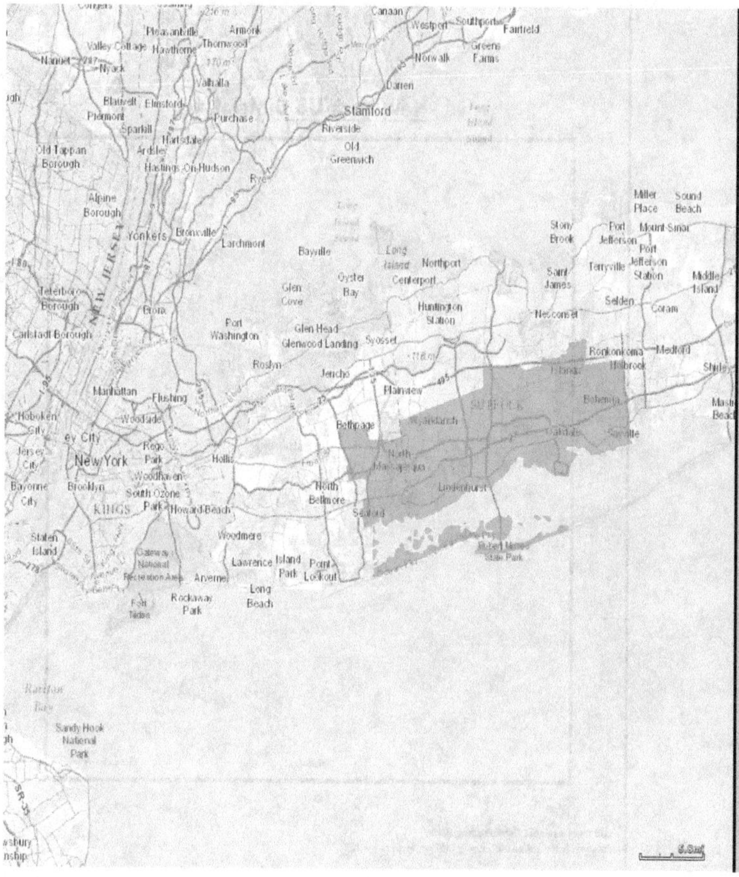

New York US District 2

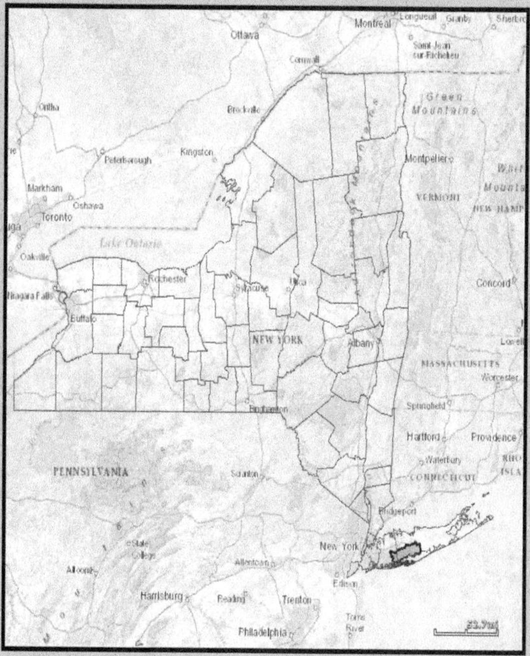

US Congressional districts since 2013
Source: http://nationalatlas.gov, 1 Million Scale project.

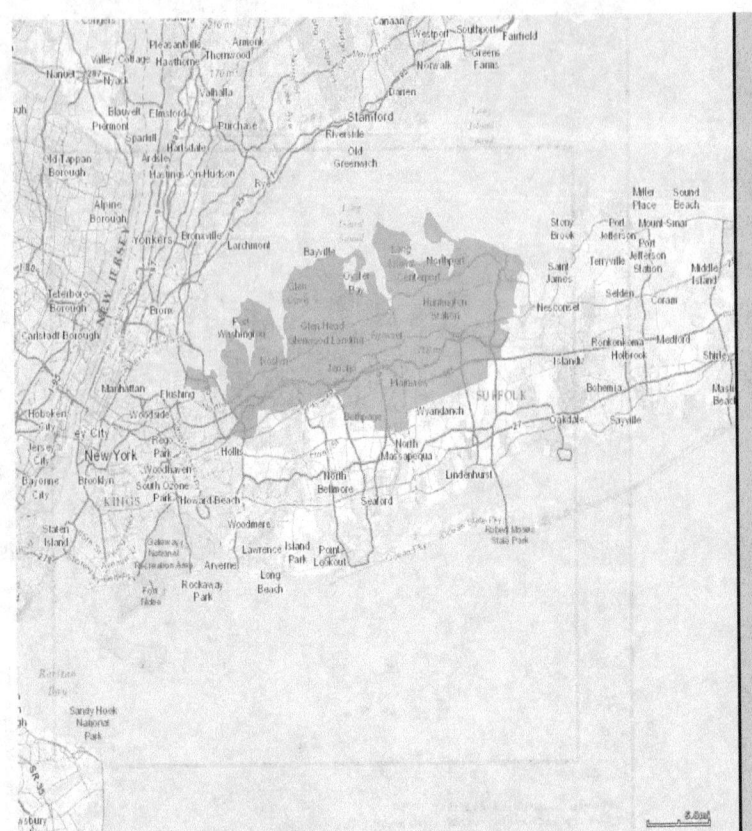

New York US District 3

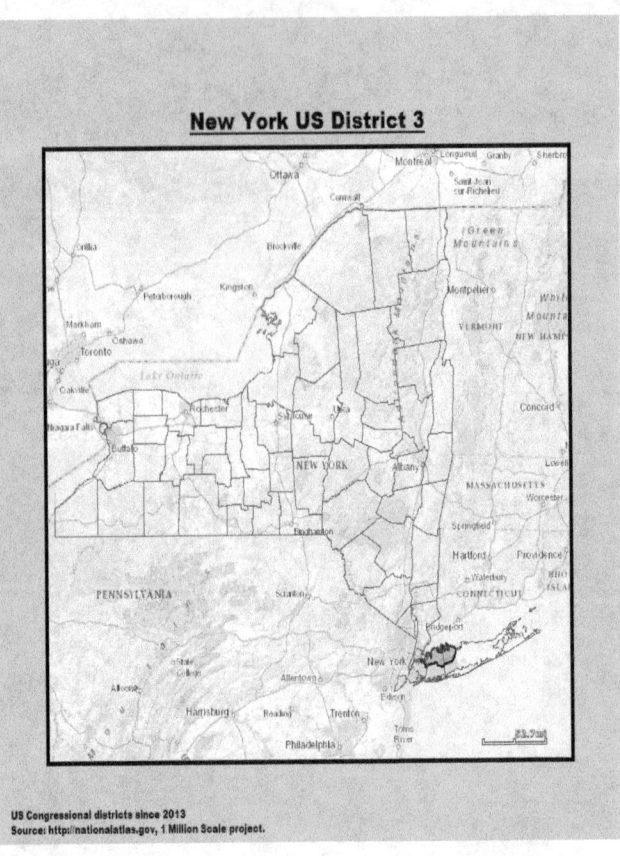

US Congressional districts since 2013
Source: http://nationalatlas.gov, 1 Million Scale project.

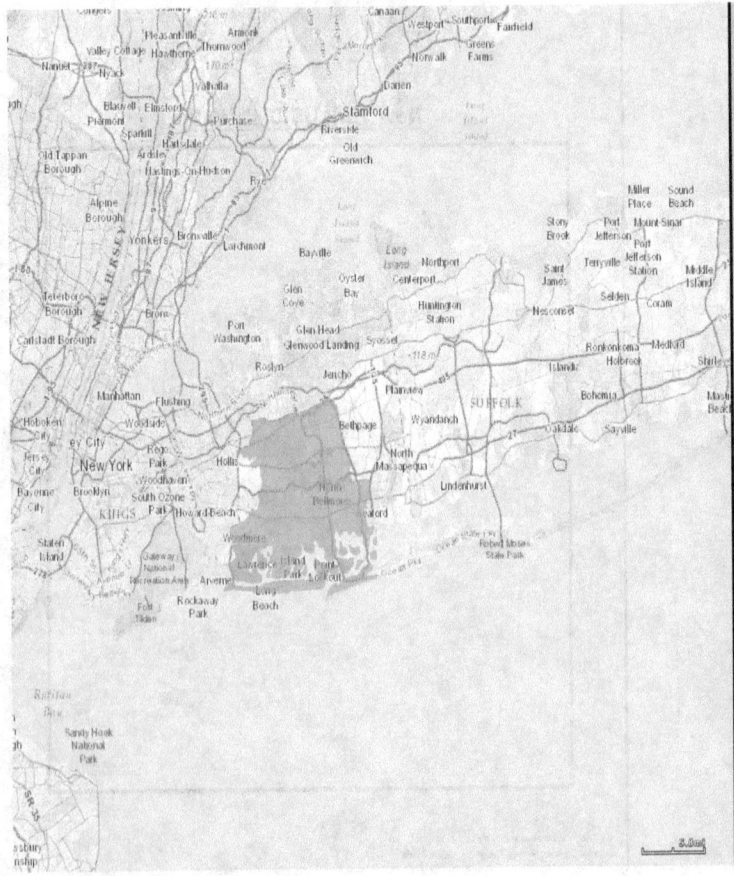

New York US District 4

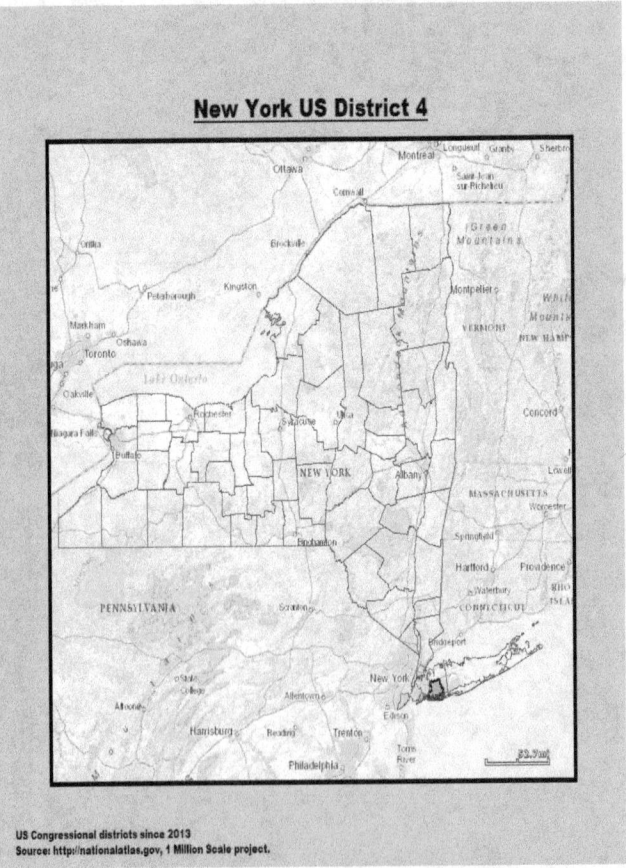

US Congressional districts since 2013
Source: http://nationalatlas.gov, 1 Million Scale project.

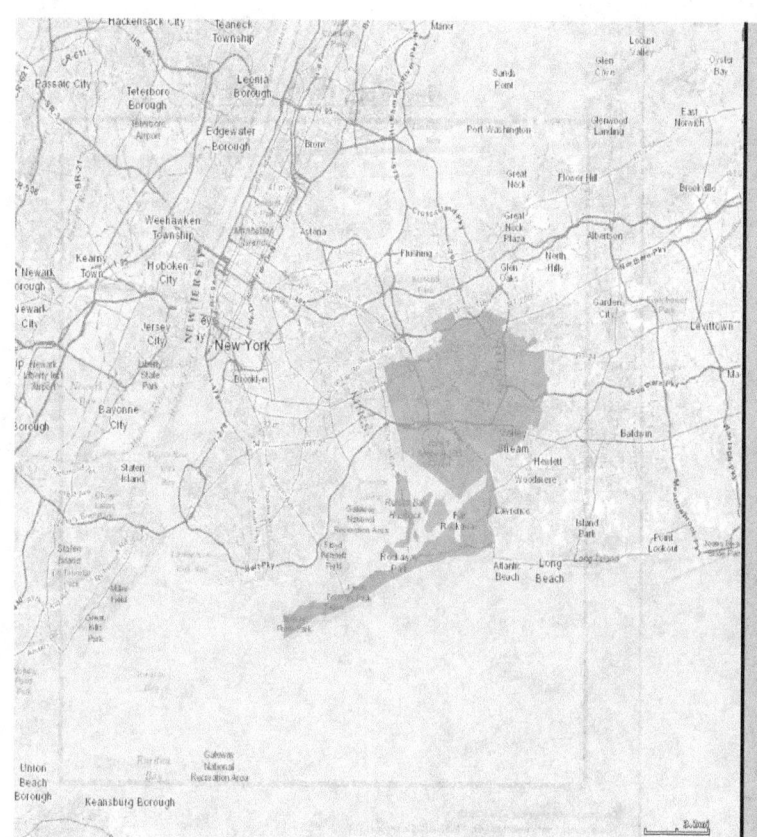

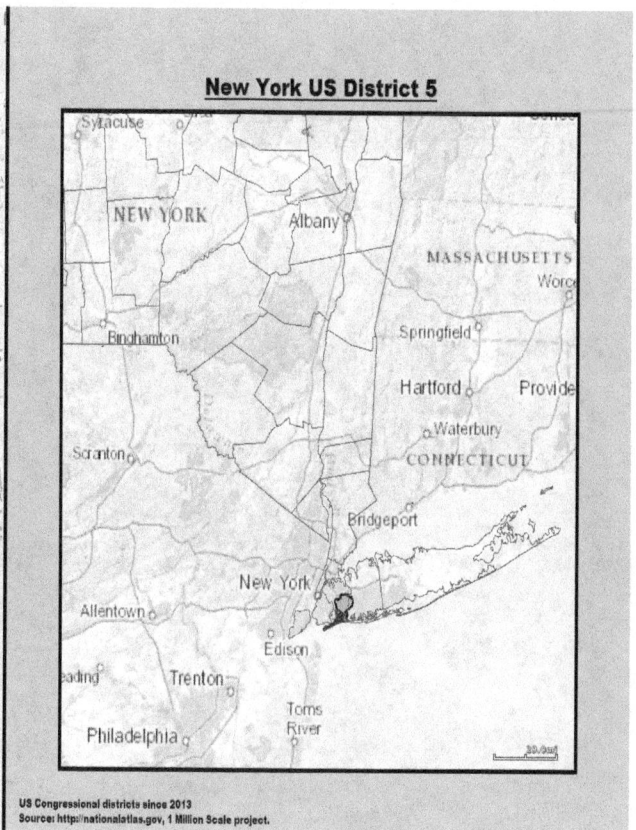

New York US District 5

US Congressional districts since 2013
Source: http://nationalatlas.gov, 1 Million Scale project.

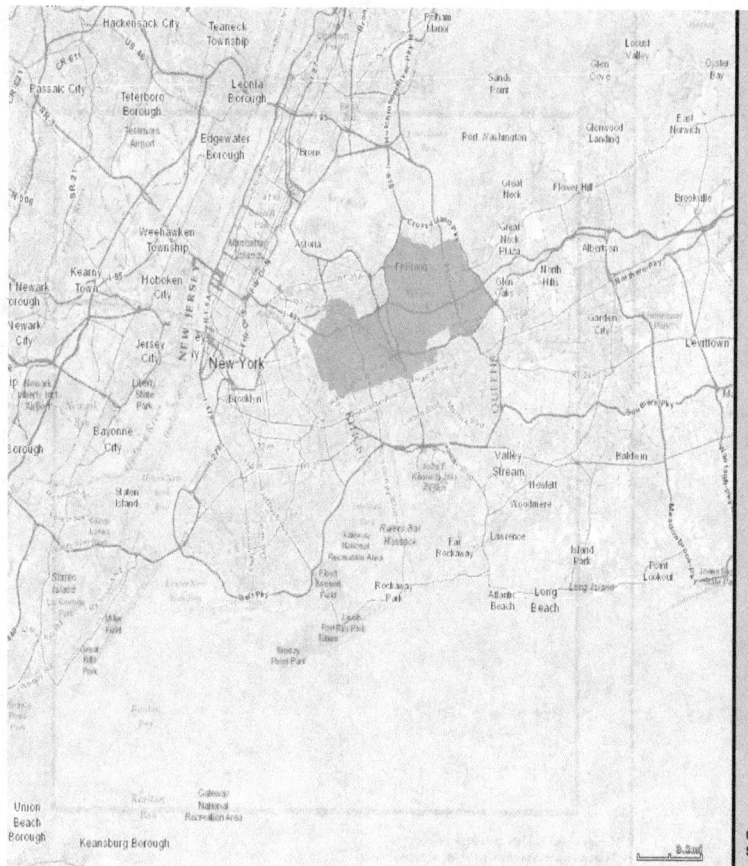

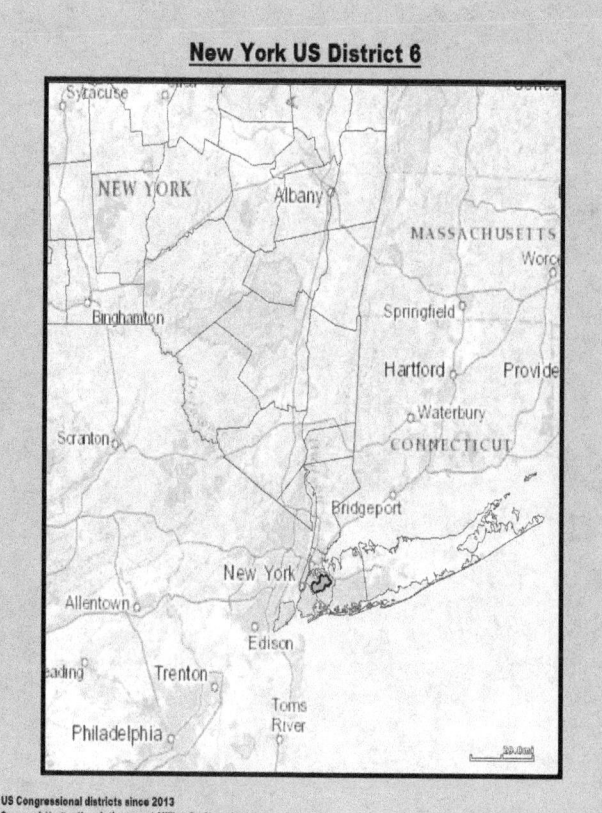

New York US District 6

US Congressional districts since 2013
Source: http://nationalatlas.gov, 1 Million Scale project.

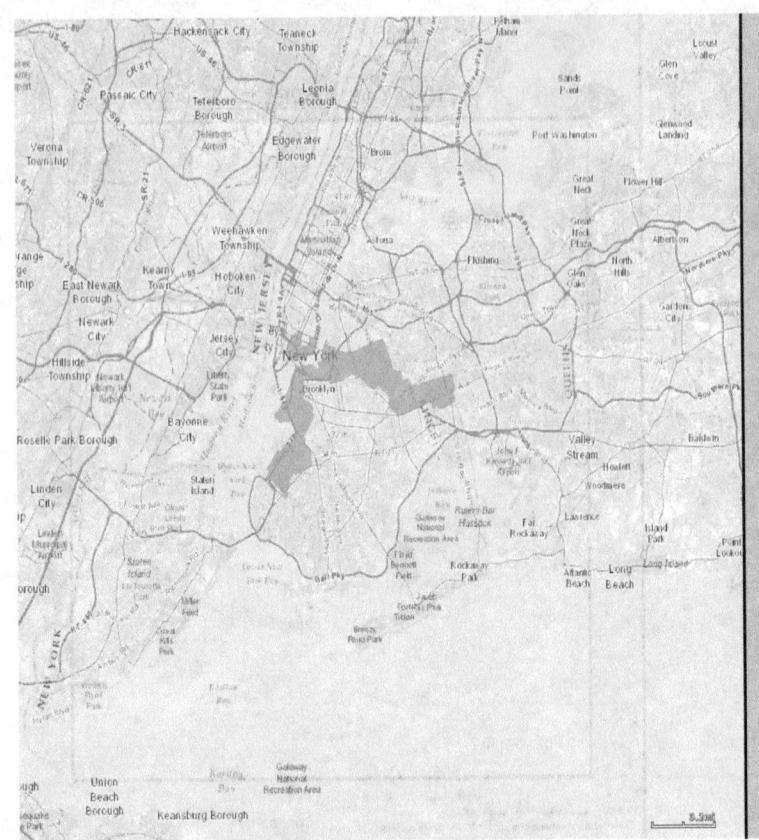

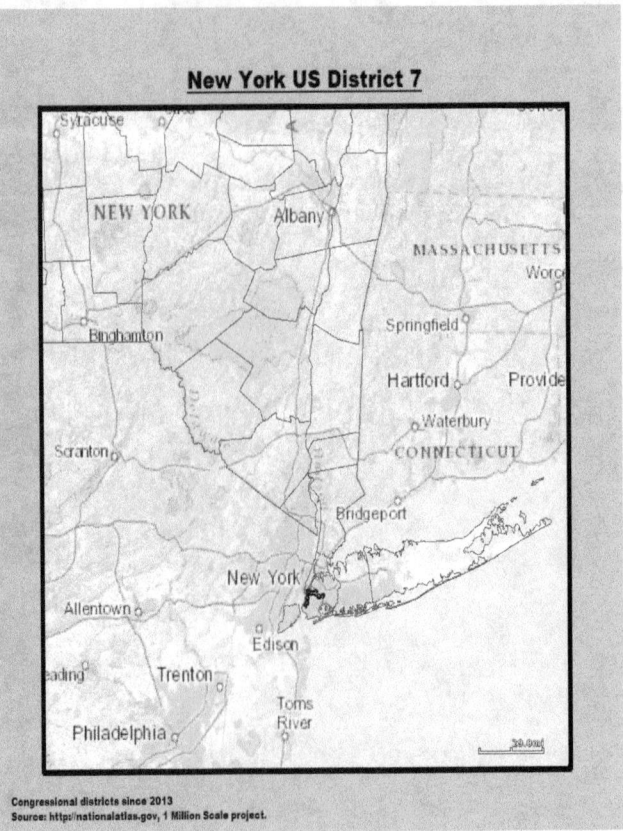

New York US District 7

Congressional districts since 2013
Source: http://nationalatlas.gov, 1 Million Scale project.

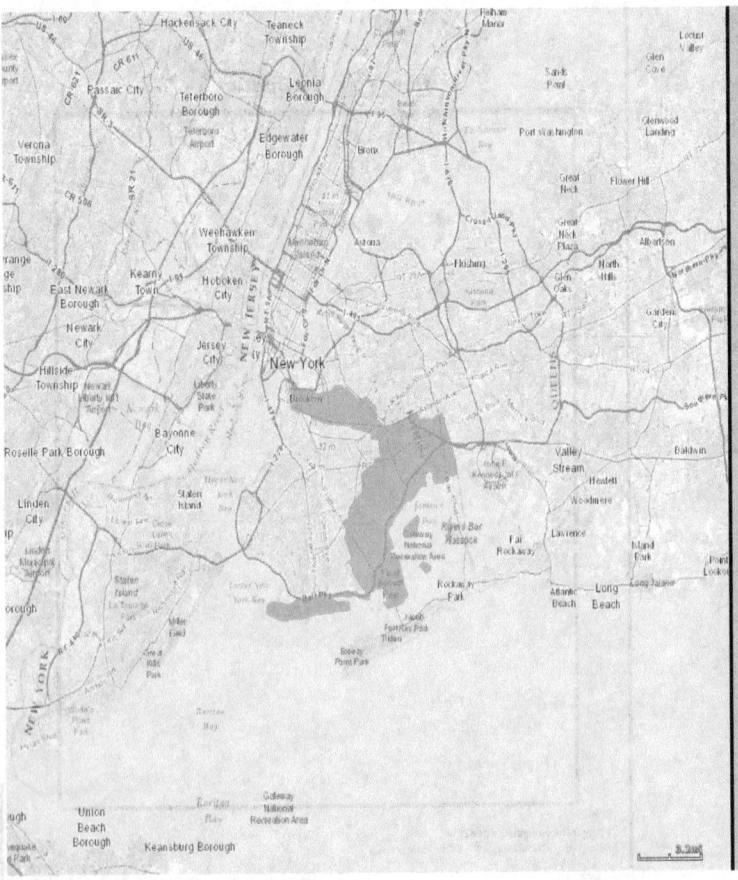

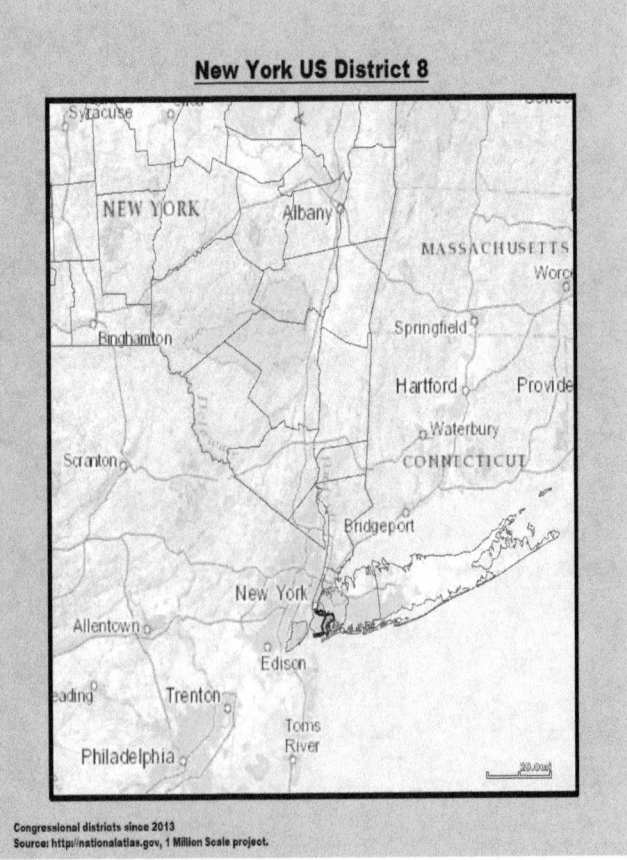

New York US District 8

Congressional districts since 2013
Source: http://nationalatlas.gov, 1 Million Scale project.

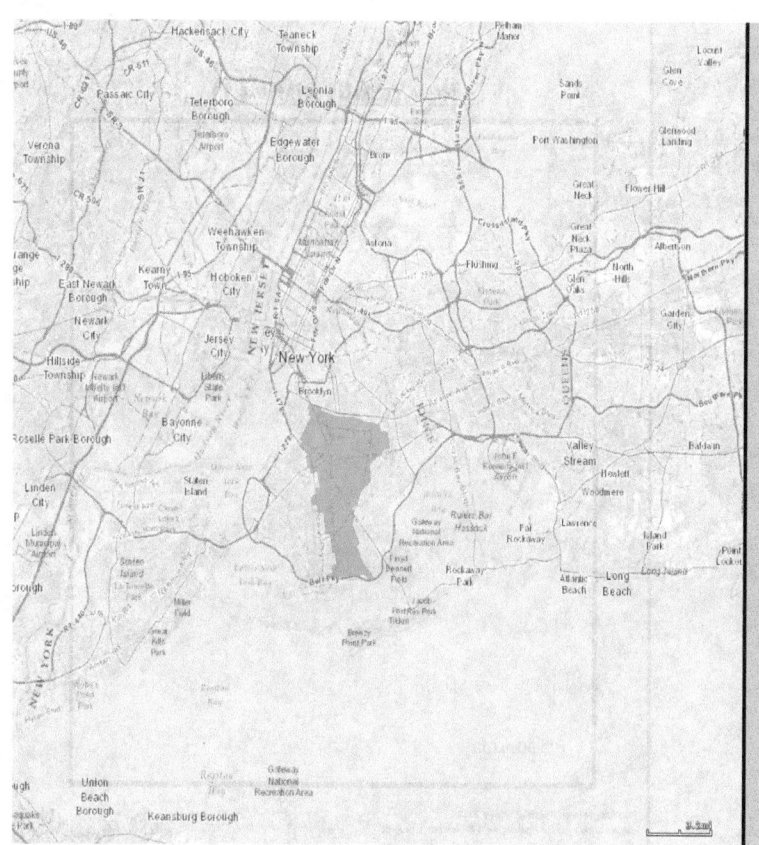

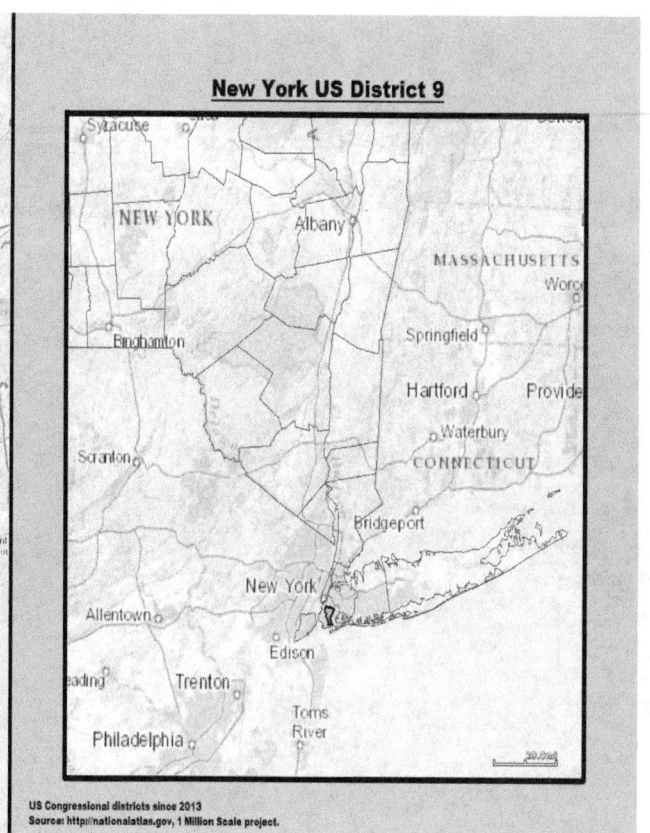

New York US District 9

US Congressional districts since 2013
Source: http://nationalatlas.gov, 1 Million Scale project.

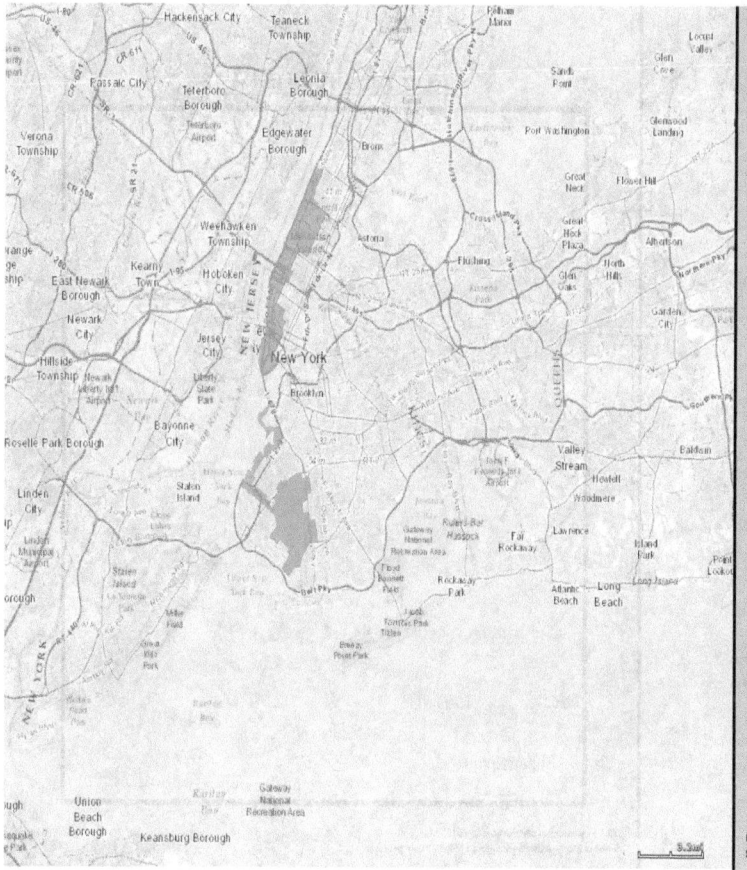

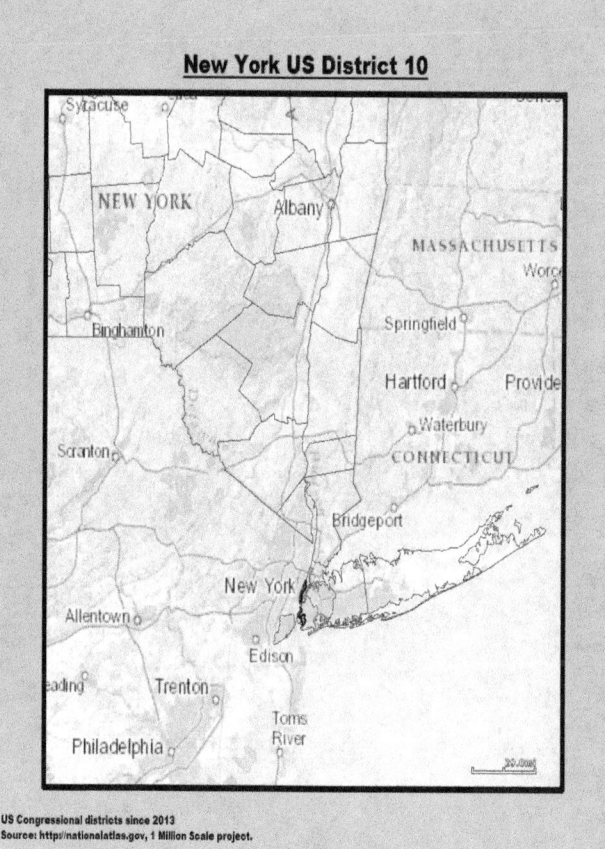

New York US District 10

US Congressional districts since 2013
Source: http://nationalatlas.gov, 1 Million Scale project.

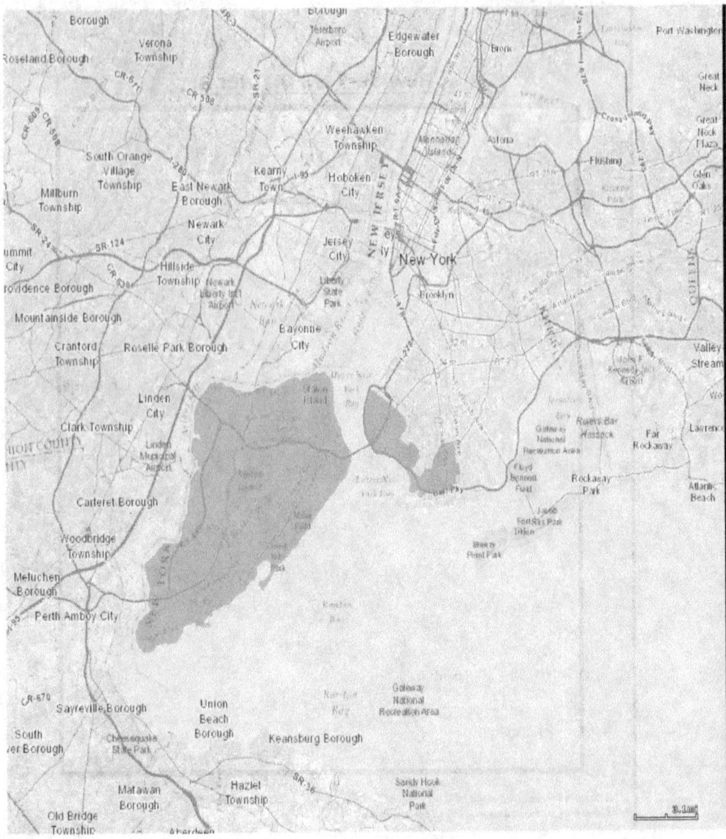

New York US District 11

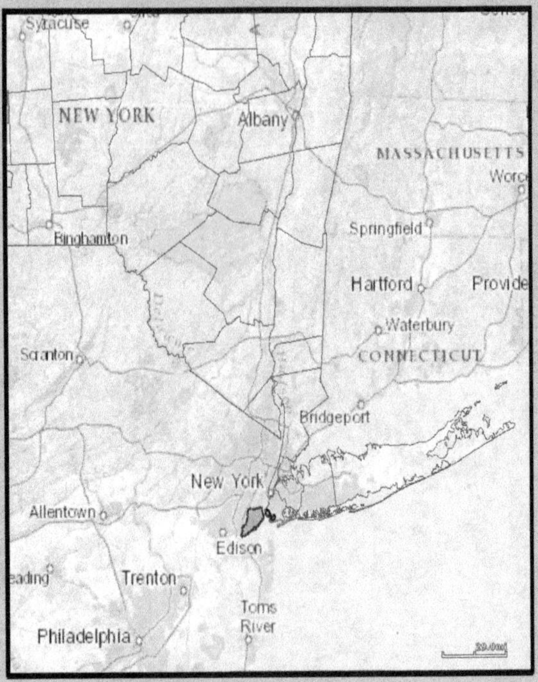

US Congressional districts since 2013
Source: http://nationalatlas.gov, 1 Million Scale project.

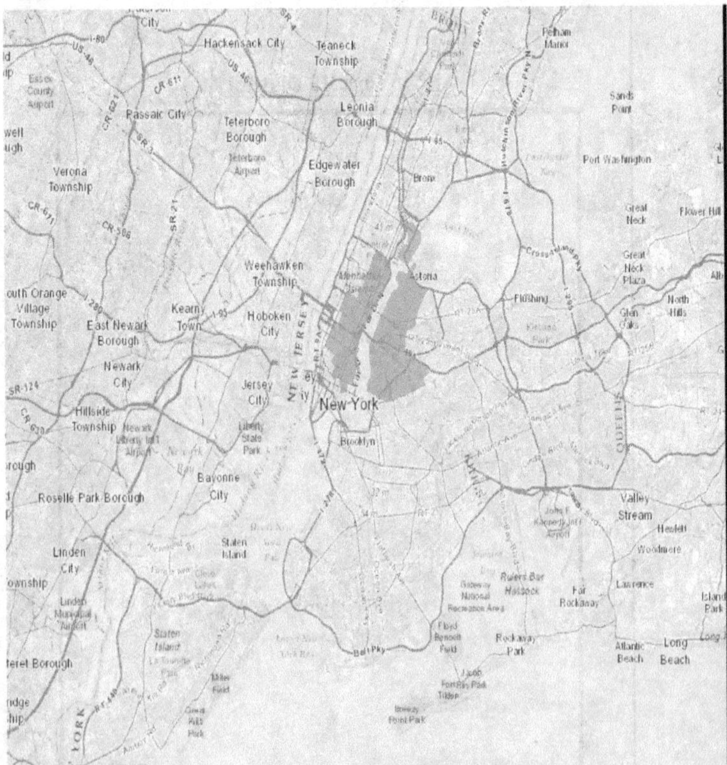

New York US District 12

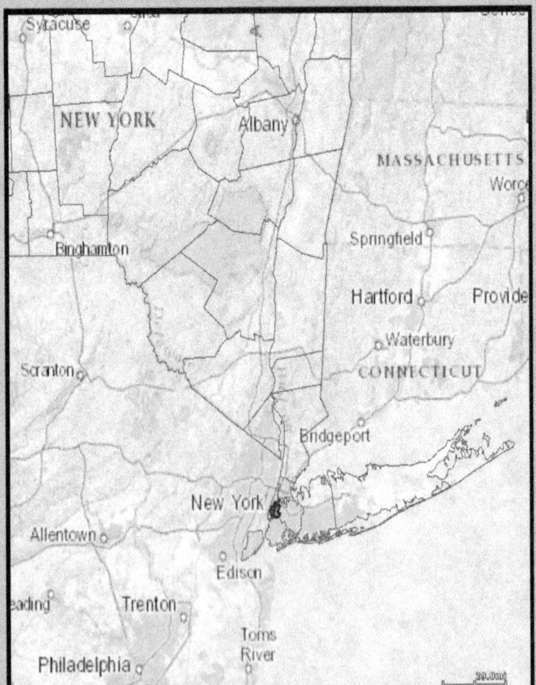

US Congressional districts since 2013
Source: http://nationalatlas.gov, 1 Million Scale project.

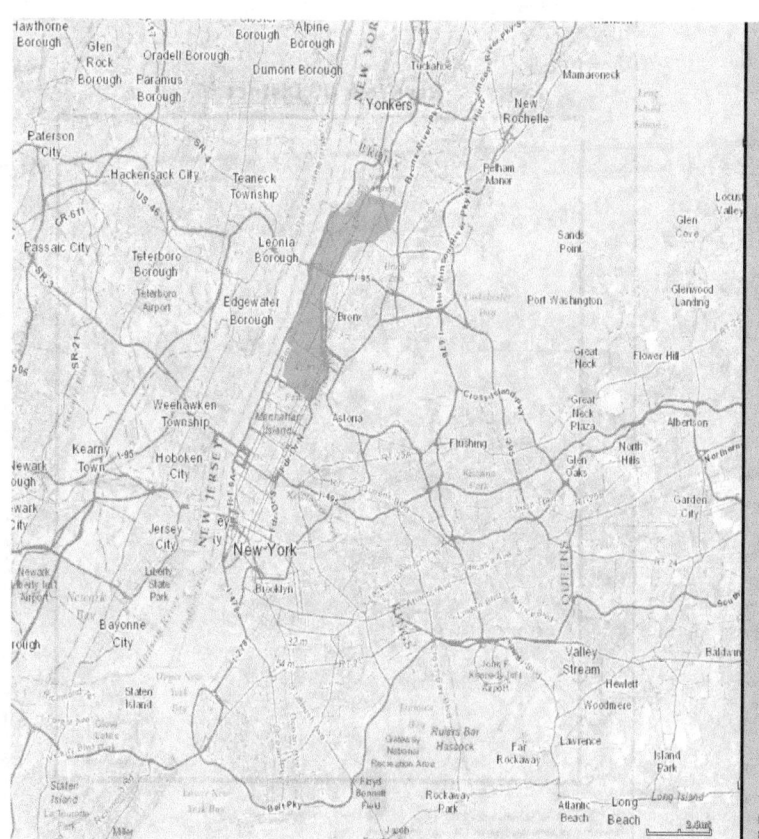

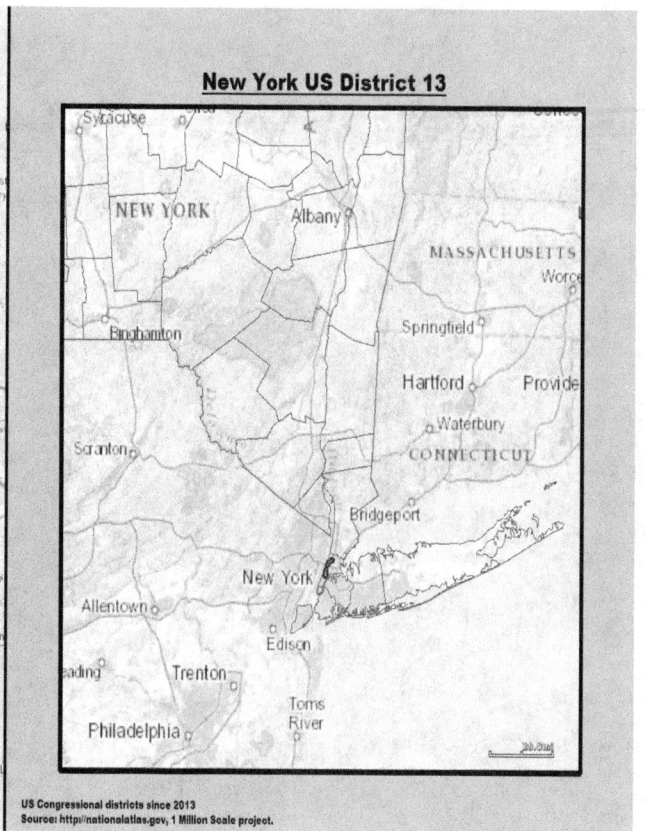

New York US District 13

US Congressional districts since 2013
Source: http://nationalatlas.gov, 1 Million Scale project.

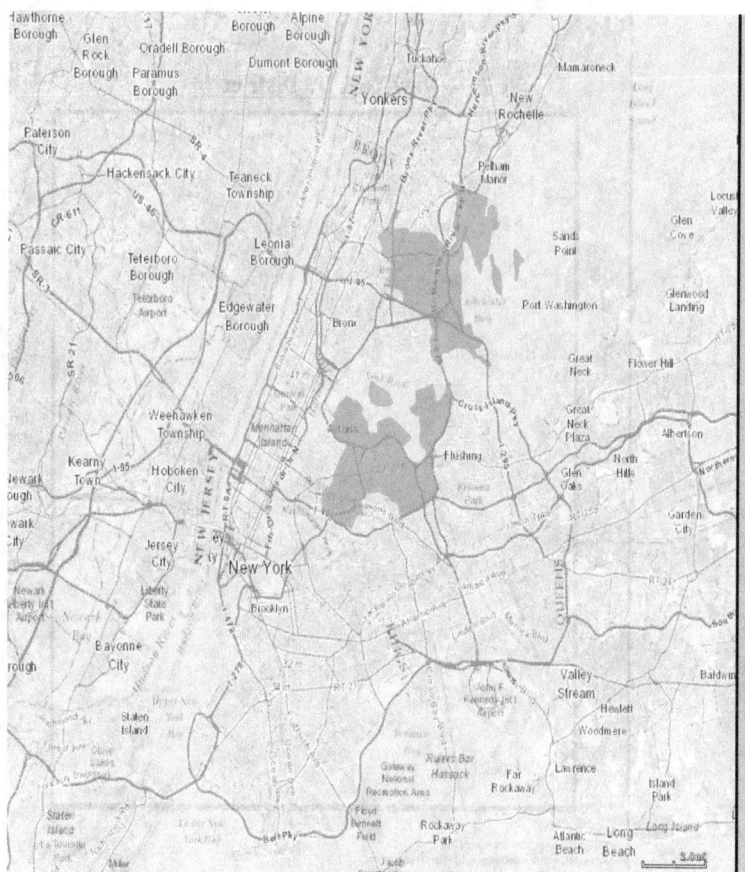

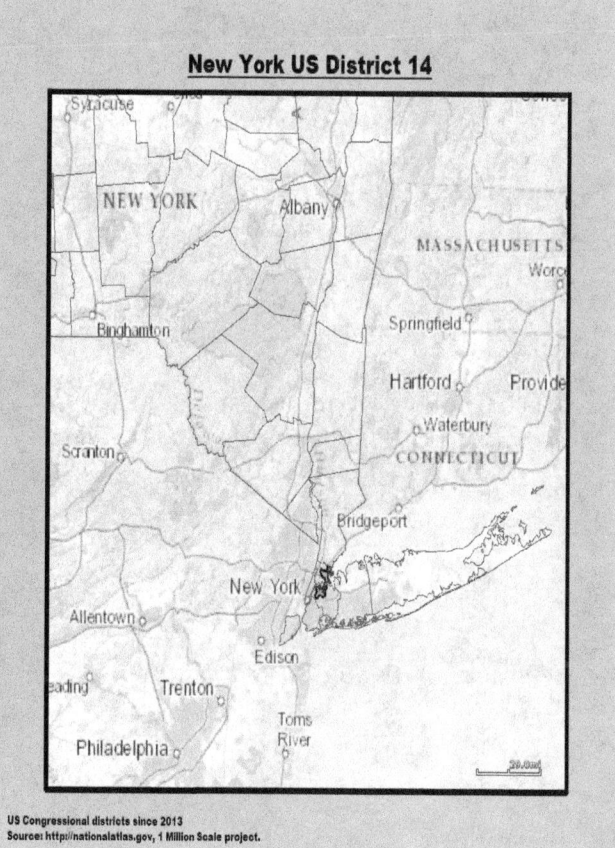

New York US District 14

US Congressional districts since 2013
Source: http://nationalatlas.gov, 1 Million Scale project.

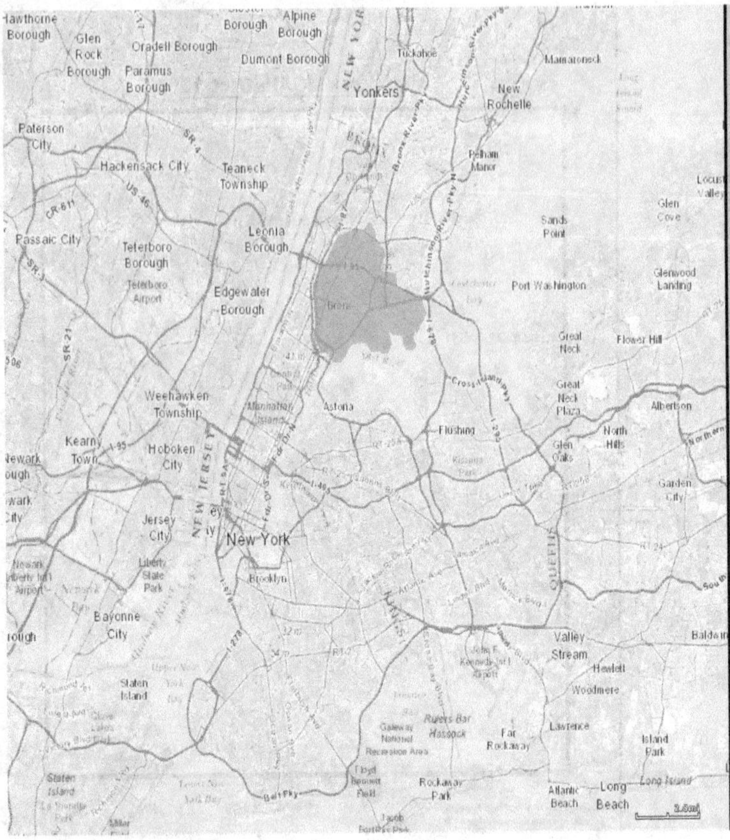

New York US District 15

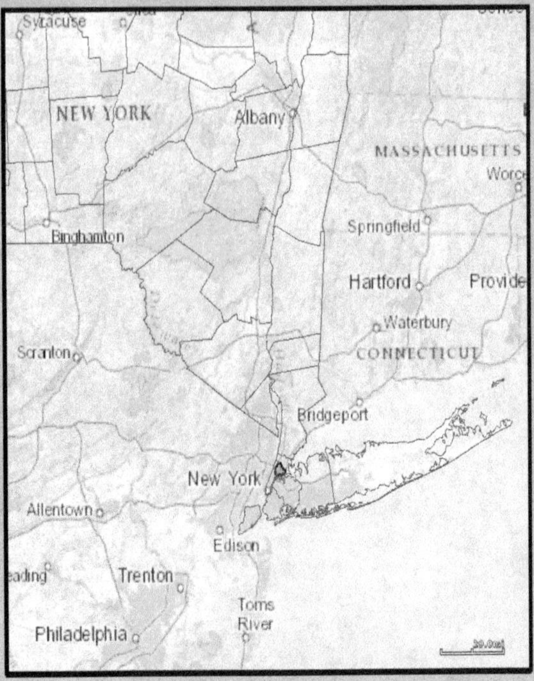

US Congressional districts since 2013
Source: http://nationalatlas.gov, 1 Million Scale project.

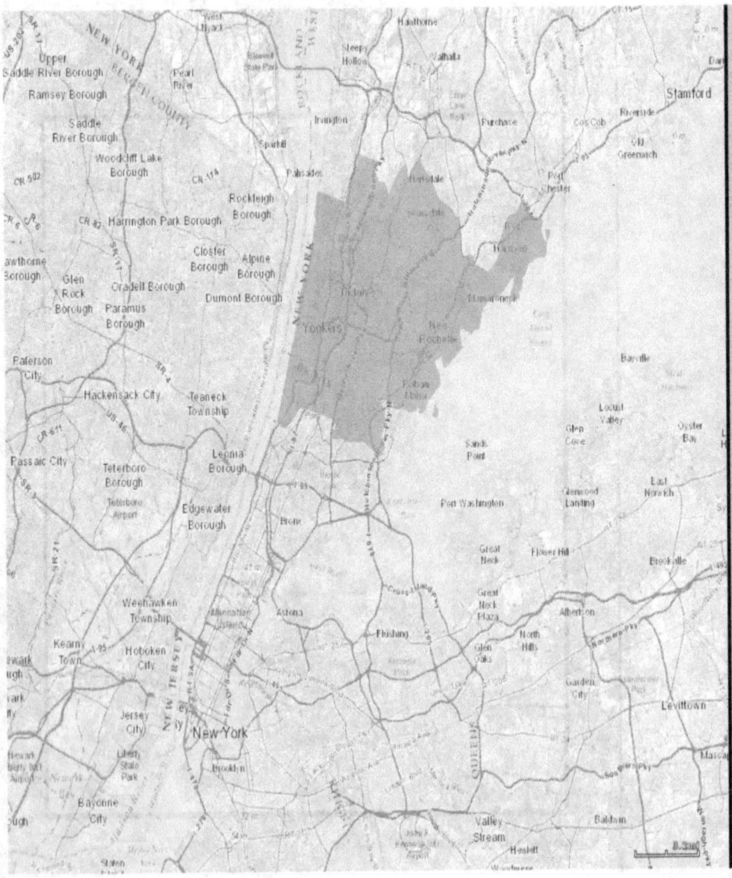

New York US District 16

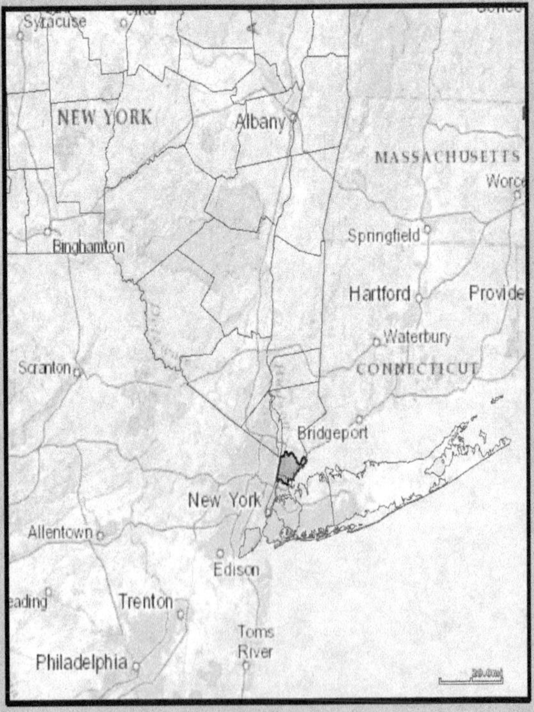

US Congressional districts since 2013
Source: http://nationalatlas.gov, 1 Million Scale project.

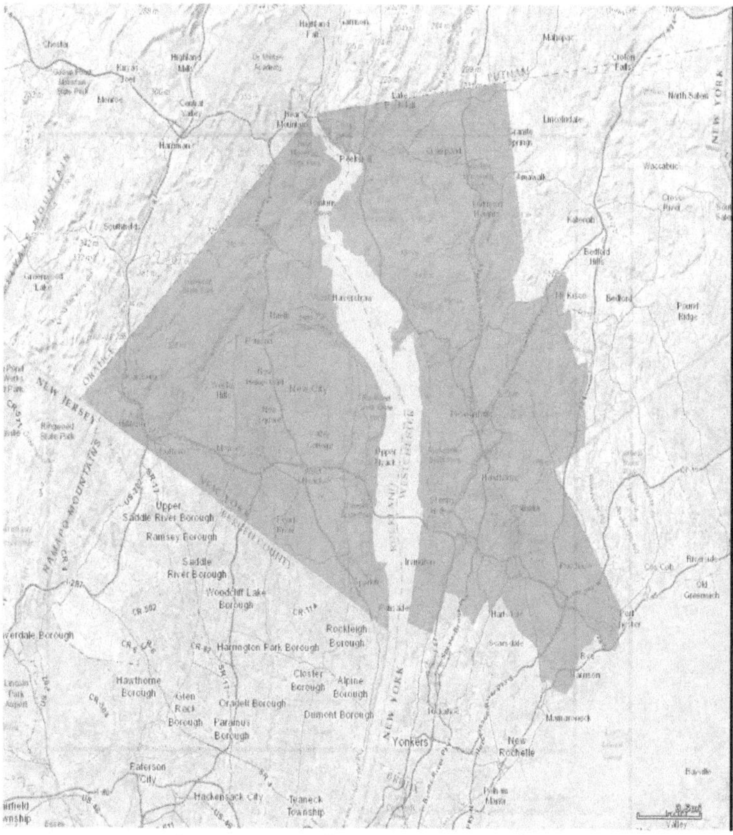

New York US District 17

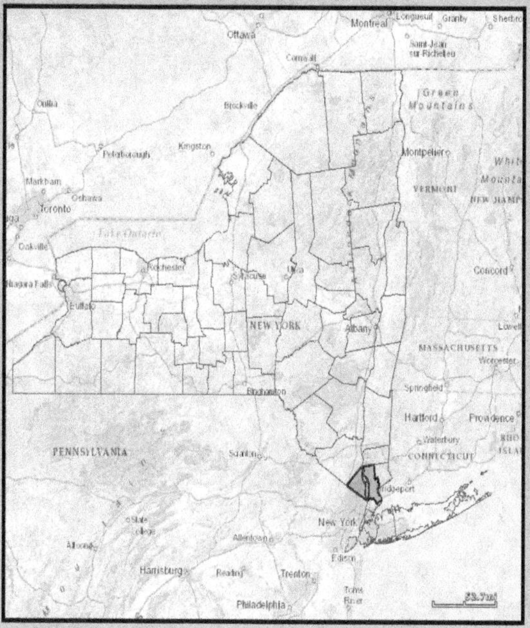

US Congressional districts since 2013
Source: http://nationalatlas.gov, 1 Million Scale project.

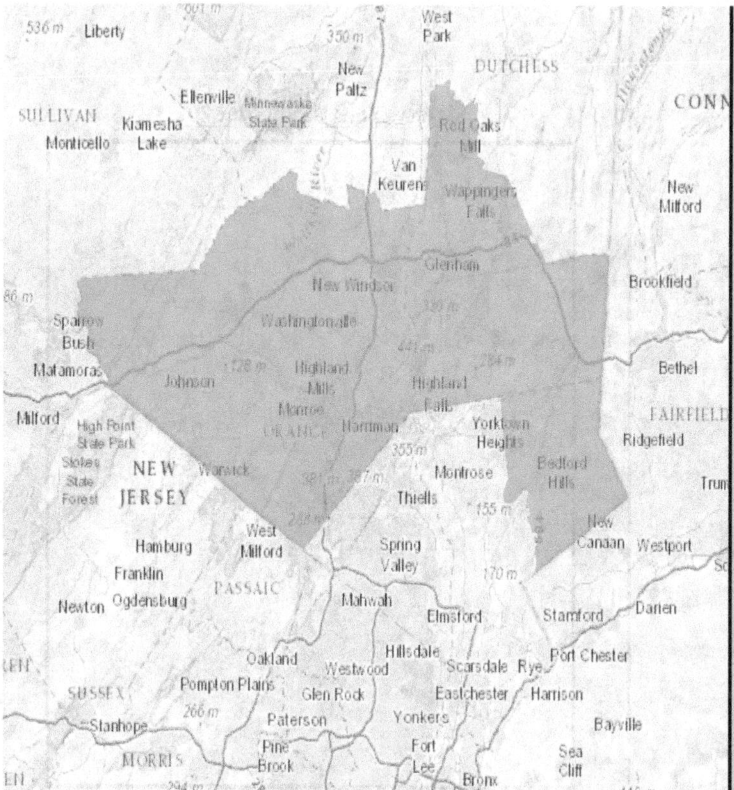

New York US District 18

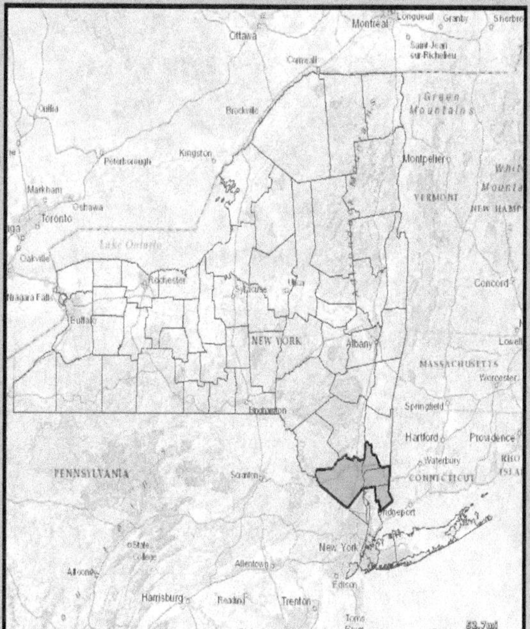

US Congressional districts since 2013
Source: http://nationalatlas.gov, 1 Million Scale project.

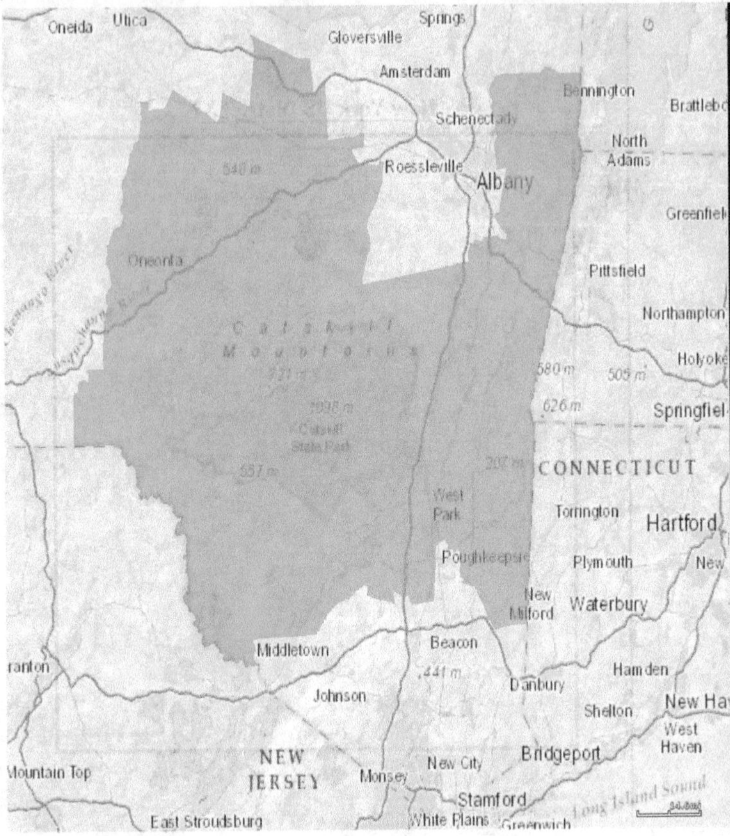

New York US District 19

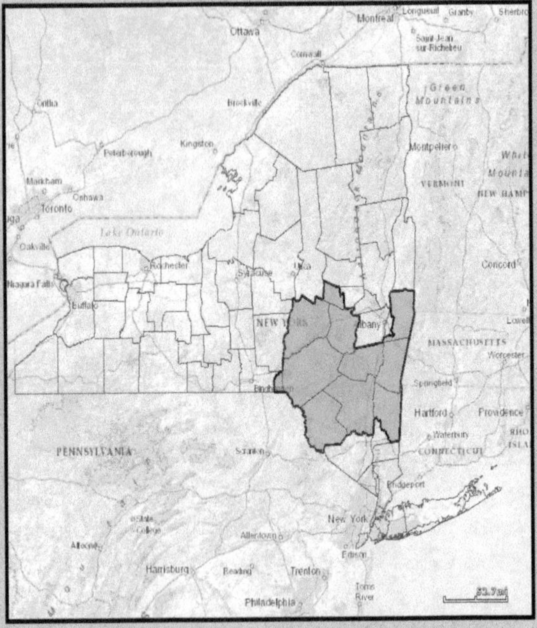

US Congressional districts since 2013
Source: http://nationalatlas.gov, 1 Million Scale project.

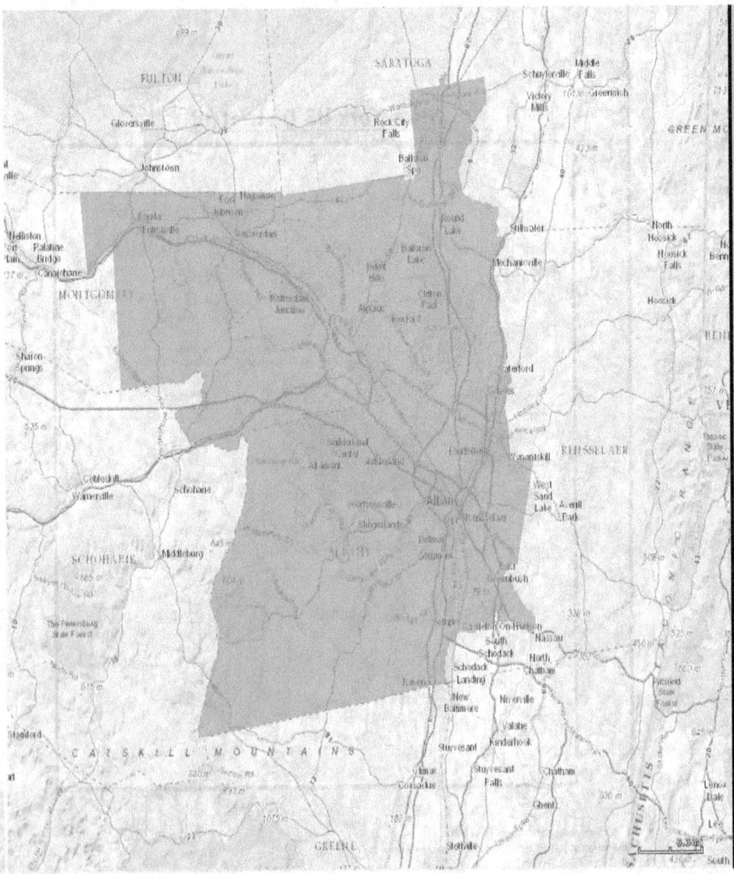

New York US District 20

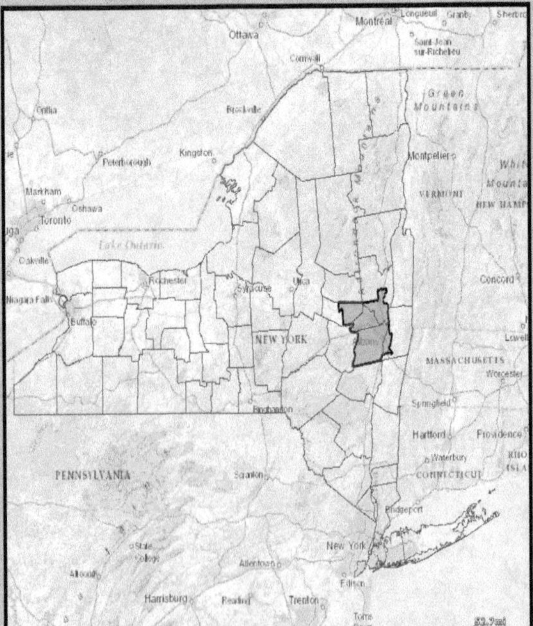

US Congressional districts since 2013
Source: http://nationalatlas.gov, 1 Million Scale project.

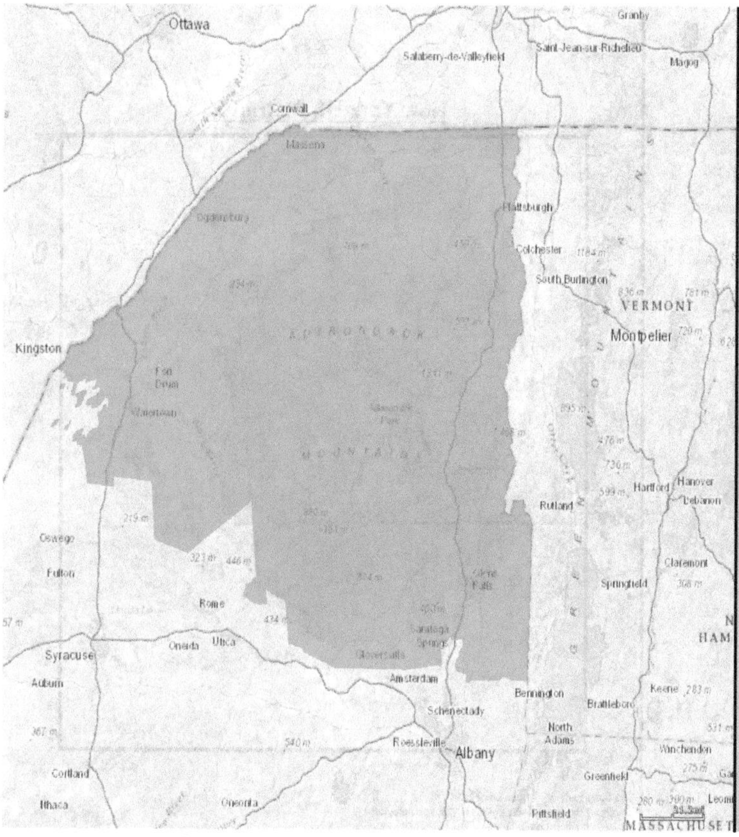

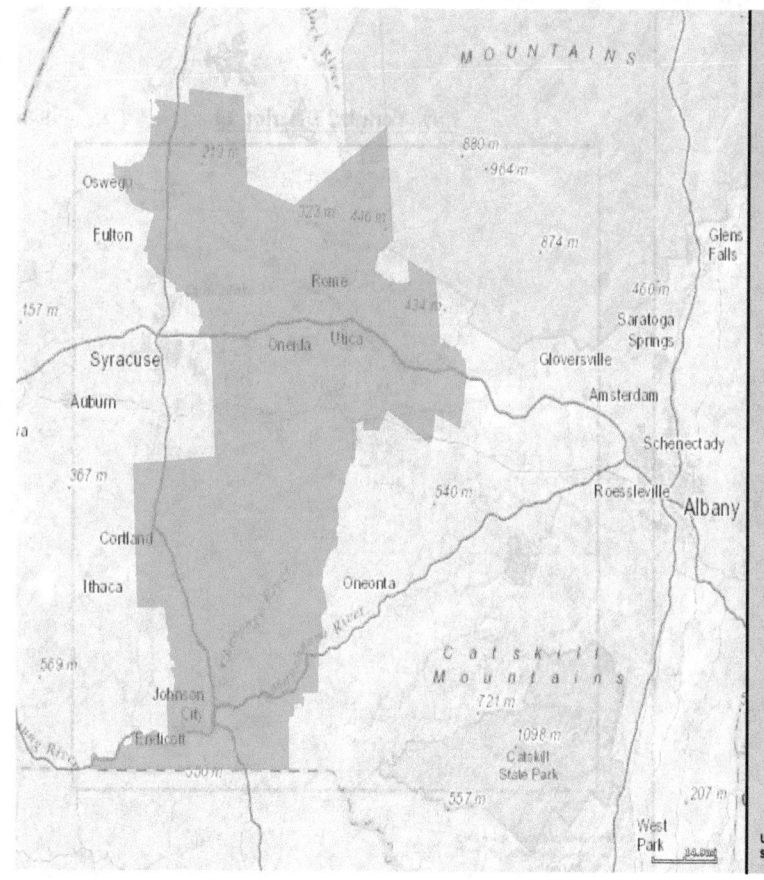

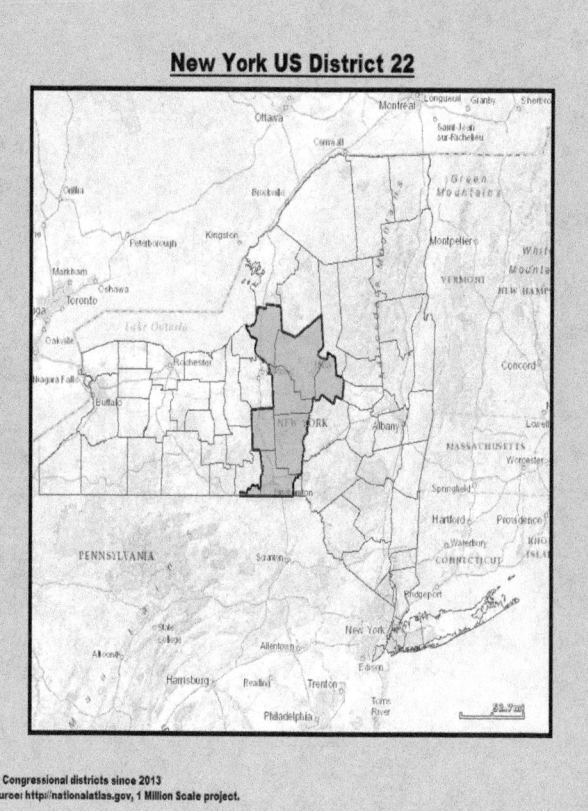

New York US District 21

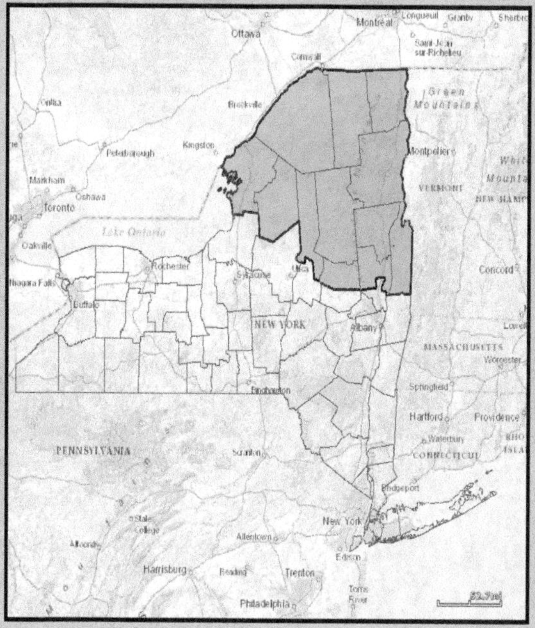

US Congressional districts since 2013
Source: http://nationalatlas.gov, 1 Million Scale project.

New York US District 22

US Congressional districts since 2013
Source: http://nationalatlas.gov, 1 Million Scale project.

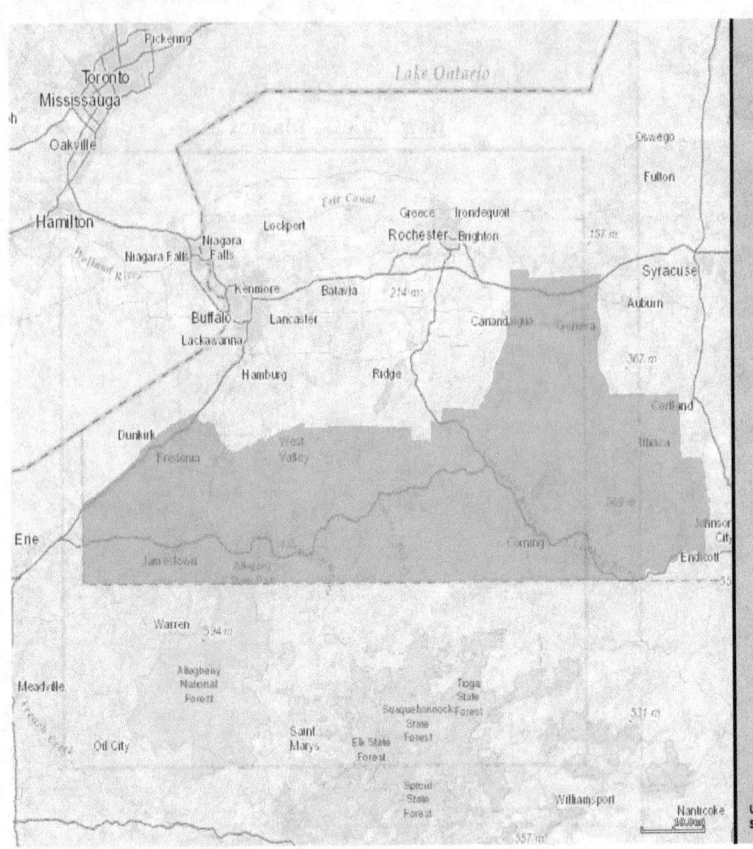

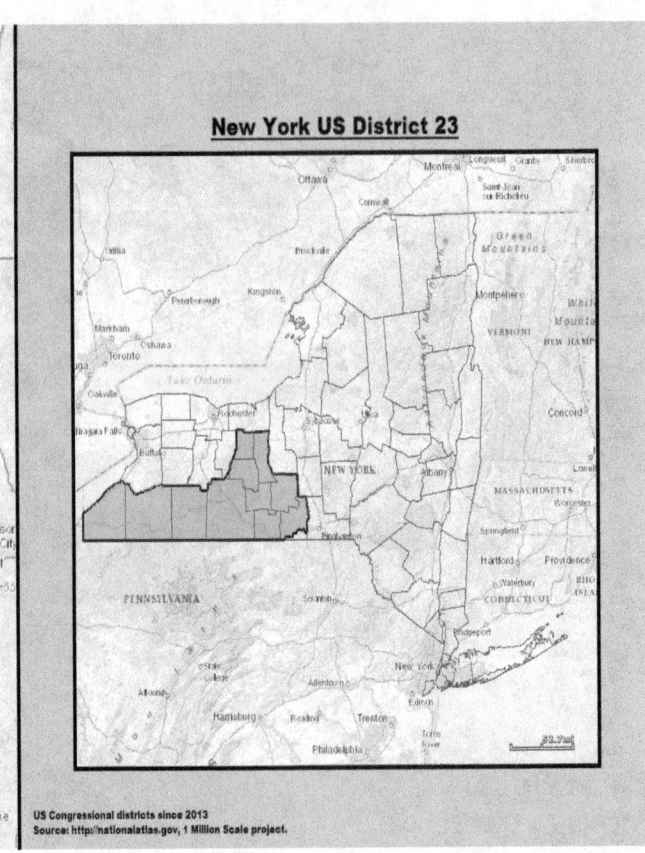

New York US District 23

US Congressional districts since 2013
Source: http://nationalatlas.gov, 1 Million Scale project.

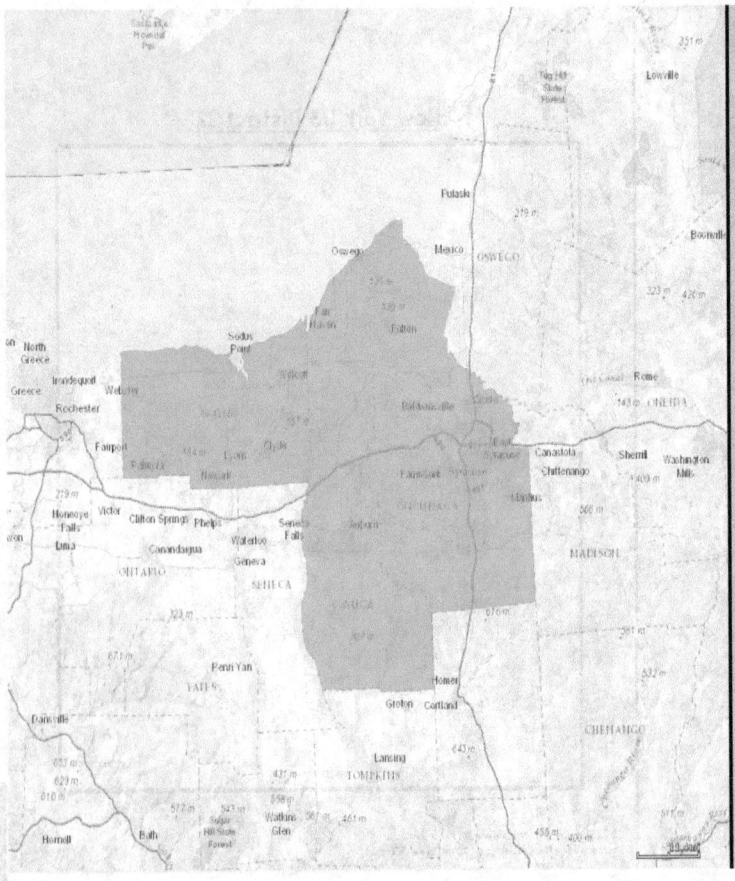

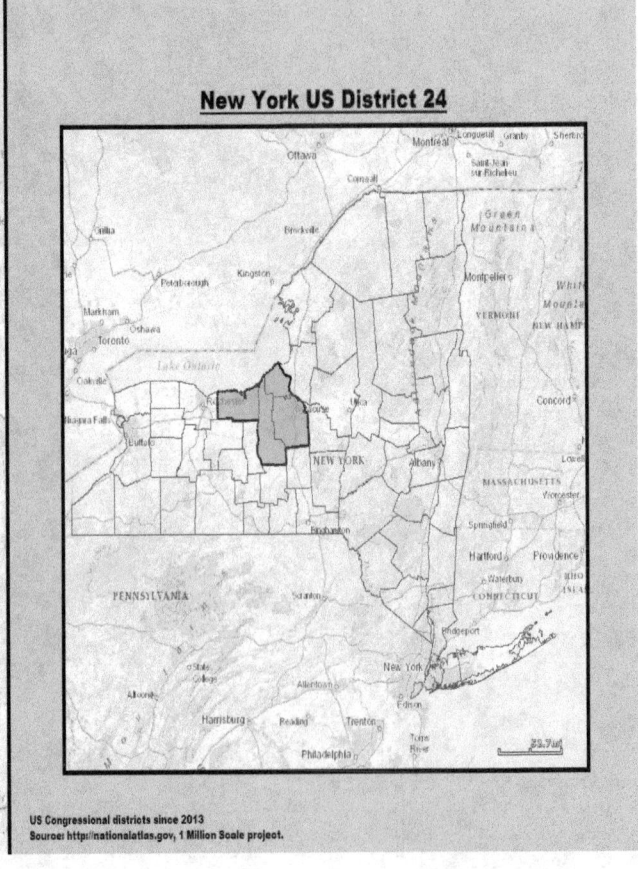

New York US District 24

US Congressional districts since 2013
Source: http://nationalatlas.gov, 1 Million Scale project.

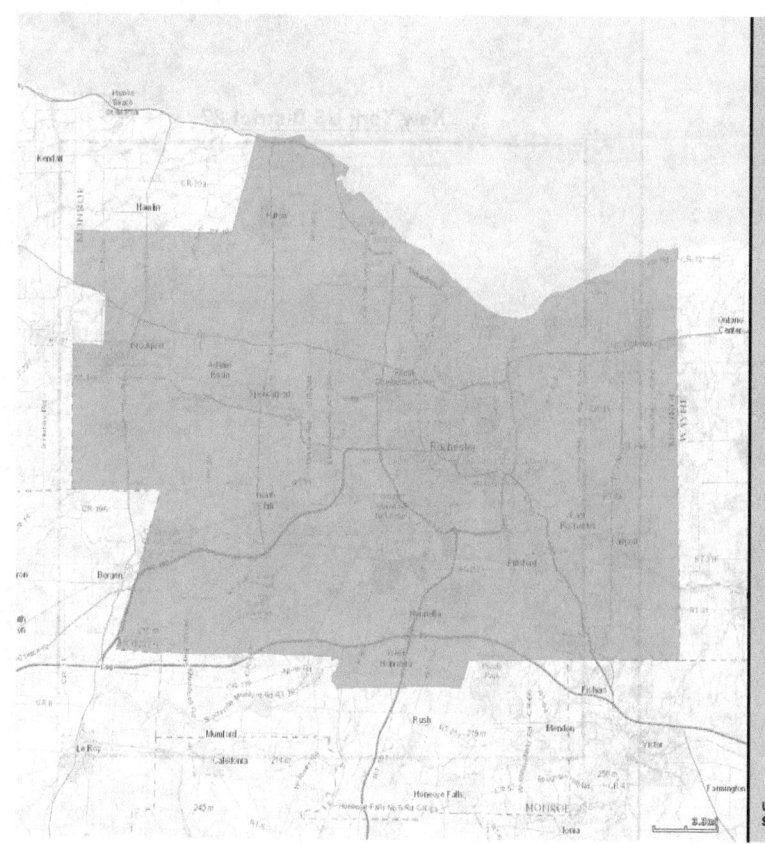

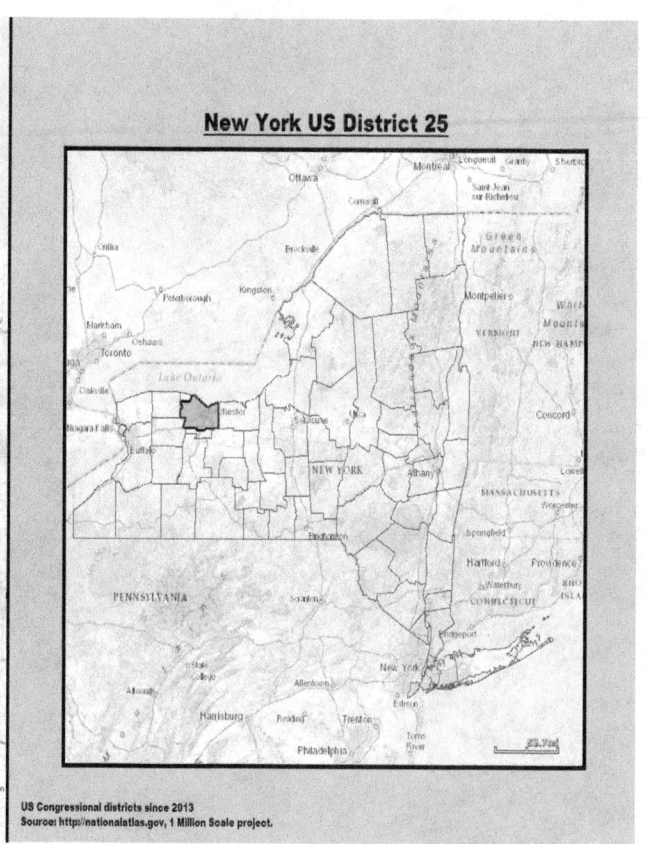

New York US District 25

US Congressional districts since 2013
Source: http://nationalatlas.gov, 1 Million Scale project.

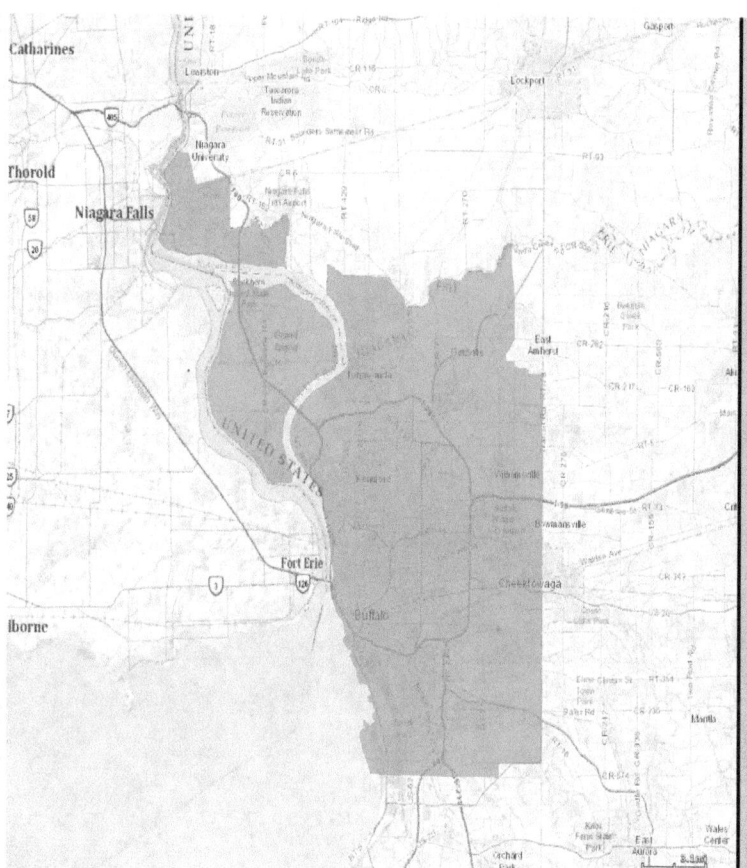

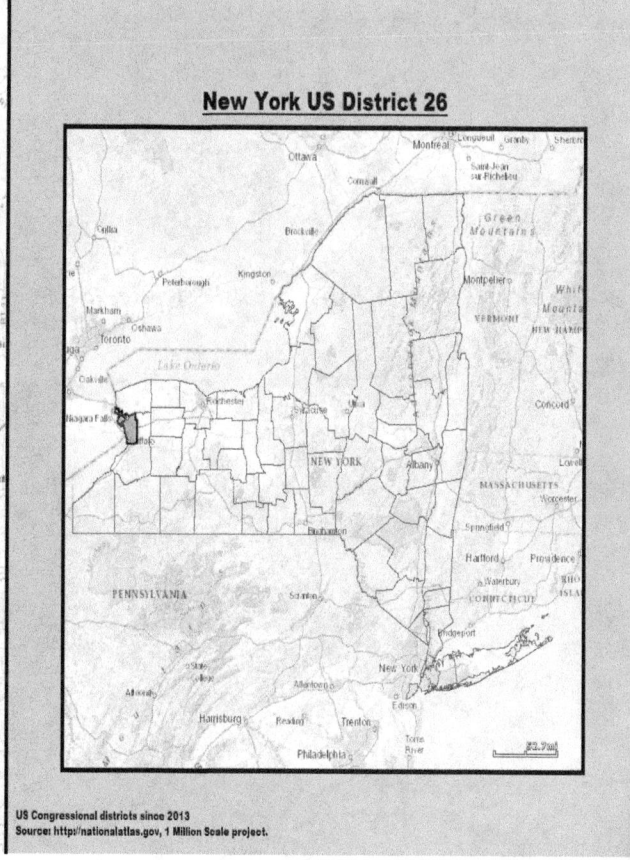

New York US District 26

US Congressional districts since 2013
Source: http://nationalatlas.gov, 1 Million Scale project.

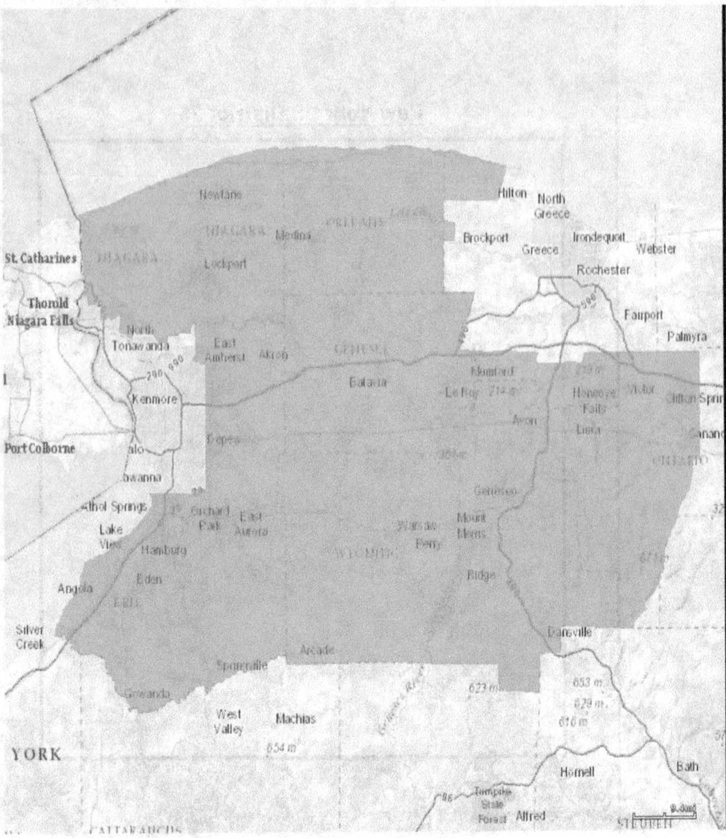

New York US District 27

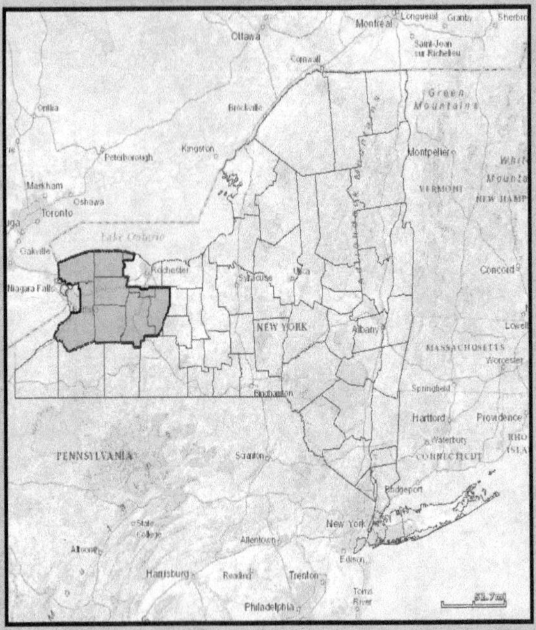

US Congressional districts since 2013
Source: http://nationalatlas.gov, 1 Million Scale project.

NEW YORK

U.S. Department of the Interior
U.S. Geological Survey

The National Atlas of the United States of America®

nationalatlas.gov™
Where We Are

FEDERAL LANDS AND INDIAN RESERVATIONS

Bureau of Indian Affairs

Department of Energy

Department of Defense
(includes Army Corps of Engineers lakes)

Fish and Wildlife Service / Wilderness

Forest Service / Wilderness

National Park Service / Wilderness

Some small sites are not shown, especially in urban areas.

MILES
0   20   40   60   80

Albers equal area projection

Abbreviations

IR   Indian Reservation
NHS   National Historic Site
NWR   National Wildlife Refuge

Appendices:
Financial Plan,
Indexes & Maps

Economic Losses from Hazard Events, 1960-2009

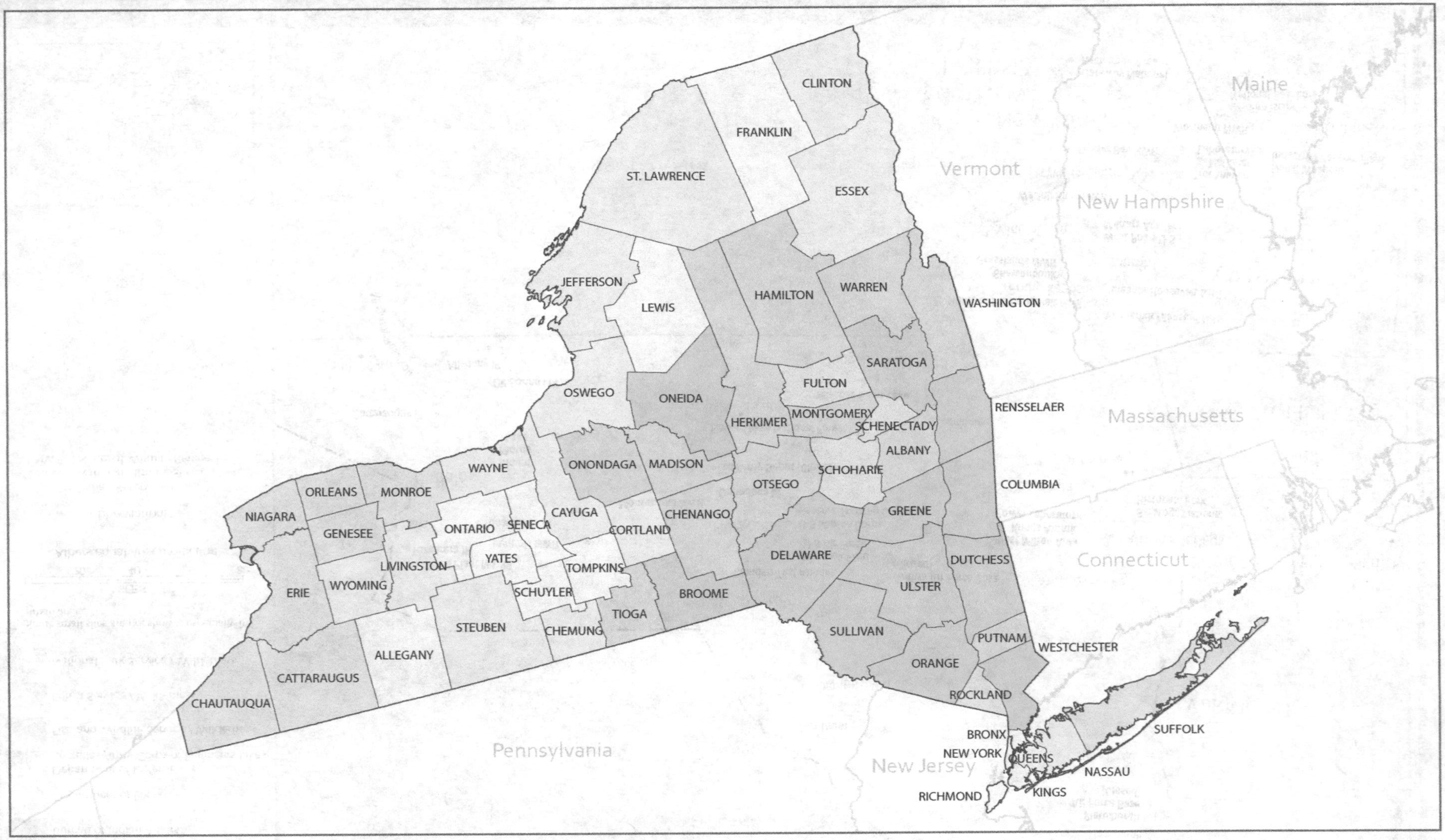

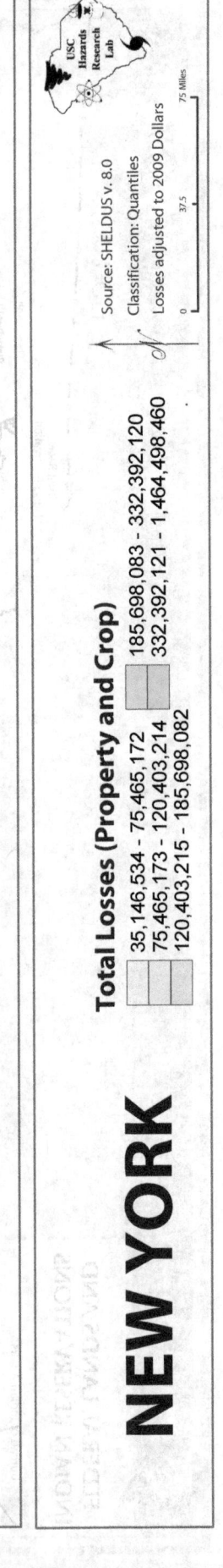

NEW YORK

Source: SHELDUS v. 8.0

Classification: Quantiles
Losses adjusted to 2009 Dollars

USC
Hazards
Research
Lab

0   37.5   75 Miles

Total Losses (Property and Crop)

- 35,146,534 - 75,465,172
- 75,465,173 - 120,403,214
- 120,403,215 - 185,698,082
- 185,698,083 - 332,392,120
- 332,392,121 - 1,464,498,460

NEW YORK
Hazard Losses, 1960-2009

Distribution of Hazard Events
(number of events)

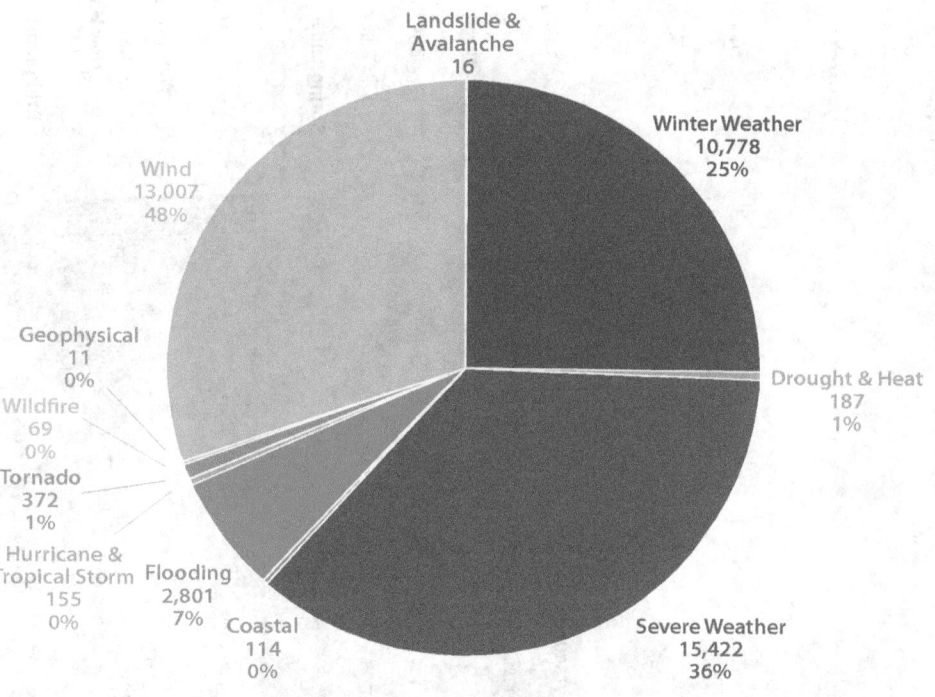

Landslide & Avalanche
16

Winter Weather
10,778
25%

Wind
13,007
48%

Drought & Heat
187
1%

Geophysical
11
0%

Wildfire
69
0%

Tornado
372
1%

Hurricane & Tropical Storm
155
0%

Flooding
2,801
7%

Coastal
114
0%

Severe Weather
15,422
36%

Distribution of Losses by Hazard Type
(in 2009 USD million)

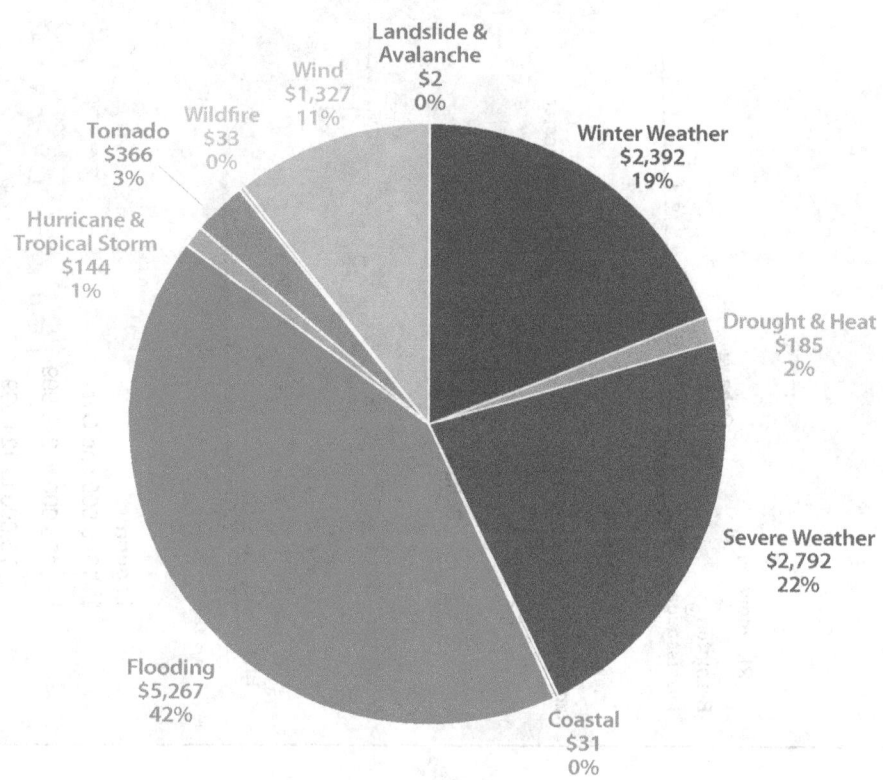

Landslide & Avalanche
$2
0%

Wind
$1,327
11%

Wildfire
$33
0%

Tornado
$366
3%

Winter Weather
$2,392
19%

Hurricane & Tropical Storm
$144
1%

Drought & Heat
$185
2%

Flooding
$5,267
42%

Severe Weather
$2,792
22%

Coastal
$31
0%

Population

Legend

	300,000 and Over
	125,000 to 299,999
	75,000 to 124,999
	50,000 to 74,999
	Under 50,000

Percent White

Legend

	95.0 and Over
	90.0 to 94.9
	85.0 to 89.9
	80.0 to 84.9
	Under 80.0

Percent Black

Legend

- 8.0 and Over
- 6.0 to 7.9
- 4.0 to 5.9
- 2.0 to 3.9
- Under 2.0

Percent Asian

Legend

	3.0 and Over
	2.0 to 2.9
	1.0 to 1.9
	0.5 to 0.9
	Under 0.5

Percent Hispanic

Legend

- 8.0 and Over
- 6.0 to 7.9
- 4.0 to 5.9
- 2.0 to 3.9
- Under 2.0

Median Age

Legend
- 41.0 and Over
- 40.0 to 40.9
- 39.0 to 39.9
- 38.0 to 38.9
- Under 38.0

Demographic & Reference Maps

Median Household Income

Legend

- 52,000 and Over
- 49,000 to 51,999
- 46,000 to 48,999
- 43,000 to 45,999
- Under 43,000

Median Home Value

Legend

- 200,000 and Over
- 175,000 to 199,999
- 150,000 to 174,999
- 125,000 to 149,999
- 100,000 to 124,999
- Under 100,000

High School Graduates*

Legend

- 89.0 and Over
- 87.0 to 88.9
- 85.0 to 86.9
- 83.0 to 84.9
- Under 83.0

College Graduates*

Legend

	27.0 and Over
	23.0 to 26.9
	19.0 to 22.9
	15.0 to 18.9
	Under 15.0

Note: *Percent of population age 25 and over with a Bachelor's Degree or higher.
Copyright © 1988-2003 Microsoft Corp. and/or its suppliers. All rights reserved. © Copyright 2002 by Geographic Data Technology, Inc.
All rights reserved. © 2002 Navigation Technologies. All rights reserved.

Percent of Population Who Voted for Barack Obama in 2012

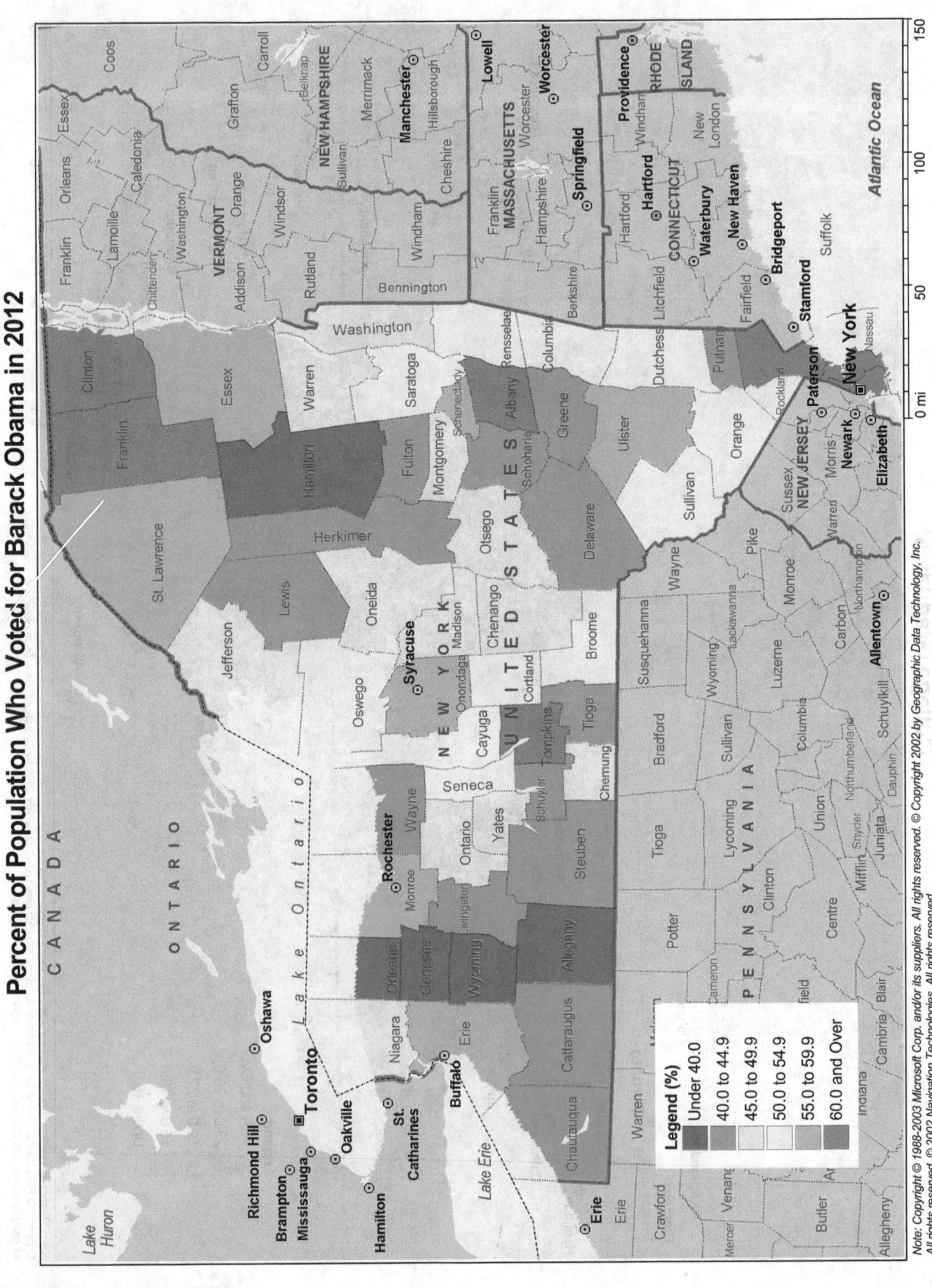

Legend (%)

Under 40.0
40.0 to 44.9
45.0 to 49.9
50.0 to 54.9
55.0 to 59.9
60.0 and Over

2015 Title List

Visit www.GreyHouse.com for Product Information, Table of Contents, and Sample Pages.

General Reference

An African Biographical Dictionary
America's College Museums
American Environmental Leaders: From Colonial Times to the Present
Encyclopedia of African-American Writing
Encyclopedia of Constitutional Amendments
Encyclopedia of Gun Control & Gun Rights
An Encyclopedia of Human Rights in the United States
Encyclopedia of Invasions & Conquests
Encyclopedia of Prisoners of War & Internment
Encyclopedia of Religion & Law in America
Encyclopedia of Rural America
Encyclopedia of the Continental Congress
Encyclopedia of the United States Cabinet, 1789-2010
Encyclopedia of War Journalism
Encyclopedia of Warrior Peoples & Fighting Groups
The Environmental Debate: A Documentary History
The Evolution Wars: A Guide to the Debates
From Suffrage to the Senate: America's Political Women
Global Terror & Political Risk Assessment
Media & Communications 1900-2020
Nations of the World
Political Corruption in America
Privacy Rights in the Digital Era
The Religious Right: A Reference Handbook
Speakers of the House of Representatives, 1789-2009
This is Who We Were: 1880-1900
This is Who We Were: A Companion to the 1940 Census
This is Who We Were: In the 1910s
This is Who We Were: In the 1920s
This is Who We Were: In the 1940s
This is Who We Were: In the 1950s
This is Who We Were: In the 1960s
This is Who We Were: In the 1970s
U.S. Land & Natural Resource Policy
The Value of a Dollar 1600-1865: Colonial Era to the Civil War
The Value of a Dollar: 1860-2014
Working Americans 1770-1869 Vol. IX: Revolutionary War to the Civil War
Working Americans 1880-1999 Vol. I: The Working Class
Working Americans 1880-1999 Vol. II: The Middle Class
Working Americans 1880-1999 Vol. III: The Upper Class
Working Americans 1880-1999 Vol. IV: Their Children
Working Americans 1880-2015 Vol. V: Americans At War
Working Americans 1880-2005 Vol. VI: Women at Work
Working Americans 1880-2006 Vol. VII: Social Movements
Working Americans 1880-2007 Vol. VIII: Immigrants
Working Americans 1880-2009 Vol. X: Sports & Recreation
Working Americans 1880-2010 Vol. XI: Inventors & Entrepreneurs
Working Americans 1880-2011 Vol. XII: Our History through Music
Working Americans 1880-2012 Vol. XIII: Education & Educators
World Cultural Leaders of the 20th & 21st Centuries

Education Information

Charter School Movement
Comparative Guide to American Elementary & Secondary Schools
Complete Learning Disabilities Directory
Educators Resource Directory
Special Education: A Reference Book for Policy and Curriculum Development

Health Information

Comparative Guide to American Hospitals
Complete Directory for Pediatric Disorders
Complete Directory for People with Chronic Illness
Complete Directory for People with Disabilities
Complete Mental Health Directory
Diabetes in America: Analysis of an Epidemic
Directory of Drug & Alcohol Residential Rehab Facilities
Directory of Health Care Group Purchasing Organizations
Directory of Hospital Personnel
HMO/PPO Directory
Medical Device Register
Older Americans Information Directory

Business Information

Complete Television, Radio & Cable Industry Directory
Directory of Business Information Resources
Directory of Mail Order Catalogs
Directory of Venture Capital & Private Equity Firms
Environmental Resource Handbook
Food & Beverage Market Place
Grey House Homeland Security Directory
Grey House Performing Arts Directory
Grey House Safety & Security Directory
Grey House Transportation Security Directory
Hudson's Washington News Media Contacts Directory
New York State Directory
Rauch Market Research Guides
Sports Market Place Directory

Statistics & Demographics

American Tally
America's Top-Rated Cities
America's Top-Rated Smaller Cities
America's Top-Rated Small Towns & Cities
Ancestry & Ethnicity in America
The Asian Databook
Comparative Guide to American Suburbs
The Hispanic Databook
Profiles of America
"Profiles of" Series - State Handbooks
Weather America

Financial Ratings Series

TheStreet Ratings' Guide to Bond & Money Market Mutual Funds
TheStreet Ratings' Guide to Common Stocks
TheStreet Ratings' Guide to Exchange-Traded Funds
TheStreet Ratings' Guide to Stock Mutual Funds
TheStreet Ratings' Ultimate Guided Tour of Stock Investing
Weiss Ratings' Consumer Guides
Weiss Ratings' Guide to Banks
Weiss Ratings' Guide to Credit Unions
Weiss Ratings' Guide to Health Insurers
Weiss Ratings' Guide to Life & Annuity Insurers
Weiss Ratings' Guide to Property & Casualty Insurers

Bowker's Books In Print® Titles

American Book Publishing Record® Annual
American Book Publishing Record® Monthly
Books In Print®
Books In Print® Supplement
Books Out Loud™
Bowker's Complete Video Directory™
Children's Books In Print®
El-Hi Textbooks & Serials In Print®
Forthcoming Books®
Large Print Books & Serials™
Law Books & Serials In Print™
Medical & Health Care Books In Print™
Publishers, Distributors & Wholesalers of the US™
Subject Guide to Books In Print®
Subject Guide to Children's Books In Print®

Canadian General Reference

Associations Canada
Canadian Almanac & Directory
Canadian Environmental Resource Guide
Canadian Parliamentary Guide
Canadian Venture Capital & Private Equity Firms
Financial Services Canada
Governments Canada
Health Guide Canada
The History of Canada
Libraries Canada
Major Canadian Cities

2015 Title List

Visit www.SalemPress.com for Product Information, Table of Contents, and Sample Pages.

Science, Careers & Mathematics

Ancient Creatures: Unearthed
Applied Science
Applied Science: Engineering & Mathematics
Applied Science: Science & Medicine
Applied Science: Technology
Biomes and Ecosystems
Careers in Business
Careers in Chemistry
Careers in Communications & Media
Careers in Environment & Conservation
Careers in Healthcare
Careers in Hospitality & Tourism
Careers in Human Services
Careers in Law, Criminal Justice & Emergency Services
Careers in Physics
Careers in Technology Services & Repair
Computer Technology Innovators
Contemporary Biographies in Business
Contemporary Biographies in Chemistry
Contemporary Biographies in Communications & Media
Contemporary Biographies in Environment & Conservation
Contemporary Biographies in Healthcare
Contemporary Biographies in Hospitality & Tourism
Contemporary Biographies in Law & Criminal Justice
Contemporary Biographies in Physics
Earth Science
Earth Science: Earth Materials & Resources
Earth Science: Earth's Surface and History
Earth Science: Physics & Chemistry of the Earth
Earth Science: Weather, Water & Atmosphere
Encyclopedia of Energy
Encyclopedia of Environmental Issues
Encyclopedia of Environmental Issues: Atmosphere and Air Pollution
Encyclopedia of Environmental Issues: Ecology and Ecosystems
Encyclopedia of Environmental Issues: Energy and Energy Use
Encyclopedia of Environmental Issues: Policy and Activism
Encyclopedia of Environmental Issues: Preservation/Wilderness Issues
Encyclopedia of Environmental Issues: Water and Water Pollution
Encyclopedia of Global Resources
Encyclopedia of Global Warming
Encyclopedia of Mathematics & Society
Encyclopedia of Mathematics & Society: Engineering, Tech, Medicine
Encyclopedia of Mathematics & Society: Great Mathematicians
Encyclopedia of Mathematics & Society: Math & Social Sciences
Encyclopedia of Mathematics & Society: Math Development/Concepts
Encyclopedia of Mathematics & Society: Math in Culture & Society
Encyclopedia of Mathematics & Society: Space, Science, Environment
Encyclopedia of the Ancient World
Forensic Science
Geography Basics
Internet Innovators
Inventions and Inventors
Magill's Encyclopedia of Science: Animal Life
Magill's Encyclopedia of Science: Plant life
Notable Natural Disasters
Principles of Chemistry
Science and Scientists
Solar System
Solar System: Great Astronomers
Solar System: Study of the Universe
Solar System: The Inner Planets
Solar System: The Moon and Other Small Bodies
Solar System: The Outer Planets
Solar System: The Sun and Other Stars
World Geography

Literature

American Ethnic Writers
Classics of Science Fiction & Fantasy Literature
Critical Insights: Authors
Critical Insights: New Literary Collection Bundles
Critical Insights: Themes
Critical Insights: Works
Critical Survey of Drama
Critical Survey of Graphic Novels: Heroes & Super Heroes
Critical Survey of Graphic Novels: History, Theme & Technique
Critical Survey of Graphic Novels: Independents/Underground Classics
Critical Survey of Graphic Novels: Manga
Critical Survey of Long Fiction
Critical Survey of Mystery & Detective Fiction
Critical Survey of Mythology and Folklore: Heroes and Heroines
Critical Survey of Mythology and Folklore: Love, Sexuality & Desire
Critical Survey of Mythology and Folklore: World Mythology
Critical Survey of Poetry
Critical Survey of Poetry: American Poets
Critical Survey of Poetry: British, Irish & Commonwealth Poets
Critical Survey of Poetry: Cumulative Index
Critical Survey of Poetry: European Poets
Critical Survey of Poetry: Topical Essays
Critical Survey of Poetry: World Poets
Critical Survey of Shakespeare's Sonnets
Critical Survey of Short Fiction
Critical Survey of Short Fiction: American Writers
Critical Survey of Short Fiction: British, Irish, Commonwealth Writers
Critical Survey of Short Fiction: Cumulative Index
Critical Survey of Short Fiction: European Writers
Critical Survey of Short Fiction: Topical Essays
Critical Survey of Short Fiction: World Writers
Cyclopedia of Literary Characters
Holocaust Literature
Introduction to Literary Context: American Poetry of the 20th Century
Introduction to Literary Context: American Post-Modernist Novels
Introduction to Literary Context: American Short Fiction
Introduction to Literary Context: English Literature
Introduction to Literary Context: Plays
Introduction to Literary Context: World Literature
Magill's Literary Annual 2015
Magill's Survey of American Literature
Magill's Survey of World Literature
Masterplots
Masterplots II: African American Literature
Masterplots II: American Fiction Series
Masterplots II: British & Commonwealth Fiction Series
Masterplots II: Christian Literature
Masterplots II: Drama Series
Masterplots II: Juvenile & Young Adult Literature, Supplement
Masterplots II: Nonfiction Series
Masterplots II: Poetry Series
Masterplots II: Short Story Series
Masterplots II: Women's Literature Series
Notable African American Writers
Notable American Novelists
Notable Playwrights
Notable Poets
Recommended Reading: 500 Classics Reviewed
Short Story Writers

Grey House Publishing | Salem Press | H.W. Wilson | 4919 Route, 22 PO Box 56, Amenia NY 12501-0056

2015 Title List

Visit www.SalemPress.com for Product Information, Table of Contents, and Sample Pages.

History and Social Science

The 2000s in America
50 States
African American History
Agriculture in History
American First Ladies
American Heroes
American Indian Culture
American Indian History
American Indian Tribes
American Presidents
American Villains
America's Historic Sites
Ancient Greece
The Bill of Rights
The Civil Rights Movement
The Cold War
Countries, Peoples & Cultures
Countries, Peoples & Cultures: Central & South America
Countries, Peoples & Cultures: Central, South & Southeast Asia
Countries, Peoples & Cultures: East & South Africa
Countries, Peoples & Cultures: East Asia & the Pacific
Countries, Peoples & Cultures: Eastern Europe
Countries, Peoples & Cultures: Middle East & North Africa
Countries, Peoples & Cultures: North America & the Caribbean
Countries, Peoples & Cultures: West & Central Africa
Countries, Peoples & Cultures: Western Europe
Defining Documents: American Revolution (1754-1805)
Defining Documents: Civil War (1860-1865)
Defining Documents: Emergence of Modern America (1868-1918)
Defining Documents: Exploration & Colonial America (1492-1755)
Defining Documents: Manifest Destiny (1803-1860)
Defining Documents: Post-War 1940s (1945-1949)
Defining Documents: Reconstruction (1865-1880)
Defining Documents: The 1920s
Defining Documents: The 1930s
Defining Documents: The American West (1836-1900)
Defining Documents: The Ancient World (2700 B.C.E.-50 C.E.)
Defining Documents: The Middle Ages (524-1431)
Defining Documents: World War I
Defining Documents: World War II (1939-1946)
The Eighties in America
Encyclopedia of American Immigration
Encyclopedia of Flight
Encyclopedia of the Ancient World
The Fifties in America
The Forties in America
Great Athletes
Great Athletes: Baseball
Great Athletes: Basketball
Great Athletes: Boxing & Soccer
Great Athletes: Cumulative Index
Great Athletes: Football
Great Athletes: Golf & Tennis
Great Athletes: Olympics
Great Athletes: Racing & Individual Sports
Great Events from History: 17th Century
Great Events from History: 18th Century
Great Events from History: 19th Century
Great Events from History: 20th Century (1901-1940)
Great Events from History: 20th Century (1941-1970)
Great Events from History: 20th Century (1971-2000)
Great Events from History: Ancient World
Great Events from History: Cumulative Indexes
Great Events from History: Gay, Lesbian, Bisexual, Transgender Events
Great Events from History: Middle Ages
Great Events from History: Modern Scandals
Great Events from History: Renaissance & Early Modern Era

Great Lives from History: 17th Century
Great Lives from History: 18th Century
Great Lives from History: 19th Century
Great Lives from History: 20th Century
Great Lives from History: African Americans
Great Lives from History: Ancient World
Great Lives from History: Asian & Pacific Islander Americans
Great Lives from History: Cumulative Indexes
Great Lives from History: Incredibly Wealthy
Great Lives from History: Inventors & Inventions
Great Lives from History: Jewish Americans
Great Lives from History: Latinos
Great Lives from History: Middle Ages
Great Lives from History: Notorious Lives
Great Lives from History: Renaissance & Early Modern Era
Great Lives from History: Scientists & Science
Historical Encyclopedia of American Business
Immigration in U.S. History
Magill's Guide to Military History
Milestone Documents in African American History
Milestone Documents in American History
Milestone Documents in World History
Milestone Documents of American Leaders
Milestone Documents of World Religions
Musicians & Composers 20th Century
The Nineties in America
The Seventies in America
The Sixties in America
Survey of American Industry and Careers
The Thirties in America
The Twenties in America
United States at War
U.S.A. in Space
U.S. Court Cases
U.S. Government Leaders
U.S. Laws, Acts, and Treaties
U.S. Legal System
U.S. Supreme Court
Weapons and Warfare
World Conflicts: Asia and the Middle East

Health

Addictions & Substance Abuse
Adolescent Health
Cancer
Complementary & Alternative Medicine
Genetics & Inherited Conditions
Health Issues
Infectious Diseases & Conditions
Magill's Medical Guide
Psychology & Behavioral Health
Psychology Basics

Grey House Publishing | Salem Press | H.W. Wilson | 4919 Route, 22 PO Box 56, Amenia NY 12501-0056

2015 Title List

Current Biography

Current Biography Cumulative Index 1946-2013
Current Biography Monthly Magazine
Current Biography Yearbook: 2003
Current Biography Yearbook: 2004
Current Biography Yearbook: 2005
Current Biography Yearbook: 2006
Current Biography Yearbook: 2007
Current Biography Yearbook: 2008
Current Biography Yearbook: 2009
Current Biography Yearbook: 2010
Current Biography Yearbook: 2011
Current Biography Yearbook: 2012
Current Biography Yearbook: 2013
Current Biography Yearbook: 2014
Current Biography Yearbook: 2015

Core Collections

Children's Core Collection
Fiction Core Collection
Middle & Junior High School Core
Public Library Core Collection: Nonfiction
Senior High Core Collection

The Reference Shelf

Aging in America
American Military Presence Overseas
The Arab Spring
The Brain
The Business of Food
Conspiracy Theories
The Digital Age
Dinosaurs
Embracing New Paradigms in Education
Faith & Science
Families: Traditional and New Structures
The Future of U.S. Economic Relations: Mexico, Cuba, and Venezuela
Global Climate Change
Graphic Novels and Comic Books
Immigration in the U.S.
Internet Safety
Marijuana Reform
The News and its Future
The Paranormal
Politics of the Ocean
Reality Television
Representative American Speeches: 2008-2009
Representative American Speeches: 2009-2010
Representative American Speeches: 2010-2011
Representative American Speeches: 2011-2012
Representative American Speeches: 2012-2013
Representative American Speeches: 2013-2014
Representative American Speeches: 2014-2015
Revisiting Gender
Robotics
Russia
Social Networking
Social Services for the Poor
Space Exploration & Development
Sports in America
The Supreme Court
The Transformation of American Cities
U.S. Infrastructure
U.S. National Debate Topic: Surveillance
U.S. National Debate Topic: The Ocean
U.S. National Debate Topic: Transportation Infrastructure
Whistleblowers

Readers' Guide

Abridged Readers' Guide to Periodical Literature
Readers' Guide to Periodical Literature

Indexes

Index to Legal Periodicals & Books
Short Story Index
Book Review Digest

Sears List

Sears List of Subject Headings
Sears: Lista de Encabezamientos de Materia

Facts About Series

Facts About American Immigration
Facts About China
Facts About the 20th Century
Facts About the Presidents
Facts About the World's Languages

Nobel Prize Winners

Nobel Prize Winners: 1901-1986
Nobel Prize Winners: 1987-1991
Nobel Prize Winners: 1992-1996
Nobel Prize Winners: 1997-2001

World Authors

World Authors: 1995-2000
World Authors: 2000-2005

Famous First Facts

Famous First Facts
Famous First Facts About American Politics
Famous First Facts About Sports
Famous First Facts About the Environment
Famous First Facts: International Edition

American Book of Days

The American Book of Days
The International Book of Days

Junior Authors & Illustrators

Tenth Book of Junior Authors & Illustrations

Monographs

The Barnhart Dictionary of Etymology
Celebrate the World
Guide to the Ancient World
Indexing from A to Z
The Poetry Break
Radical Change: Books for Youth in a Digital Age

Wilson Chronology

Wilson Chronology of Asia and the Pacific
Wilson Chronology of Human Rights
Wilson Chronology of Ideas
Wilson Chronology of the Arts
Wilson Chronology of the World's Religions
Wilson Chronology of Women's Achievements

Grey House Publishing | Salem Press | H.W. Wilson | 4919 Route, 22 PO Box 56, Amenia NY 12501-0056